We've Put It All Together For You

▶ Outstanding Student Text

▶ First-Ever Teacher's Wraparound Edition

▶ Comprehensive Support Materials

GLENCOE

A Dynamic Student Text That Grabs Their Interest and Keeps Them Involved

Understanding Psychology features a fresh new design and captivating graphics supported by high-interest content that teaches students about the relevant, practical uses of psychology in their everyday experiences.

In Your Journal requires students to use the skills of a psychologist to observe, analyze, and write about a variety of issues. A follow-up journal activity in the *Chapter Review* provides opportunities for building student portfolios, these activities also offer an alternative method of assessment.

At A Glance

IMPROVING YOUR SELF-IMAGE

If your self-image can stand a boost, try taking these steps toward greater self-confidence. As you're reading this list, remember what humanistic personality theorists believe: a positive self-image is at the heart of successful adjustment.

- Base your personal goals on an honest appraisal of your strengths and weaknesses. Trying to be something you're not can only weaken your self-image.
- Don't let guilt and shame determine your goals. Let positive thinking guide your decision making.
- Don't blame everything that goes wrong on yourself. Sometimes external events can play an equally important role.
- When others dismiss your views, keep in mind that events are interpreted in different ways by different people.
- When things go wrong, don't be too hard on yourself. Never think of yourself as a failure, stupid, or ugly.
- Accept criticism of the things you do, but don't allow people to criticize you as a person.
- Use your failures in a constructive way. They may be telling you to readjust your goals and start over in a new direction.
- Don't stay in a situation that makes you feel inadequate. If you can't change the situation, move on to something new.

Try these suggestions and you'll soon see that there's no better feeling than feeling good about yourself.

For more details, see Philip Zimbardo, Shyness: What It Is, What to Do About It, Reading, Mass.: Addison-Wesley, 1990.

CHAPTER 6

Motivation and Emotion

FIGURE 6.1 Motivation—why we do things—cannot be observed directly; it can only be inferred from goal-directed behavior.

At a Glance provides students with practical insights into human behavior based on the results of a variety of intriguing studies.

◀

▶

Using Psychology highlights fascinating details and real-world applications of the latest research and data in psychology.

High-Interest Features

Enhance Chapter Content and Promote Class Discussions

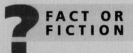

More About provides detailed information about key issues and topics.

Fact or Fiction shares intriguing information about real-life behavior.

Psychology and You reinforces the connection between psychology and students' real-life situations.

Psychology Update provides the latest findings on human behavior.

OBJECTIVES

After studying this chapter, you should be able to

- give reasons for the physiological basis of motivation.
- discuss drive reduction theory and the critiques of drive reduction theory.
- summarize the study of social motives.
- explain Maslow's hierarchy of needs.
- give examples of the physiological theories of emotion.
- give reasons for the cognitive theorists' approach to the study of emotions.

KEY TERMS

Cannon-Bard theory
drive reduction theory
fundamental needs
homeostasis
innate
James-Lange theory
lateral hypothalamus (LH)
motivation
polygraph
psychological needs
self-actualization needs
ventromedial
    hypothalamus (VMH)

Why do people climb Mount Everest or cross the Atlantic in a balloon? Why do some people spend every waking moment memorizing batting averages while others don't know the difference between the New York Yankees and the Toledo Mud Hens? And, as the song asks, why do fools fall in love?

Although all psychology is concerned with what people do and how they do it, research on motivation and emotion focuses on the underlying why of behavior.

We see Kristin studying all weekend while the rest of us hang out, and since we know she wants to go to law school, we conclude that she is "motivated" by her desire to get good grades. We see Mikko working after classes at a job he doesn't like, and since we know he wants to buy a car, we conclude that he is "motivated" to earn money for the car. Movies from *Silence of the Lambs* to *Unforgiven* have often had motives or emotions as their central theme. On the street, you hear words like "anger," "fear," "pain," "starving," and hundreds of others describing motives and

IN YOUR JOURNAL

Think about the present-day concerns and future aspirations that are most important to you. List 6 to 10 of them in any order in your journal.

133

3

Presenting the First-Ever Psychology Teacher's Wraparound Edition

Our unique **Teacher's Wraparound Edition** helps you minimize daily prep time with on-page teaching notes and lesson strategies — including a four-step lesson plan that helps you to *focus*, *teach*, *assess*, and *close* each chapter. A wealth of information presented at the point of instruction saves time while instantly preparing you to make dynamic class presentations.

Features in the Teacher's Wraparound Edition Include: ▶

NEW!

...sson Plan

TEACH

Guided Practice

■ **Demonstration.** You might introduce the subject of selective memory by calling on two volunteers to prepare short talks to be delivered simultaneously. One student should assemble detailed directions on how to get to a little-known spot in your community. The other student should talk about some "hot" topic at school, such as a recent game or concert. Tell students to pay attention to the directions. When the volunteers are done, ask class members to repeat the directions. Using information in the text, explore reasons students were able or unable to tune out the "hot-topic" speaker.
(OBJECTIVE 1)

VISUAL INSTRUCTION

Ask students to explain in their own words how people are able to "listen" to multiple messages.
Answer to caption, Figure 3.2: Selective attention: the ability to pick and choose among various inputs.

---

54   UNIT I / LEARNING AND COGNITIVE PROCESSES

TAKING IN INFORMATION

Information is any event that reduces uncertainty. For example, when a traffic light changes from red to green, it provides you with information—it reduces your uncertainty about whether you should step on the gas. Many forms of information are captured through your senses—voices, musical sounds, sweet tastes, pungent odors, colorful images, rough textures, painful stings. These and all experiences are converted into impulses in your nervous system. At any given moment a confusing array of sights, sounds, smells, and other sensations compete for your attention. If you accepted all these inputs, you would be completely overwhelmed. Two processes help people narrow sensory inputs to a manageable number: selective attention and feature extraction.

Selective Attention

Your ability to pick and choose among the various available inputs is called **selective attention.** For example, if you are at a large party where the music is turned up and everyone is talking, you can focus on a friend's voice and ignore all other sounds. In a way, selective attention is like tuning in a specific television channel.

In his *selection theory*, Donald Broadbent argued that we attend to only one of the many channels of information reaching us at any time because the channels available to interpret the information are themselves very limited. Yet, in the dichotic listening task, subjects could report hearing their name in the channel they had been instructed to

> **FIGURE 3.2**
> In a crowded setting, we cannot pay equal attention to all the sounds. Some kind of selectivity is needed. In a dichotic listening task, the subject wears earphones and listens to two different messages. **What is selective attention?**

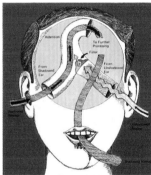

🧪 LAB EXPERIMENTS AND DEMONSTRATIONS

To illustrate feature extraction, you might hold an "index drill" in which you ask students to quickly find the first page reference for random terms that you call out. The first student to find the term should call out the page number. After doing this several times, ask: Did you read every item in the index to find the term? If not, what clues or features did you look for to find the item quickly? (*Most students will say they skimmed for initial letters.*) Next, call on students to cite other examples of how they use this practice (feature extraction) to process information in their daily lives.

54

Lab Experiments and Demonstrations promote critical thinking through hands-on activities that enable students to test hypotheses and put theories into practice.

A **Performance Assessment Activity** for each chapter provides a creative performance task to help you assess students' understanding of key concepts.

PERFORMANCE ASSESSMENT ACTIVITY

Write the following sayings by Greek writer Aeschylus and Roman orator Cicero on the chalkboard.

"Memory is the mother of all wisdom." (Aeschylus)
"Memory is the treasury and guardian of all things." (Cicero)

Ask: What do these two sayings have in common? *(the high opinion of memory)* Request students to draw posters illustrating these sayings or sayings of their own design. *(Posters should express graphically a point of view on the function or purpose of memory.)*

CHAPTER 3 / MEMORY AND THOUGHT   **55**

...ore. Others, told to ignore one channel, nevertheless could report the ...v of a complete story even though the story was switched without ...ning to the ignored channel. Based on this work in 1960, Anne Treis-...n (1964) later proposed an *attenuation theory.* She argued that Broad-...t's filter suppressed other channels but did not eliminate them. Some ...ormation was still being processed. Thus, unlike a television dial, selec-...attention does not completely block out other programs or stimuli. ...ese theories assume that when you first analyze a wide variety of in-...ming information you focus on a select few and direct most of your ...scious attention to them.

...Later, psychologists suggested we may actually be limited not in our ...lity to process information, but in our ability to respond after all infor-...tion has been processed. If you meet several friends at once in school, ...cannot say "Hello" to all of them at the same time, so you attend to each ...individually. The results of human performance in tasks such as you ...in Figure 3.3 argue that we are selecting among responses. This sug-...ts that attention registers its effects late, after the meaning of incoming ...mulation has been more or less fully processed (Treisman, 1988).

...What makes one input more important than another? Information ...ding to the satisfaction of such needs as hunger and thirst has top ...ority. You've noticed how a person who is very hungry will pay more at-...tion to his or her dinner than to the dinner-table chitchat. We also give ...ority to inputs that are strange and novel, such as an individual who ...mes to a party dressed for snorkeling. A third director of attention is in-...est: the more interested you are in something, the more likely you are ...notice it. For example, most people "tune in" when they hear their name ...ntioned; we're all interested in what other people have to say about us. ...ewise, if you become interested in chess, you will suddenly begin to no-...e newspaper articles about chess, chess sets in store windows, and ref-...nces to chess moves in everyday speech—for example, "stalemate." ...ese inputs are not new. They were there last year and the year before, ...you simply weren't interested enough to notice them.

...ature Extraction

...Selective attention is only the first step in narrowing input. The second ...p is to decide on which aspects of the selected channel you will focus. ...is process, called **feature extraction,** involves locating the outstanding ...aracteristics of incoming information (Figure 3.4). If you want to identi-...he make of a car, you look for certain features—the shape of the fend-..., the grille and so on. For the most part, you ignore such features as ...or, upholstery, and tires, which tell you little about the make of the car. ...ilarly, when you read, you focus on the important words, skimming ...r such words as *the, and,* or *for example.*

...Being able to extract the significant features of an input helps a person ...dentify it and compare it to other inputs. For example, you are able to ...tinguish faces from one another and, at the same time, see resem-...nces. You may notice that all the members of a family have similar

FIGURE 3.3

In the lists below, ignore the letters printed in green. Time yourself as you read down the list of red letters in List A. How long did it take? Now read down the list of red letters in List B. How long did it take? Read the letters now, before reading the next paragraph.

Some researchers have argued that List B takes longer. Despite being told to ignore the green letters you process them anyway and then have to suppress them as you read Lists A and B. But in List B, the green letter is the same as the red letter in the next row. To get yourself to say the red letter from the second position all the way to the bottom, you have to overcome the suppression of the green letter from the previous row, thus adding to the time it takes you to read the red letters in List B (Driver & Tipper, 1989).

List A	List B
PT	TG
VC	GT
WE	EC
HJ	HE
QP	PH
NC	CP
IX	XC
QA	AX
BL	LA
UD	DL
FT	TD
XM	MT

CONNECTIONS: PSYCHOLOGY AND LINGUISTICS

How do we determine word meanings? One answer to this question is based on the *semantic feature theory.* This theory suggests that a word is simply a cluster of features. For example, a *dog* is any organism that barks, has four legs, fur, a tail, and is usually domesticated. What about a Mexican Hairless or a Boxer with its tail removed? Are they dogs? Such semantic problems led Elinor Rosch (1973) to propose the *theory of prototypes.* According to Rosch, we understand a word by knowing the features of its prototype and recognizing that it may have only a subset of the features of its prototype. Thus a dog may not even bark, but still possess enough "dog"ness to make it a dog. Call on two of your students to research Rosch's theories further and to present her ideas on semantic feature extraction in the form of an oral report.

55

CHAPTER 3 Lesson Plan

WORKING WITH TRANSPARENCIES

Project Transparency 2 and use the guidelines given on Teaching Strategies and Activities. Assign Student Worksheet 2.

VISUAL INSTRUCTION

Have teams of students conduct the experiment in Figure 3.3. One student should watch the eye motion of the other as he or she reads the lists of green and red letters. Does it in fact take students longer to read the red letters, as believed by some researchers?

52B

Teacher's Classroom Resources, referenced at the beginning of each chapter and at each point of use, help you coordinate and implement the wealth of resources provided with the program.

Numerous other new features provide you with a wealth of fun, easy-to-do activities that challenge your students and complement your instruction:

▶ **Did You Know**

▶ **Extra Credit Activities**

▶ **Critical Thinking Activities**

▶ **Curriculum Connections**

▶ **Psychologists at Work**

▶ **Community Involvement Projects**

No Other Program Offers More Resources — or More Flexibility

Teacher's Resource Binder

Study Guide focuses students' attention on the key chapter terms and concepts. It can be used as a preview, review, or guided reading assignment.

Application Activities for each chapter help students make connections between psychology and the real world through motivating classroom activities.

Extension Activities sharpen students' critical thinking skills and enrich their understanding through in-depth readings that extend each chapter.

Review Activities reinforce the major concepts of each chapter and provide an excellent tool for reteaching or preparing students for the chapter test.

Guidebook to Advanced Placement Test provides practice activities that prepare students to pass the Psychology Advanced Placement Test.

Chapter Tests: Forms A and B allow you to offer alternative versions of a chapter test to different classes.

Reproducible Lesson Plans cross reference all the resource materials so you can focus on the important task of teaching instead of planning.

Performance Assessment Activities include implementation strategies, assessment activities, scoring rubrics, and more, to give you additional options and opportunities to meet your performance assessment requirements.

Additional Resources

Teaching Transparencies with Strategies and Activities features full-color overhead transparencies that enhance chapter content. Teaching suggestions and reproducible student activities accompany each transparency, making it a complete instructional package.

Readings in Psychology includes a collection of articles from professional journals. No other program offers this outstanding enrichment resource compiled for you in one convenient location.

Writer's Guidebook reinforces writing skills essential to communicating effectively in psychology and other disciplines.

Testmaker Software, available in Apple, IBM, and Macintosh formats, offers you the flexibility to change, delete, or add questions to the database provided. The package includes a printout of the entire database, making it easy to preview and select questions you want to use.

New SAT Test Practice provides practice questions and test-taking strategies that help your students excel on the new version of the SAT exam.

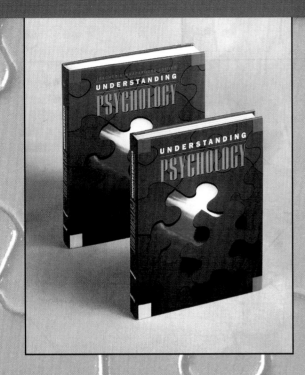
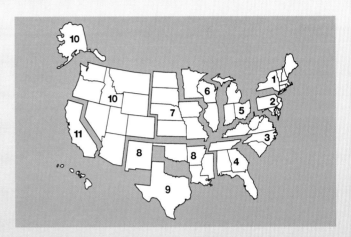

UNDERSTANDING
PSYCHOLOGY

RICHARD A. KASSCHAU, PH.D.

McGraw-Hill

New York, New York   Columbus, Ohio   Mission Hills, California   Peoria, Illinois

Author

Richard A. Kasschau, Ph.D., is Professor of Psychology at the University of Houston. Dr. Kasschau is a member of the American Educational Research Association, the American Psychological Association, and the American Psychological Society. He has written extensively for magazines, newspapers, and professional journals. An award-winning and distinguished teacher who has taught psychology for more than 20 years, Dr. Kasschau was the 1993 winner of the University of Houston's Teaching Excellence Award.

Send all inquiries to:
Glencoe/McGraw-Hill
936 Eastwind Drive
Westerville, Ohio 43081

ISBN 0-02-823155-4 (Student Edition)
ISBN 0-02-823171-6 (Teacher's Wraparound Edition)

2 3 4 5 6 7 8 9 QPK/MC   00 99 98 97 96 95

Contents

USING THE TEACHER'S WRAPAROUND EDITION

The Teacher's Wraparound Edition offers teaching suggestions on a unit-chapter basis and follows the same mode of presentation for each of the 7 units and 20 chapters of *Understanding Psychology.*

The instructional strategies in each chapter are based on a four-step teaching model—Focus, Teach, Assess, and Close.

Focus activities help make students aware of what they are supposed to be learning and why that learning is important to them.

Teach strategies are divided into Guided Practice and Independent Practice activities. Most strategies are linked to chapter objectives, allowing the teacher to guide and monitor attainment of the objectives and enabling immediate remediation of learning errors.

Assess activities first check student attainment of the chapter objectives and then evaluate student learning. Remediation is provided by review activities, and application activities help extend learning.

Close provides summary strategies that bring together the learning from the chapter objectives and require students to apply it in some way.

Contents

Alternative Presentations

Understanding Psychology is a comprehensive text that is suitable for a full-year course. Because some psychology courses are taught for only one semester, the following outlines suggest five one-semester courses, each with a different emphasis.

Outline 1

Roots of Behavior

Chapter 1	Chapter 7
Chapter 3	Chapter 8, pp. 182-196
Chapter 4	Chapter 13, pp. 316-324
Chapter 5	
Chapter 6	

Outline 2

The Work of Psychology

Chapter 1	Chapter 16
Chapter 2	Chapter 18
Chapter 11	Chapter 19
Chapter 12	Chapter 20
Chapter 15	

Outline 3

You, Others, and Society

Chapter 1	Chapter 12, pp. 303-306
Chapter 3, pp. 101-103	Chapter 13
Chapter 6	Chapter 14
Chapter 8, pp. 205-214	Chapter 17
Chapter 9, pp. 234-239	Chapter 18
	Chapter 19

Outline 4

Abnormality and Adjustment

Chapter 1, pp. 10-17	Chapter 14
Chapter 2, pp. 38-49	Chapter 15
Chapter 6	Chapter 16
Chapter 7, pp. 166-177	Chapter 17, pp. 426-437
Chapter 13	Chapter 18

Outline 5

The Individual

Chapter 1, pp. 2-10	Chapter 8
Chapter 3	Chapter 9
Chapter 4	Chapter 10
Chapter 5	Chapter 11
Chapter 6	Chapter 15
Chapter 7	

Teacher's Classroom Resources

The Teacher's Classroom Resources provide you with a wide variety of supplemental materials to enhance the classroom experience.

PROGRAM COMPONENTS INCLUDE

- Readings in Psychology
- Reproducible Lesson Plans
- Study Guide Activities
- Review Activities
- Chapter Tests
- Teaching Transparencies
- Teaching Transparencies: Strategies and Activities
- Guidebook to the Advanced Placement Test
- Application Activities
- Extension Activities

ADDITIONAL SUPPORT MATERIALS

The **Understanding Psychology Testmaker** computer software allows you to customize section, chapter, and unit tests. Use the existing data base to create tests covering one or more sections, chapters, or units. In addition, you can edit the data base questions or add your own. The software is available in Apple, Macintosh, or IBM formats.

New SAT Test Practice gives strategies and practice exercises to familiarize students with the SAT examination format.

Writer's Guidebook provides instruction and practice exercises to help students polish their writing skills.

SECTION IV
PERSONALITY AND INDIVIDUALITY

Reading 1: Personality Traits—Nature or Nurture?

The issue of whether heredity or environment plays a more important role in personality development has been hotly debated over the years. This article presents evidence in support of the importance of heredity.

The genetic makeup of a child is a stronger influence on personality than child rearing, according to the first study to examine identical twins reared in different families. The findings shatter a widespread belief among experts and laymen alike in the primacy of family influence and are sure to engender fierce debate.

The findings are the first major results to emerge from a long-term project at the University of Minnesota. Since 1979, more than 350 pairs of twins in the project have gone through six days of extensive testing that has included analysis of blood, brain waves, intelligence and allergies.

The results on personality were published in the *Journal of Personality and Social Psychology.* Although there has been wide press coverage of pairs of twins reared apart who met for the first time in the course of the study, the personality results are the first significant scientific data to be announced.

For most of the traits measured, more than half the variation was found to be due to heredity, leaving less than half determined by the influence of parents, home environment and other experiences in life.

The Minnesota findings stand in sharp contradiction to standard wisdom on nature versus nurture in forming adult personality.

Virtually all major theories [...] given far more importance t[...] nurture, than to genes, or na[...]

Even though the findings [...] influence of heredity, the f[...] the broad suggestion of pers[...] heredity. For example, a family might tend to make an innately timid child either more timid or less so. But the inference from this study is that the family would be unlikely to make the child brave.

The 350 pairs of twins studied included some who were raised apart. Among these separately reared twins were 44 pairs of identical twins and 21 pairs of fraternal twins. Comparing twins raised separately with those raised in the same home allows researchers to determine the relative importance of heredity and of environment in their development. Although some twins go out of their way to emphasize differences between them, in general identical twins are very much alike in personality.

But what accounts for that similarity? If environment were the major influence in personality, then identical twins raised in the same home would be expected to show more similarity than would the twins reared apart. But the study of 11 personality traits found differences between the kinds of twins were far smaller than had been assumed.

"If in fact twins reared apart are that similar, this study is extremely important for understanding how personality is shaped," commented Jerome [...] psychologist at Harv[...] that some aspects o[...] great degree of genet[...]

Among traits fou[...] mined by heredity w[...] prisingly, traditio[...] authority. "One woul[...]

SECTION I
LEARNING AND COGNITIVE PROCESSES

Reading 1: Molecules of Memory

In this account, researchers demonstrate that learning actually brings about physiological changes in the learner's nervous system.

In her mind, the teenage girl lying on the neurosurgeon's operating table was seven years old again, walking through a field with her brothers. The sun was shining, and she could see her brothers tramping ahead through the high grass. Then suddenly, from behind her, a man with a sack appeared and said, "How would you like to get into this bag with the snakes?" The teenager on the table screamed out in terror.

Clearly, our past lies embodied within us. The 14-year-old girl was undergoing an operation for epilepsy when an electrode probing her brain suddenly brought the terrifying childhood memory flooding back. (Although the incident sounds like some Freudian fantasy, complete with a sack full of phallic symbols, the girl's brothers attested that it really did happen; they too had witnessed it.) The event she relived with such hallucinatory vividness was evoked by electric pulses shooting through nerve cells in her cerebral cortex.

This now-famous case and others like it were first reported by American neurosurgeon Wilder Penfield in the 1930s. While they demonstrated that memories could be called up by electric stimulation of the brain, they raised far more questions than they answered: How, for example, do our experiences of the outside world—of an unmowed field in the summer sun, of a strange man with a bag of snakes—leave their traces within the cells of our brain? What miraculous substances create these cellular pieces of the past? How do we learn and remember what we learn? How, in short, do we become who we are?

In truth, the answers to these questions are still mysteries—indeed they may safely be counted among the great challenges of neuroscience. What we know is that somehow memories are kept secure within the 100 billion neurons of our brain. And we assume that the brain cells that store our memories undergo some chemical change that allows them to do so. According to today's prevailing theory, a single memory is held not within a single neuron but spread out over a vast neuronal net. Like a tile in a mosaic, each of these nerve cells represents a tiny piece of a much larger picture. But the image—the past experience—is readable only if each neuron is linked with the other relevant neurons that make up the mosaic. Destroy the connections and the memory fades into nothingness. Strengthen the connections and the memory becomes more powerful, more easily recalled.

The brain's neurons communicate with one another by pulses of electricity conducted along the fibers that stretch away from each cell. These signals in turn are passed from one nerve fiber to the next by neurotransmitters, chemical message-bearers that travel across the sliver-size gaps separating the fibers. It is at these gaps, or synapses, that the critical linkage of one nerve fiber to the next is made. And so, in some sense, it is within the pattern of signals sent across a multitude of synapses that a memory resides.

Consider the teenage girl operated on by Penfield. One summer day when she was seven, she was surprised in a field by a strange man with a bag. What happened? Light reflecting

REPRODUCIBLE LESSON PLANS let you spend less time planning and more time teaching.

Grade_____ Class(es) _____ Date(s) _____ M TU W TH F

CHAPTER 8 Lesson Plan
INFANCY AND CHILDHOOD

OBJECTIVES
_____ Describe the processes of intellectual development and Piaget's theory.
_____ Discuss the development of language.
_____ Compare the theories of social development.
_____ Summarize the cognitive-developmental theory and Kohlberg's stages of moral reasoning.

UNIT FOCUS
_____ Unit Outline, TWE, pp. 180-181
_____ Introducing the Unit, TWE, p. 180
_____ Unit Project, TWE, p. 181

CHAPTER FOCUS
_____ Motivating Activity, TWE, p. 182
_____ Meeting Chapter Objectives, TWE, p. 182
_____ Building Vocabulary, TWE, p. 182
_____ Exploring Key Ideas, TWE, p. 183
_____ In Your Journal, p. 183
_____ Extra Credit Activity, TWE, p. 183

TEACH
• GUIDED PRACTICE
_____ Activities, TWE, pp. 184-210
_____ Community Involvement, TWE, pp. 184, 204
_____ Transparencies 16, 17, 18
_____ Lab Experiments and Demonstrations, TWE, pp. 190, 192, 210-211
_____ Cooperative Learning Activities, TWE. pp. 203, 206, 208
_____ Study and Writing Skills, TWE, 189, 195, 196

Working with Graphics:
_____ Creating a Poster, TWE, p. 188
_____ Using a Time Line, TWE, p. 193
_____ Using Psychology, pp. 194, 213
_____ At a Glance, p. 203

ENT PRACTICE
E, pp. 210-213
ing Skills, TWE, p. 210
earning Activity, TWE, p. 211
Graphics:
t, TWE, p. 212
play, TWE, p. 212
in Psychology: Section 3, Reading 1

acmillan/McGraw-Hill, Inc.   **Understanding Psychology 15**

Name_____ Date _____ Class _____

CHAPTER 1 Study Guide
INTRODUCING PSYCHOLOGY

LESSON 1 pp. 2-7

Learning Key Terms
1. Write the meaning of each of the following terms:
   physiological: _____
   cognitive:_____
   norm: _____
   mnemonic devices: _____

Understanding Important Ideas
2. Write three sentences citing reasons for studying psychology. _____
_____
_____

LESSON 2 pp. 7-10

Learning Key Terms
1. Use each of the following terms in a sentence.
   psychology _____
   hypothesis _____
   applied science_____
   basic science _____
   scientific method _____

Understanding Important Ideas
2. Write four sentences describing the goals of psychologists. _____
_____
_____

LESSON 3 pp. 10-15

Learning Key Terms
1. Write the term or name that fits each description:
   a. idea that all knowledge is obtained through observation and experience_____
   b. English scientist in the 1800s who studied how heredity influences ability, character, and behavior
   _____
   c. psychologists who emphasize the investigation of observable behavior _____

Understanding Important Ideas
2. Describe how each of these individuals influenced the development of psychology.
   a. Rene Descartes_____
   b. Ivan Pavlov_____
   c. Wilhelm Wundt _____

LESSON 4 pp. 15-17

Learning Key Terms
1. Write a sentence that explains the difference between the terms "psychologist" and "psychiatrist."
_____
_____

Understanding Important Ideas
2. Name the psychologists who specialize in the fields described below.
   a. applies psychological principles to the legal system_____
   b. studies groups and the way they influence individual behavior _____
   c. develops methods to raise production and improve working conditions _____

Copyright © the Glencoe Division of Macmillan/McGraw-Hill, Inc.   **Understanding Psychology 1**

STUDY GUIDE ACTIVITIES help students master chapter information and key ideas as they read the text.

REVIEW ACTIVITIES help students focus on the main ideas and themes in each chapter.

CHAPTER 9 Review Activity

Directions: In the space at the left of each number, write the term or terms that best complete the statement.

Pages 219–229

_____ 1. The transition period between childhood and adulthood is called _____ .

_____ 2. During adolescence, individuals go through complex _____ and _____ changes.

_____ 3. _____ presented the pioneering theory of adolescence.

_____ 4. Hall characterized adolescence as a state of great " _____ and _____ ."

_____ 5. The renowned anthropologist _____ saw adolescence as a relatively smooth period in many cultures.

_____ 6. Numerous challenges or _____ face every adolescent.

_____ 7. _____ is the biological event that marks the end of childhood.

_____ 8. _____ trigger a series of internal and external changes in the adolescent.

_____ 9. The girl's first menstrual period is called the _____ .

_____ 10. In general, girls begin to mature _____ than boys.

Name _____ Date _____ Class _____

CHAPTER 5 Test

Form B

Directions: In the space at the left, write the letter of the choice that best completes the statement or answers the question. (2 points each)

_____ 1. The point at which we can discriminate two stimuli is called the
a. difference threshold
b. absolute threshold
c. Weber's Law
d. terminal threshold

_____ 2. The _____ nerve transmits sound vibrations to the brain.
a. optic   c. olfactory
b. auditory   d. semicircular

_____ 3. Which of the following is the slowest to adapt to stimulation?
a. pressure   c. cold
b. heat   d. pain

_____ 4. the absolute threshold is the amount of energy a subject can experience _____ percent of the time.
a. 100   c. 75
b. 50   d. 25

_____ 5. Weber's Law is used to measure
a. absolute thresholds
b. signal detection thresholds
c. difference thresholds
d. the response of the cones

_____ 6. Figure-ground perception is the ability to distinguish between
a. close and distant objects
b. figure and ground
c. black and white
d. reality and hallucination

_____ 7. Which of the following statements is true?
a. color blindness affects more men than women
b. color blindness is a hereditary defect affecting more women than men
c. color blindness is due to a deficiency of rods
d. color blindness is due to a deficiency in the optic nerve

_____ 8. Which of the following is not a part of signal detection theory?
a. adaptation   c. sensation
b. motivation   d. sensitivity

CHAPTER TESTS (Forms A and B) provide for evaluation of student understanding of the main facts, ideas, and critical thinking skills. The computer software Testmaker is available for Apple II, IBM, and Macintosh systems. Each of these testmakers allows you to add questions of your own.

Name _____ Date _____ Class _____

CHAPTER 17 Application Activity
TEACHER NOTES

Title:	The Influence of Image
Purpose:	To identify the messages that our clothes, posture, etc. convey.
Overview:	Students interpret the meaning that clothes, hairstyle, posture, etc. have for them and for other people.
Introduction:	Tell students that clothes, cosmetics, hairstyles, gestures, jewelry, use of perfume, etc. convey a meaning to other people. Sometimes, we intend one meaning and people perceive another.
Directions:	Tell students to list three aspects of their appearance. (The list may include clothing, jewelry, makeup, hairstyle, body language, or anything that they feel conveys a message.) For each aspect, ask students to state (1) the meaning each item is intended to convey and (2) how other people might interpret each item.
Discussion Questions:	1. After thinking about the image you present, is there anything you would like to change? (This is an open-ended question. Some students won't want to change, others will.) 2. Relate an experience in which you met somebody and immediately disliked him or her but later changed your mind. Why did you dislike the person? What changed your mind? (This is an open-ended question. Some students may say that they disliked a person initially because they were put off the person's style of dress, manner, etc. However, when they got to know the person better, they found that they liked the person.) 3. What conclusions can be drawn from this activity? (Answers will vary.)
Extension:	Point out that several popular books have been written about dressing for success in the business world. Such books are intended for men as well as women. Instruct students to read one of these books and to distinguish the suggestions that derive from principles of art and design from those that derive from psychological reasoning. Students should summarize their findings in a report on the psychology of dressing for success.

Name _____ Date _____ Class _____

CHAPTER 3 Extension Activity
PERSONALITY, COGNITION, AND MEMORY

Directions: After reading this material, answer the questions that follow.

In order to view memory and central processing of information from a clinical perspective, these functions will be described in relation to four personality types: obsessive compulsive, paranoid, hysterical, and impulsive. It should be noted that the descriptions are based on formalized categorization of actual neurotic character structures, and consequently would not be encountered in daily life in such crystallized form.

Obsessive compulsive individuals have a style of thinking marked by rigidity. While their attention is intense and sharp, it is mostly focused on detail, and they are not receptive to new facts or different points of view. This style contrasts with cognitive flexibility, which allows one to shift from the concrete and immediate to a more distant perspective and overview.

In terms of memory, obsessive compulsive individuals evidence precise, technical, and factual memories. They can assimilate and retain a high number of facts, with attention available for even the earliest memories.

The *paranoid personality* type generally manifests greater pathology than the obsessive-compulsive personality. Thinking is marked by suspiciousness coupled with a fixed and determined preoccupation with confirming such suspicious beliefs. Rigidity of thinking can be seen in the close scrutiny of new data and the intense concentration directed toward any aspect lending support to the initial suspicion. Such individuals tend to look beyond what is normally perceived, misinterpreting and distorting in rather problematic ways. Paranoid types are noted for remarkably active, intense, and searching attention narrowly directed in order to impose their own conclusions. Memory is often used in the service of collecting injustices, which are sometimes linked to an intricate system of suspicions and fears.

The *hysterical personality* type evidences a cognitive style conducive to forgetting, as it is based on global, diffuse, impressionistic perceptions. There is a general difficulty in maintaining a sharp focus of attention and concentration. Cognition is based on quick, relatively passive impressions or hunches, with a focus on the obvious or that which is immediately available. There is often a deficit in factual knowledge, and sustained intellectual curiosity is atypical.

Since memory is filtered through this type of cognitive structure, it is also impressionistic and diffuse. What is remembered may lack detail and often be embellished. This cognitive style facilitates repression, one of the basic defense mechanisms and the first to be studied by Freud.

Impulsive personality types manifest impairments in key cognitive processes, including active concentration, reflection, and abstraction. The significance of whim or impulse predominates, thus making the here-and-now a critical factor in their mental life. The initial impression becomes the final conclusion, and there is minimal shifting of attention among alternatives. The concrete and immediately impressive is focused on, and actions are executed quickly and abruptly. Impulsive people are quite deficient in goals, aims, or interest beyond immediate or short-term gratification.

Memory is discontinuous and inconsistent, as integrative and synthetic processes are minimal. Events are screened for immediate gain, and superficial involvement is evident. Distractibility prevails, and is the result of fast-paced screening.

1. Describe your own cognitive style. _____
_____
_____
_____
_____

Understanding Psychology 125

Pavlov's Experiment

Objective
° The student will understand the basis and findings of Pavlov's experiment.

Key Terms
conditioning
neutral stimulus
unconditioned stimulus
unconditioned response
conditioned stimulus
conditioned response

Introducing Transparency 1
Explain that this is an illustration of the apparatus used in Pavlov's famous st[...]
conditioning. Emphasize that the tuning fork becomes a CS (conditioned stim[...]
after training trials have paired the tuning fork and the food. In the same ma[...]
vation is called the CR (conditioned response) only after it has been conditio[...]
previously neutral stimulus like the tuning fork. Any stimulus that does not l[...]
to the intended conditioned response can become the conditioned stimulus. [...]
ever, it must be neutral with respect to the desired response.

Lesson Strategy
° Ask students to suggest other neutral stimuli that can be made to become the conditioned stimuli (instead of the tuning fork) to get the dog to salivate. (Pavlov also used a
mild electrical stimulus to the shoulder or chest of the dog.)
° Ask students to suggest stimuli that probably would not work because of the strength
of previous learning or even innate behavior. (The sound of a cat meowing or the dog's
owner whistle may elicit other responses that prevent new conditioning-they may not be
neutral.)
° Ask students to provide other examples of this kind of learning. Each student [...]
identify the original UCS, the CS, and the CR. (An example might be [...]
sound of a bell-CS-at lunchtime-UCS.)

TRANSPARENCIES vividly illuminate key ideas in psychology. Each transparency is accompanied by a Teaching Strategy page, which includes clear objectives, activities, and discussion questions. A Student Activity page allows students to analyze and evaluate each transparency.

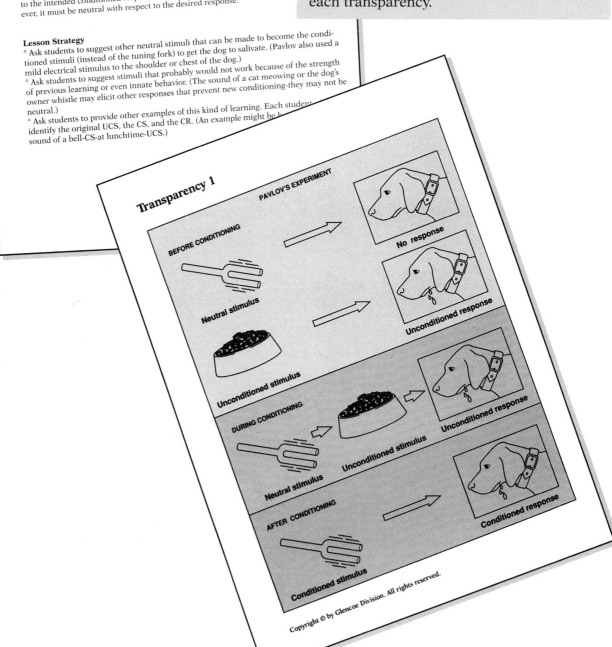

Transparency 1

PAVLOV'S EXPERIMENT

BEFORE CONDITIONING

Neutral stimulus

No response

Unconditioned response

Unconditioned stimulus

DURING CONDITIONING

Unconditioned stimulus — Unconditioned response

Neutral stimulus

AFTER CONDITIONING

Conditioned stimulus

Conditioned response

Name_____

_____Date_____

_____Class_____

STRATEGIES FOR ANSWERING ESSAY QUESTIONS

Make sure that you answer the question that has been asked. If you do not know the answer to all parts of a multipart question, answer in full those parts that you do understand and know.

Do not repeat the question when you start your answer. Each reader reads literally hundreds of essays responding to each question. All of them know the question by heart! Moreover, if you simply restate the question, you've wasted both the reader's time and your own.

Avoid repeating yourself. Write it once and move on to your next point.

Spend part of your time thinking about how your answer will be organized. It is worthwhile to outline your answer for your own benefit—perhaps on one of the back pages of your booklet. If you are unable to answer the questions completely in the time allotted, you can always refer the reader to your remaining outline, perhaps with brief notes about what additional detail you had planned to include. Although credit for outlines is not awarded, if your outline makes it clear you do understand one or more of the concepts not covered in your essay, credit may be earned.

Write your essay; do not rely on outline form. One of the things that is being graded is students' ability to express themselves effectively on a concept with psychological content. Outlines do not typically permit effective writing skill to be demonstrated.

The use of humor is fine, but try to keep it on target relative to the question you are answering.

Avoid the use of multiple examples. Readers are scoring the essays for points assigned to a master "rubric"—a listing of the important concepts, definitions, and examples that must be covered in an essay. For any intellectual point to be made, only one effective example is necessary. Multiple examples of the same concept earn no additional points, and thus waste your time.

While it is sometimes an effective strategy for students who do not know the answer to an essay question to reshape the question into one they can answer, that strategy should be avoided in the Advanced Placement essays.

You will not be able to use all of the information you have learned in developing answers for the essays. Avoid the temptation to "throw in" other information that is at best

Professional Notes

COOPERATIVE LEARNING STRATEGIES

Although Cooperative Learning is a useful teaching strategy in many subjects, it occupies a special place in the social studies curriculum because of its success in imparting the abilities needed to work effectively in a group.

Characteristics of Cooperative Learning Cooperative Learning requires careful structuring and monitoring by the teacher if it is to be something more than a group activity. Characteristics of Cooperative Learning include the following:

• Students work face to face in heterogeneous groups.
• The activity promotes a sense of positive interdependence.
• Each member of a group has individual accountability.
• The group has a common product or goal.

The Role of the Teacher Although successful Cooperative Learning groups may appear to work independently, this is no doubt due to the astute coaching of a good teacher. Students will need the teacher's help at key moments during a group project: in agreeing upon goals, in establishing a structure of accountability, and in evaluating their success.

Program Components The *Understanding Psychology* program provides many opportunities for Cooperative Learning. Every chapter includes one or more Cooperative Learning Activities designed to be completed as chapter projects.

CRITICAL THINKING SKILLS

Preparing students to think critically requires direct instruction in particular skills. Benjamin Bloom's Taxonomy of Cognitive Behavior serves as a basic organizational design that places cognitive learning into these six major hierarchal classes:

Knowledge: define, recognize, recall, identify, label, understand, examine, show, collect

Comprehension: translate, interpret, explain, describe, summarize, extrapolate

Application: apply, solve, experiment, show, predict

Analysis: connect, relate, differentiate, classify, arrange, check, group, distinguish, organize, categorize, detect, compare, infer

Synthesize: produce, propose, design, plan, combine, formulate, compose, hypothesize, construct

Evaluation: appraise, judge, criticize, decide

Since these skills build one on another, students must learn lower-level thinking skills before moving on to higher-level thinking skills.

Critical Thinking Activities To learn about a body of study in a way that prepares students to become thoughtful participants in this world, students must learn to think critically. They need to be able to evaluate and to question the meaning of what they see, read, and hear. The teacher plays a crucial role in this development by creating a classroom climate that actively encourages critical thinking. *Understanding Psychology* teaches the skills used in critical thinking, such as distinguishing between fact and opinion, identifying evidence, and interpreting point of view.

The Classroom Climate The teacher can promote critical thinking in the classroom by verbalizing the inner thought processes that take place. Asking questions such as "What do I want to achieve?" and "What do I already know?" models for students the importance of setting goals and of assessing current knowledge. Asking "Have I understood what I have read?" establishes the importance of checking one's progress as one proceeds.

AT-RISK STUDENTS

Most educators today agree that the nation's schools are facing an epidemic of students who are at risk of failure. It is difficult to define exactly what constitutes an at-risk student because being at risk is often linked to several environmental causes such as poverty, low self-esteem, substance abuse, or pregnancy. Current educational research has shown that certain teaching methods can help keep at-risk students from dropping out. One method is to maximize time-on-task to help students overcome distracting outside stimuli.

Another method is to establish high expectations and a school climate that supports learning. Many school activities involve parents in this process so that the expectations for success are not left inside the classroom after school is out. Many teachers give positive feedback at the end of each successfully completed assignment and include awards ceremonies for students who meet expectations.

Rather than emphasizing remedial techniques, many educators believe that at-risk students need to learn at a faster rate. Instruction emphasizes assets that at-risk students often bring to the classroom—interest in oral and artistic expression and kinesthetic learning abilities. For example, at-risk students may excel at dramatizations in which they also construct the sets.

THE MULTICULTURAL PERSPECTIVE

Educators use the term *multiculturalism* to describe an approach to curriculum that seeks to integrate the history and culture of different ethnic and racial groups within the framework of study. A major goal of multicultural education is to promote pride, respect, and appreciation for the cultural diversity that characterizes the United States today.

Throughout features and activities that highlight differences and similarities in human experience, *Understanding Psychology* seeks to widen students' understanding of the richness and complexity of psychology.

The following five points have been identified as some of the major goals of multicultural education:

- Promoting the strength and value of cultural diversity
- Promoting human rights and respect for those who are different from oneself
- Promoting alternative life choices for people
- Promoting social justice and equal opportunity for all people
- Promoting equity in the distribution of power among groups

PERFORMANCE ASSESSMENT

In response to the growing demand for accountability in the classroom, many educators are advocating new approaches to assessment. One such approach is authentic assessment, which measures student achievement in a more constructive and interactive manner than traditional tests. In general, authentic assessment includes performance-based assessment and portfolios.

Performance tests ask students to effectively and creatively apply the knowledge they have gained. These tests require the application of problem-solving skills rather than mere recall. Instead of using a multiple-choice test to assess knowledge of a specific battle, for example, a performance-based test asks students to write a first-person account of the battle. In designing performance-based tests, educators devise tasks that have more than one correct answer and which require more than one step to complete. A key element in scoring such tests is to analyze the **process** the students use to clarify and solve the problem. Scoring involves rating students' performance on multiple factors, resulting in a descriptive profile of performance.

The portfolio approach is often used with performance-based assessment. Portfolios contain samples of students' work collected over a period of time—an entire grading period or even a semester. Students often help choose which items will be included in their portfolios.

Portfolios allow for assessing a broader range of skills than traditional tests. Students can see how much progress they are making by comparing the work that they have completed throughout the course.

In Your Journal is a writing activity included on chapter opening pages of the student edition. This journal and the follow-up writing assignment found in every Chapter Review may be used in a portfolio approach along with other activities the teacher and students choose. In addition, an activity is presented on every chapter opening planning guide that can serve as a basis for a performance assessment activity.

UNDERSTANDING
PSYCHOLOGY

RICHARD A. KASSCHAU, PH.D.

GLENCOE
McGraw-Hill

New York, New York   Columbus, Ohio   Mission Hills, California   Peoria, Illinois

AUTHOR

Richard A. Kasschau, Ph.D., is Professor of Psychology at the University of Houston. Dr. Kasschau is a member of the American Educational Research Association, the American Psychological Association, and the American Psychological Society. He has written extensively for magazines, newspapers, and professional journals. An award-winning and distinguished teacher who has taught psychology for more than 20 years, Dr. Kasschau was the 1993 winner of the University of Houston's Teaching Excellence Award.

ACADEMIC CONSULTANTS

Samuel Cameron, Ph.D.
Department of Psychology
Beaver College
Glenside, Pennsylvania

James Devine, Ph.D.
Department of Psychology
University of Texas at El Paso
El Paso, Texas

David J. Pittenger, Ph.D.
Chair, Department of Psychology
Marietta College
Marietta, Ohio

Charles Prokop, Ph.D.
Dean of Psychology
Florida Institute of Technology
Melbourne, Florida

TEACHER REVIEWERS

Karla R. Galindo
Harlandale High School
San Antonio, Texas

Kay Geiger
Lubbock High School
Lubbock, Texas

Joe McCuistion
Auburn High School
Auburn, Washington

James J. Mills
Williamsville South High School
Williamsville, New York

Ruth C. Newhouse
Lakeview Centennial High School
Garland, Texas

Vi Stemmer
Burnsville Senior High School
Burnsville, Minnesota

Kathryn G. Williams
Richland Northeast High School
Richland County School District 2
Columbia, South Carolina

Send all inquiries to:
Glencoe/McGraw-Hill
936 Eastwind Drive
Westerville, Ohio 43081

ISBN 0-02-823155-4 (Student Edition)
ISBN 0-02-823171-6 (Teacher's Wraparound Edition)
Printed in the United States of America

2 3 4 5 6 7 8 9 10 QPK/MC   00 99 98 97 96 95 94

Contents

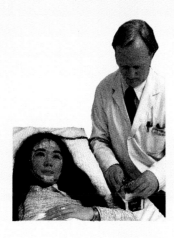 

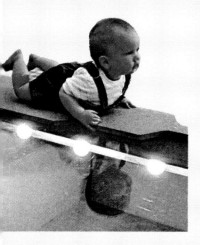

SPECIAL FEATURES

At A Glance

Using Psychology

CHAPTER 1

Introducing Psychology

TEXT TOPICS	SPECIAL FEATURES	RESOURCE MATERIALS
Why Study Psychology?, pp. 3–7		▰ Reproducible Lesson Plan; Study Guide; Review Activity
Overview of Psychology, pp. 7–10		▰ Reproducible Lesson Plan; Study Guide; Review Activity ▮ *Readings in Psychology:* Introducing Psychology, Reading 1
A Brief History of Psychology, pp. 10–15	**More about Psychology,** p. 12 **Psychology Update,** p. 14	▰ Reproducible Lesson Plan; Study Guide; Review Activity; Application Activity ▮ *Readings in Psychology:* Introducing Psychology, Reading 2
Psychology as a Profession, pp. 15–17	**Fact or Fiction?,** p. 15	▰ Reproducible Lesson Plan; Study Guide; Review Activity; Extension Activity; Chapter Tests, Form A and Form B ◉ Understanding Psychology Testmaker

PERFORMANCE ASSESSMENT ACTIVITY

Assign students to bring in a magazine picture or photo that displays some distinct kind of behavior. To guide students, you may wish to explain that the picture might show a very obvious show of emotion such as anger, fear, or happiness. Assign students to write a paragraph of at least 150 words explaining the factors that might cause or contribute to this behavior. (Most students will draw upon their own personal experience.) Collect these assignments, and redistribute them at the end of the chapter. At that time, have students look at the pictures through the eyes of a psychologist. Have them rewrite their paragraphs from this perspective. Call on students to explain any changes in the way they saw or analyzed the picture. (Comments should reflect knowledge of some of the analytical methods mentioned in the chapter.)

CHAPTER RESOURCES

Readings for the Student

Clayton, Lawrence. *Careers in Psychology.* Baltimore: Rosen Publishing Group, 1992.

McCain, G., and Segal, E. M. *The Game of Science.* Belmont, CA: Brooks/Cole, 1988.

Stratton, Peter and Hayes, Nicky. *A Student's Dictionary of Psychology.* New York: Routledge Chapman & Hall, 1993.

Readings for the Teacher

Baxter, Pam M. *Psychology: A Guide to Reference and Information Sources.* Englewood, CO: Libraries Unlimited Resources, 1993.

Hunt, Morton. *The Story of Psychology.* New York: Doubleday, 1993.

Kaplan, Harold and Sadock, Benjamin. *Comprehensive Glossary of Psychiatry and Psychology.* Baltimore: Williams & Wilkins, 1991.

Ludy, Benjamin T., Jr. *A History of Psychology: Original Sources and Contemporary Research.* New York: McGraw-Hill, 1988.

Pettijohn, Terry F., ed. *The Encyclopedic Dictionary of Psychology,* 4th ed. Guilford, CT: Duskhin Publishing Group, 1991.

Multimedia

Discovering Psychology: Past, Present, and Promise. Produced by WGBH Boston in association with the American Psychological Association (VHS).

The Evolution of a Clinical Psychologist. Jeffrey Norton (Audiotape).

Search and Research. Harvard Medical School Mental Health Training Film, Psychological Films.

For additional resources, see the bibliography beginning on page 530.

FOCUS

Motivating Activity

Students often begin their study of psychology with only a fuzzy image of a psychologist. Many assume that all psychologists deal with abnormal emotional disturbances. You might investigate student assumptions by brainstorming a list of all the traits and functions associated with the word *psychologist*. To encourage spontaneity, set a three-minute time limit. Record all student responses on the chalkboard. Based on these responses, request volunteers to complete the following sentence: "A psychologist is a person who _____ ." Save the brainstorming and sentences for review at the end of the chapter. Challenge students to identify any stereotypes that they held prior to reading.

Meeting Chapter Objectives.

Identify the main subjects in each objective on page 3. Have groups of students prepare data sheets on each of these subjects as they read Chapter 1.

Building Vocabulary.

Call on students to create or read aloud definitions of each of the Key Terms in the Glossary. Challenge volunteers to use these terms in a sentence.

Introducing Psychology

FIGURE 1.1 Studying psychology can help you gain a perspective on your own behavior.

2

TEACHER CLASSROOM RESOURCES

- Chapter 1 Reproducible Lesson Plan
- Chapter 1 Study Guide
- Chapter 1 Review Activity
- Chapter 1 Application Activity
- Chapter 1 Extension Activity

- *Readings in Psychology:*
  Introducing Psychology,
  Readings 1, 2

- Chapter 1 Test, Form A and Form B

- Understanding Psychology
  Testmaker

Exploring Key Ideas

Defining Psychology.
Copy the following definition of psychology on the chalkboard: "A scientific study of behavior and mental processes." Then dissect this definition further. Ask: What is meant by each of these phrases: *scientific study, behavior,* and *mental processes*? Next, direct students to the first two objectives on this page. What topics or questions do they expect to explore in a psychology class? Use this discussion to introduce students to "In Your Journal."

After studying this chapter, you should be able to

- describe the range of topics that are covered in an introductory course in psychology.
- cite the questions psychologists ask and describe how research is performed.
- explain important trends within psychology.
- summarize the careers and specialized fields in psychology.

applied science
basic science
cognitive
hypothesis
introspection
physiological
psychiatry
psychology

W hat is it that fascinates psychologists about ordinary behavior? What exactly do they study? One way to answer this question is to look at a slice of life through a psychologist's eyes.

Ruth, a college student, decides to have lunch at the school cafeteria. She walks to the cafeteria, gets in line, chooses tuna salad and orange juice, and pays at the counter. She then looks around for someone with whom to sit. She doesn't see any close friends, so she goes to a table by herself, sits down, and begins to eat.

A few minutes later, Gary, a fellow student in Ruth's English class, comes over to join her. When Ruth looks up at him, she no longer feels like eating. She thinks Gary is good-looking, but he never speaks to Ruth unless he has missed a class and wants to borrow her notes. She greets him coolly, but Gary sits down anyway and begins to tell a long, rambling story about *A Visit from the Little Green People,* the horror movie he stayed up to watch on TV last night. Meanwhile, Ruth remembers that Gary missed English class and catches him eyeing her notebook.

Ruth fantasizes dumping her lunch on Gary's neatly groomed hair, but instead she gets up to leave. Gary attempts a casual smile and asks to borrow her notes. Now Ruth is more than annoyed. Although her English notebook is in plain sight, she tells him curtly that she is sorry

In Your Journal

Think about your personal reasons for studying psychology. Write an entry in your journal of at least 100 words describing what you hope to gain from this experience.

In Your Journal

Explain to students that "In Your Journal" is an ongoing feature of this program. You might point out that the journal will help them to explore their own behavior and mental processes—the two main areas of psychological investigation. Encourage students to record any observations they wish during the term. Allow time during the term to have students raise issues or observations from their journals for discussion. To begin this exercise, have students imagine they are psychologists investigating the reasons students sign up for their first psychology class. Assign them to write a series of interview questions for this project. Students can either answer these questions themselves or use them to interview each other.

EXTRA CREDIT ACTIVITY

Request several students to investigate the available resources on psychology in your school or community library. Suggest that they see if the library carries special interest magazines such as *Psychology Today, American Psychologist,* or *Scientific American.* Also, tell students to check the number of books on psychology in the card catalog. Does the library have a large collection? If so, what are some of the subheadings in the card catalog? What other references can the librarian recommend? Have students report their findings to the class.

TEACH

Guided Practice

■ **Creating a Chart.** Tell students that when people use the word *behavior* they generally mean *conduct*—or the way a person acts. Next, point out that behavior can be either *voluntary* or *involuntary*. Assign students to make a chart in which they give examples of each of these categories of behavior. Then have them read or reread the opening story about Ruth. How would students classify each of the behaviors cited? (OBJECTIVE 1)

VISUAL INSTRUCTION

Ask students to imagine they are psychologists looking at this scene (the photograph on page 4). What types of behavior can they identify? What visual clues did they use to formulate their answers?

Answer to caption, Figure 1.2: One reason is to get a better understanding of ourselves and others.

FIGURE 1.2

Where we might see two people sitting and talking, a psychologist might see a sequence of complex behaviors. **Why are students attracted to the study of psychology?**

but she has left her notes in the library—to which, as a matter of fact, she must return right away. As she leaves the cafeteria, she glances back and sees Gary still sitting at the table. He looks depressed. Suddenly, she feels a bit depressed herself.

This is a simple story, but from a psychologist's point of view, the behavior was complex. First of all, Ruth decided to have lunch because of her **physiological** (physical) state—she was hungry. She may also have been motivated by **cognitive** (mental) elements—she knew she must eat now because she had classes scheduled for the next several hours. When she entered the cafeteria, she *perceived* sensory stimuli different from those outside, but she paid little attention to the new sights, sounds, and smells, except to note that the food smelled good and the line was mercifully short. She went through the line and paid for her food—*learned behavior* similar to that of a hungry rat that runs a maze for a food reward.

Ruth looked for a *social group* to join, but found none to which she belonged. She sat alone until Gary joined her. He felt free to do so because in most schools and colleges there is an informal rule, or *norm*, that students who have a class together may approach each other socially. This rule usually does not apply to looser collections of people, such as commuters who ride the same bus. Ruth *remembered* how Gary had behaved toward her in the past and realized that he was about to follow the same note-borrowing routine. This triggered the *emotional* reaction of anger. However, she did not dump her food on his head as a 2-year-old might have done, but acted in a way that was more appropriate to her stage of *development*. We can assume that her response was characteristic of her *personality:* she told the young man that she didn't have the notes (even though he had seen them) and left.

MEETING SPECIAL NEEDS

Study Strategy. Students with special learning needs may profit by getting an overview of the book's organization. Use the Table of Contents to point out major divisions and sub-divisions. Have students look for any special features or reference tools such as an index or glossary. Suppose students wanted to look up a definition of psychology. What feature of the text would they use? *(glossary)* Where would they look to find data on Sigmund Freud? *(index)* Where would they turn to find the major topics covered in the book? *(table of contents)*

If such situations occurred often, and if they were followed by depression, either student's behavior could indicate psychological *disturbance*. If Gary relied on others for help and manipulated people to get his way, his behavior might be a sign of a personality disorder. So might Ruth's, since she interprets simple requests as demands but finds herself unable either to meet or refuse the request in a direct way. However, in this context, neither student's behavior seems *abnormal*.

Viewed in this way, an apparently simple event raises many questions about why people behave and feel as they do. How is their behavior influenced by their physiological states? What motivates them to choose one action instead of another? Most topics covered in this book are reflected in the many ways psychologists analyze behavior.

WHY STUDY PSYCHOLOGY?

You might be studying psychology to gain a better understanding of people, or you might be studying it for more specific and personal reasons. As you read this book, you will discover new ways of looking at and interpreting your behavior. Daily events you might ordinarily take for granted may now become fuel for thought. Learning about psychology can help you gain a better understanding of your own behavior, knowledge about how psychologists study human and animal behavior, and practical applications for enriching your life.

Insight

Psychology can provide useful insight into behavior. For example, suppose a student is convinced that he is hopelessly shy and doomed forever to feel uncomfortable in groups. Then he learns through social psychology that different kinds of groups tend to have different effects on their members. He thinks about this. He notes that, although he is miserable at parties, he feels fine at meetings of the school newspaper staff and in the group he works with in the biology laboratory (in technical terms, he is much more uncomfortable in unstructured social groups than in structured, task-oriented groups). Realizing that he is uncomfortable only in some groups brings relief. He is not paralyzingly shy; he just does not like unstructured groups. He is not alone in his feelings—and thinking about his feelings helps him gain confidence in himself.

There is something to learn about each of us in *Understanding Psychology*. You, too, may find that because of something you read or discuss, you see yourself in a new way.

Of course, you must be careful in applying your new insight. Few people are more obnoxious than the student who has had one psychology course and proceeds to terrorize family, friends, and strangers with an analysis of every action. Many puppies and kittens have become the targets of a psychology student's newly learned training methods.

ADDITIONAL INFORMATION

More than 100 years ago, Hermann Ebbinghaus found that studying a list of new information once a day for several days led to better recall than studying that same list several times in one day. Other researchers have corroborated that *spaced practice* can result in better learning than *massed practice*. Ask students to analyze why this is so.

■ **Analyzing a Quote.** Tell students that psychologist John B. Watson once said:

Give me a dozen healthy infants . . . and my own specified world to bring them up in and I'll guarantee to take any one and train him or her to become any type of specialist I might want to select. . . .

Ask: How does this quote reflect the idea of *shaping?* Do students agree or disagree with this theory? What, if any, are the limits of shaping? If John Watson is correct, is there such a thing as free will? (OBJECTIVE 2)

VISUAL INSTRUCTION

You might have students redraw this cartoon showing negative reinforcement. **Answer to caption, Figure 1.3:** Shaping is a systematic way in which we dispense rewards and punishment.

"A little learning is a dangerous thing," according to an old cliché, but the more psychology you study, the more respect you will gain for the complexity and diversity of human and animal behavior. An introductory psychology course is just one investment in a lifelong process of education about yourself and others.

Practical Information

Most of the chapters in this book include material that has a practical application in everyday life. You will learn concrete and detailed ways to carry out a number of useful procedures psychologists have developed.

For example, Chapter 2 describes the systematic way of dispensing rewards and punishments that psychologists call *shaping* (Figure 1.3). You will definitely find this useful if you ever have to train a puppy. You may find yourself wondering how you are shaping the behavior of people around you. Perhaps you have two friends who are always happy to join you for a soda or a movie but who never bring any money along. You have loaned them money many times and, just as many times, they have failed to pay you back. You know they can afford to pay their share, and you have repeatedly told them so. They are good friends, however, so you end up paying their way again and again. In doing so, you are rewarding or reinforcing an undesirable behavior pattern. Is that what you really want to do?

Chapter 3 includes a description of several *mnemonic devices,* or memory aids, that help you retain information. The poem beginning "Thirty days has September," which helps many people remember the number of days in each month, is an example. With mnemonic devices, you usually associate each item on a list with something easier to remember, such as a picture, rhyme, or phrase. Although this may require time and effort, memory experts have shown that it is worth the trouble. The techniques described may help you memorize almost any list of words or numbers—the names of the Presidents of the United States and their dates in office (for a

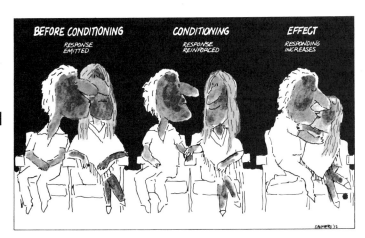

FIGURE 1.3

Kissing is a response that is subject to shaping. Here the response is emitted tentatively and would probably be repeated only after a considerable time if it produced no result. The kiss is reinforced, however, and immediately the response increases in frequency and in vigor. **How do psychologists define shaping?**

CONNECTIONS: PSYCHOLOGY AND LANGUAGE ARTS

Ask students to use a dictionary to look up the origin of the word *mnemonic.* (from the Greek *mnemonikos,* for "mindful") Challenge students to write some mnemonic device to keep the class "mindful" of the four goals of psychological research: description, explanation, prediction, and control. For tips, refer students ahead to information on mnemonic devices in Chapter 3. Hold a class vote to decide which mnemonic device students find most useful.

history course), vocabulary terms, the authors and titles of books (for an English course), telephone numbers, shopping lists, and so on.

In reading about child development in Chapter 8, you may recall similar experiences you had in your own childhood. Chapter 15, on disturbance and breakdown, may help you understand difficult periods in your own life and in the lives of those around you. Chapter 16 will tell you about the different kinds of therapy available to people who are experiencing severe or chronic difficulties. Of course, you should not jump to conclusions on the basis of this introduction to psychology. It takes a trained professional to diagnose and treat developmental and psychological problems, as explained in Chapter 16.

OVERVIEW OF PSYCHOLOGY

Defining Psychology

Psychology is the scientific study of behavior and mental processes. Such study can involve both animal and human behaviors. When applied to humans, psychology covers everything that people think, feel, and do. Psychologists differ in how much importance they place on specific types of behavior. For example, some psychologists believe that you should study only behavior that you can see, observe, or measure directly. Ruth's behavior of selecting and paying for her food, choosing a table, and refusing to lend her notes to Gary are all examples of observable behaviors. Some psychologists believe that our fantasies, thoughts, and feelings are also important, even though these behaviors are not directly observable. Ruth may infer or guess that Gary is sad by the expression on his face, but she cannot actually know his emotional reaction.

While psychologists may differ on which kinds of behavior are important, they do agree that the study of behavior must be systematic. The use of a systematic method of asking and answering questions about why people think, act, and feel as they do reduces the chances of coming to false conclusions. Consider the old story of the blind men and the elephant. A long time ago, three very wise, but blind men were out on a journey when they came across a sleeping elephant. Because they could not see the elephant, they did not know what was blocking their way so they set about to discover what they could about the obstacle. As it happened, each man put his hands on a different section of the elephant, examining it in great detail and with much thought. The first man, having felt the elephant's trunk, described a creature that was long, wormlike, and quite flexible. "No, no! You must be mistaken," said the second man who was seated astride the elephant, "This creature is wide, very round, and does not move very much." The man who was holding one of the elephant's tusks added his description of a small, hard, pointed creature. Each of these men was correct in his description of what he felt, but in order to understand the elephant fully, they needed to combine their accumulated knowledge. The study of human behavior is similar. Many different approaches are necessary to understand the complex richness of human behavior.

Many different approaches are necessary to understand the complex richness of behavior.

■ **Discussion.** Call on a volunteer to read aloud the story about the three blind men and the elephant. Ask: What is the lesson of this story in terms of the study of psychology? *(To understand people, you need to study all aspects of human behavior.)* Do students agree with the idea that dreams, feelings, and fantasies are also an important part of human behavior? Why or why not? (OBJECTIVE 2)

Teacher Note. You might introduce your students to the term *naturalistic observation.* (analyzing the behavior of humans and other animals in their environment) Ask students to assess the advantages and disadvantages of naturalistic observation. Why might some psychologists prefer *controlled observation,* or observation done under laboratory conditions? Again referring to the story about the elephant, can students think of any situations in which both types of observation might be necessary?

DID YOU KNOW?

The word *psychology* comes from the Greek word *psyche* ("mind" or "soul") and *logia* ("study").

CONNECTIONS: PSYCHOLOGY AND LITERATURE

Tell students that many fairy tales and fables end with a moral, or lesson about right or wrong behavior. Request volunteers to reread a tale told to them as a child. What behaviors can they identify in the story? What was the moral? How might the story shape a child's behavior? Call on students to share both the story and their analysis of the story with the class as a whole.

■ **Research.** Remind students that one of the goals of this course is to learn the "whys" and "hows" of psychological research. Another goal is for students to gain a better understanding of themselves and others. To give students a chance to pursue these goals, write the following question on the chalkboard: "What, if any, misconceptions do people hold about psychological research?" Then have students answer and evaluate their answers to the questions on this page.

Next, have students prepare copies of the questions for use in a survey outside the classroom. Tell students to add one additional item: "Have you ever taken a psychology course?" Assign students to use the questions to poll friends. Based on the survey, challenge students to identify common misconceptions about psychological research. How did survey results compare to their own misconceptions? Were there any differences in the responses from people with a background in psychology? What conclusions can students form on the basis of their research? (OBJECTIVE 2)

VISUAL INSTRUCTION

See activity above for suggested use of Figure 1.4.

We each like to think we understand people. We spend time observing others (and ourselves) and form conclusions about people from our daily interactions. Sometimes the conclusions we draw, however, are not accurate because we are not systematic in our "study." Check the accuracy of some of your conclusions by responding true or false to the statements in Figure 1.4. Then compare your answers with the correct ones found on page 16.

The Scientific Basis of Psychology

Psychologists rely on the *scientific method*. This means that they reach their conclusions by identifying a specific problem or question, formulating a hypothesis, collecting data through observation and experiment, and analyzing the data.

By asking specific, well-defined questions, psychologists can gain insight into the behavior they are studying. Forming a *hypothesis* to explain the behavior is also a basic method of research. A **hypothesis** is an "educated guess"—the researcher has some evidence for suspecting a specific answer. In a hypothesis, researchers state what they expect to find, expressed in such a way that it can be proved or disproved. A psychologist might, for example, make the following hypothesis: People who have similar opinions on important issues in their lives are more likely to be attracted to each other than people who have very different opinions. The psychologist would then test the hypothesis in a way that would enable him or her to collect data. A survey might be conducted, for example, or questionnaires sent out. Finally, the psychologist would analyze the data (see Chapter 20). The hypothesis might prove to be wrong—that is, the

FIGURE 1.4

Test your intuitions about behavior by answering true or false to the statements below. Turn to page 16 to check your answers.

1. The behavior of most lower animals—insects, reptiles and amphibians, most rodents, and birds—is instinctive and unaffected by learning.
2. For the first week of life, a baby sees nothing but a gray blur regardless of what he or she "looks at."
3. A child learns to talk more quickly if the adults around the child habitually repeat the word he or she is trying to say, using proper pronunciation.
4. The best way to get a chronically noisy child to settle down and pay attention is to punish him or her.
5. Slow learners remember more of what they learn than fast learners.
6. Highly intelligent people—"geniuses"—tend to be physically frail and socially isolated.
7. On the average, you cannot predict from a person's grades at school and college whether he or she will do well in a career.
8. Most stereotypes are completely true.
9. In small amounts, alcohol is a stimulant.
10. LSD causes chromosome damage.
11. The largest drug problem in the United States, in terms of the number of people affected, is marijuana.
12. Psychiatry is a subdivision of psychology.
13. Most mentally retarded people are also mentally ill.
14. A third or more of the people suffering from severe mental disorders are potentially dangerous.
15. Electroshock therapy is an outmoded technique rarely used in today's mental hospitals.
16. The more severe the disorder, the more intensive the therapy required to cure it; for example, schizophrenics usually respond best to psychoanalysis.
17. Nearly all the psychological characteristics of men and women appear to be inborn; in all cultures, for example, women are more emotional and sexually less aggressive than men.
18. No reputable psychologist "believes in" such irrational phenomena as ESP, hypnosis, or the bizarre mental and physical achievements of Eastern yogis.

STUDY AND WRITING SKILLS

After students have identified the incorrect statements in Figure 1.4, assign them to do research into one or more of these topics. Have students present their findings in a short essay entitled: "Setting the Record Straight." Each essay should begin with the incorrect statement being addressed. If possible, distribute copies of these essays to the class as a whole. Ask: How do these essays dispel commonly held misconceptions?

researcher may conclude that there are no differences between those with similar and those with opposing opinions.

There are many hypotheses, but real answers to questions such as who attracts whom are arrived at only through general agreement achieved by experts after years of research on many different aspects of a problem.

The Goals of Psychology

As psychologists go about their systematic and scientific study of humans and animals, they have several goals. Overall, psychologists seek to do four things—describe, explain, predict, and control behavior.

Description. The first task for any scientist or psychologist is to gather information about the behavior being studied and to present what is known. For example, we described Ruth's behavior in the cafeteria.

Explanation. Psychologists are not content to simply state the facts. Rather, they also seek to explain why people (or animals) behave as they do. Psychologists propose these explanations as hypotheses. As research studies designed to test each *hypothesis* are completed, more complex explanations called theories are constructed. A *theory* is usually a complex explanation, based on findings from a large number of experimental studies assembled to explain the results. Such theories change as new data improves our understanding, and a good theory becomes the source of additional ideas for experiments. Theories allow us to describe and to explain observed behavior.

Prediction. The third goal of psychologists is to predict, as a result of accumulated knowledge, what organisms will do, and in the case of humans, what they will think or feel in various situations. By studying descriptive and theoretical accounts of past behaviors, psychologists can predict subsequent behaviors.

Control. Finally, some psychologists seek to influence or control behavior in helpful ways. Other psychologists are conducting studies with a long-term goal to find out more about human or animal behavior. They are doing **basic science,** or research. Other psychologists are more interested in discovering ways to use what we already know about people to benefit others. They view psychology as an **applied science** and are using psychological principles to solve more immediate problems.

Psychologists who study the ability of infants to perceive visual patterns are doing basic research. They would not be concerned with the implication their findings might have on the design of a crib. Psychologists studying rapid eye movement in sleep research are also involved in basic science. If they discover that one individual has a sleep disturbance, they will try to understand and explain the situation, but they will not try to correct it. That is a job for applied scientists, such as clinical psychologists. An example of a psychologist involved in applying psychological principles rather than discovering them is a consultant to a toy manufacturer.

Psychologists seek to influence or control behavior in helpful ways.

■ **Creating a Chart.** Tell students that a flowchart shows the various steps in an idea or process. Based on material in "The Goals of Psychology," have students create a flowchart depicting the various stages in the psychological research process. Tell students to show the "flow" of stages with arrows. Display some of these charts around the room. For enrichment, students might write a paper applying these steps to a "slice of life" similar to Ruth's story. Step 4, control, should be an "average," or typical, slice of life. (OBJECTIVE 2)

Teacher Note. You might want to clarify differences among the terms *psychology, psychoanalysis, parapsychology,* and other fields with similar word roots. Request volunteers to design posters or charts that visually depict distinctions among these fields.

DID YOU KNOW?

Psychiatrists have an M.D. degree. Psychologists, on the other hand, have an M.A., a Psy.D., or a Ph.D. degree. Psychiatrists can dispense medical prescriptions and perform operations. Select psychologists can dispense medical prescriptions.

CRITICAL THINKING ACTIVITY

Classifying Information. Tell students that not all psychologists see psychology as a science. Some consider it an "art." Such psychologists claim that creativity and intuition play as much of a role in psychology as hard-and-fast scientific laws. Challenge students to list all the functions and tasks performed by psychologists. Then have them classify each of these functions as an "art," a "science," or some other category of activity altogether.

■ Designing a Time Line.
Distribute pieces of newsprint, posterboard, or computer paper. Working in groups, have students design a time line showing some of the major events in the history of psychology. Based on the completed time lines, ask: What major changes or trends can you identify within the field? You might compile a master time line for the wall. As the course continues, have students add pivotal dates. (OBJECTIVE 3)

VISUAL INSTRUCTION

Tell students to cover the picture caption on page 10 with their hand. Glancing quickly at the picture, what do they see? Now use the visual prompt provided in the caption. How does the cue alter student perceptions? **Answer to caption, Figure 1.5:** Looking at only one view of a problem prevents a researcher from seeing or studying other aspects of a problem. (Thus, any solutions are likely to be more limited—and perhaps less effective.)

■ Reteach.
Have students complete the Chapter 1 Study Guide Activity, pages 5–10. For extended review, assign the Chapter 1 Review Activity, pages 5–10, as homework or an in-class activity.

FIGURE 1.5

This engraving depicts a forest scene, doesn't it? If you answer yes, it may be because you looked only at the "framed area." If we had said, "Look at the muddy road," you would have seen that the forest is simply a reflection in a puddle. **What problems may occur when a researcher accepts one theoretical view?**

Although both types of psychologists are scientists, this distinction remains important. Why? Because the transfer of findings from basic to applied science can be tricky. The following example illustrates this.

Psychologists doing basic research have found that babies raised in institutions such as orphanages are seriously retarded in their physical, intellectual, and emotional development. Wayne Dennis (1960), among others, traces this to the fact that these babies have nothing to look at but a blank, white ceiling and white crib cushions, and are handled only when they need to be fed or changed. However, we have to be very careful not to apply this finding too broadly. Because children who lack stimulation tend to develop poorly does not mean that, by providing them with maximum stimulation, they will grow up emotionally sound and intellectually superior. Quite the contrary, most babies do best with a medium level of stimulation (White, 1969). Even more significantly, social interaction seems much more important than visual stimulation. Normal development is more likely to result from long-term interactions with a responsive caregiver (Shaffer, 1993). Basic science provides specific findings: what happened in one study conducted at one time and in one place. To generalize these specific findings into a list of general rules is misleading.

Understanding Psychology focuses on psychology as a basic research science. The research findings provide the foundations on which practical applications are built. However, we sample the range of applications in psychology by including many subsections called "Using Psychology."

A BRIEF HISTORY OF PSYCHOLOGY

Even though psychology is one of the newer sciences, the study of behavior began with the ancient Greek philosophers. In the fifth and sixth centuries B.C., they began to study human behavior and decided that

CONNECTIONS: PSYCHOLOGY AND THE MEDIA

Assign students to "observe" the characters in a television program, movie, or video of their own choosing. As they watch, have students record notes on some of the observed behaviors. What factors shaped these behaviors? Have students share their observations. In a follow-up discussion, ask: How did this activity influence the way you viewed the media? What was different about the way you watched this TV show or movie?

people's lives were dominated not so much by the gods as by their own minds: people were rational.

These early philosophers attempted to interpret the world they observed around them in terms of human perceptions—objects were hot or cold, wet or dry, hard or soft, and these qualities influenced people's experience of them. Although the Greek philosophers did not rely on systematic study, they did set the stage for the development of the sciences, including psychology, through their reliance on observation as a means of knowing their world.

In the mid-1500s, Nicolaus Copernicus published the idea that the earth was not the center of the universe, but revolved around the sun. In doing this, Copernicus introduced observation as a key element of the scientific procedures that began to develop. Later, Galileo Galilei used a telescope to confirm predictions about star position and movement based on Copernicus's work. Thus was introduced the modern concept of experimentation through observation.

Seventeenth century philosophers popularized the idea of *dualism*, the concept that the mind and body are separate and distinct. The French philosopher René Descartes disagreed, however, claiming that a link existed between mind and body. He reasoned that the mind controlled the body's movements, sensations, and perceptions. His approach to understanding human behavior was based on the assumption that the mind and body influence each other to create a person's experiences. Exactly how this interaction takes place is still being studied today.

"Modern science began to emerge by combining philosophers' reflections, logic, and mathematics with the observations and inventiveness of practical people" (Hilgard, 1987, p. 7). By the nineteenth century, biologists had announced the discovery of cells as the building blocks of life. Later, chemists developed the Periodic Table of elements and physicists made great progress in furthering our understanding of atomic forces. Many natural scientists were studying complex phenomena by reducing them to simpler parts. It was in this environment that the science of psychology was formed.

Psychology as a Discipline

Structuralism.   The establishment of psychology as a separate, formal field of study is widely thought to have begun in 1879 in Leipzig, Germany, when Wilhelm Wundt started his Laboratory of Psychology. Although he was trained in physiology—the study of how the body works—Wundt's real interest was in the study of the human mind. In his laboratory, he modeled his research on the mind after that in other natural sciences he had studied. He developed a method of self-observation called **introspection** to collect information about the mind. In carefully controlled situations, trained subjects reported their thoughts, and Wundt tried to map out the basic structure of thought processes. Wundt's experiments were very important historically, not so much because he advanced our understanding of the

■ **Summarizing Information.** Assign groups of students to design a basic handbook of psychology. The first part of the book should include key definitions from Chapter 1. (Encourage students to include any words that they learned in addition to those set in boldface or italicized type.) The second part of the book should list and describe the specialized fields or disciplines within psychology. The third part should summarize career options in psychology. Encourage students to illustrate at least some of the entries. (OBJECTIVE 4)

PORTRAIT

Wilhelm Wundt
1832–1920
Born in Neckarau, Germany, Wundt showed little interest in scholarship. As a child and teenager, Wundt nearly failed to finish school because of his penchant for daydreaming. Nobody could guess that in 1855 the daydreamer would rank first on the state medical examinations. Nor could they know that his "institute," as Wundt called his laboratory, would become a magnet for the leading psychologists of the day. To Wundt, all sound psychological theory rested upon experimental science. What did he think of the methods employed by his rival William James? Said Wundt: "It is literature, it is beautiful, but it is not psychology."

CRITICAL THINKING ACTIVITY

Making Comparisons. Tell students that Hippocrates, the Greek "father of medicine," once said: "Men ought to know that from the brain, and the brain only, arise our pleasures, joys, laughter, and jests, as well as our sorrows, pains, grief, and tears." Challenge students to compare this view of behavior to those of other psychological pioneers mentioned in the chapter. Which people would be *most* likely to agree with Hippocrates? Which would be *least* likely to agree?

Independent Practice

■ **Study and Writing Skills.** Read aloud the following remark made by Freud near the end of his life.

Looking back, then, over the patchwork of my life's labors, I can say that I have made many beginnings and thrown out many suggestions. . . . I can [only] . . . hope that I have opened up a pathway for an important advance in our knowledge.

Ask students how Freud opened the door to new topics of inquiry. Then assign them to research other pioneers mentioned in this chapter. In short written reports, have students describe the subjects, questions, and methods raised or introduced by each of these figures. (OBJECTIVES 1, 2)

■ **Cooperative Learning Activity.** Refer students to the special feature in the margin on this page. Then, have students work in small groups and challenge them to create a dialogue in which a physiological psychologist explains his or her methodology to Freud. As a prewriting activity, have students list some of Freud's possible questions or reactions. Request group members to share their dialogues.

MORE about . . .

Psychology as the Study of Physiological Processes. In addition to the ways psychology has been studied in the past, some psychologists today also focus on the physiological basis of behavior. Psychologists who subscribe to the physiological perspective contend that behavior can be best understood by looking at its biological or physical causes. *Physiological psychologists* (also called *biopsychologists*) believe that most or all psychological events are the result of underlying biological or chemical processes. Many physiological psychologists do research on the functioning of the nervous system, study how brain cells communicate with each other, and explore the relationship between hormones and behavior.

Physiological psychologists often conduct research on animals in order to understand basic physiological processes. These results can then be applied to the study of more complicated behavior of human beings. Successes in treating problems such as depression and schizophrenia with medication lend support to the physiological position that to understand human behavior we must understand its underlying physiological processes.

---

mind, but because his work attracted many students who carried on the tradition of psychological research.

Functionalism. A close rival for the honor of founder of psychology is the American psychologist William James. In his text *Principles of Psychology* (1890), James speculated that thinking, feeling, learning, remembering—all activities of the mind—serve one major function, to help us survive as a species. Rather than focusing on the structure of the mind as Wundt did, James focused on the functions of the conscious mind and the goals or functions of behaviors. Although James did not produce any significant experimental findings, his writings and theories are still influential. In Chapter 6, you will learn more about James's ideas on motivation and emotion.

Psychology as the Study of Unconscious Processes

Psychoanalysis. While the first psychologists were interested in understanding the conscious mind, Sigmund Freud, a physician who practiced in Vienna until 1938, was more interested in the unconscious mind. He believed that our conscious experiences are only the tip of the iceberg, that beneath the surface are primitive biological urges that are in conflict with the requirements of society and morality. According to Freud, these unconscious motivations and conflicts are responsible for most human behavior. He thought that they were responsible for many medically unexplainable physical symptoms that troubled his patients.

Freud used a new method for indirectly studying unconscious processes. In this technique, known as *free association*, a patient said everything that came to mind—no matter how absurd or irrelevant it seemed—without attempting to produce logical or meaningful statements. The person was instructed not to edit or censor the thoughts. Freud's role, that of *psychoanalyst*, was to be objective; he merely sat and listened, then interpreted the associations (Figure 1.6). Free association, Freud believed, revealed the operation of unconscious processes. Freud also believed that dreams are expressions of the most primitive unconscious urges. To learn more about these urges, he developed *dream analysis*—basically an extension of free association—in which the patient applied the same technique to his or her dreams (Freud, 1940).

While working out his ideas, Freud took careful, extensive notes on all his patients and treatment sessions. He used these records, or case studies, to develop and illustrate a comprehensive theory of personality (Ewen, 1993). Freud's theory of personality will be discussed in Chapter 11.

In many areas of psychology today, Freud's view of unconscious motivation remains a powerful and controversial influence. Modern psychologists may support, alter, or attempt to disprove it, but most have a strong opinion about it. The technique of free association is still used by psychoanalysts, and the method of intensive case study is still a major tool for investigating behavior.

 LAB EXPERIMENTS AND DEMONSTRATIONS

Tell students to write down the first thought that comes into their minds as you read aloud the following list of words:

time death red mother fear home school friend love hate

Direct students not to write their names on their papers. Also, they should remain silent so that their responses do not influence anyone else.

After the activity, collect the papers and redistribute them. Working in pairs, students should review the responses. What, if anything, can they determine about the person whose list they are reviewing? Discuss how psychologists use this technique (see text comments). Also, point out the difficulty of analyzing personality on the basis of a few responses.

Sigmund Freud (1856–1939) was founder of the theory and discipline of psychoanalysis. His discoveries about the unconscious, revolutionary in their day, were basic contributions to the science of psychology. **Why did Freud believe it is important to study unconscious processes?**

Psychology as the Study of Individual Differences

Sir Francis Galton, a nineteenth-century English mathematician and scientist, wanted to understand how heredity (inherited traits) influences a person's abilities, character, and behavior (Figure 1.7). Galton (1869) traced the ancestry of various eminent people and found that greatness runs in families. (This was appropriate, since Galton himself was considered a genius and his family included at least one towering intellectual figure, a cousin named Charles Darwin). He therefore concluded that genius or eminence is a hereditary trait. This conclusion was like the blind men's ideas about the elephant. Galton did not consider the possibility that the tendency of genius to run in eminent families might be a result of the exceptional environments and socioeconomic advantages that also tend to run in such families.

The data Galton used were based on his study of biographies. However, not content to limit his inquiry to indirect accounts, he went on to invent procedures for directly testing the abilities and characteristics of a wide range of people. These tests were the primitive ancestors of the modern personality tests and intelligence tests that virtually all of you have taken at some time.

Although Galton began his work shortly before psychology emerged as an independent discipline, his theories and techniques quickly became central aspects of the new science. In 1883 he published a book, *Inquiries into Human Faculty and Its Development,* that is regarded as the first study of individual differences. Galton's writings raised the issue of whether behavior is determined by heredity or environment—a subject that remains a focus of controversy. Galton's influence can also be seen in the current widespread use of psychological tests.

Sir Francis Galton invented procedures for testing abilities and characteristics that are still used in modern personality and intelligence tests. **What conclusions did Galton reach about genius?**

CONNECTIONS: PSYCHOLOGY AND SOCIAL STUDIES

Assign groups of students to use a world history book to investigate the times in which each of the psychologists mentioned in this chapter lived. For example, what was happening in Freud's Vienna, Austria, during the late 1800s and early 1900s? What was taking place in Galton's London, England, during the mid- and late 1800s? What, if any, events of the era may have influenced the thinking of each of these figures? Or was their thought so original that these individuals shaped the times in which they lived?

■ **Study and Writing Skills.**
Ask students to explain the
purpose of a *rebuttal*. (It is an
argument meant to refute or
overthrow another argument,
especially in law.) Next, read
aloud the following comment
by B. F. Skinner.

*We do not need to try to discover what personalities, states of
mind, feelings, traits of character, plans, purposes, [or] intentions . . . [of people] are in
order to get on with a scientific
analysis of behavior. . . . [All we
need to know] are external
causes.*

Using outside references, have
students write a rebuttal of this
point of view by a psychoanalyst, or a modern-day Freudian.
(OBJECTIVES 2, 3)

DID YOU KNOW?

Women blazed new trails
in psychology, too. In the
1920s, Leta Stetter
Hollingworth coined the
name "gifted" for unusually talented children. June
Etta Downey invented a
widely used personality
test and became the first
woman to lead a psychology department. Even
though women still entered psychology in smaller numbers than men in
the early 1900s, more entered psychology than any
other science.

PSYCHOLOGY UPDATE

Psychology in China. Psychology in modern China lags
far behind the United States,
but the roots of psychological
testing can be traced to the
ancient Chinese. Several thousand years ago, the Chinese
developed and used written
tests to evaluate abilities in
areas such as law and poetry.

In more recent times,
Chinese psychologists often
came to the United States for
training. Then, after World
War II, because of the communist orientation of the
People's Republic of China,
psychologists turned to the
Soviets. Then, in the mid-1960s, the prevailing view
that "no universal laws for
the whole human race"
existed and that each class of
society had its own rules for
its thinking led to the
removal of psychology from
university curricula.

The coming of the Cultural
Revolution led to the rebirth
of the Chinese Psychological
Society in 1977. There are
now more than 2,000 psychologists in China, though
less than half are estimated
to have doctorate degrees.
These psychologists are
encouraged to study practical
issues, especially in education
and social psychology (Blowers
& Turtle, 1987). Worldwide,
psychology continues to grow
(Sexton & Hogan, 1992).

Psychology as the Study of Observable Behavior

Behaviorism.   The pioneering work of Russian physiologist Ivan Pavlov,
who won the Nobel prize in 1904 for his studies related to the physiology
of digestion, charted another new course for psychological investigation.
In a now-famous experiment, Pavlov rang a tuning fork each time he gave
a dog some meat powder. The dog would naturally salivate when the powder reached its mouth. After Pavlov repeated the procedure several times,
the dog would salivate when it heard the tuning fork, even if no food appeared. It had been conditioned to associate the sound with the food.

The conditioned reflex was a response (salivation) elicited by a stimulus
(the tuning fork) other than the one that first produced it (food). The concept was used by psychologists as a new tool, as a means of exploring the
development of behavior. Using this tool, they could begin to account for
behavior as the product of prior experience. This enabled them to explain
how certain acts and certain differences among individuals were the result
of learning.

Psychologists who stressed investigating observable behavior became
known as *behaviorists.* Their position, as formulated by American psychologist John B. Watson (1924), was that psychology should concern itself
only with the *observable* facts of behavior. Watson further maintained
that all behavior, even apparently instinctive behavior, is the result of
conditioning and occurs because the appropriate stimulus is present in
the environment.

Although it was Watson who defined and solidified the behaviorist
position, it was B. F. Skinner, another American psychologist, who refined
and popularized it. Skinner attempted to show how, in principle, his laboratory techniques might be applied to society as a whole. In his classic novel
Walden Two (1948), he portrayed his idea of Utopia—a small town in which
conditioning, through rewarding those who display behavior that is considered desirable, rules every conceivable facet of life.

Skinner exerted great influence on both the general public and the science of psychology. His face was familiar to television audiences, and his
book *Beyond Freedom and Dignity* (1971) became a bestseller (Figure 1.8).
A number of Walden Two communities have been formed in various parts
of the country, and many people toilet-train their children, lose weight, quit
smoking, and overcome phobias by using Skinner-inspired methods.

Skinner was widely criticized, for many people were convinced that his
"manipulative" conditioning techniques are a means of limiting personal
freedom. He has also been heartily applauded as a social visionary. In any
event, his theories and methods have been highly influential in psychology. Behaviorist-inspired techniques compete with more traditional psychotherapy for use in the treatment of various psychological disorders. The
techniques of *reinforcement*, or controlled reward and punishment,
have become increasingly popular in education, and Skinner's teaching
machine was the forerunner of modern computer-assisted instruction.
Moreover, a vast number of today's psychologists use Skinner's research
methods to obtain precise findings in their laboratory experiments.

LAB EXPERIMENTS AND DEMONSTRATIONS

To understand the concept of observable behavior, ask students to watch
you (or a student volunteer) for three or
four minutes. Have students record everything that they "see." Instruct them
to be as objective as possible, avoiding
any value judgments or inferences
about your physical appearance or behavior. Sample student responses, and
point out any subjective comments or
observations. Explore the importance—
and difficulty—of objectivity as a technique of gathering information. Ask: Do
you think psychologists can learn everything they need to know about a person
by observing only their behaviors?

Humanism. Humanistic psychology developed as a reaction to the behavioral movement. Humanistic psychologists, notably Abraham Maslow, Carl Rogers, and Rollo May, describe human nature as active and creative rather than passively reacting to external stimuli. Unlike behaviorists, humanists feel that the human mind is able to influence and change the world in which it functions.

Psychology as the Study of Cognitive Processes

Another reaction to the narrow perspective of S-R (Stimulus-Response) explanations of behavior has been the growing importance—since the mid-1970s—of internal, or cognitive, explanations of behavior. Sometimes using computer-based models of behavior for their studies, cognitive psychologists recognize that some of the processes that govern human and animal behavior are internal. We perceive and interpret our world, we think about problems, we constantly assess our knowledge of ourselves and others, and we use language to communicate with one another.

If, for example, you need a favor from a brother or sister who is almost your age, you will probably ask for it. If you know, however, that he or she is studying for a big test or has just had an argument with a boyfriend or girlfriend, you are likely to delay making your request. Your knowledge of his or her condition or your memory of the results of asking for a favor last time has altered your behavior.

FIGURE 1.8

B. F. Skinner influenced large numbers of people with his techniques of conditioning behavior by rewards and punishments. **What movement developed in reaction to behaviorism?**

PSYCHOLOGY AS A PROFESSION

What is a Psychologist?

Perhaps the best way to answer this question is to ask who is not a psychologist. Although your parents may tell you they know a lot about human behavior and may have been studying your behavior all your life, they are not psychologists because of it. Psychologists are people who have been trained to observe and analyze behavior patterns, to develop theories on behavior, and to apply what they know to influence behavior. Just as there are many different branches of medicine, there are also many different fields of psychology. The principal ones are described below.

People often confuse the terms "psychologist" and "psychiatrist." These are different professions. **Psychiatry** is a specialty of medicine. After a student of psychiatry completes medical school, he or she continues training in psychiatric medicine and learns to treat people with disturbed behavior. Many psychiatrists work in hospitals, have their own private practices, and some combine both. They can prescribe medicine to treat their patients. Sometimes, a psychiatrist works with a psychologist in testing, evaluating, and treating patients. Unlike psychologists, most psychiatrists are not involved in much research; they focus their efforts primarily on helping their patients deal with emotional difficulties.

? FACT OR FICTION

Forensic psychologists apply psychology to legal issues.

Fact. *Forensic psychology* is a growing area of psychology. It attempts to apply psychological principles to the legal system. A forensic psychologist might provide testimony as an expert witness in a trial, be employed to counsel inmates at a correctional facility, or work with law enforcement authorities in solving criminal cases.

Research.
Request volunteers to collect newspapers from the nearest major city in your state. For several weeks, have them clip the help-wanted advertisements for different occupations within the field of psychology. Ask students to paste these clippings onto a poster board. Next to each clipping, tell students to name the career or occupation described in each ad. (OBJECTIVE 4)

Teacher Note. You may wish to refer students to Table 16.1 on page 396. Ask: What are some of the different kinds of therapists described? Suppose students wanted to find out if they had a problem that warranted analysis. Which of these therapists might they *first* consult? Why?

VISUAL INSTRUCTION

Ask students to identify the different types of psychology illustrated in the montage on page 17. Request volunteers to skim the yellow pages of the phone book. What other psychological services can they identify?

Readings in Psychology.
Have students read Readings 1 and 2 in the Introducing Psychology section in *Readings in Psychology* and answer the questions that follow each reading. Discuss students' reactions to the readings in class as well as their answers to the questions. Do they agree or disagree with each other? What are the reasons for the disagreements?

ANSWERS TO FIGURE 1.4

All of the statements in Figure 1.4 are false. As you read the different chapters in this book, you will learn more about the correct answers to these statements and the research that psychologists have conducted to demonstrate why these statements are false.

FIGURE 1.9

(Opposite) Psychologists at work. (a) One-to-one therapy. (b) Educational psychologists help design computer-assisted instruction. (c) Administering a standard intelligence test. (d) A therapist working with a mentally disturbed child. (e) Space vehicles designed with the help of psychologists. (f) Doing research on sleep and dreaming. (g) Clinical psychologist counseling mother and daughter.

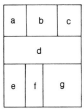

Specialty Fields in Psychology

In the process of expanding its scope, psychology has been divided into a number of subfields. *Clinical* and *counseling psychology* are the most popular. Specialists in this field are often referred to as *psychotherapists.* Clinical psychologists help people deal with their personal problems. They work mainly in private offices, mental hospitals, prisons, and clinics. Some specialize in giving and interpreting personality tests designed to determine whether a person needs treatment and, if so, what kind. Counseling psychologists usually work in schools or industrial firms, advising and assisting people with the problems of everyday life. School psychologists, educated in principles of human development, clinical psychology, and education help young people with emotional or learning problems. About one-half of all psychologists specialize in clinical psychology.

A large number of specialists study *personality, social psychology,* or *developmental psychology.* These psychologists are usually involved in basic rather than applied science. Psychologists who study personality investigate its development, personal traits, or may create personality tests. Social psychologists study groups and how they influence individual behavior. Some are particularly interested in public opinion and devote much of their time to conducting polls and surveys.

Educational psychology deals with topics related to teaching children and young adults, such as intelligence, memory, problem solving, and motivation. Specialists in this field evaluate teaching methods, devise tests, and develop new instructional devices for films, television, and classrooms. *Community psychology* is a relatively new area of community mental health. A psychologist who specializes in this area may work in a mental health or social welfare agency operated by the state or local government or by a private organization. A community psychologist may help design, run, or evaluate a mental health clinic. *Industrial/Organizational psychology* is another area of specialization. Industrial psychologists study and develop methods to boost production, improve working conditions, place applicants in jobs for which they are best suited, train people, and reduce accidents.

Finally, some psychologists are engaged in *experimental psychology.* These psychologists do everything from testing how electrical stimulation of a certain area of a rat's brain affects its behavior, through studying how disturbed people think, to observing how different socioeconomic groups vote in elections. They are basic scientists rather than applied scientists.

What psychologists think about, what experiments they have done, and what this knowledge means form the subject of this book. Psychology is dedicated to answering some of the most interesting questions of everyday life: What happens during sleep? How can bad habits be broken? Is there a way to measure intelligence? Why do crowds sometimes turn into mobs? Do dreams mean anything? How does punishment affect a child? Can memory be improved? What causes psychological breakdowns? In trying to answer such questions, psychology ties together all that has been discovered about human behavior and feelings in order to look at the total human being. The picture is far from complete, but much of what is known will be found in the chapters that follow.

COOPERATIVE LEARNING ACTIVITY

Assign small groups of students to devise lists of behavior disorders, areas of investigation, or job functions that relate to one of the fields of psychology mentioned in "Psychology as a Profession." Tell students to write each of these items on a three-by-five card. (They should keep answers on a separate master key.) Next, have the groups exchange cards. Challenge each group to guess which type of psychologist might best handle each disorder or task named. (The group that prepared the cards will check answers.)

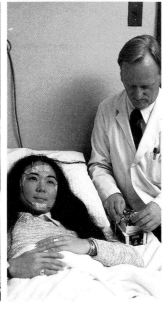

17

ASSESS

Check for Understanding

Assign students to write an essay entitled: "Psychology—Something for Everybody." In the essay, have students cover some of the diverse topics and research investigated by psychologists today.

Reteach

Have students complete the Chapter 1 Study Guide Activity, pages 10–17. For extended review, assign the Chapter 1 Review Activity, pages 10–17, as homework or an in-class activity.

Enrich

Have students complete the Chapter 1 Extension Activity and answer the questions that follow it.

Have students complete the Chapter 1 Application Activity.

Evaluate

Administer and grade the Chapter 1 Test. Two forms are available should you wish to give different tests to different students/classes.

Use the Understanding Psychology Testmaker to create a customized test.

CLOSE

On page 6, the author states an old cliche: "A little learning is a dangerous thing." Ask students if they agree or disagree with this cliche when it comes to assessing human behavior. What evidence can students cite to support their opinions?

PSYCHOLOGISTS AT WORK

Write the following statement on the chalkboard: "Warning: your personality may be hazardous to your health." Tell students that this is the advice a *health psychologist* might give to a cynical, hostile, or depressed person. As students might suspect, health psychologists believe that the mind plays an important role in many physical disorders such as ulcers, heart disease, and even cancer. They study ways people can stay healthier through a more positive outlook on life. What "prescription" might a health psychologist write for an angry person suffering from insomnia and a loss of appetite?

ANSWERS

Concepts and Vocabulary

1. gain insight and practical information

2. identifying or defining the problem

3. describe, explain, predict, and control

4. Dualism refers to the concept that the world is divided into two elements: mind and matter.

5. helped prove the importance of observation to experimentation

6. Wilhelm Wundt

7. introspection

8. All functions of the mind (thinking, feeling, learning, remembering) contributed to the survival of the human species.

9. Freud studied unconscious motivations of human behavior. He took extensive notes to compile case studies that helped him develop a comprehensive personality theory.

10. Freud's views of unconscious motivations still remain a powerful—and controversial—force.

11. Galton wanted to determine the role of heredity in shaping behavior. He helped begin the field of individual psychology and developed the first personality and intelligence tests.

12. Psychologists who investigate observable behavior are known as behaviorists. Behaviorist pioneers include B. F. Skinner, John B. Watson, and Ivan

---

SUMMARY

Use the following outline as a tool for reviewing this chapter. Copy the outline onto your own paper, leaving spaces between headings to make notes about key concepts.

   I. Why Study Psychology?

      A. Insight

      B. Practical Information

  II. Overview of Psychology

      A. Defining Psychology

      B. The Scientific Basis of Psychology

      C. The Goals of Psychology

 III. A Brief History of Psychology

      A. Psychology as a Discipline

      B. Psychology as the Study of Unconscious Processes

      C. Psychology as the Study of Individual Differences

      D. Psychology as the Study of Observable Behavior

      E. Psychology as the Study of Cognitive Processes

  IV. Psychology as a Profession

      A. What Is a Psychologist?

      B. Specialty Fields in Psychology

CONCEPTS AND VOCABULARY

1. What are some advantages of learning about psychology?

2. What is the first step in psychological research?

3. What are four goals of psychology?

4. What is the concept of dualism?

5. How did Copernicus and Galileo influence scientific procedures?

6. Who established the first psychology laboratory?

7. What method of study did Wundt develop to collect information about the mind?

8. According to William James, what was the single function of all the activities of the mind?

9. What type of motivations did Freud study? What methods did he use in his studies?

10. Is Freud's view of unconscious motivation still influential?

11. What did Sir Francis Galton want to understand? What area of psychology did he begin?

12. What is the name given to psychologists who investigate observable behavior? Can you name three of these psychologists? Who influenced the formation of communities based on learning, or conditioning, principles? What is the name given to these communities?

13. What does a forensic psychologist do? What type of psychologist usually works in schools? What type might work in a factory?

CRITICAL THINKING

1. **Synthesize.** Write your own definition of psychology. Is your definition different from one you would have written before reading the chapter? Put the definition in a safe place and take it out and read it at the end of the course to see if you still agree with it.

2. **Apply.** Write about a situation in which you were involved and reacted in a way you now know was a "psychological response." For example, like Ruth's behavior in the cafeteria or the blind men and the elephant, you may not have known your reasons at the time. Now you know possible explanations for your behavior. What did you do? What were the reasons?

3. **Evaluate.** Psychology is generally thought of as a helpful science and is expected to help people

---

Pavlov. Skinner influenced the formation of Walden Two communities—places where learning was shaped through conditioning.

13. A forensic psychologist applies the principles of psychology to the legal system. A special therapist known as a school psychologist works in schools. An industrial psychologist works in a factory.

Critical Thinking

1. Discuss with students how Chapter 1 affected their understanding of psychology. You might organize a portfolio system in which each student stores his or her journal and other items from the course of study. Encourage students to record their definition of psychology on the outside of the portfolio along with a date.

become better adjusted and more productive, with a greater understanding of interpersonal relationships. However, well-meaning people throughout history have also applied what they considered to be sound "psychological" techniques that have actually tormented or totally destroyed their intended beneficiaries. Can you see any possibilities today where psychological knowledge could be used against the best interests of an individual or society?

APPLYING KNOWLEDGE

1. Make a list of various professions or occupations. List the ways a psychologist might contribute to better functioning within the occupation or profession. What kind of psychologist do you think would be most helpful in performing each job?

2. Much of psychology is, in effect, an attempt to understand the nature of human behavior. Make a list of characteristics or behavioral tendencies that you think apply to all people. Compare your list with those of other students in your class.

3. Psychology is usually thought of as a science. Psychologists rely on the scientific method, testing hypotheses by collecting information, analyzing data, and conducting additional experiments. But is psychology a science in the same way that biology or chemistry is a science? Can you study human behavior in the same way that you study biological phenomena? Are there any characteristics or "laws" that are universally true for all humans? If so, do these characteristics or laws compare to the established laws of physics? Write an essay that argues both sides of the issue. Use what you learned in this chapter as well as your own thoughts and ideas. Begin your essay with a basic definition of science.

BEYOND THE CLASSROOM

1. Go to a library, your school's guidance office, or career resource center and ask the staff where you can find information on careers. Explain that you are doing a project for school on careers in the field of psychology. Read what you can find about the different careers that exist within the field of psychology. Choose one field and arrange an interview with a psychologist in that area. How did he or she choose the field of psychology? What education was needed? What are the most rewarding aspects of the job? Are there negative parts of the job? Which type of psychologist would you choose to be? Why?

IN YOUR JOURNAL

1. Review the journal entry that you wrote at the beginning of the chapter on your reasons for studying psychology. Based on what you have learned from studying the chapter and classroom discussions, assess the ideas you presented in the original entry.
Ask yourself:
   a. Are any of the ideas based on misconceptions, false premises, or faulty reasoning?
   b. What ideas would you revise or delete?
   c. What other ideas for studying psychology would you now include?

Write a new entry in your journal. Describe in 200 words the three biggest benefits you feel you can derive from studying psychology. Provide reasons to justify your choices.

19

2. To protect individual privacy, you might allow students to complete this assignment anonymously. If any students volunteer to share their "slice of life," you might arrange for them to do so in small group settings in which students identify factors that influenced behavioral patterns.

3. To help students organize their thoughts, suggest that they develop a pro and con chart on the application of psychology. What, if any, limits should be placed on the practice of psychology?

CHAPTER BONUS
Test Question

This question may be used for extra credit on the chapter test.
Choose the letter of the correct response.

Psychologists who work to discover ways to use knowledge to benefit others and solve immediate problems are working in
a. applied science.
b. basic science.
c. behaviorism.
d. introspection.

Answer: **a**

Applying Knowledge

1. Answers will vary. But students should include examples of the character traits suitable to some of the occupations listed.

2. Answers will vary. You might compile a master list on the chalkboard so that students can note any commonly cited behavioral tendencies. Do students hold an

optimistic or a pessimistic view of human nature?

3. Answers will vary. But students should provide evidence or examples that support their characteristics or laws.

Beyond the Classroom

1. Answers will vary. Advise students to develop interview questions before heading out into the field. Also, you might want to prepare a release form

for the interview. When students are done, have them report their findings to the class.

IN YOUR JOURNAL

If time permits, discuss journal entries individually with students.

Learning and Cognitive Processes

CHAPTER 2

Learning:
Principles and
Applications

CHAPTER 3

Memory and
Thought

Learning is involved in almost every phenomenon psychologists study and occurs in many different ways.

20

INTRODUCING THE UNIT

As a bridge between the Introduction and Unit 1, you might read aloud a remark by Morton Hunt, author of *The Story of Psychology.* "From [Greek times] to ours, explorers of the mind have been pressing ever deeper into its . . . uncharted wilderness. It has been and continues to be a voyage as challenging and enlightening as any expedition across unknown seas or lands, any space mission to far-off planets. . . ." Ask students if they agree with this remark. Then have them skim the headings in Chapters 2 and 3. Into what "uncharted wilderness" do they expect to pass?

Unit 1 in Perspective

Chapter 2 explores the three basic types of learning that psychologists have studied—classical conditioning, operant conditioning, and modeling. It also illustrates how the principles of learning are applied to human and animal behavior through such techniques as reinforcement.

Chapter 3 investigates the ways in which people receive, process, store, retrieve, and analyze information. It also underscores the creative manipulation of information that distinguishes humans from other species.

Connecting to Past Learning
Ask students to think about how they learned a particular common task, such as riding a bicycle. Have them consider various ways proficiency was attained, such as through instruction, trial and error, or observation of others. Did any one method of learning seem to work better for most of the students? Have the class members discuss why they think people have different methods of learning. What factors do they think can influence learning styles?

21

UNIT PROJECT

Assign students to keep an "I Learned" diary. On a daily basis, students should write in their journals at least one thing that they learned during a 24-hour period. Beneath the entry, students should also write down the method of learning. If students actively try to commit something to memory—like a telephone number—they should write that down, too. They might also record examples of things they totally forgot, such as a person's name. After study of Unit 1 is completed, have students share examples of some of the specific thought processes mentioned in Chapters 2 and 3.

CHAPTER 2

Learning: Principles and Applications

TEXT TOPICS	SPECIAL FEATURES	RESOURCE MATERIALS
Classical Conditioning, pp. 23–29	**At a Glance:** The Case of Little Albert, p. 26	Reproducible Lesson Plan; Study Guide; Review Activity Transparency 1
Operant Conditioning, pp. 29–37		Reproducible Lesson Plan; Study Guide; Review Activity
Factors That Affect Learning, pp. 37–38		Reproducible Lesson Plan; Study Guide; Review Activity *Readings in Psychology:* Section 1, Reading 1
Learning Strategies, pp. 38–40		Reproducible Lesson Plan; Study Guide; Review Activity
Learning Complicated Skills, pp. 40–42	**Psychology Update,** p. 40	Reproducible Lesson Plan; Study Guide; Review Activity
Modeling, pp. 42–43	**Using Psychology: Behavior Modification,** pp. 43–49 **More About Psychology,** p. 43 **Fact or Fiction?,** p. 44	Reproducible Lesson Plan; Study Guide; Review Activity; Application Activity; Extension Activity Chapter Test, Form A and Form B Understanding Psychology Testmaker

PERFORMANCE ASSESSMENT ACTIVITY

Individuals may sometimes learn more about learning by teaching others. If possible, provide opportunities for students to teach or tutor another individual or a group in some subject area or skill. To focus their teaching experiences, have students plan their lessons so that they apply one of three factors that affect learning—feedback, transfer, or practice—as described on pp. 37–38. Ask each student to keep a written log of the teaching experience. (The logs should describe the goal of the lesson, the learning principles applied, and the results of the instruction.)

CHAPTER RESOURCES

Readings for the Student

Bender, William N. *Introduction to Learning Disabilities.* Needham Heights, MA: Allyn and Bacon, 1992.

Duckworth, Eleanor. *The Having of Wonderful Ideas and Other Essays on Teaching and Learning.* New York: Teachers College Press, Columbia University, 1987.

Seligman, Martin E. P. *What You Can Change and What You Can't: The Ultimate Guide to Self-Improvement.* New York: Alfred A. Knopf, Inc., 1994.

Skinner, B. F. *About Behaviorism.* New York: Random House, Inc., 1976.

Skinner, B. F. *Walden Two.* New York: Macmillan, 1976.

Readings for the Teacher

Ackerman, Philip L. *Learning and Individual Differences.* New York: W. H. Freeman, 1989.

Bower, Gordon H., ed. *The Psychology of Learning and Motivation,* Vol. 26, *Advances in Research and Theory.* San Diego: Academic Press, 1990.

Mulcahy, Robert F., *et al.,* eds. *Enhancing Learning and Thinking.* Westport, CT: Greenwood, 1991.

Seligman, Martin E. P. *Learned Optimism.* Edited by Julie Rubenstein. New York: Pocket Books, 1992.

Multimedia

A Conversation with B. F. Skinner (23 minutes). McGraw-Hill Training Systems. In this video Skinner discusses the basic principles of behaviorism and the issues of control and freedom in human behavior.

Learned Helplessness. Jeffrey Norton. On this audiotape Martin Seligman describes laboratory experiments and the development of the concept of learned helplessness.

Token Economy (22 minutes). McGraw-Hill Training Systems. In this video token economy formats are applied.

For additional resources, see the bibliography beginning on page 530.

FOCUS

Motivating Activity

Most people react involuntarily to certain sounds. To demonstrate this point, arrange to have a telephone begin ringing during class. (You might hide a tape recorder in a desk drawer.) Pretend to ignore the sound. See how long it takes for students to feel anxious or to insist on answering the phone. Ask students to explain why they felt compelled to respond to the sound. How did they learn this behavior? Next, point out that this is an example of classical conditioning. Tell students that they will learn more about this and other kinds of learning in Chapter 2.

Meeting Chapter Objectives.

Refer students to the objectives on page 23. Organize the students into five groups. Make four of the groups each responsible for summarizing one of the objectives after the chapter has been read. Assign the fifth group to list the differences between classical conditioning and operant conditioning.

Building Vocabulary.

Assign students to use word parts to guess the definition of each of these terms as it applies to learning. After each guess, have students look up the term in the glossary. How close did they come to the real meaning?

Learning: Principles and Applications

FIGURE 2.1 Skill at a sport is learned behavior, as is almost everything else human beings do.

22

TEACHER CLASSROOM RESOURCES

■ Chapter 2 Reproducible Lesson Plan
■ Chapter 2 Study Guide
■ Chapter 2 Review Activity
■ Chapter 2 Application Activity
■ Chapter 2 Extension Activity
▯ Transparency 1
▯ Transparency Strategies and Activities

▯ *Readings in Psychology:* Section 1, Reading 1

■ Chapter 2 Test, Form A and Form B

◉ Understanding Psychology Testmaker

OBJECTIVES

After studying this chapter, you should be able to

- describe the principles and techniques of classical conditioning.
- outline the principles, techniques, and applications of operant conditioning.
- cite the factors involved in the process of learning.
- apply the principles of learning to human and animal behavior.

Learning is basic to our understanding of behavior. It is part of nearly every aspect of our lives. As an infant, you learned to hold yourself upright, to walk, and to use your hands. Later, you learned to run, ride a bicycle, and to operate a television. You learned to read, write, and study for tests. Eventually, you learned how to get people to give you what you want by asking, bargaining, being nice, or pouting. You may even have learned to be afraid of the dentist or fear taking exams. Have you learned how to overcome these fears? You also have learned how to learn. **Learning** can be defined as a relatively permanent change in behavior that results from experience.

Not all of the behaviors that we learn are acquired in the same way. Furthermore, the same behavior can be learned in different ways. You may learn, for example, to fear the dentist because you associate the dentist with the experience of pain. You may have acquired a fear of the dentist because every time you expressed your fears, your parents or friends gave you special attention and comfort. You may never have even gone to the dentist, but you may have learned to fear him or her by watching someone else's reaction. These examples represent the three basic types of learning that psychologists have studied: *classical conditioning*, *operant conditioning*, and *modeling*.

KEY TERMS

aversive control
avoidance conditioning
behavior modification
classical conditioning
conditioned response (CR)
conditioned stimulus (CS)
discrimination
escape conditioning
extinction
feedback
fixed-interval schedule
fixed-ratio schedule
generalization
learning
negative reinforcement
neutral stimulus
operant conditioning
primary reinforcers
reinforcement
response chains
secondary reinforcer
shaping
token economy
transfer
unconditioned response (UCR)
unconditioned stimulus (UCS)
variable-interval schedule
variable-ratio schedule

IN YOUR JOURNAL

Recall a situation in which you taught another person a skill or how to do a task. Write a brief account about it in your journal. Make sure to include a description of the strategy you used in teaching.

23

Exploring Key Ideas

Shaping Behavior.
Parents and other influential adults consciously try to shape children's behavior and attitudes by rewarding "good" behavior and punishing "bad" behavior. Ask students to give examples of these efforts at shaping behavior. *(giving or withholding of food or privileges; exhibiting affection or anger; showing recognition or non-recognition of an act)* Point out that the shaping of behavior may also be unintentional. For example, if a child receives continual attention as a result of crying, the crying will be reinforced. The child may thus "learn" to cry more frequently—contrary to the intentions of the parents. Challenge students to think of other examples of unintentional reinforcement of "bad" habits.

IN YOUR JOURNAL

Help students jog their memories by having the class generate a list of various ways that skills can be taught—verbal directions, demonstration, coaching, and so on. Suggest that their accounts mention any problems they may have encountered in teaching the other person.

EXTRA CREDIT ACTIVITY

Ask students to choose someone they know who has a particular skill that they would like to learn. Have students interview that person to find out how he or she acquired the skill and how long it took to reach current proficiency. Students should also find out what reinforcement the individual received while learning. Did the reinforcement come from another person or from completion of the task? Students should present their findings either in writing or in brief oral reports to the class.

TEACH

Guided Practice

■ **Understanding Cause and Effect.** To help students understand the interrelationship among the key terms involved in classical conditioning, organize the students into small groups. Ask each group to appoint a recorder. Next, direct the groups to review the pages on classical conditioning (pp. 24–29). Based on these pages, have students write a series of four or more statements that explain the cause-and-effect relationships between the different kinds of stimuli and responses. After the groups complete their statements, ask each recorder to report for the group. List the valid statements on the chalkboard. Discuss any invalid statements, and challenge students to correct these statements. (OBJECTIVE 1)

VISUAL INSTRUCTION

Pavlov spent the first half of his career studying the digestive system. His keen observations led him to discover what he called "psychical secretion." Ask students what they think Pavlov might have meant by that phrase.

Answer to caption, Figure 2.2: A neutral stimulus is one that has nothing to do with a response prior to conditioning.

CLASSICAL CONDITIONING

Like many great discoveries, Ivan Pavlov's discovery of the principle of classical conditioning was accidental. Around the turn of the century, this Russian scientist had been studying the process of digestion. Pavlov wanted to understand how a dog's stomach prepares to digest food when something is placed in its mouth. Then he noticed that the mere sight or smell of food was enough to start a dog salivating. Pavlov became fascinated with what he called "psychic secretions" that occurred before the food was presented, and decided to investigate how they worked.

Pavlov's Experiment

Pavlov (1927) began his experiments by ringing a tuning fork and then immediately placing some meat powder on the dog's tongue. He chose the tuning fork because it was a **neutral stimulus**—that is, one that had nothing to do with the response to meat (salivation) prior to conditioning. After only a few times, the dog started salivating as soon as it heard the sound, even if food was not placed in its mouth (Figure 2.2). Pavlov went on to demonstrate that a neutral stimulus will cause a formerly unrelated response if it is presented regularly just before the stimulus (here, food) that normally induces that response (salivation).

Pavlov used the term *unconditioned* to refer to stimuli and to the automatic, involuntary responses they caused. Such responses include blushing, shivering, being startled, or salivating. In the experiment, food was the **unconditioned stimulus (UCS):** an event that leads to a certain, predictable response without previous training. Food normally causes salivation. A dog doesn't have to be taught to salivate when it smells meat. This is an **unconditioned response (UCR):** a reaction that occurs naturally and automatically when the unconditioned stimulus is presented.

FIGURE 2.2

Pavlov's students used this apparatus to study conditioned salivation in dogs. The harness held the dog steady, while the tube leading from the dog's mouth deposited saliva on an arm connected to the recorder on the left, called a kymograph. Drops of saliva moved the pen, making a permanent record of the salivation response to such stimuli as food and sights or sounds associated with food. **What is a neutral stimulus?**

CRITICAL THINKING ACTIVITY

To help students understand the principle of generalization, analyze the example of the dentist's drill on pages 25 and 27. Ask students to suggest other examples from their own experience. *(For ex-ample, a person might learn to associate the smell of flowers with funerals and subsequently feel sad or uneasy in flower shops.)* (OBJECTIVE 1)

Under normal conditions, the sound of a tuning fork would not cause salivation. The dog had to be taught, or *conditioned*, to associate this sound with food. An ordinarily neutral event that, after training, leads to a response such as salivation is termed a **conditioned stimulus (CS).** The salivation it causes is a **conditioned response (CR).** A conditioned response is learned. A wide variety of events may serve as conditioned stimuli for salivation: the sight of food or an experimenter entering the room, the sound of a tone, a flash of light. Controlling an animal's or a person's responses in this way so that an old response becomes attached to a new stimulus is called **classical conditioning.** A number of different "reflex" responses that ordinarily occur automatically following a UCS can be conditioned to occur whenever the correct CS occurs. These include responses produced by the glands, such as salivation or weeping, and responses of our internal muscles, such as those of the stomach. These responses are usually controlled by the autonomic nervous system and are very much involved in your emotions, as you will see in Chapter 4.

General Principles of Classical Conditioning

Acquisition of a classically conditioned response generally occurs gradually. With each pairing of the conditioned stimulus and the unconditioned stimulus, the learned response, or CR, is strengthened. In Pavlov's experiment, the more frequently the tuning fork was paired with the food, the more often the tone elicited salivation—the conditioned response. The timing of the association between the conditioned stimulus (the tone) and the unconditioned stimulus (food) also influences learning. Pavlov tried several different conditioning procedures in which he varied the time between the conditioned stimulus and the unconditioned stimulus. Sometimes he presented the tone before the food. Other times, he presented the tone at the same time as the food, called *simultaneous conditioning*. He found that classical conditioning was most reliable and effective when the conditioned stimulus was presented just before the unconditioned stimulus. He found that presenting the CS about half a second before the UCS gave the best results.

In the same set of experiments, Pavlov also explored the phenomena of *generalization* and *discrimination*. **Generalization** occurs when an animal responds to a second stimulus similar to the original CS, without prior training with the second stimulus. When Pavlov conditioned a dog to salivate at the sight of a circle (the CS), he found that the dog would salivate when it saw an oval as well. The dog had generalized its response to include a similar stimulus. Pavlov was later able to do the opposite, to teach the dog to respond only to the circle by always pairing meat powder with the circle but never pairing it with the oval. He thus taught the dog **discrimination:** the ability to respond differently to different stimuli.

Generalization and discrimination are complementary processes and are part of your everyday life. For example, assume a friend has come to associate the sound of a dentist's drill (CS) with a fearful reaction (CR). After several exposures to a dentist's drill, your friend may find that he or she has generalized this uncomfortable feeling to the sound of other, non-dental

COOPERATIVE LEARNING ACTIVITY

Have students work in small groups to develop story boards that illustrate the steps in Pavlov's experiment or some other experiment in classical conditioning. The story boards should include both drawings (or other appropriate graphics) and captions that pertain to the three phases of classical conditioning: before, during, and after training. After the groups have presented their story boards to the class, display the works in the classroom. (Teaching Tip: Tell students to think of story boards as frames in a film or squares in a comic strip.)

WORKING WITH TRANSPARENCIES

Project Transparency 1 and use the guidelines given on Teaching Strategies and Activities. Assign Student Worksheet 1.

At A Glance

After students read "The Case of Little Albert," ask them the following questions:

1. What was the unconditioned stimulus in the experiment by Watson and Rayner? *(the noise made by the hammer striking the metal bar)*

2. How did Albert's response become generalized? *(Albert was conditioned specifically to fear rats. But his response extended to rabbits and other furry white objects that resembled rats.)*

3. Why are many psychologists critical of this experiment? *(The experimenters induced a new fear into a child and apparently made no attempt to extinguish that fear before Albert left the study.)*

MORE about...

Research with Human Participants: Ethical Principles. The Little Albert study led to questions related to research ethics. As a result of these and other questions, the American Psychological Association published a set of binding ethical principles that govern psychologists' research, revised (1992) as follows:

Planning research: Using recognized standards of competence and ethics, psychologists plan research so as to minimize the possibility of misleading results. Any ethical problems are resolved before research is started. The welfare of all subjects is to be protected.

Responsibility: Psychologists are responsible for the dignity and welfare of participants. Psychologists are also responsible for all research they perform or performed by others under their supervision.

Compliance with law and standards: Psychologists obey all state and federal laws and regulations as well as professional standards governing research with human and animal subjects.

Research responsibilities: Except for anonymous surveys, naturalistic observations, and similar research, psychologists reach an agreement regarding the rights and responsibilities

(Continued on page 27)

At A Glance

THE CASE OF LITTLE ALBERT

John B. Watson and Rosalie Rayner (1920) showed how conditioning could be used on a human infant. They experimented with a well-adjusted 9-month-old child named Albert. They presented Albert with many objects, including a rat, blocks, a rabbit, a dog, a monkey, masks with and without hair, cotton, wool, and burning newspapers. Albert showed no fear of any of these objects—they were all neutral stimuli for the fear response.

Watson and Rayner decided that, when Albert was 11 months old, they would attempt to condition him to fear rats. They began by placing a furry white rat in front of him. Albert would reach out to touch it and, each time he did, one of Watson's assistants would strike a metal bar with a hammer behind Albert. The first time the metal bar was struck, Albert fell forward and buried his head in a pillow. The next time he reached for the rat and the bar was struck, Albert began to whimper. The noise, the unconditioned stimulus, brought about a naturally unconditioned response, fear. After only a few such pairings, the rat became a *conditioned stimulus* that elicited a *conditioned response*, fear.

Five days after Watson and Rayner conditioned Albert to fear rats, they presented him with blocks, a rabbit, a rat, and a dog, each alone. They also showed him a number of other stimuli, including a Santa Claus mask. Albert reacted fearfully to all but the blocks. The degree of fear Albert showed toward these other neutral stimuli depended on how much they resembled the furry white rat. His conditioned fear response generalized to include the rabbit and all the white furry objects he was then shown but not the blocks.

One of the most frequent criticisms of the experiment was that Watson and Rayner were successful in teaching a previously healthy, well-adjusted child to be fearful. Apparently, the researchers knew at least one month ahead of time that Albert would be leaving the study and yet they made no attempt to extinguish his conditioned fears (Harris, 1979). Ethical researchers today would not repeat the Little Albert study, because of the potential psychological harm to the young child.

One of Watson's students, Mary Cover Jones (1924, 1974), developed an extinction procedure to reduce people's existing fears. Peter was a boy who was extremely fearful of rabbits. Jones helped Peter eliminate his fear by pairing the feared object (the rabbit) with pleasant experiences such as eating ice cream or receiving special attention. We will discuss these techniques in Chapter 16, "Therapy and Change."

ADDITIONAL INFORMATION

Students may wonder who Little Albert was and what eventually became of him. Albert was the son of an employee of the Phipps Clinic at Johns Hopkins University in Baltimore, where Watson and Rayner were conducting their experiments. Albert left their study when he was adopted by a family outside of Baltimore. Nothing of his subsequent history is known. If still alive today, Albert would be in his seventies. You might ask students to speculate whether extinction eventually occurred in Albert's case or whether they think Albert may still have an inexplicable fear of furry white animals.

drills. Later, your friend may learn to discriminate between the sound of a dentist's drill and other drills.

A classically conditioned response, like any other behavior, is subject to change. Pavlov discovered that if he stopped presenting food after the sound of the tuning fork, the sound gradually lost its effect on the dog. After he repeatedly struck the tuning fork without giving food, the dog no longer associated the sound with the arrival of food—the sound of the tuning fork no longer elicited this salivation response. Pavlov called this effect **extinction** because the CR had gradually died out.

Even though a classically conditioned response may be extinguished, this does not mean that you have completely unlearned the CR. After extinction, we can introduce a rest period in which the CS is not presented. The previously extinguished CR may reappear when the CS is presented again but not followed by a UCS. This *spontaneous recovery* does not bring the CR back to original strength, however. Pavlov's dogs produced much less saliva during spontaneous recovery than they did at the end of their original conditioning. Alternating lengthy rest periods and the tone without food caused more rapid loss of salivation each time and less recovery the next time the CS was presented.

A good example of extinction and spontaneous recovery is the following. Every time you are in the shower and the water pressure drops, the water suddenly turns very hot. You learn to associate the normally neutral stimulus of a drop in water pressure with your automatic startle reaction to the hot water surge. Even after you finally repair your plumbing so that hot water no longer follows a drop in water pressure, it may take several showers before you no longer react to a water pressure change. You eventually extinguish the startle reaction. Then you go away on a vacation. When you return, you again react with a startle whenever the water pressure changes. You have had a spontaneous recovery of your conditioned startle reaction. After several showers without any hot water assaults, you no longer have a reaction; it is extinguished.

Classical Conditioning and Human Behavior

Using the principle of classical conditioning, a practical solution to the problem of bedwetting was discovered by O. Hobart Mowrer and his wife Mollie (1938). One reason bedwetting occurs is that children do not wake up during the night when they have a full bladder. The Mowrers developed a device known as the *bell and pad*. It consists of two metallic sheets perforated with small holes and attached by wires to a battery-run alarm. The thin, metal sheets—wrapped in insulation or padding—are placed under the child's bed sheets. When the sleeping child moistens the sheet with the first drops of urine, the circuit closes, causing the alarm to go off and wake the child. The child can then use the bathroom. The alarm is the unconditioned stimulus that produces the unconditioned response of waking up. The sensation of a full bladder is the conditioned stimulus which, before conditioning, did not produce wakefulness. After several pairings of the full bladder (CS) and the alarm (UCS), the child is able to awaken to the sensation of a full bladder without the help of the alarm. This technique has

of both subjects and researcher(s) before research is started.

Informed consent: When consent is required, psychologists obtain a signed informed consent before starting any research with a subject. Psychologists inform participants of the nature of the research and that the participants are free to take part, decline, or withdraw from the research.

Deception in research: Deception is used only if no better alternative is available. Under no condition is there deception about (negative) aspects that might influence a subject's willingness to participate. Any such deception must be explained as soon as possible, but no later than the conclusion of the research.

Other issues covered under the ethical principles include: sharing and utilizing data, offering inducements, minimizing evasiveness, and providing participants with information about the study.

Teacher Note. A good way to illustrate the process of extinction is to connect it to a discussion of taste aversions (p. 29), which most students will have experienced. Have volunteers describe how they developed aversions to certain foods. If any students have overcome an aversion, ask them to describe the process. *(Perhaps they tried the food after a period of time and did not become ill or nauseated.)* Explain that a spontaneous recovery of the extinguished food aversion might occur again if the food later becomes reassociated with illness or nausea.

■ **Demonstrating Reasoned Judgment.** The principle of extinction is the basis for many psychological treatments aimed at alleviating irrational fears, or phobias. The psychologist systematically desensitizes the patient to the feared object or experience until the phobic response is extinguished. Ask students to design a program of steps by which a psychologist might systematically extinguish, for example, an individual's fear of heights. (OBJECTIVES 1, 2)

MEETING SPECIAL NEEDS

Learning Strategy. Active learning tasks that involve students' own experiences and prior knowledge will help them better understand the principles and techniques involved in conditioning. For example, in discussing the practical application of classical conditioning to human behavior, you might ask volunteers to explain step by step how they overcame an unwanted habit, such as tardiness or oversleeping.

Point out that both experiments demonstrate the same procedural pattern: A neutral stimulus *(tone/full bladder)* becomes a conditioned stimulus, and elements of an unconditioned response *(salivation/ awakening)* become a conditioned response.
Answer to caption, Figure 2.3: the alarm

Teacher Note. You might use a discussion of the chart on this page to review the definitions of five key terms associated with classical conditioning: neutral stimulus, unconditioned stimulus (UCS), conditioned stimulus (CS), unconditioned response (UCR), and conditioned response (CR). If necessary, have students refer to pp. 24–25 to review the definitions. Make sure, too, that students understand how classical conditioning works. Stress that a subject learns a response to a neutral stimulus that normally does not bring about that response. (OBJECTIVE 1)

FIGURE 2.3

The classical conditioning procedure involves three phases—before, during, and after training. The learner eventually responds to the neutral stimulus (the CS) with a conditioned response (the CR). **What is the unconditioned stimulus in Mowrer's experiment?**

TWO EXAMPLES OF CLASSICAL CONDITIONING

Pavlov's Experiment

	Stimulus	Response
BEFORE CONDITIONING	Tone (neutral stimulus) ⟶	Does not produce response of salivation
	Food (UCS)	Salivation (UCR)
DURING CONDITIONING	Tone (CS) paired with Food (UCS) ⟶	Salivation (UCR)
AFTER CONDITIONING	Tone (CS) ⟶	Salivation (CR)

Mowrer's Experiment

	Stimulus	Response
BEFORE CONDITIONING	Full bladder (neutral stimulus) ⟶	Does not produce response of wakening
	Alarm (UCS) ⟶	Awakening (UCR)
DURING CONDITIONING	Full bladder (CS) paired with Alarm (UCS) ⟶	Awakening (UCR)
AFTER CONDITIONING	Full bladder (CS) ⟶	Awakening (CR)

To illustrate the intensity of Pavlov's personality, you might tell students the following story. Soon after his marriage, Pavlov became immersed in a study of butterflies. Often he forgot to pick up his paycheck. Pavlov seemed not to notice that he teetered on the edge of poverty—that is, until fuel ran out and his butterflies died. When his wife pointed out the need for money, he fumed: "Oh, leave me alone, please. A real misfortune has occurred. All my butterflies have died, and you are worrying about some silly trifle."

proved to be a very effective way of treating bedwetting problems. To identify the elements in this conditioning example and compare them to Pavlov's experiment, see Figure 2.3.

Taste Aversions. Suppose you go to a fancy restaurant. You decide to try an expensive appetizer you've never had—let's say, snails. Then suppose that, after dinner, you go to a concert and become violently ill. You will probably develop a taste aversion—you will never be able to look at another snail without becoming at least a little nauseated.

Your nausea reaction to snails is another example of classical conditioning. What makes this type of conditioning interesting to learning theorists is that, when people or other animals become ill, they seem to decide, "It must have been something I ate," even if they haven't eaten for several hours. It is unlikely that the concert hall in which you were sick will become the conditioned stimulus, nor will other stimuli from the restaurant—the wallpaper pattern or the type of china used. What's more, psychologists can even predict which part of your meal will be the CS: you will probably blame a new food. Thus, if you get sick after a meal of salad, steak, and snails, you will probably learn to hate snails, even if they are really not the cause of your illness.

John Garcia and R. A. Koelling (1966) first demonstrated this phenomenon with rats. The animals were placed in a cage with a tube containing flavored water. Whenever a rat took a drink, lights flashed and clicks sounded. Then, some of the rats were given an electric shock after they drank. All these rats showed traditional classical conditioning: the lights and the sounds became conditioned stimuli, and they tried to avoid them in order to avoid a shock. The other rats were not shocked, but were injected with a drug that made them sick after they drank and the lights and sounds occurred. These rats developed an aversion not to the lights or the sounds but only to the taste of the flavored water.

This special relationship between food and illness was used in a study (Gustavson *et al.*, 1974) that made coyotes hate the taste of lamb by giving them a drug to make them sick when they ate sheep. This is an important application because sheep farmers in the western United States would like to eliminate the coyotes that threaten their flocks, while naturalists are opposed to killing the coyotes. The psychologists realized that coyotes could be trained to eat other kinds of meat, and thus learn to coexist peacefully with sheep.

OPERANT CONDITIONING

Suppose your dog is wandering around the neighborhood, sniffing trees, checking garbage cans, looking for a squirrel to chase. A kind neighbor sees the dog and tosses a bone out the kitchen door to it. The next day, the dog is likely to stop at the same door on its rounds, if not go to it directly. Your neighbor produces another bone, and another the next day. Your dog becomes a regular visitor.

■ **Forming Hypotheses.** Psychologists use the results of studies to formulate hypotheses that serve as the bases for further studies. Ask students to suggest some hypotheses that psychologists might want to test after considering the results of Gustavson's study involving coyotes and food aversion. *(Psychologists and other scientists would probably want to test how long the coyotes' aversion to lamb lasted before extinction occurred and whether the learned behavior is passed along to the coyotes' young, and, if so, to what degree.)* (OBJECTIVES 1, 4)

COOPERATIVE LEARNING ACTIVITY

Organize the students into small groups of experimenters and subjects. Tell the experimenters to follow this procedure: Sit at a table with a lamp you can easily switch on and off. Place a glass of water and a spoon within reach. Have the subject sit across from you so that you can observe his or her eyes. First, turn off the lamp to see how much your subject's eyes dilate under normal conditions. Then make the room dark enough to have the subject's eyes dilate prior to switching off the light. When this happens, immediately turn off the lamp. See the subject's eyes adapt. Switch on the lamp. Tap the glass and immediately turn off the lamp. Continue—Tap, off, watch, on. For the 11th trial, tap the glass and leave the lamp on. What happens to your subject's eyes? Explain your observation in behavioral terms.

VISUAL INSTRUCTION

An important early figure in the study of operant conditioning was Edward L. Thorndike. He devised an experiment to study the process by which cats learned to press a paddle to escape a cage and receive food. Stress the distinction that, while Thorndike taught the cats to get their food by leaving the cage, animals in the Skinner box learned to get their food by operating on their environment within the box.

Answer to caption, Figure 2.4: Operant conditioning is learning from the consequences of behavior.

Answer to caption, Figure 2.5: Reinforcements include the likelihood that the child's practice session will be repeated and that the music teacher will provide feedback.

■ **Evaluating Generalizations.** Read the following statement by B. F. Skinner to the class: "Everything we do and are is determined by our history of rewards and punishments." Ask students to evaluate this generalization and express whether they agree or disagree with it. Ask them to cite examples to support their positions. (OBJECTIVE 2)

FIGURE 2.4

A rat presses a bar in a Skinner box. The Skinner box is an artificial environment in which lights, sounds, rewards, and punishments can be delivered and controlled. Some of the animal's behaviors, such as bar pressing, can be recorded by automatic switches. **What is operant conditioning?**

Suppose you have a younger brother who is unhappy because you seem to be capturing your mother's attention. He begins to pout and act aggressively toward you. Right away your mother stops attending to you to reprimand him. Even though your mother's attention is negative, your brother seems to like it. A short time later, he is back again harassing you and earning another reprimand from your mother.

Both stories are examples of **operant conditioning**—that is, learning from the consequences of behavior. The term *operant* is used because the subject (the wandering dog and your brother in our examples) *operates* on or causes some change in the environment. This produces a result that influences whether they will operate or respond in the same way in the future. Depending on the effect of the operant behaviors, the learner will repeat or eliminate these behaviors—to get rewards or avoid punishment.

How does operant conditioning differ from classical conditioning? One difference is in how the experimenter conducts the experiment. In classical conditioning, the experimenter presents the CS and UCS independent of the subject's behavior. Reactions to the CS are then observed. In operant conditioning, the subject must engage in a behavior in order for the programmed outcome to occur. In other words, operant conditioning is the study of how behavior is affected by its consequences.

Reinforcement

B. F. Skinner (1974) has been the psychologist most closely associated with operant conditioning. He and his colleagues believe that most behavior is influenced by one's history of rewards and punishments. Suppose you want to teach a dog to shake hands. One way would be to give the animal a pat on the head or a biscuit every time it lifts its paw up to you. The biscuit or

FIGURE 2.5

Practice is an important part of learning to play a musical instrument. Beginners spend many hours practicing scales and simple tunes. Once they master the basics, they can move on to more complicated arrangements. **What are the reinforcements in this illustration?**

CONNECTIONS: PSYCHOLOGY AND LITERATURE

The notion that a Skinner box is a complete, artificially controlled environment in which rewards and punishments can be delivered has its parallels in utopian literature. An example is Aldous Huxley's *Brave New World*. Have students research synopses of various utopian novels—especially twentieth-century works—in literary reference books. Discuss these synopses in class, and have students select appropriate titles for independent reading.

pat is called a *positive reinforcer*. In this example, the dog will eventually learn to shake hands to get a reward. **Reinforcement** can be defined as a stimulus or event that affects the likelihood that an immediately preceding behavior will be repeated. The nature of the reinforcement depends on the effect it has on the learner. Examples of reinforcers that people respond to are social approval, money, and extra privileges.

Your dog will stop shaking hands when you forget to reward it for the trick and withdraw reinforcement. Extinction will occur, but it will take a period of time. In fact, for a while after you stop rewarding it, the dog will probably become impatient, bark, and paw even more insistently than it did before.

Schedules of Reinforcement

One important factor in operant conditioning is the timing and frequency of reinforcement. Behavior that is reinforced every time it occurs is said to be on a *continuous schedule* of reinforcement. You might suppose that behavior would best be acquired by reinforcing every response. Although learning occurs at a faster rate under a continuous reinforcement schedule, in the long run, the best results are not obtained in this way. When positive reinforcement occurs only intermittently or on a *partial schedule,* the responses are generally more stable and last longer, once they are learned.

Skinner discovered the strength of partial reinforcement by accident when his apparatus kept breaking down. Skinner found that the rats kept responding even though they were reinforced randomly only on every second or third lever press. In fact, the rats responded with even greater endurance.

Although intermittent reinforcement may be arranged in a number of ways, four basic methods, or schedules, have been studied in the laboratory. Schedules of reinforcement may be based either on the *number* of correct responses that the organism makes between reinforcements (*ratio* schedules) or on the *amount of time* that elapses before reinforcement is made available (*interval* schedules). In either case, reinforcement may appear on a regular, or fixed, schedule or on an irregular, or variable, schedule. The four basic schedules result from the combination of these four possibilities. People respond differently to each type.

In a **fixed-ratio schedule,** reinforcement depends on a specified quantity of responses, such as rewarding every fourth response. The student who receives a good grade after completing a specified amount of work and the typist who is paid by the number of pages completed are on fixed-ratio schedules. People tend to work hard on fixed-ratio schedules, pausing briefly after each reward. What happens if the amount of work or number of responses to be completed before the next reward is huge? In that case, the student or pieceworker is likely to show low morale and few responses at the beginning of each new cycle because there is such a long way to go before the next reinforcement.

A **variable-ratio schedule** does not require that a fixed or set number of responses be made for each reinforcement, as in the fixed-ratio schedule. Rather the number of responses needed for a reinforcement changes from

■ **Discussion.** Tell students that some factory workers are paid according to the number of items they produce, regardless of the time spent in producing them. Ask: Which schedule of reinforcement is this so-called "piecework" pay? Why might an employer be in favor of such a schedule? How might a Skinnerian psychologist justify it? What might a factory worker say for or against it?

This discussion can provide the opportunity for students to generalize from factory to classroom. What reinforcement schedules operate in the classroom? If grades are the equivalent to piecework pay, what reinforcements would operate if grades were abolished? (OBJECTIVE 2)

STUDY AND WRITING SKILLS

B. F. Skinner suggested that the behaviorist principles of operant conditioning might be put to use in improving society and the human condition. In his book *Walden Two,* Skinner describes a utopian community that runs according to operant principles. Skinner explains assumptions in this work more fully in his book *Beyond Freedom and Dignity.* Have interested students read these two books and write essays in which they consider the advantages and disadvantages of such attempts at social engineering.

one time to the next. Slot machines are a good example of a variable-ratio schedule. They are set to pay off after a varying number of attempts. Gamblers often overlook this feature of slot machines and continue to deposit coins at a steady high rate. They believe, mistakenly, that the more they do so, the sooner they will hit the jackpot. Instead, the ratio must be set so the casino operators can make a profit. Generally, organisms on variable-ratio schedules of reinforcement tend to work or respond at a steady high rate.

On a **fixed-interval schedule,** the first response after a predetermined time has elapsed since the last reinforcement is reinforced. The time interval—whether seconds, minutes, hours, or days—is always the same. Once organisms gain experience with a fixed-interval reinforcement schedule, they exhibit a "scalloped" performance curve. After reinforcement, the subject simply stops responding. This makes sense because the organism has never been reinforced immediately after gaining a reinforcer. Your teachers, for example, often give quizzes or tests on a fixed-interval schedule. It is likely that you will study feverishly the day of a test, but rarely crack a book in the subject immediately afterwards!

On a **variable-interval schedule,** the time at which the reinforcement becomes available changes throughout the conditioning procedure. If you are trying to call a friend, but the line is busy, what do you do? You keep trying. The reinforcer is gained the first time you dial after your friend has hung up, but you don't know when that's going to occur. So you fall into a slow, deliberate style of dialing every few minutes. The usual response rate on a variable-interval schedule is slow, but steady—slower than on any other schedule of partial reinforcement. In fact, your eagerness to reach your friend probably will determine roughly how often you try the phone again . . . and again. Similarly, a pigeon (such as the one in Figure 2.6) that is on a variable-interval schedule tends to peck at a key on a much more

FIGURE 2.6

This pigeon is showing signs of emotional upset common in extinction of an operantly conditioned response. Experimenters used a variable-interval schedule to train the bird to obtain food from the square hole by pecking at the key in the round hole. When the experimenter switched off the circuit that made the arrangement work, the bird pecked the key for a while and then, finding no food, began to jump around and flap its wings. **What is the difference between ratio schedules and interval schedules?**

steady basis than an animal on a fixed-interval schedule, because the amount of time it will take to be reinforced is unknown.

In summary, ratio schedules are based on numbers of responses, while interval schedules are based on time. Responses are learned better and are more resistant to extinction when reinforced on a variable rather than on a fixed schedule. However, to be most effective, the reinforcement must be consistent for the same type of behavior, although it may not occur each time the behavior does. The complexity of our behavior means that most reinforcers in human relationships are on a variable schedule. How people will react cannot always be predicted.

Stimulus Control

In operant conditioning, stimuli that are associated with receiving rewards or punishment become *signals* for particular behaviors. For example, we learn to cross a street only when the traffic light is green and to answer the phone only when it rings. These signals simply indicate that if you cross the street or answer the phone, a reinforcer is likely to follow in the form of safe arrival on the other side of the street or of a voice on the phone. These signals often control your behavior.

Organisms generalize among and discriminate between conditioned stimuli in classical conditioning, and stimuli that serve as signals in operant conditioning. For example, the child who has been rewarded for saying "doggie" every time he or she sees the family's basset hound may generalize and say "doggie" when he or she sees a sheep, a cow, or a horse. These animals are similar enough to the hound for them to become signals that "doggie" will produce a reward. Discrimination results when "doggie" fails to produce a reward in these other cases. The child learns to confine the use of the word to dogs and to respond differently when seeing sheep, cattle, or horses.

Because signals are guides to future rewards and punishments, they often become rewards or punishers in themselves. In such cases, the signal is called a **secondary reinforcer,** or conditioned reinforcer, because without the conditioning process, it would be a neutral stimulus having no positive or negative value to a person. With conditioning, almost any stimulus can acquire almost any value.

One experimenter (Wolfe, 1936) demonstrated this with chimpanzees. Poker chips have no value for chimps—they aren't edible and they aren't very much fun to play with. This experimenter, however, used operant conditioning to teach chimps to value poker chips as much as humans value money. He provided the animals with a "Chimp-O-Mat" that dispensed peanuts or bananas, which are **primary reinforcers** that satisfy or reduce a basic, natural need, such as hunger. To obtain food, the chimps had to pull down on a heavily weighted bar to obtain poker chips, then insert the chips in a slot in the machine (Figure 2.7). With repetition, the poker chips became conditioned reinforcers. Their value was evident from the fact that the chimpanzees would work for them, save them, and sometimes try to steal from one another.

■ **Discussion.** Ask for volunteers to provide examples of primary and secondary reinforcers. *(Answers will vary. Sample responses might include: primary—water, food, pain reduction; secondary—smiles, praise, frowning.)* Stress that a reinforcer is very subject-specific. In other words, a stimulus that acts as a reinforcer for one subject might have no effect on another subject. (OBJECTIVE 2)

DID YOU KNOW?

Millions have read *Walden Two*, B. F. Skinner's best-known work. One small group created a community in Virginia based on the Walden Two model. Although what became known as the Twin Oaks Community has survived, its members have long given up trying to shape behavior based on Skinner's reinforcement methods.

CONNECTIONS: PSYCHOLOGY AND THE MEDIA

Organize the students into small groups. Point out that advertisements often associate products with appealing and enjoyable events or situations—what Vance Packard called "hidden persuaders." Although such associations are arbitrary in terms of the product's actual effects, advertisers use the associations to try to shape consumers' feelings toward the product. Have students find various examples of advertisements in the print and electronic media in which hidden persuaders are at work. Ask students to identify the operant conditioning techniques evident in the advertising appeals.

Make sure that students understand the distinction between primary reinforcers *(natural rewards)* and conditioned reinforcers *(stimuli that acquire value because of conditioning).*
Answer to caption, Figure 2.7: The chimpanzee learned to value the poker chips through conditioning. Without the conditioning process, the chips would have no positive or negative value.

■ **Discussion.** Many of our routine activities are the result of operant conditioning. Challenge students to brainstorm typical daily activities that are a result of some sort of conditioning (such as bathing, grooming, completing homework assignments). Record student responses on the chalkboard. Then ask them to identify the specific type of conditioning involved for each item. What conclusion can be drawn? Is most reinforcement in our lives positive or negative? (OBJECTIVE 2)

FIGURE 2.7

The chimpanzee uses poker chips obtained by pulling down on a heavily weighted bar to "buy" peanuts and bananas. Through operant conditioning, the chimp then learned to value something that is neither fun to play with nor edible. **Why are the poker chips in this experiment called conditioned reinforcers?**

There is no need to look only to animals for examples of this phenomenon. Smiles have little value for newborn babies, and words of approval have no meaning. In time, however, babies learn that these expressions and sounds mean that an adult is about to pick them up, cuddle them, perhaps feed them (primary reinforcers). The smiles and sounds of approval signal a reward. In time, children begin to value smiles, praise, and other forms of social approval in and of themselves.

Aversive Control

People often use the word *reinforcement* to refer only to the pleasant consequences of behavior. Psychologists, however, use it to refer to anything that increases the frequency of an immediately preceding behavior. Unpleasant or aversive consequences (as opposed to pleasant ones) influence much of our everyday behavior. **Aversive control** refers to this type of conditioning, or learning. There are two ways in which unpleasant events, or aversive stimuli, can affect our behavior: as negative reinforcers or as punishers.

If possible, have students observe how very young children are handled by adults in a day-care center or a similar facility for children. What evidence of secondary reinforcement can the students identify? What other kinds of operant conditioning can they spot? Ask students to keep a careful log of their observations and to prepare oral reports of their findings for the class. As a related assignment, the students might interview the caregivers regarding their attitudes toward child rearing. Are the adults consciously trying to condition the children's behavior? (Teaching Tip: Before carrying out either of these assignments, obtain release forms for the children/interviewees.)

Negative reinforcement. In **negative reinforcement,** a painful or unpleasant stimulus is removed or is not applied at all. The removal of unpleasant consequences increases the frequency of a behavior (Figure 2.8). It may help you to understand negative reinforcement if you remember that it *follows* and takes away, or *negates,* an aversive stimulus. B. F. Skinner provided this example: If walking with a stone in your shoe causes you to limp, removing the stone (negating it) allows you to walk without pain. Two types of negative reinforcement that psychologists have studied in detail are *escape conditioning* and *avoidance conditioning.* In **escape conditioning,** a person's behavior causes an unpleasant event to stop. Consider the case of a child who hates liver and is served it for dinner—a thoroughly repulsive experience. She whines about the food and gags while eating it. At this point, her mother removes the liver. The gagging and whining behavior has been thus negatively reinforced, and the child is likely to gag and whine in the future when given an unpleasant meal. This kind of learning is called escape conditioning because the behavior has enabled the child to escape the liver meal.

In **avoidance conditioning,** the person's behavior has the effect of preventing an unpleasant situation from happening. In our example, if the girl's past whining and gagging behavior had stopped the mother from even serving the liver, we would identify the situation as avoidance conditioning; the child would have avoided the unpleasant consequences in advance. The reinforcer here is the reduction of the girl's disgust.

Punishment. The most obvious form of aversive control is not negative reinforcement, but punishment. If you want to stop a dog from pawing at you when it wants attention, you should loudly say, "NO!" when it paws at you. Such actions are called *punishers.* In fairness, you

FIGURE 2.8

A rat makes the correct choice on the jump stand. Learning is rapid in this apparatus because an incorrect choice produces aversive consequences: The rat bumps its nose on the closed door (horizontally striped in this case) and falls into the net below. **In what two ways do aversive stimuli affect behavior?**

Teacher Note. In discussing negative reinforcement, make sure students understand the distinction between escape conditioning *(when behavior makes an unpleasant situation stop)* and avoidance conditioning *(when behavior prevents the unpleasant situation from happening).* Challenge students to think of examples of each. *(Escape: a subject's crying stops a friend from arguing; the subject may resort to crying whenever confronted with an argument. Avoidance: a friend gets angry whenever the subject offers advice; the subject avoids making the friend angry by no longer offering advice.)* (OBJECTIVE 2)

VISUAL INSTRUCTION

Point out that the jumping stand has been a widely used device in psychological experiments, particularly in studies of discrimination and choice behavior. **Answer to caption, Figure 2.8:** as negative reinforcers and as punishers

COOPERATIVE LEARNING ACTIVITY

Organize the class into teams of experimenters and subjects. Tell students that they will be conducting a simple experiment in both avoidance conditioning and classical conditioning. Ask the subject to sit at a table about two feet from the experimenter. The subject should then place his or her right hand on the table, palm down. Using a ruler, the experimenter should lightly tap the table with it every few seconds. Periodically, the ruler should be tapped twice against the table and then gently on the subject's knuckles. After a few repetitions of this procedure, the subject should begin to show avoidance responses by either withdrawing the hand after the two taps or by anticipating them.

VISUAL INSTRUCTION

Ask students to explain what is happening in the cartoon's last panel. How have the behaviors of the child and parents become generalized? *(The child is considering resorting to a tantrum to get what he wants—a new bicycle. The parents, fearing a tantrum, are probably considering buying their child a bicycle to avoid a possible tantrum.)* **Answer to caption, Figure 2.9:** Aversive stimuli may produce unwanted side effects, and the subject or subjects may learn to avoid the person delivering the aversive consequences.

■ **Discussion.** After students have examined the cartoon and read the section on punishment, ask them to explain why some psychologists would be against the following maxim: "Spare the rod and spoil the child." Why might some psychologists be in favor of this advice?

As a follow-up to the discussion, you might assign the students to imagine that they are editorial writers for a popular magazine geared toward young parents. They should write a short persuasive essay making a case either for or against spanking. Encourage those students who are inclined to use humor and satire to use these techniques to strengthen their arguments. (OBJECTIVE 2)

FIGURE 2.9

In the cartoons, the child is about to engage in a positively reinforcing activity (playing in the mud), but his parents stop him. He punishes their forbidding behavior with an aversive stimulus (a violent tantrum). Their forbidding behavior decreases in strength and they give in. The parents' giving-in behavior is now negatively reinforced of the removal of the aversive tantrum. The child's tantrum is positively reinforced by playing in the mud. The results of this conditioning process are that tantrums are now more likely, forbidding is less likely, and giving in is more likely. The new behavior may generalize to a new yet similar situation. **What are disadvantages in using aversive stimuli to change behavior?**

should positively reinforce desirable forms of attention-seeking when they occur.

As with reinforcers, the events or actions that serve as punishers depend on their effect on the learner. In the example on operant conditioning you read earlier, the mother's reprimands were meant to be punishers. Actually, the reprimands were reinforcers because of the effect they had on the boy, who wanted attention. Perhaps sending him to his room every time he harassed you would have been an appropriate punisher; this unpleasant stimulus would have discouraged him from repeating the behavior.

In punishment, an unpleasant consequence occurs and decreases the frequency of the behavior that produced it. Negative reinforcement and punishment operate in opposite ways. In negative reinforcement, escape or avoidance behavior is *repeated*, and increases in frequency. In punishment, behavior that is punished decreases or is *not repeated*.

CRITICAL THINKING ACTIVITY

Problem Solving. Have students reexamine the various kinds of conditioning taking place in the cartoon on page 36. In their opinion, has the child become a "spoiled brat"? What advice would they give to the parents to help modify their child's behavior? After the students have formulated their advice, you might extend the activity by requesting volunteers to role-play the encounter between the parents and their child as they engage in behavior modification. The role plays should cover the three procedural stages of conditioning: before, during, and after.

Psychologists have found several disadvantages in using aversive stimuli to change behavior. For one thing, aversive stimuli can produce unwanted side effects such as rage, aggression, and fear. Then, instead of having to change only one problem behavior, there may be two or more. For example, children whose parents rely on spanking to control disobedience may also have to deal with the problem of their children's increased aggressiveness toward other children.

A second problem with aversive stimuli is that people learn to avoid the person delivering the aversive consequences. Children learn to stay away from parents or teachers who punish often. One consequence of this is that such parents and teachers have less opportunity to correct the children's inappropriate behavior. Also, punishment is likely to merely suppress rather than eliminate such behaviors. The punished behavior is likely to occur at some other time or in some other place.

FACTORS THAT AFFECT LEARNING

Studies of more complex forms of learning have revealed that several factors can help or hinder the process. Among them are feedback, transfer, and practice.

Feedback

Finding out the results of an action or performance is called **feedback.** Without feedback, you might repeat the same mistakes so many times that you develop a skill incorrectly—you would never learn what you were doing wrong. Even if you were performing correctly, you would not be receiving reinforcement for continuing. If, for example, you always wore earplugs while you practiced the piano, you would never know just how bad your version of "Chopsticks" sounded.

Transfer

Often a skill that you have already learned can help you to learn a new skill. For example, if you have learned to play the saxophone, it will be much easier for you to learn to play the clarinet. You can **transfer** skills you already have, such as reading notes and converting them into responses of your lips, tongue, and fingers to the clarinet. When previously learned responses help you learn to master a new task, it is called *positive* transfer.

When a previously learned task hinders learning, *negative* transfer is occurring. An American may find driving in England to be difficult. In England the steering wheel is on the opposite side of the car, and people drive on the opposite side of the road. The learned skill of driving American style makes it difficult to perform the necessary new mental and motor tasks. An American's responses in England may be the exact opposite of what is needed—an example of negative transfer.

■ **Creating a Chart.** Write the headings **Feedback, Transfer,** and **Practice** on the chalkboard. Then have the class brainstorm as many practical examples of each factor as they can. Next, analyze the lists with the class. In looking at the **Feedback** column, for example, distinguish between feedback from others and feedback as the result of actions. *(A basketball player might get feedback in the form of advice from a coach. However, the player also gets feedback whenever the ball goes through the hoop.)* Follow the same procedure with items in the other two columns. For the **Transfer** column, distinguish between examples of positive and negative transfer. For items in the **Practice** column, distinguish between examples of physical and mental practice. *(If students have failed to come up with enough items for comparison, repeat the brainstorming until the chart is completed.)* (OBJECTIVE 3)

■ **Readings in Psychology.** Have students read the Section 1, Reading 1 selection in *Readings in Psychology* and answer the questions that follow the reading.

LAB EXPERIMENTS AND DEMONSTRATIONS

Bring a clean trash can and three beanbags into class. Demonstrate for students how to throw the beanbag over your shoulder into the trash can, which should be set up approximately 6 to 8 feet behind you. Then ask for three volunteers to replace you. Have them each throw the beanbag without feedback. Next, allow the class to give minimum feedback on how to throw it ("to the right," "a little further," etc.). Repeat a second and third time, each with more specific feedback. Discuss the effect of the feedback on the students' performances. Ask: How does immediate, specific feedback help you to learn a particular skill? (Relate the effects of feedback to something learned in school, sports, work, and so on.)

■ **Creating a Flowchart.**
Remind students that a flowchart shows the steps or stages in a process or idea. Working in small groups, have students design flowcharts showing how feedback, transfer, and practice may work in learning a particular skill, such as mastering a video game. When students complete the activity, have each group present its chart. Encourage other groups to practice "feedback" by verbally commenting on the charts. (OBJECTIVE 3)

■ **Research.** Ask students to go to the library and find articles on the application of behavior modification techniques to particular areas of human behavior. *(Common uses of behavior modification include smoking, weight loss, child rearing, assertiveness.)* Instruct students to read several articles related to their chosen area and to prepare oral reports analyzing the techniques used to change behavior. In concluding remarks, students should offer their assessment on the effectiveness of these techniques. (OBJECTIVE 4)

Practice

Practice, the repetition of a task, helps to bind responses together. It is the key element that makes for smooth and fluent movement from response to response.

Because practice takes time, psychologists have been interested in determining how to use that time most efficiently. They have found that whatever type of skill a person is learning, it is usually better to practice over a period of time rather than do it all at once.

It is possible to practice by imagining oneself performing a skill. Athletes imagine themselves making golf swings over and over again or mentally shooting free throws in basketball to improve their performance. Psychologists call such effort *mental practice*. Although it is not as effective as the real thing, it is better than nothing at all.

LEARNING STRATEGIES

It would be difficult to solve problems if people had to start from the beginning each time a new problem occurred. Fortunately, when you learn to solve one problem, some of the problem-solving experiences may transfer to other, similar problems. Once you learn certain strategies for solving problems and learning tasks, you will usually have an easier time on your next attempts. (Such problem-solving strategies are also discussed in Chapter 3.) Strategies are affected by their consequences just as less complex reasons are. If a strategy works, the person or animal is likely to use it again. Many learned principles for dealing with life are valuable; others may actually be handicaps.

Learning to Learn

Harry Harlow (1949) showed that animals can learn to learn—they can learn to use strategies for solving similar problems and tasks. He gave a monkey the problem of finding a raisin under one of two wooden lids, one red and one green (Figure 2.10). The raisin was always hidden under the green lid. Because the experimenter kept changing the position of the lids, eventually the monkey began to realize that color was important, not location.

When the monkey had learned always to pick the green lid, the experimenter changed the problem. Now the monkey had to choose between triangular and circular lids. The raisin was always placed under the circular lid, and the experimenter again changed the location of the lids on each trial. As before, it took several tries for the monkey to learn that the shape of the lid, not its location, indicated where the raisin would be. After doing a number of problems like these, the monkey began to learn that the difference between the two lids always contained the key to the problem. Eventually after solving several hundred problem sets, the monkey could solve any similar two-choice problem with, at most, one error.

PSYCHOLOGISTS AT WORK

People usually associate psychologists with therapists and similar counselors who offer advice to patients and clients. Point out to students that most of the psychologists whose studies are described in this chapter are *experimental psychologists.* These professionals perform most of their work in laboratories and adhere to strictly controlled scientific procedures. Unlike therapists, experimental psychologists are involved in "pure research" and do not immediately apply their knowledge beyond the laboratory. Such specialists generally hold doctoral degrees and are proficient in mathematics because they must be able to analyze the data they collect according to statistical procedures.

The learning of strategies and principles is extremely important in human behavior. In school you practice such skills as reading books, writing essays, and taking tests. In many cases the particular things you have learned will be less important in the long run than what you have learned about learning generally. Learning to extract information from a book, for example, will be helpful whether the book is about physics, grammar, or cooking. Just as Harlow's monkey acquired a general method for quickly solving particular problems, you are acquiring a general strategy for learning particular pieces of information.

Learned Helplessness and Laziness

Psychologists have shown that general learning strategies can affect a person's relationship to the environment. For example, if a person has numerous experiences in which his actions have no effect on his world, he may learn a general strategy of helplessness or laziness.

In the first stage of one study (Hiroto, 1974), one group of college students were able to turn off an unpleasant loud noise, while another group had no control over the noise. Later, all were placed in a situation in which they merely had to move a lever to stop a similar noise. Only the ones who had control over the noise in the first place learned to turn it off. The others did not even try!

It is not hard to see how these results can apply to everyday situations. In order to be able to try hard and to be full of energy, people must learn that their actions *do* make a difference. If rewards come without effort, a person never learns to work (learned laziness). If pain comes no matter how hard one tries, a person gives up (learned helplessness).

Martin Seligman believes that learned helplessness is one major cause of depression. He has revised his theory (Abramson, Seligman, and Teasdale, 1978; Miller and Seligman, 1982) so that it is now somewhat more detailed than his earlier theory, which was based primarily on animal studies. He reasons that, when people are unable to control events in their lives, they generally respond in one of the following ways. They may be less motivated to act and thus stop trying. They may experience a lowered sense of self-esteem and think negatively about themselves. They may also feel depressed.

Seligman identified three important elements of learned helplessness: *stability*, *globality*, and *internality*. Stability refers to the person's belief that the state of helplessness results from a permanent characteristic. For example, a student who fails a math test can decide that the problem is either temporary ("I did poorly on this math test because I was sick") or *stable* ("I never have done well on math tests and never will"). Similarly, the person can decide that the problem is either specific ("I'm no good at math tests") or *global* ("I'm just dumb"). Both stability and globality focus on the student—on *internal* reasons for failure. The student could have decided that the problem was external ("This was a bad math test") instead of internal. People who attribute an undesirable outcome to their own inadequacies

FIGURE 2.10

Harry Harlow presented monkeys with pairs of lids and required them to learn strategies for determining which lid in each pair covered a morsel of food. After being presented with a few hundred such problems, the monkeys learned to use the same strategy for dealing with each new pair. **Why is it important that problem-solving experiences can be transferred to other, similar problems?**

STUDY AND WRITING SKILLS

At the opposite end of the spectrum from learned helplessness seems to be a certain brand of heroism. Some heroes seem to defy the odds and do not give up even though pain comes. Have students write a story or narrative poem about such a person struggling against overwhelming adversity. What inner resources give the hero the strength to avoid a state of learned helplessness? Encourage students to portray their heroes in real-life, contemporary situations or in an actual historical setting.

■ **Analyzing Passages.** In 1928 John B. Watson and Rosalie Rayner—the team noted for the classical conditioning of Little Albert—published a best-selling book entitled *Psychological Care of Infant and Child.* Read aloud the following passage from the book:

There is a sensible way of treating children. Treat them as though they were young adults. Dress them, bathe them with care and circumspection. Let your behavior always be objective and kindly firm. Never hug or kiss them, never let them sit on your lap. If you must, kiss them on the forehead when they say goodnight. Shake hands with them in the morning. Give them a pat on the head if they make an extraordinary good job of a difficult task.

Ask students what type of principles and techniques this passage recommends to shape human behavior. What do they think are the strengths and shortcomings of this method? (OBJECTIVES 1, 4)

PSYCHOLOGY UPDATE

Shaping Complicated Behaviors in Animals. Psychologists have used shaping to condition very complicated behavior patterns in animals. Pigeons have been taught to play Ping-Pong and peck out songs on a small piano. During World War I, the British trained sea gulls to detect enemy submarines in the English Channel. To train them, the British sent their own submarines out in the Channel while dropping food on the surface. Soon the sea gulls would follow subs from the air without food, and sighting sea gulls over the Channel signaled the possible presence of German submarines.

During World War II, B. F. Skinner was involved in a project that trained pigeons to guide missiles to enemy targets. The pigeons were gradually reinforced for pecking at images of enemy targets projected on a screen. Although these "top gun" pigeons were quite accurate, they were never actually used in real combat.

More recently, the U.S. Navy has trained dolphins to detect enemy divers and locate undersea mines. Also, sea lions have been taught to recover antisubmarine rockets so that the Navy can evaluate the rockets' performance.

will probably experience depression along with guilt and self-blame. Those who attribute their problems to their own inadequacies and see these personal shortcomings as enduring traits that apply to all situations are likely to suffer from severe depression.

The revision of Seligman's theory is important because it is a good example of important trends in behaviorism. As learning theorists begin to study people rather than animals, they are finding that some of the old behavior models are too simple because they focus simply on what people *do.* What people *think* is also important.

LEARNING COMPLICATED SKILLS

When you acquire a skill such as knitting, photography, shooting a basketball, or talking persuasively, you learn more than just a single new stimulus-response relationship. You learn a large number of them, and you learn how to put them together into a large, smooth-flowing unit. Psychologists have devoted considerable attention to how new responses are acquired and to how they are put together in complex skills.

Shaping is a process in which reinforcement is used to sculpt new responses out of old ones. An experimenter can use this method to teach a rat to do something it has never done before and would never do if left to itself. He or she can shape it, for example, to raise a miniature flag. The rat is physically capable of standing on its hind legs and using its mouth to pull a miniature flag-raising cord, but at present it does not do so. The rat probably will not perform this unusual action by accident, so the experimenter begins by rewarding the rat for any action similar to the wanted responses, using reinforcement to produce successive, or closer and closer, approximations of the desired behavior.

Imagine the rat roaming around on a table with the flag apparatus in the middle. The rat inspects everything and finally sniffs at the flagpole. The experimenter immediately reinforces this response by giving the rat a food pellet. Now the rat frequently sniffs the flagpole, hoping to get another pellet, but the experimenter waits until the rat lifts a paw before he gives it another reward. This process continues, with the experimenter reinforcing close responses and then waiting for even closer ones. Eventually, he has the rat on his hind legs nibbling at the cord. Suddenly the rat seizes the cord in its teeth and yanks it. Immediately the rat is rewarded, and it begins pulling rapidly on the cord. A new response has been shaped.

Shaping has been used to teach language skills to impaired children. Psychologists at first reward the children for simple sounds, such as "bah." Later the children are rewarded only for complete words, such as "beans," and later for complete sentences, such as "Beans, please." Many such children have successfully learned to use some language by this method (Lovaas *et al.*, 1967).

COOPERATIVE LEARNING ACTIVITY

Have students work in small teams of writers, artists, and editors to develop an illustrated children's book depicting the story of the rat learning to raise the flag on the pole. Remind students that their books are intended for a young audience and should be entertaining. However, they should also demonstrate an understanding of the process of shaping. Tell them to consider using the point of view of the rat in telling the story. After the teams have produced their books, arrange to have the stories read to a group of young children. Afterwards, have students discuss the children's reactions to the stories.

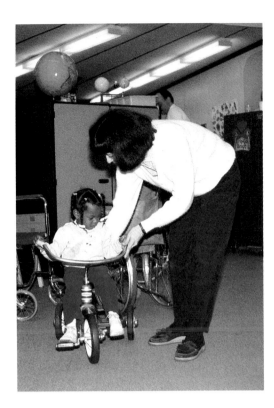

FIGURE 2.11

Psychologists shape behavior by using reinforcement to sculpt new responses out of old ones. This instructor is shaping behavior as she teaches a physically impaired preschooler to ride a tricycle. **What are response chains?**

Combining Responses: Chaining

In order to learn a skill, a person must be able to put various new responses together. Responses that follow one another in a sequence are put together in **response chains.** Each response produces the signal for the next one. For example, to hammer a nail into a board, you would have to put together the following chain of responses: pick up the hammer, pick up the nail, position the nail, swing the hammer, hit the nail, swing the hammer, hit the nail, and so on until the nail is completely sunk in. Each hit of the nail is a signal that you are striking it correctly, and the nail's being flush with the board's surface is a signal that no further action is required.

In learning, chains of responses are organized into larger *response patterns*. For example, the complex skill of swimming has three major chains that are combined to make up the whole swimming pattern: an arm-stroking chain, a breathing chain, and a leg-kicking chain (Figure 2.12). After much practice, you no longer have to think about the different

■ **Discussion.** In discussing the principles of modeling, you might mention that psychologist Albert Bandura coined the term *observational learning*. This term referred to the learning that takes place by having the learner observe someone else perform a task or tasks. The importance of observational learning is that it shows how new responses can be learned without shaping and conditioning. For example, Bandura notes that a polite request acts as a very powerful reinforcer. Similarly, a request to discontinue a particular behavior produces instantaneous extinction. Do students think such direct requests would be considered legitimate reinforcers by adherents of operant conditioning? Why or why not? (OBJECTIVES 2, 4)

steps involved. The behavior takes on a rhythm of its own: the chains of responses flow naturally as soon as you dive into the water.

It is often necessary to learn simple responses before mastering the complex pattern. If you cannot hit a nail with a hammer, you certainly cannot build a house. Therefore, before a person can learn to perform a particular skill, he or she must learn all the subordinate skills that make the larger skill possible.

MODELING

Up to this point it would seem that classical and operant conditioning are the only two types of learning. However, the informal observations you have been making all your life concerning learning probably suggest to you that there is more to learning than this—that, in fact, we most often learn by imitating others. This is especially true of social responses—when we learn how to behave in a new situation by watching how others behave. When you go to a concert for the first time, you may be very hesitant about where to go, when to enter (especially if you are late), when to clap, how to get a better seat after the first intermission, and so on. So you observe others, follow them, and soon you are an "old hand." This illustrates a third type of learning, observation and imitation.

We would expect imitation to be responsible for more basic forms of behavior as well, when the proper response is essential for life. Trial-and-error learning is not useful if the punishment for failure to emit the re-

FIGURE 2.12

In learning a skill, responses that follow one another in sequence are put together in chains, and the chains are then organized into response patterns. **What are the three major response chains that the swimmer is using?**

sponse is to be eaten by a predator. Thus, correct avoidance behavior often must be learned by imitating.

The general term for this kind of learning is *modeling*. It includes three different types of effects. In the simplest case the behavior of others simply increases the chances that we will do the same thing. We clap when others do, look up at a building if everyone else is looking there, and copy the styles and verbal expressions of our peers. No learning occurs in this case, in the sense of acquiring new responses. We simply perform old responses that we otherwise might not be using at the time.

The second type of modeling is usually called *observational learning*, or simply, imitation. In this sort of learning an observer watches someone perform a behavior and is later able to reproduce it closely, though the observer was unable to do this before observing the model. An example is watching someone do an unfamiliar dancestep, either live or on film, and afterward being able to do the dancestep yourself.

A third type of modeling involves disinhibition. When an observer watches someone else engage in a threatening activity without being punished, the observer may find it easier to engage in that behavior later. For example, someone with a snake phobia may watch another person handling snakes. Such observation may help to alleviate the phobia. This procedure is used in clinical work, as we will see in the chapter on therapies.

What happens when an observer learns by watching? Early theorists believed that we have some sort of "instinct" for imitation and, indeed, it is probable that some animals do imitate automatically, especially when they are very young and have good models constantly around them: their parents. Operant-conditioning theorists such as Skinner have suggested that imitation itself is a kind of response, one that is often reinforced because it works so well. That is, the behavior of others comes to function as a stimulus for a matching behavior, which is then reinforced because it works on the environment, or because other persons tend to reinforce such matching (as when a mother praises her child for correctly imitating her words).

MORE about . . .

Spatial Learning. Both classical and operant conditioning revolve around time. In Pavlov's demonstration of classical conditioning, the sound of a tuning fork came before food. In operant conditioning, a dog lifting a paw before being given a biscuit learns to "shake hands."

In addition to these types of conditioning, psychologists have studied spatial learning, which involves learning the location of things in the environment. Psychologists who study spatial learning claim that humans explore their environment and form internal cognitive maps. These maps help us to master new environments. Do you remember how confusing school was on your first day? You quickly formed a cognitive map, and this spatial learning explains why by now you could probably find your way around blindfolded.

Psychologists have found that spatial learning occurs not only in humans, but also in animals. They believe that cognitive maps account for the facts that chimps quickly learn to detect food hidden in an area, rats learn their way around a maze, and honeybees find their way back to the hive.

Using Psychology

Behavior Modification

The term *behavior modification* often appears in magazine articles describing research on changing people's behavior through drugs, "mind control," or even brain surgery. In fact, it is none of these things. **Behavior modification** refers to the systematic application of learning principles to change people's actions and feelings.

Independent Practice

■ **Discussion.** After students have read the *More About* feature, ask students to define spatial learning and cognitive maps. Then ask those who own cats and dogs to comment on whether they have ever observed evidence of such learning in their animals. (OBJECTIVE 4)

■ **Study and Writing Skills.** Request volunteers to check television listings for nature programs on an educational channel. When such a program appears, students should watch the program for examples of the way animals rear their young. Students should present their findings in the form of a written case study on the particular animal(s) observed. (OBJECTIVE 4)

Using Psychology

After students have read the information on behavior modification in paragraph 1, ask them to speculate on ways misinformation on behavioral modification may have spread. (You might refer students back to the discussion on p. 8 of Chapter 1.) Then assign students to find out the "real story" behind behavior modification by reading the rest of the feature. Based on this feature, challenge students to write an article on "behavior mod" that might run in a popular magazine. The purpose of the article is to explode some of the myths surrounding this technique of learning.

STUDY AND WRITING SKILLS

Tell the class that when we think of learning skills, we usually think of physical skills *(such as driving a car, sewing, playing basketball)* or mental skills *(such as mastery of mathematics or a new language)*. Learning, however, also involves acquisition of social skills, and it is obvious some people learn them better than others do. Ask students to discuss a specific social skill in a written report. How do the principles of learning outlined in this chapter apply to the acquisition of that skill?

■ **Distinguishing Fact from Fiction.** After students have read the *Fact or Fiction* feature, point out that the findings of scientific studies, such as those regarding alcoholism, sometimes yield conflicting results. Ask: What is meant by the phrase "weight of evidence"? *(a sufficient body of observations for study and testing from which reasoned conclusions can be drawn)* How much "weight of evidence" should psychologists have before implementing a course of treatment aimed at modifying a patient's behavior—in this case, abuse of alcohol? (OBJECTIVE 4)

■ **Analyzing Passages.** Have students read paragraphs 1–3 on page 44, and ask them to consider the steps involved in behavior modification. Request volunteers to prepare a poster with the following question written across the top: "What are the important steps in modifying behavior?" A list might include:

- Define the problem.
- Identify goals and/or target behaviors.
- Select the strategy.
- Design a data-recording system.
- Record data.
- Implement the strategy.
- Evaluate the strategy.
- Change the strategy if necessary.

If possible, encourage students to illustrate some of the items on their poster with either original art or clippings from magazines. (OBJECTIVES 2–4)

FACT OR FICTION

Most psychologists believe that alcoholics can "learn" to be social drinkers.

Fiction. Although attempts have been made to use behavior modification on alcoholics to teach them to be social drinkers, these attempts have generally been unsuccessful. Most psychologists believe that alcoholics simply cannot learn to drink in moderation. Thus, attempts at behavior modification usually involve abstaining completely from alcohol as a first and necessary step on the road to recovery.

When you give your little brother a quarter to leave you alone, that is very much like behavior modification. What distinguishes behavior modification from common-sense approaches is the fact that it involves a series of well-defined steps to change behavior. The success of each step is carefully evaluated to find the best solution for a given situation.

The behavior modifier usually begins by defining a problem in concrete terms. For example, Johnnie's mother might complain that her son is messy. If she used behavior modification to reform the child, she would first have to define "messy" in such objective terms as: he does not make his bed in the morning, he drops his coat on the couch when he comes inside. She would not worry about where his bad habits come from. Rather she would work out a system of rewards and punishments aimed at getting Johnnie to make his bed, hang up his coat, and so on.

Modeling, operant-conditioning, and classical-conditioning principles have been used in behavior modification. Classical-conditioning principles are particularly useful in helping people to overcome fears, and we shall discuss them when we consider the problem of treating abnormal behavior (Chapter 16). Modeling is often used to teach desired behaviors. In addition, as you will see in the following examples, operant-conditioning principles have also been applied to everyday problems.

Computer-Assisted Instruction

The famous Greek teacher Socrates taught his students by a conversational method very similar to what *computer-assisted instruction (CAI)* is using today. CAI is a refinement of the concept of programmed instruction that was introduced by S. L. Pressey (1926) and refined by B. F. Skinner in the 1950s.

The essential concept of programmed instruction is based on operant conditioning. The material to be learned is broken down into simpler units called "frames"; each time the student demonstrates that she or he has learned the information in a frame, the student is given positive reinforcement in the form of new information, choices, or point rewards similar to those used in video games. Each question, or "prompt," builds on information already mastered. The computer retains (as does the student) exactly what the learner understands on the basis of the student's answers to questions. These questions can be multiple choice, true or false, fill-in-the-blank, or conversational in format.

There are several advantages to this system of instruction over conventional classroom methods. The learner has immediate feedback about whether he or she understands the material. The learn-

CONNECTIONS: PSYCHOLOGY AND LITERATURE

The popular notion of behavior modification as "mind control" is central to many works of science fiction. In George Orwell's *Nineteen Eighty Four* (1946), the main character, Winston Smith, is conditioned to become a passive member of the proletariat. In Anthony Burgess's *A Clockwork Orange* (1963), a violent street thug is conditioned to respond negatively to violence. Ask: What negative connotations regarding behavior modification does Burgess's title convey? *(that science can take a living organism—an orange—and turn it into something mechanical—a clockwork)*

FIGURE 2.13

A modern technique in teaching is computer-assisted instruction (CAI). Computers ask the student a question, get a response, and tell the student if the answer is right or wrong.

er reviews only material he or she does not understand. There is constant incentive to learn because of many positive reinforcements. This method also avoids aversive aspects of classroom learning, including a sense of failure for wrong answers. The student can progress at an individual rate, depending on how well rather than how fast he or she learns.

In most variations of CAI, the student can "talk" with the computer by typing in various comments or writing on the screen with a special pen. In the *branching* system of information delivery, the student can choose between paths of instruction after she or he makes a response. The paths can be remedial or supplementary. If the student responds incorrectly, she or he is taken back to the original question that led to the path she or he was on. There is also a simpler, *linear*, system in which such choices are not included.

After completing a course taught by CAI, the student is either given a letter grade automatically (according to how much of the course was completed) or takes a test to see how much information was retained.

CRITICAL THINKING ACTIVITY

Predicting Alternative Futures. Ask students to explain whether they believe computers will ever think like humans. You might use the depictions of HAL in *2001: A Space Odyssey* and of Data in *Star Trek: The Next Generation* as starting points for discussion. There is some evidence that computers will indeed be able to think and learn as people do. According to recent psychological studies (see Silfe & Rubenstein, 1992; Pollack, 1987), few psychologists believe that computers would think differently from humans.

Teacher Note. Make sure students understand that a token economy operates according to three principles:

1. The subject is reinforced with tokens for appropriate behavior.
2. The number of tokens is proportional to the requirements of the response (i.e., more tokens for more or better work).
3. The tokens may be cashed in for rewards.

■ **Discussion.** Ask students to explain the advantages of token economies. *(Answers will vary, but students should note that a token economy sets clear goals and specific guidelines to reach those goals.)* Next, ask students to speculate on what might happen to a learner or patient who either leaves the setting where a token economy is used or must remain where it has been discontinued. *(Answers will vary. Some learners and patients would likely revert to their old behaviors; others would probably be able to provide their own reinforcement and continue their new behavior.)* Ask: Are there any parallels between the tokens in a token economy and the allowance some parents give their children? (OBJECTIVE 4)

Almost every study comparing this method of instruction with conventional classroom methods has shown it to be superior in student retention of the material. One problem sometimes experienced with CAI is that students may not finish the courses when there is no set timetable of instruction. Other disadvantages are expense and lack of human interaction.

Several principles of learning psychology are at work in CAI. The student is learning complex material through a response chain. She or he is reinforced constantly on a fixed schedule. Knowledge is being shaped in a systematic and predictable way. The student is able to have a dialogue with the instructor on every point, which is impossible for a class of students in a conventional setting.

Token Economies

Psychologists tried an experiment with a group of extremely disenchanted boys in Washington, D.C. In fact, the boys had been labeled "uneducable" and placed in the National Training School. The experimenters used what is known as a **token economy** to motivate the boys. The youngsters received points for good grades on tests. They could "cash" these points in for such rewards as snacks, lounge privileges, or items in a mail-order catalog. In other words, they created a system that worked like the Chimp-O-Mat, discussed earlier. Within a few months, a majority of the students showed a significant increase in IQ scores (an average gain of twelve-and-a-half points). The boys continued to improve in the months that followed, showing that they were, indeed, educable (Cohen and Filipczak, 1971).

In another experiment teachers used a token economy to teach preschoolers in a Head Start program to write, and compared their scores on writing tests with those achieved by children who did not participate in a token economy. The youngsters who received tokens, which they could exchange for food, movies, and other rewards, improved dramatically. Equally important, they seemed to develop a very positive attitude toward school. The youngsters who did not receive tokens made very little progress (Miller and Schneider, 1970).

Thus, in token economies, people are systematically paid to act appropriately. In the real world, behaviorists argue, the rewards are just as real; they are simply less systematic. In overcrowded mental hospitals, for example, the only way some patients can get attention is by "acting crazy." Most staff members simply don't have time to bother with people who are not causing trouble. Since attention from the staff is reinforcing for these patients, in effect people are rewarded for undesirable behavior. By systematically

CRITICAL THINKING ACTIVITY

Predicting Consequences. Lack of human interaction is one of the disadvantages of computer-assisted instruction. Have students predict the likely consequences of an entire generation of students educated entirely through CAI. *(One set of possible consequences would be people who work well with computers but have difficulty interacting harmoniously with other people because they have not learned the necessary social skills. On the positive side, these people might have a higher level of self-esteem because of CAI feedback.)*

rewarding only desirable behavior, token economies have been set up in prisons, mental hospitals, halfway houses, and classrooms. (See also Chapter 16.)

Self-Control

In token economies, a psychologist sets up an elaborate system of reinforcers to get people to act the way he or she wants. One of the most important features in behavior modification is an emphasis on asking people to set up personal systems of rewards and punishments to shape their own thoughts and actions.

In the past, behaviorists limited their studies to observable behavior (Chapter 1), and made little attempt to observe or change the way people thought. Then, as more learning researchers began to study humans (instead of focusing exclusively on animals), it became obvious that what people *do* is only part of the story. As we described earlier, for example, Martin Seligman expanded his theory of learned helplessness to try to explain why some people develop long-lasting depressions while others seem to get over them. Part of the difference, Seligman argues, is based on what people *think*—that is, how they interpret their failures.

As in any application of behavior modification, the first step in self-control is to define the problem. People who smoke too much would be encouraged to actually count how many cigarettes they smoked every hour of the day and note what kinds of situations led them to smoke. (After a meal? When talking to friends? Driving to work?) Similarly, people who had a very poor opinion of themselves would have to define the problem more concretely. They might begin by counting the number of self-deprecating remarks they made and thoughts they had. Researchers have found that just keeping track of behavior in this way often leads a person to start changing it.

The next step may be to set up a behavioral contract. One soda lover who had trouble studying decided that she would allow herself a soda only after she studied for half an hour. Her soda addiction remained strong, but her study time increased dramatically under this system. A behavioral contract simply involves choosing a reinforcer (buying a new shirt, watching a favorite TV program) and making it depend on some less desirable but necessary act such as getting to work on time or washing the kitchen floor. These contracts are most likely to succeed if you also use successive approximations—starting with an easy task and gradually making it more difficult. For example, you might begin by studying 10 minutes before rewarding yourself, and gradually increase it to an hour.

Teacher Note. It might interest students to know that Martin Seligman began developing his theory of learned helplessness when he was a 21-year-old graduate student at the University of Pennsylvania. Since then, Seligman and his colleagues have continued to investigate the theory as well as work in other areas, including studies on the influence of personality on health and contentment.

DID YOU KNOW

Each year in the United States, more than 10 million adults are affected by serious depression.

COOPERATIVE LEARNING ACTIVITY

Have students work in small groups to research some of the many techniques that psychologists have developed to help people learn self-control. Then ask each group to draw up a formal behavioral contract (somewhat like a legal document) intended to help someone overcome a simple behavioral problem, such as watching too much television or chronic tardiness. Tell students that they should check their contracts to be sure they include appropriate reinforcers and use successive approximations.

Teacher Note. Students who need to improve their study skills might find it useful to work with a classmate to devise a procedure like the one described on this page. The classmate should keep a record of the subject's progress. At the end of the program period, the pair should prepare a final report analyzing the procedure's effectiveness. You might encourage students to present their "experiment" to the class as a whole.

ASSESS

Check for Understanding

Ask students to summarize the three general types of learning described in this chapter and to describe how feedback, transfer, and practice affect learning. As a tip, tell students that a summary condenses information to highlight the main point(s).

Reteach

Have students complete the Chapter 2 Study Guide Activity. For extended review, assign the Chapter 2 Review Activity as homework or an in-class assignment.

Enrich

Have students complete the Chapter 2 Extension Activity and answer the questions that follow it.

Have students complete the Chapter 2 Application Activity.

Behavior modifiers have developed and tested a wide variety of techniques to help people learn to control themselves.

Improving Your Study Habits

One psychologist designed a program to help students improve their study habits and tried it on a group of volunteers. The students were told to set a time when they would go to a small room in the library they had not used before, taking only the materials they wanted to study. They were then to work for as long as they remained interested—and *only* for as long as they were interested. As soon as they found themselves fidgeting, daydreaming, becoming drowsy or bored, they were to make the decision to stop studying. There was only one condition. They had to read one more page, or solve one more simple problem, before they left. Even if this made them want to study longer, they were instructed to hold to their decision to leave the library, go for a cup of coffee, call a friend, or do whatever they wanted to do.

The next day they were asked to repeat the same procedure, adding a second page to the amount they read between the time they decided to leave and the time they actually left the library. The third day they added a third page, and so on. Students who followed this procedure found that in time they were able to study for longer periods than before, that they were studying more effectively, and they didn't mind studying so much.

Why did this procedure work? Many students force themselves to study. One common technique is to go to the library to avoid distractions. The result may be hours spent staring at a book without really learning anything. Repeated failures to get anything accomplished and sheer discomfort turn studying into a dreaded chore. The library becomes a conditioned aversive stimulus—you hate it because you've spent so many uncomfortable hours there. The procedure was designed to change these feelings.

Requiring students to leave as soon as they felt distracted helped to reduce the negative, punishing emotions associated with studying. The students stopped when these feelings began. Studying in a new place removed the conditioned aversive stimulus. Thus, aversive responses were not conditioned to the subject matter or the room, as they are when students force themselves to work.

Second, the procedure made use of successive approximations. The students began by reading just one page after they became bored, and only gradually increased the assignment. This also reduced the aversive response to studying. The task no longer seemed so difficult.

MEETING SPECIAL NEEDS

Sequencing Skills. Students with learning problems need concrete examples to help them understand abstract concepts, such as successive approximations. Ask students to identify the successive approximations used in the program that the psychologist developed to improve study skills (*gradually* *increasing the number of pages read*). Have students suggest other examples of successive approximations in other learning improvement procedures, such as those track and field athletes might use.

FIGURE 2.14

The library need not become a conditioned aversive stimulus if you learn how to build positive reinforcement into your studying routine. Try to devise appropriate methods to organize the routine of studying and improve your study habits.

The experimenter's procedure also worked because it strengthened a conditioned response by reinforcing the response with a positive or pleasant stimulus. In this experiment, the students received different kinds of positive reinforcement when they completed their task. First, they had the satisfaction of knowing they had followed the procedure and they had completed an assignment; in this case, they had read one more page. Finally, the students rewarded or reinforced themselves for however much studying they did (Fox, 1966). You might try this procedure.

Evaluate

Administer and grade the Chapter 2 Test. Two forms are available should you wish to give different tests to different students/classes.

Use the Understanding Psychology Testmaker to create a customized test.

VISUAL INSTRUCTION

Ask students to summarize how the various behavior modification techniques described in the *Using Psychology* feature (pages 43–49) can be applied to improving basic study habits.

CLOSE

Ask students to think back to the ringing telephone they heard at the beginning of the lesson. What other events in daily life can they now associate with conditioning and the other concepts of learning covered in this chapter?

COMMUNITY INVOLVEMENT

Arrange to have students visit a counseling session or support group in your community that is open to the general public, at which self-control and other self-improvement techniques are taught. Students should record their observations afterward. Make it clear that they cannot take notes during the session. They should look for the following stages/techniques: definition of the problem, establishment of behavioral contracts, and application of reinforcers in a program of successive approximations. Ask students to summarize their findings in a brief paper.

ANSWERS

Concepts and Vocabulary

1. This type of learning is classical conditioning. In Pavlov's experiments, food was the unconditioned stimulus; the dog's salivation upon ingesting food was the unconditioned response; the sound of the tuning fork was the conditioned stimulus; the salivation response to the sound of the tuning fork was the conditioned response. Pavlov used the term extinction.

2. B. F. Skinner; classical conditioning

3. reinforcement; punishers; To have a behavior repeated, you can reward the behavior or remove unpleasant consequences. To prevent a behavior from being repeated, you can use punishment or stop rewarding the behavior.

4. The four types include fixed-ratio, variable ratio, fixed-interval, variable interval.

5. Examples of primary reinforcers include food, warmth, and water. Money is a conditioned reinforcer. Physical, psychological, and symbolic reinforcers respectively include food, praise, and smiles.

6. Aversive stimuli can be used as negative reinforcers or as punishers. In negative reinforcement, a painful or unpleasant stimulus is removed or not applied at all if a certain behavior occurs. With punishment, an unpleasant consequence is applied when a certain behavior occurs. In avoidance

SUMMARY

Use the following outline as a tool for reviewing this chapter. Copy the outline onto your own paper, leaving spaces between headings to make notes about key concepts.

I. Classical Conditioning
   A. Pavlov's Experiment
   B. General Principles of Classical Conditioning
   C. Classical Conditioning and Human Behavior

II. Operant Conditioning
   A. Reinforcement
   B. Schedules of Reinforcement
   C. Stimulus Control
   D. Aversive Control

III. Factors that Affect Learning
   A. Feedback
   B. Transfer
   C. Practice

IV. Learning Strategies
   A. Learning to Learn
   B. Learned Helplessness and Laziness

V. Learning Complicated Skills
   A. Combining Responses: Chaining

VI. Modeling

CONCEPTS AND VOCABULARY

1. What type of learning is involved when an old response becomes attached to a new stimulus? What terms did Pavlov use for each of the following elements in his experiments with dogs: food, the dog's salivation response at the sight of food, the sound of the tuning fork, the ani-

mal's salivation response to the sound of the tuning fork? What term did he use to explain the effect of repeatedly striking the tuning fork without providing food?

2. Who is the psychologist closely associated with operant conditioning? Which type of learning—operant conditioning or classical conditioning—emphasizes that the stimulus elicits the response?

3. What are positive consequences called? Negative consequences? Can you name two ways to have a behavior repeated and two ways to prevent a behavior from being repeated?

4. What are the four types of schedules of partial reinforcement?

5. What are some examples of primary reinforcers? What type of reinforcer is money? Make a list of reinforcers that could be labeled physical, psychological, and symbolic.

6. Aversive stimuli can be used in two ways. What are they? How are they different? People can avoid unpleasant events or escape from them. Can you explain the difference?

7. How did Martin Seligman develop learned helplessness in animals? A person who has learned helplessness is more likely to be depressed. If a person feels helpless and depressed after taking an exam, what things is this person likely to be thinking about?

8. What is the process in which a person is reinforced for closer and closer approximations of the desired behavior? What is the name of the sequence in which one response produces the signal for the next response?

9. What are the three types of modeling?

CRITICAL THINKING

1. Analyze. Which of the schedules of reinforcement do your instructors generally use in conducting their classes? How would your classes

conditioning, people can avoid unpleasant events by engaging in a behavior that prevents the unpleasant event from happening. In escape conditioning, the person can escape from the unpleasant event by engaging in a particular behavior.

7. Answers will vary, but students might note: by setting up experiments in which the animals' actions made no dif-

ference. A person who feels helpless after failing an exam would be thinking, "I never have done well on math tests and never will" and "I'm just dumb."

8. shaping; response chain

9. the behavior of others simply increases the chances we will do the same thing; observational learning; disinhibition

be different if they used the other schedules? Give examples for your answers and justify your reasoning.

2. **Apply.** Businesses often make use of conditioning techniques in their commercials. They associate the name of their product with pleasant tunes or exciting scenes, so that the name alone will elicit conditioned relaxation or excitement. Think of specific ads that use these techniques. Describe several selling methods that use operant conditioning.

3. **Analyze.** In an experiment on learned helplessness (Seligman, 1978), animals that were unable to change their situation for long periods seemed unable or unwilling to change when the possibility was opened to them. What implications do such experiments have for humans? Can you think of situations in your life that have had the effect of learned helplessness?

APPLYING KNOWLEDGE

1. Select some particular task that you find difficult or unpleasant. Whenever you begin to work at this task, play one of your favorite tapes or CDs as you work. Do this for two weeks and then analyze your reactions. Have your feelings toward the music become associated with the task? Do you find it easier to work and complete the task? Explain your findings in light of what you know about conditioning techniques.

2. Much has been written about the deficiencies in American education today. Some commentators cite the decline in test scores as evidence that the students of today do not measure up to their peers of a generation ago. Many reasons are given, including the amount of time spent watching television rather than reading or studying. Others argue that television has had little or no impact on the quality of education in America. Write an essay supporting both viewpoints. Be sure to include what you have learned from the chapter about how people learn. Read recent magazine and newspaper articles for more information on the causes of the decline in the American educational system.

BEYOND THE CLASSROOM

1. Go to a public place where you can watch parents and children interacting with each other. Shopping malls, fast food restaurants, and supermarkets are ideal settings to observe parents attempting to control children *and* children attempting to control parents. Watch a parent-child interaction long enough to identify an aversive stimulus the parent or child may be using to control behavior. What particular behavior of the child is the parent attempting to change? What particular behavior of the parent is the child attempting to change? Are they successful? Can you identify the disadvantages to both parent and child of using aversive stimuli in the situation you have observed? What changes would you recommend?

IN YOUR JOURNAL

1. Reread the journal entry in which you described your attempts to teach a skill or task. Identify the kind or kinds of learning techniques you used. Would you classify them as based on classical conditioning, operant conditioning, modeling, or combinations of all three?

   Make a new entry in your journal in which you describe and identify the learning techniques. Explain why your teaching strategy was successful or unsuccessful. Be sure to include examples of other strategies you would use in a similar situation.

2. Answers will vary. Responses should deal adequately with both sides of the issue, cite references in support of arguments, and indicate an understanding of how people learn.

Beyond the Classroom

1. Answers will vary. Students should keep careful notes of their observations and respond as completely as possible to each of the five questions in the assignment.

IN YOUR JOURNAL

If time permits, discuss journal entries individually with students. Make sure each correctly identifies the various learning techniques used and provides valid reasons for new strategies.

Critical Thinking

1. Be sure students start by analyzing the reinforcement schedule currently in use and then explain how their classes would be different under each of the other three schedules.

2. Encourage students to bring clippings or videotapes of current ads to class for discussion. One example of operant conditioning in advertising is the use of coupon promotions.

3. Since some students may not feel comfortable discussing their private lives, guide the discussion toward common experiences. One example would be people who have interviewed for many jobs but received no offers.

Applying Knowledge

1. Answers will vary. Students should demonstrate an understanding of conditioning techniques.

CHAPTER BONUS
Test Question

This question may be used for extra credit on the chapter test.
Choose the letter of the correct response.

When reinforcement occurs after a set time period, the schedule is:
a. variable ratio.
b. fixed interval.
c. variable interval.
d. fixed ratio.

Answer: **b**

CHAPTER 3
Memory and Thought

TEXT TOPICS	SPECIAL FEATURES	RESOURCE MATERIALS
Taking in Information, pp. 53–56		Reproducible Lesson Plan; Study Guide; Review Activity Transparency 2
Storing Information, pp. 56–61		Reproducible Lesson Plan; Study Guide; Review Activity Transparencies 3, 4
Retrieving Information, pp. 61–69	**Using Psychology:** Eyewitness Testimony, pp. 61–62 **Psychology Update,** p. 61 **At a Glance:** Remembering High School Classmates, p. 65 **Fact or Fiction?,** p. 66 **Using Psychology:** Mood and Memory, pp. 66–67 **Psychology and You,** p. 67	Reproducible Lesson Plan; Study Guide; Review Activity *Readings in Psychology:* Section 1, Readings 2, 3
Central Processing of Information, pp. 69–75	**More about Psychology,** p. 69	Reproducible Lesson Plan; Study Guide; Review Activity; Application Activity; Extension Activity; Chapter Test, Form A and Form B Understanding Psychology Testmaker

PERFORMANCE ASSESSMENT ACTIVITY

Write the following sayings by Greek writer Aeschylus and Roman orator Cicero on the chalkboard.

"Memory is the mother of all wisdom." (Aeschylus)
"Memory is the treasury and guardian of all things." (Cicero)

Ask: What do these two sayings have in common? *(the high opinion of memory)* Request students to draw posters illustrating these sayings or sayings of their own design. *(Posters should express graphically a point of view on the function or purpose of memory.)*

CHAPTER RESOURCES

Readings for the Student
Adler, Bill, Jr. *The Student's Memory Book: Easy-to-Master Memory Techniques That Will Revolutionize Your Study Habits.* New York: Doubleday and Co., 1988.

Gallant, Roy A. *Memory: How It Works and How to Improve It.* New York: Macmillan Children's Book Group, 1984.

Schafer, Edith N. *Our Remarkable Memory.* Washington, D.C.: Starrhill Press, 1992.

Wartik, Nancy. *Memory and Learning.* New York: Chelsea House, 1992.

Readings for the Teacher
Higbee, Kenneth L. *Your Memory: How It Works and How to Improve It.* New York: Paragon House, 1993.

Johnson, George. *In the Palace of Memory: How We Build the Worlds Inside Our Heads.* New York: Random House, 1992.

Kail, Robert. *The Development of Memory in Children.* New York: W. H. Freeman, 1989.

Loftus, E. F. *Eyewitness Testimony.* Cambridge, MA: Harvard University Press, 1980.

Multimedia
Computers and Human Behavior (29 minutes). Indiana University. This video display attempts to use the computer to understand human cognitive processes.

Learning and Memory (60 minutes, 3/4″ or 1/2″ video). Films Incorporated Educational. This shows the operation of memory in the learning process.

Memory (30 minutes, 3/4″ or 1/2″ video). McGraw-Hill Training. This shows proven methods for improving memory by categorizing and referencing memories.

FOCUS

Motivating Activity

Working individually, have students write down at least three memorable experiences in their lives. As a prompt, you might ask them to recall some "famous firsts." To encourage self-reflection, tell students that the list will not be collected. Based on items chosen, challenge students to suggest some of the factors that make an experience memorable. *(Being a "first," for example, often sets an experience apart.)* Suggest students review their ideas as they read the chapter.

Meeting Chapter Objectives.

Refer students to the objectives on page 53. Working individually or in small groups, have students skim the heads in this chapter. Ask: On what pages would you expect to find information on each of these objectives? What clue words led you to this answer? Then ask a volunteer to read the margin feature on page 67 aloud to the class. Ask: What part of the SQ3R method have you just completed? *(S)* Next, have students complete the "Q" part by forming each objective into a question. Plan with students how they might best complete the "3R" parts of the SQ3R method.

Building Vocabulary.

Assign groups of students to prepare crossword puzzles using at least 20 of the Key Terms. Have the groups exchange their puzzles with each other.

Memory and Thought

FIGURE 3.1 No mysteries are more fundamental than how we think, remember, solve problems, and create ideas.

52

TEACHER CLASSROOM RESOURCES

- Chapter 3 Reproducible Lesson Plan
- Chapter 3 Study Guide
- Chapter 3 Review Activity
- Chapter 3 Application Activity
- Chapter 3 Extension Activity

- Transparencies 2–4 Transparency Strategies and Activities

- *Readings in Psychology:* Section 1, Readings 2, 3

- Chapter 3 Test, Form A and Form B

- Understanding Psychology Testmaker

The Purposes of Memory. Write the word *cognitive psychologist* on the chalkboard. Ask: What do you think is the specialty of this psychologist? *(the study of cognition, or the process of "knowing" through perception and memory)* Then read aloud the following comment by a cognitive psychologist James McGaugh:

Memory is essential for our behavior. There is nothing of significance that is not based fundamentally on memory. Our consciousness and our actions are shaped by our experiences. And, our experiences shape us only because of their lingering [memories].

Ask: What purpose does McGaugh say memory serves? Do you agree or disagree with this point of view? What examples from your own life could you use to support your opinion?

OBJECTIVES

After studying this chapter, you should be able to

- describe the concept of information processing.
- identify the different types of memory systems.
- explain the different theories that account for memory.
- describe the psychological perspective on thought, the units of thought, and the basic types of thought.
- define problem solving and outline the development of problem-solving strategies.

I s anything more complex than the human mind?

Consider all the material stored in your memory: your social security number, the capital of South Dakota, "The Star-Spangled Banner," your first love's phone number, the important generals of the Civil War, the starting lineup for the Boston Red Sox, your best friend in first grade, and so on. What kind of incredible filing system allows you to instantly recover a line from your favorite movie? How does all that information fit in your head?

Going beyond memory, how do we think? How do we solve problems? How do we create ideas? No mysteries are more fundamental, and researchers are just beginning to investigate human thought. Psychologists refer to all cognitive and mental activities—from memorizing lists of numbers to writing poems and inventing new technologies—as *information processing*. This involves three steps: input, central processing, and output. **Input** is the information people receive from their senses. **Central processing** is the storing (in memory) and sorting (by thought) of this information in the brain. **Output** refers to the ideas and actions that result from processing.

KEY TERMS

central processing
concept
confabulation
creativity
directed thinking
eidetic memory
feature extraction
image
input
insight
long-term memory
memory
metacognition
mnemonic devices
nondirected thinking
output
proactive interference
recall
recognition
recombination
repression
retrieval
retroactive interference
rule
selective attention
sensory storage
set
short-term memory
symbol

IN YOUR JOURNAL

Think back to your childhood and recall your earliest memory. Describe this memory in your journal.

IN YOUR JOURNAL

You might begin this activity by telling the story behind Alex Haley's bestselling book *Roots*. As an adult, Haley wanted to find out more about the "furthest-back person" known to his family—an enslaved African named Kunta Kinte. To find out about Kinte, Haley had to search the "furthest-back" memories of people on both sides of the Atlantic. Tell students to recall their "furthest-back" memories, including stories told by their families. What roles do such memories serve in shaping an individual's identity?

EXTRA CREDIT ACTIVITY

Many popular songs, both past and present, deal with the theme of memories—some pleasant, some painful. Request groups of students to go through their CD or tape collections to find songs that focus on memories. They might also ask their family or friends for suggestions. (An example of an older tune is the Beatles' song "In My Life.") Have these students put together an oral report, illustrated with relevant song lyrics, that assess what seem to be the most common memories recounted in popular music. Have class members find information that explains why people hang on to such memories.

TEACH

Guided Practice

■ **Demonstration.** You might introduce the subject of selective memory by calling on two volunteers to prepare short talks to be delivered simultaneously. One student should assemble detailed directions on how to get to a little-known spot in your community. The other student should talk about some "hot" topic at school, such as a recent game or concert. Tell students to pay attention to the directions. When the volunteers are done, ask class members to repeat the directions. Using information in the text, explore reasons students were able or unable to tune out the "hot-topic" speaker. (OBJECTIVE 1)

VISUAL INSTRUCTION

Ask students to explain in their own words how people are able to "listen" to multiple messages.
Answer to caption, Figure 3.2: Selective attention: the ability to pick and choose among various inputs.

TAKING IN INFORMATION

Information is any event that reduces uncertainty. For example, when a traffic light changes from red to green, it provides you with information—it reduces your uncertainty about whether you should step on the gas. Many forms of information are captured through your senses—voices, musical sounds, sweet tastes, pungent odors, colorful images, rough textures, painful stings. These and all experiences are converted into impulses in your nervous system. At any given moment a confusing array of sights, sounds, smells, and other sensations compete for your attention. If you accepted all these inputs, you would be completely overwhelmed. Two processes help people narrow sensory inputs to a manageable number: selective attention and feature extraction.

Selective Attention

Your ability to pick and choose among the various available inputs is called **selective attention.** For example, if you are at a large party where the music is turned up and everyone is talking, you can focus on a friend's voice and ignore all other sounds. In a way, selective attention is like tuning in a specific television channel.

In his *selection theory,* Donald Broadbent argued that we attend to only one of the many channels of information reaching us at any time because the channels available to interpret the information are themselves very limited. Yet, in the dichotic listening task, subjects could report hearing their name in the channel they had been instructed to

FIGURE 3.2

In a crowded setting, we cannot pay equal attention to all the sounds. Some kind of selectivity is needed. In a dichotic listening task, the subject wears earphones and listens to two different messages. **What is selective attention?**

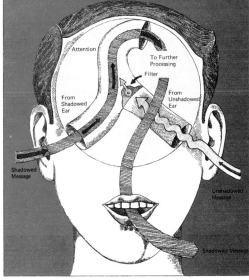

🧪 LAB EXPERIMENTS AND DEMONSTRATIONS

To illustrate feature extraction, you might hold an "index drill" in which you ask students to quickly find the first page reference for random terms that you call out. The first student to find the term should call out the page number. After doing this several times, ask: Did you read every item in the index to find the term? If not, what clues or features did you look for to find the item quickly? *(Most students will say they skimmed for initial letters.)* Next, call on students to cite other examples of how they use this practice (feature extraction) to process information in their daily lives.

ignore. Others, told to ignore one channel, nevertheless could report the flow of a complete story even though the story was switched without warning to the ignored channel. Based on this work in 1960, Anne Treisman (1964) later proposed an *attenuation theory.* She argued that Broadbent's filter suppressed other channels but did not eliminate them. Some information was still being processed. Thus, unlike a television dial, selective attention does not completely block out other programs or stimuli. These theories assume that when you first analyze a wide variety of incoming information you focus on a select few and direct most of your conscious attention to them.

Later, psychologists suggested we may actually be limited not in our ability to process information, but in our ability to respond after all information has been processed. If you meet several friends at once in school, you cannot say "Hello" to all of them at the same time, so you attend to each one individually. The results of human performance in tasks such as you see in Figure 3.3 argue that we are selecting among responses. This suggests that attention registers its effects late, after the meaning of incoming stimulation has been more or less fully processed (Treisman, 1988).

What makes one input more important than another? Information leading to the satisfaction of such needs as hunger and thirst has top priority. You've noticed how a person who is very hungry will pay more attention to his or her dinner than to the dinner-table chitchat. We also give priority to inputs that are strange and novel, such as an individual who comes to a party dressed for snorkeling. A third director of attention is interest: the more interested you are in something, the more likely you are to notice it. For example, most people "tune in" when they hear their name mentioned; we're all interested in what other people have to say about us. Likewise, if you become interested in chess, you will suddenly begin to notice newspaper articles about chess, chess sets in store windows, and references to chess moves in everyday speech—for example, "stalemate." These inputs are not new. They were there last year and the year before, but you simply weren't interested enough to notice them.

Feature Extraction

Selective attention is only the first step in narrowing input. The second step is to decide on which aspects of the selected channel you will focus. This process, called **feature extraction,** involves locating the outstanding characteristics of incoming information (Figure 3.4). If you want to identify the make of a car, you look for certain features—the shape of the fenders, the grille and so on. For the most part, you ignore such features as color, upholstery, and tires, which tell you little about the make of the car. Similarly, when you read, you focus on the important words, skimming over such words as *the, and,* or *for example.*

Being able to extract the significant features of an input helps a person to identify it and compare it to other inputs. For example, you are able to distinguish faces from one another and, at the same time, see resemblances. You may notice that all the members of a family have similar

---

FIGURE 3.3

In the lists below, ignore the letters printed in green. Time yourself as you read down the list of red letters in List A. How long did it take? Now read down the list of red letters in List B. How long did it take? Read the letters now, before reading the next paragraph.

Some researchers have argued that List B takes longer. Depite being told to ignore the green letters you process them anyway and then have to suppress them as you read Lists A and B. But in List B, the green letter is the same as the red letter in the next row. To get yourself to say the red letter from the second position all the way to the bottom, you have to overcome the suppression of the green letter from the previous row, thus adding to the time it takes you to read the red letters in List B (Driver & Tipper, 1989).

List A	List B
RT	TG
VC	GT
WE	EC
HH	HE
GP	RH
NC	GP
IX	XC
QA	AX
BL	LA
UD	DL
FT	TD
XM	MT

CONNECTIONS: PSYCHOLOGY AND LINGUISTICS

How do we determine word meanings? One answer to this question is based on the *semantic feature theory.* This theory suggests that a word is simply a cluster of features. For example, a *dog* is any organism that barks, has four legs, fur, a tail, and is usually domesticated. What about a Mexican Hairless or a Boxer with its tail removed? Are they dogs? Such semantic problems led Elinor Rosch (1973) to propose the *theory of prototypes.* According to Rosch, we understand a word by knowing the features of its prototype and recognizing that it may have only a subset of the features of its prototype. Thus a dog may not even bark, but still possess enough "dog"ness to make it a dog. Call on two of your students to research Rosch's theories further and to present her ideas on semantic feature extraction in the form of an oral report.

■ **Demonstration.** To illustrate sensory memory storage, completely darken the classroom for several minutes. While the lights are out, tape up a large block of black print on a white background or on the chalkboard or wall. Tell students to look in that direction as you flick on the light switch for a second or less. Ask: What part of the letter block did you "see" when the lights went off again? *(Some students may have seen a blur; others may have retained an "image" of the letters.)* Have students write a short paragraph in which they explain how this activity illustrated the principle of sensory storage. (OBJECTIVE 2)

VISUAL INSTRUCTION

Ask students what features they used to "extract" the hidden faces from the picture.

Answer to caption, Figure 3.4: Answers will vary. Lead students to understand that feature extraction can help individuals to identify, compare, or distinguish items.

FIGURE 3.4

Can you spot the hidden faces in this picture? To find them, it is necessary for you to extract those features that define a human face from a large amount of irrelevant information.
Why is feature extraction helpful?

noses, yet you are able to recognize each person on the basis of other features.

Obviously, feature extraction depends to some extent on experience—on knowing what to look for. This is especially true where fine distinctions must be made. It takes considerable expertise to distinguish an original Rembrandt from a skillful forgery. Most of us cannot distinguish between two grades of diamonds, but an expert who knows what to look for can make this distinction easily.

Like selective attention, feature extraction is an evaluative process. If you are reading a novel for pleasure, you may look for the "juicy" parts. If you're reading a historical biography to prepare for an exam, you'll probably still look for the juicy parts. When you don't find any, you go ahead and concentrate on the other facts.

STORING INFORMATION

In order to be used, the inputs that reach the brain must be registered, held onto, perhaps "filed" for future reference. We call the storage of inputs **memory.** Psychologists distinguish among three kinds of memory, each of which has a different purpose and time span. **Sensory storage** holds information for only a second or so; **short-term memory** keeps it in mind as long as you repeat it; **long-term memory** can store it indefinitely.

Sensory Storage

The senses of sight and hearing seem to be able to hold an input for a fraction of a second before it disappears. For example, when you watch a motion picture, you do not notice the gaps between frames. The actions seem smooth because each frame is held in sensory storage until the next frame arrives.

Sperling (1960) demonstrated this phenomenon in an ingenious experiment. He used a tachistoscope (a device that presents a picture for a very brief time) to present a group of letters and numbers to people for a twentieth of a second. Previous studies had shown that if you present a stimulus like this

7	1	V	F
X	L	5	3
B	7	W	4

people will usually be able to tell you four or five of the items. Sperling believed that people took a mental photograph of the letters, and were able to read back only a few before the picture faded. He told the people in his experiment that after he flashed the letters on the tachistoscope screen, he would present a tone. Upon hearing a high tone, the subjects were to tell him the top row, a medium tone the middle row, and a low tone the bottom row. Once people learned this system, they were indeed able to remember about 75 percent of any one row. Thus, he proved that the subject retains a brief image of the whole picture so that he or she can still read off the items in the correct row *after* the picture has left the screen.

 LAB EXPERIMENTS AND DEMONSTRATIONS

Ask four student volunteers to act as subjects for a demonstration on sensory storage and short-term memory. Read a list of 10 two-digit numbers. Wait three seconds, and ask the first student to write down the numbers. After five seconds, ask the second student to write the numbers. After 15 seconds, ask the third student to write them down. After 30 seconds, ask the fourth student to do the same. Graph the results, recording time along one of the coordinates and the number of items recalled along the other. Ask: What conclusions can you draw about information storage based upon this demonstration?

The information held momentarily by the senses has not yet been narrowed down or analyzed. It is like a short-lived but highly detailed photograph or tape recording that fades rapidly. However, by the time information gets to the next stage—short-term memory—it has been analyzed, identified, and simplified so that it can be conveniently stored and handled for a longer time.

Short-Term Memory

The things you have in your conscious mind at any one moment are being held in short-term memory. Short-term memory does not necessarily involve paying close attention. You have probably had the experience of listening to someone only partially and then having that person accuse you of not paying attention. You deny it and, in order to prove your innocence, you repeat, word for word, the last words he or she said. You can do this because you are holding the words in short-term memory. Usually, however, the sense of what that person was saying does not register until you repeat the words out loud. Repeating the words makes you pay attention to them. This is what psychologists mean by rehearsal.

Rehearsal.   To keep information in short-term memory for more than a few seconds, you have to repeat it to yourself, in your mind or out loud. When you look up a telephone number, for example, you can remember the seven digits long enough to dial them *if* you repeat them several times. If you are distracted or make a mistake in dialing, the chances are you will have to look the number up again. It has been lost from short-term memory.

Psychologists have measured short-term memory by seeing how long a subject can retain a piece of information without rehearsal. The experimenter shows the subject 3 letters, such as *CPQ*, replaced by 3 numerals, such as 798, one second later. To prevent rehearsal, the subject has been instructed to start counting backward by threes and reporting the result in time with a metronome striking once per second. If the subject performs this task for only a short time, she or he will usually remember the letters. If kept from rehearsing for 18 seconds, however, recall will be no better than a random guess; the information is forgotten. Short-term memory lasts a bit less than 20 seconds without rehearsal.

Chunking.   Short-term memory is limited not only in its duration, but in its capacity as well. It can hold only about seven unrelated items. Suppose, for example, someone quickly reels off a series of numbers to you. You will be able to keep only about seven or eight of them in your immediate memory. Beyond that number, confusion among them will set in. The same limit is there if the unrelated items are a random set of words. We may not notice this limit to our capacity because we usually do not have to store so many unrelated items in our immediate memory. Either the items are related (as when we listen to someone speak) or they are rehearsed and placed in long-term memory.

Short-term memory can hold only about seven unrelated items.

■ **Discussion.** Tell students that George Miller first presented his landmark ideas on memory in a 1955 address called "The Magical Number Seven, Plus or Minus Two." He began his talk by saying, "My problem is that I have been persecuted by an integer [number]." That integer, explained Miller, was seven. Based on information on this page, have students assess why Miller might have described seven as "magical." *(It is the maximum number of digits that most people can hold in immediate memory.)* Why might he have been "persecuted" by that same number? *(Miller could not figure out a way to increase the memory limit beyond seven until he tried chunking.)* (OBJECTIVE 3)

VISUAL INSTRUCTION

Ask students why this experiment is a demonstration of short-term memory. *(because they will soon forget how many dots they saw in either figure)*
Answer to caption, Figure 3.5: The organization of dots into a small number of chunks makes it easier to process the information.

FIGURE 3.5

Glance quickly at the left figure in this pair, then look away. How many dots did you see? Now do the same with the right figure. You were probably more sure and more accurate in your answer for the right figure. **Why is this so?**

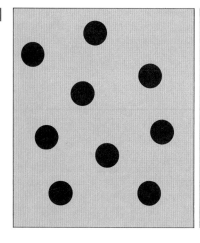
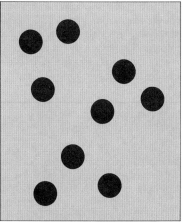

The most interesting aspect of this limit, discovered by George Miller (1956), is that it involves about seven items of any kind. Each item may consist of a collection of many other items, but if they are all packaged into one "chunk" then there is still only one item. Thus we can remember about seven unrelated sets of initials, such as COMSAT, DDT, SST, or the initials of our favorite radio stations, even though we could not remember all the letters separately. This occurs because we have connected, or "chunked," them together previously, so that DDT is one item, not three.

One of the tricks of memorizing a lot of information quickly is to chunk together the items as fast as they come in. If we connect items in groups, we have fewer to remember. For example, we remember new phone numbers in two or three chunks (555–6794 or 555–67–94) rather than as a string of seven digits (5–5–5–6–7–9–4). As Figure 3.5 illustrates, we use chunking to remember visual as well as verbal inputs.

Even with chunking, storage in short-term memory is only temporary. It contains information that is "of possible interest." Information worth holding onto must be rehearsed—with intent to learn—to transfer it to long-term memory. Rehearsal without intent to learn yields no transfer.

Long-Term Memory

Long-term memory is where we store information for future use. Information is apparently stored by features; it is not stored like a piece of paper in a filing cabinet. You reconstruct what you must recall when you need it. When you say a friend has a good memory, you probably mean he or she can recall a wide variety of information accurately. Long-term memory contains representations of countless facts, experiences, and sensations. You may not have thought of your childhood home for years, but you can probably still visualize it.

Long-term memory involves all the processes we have been describing. Suppose you go to see a play. As the actors say their lines, the sounds flow

LAB EXPERIMENTS AND DEMONSTRATIONS

To demonstrate how chunking can increase retention of information, pass out the following lists of words. Type or write the words in vertical columns. Slash marks in List A show the "chunks".

List A: dogs cats birds horses/ purple yellow red blue/ Dolphins Saints Eagles Cowboys/ Temple Princeton UCLA Notre Dame/ MCI NFL NBC IBM

List B: Temple dogs purple IBM Saints Princeton horses red blue NFL Cowboys yellow cats UCLA Dolphins birds MCI Eagles Notre Dame NBC
(continued on page 59)

through your sensory storage. Selective attention screens out other sounds, and feature extraction turns sounds into recognizable words. These words accumulate in short-term memory and form meaningful phrases and sentences.

You attend to the action and changing scenery in much the same way. Together, they form chunks in your memory. An hour or two later, you will have forgotten all but the most striking lines, but you have stored the *meaning* of the lines and actions in long-term memory. The next day, you may be able to give a scene-by-scene description of the play. Throughout this process, the least important information is dropped and only the essentials are retained (Figure 3.6). A month or two later, without much rehearsal, you may remember only a brief outline of the plot and perhaps a few particularly impressive moments. In time you may not remember anything about the play. Other, more recently stored items block access to earlier memories or may even replace them. But if you see the play again, you will probably recognize the lines of the play and anticipate the actions. Although it has become less accessible, elements of the play are still stored in long-term memory.

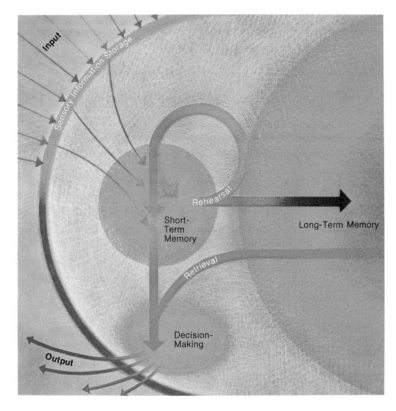

FIGURE 3.6

Input to the senses is stored temporarily, and some of it is passed on into short-term memory. Information may be kept in short-term memory by rehearsal, or it may be passed on to long-term memory. Material stored in both short- and long-term memory is used in making decisions. **What is the capacity of short-term memory?**

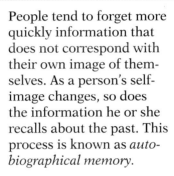

■ **Identifying Points of View.**
Read aloud the following excerpt from an essay by Ulric Neisser entitled: "Memory—What Are the Important Questions?"

The psychologists who . . . [study memory] . . . have always hoped that their work would have wide applicability sooner or later. Their preference for artificial tasks has a rational basis: one can control variables and manipulate conditions more easily in the lab than in natural settings. . . .

We would like to understand how this happens under natural conditions . . . in schools and at home, on the job, and in the course of thought. . . .

Ask: What issue is Neisser discussing? *(value of laboratory research on memory)* What is his point of view on this issue? *(prefers studies in naturalistic settings)* Do you agree with Neisser? Why or why not? (OBJECTIVES 2, 3)

Other Models of Memory

For almost a century, the study of memory focused on how long information was stored for usage. Then a Canadian psychologist, Endel Tulving (1972), proposed that we have two types of memory. *Semantic memory* is our knowledge of language, including its rules, words, and meanings. We share that knowledge with other speakers of our language. *Episodic memory* is our memory of our own life—such as when you woke up this morning. Stored here are things where time of occurrence is important.

L. R. Squire (1987) proposed a related model of memory. *Declarative memory*, sometimes called *explicit memory*, involves both episodic and semantic memory. This knowledge you call forth consciously and use as you need it. *Procedural memory*, sometimes called *implicit memory* (Roediger, 1990), does not require conscious recollection to have past learning or experiences impact our performance. One form of procedural memory involves *skills*, learned as we mature—including both complex skills such as swimming or driving a car, and simple skills such as tying a tie. Ask a male to describe to you—in as little time as it would take him to do it—how to tie a tie. Most will fail your test! As we gain skill, we gradually lose the ability to describe what we are doing. Trying to do so will actually slow us down! It's unconscious; it's much faster to show someone how.

Another form of procedural memory is *priming*. Suppose you are shown such words as *assassin, barrel,* and *monkey* in a very long list. Later we give you cues such as: _ss_ss_ _, barr_ _, and mo_ _ey. You will be able to recognize these words with much greater accuracy and speed than will anyone who has not seen the list. People with amnesia perform just as well as the rest of us on this kind of priming task. Yet, if they are then asked to identify which words were used on puzzles in the second part of the study, they will do much worse than those without amnesia. Implicit memory—influenced by the effects of priming—is unaffected by amnesia. Amnesia affects only explicit memory. *Conditioning* can occur in which humans learn responses without being consciously aware that their responding has been affected.

Memory and the Brain

What happens in the brain when something is stored in long-term memory? This question is highly controversial. Although psychologists agree that some physiological changes occur in the brain, they are only beginning to identify how and where memories are stored.

What physiological changes occur when we learn something? Some psychologists theorize it is change in the neuronal structure of nerves. Others contend that learning is based on molecular or chemical changes in the brain. The evidence is more and more clear that both sides are correct. What changes occur depend on the level at which you are examining the changes learning creates.

Where does learning occur? There is growing evidence that formation of procedural memories involves activity in an area of the brain called the *striatum*, deep in the front part of our *cortex*. Declarative memories result

CONNECTIONS: PSYCHOLOGY AND SOCIAL STUDIES

Some psychologists study the *flashbulb memory phenomenon*. This type of memory centers around a specific, important, or surprising event. The memory is so vivid that it represents a mental snapshot. For many people, especially members of the "Baby Boom" generation, the Kennedy assassination is a flashbulb memory. Assign students to explore the effect of the Kennedy assassination on members of their parents' era. Suggest that they read articles commemorating the 30th anniversary of Kennedy's death in news magazines such as the November 1993 issues of *TIME* or *U.S. News & World Report*. Ask: What evidence of the "flashbulb memory phenomenon" can you find in these stories?

from activity in the *hippocampus* and the *amygdala* (Mishkin & Petri, 1984). Further discussion of the location of these and other structures is in Chapter 4. Richard Thompson (1987) has studied brain activity caused by classical conditioning of the nictitating membrane—a second eyelid located just under the visible eyelid—in the eyes of rabbits. Thompson's CS is a tone; his UCS is an air puff to one of the rabbit's eyes. Once the rabbit has been conditioned, Thompson has identified cells that are active only if the tone sounds first, but not if the air puff is delivered without warning. Removal of these cells in the cerebellum causes the rabbit to lose the CR. The rabbit can be reconditioned using the other eye, but it never again learns the CR with the original eye, though it still blinks to any air puff and can hear the tone.

It is not clear yet how individual nerve cells—called *neurons*—establish connections with one another when learning occurs. What is clear is that a very complex chemical process precedes the formation of new connections between neurons. Some have credited increases in calcium. Others talk of decreased potassium flow. Processes as diverse as increased protein synthesis, heightened levels of glucose, and other biochemical processes are involved (Kalat, 1992). Exactly how it all fits together remains an active area of psychological research.

RETRIEVING INFORMATION

Stored information is useless unless it can be retrieved from memory. Once you've forgotten to send a card for your mother's birthday, it's not very

U sing Psychology

Eyewitness Testimony

One situation in which recognition is extremely important (sometimes a matter of life or death) is in the courtroom. It is very convincing to a judge or jury when an eyewitness points to someone in the room and says, "He's the one who did it."

A psychologist who remains deeply involved in the issue of eyewitness testimony is Elizabeth Loftus. She has shown (1974) that even after it had been proved that the eyesight of a witness was too poor for her to have seen a robber's face from where she stood at the scene of a robbery, the jury was still swayed by her testimony.

Lawyers can cite many cases of people falsely accused by eyewitnesses whose testimonies later proved to be inaccurate. In one such case, 14 eyewitnesses agreed that the defendant had robbed a Cal-

PSYCHOLOGY UPDATE

Selective Memory Problems. Memory problems can sometimes take a surprising twist. One example is the peculiar condition known as *prospagnosia*, in which the patient is unable to recognize familiar faces—even his or her own face. People who have this condition can still perceive other aspects of faces, however, such as whether a person's expression is happy or sad.

Prospagnosia usually results from a stroke or head injury, and it illustrates how remarkably narrow or selective memory problems can sometimes be.

As another example of a selective problem, consider the case of a 34-year-old man who suffered a stroke. He recovered and regained his previous abilities—except that he found it nearly impossible to name common fruits and vegetables. He could, however, pick out the objects if the names were read to him. Selective problems such as this suggest that memories are organized into categories. Somehow, an individual category may become disconnected from the memory system as a whole.

■ **Discussion.** After students have read the margin feature on this page, ask the following questions.

1. What is prospagnosia? *(inability to recognize familiar faces)*
2. What theory does the writer use to explain selective memory problems? *(Memory is organized into categories. An individual category may become disconnected from the memory system.)* (OBJECTIVE 3)

U sing Psychology

You might introduce an activity based on this feature by writing the following phrase on the chalkboard: "Seeing is believing." Explore with students the shortcomings of this statement. *(Emphasize the role of selective attention in short- and long-term memory.)* After students have read the feature, ask: What factors may lead to inaccurate eyewitness testimony? *(Sample answers: shocking events may hamper our ability to form a strong memory; phraseology of a question may mislead a witness; speed at which an event occurred prevents storage of certain details.)*

PSYCHOLOGISTS AT WORK

Like experimental psychologists (see Chapter 2), *neuropsychologists* also study basic physical processes of the brain. However, these scientists focus on those processes controlled by the nervous system. They are particularly interested in understanding the neurological basis of human behavior. In recent years, neuropsychologists have probed deeply into the causes of the memory breakdown associated with old age. They have also explored the neurological basis of hyperactivity, looking for ways to control body movement and attention spans.

Neuropsychologists often work in hospitals and universities. However, they have also found employment in pharmaceutical companies. Here they assess and develop new drugs for psychological care and treatment.

VISUAL INSTRUCTION

Refer students to the three photos of the "Son of Sam." Ask: Why do you think these pictures differ? *(Emphasize the effect of stress and violence upon memory.)* Tell students to imagine they are criminologists—experts who study crime—assigned to the police department. What, if any, details do these sketches have in common? *(As a tip, have students reread the information on feature extraction on pp. 55-56.)* What would they tell police officers to look for as they patrolled the streets?

Readings in Psychology.
Have students read the Section 1, Reading 2 selection in *Readings in Psychology* and answer the questions that follow the reading.

DID YOU KNOW?

Psychologists use a machine called a *tachistoscope* to measure the length of sensory storage. This apparatus allows a psychologist to present an image as briefly as a few hundredths of a second!

ifornia supermarket and shot a policeman. However, later evidence proved that he was nowhere near the scene of the crime.

Loftus and Palmer (1974) have done a fascinating series of experiments showing that when people are asked to recall the details of auto accidents, they, too, are likely to distort the facts. After groups of college students saw a filmed accident, they asked some of them, "About how fast were the cars going when they contacted each other?" The average estimate was under 32 miles per hour. When they substituted the word *smashed* for *contacted* in the above question, another group of students remembered the same accident with the cars going significantly faster—41 miles per hour.

FIGURE 3.7

Three sketches of the "Son of Sam" killer show that eyewitnesses have different memories of his appearance.

Sam: the latest sketches
Cops' update alters description

Loftus (1979, 1980) has also found that a person's memory of an event can be distorted in the process of remembering it. Shocking events, such as those involving violence, can disrupt our ability to form a strong memory. Without a strong, clear memory of the event, the eyewitness is more likely to incorporate misinformation into the recall. For example, if a police officer asks a witness to describe the gun used in a robbery, the witness may recall a gun even though the robber never revealed a weapon.

Defense attorneys are well aware of the effects that leading questions can have on people's memories. Expert testimony by psychologists on the nature of human memory and on the factors that influence the accuracy of an identification may be needed to convince jurors to be more critical in their appraisal of eyewitness testimony. Even after being cautioned by experts on human memory, however, jurors still tend to believe erroneously that the eye is a camera and that recall is like a videotape.

CONNECTIONS: PSYCHOLOGY AND LANGUAGE ARTS

The Using Psychology feature provides an opportunity to show how *loaded words* can shape attitudes, opinions, and behavior. Tell students that loaded words are terms or phrases packed with emotional and/or double meanings. Refer students to the effect that substituting "smashed" for "contacted" had on the answers of eyewitnesses. Working in small groups, have students rewrite any three statements in this chapter to include at least one loaded word. Call on volunteers to read the original and altered statements. Have the rest of the class identify the loaded word(s). Ask: How does the addition of the word(s) change the impact of the statement? At the end of class, ask students to write down as many of the original and altered words as they can. On the following day, tally and report: Were more loaded or unloaded words recalled?

consoling to prove that you have the date filed away in your brain. We've all experienced the acute embarrassment of being unable to remember a close friend's name. There are few things in life more frustrating than having a word "on the tip of your tongue," but just not being able to remember it.

The problem of memory is to store many thousands of items in such a way that you can find the one you need when you need it. The solution to **retrieval** is organization. Since human memory is extraordinarily efficient, it must be extremely well organized. Psychologists do not yet know how it is organized, but they are studying the processes of retrieval for clues.

Recognition

Human memory is organized in such a way as to make recognition quite easy—people can say with great accuracy whether or not something is familiar to them. If someone asked you the name of your first-grade teacher, for example, you might not remember it. But chances are that you would recognize the name if you heard it. Similarly, a multiple-choice test may bring out knowledge that a student might not be able to show on an essay test. The ability to recognize suggests that much more information is stored in memory than one might think.

The process of **recognition** provides insight into how information is stored in memory. We can recognize the sound of a particular musical instrument (say, a piano) no matter what tune is being played on it. We can also recognize a tune no matter what instrument is playing it. This pattern of recognition indicates that a single item of information may be "indexed" under several "headings" so that it can be reached in a number of ways. Thus, "the attractive teller at the Five Cents Savings Bank" might be indexed under "Five Cents Savings Bank," "service people," "potential friends," and "blondes." A person's features may be linked to a large number of categories. The more categories an item is filed in, the more easily it can be retrieved.

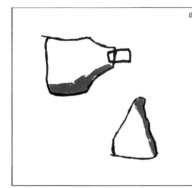

Memories may be simplified, enriched, or distorted over time.

FIGURE 3.8

Children between the ages of 5 and 7 were shown a bottle half filled with colored water and suspended at an angle, such as is shown in this drawing. After the children had seen this arrangement, they were asked to draw it from memory. Some of the results of the experiment are shown in Figure 3.9.

FIGURE 3.9

The drawing produced immediately after seeing the original and those produced a week later were very similar. An interesting change developed, however, when the children were asked 6 months later to reproduce the figure again. Most of the children's drawings, 58 percent, showed no change; 12 percent drew less sophisticated reproductions, but 30 percent of the drawings were a more accurate depiction. **What is involved in recall?**

🧪 LAB EXPERIMENTS AND DEMONSTRATIONS

Review the information on recognition patterns on this page. Then hand out three-by-five index cards or slips of paper to students. Challenge them to devise the "headings" under which they might file you. (*Samples include "high school teacher," "psychology class," "good friend of the English* teacher," "husband/wife/mother," *and so on.*) Compile a master list of headings on the chalkboard, and ask how such headings are used to retrieve information. For example, suppose students wanted to find your friend the English teacher. They would pull up that heading, which in turn would send them to you for help.

■ **Analyzing a Quote.** Read the following comment by William James to the students:

Forgetting is as important as remembering. . . . If we remembered everything, we should be as ill off as if we remembered nothing. It would take as long for us to recall a space of time as it took the original time to elapse, and we should never get ahead with our thinking.

Ask: According to James, what is the function of forgetting? *(allows people to spend less time sorting through data)* What other functions can students suggest? OBJECTIVES 3, 4)

Recall

More remarkable than the ability to recognize information is the ability to recall it. **Recall** is the active reconstruction of information. Just think about the amount of recall involved in a simple conversation. Each person uses hundreds of words involving all kinds of information, even though each word and bit of information must be retrieved separately from the storehouse of memory.

Recall involves more than searching for and finding pieces of information, however. It involves a person's knowledge, attitudes, and expectations. This was demonstrated in the experiment illustrated in Figures 3.8 and 3.9. Despite six months to forget, apparently many of the children later had a better idea of what a tilted bottle *should* look like (Inhelder, 1969). Our recall seems to result from an act of reconstruction. Our memories may be simplified, enriched, or distorted, depending on our experiences and attitudes. One type of mistake is called **confabulation;** a person "remembers" information that was never stored in memory. If our reconstruction of an event is incomplete, we fill in the gaps by making up what's missing. Sometimes we may be wrong.

About 5 percent of all children do not seem to reconstruct memories actively. They have an **eidetic memory**—or "photographic memory"—an ability shared by few adults. Children with eidetic memory can recall very specific details from a picture, a page, or a scene briefly viewed.

Relearning

While recognition and recall are measures of explicit memory, *relearning* is a measure of implicit memory. Suppose you learned a poem as a child, but have not rehearsed it in years. If you can relearn the poem with fewer recitations than someone with ability similar to yours, you are benefitting from your childhood learning.

Forgetting

Everyone experiences a loss of memory from time to time. You're sure you've seen that person before but can't quite place her. You have the word on the tip of your tongue, but. . . . When information that once entered long-term memory cannot be retrieved, it is said to be forgotten. Forgetting may involve decay, interference, or repression.

Some inputs may fade away, or decay, over time. Items quickly decay in sensory storage and short-term memory, as indicated earlier. It is not certain, however, whether long-term memories can ever decay. We know that a blow to the head or electrical stimulation of certain parts of the brain can cause loss of memory. The memories lost are the most recent ones, however; older memories seem to remain (see feature on page 65). The fact that apparently forgotten information can be recovered through meditation, hypnosis, or brain stimulation suggests that at least some memories never decay. Rather, interference or repression causes people to lose track of them.

CONNECTIONS: PSYCHOLOGY AND SCIENCE

Assign interested students to investigate the ground-breaking work being done on Alzheimer's disease. In 1993, neuropsychologists released two theories that turned the entire field upside down. One group of researchers proposed a genetic link to Alzheimer's. Another group proposed a theory to explain how inheritance of the gene results in the disorder. Tell students to use the *Readers' Guide to Periodical Literature* to locate articles that describe how science and psychology are working together to solve this heart-breaking riddle.

(Note: For students who have access to *The New York Times*, they might consult "Scientists Propose Novel Explanation for Alzheimer's," November 9, 1993, p. C3.)

At A Glance

REMEMBERING HIGH SCHOOL CLASSMATES

Few of us will ever forget our high school days, with all their glory and pain. But how many of us will remember the names and faces of our high school classmates 10, 20, 30, and even 40 years after graduation? According to one study, apparently more of us than you might think.

To find out just how long our long-term memory is, researchers showed nearly 400 high school graduates, ranging in age from 17 to 74, pictures from their high school yearbooks. Here are some of the surprising results:

- Thirty-five years after graduation, people could identify the faces of 9 out of 10 of their classmates. The size of the high school made no difference in their response.
- Fifteen years after graduation, subjects could recall 90 percent of their classmates' names.
- Name recall began to fade to between 70 and 80 percent by the time people reached their late 30s.
- Women generally had better memories for names and faces than men.

Researchers explain these amazing results by looking to the way we collect this information in the first place. Our storehouse of names and faces is built over our four-year high school career, and continual repetition helps cement this knowledge in our memories for decades.

So if you're afraid you're going to forget all the classmates you will leave behind, take heart. They'll probably be part of your memory for a very long time.

For more details, see Harry P. Bahrick, Phyllis O. Bahrick, and Roy P. Wittinger, "Those Unforgettable High School Days," *Psychology Today,* December 1974. Kolata, G. "Does Brain Exercise Work?" *Reader's Digest,* 142: 108–110, February 1993.

Interference refers to a memory being blocked or erased by previous or subsequent memories. This blocking is of two kinds: proactive and retroactive. In **proactive interference** an earlier memory does the blocking. In **retroactive interference** a later memory does the blocking. Suppose you move to a new home. You now have to remember a new address and phone number. At first you may have trouble remembering them because the memory of your old address and phone number gets in the way (proactive interference). Later, you know the new information, but have trouble remembering the old data (retroactive interference).

It may be that interference actually does erase some memories permanently. In other cases the old data have not been lost. The information is in

At A Glance

After students have read the feature, ask the following questions.

1. What is the main finding, or conclusion, of researchers who conducted the study? *(that we remember high school classmates for a long time)*

2. What factors encouraged such long-term memory and recall? *(continued repetition over a four-year period)*

3. What other factors do you think might encourage people to remember their high school classmates? *(Answers will vary, but students may suggest the emotional impact of experiencing early steps into adulthood for the first time.)*

Teacher Note. While exploring the subject of forgetting, you might tell students about *Alzheimer's disease.* Described for the first time in the early 1900s by Alois Alzheimer, this degenerative disease primarily affects people over age 60. Today about 4 million Americans suffer from the disease, including some people less than 50 years old. Volunteers may wish to conduct research to find more information on this incurable disorder.

COMMUNITY INVOLVEMENT

Request volunteers to find older friends and relatives who have their high school yearbooks readily available. Have students ask these people to "walk" them through the yearbook. (Students should tell the people that the exercise is part of a school assignment. But, if possible, they should not mention its purpose or the subject for which it will be used.) Tell students to observe the process by which each person recalls the past. Have students share their observations with the class. Ask: How did this experiment compare with the results in At a Glance?

Using Psychology

After students have read this feature, ask the following questions.

1. What is state-dependent memory? *(memory that can be recalled when a person is put back in the same state)*

2. What is mood-dependent recall? *(memory stored and associated with a particular mood; that mood often serves as a cue for recall)*

3. According to Bower, what is the best way to use mood-dependent recall to study for a test? *(match the mood for test taking with the mood of studying)*

4. Based on your experience, is Bower's theory correct? *(Answers will vary. Have students recall how their study time measures up to the test situation in terms of feelings or mood.)*

? FACT OR FICTION

A pleasant fragrance can help you recall enjoyable experiences.

Fact. In one experiment, people were asked to recall events associated with various words. When a pleasant odor was present in the room, people were more likely to remember positive events than negative events.

your memory somewhere, if only you could find it. According to Sigmund Freud, sometimes blocking is no accident. A person may subconsciously block memories of an embarrassing or frightening experience. This kind of forgetting is called **repression.** The material still exists in the person's memory, but it has been made inaccessible because it is so disturbing. We discuss repression further in Chapter 11.

Improving Memory

Techniques for improving memory are based on efficient organization of the things you learn and on chunking information into easily handled

Using Psychology

Mood and Memory

In 1968, Sirhan Sirhan assassinated Senator Robert Kennedy, brother of former President John F. Kennedy, in a Los Angeles hotel. Sirhan was in a highly agitated state when he killed Kennedy. When questioned about it immediately afterward, he had no recollection of the event. A hypnotist was called in. The hypnotist recreated the events of the murder. As Sirhan listened, he became agitated and recalled more and more details of the murder. Sometimes while he was in a trance he described events aloud; at other times he recorded his memories by writing them down automatically, without being aware of what he was writing (Bower, 1981). In his non-hypnotized state, Sirhan was never conscious of these memories and even denied that he had committed the murder.

Sirhan Sirhan's case is a dramatic example of *state-dependent memory.* The theory of this type of memory is based on the assumption that events learned in a certain emotional state can be remembered better when one is put back into the same state.

To learn more about the influence of mood on memory, psychologist Gordon Bower conducted a series of laboratory experiments. In one study, he hypnotized a group of subjects and made them feel happy. While they were in that happy state, he gave them a list of words to learn. At another session, he hypnotized them again, but put them in a sad mood and gave them a different list of words to learn. Later, the subjects were hypnotized again and were asked to recall one of the lists they had been given previously. Bower found that the subjects who tried to recall a list in the same mood as that in which they learned it could remember more of the words than subjects who tried to recall the list they had learned while in the other mood.

🧪 LAB EXPERIMENTS AND DEMONSTRATIONS

Bring a mix of 20 objects, both familiar and unfamiliar, into class in a bag. Record these items on a list jumbled among another 10–15 items. Quickly pull each of the items out of the bag. Then tell half the students to write down what they saw on a blank sheet of paper. Have the other half circle the items on the prepared list. Compare the results. Ask: How does *prompting* improve the process of recall? How would prompting help improve such tasks as studying for tests? *(Clue words could trigger the recall of information in rehearsal for the same task on a test.)*

Bower also had subjects keep daily records of the emotional events in their lives. Later, he hypnotized them and asked them to recall the incidents they had recorded. Bower found that subjects who were placed in a sad mood recalled more unpleasant events in their daily lives than subjects who were hypnotized to be in a happy mood. Also, subjects recalled more unpleasant events from their childhood when they were in a sad mood than they recalled happy events when in a happy mood.

One explanation for this mood-dependent recall offered by Bower is that mood serves as a cue for retrieving information. When a memory is stored, it is associated with a specific emotion as well as with specific actions or people. The emotional state later functions as a marker in our memory of the specific event. When we are in the same mood, we are more likely to be able to find the memory thus marked.

If you want to maximize your recall of material, one way to do so is to recall the material in a circumstance or emotional context similar to the one in which the material was learned. For example, if you match a mood of tension while studying for an exam with a tense mood while taking an exam, you can expect to do better in recalling the studied material. Often, students are relaxed while studying for an exam, but anxious while taking it—a bad match for recall, according to Bower.

packages. Meaningfulness, association, lack of interference, and degree of original learning all influence your ability to retrieve data from memory.

The more meaningful something is, the easier it will be to remember. For example, you would be more likely to remember the six letters *DFIRNE* if they were arranged to form the word *FRIEND*. Similarly, you remember things more vividly if you associate them with things already stored in memory or with a strong emotional experience. As pointed out earlier, the more categories a memory is indexed under, the more accessible it is. If an input is analyzed and indexed under many categories, each association can serve as a trigger for the memory. If you associate the new information with strong sensory experiences and a variety of other memories, any of these stimuli can trigger the memory. The more senses and experiences you use when trying to memorize something, the more likely it is that you will be able to retrieve it—a key to improving memory.

For similar reasons, a good way to protect a memory from interference is to *overlearn* it—to keep on rehearsing it even after you think you know it well. Another way to prevent interference while learning new material is to

PSYCHOLOGY and YOU

SQ3R. "SQ3R" is an effective study method that can be applied to textbooks. It involves five steps. Step one is to *Survey*. When beginning a chapter, read through the section headings quickly to see what is going to be covered. Next comes *Question*. Change each section heading into a question. This helps you keep in mind what is to be learned. For example, the title of the adjacent section in this book is "Improving Memory." You might, therefore, pose the question, "How can my memory be improved?" For maximum benefit, make your questions personally important to you. Step three is to *Read* the chapter. As you do, try to answer the questions you posed. In step four, *Recite*, either write brief notes covering the highlights of the reading or recite the main points out loud. Since you get credit on exams only for what you can recall and apply under pressure, spend more of your time reciting, not reading. Finally, *Review* the main points by asking the questions again and then writing or reciting the answers. By the time you finish doing all the steps, you should have learned much about the text, partly because, by using the SQ3R method, you have actively thought about the material.

Teacher Note. You might introduce students to the concept of *dissociation*. Point out that in times of extreme distress people often report a sense of detachment from their surroundings. After the 1989 San Francisco earthquake, researchers interviewed 101 graduate students in psychology and medicine. More than 50 percent reported a feeling of dissociation from the earthquake. According to Martin Roth, such a feeling is a "built-in cerebral response for survival in the face of danger." Challenge students to explore the meaning of Roth's comment. (*Lead them to understand how dissociation allows people to deal with overwhelming events until they are emotionally ready to process them.*)

Readings in Psychology. Have students read the Section 1, Reading 2 selection in R*eadings in Psychology* and answer the questions that follow the reading.

MEETING SPECIAL NEEDS

Reading Disability. Some students may have difficulty with the "R" (Read) part of the SQ3R method. You might use the CLOZE technique to assess student reading comprehension. Recopy part of the margin feature, and remove every sixth, seventh, or eighth word. Do not omit proper names or technical terms. Have students fill in the blank spaces so that the passage makes sense. For example: ""SQ3R" is an effective study _____ that can be applied to textbooks. It involves five _____ . Step _____ is to *Survey*." Poor student performance may signal reading comprehension difficulties.

■ **Research.** Chapter 1 already introduced students to the concept of mnemonic devices. You might have students do additional research into some other mnemonic devices. *(Suggest that they look up the topic of memory in the card catalog or in psychology texts.)* Have students present their favorite or most bizarre mnemonic in the form of a poster. Some common examples include:

1. A Rat in the House May Eat Tommy's Ice Cream. *(Spelling of arithmetic.)*
2. Georgie eats old grey rats and paints houses yellow. *(Spelling of geography.)*
3. Men Very Easily Made Jugs Serve Useful Nocturnal Purposes. *(Names of the planets—Mercury, Venus, Earth, Mars, Jupiter, Saturn, Uranus, Neptune, Pluto.)*
4. Flabby Butlers Feel Losing Weight Makes Light Housekeeping Healthier. *(Weight classifications in boxing—flyweight, bantamweight, featherweight, lightweight, welterweight, middleweight, light heavyweight, and heavyweight.)*

VISUAL INSTRUCTION

Ask students to identify examples of how the artist used humor and symbols to reinforce learning.
Answer to caption, Figure 3.10: techniques for using associations to memorize information

---

avoid studying similar material together. Instead of studying history right after political science, study biology in between. Still another method is to space out your learning. Trying to absorb large amounts of information at one sitting results in a great deal of interference. It is far more effective to study a little at a time.

Mnemonic Devices.   **Mnemonic devices** are techniques for using associations to memorize information. The ancient Greeks memorized speeches by mentally walking around their homes or neighborhoods and "placing" each line of a speech in a different spot—called the *Method of Loci.* Once they made the associations, they could recall the speech by mentally retracing their steps and "picking up" each line. The rhyme we use to recall the number of days in each month ("Thirty days has September") is a mnemonic device. In the phrase "Every Good Boy Does Fine," the first letters of the words are the same as the names of the musical notes on the lines of a staff (E, G, B, D, and F); the notes between the lines spell FACE.

Another useful mnemonic device is to form mental pictures containing the information you want to remember—the sillier the better. Suppose you have trouble remembering the authors and titles of books, or which artists belong to which schools of painting. To plant the fact in your mind that John Updike wrote *Rabbit, Run,* you might picture a RABBIT RUNning UP a DIKE. To remember that Picasso was a Cubist (Figure 3.10), picture someone attacking a giant CUBE with a PICKAX, which sounds like Picasso (Lorayne and Lucas, 1974: pp. 166–169).

FIGURE 3.10

Here is a mnemonic device for remembering that Picasso (which sounds like "pickax") was a Cubist. Often, the sillier the mental picture, the better it is for retrieving the information you have trouble remembering. **What are mnemonic devices?**

CONNECTIONS: PSYCHOLOGY AND ART

Working individually or in groups, have students design a visual mnemonic to remember the artistic style of another famous artist in world history. Examples might include: Mary Cassatt and Impressionism, Roy Lichtenstein and Pop Art, Georges Seurat and Pointillism. (Suggest that students consult an art history book in the library for additional ideas.) You might arrange for students to present their graphic learning devices to some of the world history classes in your school.

Mnemonic devices are not magical. Indeed, they involve extra work—making up words, stories, and so on. But the very effort of trying to do this may help you to remember things.

CENTRAL PROCESSING OF INFORMATION

If storage and retrieval were the only processes we used to handle information, human beings would be little more than glorified cameras and projectors. But, in fact, we are capable of doing things with information that make the most complex computers seem simple by comparison. These processes—thinking and problem solving—are most impressive when they show originality or creativity.

Thinking

Thinking may be viewed as changing and reorganizing the information stored in memory in order to create new information. By thinking, humans are able to put together any combination of words from memory and create sentences never devised before—such as this one.

Units of Thought.   The processes of thought depend on several devices or units of thought: images, symbols, concepts, and rules.

The most primitive unit of thought is an **image,** a mental representation of a specific event or object. The representation is not usually an exact copy; rather, it contains only the highlights of the original. For example, if an adult tries to visualize a grandmother who died when he was seven, he would probably remember only a few details—perhaps the color of her hair or a piece of jewelry that she wore.

A more abstract unit of thought is a **symbol,** a sound or design that represents an object or quality. The most common symbols in thinking are words: every word is a symbol that stands for something other than itself. An image represents a specific sight or sound, but a symbol may have a number of meanings. The fact that symbols differ from the things they represent enables us to think about things that are not present, to range over the past and future, to imagine things and situations that never were or will be. Numbers, letters, and punctuation marks are all familiar symbols of ideas that have no concrete existence.

When a symbol is used as a label for a class of objects or events with certain common attributes, or for the attributes themselves, it is called a **concept.** "Animals," "music," "liquid," and "beautiful people" are examples of concepts based on the common attributes of the objects and experiences belonging to each category. Thus the concept "animal" separates a group of organisms from such things as automobiles, carrots, and Roquefort cheese. Concepts enable us to chunk large amounts of information. We do not have to treat every new piece of information as unique since we already know something about the class of objects or experiences to which the new item belongs.

MORE about...

The Memory. One of the best documented cases of a man with an astounding memory is presented in A.R. Luria's book *The Mind of a Mnemonist* (1968). In the 1920s, a newspaper reporter came to Luria's laboratory to participate in a memory experiment. Luria was amazed to learn that S. (as he called the reporter) could easily repeat lists of 70 numbers—backward or forward with equal ease—after he heard them once. Fifteen years later, when asked to recall these early lists, S. could still do so!

How did he do it? Every word or number would conjure up rich visual images that S. easily remembered. After starting a career as a professional mnemonist, S. discovered that one of his biggest problems was learning to forget. His brain was cluttered with old lists of words, numbers, and letters. When relaxing, S. was flooded with past images. He had trouble reading because each word brought vivid images from the past, obscuring the meaning of what he read. Dr. Luria wrote, "S. struck one as a disorganized and rather dull-witted person."

■ **Making a Chart.** Working in small groups, have students design a chart classifying examples of the four units of thought: images, symbols, concepts, and rule. Encourage students to illustrate at least some of the entries. After students have shared their charts, point out that to complete this assignment they used a critical thinking skill known as classification. Ask: Is classification an example of directed or nondirected thinking? *(directed)* (OBJECTIVE 4)

■ **Problem Solving.** You might point out that problem solving involves a series of thought processes. These include:

- Defining the problem.
- Identifying alternative solutions.
- Predicting alternative outcomes.
- Comparing alternative outcomes.
- Choosing an alternative.
- Preparing a plan of action.
- Evaluating the decision.

Assign students to work in small groups to apply these steps to a problem such as the ones used on page 71. Students may record the problem-solving process either in a written or oral report or in the form of story boards. (OBJECTIVE 5)

CRITICAL THINKING ACTIVITY

Evaluating Information. Read aloud the quote by William James in the Analyzing a Quote feature on page 64. Then have students read the margin feature on memory. Ask: Does this case study confirm or disprove James's theory? What evidence supports your answer? As a writing exercise, you might have students imagine they are James. Assign them to write a letter to A. R. Luria in which James evaluates the premise in *The Mind of a Mnemonist.*

VISUAL INSTRUCTION

Request a volunteer to read De Bono's problem aloud. Then challenge students to solve it within two minutes. Have class members present their answers. **Answer to caption, Figure 3.11:** when they are relaxing or trying to escape from stress or boredom

Independent Practice

■ **Making Comparisons.** As students have read, psychologists refer to human cognitive activities as "information processing." This is the same term used to describe the work of computers. Computers perform three main functions—input, central processing, and output—in handling, or processing, data. Working in small groups, have students research and write papers that compare information processing in the human brain with information processing in the computer. (OBJECTIVES 1, 4, 5)

FIGURE 3.11

This problem was devised by psychologist Edward De Bono, who believes that conventional directed thinking is insufficient for solving new and unusual problems. His approach to problem solving requires use of nondirected thinking in order to generate new ways of looking at the problem situation. The answer to this problem is provided in Figure 3.16. **When are people most likely to engage in nondirected thinking?**

n old money-lender offered to cancel a merchant's debt and keep him from going to prison if the merchant would give the money-lender his lovely daughter. Horrified yet desperate, the merchant and his daughter agreed to let Providence decide. The money-lender said he would put a black pebble and a white pebble in a bag and the girl would draw one. The white pebble would cancel the debt and leave her free. The black one would make her the money-lender's, although the debt would be canceled. If she refused to pick, her father would go to prison. From the pebble-strewn path they were standing on, the money-lender picked two pebbles and quickly put them in the bag, but the girl saw he had picked up two black ones. What would you have done if you were the girl?

The fourth and most complex unit of thought is a **rule,** a statement of a relation between concepts. The following are examples of rules: a person cannot be in two places at the same time; mass remains constant despite changes in appearance.

Images, symbols, concepts, and rules are the building blocks of mental activity. They provide an economical and efficient way for people to represent reality, to manipulate and reorganize it, and to devise new ways of acting. A person can think about pursuing several different careers, weigh their pros and cons, and decide which to pursue without having to try every one of them.

Kinds of Thinking.   People think in several ways. **Directed thinking** is a systematic and logical attempt to reach a specific goal, such as the solution of a problem. This kind of thinking, also called convergent thinking, depends heavily on symbols, concepts, and rules. Another type, called **nondirected thinking** (or divergent thinking), consists of a free flow of thoughts with no particular goal or plan, and depends more on images (Figure 3.11).

Nondirected thinking is usually rich with imagery and feelings such as daydreams, fantasies, and reveries. People often engage in nondirected thought when they are relaxing or escaping from boredom or worry. This kind of thinking may provide unexpected insights into one's goals and be-

CONNECTIONS: PSYCHOLOGY AND MUSIC

You might bring a tape into class. The recording should have no words. It can use music or a combination of music and sounds from nature (such as waves, whale songs, and so on). Lower the lights, and tell students to let their minds wander. After 10 minutes, stop the tape and tell students to write down their random thoughts as they listened to the tape. (To protect student privacy, do this exercise anonymously.) When students are done, request volunteers to share how divergent, or nondirected, thinking provides a method of relaxation or escape. If students want to share some of their specific thoughts, allow them to do so.

liefs. Scientists and artists say that some of their best ideas emerge from drifting thoughts that occur when they have set aside a problem for the moment.

In contrast, directed thinking is deliberate and purposeful. It is through directed thinking that we solve problems, formulate and follow rules, and set, work toward, and achieve goals.

A third type of thinking is **metacognition,** or thinking about thinking. When you tackle an algebra problem and cannot solve it, thinking about your strategy may cause you to change to another strategy.

Problem Solving

One of the main functions of directed thinking is to solve problems—to bridge the gap, mentally, between a present situation and a desired goal. The gap may be between hunger and food, a column of figures and a total, lack of money and bills to pay, or cancer and a cure. In all these examples, getting from the problem to the solution requires some directed thinking.

Strategies.   Problem solving depends on the use of strategies, or specific methods for approaching problems. One strategy is to break down a complex problem into a number of smaller, more easily solved problems. For example, it is the end of the semester and your life is falling apart. You don't even have time to tie your shoelaces. You solve the problem by breaking it down into small pieces: studying for a science exam; finishing that overdue paper; canceling your dinner date; scheduling regular study breaks to maintain what's left of your sanity; and so on.

For some problems, you may work backward from the goal you have set. Mystery writers often use this method: They decide how to end the story ("who did it") and then devise a plot leading to this conclusion.

Another problem may require you to examine various ways of reaching a desired goal. Suppose a woman needs to be in Chicago by 11 A.M. on July 7 for a business conference. She checks train departures and arrivals, airline schedules, and car-rental companies. The only train to Chicago that morning arrives at 5 A.M. (too early), and the first plane arrives at 11:30 A.M. (too late). So she decides to rent a car and drive.

To determine which strategy to use, most of us analyze the problem to see if it resembles a situation we have experienced in the past. A strategy that worked in the past is likely to work again. We tend to do things the way we've done them before, and shy away from new situations that call for new strategies. The more unusual the problem, the more difficult it is to devise a strategy for dealing with it.

Set.   There are times when certain useful strategies become cemented into the problem-solving process. When a particular strategy becomes a habit, it is called a **set**—you are "set" to treat problems in a certain way. For example, a chess player may always attempt to control the four center squares of the chessboard. Whenever her opponent attacks, she responds by looking for ways to regain control of those four squares. She has a "set" for this strategy. If this set helps her to win, fine. Sometimes, however, a set

■ **Problem Solving.** Tell students to solve problems, people often have to retrieve (recall) information from long-term memory. To illustrate this, challenge volunteers to devise a word game entitled "What's This Word?" (All students might receive a "prize" in the form of extra credit.) Assign some students to be game show writers, others to be the host/hostess, and still others to be contestants. The game show writers should come up with a series of familiar words. On the chalkboard have them list blanks for the number of letters in each word (like the game show "Wheel of Fortune"). Student contestants can guess only consonants. Every time they miss, their opponent gets a free letter or guess. Continue until you hold several playoffs among winning "contestants."

When the activity is completed, ask what types of memory retrieval they used to guess words. Also, ask the contestants who played several rounds about the kind of "sets" they developed. That is, what problem-solving process did they develop? *(For example, most students probably stayed away from uncommon consonants such as "x," "q," or "z.")* (OBJECTIVES 2, 3, 5)

■ **Cooperative Learning Activity.** Organize the students into small groups. Tell students to imagine they are a team of child-care workers at a new learning center for young children. Challenge them to write a list of "Dos" and "Do Nots" on a poster entitled "Creating Creativity." Next, assign students to develop a list of activities and/or games that might encourage creativity. Have a member from each group share its plan with the class. (OBJECTIVE 5)

CRITICAL THINKING ACTIVITY

Problem Solving. Request volunteers to play a game of charades for the class. Each volunteer should think of a phrase to act out through gestures. The rest of the class should use the techniques of memory retrieval—such as recall and recognition—to solve the problem of interpreting "wordless communication."

When the exercise is done, ask students if they devised a "set" of strategies to approach the charades. Also, did any students experience the feeling of "aha" (insight) in figuring out the answer?

VISUAL INSTRUCTION

Ask students to devise solutions to the problems presented in Figures 3.12 and
3.13.
**Answer to caption, Figure
3.12:** the inability to imagine new functions for familiar objects
**Answer to caption, Figure
3.13:** flexibility and
recombination

■ **Demonstration.** Using a
spinoff of the paper clip exercise mentioned in the text on
page 73, bring in a familiar everyday object such as a soda
can, paper cup, or newspaper.
Working in groups, challenge
students to think of as many
uses for the object as possible.
*(You might want to remind stu-
dents that each of these items
can be recycled.)* Call on students to share their ideas. If
any group members experi-
enced rigidity in thought, encourage them to share how
they overcame it.
(OBJECTIVE 5)

FIGURE 3.12

Given the materials pictured here,
how would you go about mounting a
candle vertically on a wooden wall in
such a way that it can be lit? This was
one of the many problems German
psychologist Karl Duncker formulated
to test creative thinking. The solution
is presented in Figure 3.16. **What is
functional fixedness?**

FIGURE 3.13

Draw this figure on a separate sheet
of paper. Then, connect the dots with
four straight lines without lifting your
pencil. The solution appears in Figure
3.16. **What are two characteristics
of creative thinking?**

interferes with problem solving, and then it is called *rigidity*. You probably know the old riddle, "What is black, white, and read all over? A newspaper." When you say the riddle, the word *read* sounds like *red*, which is
why some people cannot guess the answer. *Read* is heard as part of the
black and white set—it is interpreted as being a color. If you asked, "What
is read by people every day and is black and white?" the correct answer
would be obvious. And boring.

One form of set that can interfere with problem solving is functional
fixedness—the inability to imagine new functions for familiar objects. In
experiments on functional fixedness, people are asked to solve a problem
that requires them to use a familiar object in an unfamiliar way (Duncker,
1945). Because they are set to use the object in the usual way, people tend
to pay attention only to the features of the object that relate to its everyday
use (see Figure 3.12). They respond in a rigid way.

Another type of rigidity occurs when a person makes a wrong assumption about a problem. In Figure 3.13, for example, the problem is to connect
the dots with four straight lines without lifting your pencil. Most people
have trouble solving this puzzle because they falsely assume that they must
stay within the area of the dots.

People trying to solve the kind of problem shown in Figure 3.14 experience a third kind of rigidity. Most people look for direct methods of solving
problems and do not see solutions that require several intermediate steps.

Rigidity can be overcome if the person realizes that his or her strategy is
not working and looks for other ways to approach the problem. The more
familiar the situation, the more difficult this will be. Rigidity is less likely to
occur with unusual problems.

Creativity

Creativity is the ability to use information in such a way that the result is
somehow new, original, and meaningful. All problem solving requires
some creativity. Certain ways of solving problems, however, are simply
more brilliant or beautiful or efficient than others. Psychologists do not
know exactly why some people are able to think more creatively than

🧪 **LAB EXPERIMENTS AND DEMONSTRATIONS**

You might try a joke used by some
psychologists to determine whether a
person is a literal thinker. On a sheet
of paper, have students quickly write
down the answer to these questions:
What is the color of snow? *(white)*
What do cows drink? *(the answer is
"water," but a surprising number of*
students will say "milk") Explain to
students that linear thinkers may not
answer the question spontaneously.
They will think it through and come
up with the correct answer—water.
Students who respond with their first
free association will probably say
milk (which links white and cows).
Debate which method of thinking students think may be the most creative.

FIGURE 3.14

How would you go about solving this problem? Eight soldiers need to cross a river, but the only way to cross is in a small boat in which two children are playing. The boat can carry at most two children or one soldier. How do the soldiers get across? You'll find the answer in Figure 3.16. **How can rigid thinking be overcome?**

others, although they have identified some of the characteristics of creative thinking—including flexibility and the ability to recombine elements to achieve insight.

Flexibility. Flexibility is, quite simply, the ability to overcome rigidity. Psychologists have devised a number of ingenious tests to measure flexibility. One test is shown in Figure 3.15. The individual is asked to name a word that the three words in each row have in common. To do this, a person must be able to think of many different aspects of each of these words. Another test of flexibility is to ask people how many uses they can imagine for a single object, such as a brick or a paper clip. The more uses a person can devise, the more flexible he or she is said to be. Whether such tests actually measure creativity is debatable. Nevertheless, it is obvious that inflexible, rigid thinking leads to unoriginal solutions, or no solutions at all.

Recombination. When the elements of a problem are familiar but the required solution is not, it may be achieved by **recombination,** a new mental arrangement of the elements. In football and basketball, for example, there are no new moves—only recombinations of old ones. Such recombination seems to be a vital part of creativity. Many creative people say that no truly great poem, no original invention, has ever been produced by someone who has not spent years studying his or her subject. The creative person is able to take the information that he or she and others have compiled and put it together in a totally new way. The brilliant philosopher and mathematician Sir Isaac Newton, who discovered the laws of motion, once said, "If I have seen further, it is by standing on the shoulders of giants." In other words, he was able to recombine the discoveries of the great scientists who had preceded him to uncover new and more far-reaching truths.

FIGURE 3.15

In this test devised to measure flexibility in thinking, the task is to name a single word that all three words on a line have in common. The answer to the first item is *foot.* The other answers are given in Figure 3.16. **What is recombination?**

1.	stool	powder	ball
2.	blue	cake	cottage
3.	man	wheel	high
4.	motion	poke	down
5.	line	birthday	surprise
6.	wood	liquor	luck
7.	house	village	golf
8.	card	knee	rope
9.	news	doll	tiger
10.	painting	bowl	nail
11.	weight	wave	house
12.	made	cuff	left
13.	key	wall	precious
14.	bull	tired	hot
15.	knife	up	hi
16.	handle	hole	police
17.	plan	show	walker
18.	hop	side	pet
19.	bell	tender	iron
20.	spelling	line	busy

VISUAL INSTRUCTION

Ask students to devise solutions to the problems presented in Figures 3.14 and 3.15.
Answer to caption, Figure 3.14: by realizing that a strategy is not working; by looking for alternative solutions
Answer to caption, Figure 3.15: the ability to take information and put it together in a new way

ASSESS

Check for Understanding

Assign groups of students to write down two or three statements about each of the topics listed under the four main heads in the outline on page 76.

Reteach

Have students complete the Chapter 3 Study Guide Activity and share responses with each other. For extended review, assign the Chapter 3 Review Activity as homework or an in-class assignment.

CONNECTIONS: PSYCHOLOGY AND SOCIAL STUDIES

The paragraph on recombination mentions Isaac Newton. You might assign students to research other famous inventors or geniuses. Examples include: Marie Curie, Albert Einstein, Thomas Edison, or Henry Ford. In a written biography, have students present the original solution, idea, or invention developed by each person. Then have them assess some of the character traits that encouraged creativity in each of these individuals. In a follow-up discussion, repeat a comment by English poet John Dryden. Said Dryden: "Genius must be born, and never taught." In terms of psychology, do students agree? Why or why not? Edison reportedly said, "Genius is 10 percent inspiration and 90 percent perspiration." Ask: Is Dryden's statement or Edison's more valid? Defend your answer.

For a class project, you might organize the class into five groups. Have each group administer one of the problems depicted in this chapter to at least four friends. Tell students to record observations of how their friends solved or failed to solve the problem. Direct them to pay particular attention to rigidity or creativity. Have students share their findings with the class.

Enrich

Have students complete the Chapter 3 Extension Activity and answer the questions that follow it.

Have students complete the Chapter 3 Application Activity.

Evaluate

Administer and grade the Chapter 3 Test. Two forms are available should you wish to give different tests to different students/classes.

Use the Understanding Psychology Testmaker to create a customized test.

Another result of recombination is Samuel Taylor Coleridge's unusual poem "Kubla Khan." Scholars have shown that almost every word and phrase came directly from Coleridge's past readings and personal experiences. Coleridge recombined these elements during a period of non-directed thinking—drug-induced sleep. He awoke with the entire poem in his mind, but was able to commit only part of it to paper before he was interrupted by a knock at his door. When Coleridge went back to his poem, it had vanished from his mind.

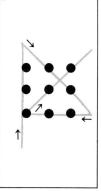

1. foot   11. light
2. cheese   12. hand
3. chair   13. stone
4. slow   14. dog
5. party   15. jack
6. hard   16. man
7. green   17. floor
8. trick   18. car
9. paper   19. bar
10. finger   20. bee

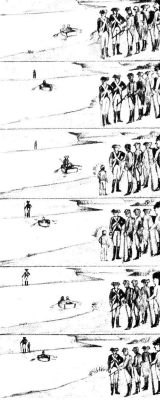

FIGURE 3.16

Note that each solution requires breaking certain habits of thought. (a) In the De Bono problem, it is difficult to imagine that control of the situation can be taken out of the hands of the powerful moneylender. (b) Solving the Duncker candle problem requires the solver to look at the matchbox and candle box as more than containers to be discarded. The presence of the useless piece of string usually serves to confuse problem solvers. (c) As the text points out, the solution to this problem is blocked if the person avoids going beyond the boundaries of the dots. (d) The answers to the test of flexibility require that the individual ignore common associations and look for unusual ones. (e) Once solvers discover the first step in the problem's solution, they may become further bogged down if they do not realize the lengthy cyclical nature of the process required.

Assign students to interview people in different careers or fields of work. Tell students to use the following questions.

1. What type of problems do you encounter in your daily work?
2. What problem-solving strategies do you use to resolve these dilemmas?
3. Which strategy do you find most effective?

After students complete the assignment, have them present their findings. Ask: Can you see any common approaches to problem solving regardless of a person's profession? Do any approaches seem more useful in certain fields than in others? (*Students should back up their answers with examples from the interviews.*)

FIGURE 3.17

Most of us have experienced insight or the "aha" experience at some time. Can you recall the most recent time you experienced frustration, abandoned the task for a while, and suddenly the solution seemed to come out of nowhere? **What elements are involved in insight?**

Insight.   The sudden emergence of a solution by recombination of elements is called **insight.** Insight usually occurs when problems have proved resistant to all problem-solving efforts and strategies. The scientist or artist reaches a point of high frustration and temporarily abandons the task. But the recombination process seems to continue on an unconscious level. When the person is absorbed in some other activity, the answer seems to appear out of nowhere. This sudden insight has appropriately been called the "aha" experience.

Certain animals appear to experience this same cycle of frustration, temporary diversion (during which time the problem "incubates"), and then sudden insight. For example, Wolfgang Köhler (1925) placed a chimpanzee in a cage where a cluster of bananas was hung out of its reach. Also in the cage were a number of wooden boxes. At first the chimpanzee tried various unsuccessful ways of getting at the fruit. Finally it sat down, apparently giving up, and simply stared straight ahead for a while. Then suddenly it jumped up, piled three boxes on top of one another, climbed to the top of the pile, and grabbed the bananas.

VISUAL INSTRUCTION

Ask students to share instances when a solution to a seemingly unsolvable problem came out of "nowhere." **Answer to caption, Figure 3.17:** a sudden recombination of elements

PROFILE

Wolfgang Köhler
1887–1967
Born in Estonia, and reared in Wolfenbuttel, Germany, Wolfgang Köhler's life became intertwined with Max Wertheimer and Kurt Koffka. Together they founded what became known as Gestalt psychology (see page 120).

Köhler paved the way for Gestalt through experiments with a female chimpanzee named Tschego. He discovered that Tschego could solve problems (get out-of-reach bananas) through *insight.* "Insight," said Köhler, "is the appearance of a complete solution with reference to the whole layout of the problem." The idea that learning could occur without response-stimuli turned psychology upside down. Köhler threw out a challenge to Thorndike and other behaviorists of his day.

ADDITIONAL INFORMATION

Psychologists at Teacher's College, Columbia University, confirmed Köhler's findings (A. Alpert, 1928). They put children ages 1–4 inside a playpen. They scattered toys outside the playpen and placed several sticks inside. After fumbling around with the sticks, the children began to use the tools to move the more desirable toys within reach. Without instruction or reward, they exhibited insight as a method of problem solving. The children also showed *positive transfer* when the toys were later placed up on a shelf. In this case, the children used the sticks to knock the toys onto the floor.

CLOSE

Ask students to review the earliest memories that they recorded in their journals. Based on information in this chapter, what techniques did students use to recall these memories?

ANSWERS

Concepts and Vocabulary

1. The three steps involved are input (the information people receive from their senses), central processing (the sorting by thought of this information in the brain), and output (the ideas and actions that result from processing).

2. selective attention and feature extraction

3. Information leading to the satisfaction of needs receives top priority. Inputs that are strange and novel also receive attention.

4. sensory storage, short-term memory, and long-term memory

5. include rehearsal and chunking

6. One theory suggests that memory is due to changes in the form of protein molecules in the brain. Another theory focuses on chemical-electrical changes in the brain. It is possible that memory develops when the characteristics of the synapses change chemically.

7. Implicit memory includes learned skills. Explicit memory includes episodic memory, memory of our own lives, and semantic memory. Implicit memory does not require conscious recollection to have past experiences impact performance.

8. proactive and retroactive interference; one possible mnemonic would be

CHAPTER
3 Review

SUMMARY

Use the following outline as a tool for reviewing this chapter. Copy the outline onto your own paper, leaving spaces between headings to make notes about key concepts.

I. Taking In Information
  A. Selective Attention
  B. Feature Extraction

II. Storing Information
  A. Sensory Storage
  B. Short-Term Memory
  C. Long-Term Memory
  D. Other Models of Memory
  E. Memory and the Brain

III. Retrieving Information
  A. Recognition
  B. Recall
  C. Relearning
  D. Forgetting
  E. Improving Memory

IV. Central Processing of Information
  A. Thinking
  B. Problem Solving
  C. Creativity

CONCEPTS AND VOCABULARY

1. Information processing involves three steps. List and define them.

2. What are the first two processes that help people narrow sensory inputs?

3. What factors make one input more important than another?

4. Name the three types of memory based on length of storage.

5. List two strategies for expanding the limits of short-term memory.

6. What are the two theories that explain the activities in the brain when something is stored in long-term memory?

7. What are the differences between implicit memory and explicit memory? What types of memory activities affect implicit memory? What types impact explicit memory?

8. What are the two types of interference that block memory? Can you develop a mnemonic device to remember their definitions?

9. Describe six methods you can use to improve your memory.

10. List the four units of thought in order of increasing complexity.

11. What are the two kinds of thinking?

12. When a problem-solving strategy becomes a habit, what is it called? Give one example of how this can interfere with problem solving.

13. What are three characteristics of creative thinking?

CRITICAL THINKING

1. **Analyze.** In the middle of an ordinary activity, like reading a book, stop for a moment and listen for sounds you normally block out. Jot down the sounds you hear and try to identify them. Why don't you usually hear them? Under what circumstances would you notice them?

2. **Analyze.** Relax and engage in nondirected thinking—let your thoughts wander. Things may come into your mind that you thought you had forgotten or that you didn't know you knew. Or reflect on a recent dream you had—where might the various images have come from?

3. **Evaluate.** Suppose you wanted to put together a jigsaw puzzle. What are the problem-solving strategies you might use? Which one do you think would work best?

4. **Synthesize.** Try to remember what you were doing on your last birthday. As you probe your memory, verbalize the mental steps you are going through. What does this exercise tell you about your thought processes?

"PEARL." (Proactive Earlier and Retroactive Later)

9. Six methods for improving your memory are meaningfulness, association, lack of interference, degree of original learning, association with more than one sense, and use of mnemonics.

10. image, symbol, concept, and rule

11. directed thinking and nondirected thinking

12. a set; for example, suppose someone always takes the same route to work. The strategy of how to get to work becomes a set. When a traffic jam occurs, the set prevents the person from seeking an alternative route.

13. Characteristics include: flexibility, recombination, and insight.

1. Mentally determine where the light switches in your home are located and keep track of them in your head. Do you have to use visual images to count the switches? To keep track of the number? If not, could you do it with images if you wanted to?

2. Try this simple learning task on your friends. Give them a list of numbers to memorize: 6, 9, 8, 11, 10, 13, 12, 15, 14, 17, 16, and so on. Tell some of them simply to memorize the material. Tell others that there is an organizational principle behind the number sequence, and to memorize the number with the aid of the principle (which they must discover). In the sequence above, the principle is "plus 3, minus 1." Is one group better at remembering the list than the other? Based on what you know from the chapter, why do you think this is so?

3. Try the following game to demonstrate the reconstructive aspects of recall. (You will need at least seven or eight people.) Before you gather the group together, write or copy a very short story containing a fair amount of descriptive detail. Memorize, as best you can, the story, and whisper it to one member of the group, making sure the others are out of earshot. Then instruct your listener to whisper the story to another player, and so on until all the players have heard it. When the last person has been told the story, have him or her repeat it aloud to the entire group. Then read the original story from your written copy. Chances are good that the two versions are quite a bit different. Discuss among yourselves how, when, and why the story changed.

ANALYZING VIEWPOINTS

1. This text discusses the validity of eyewitness testimony in court cases. When an eyewitness identifies an individual as the person who committed the crime, the evidence can be very con-vincing to the jury. However, there are many cases of people who are falsely accused by eye-witnesses. In fact, innocent people have served time in jail for crimes they did not commit be-cause of inaccurate eyewitness testimony. Should eyewitness testimony be used in the courtroom? Why or why not? Write a paper that argues both sides of the issue. Use what you know about the nature of human memory and studies of eyewitness testimony. You may also want to look for magazine and newspaper articles that report on specific crimes where eyewitness testimony was used.

BEYOND THE CLASSROOM

1. Think of a significant news event that has happened in the past 10 years, such as the explosion of the *Challenger* space shuttle, or the tearing down of the Berlin Wall. Ask people of different ages what they remember about the event. After they have described their memories, ask them how they went about trying to recall the event. What do their answers tell you about long-term memory? What do their answers tell you about how people retrieve information from memory? Did you find any differences in the memories of teenagers, adults, or the elderly? How can these differences be explained?

IN YOUR JOURNAL

1. Reread the journal entry you wrote about your earliest memory. Write an analysis explaining why you think this is your first memory and why it continues to stay in your mind. Explain whether any confabulation might be involved in this memory. Were other people involved? Is their recall of the memory consistent with the way you remember it? Explain.

Critical Thinking

1. Student answers should focus on aspects of selective attention.

2. Some students may be uncomfortable sharing personal thoughts. Request volunteers or explore more generalized images or feelings.

3. Answers will vary. Students might mention associating puzzle pieces by color, shape, and so on.

4. Students may be uncomfortable sharing personal memories. In such cases, focus instead on the thought processes involved, such as the influence of mood upon recall and so on.

Applying Knowledge

1. Answers will vary. Students should note that the visual images act as retrieval cues.

2. Answers will vary. Students should note the connection between organization and memory.

3. Answers will vary. Students may note that many of the

CHAPTER BONUS
Test Question

This question may be used for extra credit on the chapter test.
Choose the letter of the correct response.

Transfer of materials from short- to long-term memory by repetition is:

a. encoding.
b. retrieval.
c. rehearsal.
d. chunking.

Answer: **c**

items in sensory storage and short-term memory faded quickly. Some of the subjects may have filled in the gaps by making up the rest.

Analyzing Viewpoints

1. Answers will vary. Students should show a knowledge of the memory processes—and limitations.

Beyond the Classroom

1. Answers will vary.

IN YOUR JOURNAL

If time permits, discuss journal entries individually with students.

The Workings of Mind and Body

Understanding human behavior requires knowledge of the underlying biological influences.

INTRODUCING THE UNIT

You might open the unit by having students brainstorm all the types of sensory data that they must process—or ignore—on a daily basis. To encourage spontaneity, set a three-minute time limit. Also, call on three volunteers to record all the items on the chalkboard. When students finish, have them categorize this data by the main sense through which it is received: sight, sound, smell, taste, or feel. Tell students that this unit will explain, among other things, the conscious and unconscious processes that allow us to handle all this data.

Connecting to Past Learning
Write the following labels on
the chalkboard: *Physical
States, Emotional States, Mental States*. Request volunteers
to cite examples of each of
these states that they might experience in a typical 24-hour
period. To trigger discussion,
ask where students would
place each of the following
terms—sleep, hunger, fear,
daydreaming, and anger.

UNIT PROJECT

Parts of Unit 2 connect human behavior
with physiological processes. Assign
groups of students to prepare a large
anatomical wall chart showing the
structure of two key systems: the central nervous system (including the
brain) and the endocrine system. Post
this chart on the wall for reference or
addition throughout the unit.

CHAPTER 4
Body and Behavior

TEXT TOPICS	SPECIAL FEATURES	RESOURCE MATERIALS
The Nervous System, pp. 81–89	**Fact or Fiction?,** p. 82 **At a Glance:** Which Way Do the Eyes Move?, p. 89	Reproducible Lesson Plan; Study Guide; Review Activity; Application Activity *Readings in Psychology:* Section 2, Reading 1 Transparencies 5, 6
How Psychologists Study the Brain, pp. 90–93	**At a Glance:** The Courts and Psychosurgery, p. 93	Reproducible Lesson Plan; Study Guide; Review Activity
The Endocrine System, pp. 93–96	**Psychology Update,** p. 94 **Using Psychology:** Psychosurgery, pp. 94–95	Reproducible Lesson Plan; Study Guide; Review Activity
The Relationship Between Humans and Animals, pp. 96–101	**More About Psychology,** p. 98	Reproducible Lesson Plan; Study Guide; Review Activity
Heredity and Environment, pp. 101–103		Reproducible Lesson Plan; Study Guide; Review Activity; Extension Activity; Chapter Test, Form A and Form B *Readings in Psychology:* Section 2, Reading 2 Understanding Psychology Testmaker

PERFORMANCE ASSESSMENT ACTIVITY

Many of the most exciting developments in psychology are occurring in biological psychology. Assign students to find recent magazine and newspaper articles describing advances in this field, especially articles on discoveries about the workings of the brain and on psychosurgery. Have students contribute their articles to a class anthology, which can be used for reference. Ask each student to write a one-paragraph summary to accompany their contributions. *(Summaries should cover all main ideas.)*

CHAPTER RESOURCES

Readings for the Student
Gibbons, A. "New Maps of the Human Brain." *Science,* 249 (July 30, 1990): 122–123.

Marx, J. L. "Brain Protein Yields Clues to Alzheimer's Disease." *Science,* 243 (March 31, 1989): 1664–1666.

Ornstein, R., and Thompson, R. F. *The Amazing Brain.* Boston: Houghton Mifflin, 1984.

Sacks, O. *The Man Who Mistook His Wife for a Hat.* New York: Harper and Row, 1987.

Readings for the Teacher
Gazzaniga, M. S. "Right-Hemisphere Language Following Brain Bisection: A Twenty Year Perspective." *American Psychologist,* 38 (1983): 525–537.

Kety, S. S. "Disorders of the Human Brain." *Scientific American,* 241 (1979); 202–214.

Lewontin, R. C., Rose, S., and Kamin L. J. *Not in Our Genes.* New York: Pantheon, 1984.

Rosenzweig, M. R., and Leiman, A. L. *Physiological Psychology* (2nd ed.). New York: McGraw-Hill, 1989.

Multimedia
Emotion, Mind and Body (30 minutes, 3/4" or 1/2" video). Wisconsin Foundation for Vocational Technical and Adult Education. This shows the effects emotional stress has on health.

Miss Goodall and the Wild Chimpanzees (28 minutes). National Geographic. This video describes Jane van Lawick-Goodall's studies of the wild chimpanzees in East Africa.

Stress (11 minutes). National Film Board of Canada. Hans Selye explains his theory that stress is the cause of many illnesses, especially in people who are not prepared to cope.

For additional resources, see the bibliography beginning on page 530.

Body and Behavior

FOCUS

Motivating Activity
Have students consider the ways in which psychology is connected with biology. Ask them to brainstorm examples of how human behavior is affected by the functions of the body and by the genes with which people are born. List student responses on the chalkboard. Ask: Are any of the behaviors named determined more by environment than by physical functions? If so, why? Tell students that they will learn more about the relationship between body and behavior in this chapter.

Meeting Chapter Objectives.
Point out the objectives on page 81 to students. Have them rephrase the objectives in question form. Then, assign each question to a group of students to answer as they read Chapter 4.

Building Vocabulary.
Many of the key terms in this chapter, especially those for parts of the brain, are derived from Latin and Greek. As a study aid, have students check the etymologies of these words in a dictionary. Call on them to discuss the connection between the etymological roots and the modern definitions. For example, *pons* is Latin for "bridge"; the pons is a bridge of white matter at the base of the brain.

FIGURE 4.1   The control of our bodies rests with our brains. It is the brain and the nervous system that enable us to sit, stand, skate, run—and to think and plan.

80

TEACHER CLASSROOM RESOURCES

Chapter 4 Reproducible Lesson Plan
Chapter 4 Study Guide
Chapter 4 Review Activity
Chapter 4 Application Activity
Chapter 4 Extension Activity

Transparencies 5, 6
Transparency Strategies and
    Activities

Readings in Psychology: Section 2,
    Readings 1, 2

Chapter 4 Test, Form A and Form B

Understanding Psychology
    Testmaker

Exploring Key Ideas

To demonstrate how the physical properties of the brain control behavior, have students research information on the effects of various types of brain injuries. In class discussion, develop a catalog of brain injuries, relating the symptoms to the particular area of the brain affected. Explain that brain injuries can have widely varying effects, depending on the part of the brain injured.

PORTRAIT

Hippocrates
ca. 460–ca. 370 B.C.
Born on a Greek island off the coast of Turkey, Hippocrates is called "the Father of Medicine." He was the first physician to insist that treatment be based on observation and deductive reasoning. More importantly, he credited all diseases to natural causes, rather than the workings of the gods. In so doing, he separated medicine from religion and philosophy, making it a separate empirical science. Although he ascribed mental illness to an imbalance in the four bodily humors, he was not far from the mark: Many mental illnesses are indeed the result of biochemical imbalances.

OBJECTIVES

After studying this chapter, you should be able to

- name the parts and functions of the nervous system.
- identify the structure and functions of the human brain.
- discuss the different ways psychologists study the brain.
- describe the endocrine system.
- summarize research on the effects of heredity and environment.

You are your brain. Your pleasant personality, your wry sense of humor, and your favorite color are all coded in the billions of nerve cells of your brain. Ordinarily, we pay no attention to our biological nature. But your reliance on the physical properties of the nervous system would become painfully obvious if you were involved in a car accident that damaged your brain: your personality, your memories, and even your sense of humor might be affected.

The Greek physician Hippocrates was the first to notice that head injuries often disturbed thought and behavior. In the 24 centuries since his observations, many attempts have been made to explain how this mass of soggy gray tissue could create the theory of relativity, the Sistine Chapel ceiling, and the energy crisis. But the mind remains a mystery to itself.

Some of the most exciting developments in psychology are going on in biological psychology, and this chapter will help you to understand the newspaper and magazine articles reporting new discoveries that you will be reading into the twenty-first century. In addition to describing the organization of the nervous system, we will discuss studies of animals and the possible role of genes in complex human behavior.

KEY TERMS

adrenal glands
autonomic nervous system (ANS)
central nervous system (CNS)
cerebellum
cerebral cortex
cerebrum
corpus callosum
endocrine system
ethology
forebrain
hindbrain
hormones
hypothalamus
lobes
medulla
midbrain
neurons
peripheral nervous system (PNS)
pituitary gland
pons
sociobiology
somatic nervous system (SNS)
species-specific behaviors
spinal cord
synapses
thalamus
thyroid gland

IN YOUR JOURNAL

Ask yourself why it is important for psychologists to study the brain and nervous system. Write your answer to this question in your journal and justify your response.

81

EXTRA CREDIT ACTIVITY

Help students arrange to interview someone who suffers from a brain ailment or endocrine imbalance that affects behavior, such as a seizure disorder or hyperactive thyroid. Students should ask questions to learn about symptoms, diagnostic procedures, and treatment. Students should also find out if the subject has experienced discrimination because of the condition. Ask students to present their findings as a brief oral report to the class. *(You might arrange for release forms requesting permission to use comments by any interviewees.)*

IN YOUR JOURNAL

Remind students that the assignment asks them to justify their responses. Suggest that they recall the lists generated during the Motivating Activity to find ample justification.

81

TEACH_____

Guided Practice

■ **Discussion.** In discussing receptors and effectors, ask the students to give other examples of how the brain automatically controls the body's responses to certain external stimuli. *(for example, swatting a stinging insect, jumping when we hear a sudden noise, freezing when we see a snake)* (OBJECTIVE 1)

Teacher Note. Stress that the nervous system is the body's communication network and control center. Make sure that students comprehend that the nervous system has two main divisions—the central and the peripheral nervous system, and that the latter can be subdivided into subsets of even more specific nervous systems.

VISUAL INSTRUCTION

Ask students to identify actions that the somatic nervous system controls. *(Answers may include any voluntary action.)* **Answer to caption, Figure 4.2:** the part of the peripheral nervous system that controls voluntary activities

Teacher Note. To illustrate the all-or-none principle of neurons, you might use the example of a balloon subjected to the "stimulus" of increasing pressure until it reaches the threshold at which it explodes.

? FACT OR FICTION

Once a neuron begins to "fire," it can be stopped if the original stimulation is weak.

Fiction. Transmission between neurons or nerve cells occurs whenever the cells are stimulated past a minimum point and emit a signal. The neuron is said to "fire." The firing of neurons occurs in line with the *all-or-none principle*, which states that when a neuron fires it does so at full strength. If a neuron is not stimulated past the minimum, or *threshold* level, it does not fire at all.

THE NERVOUS SYSTEM

In some ways, the nervous system is like the telephone system in a city. Messages are constantly traveling back and forth. As in a telephone system, the messages are electrical for most of their journey. They travel along prelaid cables, linked with one another by relays and switchboards. In the body, the cables are *nerve fibers*. The connections, the gaps that occur between individual nerve cells, are **synapses.** The switchboards are special cells that are found along the lines of communication (called *interneurons*) and the networks of nerve cells found in the brain and spinal cord. One major difference is that a telephone system simply conveys messages, while the nervous system actively helps to run the body.

The brain monitors what is happening inside and outside the body by receiving messages from *receptors*—cells whose function is to gather information. The brain sifts through these messages, combines them, and sends out orders to the *effectors*—cells that work the muscles and internal glands and organs. For example, receptors in your eye may send a message to the brain such as "Round object. Size increasing. Distance decreasing rapidly." Your brain instantly connects this image with information from memory to identify this object as a baseball. Almost simultaneously, your brain orders the effectors in your arms to position themselves so you don't get beaned.

How the Nervous System Works

Messages to and from the brain travel along the nerves, which are strings of long, thin cells called **neurons** (see Figure 4.2). Chemical-electrical sig-

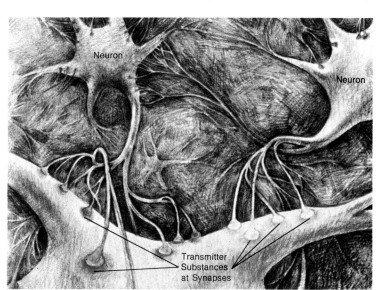

FIGURE 4.2

The human body contains billions of neurons. Neurons connect with each other at the synapses, where chemical substances cross the gap from one nerve cell to another. In that way, messages can travel through the body. **What is the somatic nervous system?**

CONNECTIONS: PSYCHOLOGY AND ANATOMY

Until the sixteenth century, when anatomists began dissecting cadavers to explore the workings of the body, the views of the Greco-Roman physician Galen (ca. 130–ca. 200) concerning the brain and nervous system went virtually uncontested. Have students research what early physicians, scientists, and philosophers believed about the brain and its functions. Ask interested students to research specific questions, such as: How did the works of the Flemish anatomist Andreas Vesalius (1514–1564), for example, overturn many of Galen's doctrines? What obstacles *(continued on page 83)*

nals travel down the neurons much as flame travels along a firecracker fuse. The main difference is that the neuron can "burn" over and over again, hundreds of times a minute.

Each neuron is long and thin, with branching or brushlike extensions (Figure 4.2). One end receives the message and the other, which can be as much as three feet away, transmits the message chemically to the next neuron. That next neuron picks up chemicals called *neurotransmitters* from across the synapse (gap). The neurotransmitters can excite the next neuron or stop it from transmitting (inhibition). The neurotransmitters are like the valves in a water system that allow flow in only one direction.

The intensity of activity in each neuron depends on how many other neurons are acting on it. Each individual neuron is either ON or OFF, depending on whether the majority of neurons acting on it are exciting it or inhibiting it. The actual destination of nerve impulses produced by an excited neuron, as they travel from one neuron to another, is limited by what tract in the nervous system they are on. Ascending tracts carry sensory impulses to the brain; descending tracts carry motor impulses from the brain.

Some of the actions that your body takes in response to impulses from the nerves are voluntary acts, such as lifting your hand to turn a page (which actually involves many impulses to many muscles). Others are involuntary acts, such as changes in the heartbeat, in the blood pressure, or in the size of the pupils. The term **somatic nervous system (SNS)** refers to the part of the peripheral nervous system that controls voluntary activities. The term **autonomic nervous system (ANS)** refers to the part of the nervous system that controls involuntary activities—those that ordinarily occur "automatically," such as heartbeat, stomach activity, and so on.

The autonomic nervous system itself has two parts: *sympathetic* and *parasympathetic*. The sympathetic nervous system prepares the body for dealing with emergencies or strenuous activity. It speeds up the heart to hasten the supply of oxygen and nutrients to body tissues. It constricts some arteries and relaxes others so that blood flows to the muscles, where it is most needed in emergencies and strenuous activity. It increases the blood pressure and suspends some activities, such as digestion. In contrast, the parasympathetic nervous system works to conserve energy and to enhance the body's ability to recover from strenuous activity. It reduces the heart rate and blood pressure and helps bring the body back to normal.

All of this takes place automatically. Receptors are constantly receiving messages (hunger, the need to swallow or cough) that alert the autonomic nervous system, via the *thalamus* in the brain, to carry out routine activities. Imagine how difficult it would be if you had no autonomic nervous system and had to think about it every time your body needed to digest a sandwich or perspire.

Structurally, the nervous system is divided into two parts (Figure 4.3): the brain and **spinal cord** (the **central nervous system (CNS)**); and smaller branches of nerves that reach the other parts of the body (the **peripheral nervous system (PNS)**). More than three-fourths of your body's neurons are in the brain, which weighs about 2 ⅔–3 pounds. The nerves of the peripheral system that branch out from the spinal column are about as thick

FIGURE 4.3

The nervous system is divided into two parts: the central nervous system (CNS) and the peripheral nervous system (PNS). **What are the two main parts of the central nervous system?**

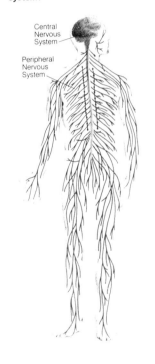

Central Nervous System

Peripheral Nervous System

■ **Discussion.** This problem should be an interesting one for students to figure out: How can a neuron that fires all or none relay different levels of stimulation? There are two means: First, an excitatory cell that is stimulated more heavily fires more rapidly. Second, if stimulation is heavy, a larger number of neurons will fire. To illustrate these concepts, you might use the example of a pencil (eraser end) applied to the skin: As pressure is increased, the level of pressure experienced increases. This is because the neurons are firing more rapidly and in greater number, sending pressure signals to the brain. (OBJECTIVE 1)

VISUAL INSTRUCTION

Point out that the PNS connects the CNS to other parts of the body through 43 pairs of nerves that extend from the CNS.
Answers to caption, Figure 4.3: the brain and spinal cord

Enrich. Have students complete the Chapter 4 Application Activity.

CONNECTIONS: PSYCHOLOGY AND ANATOMY

did Vesalius and other anatomists of his day have to overcome? Encourage students to incorporate their findings with graphics for display in the classroom.

Displays might include some of Vesalius's anatomical drawings of the nervous system.

■ **Demonstration.** Locate a model of the brain (one may be available in the school's biology lab). Review the structure of the brain with the class, and point out or have students name all the major parts. If available, bring brain models for other species as well so that students can compare brain size, parts, and functions of the human brain with those of other animals. Notice, for example, the declining size of the cortex in less sophisticated animals. (OBJECTIVE 2)

VISUAL INSTRUCTION

Point out that about 85 percent of the brain's weight is made up of the "new brain," the part of the brain associated with thinking and memory.
Answer to caption, Figure 4.4: The cerebellum controls posture and balance.
Answer to caption, Figure 4.5: The motor cortex sends information to control body movement.

as a pencil. Those in the extremities, such as the fingertips, are invisibly small. All parts of the nervous system are protected in some way: the brain by the skull and several layers of sheathing; the spinal cord by the vertebrae; and the peripheral nerves by layers of sheathing. The bony protection of the spinal cord is vital. An injury to the spinal cord could prevent the transmittal of messages between the brain and the muscles, and could result in paralysis.

The brain is composed of three parts, the hindbrain, midbrain, and forebrain. The **hindbrain,** located at the rear base of the skull, includes the **medulla** and the **pons.** The medulla controls breathing and a variety of reflexes while the pons is concerned with balance, hearing, and other functions. Another part of the hindbrain, the **cerebellum,** located behind the spinal cord, helps control posture and balance. The **midbrain** is a small part of the brain above the pons that integrates sensory information and relays it upward. The medulla, pons, and midbrain compose most of the brain stem, and the reticular activating system (RAS) spans across all these structures. The RAS serves to alert the rest of the brain to incoming signals. The **forebrain,** located above the brain's central core, includes the thalamus, which integrates sensory input, and the hypothalamus, which monitors emotion, sleep, and other bodily processes.

The "higher" thinking processes are housed in the forebrain. The outer layer of the forebrain consists of the **cerebral cortex.** The inner layer is the **cerebrum.** The cerebral cortex and cerebrum surround the hindbrain and

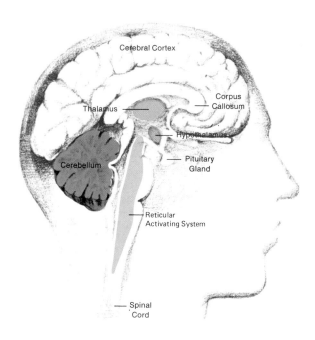

FIGURE 4.4

The brain is the largest, most complex part of the nervous system. **What are functions of the cerebellum?**

COOPERATIVE LEARNING ACTIVITY

Organize the class into small groups. Instruct each group to select a part of the brain and prepare a short skit to present to the class. The skit should convey the function of the particular part and how it interacts with other parts of the body. On a larger scale, you might have different groups collaborate to show how the various parts of the brain interact. Encourage students to develop props, such as signs and drawings, to aid in their presentations.

brain stem much like the way a halved peach surrounds the pit. The cerebral cortex gives you the ability to learn and store complex and abstract information, and to project your thinking into the future. It is your cerebral cortex that allows you to see, read, and understand this sentence. The cortex, or bark, of the cerebrum is the site of the conscious thinking processes, yet it is less than a half-inch thick.

Precisely which areas of the cerebral cortex control which activities is not completely known, but information is being gathered and brain maps are being made. To help them describe the location of certain activities, scientists refer to sites on different **lobes,** or regions, of the brain (Figure 4.5). The information that is available is based on observations of people and laboratory animals with brain or nerve damage. Scientists have also gathered information by stimulating parts of the brain during surgery, which is painless since there are no touch receptors in the brain, and by conducting tests that measure the activity in different areas of the brain.

Some areas of the cortex receive information from the skin senses and from muscles. The amount of brain tissue connected to any given body part determines the sensitivity of that area, not its size (Figure 4.6). For example, the highly developed sense of touch in the hand involves a much larger brain area than that of the relatively insensitive calves. The part of the cortex that receives information is called the somatosensory cortex. The motor cortex sends information to control body movement. The motor cortex is also divided according to need. The more sophisticated the move-

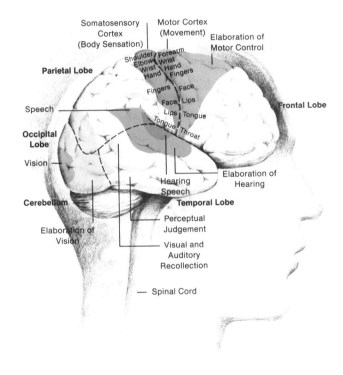

FIGURE 4.5

The functions of the cerebral cortex are not fully understood. Some areas whose behavioral importance is known are indicated. **What is the function of the motor cortex?**

Teacher Note. Point out that each lobe is named after the bone in the skull that protects it. Explain that "temporal" in this context does not refer to time, but to the temples on either side of the head.

■ **Discussion.** In discussing the different lobes and the locations of certain activities, ask students if they recall reading about lobotomies in the plays (and life) of Tennessee Williams or in the well-known novel *One Flew Over the Cuckoo's Nest*. What was the purpose of such operations? *(to rid the patient of certain severe disturbances and violent behavior)* (OBJECTIVE 2)

WORKING WITH TRANSPARENCIES

Project Transparencies 5 and 6 and use the guidelines given on Teaching Strategies and Activities. Assign Student Worksheets 5 and 6.

CONNECTIONS: PSYCHOLOGY AND HISTORY

The pseudoscience of phrenology was an offshoot of scientific attempts to map the brain. Phrenologists believed that traits were localized in specific surface areas of the brain and that well-developed traits caused small bumps to appear on the skull. Less-developed traits supposedly manifested themselves with indentations. Accordingly, anyone's personality could be charted by studying the bumps on that person's skull. Phrenology became a fad in the mid-1800s, and phrenological charts were even published for the presidential candidates in the 1860 election. Some businesses required phrenological examinations for prospective workers. If students think such pseudoscience is a thing of the past, remind them of astrology's claims to chart behavior.

FIGURE 4.6

Two views of the same half of the brain, sliced in half between the parietal and frontal lobes (along the groove that separates the somatosensory cortex from the motor cortex) are illustrated. The areas of greatest sensitivity (left) and motor control (right) are listed. The funny little figures depict how the body would look if areas of greatest sensitivity and motor control were proportionate in the body to their size in the brain. **What is the function of the somatosensory cortex?**

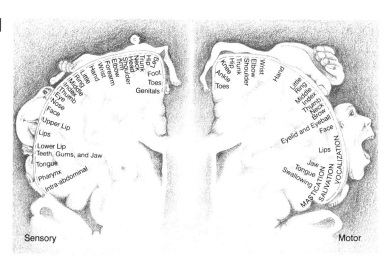

FIGURE 4.7

This drawing was adapted from one of the sketches made by the doctor who attended Phineas Gage. It shows the path taken by the iron stake that was propelled through Gage's skull. **According to some studies, what do the frontal lobes control?**

ments have to be (such as those used in speaking), the bigger the brain area involved. The *association areas* mediate between the other two and do most of the synthesizing of information.

The brain processes a vast number of incoming and outgoing messages every second, but not all of them reach the cerebral cortex. Some parts of the lower brain (such as the reticular activating system and the **thalamus**) filter out all but the most important messages. Exactly how the parts of the brain process so much information is being studied. It seems that patterns of stimuli and appropriate responses are stored in the memory. So when a pattern of incoming impulses is screened by the lower parts of the brain, it is compared to other, previous patterns. This is an ongoing process.

The brain's ability to process many experiences at once makes it so superior to the most sophisticated computer that scientists can never hope to match its capabilities. Researchers are still trying to determine the different functions and interactions of the parts of the brain. Some studies suggest that the frontal lobes control creativity and personality: they enable people to be witty, sensitive, or easygoing. Evidence for this theory is provided by the case of Phineas Gage. A railroad crew foreman, he was injured in an explosion in the mid-1800s. The force of the blast drove an iron stake through Gage's head, damaging the frontal lobes (Figure 4.7). Remarkably, Gage survived and was back at work in a few months. The accident did not impair his bodily functions, or his memory or skills. However, Gage's personality changed dramatically. This once trustworthy and dependable man became childish, fitful, impatient, and capricious. Later studies of large numbers of people with similar brain damage suggest that planning future action, emotional control, and the ability to pay attention depend on the frontal lobes.

The Hemispheres of the Brain

The cortex is divided into two hemispheres that are roughly mirror images of each other. (Each of the four lobes is present in both hemispheres.) The two hemispheres are connected by a band of nerves called the **corpus callosum,** which carries messages back and forth between the two. Each hemisphere is connected to half of the body in a crisscrossed fashion. The motor cortex of the left hemisphere of the brain controls most of the right side of the body; the right hemisphere motor cortex controls most of the left side of the body. Thus a stroke that causes damage to the right hemisphere will result in numbness or paralysis on the left side of the body. Researchers have also found a number of more subtle differences between the sides of the brain: in right-handed people, the left hemisphere usually controls language, while the right hemisphere is involved in spatial tasks.

Many psychologists became interested in differences between the cerebral hemispheres when "split brain" operations were tried on epileptics like Harriet Lees. For most of her life Ms. Lees's seizures were mild and could be controlled with drugs. However, at age 25 they began to get worse, and by 30 Lees was having as many as a dozen violent seizures a day. An epileptic seizure involves massive uncontrolled electrical activity that begins in either hemisphere and spreads to the other. To enable this woman to live a normal life, doctors decided to sever the corpus callosum so that seizures could not spread.

Not only does the operation reduce the severity of seizures, it also results in fewer seizures (Kalat, 1992). But psychologists were even more interested in the potential side effects of this operation. Despite the fact that patients who had this operation now had "two separate brains," they seemed remarkably normal. Researchers went on to develop a number of techniques to try to detect subtle effects of the operation. To understand the procedures, you need to know a little about brain anatomy. For example, the right visual field is connected to the left hemisphere of the brain and the left visual field is connected to the right hemisphere. To get a message to only one hemisphere at a time, the researchers asked each split-brain patient to stare at a dot while they briefly flashed a word or a picture on one side of the dot. If the word "nut" was flashed to the right of the dot, it went to the left hemisphere. The patient could usually read it quite easily under these circumstances, because the left hemisphere controls language for most right-handed people.

But when the same word was flashed to the left visual field, stimulating the right hemisphere of the brain, the patient was not able to repeat it. For an ordinary person, the word "nut" would quickly go from one side of the brain to the other via the corpus callosum. Since this patient's corpus callosum had been cut, however, the message could not get from the nonverbal right hemisphere to the verbal left. Even more amazing was the fact that the patient really did recognize the word: with her left hand (which is also connected to the right hemisphere), she could pick out a nut from a group of objects hidden behind a screen. But even after she correctly picked out the nut and held it in her hand, still she could not remember the word!

CRITICAL THINKING ACTIVITY

Demonstrating Reasoned Judgment. Point out that epileptics have for centuries been subject to discrimination because of their ailment and the way it affects behavior. For example, at one time, epileptics were believed to be possessed by evil spirits or presumed to be "crazy" or of subnormal intelligence and therefore unfit for employment. Ask students to discuss how knowing the physiological causes of behavior might breed greater tolerance for those afflicted with epilepsy and similar ailments. (You might have students contact the Epilepsy Foundation for additional information.)

DID YOU KNOW?

After observing that injury to one side of the head often produces paralysis on the opposite side of the body, Hippocrates concluded that the right side of the body is controlled by the left side of the brain, and vice versa.

VISUAL INSTRUCTION

Explain that the word *chiasm* in the phrase *optic chiasm* comes from *chi*, the Greek letter that resembles our letter X.

Answer to caption, Figure 4.8: In right-handed people, the left hemisphere usually controls language, while the right hemisphere is involved in spatial tasks.

■ **Discussion.** Some psychologists contend that the left hemisphere tends to process information sequentially, while the right hemisphere considers information globally. Ask students to explain why these tendencies make sense, considering the activities that each hemisphere controls. *(We generally process language sequentially, one word at a time, whereas we usually consider an object in space as a whole.)* (OBJECTIVE 2)

■ **Readings in Psychology.** Have students read the Section 2, Reading 1 selection in *Readings in Psychology* and answer the questions that follow the reading.

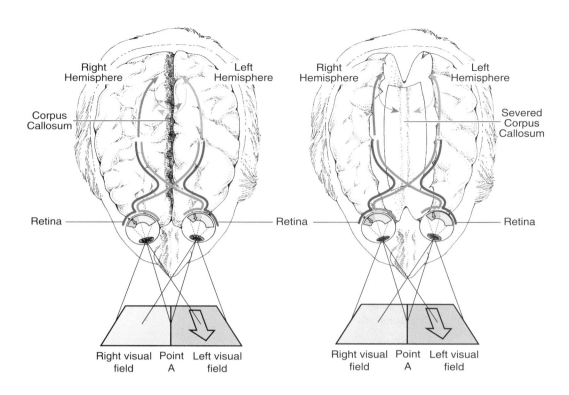

FIGURE 4.8

At the back of each eye is a large nerve cable called the optic nerve that connects the eye with the brain. Because the optic nerve coming from each eye splits at the optic chiasm, the image to a person's right is sent to the left side of the brain, and the image to a person's left is transmitted to the right side of the brain. **What are the differences between the hemispheres of the brain in right-handed people?**

In another experiment, a picture of a nude woman was flashed to the right hemisphere (via the left visual field) of another split-brain patient. This woman laughed but said she saw nothing. Only her left hemisphere could speak and it did not see the nude. The right hemisphere, which did see the nude, produced the laugh. When the woman was asked why she laughed, she acted confused and couldn't explain it.

Right-handed children are genetically predisposed to develop verbal left hemispheres, but the actual specialization develops over the years. If a child suffers damage to the left hemisphere, the right hemisphere will take over the function of speech. The child may learn more slowly than other children, but he or she will learn to speak. However, almost all adults who suffer damage to the left hemisphere have extreme difficulty speaking—if they can speak at all. The effects of right-hemisphere damage are less clear, but they probably include problems with spatial abilities.

Though this specialization of labor is particularly relevant for people with brain damage, it also involves normal people. One group of studies, for example, has looked at the brain waves of right-handed people as they perform verbal and spatial tasks. The brain waves show greater activity in the right hemisphere for spatial tasks like memorizing geometrical designs, remembering faces, or imagining an elephant in a swing. But when the same people were asked to perform verbal tasks—writing a letter in their

LAB EXPERIMENTS AND DEMONSTRATIONS

Researchers have developed the following lists of dominant traits/preferences to determine if an individual is "right brain dominant" or "left brain dominant." Students might use these traits as a checklist to determine their own hemispheric inclination. *(Tell students that this is only an informal indication of which hemisphere may be dominant for them.)*

Left Brain Characteristics
1. rational thinker
2. sequential
3. structured/planned
4. makes objective judgments
5. prefers talking and writing
6. time-oriented
7. thinks concretely
8. controls feelings
9. is logical
10. looks for differences
11. needs to be in control
(continued on page 89)

At A Glance

WHICH WAY DO THE EYES MOVE?

Did you know that the direction your eyes move when you think about a question may indicate which side of the brain you are using for the answer?

Ask a friend the following four questions, and secretly watch whether she first looks to the right or the left as she considers each:

1. Make up a sentence using the words "code" and "mathematics."
2. Picture the last automobile accident you saw. In which direction were the cars going?
3. What does the proverb "Easy come, easy go" mean?
4. Picture and describe the last time you cried.

Questions 1 and 3 are verbal, nonemotional questions; a right-handed person should use the left hemisphere to answer and, as a result, tend to look to the right. Questions 2 and 4 are spatial-emotional questions that require the right hemisphere and should, on the average, yield more eye movements to the left than the right.

For more details, see G. E. Schwartz, R. Davidson, and F. Maer, "Right Hemisphere Lateralization for Emotion in the Human Brain: Interactions with Cognition," *Science*, 190 (1975): 286–288.

heads, thinking of words that begin with "t," and listening to boring passages from the *Congressional Record*—their brain waves showed relatively greater activity in the left hemisphere (Hassett, 1978). Even more interesting, and far easier to observe, is the fact that normal people tend to move their eyes in a certain way depending on which hemisphere they are using.

These clear differences between the hemispheres apply primarily to right-handed people. Some left-handers have the opposite pattern of cerebral dominance—language is found in the right hemisphere. More commonly, lefties have less dramatic differences between the halves of the brain, but thicker corpus callosums aiding communication between the hemispheres (Witelson, 1985).

One by-product of all the research on cerebral dominance has been an increased interest in the phenomenon of handedness. About 9 out of 10 people prefer to use their right hand, and this seems to be a distinctly human characteristic with a long history. Even the people pictured in Egyptian tomb paintings usually use their right hand (Figure 4.9). Jeannine Herron (1976) has argued that left-handers, a clear minority, are often the subject of discrimination. Teachers sometimes try to get young children to use their right hands. The French word for left is *gauche*, which in English means *clumsy* or *socially inept*, as in "left-handed compliment." There is no scientific basis, Herron argues, for believing that right-handed is better.

About 9 out of 10 people are right-handed.

At A Glance

Have students try the test described in the feature on friends outside of class and report their findings.

■ **Discussion.** Have the students consider the functions of the left and right hemispheres of the brain. Give the class the following list of occupations, and ask which hemisphere they would expect to be dominant in each: engineer, artist, lawyer, musician, architect, surgeon, mechanic, editor, bus driver. Inform students that although much is known about left-brain, right-brain differences (technically called *hemispheric asymmetry*), most of the research was done with right-handed subjects. Much less is known about the organization of brains of left-handed individuals. (OBJECTIVE 2)

■ **Discussion.** Point out that scissors are generally designed for use by right-handed people. Ask students to think of other implements or objects intended for right-handed use. Have the left-handed students in class discuss problems they may have experienced in adjusting to a right-handed environment. (OBJECTIVE 2)

LAB EXPERIMENTS AND DEMONSTRATIONS

Right Brain Characteristics
1. intuitive
2. holistic
3. spontaneous
4. makes subjective judgments
5. prefers drawing and working with objects
6. ignores deadlines

7. prefers the elusive, uncertain
8. lets feelings go
9. is analogic
10. looks for similarities
11. takes more risks

For more about hemispheric preferences, students might read *Learning to Learn: Strengthening Study Skills*

and Brain Power, by Gloria Frender (Incentive Publications, 1990).

FIGURE 4.9

An Egyptian tomb painting shows people at work, using their right hands. **What is the ratio of right-handed people to left-handed people?**

HOW PSYCHOLOGISTS STUDY THE BRAIN

Mapping the brain's mountains, canyons, and inner recesses has supplied scientists with fascinating information about the role of the brain in behavior. Psychologists who do this kind of research are called *physiological psychologists*. Among the methods they use to explore the brain are recording, stimulation, and lesioning.

Recording

By inserting wires called electrodes into the brain, it is possible to detect the minute electrical changes that occur when neurons fire (Figure 4.10). The wires are connected to electronic equipment that amplifies the tiny voltages produced by the firing neurons. Even single neurons can be monitored. For example, two researchers placed tiny electrodes in the sections of cats' and monkeys' brains that receive visual information. They found that different neurons fired, depending on whether a line, an edge, or an angle was placed before the animal's eyes (Hubel and Wiesel, 1962).

The electrical activity of whole areas of the brain can be recorded with an electroencephalograph (EEG). Wires from the EEG machine are taped to the scalp so that millions upon millions of neurons can be monitored at the same time (Figure 4.11). Psychologists have observed that the overall

PSYCHOLOGISTS AT WORK

Physiological psychologists are specialists within the broader field of experimental psychology (see Psychologists at Work, p. 38). These specialists perform "pure research" in laboratory settings. Their work requires expert knowledge of the anatomy of the nervous system as well as the techniques of brain surgery and the application of biochemical methods. Subspecialties within the field of physiological psychology include neuropsychology and psychophysiology.

FIGURE 4.10

This rat has an electrode implanted in an area of its brain. Each time the animal presses the lever, a tiny pulse is delivered to its brain. The extremely high rates of lever-pressing performed by animals with such implants indicate that a "pleasure center" is probably being stimulated by the electricity. Rats will often continue to press the lever rather than respond to any other needs, such as hunger, thirst, or sleep. **What methods do physiological psychologists use to explore the brain?**

electrical activity of the brain rises and falls rhythmically and that the pattern of the rhythm depends on whether a person is awake, drowsy, or asleep (as illustrated in Chapter 7). These rhythms, or brain waves, occur because the neurons in the brain tend to increase or decrease their amount of activity in unison.

EEGs can be used to monitor the brain malfunction that causes epilepsy, now usually called a *seizure disorder*. When an epileptic seizure occurs, abnormal electrical activity begins in a small piece of damaged brain tissue and then spreads to neighboring areas of the brain. By monitoring brain waves on an EEG, doctors can determine what kind of surgical procedure (if any) would reduce violent seizures. Another test has been developed that measures brain activity by revealing the amount of glucose consumed by neurons in the brain. This technique, called a *positron emission tomography (PET)* scan, can be used to locate tumors and seizure activity.

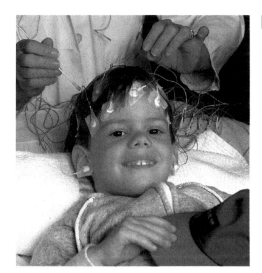

FIGURE 4.11

Scientists use an electroencephalograph (EEG) machine to measure brain waves. **What have psychologists observed about the electrical activity of the brain?**

■ **Debating an Issue.** Psychosurgery and stimulation techniques that alter human behavior raise many ethical and legal questions, especially when the rights of prisoners, minors, and the mentally incompetent are involved. Have the class research both sides of this controversy. Based on this research, have the class debate the following topic: *Resolved—* That a prisoner serve the full term of his or her sentence even if psychosurgery has successfully eliminated the prisoner's tendency toward criminal behavior. (OBJECTIVE 3)

Stimulation

Electrodes may be used to set off the firing of neurons as well as to record it. Brain surgeon Wilder Penfield stimulated the brains of his patients during surgery to determine what functions the various parts of the brain perform. In this way he could localize the malfunctioning part for which surgery was required, for example, for epilepsy. When Penfield applied a tiny electric current to points on the temporal lobe of the brain, he could trigger whole memory sequences. During surgery, one woman heard a familiar song so clearly that she thought a record was being played in the operating room (Penfield and Rasmussen, 1950).

Using the stimulation technique, other researchers have shown that there are "pleasure" and "punishment" centers in the brain. One research team implanted electrodes in certain areas of the "old brain" of a rat, then placed the rat in a box equipped with a lever that the rat could press. Each time the rat pressed the lever, a mild electrical current was delivered to its brain. When the electrode was placed in the rat's "pleasure" center, it would push the lever several thousand times per hour (Olds and Olds, 1965).

Scientists have used chemicals as well as electricity to stimulate the brain. In this method, a small tube is implanted in an animal's brain so that the end touches the area to be stimulated (Figure 4.12). Chemicals can then be delivered through the tube to the area of the brain being studied. Such experiments have shown that different chemicals in the hypothalamus can affect hunger and thirst in an animal.

Stimulation techniques have aroused great medical interest. They have been used with terminal cancer patients to relieve them of intolerable pain without using drugs. A current delivered through electrodes implanted in certain areas of the brain seems to provide a sudden temporary relief (Delgado, 1969). Furthermore, some psychiatrists have experimented with similar methods to control violent emotional behavior in otherwise uncontrollable patients.

Lesions

Scientists sometimes create lesions by cutting or destroying part of an animal's brain. If the animal behaves differently after the operation, they

FIGURE 4.12

This technique is used to stimulate the inside of a rat's brain with chemicals. (a) The rat is prepared for brain surgery. (b) A small funnel at the top of a tiny tube is permanently implanted in the rat's skull. The other end of the tube is deep inside the brain. (c) A measured amount of some chemical that affects the nervous system is passed into the tube in a solution of water. **How have stimulation techniques been used to help cancer patients?**

a
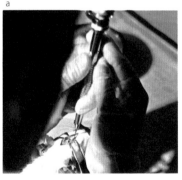
b

c

At A Glance

THE COURTS AND PSYCHOSURGERY

In 1973, a Michigan court made an important decision that limited psychosurgery. L.S., a criminal who had been charged with first-degree murder and rape, had been confined to a Michigan mental hospital for 18 years when he agreed to have brain surgery to try to make him less violent. A legal services lawyer brought suit to prevent the operation.

Both L.S. and his parents had given written consent for the operation. But it became clear in court that neither completely understood the implications of the procedure. Furthermore, L.S. suspected that he might be released earlier if he went along with the operation.

The court ruled that the operation should not be done even though L.S. had said he wanted it. Involuntarily confined patients, the court said, simply cannot give legally adequate consent to experimental high-risk procedures like psychosurgery.

A related case in Texas involved a prisoner repeatedly jailed for sex crimes. He requested castration as a means to assure that he could safely be released. His suggestion was ultimately rejected by the court because of a lack of confirming evidence that the operation would have the intended effect. Thus, the legal status of various forms of surgery intended to alter behavior has been seriously challenged in court.

For more details, see Carole Wade Offir, "The Movement to Pull Out the Electrodes," *Psychology Today,* 7 (May 1974): 69–70, and *Houston Chronicle* (1992). Rodgers, Joann E. *Psychosurgery: Damaging the Brain to Save the Mind.* New York: Harper Collins, 1992.

assume that the destroyed brain area is involved with that type of behavior. For example, in one classic lesion study, two researchers removed a certain area of the temporal lobe from rhesus monkeys. Normally, these animals are aggressive and vicious, but after the operation they became less fearful and at the same time less violent (Klüver and Bucy, 1937). The implication was that this area of the brain controlled aggression. The relations revealed by this type of research are far more subtle and complex than people first believed.

THE ENDOCRINE SYSTEM

The nervous system is one of two communication systems for sending information to and from the brain. The second is the endocrine system. The **endocrine system** sends chemical messages, called **hormones.** The hormones are produced in the endocrine glands and are distributed by the blood and other body fluids. (The names and locations of these glands are shown in Figure 4.13.) The hormone messages are like letters in a

At A Glance

After students have read the At a Glance feature, ask them the following questions:
1. Why did the court ultimately deny L.S. his request to have brain surgery to make him less violent? *(Neither he nor his parents fully understood the implications of the procedure; furthermore, L.S. suspected having the operation would lead to his early release.)*
2. Why did the court deny the sex offender his request to be castrated? *(The court accepted evidence that the operation would not prevent him from committing sex crimes in the future.)*

■ **Drawing Conclusions.** Ask students to decide which of the three methods for exploring the brain promises to yield the most practical benefits for treating human behavioral problems. *(Answers will vary. All three methods have the potential for yielding significant benefits.)* (OBJECTIVE 3)

STUDY AND WRITING SKILLS

Psychosurgery involving prisoners remains controversial, not only because of legal questions related to informed consent and effectiveness, but also because of societal attitudes over the proper role of prisons. Are they intended to rehabilitate or to punish? If the former, are taxpayers morally obligated to fund expensive psychosurgical procedures that may rehabilitate prisoners? Ask students to take a stand on these issues and to write a persuasive essay in which they use psychological knowledge to support their opinions.

Teacher Note. After students read the Psychology Update, point out that brain cells, unlike most of the other cells in the body, do not regenerate once they are destroyed. This fact explains the importance of quick action following a stroke or other head trauma to reduce neuronal activity.

Using Psychology

After students read the special feature, point out that, as technology has developed, significant advances have been made in the precision of psychosurgery. In 1993, for example, surgeons successfully used microwaves to destroy a small patch of cells in a man's brain that caused him to suffer from frequent, uncontrollable panic attacks. However, since such procedures are usually experimental, risky, and very expensive, they have not been covered by traditional medical insurance policies. This situation partially accounts for the low number of psychosurgeries performed in the United States today.

■ **Discussion.** Ask students to discuss whether they would opt for invasive, risky psychosurgery if they suffered from a serious behavioral problem (such as panic attacks) that could not be treated effectively with drugs. Ask: Would your answer change if you knew that the problem could potentially be cured through psychotherapy? (OBJECTIVE 3)

PSYCHOLOGY UPDATE

Brain Damage. Strokes or head injuries often cause brain damage. Within several minutes, brain cells begin to die. Since this process happens so quickly, it had been thought that little could be done to prevent permanent brain damage. Neuroscientists now believe, however, that neurons die in two ways. First, neurons that are cut off from their supply of oxygen die from suffocation. Second, neurons also die from overstimulation. Active cells consume their resources; if those resources are not replaced, the cell dies. Thus, an effective reduction of cell activity in stroke victims should lead to a reduction in the number of neurons destroyed.

Research with rats confirms that cell death can be reduced considerably by injecting magnesium, which blocks transmission at the synapse, or by injecting drugs to block the action of glutamate at synapses sensitive to that excitatory chemical in the brain. Injecting insulin slows all activity of neurons, as will lowering body temperature. All of these procedures reduce stroke damage by reducing neuronal activity, especially near the site of the stroke (Kalat, 1992).

Using Psychology
Psychosurgery

We have already discussed the use of lesions in treating violent seizure disorders (by severing the corpus callosum). Experiments with animals suggested to some researchers that it might be possible to treat certain behavioral problems with similar operations. Brain surgery aimed at changing people's thoughts and actions is called psychosurgery.

The first great wave of psychosurgery was from about 1935 to 1955. A number of studies had shown that monkeys were less upset by frustration after portions of the frontal lobe of their brains were destroyed. A similar operation, called a prefrontal lobotomy, was tried on about 50,000 mental patients in the United States and Great Britain. These operations often seemed to help people who had serious mental problems. But they also had some undesirable side effects.

After the frontal lobes were destroyed, many patients lost the ability to deal with new information or pursue goals. For example, a woman who was a very innovative cook before her operation had trouble with new recipes afterward. Even more distressing was the fact that when she went out food shopping, she would sometimes get distracted and would forget why she had left the house (Valenstein, 1973). But it is hard to draw a firm conclusion about the overall effects of frontal lobotomies. After reviewing all the available evidence, Elliot Valenstein wrote: "There is certainly no grounds for either the position that all psychosurgery necessarily reduces people to a 'vegetable status' or that it has a high probability of producing miraculous cures. The truth, even if somewhat wishy-washy, lies in between these extreme positions. There is little doubt, however, that many abuses existed" (Valenstein, 1973: p. 315). But the matter became academic in the mid-1950s because new drugs were introduced that became the treatment of choice in mental hospitals.

By the early 1970s, new operations had been introduced. Instead of destroying large portions of the brain, sophisticated procedures were used to destroy very small areas of tissue deep inside the brain. Controversy arose and the federal government issued a list of the correct procedures for obtaining informed consent from those offered psychosurgery (Brown, Wienckowski, & Bivens, 1973), to protect the rights of the patients. The National Association of Mental Health argued that psychosurgery should be a therapy of last resort ("Psychosurgery: An NAMH Position Statement," 1974).

BEYOND THE CLASSROOM

In discussing psychosurgery, explain that other approaches aimed at changing people's thoughts and actions involve drug therapy and electroconvulsive shock therapy. You might have students research these two alternative approaches and prepare oral reports for the class. Students should describe these therapies, discuss the degree to which they are effective, and explain any controversies or popular misconceptions connected with them.

By 1985 it was estimated that less than 100 psychosurgeries were performed annually in the United States (Kaplan & Saddock, 1985).

Public attention brought psychosurgery into the courts and the political arena. In 1974, Congress appointed the 11 member National Commission for the Protection of Human Subjects of Biomedical and Behavioral Research to study several controversial areas. In October 1976, they released their report on psychosurgery. At this time, public and scientific opinion was generally opposed to psychosurgery. The commission's conclusions were, in the words of one reporter (Culliton, 1976), "surprisingly favorable." They did not approve the older technique of frontal lobotomy, but they did say that some of the newer operations seemed to work. For example, an operation called a cingulotomy (destruction of a major subcortical structure) seems to be very helpful for some people who suffer from pain and severe depression.

The complexity of these operations on the brain and the philosophical issues raised by the idea of changing the way people act by changing their brains guarantees that psychosurgery will remain controversial for some time to come. Because of these controversies, an increase in the use of psychosurgery is not very likely (Valenstein, 1986).

postal system. They can circulate throughout the bloodstream, but they will be properly received only at a specific address: the particular organ of the body that they influence. The endocrine glands are also called ductless glands because they release hormones directly into the bloodstream. In contrast, the *duct glands*, or *exocrine glands*, release their contents through small holes, or ducts, onto the surface of the body, or into the inside of the digestive system. Examples of duct glands are sweat glands, tear glands, and salivary glands.

Under the direction of the **hypothalamus** in the brain, the **pituitary gland** acts as the "master gland." The pituitary gland secretes a large number of hormones, many of which control the output of hormones by other endocrine glands. The hypothalamus monitors the amount of hormones in the blood and sends out messages to correct imbalances.

What do these hormone messages tell the body to do? They carry messages to organs involved in regulating and storing nutrients so that, despite changes in conditions outside the body, cell metabolism can continue on an even course. They also control growth and reproduction, including ovulation and lactation (milk production) in females.

The **thyroid gland** produces the hormone thyroxin. Thyroxin stimulates certain chemical reactions that are important for all tissues of the body. Too little thyroxin makes people feel lazy and lethargic; too much makes them overactive. The **adrenal glands** become active when a person

FIGURE 4.13

The endocrine system, which consists of ductless glands and the hormones they produce, works closely with the nervous system in regulating body functions. **What is the function of the pituitary gland?**

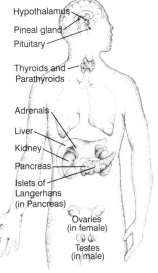

Hypothalamus
Pineal gland
Pituitary
Thyroids and Parathyroids
Adrenals
Liver
Kidney
Pancreas
Islets of Langerhans (in Pancreas)
Ovaries (in female)
Testes (in male)

CONNECTIONS: PSYCHOLOGY AND HEALTH

Another promising area of psychosurgery involves tissue implants—the grafting of healthy nerve tissue from a donor into a patient's brain. Unlike lesioning, which severs or destroys tissue, implanting attempts to replace damaged brain tissue (which cannot regenerate on its own) with functioning cells that will lessen or eliminate the symptoms of such ailments as Parkinson's disease and multiple sclerosis. Though marginally successful up to now, researchers are continuing their attempts to improve implanting procedures.

CHAPTER 4 Lesson Plan

VISUAL INSTRUCTION

Point out that scientists have discovered more than 30 different hormones in the human body.
Answer to caption, Figure 4.13: This "master gland" regulates the other endocrine glands.

■ **Creating a Chart.** Using Figure 4.13 as a basis, have students work in groups to design, illustrate, and annotate a life-size chart of the human body showing the endocrine system and explaining how the various glands affect human behavior. Display the completed charts in the classroom. (OBJECTIVE 4)

DID YOU KNOW?

Nerve impulses travel from head to foot in about 1/50 of a second (250 mph). Hormonal messages travel at the speed of blood—little more than one foot per second in the arteries and at a slower speed in the capillaries and veins.

to explain the major difference in how the nervous and endocrine systems work to help the brain monitor and control most human behavior. *(The nervous system works by transmitting chemical-electrical messages along nerves; the endocrine system works by sending chemical messages through the blood and other body fluids.)* (OBJECTIVE 4)

VISUAL INSTRUCTION

Point out that, in *The Expression of the Emotions in Man and Animals* (1872), Darwin suggested that emotions evolved because they increase a creature's chance to survive. Ask students to provide examples of animal and human behavior that Darwin might have cited to prove his point. *(Answers will vary, but appropriate examples include: a wolf baring fangs, a cat bristling fur, a gorilla beating its chest, and a human sneering at a foe.)* **Answer to caption, Figure 4.14:** the study of the natural behavior patterns of all species of animals from a biological point of view

is angry or frightened. They release adrenalin into the bloodstream. The adrenalin causes the heartbeat and breathing to increase. These and other changes help a person generate the extra energy he or she needs to handle a difficult situation.

Through the combined action of the nervous and endocrine systems, the brain monitors and controls most human behavior. Later we will see how the endocrine system influences behavior we normally attribute to psychological causes—emotion and motivation.

THE RELATIONSHIP BETWEEN HUMANS AND ANIMALS

Much of the research described in this chapter has been done primarily with other animals. The research that has been done on humans has either occurred as a part of some necessary medical operation or has involved observing people who have suffered an injury.

It is now commonly accepted that the study of animals can help in the study of human beings, even though direct experiments on humans would be even more useful if they could be done. Animal studies are especially valuable in medicine and physiology. Medicine, vaccines, and new forms of surgery are regularly tested on animal subjects. Such research is considered useful because human beings are believed to have evolved from more primitive animal origins, and their bodies are therefore similar to the bodies of other animals.

The Evolution of Behavior

Some scientists believe that the theory of evolution applies not only to anatomy and physiology, but also to behavior. Charles Darwin, the biolo-

FIGURE 4.14

There are many similarities between human behavior and animal behavior. At this penguin gathering, for example, there are penguins in pairs and by themselves. Some appear aloof, some seem to enjoy the sunshine, and some are simply observing the scene. **What is ethology?**

STUDY AND WRITING SKILLS

Have students read a biography or view a film about Charles Darwin, especially one that focuses on his voyages on the *H.M.S. Beagle* and his discoveries in Patagonia and the Galapagos Islands. Ask students to write a brief biological sketch of Darwin, explaining why his theories were considered so revolu- tionary. To expand the activity, have students supplement their sketches with relevant excerpts from Darwin's writings.

gist who in 1859 published his theory of evolution, believed that all animal species are related to one another. Consequently, the structure of their bodies and their behavior patterns can be distinguished and compared, just as one may compare a child's nose or his temper to that of his father. The bones in a bird's wing are different, but comparable to the bones in a human arm; the way birds flock together can be compared to the way humans gather in groups (Figure 4.14). Just as the parts of a chimpanzee's brain can be compared to a human's, so can a chimpanzee's ability to solve problems be compared to human thinking ability.

Darwin's theory does not mean that humans do not possess unique qualities. It does, however, make it possible to think of humans as members of a particularly complex, interesting species rather than as totally different from other animals.

Ethology

Ethology, the study of the natural behavior patterns of all species of animals from a biological point of view, is an outgrowth of Darwin's theory of evolution. Ethologists study how these patterns have evolved and changed, and how they are expressed in humans. Ethologists call these natural patterns **species-specific behaviors,** behaviors that are characteristic of a particular animal species. By observing animals in their natural environment, ethologists hope to discover the links between a species' surroundings and its behaviors and to understand the biological mechanisms on which the behavior is based.

Ethologists have found that the behavior and experience of more primitive animals, such as insects or fish, are less flexible, or more stereotyped, than the behavior of more complex animals, such as apes or humans. Stereotyped behaviors consist of patterns of responses that cannot change readily in response to changes in the environment. They work well only if the environment stays as it was when the behavior pattern evolved.

For example, when a horse is confronted with danger and requires a quiet escape, it is impossible for it to tiptoe away. Its escape behavior consists of only three patterns: walking, trotting, and galloping. Each pattern is a distinct series of movements that vary little from one horse to another, and all normal horses display these patterns. These are called *fixed action patterns* because they are inflexible—an animal can react to certain situations only in these ways.

Fixed action patterns are one kind of instinct—a behavior pattern that is inborn rather than learned. People often misuse the word *instinct* to refer to behaviors that become automatic after long practice. A professional baseball player may be described as *instinctively* making the right play, for example. But ethologists use the term *instinct* to refer only to those abilities that seem to be inherited.

Ethologists have found that animals are born with special sensitivities to certain cues in the environment, as well as with special ways of behaving. These cues are called sign stimuli, or releasers. For example, Niko Tinbergen showed that the male stickleback, a small fish, will attack a model of another stickleback if it has a red belly. Even if the model is distorted, as

FIGURE 4.15

The bright red belly of the male stickleback is a sign stimulus for attack from other sticklebacks. They will attack red-bellied models like the ones below before they will respond to a realistic model of a stickleback that does not have a red belly. **What is the term for behaviors that are characteristic of a particular species?**

VISUAL INSTRUCTION

Have the students think of other examples of fixed action patterns in animals. *(Answers will vary, but examples include: the instinctive tendency of male Siamese fighting fish to attack other males of the species; the tendency of moths to fly toward lights; the tendency of opossums to play dead when confronted with aggression.)* **Answer to caption, Figure 4.15:** species-specific behaviors

■ **Discussion.** Remind students that instincts are inborn behavior patterns, not behaviors that become automatic after long periods of practice or conditioning. Ask students to give examples of human behaviors that they think are instinctual, such as an adult's tendency to react to an infant's cries. Does everyone agree? Or might the behaviors be the result of environmental factors? (OBJECTIVE 5)

BEYOND THE CLASSROOM

As an introduction to ethology, students might enjoy reading Elizabeth Marshall Thomas's short best-seller *The Hidden Life of Dogs* (Davison/Houghton Mifflin, 1993). In this work, Thomas interprets the behavior patterns of her dogs, whose roamings and interactions she observed over a course of many years.

If you assign this reading to the entire class, you might afterward ask students to discuss whether Thomas proves her claim that dogs live richly textured emotional and intellectual lives.

■ **Discussion.** After students read the More About feature, ask them to identify other behaviors that might be of interest to human ethologists. *(Answers will vary, but might include the human tendency to raise an open hand in greeting or to perform mutual grooming to strengthen social bonds.)*

■ **Analyzing Information.** Ask students to consider the analogy between a soldier ant that sacrifices itself to protect the colony from predators and an immune-system cell that dies in fending off an infection in the body. Which is performing an act of altruism? *(Answers will vary. Students might answer that the ant is no more altruistic than the body cell is. Both are incapable of making any other choice than self-sacrifice.)* Point out that critics of sociobiology see problems in applying the genetically ordained behaviors of lower-order organisms to explain the actions of higher organisms, such as primates.
(OBJECTIVE 5)

MORE about...

Using Ethology to Study Human Behavior. Human ethology is the study of human behavior as it naturally occurs. Ethologists make comparisons between human and animal behaviors as part of their investigations.

One study investigated whether people crossing the street looked both ways before they crossed. When males and females crossed together, males looked both ways more often than females. Human ethologists see a similarity between this finding and the behavior of monkey and baboon troops living in the wild, whose adult males serve as lookouts.

Basketball fans know that Michael Jordan stuck out his tongue when he attempted a difficult shot. Similarly, it has been found that expert billiard players stick out their tongues more often when making hard shots than when attempting relatively easy shots. According to ethologists, a tongue display acts as a nonverbal sign that interaction is not desired. For humans, the tongue displays seem to indicate that the person does not want to be interrupted because of the need to concentrate in a difficult situation.

in Figure 4.15, the male will still attack. Yet if it sees a very lifelike model of a stickleback without a red belly, the male will leave it alone. In this case, the sign stimulus that triggers attack is the color red. In other species other sign stimuli can trigger certain behaviors. Complex patterns of behavior may unfold as one behavior becomes a sign for the next.

Do sign stimuli occur in humans? Although instincts are less common and less powerful in human behavior, there is evidence that some stereotyped behaviors exist. For example, Konrad Lorenz found that a "parental instinct" seems to be aroused by the appearance of the human baby. When he compared human infants to other young animals, he noticed that they all seem to display a similar set of sign stimuli that appear to stir up parental feelings. Short faces, prominent foreheads, round eyes, and plump cheeks all seem to arouse the parental response.

Sociobiology

Closely related to ethology is another discipline that studies the hereditary basis of social behavior in animals and humans. This science, known as **sociobiology,** draws on the findings of biology, anthropology, and psychology. It has attracted a great deal of attention, and an even greater amount of controversy. In 1975, Harvard zoologist Edward O. Wilson published *Sociobiology: A New Synthesis*, in which he defined the new discipline as "the systematic study of the biological basis of all social behavior." Wilson surveyed the social behavior of all known primates. He identified certain traits that humans share with almost all other primates—prolonged maternal care of offspring, for instance, and male dominance over females. Wilson suggested that these behaviors may have been passed along to us in our genes.

Sociobiologists regard their discipline as the last phase of the revolution begun by Charles Darwin. It tries to fill a major gap in Darwin's theory of natural selection: nature's goal is individual survival and reproduction, yet several traits of humans and other animals seem to work directly against this goal. Soldier ants will fight to the death, thus contributing to saving their group from invaders. A bird will often call out a warning to other birds that a predator is nearby, though the warning call itself alerts the enemy to that particular bird's whereabouts and risks the bird's life. Dolphins have been known to band together and support a stricken companion on the surface of the water where it can breathe. And, of course, among humans, parents die rescuing their children from fires, and soldiers throw themselves on grenades to save their buddies.

Sociobiologists fit all these acts of self-sacrifice into nature's economy. They explain that altruism itself favors genetic gain: the individual risks itself, but the result of this behavior is that other individuals who share its genes may survive (Figure 4.16). The soldier ant, which is sterile, protects its queen, which then lives to produce more of the soldier ant's kind. The bird who calls a warning in effect also protects its kind, and this increases the chance that its genes will survive, as does the behavior of the mother who saves her baby. The battlefield hero dies confident that the nation will keep his family safe to reproduce—and thus to perpetuate his own genes.

CRITICAL THINKING ACTIVITY

Determining Cause and Effect. Altruism—unselfish concern for the welfare of others—takes many forms. Ask students to think of other examples of altruistic behavior than those mentioned in the text. Compile a list on the chalkboard that includes both human and animal behaviors. Can students ascribe a genetic cause to each example (as sociobiologists would contend)? Or do some altruistic acts seem to be truly selfless? (Consider, for example, if the dolphins had saved a drowning child.)

FIGURE 4.16

Sociobiologists explain firefighters risking their lives to save others as yet another aspect of natural selection: the individual risks itself, but the species survives. **What is sociobiology?**

VISUAL INSTRUCTION

Point out that the theory of natural selection was first proposed by Charles Darwin and Alfred Wallace in 1858. You might also find it helpful to explain that just because a body of knowledge is called a theory does not mean it is unsubstantiated and, therefore, untrue. Theories, when sufficiently tested and backed up with scientific evidence, attain validity. You might have volunteers assess the validity of Darwin's theory.
Answers to caption, Figure 4.16: the study of the hereditary basis of social behavior in animals and humans

The noted British biologist J. B. S. Haldane once joked that he would give his life for his two brothers, each of whom shares about half his genes, or for eight cousins (cited in *Time*, August 1, 1977, p. 56).

Sociobiology seeks to explain other social behaviors, even aggression, in terms of genetic advantage. The bully who kicks sand in the weakling's face is actually sending a message to the weakling's girlfriend: "I have strong genes. You ought to choose me instead."

The idea that genes determine human behavior has been controversial. Some critics, notably Richard Lewontin, Stephen Gould, and other members of the Harvard-based Sociobiology Study Group, have expressed fear that sociobiology can be used to support the political, economic, and legal status quo. According to the logic of sociobiology, these must have been determined by our genes (reported in Wade, 1976).

Other critics point out that there is no hard evidence that specific genes exist for altruism, aggression, or other social behaviors, but only theories and guesswork (Washburn, 1978). They also point out that animals may behave very selfishly indeed. Among the lions of the Serengeti plain in East Africa, lionesses have been observed driving their own cubs away from food if the catch was small; many of these cubs have died of starvation. Of 1,400 herring gull chicks studied during one period, 23 percent were killed by attacks from adults of their own species as they strayed from the nest (Marler, 1976).

Along the same lines, anthropologists have repeatedly contested the popular belief that human males are innately aggressive and dominant

STUDY AND WRITING SKILLS

Ask students to explain the meaning of J.B.S. Haldane's joking assertion that he would give his life "for eight cousins." Why eight instead of four or twelve? Have students research how a person's genes are shared among cousins, and assign them to write an explanatory paragraph or to illustrate in chart form exactly what Haldane meant.

VISUAL INSTRUCTION

Point out that scientists who study animal social behavior in the wild must take great care not to alter the animals' environment through their presence. For example, providing animals with food in order to attract them might have the effect of altering their normal patterns of hunting or foraging. **Answer to caption, Figure 4.17:** Genes are an important part, but cannot solely determine human behavior.

Independent Practice

■ **Research.** Explain that brain injuries can have widely varying effects, depending on the part of the brain that was injured. Instruct students to look in medical encyclopedias and periodicals to find information on injuries to the brain, especially those involving people in such high-risk professions as boxing, race-car driving, and the military. Ask students to select one such victim. Have them write a brief report on his or her injury and on the effects and changes it produced. (OBJECTIVES 1–3)

FIGURE 4.17

Although many people believe that primate males dominate females, relations between the sexes are actually quite complicated. **What role do genes play in human behavior?**

over females. The supporters of this argument often cite studies of baboons that document male aggression and dominance over females. Opponents point out that the baboons observed in these studies were in a game park, an abnormal environment that exposed them to a heavy concentration of predators (especially human ones) and to a high level of tension. Among baboon troops that live undisturbed in the forest, however, it is female baboons who determine the troop's movements. Males exhibit very little aggression and little dominance (Pilbeam, 1972). The relationship between male and female baboons is much more balanced and complex than previously thought. Also, there may be more male involvement with infants in the wild (Hrdy, 1988).

If baboon behavior can vary so widely in different environments, it is even more likely that human behavior will do so. Genes may very well be an important component of human social behavior, but they cannot entirely determine it. If the children of two great athletes are never permitted to exercise, their genes will never make them athletes. Indeed, the flexibility of human social behavior, the extreme differences in various cultures and in different contexts, is uniquely human (Pilbeam, 1972). Only human beings construct cultures, passing on large and growing accumulations of learning from generation to generation and thereby to a certain extent overcoming the slow process of genetic evolution. Only human beings exhibit a wide variety of culturally determined behaviors, such as wearing black to funerals in some countries and white in others.

The question of the extent to which heredity does determine human social behavior is far from settled. But Wilson and some other sociobiologists believe that humankind is flexible and must be so, and that genetic inclinations need not always be obeyed and sometimes should not be. Some believe that evolution takes place so slowly that we may still be inheriting behavior patterns that were adaptive in prehistoric times but that are no longer useful in our radically different world. In the Stone Age it may well have been important to raise as many healthy children as possible; on today's crowded planet it is not. When humans lived in hunter-gatherer

DEMONSTRATION

Ask students to evaluate the effects of heredity and the environment on each of the following characteristics, using a percentage rating system (e.g., intelligence: environment 60 percent; heredity 40 percent). Remind students that each rating should add up to 100%.

1. Body build
2. Intelligence
3. Personality
4. Height
5. Musical ability
6. Mathematical ability
7. Baldness
8. Handedness
9. Sense of humor
10. Longevity

When students finish, ask them to compare their ratings. Request volunteers to explain why they rated each characteristic as they did.

societies, it might have been necessary to wage war against all foreigners in order to survive; now war could mean the end of humankind (Wilson, 1975). The major contribution of sociobiology has been to remind us that genes do count, but that human beings have the capacity to learn a wide range of behaviors and to unlearn those that cease to be adaptive.

HEREDITY AND ENVIRONMENT

People often argue about whether human behavior is instinctive (due to heredity) or learned (due to environment). Do people learn to be good athletes, or are they born that way? Do people learn to do well in school, or are they born good at it? Do people learn to be homosexual, or are they born that way? The reason for the intensity of the argument may be that many people assume that something learned can probably be changed, whereas something inborn will be difficult or impossible to change. The issue is not that simple, however. Inherited factors and environmental conditions always act together in complicated ways. Asking whether heredity or environment is responsible for something turns out to be like asking "What makes a cake rise, baking powder or heat?" Obviously, an interaction of the two is responsible.

The argument over the nature-nurture question has been going on for centuries. Sir Francis Galton, a cousin of Charles Darwin, was one of the first to preach the importance of nature in the modern era. In 1869 he published *Hereditary Genius*, a book in which he analyzed the families of over 1,000 eminent politicians, religious leaders, artists, and scholars. He found that success ran in the families and concluded that heredity was the cause.

But most psychologists have emphasized the importance of the environment. The tone was set by John Watson, the founder of behaviorism, who wrote in 1930: "Give me a dozen healthy infants, well-formed, and my own specified world to bring them up in and I'll guarantee to take any one at random and train him to become any type of specialist I might select—doctor, lawyer, artist, merchant-chief, and, yes, even beggarman and thief, regardless of his talents, penchants, tendencies, abilities, vocations, and race of his ancestors" (Watson, 1930, p. 104).

Watson's view now seems a bit extreme. Studies that examined evidence of genetic influence on human traits have focused on three general areas: cognitive abilities (like IQ), mental illness, and personality. The argument over IQ (see Chapter 12) has been particularly loud and long, but each of the other areas is also controversial.

One way to find out whether a trait is inherited is to study twins. Identical twins develop from a single fertilized egg (thus, they are called monozygotic) and share the same genes. Fraternal twins develop from two fertilized eggs (thus, dizygotic), and their genes are not more similar than those of brothers or sisters.

Inherited factors and environmental conditions always act together in complicated ways.

■ **Descriptive Writing.** Organize the students into small groups. Tell them to imagine they are research teams involved in studying the brain. They must present a research proposal to a funding agency. The proposals should include a description of the team's goals and of the methods to be used in gathering data—such as recording, stimulation, and lesioning. (OBJECTIVE 3)

■ **Research.** Ask students to select one of the endocrine glands mentioned in the text and to do in-depth research for a brief oral report on that gland's connection to general health and behavior. Reports should include a description of the gland, its location, and the hormones it secretes, the role it plays in the body, and an overview of the problems that may occur if it malfunctions. (OBJECTIVE 4)

■ **Analyzing a Passage.** Ask students to read the quotation by John Watson. Challenge them to explain what this view—if it were true—would mean in the nature-versus-nurture argument. *(that nurture determines behavior, not nature; that nurturing can override hereditary behavior)* (OBJECTIVE 5)

CRITICAL THINKING ACTIVITY

Analyzing Information. Have students locate other recent psychological studies involving twins and the nature-nurture debate. What, for example, do recent studies involving twins reveal about the probable causes of homosexuality and other behaviors considered abnormal? Ask students to explain why such studies involving the nature-nurture question stir up such controversy. *(because they sometimes challenge the legitimacy of traditional cultural values)*

VISUAL INSTRUCTION

To help students in their readings in the literature of psychology, point out that there are many nearly interchangeable terms for *hereditary*: *genetic, biological, natural, inborn, inherited,* and *innate*.

Answer to caption, Figure 4.18: the debate over whether heredity or environment makes greater contributions to the makeup of an organism

■ **Expository Writing.** After students have read and discussed the theories pertaining to the effect of nature versus nurture, ask them to write an essay expressing their own theory on how much influence the environment has, in relation to heredity, on the development of personality traits. (OBJECTIVE 5)

DID YOU KNOW?

In the 1920s Chinese psychologist Zing-Yang Kuo contended it is possible to have a "psychology without heredity." Kuo raised kittens and rats together as well as kittens and birds. These animals showed affection toward one another. The birds sometimes rode around the laboratory on the cats' backs.

FIGURE 4.18

Because identical twins share the same genes as well as the same environment, studying them is one way to find out whether a trait is inherited or learned. **What do psychologists mean by the "nature-nurture question"?**

Twins growing up in the same house share the same general environment. But identical twins also share the same genes. So, if identical twins who grow up together, prove to be more alike on a specific trait than fraternal twins do, it probably means that genes are important for that trait.

For example, many twin studies have been done on the inheritance of mental disease. Schizophrenia is the most common form of serious mental illness. Some data suggest that if one twin becomes schizophrenic, the other twin is more than three times as likely to become schizophrenic if he or she is an identical twin rather than a fraternal twin (Gottesmann & Shields, 1982). Adults raised as children in adoptive homes are more likely to share the development of schizophrenia and other serious disorders with their genetic brothers and sisters than they are with their adoptive brothers and sisters (Plomin, 1990). Thus, schizophrenia is at least partly genetic. However, it is also clear that in many cases, one identical twin develops schizophrenia and the other does not. Thus, environmental factors are also important.

There are several other ways of studying the nature-nurture problem in humans. In a few cases, identical twins have been separated at birth. These twins show the effects of the same genes in different environments. Such rare cases are important for science. It is also possible to see whether adopted children more closely resemble their biological parents or their adoptive parents. Although many such studies are going on, the nature-nurture question will probably continue to be controversial, at least until people gain a more sophisticated understanding of how heredity and environment interact to produce behavior.

 LAB EXPERIMENTS AND DEMONSTRATIONS

Have students bring in pictures of themselves and other family members (especially, if possible, from earlier generations). As an anonymous activity, ask students to develop a list of physical or personality traits that they feel connect them to their family in some way. After each trait, instruct students to write *I* if they feel the trait was inherited or *E* if the trait was environmentally learned. Request volunteers to share their lists and photos with the class.

Psychologists at the University of Minnesota have been studying identical twins who were separated at birth and reared in different environments (Holden, 1980). One of the researchers, Thomas Bouchard, reports that despite very different social, cultural, and economic backgrounds, the twins shared many common behaviors. For example, in one set of twins (both named Jim), both had done well in math and poorly in spelling while in school, both worked as deputy sheriffs, vacationed in Florida, gave identical names to their children and pets, bit their fingernails, had identical smoking and drinking patterns, and liked mechanical drawing and carpentry. These similarities and others suggest that heredity may contribute to behaviors that we normally associate with experience.

Many researchers now believe that many of the differences among people can be explained by considering heredity as well as experience. Contrary to popular belief, the influence of genes on behavior does not mean that nothing can be done to change the behavior. Although it is true that it is difficult and may be undesirable to change the genetic code that may direct behavior, it is possible to alter the environment in which the genes operate. The genetic disorder phenylketonuria (PKU) is a case in point. PKU is a single gene defect which, if undetected and untreated, can result in severe mental retardation. A simple blood test at birth (Figure 4.19) can reveal the presence of PKU, which afflicts about 1 in 20,000 whites (it is rare among blacks). Afflicted infants can be placed on a special diet until the brain develops and is no longer in danger. Thus, although PKU is inherited, its effects can be changed by controlling the environment.

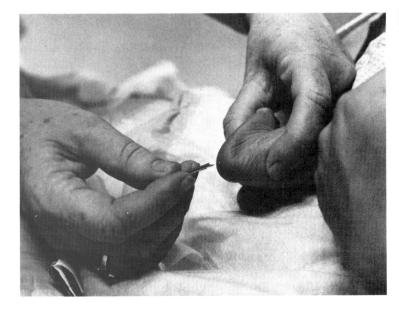

FIGURE 4.19

The test for PKU, a simple prick on the heel, is now given automatically to all newborns, since early detection and treatment can prevent the ravages of this congenital disease.

CONNECTIONS: PSYCHOLOGY AND SCIENCE

Ask a science teacher or a representative of the March of Dimes to help students research genetic disorders related to the central nervous system. Have students learn about the following: genetic mapping; amniocentesis; and genetic disorders resulting from the age of a woman during pregnancy, from poor prenatal care, and from substance abuse (tobacco, alcohol, marijuana, cocaine, etc.) during pregnancy.

ASSESS

Check for Understanding

Ask students to explain briefly how the brain works through the nervous and endocrine systems to control body functions and behavior. Then have them summarize the role of heredity and environment in determining behavior.

Reteach

Have students complete the Chapter 4 Review Activity and share responses with each other.

Enrich

Have students complete the Chapter 4 Extension Activity and answer the questions that follow it.

Evaluate

Administer and grade the Chapter 4 Test. Two forms are available should you wish to give different tests to different students/classes.

Use the Understanding Psychology Testmaker to create a customized test.

CLOSE

Now that they have completed the chapter, ask students to list as many examples as they can of ways in which the body and behavior interact. Did they expect that biology would play such a significant role in determining behavior? Why or why not?

ANSWERS

Concepts and Vocabulary

1. Messages travel along the nerves, which are strings of cells called neurons. Neurotransmitters are chemicals that carry the signal across the synapses between neurons or inhibit it.

2. the central and the peripheral nervous systems; the CNS

3. voluntary activities

4. the sympathetic and parasympathetic nervous systems; the sympathetic

5. the somatosensory cortex

6. The reticular activating system and thalamus work as filters. The brain seems to process information by filtering patterns of stimuli through the lower brain and then comparing them to previous patterns already stored in memory.

7. mainly controls posture and balance

8. The parietal controls speech; the occipital, vision; the temporal, hearing; and the frontal influences motor control, planning, and attentiveness.

9. The left hemisphere controls the right side of the body, and vice versa. In right-handed people, the left hemisphere controls language, and the right, spatial tasks. The corpus callosum carries messages between the two.

10. recording, stimulation, and lesioning

11. the endocrine system; via hormones released directly

SUMMARY

Use the following outline as a tool for reviewing this chapter. Copy the outline onto your own paper, leaving spaces between headings to make notes about key concepts.

I. The Nervous System
   A. How the Nervous System Works
   B. The Hemispheres of the Brain

II. How Psychologists Study the Brain
   A. Recording
   B. Stimulation
   C. Lesions

III. The Endocrine System

IV. The Relationship Between Humans and Animals
   A. The Evolution of Behavior
   B. Ethology
   C. Sociobiology

V. Heredity and Environment

CONCEPTS AND VOCABULARY

1. Explain how messages travel to and from the brain through the nervous system. What are the neurotransmitters?

2. Name the two types of nervous systems. To which system does the spinal cord belong?

3. What activities does the somatic nervous system control?

4. Name the two parts of the autonomic nervous system. Which part uses up the energy in the body?

5. What is the part of the cortex that receives information?

6. What two parts of the lower brain work to filter out all but the most important messages before they reach the cerebral cortex? How do

parts of the brain process such a large amount of information?

7. Describe one of the main functions of the cerebellum.

8. What are the four lobes of the cerebral cortex? What is the main function of each?

9. The cortex of the brain is divided into the left and the right hemispheres. Which side of the body does each hemisphere control? What kinds of tasks does each hemisphere control in right-handed people? What is the function of the corpus callosum?

10. Describe three of the methods used to study the brain.

11. What is the name of the chemical system of communication between the body and the brain? How are the messages of this system transmitted? Which gland is the center of control for this system? What other gland helps in regulating general bodily activity?

12. What is the study of the natural behavior patterns of animals from a biological point of view?

13. How do ethologists use the term *instinct*?

14. What is the name of the science that studies the hereditary basis of social behavior? What is the major contribution of this science?

15. One way to find out whether a trait is inherited is to compare the behavior of identical and fraternal twins. Explain how this works.

CRITICAL THINKING

1. **Synthesize.** Suppose a person suffers a stroke that causes damage to the frontal lobes. What aspects of the person's behavior would you expect to see change? What if the damage occurred in the occipital lobe instead? What problems would you expect the person to experience?

2. **Evaluate.** What aspects of your personality, your way of acting, and your appearance seem

into the bloodstream. The pituitary is the "master gland;" the thyroid helps regulate general body activity

12. ethology

13. to refer to inborn behavior

14. Sociobiology; its major contribution is to remind us that genes do play a role in determining social behavior, but that humans have the capacity to learn and unlearn behaviors.

15. Identical twins share the same genes, while fraternal twins do not. Twins growing up in the same house share the same environment. Identical twins who grow up together share both environment and genes. If identical twins prove to be more alike on a specific trait, it probably means that genes are more important than environment for that trait.

obviously the result of heredity? Which seem to be more related to your environmental up-bringing? What factors make it difficult to decide whether hereditary or environmental factors are of greatest influence?

APPLYING KNOWLEDGE

1. Ask several of your friends to perform some mental task, such as multiplying 31 by 24 in their heads, or counting the number of letters in a simple phrase (such as "early to bed"). Observe which way their eyes shift as they begin to think about the problem. If their eyes shift to the right, which hemisphere is being used to do the counting? Which hemisphere is doing the counting if their eyes shift to the left?

2. Observe species-specific behaviors in cats, dogs, or any other animals you see regularly. If you have an animal that you can observe carefully, try to identify fixed action patterns that are common to the animal's species. Do they exist in any form in yourself?

ANALYZING VIEWPOINTS

1. Within the field of psychology, there is a debate about the role that heredity plays in determining behavior as compared to the role of the environment. Some psychologists argue that behavior is genetically predetermined. For example, they believe that great athletes are born with the talent and drive to succeed. On the other hand, some psychologists believe that behavior is determined more by environmental factors. These psychologists argue that someone born with average athletic abilities could be developed into a great athlete with the proper exercise and coaching. Write a two-page paper supporting each side of the issue. Use what you learned about the contributions of heredity and environment to human behavior. You may also want to read magazine articles or biographies of athletes to gather more information.

2. Much of what we know about the brain and its functioning has come from studies performed on animals. Animal rights groups protest the use of animals in experiments, citing the inhumane treatment of animals used in laboratory experiments. List the pros and cons of using animals for psychological research. Read recent articles for more information.

BEYOND THE CLASSROOM

1. Choose the family of a friend or neighbor that you know well. Ask the family for permission to study and report on the family members before you begin this project. Spend several hours visiting with the family. Carefully observe the personalities and behaviors of the parents and different siblings. Try to identify the dominant traits and characteristics of each family member. What is each family member's personality? Do family members have similar personalities, or is one person easygoing and another nervous and tense? Are there vast differences in personality between the oldest and the youngest child? What does each family member do better than most people? Is there a special ability, such as musical talent, that all family members share? Which of the traits and characteristics you identified are due to heredity? Which do you think are due to environmental factors? What evidence did you find of the interaction of heredity and the environment in determining personality and behavior?

IN YOUR JOURNAL

1. Think about two of your friends. Speculate on how they appear to differ in the extent to which their right or left hemisphere dominates. Write your findings in your journal.

Critical Thinking

1. Damage to the frontal lobes might cause severe personality change. Damage to the occipital lobe would impair vision and perhaps balance and posture.

2. Answers will vary. Traits and characteristics common to several family members over several generations would indicate hereditary influences. Those common to family members living together but not common to those reared or living apart would indicate environmental influences. It is difficult to separate their roles because the two are constantly interacting to produce personality and behavior.

Applying Knowledge

1. If the eyes shift to the right, he or she is using the left hemisphere, and vice versa.

2. Answers will vary. Students should provide examples.

CHAPTER BONUS
Test Question

This question may be used for extra credit on the chapter test.
Choose the letter of the correct response.

The basic elements of the nervous system are specialized cells that carry messages called:
a. axons.
b. pons.
c. dendrites.
d. neurons.

Answer: **d**

Analyzing Viewpoints

1. Answers will vary. Responses should deal adequately with both sides of the issue.

2. Answers will vary, but responses should reflect both sides of the controversy.

Beyond the Classroom

1. Answers will vary.

IN YOUR JOURNAL

If time permits, discuss journal entries individually with students.

CHAPTER 5

Sensation and Perception

TEXT TOPICS	SPECIAL FEATURES	RESOURCE MATERIALS
Sensation, pp. 107–115	**More About Psychology,** p. 108 **Psychology and You,** p. 109 **Using Psychology:** Subliminal Advertising, pp. 109–110 **Psychology Update,** p. 112 **At a Glance:** Phantom Limb Pain, p. 112	Reproducible Lesson Plan; Study Guide; Review Activity Transparency 7
The Senses, pp. 115–120		Reproducible Lesson Plan; Study Guide; Review Activity; Application Activity Transparencies 8, 9
Perception, pp. 120–126	**Fact or Fiction?,** p. 124	Reproducible Lesson Plan; Study Guide; Review Activity Transparencies 10, 11 *Readings in Psychology,* Section 2, Readings 3, 4
Extrasensory Perception, pp. 126–128		Reproducible Lesson Plan; Study Guide; Review Activity Chapter Test, Form A and Form B Understanding Psychology Testmaker

PERFORMANCE ASSESSMENT ACTIVITY

Have groups of students clip pictures of 10 different faces from magazines and newspapers. Ask students to paste these pictures on poster board. Based on physical characteristics, have students assign some of the labels given to people in high school yearbooks such as: "Most Likely to Succeed," "Best Looking," "Class Clown," "Most Studious," and so on. Call on students to share their posters and labels. Ask: What physical characteristics did you use to make each of your decisions? Have students write a paragraph explaining what they learned from this activity. *(Encourage students to see how mental images or stereotypes can order physical perception.)*

CHAPTER RESOURCES

Readings for the Student

Bouldin, Don. *Ears to Hear, Eyes to See.* Nashville: Broadman Press, 1991.

Caras, Roger A. *A Dog is Listening: The Way Some of Our Closest Friends View Us.* New York: Summit Books, 1992.

De Bono, Edward. *I Am Right, You Are Wrong.* New York: Viking Penguin, 1992.

Gardner, Martin. *The Book of Visual Illusions.* New York: Dover Publications, 1993.

Readings for the Teacher

Frisby, J. P. *Seeing: Illusion, Brain, and Mind.* New York: Oxford University Press, 1980.

Rhine, J. B. *Extra-Sensory Perception.* Boston: Branden Publishing Co., 1983.

Schlossberg, Edwin. *Atlas of Perception.* New York: Random House, Inc., 1992.

Multimedia

ESP and the Soviet Union (30 minute audiotape). *Psychology Today* (reader service). In a tape of historical significance, Stanley Krippner discusses Soviet research into ESP.

Introduction to Visual Illusions. (18 minutes, 3/4" or 1/2" video). Pyramid Film and Video. More than 20 visual illusions are illustrated.

Perception. (27 minutes, 3/4" or 1/2" video). McGraw-Hill Films. This shows how human perception is shaped by cultural, physiological, and psychological forces.

For additional resources, see the bibliography beginning on page 530.

FOCUS

Motivating Activity

Show students 4 or 5 slides or photographs depicting people involved in a variety of activities and settings. (The visuals might be from your own collection or clippings from magazines.) Working independently, ask students to write a short description of each scene. Compare these descriptions, and discuss any differences. Challenge students to explain how a group of people can all look at the same picture and *perceive* it differently. Record student answers on the chalkboard. As they work through the chapter, have them modify their list, erasing incorrect answers, expanding upon incomplete ones, and adding entirely new explanations.

Meeting Chapter Objectives.

Write the "reporter's questions" on the chalkboard: *Who? What? Where? When? Why? How?* Tell students to use these words to turn the chapter objectives into as many questions as possible. To encourage creativity, tell students that objectives can be broken apart and rephrased. Compile a master list of questions for students to answer as they read the chapter.

Building Vocabulary.

Have pairs of students write a sentence that makes use of a synonymous word or phrase for each term in the list. Read these sentences aloud, and have the rest of the class guess the term. (Students may consult the Glossary and/or a class dictionary.)

Sensation and Perception

FIGURE 5.1 We "take in" information through our senses. Through sight, sound, touch, and smell we perceive the world around us.

106

TEACHER CLASSROOM RESOURCES

Chapter 5 Reproducible Lesson Plan
Chapter 5 Study Guide
Chapter 5 Review Activity
Chapter 5 Application Activity
Chapter 5 Extension Activity

Transparencies 7–11
Transparency Strategies and Activities

Readings in Psychology: Section 2, Readings 3, 4

Chapter 5 Test, Form A and Form B

Understanding Psychology Testmaker

OBJECTIVES

After studying this chapter, you should be able to

- describe the field of study known as psychophysics.
- define and discuss threshold, Weber's law, and signal detection.
- describe the nature and functioning of the sense organs.
- outline the principles involved in perception.

I n the next few seconds, something peculiar will start hap pening to the material youa rereading. Iti soft ennotre alized howcom plext heproces sof rea ding is. Afe w sim plerear range mentscan ha veyoucomp lete lycon fused!

As you can see, your success in gathering information from your environment, interpreting this information, and acting on it depends considerably on its being organized in ways you expect.

Your knowledge of the external world—and of your internal state as well—comes entirely from chemical and electrical processes occurring in the nervous system, particularly in the brain. Physical change in the external or internal environment triggers chemical, electrical, and mechanical activity in sense receptors. After complex processing in the nervous system, a pattern of activity is produced in certain areas of the brain. This initial electrical activity is a **sensation**—created by colors, forms, sounds, smells, tastes, and so on. Usually you experience some individual stimuli— you see Wayne Gretzky play, hear Whitney Houston's voice, smell an old, dirty sock—rather than a collection of sensations. The organization of sensory information into meaningful stimuli is known as **perception.**

This process can be seen in the act of eating. When someone puts two hamburgers in front of you, receptors in your eyes send a message to the

KEY TERMS

absolute threshold
auditory nerve
binocular fusion
cones
constancy
decibels
difference threshold
extrasensory perception (ESP)
Gestalt
illusions
kinesthesis
lens
motion parallax
olfactory nerve
optic nerve
perception
pitch
psychophysics
pupil
referred pain
retina
retinal disparity
rods
sensation
signal-detection theory
stereopsis
subliminal advertising
vestibular system
Weber's law

IN YOUR JOURNAL

Think about an occasion in which you were in a crowded and noisy setting. Did you find yourself listening to or picking up part of another conversation? Write an explanation for this phenomenon in your journal.

Exploring Key Ideas

You might start off discussion of Chapter 5 by repeating these two popular sayings:

- "Beauty is in the eye of the beholder."
- "Is your glass half empty or half full?"

Request volunteers to explain the meaning behind each of these sayings. *(Lead students to understand that both sayings emphasize that perception rests with the individual.)* Tell students that this chapter examines how and why we see the world as we do. It all starts with the senses. Before turning to the chapter, ask students to define and identify the senses.

IN YOUR JOURNAL

To provoke student thought, ask them to imagine the following scene: You're sitting in the lunch room listening to a friend's story. Two tables away, you hear a couple of students mention your name and suddenly you hear nothing that your friend says. What triggered this response? Use student discussion as a springboard into the journal-writing activity.

EXTRA CREDIT ACTIVITY

Encourage interested students to locate examples of artwork and photos that illustrate Gestalt principles of organization. *(The Batman symbol is one example. It can be perceived as both a bat and an open-toothed mouth. Other examples include the picture games that challenge people to find hidden faces or objects.)*

Suggest that students start their search by looking up *Gestalt* in the card catalog or in standard library references. Using an opaque projector, have students challenge the rest of the class to describe what they see upon first glimpse.

TEACH

Guided Practice

■ **Discussion.** Distribute copies of the following questions asked by James J. Gibson, one of the leading perception psychologists of the post-World War II era.

- "Why do things look as they do?"
- "How do we see where we are in the environment?"
- "How do we see whether or not we're moving, and, if we are, where we are going?"
- "How do we see how to do things?"

Organize the students into groups and tell them to imagine they are psychophysicists. Based on information in the text, what tentative answers can they pose to each of these questions? Have students share their findings with the class. (OBJECTIVE 1)

MORE about. . .

Sensation Versus Perception. Sensation is usually thought of as a simple input process involving stimulation of a receptor. It may also include relaying a neural message upward in the nervous system.

The problem is that there are some cells on the receptor surface of the eye that only fire when visual stimuli are moving left to right; others fire only in response to a stimulus moving right to left. So, even in the act of firing, such receptors have already initiated the process of perception.

---

brain: the all-beef patties are stacked together in the sesame seed bun, along with some lettuce. Receptors in your nose may tell you there's ketchup and cheese inside, while other receptors in your mouth send messages about pickles and some mysterious sauce. As you grasp this gourmet delight in your hands, receptors in your fingers tell you that the roll is soft and warm. And the brain combines all these inputs into one unified perception: it's a Big Mac.

In this chapter we will look at each of these steps more closely, focusing on how each organ converts physical changes into chemical-electrical signals to the brain and how perceptions are built from this information. In the last section we will discuss the possibility of gaining information without the known senses—through the process of extrasensory perception.

SENSATION

The world is filled with physical changes—an alarm clock sounds; the flip of a switch fills a room with light; you stumble against a door; steam from a hot shower billows out into the bathroom, changing the temperature and clouding the mirror. Any aspect of or change in the environment to which an organism responds is called a stimulus. An alarm, an electric light, and an aching muscle are all stimuli for human beings.

A stimulus can be measured in many physical ways, including its size, duration, intensity, or wavelength.

Stimuli are physical events usually in the world beyond your body. A *sensation* occurs any time a stimulus activates one of your receptors. The sensation may be combined with other sensations and your past experience to yield a *perception*. A stimulus and a sensory experience are not the same. Stimuli precede sensations, but the boundary between a sensation and a perception is fuzzy at best. The distinction is more a matter of convenience than of importance.

Psychologists are interested in the relationship between physical stimuli and sensory experiences. In vision, for example, the perception of color corresponds to the wavelength of the light, whereas brightness corresponds to the intensity of this stimulus.

What is the relationship between color and wavelength? How does changing a light's intensity affect your perception of its brightness? The psychological study of such questions is called **psychophysics.** The goal of psychophysics is to develop a measurable relationship between stimuli from the world (such as frequency and intensity) and the sensory experiences (such as pitch and loudness) produced by them.

Threshold

In order to establish laws about how people sense the external world, psychologists first try to determine how much of a stimulus is necessary for a person to sense it at all. How much energy is required for someone to hear a sound or to see a light? How much of a scent must be in the room

---

STUDY AND WRITING SKILLS

Challenge students to write a help-wanted advertisement for the job of psychophysicist. For ideas on scientific qualifications, you might encourage students to talk with you, another psy- chology student or teacher, or with a physics student or teacher. Post these ads on the bulletin board. (OBJECTIVE 1)

before one can smell it? How much pressure must be applied to the skin before a person will feel it?

To answer such questions, a psychologist might set up the following experiment. First, a person (the subject) is placed in a dark room and is instructed to look at the wall. He is asked to say "I see it" when he is able to detect a light. The psychologist then uses an extremely precise machine that can project a low-intensity beam of light against the wall. The experimenter turns on the machine to its lowest light projection. The subject says nothing. The experimenter increases the light until finally the subject responds, "I see it." Then the experimenter begins another test in the opposite direction. He starts with a visible, but faint, light and decreases its intensity until the light seems to disappear. Many trials are completed and averaged. The **absolute threshold**—the minimum amount of physical energy required to produce a sensation—can be detected. It is usually accepted that the absolute threshold is the level that produces a response 50 percent of the time.

Interestingly enough, thresholds determined in this way are not absolute. The point at which the person says "I see it" may vary with the instructions he is given. "Say you see it only if you're absolutely certain" yields

PSYCHOLOGY and YOU

Avoiding Motion Sickness. One sensation you may be familiar with is "motion sickness." This condition occurs when a person's body is in motion and the inner ear becomes overstimulated or confused. Here are some things you can do to avoid motion sickness:

When you are flying try to position yourself where there is the least movement. Airline passengers sitting next to the wings have the smoothest ride. Recline your seat if possible. Avoid large meals, but try to take frequent small amounts of fluids and simple foods.

If you are riding in a car, avoid reading. You are less likely to get sick if you watch the ground some distance away from the car, or watch the horizon. The visual input helps you maintain equilibrium. One reason that small children are especially prone to motion sickness is that they cannot see out of the car and so they lose visual contact with their environment. The back seat is often the worst place for children to ride, especially in cars with small or high rear side windows that block the view.

Using Psychology

Subliminal Advertising

In the late 1950s, an advertising executive held a press conference to announce a revolutionary breakthrough in marketing techniques: **subliminal advertising.** The word "subliminal" comes from the Latin: *sub* ("below") and *limen* ("threshold"). The words "Eat Popcorn" and "Coca-Cola" had been flashed on a movie screen in a New Jersey theater on alternate nights for six weeks, according to the executive. Although the flashes were so brief (1/3,000 of a second, once every five seconds) that none of the moviegoers even seemed to notice them, the sale of popcorn and Coca-Cola rose dramatically.

The public response to this announcement was long, loud, and hysterical. In a TV interview, Aldous Huxley predicted that it would be possible to manipulate people politically with this technique "by about 1964" (quoted in Brown, 1963: p. 184). Congressional representatives called for FCC regulations, while several state legislatures passed laws banning subliminal ads.

Meanwhile, more test results began to appear. When the man who made the original claims staged another test for the FCC a

■ **Discussion.** After students read the margin feature on motion sickness, ask the following questions.

1. What should a person do to avoid motion sickness on an airplane? *(sit next to a wing, recline the seat, avoid large meals, regularly take in small amounts of fluid)*
2. Why are small children especially prone to motion sickness? *(Since they cannot see out of the window, they lose visual contact with the environment.)*

Using Psychology

To guide student reading of the feature, ask the following questions.

1. What is subliminal advertising? *(advertising aimed at influencing someone without the person's conscious awareness)*
2. Why was there a mass outcry over the use of subliminal messages? *(because people feared these messages shaped behavior without their conscious knowledge)*
3. How do most psychologists view this technique today? *(They think that it has minimal, if any, effect.)*

CRITICAL THINKING ACTIVITY

Identifying Cause and Effect. Tell students that *sensory deprivation* occurs whenever a person is denied use of one or more of his or her senses. Deprivation could be minor, such as when a person loses a sense of smell because of a cold. Or it could be serious, such as when someone is trapped in a cave or confined as a prisoner of war. Challenge students to brainstorm a list of situations that could qualify as sensory deprivation. Have them rank these from serious to most serious. Ask: What psychological effects could be caused by severe sensory deprivation? In the case of a prisoner of war, how might sensory deprivation further "brainwashing"?

■ Evaluating Data. Distribute copies of the following examples of absolute thresholds. (Galanter, 1962)

- A candle flame can be seen 30 miles away on a dark, clear night. *(sight)*
- The ticking of a watch can be heard 20 feet away under quiet conditions. *(hearing)*
- Sugar can be tasted when 1 teaspoon is dissolved in 2 gallons of water. *(taste)*
- Perfume can be detected when one drop is put in a three-room apartment. *(smell)*
- A bee's wing falling from a distance of 1 centimeter can be felt on a cheek. *(touch)*

Using this data, have students write a short paper in which they defend the text statement on this page: "Under ideal conditions, the senses have very low absolute thresholds." (OBJECTIVE 2)

If the ear were any more sensitive, you might hear the sound of air molecules bumping into each other.

few months later, the results were equivocal. Later, WTWO-TV in Bangor, Maine, flashed the words "If you have seen this message, write WTWO" on the screen for 1/60 of a second every day for a week. Nobody wrote. A Seattle radio station experimented with auditory subliminal ads. During regular programming, a very low whisper in the background repeated "TV's a bore" and "Isn't TV dull?" There is no reason to believe that these ads had any effect.

The heavy metal group *Judas Priest* released an album entitled *Stained Class*. Two families sued the group, alleging that subliminal messages in the music encouraged their sons' suicides. The musicians' lawyers cited evidence showing the lack of a causal link between subliminal messages and behavior. The group denied that it was a planned message, and they were acquitted.

The idea for subliminal ads was a natural outgrowth of a long series of controversial studies on *subliminal perception*—the ability to notice stimuli that affect only the unconscious mind. Most of these earlier studies involved presenting verbal or visual material at intensities that were considered too low for people to perceive. However, a more critical look at the studies revealed several flaws in the way they were designed and carried out. For example, the original New Jersey study was done by nonpsychologists working for the Subliminal Projection Company. No attempt was made to assess or control factors other than the subliminal message that might have influenced the purchase of Coke or popcorn. The temperature in the theater or the length of the movie might have contributed to the increase in sales. Unfortunately, the study was not presented in enough detail to be evaluated by scientists.

Even if it is possible for people to perceive information at very low levels of intensity, there is no clear evidence that these weak, often limited, messages would be more powerful than conscious messages in influencing people. The idea may be appealing to some advertising executives looking for a way to increase sales. There is a consensus among psychologists who have done well-controlled studies, however, that subliminal advertising does not work (Bornstein, 1989).

fewer responses than "If there's any doubt, say you see it." Even the order in which the stimuli are presented may affect the subject's responses.

Under ideal conditions, the senses have very low absolute thresholds. That is, sensations will be experienced with very small amounts of stimulation. For example, your ear registers a sound if your eardrum moves as little as 1 percent of the diameter of a hydrogen molecule. If the ear were

ADDITIONAL INFORMATION

You might tell students about a test done by Anthony Greenwald and his colleagues in 1990. They switched the labels on two subliminal tapes—one aimed at improving the memory, the other at improving self-esteem. At the end of one month, participants in the study reported an improvement in whatever area the label promised. Ask students what conclusions they can draw from this experiment. *(Subliminal messages have little effect, especially when compared to the power of suggestion.)*

any more sensitive, you might hear the sound of air molecules bumping into each other (Geldard, 1972).

Sensory Differences and Ratios

Another type of threshold is the **difference threshold** or just noticeable difference. This refers to the minimum amount of physical energy change required to produce a change in sensation. To return to our example of the person tested in a dark room, a psychologist would test for the difference threshold by gradually increasing the intensity of a visible light beam until the person says, "Yes, this is brighter than the light I just saw." With this technique, it is possible to identify the smallest increase in light intensity that will be noticeable to the human eye.

Psychologists also have found that a particular sensory experience depends more on *changes* in the stimulus than on the absolute size or amount of the stimulus. For example, if you put a 3-pound package of food into an empty backpack, the perceived weight will be greatly increased. But if you add the same amount to a backback with a 100-pound weight in it, your perception will hardly increase at all. This is because the perception of the added weight reflects a proportional change—and 3 pounds does not provide much change in a 100-pound load.

In psychophysics, this idea is known as **Weber's law:** the larger or stronger a stimulus, the larger the change required for an observer to

FIGURE 5.2

A change in sensory experience is proportional to the amount of physical change. In this case, each time the amount of sugar triples, the perceived sweetness of the lemonade doubles. **What is Weber's law?**

UNSWEETENED   SWEET   TWICE AS SWEET   FOUR TIMES AS SWEET

■ **Demonstration.** To illustrate points made in the margin feature on this page, bring in several sheets of brightly colored fabric or paper to class. Have students look at these materials with the lights on. Then switch off the lights. Ask: How has your sense of color diminished? What physiological factors account for this? *(Cones need illumination to function. When light is diminished, "rod vision" takes over.)* There may be more light reflecting off black shoes in direct sunlight than off a white shirt or blouse in a darkened school room. Yet, in both instances, the shirt or blouse is perceived as brighter. Ask: What does this illustrate? *(Lead students to understand that this illustrates brightness constancy.)*

At A Glance

Tell students that people often combine nouns to form entirely new words or phrases. Have students look up the definition of each of the nouns in the phrase "phantom limb pain." Using this information and data in the feature, have students write a definition for phantom limb pain that might appear in an encyclopedia of neurosciences.

PSYCHOLOGY UPDATE

Seeing in the Dark. Certain workers, such as radar operators, sometimes need to keep their eyes adapted to darkness, even when they take a rest break in a well-lit room. They can do this by wearing goggles that admit only red light. The red goggles work because the eye has two kinds of receptor cells, called rods and cones. It is the cones that allow us to see colors. Since the red light admitted by the goggles stimulates only the cones, the adaptation level of the rods is not affected. It is, in fact, as if the rods were still in darkness.

When the worker returns to a dim room and removes the goggles, the rods will be highly sensitive and night vision will be good. Though the cones are now light-adapted, they will not interfere with vision unless the perception of color becomes especially important. Moreover, the cones will adapt to the dark in only 8 minutes or so.

At A Glance

PHANTOM LIMB PAIN

Every night Andy woke covered in a cold, soaking sweat. The pain that filled his left hand was more than he could bear. It felt like a razor-sharp scalpel was being jabbed deeper and deeper into the palm of his hand. No one had prepared him for this pain—not even the doctors who had amputated his left hand two years before.

The *phantom limb pain* we've just described is one of the most bizarre phenomena in medicine. It may take the form of tingling feelings, warmth, coldness, heaviness, or intense pain perceived in a limb that is no longer there.

About one-third of all amputees report phantom limb pain, which in most cases continues for about a year. But as doctors and some unfortunate amputees know, pain may last for decades.

Evidence suggests that phantom limb pain has no single cause. Irritation of the stump, abnormal sympathetic nervous system activity, and emotional disturbance may all play a role. But no one is sure exactly how these factors contribute to the pain or how to rid an amputee of the agony he feels in a limb that is no longer there.

For more details, see Ronald Melzack, "Phantom Limbs and the Concept of a Neuromatrix," *Trends in Neurosciences,* 13 (1990): 88–92.

notice that anything has happened to it, that is to experience a just noticeable difference (Weber, 1834).

The amount of stimulus change necessary to produce some increase in sensory experience is different for different cases, but in the middle range it is almost always proportional. Suppose, for example, that you have a glass of unsweetened lemonade. In order to make it sweet, you add 2 spoonfuls of sugar. Now to make the lemonade taste "twice as sweet," you must add 6 spoonfuls—3 times the original amount of sugar. Then you discover that in order to make the lemonade "four times as sweet," you must add a total of 18 spoonfuls (Figure 5.2). Each time the sweetness doubles, the amount of sugar triples (see Stevens, 1962).

By experimenting in this way with variations in sounds, temperatures, pressures, colors, tastes, and smells, psychologists are learning more about how each sense responds to stimulation. Some senses produce huge increases in sensation in response to small increases in energy. For example, the pain of an electric shock can be increased more than eight times by doubling the voltage. On the other hand, the intensity of a light must be increased many times to double its brightness.

CONNECTIONS: PSYCHOLOGY AND THE MEDIA

Tell students that psychologists usually apply Weber's law to one of the five senses, such as taste. Ask: Do you think the same law can be applied to the effects of the media upon behavior? For example, does the prevalence of violence on television make people less shocked by violence in general? Or does the use of flip, disrespectful language make people less courteous in their day-to-day lives? Assign students to find articles on this subject, such as the criticism of the media leveled by Attorney General Janet Reno in late 1993.

Sensory Adaptation

Psychologists have focused on people's responses to changes in stimuli because they have found that the senses are tuned to change. Senses are most responsive to increases and decreases, to new events rather than to ongoing, unchanging stimulation. This is because our senses have an ability to adapt, or adjust themselves, to a constant level of stimulation. They get used to a new level and respond only to changes away from it.

A good example of this process of adaptation is the increase in visual sensitivity that you experience after a short time in a darkened movie theater. At first you see only blackness, but after a while your eyes adapt to the new level, and you can see seats, faces, and so on. Adaptation occurs for the other senses as well. Receptors in your skin adapt to the cold water when you go for a swim; disagreeable odors in a lab seem to disappear after a while; street noises cease to bother you after you've lived in a city for a time. Without sensory adaptation, you would feel the constant pressure of the clothes on your body, and other stimuli would seem to be bombarding all your senses at the same time.

Motivation and Signal-Detection Theory

Sensory experience does not depend on the stimulus alone. A person's ability to detect a stimulus also depends on motivation. The individual does not simply receive a signal passively. Rather, the individual makes a decision

FIGURE 5.3

Air-traffic controllers must be able to detect an airplane on the radar screen even when the plane's blip is faint and difficult to distinguish from blips caused by natural phenomena such as flocks of birds or bad weather. **What is signal-detection theory?**

Teacher Note. You might point out the difference between *adaptation* and *habituation*. Both terms can be used to describe a decrease in response after prolonged exposure to a stimulus. However, adaptation refers to a change in a sensory receptor. Habituation involves the central nervous system and could be a simple type of learning (as in picking up a good or bad habit). Habituation also refers to increased tolerance to a drug or chemical.

VISUAL INSTRUCTION

Point out that signal-detection theory also involves the study of psychological factors that affect our ability to identify stimuli.
Answer to caption, Figure 5.3: the study of the mathematical relationship between motivation, sensitivity, and sensation

ADDITIONAL INFORMATION

Tell students that it would be dangerous if our vision adapted too much. For example, a steelworker would be at great risk if the edge of the girder faded away after he or she stared at it for a long time. Luckily, the eye prevents such adaptation through a process known as *physiological nystagmus*, or what amounts to a constant series of tremors. To see how this process works, instruct students to stare at one of the letters on this page. Most students will soon notice that they have trouble keeping their eyes focused because of the tremors that prevent the receptor cells from adapting.

■ **Discussion.** Tell students that psychologists have applied the signal-detection theory to the criminal justice system. Explain that biases and expectations sometimes influence the ability of a witness to identify criminals from mug shots or a lineup. Using signal-detection theory, psychologists have been able to increase accuracy of witness identification. Ask students how each of the following tips helps achieve this goal. (Buckhout, 1976)

• Telling a witness that the criminal may not be in a lineup. *(lessens pressure to perceive one of the persons as a criminal)*
• Including equally dissimilar people in a lineup. *(reduces the chances of guessing)*
(OBJECTIVE 2)

VISUAL INSTRUCTION

Tell students that the word "blind spot" has another meaning when applied to human relationships. Can students guess what it is? *(insensitivity, ignorance, or prejudice)*
Answer to caption, Figure 5.4: to change light energy into chemical and electrical impulses

as to its presence, though the decision-making process is usually entirely unconscious.

Thus the nervous new radar operator may see blips on his screen when there are none while the overrelaxed veteran may not notice the unexpected. To use a more complex example, if you've been thinking about your old boyfriend, you may think you see him walking down the street when it's really somebody else. On the other hand, you probably wouldn't expect to meet your piano teacher at a football game, and you might not notice him if he showed up there. Thus, feelings, expectations, and motivation influence whether or not you perceive a stimulus.

Signal-detection theory studies the mathematical relations between motivation, sensitivity, and decision-making (Green and Swets, 1966). Detection thresholds involve recognizing some stimulus against a background of noise. A radar operator must be able to detect an airplane on a radar screen even when the plane's blip is faint and difficult to distinguish from blips caused by flocks of birds or bad weather, which can produce images that are like visual "noise" (Figure 5.3). Consider radar operators watching a screen in wartime during a storm. How do they decide whether a blip on the screen is an enemy plane or a patch of noise? If they were to call out massive armed forces for every blip, they would create chaos. But if one bomber was mistakenly identified as noise, the results could be disastrous. The radar operator's judgment will be influenced by many factors, and different operators appear to have different sensitivities to blips. Moreover, a specific individual's apparent sensitivity seems to fluctuate, depending on the situation. For example, being watched by a superior will probably affect the operator's performance, as will fatigue or other distractions.

In studying the difficulties faced by radar operators, psychologists have reformulated the concept of absolute threshold to take into account the many factors that affect detection of minimal stimuli. As a result, signal-detection theory abandons the idea that there is a single true absolute threshold for a stimulus. Instead it is based on the notion that the stimulus, here called a signal, must be detected in the presence of noise, which

FIGURE 5.4

A cross-section of the human eye (a) shows the passage of light. Note that the retina receives an inverted image of the external world, although people are never aware of this inversion. The place where the optic nerve leaves the eye is called the blind spot because it is the only spot on the retina where there are no receptors. In the cell structure of the retina (b), the light-sensitive cells (the rods and cones) are those farthest from the light, not the closest. Light arriving at the retina must pass through other cells before striking the rods and cones. **What is the main function of the rods and cones?**

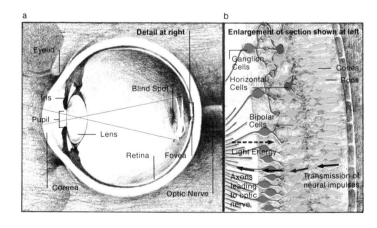

🧪 LAB EXPERIMENTS AND DEMONSTRATIONS

Select several students to act as experimenters and select one to act as a subject. Give the subject some type of visual brainteaser to solve, such as Rubik's cube. Instruct the experimenters to stare intently at the subject (an overexaggerated version of the supervisor watching the radar operator).

After several minutes, ask the subject to describe the effect of the experimenters' gazes upon his or her ability to solve the puzzle. That is, did their presence interfere with the ability to detect visual signals or clues? Why or why not?

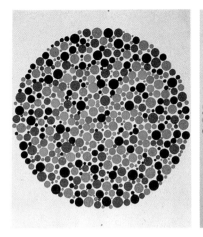 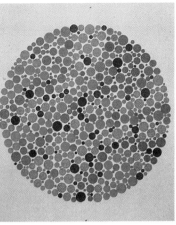

FIGURE 5.5

Can you see numerals in the dot patterns that make up these two figures? If you cannot distinguish a number in the circle to the left, you may be color-deficient. Viewing the circle on the right, those with normal vision will see only random patches of color. Those with red-green deficiency will see a number. **What is the cause of color deficiency?**

can interfere with detection of the signal. Thus signal detection is similar to standing in a noisy bus terminal, listening for the announcement of your bus departure time over the loudspeaker. Although the volume of the loudspeaker remains constant, you will have more or less difficulty in detecting your "signal," depending on the amount of noise in the bus terminal.

THE SENSES

Although people are thought to have five senses, there are actually more. In addition to vision, hearing, taste, smell, and touch, there are several skin senses and two "internal" senses: *vestibular* and *kinesthetic*.

Each type of sensory receptor takes some sort of external stimulus—light, chemical molecules, sound waves, pressure—and converts it into a chemical-electrical message that can be understood by the brain. So far, we know most about these processes in vision and hearing. The other senses have received less attention and are more mysterious in their functioning.

Vision

Vision is the most studied of all the senses, reflecting the high importance we place on our sense of sight. Vision provides us with a great deal of information about our environment and the objects in it—the sizes, shapes, and locations of things, and their textures, colors, and distances.

How does vision occur? Light enters the eye through the **pupil** (see Figure 5.4a) and reaches the **lens,** a flexible structure that focuses light on the **retina.** The retina contains two types of light-sensitive receptor cells: **rods** and **cones** (see Figure 5.4b). These cells are responsible for changing light energy into neuronal impulses, which then travel over the **optic nerve** to the brain.

■ **Demonstration.** Rods only exist on the outer part of the retina (no cones). To illustrate this, organize students into subjects and experimenters. Give the experimenters red, blue, yellow, and green pencils. Tell subjects to stare straight ahead at some fixed spot without moving their eyes. Then have experimenters move each pencil from the back toward the front of the subject's head. Have the subject say when he or she sees the pencil *and* when he or she can identify the color. Instruct experimenters to record the results with each color pencil. *(Students will see the pencil before the color. Also, because blue and yellow cones extend farther into the periphery, students should see these colors sooner than they will see reds and greens.)* (OBJECTIVE 3)

WORKING WITH TRANSPARENCIES

Project Transparency 8 and request volunteers to explain the path of sound to brain centers where the message is interpreted. For further study, assign Student Worksheet 8.
Answer to caption, Figure 5.6: binocular fusion
Answer to caption, Figure 5.7: carries impulses from the inner ear to the brain, resulting in the sensation of sound

FIGURE 5.6

To experience stereoscopic depth perception, take a tall, thin piece of cardboard and place it perpendicular to the page on the line that marks the separation of the two pictures. Then, with the edge of the cardboard resting between your eyes (as shown in the drawing), look at the left photo with your left eye and the right photo with your right eye and try to let the two images come together as one. (It helps to concentrate on the white dot.) If you are successful in fusing the images, the scene will suddenly have a third dimension, depth. **What is the name of the process by which a viewer combines two images into one?**

Cones require more light than rods before they begin to respond; they work best in daylight. Since rods are sensitive to much lower levels of light than cones, they are particularly useful in night vision. There are many more rods (75 to 150 million) than there are cones (6 to 7 million), but only cones are sensitive to color. Rods and cones can be compared to black-and-white and color film. Color film takes more light and thus works best in daylight like our cones; sensitive black-and-white film works not only in bright light but in shadows, dim light, and other poor lighting conditions, just like our rods.

Color Deficiency. When some or all of a person's cones do not function properly, he or she is said to be color-deficient. There are several kinds of color deficiency; most color-deficient people do see *some* colors (Figure 5.5). For example, some people have trouble distinguishing between red and green. Fewer people have no trouble with red and green but cannot dis-

FIGURE 5.7

Sound vibrations in the air strike the eardrum and set in motion a chain of three bones—the malleus (hammer), the incus (anvil), and the stapes (stirrup). The stapes strikes another drum on the cochlea—a long, coiled, fluid-filled tube with two skin-like membranes running down the middle of it. **What is the function of the auditory nerve?**

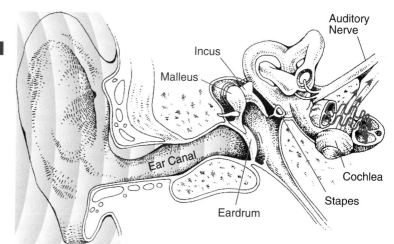

PSYCHOLOGISTS AT WORK

The growth of the environmental movement in the 1960s and 1970s gave birth to a new field of psychological specialization known as environmental psychology. *Environmental psychologists* focus on the relationships between people and their physical or social surroundings. They study such things as the effect of high-rise buildings upon city dwellers. They also study the effects of noise pollution upon behavior. Because of the broad range of their studies, environmental psychologists often work hand-in-hand with specialists in other fields such as architects, urban planners, and sociologists.

tinguish between yellow and blue. A very few people are totally color-blind. They depend on their rods, so to them the world looks something like black-and-white television programs—nothing but blacks, whites, and shades of gray.

Color deficiency affects about 8 percent of American men and less than 1 percent of American women. It results from a hereditary defect in the cones. This defect is carried in the genes of women whose vision is usually normal. These women pass these genes on to their sons, who are born color-deficient (see Wald, 1964).

Binocular Fusion and Stereopsis. Because we have two eyes, located about 2.5 inches (6.4 cm) apart, the visual system receives two images. But instead of seeing double, we see a single image, probably a composite of the views of two eyes. The combination of the two images into one is called **binocular fusion.**

Not only does the visual system receive two images, but there is a difference between the images on the retinas. This difference is called **retinal disparity.** You can easily observe retinal disparity by bringing an object such as an eraser close to your eyes. Without moving it, look at the eraser first with one eye, then with the other. You will see a difference in the two images because of the different viewpoint each eye has. When you open both eyes you will no longer see the difference, but will instead see the object as solid and three-dimensional, if you have good binocular vision. **Stereopsis** refers to the phenomenon of seeing depth as a result of retinal disparity (Figure 5.6).

Hearing

Hearing depends on vibrations of the air, called sound waves. Sound waves from the air pass through various bones and fluids (shown in Figure 5.7) until they reach the inner ear, which contains tiny hairlike cells that move back and forth (much like a field of wheat waving in the wind). These hair cells change sound vibrations into neuronal signals that travel via the **auditory nerve** to the brain.

The perception of loudness depends on the amplitude of the vibrations in the air. This strength, or sound-pressure energy, is measured in **decibels.** The sounds we hear range upward from 0 decibels, the softest sound the human ear can detect, to about 140 decibels, which is roughly as loud as a jet plane taking off. Any sound over 110 decibels can damage hearing as can persistent sounds as low as 80 decibels. Any sound that is painful when you first hear it *will* damage your hearing if you hear it often enough. Figure 5.8 lists the decibel levels of some common sounds.

Pitch depends on sound-wave frequency, or the rate of the vibration of the medium through which the sound wave is transmitted. Low frequencies produce deep bass sounds; high frequencies produce shrill squeaks. If you hear a sound composed of a combination of different frequencies, you can hear the separate pitches even though they occur simultaneously. For example, if you strike two keys of a piano at the same time, your ear can detect two distinct pitches.

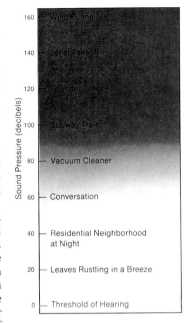

FIGURE 5.8

Sound actually becomes painful at about 130 decibels. Decibels represent ratios: a 20-decibel difference between 2 sounds indicates that one sound wave is physically 10 times more powerful than the other. Thus a vacuum cleaner puts 10 times as much pressure on your eardrums as conversation does. A 10-decibel increase means the sound is perceived to be twice as loud (Stevens, 1955). **What is the measurement in decibels of a subway train?**

MEETING SPECIAL NEEDS

Hearing Impairments. You might keep these tips in mind when communicating with the hearing impaired.
- Do not assume that a hearing aid corrects a hearing loss.
- Make sure you have the person's attention before you begin speaking.
- Face the hearing-impaired person and maintain eye contact.
- Make sure he or she can clearly see your mouth and face.
- Speak and enunciate clearly.
- Use your voice, but don't shout.
- Be sensitive to whether the hearing-impaired person understands or is just being polite.

VISUAL INSTRUCTION

Tell students that about 10 million Americans are regularly exposed at work to noises loud enough to cause permanent hearing damage. **Answer to caption, Figure 5.8:** 100 decibels

Tell students that about 9,000 taste buds cover the tongue.
Answer to caption, Figure 5.9: Chemicals stimulate receptors in the taste buds on the tongue. Taste information is then relayed to the brain.

■ **Demonstration.** Organize the class into small groups. Have half the members of each group blindfold themselves. The other half should give the subjects something to taste such as a cookie while holding a perfume-scented cloth or onion to their noses. Ask the subjects to describe what they tasted. After a few minutes, have the experimenters repeat the same taste test *without* holding anything up to the subjects' noses. Have them again describe the food's taste. Compare responses with the class as a whole. Ask: Did the experiment prove or disprove the text statement on this page: "Much of what is referred to as taste is actually produced by the sense of smell." (OBJECTIVE 3)

Review. Have students complete the Chapter 5 Application Activity.

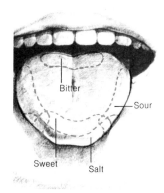

This map indicates the areas that seem more sensitive to one kind of stimulation than to others. Interestingly, it is possible to be taste-deficient as well as color-deficient. A chemical called phenylthiocarbamide (PTC) tastes extremely bitter to some people and is quite tasteless to others. **How does the sense of taste work?**

Sources of sounds can be located when your ears work together. When a noise occurs on your right, for example, the sound wave comes to both ears, but it reaches your right ear a fraction of a second before it reaches the left. It is also slightly louder in the right ear. These differences tell you from which direction it is coming.

Smell and Taste

Smell and taste are known as the chemical senses because their receptors are sensitive to chemical molecules rather than to light energy or sound waves. For you to smell something, the appropriate molecules must come into contact with the smell receptors in your nose. These molecules enter your nose in vapors, which reach a special membrane in the upper part of the nasal passages on which the smell receptors are located. These receptors send messages about smells via the **olfactory nerve** to the brain.

For you to taste something, appropriate chemicals must stimulate receptors in the taste buds on your tongue. Taste information is relayed to the brain along with data about the texture and temperature of the substance you have put in your mouth.

Studies show that four primary sensory experiences—sour, salty, bitter, and sweet—make up taste (Beebe-Center, 1949). One of the older theories of smell proposed that all smells are made up of six qualities: flowery, fruity, spicy, resinous, putrid, and burned (Henning, 1916). One theory (Buck & Axel, 1991) notes that there may be a thousand olfactory receptors, each responding only to a very limited number of gaseous molecules. At this point, we cannot draw any conclusions.

Much of what is referred to as taste is actually produced by the sense of smell. You have undoubtedly noticed that when your nose is blocked by a cold, foods usually taste bland. Sensations of warmth, cold, and pressure also affect taste. Try to imagine eating cold chicken soup or drinking a hot Pepsi, and you will realize how important temperature is to the sense of taste. Now imagine the textural differences between a spoonful of pudding and a crunchy chocolate bar, and you will see how the texture of food also influences taste.

The chemical senses seem to play a relatively unimportant role in human life when compared to their functions in lower animals. Insects, for example, often depend on smell to communicate with one another, especially in mating. In humans, smell and taste have become more a matter of esthetics than of survival.

The Skin Senses

Receptors in the skin are responsible for providing the brain with at least four kinds of information about the environment: pressure, warmth, cold, and pain.

Sensitivity to pressure varies from place to place in the skin. Some spots, such as your fingertips, are densely populated with receptors and are, therefore, highly sensitive. Other spots, such as the middle of your back or the back of your calf, contain relatively few receptors. Pressure sen-

 LAB EXPERIMENTS AND DEMONSTRATIONS

To apply Weber's law to smell, bring a bottle of perfume or cologne to class. Open the bottle and place several drops on your wrist. Ask students to indicate by a show of hands how many smell it. Record the result. In the next class session, put a much larger amount of the scent on a handkerchief or bandanna.

After students settle down, place several drops on your wrist. Do any of them notice the difference? If so, how did it compare to the sensation felt the prior day? Use this experiment to discuss adaptation of smell.

sations can serve as protection. For example, feeling the light pressure of an insect landing on your arm warns you of the danger of being stung.

Some skin receptors are particularly sensitive to hot or cold stimuli. In order to create a hot or cold sensation, a stimulus must have a temperature greater or less than the temperature of the skin. If you plunge your arm into a sink of warm water on a hot day, you will experience little or no sensation of its heat. If you put your arm in the same water on a cold day, however, the water will feel quite warm.

Many kinds of stimuli—scratches, punctures, severe pressure, heat, and cold—can produce pain. What they have in common is real or potential injury to bodily tissues. Pain makes it possible for you to prevent damage to your body—it is an emergency system that demands immediate action.

Because pain acts as a warning system for your body, it does not easily adapt to stimulation—you rarely get "used to" pain. Pain tells you to avoid a stimulation that is harmful to you. Without this mechanism, you might "adapt" to a fire when you stand next to it. After a few minutes you would literally begin to cook, and your tissues would die.

Balance

The body's sense of balance is regulated by the **vestibular system** inside the inner ear. Its prominent feature is the three *semicircular canals*. Hair cells project into the fluid within each of the canals. When you turn your head, the canals, attached to your head, also move. Inertia causes the fluid within at least one canal to be slow moving, which bends receptor hair cells projecting into the fluid (Figure 5.10).

The stimuli for vestibular responses include movements such as spinning, falling, and tilting the body or head. Overstimulation of the vestibular sense by such movements can result in dizziness and "motion sickness," as you probably have experienced by going on amusement-park rides or by spinning around on a swivel stool. Although you are seldom directly aware of your sense of balance, without it you would be unable to stand or walk without falling or stumbling.

Body Sensations

Kinesthesis is the sense of movement and body position. It cooperates with the vestibular and visual senses to maintain posture and balance. The sensation of kinesthesis comes from receptors in and near the muscles, tendons, and joints. When any movement occurs, these receptors immediately send messages to the brain.

Without kinesthetic sensations, your movements would be jerky and uncoordinated. You would not know what your hand was doing if it went behind your back, and you could not walk without looking at your feet. Furthermore, complex physical activities, such as surgery, piano playing, and acrobatics, would be impossible.

Another type of bodily sensation comes from receptors that monitor internal body conditions. These receptors are sensitive to pressure, temperature, pain, and chemicals inside the body. For example, a full stomach

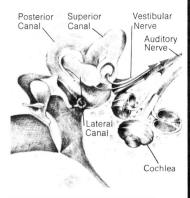

FIGURE 5.10

The organs of balance consist of three semicircular canals at right angles to each other, filled with a freely moving fluid. Continuous motion in a straight line produces no response in this system. However, starting, turning, and speeding up cause the inertia of the fluid to lag behind the movement of at least one of your canals. This bends the hair cells that project into the fluid. If the fluid "catches up" with the canal as you continue to start, turn, or accelerate, then you experience movement in the opposite direction when you slow down or stop. Once moving, inertia causes the fluid to keep moving as your canal is decelerating, which bends hair cells in the opposite direction and yields the opposite experience. These hair cells convert the movement into neural impulses that are sent to the brain via the auditory nerve. **What are the three canals of the inner ear?**

STUDY AND WRITING SKILLS

Tell students that 10 percent of all Americans suffer from *dyslexia*—a reading disability with a perceptual base. People with dyslexia reverse letters and numbers. They also have a hard time discerning left from right and experience difficulty with physical coordination. Underscore that dyslexia is unrelated to intelligence. Mention some famous past and present dyslexics—Thomas Edison, Woodrow Wilson, Cher, and Tom Cruise. Assign students to prepare a written report on some of the new advances being made in the treatment of dyslexia.

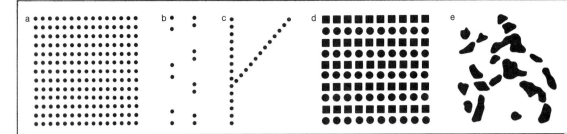

FIGURE 5.11

Humans see patterns and groupings in their environment rather than disorganized arrays of bits and pieces. It is impossible to look, for example, at the array of dots in (a) without seeing shifting patterns of squares and lines. In (b), elements that are close to one another seem to belong together. As (c) shows, however, continuity can be more important. Although the bottom dot in the inclined series is closer to the vertical series, it is not seen as belonging to the vertical row, it is seen as a continuation of the inclined row and therefore as part of it. Similar elements seem to belong to one another (d) and therefore one sees the array as a set of horizontal rows rather than vertical columns, as one might if all the elements were the same. In (e) a principle known as closure is demonstrated. The breaks are ignored; what is seen is a "whole." **What is perception?**

stretching these internal receptors informs the brain that you have ingested too much.

Little is known about pain from the interior of the body except that it seems to be deep, dull, and much more unpleasant than the sharply localized pain from the skin. In some cases, internal pain receptors may send inaccurate messages. They may indicate, for example, that pain is located in the shoulder when in reality the source of irritation is in the lower stomach. Such sensation of pain in an area away from the actual source is called **referred pain.**

PERCEPTION

People do not usually experience a mass of colors, noises, temperatures, and pressures. Rather we see cars and buildings, hear voices and music, and feel pencils, desks, and close friends. We do not merely have sensory experiences; we perceive objects. The brain receives information from the senses and organizes and interprets it into meaningful experiences—unconsciously. This process is called perception.

Principles of Perceptual Organization

Through the process of perception, the brain is always trying to build "wholes" out of the confusion of stimuli that bombards the senses. The "whole" experience that comes from organizing bits and pieces of information into meaningful objects and patterns is called a **Gestalt.** Here, the whole is greater than the sum of the parts. ("Gestalt" is a German word meaning pattern or configuration.)

Gestalt psychologists have tried to identify the principles the brain uses in constructing perceptions (Koffka, 1963). Some of the principles they have discovered are demonstrated in Figure 5.11. For example, they have found that people tend to see dots in patterns and groups. Thus, when you look at Figure 5.11a, you see shifting patterns of lines and rectangles, not just an array of dots. Three principles that people use in organizing such patterns are proximity, continuity, and similarity. If the elements of the pattern are close to one another or are similar in appearance, they tend to be perceived as belonging to one another. These principles are demonstrated in Figures 5.11b, c, and d.

The Gestalt principles of organization help to explain how we group our sensations and fill in gaps in order to make sense of our world. In music, for instance, you tend to group notes on the basis of their closeness, or proximity, to one another in time—you hear melodies, not single notes. Similarity and continuity are also important. They allow you to follow the sound of a particular voice or instrument even when many other sounds are occurring. For example, you can follow the sound of a bass guitar through a song.

Figure-Ground Perception

One form of perceptual organization is the division of experience into figure and ground. Look at Figure 5.12. What do you see? Sometimes the figure looks like a white vase against a black background. At other times it appears to be two black faces nose to nose against a white background.

Figure-ground perception is the ability to discriminate properly between figure and ground. When you look at a three-dimensional object against the sky, you have no trouble distinguishing between the object and its background. It is when something is two-dimensional, as in Figure 5.12, that you may have trouble telling the figure from the ground. Nevertheless, such figure-ground perceptions give clues as to the nature of perception. The fact that a single pattern can be perceived in more than one way demonstrates that we are not passive receivers of stimuli.

Figure and ground are important in hearing as well as in vision. When you follow one person's voice at a noisy meeting, that voice is a figure and all other sounds become ground. Similarly, when you listen to a piece of music, a familiar theme may "leap out" at you: the melody becomes the figure, and the rest of the music merely background.

FIGURE 5.12

What did you see the first time you looked at this illustration? Whatever you saw, you saw because of your past experiences and current expectations. People invariably organize their experience into figure and ground. **What does the fact that we perceive a single pattern more than one way demonstrate?**

FIGURE 5.13

Even though you cannot see it, you assume that the road will continue beyond the slight rise—not stop abruptly at the limits of your vision from the car. **On what is perceptual inference based?**

CONNECTIONS: PSYCHOLOGY AND MUSIC

You might illustrate the ability to fill in gaps in what our senses tell us by organizing a game of "Name That Tune." Request several students to bring in tapes or CDs of well-known songs. Instruct these "DJs" to play only a few notes at a time. Record how many notes it takes before a class member can guess the name of the song. Ask students to identify the auditory clues that provided them with their answers. *(artist's voice, beat, lyrics, instrumentation, and so on)*

■ **Study and Writing Skills.**
Assign students to keep a log of perceptual inferences that they make over a 24-hour period. For example, they might hear the sound of the school bus before actually seeing it. But, based on past experience, they will perceive this auditory stimulus as a school bus. When students are done, call on volunteers to share their entries with the class. Ask: How does perceptual inference help people to function more effectively? *(To trigger discussion, focus on the example of the seat in a dark movie theater. Ask: Suppose people had to check out the seat every time they sat down? Or suppose people had to stop the car to look over every hill to make sure the road continued?)*

VISUAL INSTRUCTION

Point out that infants also have a sense of height. When picked up, they instantly exhibit recognition of being lifted off a solid—and safe—surface.
Answer to caption, Figure 5.14: that the infant perceives depth

Perceptual Inference

Often we have perceptions that are not based entirely on current sensory information. When you hear barking as you approach your house, you assume it is your dog—not a cat or a rhinoceros or even another dog. When you take a seat in a dark theater, you assume it is solid and will hold your weight even though you cannot see what supports the seat. When you are driving in a car and see in the distance that the road climbs up a steep hill then disappears over the top, you assume the road will continue over and down the hill, not come to an abrupt halt (Figure 5.13).

This phenomenon of filling in the gaps in what our senses tell us is known as perceptual inference (Gregory, 1970). Perceptual inference is largely automatic and unconscious. We need only a few cues to inform us that a noise is our dog barking or that a seat is solid. Why? Because we have encountered these stimuli and objects in the past and know what to expect from them in the present. Perceptual inference thus often depends on experience. On the other hand, we are probably born with some of our abili-

FIGURE 5.14

An infant of crawling age (about 6 months) will usually refuse to cross the glass surface over the "deep" side even if his mother is on the other side urging the child to join her. The infant is perfectly willing to cross the "shallow" side to reach his mother, however. **What does this experiment demonstrate?**

COMMUNITY INVOLVEMENT

If any students have relatives or friends with an infant less than one year old, you might ask them to request permission to videotape or borrow a videotape of the infant. Have students explain that the tape will be used to study the way humans learn to perceive the world. (You might help students design a letter of explanation and a release form to show the tape.) Have the class observe these tapes carefully, looking for examples of perceptual inference or sensory development. For additional observation cues, refer students to the discussion of insight in Chapter 3. Assign students to summarize their observations in the form of a written report.

FIGURE 5.15

A cut-away view of the apparatus shows that active involvement is necessary for perceptual learning. Both kittens are receiving roughly the same visual input as they move in relation to the vertical stripes painted on the walls of the cylinder. One kitten, however, is producing the changes in what it sees by its own muscular movements. The other kitten sees similar changes because of the way it is harnessed to the first kitten, but what it sees has nothing to do with its own movements. **How did the two kittens differ in their development of depth perception?**

ty to make perceptual inferences. For example, experimenters have shown that infants just barely able to crawl will avoid falling over what appears to be a steep cliff—thus proving that they perceive depth (Gibson and Walk, 1960). (See Figure 5.14.)

Learning to Perceive

In large part, perceiving is something that people *learn* to do. For example, infants under one month will smile at a nodding object the size of a human face, whether or not it has eyes, a nose, or other human features. At about 20 weeks, however, a blank oval will not make most babies smile, but a drawing of a face or a mask will. The baby has learned to distinguish something that looks like a person from other objects. Babies 28 weeks and older are more likely to smile at a female than a male face. By 30 weeks most smile more readily when they see a familiar face than when they see someone they do not know. But it takes 7 or 8 months for babies to learn to recognize different people (Ahrens, 1954).

Experiments show that people and animals must be actively involved in their environments to develop perception. An experiment with newborn kittens demonstrates this. A number of kittens were raised in the dark until they were 10 weeks old. Then they were divided into 2 groups: actives and passives.

For 3 hours a day an active kitten and a passive kitten were linked together, as shown in Figure 5.15. The kittens were harnessed in such a way that every action of the active kitten moved the passive kitten an equal distance, forward, backward, up, down, and from side to side. The visual stimulation for the two kittens was approximately the same, but the active animal produced its *own* changes in stimulation (by walking, for example). The other kitten was merely a passive receiver of stimulation. When the kittens were tested later, the passive one was not able to discriminate depth—to judge how close or far away various objects were. But the active kitten developed this ability normally. Not until the passive kitten had been al-

■ Evaluating Visual Data.

Request students to collect samples of children's art. (Or arrange to get some pictures from one of the elementary teachers in your community.) Post these pictures around the classroom. Tell students that many different factors, including the age of development, play a role in shaping children's art. In this case, however, students should focus on what these pictures reveal about children's perceptions of the environment. What do proportional sizes, colors, and shapes tell students about how children see the world? What stimuli captured the children's attention? How do the children depict depth (if at all)? Based on such questions, have students summarize findings in a short written report. (OBJECTIVES 2–4)

■ Study and Writing Skills.

Tell students that one of the basic questions facing perception psychologists is this: "How do we see the world as three-dimensional when our main source of visual information—the retina—is two-dimensional?" Using information on page 124, challenge students to write a short essay answering this question. (OBJECTIVES 3, 4)

? FACT OR FICTION

By feeling people's faces, blind people can visualize how they look.

Fiction. Visualization is based on the memory of things we have seen. If a person has been blind since birth, he or she has no such memories.

Depth perception develops in infancy.

---

lowed to live normally for 2 days—to move around in a visual environment of its own—did it develop normal depth perception (Held and Hein, 1963).

Experiments with human beings have also shown that active involvement in one's environment is important for accurate perception. People who have been blind from birth and who have had their sight restored by an operation (which is possible in only a few cases) have visual sensations, but initially they cannot tell the difference between a square and a circle or see that a red cube is like a blue cube (Valvo, 1971). In fact some had difficulty making such simple distinctions six months after their vision was restored.

Depth Perception

Depth perception—the ability to recognize distances and three-dimensionality—develops in infancy. If you place a baby on a large table, he or she most likely will not crawl over the edge. The baby is able to perceive that it is a long distance to the floor. Psychologists test depth perception in infants with a device called the visual cliff (Gibson and Walk, 1960).

People use many cues to perceive distance and depth. There are at least a half-dozen cues external to us that we use. In the absence of any other cues, the *size* of an object—bigger is nearer—will be used. *Interposition* causes us to view the object we can see in its entirety to be closer than one whose outline is interrupted by another object. *Shadows*—whether *attached* or *cast*—yield information about an object's shape and size. *Texture-density gradient* means that the further removed an object is, the less detail we can identify. *Aerial perspective*, or blueing, makes faraway objects look bluer. A related process, *atmospheric perspective*, or graying, uses pollution in the air as a gauge of relative distance. *Linear perspective* (Figure 5.17c) suggests that parallel lines do meet somewhere in the distance. Blurring occurs to near objects if you look beyond them and to far objects if you look in front of them. *Accommodation* occurs when the lens in your eye thickens as you look at nearby objects, and thins to view distant objects.

There are also a number of cues based on internal processes. *Convergence* is the process by which your eyes turn inward to look at nearby objects. Another is the information provided by retinal disparity, as discussed earlier in the chapter. A third is **motion parallax**—the apparent movement of objects that occurs when you move your head from side to side or when you walk around. You can demonstrate motion parallax by looking toward two objects in the same line of vision, one near you and the other some distance away. If you move your head back and forth, the near object will seem to move more than the far object. In this way, motion parallax gives you clues as to which objects are closer than others.

A final related cue is *relative motion*. When you are riding in a car, for example, and look at distant mountains, the objects in a nearby field seem to be moving in the opposite direction to your movement. Yet, when you look at an animal in a nearby field, the mountains or land beyond the animal seem to be moving in the same direction you are.

ADDITIONAL INFORMATION

Tell students that in 1977 perceptual psychologist O. A. Favreau found that in nearly 20 textbooks the longer line in the Müller-Lyer illusion was really longer. Tongue-in-cheek, Favreau said, "I'm disillusioned about the illusion." She then set out to see if the "Müller-Liar" illusion worked. Favreau drew two parallel lines 31 and 31.5 millimeters long. She placed the outward fins on the shorter line and the inward fins on the longer line. How did people perceive the lines? They said the shorter line was longer, restoring Müller-Lyer to its place in the history of psychology.

Constancy

When we have learned to perceive certain objects in our environment, we tend to see them in the same way, regardless of changing conditions. You probably judge the whiteness of the various portions of these pages to be fairly constant, even though you may have read the book under a wide range of lighting conditions. The light, angle of vision, distance, and, therefore, the image on the retina all change, but your perception of the object does not. Thus despite changing physical conditions, people are able to perceive objects as the same by the processes of size, shape, and brightness **constancy** (Figure 5.16).

An example of size constancy will illustrate how we have an automatic system for perceiving an object as being the same size whether it is far or near. A friend walking toward you does not seem to change into a giant even though the images inside your eyes become larger and larger as she approaches. To you, her appearance stays the same size because even though the size of your visual image is increasing, you are perceiving an additional piece of information: distance is decreasing. The enlarging eye image and the distance information combine to produce a perception of an approaching object that stays the same size.

Distance information compensates for the enlarging eye image to produce size constancy. If information about distance is eliminated, your perception of the size of the object begins to correspond to the actual size of the eye image. For example, it is difficult for most people to estimate the size of an airplane in the sky because they have little experience judging such huge sizes and distances. Pilots, however, can determine whether a flying plane is large and far away or small and close because they are experienced in estimating the sizes and distances of planes.

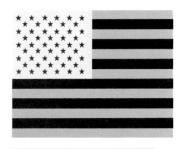

FIGURE 5.16

Stare steadily at the lowest right-hand star for about 45 seconds, or until the colors start to shimmer. Then stare at a blank piece of paper. After a second or two, you should see a negative afterimage of this figure in which the flag shows the normal colors. This occurs because the receptors for green, black, and yellow become fatigued, allowing the complementary colors of each to predominate when you stare at the white paper. Since these complements are, respectively, red, white, and blue, you see a normal American flag. Now shift your glance to a blank wall some distance away. Suddenly the flag will appear huge. **Why did this occur?**

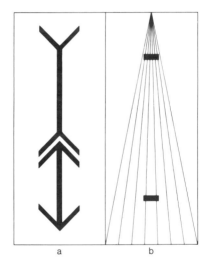

FIGURE 5.17

The Müller-Lyer illusion (a) and the Ponzo illusion (b) are two of the most famous illusions in psychology. The lines between the arrowheads in (a) are exactly the same length, as are the heavy black lines in (b). Some psychologists believe that the reason the lines in (a) seem of different lengths is because they are interpreted as offering different cues to their distance from the viewer. The lines in (b) may appear to be different in length because the brain interprets this diagram as though it is from a scene such as that in (c). **What are illusions?**

a   b   c

CONNECTIONS: PSYCHOLOGY AND SCIENCE

Assign students to prepare an oral report on *mirages*—atmospheric optical illusions in which an observer sees a nonexistent body of water or an image of some distant object. Mirages project such a solid image that they have even been photographed. Have students explain the scientific facts behind this natural illusion. If possible, encourage them to show some pictures of mirages. *(Examples include a shimmering pool of water in a desert or an inverted ship seen in the sky while at sea.)* Stress that they are not illusions, hallucinations, or extrasensory perceptions, but natural, physical phenomena.

VISUAL INSTRUCTION

Have students compare the optical illusion in Figure 5.18 with the Gestalt art in Figure 5.12. Both of these pieces of art play perceptual tricks. Yet they illustrate two very different principles in the psychology of perception. Ask students to summarize these differences. **Answer to caption, Figure 5.18:** Answers will vary, but students should note that misinterpretations are caused by errors in visual processing and the way the brain interprets its information and also by our prior knowledge about the world and how we perceive it. (OBJECTIVE 4)

FIGURE 5.18

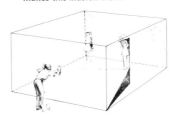

These two individuals appear to be a giant and a very small person in an ordinary room. In fact, they are ordinary-sized people in a very peculiar room. This room, the true design of which is shown in the accompanying diagram, was constructed by psychologist Adelbert Ames. **What makes this illusion work?**

Illusions

Illusions are incorrect perceptions that occur when sensations are distorted. For example, look at the lines in Figure 5.17. Which lines are longer? Measure the lengths of the pairs of lines with a ruler, then look again. Do the lines *look* as long now that you *know* they are the same? For most people, the answer is no.

A possible explanation of this type of illusion is that even though the patterns are two-dimensional, your brain treats them as three-dimensional. These illusions have features that usually indicate distance in three-dimensional space. The top line in Figure 5.17a, for example, can be thought of as the far corner of a room; the bottom line is like the near corner of the building. In Figure 5.17b and Figure 5.17c the converging lines create the illusion of distance so that the lower bar looks nearer and shorter than the upper bar. This "perceptual compensation" seems to be unconscious and automatic.

Figure 5.18 shows two individuals in a room. Their sizes look dramatically different because you perceive the room as rectangular. In fact, the ceiling and walls are slanted so that the back wall is both shorter and closer on the right than on the left. But even when you know how this illusion was achieved, you still accept the peculiar difference in the sizes of the two people because the windows, walls, and ceiling appear rectangular. Your experience with rectangular rooms overrides your knowledge of how this trick is done.

EXTRASENSORY PERCEPTION

In this chapter, we have discussed the perception of tangible and measurable aspects of our environment. But humans are rarely content with un-

LAB EXPERIMENTS AND DEMONSTRATIONS

Your students might be interested in trying out a simple experiment in ESP. Select several "senders" to sit at the front of the room with the numbers 1–5 written on three-by-five cards. Have the senders arrange these cards in a shuffled, random, prerecorded order. Then, with their backs turned to the class, have students "send" an image of these cards to the "receivers" behind them. Tell other students to concentrate and write down the messages that they receive. After several seconds, determine if any students got the numbers in order. Debate whether the results did or did not demonstrate ESP. What happens if the series is repeated with reshuffled cards?

FIGURE 5.19

Dr. J. B. Rhine administers an ESP test to two subjects using a special deck of cards. **What do parapsychologists do?**

derstanding only what can be seen and directly measured. We are fascinated by things that can't be seen, easily explained, or often even verified—flying saucers, atoms, genes, and extrasensory perception.

Extrasensory perception (ESP)—receiving information about the world through channels other than the normal senses—is a hotly debated topic. Many people are convinced that ESP exists because of an intense personal experience that can never be scientifically validated. For instance, we all have some fears before traveling, and we imagine the worst: our plane will crash, our train will be derailed, or we will have an automobile accident. These events almost never happen, and we easily forget about our frightening premonitions. However, if the improbable should actually take place, our premonitions turn into compelling evidence for the existence of precognition. Such coincidences sometimes become widely publicized evidence supporting paranormal phenomena, and we may quickly forget all the occasions when our premonitions were completely wrong. However, if we are truly interested in validating the existence of ESP, we must keep track of the frequency of its failures as well as its successes.

Scientists have been investigating ESP since the turn of the century. Probably the most famous parapsychologist (as these researchers into the supernatural are called) is J. B. Rhine. Around 1930, Rhine began a series of precise statistical tests of ESP. In tests of telepathy, for example, a "sender" focuses one at a time on each of 25 cards in a special deck. (The deck includes 5 cards for each of 5 different symbols.) A "receiver" locked in a distant room states which card he thinks the sender is focusing on. With luck alone, the receiver will guess about 5 cards correctly, sometimes a few more, sometimes a few less. Yet thousands of tests have shown that some people consistently respond above the average.

Some ESP researchers have concluded that these people are receiving information through senses or other channels we do not know about.

STUDY AND WRITING SKILLS

Assign interested students to research ESP in their school or community library. Based on this research, have them prepare a chart showing the different types of ESP experiences that they uncovered. Have them present this chart—and an overview of opinions on ESP—in an oral presentation to the class. Ask students whether they think parapsychology is a legitimate offshoot of psychology. *(Some students may argue that it is a hoax. Others may argue that anything affecting human beliefs belongs in psychology.)*

■ **Debating an Issue.** Organize teams to debate the following issue: *Resolved*—That parapsychology is a lot of bunk. Encourage students to do outside research in preparation for the debate. (OBJECTIVE 4)

ASSESS

Check for Understanding

Assign students to write a short paragraph explaining the link between sensation and perception.

Reteach

Have students complete the Chapter 5 Study Guide Activity and share responses with each other. For extended review, assign the Chapter 5 Review Activity as homework or an in-class assignment.

Enrich

Ask students to complete the Chapter 5 Extension Activity and answer the questions that follow it.

Readings in Psychology. Have students read the Section 2, Readings 3 and 4 selections in *Readings in Psychology* and answer the questions that follow the reading.

Evaluate

Administer and grade the Chapter 5 Test. Two forms are available should you wish to give different tests to different students/classes.

Use the Understanding Psychology Testmaker to create a customized test.

CLOSE _____

At the end of the chapter, you might have students explore what new data from Chapter 5 made its way into their long-term memory (see Chapter 3). Without consulting their textbooks, have students write down five new things that they learned from this chapter. Call on students to share their answers. With the class, analyze some of the responses. Ask: Why do you think some data made a bigger imprint on memory than other data?

The results found in these studies are indeed statistically unlikely, but in other ways they are not nearly as impressive. For example, in one study (described in Chance, 1976), Charles Tart screened 1,500 college students and found 25 who seemed to have ESP. The students were shown a machine that randomly turned on one of four lights. They had to guess which light would come on next. They guessed nearly 7,500 times, and were right 26.8 percent of the time. Since one would expect people without ESP to be right only 25 percent of the time (one out of four), and since they guessed so many times, the result was statistically significant: the odds were more than 2,500 to 1 against this performance occurring by chance. These are impressive odds, but they are not particularly impressive results. This minimal ESP would not be particularly useful for playing the stock market or a football pool. There is one more problem with Tart's experiment: Unsupervised undergraduates collected the data. Many studies have shown that experimenters who believe in ESP tend to make errors supporting their belief, just as skeptics make errors showing that it does not exist.

Another problem is intentional fraud. It would not be the first time a student falsified data to please his professor or to get a good grade. And there have been several rather spectacular cases of fraud in ESP research.

Another reason many scientists do not accept the results of experiments supporting ESP is that the findings are highly unstable. One of the basic principles of scientific research is that one scientist should be able to replicate another scientist's results. Not only do different ESP experiments yield contradictory findings, but the same individual seems to show ESP on one day but not on the next.

Perhaps the most telling argument against ESP is that when strict controls are used in an ESP experiment, there is little likelihood of demonstrating ESP. This is, of course, exactly contrary to what one normally expects when trying to demonstrate a phenomenon under strictly controlled conditions.

Proponents of ESP argue that this type of research cannot be consistently replicated because the special abilities are stifled in a laboratory situation. They say that ESP responses are best generated in highly emotional or relevant situations. Laboratory experiments that test people's ability to sense which symbols appear on cards are irrelevant to most people's lives, and far from being highly emotional, are usually a boring way to spend an afternoon. According to this viewpoint, it is remarkable that ESP has been reported to appear in the laboratory setting at all.

Although ESP may indeed be a very fragile phenomenon, the inability to replicate results and the difficulty of verifying ESP events are crucial problems. Many will remain skeptical about the existence of ESP until these problems are solved. However, such skepticism has often been overcome in the past. For example, just a century or so ago, the suggestion that many diseases were caused by invisible organisms was greeted with disbelief. Only after the work of Pasteur and other researchers proved that a clear relationship existed between these organisms and illness, was the "germ theory" of disease accepted. Perhaps the development of appropriate techniques for testing ESP could similarly lead to establishing the existence of paranormal phenomena—and perhaps they won't.

STUDY AND WRITING SKILLS

Assign groups of students to write a personal essay entitled: "Seeing Is Believing—Or Is It?" Based on information in this chapter, have students evaluate the meaning of this topic from the point of view of a perceptual psychologist. Tell students that they might use humor or irony to get their point across. As models, suggest that students look at the back-page essays in many news magazines.

SUMMARY

Use the following outline as a tool for reviewing this chapter. Copy the outline onto your own paper, leaving spaces between headings to make notes about key concepts.

I. Sensation
   A. Threshold
   B. Sensory Differences and Ratios
   C. Sensory Adaptation
   D. Motivation and Signal-Detection Theory

II. The Senses
   A. Vision
   B. Hearing
   C. Smell and Taste
   D. The Skin Senses
   E. Balance
   F. Body Sensations

III. Perception
   A. Principles of Perceptual Organization
   B. Figure-Ground Perception
   C. Perceptual Inference
   D. Learning to Perceive
   E. Depth Perception
   F. Constancy
   G. Illusions

IV. Extrasensory Perception

CONCEPTS AND VOCABULARY

1. Define a stimulus. Give several examples.

2. What field of psychology tries to quantify the relationship between stimuli from the world and the sensory experiences produced by them? Describe a sample experiment.

3. Compare and contrast an absolute threshold with a difference threshold.

4. Give the current view of the ability of subliminal advertising to influence a person's behavior.

5. Name a psychological principle that explains why you are more likely to notice when a single light bulb burns out in a room with three lamps than when a single light bulb burns out in a sports arena.

6. Give several possible explanations for phantom limb pain.

7. Which sense has received the most research? Why?

8. What is believed to be the cause of color deficiency?

9. Name the cues we use to determine distance and depth in vision. What cues do we use to determine direction of sounds?

10. Why are the senses of taste and smell known as the chemical senses?

11. List four kinds of information we receive from our skin.

12. Name the sensory system that results in dizziness. How does it work?

13. What sources of sensory information would a person use when dancing?

14. Gestalt psychologists have identified several principles that we use in organizing our perceptions. What are some of these principles?

15. If you took two books of the same size and placed one at the far end of the room and the other on a table in front of you, you would conclude that they are the same size, even though the farther one creates a much smaller image on your retina. Why do you perceive them as the same size?

16. How do psychologists react to the available evidence for the existence of ESP?

CRITICAL THINKING

1. **Analyze.** To appreciate the importance of visual sensations in your daily life, try doing some of your daily activities while blindfolded. You

129

ANSWERS

Concepts and Vocabulary

1. A stimulus is any aspect of, or change in, the environment to which an organism responds.

2. The field is psychophysics. A sample experiment might be a test for the absolute threshold of light.

3. An absolute threshold is the smallest amount of energy that will produce a sensation. The difference threshold is the smallest change in a stimulus that will produce a change in sensation.

4. Most psychologists believe that subliminal advertising has little or no effect on the unconscious mind.

5. Weber's law suggests that the larger or stronger a stimulus, the larger the change required for an observer to notice that anything has happened to it. In other words, in a larger arena, it would take a larger change, such as 100 light bulbs burning out, for the observer to notice it.

6. Explanations include: irritation of the stump, abnormal sympathetic limb pain, nervous system activity, or an emotional disturbance.

7. Vision has received the most research because of the importance that humans place on sight.

8. Color deficiency is believed to result from a hereditary defect in the cones of the eye.

9. Depth results from information provided by retinal

disparity. Distance results from motion parallax. Direction results from selective listening in one ear.

10. The receptors from sense and taste are sensitive to chemical molecules rather than to light energy or sound waves.

11. Information includes: pressure, warmth, cold, and pain.

12. The vestibular system results in dizziness. When people turn their heads, the liquid in three semicircular canals moves, bending the endings of receptor hair cells. These cells connect with the vestibular nerve, which joins the auditory nerve with the brain. Overstimulation of the vestibular sense causes dizziness.

13. When dancing, a person is likely to use kinesthesis, the sense of movement, and body posture. A dance would also use hearing to match movement to rhythm.

14. Principles include: proximity, similarity, continuity, and closure.

15. The books would be perceived as the same size because of the idea of constancy. We have learned to perceive certain objects in the environment as the same size, regardless of the environmental circumstances.

16. Many question ESP because of the inability to replicate experimental results and the difficulty in verifying ESP events.

Critical Thinking

1. Students may report that their other senses seem more intense. This is in part because students are relying on these senses to a greater degree than when vision was present. In citing cues, students may mention visual maps stored in memory or use of the sense of touch to feel where things were located.

2. Students might mention the lack of choice in subliminal advertising. Unlike other forms of advertising, people aren't aware of the messages, so they can't switch them off.

3. Some students may report feeling pressure or seeing colors. They may suggest a sense of vision from light energy left in the eye. They may also speculate that pressure causes the rods to send impulses to the brain.

4. Students should describe the experiment and report their discoveries. One experiment is to turn the textbook upside down and read it that way. Continue reading until it gets easier. Then turn the book right

will need the help of a friend who can serve as your watchdog to prevent injury. While you are blindfolded, notice your sensations of taste, sound, and touch. How is your use of these sensations different from what it normally is? What cues do you use to guide your walking? How do you rely on your past experiences to help you "see" while blindfolded?

2. Evaluate. One of the objections to the use of subliminal advertising techniques is that they could be used to manipulate or influence large numbers of people without their knowing it. Evaluate whether you think this is an important objection. Use a description of a research design of your own or the data from another experiment to defend your opinion about the use of subliminal advertising techniques.

3. Apply. Close your eyes and gently press on one of your eyeballs at the outer edge. What sensation do you experience? Do you "see" anything? How can you explain the visual experience in the absence of light rays?

4. Synthesize. Sensory adaptation refers to the ability of the senses to adjust themselves to a constant level of stimulation. A sense gets used to a new level and responds only to changes from it. Create a simple experiment to test for sensory adaptation.

APPLYING KNOWLEDGE

1. Have a friend stand with his or her back to you. Touch various parts of the friend's back with one pencil or with two pencils held together. Each time you touch the back, ask how many points he or she felt. Now touch the points to the friend's hand or arm, again asking how many points he or she feels. What are the results? What accounts for the results?

2. To demonstrate the information shown in Figure 5.9, prepare solutions of salt water (salty), lemon juice (sour), baking soda (bitter), and sugarwater (sweet). Using a different cotton

swab for each solution, dab each on various points on your tongue, and see if you can verify which area of the tongue is predominately sensitive to each of these major tastes.

3. Perform the following experiment to test one kind of sensory adaptation. Write a sentence while looking at your writing in a mirror. Do this until it begins to feel natural. Then write the sentence normally. Does normal writing now feel strange?

4. Try the following experiment to demonstrate an illusion of the sense of touch. Stretch a one-square-foot piece of chicken wire tautly over a frame. Blindfold your subject and ask him or her to hold the thumb and forefinger of his or her hand to lightly touch each side of the chicken wire. Slide the wire rapidly back and forth between his or her fingers. Ask your subject to report the sensation he or she feels. Most people report feeling a continuous slippery or oily surface. This illusion will probably be stronger if the subject does not know in advance the actual nature of the material he or she is feeling.

5. Station yourself behind a window or glass door (to eliminate sounds and smells that you might give off) and stare intently at someone who has his or her back toward you. Pick someone who is within a ten-yard range and who is not engaged in any particular activity at the moment. Does the person turn around and look at you? If so, how long does it take him or her to "sense" your presence? In what ways can you explain this phenomenon?

6. Hold a pencil about 12 inches in front of your face. Look at it with your left eye closed, then with your right eye closed. Notice how the pencil seems to jump around. What happens when you look at the pencil with both eyes? What principle does this experiment demonstrate?

7. Fill three bowls with water—warm tap water in one, cool in another, and lukewarm in the third. Put one hand in the cool water and the other in the warm water. Leave them there for 30

side up and read. Reading the normal way will probably feel strange at first. This illustrates how our senses adapt to new conditions and must readapt to old conditions.

Applying Knowledge

1. Answers will vary. But most students will have less feeling in their back because of the lack of receptors (when compared with the hand).

2. For most students, areas will roughly correspond to those shown in the figure.

3. Answers will vary, but should deal with sensory adaptation.

4. After students have felt the wire blindfolded, have them touch it while using their sense of vision. Do they experience any differences in touch? If so, have students suggest reasons for variations in sensation.

seconds. Now put both hands in the lukewarm water at the same time. What do you feel? How does this demonstrate the principle of sensory adaptation?

8. Get a fresh potato and peel it. Do the same with an apple. Now have a friend close his eyes and smell a fresh onion while he takes a bite of each one. Can he tell which food is which without his sense of smell? Try this experiment with various people, using different foods that have similar textures.

9. To illustrate the importance of two retinal images for depth perception, try out the following demonstration with the help of a friend. You will need to construct a pendulum using a 3- to 4-foot piece of string with a weight attached. Secure your pendulum to the middle of the top part of a door frame. With the door open, set the pendulum in motion swaying back and forth parallel to the door frame. Now have your friend stand in front of the doorway wearing a patch over one eye. Ask your friend to describe the motion of the pendulum. In what direction does it move? Now have your friend switch the patch to the other eye and describe the pendulum movement again. What differences are there in the two descriptions?

10. Put a backpack that has been filled with 10 pounds of materials. Arrange a series of objects that differ in weight from very light (a piece of paper) to medium weight (a paperback book) to heavy (a pound of candy or a 2-pound weight). Have a friend insert these objects into the backpack one at a time, in increasing order of weight. Be sure you cannot see which object is being placed in the pack. After each object is placed in the pack, give a report of the perceived difference in weight. At what point do you notice the difference in the weight of the pack? Explain your experience by referring to the concept of difference thresholds.

ANALYZING VIEWPOINTS

1. If perception is based entirely on signals in the brain that are subject to interpretation, does everyone experience the world differently? Write a one-page paper that argues that everyone experiences the world differently. Then, write an essay that argues that everyone experiences the world in the same way. Use what you have learned from the chapter.

2. Does extrasensory perception exist? Some people believe it does, but the scientific community has strong doubts. Write a one-page paper that presents a case for both sides of this issue. Use what you learned from the chapter.

BEYOND THE CLASSROOM

1. Arrange to watch a movie with your parents or grandparents. As soon as the film is over, ask each person to write a paragraph describing the last scene in the movie. After the paragraphs have been written, read each one aloud. Did everyone have the same perception of the scene, or did some people perceive it differently? If there are differences, ask people to talk about what they perceived. How could you explain these differences?

IN YOUR JOURNAL

1. Reread your journal entry about hearing another conversation in a crowded setting. Is your explanation still valid? If necessary, how would you change it?
2. Think about what it would be like if our senses did not have the limits they do. What visual problems might we have? What would we hear if our sense of hearing had a different range? Write answers to these questions in your journal.

5. Ask students if they have heard the expression "you must have eyes in the back of your head." How do results from this activity yield insight into the origins of this saying?

6. If students have trouble assessing this activity, refer them to the material on *binocular vision*.

7. The hand that was in warm water will feel cool; the hand that was in cold water will feel warm. The experiment shows how the receptors in each hand adapted to differences in water temperatures.

8. Most people will have trouble identifying the taste of food if they are smelling a stronger odor.

9. If students have trouble assessing this activity, refer them to the discussion of *relative motion*.

10. If students have trouble assessing this activity, refer them to *Weber's law*.

CHAPTER BONUS
Test Question

This question may be used for extra credit on the chapter test.
Choose the letter of the correct response.

Visual illusions are most likely caused by:
a. architectural mistakes.
b. distortions of memory.
c. retinal image distortions.
d. errors in interpretation of sensations.

Answer: **d**

Analyzing Viewpoints

1. As an alternative approach, assign each student to defend one of the positions cited. Then have students exchange essays to assess each other's arguments.

2. Follow the same basic procedure as above.

Beyond the Classroom

1. Lead students to understand how this experiment illustrates the principle of selective attention.

IN YOUR JOURNAL

If time permits, discuss journal entries individually with students.

CHAPTER 6

Motivation and Emotion

TEXT TOPICS	SPECIAL FEATURES	RESOURCE MATERIALS
Biological Motives, pp. 133–139	**Psychology Update,** p. 134 **At a Glance:** Losing Weight, p. 137	▬ Reproducible Lesson Plan; Study Guide; Review Activity *Readings in Psychology:* Section 2, Reading 5 Transparency 12
Social Motives, pp. 139–144	**At a Glance:** Is It Learned? Is It Physiological? p. 139	▬ Reproducible Lesson Plan; Study Guide; Review Activity Transparency 13
Emotion, pp. 144–153	**Fact or Fiction?,** p. 145 **Using Psychology:** Lie Detection, pp. 149–151 **More About Psychology,** p. 150	▬ Reproducible Lesson Plan; Study Guide; Review Activity; Extension Activity; Chapter Test, Form A and Form B *Readings in Psychology:* Section 2, Reading 6 Transparency 14 Understanding Psychology Testmaker

PERFORMANCE ASSESSMENT ACTIVITY

Assign students to find photographs in magazines and newspapers that depict various emotional states (such as joy or sadness) or the result of some motivation (such as the desire to earn money). Combine students' photographs into one classroom display. Have students create titles and captions that describe the emotions and motivations expressed in the pictures. Ask students to work in small groups to write a one-paragraph introduction to the display, in which they explain what the relation is between human emotions and motivations. *(The paragraphs should take into consideration one or more of the theories discussed in this chapter.)*

CHAPTER RESOURCES

Readings for the Student

Chernin, K. *The Obsession: Reflections on the Tyranny of Slenderness.* New York: Harper & Row, 1981.

Maslow, A. H. *The Farther Reaches of Human Nature.* New York: Viking Press, 1971.

McClelland, David. *The Achieving Society.* New York: Von Nostrand Reinhold, 1961.

Readings for the Teacher

Izard, C. E., Kagan, J., and Zajonc, R. B. *Emotions, Cognition, and Behavior.* New York: Cambridge University Press, 1984.

Scheier, M. F., and Carver, C. S. "Optimism, Coping, and Health." *Health Psychology,* 4 (1985); 219–247.

Scherer, K. R., and Ekman, P. *Approaches to Emotion.* Hillsdale, NJ: Lawrence Erlbaum, 1984.

Multimedia

Emotions and Mental Health (45 minutes, 1/2" video). Human Relations Media Video. Case studies used in this video show healthy and unhealthy handling of emotions. The major theories of emotion are presented with reference to James, Cannon, and Freud.

The Need to Achieve—Motivation and Personality. (29 minutes). Focus on Behavior Series, Indiana University. In this video David McClelland explains his psychological theory—that the economic growth or decline of nations is dependent to a large extent on the entrepreneurs of those nations. He seeks to substantiate his theory through motivational tests.

For additional resources, see the bibliography beginning on page 530.

FOCUS

Motivating Activity

Ask students to brainstorm reasons people might marry. *(The list might include such factors as love, desire for long-term companionship, feeling of security, family pressure, sex.)* Then ask students to categorize the motives as either biological or social. Which factors might be described as purely emotional? Tell students that they will learn more about people's motivations and emotions in this chapter.

Meeting Chapter Objectives

Point out the six objectives on page 133, and have students identify the pages in the text that correspond to each one. Then assign groups of students to carry out the direction(s) in each objective as they read Chapter 6.

Building Vocabulary.

Have students preview the list of key terms and offer definitions for any expressions they feel they already know, such as *motivation*. Next, ask them to guess what they think the distinction is between *fundamental* and *psychological needs*. After each guess, have students look up the terms in the Glossary. How close did they come to the real meanings?

Motivation and Emotion

FIGURE 6.1   Motivation—why we do things—cannot be observed directly; it can only be inferred from goal-directed behavior.

132

TEACHER CLASSROOM RESOURCES

- Chapter 6 Reproducible Lesson Plan
- Chapter 6 Study Guide
- Chapter 6 Review Activity
- Chapter 6 Application Activity
- Chapter 6 Extension Activity

 Transparencies 12, 13, 14
Transparency Strategies and Activities

- *Readings in Psychology:* Section 2, Readings 5, 6

- Chapter 6 Test, Form A and Form B

- Understanding Psychology Testmaker

OBJECTIVES

After studying this chapter, you should be able to

■ give reasons for the physiological basis of motivation.

■ discuss drive reduction theory and the critiques of drive reduction theory.

■ summarize the study of social motives.

■ explain Maslow's hierarchy of needs.

■ give examples of the physiological theories of emotion.

■ give reasons for the cognitive theorists' approach to the study of emotions.

KEY TERMS

Cannon-Bard theory
drive reduction theory
fundamental needs
homeostasis
innate
James-Lange theory
lateral hypothalamus (LH)
motivation
polygraph
psychological needs
self-actualization needs
ventromedial
   hypothalamus (VMH)

W hy do people climb Mount Everest or cross the Atlantic in a balloon? Why do some people spend every waking moment memorizing batting averages while others don't know the difference between the New York Yankees and the Toledo Mud Hens? And, as the song asks, why do fools fall in love?

Although all psychology is concerned with what people do and how they do it, research on motivation and emotion focuses on the underlying why of behavior.

We see Kristin studying all weekend while the rest of us hang out, and since we know she wants to go to law school, we conclude that she is "motivated" by her desire to get good grades. We see Mikko working after classes at a job he doesn't like, and since we know he wants to buy a car, we conclude that he is "motivated" to earn money for the car. Movies from *Silence of the Lambs* to *Unforgiven* have often had motives or emotions as their central theme. On the street, you hear words like "anger," "fear," "pain," "starving," and hundreds of others describing motives and

IN YOUR JOURNAL

Think about the present-day concerns and future aspirations that are most important to you. List 6 to 10 of them in any order in your journal.

Exploring Key Ideas

The Purpose of Emotions.
Ask students to speculate what human society would be like if people had no emotions—if they never expressed love, anger, disgust, envy, happiness, fear, or sadness. Would people in such a world be motivated to do anything, such as raise a family, participate in government, or create a work of art? Would such a world be free of crime and war? Have students list as many reasons as they can that people have emotions.

IN YOUR JOURNAL

Help students get started by suggesting they list not only concrete concerns (such as "I'd like to have my own car") but also more abstract concerns (such as "I'd like to be admired for my accomplishments as an athlete").

EXTRA CREDIT ACTIVITY

Point out to students that in late medieval times morality plays became a popular form of drama. In these plays the characters portrayed various virtues and vices battling for possession of a person's soul. Ask students to write a skit or one-act "emotion play" in which a central character's emotions come to life and interact in some sort of dramatic or comic situation. If time permits, arrange to have the plays staged for the class.

133

TEACH

Guided Practice

■ **Discussion.** Point out that much human behavior is obviously not related to primary reinforcers, such as thirst, hunger, and sex. Ask students why they think, for example, that a miser continues to hoard money even when there is no need to do so. Ask students to think of examples of their own behavior that could be considered independent of the rewards that originally gave rise to those behaviors. Have them speculate on motivations for those behaviors. (OBJECTIVE 1)

■ **Critical Thinking Activity.** After students have read the special feature, ask them to define, in their own words, the terms *anorexia nervosa* and *bulimia*. What does the fact that these conditions affect mainly young women suggest about their cause? *(that the cause may be genetic, hormonal, or the result of conditioning)* You might assign students to research these eating disorders thoroughly and prepare oral reports for the class. (Suggest that students include sources of help for these disorders.) (OBJECTIVE 1)

PSYCHOLOGY UPDATE

Anorexia Nervosa and Bulimia. Anorexia nervosa and bulimia are serious eating disorders. Both syndromes are found mostly in young females. They rarely occur in males.

A person suffering from anorexia nervosa stops eating to the point of starvation. The disorder is typically associated with extreme dieting. Symptoms of anorexia include body weight at least 15 percent below normal, an extreme fear of gaining weight, and a misperception that one's body is too heavy or out of shape. Psychologists estimate that 1 out of 250 women between 12 and 18 years of age are anorexic, and the number is increasing (Mitchell & Eckert, 1987).

Bulimia is a more common eating disorder. It is characterized by alternating periods of uncontrolled eating followed by purging—self-induced vomiting, taking of laxatives, or fasting. This is why bulimia is also referred to as binge-purge syndrome. Contrary to what you might expect, it is the extended periods of hunger caused by purging that leads to eating binges, not the other way around (Polivy & Herman, 1987). Bulimia can result in ulcers, tooth decay, and electrolyte imbalance, which may cause heart problems.

emotions. Conceptions of motivation in psychology are in many ways similar to those expressed in everyday language. Since motivation cannot be observed directly, psychologists, like the rest of us, infer motivation from goal-directed behavior.

BIOLOGICAL MOTIVES

Some behavior is determined by the physiological state of the organism. Like other animals, human beings have certain survival needs. The nervous system is constructed in such a way that dramatic variations in blood sugar, water, oxygen, salt, or essential vitamins lead to changes in behavior designed to return the body to a condition of chemical balance. The first part of this section discusses the role of such physiological factors in motivating behavior.

But many human motives, such as Kristin's desire to get into law school or Mikko's desire to buy a car, do not have a simple physiological basis. Although not all psychologists would be able to agree on an explanation of these behaviors, none would say that they were the result of physiological deficits. The rest of this section discusses some approaches to analyzing the motivational basis of these kinds of human activities.

The Biology of Motivation

All organisms, including humans, have built-in regulating systems that work like thermostats to maintain such internal processes as body temperature, the level of sugar in the blood, and the production of hormones. As we saw in Chapter 4, when the level of thyroxin in the bloodstream is low, the pituitary gland secretes a thyroxin-stimulating hormone. When the thyroxin level is high, the pituitary gland stops producing this hormone. Similarly, when your body temperature drops below a certain point, you start to shiver, your blood vessels constrict, and you put on more clothes. All these activities reduce heat loss and bring body temperature back to the correct level. If your body heat rises above a certain point, you start to sweat, your blood vessels dilate, and you remove clothes. These processes cool you.

The tendency of all organisms to correct imbalances and deviations from their normal state is known as **homeostasis.** Several of the drives that motivate behavior are homeostatic—hunger, for example.

Hunger. What motivates you to seek food? Often you eat because the sight and smell of, say, pizza tempts you into a store. Other times you eat out of habit because you always have lunch at 12:30 or to be sociable because a friend invites you out for a snack. But suppose you are working frantically to finish a term paper. You don't have any food, so you ignore the fact that it is dinner time and you keep working. But at some point your

CRITICAL THINKING ACTIVITY

Identifying Central Issues. As students read the chapter, ask them to relate Maslow's hierarchy to the ideas used in recovery programs and by self-help proponents. Which level of needs are they addressing? How will this help people recover and go on to meet the next set of needs?

body will start to demand food. You'll feel an aching sensation in your stomach. What produces this sensation? What makes you feel hungry?

Your body requires food to grow, to repair itself, and to store reserves. To what is it responding? If the portion of the hypothalamus called the **lateral hypothalamus (LH)** is stimulated with electrodes, a laboratory animal will begin eating, even if it has just finished a large meal. Conversely, if the LH is removed surgically, an animal will stop eating and eventually die of starvation if it is not fed artificially. Thus the LH provides the "go" signals: it tells you to eat.

If a different portion of the hypothalamus called the **ventromedial hypothalamus (VMH)** is stimulated, an animal will slow down or stop eating altogether, even if it has been kept from food for a long period. However, if the VMH is removed, the animal will eat everything in sight until it becomes so obese it can hardly move. This indicates that the VMH provides the "stop" signals: it tells you when you have had enough food.

Some research suggests that the impact of the LH and VMH on eating may be indirect at best (Logue, 1986). All that may happen is that LH firing increases your general drive level. If food is available, you eat. In addition, the hypothalamus responds to temperature. The LH, or "go" signal, is more active in cold temperatures; the VMH, or "stop" signal, more active in warm temperatures (presumably because people and other animals need to eat more in cold weather).

Other factors also influence your hunger. The *glucostatic theory* suggests that the hypothalamus monitors the amount of glucose, or ready energy, available in the blood. As the blood glucose entering cells drops, the LH fires to stimulate you to start eating. At the same time, the pancreas releases *insulin* to convert the incoming calories into energy—whether to be consumed by active cells or converted to stored energy in the form of fat for use later (Woods, 1991). After your meal—as your blood glucose drops—the pancreas secretes *glucagon*, which helps convert the stored energy back into useful energy. Some believe that glucostatic receptors in the liver play a role in stimulating the LH.

Another factor affecting eating is the *set-point*—the weight around which your day-to-day weight tends to fluctuate. Although your daily calorie intake and expenditure of energy varies, your body maintains a very stable weight over the long run. For many, the classic binge meal is Thanksgiving dinner. Many of us experience a lesser appetite for several days after that meal. Some evidence suggests that the VMH plays a role in the level at which your set-point is maintained, because rats whose VMH has been destroyed do not eat so much that they explode. Certainly, they increase to 4 or 5 times their normal weight, but they do not continue to add weight beyond that point.

In summary, the hypothalamus "interprets" at least three kinds of information: the amount of glucose entering the cells of your body, your set-point, and your body temperature. These determine whether the hypothalamus will contribute to causing you to eat or not.

Obesity. Stanley Schachter (1971) and his colleagues at Columbia University conducted a number of ingenious studies which show that obese

Teacher Note. As students have already seen, the names for many body parts and conditions are derived from Latin and Greek. You might point out, for example, a condition known as *aphagia* results when the lateral hypothalamus is damaged. *Aphagia* in Greek simply means "not eating." *Hyperphagia*—literally, "overeating" in Greek—results when the ventromedial hypothalamus is damaged.

■ **Discussion.** Have volunteers describe the food choices they make when they are angry, sad, or frustrated. Ask them if their choices are different when they are happy or excited. If so, ask them to describe how they are different and to explain in terms of the theories discussed on this page why they think this change occurs. (OBJECTIVE 1)

▊ **Readings in Psychology.** Have students read the Section 2, Reading 5 selection in *Readings in Psychology* and answer the questions that follow the reading.

CRITICAL THINKING ACTIVITY

Demonstrating Reasoned Judgment. Point out that homeostatic drives are ones that are controlled primarily by physiological processes over which an individual has no conscious control, such as the drive to quench a thirst. Nonhomeostatic drives, such as sexual behavior, fear, and aggression, are greatly influenced by social and psychological factors. To some extent, they can be consciously controlled. Ask students to give several examples of such nonhomeostatic behavior. *(A soldier's bravery despite the terror of battle is one example of such conscious control.)*

■ **Discussion.** Ask students to recall messages they received as they were growing up concerning eating. Examples might include giving candy or other sweets as a reward, forcing vegetables on children as punishment, requiring that children eat everything on their plates before leaving the table, or disciplining children by sending them to bed hungry. Have students discuss the impact these early experiences might have on present food choices and behaviors. (OBJECTIVE 1)

Obese people eat not because they are hungry, but because they see something tempting or their watches say it's time.

people respond to external cues—they eat not because they are hungry, but because they see something good to eat or their watches tell them it's time.

To prove this, Schachter first set up a staged taste test in which people were asked to rate five kinds of crackers. The goal was to see how many crackers normal-weight and overweight people would eat. Each person, instructed to skip lunch, arrived hungry. Some were told that the taste test required a full stomach; they were given as many roast beef sandwiches as they wanted. The rest stayed hungry. Schachter predicted that normal-weight people eat because they're hungry, while obese people eat whether they are hungry or not. This was true. People of normal weight ate more crackers than overweight people did when both groups were hungry, and fewer crackers after they had eaten the roast beef.

In another study, Schachter put out a bowl of almonds that people could eat while they sat in a waiting room. Overweight people ate the nuts only when they didn't have to take the shells off. Thus, again, they ate simply because the food was there. People of normal weight were equally likely to try a few nuts whether they were shelled or not.

In summary, Schachter argues that overweight people respond to external cues (for example, the smell of cookies hot from the oven) while normal-weight people respond to internal cues, such as the stomach contractions of hunger. His work shows that, for people, even physiological needs like hunger are influenced by complex factors.

Other factors are also important. Anxiety and depression are not a cause of overeating. These conditions occur just as frequently among people of normal weight as among those who are overweight (Wadden & Stunkard, 1987). Exercise leads to weight loss unless you start eating more as your exercise increases. Obviously then, another cause of weight gain is too little exercise in proportion to the amount of food you eat.

Drive Reduction Theory

Drive reduction theory emerged from the work of experimental psychologist Clark Hull (1943) who traced motivation back to basic physiological needs. According to Hull, when an organism is deprived of something it needs or wants (such as food, water, or sex) it becomes tense and agitated. To relieve this tension, it engages in more or less random activity. Thus biological needs *drive* an organism to act.

If a behavior reduces the drive, the organism will begin to acquire a habit; that is, when the drive is again felt, the organism will first try the same response again. Habits channel drives in certain directions. In short, **drive reduction theory** states that physiological needs drive an organism to act in either random or habitual ways until its needs are satisfied.

Hull and his colleagues suggested that all human motives—from the desire to acquire property to striving for excellence and seeking affection or amusement—are extensions of basic biological needs. For example, people develop the need for social approval because as infants they were fed and cared for by a smiling mother or father. Gradually, through conditioning and generalization, the need for approval becomes important in itself. So, according to Hull, approval becomes a learned drive. The results of subse-

ADDITIONAL INFORMATION

You might find it helpful to present the following information relating to eating: A dog was operated on to divert its esophagus through a U-shaped tube attached to its neck. With the tube in place, the dog could eat normally. Removing the tube and attaching a receptacle would allow the dog to salivate, chew, and swallow, but the food simply dumped into the receptacle. And what happened? The dog would eat about what it would normally eat and then stop. About 30 minutes later it would do the same thing. If the pre-chewed food was loaded into the dog's stomach, *(continued on page 137)*

At A Glance

LOSING WEIGHT

If you want to lose weight, begin by keeping detailed records of everything you eat for a week or two. Get a good book on nutrition and analyze your eating habits, particularly the number of fat grams you consume on an average day.

Once you figure out what you are eating and what you should be eating, all that's left is the hard part—doing something about it. Set up a system of rewards for sticking to your diet and punishments for sneaking off for hot fudge sundaes. Continue to monitor what and when you eat and chart your progress. Have someone lose weight with you. Have someone compliment and reward you when you do well, and remind you when you need to do something—but not punish you.

For more details, see D.L. Watson & R.G. Tharp, *Self-Directed Behavior: Self-Modification for Personal Adjustment,* 6th ed. Pacific Grove, CA: Brooks/Cole Publishing Company, 1993.

quent experiments suggested, however, that Hull and his colleagues had overlooked some of the more important factors in human—and animal—motivation. According to drive reduction theory, infants become attached to their mothers because mothers usually relieve such drives as hunger and thirst. Harry Harlow (among others) doubted that this was the only or even

FIGURE 6.2

What motivates a hard-driven executive? Researchers suggest a variety of factors may be involved, including the desire to lead others, to earn more money, and to gain recognition and praise. **What is drive reduction theory?**

At A Glance

Invite dieticians or spokespersons from the American Heart Association or the American Cancer Society to talk to the class about eating for good health. Ask speakers to discuss nutrients in food, the relationship between diet and health, and guidelines for healthful eating.

WORKING WITH TRANSPARENCIES

Project Transparency 12 and use the guidelines given on Teaching Strategies and Activities. Assign Student Worksheet 12.

After students have answered the question in the caption, ask them to explain how drive reduction theory might apply to the hard-driven executive. *(According to the theory, the need for social approval drives the executive to strive for success.)* Point out that one of the arguments against drive reduction theory is intrinsic motivation, which theorizes that humans and other animals have an innate need to deal effectively with their environment and to master new challenges.
Answer to caption, Figure 6.2: the hypothesis that physiological needs drive an organism to act in ways, either random or habitual, until its needs are satisfied

ADDITIONAL INFORMATION

it would eat about half of a normal meal. And the conclusion? It seems that our experience in how much we normally eat combines with our assessment as to how hard our jaw has worked to get us to stop eating in the short term. Long-term, the readjustment of our internal body chemistry prevents us from going back to eat. If we eat as little as 5 percent too much, we will gain 15 pounds in a year; if we eat 5 percent too little, eventually we will die (Jequier, 1987). The body maintains a very delicate balance to remain healthy.

In discussing the arguments against drive reduction theory, ask students to give examples of inherently pleasurable experiences that do not seem to reduce biological drives (*e.g., pausing to watch a beautiful sunset*). **Answer to caption, Figure 6.3:** It indicated that the inherently pleasurable feeling of hugging something soft, especially in times of stress, took precedence over the biological drive to reduce hunger. **Answer to caption, Figure 6.4:** They propose no general theory of motivation of the type Hull suggested, but a hybrid in which innate physiological drives vie with many others, such as curiosity and the desire for contact with soft things.

FIGURE 6.3

The monkeys in Harlow's study spent most of their time with the terrycloth mother even though they fed from the wire mother. The terrycloth mother was also a security base when they were frightened. **What did this experiment indicate?**

FIGURE 6.4

This monkey worked for the privilege of watching an electric train, but it would be difficult to say what drive is reduced as a result. **What do some psychologists propose as replacements for drive reduction theory?**

the main source of an infant's love for its mother. Harlow took infant monkeys away from their mothers and put them alone in cages with two surrogate "mothers" made of wire (Figure 6.3). One of the wire mothers was equipped with a bottle. If drive reduction theory were correct, the monkeys would become attached to this figure, because it was their only source of food. The other wire mother was covered with soft cloth but could not provide food and relief from hunger. In test after test, the small monkeys preferred to cling to the cloth mother, particularly when strange, frightening objects were put into their cages (Harlow and Zimmerman, 1959).

Some drive theorists overlooked the fact that some experiences (such as hugging something or someone soft) are inherently pleasurable. Although they do not seem to reduce biological drives, these experiences serve as incentives or goals for behavior. Another factor that drive theorists overlooked was the pleasure humans and related animals derive from stimulation or arousal (Figure 6.4). Just think about how dogs love to be petted or how children love rides at amusement parks that are designed to terrify them. In the end, then, a drive *for* stimulation looked as plausible as a drive to *reduce* stimulation.

Adults do not solve crossword puzzles or engage in competitive sports to reduce a drive during competition, nor do children play to reduce a drive. James Olds (1960) discovered a pleasure center in the hypothalamus. He showed that rats would bar-press in a Skinner Box until they dropped from exhaustion to gain a brief stimulation from an implanted electrode—rather than partake in available food, water, sex, or rest. Finally, humans learn through observation with no identifiable reward. All of these findings, combined with Harlow's work, led many psychologists to conclude that there

Assign the class to create a primer for children learning the alphabet. Tell the students to illustrate the primer with pictures of pleasurable experiences that do not apparently reduce biological drives. For example, the letter C might be represented by the word *cuddling* and show a child cuddling with a parent or teddy bear. Remind students that topics and pictures should be suitable for small children. Display the 26 pages in class when they are finished and afterwards have them bound in book form.

At A Glance

IS IT LEARNED? IS IT PHYSIOLOGICAL?

Which of your motives is the most purely physiological or inherited? You might say hunger or thirst. Both are inherited, present at birth, and appear without any evidence of a need to practice how to respond to them. Physiological motives are inherited needs satisfied only by specific goals—food for hunger and water for thirst. Yet, we quickly develop "tastes" for certain foods and dislikes for others. So, what is the role of learning and the environment in our motives?

Consider arranging your motives on a continuum from those most purely inherited to those most purely learned. Hunger and thirst would be at one end, and certainly motives like achievement and social approval would fall at the other end. But what of a motive like avoiding pain?

Pain avoidance seems inborn, yet Melzack and Wall (1965) raised Scottish terriers in gentle, padded isolation so that they had no experience with pain. The result was dogs that would burn their noses not once but repeatedly, putting out a match struck in front of them. Pain has two components—information that is supplied by an inherited nervous system and emotion that is supplied by experience. Both are important to a full understanding of pain.

In the middle of the continuum, then, we could list such motives as pain avoidance, sex, and the need for stimulation. Here, physiology clearly plays a role, yet learning is crucial to our effective response to such "mixed" motives. Finally, motives such as achievement and social approval certainly are most subject to the ultimate effects of experience. For these learned or social motives, the satisfying goals are much more diverse. A sense of achievement can be gained from writing a paper, solving a problem, or driving home safely.

could be no general theory of motivation of the type Hull suggested. Instead of a drive reduction theory, we are left with a list of unlearned, innate drives that include hunger and thirst, but also curiosity, contact with soft things, and many others.

SOCIAL MOTIVES

Many psychologists have concentrated their research on social motives rather than on the unlearned, biological motives we have been discussing. Social motives are learned from our interactions with other people.

FIGURE 6.5

In his formulation of a theory of human personality, Henry Murray distinguished between a class of primarily physical needs and a much larger class of psychological needs (see list below). **How do we learn social motives?**

Acquisition
(to gain possessions and property)
Conservance
(to collect, repair, clean, and preserve things)
Order
(to arrange, organize, put away objects)
Construction
(to organize and build)
Achievement
(to overcome obstacles, to exercise power, to strive to do something difficult as well and as quickly as possible)
Recognition
(to excite praise and commendation)
Defendance
(to defend oneself against blame or belittlement)
Dominance
(to influence or control others)
Autonomy
(to resist influence or coercion)
Aggression
(to assault or injure)
Affiliation
(to form friendships and associations)
Rejection
(to snub, ignore, or exclude)
Nurturance
(to nourish, aid, or protect)
Succorance
(to seek aid, protection, or sympathy)
Play
(to relax, amuse oneself, seek diversion and entertainment)
Cognizance
(to explore)

At A Glance

After students have read the special feature, have them brainstorm a list of all the motives that propel them through a typical day. Next, have students work individually to arrange all the motives on a continuum from those most purely inherited (such as hunger) to those most purely learned (such as desire for achievement). Finally, have the students compare their continua. Are they in general agreement about the nature of their motives? Discuss any major discrepancies. (OBJECTIVE 2)

VISUAL INSTRUCTION

Have students think of specific, everyday activities that might fulfill each of the psychological needs in Murray's list shown in Figure 6.5. For example, planting a flower garden might fall under the category of Construction. **Answer to caption, Figure 6.5:** from our interactions with other people

---

STUDY AND WRITING SKILLS

Among the other psychological needs formulated by Henry Murray are Retention, Superiority, Exhibition, Inviolacy, Avoidance of Inferiority, Counteraction, Deference, Contrariness, Abasement, Avoidance of Blame, and Exposition. Have students find definitions of these terms in a psychology text or reference book. As a follow-up to your discussion of Figure 6.5, assign students to work individually or in teams to create an alphabetical glossary of all of Murray's categories, giving definitions and specific examples for each term.

CHAPTER 6 Lesson Plan

In Chapter 11 we will discuss the theories of several psychologists who sought to explain the development of personality. One such psychologist was Henry Murray, whose theory of personality identifies 16 basic needs (see Figure 6.5). Note that most of these are social motives rather than biological needs (see Murray *et al.*, 1934). Hundreds of studies have been performed on just one of these needs, the need for achievement.

Measuring the Need for Achievement

One reason the achievement motive has been so well researched is that David McClelland became interested in finding some quantitative way of measuring social motives (McClelland *et al.*, 1953). His main tool for measuring achievement motivation was the Thematic Apperception Test

FIGURE 6.6

This is a picture of the sort that might be used in the measurement of the need for achievement. Examples of stories that would be scored from fairly high to low are given below. The portions of the stories printed in italics are the kinds of themes considered to reflect the need for achievement.

This guy is just getting off work. These are all working guys and they don't like their work too much either. The younger guy over on the right knows the guy with the jacket.

Something bad happened today at work—*a nasty accident that shouldn't have happened.* These two guys don't trust each other *but they are going to talk* about it. *They mean to put things to rights. No one else much cares,* it seems.

The guy with the jacket is *worried.* He feels that *something has to be done. He wouldn't ordinarily talk* to the younger man *but now he feels he must.* The young guy is ready. He's *concerned* too but doesn't know what to expect.

They'll both realize after talking that you never know where your friends are. *They'll both feel better* afterward because they'll feel they have someone they can rely on next time there's trouble.

Harry O'Silverfish has been working on the Ford assembly line for thirteen years. Every morning he gets up, eats a doughnut and cup of coffee, takes his lunch pail, gets in the car, and drives to the plant. It is during this morning drive that his mind gets filled with *fantasies of what he'd like to be doing* with his life. Then, about the same time that he parks his car and turns off his ignition, he also *turns off his mind*—and it remains turned off during the whole working day. In the evenings, he is *too tired and discouraged to do much more* than drink a few beers and watch TV.

But this morning Harry's mind didn't turn off with the car. He had witnessed a car accident on the road—in which two people were killed—soon after leaving home. Just as he reaches the plant gate, Harry suddenly turns. Surprised, he discovers that he has made a *firm decision* never to enter that plant again. He knows that *he must try another way* to live before he dies.

These are hard-hats. It's the end of the shift. There is a demonstration outside the plant and the men coming out are looking at it. Everyone is just walking by. They are not much interested. One person is *angry* and *wants to go on strike*, but this does not make sense to anyone else. He is out of place. Actually he is not really angry, he is just bored. He looks as though he might do a little dance to amuse himself, which is more than the rest of them do. *Nothing will happen* at this time *till more people join* this one man in his needs.

PSYCHOLOGISTS AT WORK

Edwin Garrigues Boring once described all psychologists as falling into two groups: biotropes and sociotropes—that is, those leaning toward biology and those leaning toward sociology. As a branch of psychology, *social psychology* is the study of the behavior of individuals in a social context. Psychologists involved in this subdiscipline conduct research on such topics as worker performance, group dynamics, and group decision processes.

(TAT). This test consists of a series of pictures. Subjects are told to make up a story that explains each picture. Tests of this sort are called projective tests, and we will describe them in detail in Chapter 12. At this point, it is only important to know that there are no right or wrong answers. Since the test questions are ambiguous, the answers must be created from the test-taker's own beliefs, motives, and attitudes. Each story is "coded" by looking for certain kinds of themes and scoring these themes according to their relevance to various types of needs, such as achievement.

Based on these tests, McClelland developed a scoring system for the TAT. For example, a story would be scored high in achievement imagery if the main character was concerned with standards of excellence and a high level of performance, with unique accomplishments (such as inventions and awards), or with the pursuit of a long-term career or goal. Coding has been refined to the point where trained coders agree about 90 percent of the time. Figure 6.6 shows an example of how need for achievement might be measured.

People who scored high and low in achievement on the TAT were compared in a variety of situations. McClelland followed up the careers of some students at Wesleyan University who had been tested with the TAT in 1947. He wanted to see which students had chosen entrepreneurial work—that is, work in which they had to initiate projects on their own. He found that 11 years after graduation, 83 percent of the entrepreneurs (business managers, insurance salesmen, real estate investors, consultants, and so on) had scored high in achievement, but only 21 percent of the nonentrepreneurs had scored that high (McClelland, 1965).

McClelland does not believe we should all train ourselves as high achievers. In fact, he has said that such persons are not always the most interesting, and they are usually not artistically sensitive (McClelland and Harris, 1971). They would also be less likely to value intimacy in a relationship. Studies have shown that high achievers prefer to be associated with experts who will help them achieve instead of with more friendly people.

Fear of Success. McClelland's work inspired a wide variety of research on other aspects of motivation. Matina Horner (1970, 1972) asked 89 men to write a story beginning with the line, "After first term finals, John finds himself at the top of his medical school class." Substituting the name Anne for John in the opening line, she also asked 90 women to write a story. Ninety percent of the men wrote success stories. However more than 65 percent of the women predicted doom for Anne.

On the basis of this study Horner identified another dimension of achievement motivation, the *motive to avoid success*. Females in our society are (or were) raised with the idea that being successful in all but a few careers is odd and unfeminine. Thus, a woman who is a success in medicine, law, and other traditionally male occupations must be a failure as a woman. It might have been all right for Anne to pass her exams, but the fact that she did better than all the men in her class made the female subjects anxious.

Horner discovered that bright women, who had a very real chance of achieving in their chosen fields, exhibited a stronger fear of success than

■ **Discussion.** Point out that, according to a study by John Atkinson and George Litwin, high achievers will take moderate risks when asked to perform a task that will bring some form of reward or punishment. Subjects with a high fear of failure will either take little risk (ensuring success) or very great risk (making it almost impossible to succeed and thereby lowering their anxiety). Request volunteers to discuss whether the theories have any applicability to their own behaviors. (OBJECTIVE 3)

CRITICAL THINKING ACTIVITY

Demonstrating Reasoned Judgment. Have students discuss how Horner's theory about the fear of success might operate in a school setting. For example, why might a student actually fear getting good grades? *(One possible motive might be fear of being ostracized by peers and being labeled an "egghead." Another might be fear of having to continually live up to the high expectations of teachers.)* Ask students to recommend ways that someone might overcome fear of success.

Teacher Note. In discussing competency theory, you might point out that studies indicate that people who score high in the need for achievement persist longer on difficult tasks—and do better—than most lower-scoring individuals. These individuals are also more likely to set challenging but realistic goals.

■ **Testing a Hypothesis.** Ask students to work in groups to devise experiments like the one described in Figure 6.7. Remind students of the research goal: To test the hypothesis that adding an extrinsic motivation to a task that has been performed perfectly well for its intrinsic motivation may lead to a drop in performance. Have the groups write up descriptions of their experiments before they initiate the actual experiments. Guide the students in adhering to scientific procedures. After the experiments have been conducted, discuss the groups' findings in class.
(OBJECTIVE 3)

did women who were average or slightly above average. Expecting success made them more likely to avoid it, despite the obvious advantages of a rewarding career. This seemed to confirm Horner's belief that success involves deep conflicts for women.

Other researchers then set out to verify Horner's findings. They quickly found that the picture was more complicated than Horner's study suggested. For one thing, it's very hard to define success. Being a mother might be quite satisfying for one woman, but a sign of failure for someone who would have preferred a career outside the home. Also, it is often hard to tell whether a person who doesn't try something is more afraid of success or failure.

In the late 1960s, when Horner's study was conducted, medical school was still dominated by males. Likewise, nursing school was dominated by females. What if females write about males and vice versa? What if females or males write about males' success in a female-dominated occupation? Then we find both men and women write stories reflecting Horner's "fear of success" (Cherry & Deaux, 1978). Later, researchers analyzed 64 studies bearing on the issue that Horner had raised. Measured on a mean rate, 45 percent of the men expressed a fear of success, while 49 percent of the women did—a small difference (Paludi, 1984). So, fear of success is found in both men and women.

Other Theories.   J.W. Atkinson developed an *expectancy-value* theory to explain goal-directed behavior. *Expectancy* is your estimated likelihood of success; *value* is simply what the goal is worth to you.

Others have argued instead for a *competency* theory. Too easy a task means we don't learn anything about how competent we are, any more than we learn from an impossibly difficult task. So, to prove and improve our competency, we choose moderately difficult tasks where both successes and failures may be instructive (Schneider, 1984).

In a ring-toss game, children could choose to stand 1 to 15 feet away from the stake onto which they tried to toss rings as a group watched. Those with a high need for achievement were up to 10 times more likely to choose an intermediate distance from the stakes than to choose ridiculously easy or impossibly difficult distances (McClelland, 1958).

Being a mother might be quite satisfying for one woman, but not for another.

Intrinsic and Extrinsic Motivation.   When you read a mystery, you read it for the pleasure it gives you. The knowledge you gain and fun you have is reward enough for your effort—this is *intrinsic motivation*. If you are paid, however, to read mysteries, you are responding to *extrinsic motivation*—a reward that is external to you. What happens if we add extrinsic motivation to a task you were performing perfectly well for its intrinsic motivation? Sometimes, this leads to a drop in performance (see Figure 6.7).

Luckily, some forms of extrinsic motivation will increase your intrinsic motivation. External rewards such as money or access to power are controlling rewards. By contrast, praise—"You did an excellent job on the essay. Keep up the good work!"—is an informative reward that will often increase our intrinsic motivation (Deci & Ryan, 1987).

COMMUNITY INVOLVEMENT

Assign students to watch children in a playground as they practice trying to master some game or sport, such as shooting baskets or jumping rope. What evidence can they observe to prove the competency theory that people choose moderately difficult tasks in which both successes and failures can be instructive? Students should keep an accurate log of their observations and report their findings and conclusions in either written or oral form.

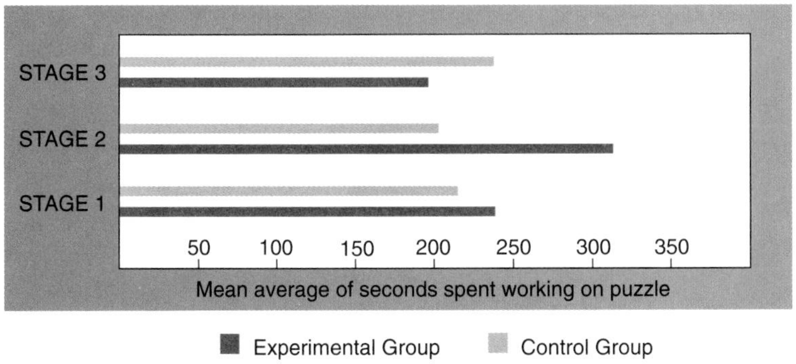

FIGURE 6.7

Mean average of seconds spent working on puzzle

■ Experimental Group ▨ Control Group

In one study, researchers introduced a puzzle to students. In Stage 1, students in both the experimental group and the control group played similar amounts of time with the puzzle. Before Stage 2, researchers informed members of the experimental group that they would be paid $1 for every correct solution. There was no reward for the members of the control group. Then, in Stage 3, neither group was rewarded (from Deci, 1971). **Why did the experimental group spend less time on the puzzle during Stage 3?**

Maslow's Hierarchy of Needs

Abraham Maslow, one of the pioneers of humanistic psychology, believed that *all* human beings need to feel competent, to win approval and recognition, and to sense that they have achieved something. He placed achievement motivation in the context of a hierarchy of needs all people share.

Maslow's scheme, shown in Figure 6.8, incorporates all the factors we have discussed so far in this chapter, and goes a step further. He begins with biological drives, including the need for physical safety and security. In order to live, he asserted people have to satisfy these **fundamental needs.** If people are hungry, most of their activities will be motivated by the drive to acquire food, and their functioning on a higher level will be hindered.

The second level in Maslow's hierarchy consists of **psychological needs:** the need to belong and to give and receive love, and the need to acquire esteem through competence and achievement. Maslow suggests that these needs function in much the same way that biological needs do, and that they can be filled only by an outside source. A lack of love or esteem makes people anxious and tense. There is a driven quality to their behavior. They may engage in random, desperate, and sometimes maladaptive activities to ease their tensions.

Self-actualization needs are at the top of Maslow's hierarchy. These may include the pursuit of knowledge and beauty, or whatever else is required for the realization of one's unique potential. Maslow believed that, although relatively few people reach this level, we all have these needs. To be creative in the way we conduct our lives and use our talents, we must first satisfy our fundamental and psychological needs. The satisfaction of these needs motivates us to seek self-actualization.

Maslow thus added to motivation theory the idea that some needs take precedence over others and the suggestion that achieving one level of satisfaction releases new needs and motivations.

Others' research does not support Maslow's conclusion that one need must be satisfied before another can be (Inglehart & Hildebrandt, 1990). Christopher Columbus, for example, may have achieved self-actualization, but he certainly put his (and many others') need for safety at risk in opting to seek a new route to China on what was, at the time, thought to be a flat earth. Wouldn't we conclude that his need for esteem was dominant in his

VISUAL INSTRUCTION

Point out that according to standard scientific procedures, the control group exists to serve as a standard of comparison for verifying or checking the findings of an experiment.
Answer to caption, Figure 6.7: Answers will vary, but may include: The experimental group clearly has less intrinsic motivation to play with the puzzle after their experience with extrinsic reward in the previous stage.

Teacher Note. Maslow's concept of self-actualization is discussed in more detail in Chapter 11.

■ **Evaluating Conclusions.**
Ask students to consider the validity of the example of Christopher Columbus given at the bottom of this page. What assumption does it make regarding Columbus's attitude toward seafaring and exploration? *(that he believed they were intrinsically dangerous pursuits)* How might the example of Columbus be reinterpreted to prove Maslow's conclusion? *(A biography might reveal that Columbus did not believe he was putting himself and others at extraordinary risk and that he was secure in his need for safety. On his first voyage, Columbus felt secure in his calculations and his well-provisioned ships and sea-tested sailors.)* (OBJECTIVE 4)

CONNECTIONS: PSYCHOLOGY AND SOCIAL STUDIES

Ask students to go to the library and research a political or historical figure of their choosing. The purpose of the research is to identify the motivations behind that individual's success or rise to power or prominence. Ask the students to write a short informative essay explaining the individual's motivations in terms of one or more of the theories of motivation: drive reduction, McClelland's need for achievement, and Maslow's hierarchy.

WORKING WITH TRANSPARENCIES

Project Transparency 13 and use the guidelines provided in Teaching Strategies and Activities. Assign Student Worksheet 13.

VISUAL INSTRUCTION

Point out that Maslow contended that the lower the need in the hierarchy, the more potent it becomes if unfulfilled. A person who is starving, for example, will show little regard for self-esteem. **Answer to caption, Figure 6.8:** fundamental needs

■ **Discussion.** Ask the students to make a list of what they consider most important in their lives—either present-day concerns or future aspirations. When the lists are completed, have the students evaluate the items in terms of Maslow's hierarchy and classify them in terms of fundamental, psychological, and self-actualization needs. Request volunteers to discuss their rationale for classifying individual items. (OBJECTIVE 4)

FIGURE 6.8

According to Maslow, only after satisfying the lower levels of needs is a person free to progress to the ultimate need of self-actualization. Others have argued against this organization. **Into what category in the hierarchy do biological needs fall?**

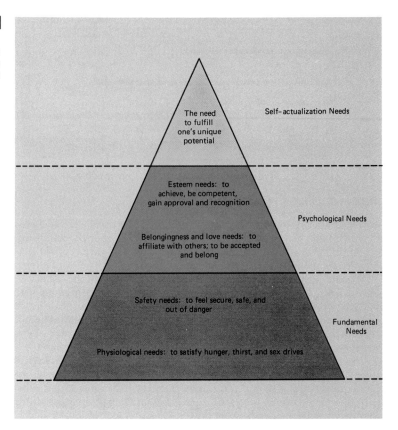

search? It should not be asserted that starving people anywhere in the world lack a need for love and self-esteem—those may be all they can achieve (Neher, 1991).

These researchers are suggesting that perhaps Maslow identified types of needs that may operate in all of us, but there is no guarantee that the needs must be satisfied in order. Any one need may dominate at a particular time, even as the organism is seeking to respond to others among his or her dominant needs. A need may be dominant in any of us at a particular moment, without necessarily meaning the other needs are not present and influencing our behavior at some level.

EMOTION

It is difficult to draw a clear line between motives and emotions. When a person needs food, the stomach contracts, the level of sugar in the blood drops, neural and endocrine systems are thrown slightly off balance, and taste buds become more sensitive. When a person is frightened, heart and breathing rates quicken, energy level rises, the senses mobilize, and blood

COOPERATIVE LEARNING ACTIVITY

Organize the students into groups of four or five. Have each group create a television commercial for a product (and videotape it if possible). Explain that each group should establish roles for its members and make sure that everyone is involved. Tell the groups that the commercial should attempt subtly to persuade people that one or more of their needs will be satisfied if they buy the product. After the groups make their presentations, ask which needs the commercials were directed toward and how successful the commercials were in promising to satisfy those needs.

rushes away from the stomach into the brain, heart, and other muscles. Of course, a poet might diagnose a pounding heart, loss of appetite, and heightened awareness of the moonlight and scented breezes as love. Why, if all three involve identifiable physiological changes, do we call hunger a biological drive, and fear and love emotions?

It depends on whether we are describing the source of our behavior or the feelings associated with our behavior. When we want to emphasize the needs, desires, and mental calculations that lead to goal-directed behavior, we use the word "drive" or "motivation." When we want to stress the feelings associated with these decisions and activities, we use the word "emotion" or "affect."

Clearly, the two are intertwined. We frequently explain our motives in terms of emotions. Why did you walk out of the meeting? I was angry. Why do you go to so many parties? I enjoy meeting new people and love to dance. Why did you lend your notes to someone you don't particularly like? I felt guilty about talking behind her back.

As these examples demonstrate, emotions push and pull us in different directions. Sometimes emotions function like biological drives: our feelings energize us and make us pursue a goal. Which goal we pursue may be determined by our social learning experiences. Other times we do things because we think they will make us feel good: anticipated emotions are the incentive for our actions. The consequences of striving for one goal or another also evoke emotions.

Expressing Emotions: Innate and Learned Behavior

In *The Expression of the Emotions in Man and Animals* (1872), Charles Darwin argued that all people express certain basic feelings in the same ways. Without knowing a person's language, you can tell whether he or she is amused or infuriated just by looking at that person's face. One group of researchers selected a group of photographs they thought depicted surprise, anger, sadness, and happiness. Then they showed the photographs to people from five different cultures and asked them to say what the person in each photograph was feeling. The results of this experiment are shown in Figure 6.9. The overwhelming majority of the subjects identified the emotions as the researchers expected they would. Was this simply because they had met Americans, or at least seen American television shows and movies, and so learned how to "read" our facial expressions? Apparently not. A second study was conducted in a remote part of New Guinea, with people who had relatively little contact with outsiders and virtually no exposure to mass media. They too were able to identify the emotions being expressed (Ekman, Friesen, and Ellsworth, 1972).

These studies imply that certain basic facial expressions are **innate**—that is, part of our biological inheritance. Observations of children who were born without sight and hearing lend support to this view. These youngsters could not have learned how to communicate feelings by observing other people. Still, they laugh like other children when they're happy, pout and frown to express resentment, clench their fists and teeth in anger (Goodenough, 1932).

? FACT OR FICTION

A person who is in a good mood is more likely to be helpful.

Fact. Positive emotional states are associated with greater helping. It has been found that the "glow of good will" occurs even when being in a good mood is caused by a minor event. Thus, people who find change left in phone booths or have cookies placed on their study tables in the library are more generous when asked for help.

■ **Making Inferences.** After students have read the special feature, poll the class to see if they agree that a good mood translates into goodwill toward others. In their experience, is the opposite also true—that a bad mood translates into indifference or ill will toward others? Ask students to give concrete examples either proving or disproving these tendencies in human behavior.

■ **Evaluating a Generalization.** Charles Darwin believed that emotions develop because they have survival value. Have students discuss the validity of this generalization. What are the survival values of emotions, such as hate, anger, joy, love, fear, and empathy? If emotions are indeed linked to survival, do animals have emotions? (OBJECTIVE 5)

■ **Discussion.** Ask the students to consider to what extent human fear and aggression are innate, unlearned forms of behavior. Have them give examples of situations and stimuli that trigger these responses in humans. If such behaviors are innate, what are the implications for eliminating crime and war? (OBJECTIVE 5)

🧪 LAB EXPERIMENTS AND DEMONSTRATIONS

Provide paper and pencils to the students and instruct them to work in pairs to draw the facial expressions that they associate with the following emotions: confusion, excitement, love, hate, disappointment, frustration. Remind students that they should pay attention to the shapes of the eyebrows, eyes, and mouth in each facial expression. Have students share their drawings and discuss to what degree the expressions are similar for each emotion. You may wish to keep some of the more interesting samples to use as examples for future classes.

VISUAL INSTRUCTION

First, you might poll the class to see how their judgments correspond to the percentages in the table, and discuss what other emotions might be assigned to the photographs other than those listed. *(For example, the boy might be expressing determination rather than anger, and the woman on the right might be expressing pain rather than fear.)* As a follow-up, you might ask for volunteers to work as a team to poll the school population for their judgments of the six photographs. Have the class analyze the results. Discuss the factors that might skew the students' data. *(Data might vary depending on the degree of cultural diversity within the school population.)*
Answer to caption, Figure 6.9: Chileans, 94 percent; Americans, 67 percent.

Photograph Judged						
Judgment	Happiness	Disgust	Surprise	Sadness	Anger	Fear
Culture			Percent Who Agreed with Judgment			
99 Americans	97	92	95	84	67	85
40 Brazilians	95	97	87	59	90	67
119 Chileans	95	92	93	88	94	68
168 Argentinians	98	92	95	78	90	54
29 Japanese	100	90	100	62	90	66

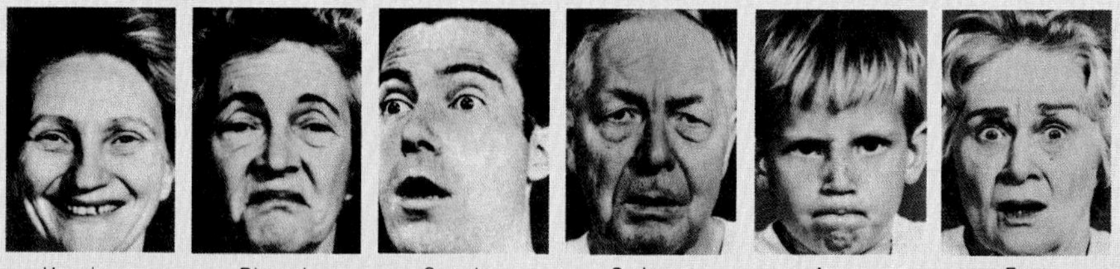

FIGURE 6.9

The data shows that substantial agreement exists among the members of different cultures about the meaning of various facial expressions. The muscular movements that produce these expressions are probably innate human responses. (After Ekman, Friesen, and Ellsworth, 1972). **What was the lowest and highest percent of agreement among the cultures for the facial expression showing anger?**

Psychologist Carroll Izard and his colleagues (Trotter, 1983) developed a coding system for assessing emotional states in people. By noticing changes in different parts of the face, such as the eyebrows, eyes, and mouth, they have been able to identify 10 different emotional states. For example, anger is indicated when a person's eyebrows are sharply lowered and drawn together, and the eyes narrowed or squinted. Izard has used his coding system to study emotional expressions in infants. Trained coders watching videotaped segments of an infant's face assess the emotional state of the baby. This technique is especially useful for studying emotions in young children who cannot verbally report what they are feeling. Izard's work also enables psychologists to study how effectively parents are able to read their babies' faces and figure out what they are feeling. Not only are parents watching their babies, but the reverse is also true. Babies spend a lot of time watching their parents. Infants have many opportunities to learn about and express emotions by using the parents' faces as models.

Learning is an important factor in emotional expression. James Averill (1983) believes that many of our everyday emotional reactions are the result of social expectations and consequences. He believes that emotions are responses of the whole person and that we cannot separate an individual's physical or biological experience of emotions from that person's thoughts or actions associated with those emotions. We learn to express and experience emotions in the company of other people and we learn

STUDY AND WRITING SKILLS

Ask students to choose one of the photographs in Figure 6.9 and write a one-paragraph, detailed description of the facial expression without specifically mentioning the emotion it represents. Instruct students to avoid using such revealing words as *smile* and *frown* in their descriptions. After students have finished their paragraphs, read samples to the class. How many students can identify the emotion based on the description of the facial expression alone?

that emotions can serve different social functions. Parents, for example, modify their children's emotions by responding angrily to some outbursts, by being sympathetic to others, and on occasion by ignoring their youngsters. In this way, children are taught which emotions are considered appropriate in different situations.

Learning explains the differences we find among cultures once we go beyond such basic expressions as laughing or crying. For example, in Victorian English novels, women closed their eyes, opened their mouths with a gasp, and fainted when they were frightened or shocked. In Chinese novels, men fainted when they became enraged. Medical records from the period indicate that Chinese men did indeed faint from anger (Klineberg, 1938). What these findings suggest is that all of us are born with the capacity for emotion and with certain basic forms of expression, but when, where, and how we express different feelings depend in large part on learning.

Analyzing facial expressions helps us to describe emotions, but it does not tell us where emotions come from. Some psychologists believe emotions derive from physical changes; others, that emotions result from mental processes.

Physiological Theories

In *Principles of Psychology*, a classic work published in 1890, William James attempted to summarize the best available literature on human behavior, motivations, and feelings. When it came to drawing up a catalogue of human emotions, James gave up; he felt there were too many subtle variations. But he was struck by the fact that nearly every description of emotions he read emphasized bodily changes. James's observations of his own and other people's emotions confirmed this point. We associate feelings with sudden increases or decreases in energy, muscle tension and relaxation, and sensations in the pit of our stomach.

The James-Lange Theory. After much thought James concluded that we use the word "emotion" to describe our visceral or "gut" reactions to the things that take place around us. In other words, James (1890) believed that emotions are the perception of certain internal bodily changes.

> My theory . . . is that *the bodily changes follow directly the perception of the exciting fact, and that our feeling of the same changes as they occur IS the emotion.* Commonsense says, we lose our fortune, are sorry and weep; we meet a bear, are frightened and run; we are insulted by a rival, are angry and strike. . . . [T]he more rational statement is that we feel sorry because we cry, angry because we strike, afraid because we tremble. . . . Without the bodily states following on the perception, the latter would be . . . pale, colorless, destitute of emotional warmth.

In a sense, James was putting the cart before the horse. Other psychologists had assumed that emotions trigger bodily changes; James ar-

LAB EXPERIMENTS AND DEMONSTRATIONS

To demonstrate the physiological aspects of emotions, instruct students to tense the muscles in their upper body for several seconds. As they do, tell them to pay careful attention to their bodily reactions and sensations, and have them describe what they are experiencing. Ask whether these reactions and sensations are similar to any feelings they have while experiencing a particular emotion. Point out that tension in the upper body due to raised blood pressure is associated with the physiological reaction of anger.

■ **Discussion.** In discussing cognitive theories, begin by having students look up *cognition* (the process of knowing in the broadest sense) in the dictionary. Emphasize that knowing what is going on within and around us affects physiological arousal. As an example, pose this scenario: Two men are videotaping a political event with hand-held recorders. One is a saboteur and knows a bomb will go off; the other is an innocent bystander. Whose videotape do students suspect will show greater evidence of jolting at the moment the bomb detonates? Whose videotape would more likely show evidence of shaking before the bombing? *(The bystander would be more surprised at the bombing and respond with a greater jolt. The saboteur, on the other hand, might be nervous with anticipation and would therefore tend to shake.)* (OBJECTIVE 5)

Independent Practice

■ **Research.** Have students keep a 24-hour record of their behaviors and afterward classify them according to Maslow's hierarchy. Ask students to analyze their findings by responding to the following questions in writing. (1) How much time was spent fulfilling each type of need? (2) Do any patterns emerge in needs fulfillment? (3) Is Maslow's scheme particularly useful for classifying human needs? Or are there better ways of classification? (OBJECTIVES 1–4)

gued that the reverse is true. Because Carl Lange came to the same conclusion about the same time, this position is known as the **James-Lange theory** (Lange and James, 1922). Izard's (1972) theory of emotions bears a striking resemblance to the James-Lange theory. He believes that our conscious experience of emotion results from the sensory feedback we receive from the muscles in our faces. You can check this out by noticing the difference in your emotional experience when you smile for two minutes as opposed to when you frown for two minutes. According to Izard's view, if you continue to frown, you will experience an unpleasant emotion.

The Cannon-Bard Theory. Techniques for studying bodily changes improved over the next three decades, and evidence that contradicted the James-Lange theory began to grow. For example, the physiological changes that occur during emotional states also occur when people are not feeling angry or sad—or anything. In fact, injecting a drug that produces physiological arousal of the body does not necessarily produce changes in emotions. (If James and Lange had been correct, such physiological changes would always produce emotions.) Also the internal state of the body changes only slowly. "Gut" reactions could not produce the rushes of emotion we all experience from time to time. Indeed, if bodily changes were the seat of emotion, we would all be rather dull.

In 1929, Walter B. Cannon published a summary of the evidence against the James-Lange theory. Cannon argued that the thalamus (part of the lower brain) is the seat of emotion—an idea Philip Bard (1934) expanded and refined. According to the **Cannon-Bard theory,** certain experiences activate the thalamus, and the thalamus sends messages to the cortex and to the body organs. Later, more sophisticated experiments showed that the thalamus is not involved in emotional experience, but the hypothalamus is. Thus, when we use the word "emotion," we are referring to the *simultaneous* burst of activity in the brain and "gut" reactions. In Cannon's words, "The peculiar quality of emotion is added to simple sensation when the thalamic processes are aroused" (1929).

Cannon also emphasized the importance of physiological arousal in many different emotions. He was the first to describe the "fight or flight" reaction to the sympathetic nervous system that prepares us for an emergency. Some of the signs of physiological arousal are measured in one of the most famous applications of psychological knowledge: lie detection.

Cognitive Theories

Cognitive theorists believe that bodily changes and thinking *work together* to produce emotions. Physiological arousal is only half of the story. What you feel depends on how you interpret your symptoms. This, in turn, depends on what is going on in your mind and in your environment.

The Schachter-Singer Experiment. Stanley Schachter and Jerome Singer designed an experiment to explore this (1962). They told all their subjects they were testing the effects of vitamin C on eyesight. In reality, most received an adrenalin injection. The informed group was told that the

---

CRITICAL THINKING ACTIVITY

Evaluating a Hypothesis. After the students have read about the Schachter-Singer experiment, instruct them to work in small groups to devise another scenario that might be used to test the validity of the theory. That is, do internal components of emotion affect a person differently, depending on his or her interpretation or perception of the social situation? After each group has presented its scenario to the class, ask the students to decide which scenario would be the best test of the theory.

FIGURE 6.10

The polygraph measures sweating of the skin, breathing, blood pressure, and heart rate. **What is another name commonly used for the polygraph test?**

"vitamin" injection would make their hearts race and their bodies tremble (which was true). The misinformed group was told that the injection would make them numb. An uninformed group was not told anything about how their bodies would react to the shot. And a control group received a neutral injection that did not produce any symptoms. Like the third group, these subjects were not given any information about possible side effects.

After the injection, each subject was taken to a reception room to wait for the "vision test." There they found another person who was actually part of the experiment. The subjects thought the accomplice had had the same injection as theirs. With some subjects, the accomplice acted wild and

Cognitive theorists believe bodily changes and thinking work together to produce emotions.

Using Psychology

Lie Detection

Most of us associate lie detection with shifty-eyed criminals accused of murdering their grandmothers. At one time, however, American industry used the lie detector far more often than the police. No one knows exactly how many polygraph tests (**polygraph** is another name for a lie detector) were given each year, but one

Using Psychology

After students have read the special feature, explain that, in addition to the recording devices mentioned in the text, a polygraph can also be set up to measure a number of different physiological responses at the same time: An electrocardiogram (EKG) can measure changes in the heart rate; an electroencephalogram (EEG) can measure brain activity; and an electromyogram (EMG) can record changes in facial muscle action. If possible, arrange for a polygrapher to visit the class and explain how the various graphs are interpreted in light of the subject's verbal responses to the questions posed during the course of the examination.

DEBATING AN ISSUE

Lie detection continues to have its advocates and detractors. Have students research to what extent the results of lie detector tests are admissible as evidence in courts of law. Based on this research, have the class debate the following topic: *Resolved*—polygraphs should be admissible evidence in determining a defendant's guilt or innocence.

DID YOU KNOW?

Centuries ago in some parts of Asia, officials used a form of lie detection based on the lessening of salivation under nervous stress. Suspects were ordered to fill their mouths with dry rice. The suspect who had the most difficult time spitting out the rice was judged the guilty party.

■ **Testing Hypotheses.** You might have students work in groups to devise experiments to test the hypothesis that males are better liars than females. Stress that experiments are to adhere to Hippocrates' primary principle: "First do no harm." If possible, have the groups involve the entire class in their experiments.

■ **Readings in Psychology.** Have students read the Section 2, Reading 6 selection in *Readings in Psychology* and answer the questions that follow the reading.

MORE about...

Men, Women, and Lying. A psychologist who has conducted research on conflict between men and women has found that many women get upset about men's lack of emotional expression.

Women seem to express emotions more often than men. This may explain another research finding: Men are better liars than women. One study found that videotapes of male college students instructed to lie were seen as sincere. However, women's lies were more easily detected.

Why are women worse liars than men? One possibility has to do with women being better at expressing their emotions than men. Since women appear to be better at expressing themselves and do so more often than men, they may find it difficult when required to hide what they truly feel. Men, on the other hand, tend to limit their emotional expressions. They also believe that the expression of most emotions is controllable. Thus, expressing an emotion that one does not feel may come more easily for many males.

psychologist (Lykken, 1974) placed the number at several million. Companies used these tests for everything from finding out whether a job applicant had ever been in trouble to seeing who had his or her hand in the till at the local fast-food restaurant.

The first modern "lie detector" was invented by Leonarde Keeler, a member of the Berkeley, California, police force in the 1920s. As you can see in Figure 6.10, a polygraph includes electrodes for measuring the electrical resistance of the skin (often called the GSR, this is a measure of sweating), a tube that is tied around the chest to measure upper- and lower-chest breathing, and an inflatable cuff that measures blood pressure and heart rate. There is no single physiological change that always goes along with a lie. Rather, the lie-detection expert looks for general signs of the activation of the sympathetic nervous system: an irregular breathing pattern, high heart rate and blood pressure, and increased sweating (indicated by decreases in the electrical resistance of the skin).

Surprisingly, almost all of the people who become lie-detection experts have backgrounds not in psychology but in law enforcement. The way they cross-question a person is at least as important as the machine itself. To illustrate this point, polygraphers sometimes tell an old tale about a medieval prince who wanted to find out which of his servants had stolen some food. He called all his servants together and announced that he had a sacred donkey in the next room. The donkey would bray only when the guilty man pulled his tail. One by one, the servants went by themselves into a dark room with the donkey, pulled his tail, and returned to the prince. Finally, the last man returned and still the ass had not made a sound. The prince then told the servants to hold out their hands. He had covered the donkey's tail with soot. Only the guilty man had been afraid to pull the tail, and so only his hands were clean. Similarly, some experts say that if a person believes in the lie detector, it can be used to make him or her tell the truth. Indeed, many people confess during an interview that usually takes place before the machine is even plugged in.

The polygrapher tries to develop three different kinds of questions for the actual tests. Some are nonemotional (for example "Is your name Bill Clinton?"); some are emotional but not relevant to the investigation ("Have you ever lied to your parents?"); a few are related specifically to the investigation.

Benjamin Kleinmuntz and Julian Szucko (1984) examined lie-detection tests administered to 50 suspects who confessed to a crime and 50 who were proven innocent when others confessed. The study showed that 37 percent of six judges' ratings of 50 innocent people were wrong. These are called *false positives*. The researchers also studied *false negatives* (the guilty who are declared

COMMUNITY INVOLVEMENT

Have the class poll 100 people in the community on the subject of polygraph tests to determine the public's attitude toward the accuracy of the tests. To help students figure responses by percentage, suggest that they use the following forced-choice answers: always accurate, highly accurate, moderately accurate, or seldom accurate. The students should also ask those polled to explain why they feel as they do about polygraphs. Ask for volunteers to tabulate all the data and prepare a report for the class.

innocent) and showed that about 20 percent of those who are guilty gain their freedom. Partly because the tests are unreliable, Congress voted in 1988 to prohibit continued use of lie detectors in most employee hiring practices.

One alternative, the *guilty-knowledge test* has yielded better results. In this form of lie detection, the subject is asked a variety of questions regarding details of a crime as well as a selection of questions about other facts not related to the crime. "Did the thief use a gun?" "Did the thief use a knife?" "Did the thief use a pipe?" The innocent would not know the "right" from the "wrong" answer, whereas the person(s) who committed the theft would know. Under these conditions, about 20 percent of the actual thieves are still missed, but it is very rare to tag an innocent person falsely guilty (Lykken, 1988).

crazy—dancing around, laughing, making paper airplanes with the questionnaire they'd been asked to fill out. Other subjects had to fill out a long and offensive questionnaire that asked, for example: "With how many men (other than your father) has your mother had extramarital relationships? 4 and under ___; 5–9 ___; 10 and over ___." The accomplice for this group acted more and more angry as the subject filled out the questionnaire.

Subjects from the first group, who had been told how the injection would affect them, watched the accomplice with mild amusement. So did subjects who had received the neutral injection. However, those from the second and third groups, who either had an incorrect idea or no idea about the side effects, joined in with the accomplice (Figure 6.11). If he was euphoric, so were they; if he was angry, they became angry.

What does this experiment demonstrate? That internal components of emotion (such as those adrenalin produces) affect a person differently, depending on his or her interpretation or perception of the social situation. When people cannot explain their physical reactions, they take cues from their environment. The accomplice provided cues. But when people knew that their hearts were beating faster because of the shot, they did not feel particularly happy or angry. The experiment also shows that internal changes are important—otherwise the subjects from the neutral group would have acted in the same way as those from the misinformed groups. Perception and arousal *interact* to create emotions.

Opponent-Process Theory. Physiological processes, discussed earlier in the chapter, clearly are controlled by homeostatic mechanisms that keep the body within certain narrow limits. Emotions, such as being in love, are

■ **Cooperative Learning Activity.** Assign each students to bring in a photo showing women and men in various work situations. Collect all the photos and redistribute them at random. Tell students to write a short narrative explaining what is happening in the picture they were given. After students have finished, ask for volunteers to show their pictures to the class and read their stories aloud. Tell the class to listen closely and to identify any themes that reflect the need for achievement. Can they find any evidence for the motive to avoid success? Have the class discuss their findings, taking into account Horner's research on the fear of success. (OBJECTIVE 3)

■ **Research.** Instruct students to interview two adults they know who are working in different types of jobs to learn the rewards that the adults derive from their work. They should ask the adults to rate the following job-related factors on a 1–5 scale: money, enjoyment, helping people, working with friendly people, job security, responsibility, and prestige. After they have collected their data, have students analyze the responses and classify the jobs according to Maslow's hierarchy. For example, a job rated high on helping others and working with friendly people could be classified as meeting belongingness and love needs. (OBJECTIVE 4)

CRITICAL THINKING ACTIVITY

Evaluating Generalizations. Ask students to evaluate the contention that any extreme emotion is disabling to normal activity. To what extent is this generalization true? Suggest that students consider such "extreme" emotions as falling head over heels in love or harboring a grudge over an extended period of time. In light of the opponent-process theory, is it possible to sustain such emotions indefinitely? *(According to the theory, it is not possible.)*

just as disabling to normal activity. Why wouldn't the body develop a homeostatic mechanism to control the effects of extreme emotions?

Psychologists Richard Solomon and John Corbit (1974) proposed an opponent-process theory—a homeostatic theory of emotional reactions. They proposed that any intense emotion will, with repeated exposure, bring about an internal counterforce of similar magnitude. If the external, emotion-arousing event is State A, the internal force is labeled State B.

Suppose you meet someone on the first day of school and, from the start, you like each other. The two of you stun your English teacher with sharp questions and quick answers when challenged. Later, you share a wonderful lunch—both of you love the same four-topping pizza at the hangout on Third Street. An afternoon in the park was glorious; and doing homework assignments together are fun and easy. Then, a week later, your friend tells you that his or her family is moving to the coast—gone forever. You are annoyed . . . but let's face it, the next day you're back out looking for another special person. The opponent-process theory would indicate that with this person you were subjected to State A which aroused your emotions, but no State B had developed.

Now let's put a different slant on the ending. Your friend did not move away. You marry and enjoy a loving relationship and a long, healthy life together. One morning, however, your spouse dies. Your years together had produced a strong countering State B, which occurred any time you were in the presence of your beloved. It kept your emotions near neutral and allowed you to get on with your daily activities. But now that your spouse is gone, you are left with only the incredibly depressing effects of the re-

FIGURE 6.11

Shown here are two of the conditions in Schachter and Singer's experiment on emotion. (a) A subject is misled about the effects he should expect from an adrenalin injection. Placed with an accomplice who joyfully flies airplanes around the room, he attributes his state of arousal to a similar mood in himself and joins in. (b) A subject is told exactly what to expect from the injection. **How does this subject react?**

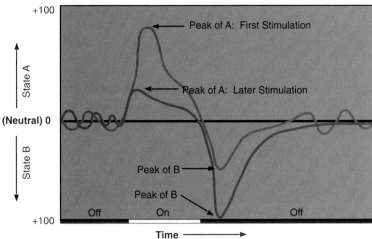

FIGURE 6.12

This illustration shows part of Solomon and Corbit's opponent-process theory in graph form. The psychologists label the external, emotion-arousing event State A and the internal force that it brings about State B. **Why does State A reach its peak during the first stimulation but not during later stimulations?**

maining State B. Have you ever had the misfortune of watching one of your grandparents lose the partner to whom he or she was deeply devoted? Then you must recognize that you now face a long, painful process of readapting your emotions to a world without your spouse, just as the opponent-process theory of emotion would predict.

The significance of this theory is that if the State A event is a terrifying one—such as your first parachute jump—it still predicts what will happen. You simply flip the chart in Figure 6.12 180 degrees. Novice parachutists are terrified coming out of a plane and briefly, but wildly delighted when they return to the ground; they are subject to State A. An experienced jumper knows that how he or she packs the chute is crucial, how they coordinate during the fall is important, and it's important that they know how to land. The jump is eventually only a bit stressful—thanks to State B. They usually jump for the long-term satisfaction that is generated—again, thanks to the aftereffects of State B—once the jump itself is completed.

In fact, other emotion researchers believe that emotion may play an important role in our survival as human beings and in our ability to achieve goals, precisely because it spurs us to action. Take the example of a car rushing toward you. If you do not jump out of the way, you may not live to see another day. On less extreme levels, emotions may serve to help us achieve difficult goals. Suppose you want your own car, but your parents say no. You may feel angry with them, or embarrassed because all your friends have cars. These emotions may spur you to get a job to earn money for a car, or to explore other options with your parents. Either way, you are responding to an emotion by acting to achieve a goal.

Emotions and physical changes are intertwined. It will probably be many years before we understand all the complex ways in which the two interact in human behavior.

CONNECTIONS: PSYCHOLOGY AND ART

Assign students to find examples of modern abstract paintings—such as those by Rothko, Pollock, and Frankenthaler—that they feel express particular emotions through shape and color alone. If possible, display the examples in the classroom, and poll the students to see how many agree that the paintings express identifiable emotions. You may also wish to have students name the emotion being depicted before knowing the painting's title.

VISUAL INSTRUCTION

Remind students that Solomon and Corbit hypothesized that every state of positive feeling is followed by a contrasting feeling. Conversely, a state of negative feeling leads to a positive feeling. **Answer to caption, Figure 6.12:** because no State B has yet developed

ASSESS

Check for Understanding

Ask students to summarize the various ways that motivations and emotions are intertwined.

Reteach

Have students complete the Chapter 6 Study Guide Activity. For extended review, assign the Chapter 6 Review Activity as homework or an in-class assignment.

Enrich

Ask students to complete the Chapter 6 Extension Activity and answer the questions that follow it.

Evaluate

Administer and grade the Chapter 6 Test. Two forms are available should you wish to give different tests to different students/classes.

CLOSE

Ask students to recall the discussion about the motives for marriage. Have them discuss the motivations and emotions involved in terms of the various theories that they read about in this chapter.

CHAPTER 6

ANSWERS

Concepts and Vocabulary

1. The hypothalamus monitors blood sugar levels, amount of food in the stomach, and body temperature to determine when to signal you with internal hunger cues. Overweight people respond to external cues, while others respond to internal cues.

2. Hunger and the need for oxygen are consistent with Hull's theory because they are physiological needs. The other examples are inconsistent since none is a biological need.

3. drive reduction theory

4. Harlow's experiment showed that a monkey prefers soft contact rather than a mother figure that provides relief from hunger.

5. through Thematic Apperception Tests (TATs); Such a person is more likely to be an entrepreneur and prefer the association of experts, and less likely to be artistically inclined and to value intimacy in a relation.

6. physiological needs, safety, belongingness and love, esteem, self-actualization

7. Physiological and safety needs must be satisfied first. Self-actualization needs are satisfied after all others.

8. Motivations are needs, desires, and mental calculations that lead to goal-directed behavior. Emotions are feelings

154

CHAPTER 6 Review

SUMMARY

Use the following outline as a tool for reviewing this chapter. Copy the outline onto your own paper, leaving spaces between headings to make notes about key concepts.

I. Biological Motives

   A. The Biology of Motivation

   B. Drive Reduction Theory

II. Social Motives

   A. Measuring the Need for Achievement

   B. Maslow's Hierarchy of Needs

III. Emotion

   A. Expressing Emotions: Innate and Learned Behavior

   B. Physiological Theories

   C. Cognitive Theories

CONCEPTS AND VOCABULARY

1. Enumerate the physiological processes that determine whether or not we "feel hungry." How do normal-weight and overweight people differ in their sensitivity to these cues?

2. Explain why each of the following is or is not consistent with Hull's drive reduction theory: hunger, curiosity, the need for oxygen, taking risks, children playing.

3. Which theory of motivation suggests that all human motives are extensions of basic biological needs?

4. How did Harlow's experiment challenge drive reduction theory?

5. How does McClelland measure a person's need for achievement? What kind of person has a high need for achievement?

6. Describe the five levels of needs in Maslow's hierarchy.

154

SUMMARY

7. According to Maslow's hierarchy of needs, which needs must be satisfied first? Which needs are satisfied after all others?

8. How do psychologists try to distinguish between motivation and emotion?

9. What research evidence suggests that our expression of emotions is universal across different societies and cultures and may be innate? What evidence suggests that emotions are affected by learning?

10. How does the Cannon-Bard theory of emotion differ from the James-Lange theory?

11. What did Schachter and Singer's experiment demonstrate?

12. What did Soloman and Corbit's experiment demonstrate?

CRITICAL THINKING

1. **Evaluate.** Try going without bread in your meals for several days a week. Do you find that you are beginning to think about bread more often, even dream about it? Are you becoming more aware of advertisements for bread? Compare your experience with the description of drive reduction behavior in this chapter.

2. **Analyze.** Write down several activities or behaviors you do when your time is your own. In which level of Maslow's hierarchy of needs would you place each of these activities or behaviors; that is, what really motivates you to engage in each of them? Perhaps you will discover a different kind of motive, one that doesn't seem to fit in with Maslow's set. Check the chapter on personality and the Maslow readings to see whether or not it might fit. If none of the activities on your list seems to be motivated by self-actualization, can you imagine activities that would be, and that you might enjoy doing?

associated with these decisions and activities.

9. Research involving facial expressions suggests that certain emotional behaviors are universal and innate. Averill has shown that people learn to adapt their emotions to serve different social functions. For example, parents help children learn to control emotional outbursts.

10. The James-Lange theory concluded that emotions are the perception of certain internal bodily changes. The Cannon-Bard theory argues that bodily changes are not the origin of all emotions, but that emotions are the result of simultaneous bursts of activity in the brain and "gut" reactions.

11. It demonstrated that perception and arousal interact to create emotions.

154

APPLYING KNOWLEDGE

1. With a partner or as a group, select 10 emotions to express. Then play a variation of charades, with one person attempting to convey each of these emotions by facial expression alone. Are some emotions harder to convey than others? Are there consistent differences in interpretation between individuals? How important do you think context (the social situation in which the facial expression occurs) is in perceiving other people's emotions?

2. Ask students in other classes to write stories. Each person should write several stories, possibly around a set of ambiguous pictures. Names should not be placed on stories (so as to ensure privacy), but each person should mark male or female on the manuscript. Then compare the goals and dreams of males and females for the achievement motive. Are there differences? Do you think there have been changes in this factor in the last few years?

3. If you are interested in the achievement motive, you might try the story-writing techniques described in this chapter. Try writing stories with and without achievement themes. Include themes related to the three aspects of achievement motivation. After you have written several stories, think about whether this exercise has made you more aware of achievement. Do you think doing the exercise increased your ability to achieve?

ANALYZING VIEWPOINTS

1. As you know from reading the chapter, lie detectors, while usually accurate, can make mistakes. Should lie detectors be used by businesses as part of interviewing prospective job candidates? Write a paper that argues both issues. Include both psychological and ethical reasons in your report.

BEYOND THE CLASSROOM

1. Attend a sporting event at your school or in your community. Observe the event for at least 30 minutes. Watch for evidence of achievement motivation in the participants. Do some players appear to be more motivated than others? How can you tell? If possible, talk with the coach after the game. Ask the coach what techniques he or she uses to motivate the players. Does one technique work for all the players, or does the coach use different techniques for different players? What suggestions would you make for increasing the players' motivation? Interpret your observations in light of the theories of motivation presented in the chapter.

IN YOUR JOURNAL

1. Analyze the list of concerns and aspirations you wrote in your journal. Evaluate these items in terms of Maslow's hierarchy of needs. In other words, classify the items in terms of fundamental needs, psychological needs, and self-actualization needs. In your journal, write a rationale for classifying the individual items as you did.

2. To gain a clearer understanding of the range of emotional reactions you experience, keep an "emotion diary" for one day. Try to jot down in your journal what you felt, how you interpreted your feelings, and what brought on your reaction. At the end of the day, analyze your diary to determine the differences in physiological reactions that you experienced in response to each situation. What conclusions can you draw about your emotional responses on that day?

155

12. It demonstrated that any intense emotion will, with repeated exposure, bring about an internal counterforce of similar magnitude.

Critical Thinking

1. Encourage students to consider how realistic dieting really is in light of drive reduction theory.

2. After students have discussed what they do when their time is their own and have analyzed their motives according to Maslow's hierarchy, ask them to explain what self-actualization means to them and to compare their answers to Maslow's definition.

Applying Knowledge

1. Answers will vary. Students may find that learned emotions, such as sympathy, are more difficult to express than innate ones.

2. Answers will vary.

3. Answers will vary.

CHAPTER BONUS
Test Question

This question may be used for extra credit on the chapter test.
Choose the letter of the correct response.

Desired goals that prompt behavior are called:
a. emotions.
b. motives.
c. set points.
d. channels.

Answer: **b**

Analyzing Viewpoints

1. Answers will vary, but should include valid arguments.

Beyond the Classroom

1. Answers will vary, but should include evidence of firsthand observation and should interpret those observations in light of theories of motivation.

IN YOUR JOURNAL

If time permits, discuss journal entries individually with the students.

CHAPTER 7
Altered States of Consciousness

TEXT TOPICS	SPECIAL FEATURES	RESOURCE MATERIALS
Sleep and Dreams, pp. 157–163	**More About Psychology,** p. 160 **At a Glance:** Insomnia, p. 160 **Fact or Fiction?,** p. 161 **Readings in Psychology:** Freud on Dreams, p. 162 **Psychology Update,** p. 163	▬ **Reproducible Lesson Plan; Study Guide; Review Activity Transparency 15**
Hypnosis, pp. 163–165	**More About Psychology,** p. 165	▬ **Reproducible Lesson Plan; Study Guide; Review Activity** *Readings in Psychology:* **Section 2, Reading 7**
Hallucinations, pp. 165–166		▬ **Reproducible Lesson Plan; Study Guide; Review Activity**
Sensory Deprivation, p. 166		▬ **Reproducible Lesson Plan; Study Guide; Review Activity**
Psychoactive Drugs, pp. 166–172	**Psychology Update,** p. 166	▬ **Reproducible Lesson Plan; Study Guide; Review Activity**
Biofeedback, pp. 173–174		▬ **Reproducible Lesson Plan; Study Guide; Review Activity**
Meditation, pp. 174–176	**Using Psychology:** Lowering Blood Pressure, pp. 176–177	▬ **Reproducible Lesson Plan; Study Guide; Review Activity; Application Activity; Extension Activity; Chapter Test, Form A and Form B** *Readings in Psychology:* **Section 2, Reading 8** **Understanding Psychology Testmaker**

PERFORMANCE ASSESSMENT ACTIVITY

Assign students to contact the county mental health agency for pamphlets on the recognition, effects, and treatment of substance abuse. Using these materials, direct students to design posters showing how use of drugs or alcohol alters normal thinking processes.

Arrange the pamphlets and posters in a classroom display entitled: "Think—While You Still Can." *(The display should reflect some of the mental changes that take place when alcohol and drugs are abused.)*

CHAPTER RESOURCES

Readings for the Student

Arnheim, Rudolf. *Art and Visual Perception: A Psychology of the Creative Eye.* Berkeley, CA: University of California Press, 1974.

Eckholm, E. "Exploring the Forces of Sleep." *The New York Times Magazine* (April 17, 1988): 26–34.

Palladino, J. J., and Carducci, B. J. "Students' Knowledge of Sleep and Dreams." *Teaching of Psychology, 11* (1984): 189–191.

Shafer, R. G. "An Anguished Father Recounts the Battle He Lost—Trying to Rescue a Teenage Son from Drugs." *People Weekly* (March 12, 1990): 81–83.

Readings for the Teacher

Baker, T. B., and Cannon, D. (eds.) *Addictive Disorders: Psychological Research on Assessment and Treatment.* New York: Praeger, 1987.

Brickman, P. *et al.* "Models of Helping and Coping." *American Psychologist, 37* (1984): 368–384.

Mahowald, M. W., and Schenck, C. H. "REM Sleep Behavior Disorder." In *Principles and Practice of Sleep Medicine,* M. H. Kryger, T. Roth, and W. C. Dement (eds.) Philadelphia: Saunders, 1989.

Multimedia

Altered States of Consciousness. (29 minutes, 3/4" video). Coast District Telecourses. This video shows how drugs affect neural processes after background of nature of sleep and consciousness.

Objective Indicators of Dreaming. (19 minutes). Jeffrey Norton. In this audiotape Calvin Hall gives an overview of research into REM and brain waves in the study of dreaming.

Objective Methods for Analyzing Dreams. (20 minutes). Jeffrey Norton. Calvin Hall discusses quantifiable methods employed in the analysis of dream contents in this audiotape.

For additional resources, see the bibliography beginning on page 530.

FOCUS

Motivating Activity

You might open this chapter by asking students to write a definition of "consciousness." *(state of awareness, including a person's feelings, sensations, ideas, and perceptions)* Next, have students speculate on what is meant by the phrase "altered state of consciousness." *(change in mental processes)* Challenge students to brainstorm examples of altered states of consciousness *(daydreams, meditation, hypnosis, and so on).* Have a volunteer record student responses for use at the end of the lesson. (See Close on page 177.) Tell students that Chapter 7 will provide data to assess the accuracy of their speculations.

Meeting Chapter Objectives.
Identify the main subjects of each objective on page 157. Have groups of students prepare data sheets on each of these subjects as they read Chapter 7.

Building Vocabulary.
Have students look up each term in the Glossary or dictionary. Then assign them to write a sentence using a synonymous word or expression for each term. Read these sentences aloud, and have the rest of the class guess the term.

Altered States of Consciousness

FIGURE 7.1 An altered state of consciousness, like meditation, involves a change in mental processes. Sensations, perceptions, and thought patterns actually change.

156

TEACHER CLASSROOM RESOURCES

- Chapter 7 Reproducible Lesson Plan
- Chapter 7 Study Guide
- Chapter 7 Review Activity
- Chapter 7 Application Activity
- Chapter 7 Extension Activity

- Transparency 15
  Transparency Strategies and
  Activities

- *Readings in Psychology:* Section 2,
  Readings 7, 8

- Chapter 7 Test, Form A and
  Form B

- Understanding Psychology
  Testmaker

Assessing Consciousness. Conduct a session in which students sit in a darkened room for 10 minutes. During this time, direct students to "watch" their thoughts and bodily perceptions (such as the sound of a heartbeat). Challenge students to let go quickly of every thought or physical sensation. Instead, they should try to focus on the pattern of their breathing—in, out, in, out.

End the session with the sound of a hand clap. Then slowly open the window shades or turn on a light. Request volunteers to describe their feelings. Do any students think they would describe these feelings as an "altered state of consciousness"? Why or why not? (*As a tip, you might ask: How did your mental processes differ from "normal" during the demonstration? Some researchers would argue the same effects are achieved simply by relaxing. Do students think they were meditating or relaxing? Ask: How can you prove it?*)

OBJECTIVES

After studying this chapter, you should be able to

- describe the research related to sleep and dreaming.
- define altered states of consciousness, including hypnosis and hallucination.
- discuss the effects of drug states and such substances as marijuana and alcohol.
- describe research into such techniques as biofeedback and meditation.

KEY TERMS

biofeedback
consciousness
hallucinations
hallucinogens
hypertension
hypnosis
LSD
marijuana
meditation
posthypnotic suggestion
REM sleep

As you read this sentence you are conscious of the words on this page. Perhaps, however, your awareness is drifting to that attractive classmate sitting across from you in the library. In either case, everything you think and feel is part of your conscious experience.

You might expect, then, that normal states of **consciousness** would be one of the most active areas of research in psychology. But this is not the case. Although some of the earliest researchers defined psychology as the study of conscious experience, consciousness proved to be a difficult topic to analyze scientifically. Behaviorism—with its emphasis on studying only what people do, not what they think or feel—became popular partly because studying consciousness had proved to be so difficult.

But a related area that *has* been the subject of a great deal of research in recent years is the study of altered states of consciousness. An altered state of consciousness involves a change in mental processes, not just a quantitative shift (such as feeling more or less alert).

Since at least 1960, psychologists have been studying altered states of consciousness by having people sleep, meditate, undergo hypnosis, or take drugs during laboratory experiments. In the laboratory, researchers can observe changes in behavior and measure changes in breathing, pulse

IN YOUR JOURNAL

What is the purpose of sleep? Do you think it would be possible or desirable to perfect a way to eliminate sleep or dreams? Write a one-page essay in your journal answering these questions.

EXTRA CREDIT ACTIVITY

Instruct students to research books and articles on the interpretation of dreams. Possible magazine sources include: *Psychology Today, Omni,* and *Discover.* A possible book is *The Dream Game* by Anne Faraday. Based on this information, challenge students to write a position paper attacking or defending the usefulness of dreams as a psychological tool.

IN YOUR JOURNAL

Request volunteers to describe what happens to their attitudes, emotions, or ability to perform if they fail to get enough rest. Suppose the mind functioned in a state of wakefulness around the clock. Do students think their lives would be richer? Or is sleep needed to prevent sensory overload? Explain.

TEACH
Guided Practice

DID YOU KNOW?

In rare cases, people do *not* lose the muscle tone normally associated with REM sleep. Instead they physically act out their dreams. This condition, known as *REM Behavior Disorder,* differs from sleepwalking, which starts in non-REM sleep and occurs most often in childhood. REM Behavior Disorder frequently results from neurological damage (such as a stroke) and most commonly occurs in men over age 60. One 67-year-old man, for example, grabbed his wife's neck while dreaming he was choking a deer.

FIGURE 7.2

This girl may be conscious of several things—the sound of the rain on the window, the sight of a tree bending in the wind, her mother standing next to her, and voices in a nearby room. **What makes up our conscious experience?**

FIGURE 7.3

Yoga stretches and tones muscles, but it's also a mental discipline that some say allows practitioners to achieve an altered state of consciousness. **What is the most common altered state of consciousness?**

rate, body temperature, and brain activity. (Brain activity, or "waves," can be recorded with a device known as an electroencephalograph, or EEG, which was discussed in Chapter 4.) The subjects' own reports of how they feel or what they remember supplement these data. What have psychologists learned about these phenomena? We begin with sleep.

SLEEP AND DREAMS

Most people think of sleep as a state of unconsciousness, punctuated by brief periods of dreaming. This is only partially correct. Sleep is a state of *altered* consciousness, characterized by certain patterns of brain activity.

Although sleep is a major part of human and animal behavior, it has been extremely difficult to study until recently. A researcher cannot ask a sleeping person to report on the experience without first waking the person. The study of sleep was aided by the development of the EEG machine for recording the electrical activity of the brain. By observing sleeping subjects and by recording their brain and body responses, researchers have discovered two different types of sleep patterns—*quiet sleep* and *active sleep.* There are four different stages of quiet sleep.

Stages of Sleep

As you begin to fall asleep, your body temperature declines, your pulse rate drops, and your breathing grows slow and even. Gradually, your eyes close and your brain briefly emits alpha waves, as observed on the EEG, which are associated with the absence of concentrated thought and with relaxation (Figure 7.4). Your body may twitch, your eyes roll, and brief visual images flash across your mind (although your eyelids are shut) as you enter Stage I sleep, the lightest level of sleep.

In Stage I sleep, your pulse slows a bit more and your muscles relax, but your breathing becomes uneven and your brain waves grow irregular. If you were awakened during this stage, you would report that you were "just drifting." This phase lasts for about 10 minutes. At this point, your brain waves occasionally shift from low-amplitude, high-frequency waves to high-amplitude, low-frequency waves—a pattern that indicates you have entered Stage II sleep. Your eyes roll slowly from side to side. Some 30 minutes later, you drift down into a deeper level of Stage III sleep, and large-amplitude delta waves begin to sweep your brain every second or so.

Stage IV is the deepest sleep of all; it is difficult to waken a sleeper in this stage. Large, regular delta waves—occurring more than 50 percent of the time—indicate you are in a state of oblivion. If you are awakened by a loud noise or sudden movement, you may feel disoriented. Talking out loud, sleepwalking, and bed-wetting—all of which may occur in this stage—leave no trace on memory. Deep sleep is important to your physical and psychological well-being. Perhaps this is why people who are able to sleep only a few hours at a time descend rapidly into Stage IV and remain there for most of their nap.

On average a person spends 75 percent of sleep time in Stages I through IV. At this point, something curious happens. Although your muscles are

 LAB EXPERIMENTS AND DEMONSTRATIONS

Tell students that before slipping into Stage I sleep, people experience what is known as the *hypnagogic state.* Request several volunteers to conduct research into this state over a period of several nights. Tell the researchers to put a notebook and pen next to the bed. When they lie down, they should prop up their elbow in a comfortable position so that their arm dangles in the air. As they slip into hypnagogic sleep, their arm should fall, jarring them awake. When they awake, students should quickly write down whatever images or thoughts they experienced before their arm fell. Call on volunteers to share their journals. What, if any, common experiences help to define this short altered state of consciousness? (*For example, how do hypnagogic dreams compare with daydreams and deep-sleep dreams?*)

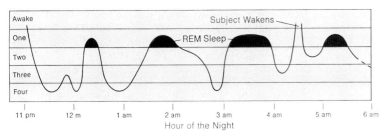

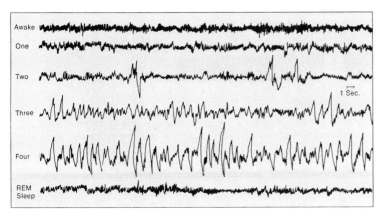

FIGURE 7.4

A diagram (top) shows the passage of a sleeper through the various stages of sleep over a seven-hour period. The second diagram shows the patterns of electrical activity (EEGs) in the brain that correspond to the various states of sleep. The EEG pattern shown for being awake is one that occurs when the person is resting quietly with eyes closed. **What percentage of sleep is spent in Stages I–IV?**

even more relaxed than before, your eyes begin to move rapidly. You have entered a more active type of sleep characterized by rapid eye movement. This is called **REM sleep.** Your pulse rate and breathing become irregular, and the levels of adrenal and sexual hormones in your blood rise—as if you were in the middle of an intensely emotional or physically demanding activity. Often, your face or fingers twitch and the large muscles in your arms and legs are paralyzed. Your brain sends out waves that closely resemble those of a person who is fully awake. For this reason, REM sleep is called active sleep. States I through IV are sometimes referred to as NREM (non REM) or quiet sleep because of the absence of rapid eye movement, which is accompanied by the slower pattern of brain waves. It is during REM sleep that almost all dreaming normally takes place.

REM sleep lasts for about 10 minutes, after which you retrace the descent to Stage IV. You go through this cycle every 90 minutes or so. Each time the period of Stage IV sleep decreases and the length of REM sleep increases—until you eventually wake up. But at no point does your brain become inactive.

How Much Sleep?

The amount of sleep a person needs in order to function effectively varies considerably from individual to individual and from time to time within a

LAB EXPERIMENTS AND DEMONSTRATIONS

Assign students to log the number of hours that they sleep each night for at least one week. If possible, have them request that other members of their household do the same. (If anyone has an infant in their family, encourage them to track the number of hours that he or she sleeps.) When students are done, have them compile averages for each person in their household by the following age ranges: infants, 2–12, 13–20, 21–30, 31–40, 41–50, 51–60, and 60+. Then compile a class average for these ages. Ask: What, if any, age-related sleeping patterns can you identify? How does your sleeping pattern compare with those of the rest of the class? How does it compare with figures mentioned in the textbook?

At A Glance

After students have read the special feature, ask them to recall the principles behind conditioned behavior. (If students have trouble, allow them to review Chapter 2.) Then ask the following questions.

1. Which of the steps for dealing with insomnia reflect efforts at conditioning?

2. Do you think that sleeping patterns are biologically programmed? Or can they indeed be relearned? Explain.

3. Have you ever tried any of these suggestions? If so, have they worked?

■ **Discussion.** Tell students that Alfred the Great (871–899) recommended that a person work eight hours a day, play eight hours a day, and sleep the rest of the time. Request volunteers to explain how this advice compares to their own ideas on sleep (and life). Suppose students were psychologists who specialized in sleeping patterns. How would they respond to Alfred? (OBJECTIVE 1)

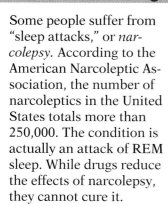

DID YOU KNOW?

Some people suffer from "sleep attacks," or *narcolepsy.* According to the American Narcoleptic Association, the number of narcoleptics in the United States totals more than 250,000. The condition is actually an attack of REM sleep. While drugs reduce the effects of narcolepsy, they cannot cure it.

MORE about . . .

The Function of Dreams. Contrary to the view that dreams serve no function, one theorist suggests that dreams are the brain's way of "unlearning" or removing certain unneeded memories. In other words, dreams are a form of mental housecleaning.

Such mental housecleaning might be necessary because it is not useful to remember every single detail of your life. Instead we tend to remember *important* things and somehow forget the rest. If the theory is correct, then those things that need to be forgotten are included in dreams, and the very act of dreaming somehow helps to erase them.

This idea has been proposed by Francis Crick, Nobel Prize winner and co-discoverer of DNA. Crick believes that if it were not for the helpful effects of dreams, evolution could not have produced the highly refined human brain. He theorizes that a brain so complex as ours could not work properly without a cleaning-up mechanism.

person's life. Newborns spend an average of 16 to 18 hours a day sleeping, almost half of it in REM sleep. Sixteen-year-olds may spend as much as 10 to 11 hours asleep each night. Students in graduate school average 8 hours a night.

Men and women who are 70 years old or older may need only 5 hours of sleep (Hobson, 1989). Adults average about 25 percent of their time in REM sleep, and 75 percent in NREM sleep. Although the amount of sleep a person needs may vary, it does appear that everyone sleeps and that both types of sleep are important to normal functioning.

At A Glance

INSOMNIA

Everyone has had a sleepless night at one time or other—a night where nothing you do brings the calm, soothing peace you want. Some people have sleep problems like this all the time, and they rarely get more than an hour or two of uninterrupted sleep a night. To help these insomniacs, psychologists Richard R. Bootzin and Perry M. Nicassio have developed a behavior modification program to strengthen the bed as a cue for sleep and weaken it as a cue for sleep-interfering activities.

They suggest that insomniacs follow these instructions:

1. Lie down to sleep only when you feel sleepy.
2. Don't use the bed for any activity other than sleep. That means no eating, reading, watching television, listening to the radio, or worrying in bed.
3. If after you're in bed for about 10 minutes you find that you can't sleep, get up and go into another room. This will help you associate your bed with falling asleep quickly and dissociate it with tossing and turning. Return to your bed when you feel sleep coming on.
4. Repeat step 3 if you still can't sleep. Get out of bed as many times as necessary during the night.
5. Get up at the same time every morning no matter how little sleep you had the night before. This will help you develop a consistent sleep pattern.
6. Don't nap during the day.

Laboratory studies have shown the effectiveness of these techniques in helping insomniacs fall asleep and stay asleep. If you have a problem, they may work for you.

For more details, see Richard R. Bootzin, Behavior Modification and Therapy: An Introduction. Cambridge, Mass.: Winthrop, 1975. Sweeney, Donald R. *Overcoming Insomnia.* New York: Bantam Books, 1991.

ADDITIONAL INFORMATION

Ask students to explain what is meant by the term "cramming." *(studying in a condensed period of time)* Point out that people commonly think that the biggest danger of cramming is sleep deprivation, which reduces alertness on a test. But, in terms of testing, cramming actually has a riskier side effect—anxiety.

To reduce anxiety, many experts recommend short catnaps to break the tension. They also suggest avoidance of all stimulants, including caffeine. A sense of calm can increase test scores more than a cup of coffee.

CHAPTER 7 Lesson Plan

Teacher Note. You might want to give students the following tips for remembering dreams.

- Always keep a pad and pen by your bed.
- Keep a light switch or flashlight in easy reach.
- Before sleeping, repeat several times "I will dream."
- Sit up slowly after a dream. Fast motions will jolt or blur the image.
- Write down your dream immediately, with as much detail as possible.
- In the morning, write down whatever dream states you remember. Do not wait until later.

VISUAL INSTRUCTION

Point out that some psychologists use the phrase *D sleep* instead of REM sleep. This phrase stands for the *dreaming stage.* It also stands for *desynchronized* EEG patterns, the wave form during REM sleep. *S sleep,* on the other hand, stands for the *slow, synchronized,* and *steep* waves of NREM sleep. **Answer to caption, Figure 7.5:** REM sleep

Dreams

We call the mental activity that takes place during sleep dreaming. Everybody dreams, although most people are able to recall only a few, if any, of their dreams. Sleep researchers sometimes make a point of waking subjects at regular intervals during the night to ask them about their dreams. The first few dreams are usually composed of vague thoughts left over from the day's activities. A subject may report that she was watching television, for example. As the night wears on, dreams become longer and more vivid and dramatic, especially dreams that take place during REM sleep. Since the amounts of time spent in REM sleep increase during the night, the last dream is likely to be the longest and the one people remember when they wake up, although people can rarely recall more than the last 15 minutes of a dream when they are awakened (Dement & Wolpert, 1958). Researchers have found that, after people have been deprived of REM sleep, they subsequently increase the amount of time they spend in REM sleep. Thus it appears that a certain amount of dreaming each night is necessary (Dement, 1976).

The Content of Dreams. When people are awakened randomly during REM sleep and asked what they had just been dreaming, the reports generally are commonplace, even dull (Hall and Van de Castle, 1966). The dreams we remember and talk about "are more coherent, sexier, and generally more interesting" than those collected in systematic research (Webb, 1975: p. 140).

Researchers who have recorded the contents of thousands of dreams have found that most—even the late-night REM adventures—occur in such commonplace settings as living rooms, cars, and streets. Most dreams involve either strenuous recreational activities or passive events such as

Everybody dreams, but most people can recall very few of their dreams.

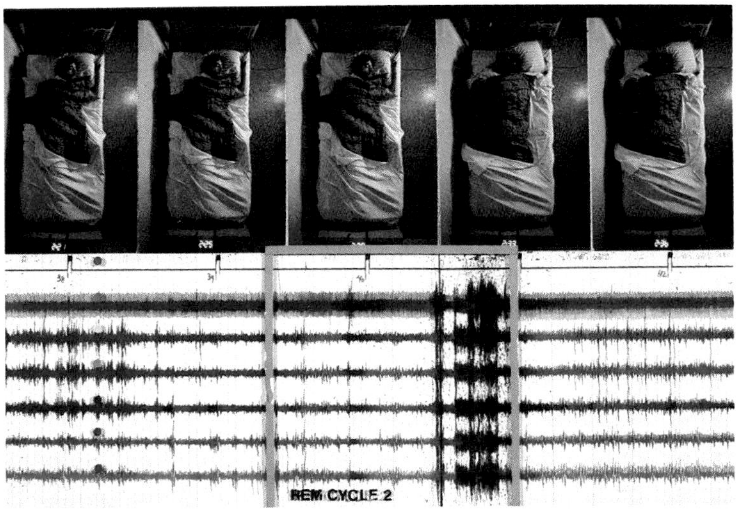

FIGURE 7.5

In recent years, psychologists have done much research on sleep in order to increase our knowledge of the various states of consciousness. **During which stage of sleep does most dreaming take place?**

CONNECTIONS: PSYCHOLOGY AND ART

Tell students that a group of painters known as the *surrealists* believed that a dream could be transposed directly from the unconscious mind onto the canvas. Marcel Duchamp and his followers defined the movement as: "pure psychic automatism . . . intended to express . . . the true process of thought." In creating their works, the surrealists borrowed heavily from the psychoanalysis started by Freud. Request volunteers to find paintings by surrealist painters such as Salvador Dali, Marc Chagall, Joan Miro, or Max Ernst. Show these works to the class as a whole. Ask: What can you infer about the surrealist view of dreams? How does it match your own vision of dreams?

Readings in Psychology.

To guide student reading, you might ask the following questions.

1. What did Freud mean when he called dreams "the royal road to the unconscious"? *(They gave insight into unconscious wishes—both fulfilled and unfulfilled.)*

2. According to Freud, what was the relationship between dreams and daily life? *(He saw all dreams as a reflection of past and present experiences.)*

3. What was Freud's lasting legacy to psychology? *(He opened the door for the scientific study of dreams and introduced the concepts of the unconscious, neurosis anxiety, and defense mechanisms.)*

VISUAL INSTRUCTION

Read aloud Freud's landmark conclusion in *The Interpretation of Dreams:* "The dream represented a particular state of affairs as I should have wished it to be. Thus its content was the fulfillment of a wish and its motive was a wish." Explore students' personal feelings about Freud's theory.

Answer to caption, Figure 7.6: the content of a dream that expresses an individual's unconscious wishes

READINGS IN PSYCHOLOGY

Freud on Dreams

Dreams are not meaningless, they are not absurd . . . . On the contrary, they are psychical phenomena of complete validity—fulfillments of wishes . . . .

If I eat anchovies or olives in the evening . . . I develop thirst during the night which wakes me up. But my waking is preceded by a dream . . . that I am drinking.

Dreams which can only be understood as fulfillments of wishes and which bear their meaning upon their faces without disguise are to be found under the most frequent and various conditions. They are mostly short and simple dreams . . . .

But in cases where the wish-fulfillment is unrecognizable, where it has been disguised, there must have existed some inclination to put up a defense against the wish; and owing to this defense the wish was unable to express itself except in a distorted shape . . . .

A young physician had sent in his income tax return, which he had filled in perfectly honestly, since he had very little to declare. He then had a dream that *an acquaintance of his came to him from a meeting of the tax commissioners and informed him that, while no objection had been raised to any of the other tax returns, general suspicion had been aroused by his and a heavy fine had been imposed on him.* The dream was a poorly disguised fulfillment of his wish to be known as a doctor with a large income . . . .

Before Freud wrote his treatise on dreams in 1900, there had been no modern attempt to investigate dreams. Freud believed that dreams often represented disguised fulfillment of repressed wishes. In Freudian dream interpretation, every dream has a *manifest content* that comes from the events of the day, sensations during sleep, and early memories, and a *latent content* that comes from the person's unconscious wishes. Freud was particularly interested in wishes involving childhood psychosexual conflicts.

Very few psychologists still use Freud's system of dream interpretation, but it opened the door for the scientific study of dreams.

From Sigmund Freud, *The Interpretation of Dreams.* Translated from the German and edited by James Strachey. Third English edition. New York: Avon Books, 1965.

FIGURE 7.6

Sigmund Freud was the first psychologist to study dreams thoroughly. He hypothesized that dreams express impulses and thoughts, often in highly symbolic form, that are unacceptable at the conscious level. **What did Freud mean by the "latent content" of dreams?**

sitting and watching, not work or study. A large percentage of the emotions experienced in dreams are negative or unpleasant—anxiety, anger, sadness, and so on. Contrary to popular belief, dreams do not occur in a split second; they correspond to a realistic time scale.

Often we incorporate our everyday activities into our dreams. Some sleep researchers have attempted to manipulate the content of a person's dreams by exposing the dreamer to either a light water spray, a flashing light, or a five-second tone. They found that the water was incorporated into 42 percent of the dreams, the light into 23 percent, and the tone into 9 percent (Dement and Wolpert, 1958). Some people maintain that their creative ideas or inspiration come from dreaming. Samuel Taylor Coleridge, for example, is said to have composed his poem "Kubla Khan" while dreaming.

Only a small proportion of dreams are negative enough to be considered nightmares. Nightmares often have such a frightening quality that we awaken in the middle of them. The sense of dread in nightmares may

CRITICAL THINKING ACTIVITY

Analyzing a Quote. Read aloud the following remark made by Freud near the end of his life.

Looking back, then, over the patchwork of my life's labors, I can say that I have made many beginnings. . . . Something will come of them in the future, though I cannot myself tell whether it will be much or little. I can, however, express a hope that I have opened up an important advance in our knowledge.

Ask: Based on information in the text, what were some of Freud's many "beginnings"? What "important advance" did he make in our knowledge of dreams?

be related to the intensity of brain activity and to the stimulation of those parts of the brain responsible for emotional reactions. The emotional reaction of dread may then influence the content of the dream. For example, you may dream that you are about to open a door and you experience a sense of dread. Once you are emotionally aroused in the dream, you may create images in the dream to justify your feelings.

Dream Interpretation

Although dreams may contain elements of ordinary, waking reality, these elements are often jumbled in fantastic ways. The dreamer may see people in places they would never go, wander through strange houses with endless doors, find herself or himself transported backward in time. The dreamer may be unable to speak—or able to fly. What do these distortions mean?

Dream interpretations have been discovered dating back to 5000 B.C. Sigmund Freud was the first theorist in the modern era to argue that dreams are an important part of our emotional lives (see Figure 7.6).

Freud believed that no matter how simple or mundane, dreams may contain clues to thought and desires the dreamer is afraid to acknowledge or express in his or her waking hours. Indeed, he maintained that dreams are full of hidden meanings and disguises.

However, some social scientists are skeptical of dream interpretations. Nathaniel Kleitman, one of the pioneers who discovered REM sleep, wrote in 1960: "Dreaming may serve no function whatsoever." According to this view, the experience of a dream is simply an unimportant by-product of stimulating certain brain cells during sleep. McCarley (1978), for example, argues that the common experience of feeling paralyzed in a dream simply means that brain cells that inhibit muscle activity were randomly stimulated.

HYPNOSIS

Hypnosis is a form of altered consciousness in which people become highly suggestible and do not use their critical thinking skills. By allowing the hypnotist to guide and direct them, people can be made conscious of things they are usually unaware of and unaware of things they usually notice. (Subjects may recall in vivid detail incidents they had forgotten, or feel no pain when pricked with a needle.)

Hypnosis does not put the subject to sleep, as many people believe. A hypnotic trance is quite different from sleep. In fact, subjects become highly receptive and responsive to certain internal and external stimuli. They are able to focus their attention on one tiny aspect of reality and ignore all other inputs. The hypnotist induces a trance by slowly persuading a subject to relax and to lose interest in external distractions. Whether this takes a few minutes or much longer depends on the purpose of the hypnosis, the method of induction, and the subject's past experiences with hypnosis.

In an environment of trust, a subject with a rich imagination can become very susceptible to the hypnotist's suggestions. Subjects function as de-

PSYCHOLOGY UPDATE

REM Sleep. Theories about REM sleep and why we dream seem almost as bountiful and different as dreams themselves. Certainly the link between REM sleep and dreaming is well established. All of us dream, but why do we need REM sleep?

One theorist argues that REM sleep aids consolidation of long-term memory. Another contends that REM sleep serves to purge the brain of unneeded information—a form of mental housecleaning.

Others argue that REM sleep is necessary to provide occasional stimulation to the brain through the sleeping hours. Still others believe it is necessary for brain growth, while another theorist claims that REM sleep reduces the impact of unusually strong motivations.

Supporting evidence for each of these ideas is mixed at best. So, the understanding of the role and the importance of REM sleep and dreaming remains a highly significant research topic, many years after the original discovery of the link between REM sleep and dreaming.

PORTRAIT

Sigmund Freud
1856–1939
Praise and condemnation have been heaped on Freud—one of the giants of 20th-century intellectual thought. Raised in Vienna, Austria, Freud experienced the anti-Semitism of his era. Even so, he stayed in his homeland until Hitler's invasion drove him to England.

Freud's greatest accomplishment rests upon his recognition of the unconscious mind. He rejected hypnosis in favor of free association, one of the bases of modern-day psychoanalysis. Freud also held that repression formed the cornerstone of all psychotherapy.

Not everyone accepts Freud's ideas today, but few refute his lasting imprint on our culture. On his 80th birthday, some 200 intellectuals sent Freud a message that read in part:

This courageous seer and healer has for two generations been a guide to hitherto undreamed-of regions of the human soul. . . . Even should the future remold and modify one result or another of his researches, never again will the questions be stilled which Sigmund Freud put to humankind. . . .

Readings in Psychology. Have students read the Section 2, Reading 7 selection in *Readings in Psychology* and answer the questions that follow the reading.

CRITICAL THINKING ACTIVITY

Identifying a Central Issue. Have students reread "Dream Interpretation." Ask: What was the central issue in the different views of dreams held by Freud and Kleitman? *(whether dreams served a purpose)* Next, organize a debate of the following topic: *Resolved*—That dreams hold no special meaning whatsoever.

They are merely a jumble of events recalled by stimulated brain cells. If possible, encourage students to do outside research in preparation for the debate.

VISUAL INSTRUCTION

According to some studies (Lynn, *et al.*, 1991; Sabourin, *et al.*, 1990), about 15 percent of the population can be very easily hypnotized. Between 5 and 20 percent are not susceptible to hypnotic suggestion. **Answer to caption, Figure 7.7:** that subjects are under a hypnotist's power once they are hypnotized

DID YOU KNOW?

Hypnosis came from the term "neuro-hypnology," which in turn came from the Greek *neuron* for "nerve" and *hypnos* for "sleep".

■ **Study and Writing Skills.** Tell students that the story of hypnosis starts with Franz Anton Mesmer (1734–1815), a German-born physician. He worked with a cure known as "animal magnetism." Using magnets or magnetized fluids, Mesmer attempted to cure people by reorganizing bodily fluids. Assign students to investigate the *mesmerists,* as Mesmer's followers became known, and write a short report on the movement. Instruct students to find out how the power of suggestion played a role in mesmerism. Also, have them look into reasons mesmerism initially stigmatized hypnosis as another "pseudoscience." (You might have students deliver their papers before completing the Community Involvement activity on this page.) (OBJECTIVE 2)

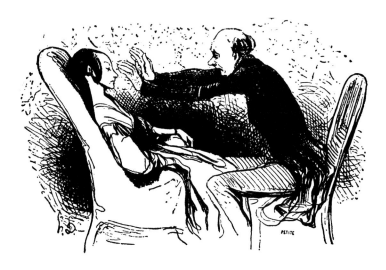

FIGURE 7.7

The nineteenth-century painter and caricaturist Daumier drew this sketch of a hypnotist. **What are some of the misconceptions about hypnotism?**

A subject must cooperate in order to be hypnotized; he or she is not under the hypnotist's "power."

scribed in the feature on page 165. Psychologists who use hypnosis stress that the relationship between the hypnotist and subject involves cooperation, not domination. The subject is not under the hypnotist's "power" and cannot be forced to do things against his or her will. Rather, the person is simply cooperating with the hypnotist. *Together* they try to solve a problem or to learn more about how the subject's mind works. Anyone can resist hypnosis by simply refusing to open his or her mind to the hypnotist, and people under hypnosis cannot be induced to do things they would not do when "awake" unless they want to.

Hypnotists can also suggest things for their subjects to remember when the trance is over, a phenomenon known as **posthypnotic suggestion.** For example, the hypnotist can suppress memory by suggesting that, after the person is awakened, she will be unable to hear the word "psychology." When she comes out of the trance, the subject may report that some people around her are speaking strangely. They seem to leave out some words occasionally, especially when they are talking about topics involving the taboo word "psychology." The subject is not aware that part of her consciousness has been instructed to block out that word. Memory can also be aided or enhanced through posthypnotic suggestion. Posthypnotic suggestion has been found to be particularly helpful in changing unwanted behaviors, such as smoking or overeating.

Psychologists do not agree about the nature of hypnosis. Some, like Theodore Barber (1965), argue that hypnosis is not a special state of consciousness, but simply the result of suggestibility. If people are just given instructions and told to try their hardest, they will be able to do anything that hypnotized people can do. Barber has shown that unhypnotized people can hold a heavy weight at arm's length for several minutes; they can lie stiff as a board with only one chair under their shoulders and another under their feet to support them; they can even stick needles through their hands.

COMMUNITY INVOLVEMENT

Arrange for a hypnotist or someone well-versed in hypnosis to visit the class. Have the visitor explain the uses and techniques of hypnosis. Prior to the visit, assign students to formulate questions to ask the visitor. Have the class assess these questions for relevance. After the visit, instruct students to summarize how the visitor affected their opinion of hypnosis as a psychological tool.

Others, like Ernest Hilgard (1986), believe that there is something special about the hypnotic state. People who are hypnotized are very suggestible; they go along with the hypnotist and do not initiate activities themselves; and they can more easily imagine and remember things. Hilgard believes that consciousness includes many different aspects that may become separated, or dissociated, during hypnosis. This view is called neodissociation theory, which includes a "hidden observer"—a portion of the personality that watches and reports what happens to the hypnotized person.

Another explanation of hypnosis is based on the importance of suggestibility in the hypnotic induction. According to some theorists (Sarbin and Coe, 1972, 1979), hypnotized people behave as they do because they have accepted the role of a hypnotized subject. We expect that hypnotized individuals will forget certain things when told, or will recall forgotten material, and we play the role. Many stage hypnotists entertain their audiences with dramatic hypnotic demonstrations by carefully selecting volunteers who appear most willing to play the role (Bowers, 1976).

Whether hypnosis is a special state of consciousness or not, it does reveal that people often have potential abilities that they don't use. Continued study may help us to understand where these abilities come from and how to use them better.

HALLUCINATIONS

Hallucinations are perceptions that have no direct external cause—seeing, hearing, smelling, tasting, or feeling things that do not exist.

Hypnosis, meditation, certain drugs, withdrawal from a drug to which one has become addicted, and psychological breakdown may produce hallucinations. (We discuss the hallucinations associated with drug withdrawal and mental breakdowns in Chapter 15.) But they also occur under "normal" conditions. People hallucinate when they are dreaming and when they are deprived of the opportunity to sleep. Periods of high emotion, concentration, or fatigue may also produce false sensations and perceptions. For example, truck drivers on long hauls have been known to swerve suddenly to avoid stalled cars that do not exist. Even daydreams involve mild hallucinations.

Interestingly enough, it seems that hallucinations are very much alike from one person to the next. Soon after taking a drug that causes hallucinations, for example, people often see many geometric forms in a tunnel-like perspective. These forms float through the field of vision, combining with each other and duplicating themselves. While normal imagery is often in black and white, hallucinations are more likely to involve color.

When Seigel (1977) traveled to Mexico's Sierra Madre to study the reactions of Huichol Indians who take peyote, he found that their hallucinations were much like those of American college students who took similar drugs. Seigel believes that these reactions are similar because of the way

MORE about...

Hypnotic States. One researcher (Gilligan, 1987) listed 12 trance experiences that are associated with the hypnotic condition.

When you are hypnotized, you may experience:

1. *total attentiveness* to your current state. You can block out irrelevant stimuli.

2. *effortless expression* in which no apparent effort is required to perform a task.

3. *reduction of critical evaluating skills*.

4. *willingness to experiment* or try new or unusual things.

5. *flexibility in your relation to time and space*. You think age regression or progression is quite possible.

6. *altered sensory experience* in which perception of your body or of visual and auditory cues may be altered.

7. *fluctuations in level of involvement* from shallow to quite deep.

8. *inhibition of verbal and motor skills*. You can move, but think it's unnecessary.

9. *trance logic* in which you find nothing bizarre.

10. *processing experience as a metaphor*. What happens to others is experienced as if happening to you.

11. *time distortion*.

12. *amnesia* may cause you to have no memory of events while hypnotized.

■ **Lab Experiments and Demonstrations.** To illustrate the power of suggestion, request a team of students to conduct a "yawn poll." Have them start to yawn as they talk to friends or family. How many times do they have to yawn before the other person also yawns? How many people are immune to the yawn? Tell students to tally the results and report to the class. Use this experiment as a basis to explore the role of suggestion in hypnosis.

DID YOU KNOW?

Many people in the path of a total eclipse experience a dramatic non-chemical "high" in which reality becomes dreamlike. Research reveals that this unique altered state of consciousness is produced by the effect of the unique light of an eclipse upon the cornea (Andrew Weil, 1977). The sense of euphoria has led people to chase eclipses around the world to duplicate the feeling.

CRITICAL THINKING ACTIVITY

Interpreting a Political Cartoon. Tell students that the purpose of a political cartoon is to convey an opinion and to influence the opinions of others. A cartoonist's tools include the use of symbols, caricatures (exaggerated features), satire, and so on. Have students study the political cartoon by Daumier in Figure 7.7. Ask: What is Daumier's opinion of hypnosis? What techniques or details does he use to get the opinion across? As a follow-up exercise, have students design political cartoons to express their own ideas on hypnosis.

■ **Creative Writing.** Tell students to imagine they are part of the sensory deprivation team described on this page and shown in Figure 7.8. Working in small groups, challenge students to write a stream-of-consciousness monologue that recreates the experience. (Tell students that stream-of-consciousness is a writing technique in which a story is told through the voice of a single character, often with one thought flowing into another.) The monologue might trace initial expectations of rest, descriptions of limited sensations, detachment from reality, and request to be released from the project. Call on volunteers to read their stories aloud. Then have students answer the caption question for Figure 7.8. (OBJECTIVE 2)

■ **Psychology Update.** After students read the margin feature, ask the following questions.

1. How was cocaine first used? *(as a painkiller)*
2. What are the effects of cocaine? *(Lead students to understand that the drug's addictive properties ultimately produce mental, emotional, and physical deterioration.)*
3. What treatments are prescribed for cocaine addiction? *(hospitalization during withdrawal, counseling, social support)*

PSYCHOLOGY UPDATE

"Crack" Cocaine. When pure cocaine was first isolated in the late 1800s, its painkilling properties revolutionized medicine. But when the addictive effects of cocaine became clear in the early 1900s, laws were passed to make it illegal.

By the mid-1980s, the use of cocaine and the variation called "crack" was epidemic, with crack easily available on the streets to anyone with $5 to $10 (Payne, Hahn, & Pinger, 1991). The immediate cocaine "high" is followed by extreme depression and desire for more of the drug. Other psychological effects include nervousness, confusion, and paranoid thoughts.

So far there are no proven pharmacological "cures" for cocaine addiction. Current treatments involve hospitalization during the withdrawal period, followed by long-term counseling and peer, family, or spouse support. Social support is vital, because drug users in healthy relationships are better able to handle stress and depression without returning to drugs.

such drugs affect the brain: portions of the brain that respond to incoming stimuli become disorganized while the entire central nervous system is aroused.

SENSORY DEPRIVATION

Donald Hebb began a series of experiments on the effects of boredom. As one of the researchers (Heron, 1957: p. 52) later described it: "The aim of this project was to obtain basic information on how human beings would react in situations where nothing at all was happening."

Male college students were paid to lie all day on a comfortable bed—they could get up only for meals and to go to the bathroom. Plastic visors over their eyes kept them from seeing anything but diffuse light; U-shaped foam-rubber pillows around their heads and the hum of a small air conditioner muted any sounds; and cotton gloves and long cardboard cuffs restricted the sense of touch (see Figure 7.8). In short, the subjects could see, hear, or touch only severely limited stimuli—they were in a state of sensory deprivation.

Most people had signed up for the experiment hoping to catch up on their work—planning term papers, lectures, and so on. How long could you last? Most lasted only into the second day. Under these conditions they quickly became irritable and found that they had trouble concentrating. After a while, some of them even began to hallucinate.

Other studies of sensory deprivation have also been performed using a variety of techniques for restricting sensory input. One study involved submerging completely in a pool heated to body temperature while wearing nothing but a diving helmet to supply oxygen. Not all techniques and conditions had the same effects. Hallucinations were generally not as common in later experiments, but extended periods of sensory deprivation did consistently lead to irritability, restlessness, and emotional upset. One of the early researchers, John Lacey, now markets a small, body-size version of the flotation chamber as an aid to relaxation!

PSYCHOACTIVE DRUGS

The drugs of interest for the study of consciousness are those that interact with the central nervous system to alter a person's mood, perception, and behavior. These are called psychoactive drugs, and range from the caffeine in coffee and in cola drinks to powerful consciousness-altering substances like marijuana, alcohol, amphetamines, and LSD (see Table 7.1).

Marijuana

Marijuana has been used as an intoxicant among Eastern cultures for centuries. In some societies it is legally and morally acceptable, whereas alcohol is not. Before 1960, marijuana use in the United States was common

CONNECTIONS: PSYCHOLOGY AND MUSIC

Tell students that in some Spanish-speaking neighborhoods people compose *plenas*, a kind of musical newspaper. Then repeat the following lines from a *plena* written about crack. Declares the composer: "Be careful of crack, you shouldn't smoke it. This sorry atrophy *[waste]*, if you do not look out, will crack *you!*" Challenge students to write their own *plenas* about the dangers of one of the psychoactive drugs described in this chapter. Call on volunteers to read the lyrics aloud. (If you have any Spanish-speaking students, have them write the *plenas* in Spanish—the language that gave birth to the *plena*.)

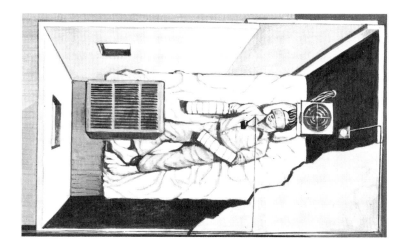

FIGURE 7.8

In an experiment on the effects of boredom, gloves and cotton cuffs prevented input to the hands and fingers. A plastic visor diffused the light coming into the eyes. A foam pillow and the continuous hum of the air conditioner and fan made input to the ears low and monotonous. Except for eating and using the bathroom, the subjects did nothing but lie on the bed. (After "The Pathology of Boredom" by Woodburn Heron. © 1957 by Scientific American, Inc. All rights reserved.) **How do the subjects usually react during sensory deprivation?**

FIGURE 7.9

Addictive drugs, like cocaine, produce a biological or psychological dependence in the user. **What are psychoactive drugs?**

VISUAL INSTRUCTION

Point out that sensory deprivation and drug addiction are altered states of consciousness. Ask: How do the two conditions differ? (*Lead students to understand that sensory deprivation results from restricted sensory input. In the case of drug addiction, sensory input may not be reduced. However, perception is chemically disrupted or altered by drugs.*) **Answer to caption, Figure 7.8:** with mood swings, restlessness, and eventually hallucinations **Answer to caption, Figure 7.9:** drugs that interact with the central nervous system to change mood, perception, and behavior

DID YOU KNOW?

Most psychologists consider alcohol, nicotine, and caffeine psychoactive drugs because they alter a person's psychological state in some way.

PSYCHOLOGISTS AT WORK

To help people overcome the addiction to drugs or alcohol, training is now offered to help people become either *substance abuse counselors* or *certified alcohol counselors* (CACs). To enter this field, people need a concentration of courses recommended by licensing agencies in most states. They also have to work a set number of hours—often more than 1,000—in a licensed treatment center. Many substance abuse counselors and CACs hold Masters in Social Work (MSW) degrees or advanced degrees in psychology. Today a number of public schools around the nation hire these specialists to work as part of the guidance department.

■ **Cooperative Learning Activity.** Organize the class into small groups. Give each group a sheet of newsprint and a felt-tip pen. Instruct the groups to select what they consider to be the 10 most dangerous psychoactive drugs listed in Table 7.1. Then have students rank these drugs from 1 to 10, with 1 being assigned to the most dangerous drug. (Remind students that some narcotics have medical value in cases of extreme pain.) Have students record their rankings on the newsprint. Call on volunteers to explain the criteria used for rating the various drugs. Point out that students generated social as well as medical bases for evaluating the drugs. (OBJECTIVE 3)

■ **Identifying Cause and Effect.** Read aloud the following description of marijuana (cannabis) use written by J. R. Tinkleman (1975).

Initial effects of cannabis at low doses usually include euphoria, heightening of subjective sensory experiences, alterations in time sense, and the [feeling] . . . *of a relaxed . . . passivity. With time, . . . these effects are intensified with impaired memory function, disturbed thought patterns, lapses of attention, and a . . . feeling of unfamiliarity.*

Based on this quote, have students speculate on some of the physical causes of dependency upon marijuana. Ask: What are some of the effects of that dependency? Does the chart uphold Tinkleman's statement? (OBJECTIVE 3)

TABLE 7.1 • Drugs and Their Effects

Name of Drug or Chemical	Duration of Action (hours)	Habituation Potential (Psychological Dependence)	Tolerance Potential (Leading to Higher Dose)	Addiction Potential (Physical Dependence)
Depressants Barbiturates (Amytal, Nembutal, phenobarbital, Seconal) Quaaludes	4–6	Moderate to high	Yes	Yes
Valium/Librium	4–6	Moderate to high	Yes	Yes
Alcohol	2–4	High	Yes	Yes
Opiates Narcotics (opium, heroin, morphine, codeine, Percodan, Demerol, methadone)	4–6	High (Very high in codeine injected)	Yes	Yes
Stimulants (amphetamines, Benzedrine, Methedrine, Dexedrine, Ritalin, Preludin)	4–8	Very high (injected) Moderate (oral)	Yes	Yes
Cocaine (crack)	1–2	High	Yes	Yes
Caffeine	2–4	Moderate	Yes	Yes
Nicotine	1–2	High	Yes	Yes
Psychedelics LSD	10–12	Low	Yes	No
Psilocybin	6–8	Low	Yes	No
Mescaline	12–14	Low	Yes	No
PCP	Variable	High	Yes	Yes
Marijuana (cannabis)	2–4	Moderate	Yes	Low
Hashish	2–4	Moderate	Yes	Low
Antidepressants Lithium Dibenzapines MAO inhibitors	8–12	Low	No	No
Inhalants (hydrocarbons, nitrous oxide, chlorohydrocarbons)	1–2	Moderate	Unknown	Unknown

ADDITIONAL INFORMATION

Assign interested students to locate the following article in the periodical section of their local library: "The End of Addiction," by Marc Galanter, *Psychology Today* (November/December 1992). Based on this article, have students write an essay that answers the following questions. (1) What type of substance abuser does Galanter feel would be most successful at "network therapy"? (2) For what types of people is this therapy usually least successful? (3) How does "network therapy" compare to anonymous twelve-step programs such as Alcoholics Anonymous (AA) or Narcotics Anonymous (NA)?

Possible Short-Term Effects	Possible Long-Term Effects
CNS depressants; sleep induction; relaxation (sedation); confusion; drowsiness; impaired judgment, reaction time, coordination, and emotional control; relief of anxiety-tension; lethargy; suppression of hallucinations; hallucinations	Irritability; weight loss; addiction with severe withdrawal illness; drowsiness; blurred vision; jaundice; habituation; possible death
CNS depressant; relaxation (sedation); confusion; drowsiness; impaired judgment, reaction time, coordination, and emotional control; frequent aggressive behavior	Diversion of energy and money from more creative and productive pursuits; habituation; possible obesity with chronic excessive use; irreversible damage to brain and liver; addiction; DTs; death
CNS depressants; sedation; relief of pain; apathy; impaired intellectual functioning and coordination; nausea and drowsiness	Constipation; loss of appetite and weight; temporary impotence or sterility; habituation; addiction with unpleasant and painful withdrawal illness; death
CNS stimulants; increased alertness, reduction of fatigue; loss of appetite; insomnia; increased respiration and heart rate	Restlessness; insomnia; irritability; weight loss; paranoia; gastric irritation; habituation; death
CNS stimulant; often elevates mood; increased heart rate and respiration; drying of the nose; laxative; depression and fatigue after effects wear off	Restlessness; irritability; destruction of nasal walls; habituation; diversion of energy and money; weight loss; paranoia; death
CNS stimulant; increased alertness; reduction of fatigue; increased pulse rate	Sometimes insomnia, restlessness, gastric irritation; habituation
CNS stimulation; relaxation; constriction of blood vessels; impaired breathing	Heart and blood vessel disease; respiratory diseases; habituation
Effects are unpredictable but can include intense visual imagery; increased sensory awareness; feeling of consciousness expansion; anxiety; rapid mood changes; nausea; increased pulse rate and blood pressure; very violent behavior with PCP	Sometimes precipitates or intensifies an already existing psychosis. Other effects include panic reaction; distorted judgment and perception; flashbacks; possible brain damage and genetic damage
Distortion of thoughts and perception; short-term memory loss; impaired coordination; panic reaction; increased appetite; hallucination in larger doses	Impaired judgment; apathy; temporary sterility and infertility; brain damage; lung cancer; possible genetic damage; habituation; hinders long-term memory
Relief of depression (elevation of mood); stimulation	Basically the same as tranquilizers
Euphoria; shortness of breath; nausea; headache; dizziness; fainting	Unknown

(includes information from Ray & Ksir, 1993)

DID YOU KNOW?

In the late 1800s, the addictive effects of narcotics such as opium and morphine sent researchers looking for a non-addictive painkiller. One of the new "miracle drugs" of this era was aspirin, invented in the 1870s by Heinrich Dreser.

■ **Evaluating Data.** Tell students to imagine they work in the emergency department. A jittery, underweight patient complains of a lack of appetite and chronic insomnia. Vital signs reveal increased respirations and a rapid heart rate. The irritable patient admits taking a drug to keep up with two jobs. Ask: Based on Table 7.1, what class of drugs would you suspect? *(stimulants)*

MEETING SPECIAL NEEDS

Visual Disability. Tables and charts sometimes present special problems for students who have difficulties with visual materials and spatial organization. Using Table 7.1, show students how the tabular material is organized. Point out the title first. Ask: What does this tell you about the selection of data for the table? Next, guide students through the various horizontal column heads. Then look at the vertical column heads. Ask: Suppose you wanted to find information on the effects of caffeine. How would the column heads help you to find this information?

■ Analyzing a Quote. Read aloud the following quote by a teenager named Lisa who entered a recovery program for drug addiction in 1993.

Some of my friends smoked [marijuana] and seemed to have a good time. So I decided to try it too. Where we hung out, you could buy other drugs. But I stayed away from them—that is, until I thought it wouldn't hurt to try crack just once. Once—ha! Before I knew it, I was wacked [crazy]. I was a 15-year-old with a habit. My parents found a hospital where I could get help. You know what I learned there? 'A drug is a drug is a drug.' That includes alcohol. Sometimes it's tough, but I just remember the look in my parents' eyes when they dropped me off at the hospital. That keeps me straight.

Based on this quote, ask students how Lisa would probably view marijuana. *(as a dangerous drug)* Her story reveals a possible side effect of marijuana that can't be easily measured in a laboratory. Ask: What is that side effect? *(the temptation of trying a stronger drug)*

only among members of certain subcultures, such as jazz musicians and artists in big cities. Marijuana use increased throughout the 1960s and most of the 1970s, but then began to decline. The U.S. National Institute on Drug Abuse in the early 1990s classified 13 percent of 18 to 25 year olds as current users, down from 25 percent in 1974.

The active ingredient in marijuana is a complex molecule called tetra-hydrocannabinol (THC), which occurs naturally in the common weed *Cannabis sativa*, or Indian hemp. Marijuana is made by drying the plant; hashish is a gummy powder made from the resin exuded by the flowering tops of the female plant. Both marijuana and hashish are usually smoked, but they can also be cooked with food and eaten.

The effects of the drug vary somewhat from person to person and also seem to depend on the setting in which the drug is taken and the user's past experience. But, in general, most sensory experiences seem greatly augmented—music sounds fuller; colors look brighter; smells are stronger; foods have stronger flavors; and other experiences are more intense than usual. Users may feel elated, the world may seem somehow more meaningful, and even the most ordinary events may take on an extraordinary significance. A person who is high on marijuana may, for example, suddenly become aware of the mystical implications of a particular painting. The sense of time is greatly distorted. A short sequence of events may seem to last for hours. Users may become so obsessed with an object that they sit and stare at it for many minutes. A musical phrase of a few seconds' duration may seem to stretch out in time until it becomes isolated from the rest of the composition.

As many users of marijuana have discovered, the drug can instill or heighten a variety of unpleasant experiences. If a person is in a frightened, unhappy, or depressed mood to begin with, the chances are excellent that taking the drug will blow the negative feelings out of proportion, so that the user's world, temporarily at least, becomes very upsetting. Cases have been reported in which marijuana appears to have helped bring on psychological disturbances in people who were already unstable before they used it.

Despite the obvious need for careful research on marijuana, the first well-controlled scientific studies of its effects did not appear until the late 1960s, scarcely anticipating its surging popularity in the 1970s and 1980s. Some of these studies have suggested that heavy and prolonged use of marijuana may impair testosterone hormone levels in males and produce lower sperm counts, but the results, so far, are inconsistent, and thus questionable. Other studies suggest that marijuana use is more damaging to the lungs than cigarette use. Although there is no direct evidence that marijuana use causes lung cancer, the tar and other chemicals in marijuana smoke are drawn deep into the lungs and held 20 to 40 seconds, adding to the drug's potential for hindering lung function (Ray & Ksir, 1993).

Hallucinogens

Hallucinogens—so-called because their main effect is to produce hallucinations—are found in plants that grow throughout the world. They have

COOPERATIVE LEARNING ACTIVITY

Organize the class into groups. Tell students that they have been chosen as part of a special presidential youth commission to develop materials for the war against drugs. Challenge each group to create a series of posters, brochures, and newspaper advertisements to discourage drug abuse among teenagers. Suggest that students go beyond library research to contact local health organizations already involved in combating substance abuse. You might arrange to have students display their various materials on the wall and a table outside the guidance office, gym, or health class.

FIGURE 7.10

Because drug dependence is almost impossible to cure on one's own, people who suspect that they have a problem should seek immediate attention from a psychologist, physician, or counselor. **What are hallucinogens?**

VISUAL INSTRUCTION

Tell students that recovery programs often stress repetitive routines and slogans. Based on what students have read about learned behavior, why do they think these techniques are used to break a drug dependency? *(Answers will vary, but lead students to understand that it is much harder to break a habit—especially an addictive habit—than it was to learn it.)* **Answer to caption, Figure 7.10:** drugs that produce hallucinations

DID YOU KNOW?

In 1991, researchers at the University of Michigan surveyed 15,500 high school seniors at 136 high schools. Findings showed that illicit drug use had dropped from 33 percent to 29 percent since 1990. This figure contrasted sharply to the 54 percent recorded by researchers in the peak year of 1979.

been used for their effects on consciousness since earliest human history (Schultes, 1976). These drugs are also called "psychedelic" (mind-manifesting) because they are seen as demonstrating the ways in which the mind has the potential to function.

Among the more common hallucinogenic plants are belladonna, henbane, mandrake, datura (jimson weed), one species of morning-glory, peyote, many kinds of mushrooms, and also cannabis. While we still do not know the exact chemical effects of hallucinogens on the brain, some contain chemical compounds that seem to mimic the activity of certain neurotransmitters, the chemical messengers that regulate brain-cell activity.

LSD (lysergic acid diethylamide), the best-known and most extensively studied of the hallucinogens, is also the most potent; in fact, it is one of the most powerful drugs known. LSD, which is a synthetic substance, is 100 times stronger than psilocybin, which comes from certain mushrooms, and 4,000 times stronger than mescaline, which comes from the peyote. A dose of a few millionths of a gram has a noticeable effect; an average dose of 100

STUDY AND WRITING SKILLS

Assign interested students to investigate the non-chemical hallucinations sought in some Native American religions. An example includes the sweat lodges of the Lakota (Sioux). After an intense steam bath, sweat bathers are doused with icy cold water—much like the process in Scandinavian saunas. The bathers report a euphoria more intense than any state induced by a psychedelic drug.

Teacher Note. Point out to students that alcohol depresses the central nervous system, much like a sedative. It works first on those parts of the brain that affect self-control and other learned behaviors. When pregnant women drink more than three ounces of alcohol a day, it also affects the brain of the unborn child. The result can be a condition known as *Fetal Alcohol Syndrome (FAS)*. FAS babies often have brain defects, problems in speaking, and other developmental disabilities. (Cole, *et al.*, 1987) Additional information on alcohol abuse can be found in Chapter 15.

■ **Interpreting Statistics.** Distribute copies of the following figures on the percentage of high school seniors who have tried alcohol.

1975 90.4%		**1980** 93.2%
1985 92.6%		**1990** 89.5%
1991 88%			

Based on these figures, what generalizations can students form about alcohol use among students their age? *(Answers will vary, but might note that most have tried it at some time; that alcohol use is dropping)*

to 300 micrograms produces a "trip" that lasts from 6 to 14 hours. To control such small doses, LSD is often dissolved into strips of paper or sugar cubes.

During an LSD trip a person can experience any number of mood states, often quite intense and rapidly changing. The person's "set"—expectations, mood, beliefs—and the circumstances under which he or she takes LSD can affect the experience, often making it terrifying. Perceptual hallucinations are very common with LSD. Hallucinatory progressions may be experienced in which simple geometric forms evolve into surrealistic impossibilities. The user may encounter such distortions that familiar objects become almost unrecognizable. A wall, for example, may seem to pulsate or breathe. One's senses, too, seem to intermingle; sounds may be "seen" and visual stimuli may be "heard." A person may experience a dissociation of the self into one being who observes and another who feels. Distortions of time, either an acceleration or a slowing down, are also common. A single stimulus may become the focus of attention for hours, perceived as ever-changing or newly beautiful and fascinating.

As measured by the ability to perform simple tasks, LSD impairs thinking, even though users may feel they are thinking more clearly and logically than ever before. Panic reactions are the most common of LSD's unpleasant side effects. Those who experience panic and later describe it often say that they felt trapped in the experience of panic and were afraid that they would never get out or that they would go mad. Use of LSD peaked in the 1960s. The likelihood of *flashback* experiences, even months after taking LSD and public fears of chromosome damage—not confirmed by subsequent research—probably led to LSD's declining popularity (Ray & Ksir, 1993).

Alcohol

The most widely used and abused mind-altering substance in the United States is alcohol. The consumption of alcohol is encouraged by advertisements and by social expectations and traditions. The immediate effect of alcohol is a general loosening of inhibitions. Despite its seeming stimulating effect, alcohol is actually a depressant that serves to inhibit the brain's normal functions. When people drink, they often act without the social restraint or self-control they normally apply to their behavior.

In small doses, alcohol use can have a temporarily pleasant effect. The effects of alcohol consumption, however, depend on the amount and frequency of drinking. As the amount consumed increases within a specific time, the drinker's ability to function diminishes. The person experiences slurred speech, blurred vision, and an impairment in judgment and memory. Permanent damage to the brain and liver and a change in personality can result from prolonged heavy use of alcohol.

Several studies suggested that not all of the early effects of drinking are the result of the alcohol alone; some are social effects. People expect to feel a certain way when they drink. In one study, men who were led to believe they were drinking alcohol when they were, in fact, drinking tonic water, became more aggressive. They also felt more sexually aroused and were less anxious in social situations (Marlatt and Rohsenow, 1981).

ADDITIONAL INFORMATION

In recent years, researchers have developed a method for detecting intoxication by sampling gases released from the fluids that moisten the eye. Alcohol is one of the few intoxicants that is released in this way. The machine works by placing an eyecup over the eye and testing the emitted gases. As of 1993, results of the test had not been accepted as evidence in courts of law. But most researchers think it promises to be a more accurate means of testing than the breathalizer.

FIGURE 7.11

Biofeedback is a process by which an individual learns to control internal physiological states. **Why do people practice biofeedback?**

BIOFEEDBACK

Biofeedback involves learning to control your internal physiological processes with the help of feedback from these physiological states. For example, you can be hooked up to a biofeedback machine so that a light goes on every time your heart rate goes over 80 (Figure 7.11). You could then learn to keep your heart rate below 80 by trying to keep the light off. How would you do it? When researcher David Shapiro (1973) asked a participant in one of his experiments how he changed his heart rate, the subject asked in return, "How do you move your arm?"

However people do it, biofeedback has been used to teach people to control a wide variety of physiological responses, including brain waves (EEG), heart rate, blood pressure, skin temperature, and sweat-gland activity (Hassett, 1978a). The basic principle of biofeedback is simple: feedback makes learning possible. Imagine trying to learn to play the saxophone if you were deaf. If you couldn't hear all the squeals and honks you made by mistake, your version of "The Star-Spangled Banner" would probably cause all your neighbors to move. It is only through the feedback of hearing your errors that your playing improves.

But our bodies are not designed to provide subtle feedback about internal physiological states. I have no idea whether my heart rate is now 60, 80, or 100 unless I take my pulse. Biofeedback involves using machines to tell people about very subtle, moment-to-moment changes in the body.

■ **Discussion.** After students have read the information on biofeedback and meditation, ask students the following questions.

1. How has biofeedback and meditation raised questions about certain physiological functions? *(They have shown that some involuntary functions might be subject to personal control.)*
2. Which method places greater reliance on technological aids? *(biofeedback)* Why? *(to report physiological changes sought by many people)*
3. Why might both techniques induce a state of well-being in the practitioner? *(Answers will vary. For example, some students may cite the sense of control over, or detachment from, certain bodily processes.)*
(OBJECTIVE 4)

VISUAL INSTRUCTION

Answer to caption, Figure 7.11: control physiological responses and improve health

Independent Practice

■ **Making a Chart.** Assign students to make a chart showing the various altered states of consciousness mentioned in the text. Column heads should include: name of the altered state, cause of the condition, physical/psychological characteristics of the condition. Encourage students to research information beyond the text, adding column heads of their own design. Also, based on library references, have them add additional types of altered states of consciousness.
(OBJECTIVES 1–4)

CONNECTIONS: PSYCHOLOGY AND SOCIAL STUDIES

Remind students of the efforts to curb alcohol abuse through Prohibition. Have them review the provisions of Amendments 18 and 21 to the Constitution. Assign students to summarize the experiment in a short paragraph. Then ask them to debate whether they think it is possible to curb substance abuse through the use of laws. Why or why not? As an extending activity, you might have students draw up a new amendment banning the sale of all mind-altering substances. Direct them to poll reactions to this proposal among the school community. What is the prevailing opinion ?

■ **Research.** Many gyms use equipment that provides biofeedback on heart rates, muscle tension, and so on. If you have a gym or YWCA/WMCA in your community that has such equipment, request volunteers to interview physical trainers on use of these devices. How does biofeedback facilitate or improve training? Have students report their findings in the form of an oral report to the class. (OBJECTIVE 4)

■ **Readings in Psychology.** Have students read the Section 2, Reading 8 selection in *Readings in Psychology* and answer the questions that follow the reading.

People can then experiment with different thoughts and feelings while they watch how each affects their bodies. In time, people can learn to change their physiological processes.

Before biofeedback, scientists believed that responses like heart rate and sweat-gland activity were involuntary, that people could not consciously control them. When researchers in the 1960s began to find that people could, there was a great deal of excitement about the potential of the nervous system. Many began experimenting with biofeedback to cure medical and stress-related conditions like high blood pressure, migraine headaches, and tension headaches. At first, many biofeedback cures were reported in the press. But doctors are very familiar with the fact that patients often improve when they believe in a treatment, even if it's only a sugar pill. Psychologists were suspicious that these miraculous cures had more to do with the power of suggestion than with biofeedback itself.

Therefore, more careful studies were started to see what medical conditions could be helped by biofeedback. Some of the best-documented biofeedback cures involve special training in muscular control. Tension headaches often seem to result from constriction of the frontalis muscle in the forehead. Thomas Budzynski and others (1973) used biofeedback to teach people to relax this specific muscle. The practice went on for several weeks while other people were given similar treatments without biofeedback. Only the biofeedback group improved significantly.

Migraine headaches have been successfully treated by a more controversial process—biofeedback for hand warming. People watch a meter that gives a very precise reading of the temperature of their fingers and gradually learn to warm up their hands slightly. Some researchers believe that this works because it changes the pattern of blood flow in the body, decreasing circulation to arteries in the forehead. Others think that the technique simply relaxes people. A third group continues to wonder whether the power of suggestion isn't the most important element in this particular cure.

As a result, using biofeedback to treat conditions from partial paralysis to epilepsy is a very active area of research; but it will take at least several years to discover the problems for which biofeedback is the best solution medical science can offer.

MEDITATION

In the 1960s, psychologists began to study **meditation,** focusing attention on an image or thought with the goal of clearing one's mind and producing an "inner peace." In one of the first experiments, people were simply asked to concentrate on a blue vase.

The participants soon reported that the color of the vase became very vivid and that time passed quickly. The people could not be distracted as easily as they normally might. Some people felt themselves merging with the vase. Others reported that their surroundings became unusually beautiful, filled with light and movement. All the meditators found the experi-

---

ADDITIONAL INFORMATION

Point out that biofeedback involves learning how to use the mind to control biological responses such as blood pressure, muscle tension, and heart rate. The technique relies on the assumption that internal organs rapidly adjust to ongoing environmental events. Researchers have shown, for example, that the heart rate of factory workers picks up at the end of a coffee break in anticipation of a return to heavy labor. Encourage students to share personal experiences with this phenomenon. For example, have any students ever experienced a dry mouth or sweaty palms in anticipation of a public speech? Discuss the implications of such reactions for the use of biofeedback in treating psychosomatic illnesses.

ence pleasant. After 12 sessions they all felt a strong attachment to the vase and missed it when it was not present during the next session (Deikman, 1963).

Other researchers went on to show that when people meditated, their physiological state changed. Robert Keith Wallace at UCLA (1970) measured the brain waves (EEG), heart rate, oxygen consumption, and sweat-gland activity of 15 people as they practiced Transcendental Meditation, a Westernized version of yoga meditation techniques, developed by the Maharishi Mahesh Yogi. For two 20-minute periods each day, meditators sit in a comfortable position and repeat a special word—called a *mantra*—over and over again. Wallace found that when people did this, electrical measurements of their bodies proved that they were deeply relaxed.

Further studies suggested that the regular practice of meditation was physically relaxing (Woolfolk, 1975), but also led to changes in behavior such as decreased drug use (Benson and Wallace, 1972). Researchers generally agree that most people can benefit from the sort of systematic relaxation that meditation provides. The issue is not clear-cut, however. Only people who benefit from meditation may continue to use it. Thus, the reported benefits may come from a biased, self-selected sample of successful practitioners. Others have reported data that suggest that, while meditating, some people may actually be sleeping. If so, the reported benefits of meditation may result simply from relaxation.

There is some controversy over how meditation techniques differ and what their specific effects are. In his best-selling book *The Relaxation Response*, Herbert Benson (1975) argued that most forms of meditation produce the same result, which he called the "relaxation response." Benson believes that all through recorded history, people have been using various

FIGURE 7.12

The *mandala* is a symbol of the universe used as an aid to meditation. This one is Tibetan and is now in the Newark Museum. **What is a mantra?**

■ **Demonstration.** Point out that one of the tools of meditation is known as a *koan*—a riddle or question that has no answer. Its purpose is to provoke concentration and self-control. To illustrate the use of a koan, challenge students to reflect on one of the following well-known examples. Tell them there is no right or wrong answer. In fact, all answers are irrelevant.

- "What is the sound of one hand clapping?"
- "What did your face look like before your parents were born?"

Request volunteers to explain how concentration on the koan helps induce an altered state of consciousness. As a follow-up activity, you might encourage students to write some of their own koans.

 LAB EXPERIMENTS AND DEMONSTRATIONS

Challenge students to develop a hypothesis about the following problem: How would relaxation exercises and/or meditation affect your pulse rate? Next, have students take their pulse (number of beats per minute) and record it. After about 10 minutes into the lesson on meditation, have them take it again. Then switch off the lights and tell students to relax, breathing in and out at a carefully paced rate. You might play a meditation tape or talk calmly to students. After 10 minutes, have them take their pulses again. Ask students whether the experiment supported or did not support their hypotheses. What variables might have affected the relaxation exercise in the classroom? (For example, how might a neighbor's giggles influence their pulse?)

■ Cooperative Learning Activity.

Organize the class into six research groups. Tell students that each group must compete for a $400,000 grant to investigate one of the following altered states: sleep and dreams, hypnosis, hallucinations, psychoactive drugs, biofeedback, and meditation. Their task is to prepare a presentation for the board awarding the grant. Each group's presentation should include a description of the altered state, reasons for studying it further, and a proposed research topic or project. Allow time for each group to deliver its presentation. If possible, have a panel of teachers select the "grant winner."

Using Psychology

To guide student reading of the feature, you might ask the following questions.

1. What do most experts think causes blood pressure to rise? *(stress, stimulants, suppressed emotions)*
2. What is hypertension? *(a condition of persistently high blood pressure)*
3. Why is blood-pressure biofeedback only a partial answer to reducing blood pressure? *(Complex, expensive equipment limits its use.)*
4. What other techniques are researchers using to lower blood pressure? *(muscle-tension feedback and meditation)*

techniques to elicit the relaxation response. He cites many examples, including the contemplative practices of St. Augustine and Martin Luther's instructions for prayer.

The opposite of Walter Cannon's famous "fight or flight" response, the relaxation response is said to be physiologically distinct from more casual states of relaxation or sleep. Four basic elements are required to elicit the relaxation response: a quiet environment, a comfortable position, a "mental device"—such as a word that is repeated over and over again, or a physical object that the meditator concentrates on—and a passive attitude. Although not all psychologists agree that the relaxation response is entirely different from sleep or that all relaxation yields the same physical pattern, most do believe that Benson's technique can be helpful for many people. It is described in detail in his book.

Using Psychology

Lowering Blood Pressure

One out of every three American adults has high blood pressure. More than 90 percent of these cases are diagnosed as essential **hypertension**—a euphemism that means nobody really knows what is causing it. Traditionally, physicians have treated this problem with pills. But now doctors are shifting their emphasis from pills to people. Patients with high blood pressure are being taught to relax, often with the help of meditation and biofeedback (Hassett, 1978b).

Blood pressure is the force of the blood moving away from the heart, pushing against the artery walls. It changes from instant to instant, peaking as the heart beats and blood spurts through the arteries, and gradually decreasing to a minimum just before the next beat. Blood pressure is expressed as two numbers: systolic pressure (the maximum value when the heart beats) over diastolic pressure (the minimum pressure between beats). It is measured in millimeters of mercury (abbreviated mmHg), a standard unit of force. Normal blood pressure is somewhere around 120/80 mmHg.

Blood pressure varies constantly and increases under stress. Visiting the dentist, taking an examination, thinking about trying out skydiving with the new friend you're trying to impress, even drinking a cup of coffee (a mild stimulant) will increase your blood pressure temporarily. Strong emotions, particularly suppressed anger, will also raise blood pressure.

When blood pressure goes up and stays up, the medical condition is called hypertension. Definite hypertension refers to a blood

CONNECTIONS: PSYCHOLOGY AND WORLD CULTURES

Request interested students to investigate the role of meditation in one of the Buddhist sects, such as Zen or Tibetan Mahayana. Encourage them to locate examples of mantras, chants, and so on. Allow time for students to share their research with the class. If possible, encourage students to conduct a meditation session similar to one that might be found in one of the Buddhist monasteries now found in the United States. You might also have students read aloud from a sample dharma discourse, or lesson, found during their research.

pressure greater than 160/95. Hypertension is called the silent killer because it usually produces no pain, no other symptoms or warnings before causing severe damage to the cardiovascular system or other organs. But a killer it is. It is a primary cause of stroke (blood-vessel damage in the brain) and, like smoking and high cholesterol levels, increases the risk of suffering heart attacks and coronary-artery disease.

After researchers discovered that healthy people could raise and lower their blood pressure with the help of biofeedback, it was but a small step to the idea that hypertensives could be taught to lower their blood pressure. In 1971, Harvard researchers Herbert Benson, David Shapiro, Bernard Tursky, and Gary Schwartz reported in *Science* that they had done just that. Five essential hypertensives had learned to lower their systolic pressure over the course of several weeks of training. Since then, others have found that biofeedback can be used to reduce both systolic and diastolic blood pressure.

Even in the first study, however, there were hints that biofeedback's effects don't always last after the subject leaves the laboratory. Gary Schwartz, for example, noticed that one man had a puzzling pattern of successes and failures. Five days a week, this hypertensive man faithfully attended training sessions, collecting $35 every Friday for his success in lowering his systolic pressure. When he returned each Monday morning, however, he again had high blood pressure. After several weeks of this, Schwartz took the patient aside and asked him for an explanation. It seemed that Saturday nights the man took his biofeedback earnings to the race track, gambled, and lost both his money and his controlled level of blood pressure!

So it was clear from the start that biofeedback was not a magical cure, only part of the answer. Since blood-pressure biofeedback requires complex and expensive equipment, it wasn't practical to use it with large numbers of patients. Other researchers therefore experimented with teaching hypertensives to relax their muscles, using a simpler form of biofeedback. This too led to lower blood pressure, at least temporarily.

Herbert Benson has shown that meditation is successful as a partial treatment for reducing high blood pressure. Surwit, Shapiro, and Good (1978) directly compared the effects of blood-pressure biofeedback, muscle-tension biofeedback, and meditation. All three reduced blood pressure, with no significant differences among the groups. Others have shown that meditation will cut the heart's pumping rate (Dillbeck & Orme-Johnson, 1987), reduce feelings of chronic anxiety (Eppley, Abrams, & Shear, 1989), and boost feelings of self-worth (Alexander, Rainforth, & Gelderloos, 1991).

ASSESS

Check for Understanding

Assign students to write a short essay in which they identify healthy and unhealthy altered states of consciousness. Instruct them to support their answers with examples from the text.

Reteach

Have students complete the Chapter 7 Study Guide Activity. For extended review, assign the Chapter 7 Review Activity as homework or an in-class assignment.

Enrich

Have students complete the Chapter 7 Extension Activity and answer the questions that follow it.

Have students complete the Chapter 7 Application Activity.

Evaluate

Administer and grade the Chapter 7 Test. Two forms are available should you wish to give different tests to different students/classes.

CLOSE

Direct students to assess their brainstorming at the start of the chapter. (See the Motivating Activity on page 156.) Ask: What, if any, items would you delete from the list? What items would you add? What characteristics do altered states of consciousness share in common?

CONNECTIONS: PSYCHOLOGY AND ARCHITECTURE

Write the word *transcendental* on the chalkboard. Ask students to define the term or look it up in a dictionary. (Lead students to understand the term in its spiritual/philosophical meaning—that is, as an effort to rise above, or transcend, the physical world.) Using an opaque projector, show students examples of Gothic cathedrals such as Notre Dame or Chartres. Ask: What elements of architecture might be described as transcendental? *(soaring vaults, stained glass windows, etc.)* How might such structures promote meditation and prayer?

ANSWERS

Concepts and Vocabulary

1. Stage 1—lightest level of sleep in which muscle relax, pulse slows, and breathing and brain waves become irregular. Stage 2—eyes roll from side to side. Stage 3—low-voltage waves sweep brain every second or so. Stage 4—deepest state of sleep with large, regular delta waves. REM sleep occurs in a separate stage.

2. 25 percent

3. Techniques include: try to sleep only when sleepy; avoid eating, watching TV, listening to the radio, or worrying in bed; get up if sleep does not come; don't nap during the day; get up the same time every morning.

4. may be related to the intensity of brain activity and to stimulation of parts of brain responsible for emotional reactions

5. Freud saw dreams as the road into the unconsciousness. Others, such as Kleitman, believe dreams serve no function at all.

6. A person becomes highly receptive to internal/external stimuli. The hypnotist induces a trace by persuading a subject to relax and lose interest in external distractions. Barber argues that hypnosis is not an altered state, while Hilgard believes there is something special about the hypnotic state.

7. phenomenon in which the hypnotist suggests things for the subject to remember when the trance is over

178

SUMMARY

Use the following outline as a tool for reviewing this chapter. Copy the outline onto your own paper, leaving spaces between headings to make notes about key concepts.

I. Sleep and Dreams
  A. Stages of Sleep
  B. How Much Sleep?
  C. Dreams
  D. Dream Interpretation
II. Hypnosis
III. Hallucinations
IV. Sensory Deprivation
V. Psychoactive Drugs
  A. Marijuana
  B. Hallucinogens
  C. Alcohol
VI. Biofeedback
VII. Meditation

CONCEPTS AND VOCABULARY

1. Describe each of the four stages of sleep. During which stage is it most difficult to awaken someone? During which stage do we dream and display REM?

2. What percentage of sleep time do adults usually spend in REM sleep?

3. Describe techniques that insomniacs can use to help them fall asleep and stay asleep.

4. Provide one possible explanation for the sense of dread people usually experience during a nightmare.

5. Explain Freud's view of the meaning of dreams. Give some other views of dreams.

178

6. Describe what happens when someone is hypnotized. What does Barber say about hypnosis being an altered state of consciousness? How do Sarbin and Coe view hypnosis? How does Hilgard view hypnosis?

7. Explain and describe the phenomenon of posthypnotic suggestion.

8. Define hallucination. Give some possible causes of hallucination.

9. Detail some of the typical effects of sensory deprivation on people.

10. Which consciousness-altering drugs have a high potential for psychological dependence?

11. Characterize the typical reactions caused by LSD.

12. Describe the possible consequences of prolonged heavy use of alcohol.

13. List some health problems that biofeedback can potentially help.

14. Give the basic elements of the relaxation response.

15. Can you name the most widely used and abused mind-altering substance in the United States?

CRITICAL THINKING

1. **Analyze.** What behaviors do you perform automatically? Pick one of your automatic behaviors and pay close attention to how you perform it. What are the individual parts that make up the behavior? How does consciously thinking about the behavior affect your performance of it?

2. **Evaluate.** Keep a diary of your dreams for at least a week. Dreams are difficult to remember, so keep a paper and pencil by your bed. When you wake up after a dream, keep your eyes closed and try to remember it in your mind. Then write it down, including as much detail as you can. Also write down any ideas you may

8. sensations or perceptions that have no direct external cause; high emotion, concentration, fatigue, or drugs

9. Common effects of sensory deprivation include irritability, restlessness, and emotional upset.

10. Answers will vary, but may include alcohol, nicotine, sedatives, narcotics, stimulants, and PCP.

11. Typical reactions include changing mood states, perceptual hallucinations, dissociation, distortions of time, and panic reactions.

12. damage to the brain and liver; personality changes

13. tension headaches, migraine headaches, possibly partial paralysis and epilepsy

14. a quiet environment, a comfortable position, a "mental device," and a passive attitude

15. alcohol

have about what the dream means and any feelings you may have about the dream. After you have kept track of your dreams for several days, ask yourself: Am I able to consciously control my dreams in any way? Am I better able to understand myself by examining my dreams?

3. **Analyze.** One way of becoming aware of your consciousness is through meditation. Meditation is not concentration in the normal sense of the word. It is opening up one's awareness to the world at the present. Try the following for 10 to 15 minutes a day. Find a quiet spot without distractions. Listen quietly without making any generalizations on what you hear. Listen for the sounds without naming them. After each period, write down your observations. Which sounds did you "hear" for the first time?

4. **Synthesize.** Have you ever hallucinated a sight or sound—perhaps when you were very tired or upset? What did you experience? Why do you suppose you created this particular hallucination?

APPLYING KNOWLEDGE

1. Hypnosis is a form of suggestibility. You may discover which of your friends is susceptible to hypnosis by doing the following test in hypnosis. Have your subjects place a coin in their open palm and shut their eyes. Repeatedly suggest to them that they feel the palm slowly turning over, until the coin falls out of the palm. You may be surprised at the results.

2. Choose any word and say it at least 100 times. What happens?

3. Some of the mind-altering chemicals that people use during the day are not ordinarily thought of as drugs. These include caffeine and nicotine. Observe your family and/or friends for a 24-hour period. Which drugs or chemicals did you see used? In what quantities were they used? Did you notice any changes in the per-

son's mood or behavior? What do your observations tell you about the effects of these drugs or chemicals on people's behavior and moods?

BEYOND THE CLASSROOM

1. In recent years, efforts to send an anti-drug message to teenagers have taken many forms. One strategy is to place anti-drug ads in magazines teenagers are likely to read, such as *Rolling Stone, Seventeen, US,* or *YM.* Look through recent magazines for advertisements against the use of drugs. Photocopy or cut out any ads you find. Bring the ads to class and ask class members to react to each ad. Ask your classmates which ads they think are effective. Then ask your classmates which ads they think are ineffective. Using the feedback you received from your classmates, come up with several ideas for new ads that would effectively convey an anti-drug message to teenagers. Present these ads to members of the class for additional feedback.

IN YOUR JOURNAL

1. Since Freud's pioneering work on dreams, many psychologists have theorized that by interpreting the content of our dreams, we can better understand our unconscious desires. Other social scientists have maintained a more commonplace view of dreams. They suggest that our dreams reflect more about what we were thinking about or doing on a particular day than what our unconscious desires may be. Write a two-page essay in your journal that presents a case for both viewpoints. You may want to look for recent magazine articles on dreams. If possible, use a recent dream that you remember as an example to support one of the viewpoints.

Critical Thinking

1. By breaking down the behavior into components, they will become more conscious of it. Students will then assess whether consciousness improves or hinders the action the behavior helps to perform.

2. You might focus on whether students felt the dreams gave them insight or just provided a rehash of everyday events.

3. Lead students to understand the heightened sense of perception caused by intense concentration.

4. Point out that some hallucinations are induced by fatigue or stress.

Applying Knowledge

1. Ask students if the results indeed surprise them. Why or why not?

2. Answers will vary.

CHAPTER BONUS
Test Question

This question may be used for extra credit on the chapter test.
Choose the letter of the correct response.

Meditation and hypnosis are similar in that both states:

a. produce total relaxation.

b. are accompanied by changes in brain activity.

c. are based on Eastern religious practices.

d. decrease blood pressure.

Answer: **b**

3. Respect student confidentiality in reporting specific family observations.

Beyond the Classroom

1. Encourage students to identify specific techniques used by advertisers such as the "bandwagon approach," "glittering generalities," and so on.

IN YOUR JOURNAL

If time permits, discuss journal entries individually with students.

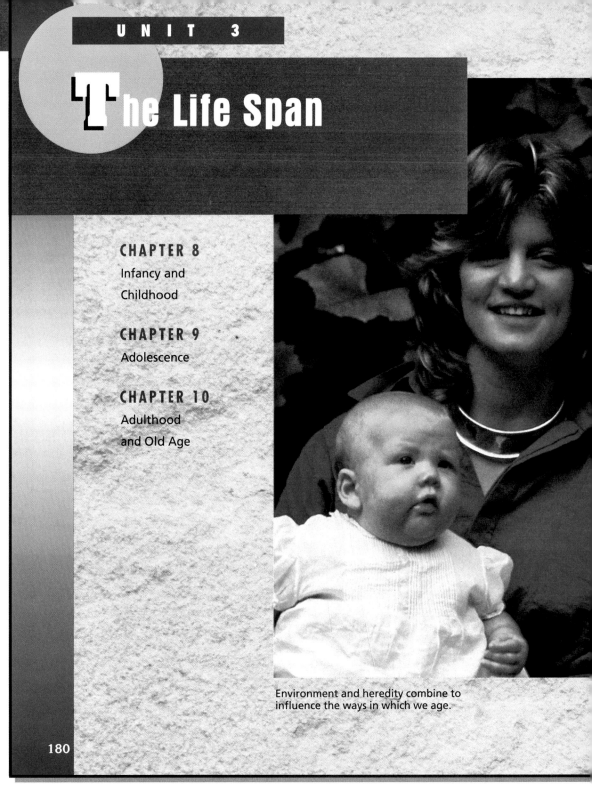

The Life Span

Environment and heredity combine to
influence the ways in which we age.

180

INTRODUCING THE UNIT

Tell students that Unit 3 investigates two themes present in all our lives—growth and change. Next, using long sheets of computer paper, have students prepare time lines broken into five-year intervals from 0–100. In blue pen, have students plot some of the physical, emotional, and intellectual milestones in their lives thus far. In red pen, have them predict events to take place in the years ahead. Call on volunteers to share what they consider to be the most important changes experienced by humans from birth to death.

181

Unit 3 in Perspective

Chapter 8 begins the story of human development by looking at both the physiological and behavioral changes that take place from birth to age 12. Within this context, the chapter explores the theories of pioneers in developmental psychology.

Chapter 9 continues the story of human development through the adolescent years, presenting facts and theories about bodily, intellectual, and emotional growth during the years 13–19.

Chapter 10 presents the closing chapters in life of any human—early adulthood, middle adulthood, old age adulthood, and death.

Connecting to Past Learning
Ask students to think about the influences that shape development. Ask: What factors do you think are most influential in shaping what and how you develop during your adolescent years? How have these factors changed since your early childhood?

UNIT PROJECT

Assign groups of students to clip pictures from magazines or bring in personal photographs that illustrate each of the developmental stages covered in this unit. You might arrange these visuals displayed on students' personal time lines along walls around the room or in one large bulletin board display.

181

CHAPTER 8
Infancy and Childhood

TEXT TOPICS	SPECIAL FEATURES	RESOURCE MATERIALS
The Beginning of Life, pp. 183–185	**More About Psychology,** p. 184	▬ Reproducible Lesson Plan; Study Guide; Review Activity
How Do Babies Grow?, pp. 185–188	**More About Psychology,** p. 186 **At a Glance:** Ethnic Differences in Infants, p. 186 **Psychology Update,** p. 188	▬ Reproducible Lesson Plan; 🔲 Study Guide; Review Activity 📦 Transparency 16
Intellectual Development, pp. 188–197	**Using Psychology:** Children and Television, pp. 194–197	▬ Reproducible Lesson Plan; 🔲 Study Guide; Review Activity 📦 Transparency 17
Mental Retardation, pp. 197–198		▬ Reproducible Lesson Plan; Study Guide; Review Activity
The Development of Language, pp. 198–200		▬ Reproducible Lesson Plan; Study Guide; Review Activity
Emotional Development, pp. 201–205	**At a Glance:** Imaginary Playmates, p. 203	▬ Reproducible Lesson Plan; Study Guide; Review Activity
Socialization, pp. 205–214	**Psychology Update,** p. 212 **More About Psychology,** p. 213 **Using Psychology:** Child Abuse, pp. 213–214 **Fact or Fiction?,** p. 214	▬ Reproducible Lesson Plan; Study Guide; Review Activity; Application Activity; 🔲 Extension Activity 📦 Transparency 18 📖 *Readings in Psychology:* Section 3, Readings 1, 2 ▬ Chapter Test, Form A and Form B ⊙ Understanding Psychology Testmaker

PERFORMANCE ASSESSMENT ACTIVITY

Ask students to work in pairs or in small groups to role-play a demonstration of a specific principle or theory of child development. For example, a pair of students might role-play the process involved in a child's developing awareness of object permanence.

Or a group of students might demonstrate the kind of learning that occurs when small children invent a game. *(The role plays should be well rehearsed and structured to convey a clear picture of the specific developmental processes involved.)*

CHAPTER RESOURCES

Readings for the Student

Bower, T. G. R. *Development in Infancy.* San Francisco: Freeman, 1982.

Gilligan, C. *In a Different Voice: Psychological Theory and Women's Development.* Cambridge MA: Harvard University Press, 1982.

Pines, Maya. *Revolution in Learning: The Years from Birth to Six.* New York: Harper and Row, 1966.

Readings for the Teacher

Bartholet, Elizabeth. *Family Bonds: Adoption and the Politics of Parenting.* Boston: Houghton Mifflin, 1993.

Hearn, Barbara. "Literacy and Reading Development: A Review of Theories and Approaches." *Early Child Development and Care,* 86 (1993): 131–146.

Kagan, J. *The Nature of the Child.* New York: Basic Books, 1984.

Monaco, Nanci M., and Gaier, Eugene L. "Developmental Level and Children's Understanding of the Gulf War." *Early Child Development and Care,* 79 (1992): 29–38.

Multimedia

Childhood—The Enchanted Years (two parts of 26 minutes each, 3/4″ or 1/2″ video). Films Incorporated, Education. This video shows the development of children from birth to four years, including reaching, perception, walking, and talking.

Cognitive Development (22 minutes, 3/4″ or 1/2″ video). McGraw-Hill Training. Piaget's theory of cognitive development is explained through animation. The behaviorist view is also presented.

For additional resources see the bibliography beginning on page 530.

CHAPTER 8
Lesson Plan

FOCUS

Motivating Activity

People learn faster and learn more in their early years than at any other time in their lives. Explore any preconceptions that students might have about infancy and childhood. For example, how much of the world do the students believe babies might comprehend? What are the earliest memories that students recall? Tell the class that in this chapter they will learn about how infants and young children develop.

Meeting Chapter Objectives.

Point out the objectives on page 183 to the students in previewing the chapter content. Have students rephrase each objective in question form. Then, assign students to answer the questions as they read Chapter 8.

Building Vocabulary.

Have students examine the list of key terms for words that they recognize. Ask volunteers to offer psychological definitions of those terms. Then have them check the Glossary for accuracy. Which words in the list were unfamiliar? Tell students to look for context clues that help define these terms as they read the chapter.

Infancy and Childhood

FIGURE 8.1 Childhood is a time of rapid learning. We change faster and learn more in these years than we ever will again.

182

TEACHER CLASSROOM RESOURCES

- Chapter 8 Reproducible Lesson Plan
- Chapter 8 Study Guide
- Chapter 8 Review Activity
- Chapter 8 Application Activity
- Chapter 8 Extension Activity

- Transparencies 16, 17, 18 Transparency Strategies and Activities

- *Readings in Psychology:* Section 3, Readings 1, 2
- Chapter 8 Test, Form A and Form B

- Understanding Psychology Testmaker

OBJECTIVES

After studying this chapter, you should be able to

■ describe the processes of intellectual development and Piaget's theory.

■ discuss the development of language.

■ compare the theories of social development.

■ summarize the cognitive-developmental theory and Kohlberg's stages of moral reasoning.

The young child lives in a strange world of wonders and delights. A door-knob or the leg of a table is a mysterious object that an infant will fondle and taste for hours. Mommy and Daddy are the source of all life's great pleasures, and many of its pains. Each day there is something new to be learned.

It is hard to believe that less than 15 years ago, you were probably only 2 feet tall and were taking your first step. Just a year or two after that, you spent your days intently playing house, cops and robbers, and doctor. Most of those events from your life are long forgotten, but you changed faster and learned more in childhood than you ever will again.

Developmental psychology is the study of the changes that occur as people grow up and grow older. It covers the entire life cycle, from conception to death. What does the newborn know? How does the infant respond in the early years of life? How do we learn to walk and talk, to think and feel? How do we develop our unique personalities? These are some of the many questions developmental psychologists seek to answer.

In this chapter we describe the variety of psychological processes experienced from infancy through childhood. In the next chapters we will look at adolescence, adulthood, and old age.

KEY TERMS

accommodation
anal stage
assimilation
conservation
critical period
developmental psychology
Electra complex
genital stage
grasping reflex
identification
imprinting
latency stage
maturation
object permanence
Oedipal conflict
oral stage
phallic stage
representational thought
role taking
rooting reflex
schemes
separation anxiety
socialization
sublimation
telegraphic speech

IN YOUR JOURNAL

Observe a group of 2-year-old children. Record in your journal the two-word sentences you hear.

183

Exploring Key Ideas

Innate and Learned Behavior.

Help students make connections with past learning by reminding them that they have already studied the general ways that people learn (Chapter 2). They have also explored many of the physiological, social, and cognitive factors that affect behavior, especially motivations and emotions. Point out that childhood development involves all of these factors. You might put the headings Conditioned, Innate, Social, and Cognitive on the chalkboard, and have students list examples of each kind of development under the appropriate heading as they read the chapter.

IN YOUR JOURNAL

Suggest that students observe several different children in a variety of settings as they interact with parents, peers, and strangers.

EXTRA CREDIT ACTIVITY

Ask students to interview a child psychologist to learn about the various developmental problems he or she studies and treats. Students should find out what kind of special training the psychologist has had and if he or she specializes in any particular area of developmental psychology. Students should present their findings either in writing or in brief oral reports to the class.

TEACH

Guided Practice

■ **Discussion.** Point out that learning begins from the moment of birth, as newborns direct their gazes toward bright patterns and faces. Have the class brainstorm a list of sensations that a typical newborn might experience within the first few days of life. (OBJECTIVE 1)

■ **Discussion.** After students read the margin feature, ask them the following questions.

1. What do you suppose is the purpose of the startle reflex? (*Answers will vary. It may facilitate the child's being scooped up by the mother in times of danger.*)
2. What do you suppose is the purpose of the Babinski reflex? (*Answers will vary.*)
3. With what other reflexes are children born? (*Answers will vary, but might include the gag reflex to clear the throat.*)

FIGURE 8.2

(a) The strength of the grasping reflex is demonstrated in a baby only a few days old. (b) This infant is responding to a touch on the cheek by opening his mouth and turning his head. **What is this response called?**

MORE about...

Reflexes. The *rooting* and *sucking* reflexes, present in all human infants, gradually decline in strength. The *grasping* reflex disappears during the first half year in those infants where it is present at birth.

The Moro, or *startle*, reflex is quite unusual. An infant lying on its back, when startled by a loud noise out of sight above his or her head, will show a very complex response. The arms will spread out at right angles to the body and grasp upwards. The legs will spread outward.

Now consider this situation. What would happen if someone ran a thumbnail right up the center bottom of your foot? Your toes would curl, and your foot would withdraw. Before her first birthday, an infant will do exactly the opposite—the toes flare outward, and the foot presses against the stimulus. This is called the *Babinski* reflex. Pediatricians use the shift in the Babinski from infantlike to adultlike form around the first birthday as a sign of normal neurological development.

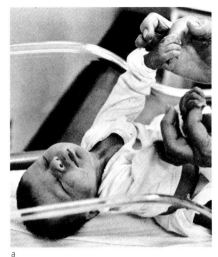
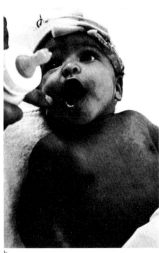

a   b

THE BEGINNING OF LIFE

Development begins long before an infant is born. Expectant mothers can feel strong movement and kicking—even hiccuping!—inside them during the later stages of pregnancy. It is common for a fetus (an unborn child) to suck its thumb, even though it has never suckled at its mother's breast or had a bottle.

Birth puts staggering new demands on a baby's capacity to adapt and survive. He goes from an environment in which he is totally protected from the world to one in which he is assaulted by lights, sounds, touches, and extremes of temperature. The newborn is capable of certain inherited, automatic, coordinated movement patterns, called reflexes, that can be triggered by the right stimulus (Figure 8.2). The **grasping reflex,** for example, is a response to a touch on the palm of the hand. Infants can grasp an object, such as a finger, so strongly that they can be lifted into the air. We suspect this reflex is left over from an earlier stage in human evolution, when babies had to cling to their apelike mothers' coats while their mothers were climbing or searching for food.

Also vital is the **rooting reflex.** If an alert newborn is touched anywhere around the mouth, he will move his head and mouth toward the source of the touch. In this way the touch of his mother's breast on his cheek guides the baby's mouth toward her nipple. The sucking that follows contact with the nipple is one of the baby's most complex reflexes. The baby is able to suck, breathe air, and swallow milk twice a second without getting confused. This is at least as difficult as learning to walk and chew gum at the same time.

Besides grasping and sucking, newborns look at their bodies and at their surroundings. From birth, unless they are sleeping, feeding, or crying, they direct their gazes toward bright patterns and faces, tracing the outlines of those patterns with their eye movements.

How do newborn infants, lying in a hospital nursery, perceive the world? Do they see a roomful of stable objects and hear distinct sounds? Or is the sensory world of newborns an ever-changing chaos of meaningless shapes and noises—as William James put it, "one great booming, buzzing confusion"?

These are difficult questions to answer. How do we measure the capabilities of newborn infants who cannot speak or understand the questions of curious psychologists? One reasonable approach is to take advantage of the things infants *can* do. And what they can do is suck, turn their heads, look at things, cry, smile, and show signs of surprise or fright. The vigor of a baby's sucking, the patterns of eye movements, and expressions of pleasure and displeasure are all closely tied to how the baby is being stimulated. By measuring these behaviors while stimulating the baby in different ways, we can infer how the infant perceives the world. For example, infants spend less time looking at out-of-focus movies than they do looking at the same movies in focus. Moreover, infants quickly learn to suck vigorously on a pacifier attached to the focusing mechanism of a movie projector in order to cause an out-of-focus picture to become more sharply defined (Figure 8.3). This suggests that babies are attuned to distinct edges; if the visual world were a blurry confusion for infants, they would not care that a movie was slightly blurry (Kalmis and Bruner, 1973). Studies like this have refuted the notion that the world is essentially disorganized and chaotic to a baby.

HOW DO BABIES GROW?

In the space of two years, this grasping, rooting, searching infant will develop into a child who can walk, talk, and feed herself or himself. This transformation is the result of both maturation and learning.

Maturation

To some extent a baby is like a plant that shoots up and unfolds according to a built-in plan. Unless something is wrong with an infant, she will begin to lift her head at about 3 months, smile at 4 months, and grasp objects at 5 to 6 months. Crawling appears at 8 to 10 months. By this time the baby may be able to pull herself into a standing position, although she will fall if she lets go. Three or four months later she will begin to walk, tentatively at first, but gradually acquiring a sense of balance.

Psychologists call internally programmed growth **maturation.** Maturation is as important as learning or experience, especially in the first years. Unless a child is persistently underfed, severely restricted in her movements, or deprived of human contact and things to look at, she will develop more or less according to this schedule. Purely as a matter of efficiency, it is worth a parent's time to wait until infants reach *maturational readiness*

FIGURE 8.3

This 4-month-old baby sucks on the pacifier to keep the pattern in focus. **How do psychologists define maturation?**

■ **Discussion.** In discussing maturational readiness, ask students to speculate about psychological drawbacks of pushing a small child to master new skills too soon. (*Answers will vary. For example, the child might experience the kind of frustration associated with learned helplessness.*) (OBJECTIVE 1)

PSYCHOLOGISTS AT WORK

The nature-versus-nurture question is of fundamental concern to *developmental psychologists*. In general, they study the interrelation between biologically predetermined maturational behaviors and the dynamics of environment. They also study how heredity and genetic makeup either enhance or limit development and how environmental factors work to promote or hinder innate capabilities. In addition, they conduct research to determine how children can be encouraged to develop their full potential within society.

At A Glance

After students have read the special feature, ask them to draw a conclusion about the cause of some of the ethnic differences in children's response patterns. (*that some differences are the result of evolution and genetic programming*)

■ Making Comparisons.

After students read the margin feature, ask them to compare the results of Freedman's study regarding ethnic differences in infants to findings in the study of the Gusii and Boston mothers. (*Whereas Freedman's study revealed genetic differences, Richman, Miller, and Le Vine's study showed that cultural factors affect the development of different responses in children.*)

WORKING WITH TRANSPARENCIES

Project Transparency 16 and use the guidelines provided in Teaching Strategies and Activities. Assign Student Worksheet 16.

MORE about...

Ethnic Differences. Studying ethnic differences in mothers' responsiveness to their children, Richman, Miller and Le Vine (1992) visited homes of the Gusii in rural Kenya and the homes of middle-class whites in the suburbs of Boston. They observed how mothers interacted with their second- (or later-) born infants. The researchers recorded the amount of holding or touching between infant and mother as well as episodes of talking.

Though equally responsive when their children were distressed, the methods of response were markedly different. When an infant cried, Gusii mothers made physical contact with them 58 percent of the time and talked to them about 8 percent of the time. Boston mothers held or touched their infant about 35 percent of the time when they cried and talked to them about 25 percent of the time.

The cultural differences studied here show that people value and support development of different responses in the children. Not only do babies start out differently, they are raised differently around the world.

At A Glance

ETHNIC DIFFERENCES IN INFANTS

It probably won't surprise you to learn that different breeds of puppies show striking differences in temperament and behavior. Young beagles, for example, are irrepressibly friendly; wire-haired terriers are tough and aggressive. But it probably will raise both your eyebrows to discover that newborn infants belonging to different ethnic groups start out life with different sets of responses that seem to relate more to their genes than to their individual personalities.

To learn how important ethnic differences are in the way we respond, psychologist Daniel G. Freedman studied the responses of newborn Chinese and Caucasian babies. His results show that in many ways Chinese and Caucasian babies behave like two different breeds.

Here are some examples of the differences Dr. Freedman found. The Chinese babies were far more adaptable than the Caucasians. They cried less easily and were easier to console. In addition, they seemed comfortable in almost any position they were placed, while the Caucasian infants tossed and turned until they were satisfied. When a cloth was briefly placed against the babies' noses, the Caucasian infants responded with a fight; they immediately turned their faces or swiped at the cloth with their hands. The Chinese babies adapted to the cloth's presence in the simplest possible way—by breathing through their mouths. As Dr. Freedman points out, "It was as if the old stereotypes of the calm, inscrutable Chinese and the excitable, emotionally changeable Caucasian were appearing spontaneously in the first 48 hours of life."

For more details, see Daniel G. Freedman, "Ethnic Differences in Babies," *Human Nature,* January 1979.

before pushing them into mastering new skills. No amount of coaching will push a child to walk or speak before she is physiologically ready.

This was demonstrated in an experiment with identical twins (Gesell and Thompson, 1929). One twin, but not the other, was given special training in climbing stairs, building with blocks, and the like. This child did acquire some skill in these areas. But in a short time the second child learned to climb and build just as well as his twin—and with much less practice. Why? Because he had matured to the point where he could coordinate his legs and hands more easily.

The process of maturation becomes obvious when you think about walking. An infant lacks the physical control walking requires. However, by the end of the first year the nerves connected to the child's muscles have grown. He or she is ready to walk.

ADDITIONAL INFORMATION

Heredity places limits on development despite all the efforts that a person may make to improve the environment in which a child is nurtured. For example, no diet or program of education will significantly increase the general level of intelligence with which a normal child is born. Similarly, heredity limits the height a child will attain and puts a cap on physical performance. No child alive today, for example, will ever be capable of high-jumping 50 feet. At best, nurturing allows hereditary potentials to emerge fully.

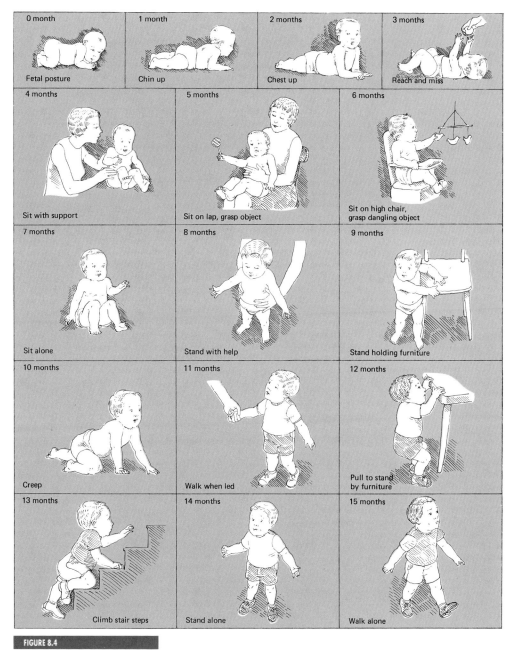

FIGURE 8.4

This artwork illustrates the sequence of motor development. The age given for the appearance of each skill is approximate; there is a wide range of individual differences. **When do most infants begin to walk on their own?**

VISUAL INSTRUCTION

If any students have young siblings at home, ask them to describe their experiences in observing motor development in infants. Point out that the sequence of motor skills involves increasingly complex patterns of muscular control. What can students infer will be the next skill in the sequence pictured here? (*running*)
Answer to caption, Figure 8.4: 15 months

DID YOU KNOW ?

Studies have shown that the quantity of time that a parent spends with a child is less important for development than the quality of that time. This is good news for working parents. (Hetherington & Park, 1986)

COMMUNITY INVOLVEMENT

Arrange for students to visit a pediatrician's office or clinic to interview mothers regarding their babies' development. Students should ask how old the infant is and find out what motor skills he or she has just mastered. Students should also try to learn if any of the motor skills pictured in Figure 8.4 developed earlier than expected or are delayed. Have students prepare oral reports of their findings for the class. (You might arrange for release forms giving students permission to use mothers' comments.)

Teacher Note. After students read the margin feature, point out that more than alcohol, tobacco, and illicit substances pose risks to the unborn. Other factors include: certain medications that the mother may be taking, environmental pollutants, and deficiencies in the mother's general diet.

■ **Creating a Poster.** Have students interview obstetricians and pharmacists to learn about substances that women should avoid during pregnancy and about things that women can do to promote the general well-being of the unborn child. Have students work with artists in the class to present their findings of dos and don'ts in an eye-catching poster. (OBJECTIVE 1)

PSYCHOLOGY
UPDATE

Drugs and Pregnancy. A child's mental and emotional development can be seriously affected by the mother's lifestyle, even before the child is born. The use of alcohol, tobacco, or other drugs by a mother-to-be has been linked to developmental problems.

Children born to women who drink large amounts of alcohol during pregnancy may suffer from *fetal alcohol syndrome*. These children are characterized by mental retardation, poor motor development, and unusual facial features such as a flat nose and widely spaced eyes. (Waterson & Murray-Lyon, 1990).

The child of a woman who smoked regularly during pregnancy averages 9 ounces less than a nonsmoker's child, and will likely be shorter both at birth and during maturation. Smoking increases the likelihood of tubal pregnancy as well as problems with breathing and, later in childhood, verbal processes such as spelling and reading (Moessinger, 1989; Fried & Watkinson, 1990).

The use of crack or of other psychoactive drugs during pregnancy causes a range of developmental problems. A major problem is that babies born to drug users may be addicted to the drug by the time they are born.

By recording the ages at which thousands of infants first began to smile, to sit upright, to crawl, and to try a few steps, psychologists have been able to draw up an approximate timetable for maturation (Figure 8.4). This schedule helps doctors and other professionals to spot problems and abnormalities. If a child has not begun to talk by the age of 2½, a doctor will recommend tests to determine if something is wrong.

However, one of the facts to emerge from this effort is that the maturational plan inside each child is unique. On the average, babies start walking at 12 to 13 months. However, some are ready at 9 months, and others delay walking until 18 months. Each baby also has his or her own temperament. Some infants are extremely active from birth and some quiet. Some are cuddly and some stiff. Some cry a great deal while others hardly ever whimper. No two babies are exactly alike, and no two mature according to the same timetable. Explaining these differences is the challenge for developmental psychologists.

Learning

Maturation is only part of the process of growing up. Infants and small children are exceptionally responsive. Each experience changes the child, teaches him something, pushes him in some direction. The child learns to make associations, to expect certain events—such as mother and food—to come together. Children learn to do things that produce rewards and to avoid doing things that produce punishments. They also learn by imitating other people.

Infants too are able to learn new behaviors. Even newborn babies change their behavior in response to the environment—which, as you will recall from Chapter 2, is the basic definition of "learning." One team of psychologists taught 2- and 3-day-old infants to turn their heads at the sound of a buzzer by rewarding them with a bottle each time they did so.

Another researcher built a small theater for 4- to 5-week-old babies. The infants were placed in a well-padded seat opposite a blank wall that served as a movie screen, and were given pacifiers. The pacifiers were connected to the projector. As we described earlier, the infants had to suck on the pacifiers to focus the picture. Soon the babies had learned the trick and sucked hard, pausing for only a few seconds to catch their breath. When the researcher reversed the procedure, so that sucking blurred the picture, they quickly learned to lengthen the pause to 8 seconds (Pines, 1970). We can assume that infants are just as responsive to everyday events as they are to the stimuli in experiments.

Clearly, then, learning is an important part of the process of growing up. In the pages that follow we will show how inner plans and outside influences—maturation and learning—work together in the development of intellect, language, love, and morality.

INTELLECTUAL DEVELOPMENT

If you have a younger brother or sister, you may remember times when your parents insisted that you let the little one play with you and your

CONNECTIONS: PSYCHOLOGY AND MUSIC

After students have read about the experiment involving the pacifiers and movies (Pines, 1970), you might play Stephen Sondheim's song "Children Will Listen" from the Broadway musical *Into the Woods*. What common-sense and psychological advice would students have for parents whose attitude is "Don't worry, the baby doesn't understand what's going on"?

friends. No matter how often you explained hide-and-seek to your 4-year-old brother, he spoiled the game. Why couldn't he understand that he had to keep quiet or he'd be found right away?

This is a question Swiss psychologist Jean Piaget set out to answer more than 60 years ago. Of the several theories of intellectual development, Piaget's is the most comprehensive and influential. Common sense told him that intelligence, or the ability to understand, develops gradually as the child grows. The sharpest, most inquisitive 4-year-old simply cannot understand things a 7-year-old grasps easily. What accounts for the dramatic changes between the ages of 4 and 7?

Piaget spent years observing, questioning, and playing games with babies and young children—including his own. He concluded that younger children aren't "dumb" in the sense of lacking a given *amount of information*. Rather, they think in a different *way* than older children and adults; they use a different kind of logic. A 7-year-old is completely capable of answering the question "Who was born first, you or your mother?" but a 4-year-old isn't (Chukovsky, 1963). Intellectual development involves quantitative changes (growth in the *amount* of information) as well as qualitative changes (differences in the *manner* of thinking).

In time Piaget was able to detail the ways in which a child's thinking changes, month by month, year by year. Although the rate at which different children develop varies, every child passes through the same predictable stages. Each stage builds on the last, increasing the child's ability to solve more complex problems.

How Knowing Changes

Understanding the world involves the construction of **schemes,** or plans for knowing. Each of us is an architect and engineer in this respect, con-

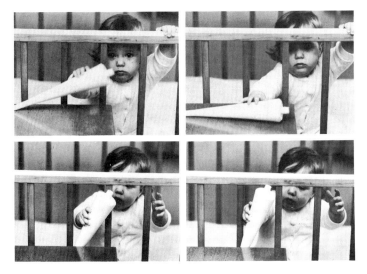

FIGURE 8.5

This child possesses a scheme for grasping objects and pulling them to her that does not adequately match the features of the environment she is trying to assimilate. At first, her scheme will not get the toy through the bars of the playpen. Finally, the addition of turning the objects to grasping and pulling achieves a state of equilibrium. **What is accommodation?**

VISUAL INSTRUCTION

Ask students what they imagine the world would be like if people never developed object permanence—i.e., if "out of sight, out of mind" were the norm. You might ask students to develop a short skit of such a world grounded in the here and now.

Answer to caption, Figure 8.6: the awareness that objects exist even when they are out of sight

Teacher Note. Point out to the students that, according to Piaget, both the concept of object permanence and the motor skills pictured in Figures 8.4 and 8.5 develop during the first, or sensorimotor, stage of cognitive development.

WORKING WITH TRANSPARENCIES

Project Transparency 17 and use the guidelines provided in Teaching Strategies and Activities. Assign Student Worksheet 17.

FIGURE 8.6

This infant of about 6 months cannot yet understand that objects have an existence of their own, away from her presence. (a) The infant gazes intently at a toy elephant. (b) When the elephant is blocked from view, she gives no indication that she understands the toy still exists. **What is object permanence?**

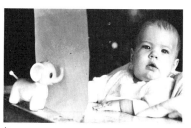

a   b

structing intellectual schemes, applying them, and changing them as necessary. When we put a scheme into action, we are trying to understand something. In the process of **assimilation,** we try to fit the world into our scheme. In the process of **accommodation,** we change our scheme to fit the characteristics of the world.

According to Piaget, newborns have a set of ready-made responses. They respond to bright lights by blinking, to objects in their hands by grasping, to a sudden loss of support by throwing out their arms and legs, and to an object in the mouth by sucking. These reflexes let babies understand and cope with things. In grasping a block, babies assimilate it to their grasping scheme after accommodating it—changing their grasp to fit it.

Assimilation and accommodation work together to produce intellectual growth. When events do not fit into existing schemes, new and grander schemes have to be created. The child begins to see and understand things in a new light. Progressive changes in the way a baby perceives objects illustrate this.

Object Permanence. A baby's understanding of things lies totally in the here and now. The sight of a toy, the way it feels in her hands, the sensation it produces in her mouth are all she knows. She does not imagine it, picture it, think of it, remember it, or even forget it. How do we know this?

When an infant's toy is hidden from her, she acts as if it had ceased to exist (Figure 8.6). She doesn't look for it; she grabs whatever else she can find and plays with that. Or she may simply start crying. At 7 to 12 months, however, this pattern begins to change. When you take the baby's toy and hide it under a blanket—while she is watching—she will search for it under the blanket. However, if you change tactics and put her toy behind your back, she will continue to look for it under the blanket—even if she was watching you the whole time.

You can't fool a 12- to 18-month-old baby quite so easily. A child this age watches closely and searches for the toy in the last place she saw you put it. But suppose you take the toy, put it under the blanket, conceal it in your hands, and then put it behind your back. A 12-month-old will act surprised when she doesn't find the toy under the blanket—and keep searching there. An 18- or 24-month-old will guess what you've done and walk behind you to look (Figure 8.7). She knows the toy must be somewhere (Ginsburg and Opper, 1969).

This is a giant step in intellectual development. The child has progressed from a stage where she apparently believed that her own actions

 LAB EXPERIMENTS AND DEMONSTRATIONS

Have students research their own maturation process by interviewing their parents or other family members and by collecting pictures of themselves at various ages from birth through adolescence. Students should find out specific things about their physical, motor, emotional, and language development. Baby books are an excellent source. Some of the facts they should try to uncover include: height and weight at birth and at various stages of development; age when they first crawled, walked, rode a bicycle, played a sport; age when they spoke their first word and what it was; age when they developed special skills, such as dancing, drawing, or singing. Have students present their findings in notebook format, collage, or combined in a bulletin board display.

created the world, to a stage where she realizes that people and objects are independent of her actions. This new scheme, **object permanence,** might be expressed: "Things continue to exist even though I cannot see or touch them." The child now conceives of a world of which she is only a part.

Representational Thought. The achievement of object permanence suggests that a child has begun to engage in what Piaget calls **representational thought.** The child's intelligence is no longer one of action only. Now, children can picture (or represent) things in their minds. At 14 months of age, Piaget's daughter demonstrated this. When she was out visiting another family, she happened to witness a child throwing a temper tantrum. She had never had a tantrum herself, but the next day she did— screaming, shaking her playpen, and stamping her feet as the other child had. She had formed so clear an image of the tantrum in her mind that she was able to create an excellent imitation a day later (Ginsburg and Opper, 1969). To Piaget, this meant that his daughter was using symbols. Soon she would learn to use a much more complex system of symbols—spoken language. The infant is limited to solving problems with his or her actions. The older child can mentally represent the problem and use language to think it through. Thinking with actions, in other words, comes before thinking with language.

The Principle of Conservation. More complex intellectual abilities emerge as the infant grows into childhood. Somewhere between the ages

FIGURE 8.7

By the age of 2, a child realizes that the disappearance of an object does not mean that it no longer exists. In fact, if an object is concealed, a child will search for it because he or she knows it still exists somewhere. **What did Piaget mean by representational thought?**

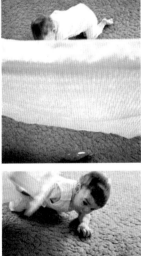

CHAPTER 8 Lesson Plan

■ **Discussion.** Ask students to explain in their own words why the anecdote about Piaget's daughter throwing a tantrum is an example of representational thought. (OBJECTIVE 1)

VISUAL INSTRUCTION

Ask students if they have ever observed the concept of object permanence operating in animals, such as pet dogs. A puppy, for example, will not miss a toy ball if the owner hides it. An older dog, however, may begin searching through the house for its toy when it feels like playing. It knows the ball exists even though it cannot see or smell it.
Answer to caption, Figure 8.7: the ability to picture (or represent) things in the mind

ADDITIONAL INFORMATION

A characteristic of the preoperational stage of cognitive thinking is egocentric thought. The child thinks that everyone is attuned to his or her own particular perspective and knows precisely what he or she knows. Accordingly, the child's explanations can be vague and full of narrative gaps. Another example of egocentric thought is similar to the proverbial image of the ostrich hiding its head in the sand. The preoperational children may "hide" in plain view by covering their eyes, thinking that if they can't see then no one can see them.

192

VISUAL INSTRUCTION

Point out that there are several other types of conservation problems that psychologists use to test cognitive development. You can easily demonstrate two of these. (1) Place four playing cards on a table so that they form a single rectangle. Now move the cards apart somewhat so that there is space between them. A child who does not understand conservation will perceive a change in total surface area. (2) Place 20 pennies spaced apart in two parallel lines of equal length. Now move the pennies in one line closer together. The young child will think there is a change in number.

Answer to caption, Figure 8.8: during the concrete operational stage

FIGURE 8.8

The girl taking part in this demonstration thinks there is more water in the graduated cylinder; she has not yet acquired the principle of conservation. Although she has seen the liquid poured from one beaker to another, she bases her decision on the height of the column of water and ignores its diameter. **During which of Piaget's four stages of cognitive development do most children acquire the ability to understand conservation problems?**

of 5 and 7, most children begin to understand what Piaget calls **conservation,** the principle that a given quantity does not change when its appearance is changed. For example, if you have two identical short, wide jars filled with water and you pour the contents of one of these jars into a tall, thin jar, a child under 5 will say that the tall jar contains more water than the short one. If you pour the water back into the short jar to show the amount has not changed, the child will still maintain that there was more water in the tall container. Children under 5 do not seem to be able to think about two dimensions (height and width) at the same time. That is, they do not understand that a change in width is made up for by a change in the height of the tall glass (Figure 8.8).

By age 7, the same child will tell you that the second jar contains the same amount of water as the first. If you ask why, he may say because the short jar is fatter than the tall jar—indicating that he is able to coordinate his perceptions of height and width. Or the child may point out that if you poured the water back into the short jar, it would be the same—indicating that he is able to think in reverse, to retrace the steps of the experiment. Younger children generally cannot do this.

Another type of conservation experiment begins when a child is shown two identical balls of clay. Then, the child watches the experimenter flatten one ball and roll it into the shape of a sausage. Again, the young child believes that the amount of clay has changed. The older child shows knowledge of the principle of conservation. That is, the child recognizes that the amount of clay is unaffected by the change in appearance.

Many such cognitive advances take place between the ages of 5 and 12. This is the stage when children develop a working knowledge of the world. They develop skills in the trial-and-error approach to problem solving. But in general, their thinking is extremely concrete. They need to try solutions out; they cannot work through problems in their heads, and have difficulty thinking about hypothetical situations or abstract reasoning.

Piaget described the changes that occur in children's understanding in four stages of cognitive development (Table 8.1). During the *sensori-*

LAB EXPERIMENTS AND DEMONSTRATIONS

Have students test Piaget's theory regarding the principle of conservation by conducting either of the two experiments described in the text—either the one with the jars of water or the one with the balls of clay. Students should test the theory with a child under the age of five and with one around the age of seven. They should record each child's response according to age and compare their findings with those of their classmates.

TABLE 8.1 • Piaget's Stages of Cognitive Development

SENSORIMOTOR STAGE (birth to 2 years): Thinking is displayed in action, such as the grasping, sucking, and looking schemes. Child gradually learns to discover the location of hidden objects at about 18 months, when the concept of object permanence is fully understood.

PREOPERATIONAL STAGE (2 to 6 years): Beginning of symbolic representation. Language first appears; child begins to draw pictures that represent things. Child cannot represent a series of actions in his or her head in order to solve problems.

CONCRETE OPERATIONAL STAGE (6 to 12 years): Ability to understand conservation problems. Ability to think of several dimensions or features at same time. Child can now do elementary arithmetic problems, such as judging the quantity of liquid containers and checking addition of numbers by subtraction.

FORMAL OPERATIONAL STAGE (12 years to adulthood): Thinking becomes more abstract and hypothetical. The individual can consider many alternative solutions to a problem, make deductions, contemplate the future, and formulate personal ideals and values.

motor stage, the young infant uses schemes that primarily involve his body and sensations. The *preoperational stage* emerges when the child begins to use mental images or symbols to understand things. By the third, *concrete operational stage*, children are able to use logical schemes, but their understanding is limited to concrete objects or problems. In the *formal operational stage*, the person is able to solve abstract problems. According to Piaget, a person's development through these four stages depends on both the maturation of his or her nervous system and on the kinds of experiences he or she has had. Everyone goes through the stages in the same order, but not necessarily at the same age.

Some Implications of Intellectual Development

A clear picture of the development of cognitive abilities sheds light on some of the other areas of child behavior. For example, at about 10 or 12 months, many children go through a period of **separation anxiety.** They become extremely upset when their mothers take them to a friend's or relative's house and leave without them. A 5-month-old baby does not react this way. Why does a 1-year-old?

Perhaps the answer is that the older child is more confused by Mom's disappearance. One study consistent with this view found that infants were not particularly upset when their mothers left a room through a familiar exit, like the nursery door. But when Mom left in a surprising way—for example, by stepping into a closet—the baby became upset. Thus, separation anxiety arose when the mother's disappearance led to uncertainty.

Piaget's theory also helps explain why 7- and 8-year-olds are more conscious of sexual identity than younger children are. If you've worked with children, you will know that 4- or 5-year-old boys object loudly to playing baseball with girls—and vice versa. Why?

COOPERATIVE LEARNING ACTIVITY

Instruct students to work in teams to convert Table 8.1 into visual form. Encourage students to consider various media. They may, for example, create a short educational videotape that explains each of Piaget's four stages of cognitive development. They might also design and publish an illustrated brochure geared for an audience of young parents. Have students present their finished works to the class for discussion and evaluation.

Using Psychology

After students read the special feature, suggest that they track over the course of a week instances of violence and aggression that they observe while watching television. Instruct the class to keep a log of their observations that identifies the network, program, time of day, and nature of the violent or aggressive act. Have students analyze their findings: Is there more violence on one network than another, or at a particular time of day?

DID YOU KNOW

In 1993, public outcry over television violence increased after a child set fire to his home after allegedly watching cartoon characters playing with fire. After Congress threatened to enact legislation limiting such programming, the entertainment industry promised to curtail violence voluntarily, especially during hours when small children are likely to be watching.

Using Psychology

Children and Television

Today, more than 95 percent of American families have at least 1 television set—many have 2 or more—and children spend a significant amount of time watching TV. One estimate is that children under 2 spend an average of 2.5 hours a day in front of the television. This amount increases to 4 hours a day for children 8 to 10 years old (Liebert, Sprafkin, and Davidson, 1982). By the time you graduate from high school, you will have spent an estimated 15,000 hours watching TV. That means the average high school graduate has spent more time in front of a television than in school since entering elementary school! Clearly, television is an important force in children's lives. In what specific ways does television viewing affect children's development? This question has generated much debate and research.

The most controversial and studied issue is the effect of watching television violence and aggression on children's behavior. The results of research studies consistently support the view that violence on television leads to aggressive behavior in children. By observing highly attractive models engaging in a variety of aggressive and physically violent behaviors, children are encouraged to act in a similar way.

Huston *et al.* (1989) summarized earlier research, which finds that children's television viewing peaks at ages 10 to 12. Below age 8 children are unable to identify the purpose of advertisements or separate them from program content, suggesting a need to monitor what children are viewing. When parents watch aggressive or violent shows with their children and discuss the events afterwards, the negative effects seem to be reduced and the positive effects enhanced.

When children watch television, they are forming beliefs about what the world is like. Their views of reality, including their views of how people act toward one another, are influenced by the characters they see portrayed on television. Often, adult TV themes include negative motives, such as jealousy, revenge, corruption, and violence. While adults may view these programs as entertainment and not base conclusions about their social world on them, children—especially those 5 and younger—do not have the cognitive sophistication to separate television "reality" from everyday experience.

Another potent way in which television affects social behavior is through the presentation of sex role models and ethnic stereotypes.

CONNECTIONS: PSYCHOLOGY AND THE MEDIA

Have students work in small groups to select a popular children's program that they have viewed on television and that they have judged as particularly violent. Instruct the students to compose a letter to the program's producers asking them to justify the program's violent content in light of recent psychological research. Be sure that the groups do not duplicate their efforts. Discuss in class the responses that the students receive. Do the responses intelligently address the students' concerns, or do they avoid the issue?

VISUAL INSTRUCTION

Have students recall their early years of television watching. What were their favorite programs? Do they think that being exposed to violent programming affected their development and attitudes toward violence? Do they think that programs like *Sesame Street* have a positive influence on children? Why or why not?

FIGURE 8.9

Television shows available to children on weekdays are targeted at a wide variety of ages, with very different activities and learning objectives.

STUDY AND WRITING SKILLS

Instruct students to watch a Saturday morning children's program. Ask them to write two capsule reviews for the program. (To get an idea of the length and style of capsule reviews, suggest that students read a few in *People* magazine's Picks & Pans column or from some other periodical or newspaper.) Tell students that one of their reviews should be aimed at an audience of children; the other should be aimed at parents. Have students share their reviews in class.

■ **Identifying Bias.** Have students record on videotape examples of racial, ethnic, and sex-role stereotyping in television programming and advertising. View the examples in class. Do the students agree with the assertion in the Using Psychology feature? That is, do they think TV now provides more representational depictions while commercials still flagrantly reinforce social stereotypes? If students disagree, ask why. If they agree, have them discuss why advertisers might rely on stereotypes to sell their products. (OBJECTIVE 1)

Girls who consistently see women portrayed as helpless victims or housewives are likely to accept this view of women as part of their sex role. Concerns over the racial, ethnic, and sex role stereotypes on television have resulted in a more representative depiction of people on television. However, commercials still seem to flagrantly reinforce limiting social stereotypes. Television presents a distorted view of our " . . . social world in which being male, youthful, beautiful, and white are valued and being female, old, handicapped, dark-skinned, or foreign are not valued" (Huston *et al.*, 1989, p. 425).

Special attention has been given to the format of children's television programs. Programs are carefully produced to capture and hold the viewer's attention. The format of commercial television programs, particularly children's shows, contains rapid-fire, action-packed sequences that are highlighted by audio and visual special effects. Children's attention is especially guided by the television format of cartoons (Wright and Huston, 1983). Children spend countless hours, particularly on Saturday morning, watching the humorous (and often violent and aggressive) adventures of cartoon characters. The faster the pace of the program, the more receptive children are to it. Yet, television is now blamed even for leading to obesity among its most dedicated youthful viewers. They are deluged with and responsive to commercials for sugar- and fat-laden products, eating snacks while they watch, and burning many fewer calories than if they were playing (Klesges, 1993).

On the positive side, TV has a rich and largely untapped potential for educating and enhancing children's development (Singer and Singer, 1983). Television is an excellent vehicle for presenting new information about the world beyond the child's or adult's immediate experience. Also, some children's programs attempt to help children deal more effectively with their fears. For example, by watching a television character overcome a fear of animals, children are able to deal more effectively with similar fears of their own.

In 1982, the United States government conducted a review of studies on the impact of television on social behavior (Pearl, *et al.*, 1982). On the basis of over 20 years of research and 3,000 scientific studies, the reviewers concluded:

> Television can no longer be considered a casual part of daily life, an electronic toy. Research findings have long since destroyed the illusion that television is merely innocuous entertainment. While the learning it provides is mainly incidental rather than direct and formal, it is a significant part of the total acculturation process (Pearl, 1982, 1:87).

The conclusion remains as true today as when it was written. Television programs are an important issue for psychologists, edu-

STUDY AND WRITING SKILLS

As a concluding activity in their investigation of children's television programming, ask students to write a "Guide for Your Children's TV Viewing." Tell the students that their guides should be geared for an audience of young parents and should include a list of practical dos and don'ts for the adults to follow in structuring their children's viewing time. Have students share their guides with the class.

cators, and parents. The American Psychological Association issued a statement supporting the view that exposure to violence on television promotes aggressive behavior. With more responsible attitudes toward TV programs, we can use them as an important vehicle for education, social learning, and merchandising.

Four-year-old children can tell you whether they are boys or girls, and many are fully informed about anatomical differences. Yet if you question children at this age, you'll find that they believe people can change their sex by wearing clothes designed for the opposite sex, changing their haircut, playing games associated with the opposite sex, and similar external changes. In other words, if you pour a boy into a female container, he'll change. Only when they understand conservation do they realize that one's sex is permanent. It is at this point that children become concerned about their own sexual identity.

MENTAL RETARDATION

The term "mentally retarded" is applied to people who have, since childhood, been less able to learn and understand things than most people of the same age. Retarded children have difficulty learning new skills, cannot keep up with regular classroom instruction in schools, and sometimes lack the necessary motor skills to join in games.

Mental retardation is an intellectual disability rather than an emotional one. But it is possible for retarded people to find the world so unpleasant that they withdraw from it. Retarded people are often made worse by the way other people treat them. Most retarded people are capable of living relatively normal lives if given the chance. They must, however, be given special attention, affection, and understanding if they are to reach their full potential as human beings.

Unfortunately, retarded people are often treated as if they were unseeing, unhearing, uncomprehending "objects." The presence of a retarded child in a household may cause a great deal of friction and resentment among members of the family. This situation does not go unnoticed by the retarded child. Despite his intellectual handicaps, the child is a sensitive human being who understands the meaning of anger and resentment as well as love and acceptance. Conflict and rejection can rob the child of the supportive environment necessary for his maximum development.

Only a small portion of the 7 million people who are called mentally retarded in the United States have a known organic or medical cause, such as the genetic disorder Down's syndrome or infectious disease. Many mentally retarded people may be handicapped by a combination of genetic and environmental factors.

■ **Making Inferences.** Have the students reread the last paragraph on page 197. Ask them to consider how government initiatives and other social programs might contribute to a radical decline in mental retardation in the United States. Programs that students might discuss include those aimed at improving prenatal care, nutrition, and vaccination; eliminating poverty; promoting public tolerance of neighborhood group homes for the mentally disabled; and guaranteeing the quality of care in public institutions. (OBJECTIVE 1)

COMMUNITY INVOLVEMENT

Arrange to have students visit a group home for the mentally disabled or some other community center where the mentally disabled are given the opportunities and encouragement to develop their potential. Students should keep a record of their impressions and afterwards discuss their observations in class. Encourage students to discuss the prejudices that the mentally disabled face in society.

If any of your students know American Sign Language, arrange a demonstration for the class. As an alternative, you might ask students to demonstrate some common examples of unspoken language communicated through hand signs and other body movements. How, for example, would students indicate "Come here," "Calm down," and "I don't know"?
Answer to caption, Figure 8.10: involve use of symbols

Teacher Note. You might mention another famous instance of language use in animals. Like Washoe, the gorilla Koko mastered sign language and could put signs together to create new meanings. For example, when she was given a kitten as a pet, she independently named it All Ball (and grieved when it was killed by a car).

FIGURE 8.10

A common form of communication for the hearing impaired is sign language. In fact, the language known as American Sign Language is the fourth most common language in the United States. **In what way are language and thought intertwined?**

The majority of people who are called retarded are people who seem never to have learned to use their minds. They may have been brought up in lonely, dull, or frightening environments in which there was no opportunity or reward for thinking. This situation occurs most often with children born into poor or unstable families and reared in slums or orphanages. If such children are given the opportunity and the encouragement to use their minds early enough, they are often able to live normal lives. We will discuss the testing of intellectual abilities in Chapter 12.

THE DEVELOPMENT OF LANGUAGE

Language and thought are closely intertwined. Both abilities involve using symbols, as we saw in Chapter 3. We are able to think and talk about objects that are present and about ideas that are not necessarily true. A child begins to think, to represent things to himself, before he is able to speak. But the acquisition of language propels the child into further intellectual development (Piaget, 1926). We have been able to learn a good deal about the acquisition of language from our nearest relative in the animal kingdom, the chimpanzee.

Can Animals Use Language?

Psychologists believe that chimpanzees must develop at least as far as 2-year-old humans because, like 2-year-olds, they will look for a toy or a bit of food that has disappeared. They can represent the existence of that toy or bit of food in their minds. Can they be taught to "talk" about it? One husband-and-wife team, the Gardners, raised a baby chimp named Washoe in their home and—since chimps are very good with their hands—taught her to use the American Sign Language for the deaf (Figure 8.10). At 3½ years of age, Washoe knew at least 87 signs for words like "food," "dog," "toothbrush," "gimmee," "sweet," "more," and "hurry." By age 5, Washoe knew and used more than 160 signs.

Making these signs at the appropriate times would not be enough to be called language, though. A dog or a parrot might make signs that its owner could interpret as demands for a walk or for food. Washoe's remarkable achievement was that some of her signs had abstract meanings and that she could put signs together in new ways to produce new meanings. Productivity is a key feature of language use. For example, she learned the sign for "more" (putting her fingertips together over her head) because she loved to be tickled and wanted more. But she was not simply doing something like a dog does when it rolls over to be tickled; she was able to use the same sign later in entirely new circumstances—asking for more food or more hair brushing.

Since the original experiments with Washoe, several chimpanzees have been taught to "talk" in other ways. Lana the chimpanzee was trained on a special typewriter connected to a computer. The machine has 50 keys, each marked with a different symbol which stands for a word in Yerkish, a special monkey language devised just for this study. When Lana presses a key, the symbol appears on the screen in front of her. Lana has learned to type out sentences and thus converse with the experimenters. Sometimes, she types a word out of order, reads the sentence on the screen, and erases it (by pressing the erase key) before she has been corrected. In other cases, Lana has made up phrases to describe objects she's never seen before. For example, the first time Lana saw a ring, she identified it as a "finger bracelet."

The ability to arrange symbols in new combinations to produce new meanings is especially well developed in the human brain. The rules for such organization of symbols are called *grammar*. Grammatical rules are what make the sentence "the rhinoceros roared at the boy" mean the same thing as "the boy was roared at by the rhinoceros." On the surface, these sentences appear different because the word position is changed. But on a deeper level, we know that the first is an active sentence and the second a

FIGURE 8.11

A 2-year-old's speech leaves out words but still gets the message across. **What are important steps in learning language?**

Teacher Note. You may wish to present the following as a basis for discussion: The fact that chimpanzees such as Washoe and Lana could learn language and communicate with humans challenges the theories of Noam Chomsky, who argued that the phenomenon of language is uniquely human. According to Chomsky, the brain has neural structures specifically geared for the acquisition of language, which begin to operate as a function of maturation.

VISUAL INSTRUCTION

Ask students to provide instances when small children have put two words together to create a new meaning (as Lana did when she called a ring a "finger bracelet"). **Answer to caption, Figure 8.11:** First, one must learn the signs, then give them meaning, and finally learn grammar.

■ **Discussion.** Discuss the significance of coinages to language development. Point out that *neologisms* (new words) and new meanings for old words (such as the computer term "bit") are constantly being created as part of our capacity for language. Ask students to brainstorm to generate a list of examples. (OBJECTIVE 2)

CONNECTIONS: PSYCHOLOGY AND SCIENCE

Speech is only one kind of language, and, as students have seen, American Sign Language is another. Have students discuss the characteristics of some of the other "languages" they may know, such as algebra, calculus, chemical formulas, and computer languages.

To what extent can each be said to have "words" and some form of "grammar"?

Teacher Note. Some students may not be familiar with the notion of telegrams. Explain that, as with classified ads, people are charged by the word and, therefore, pare down their messages to the bare essentials—sometimes presenting the recipient with a challenging puzzle.

FIGURE 8.12

Baby geese follow psychologist Konrad Lorenz. **What is imprinting?**

passive transformation of it. It may be in our ability to use such grammatical rules that we surpass the simpler language of the chimpanzee.

How Children Acquire Language

The example of Washoe shows that there are several steps in learning language. First, one must learn to make the signs—whether by hand or by mouth. Then, one must give them meaning; and finally, one must learn grammar. Each child takes these steps at his or her own rate. During the first year of life, the average child makes many sounds. Crying lessens, and the child starts making mostly cooing sounds, which develop into a babble that includes every sound humans can make—Chinese vowels, African clicks, German rolled *r*'s, and English *o*'s.

Late in the first year, the strings of babbles begin to sound more like the language that the child hears. Children imitate the speech of their parents and their older brothers and sisters, and are greeted with approval whenever they say something that sounds like a word. In this way children learn to speak what becomes their native language even though they could just as easily learn any other.

The leap to using sounds as symbols occurs some time in the second year. The first attempts at saying words are primitive, and the sounds are incomplete: "Ball" usually sounds like "ba," and "cookie" may even sound like "doo-da." The first real words usually refer to things the infant can see or touch. Often they are labels or commands ("dog!" "cookie!").

By the time children are 2 years old, they have a vocabulary of at least 50 words. Toward the end of the second year, children begin to express themselves more clearly by joining words into two-word phrases. (Figure 8.11). From about 18 months to 5 years of age, children are adding approximately 5 to 10 words a day to their vocabulary (Carey, 1978).

But at age 2, a child's grammar is still unlike that of an adult. Children use what psychologists call **telegraphic speech**—for example, "Where my apple?" "Daddy fall down." They leave out words but still get the message across. As psychologists have discovered, 2-year-olds already understand certain rules (Brown, 1973). They keep their words in the same order adults do. Indeed, at one point they overdo this, applying grammatical rules too consistently. For example the usual rule for forming the past tense of English verbs is to add "ed." But many verbs are irregular: "go"/"went," "come"/"came," "swim"/"swam," "fall"/"fell." At first children learn the correct form of the verb: "Daddy went yesterday." But once children discover the rule for forming past tenses, they replace the correct form with sentences like "Daddy *goed* yesterday." Although they have never heard adults use this word, they construct it in accordance with the rules of grammar that they have extracted from the speech they hear. "Goed" is a positive error because it indicates the child is applying rules. When the correct form appears, the child has shifted from imitation through *overgeneralization* to rule-governed language.

By the age of 4 or 5, children have a vocabulary of several thousand words. Their ability to use words will continue to grow with their ability to think about and understand things.

CRITICAL THINKING ACTIVITY

Demonstrating Reasoned Judgment. Have students consider this scenario: A baby boy is cooing and making goo-goo noises in his crib. The parents are delighted with the baby's efforts at speech and begin making goo-goo noises back at the baby. Are the parents helping or hindering the baby's language development? *(To the extent that the baby's development is maturational, the parents are not hindering development. However, to the extent that the baby is learning by reinforcement and imitation, the parents' goo-gooing may not be helpful.)* Ask students to discuss how the ways in which adults speak to a child can affect the child's language development.

EMOTIONAL DEVELOPMENT

While the child is developing his ability to use his body, to think and to express himself, he is also developing emotionally. He begins to become attached to specific people and to care about what they think and feel. In most cases, the child's first relationship is with his mother.

Experiments with Animals

The early attachment of a child to his mother and the far-reaching effects of this attachment provide a good example of the way in which maturation and learning work together in development. Experiments with baby birds and monkeys have shown that there is a maturationally determined time of readiness for attachment early in life. If the infant is too young or too old, the attachment cannot be formed. But the attachment itself is a kind of learning. If the attachment is not made, or if an unusual attachment is made, the infant will develop in an unusual way as a result.

Imprinting.   Konrad Lorenz, a student of animal behavior, was a pioneer in this field. Lorenz discovered that infant geese become attached to their mothers in a sudden, virtually permanent learning process called **imprinting.** A few hours after they struggle out of their shells, goslings are ready to start waddling after the first thing they see that moves. Whatever it is, they usually stay with it and treat it as though it were their mother from that time on. Usually, of course, the first thing they see is the mother goose, but Lorenz found that if he substituted himself or some moving object like a green box being dragged along the ground, the goslings would follow that (Figure 8.12). Goslings are especially sensitive just after birth, and whatever they learn during this **critical period,** about 13 to 16 hours after birth, makes a deep impression that resists change. If they have been imprinted with a human being instead of a goose, they will prefer the company of human beings to other geese. However, Hess (1958; 1972) raised some goslings who had imprinted on him. Later, given the opportunity to switch allegiance to their natural mother, they did so. Others, imprinted on their natural mother, would not switch allegiance to Hess.

Surrogate Mothers.   Lorenz's experiments showed how experience with a mother—whether real or a substitute—can determine an infant bird's entire view of itself or others. An American psychologist, Harry Harlow, went on to study the relationship between mother and child in a species closer to humans, the rhesus monkey. His first question was: What makes the mother so important? He tried to answer this question by taking baby monkeys away from their natural mothers as soon as they were born, as described in Chapter 6. To review: Harlow raised the monkeys with two surrogate, or substitute, mothers. Each monkey could choose between a mother constructed of wood and wire and a mother constructed in the same way but covered with soft, cuddly terry cloth. In some cages, the cloth mother was equipped with a bottle; in others, the wire mother was.

FIGURE 8.13

Harry Harlow was one of the first psychologists to study the nature of attachment between mother and child. In this experiment, an infant rhesus monkey is raised with two surrogate mothers. **What were Harlow's findings?**

CONNECTIONS: PSYCHOLOGY AND ZOOLOGY

When zoologists work with endangered species in recovery programs, they often must guard against letting the newborn animals become imprinted with the images of their human caregivers. Instruct students to investigate one of the following two programs aimed at species recovery: (1) recovery of California condor eggs from the wild to raise and release endangered birds; (2) breeding and reintroduction of the red wolf into the Southeastern woodlands. Ask: Why do the zoologists ensure that the condor chicks or wolf pups do not become accustomed to living among humans? Have the students present their findings in either written or oral reports.

Poll the class to see how many of the students grew up in households with siblings and how many were only children. Do the only children feel that the others had greater advantages in growing up, or vice versa? **Answer to caption, Figure 8.14:** at about 6 months

■ **Discussion.** Ask students to explain why attachment to a mother and interaction with peers is essential to normal development, at least in monkeys. *(Attachment and interaction promote the development of independence and learning as well as socialization.)* Have the students discuss to what extent these findings can be applied to human babies. *(Disrupted attachment, according to some studies, does not seem to have a detrimental effect on the normal development of children.)* (OBJECTIVE 3)

FIGURE 8.14

One of Harry Harlow's series of experiments with monkeys showed the importance of early peer contact for normal development. **At what age do most infants form attachments to their mothers?**

The results were dramatic. The young monkeys became strongly attached to the cloth mother, whether she gave food or not, and for the most part ignored the wire mother (Figure 8.13). If a frightening object was placed in the monkey's cage, the baby monkey would run to the terry-cloth mother for security, not to the wire mother. It was the touching—physical contact comfort—that mattered, not the feeding.

Effects Later in Life. In another set of experiments, Harlow discovered that monkeys raised without real mothers grew up with serious emotional problems. As adults they did not seem to know how to play or defend themselves or even mate, although they tried. In fact, when frightened by a strange human they often attacked their own bodies instead of making threatening signs of aggression as normal monkeys do.

The monkeys who had cloth mothers with bottles grew up more normally than the others, but even they were not well adjusted to normal monkey life. A partially adequate substitute for a mother turned out to be peers–other baby monkeys. Infant monkeys who played with other monkeys like themselves grew up fairly normally even if they never saw their mothers. To grow up completely normally, however, both mother *and* peers were necessary (Figure 8.14). Why were real mothers and other infant monkeys so essential?

One possible answer is that no matter how much contact comfort the cloth mother could provide, "she" could not encourage independence. A normal mother, brother, or sister often becomes annoyed at an infant's clinging as he gets older, forcing him to stand on his own two feet. The cloth mother, however, is always available. The encouragement of independence is only one factor. Interactions with mother and peers also allow the baby to see and learn from the behavior of other monkeys and to experience the effect of its own behavior on other monkeys. The silent surrogate provided no such opportunities.

Human Babies

Can these findings be applied to human babies? Is there a critical period when infants need to become attached to a caregiver, as Lorenz's experiments suggest? Do children who are temporarily or permanently separated from their mothers or raised in institutions without benefit of a single caregiver develop abnormally, as Harlow's monkeys did?

Some psychologists would answer these questions with a firm "yes." Babies begin to form an attachment to their mothers (or to a surrogate mother) at about 6 months, when they are able to distinguish one person from another and are beginning to develop object permanence. This attachment seems to be especially strong between the ages of 6 months and 3 years. By 3 years, the child has developed to the stage where he is able to remember and imagine his mother and maintain a relationship with her (in fantasy) even if she is absent.

CRITICAL THINKING ACTIVITY

Demonstrating Reasoned Judgment. As the text indicates, surrogate mothers can be beneficial in a child's development—up to a point. Ask students to consider other kinds of surrogate attachments that children form. To what extent are a child's attachments to pets, dolls, and stuffed animals, for example, a replacement for interactions between the child and other humans? Do students see any danger in a child's preferring the company of a doll over that of a peer? Have students give reasons drawn from the text to support their opinions.

At A Glance

IMAGINARY PLAYMATES

There's nothing new about polka dot elves, pink teddy bears, and other imaginary playmates; children have had them since childhood began. But there's a lot new in our understanding of the role these invisible, mysterious friends play in the normal development of children.

When Dr. Jerome L. Singer and Dr. Dorothy G. Singer studied a group of 3- and 4-year-olds, they found a number of striking differences between children with imaginary playmates and those without. Here are some of their results:

- Imaginary playmates are more common than you might think; more than half the children had them.
- Children with imaginary playmates are less aggressive and more cooperative than other children.
- They are rarely bored and have a rich vocabulary, far advanced for their age.
- They watch fewer hours of television than other children, and the programs they watch have fewer cartoons and violence.
- They have a greater ability to concentrate than other children.

Above all, imaginary playmates are true companions to children. They are always there to listen and talk, to be supportive and forever loyal. They seem to fill a gap in children's lives and are especially important to children who are first-born or who have no brothers and sisters. They are an adaptive mechanism that helps children get through the boring times in life.

Instead of worrying that imaginary playmates are a sign of insecurity and withdrawal, we should all look in wonderment at how creative and adaptive a healthy child can be.

For more details, see Maya Pines, "Invisible Playmates," *Psychology Today*, September 1978. Cohen, David and MacKeith, Stephen. *The Development of Imagination: The Private Worlds of Childhood.* New York: Routledge, Chapman, and Hall, Inc. 1993.

According to one psychologist, children who are separated from their mothers during this period may never be able to form attachments to other people. Suppose a child is hospitalized for an extended period. At first she will show signs of intense distress, crying and fussing as if she were trying to bring her mother back. When this fails, she will lapse into a state of apathy, which may last for several days. If the separation continues, she will begin to respond to attention and to act cheerfully, but her relations with others take on a superficial quality. She does not become attached to any one person (Bowlby, 1960-1961).

An infant begins to develop a strong attachment to its mother by the age of 6 months.

At A Glance

After students have read the special feature, poll the class to see how many had imaginary playmates. Of these, find out how many were first-born or had no siblings. Can these students remember when they no longer had a need for their imaginary playmates? *(probably when they began interacting more fully with peers)* Discuss with students under what circumstances a parent might begin to worry about a child's attachment to an imaginary playmate. *(when the child continually resists socializing with real playmates)* (OBJECTIVE 3)

DID YOU KNOW?

Though the long-term effects of day-care centers on the development of children have not yet been determined, the psychological research conducted thus far suggests that children who attend well-run programs are more sociable and considerate than children who stay at home. In addition, children from poor or disadvantaged backgrounds tend to develop better intellectually because of the stimulating environment of day-care centers.

COOPERATIVE LEARNING ACTIVITY

Have students work together in small groups to create an illustrated children's story in which the main character has (or is) an imaginary playmate. Tell students that their stories should depict the child and the playmate engaged in an adventure in which the child demonstrates the characteristics listed in the At a Glance feature. Ask the students to consider, for example, how "a greater ability to concentrate" might help the child overcome some obstacle or challenge. Have the finished stories displayed in class or read to a group of small children. Invite the children to critique the stories.

Point out that, according to ethologists, infants have an innate need to attach themselves to their mothers. In contrast, social theories of learning stress that attachment is learned when mothers dispense rewards that encourage dependency in the child.
Answer to caption, Figure 8.15: at 10–12 months

■ **Debating an Issue.** Assign students to research some of the studies that have been done to determine the effect on children of having mothers work outside the home. Debate the following issue: *Resolved—* Mothers should remain in the home to ensure the normal development of their children. (OBJECTIVES 1–3)

FIGURE 8.15

Exposure to a variety of stimulating activities and situations can aid in the development of a child's cognitive and motor skills. **At what age do infants usually develop separation anxiety?**

Some psychologists believe that institutionalization causes intellectual as well as psychological damage, retarding children's ability to use words and solve problems (Spitz & Wolff, 1946). Other research, however, suggests that the main factor is not just being in an institution, but the institution's quality of care (Vandell, Henderson, & Wilson, 1988). One team of psychologists found that, although infants in an orphanage were slow to develop, they caught up with children raised at home by the age of 4 or 5 (Thompson & Grusec, 1970).

This also raises questions about the role of mothers in the quality of life achievable by their children. How wise is it for mothers to work outside the home? Results generally suggest that quality time spent with children, combined with quality care, is not a detriment (Hoffman, 1974). Is infant-mother attachment crucial to a child's later success? Probably not. Infants raised in one home until they were 6 to 18 months old and then moved to an adopting foster home showed no detrimental effects at age 10 of the disrupted attachment to their original foster mother. (Yarrow & Goodwin, 1973).

COMMUNITY INVOLVEMENT

If possible, arrange to have the students visit a day-care center to observe the activities taking place. Have students keep a log of their observations, noting how each activity might aid in a child's development. Do the students observe any behaviors among the children that critics of day care might cite as evidence to support their contention that children are better off at home with their mothers? Have students discuss their observations and conclusions in class.

The debate over this issue is likely to continue for some time. What we do know is that up to 6 or 7 months, most infants are indiscriminate. They respond to strangers as readily as they respond to their mothers and other familiar people; they will coo or whine at just about anyone. At 6 months, however, they begin to develop a strong attachment to their mother (or whoever is caring for them). In fact, at about 8 months many babies rather suddenly develop an intense fear of strangers—crying, hiding against their mothers, and showing other signs of distress when someone they do not know or remember approaches them. Separation anxiety, which appears at 10 to 12 months, is further proof of attachment. Children do not remain exclusive for long, however. By 18 months nearly all babies have developed attachments to their father, siblings, grandparents, or other people who play an active role in their lives (Maccoby and Masters, 1970).

SOCIALIZATION

Learning the rules of behavior of the culture in which you are born and grow up is called **socialization.** To live with other people, a child has to learn what is considered acceptable and unacceptable behavior. This is not

FIGURE 8.16

Learning the difference between acceptable and unacceptable behavior is part of socialization. **Are the rules of society fixed and inflexible?**

CRITICAL THINKING ACTIVITY

Problem Solving. Have students consider the following situation: A 3-year-old child has an almost exclusive attachment to her mother. When the mother tries to leave the girl for a while to play alone or with other children, the girl either cries or tries to go after the mother. The mother usually gives in and allows the girl to stay at her side. In fact, the mother has quit her part-time job because, whenever the girl was left at day care or at her grandmother's house, she threw tantrums or remained withdrawn. What advice would the students give to the mother?

■ **Discussion.** After students have read the first two full paragraphs on p. 206, have them identify the three stages or dimensions of socialization. *(learning the rules, acquiring an identity, learning to live with others and with oneself)* Ask the students to enumerate some of the difficulties children might have at each step, and discuss how socialization can be an ongoing, lifelong process. (OBJECTIVE 3)

■ **Research.** Although Freud remains a household name, his theories have come under increasing attack with the passage of time. Ask students to research some of these recent challenges (see, for example, *TIME*, Nov. 29, 1993) and to write a summary of the controversial issues involved. Have students discuss their findings in class. (OBJECTIVE 3)

as easy as it sounds. Some social rules are clear and inflexible. For example, you are not permitted to have sexual relations with members of your immediate family.

Most social rules leave room for individual decisions, so that sometimes there seems to be a "gray area" between right and wrong. Some rules change from situation to situation. Some apply to certain categories of people. For example, the rules for boys in our society are different from the rules for girls. We tend to encourage boys to express aggression but not fear; traditionally, girls have been raised to express emotions but not ambitions. Of course the rules for feminine behavior change over the years. We do not expect adolescent girls to act like little girls, or middle-aged women to act like adolescents. To complicate matters, we require different behavior from single and married women, housewives and career women, female executives and female secretaries. Learning what the rules are, when to apply and when to bend them, is, however, only part of socialization. Every society has ideas about what is meaningful, valuable, worth striving for, and beautiful. Every society classifies people according to their family, sex, age, skills, personality characteristics, and other criteria. Every culture has notions about what makes individuals behave as they do. In absorbing these notions, a child acquires an identity as a member of a particular society, a member of different social categories, a member of a family—and an identity as an individual. This is a second dimension of socialization.

Finally, socialization involves learning to live with other people and with yourself. Anyone who has seen the shock of a 2-year-old's face when another child his age takes a toy he wants, or the frustration and humiliation a 4-year-old experiences when she discovers she can't hit a baseball on the first try, knows how painful it can be to discover that other people have rights and that you have limitations.

In the pages that follow, we examine several theories about how the child becomes socialized. We begin with Freud's theory of psychosexual development, which has been a major influence on our understanding and interpretation of socialization.

Freud's Theory of Psychosexual Development

Freud believed that all children are born with powerful sexual and aggressive urges that must be tamed. In learning to control these impulses, children acquire a sense of right and wrong. They become "civilized." The process—and the results—are different for boys and girls.

In the first few years of life, boys and girls have similar experiences. Their erotic pleasures are obtained through the mouth, sucking at their mother's breast. Weaning is a period of frustration and conflict—it is the child's first experience with not getting what he wants. Freud called this the **oral stage** of development. Later the anus becomes the source of erotic pleasure, giving rise to what Freud called the **anal stage.** The child enjoys holding in or pushing out his feces until he is required, through toilet training, to curb this freedom, and learn social control.

COOPERATIVE LEARNING ACTIVITY

Remind students that acquiring an identity and learning to live with oneself are important elements of socialization. Next, have students work in small groups to list specific phrases, events, body language, etc., that would build a positive self-image in a child. Then ask them to list things that would promote a negative self-image. After their lists are complete, have each group discuss these questions: (1) Should parents say and do only things that promote a positive self-image? (2) What are some disciplinary techniques that would not damage a child's self-image but would change his or her behavior? (3) Can a child affect his or her own self-image? How?

FIGURE 8.17

Socialization is a process that begins almost immediately after birth. Through it, children learn how to behave with others and how to use certain behaviors to get their own way. **According to Erikson, at what age do children face the crisis of initiative versus guilt?**

Teacher Note. You might want to point out that one of the major criticisms of Freudian theory is that it is not supported by compelling scientific research. Nevertheless, Freud's ideas have had a profound and lasting impact on how people think about the unconscious forces that affect our lives.

The major conflict comes between the ages of 3 and 5, when children discover the pleasure they can obtain from their genitals. As a consequence, they become extremely aware of the differences between themselves and members of the opposite sex. In this **phallic stage,** according to Freud, the child becomes a rival for the affections of the parent of the opposite sex. The boy wants to win his mother for himself and finds himself in hostile conflict with his father. The girl wants her father for herself and tries to shut out her mother. These struggles take place on an unconscious level; generally the child and the parents do not have any clear awareness that it is going on.

Freud called this crisis the **Oedipal conflict,** after Oedipus, the king in Greek tragedy who unknowingly killed his father and married his mother. Freud believed that the boy's feelings for his mother create intense conflicts. The boy finds that he hates his father and wishes him gone or dead. But his father is far stronger than he is. The boy fears that his father will see how he feels and punish him, perhaps by castrating him. (A parent telling the child that masturbation is nasty, or perhaps that it will make him sick, merely confirms his fears.) To prevent this horrible punishment, the boy buries his sexual feelings and tries to make himself "good." He tries to become as much like his father as possible so that his father will not want to hurt him. He satisfies himself with becoming *like* the person who possesses mother, instead of trying to possess her himself. In this process, which is called **identification** with the aggressor, the boy takes on all his father's values and moral principles. Thus, at the same time that he learns to behave like a man, he internalizes his father's morality. His father's voice becomes a voice inside him, the voice of conscience.

CONNECTIONS: PSYCHOLOGY AND LITERATURE

You might assign some of your more able students to read the cycle of myths and legends about Oedipus and Electra, especially as they are portrayed by the great Greek tragedians in their plays. If possible, have the students view a performance of Sophocles' *Oedipus Rex* or Igor Stravinsky's opera based on the play.

Have students discuss why they think Freud chose such thoroughly tragic characters to symbolize stages in child development. What are students' own opinions of Freud's use of these figures?

■ **Discussion.** In reviewing Erikson's stages of psychosocial development, instruct students to supply a specific example for each kind of behavior. *(For example, a teenager's decision to wear ethnic clothing, while trying to maintain ties with a culturally diverse group of friends, would be an illustration of identity.)* (OBJECTIVE 3)

Freud believed that in girls the Oedipal conflict, called the **Electra complex,** after a Greek heroine who encouraged her brother to kill their mother, takes a different form. The girl finds herself in the similarly dangerous position of wanting to possess her father and to exclude her mother. To escape punishment and to possess the father vicariously, she begins to identify with her mother. She feels her mother's triumphs and failures as if they were her own, and she internalizes her mother's moral code. At the same time, the girl experiences what Freud called penis envy. Whereas the boy is afraid of being castrated, the girl suspects that her mother has removed the penis she once had. To make up for this "deficiency," she sets her sights on marrying a man who is like her father and develops the wish to have babies.

Freud believed that at about age 5 children enter a **latency stage.** Sexual desires are pushed into the background, and children busy themselves with exploring the world and learning new skills. This process of redirecting sexual impulses into learning tasks is called **sublimation.** Although children this age often avoid members of the opposite sex, sexual interest reappears in adolescence. The way in which a person resolves the Oedipal or Electra conflict in childhood influences the kind of relationships he or she will form with members of the opposite sex throughout life. Ideally, when one reaches the **genital stage** at adolescence, one derives as much satisfaction from giving pleasure as from receiving it. For Freud, personality development is essentially complete as we enter adolescence.

Today relatively few psychologists believe that sexual feelings disappear in childhood, that all young girls experience penis envy, or that all young boys fear castration. Freud was attempting to set off a revolution in our thinking about childhood. Like many revolutionaries, he probably overstated the case. Yet the idea that children have to learn to control powerful sexual and aggressive desires, and the belief that such early childhood experiences can have a long-term effect on adult personality and behavior, would be difficult to deny. We shall return to Freud in the chapter on personality theories.

Erikson's Theory of Psychosocial Development

To Erik Erikson, socialization is neither so sudden nor so emotionally violent. Erikson takes a broader view of human development than Freud in terms of both time and scope. Although he recognizes the child's sexual and aggressive urges, he believes that the need for social approval is just as important, hence his term, psychosocial development. And although he believes that childhood experiences have a lasting impact on the individual, he sees development as a lifelong process.

We all face many "crises" as we grow from infancy to old age, as we mature and people expect more from us. Each of these crises represents an issue that everyone faces. The child—or adolescent or adult—may develop more strongly in one way or another, depending on how other people respond to his or her efforts.

For example, the 2-year-old is delighted with his new-found ability to walk, to get into things, to use words, and to ask questions. The very fact

COOPERATIVE LEARNING ACTIVITY

Assign two groups of students to prepare a panel discussion arguing the respective strengths of Freud's psychosexual and Erikson's psychosocial theories of development. To generate discussion, you might encourage panelists to view a movie scene in which a small child is in conflict with parents.

(One choice is *My Life as a Dog*, in which a child goes in search of a dog taken away from him.) Tell students to explain why their particular assigned theory is more appropriate than the other for explaining the child's behavior.

that he has acquired these abilities adds to his self-esteem. He's eager to use them. If the adults around him applaud his efforts and acknowledge his achievements, he begins to develop a sense of autonomy, or independence. However, if they ignore him except to punish him for going too far or being a nuisance, the child may begin to doubt the value of his achievements. He may also feel shame because the people around him act as if his new desire for independence is bad.

This is the second of eight stages in Erikson's theory. Each stage builds on the last. A child who has learned to trust the world is better equipped to seek autonomy than one who is mistrustful; a child who has achieved autonomy takes initiative more readily than one who doubts himself; and so on. The basic question in each stage is whether the individual will find ways to direct his needs, desires, and talents into socially acceptable channels and learn to think well of himself.

Erikson's eight crises are outlined in Table 8.2. We will refer to this theory as we continue our discussion of the life cycle in the next chapter.

TABLE 8.2 • Erikson's Stages of Psychosocial Development

Approximate Age	Crisis
0-1	**TRUST VS. MISTRUST**: If an infant is well cared for, she will develop faith in the future. But if she experiences too much uncertainty about being taken care of, she will come to look at the world with fear and suspicion.
2-3	**AUTONOMY VS. DOUBT:** Here the child learns self-control and self-assertion. But if he receives too much criticism, he will be ashamed of himself and have doubts about his independence.
4-5	**INITIATIVE VS. GUILT:** When the child begins to make her own decisions, constant discouragement or punishment could lead to guilt and a loss of initiative.
5-Puberty	**INDUSTRY VS. INFERIORITY:** The child masters skills and takes pride in his competence. Too much criticism of his work at this stage can lead to long-term feelings of inferiority.
Adolescence	**IDENTITY VS. ROLE CONFUSION:** The teenager tries to develop her own separate identity while "fitting in" with her friends. Failure leads to confusion over who she is.
Early Adulthood	**INTIMACY VS. ISOLATION:** A person secure in his own identity can proceed to an intimate partnership in which he makes compromises for another. The isolated person may have many affairs or even a long-term relationship, but always avoids true closeness.
Middle Age	**GENERATIVITY VS. STAGNATION:** A person who becomes stagnated is absorbed in herself and tries to hang onto the past. Generativity involves a productive life which will serve as an example to the next generation.
Later Adulthood	**INTEGRITY VS. DESPAIR:** Some people look back over life with a sense of satisfaction, and accept both the bad and the good. Others face death with nothing but regrets.

■ **Discussion.** Ask students to compare Freud's and Erikson's theories. What major differences do they find? *(Answers might include: Freud focused on the sexual and aggressive urges underlying personality development, whereas Erikson focuses on social forces. Freud considered personality development as virtually complete by adolescence; Erikson views it as a lifelong process.)* (OBJECTIVE 3)

WORKING WITH TRANSPARENCIES

Project Transparency 18 and use the guidelines provided in Teaching Strategies and Activities. Assign Student Worksheet 18.

 LAB EXPERIMENTS AND DEMONSTRATIONS

To help students review learning by conditioning and imitation, request a volunteer to stand facing you. Have the student extend his or her arms from the elbows, palms up, keeping the upper arms flush against the body. Place your palms about an inch above the subject's palms. Indicate each new trial by asking, "Are you ready?" When the student says yes, begin to raise your right hand as you slap his or her right hand with your left hand. Continue until the student is conditioned to remove (even slightly) his or her hand before you make contact. Now repeat the demonstration with another *(continued on page 210)*

■ **Discussion.** As an example of conditioning, discuss the practice in American society of dressing baby boys in blue and girls in pink. Do students think that if the practice were reversed it would affect the way children develop? Ask students to support their opinions in terms of learning theory—that children are rewarded for conforming to adult expectations. *(Dressing girls in blue and boys in pink might affect social development insofar as adults conditioned to the usual color scheme might treat the blue-dressed baby girls as if they were boys and vice versa.)*

Independent Practice

■ **Informative Writing.** Assign students to bring a variety of toy catalogs to class. Have students work in small groups to select four toys from the catalogs—one for each of Piaget's stages of cognitive development. Students should develop an ad for each toy that tells parents why it is appropriate for their child's particular stage of development. Ads should mention the age range that the toy is designed for as well as what concepts it is designed to teach. (OBJECTIVE 1)

Learning Theories of Development

Both Freud and Erikson stress the emotional dynamics of social development. Their theories suggest that learning social rules is altogether different from learning to ride a bicycle or to speak a foreign language. Many psychologists disagree. They believe children learn the ways of their social world because they are rewarded for conforming and because they copy older children and adults in anticipation of future rewards. In other words, social development is simply a matter of conditioning and imitation.

Conditioning. Adults—especially parents and teachers—have the power to reward and punish. Consciously and unconsciously they use praise, smiles, and hugs to reward a child for behaving in ways they consider good and for expressing attitudes that support their own. They tend to ignore or to be hostile toward the expression of opinions that are contrary to their own and toward behavior of which they disapprove.

Sex-role training provides obvious examples of this. At home and in school, boys are encouraged to engage in athletics and to be assertive. Girls are discouraged from doing these things, but are rewarded for being helpful and nice, looking neat, and acting cute. Even the rewards children receive are usually sex-typed. How many girls receive footballs or tool kits as presents? How many boys get dolls or watercolor sets?

These are some of the ways in which adults use conditioning to shape a child's development. Children gradually learn to behave in the way that leads to the greatest satisfaction, even when no one is watching. To avoid punishment and gain rewards from those around them, they learn to reward and punish themselves. A child may criticize herself for making a mistake that has led to punishment in the past. The mistake may be a moral one—lying, for example. A boy may learn to be hard on himself for showing sensitivity, because in the past his tears were met with laughter.

This is not to say that children always do as they are told. Adults also teach how to get away with misbehavior—for example, by apologizing or by giving a present to someone they have wronged. In this way, some children learn that they may, at small cost, receive praise instead of punishment for bad conduct.

Imitation. A second way in which children learn social rules is by observing other people. When youngsters see another child or an adult being congratulated for behaving in certain ways or expressing certain attitudes, they are likely to imitate that person in the hope of obtaining rewards themselves. Albert Bandura's experiments indicate that children are very quick indeed to imitate other people's behavior (Bandura and Walters, 1963). Bandura's basic technique is to show children movies of a person reacting to a situation. He then puts the children in the same situation to see how they behave.

In one experiment Bandura showed a film of a frustrated adult taking out her anger on a "Bobo" doll. The woman assaulted the doll—yelling, kicking, and punching it with all her might. After the film, children who had been deliberately frustrated with broken promises and delays were led to a

LAB EXPERIMENTS AND DEMONSTRATIONS

volunteer. Usually, the second subject will remove his or her hand before personally experiencing a slap. Point out that the first student learned through reinforcement, while the second learned through observation and imitation.

room that contained an identical doll. Taking their cue from the film, they launched furious attacks.

Later Bandura added two different endings to the film. In one the actress was praised and given candy and soft drinks after she had attacked the doll. In the other she was severely scolded for her behavior. Most of the children who saw the second version learned from the actress's experience and did not attack the doll so they would not be punished. What this suggests is that conditioning and modeling work together. Children do not imitate everything they see, only the behavior that seems to bring rewards. But when rewarded for doing so, children could model the aggression in Bandura and Walters' study regardless of its consequences for the actress.

The Cognitive-Developmental Approach

Theorists who emphasize the role of cognition or thinking in development view the growing child quite differently. Learning theory implies that the child is essentially passive—a piece of clay to be shaped. The people who administer rewards and punishments and serve as models do the shaping. Cognitive theorists see the *child* as the shaper. Taking their cue from Piaget, they argue that social development is the result of the child's acting on the environment and trying to make sense out of his experiences. The games children play illustrate this.

FIGURE 8.18

Children's games are not just fun. Seeing the need for and making rules, trying on adult roles, and learning the dimensions of competition are all part of the developmental process. **How do cognitive theorists differ in their view of development from learning theorists?**

CONNECTIONS: PSYCHOLOGY AND ART

Your students might enjoy having a close look at *Children's Games*, by Peter Breughel the Elder. (Hundreds of games are depicted on a single canvas.) Use an opaque projector to show a copy of the painting to the class. Have students try to find examples of children trying on adult roles and learning the dimensions of competition in the games that Breughel depicts.

■ **Comparing Ideas.** After students read the margin feature, ask them to summarize the male/female difference at the core of Gilligan's criticism of Kohlberg's theory. *(Males tend to emphasize individual rights in moral judgments; females tend to be less judgmental and to stress concern with the needs of others.)*

■ **Making a Chart.** After students have read about Heinz's moral dilemma on p. 212, have them complete a chart on the chalkboard, summarizing each of the six stages in Kohlberg's theory of moral development. Additionally, students could be encouraged to justify pro and con arguments using styles consistent with each of the six stages. (OBJECTIVE 4)

■ **Creating a Display.** Have students bring in photographs or reproductions of paintings for a bulletin board display showing children learning social rules by observing others. (OBJECTIVE 4)

PSYCHOLOGY UPDATE

Kohlberg and Critics. One criticism leveled at Kohlberg suggested his theory was based only on the study of males, but incorrectly applied to males and females alike. Carol Gilligan (1982) suggested that males are brought up to emphasize different orientations to problem solving than are females. Males stress being concerned with the rights of others, specifically not interfering with those rights; females stress concern with the needs of others.

Gilligan asserts that females tend to be less judgmental in moral situations, seeking instead to find a compromise. Traditional scoring on Kohlberg's system would score this approach at a lower stage of moral reasoning. There is some evidence to support Gilligan's assertion. She suggests, however, that during the course of a lifetime, males who start with an emphasis on individual rights, and females who start with a concern and focus on interpersonal relationships, tend to mature toward similar resolutions of moral dilemmas as they age (Gilligan & Attanucci, 1988).

Play. Children's games are serious business. When left to their own devices, youngsters spend a great deal of time making up rules. This enables them to learn for themselves the importance of agreeing on a structure for group activities. A child can relax and enjoy himself without fear of rejection as long as he does not break the rules. The world of play thus becomes a miniature society, with its own rules and codes.

Another function of most games is to teach children about aspects of adult life in a nonthreatening way. In young children's games, it is the experience of playing, not winning, that counts. Children can learn the dimensions of competition of various kinds, including testing themselves against their outer limits, but they will not be hurt by comparison as they may be in win-or-lose situations.

Much of the children's play involves **role taking**. Youngsters try on such adult roles as mother, father, teacher, storekeeper, explorer, and rock star. Role taking allows them to learn about different points of view firsthand. Suppose a child plays a mother opposite another child who plays a whiny, disobedient baby. When she finds herself totally frustrated by the other child's nagging she begins to understand why her mother gets mad. You can't cook even a pretend meal when the baby keeps knocking over the pots and pans.

Moral Development. Lawrence Kohlberg's studies show just how important being able to see other people's points of view is to social development in general and to moral development in particular. Kohlberg (1968) studied the development of moral reasoning—deciding what is right and what is wrong—by presenting children of different ages with a series of moral dilemmas. For example:

> In Europe, a woman was near death from cancer. One drug might save her, a form of radium that a druggist in the same town had recently discovered. The druggist was charging $2,000, ten times what the drug cost him to make. The sick woman's husband, Heinz, went to everyone he knew to borrow the money, but he could only get together about half of what it cost. He told the druggist that his wife was dying and asked him to sell it cheaper or let him pay later. But the druggist said "No." The husband got desperate and broke into the man's store to steal the drug for his wife. Should the husband have done that? Why?

At every age, some children said that the man should steal, some that he should not. What interested Kohlberg, however, was how the children arrived at a conclusion. He wanted to know what sort of reasoning they used. After questioning 84 children, Kohlberg identified six stages of moral development. He then replicated his findings in several different cultures.

In stage one, children are totally egocentric. They do not consider other people's points of view and have no sense of right and wrong. Their main concern is avoiding punishment. A child in this stage will say that the man should steal because people will blame him for his wife's death if he does not, or that he should not steal because he might go to prison.

 LAB EXPERIMENTS AND DEMONSTRATIONS

Instruct students to work in small groups to devise a moral dilemma (similar to the one in the text about Heinz) to which young children can easily relate. Have the students pose their moral dilemmas to several children of various ages. The students should record the children's responses, paying close attention to their reasons for the way they resolve the dilemma. Have students analyze the responses to identify each respondent's stage of moral development according to Kohlberg's theory.

Using Psychology

Child Abuse

While many parents provide a warm and safe environment for their children, there are an alarming number of cases reported in which children are physically, sexually, or psychologically abused or neglected by their parents or stepparents (Parke and Lewis, 1980). *Child abuse* includes the physical or mental injury, sexual abuse, negligent treatment, or mistreatment of children under the age of 18 by adults entrusted with their care. Accurate statistics are difficult to compile, since many incidents of child abuse go unreported. One estimate, however, is that in 1988 1 out of every 40 children in the United States under the age of 14 was abused (National Center on Child Abuse and Neglect, 1988).

Child abuse is viewed as a social problem resulting from a variety of causes. Many abusive parents were themselves mistreated as children, suggesting that these parents may have learned an inappropriate way of caring for children. Such parents tend to use the harsh physical discipline that they saw their own parents using. Many abusive parents have little patience with their children. Often they have unrealistic expectations for them.

Overburdened and stressed parents are more likely to abuse their children. Low-birthweight infants and those children who are hyperactive or mentally or physically disadvantaged have a higher than normal incidence of abuse. One reason for this higher incidence may be that such children are less responsive and more difficult to care for, thus making greater demands on and fewer rewards for the parents (Belsky, 1984; Pianta, Egelands, & Erikson, 1989). Social-cultural stresses such as unemployment and lack of contact with family, friends, and groups in the community are associated with child abuse.

The most effective way of treating child abuse is to prevent future incidents. Parent education for abusive parents allows them to learn new ways of dealing with their children. By providing information about resources and a support system for these families, communities may reduce the incidence of child abuse. Such support services as employment and educational opportunities for both parents and children, support groups for parents, child care facilities, homemaker services, and hotlines help reduce child abuse (Parke and Slaby, 1983).

One especially troubling form of child abuse is sexual abuse, and more than 90 percent of those who abuse children are men. Perhaps the most devastating effect of sexual abuse is that the child is

MORE about...

Kohlberg and Bias. Not everybody agrees with Kohlberg. Critics accuse him of being overly influenced by Western culture. They say that he sees moral reasoning through the eyes of someone brought up in Europe or America. Children from other cultures, they say, would not necessarily follow Kohlberg's six stages of moral development.

For example, we are raised to believe that we are responsible for ourselves and for our families, and that we must make our own decisions. Other cultures, in contrast, place the community first, and the individual second. Thus, a child from an Israeli kibbutz, or from a Chinese village, would look at Heinz's situation in a different way. The child might say that Heinz should consult his community before making a decision. Or the child might ask why the community is not helping Heinz in the first place.

Although it seems that children throughout the world go through Kohlberg's first stages, their later stages may be influenced by their particular culture.

■ **Discussion.** After students have read the More About feature, discuss how cultural bias can skew the results of psychological research such as Kohlberg's. Point out that simple, elegant theories applicable to all behavioral development are rare. As a result, researchers keep testing psychological theories to refine them and to determine *to what extent* they can be applied.

Readings in Psychology. Have students read the Section 3, Reading 1 selection in *Readings in Psychology* and answer the questions that follow the selection.

Using Psychology

After students have read the special feature, ask them to apply what they know about conditioning and imitation to create ways that abusive parents might learn patience with their children. Students might suggest, for example, that such parents, once they have acknowledged the problem, set up a system of rewards for themselves whenever they successfully maintain their patience in a trying situation.

CONNECTIONS: PSYCHOLOGY AND THE LAW

Many states have strict laws aimed at protecting children against abuse. Have volunteers interview criminal lawyers, social workers, or law enforcement officers to learn what laws have been enacted in your state to curtail child abuse. For example, are doctors in your state required to report suspected instances of abuse? Have students prepare oral reports of their findings for presentation to the class. (Arrange for the appropriate release forms.)

ASSESS

Check for Understanding

Ask students to summarize the developmental theories of Piaget, Freud, Erikson, and Kohlberg in chart form.

Reteach

Have students complete the Chapter 8 Review Activity and share responses with each other.

Enrich

Have students complete the Chapter 8 Extension Activity and answer the questions following it.

Have students complete the Chapter 8 Application Activity.

Evaluate

Administer and grade the Chapter 8 Test. Two forms are available should you wish to give different tests to different students/classes.

Use the Understanding Psychology Testmaker to create a customized test.

CLOSE

Have the students recall several early learning experiences, such as learning to whistle, tie shoes, ride a bicycle, etc. How did they feel about these accomplishments? How did they learn to perform each task? Who or what helped them learn? Ask students to explain their experiences in terms of the development theories they studied in this chapter.

? FACT OR FICTION

Abusive parents abuse all their children.

Fiction. Studies indicate that abusive parents often focus on only one child. That child usually has had physical or behavioral problems from an early age. And while that one child may be grossly maltreated, other siblings may not be abused by the parents at all.

often tricked into participating in the activity but later believes the act to be his or her fault. If the offender is someone the child knows well, the child not only experiences the trauma and stress of abuse, but is also forced to keep the incident a secret for fear of getting the grownup in trouble. Often, parents and other usually responsible adults unintentionally dismiss the child's attempts to tell about the incident because the idea of sexual abuse is too horrifying for them to accept. Fortunately, there is some evidence that child abuse may be less prevalent now than in former generations. Especially in studies that ask adults about whether they were abused during their childhood, instances of such reports are on the decline (Simons, *et al.*, 1991).

Children in stage two have a better idea of how to "work the system" to receive rewards as well as to avoid punishment. Kohlberg calls this the "marketplace orientation." Youngsters at this level interpret the Golden Rule as "help someone if he helps you, and hurt him if he hurts you." They are still egocentric and premoral, evaluating acts in terms of the consequences, not in terms of right and wrong.

In stage three, children become acutely sensitive to what other people want and think. A child in this stage will say that the man in the story should steal because people will think he is cruel if he lets his wife die, or that he should not steal because people will think he is a criminal. In other words, children want social approval in stage three, so they apply the rules other people have decreed literally and rigidly.

In stage four, a child is less concerned with the approval of others. The key issue here is "law and order"—a law is seen as a moral rule and is obeyed because of a strong belief in established authority. Many people remain at the fourth stage of moral development for their whole lives. Moral thinking here, as at stage three, is quite rigid.

In the remaining two stages, people continue to broaden their perspective. The stage-five person is primarily concerned with whether a law is fair or just. He believes that laws must change as the world changes, and they are never absolute. The important question is whether a given law is good for society as a whole. Stage six involves an acceptance of ethical principles that apply to everyone, like the Golden Rule: "Do unto others as you would have them do unto you." Such moral "laws" cannot be broken; they are more important than any written law.

To reach the highest levels of moral development, a child must first be able to see other people's points of view. But this understanding is no guarantee that a person will respect the rights of others. Thus, cognitive abilities influence moral development, but there is far more to morality than simple understanding.

CRITICAL THINKING ACTIVITY

Identifying Alternatives. Parenting is perhaps the most important responsibility a person can have, and yet most people receive little or no formal training for this responsibility. Instead, people tend to parent in the way that they themselves were parented. Ask students to suggest what should be done to improve parenting skills in American society. Should high school students be required to take courses in parenting? Encourage students to identify community resources that might already be in place to help people become more effective parents.

8 Review

CONCEPTS AND VOCABULARY

1. Describe the behaviors that newborn babies display.

2. Define maturation. How does it explain why a 4-month-old baby cannot be taught to walk?

3. What evidence is there that a young baby can learn to do some things?

4. According to Piaget, what two processes are the basis for intellectual development in children?

5. Describe the stages that a child goes through when developing object permanence.

6. Explain the principle of conservation. At what age do children acquire it?

7. Describe the process by which children learn to talk.

8. How are the first 6 months of life different from the second 6 months in terms of a child's emotional and interpersonal development?

9. Define socialization. Why is it so important to development?

10. How do Freud's and Erikson's theories of development differ?

11. What role does play assume in the development of children?

12. List and explain Kohlberg's stages of moral development.

CRITICAL THINKING

1. **Analyze.** What do you assume might happen when a boy plays with action-figure dolls? How does this behavior fit into the concept of modeling? Is this behavior liberating to boys, or does it feminize their behavior? Explain your answer. What would be the effect of girls playing football? Explain the difference(s) between your answers about boys and girls.

2. **Synthesize.** How are sex roles communicated to people in American society? Look carefully through magazines and newspapers, watch television commercials, and listen to the radio. What activities, interests, worries, virtues, weaknesses, physical characteristics, and mannerisms are presented as attributes of typical men and women? Are sex roles portrayed dif-

215

ANSWERS

Concepts and Vocabulary

1. They display reflexes, such as grasping and rooting; turn their heads to gaze at bright patterns and faces; cry, smile, show signs of surprise or fright.

2. internally programmed growth; a 4-month-old maturationally lacks the control needed to walk

3. Researchers taught infants to focus a movie by sucking on a pacifier.

4. assimilation, accommodation

5. First, an infant will forget about an object if someone hides it. At 10–12 months, if the infant sees it being hidden, he or she will look for it there. However, if it is then hidden somewhere else, he or she will continue to look in the first location. At 12–18 months, the child must be tricked to keep looking for the object in a place where it was not hidden. At 18–24 months, the child will perceive the trick and keep searching for the object in various places.

6. conservation: that a given quantity does not change when its appearance is changed; age 5 to 7

7. cooing, then babbling strings of sounds; by age 2, words, followed by 2-word phrases; mastery of the basics of language by 4–5

8. 1–6 months: indiscriminate responses to people; after 6 months: attachment to the

mother; at 8 months: fear of strangers; at 10–12 months: separation anxiety

9. Socialization is learning the rules of a culture in which you live. It is important because it involves acquiring an identity and learning how to live with others.

10. Freud: five stages involving sexual and aggressive impulses; personality complete by adolescence. Erikson:

agreed with Freud, but also saw importance of need for social approval; development as a lifelong process

11. Play promotes social development. The game becomes a microcosm of society in which children learn about rules, competition, viewing life from other perspectives.

12. Stage 1: egocentrism. 2: "working the system" to get rewards and avoid punishment. 3: need for social approval.

4: "law and order." 5: concern that a law is just.
6: acceptance of ethical principles that apply to everyone

Critical Thinking

1. Students should begin by considering how the behaviors are regarded both by the boys and girls themselves and by society—negatively or positively.

2. Encourage students to give specific examples for each assessment of stereotyping.

3. Avoid prying, but encourage students to evaluate events that span their entire lives.

4. Some students may not wish to discuss some of these issues. Ask volunteers to name areas of agreement and disagreement and to discuss the various factors that shaped their beliefs, thinking, and preferences.

Applying Knowledge

1. Answers will vary, but student responses should include a detailed log of observations and demonstrate an understanding of the principles of child development.

2. Answers will vary, but students should note especially errors involving formation of plurals and past tenses.

3. Answers will vary, but student responses should indicate that scientific procedures were followed for each step in the experiment.

4. Answers will vary, but student responses should demonstrate an understanding of the principles of object permanence, conservation, and operational thinking.

216

ferently in different media? Are there various stereotypes within each sex? About each sex?

3. **Evaluate.** What are the events that you feel have been the most significant in your life? What have been the main influences on your social and emotional development?

4. **Analyze.** Do you and your parents share the same religious beliefs? Political orientation? Feelings about violence? Attitudes toward sex? Goals for living? Opinions about money? Views on drugs? Do you have similar tastes in clothing colors and styles? Music? Pets? Housing? Furniture? Foods? Cars? Entertainment? After asking yourself these questions, determine how well your beliefs, opinions, and tastes agree with those of your parents. How important do you think your early social training was for what you believe, think, and like?

APPLYING KNOWLEDGE

1. Observe an infant under 18 months of age, and keep a log of the baby's activities. Compare your notes with the developmental descriptions in this chapter. How closely does the baby follow the norm? What differences did you note?

2. Talk with children who are under 5 years old, paying particular attention to their grammar. What kinds of errors do they make? What kinds of grammatical rules do they already seem to know?

3. If you have an infant brother or sister, or a pet dog or cat, perform a simple experiment to test for object permanence. Be sure to use several different objects for your test, and be certain that the baby or animal is not afraid of, or uninterested in, the object. Most dogs or cats will probably search for vanished objects.

4. Ask children of different ages the following questions: Where does the sun go at night? Could you become a girl (a boy) if you wanted to? Does your brother (sister) have any brothers (sisters)? What makes leaves fall off trees? If

you find some of their theories interesting, it is easy to think of many other questions.

5. Observe a father with a 1- or 2-year-old for signs of emotional attachment. A day care center, a church nursery, a pediatrician's waiting room, or a play area in a shopping mall are good places to locate a father-child pair. Ideally, you want to find a place where the toddler is allowed some freedom to move about while in the presence of the father. How often does the child make contact with his or her father? Does the child move away and explore? How does the child respond to unfamiliar people or objects? Besides physical contact, in what ways do the father and child stay in contact with each other? If the father happens to leave for a moment, what is the child's reaction?

6. Child abuse is a growing concern in our culture; everyday examples of the problem can be found in your local newspapers, in magazines, or on television news reports. Keep a record of these accounts for a period of time. What kinds of abuse are being reported? How old are the children involved? Who are the abusers? What legal action was taken? How was the abuse detected? What state or local agencies are involved with the care of the children?

7. Watch children's television programs on Saturday morning. Pay attention to both the programs and the commercials. What kinds of behavior do the characters model for the children? What do the children learn about how to get along with others, about aggression, sex roles, and food? What are the differences between the television characters and real people? In what ways do you think television is good for children? A negative influence on children?

8. List 10 events or behaviors that you think are important in the first few years of a child's life. Examine the list and differentiate between maturational and learned developmental behaviors. Do you think maturational or learned behaviors are the most important for early childhood? Explain your answer.

5. Answers will vary, but student responses should include a detailed log of observations and demonstrate an understanding of attachment and separation anxiety.

6. Answers will vary, but students should document sources and summarize their findings.

7. Answers will vary, but student responses should include a detailed log of observations and include an analysis of

how children's programming might affect development.

8. Answers will vary, but student responses should indicate an understanding of the distinctions between maturational and learned developmental behaviors.

Analyzing Viewpoints

1. Answers will vary, but student responses should indicate an understanding of

ANALYZING VIEWPOINTS

1. Since 1950 the number of employed mothers with preschool children has more than tripled. These mothers regularly place their children in the care of others. The effects of day care are hotly debated by psychologists. Some say that children in day care are as healthy and soundly developed as children raised at home. Others say that day care causes emotional and behavioral problems in children. Write an essay supporting each viewpoint. Use what you have learned from the chapter about child development and attachment. Read recent magazine and newspaper articles for more information on the day care issue.

2. Psychologists have debated the effects of television on children. More recently there has been great controversy over children's use of interactive video games such as Nintendo. Supporters say that this is the age of technology and the games help sharpen children's skills. Others say that children become addicted to these games; they stop interacting with friends and engaging in more creative activities. Have you had any experience with these games? Write down the pros and cons on this issue. Use your own experience, survey adults for their opinions, and read recent articles in newspapers and magazines.

3. Some communities from time to time pass ordinances that ban the sale of toy guns because they feel that violence is provoked in large part by what we learn in the environment. Do you agree or disagree with this type of ordinance? Why? Explain your answer.

4. Tanya is a mother who works outside the home. She argues that she spends at least two to three hours of quality time with her child every evening. Her friend, Stephanie, is a mother who is not employed outside the home. She argues that these two to three hours may be quality time for Tanya, but not necessarily for her child. She thinks there are many times when two or three hours of morning time (or after-noon time) would be the time when the child is most open to quality interaction. In other words, maybe the two or three hours in the evening are an irritable time for the child, and the child benefits little from the interaction. With whom do you agree? What are your reasons for your position?

BEYOND THE CLASSROOM

1. Spend some time observing children at a park or central play area. Which children share? Which children fight over toys? Do some children play alone? Are there children playing games together? What kinds of games are being played? Are boys always more aggressive than girls? Can you associate types of play with age or gender?

2. While shopping (or in any situation where there are young children and parents), look for signs of children trying to learn. Record the children's comments and questions as well as their parents' responses. Then, in writing, give examples of parents encouraging learning and of parents discouraging learning.

3. Find out how your school system identifies and helps children with learning disabilities. Identify other sources of help for children and parents in your community.

IN YOUR JOURNAL

1. Reread your journal entry about the sentences spoken by 2-year-olds. What sorts of words are used and in what context? Can you specify the grammatical rules children of this age use in combining words? Write your answers in your journal.

217

both sides of the controversy and cite documenting evidence.

2. Answers will vary, but student responses should draw on personal experience if possible and indicate an understanding of both sides in the psychological debate.

3. Answers will vary, but student responses should take a definite stand and present an effective argument based on an understanding of child development.

4. Answers will vary, but student responses should take a definite stand in the debate over quality time and present an effective argument indicating an awareness of recent psychological research on the subject.

Beyond the Classroom

1. Answers will vary, but student responses should include a detailed log of observations (and perhaps visual documentation). Students should analyze their findings in terms of the various theories of socialization.

2. Answers will vary, but student responses should include both positive and negative examples of parent-child interaction in learning situations.

3. Answers will vary, but student responses should include an overview of the various kinds of learning disabilities that the school system and community attempt to address.

CHAPTER BONUS
Test Question

This question may be used for extra credit on the chapter test.

Choose the letter of the correct response.

The statement "Things continue to exist even though I cannot see or touch them" is an expression of:

a. imprinting.
b. object permanence.
c. the conservation principle.
d. telegraphic speech.

Answer: **b**

IN YOUR JOURNAL

If time permits, discuss journal entries individually with the students.

CHAPTER 9
Adolescence

TEXT TOPICS	SPECIAL FEATURES	RESOURCE MATERIALS
Views of Adolescence, pp. 219–223		▬ **Reproducible Lesson Plan; Study Guide; Review Activity**
Personal Development, pp. 223–234	**More About Psychology,** p. 225 **Psychology Update,** p. 228 **Psychology Update,** p. 232 **Using Psychology:** Teenage Depression and Suicide, pp. 232–233 **Fact or Fiction?,** p. 233	▬ **Reproducible Lesson Plan; Study Guide; Review Activity; Application Activity** ▯ *Readings in Psychology:* **Section 3, Reading 3**
Social Development, pp. 234–238	**At a Glance:** What Adolescents Need and Want From Their Parents, p. 235	▬ **Reproducible Lesson Plan; Study Guide; Review Activity**
Difficulties in the Transition From Late Adolescence to Early Adulthood, p. 239	**Psychology and You,** p. 239	▬ **Reproducible Lesson Plan; Study Guide; Review Activity; Extension Activity; Chapter Test, Form A and Form B** ▣ **Understanding Psychology Testmaker**

PERFORMANCE ASSESSMENT ACTIVITY

Write the following uncompleted statement on the chalkboard: "Being an adolescent today is like _____ ." Assign groups of students to copy this statement on at least five separate sheets of paper. Then have each group ask their teenage friends to complete the sentence anonymously. Caution students to tell their friends that the papers will be used in class. Have students display these responses on an illustrated poster. Based on this data, challenge students to form generalizations on how most adolescents view their lives. *(Generalizations should summarize or reflect the available data.)*

CHAPTER RESOURCES

Readings for the Student
Evans, R. I. *Dialogue with Erik Erikson.* New York: Dutton, 1967.

Inhelder, B., and Piaget, J. *The Growth of Logical Thinking: From Childhood to Adolescence.* New York: Basic Books, 1958.

Papalia, D. E., and Olds, S. *A Child's World: Infancy Through Adolescence.* New York: McGraw-Hill, 1982.

Readings for the Teacher
Conger, John J. *Adolescence and Youth.* New York: Harper and Row, 1973.

Gullone, E., and King, N. J. "The Fears of Youth in the 1990s: Contemporary Normative Data." *Journal of Genetic Psychology,* 154 (June 1993): 137–153.

Mullis, R. L., *et al.* "Adolescent Stress: Issues of Measurement." *Adolescence,* 28 (Summer 1993): 267–279.

Multimedia
Am I Worthwhile—Identity and Self-Image (29 minutes, 3/4″ and 1/2″ video). Center for Humanities. This video presents the psychological and physical changes young people go through during adolescence and the effect these changes have on their emotional adjustment.

The Sexes: What's the Difference? (28 minutes). Filmmakers Library. This audiotape explores psychological differences beginning one day after birth. It also explores parents' influence in reinforcing societal standards of male and female behavior.

CHAPTER 9
Lesson Plan

FOCUS

Motivating Activity

Read aloud the first part of the first sentence on page 219: "Adolescence is the transition period between childhood and adulthood." Organize the class into groups. Have students design a poster that illustrates this concept. Most students will probably draw figures of some kind. Save these drawings to evaluate against later discussions of (1) how adolescents view themselves and (2) stereotyped attitudes toward age and gender.

Meeting Chapter Objectives.

Point out the four objectives on page 219, and have students identify the pages in the text that correspond with each one. Then assign groups of students to carry out the direction(s) in each objective as they read Chapter 9.

Building Vocabulary.

Call on students to read aloud definitions of each of the Key Terms in the Glossary or dictionary. Then challenge students to write a paragraph on adolescence that uses at least five of these terms.

Adolescence

FIGURE 9.1 In our society, adolescence is regarded as a period of transition in which young people are expected to assume more and more adult responsibilities.

218

TEACHER CLASSROOM RESOURCES

- Chapter 9 Reproducible Lesson Plan
- Chapter 9 Study Guide
- Chapter 9 Review Activity
- Chapter 9 Application Activity
- Chapter 9 Extension Activity

- Chapter 9 Test, Form A and Form B

- Understanding Psychology Testmaker

Readings in Psychology: Section 3, Reading 3

OBJECTIVES

After studying this chapter, you should be able to

■ define adolescence.

■ describe the physical, cognitive, and ideological changes that characterize adolescence.

■ describe research related to the sexual attitudes and roles of adolescents.

■ discuss the social development of the adolescent and the role of peers and family.

KEY TERMS

androgynous
asynchrony
authoritarian families
authoritative families
conformity
democratic families
identity crisis
initiation rites
laissez-faire families
menarche
permissive families
puberty
rationalization
self-fulfilling prophecy
sex identity
sex role
social learning theory
spermarche

A dolescence is the transition period between childhood and adulthood, and while we all have an idea what adolescence is, defining it precisely is difficult. Some define it in psychological terms: a time period of mixed abilities and responsibilities in which childlike behavior changes to adult like behavior. In some societies adolescence is not recognized as a separate stage of life; individuals move directly from childhood to adulthood (see Mead, 1961). In our own society, however, adolescence is looked upon as a time of preparation for adult responsibilities (Hall, 1904). There are many **initiation rites,** or rites of passage from one age or status to another, that mark admission into adulthood. These rites include informal celebrations such as birthdays—at 16 or 18 or 21—as well as more formal events such as bar mitzvahs and bat mitzvahs, graduation from high school or college, and even weddings. Many of the new burdens of adulthood are assumed just when young people are undergoing complex physical and emotional changes that affect them both personally and socially.

Because so much is happening in these years, psychologists have focused a great deal of attention on the period of adolescence. First, we will turn our attention to some widely held views of the adolescent years.

IN YOUR JOURNAL

According to psychologist Erik Erikson, building an identity is a task that is unique to adolescence. Write in your journal two paragraphs that argue in favor of Erikson's point of view.

Exploring Key Ideas

The Meaning of Adolescence.
Most students know that adolescence is synonymous with the teen years. They also know that the term defines their stage of life. Few, however, have given conscious thought to more concrete parameters. As an introduction to this chapter, challenge students to think of events unique to this period of human development (at least in the United States). What physical, intellectual, and emotional "firsts" or changes do most teens experience? Tell students that in Chapter 9 they will look more in depth at the changes that have shaped their lives in the past few years.

IN YOUR JOURNAL

Encourage students to review information on Erikson in Chapter 8. Ask: How would Erikson view adolescence? *(as a continuation of the process of development)*

219

EXTRA CREDIT ACTIVITY

Assign students, working individually or in small groups, to design collages entitled: "U.S. Teenagers in the 1990s." Collages should include objects, clippings, pictures, and any other items that students think capture the "flavor" of what it is to be a teenager today. You might arrange to rotate these posters in a display case in the school lobby.

Guided Practice

■ **Drawing Political Cartoons.** Challenge students to draw a two-frame cartoon that captures their opinions on how adults see adolescents and how adolescents see themselves. Remind students of the tools used by political cartoonists—symbols, caricatures, exaggerated features, labels, and so on. Request volunteers to present their cartoons. Explore whether there is any consensus among student opinions. For example, how do most students feel that adults tend to view them? Why? (OBJECTIVE 1)

DID YOU KNOW?

The word *adolescence* comes from the Latin word *adolescere,* which means "to grow into maturity."

VIEWS OF ADOLESCENCE

What is it like to be an adolescent? Are the years between late childhood and early adulthood the best that life has to offer—a carefree time to act on ideals unburdened by practical concerns? Or is adolescence a time of crisis, rebellion, and unhappiness? The answer seems to depend on whom you ask. Adults, adolescents themselves, and psychologists all give different answers.

How Adults View Adolescence

Every adult has lived through the experience of adolescence. However, the teenage years of most adults do not always help them understand the concerns and difficulties of today's adolescents. Adults vary in their attitudes toward teenagers in general and certain adults have conflicting feelings about them.

Many adults admire young people. The values, music, fashions, and activities of young people are valued and heavily promoted in the mass media. Through dress, cosmetics, consumer purchases, and a variety of physical activities, some adults attempt to look and feel as healthy and active as adolescents. Studies have shown that adults dedicated to such social issues as nuclear disarmament, world hunger, and improving the environment admire young people who are active in trying to achieve progress in these areas (Rice, 1990).

Older people who live and work directly with teenagers often value the influence young people have in their lives. Teenagers help keep them connected to a larger world outside their own experience.

On the other hand, many studies have shown that some adults feel threatened by youth. Most parents are in their forties when they watch their teenage children develop physically into maturity and are themselves beginning to see the decline of their own bodies. This situation can produce negative feelings, particularly when the adults see themselves outperformed by younger people. They may regret the loss of their own youth and envy those who are still young.

While advertising contributes to a "cult of youth," the news and popular press often portray teenagers in a negative light. Young people are often depicted as disruptive or disturbed—the stories of teenage crime and misconduct are the most sensational and thus the ones the average person is likely to notice. In truth, most adolescents go through their teenage years without extreme storm and stress. Development is typically very slow and gradual; for most, adolescence is quite unremarkable (Josselson, 1980).

One of the reasons that negative images of adolescents surface is that different generations sometimes hold different ideas of morality. On controversial issues such as sexual activity or the use of nuclear weapons, the views of younger people may contrast with those of their parents, whose experiences have been different.

Also, adolescents may provoke a negative reaction from their parents by displaying traits that their parents see as a reflection of themselves

CRITICAL THINKING ACTIVITY

Much attention has been paid to the parents' perspective on conflicts with children entering the teens. In terms of socialization, however, adolescents face a set of challenges and pressures separate in many ways from their parents. These include: (1) new biological realities as their bodies change, (2) new situational realities as they shift from single-class elementary or middle schools into junior high or high schools, and (3) peer pressures from the teen subcultures of adolescents. You might ask students to brainstorm the non-family pressures of teenagers today.

that they would prefer not to see. For example, parents who are insecure about their academic abilities may feel uncomfortable if they see the same pattern emerging in their teenage children.

For one reason or another, some adults do view adolescents in an exaggerated light—either good or bad. Some idealize youth by remembering only its positive aspects. Others look on adolescence with horror, seeing only its burdens of stress, tension, conflict, or dependency. However, most adults probably do not hold extreme views, just as most young people do not fit into either extreme stereotype.

How Adolescents View Themselves

Does the overly idealized view of adolescence on the one hand and the overly negative view on the other affect the way the young see themselves? According to many psychologists, the answer is yes. Adolescents tend to regard themselves the way they think others see them. Adult stereotypes serve as a mirror for them, and they take society's reflections as authentic models for their own behavior (Anthony, 1969). Therefore, depending on the views of the adults with whom he or she interacts, an adolescent may tend to either overidealize or hold a negative image of himself or herself.

For many individuals, adolescence is a period of searching for identity. Adolescents are continually struggling with such questions as "Who am I?", "What do I want to be as a person?", and "What are the things that are important to me?" Although these questions continue to be asked during every stage of life, they take on special significance during the adolescent years.

FIGURE 9.2

The experience of adolescence varies widely among different cultures. These boys in New Guinea are undergoing the last stage of a puberty rite. When they complete the ritual and emerge from this hut, they will be adults of their tribe. **How did psychologist G. Stanley Hall view adolescence?**

COOPERATIVE LEARNING ACTIVITY

Break the class into pairs, and assign each student to answer the following questions: (1) Who are you? (2) How would your parent(s) describe you? (3) How would your teachers and/or employer describe you? (4) How would one of your close friends describe you? Direct students to exchange this information with their partners. Have students prepare short statements introducing their partners to the rest of the class. Allow each student to correct any mistaken information.

■ Cooperative Learning Activity.

Organize the students into nine teams. Assign each team one of the developmental tasks identified by Havighurst. Challenge each group to list some of the methods that adolescents can—and do—use to master these tasks. Call on a member from each group to share its list, encouraging modifications and additions from other groups. (OBJECTIVE 2)

■ Evaluating Generalizations.

Read aloud the following statement from page 223: *Perhaps the only safe generalization is that development through adolescence is a highly individual and varied matter and is not necessarily any different in that respect than life as an adult.* Challenge students to evaluate that generalization from the points of view of G. Stanley Hall, Margaret Mead, and Robert Havighurst. Ask: What are your opinions about the accuracy of the generalization? (OBJECTIVE 2)

Theories of Adolescence

The contradictory views of society at large are reflected not just in the behavior of adolescents but in the theories of psychologists. Controversy concerning the nature of adolescent experience has raged ever since 1904, when G. Stanley Hall presented his pioneering theory of adolescence. Hall, who thought in evolutionary terms, saw the adolescent as representing a transitional stage in our evolutionary development from beast to human. Being an adolescent for Hall was something like being a fully grown animal in a cage, an animal who sees freedom but doesn't know quite when freedom will occur or how to handle it. Thus, the adolescent was portrayed as existing in a state of great "storm and stress," as a marginal being, confused, troubled, and highly frustrated.

Through the years many psychologists and social scientists have supported Hall's theories, but there have been others who strongly disagreed. The latter theorists regard adolescence as a relatively smooth period of growth that is in no way discontinuous with the period of childhood that precedes and the period of young adulthood that follows.

One major proponent of this theory was Margaret Mead. In a series of classic anthropological studies in the late 1920s and early 1930s, Mead (1961) found that in some cultures adolescence is a highly enjoyable time of life and not at all marked by storm and stress.

Other studies conducted since then have tended to support Mead. They point to a relative lack of conflict in the lives of adolescents and a smooth, continuous development out of childhood.

Though adolescence may not be as crisis-ridden as some psychologists think, few would deny that there is at least some stress during that period. Great physical, mental, and emotional changes occur during adolescence. As psychologist Robert Havighurst (1972) has pointed out, every adolescent faces challenges, in the form of developmental tasks that must be mastered. Among the tasks that Havighurst lists are the following:

1. Accepting one's physical make-up and acquiring a masculine or feminine sex role
2. Developing appropriate relations with agemates of both sexes
3. Becoming emotionally independent of parents and other adults
4. Achieving the assurance that one will become economically independent
5. Deciding on, preparing for, and entering a vocation
6. Developing the cognitive skills and concepts necessary for social competence
7. Understanding and achieving socially responsible behavior
8. Preparing for marriage and family
9. Acquiring values that are harmonious with an appropriate scientific world picture

Though the tasks present a challenge, adolescents generally handle it well. Most face some stress but find ways to cope with it.

CONNECTIONS: PSYCHOLOGY AND THE MEDIA

Assign groups of students to watch at least three different television shows (or movies) that include adolescent characters. Instruct students to take notes on the decisions or activities that involve these characters. Direct them to pay particular attention to the emotional responses. Based on these programs, ask students whether the media portrayal of adolescence most closely mirrors the picture painted by G. Stanley Hall, Margaret Mead, Robert Havighurst, or a combination of these researchers.

There are, of course, exceptions. A small percentage of young people experience storm and stress throughout their adolescent years. Another small group confronts the changes all adolescents experience with no stress at all. Perhaps the only safe generalization is that development through adolescence is a highly individual and varied matter and is not necessarily any different in that respect than life as an adult.

The pattern of development a particular adolescent displays depends upon a great many factors. The most important of these include the individual's adjustment in childhood, the level of adjustment of his or her parents and peers, and the changes that occur during adolescence. It is to these changes that we now turn.

PERSONAL DEVELOPMENT

Becoming an adult involves much more than becoming physically mature, though that is an important part of the process. The transition from childhood to adulthood also involves changes in patterns of reasoning and moral thinking, and adjustments in personality and sexual behavior. Though the process is complex, most adolescents cope reasonably well with their changing circumstances.

Physical Changes

Physical Growth.   **Puberty,** or sexual maturation, is the biological event that marks the end of childhood. Hormones trigger a series of internal and external changes. These hormones produce different growth patterns in boys and girls.

At about the age of 10, girls rather suddenly begin to grow. Before this growth spurt fat tissue develops, making the girl appear chubby. The development of fat tissue is also characteristic of boys before their growth spurt. But whereas boys quickly lose it, progressing into a "string bean" or lean and lanky phase, girls retain most of this fat tissue, and even add to it, as they begin to spurt (Faust, 1977).

Once their growth spurt begins, females can grow as much as 2 to 3.5 inches (5 to 9 centimeters) a year. During this period, a girl's breasts and hips begin to fill out, and she develops pubic hair. Between 10 and 17—normally between 12 and 13—she has her first menstrual period, or **menarche.** Another 12 to 18 months will pass before her periods become regular and she is capable of conceiving a child. Yet most societies consider menarche the beginning of womanhood.

At about 12, boys begin to develop pubic hair and larger genitals. Normally, between 12 and 13 they achieve their first ejaculation, or **spermarche.** Though their growth spurt begins 24 to 27 months later than that of girls, it lasts about 3 years longer. Once their growth spurt begins, boys grow rapidly and fill out, developing the broad shoulders and thicker trunk of an adult man. They also acquire more muscle tissue than girls and

■ **Evaluating Stereotypes.** Assign students to collect advertisements or articles on the "ideal body type" portrayed by the media. Have students arrange these pictures in a wall mural. Ask: What stereotype does the media hold up in terms of body image? What, if any, pressures do you feel this body image places on adolescents? (OBJECTIVE 2)

CONNECTIONS: PSYCHOLOGY AND ANTHROPOLOGY

Assign interested students to prepare an in-depth biographical portrait of Margaret Mead. Students should mention Mead's contributions to the field of anthropology and explore how this work paved the way for Mead's speculations on developmental psychology. Have students present their portraits to the class as a whole. Ask: What variables in Mead's research created conditions unlike those addressed by Hall? Given these variables, do you think Mead's studies can still be used as a standard to judge Hall's theories on adolescence? Why or why not?

VISUAL INSTRUCTION

Request volunteers to recall how their style of dressing has changed along with their bodies. What clothing styles do they now prefer? Why? (Be sure to respect student privacy on all discussion of their physical appearance.)
Answer to caption, Figure 9.3: tend to think in more abstract terms; able to deal with hypothetical questions and philosophical principles

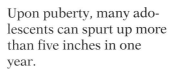

DID YOU KNOW?

Upon puberty, many adolescents can spurt up more than five inches in one year.

FIGURE 9.3

The physiological changes of puberty bring a new kind of self-awareness that did not exist in childhood. **How do thinking patterns change during adolescence?**

develop a larger heart and lungs. Their voices gradually deepen. Hair begins to grow on their faces and later on their chests. The age at which boys start to develop marks the time of greatest physical difference between boys and girls.

The rate and pattern of sexual maturation varies so widely that it is difficult to apply norms or standards to puberty. In general, however, girls begin to develop earlier than boys and for a year or two may tower over male agemates.

The period of adolescent growth can be an awkward one for both boys and girls because of **asynchrony**—the condition of uneven growth or maturation of bodily parts. For example, the hands or feet may be too large or small for the rest of the body. As the adolescent grows older, however, the

CONNECTIONS: PSYCHOLOGY AND HEALTH

This chapter discusses the physical changes that take place during the teenage years. Encourage several students to talk to the school nurse, health teacher, and/or physical education teacher about tips to make the most of these growth years. Students should compile a list of nutritional, fitness, and emotional guidelines. Suggest that they present this material in a brochure for distribution to the rest of the class. Ask students if they agree with the old adage: "Sound Body, Sound Mind." Why or why not?

bodily parts assume their correct proportions, and the clumsiness of early adolescence diminishes.

Reactions to Growth. In general, young people today are better informed than they were two or three generations ago. Most do not find the signs of their sexual maturation upsetting. Nevertheless, the rather sudden bodily changes that occur during puberty make all adolescents somewhat self-conscious. This is particularly true if they are early or late to develop. Adolescents desperately want to be accepted by their peers. They conform to ideals of how a male or female their age should act, dress, and look. For both young men and women, there is a strong correlation between having a negative body image and feelings of depression (Rierden, *et al.*, 1988). Most adolescents, especially girls, tend to evaluate themselves in terms of their culture's body ideal. In American society, for example, girls rated the attributes they seek in boys in this order: intelligence, attractiveness, and the ability to hold a conversation. When boys were asked to rank attributes in girls, attractiveness was at the top of the list, followed by friendliness, and intelligence (Hass, 1979).

Youths of both sexes are particularly sensitive about any traits they possess that appear to be sex-inappropriate. For example, boys tend to be very shy about "underdeveloped" genitalia, lack of pubic hair, or "fatty breasts," whereas girls are likely to be disturbed by "underdeveloped" breasts, or dark facial hair.

Individual differences in growth significantly affect the personality of young adolescents. For example, research indicates that boys who mature early have an advantage. They become heroes in sports and leaders in formal and informal social activities. Other boys look up to them; girls have crushes on them; adults tend to treat them as more mature. As a result they are generally more self-confident and independent than other boys. Late-maturing boys lose out not once, but twice. They watch as girls grow bigger and then they watch as boys also outgrow them. Others are leaders and move ahead, further eroding the self-confidence of late-maturing boys (Berger, 1994). Their high-pitched voices and less-than-ideal physiques may make them feel inadequate and some withdraw or rebel (Downs, 1990). The effects of late maturation for boys may last a long time.

Variations in the rate of development continue to have an effect on males even into their thirties. Those who matured earlier have been found to have a higher occupational and social status than those who matured later (Ames, 1957). The correlation weakens, however, as males enter their forties (Jones, 1965).

With girls the pattern is somewhat different. Girls who mature early may feel embarrassed rather than proud of their height and figure at first. Some begin dating older boys and become bossy with people their own age. Late-maturing girls tend to be less quarrelsome and to get along with their peers more easily. In their late teens, girls who matured early may be more popular and have a more favorable image of themselves than girls who matured slowly.

Why does physical growth have such powerful psychological effects? According to one widely held theory, the psychological reactions to physical

MORE about...

Being Early: Mixed Blessings for Girls. The early-maturing girl faces many problems. Sometimes, girls reject her and boys tease her. If permitted to date, she is likely to date older boys and, if her emotions and social skills have not kept up with her physical growth, she may face social and sexual situations she is not prepared to handle. Early pregnancy often causes a girl to delay her education, which ultimately hampers her career outside the home—a situation that can have a lingering effect (Furstenberg, *et al.*, 1987).

Later comes newfound popularity, largely because the early maturer has faced and dealt with a wide array of problems. To her peers, she is a voice of authority on matters of fashion, dating, and other matters of growing up.

■ **Weighing Alternatives.** Have students prepare a balance sheet on the pluses and minuses of early maturation for both males and females. On the whole, do students consider early maturation a biological gift or curse? (You might elicit additional input from non-threatened volunteers.) Next, focus on some of the difficulties faced by young people who mature later than their peers. Have students speculate on some of the ways these young people might compensate. *(Encourage students to think in both positive and negative terms. For example, a late-maturing teen might become the class clown. He or she might also turn small size to an advantage, becoming, for example, the coxswain on the rowing crew or a star gymnast.)* (OBJECTIVE 2)

■ **Discussion.** Tell students that less than two centuries ago the onset of puberty opened the door to adulthood—marriage, children, and so on. Ask: What economic and technological conditions have allowed U.S. society to support a chronological age group from 13–19?

CONNECTIONS: PSYCHOLOGY AND MATHEMATICS

Request students to use a recent almanac or *The Statistical Abstract of the United States* to find the breakdown of the United States population by age (based on the 1990 census). Assign students to present their findings in the form of a bar graph. Numbers (in units of tens of thousands) should appear along the vertical axis and age ranges along the horizontal axis. Distribute copies of this graph to class. Tell students that when the U.S. conducted the first census in 1790 the average American was a teenager. Ask: How do teenagers compare in numbers to the rest of the population today? In terms of the maturation process, how would you describe the U.S. population? *(Adult—in 1990, the median age was 32.9.)*

■ **Demonstration.** To illustrate thought changes in adolescence, you might duplicate "Piaget's pendulum problem." Hang a pendulum (an object suspended from a string) from the door of your classroom. Tell students that four factors can affect the swing of a pendulum: length of string, weight of the pendulum, release of pendulum from different heights, and force at which it is pushed. Working in small groups, challenge students to devise two plans: one to swing the pendulum rapidly, the other to swing it slowly. Have students carry out their plans. Next, request volunteers to conduct this same task with younger siblings or with a cooperating elementary class. What differences do students note in the way younger children approach the problem? Do their findings support comments on mental development cited in the text? Why or why not? (OBJECTIVE 2)

VISUAL INSTRUCTION

Point out that, in contrast to the egocentrism of 2- to 7-year-olds, adolescents display what David Elkind (1985) calls *social egocentrism*. In this stage, they overestimate their impact upon the immediate environment. A teen might feel invincible. An example is when a teen falls head over heels in love with someone right away, and wants to quit school and get married. **Answer to caption, Figure 9.4:** at age 11 or 12

FIGURE 9.4

During preoperational thought, children ages 2-7 are egocentric. After an adult and a child look at the same scene from different angles, the child will typically describe his or her own view as that of the adult. During the period of concrete operations (ages 7-11), children develop the ability to assume another's point of view. **When do adolescents reach the age of formal operational thinking?**

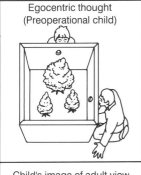
Egocentric thought
(Preoperational child)

Child's image of adult view

Adult's actual view

growth may be the result of a **self-fulfilling prophecy.** For example, the boy who believes he does not meet his culture's physical ideal may think less of himself and not pursue success as doggedly as the next person. His belief actually helps bring about the failure he feared.

Changes in Thinking

During adolescence, the thinking patterns characteristic of adults emerge. Jean Piaget has described this as "formal operational" thinking (Piaget and Inhelder, 1969). From about age 11 or 12, most people's thinking becomes more abstract and less concrete. For example, the adolescent can consider the answer to a hypothetical question like, "What would the world be like if people lived to be 200?" He or she can entertain such hypothetical possibilities in a way that a young child cannot. This ability expands the adolescent's problem-solving capacity. A teenage boy who discovers that his car's engine has a knock can consider a number of possible causes and systematically test out various adjustments and auto parts until he finds the root of the problem. This is the same ability that a scientist must have to conduct experiments.

With comprehension of the hypothetical comes the ability to understand abstract principles. Not only is this capacity important for studying higher-level science and mathematics, but it leads the adolescent to deal with such abstractions in his or her own life as ethics, conformity, and phoniness. It allows for introspection—examining one's own motives and thoughts. One adolescent noticed, "I found myself thinking about my future, and then I began to think about why I was thinking about my future, and then I began to think about why I was thinking about why I was thinking about my future."

These new intellectual capacities also enable the adolescent to deal with overpowering emotional feelings through **rationalization.** After failing a test, for example, an individual may rationalize that it happened "because I was worried about the date I might be going on next week." An eight-year-old is too tied to concrete reality to consider systematically all the reasons why he or she might have failed.

Do all adolescents fully reach the stage of formal operational thinking at the same age? As you might suspect, just as there are variations in sexual maturity, so there are variations in cognitive maturity. In general, the rate of mental growth varies greatly both among individual adolescents and among social classes in this country. One study showed that less than half of the 17-year-olds tested had reached the stage of formal operational thinking (Higgins-Trenk and Gaite, 1971).

Differences have also been noted among nations. Formal operational thinking is less prevalent in some societies than in others, probably because of differences in the amount of formal education available. People who cannot read and write lack the tools to separate thought from concrete reality and hence they cannot reach more advanced levels of thinking (Dasen & Heron, 1981).

For those who do reach that level, the change in thinking patterns is usually accompanied by changes in personality and social interactions as

CRITICAL THINKING ACTIVITY

Analyzing a Quote. Tell students that Piaget once remarked of adolescence:

The great novelty of this stage is that . . . the subject becomes capable of reasoning correctly about propositions he or she does not believe; . . . that is . . . propositions [that are] pure hypotheses. He or she also becomes capable of drawing *conclusions from truths that are merely possibilities.*

Ask: What does Piaget say is new about adolescent thought? (*abstract thinking*) Challenge students to explain how abstract thinking can be a source of stress for teens.

well. For example, adolescents tend to become very idealistic. This is related to the fact that, for the first time, they can imagine the hypothetical—how things might be. When they compare this to the way things are, the world seems a sorry place. As a result, they can grow rebellious. Some adolescents even develop a "messianic complex" and believe they can save the world from evil. In addition, the adolescents of each generation typically become impatient with what they see as the adult generation's failures. They don't understand why, for example, a person who feels a job compromises his or her principles doesn't just quit. In other words, adolescents tend to be somewhat unrealistic about the complexities of life. But at the same time, their idealism can help keep older adults in touch with ways in which the world could be improved.

Moral Development

Besides experiencing physical and cognitive changes, some adolescents, though by no means all, also go through important changes in their moral thinking. You'll recall that, according to Lawrence Kohlberg (whose theory was reviewed in Chapter 8), moral reasoning develops in stages. Young children in the early stages of their moral development are very egocentric. They consider an act right or wrong depending on whether or not it elicits punishment (Stage 1) or on whether it has positive or negative consequences for themselves (Stage 2). At later stages they judge an action by whether or not it is socially approved (Stage 3) or is sanctioned by established authority (Stage 4).

Many people never get beyond Stage 4, and their moral thinking remains quite rigid. But for those who do, adolescence and young adulthood are usually the periods of the most profound development. Individuals who progress to Stage 5 become concerned with whether a law is fair or just. They believe that the laws must change as the world changes and are never absolute. Individuals who reach Stage 6, on the other hand, accept absolute ethical principles, such as the Golden Rule, that they have worked through for themselves. Such moral laws apply to everyone, cannot be broken, and are more important than any written law.

Reaching higher levels of moral thinking involves the ability to abstract—to see a situation from another's viewpoint. That is why such moral development tends to occur in adolescence, when individuals gain the capacity for formal operational thinking. But not all adolescents who display such thinking simultaneously show higher levels of moral reasoning. In fact, only about 1 in 10 do (Kohlberg and Gilligan, 1971). Thus, formal thought, while necessary for higher moral development, does not guarantee it. Interestingly, by the mid-1980s, Kohlberg began to question whether differentiating between Stages 5 and 6 was necessary. He concluded that only one stage—combining the key features of both stages—adequately identified the most advanced form of moral development and thinking.

Overall, psychologists agree that a person's moral development depends on many factors, especially the kind of relationship the individual has with his or her parents. Evidence shows that during high school,

Children live in the present; adolescents begin to think about the future.

DID YOU KNOW

Kohlberg hypothesized that only about 10 percent of the population achieved Stage 6.

CONNECTIONS: PSYCHOLOGY AND SOCIAL STUDIES

Tell students that some people have criticized Kohlberg's Stage 6 because they feel it encourages asocial behavior. Ask: How do you think they came to this conclusion? *(because Stage 6 recognizes the right to break laws that conflict with moral principles)* Next, call on volunteers to research civil disobedience as practiced by Mohandas Gandhi and Dr. Martin Luther King, Jr. Based on their research, have students present short speeches in which Gandhi and King offer their interpretation of Stage 6.

Erik Erikson
1902–1994
Born of Danish parents, Erikson never knew his father. The Protestant Dane left Erikson's Jewish mother before he was born. His mother later married a German-Jewish pediatrician, but Erikson still felt scorned in two worlds. Mocked in synagogues because of his light features and ostracized by non-Jews because of his faith, Erikson knew firsthand the struggle of building an identity in early development.

As an art student, Erikson traveled to Rome to study the works of Michelangelo. The experience so humbled him that he entered psychoanalysis with Anna Freud (Sigmund's daughter). The success of therapy convinced Erikson to become a lay analyst.

Although Erikson never formally attained a degree in psychology, he has taught at prestigious institutions such as Harvard and Yale. His work with the Sioux and Yurok helped convince Erikson that development is a lifelong process. Erikson's major contribution to psychoanalytic theory is his identification of a life cycle comprising seven distinct stages. (See Table 8.2.)

PSYCHOLOGY UPDATE

Self-Esteem. A nationwide survey of 3,000 children revealed that girls in high school have much lower self-esteem than boys. The study found that most girls in elementary school express confidence, assertiveness, and a generally positive attitude about themselves. However, by adolescence less than one-third of the girls feel such high self-esteem. In contrast, about half of the boys feel self-assured.

Researchers also found that black high-school girls were the most self-confident, followed by Hispanics and, lastly, whites. The study concluded that black adolescent girls' self-esteem was fostered by their families and communities and not by their schools. The findings raise questions concerning our school system. Do schools undermine girls' sense of self-worth? If so, how can this be corrected?

The survey's conclusions also encourage psychologists who maintain that the psychological development of women differs greatly from that of men. Further research needs to be done to address the issues raised by this study.

adolescent moral development does not progress much. However, during college, when the individual is away from home more and therefore less under the influence of parents, more pronounced changes in moral development occur.

Personality Changes and Identity Formation

The changes adolescents undergo affect many facets of their existence, so it is hardly surprising that cumulatively they have a shaping influence on personality. Psychologists who have studied personality changes in adolescence have focused on the concept of identity. One psychologist in particular, Erik Erikson, has shown that the establishment of identity is key to adolescent development. His theory of how individuals arrive at an integrated sense of self has inspired a great deal of argument, both pro and con. Because his views have been so influential, we turn our attention now to his theory and the studies that support and challenge it.

Erikson's Theory of the Identity Crisis. According to Erikson, building an identity is a task that is unique to adolescence. Children are aware of what other people (adults and peers) think of them. They know the labels others apply to them (good, naughty, silly, talented, brave, pretty, and the like). They are also aware of their biological drives and of their growing physical and cognitive abilities. Children may dream of being this or that person and act these roles out in their play. But they do not brood about who they are or where they are going in life. Children live in the present; adolescents begin to think about the future.

To achieve some sense of themselves, most adolescents must go through what Erikson termed an **identity crisis**—a time of storm and stress during which they worry intensely about who they are (1968). Several factors contribute to the onset of this crisis, including the physiological changes and cognitive developments we have described, as well as awakening sexual drives and the possibility of a new kind of intimacy with the opposite sex. Adolescents begin to see the future as a reality, not just a game. They know they have to confront the almost infinite and often conflicting possibilities and choices that lie ahead. In the process of reviewing their past and anticipating their future, they begin to think about themselves. The process is a painful one, full of inner conflict, because they are torn by the desire to feel unique and distinctive on the one hand and to "fit in" on the other. Only by resolving this conflict do adolescents achieve an integrated sense of self.

Erikson's theory finds support in the work of another psychologist, James Marcia. According to Marcia (1966), Erikson is correct in pointing to the existence of an adolescent identity crisis. That crisis arises because individuals must make commitments on such important matters as occupation, religion, and political orientation. Using the categories of "crisis" and "commitment," Marcia distinguished four adolescent personality types: (1) *identity moratorium adolescents*, who have not experienced a crisis or made a commitment on any of the important matters facing them; (2) *identity foreclosure adolescents*, who have not had a crisis but have made

---

 LAB EXPERIMENTS AND DEMONSTRATIONS

Ask students to consider the following situation: "You are walking down the street with your best friend, and you notice a fancy car with the keys in the ignition. Your friend suggests taking the car for a ride. What would you do?" Have students answer this question from the perspective of Kohlberg's six stages of moral development. To help students, distribute the following guides. Information in parentheses indicates the motives operative at each stage.

Level 1: (to avoid punishment)
Level 2: (to receive a reward)
(continued on page 229)

a commitment based not on their own choice, but on the suggestion of others; (3) *identity confused* or *diffused adolescents,* who are in a continual search for meaning, commitment, and self-definition and thus experience life as a series of ongoing crises, and (4) *identity achievement adolescents,* who have experienced crises, considered many possibilities, and freely committed themselves to occupations and other important life matters.

These categories must not be too rigidly interpreted. It is possible for an individual to make a transition from one category to another, and it is also possible for the same individual to belong to one category with respect to religious commitment and to another with regard to political orientation or occupational choice. Marcia's main contribution is in clarifying the sources and nature of the adolescent identity crisis.

Criticism of Erikson's Theory.   Although Erikson and Marcia insist that all adolescents experience an identity crisis, not all psychologists agree. The term "crisis" suggests that adolescence is a time of nearly overwhelming stress. It also implies that the adolescent transition to maturity requires a radical break with childhood experience. As we noted earlier, many psychologists believe that adolescence is not so strife-ridden and constitutes a relatively smooth transition from one stage of life to the next.

One of the reasons Erikson may have arrived at his view is that he focused his study on disturbed adolescents who sought clinical psychiatric treatment. When adolescents attending school are selected at random and studied, critics point out, most show no sign of crisis and appear to be progressing rather smoothly through adolescence (Haan and Day, 1974).

Other Viewpoints.   Psychologists and social scientists seeking an alternative to Erikson's theory have offered several other explanations of adolescent identity formation. A.C. Peterson (1988), for example, argues that crisis is not the normal state of affairs for adolescents. When crises develop—as they do in a little more than 20 percent of all adolescent boys (Offer & Offer, 1975)—the cause is generally a change in the external circumstances of an individual's life rather than a biological factor. Thus, a divorce in the family or a new set of friends may trigger teenage rebellion and a crisis, but no internal biological clock dictates those events.

Human development, in Albert Bandura's view, is one continuous process. At all stages, including adolescence, individuals develop by interacting with others. Because of Bandura's emphasis on interaction in understanding adolescence and all other phases of human development, his approach is usually referred to as the **social learning theory** of development (Bandura, 1977).

Margaret Mead, mentioned earlier in this chapter, also stressed the importance of the social environment in adolescent identity formation. On the basis of her studies in Samoa (1961), for example, she concluded, like Bandura, that human development is more a continuous process than one marked by radical discontinuity. In that remote part of the world, adolescents are not expected to act any differently than they did as children or will be expected to act as adults. The reason is that children in Samoa are given a great deal of responsibility: They do not suddenly go from being submis-

Teacher Note. Erik Erikson came out of a school known today as the *Neo-Freudians.* This is the name given to the theorists who expanded upon and revised psychoanalytic theory from the late 1930s to the early 1950s. Neo-Freudians disagreed with Freud's emphasis on instinctual energy and childhood sexuality. They looked instead for more complex human motivations, such as societal factors.

■ **Debating an Issue.** Review the opinions held by Erikson, Marcia, Peterson, Bandura, and Mead on development during the teen years. Then organize the students into five groups. Assign the groups to prepare evidence or arguments in support of each theory. (If possible, allow a member of each group to act as a resource person who collects relevant data from the school library.) Next, organize a panel discussion in which a member from each group role-plays the psychologist assigned to the group. Conduct a panel discussion entitled: "Adolescence: How Stormy Is It?" As a follow-up activity, assign students to write short essays in which they present the theory (or theories) with which they most agree. (OBJECTIVE 3)

LAB EXPERIMENTS AND DEMONSTRATIONS

Level 3: (to win approval of others)
Level 4: (to show respect for authority)
Level 5: (to show respect for the rights of others)
Level 6: (to obey own morals and ethics)

Have students share their responses.

How do suggested actions reflect each level of moral development?

VISUAL INSTRUCTION

Students may find it easier to allow music to "do the talking" about emotional feelings. You might request volunteers to bring in CDs and tapes of songs that students think best capture the feelings of the teen years. (You might screen these songs for language and topics appropriate for class.) **Answer to caption, Figure 9.4:** genetic makeup, society, and culture

■ **Making Comparisons.** If possible, arrange for an adolescent student from another country to speak to the class. The person might be a foreign-exchange student or an immigrant who has arrived in the United States within the past few years. Assign students to explore the following questions with the speaker: (1) Does adolescence exist as a distinct stage of life in your country? If so, when does it begin and end? (2) What is the role of adolescence in regard to the family, work, and school? (3) How are male and female adolescents perceived? (4) Is there time for play? Or is adolescence a serious time of preparation for adulthood? (5) Do adolescents have the freedom to speak, dress, and act as they would like? Following the presentation, assign students to write an essay comparing adolescence in the speaker's country with adolescence in the United States. (OBJECTIVE 3)

FIGURE 9.4

Along with the physical and mental changes of adolescence come sharp increases of energy and strong emotional feelings. **What defines our sex roles?**

sive in childhood to being dominant later in life. Mead also points out that in Samoa, as in other non-industrial societies, children have sex roles similar to those of adults and therefore do not experience the onset of sexuality as an abrupt change or a traumatic experience. The identity crisis, then, is by no means a universal phenomenon.

Personality development in adolescence is a complex phenomenon. No one theory can do justice to all that is involved in the process. Erikson's emphasis on the adolescent's need for his or her own identity is an important contribution to understanding adolescent development. By focusing on individual psychology, however, he tended to ignore the influence of society and culture on the young. The studies of Bandura and Mead provide needed correctives. To arrive at a balanced picture of personality change and identity formation in adolescence, we must call upon all viewpoints.

Sexuality: Attitudes and Roles

As we noted earlier, adolescence is accompanied by puberty, when individuals mature sexually. The physical changes that occur are accompanied by changes in behavior. Adolescence is also the time when an individual develops attitudes about sex and expectations about the sex role he or she will fill.

Sexual Attitudes. Most of us have heard the term "sexual revolution" but has one actually occurred during your lifetime? In terms of behavior, the answer is "probably not." Although middle- and upper-class girls who attend college seem to be more sexually active than college girls were 30 years ago, sexual behavior in other social categories is about the same today as it

 LAB EXPERIMENTS AND DEMONSTRATIONS

Assign two groups of students to spend time in a busy public place such as a park, recreational center, or mall. Instruct one group to observe the way adults treat young girls and boys. The other group should observe interactions among male and female teenagers. Have students record behavior that re-inforces or departs from traditional sexual attitudes and/or gender roles. Ask: Which was more prevalent—traditional sexual attitudes and roles or departures from the norm? What, if any, links can be drawn between the behavior taught to children and the behavior of teens?

was then. In terms of attitudes, however, there has been a change. For example, the majority of young people believe it is morally acceptable for an engaged couple to have sexual intercourse; the majority of adults do not.

Attitudes affect the way we feel about sex and the way we respond sexually. Around the world there are wide variations in what youngsters are told about sex and how they respond. In some societies children are kept in the dark about sex until just before they are married, whereas in others preadolescent children are encouraged to engage in sexual play, even intercourse, in the belief that such play will foster mature development.

In the United States, because of our "Puritan" past, many people identify sex with sin except within marriage and with the intent of reproducing. This view is being challenged, however, by those who view sex as a source of pleasure in addition to being the means of perpetuating the species.

In the early 1970s, young women's attitudes toward premarital intercourse and pornography were still more conservative than young men's (Zubin and Money, 1973). Older adolescents are less conservative than younger ones, and, in recent years, more affluent and educated adolescents (especially young women) have become more liberated in their attitudes and behaviors than their less affluent and less educated counterparts. By the early 1990s—for the first time since data began being collected in the late 1930s—only small differences existed in the percentage of 19-year-olds who reported having premarital intercourse: 75 percent for females; 76 percent for males (Centers for Disease Control, 1991; 1992).

Sex Roles. Sex identity and sex roles are two different, though closely related, aspects of our sexual lives. **Sex identity** results from biological inheritance. Thus, if one has a vagina, one's sex identity is female; if a penis, male. Sex identity includes genetic traits we have inherited, and may include some sex-linked behaviors as well. An obvious example of a sex-linked behavior is the erection of the penis during sexual excitement.

A person's **sex role,** in contrast, is defined partly by genetic makeup but mainly by the society and culture in which the individual lives. The sex role is a standard of how a person with a given sex identity is supposed to behave. For example, in the United States, men were traditionally viewed as dominant, competitive, and emotionally reserved; women were viewed as submissive, cooperative, and emotionally responsive. These traits were considered appropriate for the different sexes.

Sex roles tell us how we are expected to behave, look, think, and feel in order to be considered by others, and to consider ourselves, "masculine" or "feminine." For example, in the past, a woman who repaired telephone lines might be considered by many people to be "unfeminine." Why? Because she does not conform to the traditional sex role requirement that women are not supposed to perform physical labor.

Sex roles vary from one society to another, and they can change over time within a given society. Sex roles give social meaning to sex identity. However, not all societies agree on the roles the sexes should assume. Indeed, anthropologists have found that some societies reverse the roles that we traditionally give to men and women, while others assign to both sexes what we might consider "masculine" or "feminine" roles. Not only do sex

■ **Categorizing Data.** To explore students' ideas on gender roles, you might ask them to recall the two most feminine women and the two most masculine men that they have known. On sheets of paper, have students list the traits that led to the selection of these individuals. With the class, compile a master list of feminine and masculine characteristics on the chalkboard. Challenge them to categorize each of these items into one or more of the following classes: Traits Defined by Biology/Genetics, Traits Assigned by Society, Traits Assigned by U.S. Culture, Non-Stereotypic Traits (i.e., traits that depart from the traditional norm). Call on volunteers to share their categorizations with the class as a whole. (OBJECTIVE 3)

Enrich. Have students complete the Chapter 9 Application Activity.

CRITICAL THINKING ACTIVITY

Identifying Stereotypes. Assign students to bring in pictures of people of all ages involved in activities that they admire or might like to take part in themselves. Pictures should be of women and men (girls and boys) in equal number. Using an opaque projector, show these pictures to the class. Identify whether the activities and/or people involved in the activities fit the stereotypic definition of *feminine* and *masculine.* Sort through the pictures, and instruct students to prepare two bulletin board displays entitled: "Traditional Role Models" and "Not-So-Traditional Role Models."

■ **Analyzing a Quote.** To illustrate the changing role of women in the workplace, you might read the following quote by Jynes Kiiskinen—a 39-year-old sheet-metal worker and mother of two teenagers.

I went into the sheet-metal trade because it offered money, opportunity, and a chance to learn a new field. I was a pre-apprentice for 2 1/2 years. They wanted to see if I'd last. Then I went to apprentice school for four years. After being out of school for 20 years I had to learn math again. I also had to learn how to weld, solder, and fashion metal into fittings, gutters, and so on. I had to carry from 4 ounces of copper to 50 pounds of metal.

Today people accept me. But 10 years ago many men thought I wouldn't last. But I carried my weight. I showed I could work with them, not against them. How do my daughter Shawna and her teenage friends feel? They see that with an education they don't have to be a secretary or nurse unless they want to be. Doors into the men's world have opened. Today there are choices.

Ask students the following questions. (1) What opportunities did the sheet-metal trade open to Jynes? (2) What gender-based attitudes did she face? (3) What lessons has her job choice taught to her adolescent daughter?

PSYCHOLOGY UPDATE

I See You're a Girl. Sandra Bem tackles the issue of sex role development at a more basic level than many. She suggests (1981; 1985; 1993) that Western culture forces children to address almost everything first in terms of sex. A child joining a neighborhood gang to play outside must first decide which activity to select in terms of whether it is appropriate for his or her sex.

Bem suggests this orientation amounts to a *lens* through which the youngster must view everything; she calls these lenses a *gender schema*. If girls go first, if boys must be brave, if . . . all of these teachings are reinforcing a more basic lesson that sex role *is* important.

Gender schema theory argues that children are active in their learning, but it encourages teachers, parents, and others to question whether sex-role stereotyping is necessary. If forced to view and organize their childhood around gender schema, won't children naturally tend to emphasize sex differences? But need they? If the education itself changed, couldn't children learn other ways to view themselves? Bem thinks so.

roles vary among societies, but they may change radically within a society, as we are witnessing today in the United States and Canada.

Sex-role stereotypes—that men should be rugged, women sensitive—have their roots deep in a time in our history when a division of labor was necessary for survival. Today, however, modern technology and birth control have freed women from duties associated with child rearing and childbearing for a large part of their lives. Sharp sex role divisions are no longer necessary or appropriate, especially in the labor force. New concepts of what it means to be "masculine" and "feminine" are becoming more widely accepted.

Partly because of the changing technology and partly as a result of affirmative action and other social and political movements, young people today have a much broader definition of what is appropriate behavior for men and women. Many people not only accept men who are to be emotionally and physically involved in the care of their children and take responsibility for other domestic duties, but expect these behaviors from them. Likewise, many women today are involved in occupations that, in the past, were reserved for men. Some of the symbols used to distinguish the sexes such as "wearing the pants" are completely obsolete. Similarly, many traditionally feminine symbols such as hair dyes and cosmetics are used by men.

Given these changing standards of acceptable sex roles, psychologist Sandra Bem argues that people should accept new **androgynous** roles—that is, roles that involve a flexible combination of traditionally male and female characteristics. She began her research by asking college students how desirable they considered various characteristics for a man and for a woman. Not surprisingly, she found that traits such as ambition, self-reliance, independence, and assertiveness were considered to be desirable for men. It was desirable for women to be affectionate, gentle, understanding, and sensitive to the needs of others.

These and other traits were then listed in a questionnaire called the Bem Sex Role Inventory. Bem asked people to rate how each of these traits applied to them on a scale from one (never or almost never true) to seven (always or almost always true). In one early report, Bem (1975) described the

Using Psychology

Teenage Depression and Suicide

Each year more than 1 million teenagers run away from home. About a million teenage girls in the United States get pregnant each year. It is estimated that more than 1.3 million American teenagers have serious drinking problems. Aside from alcohol the use of drugs, though steadily declining, remains a problem for teenagers.

COMMUNITY INVOLVEMENT

Invite men and women working in nontraditional jobs to speak to the class about their experiences. Examples of women include: plumbers, firefighters, police officers, fighter pilots, or sheet-metal workers. Examples of men include: nurses, kindergarten teachers, secretaries, or airline flight attendants. Ask the speakers to describe any problems or prejudice they may have encountered. Also, give them time to consider the following statement in the text: "New concepts of what it means to be 'masculine' and 'feminine' are becoming more commonly accepted." Request that they discuss this remark in their talk.

In the early 1990s, 10 to 15 percent of teenagers were using marijuana. These statistics highlight the seriousness of teenage depression. Many teenagers who feel helpless and hopeless use alcohol or other drugs, run away, become pregnant, or kill themselves. Suicide is among the leading causes of death among adolescents. Many accidents may, in fact, be disguised suicides. Since the 1950s, the number of suicides among those 15 to 24 years of age has quadrupled. Among high school seniors, more than 8 percent reported they have tried to commit suicide and three times that number have thought about it (Centers for Disease Control, 1991).

According to Kathleen McCoy (1982), the phenomenon of teenage depression is much more widespread then most parents or educators suspect. To many grownups who see adolescence as the best years of life, depression and youth may seem incongruous.

What events trigger depression in adolescents? One major event is the loss of a loved one through separation, family relocation, divorce or death. The adolescent may experience grief, guilt, panic, and anger as a reaction. If the teenager is not able to express these feelings in a supportive atmosphere, depression may result.

Another form of loss that causes depression is the breakdown of the family unit, often as a result of separation and divorce. Family members may be in conflict with each other and thus unable to communicate well. Adolescents may be thus deprived of the emotional support they need.

Unlike depressed adults, who usually look and feel sad or "down," depressed teenagers may appear to be extremely angry. They often engage in rebellious behavior such as truancy, running away, drinking, using drugs, or being sexually promiscuous. Often, depressed teenagers appear intensely hyperactive and frantic, traits that are frequently mistaken for normal behavior in teenagers. McCoy urges parents and educators to be aware of the warning signals of teenage depression and suicide. One warning signal is a change in the intensity and frequency of rebellious behavior. Others are withdrawal from friends, engaging in dangerous risktaking, talking about suicide, and excessive self-criticism. Often, the greatest danger of suicide occurs after a depression seems to be lifting.

The best way to deal with teenage depression is to communicate with the teenager about his or her problems. Sometimes a caring, listening parent or a responsive, sensitive friend can help the youth deal with his or her concerns. In other cases, parents and their teenage child may need professional help. This is particularly true when few channels of communication are open.

? FACT OR FICTION

Publicizing teenage suicides helps prevent more suicides.

Fiction. In the mid-1980s, leaders in communities around the country believed that talking publicly about teenage suicides as they occurred would stop other teens from taking their own lives. Unfortunately, the opposite occurred. Publicizing suicides seems to encourage more. Psychologists are trying to understand why this happens.

Using Psychology

Suicide is the second leading cause of death for people between the ages of 15 and 19. The rate of reported suicides among young people has nearly tripled in 30 years. Because of this, discussion of suicide is a particularly sensitive topic among teens. You might want to preview this activity by first exploring some of the support facilities for suicide within your community—e.g., a suicide hot line, guidance counselor, county mental health agency, and so on.

To guide students through the reading, ask the following questions.
1. What events may trigger serious depression in adolescents?
2. What are some of the warning signs of suicidal thought?
3. What actions should you take if a friend exhibits any of these signs? *(Students will mention shows of affection and "talk therapy." If they do not mention outside help, underscore that seeking adult or professional advice is not a betrayal of friendship. Point out that suicide deeply affects everyone in contact with the victim. If any of your students have experienced a suicide, you might offer to speak with them privately.)*

COMMUNITY INVOLVEMENT

Invite a counselor from a county mental health unit or a crisis center to discuss teenage suicide. If possible, request that the speaker bring written material on support services available for depressed youth or youth with drug or alcohol problems. Encourage the counselor to mention problems that most commonly overwhelm teenagers (as opposed to adults). Show the counselor the Fact or Fiction feature on this page. Have her or him comment on the feature, noting alternatives that have proven successful in curbing suicidal behavior.

■ **Discussion.** You might explore with some students the blur of gender among teenagers who adopt a non-sexed type look in clothing and/or appearance. (To kick off discussion, you might repeat the line from David Bowie's song *Rebel, Rebel:* "Your parents can't tell if you're a boy or a girl.") Ask: (1) How is non-sexed type dress a form of social rebellion? (2) According to Sandra Bem, what are some of the traits of androgynous people? (3) Do you agree with Bem that "androgyny should be our ideal"? Why or why not?

results for 1,500 Stanford undergraduates: about 50 percent stuck to "appropriate" sex roles (masculine males or feminine females), 15 percent were "cross-sex typed" (women who described themselves in traditionally male terms, or men who checked feminine adjectives), and 36 percent were androgynous people who checked off both male and female characteristics when they described themselves.

In later studies, Bem found that the androgynous people were indeed more flexible. Such women were able to be assertive when it was required, as could traditional males, but traditional females could not. Such people were also able to express warmth, playfulness, and concern as could traditional females, but traditional males could not. In our complex world, Bem argues, androgyny should be our ideal: there is no room for an artificial split between "woman's work" and "a man's world."

Androgyny is becoming an accepted ideal in our culture. One consequence of this shift is that adolescents who are developing into adults have more choices in the way they define themselves in life. In some ways, this shift toward more freedom in sex roles has resulted in greater personal responsibility. No longer limited by rigid sex role stereotypes, young people are challenged to define themselves according to their talents, temperaments, and values. At the same time, not all people within the culture accept the more androgynous sex roles. Older people, especially, may still define themselves and others in terms of more traditional and rigid sex role standards.

SOCIAL DEVELOPMENT

Adolescent development is multifaceted. In addition to the personal development just described, the adolescent also experiences changes in his or her social relationships. No longer a child though not yet an adult, the teenager must find a new role in the family—one that parents are not always ready to accept. He or she must also adjust to new, often more intense relationships with peers. The influence of family and peers on adolescent development has been the subject of much research, which is worth reviewing here.

The Family

Families in the United States experienced marked changes through the 1970s and 1980s. With many marriages ending in divorce, fewer and fewer American families have the pre-1970s norm of a wage-earning father working outside the house and a mother working within the home. Regardless of these changes, one of the principal developmental tasks for adolescents is becoming independent of their families. Unfortunately, the means of achieving this status are not always clear, either to the adolescents or to their parents. First, there are mixed feelings on both sides. Some parents have built their lifestyles around the family and are reluctant to let the child go. Such parents know they will soon have to find someone else on whom

CONNECTIONS: PSYCHOLOGY AND WORLD CULTURES

Tell students that *nuclear families* are the norm in the industrial societies of Europe and the United States. In other parts of the world, however, societies value *extended families* made up of two or more generations. Assign students to research extended families in African nations such as Kenya or Asian nations such as China or Japan. Tell them to focus on child-rearing practices and the roles assigned to people in their teens. How do students think parent-adolescent relationships might differ in extended families? What other stresses might develop within families? Have students present their findings in oral reports to the class.

At A Glance

WHAT ADOLESCENTS NEED AND WANT FROM THEIR PARENTS

Every family will experience clashes between parents and their adolescent offspring. Both parents and teenagers can benefit from having a general idea of the qualities adolescents need and want from their parents. This knowledge can help parents meet their children's needs, and it provides a yardstick against which teenagers can measure their expectations of their parents to see how realistic those expectations are. Several studies have revealed a number of qualities that adolescents most need and want in their parents.

1. Teenagers want parents to **take an interest** in their activities and to be available when they need help and support. One disappointed high school basketball player expressed this view very clearly:

I'm the star player on the school basketball team, but never once has either parent come to see me play. They're either too busy or too tired or can't get a baby-sitter for my younger sister. The crowds cheer for me, the girls hang around my locker, some kids even ask me for my autograph. But it doesn't mean much if the two most important people in my life don't care.

2. Parents should **listen** to what their teenaged children say, and should try to understand their point of view.
3. Similarly, parents should **communicate** with their children, exchanging ideas and talking with their teenagers, not at them.
4. Parents should **love and accept** adolescents as they are. Too often, teenagers feel rejected and worthless because they cannot meet their parents' too-high expectations of them.
5. Parents should **trust** their children and **respect** their privacy. Teenagers especially resent parents who open their mail, read their diaries, or eavesdrop on their phone conversations.
6. Parents should **allow** their children to learn to be **independent** by giving them leeway in such areas as choice of friends and clothing. Teenagers especially want their parents to grant them autonomy in gradually increasing amounts as they learn to handle it.
7. Parents should be **neither too strict nor too permissive.** Once the family rules are established—preferably in a democratic way—parents should be consistent in enforcing them.

For more details, see F. P. Rice, The Adolescent: Development, Relationships, and Culture, 7th ed. Boston: Allyn & Bacon, 1992, pp. 410–419; Garrod, Andrew, Adolescent Portraits. Needham Heights, MA: Allyn & Bacon, Inc., 1992.

At A Glance

As a guide to reading the feature, you might assign the following questions.
1. How do agreed-upon qualities for parenting help both parents and adolescents? *(They help parents meet their children's needs. They also provide adolescents with a yardstick of expectations.)*
2. According to several studies, what qualities in parents do teens most desire? *(Answers should reflect bold-faced qualities in the feature.)*
3. What additional qualities can you name? *(Answers will vary. For example, some students might note that parents should act as positive role models, avoiding the time-worn adage "Do as I say, not as I do.")*

■ **Discussion.** After students have read "Social Development" on pages 234–238, write the following two headings on the chalkboard: Family Influence and Peer Influence. Challenge students to brainstorm the way each of these socializing agents influences teen behavior. (You might also ask students to indicate for each item whether it is a positive or a negative influence.) Based on this list, ask: Does the family or peer group have more influence over teen development, or does each have about the same amount of influence? (OBJECTIVE 4)

PSYCHOLOGISTS AT WORK

In sorting out the problems between parents and children, many people turn to *family counselors*. Unlike other counselors, these professionals work with entire families or with individuals as members of a family unit. One of their primary tasks is to restore communications so that all parties involved set aside anger to see their own role in an issue. Family counselors work in a variety of settings—private practice, social-service agencies, and hospitals.

Independent Practice

■ **Cooperative Learning Activity.** Assign groups of students to devise a handbook on parenting the adolescent, complete with appropriate illustrations clipped from magazines. Tell students to begin the book with a definition of adolescence. The following pages should be broken into sections based upon the area of development addressed (physical, emotional, intellectual, social, and so on).

Have groups exchange their handbooks at least once for editing. "Editors" should correct more than grammar: they should also look for inappropriate teen-oriented advice. Allow students time to examine the completed handbooks. Ask: How does the advice in these handbooks reflect the guidelines in the "At a Glance" feature on page 235? Would you describe the advice in each handbook as authoritarian, democratic, or permissive? Explain. (OBJECTIVES 1–4)

■ **Applying Concepts.** As a creative writing assignment, have students write a short skit on a decision-making situation between a parent and adolescent. Call on students to read these skits aloud. Challenge the rest of the class to guess whether the skit depicts an authoritarian family, a democratic/authoritative family, or a permissive/laissez-faire family. (OBJECTIVE 4)

to shift their emotional dependence. Also, parents whose children are old enough to leave home sometimes have to wrestle with their own fears of advancing age. Many parents worry about whether their children are really ready to cope with the harsh realities of life—and so do adolescents. At the same time that young people long to get out on their own and try themselves against the world, they worry a lot about failing there. This internal struggle is often mirrored in the adolescent's unpredictable behavior, which parents may interpret as "adolescent rebellion." Against this background of uncertainty, which is almost universal, there are various family styles of working toward autonomy.

Parenting Styles

The way in which adolescents seek independence and the ease with which they resolve conflicts about becoming adults depends in large part on the parent-child relationship.

Diana Baumrind (1971, 1973) observed and interviewed nursery school children and their parents. She observed and questioned both how the children interacted with their parents, and what the parents did. Follow-up observations when the children were 8 or 9 led to several conclusions about the impact of three distinct parenting styles on children.

In **authoritarian families** parents are the "bosses." They do not feel that they have to explain their actions or demands. In fact, such parents may feel the child has no right to question parental decisions.

In **democratic** or **authoritative families** adolescents participate in decisions affecting their lives. There is a great deal of discussion and negotiation in such families. Parents listen to their children's reasons for wanting to go somewhere or do something, and make an effort to explain their rules and expectations. The adolescents make many decisions for themselves, but the parents retain the right to veto plans of which they disapprove.

In **permissive** or **laissez-faire** families children have the final say. The parents may attempt to guide the adolescents, but give in when the children insist on having their own way. Or the parents may simply give up their child-rearing responsibilities—setting no rules about behavior, making no demands, voicing no expectations, virtually ignoring the young people in their house.

Maccoby and Martin (1983) later identified a fourth parenting style: Uninvolved parents were typically very self-centered in their child rearing, seemed uncommitted to their role and quite distant from their child.

Numerous studies suggest that adolescents who have grown up in democratic or authoritative families are more confident of their own values and goals than other young people. They are more likely to want to make their own decisions with or without advice. There are several reasons for this: First, the child is able to *assume responsibility gradually*. He or she is not denied the opportunity to exercise judgment (as in authoritarian families) or given too much responsibility too soon (as in permissive families). Second, the child is more likely to *identify with parents* who love and respect him or her than with parents who treat him or her as incompetent or who

---

CONNECTIONS: PSYCHOLOGY AND THE MEDIA

Assign students to watch a popular television situation comedy or drama that involves a family with one or more children. Based on information in the text, have students decide whether the family is authoritarian, democratic/authoritative, or permissive/laissez-faire. Ask students to present their findings in the form of short oral reports. Advise them to include concrete examples to support their conclusions.

seem indifferent. Finally, through their behavior toward the child, democratic parents *present a model of responsible, cooperative independence* for the growing person to imitate.

Children raised in authoritarian families lack practice in negotiating for their desires and exercising responsibility. They tend to resent all authority and to rebel without cause. Children raised in permissive families tend to feel unwanted and to doubt their own self-worth. They often do not trust themselves or others (Conger, 1973). The children of uninvolved parents tend to be more aggressive and to have both lower self-esteem and poorer control over impulsive behavior.

It seems clear that authoritative parenting yields the best results. This seems to come from two features—the *establishment of limits* on the child and *responding* to the child with warmth and support (Bukatko & Daehler, 1992).

Although the style parents adopt in dealing with their children influences adolescent development, it would be wrong to conclude that parents are solely responsible for the way their children turn out. Adolescents themselves may contribute to the style parents embrace, with consequences for their own personal development. Parents may adopt a laissez-faire attitude simply because they find that style the easiest way to cope with a teenager who insists on having his or her own way. Adolescents experiencing rapid physical and emotional changes may force their parents to make major adjustments to the adolescent.

Conflict between adolescents and parents, even in democratic families, is not uncommon. In general, the more authoritarian a family, the more frequent such conflicts tend to be. But other factors affect the frequency of arguments. The sex of the adolescent is one such factor, with girls reporting more conflict with family members than boys. The size of the family is another. Large middle-class families, for example, experience more conflict than smaller ones (Edwards *et al.*, 1973).

Thus far in this section, we have emphasized the relationship between adolescents and parents, but there is also a flow of influence between the adolescent and other family members, especially siblings. Older siblings, for example, serve as role models for the adolescent. Younger siblings allow the adolescent to assume the role of surrogate parent, and thus to learn an array of adult roles and responsibilities. In general, siblings learn from one another—through play, sharing secrets and experiences, and through fighting—how to negotiate relationships with others and thereby to get along better in the larger world.

The Peer Group

Adolescents can trust their peers not to treat them like children. Teenagers spend much of their time with friends—they need and use each other to define themselves.

High schools are important as places for adolescents to get together. And they do get together in fairly predictable ways. Most schools contain easily recognizable and well-defined sets, or crowds. And these sets are arranged in a fairly rigid hierarchy—everyone knows who belongs to which

Adolescents need and use the peer group to define themselves.

■ **Discussion.** Tell students that the term *sibling rivalry* has become part of our everyday language. You might ask students to explore the negative and positive effects of having brothers and sisters (or none at all, if an only child). Ask: Do you think the term *sibling rivalry* has validity as a psychological term? Why or why not? (OBJECTIVE 4)

COOPERATIVE LEARNING ACTIVITY

Organize the students into groups, and assign each group to design a contract between parents and children in a democratic/authoritative family. Tell students that the contract should include a statement of rights and responsibilities for adults, teens, and preteens. You might also suggest that the contract include a "bill of rights" for the family unit as a whole. Call on a volunteer from each group to present its contract. Ask: How do you think the research team of Bukatko and Daehler might respond to these contracts? Why?

■ **Demonstration.** Request several volunteers to take part in an experiment. Ask that they dress in a manner inappropriate for their peer group. (For example, if the preferred style of dress is "grunge," then students should dress in a business suit.) Have students record reactions to their dress for a day—both from their peers and from adults. Allow time for students to share their observations with the class as a whole. Based on this demonstration, what conclusions can students reach about conformity among teenagers? (For example, what is the major force in producing conformity—parents, influential adults, or peers?) (OBJECTIVES 3, 4)

set and what people in that set do with their time. Early in adolescence the sets are usually divided by sex, but later the sexes mix. Sets usually form along class lines. Some school activities bring teenagers of different social classes together, but it is the exception rather than the rule that middle-class and lower-class adolescents are close friends.

Besides class, what determines whether an adolescent will be accepted by a peer group? Many studies have shown that personal characteristics are very important. Well-liked peers tend to be well-groomed, good-looking, outgoing, neat, fun, and adept at making others feel accepted. Unpopular peers are seen by others as irresponsible, sloppy, childish, shy, and lonely, among other negative characteristics (Hartup, 1970; Harrocks and Benimoff, 1967).

Belonging to a *clique* (a group within a set) is very important to most adolescents and serves several functions. Most obviously, perhaps, it fulfills the need for closeness with others. But, in addition, it gives the adolescent a means of defining himself or herself, a way of establishing an identity. The group does this by helping the individual achieve self-confidence, develop a sense of independence from family, clarify values, and experiment with new roles (Rogers, 1977). By providing feedback, clique members not only help define who an individual is but also who he or she is not: group membership separates an adolescent from others who are not in his or her set.

Of course, there are drawbacks to this kind of social organization. One of the greatest is the fear of being disliked, which leads to **conformity**—the "glue" that holds the peer group together. A teenager's fear of wearing clothes that might set him or her apart from others is well known. But group pressures to conform may also lead young people to do more serious things that run contrary to their better judgment.

Despite their tendency to encourage conformity, peer groups are not always the dominant influence in an adolescent's life. Both parents and peers exercise considerable influence in shaping adolescent behavior and attitudes. Peers tend to set the standards on such matters as fashion and taste in music (Munns, 1972). In addition, their advice on school-related issues may also be considered more reliable than parental counsel (Brittain, 1963, 1969).

When it comes to basic matters, however, involving marriage, religion, or educational plans, adolescents tend to accept their parents' beliefs and to follow their advice (Chand, Crider, and Willets, 1975; Kandel and Lesser, 1969). Only in a few areas touching basic values—for example, drug use or sexual behavior—are there differences. Even here the differences are not fundamental and represent only a difference in the strength with which the same basic belief is held (Lerner and Knapp, 1975).

Peer groups, then, do not pose a threat to parental authority. Even though parents spend less time with their adolescent children as the latter mature, their influence is still strong. Adolescents of both sexes tend to choose friends with values close to those of their parents, and these peer groups are of immense help in making the transition from dependent child to independent adult. Thus, generational conflict is not nearly so pronounced as some would have us believe.

MEETING SPECIAL NEEDS

Students with learning disabilities sometimes need concrete examples to understand abstract concepts. Point out the use of the word *conformity* on this page. Ask students to look up the definition in the Glossary. Then show students photos or clippings illustrating conformity, such as pictures of a group of military cadets, 1950s executives, and so on. Ask students how these pictures illustrate the concept of conformity. Then assign students to find other examples of conformity—not only in magazines, but in their own school. Is there, for example, a "uniform" to which most of their peers conform?

DIFFICULTIES IN THE TRANSITION FROM LATE ADOLESCENCE TO EARLY ADULTHOOD

As we have seen in this chapter, adolescence is a time of transition. There are many developmental tasks to be mastered, but adolescence is not distinct from other periods of life in this respect. As Erikson (1950, 1968) and Havighurst (1972) pointed out, every stage of life brings with it unique challenges that are specific to that stage, whether it is old age, early childhood, or adolescence.

When a person has mastered the tasks of adolescence, he or she is an adult, but not a "mature" adult. The developmental stage of adulthood spans many years and the end of adolescence is just the beginning of this long journey. The graduate-adolescent is a "young" adult heading toward "middle" adulthood, the phase before mature adulthood. The young adult will find that he or she now has new tasks to master unique to this stage of life.

Given the great array of profound changes the adolescent must cope with involving his or her mind, body, emotions, and social relationships, it is natural and normal that most adolescents should experience some *temporary* psychological difficulties. The great majority, however, adjust fairly quickly. Although some studies show that mental illness and suicide are relatively rare among adolescents, the rates of both have been increasing over the past several decades. The occurrence of teenage suicide has tripled over the past 20 years—and this figure may be underestimated because medical personnel sometimes label a death as an accident to protect the victim's family.

For these and other reasons, the adolescent years are the most difficult. The illusion of invulnerability—"Others may get caught, but not me!"—is a part of adolescent egocentrism. This illusion may lead adolescents to do things with their peers they would not do alone. This troubled minority often "acts out" problems in one of several ways. Acts of juvenile delinquency, running away from home, unwanted pregnancies, alcohol and drug abuse, and underachievement at school are typical. Although one-third of all arrests in the United States involve adolescents (U.S. Department of Justice, 1990), repeat offenders and the fact that many are not caught make these data hard to interpret. Talking to and studying adolescents reveals another view. As many as 80 percent have committed crimes, such as vandalism, for which they could have been arrested (Binder *et al.*, 1988). Most of us outgrow these tendencies as we mature.

Unfortunately, troubled adolescents do not simply "outgrow" their problems, but carry them into later life if they are not treated. Adults, therefore, should be concerned about troubled teenagers. It is important to note, however, that abnormal behavior should be seen as a more intense form, or a more extreme degree, of normal behavior. It should not be considered a different *kind* of behavior. For example, teenagers who experiment with drugs—or even become drug abusers—need understanding. By not labeling the teenaged drug abuser "strange" or "different," we can better meet his or her psychological needs.

PSYCHOLOGY and YOU

Teenagers and Work. By high school graduation, more than 80 percent of students have had some kind of job. Most take low-skilled jobs that provide an opportunity to make some extra money. While most people tend to believe that any kind of job experience is good, research indicates that such work can, in fact, be harmful.

One reason for this is that students who work evenings or weekends have less time to study. If you work, you need to set time aside for school work. Another is that students might gain a false impression of the workplace from their work experience. The jobs they take tend to be low-paying, boring, and unchallenging.

Finally, working while still in school can create false ideas about money. Most students work to pay for luxury items such as brand-name clothes or concert tickets. There's a danger that they will experience "premature affluence" because what they earn is spending money; they don't have to pay for necessities such as food and rent. Realizing that spending money may, in fact, be less available when you take a full-time job will help you avoid this trap.

ASSESS

Check for Understanding

Organize the class into groups, and assign each group to prepare a data sheet on one of the main headings in the outline on page 240. Reassemble the groups, and compile a master outline.

Reteach

Have students complete the Chapter 9 Study Guide Activity. For extended review, assign the Chapter 9 Review Activity as homework or an in-class assignment.

Enrich

Ask students to complete the Chapter 9 Extension Activity and answer the questions that follow it.

Readings in Psychology. Have students read the Section 3, Reading 3 selection in *Readings in Psychology* and answer the questions that follow the selection.

Evaluate

Administer and grade the Chapter 9 Test. Two forms are available should you wish to give different tests to different students/classes.

CLOSE

Ask students to review the statements and/or posters compiled in the Motivating Activity on page 218. Using information in this chapter, have students identify examples in the statements of some of the challenges, stresses, and changes associated with adolescence.

COOPERATIVE LEARNING ACTIVITY

Challenge the class to brainstorm situations or conditions that create stress on adolescents today. Have students agree on the top 10 items. Then assign teams of students to list these items on index cards or sheets of paper. Working in teams, have students conduct a survey in which teenagers in their school or community rank these items in order of importance in terms of their lives. Have the teams tally the number of students polled and the overall results. Based on this poll, what do students think are the two most important issues facing teens today?

ANSWERS

Concepts and Vocabulary

1. Many either idealize teens or feel threatened by them.

2. Answers will vary, but may include: generational differences on morality, reminder of undesirable traits that adults possess themselves, internalization of negative images presented by the media, resentment of adolescent youthfulness

3. Hall saw adolescence as a transitional time of "storm and stress." Mead's research did not support Hall. She saw adolescence as a part of the ongoing development process.

4. See page 225.

5. more abstract than early stages of thinking; can comprehend hypothetical ideas and contemplate ideals

6. stages at which people judge laws on the basis of their morality and justice; flexible thought and ability to abstract principles

7. moratorium adolescents, identity foreclosure adolescents, identity confused or diffused adolescents, and identity achievement adolescents; argue that not all adolescents experience an identity crisis

8. Sex identity results from biological/genetic inheritance; sex roles result largely from societal and cultural conditioning. Androgyny is a sex role.

9. authoritarian, democratic or authoritative, and permissive/laissez-faire; probably the democratic style

10. marriage, religion, and educational plans

11. answers will vary; have a more intense or extreme behavior rather than being different

---

9 Review

SUMMARY

Use the following outline as a tool for reviewing this chapter. Copy the outline onto your own paper, leaving spaces between headings to make notes about key concepts.

I. Views of Adolescence
   A. How Adults View Adolescence
   B. How Adolescents View Themselves
   C. Theories of Adolescence

II. Personal Development
   A. Physical Changes
   B. Changes in Thinking
   C. Moral Development
   D. Personality Changes and Identity Formation
   E. Sexuality: Attitudes and Roles

III. Social Development
   A. The Family
   B. Parenting Styles
   C. The Peer Group

IV. Difficulties in the Transition from Late Adolescence to Early Adulthood

CONCEPTS AND VOCABULARY

1. Describe two common views that adults have toward adolescents.

2. List at least four reasons that may explain why some adults view adolescents in a negative light.

3. Describe G. Stanley Hall's theory of adolescence. Does the research of Margaret Mead support his position? Explain why or why not.

4. Do early-maturing adolescent boys have a more positive view of themselves than late maturers? Is this difference the same for early- and late-maturing girls?

5. Explain what Piaget means by "formal operational" thinking. How does this change in cognitive ability affect an adolescent?

6. According to Kohlberg, what are the fifth and sixth stages of moral development? What other change is necessary in order for persons to achieve these advanced stages of moral development?

7. Based on Erikson's concept of identity crisis, what are the four adolescent personality types presented by Marcia? Why do some psychologists disagree with Erikson and Marcia?

8. How does sex role differ from sexual identity? When Sandra Bem discusses androgyny, is she talking about sex role or sexual identity?

9. Describe three types of family interaction patterns. Which style would you use if you wanted your children to act independently and have confidence in their personal decisions?

10. In what areas do adolescents tend to follow the beliefs and advice of their parents?

11. What percentage of adolescents have a very difficult time mastering the developmental tasks of this period in their lives? Are these persons "different" from other adolescents who have less difficulty?

CRITICAL THINKING

1. **Evaluation.** First, write five words or phrases that, in your opinion, characterize adolescence. Then, ask an adult (for example, a parent) to also write five words or phrases. What are the similarities and differences? In your opinion, what are some reasons for the differences?

2. **Analyze.** Erikson and Marcia insist that all adolescents experience an identity crisis. Do you agree? Have you experienced an identity crisis? If so, can you relate what happened to what you have learned in your reading and class discussions?

Critical Thinking

1. Analysis of similarities and differences should take into account material on pp. 220–223.

2. Respect student confidentiality when discussing an identity crisis. Also, remind students that not all psychologists feel such crises occur. (You might request volunteers to explain if they think some teens do in fact escape the so-called crisis period.)

APPLYING KNOWLEDGE

1. Pretend you are a high school psychology teacher. Describe what you would plan to teach in the course, reasons for your selections, and how you would plan to teach this material. Would you use an experiential or a cognitive approach? Which topics of importance to adolescents would you specifically include?

2. If you were a parent, which family structure would you choose to have in your home—authoritarian, authoritative, or permissive? What behaviors would you engage in to ensure that the family structure actually existed?

3. It has often been said that American culture is preoccupied with youthfulness and remaining young. The values, music, fashion, and activities of young people are heavily publicized in the mass media. Find as many examples as you can of America's fascination with youth. Be sure to examine newspapers, magazines, radio, television, and popular music when you search for examples. Pay particular attention to advertising that emphasizes the marketing of youthful values. Cut out examples as evidence.

4. Some psychologists believe that men and women should accept androgynous sex roles. Androgynous sex roles consist of a combination of characteristics that are both masculine and feminine. Think of some traits that you consider to be masculine or feminine. Then think of people who possess mostly all masculine or all feminine traits. Next, think of people who possess both masculine and feminine characteristics. Your examples can be people you know, or they can be people from television, movies, or music. Do people with either mostly masculine or mostly feminine characteristics behave differently from people with both masculine and feminine traits? If so, in what type of sit-

uation? Do you think someone with an androgynous sex role is healthier than someone with a traditional sex role? Explain your reasoning.

5. Belonging to a group is often a very important part of adolescence. Identify three different groups in your school. How would you characterize the people who belong to each group? What keeps groups together? Are you part of any group? Why or why not? Do others think you are?

BEYOND THE CLASSROOM

1. Many communities and mental health centers sponsor suicide hot lines. Ask your guidance counselor or school nurse if he or she knows of a hot line in your area. Check with your teacher, and, if possible, contact someone at the hot line and ask the person to come to your school and speak about how the hot line works. Have the person explain what type of training is required to become a phone counselor; how many calls come in on a typical night; what is the busiest time of day; day of the week, and time of year. If you are unable to find a hot line in your area, look for articles on teen suicide and what is being done to prevent it.

IN YOUR JOURNAL

1. Reread the journal entry that you wrote at the beginning of the study of Chapter 9. Other social scientists have suggested that building an identity is a lifelong process, and that changes to the identity occur at different times. Write a journal entry that argues that building an identity is a lifelong experience. Support your arguments with evidence from the chapter as well as evidence from your own experience. Finally, reread both entries and write a short summary explaining whether you think one position is more valid than the other.

Applying Knowledge

1. You might assign groups of students to prepare a psychology curriculum, using topics in this textbook as a guide. Focus in particular on adolescence. What topics, if any, do students think were left out? Which, if any, were covered in too much depth?

2. In choosing their plan of behavior, have students weigh day-to-day family management against long-term child-rearing goals. For example, authoritarian families might have more order, but do they produce independent children?

3. In preparing this activity, encourage students to investigate publications for a broad-based audience, such as *TIME*, *Newsweek*, or *Family Circle*. You might have some students look at age-geared publications such as *Lear's*. Ask: Have models gotten older along with the baby boomers? Or are ads still youth-oriented?

CHAPTER BONUS
Test Question

This question may be used for extra credit on the chapter test.
Choose the letter of the correct response.

Families in which there are few rules and little direction for the children may be categorized as:

a. authoritative.
b. authoritarian.
c. laissez-faire.
d. all of the above.

Answer: **c**

---

4. You might approach this activity by looking at the positive and negative effects of sex roles. Ask: Is there any way to have feminine and masculine roles without stereotypes and prejudice? If so, how?

5. Respect student privacy in this activity. Some students may not belong to any groups at all. They might take pride or shame in their role as an "outsider."

Beyond the Classroom

1. Assign students to summarize information from the speaker and/or research in the form of a written report.

IN YOUR JOURNAL

If time permits, discuss journal entries individually with students.

CHAPTER 10

Adulthood and Old Age

TEXT TOPICS	SPECIAL FEATURES	RESOURCE MATERIALS
Adulthood, pp. 243–254	**More About Psychology,** p. 244 **Fact or Fiction?,** p. 253	■ **Reproducible Lesson Plan; Study Guide; Review Activity Transparency 19** *Readings in Psychology:* **Section 3, Reading 4**
Old Age, pp. 254–258	**Psychology Update,** p. 254 **More About Psychology,** p. 256; p. 258	■ **Reproducible Lesson Plan; Study Guide; Review Activity; Application Activity** *Readings in Psychology:* **Section 3, Reading 5**
Death and Dying, pp. 259–261	**Using Psychology:** Hospices, pp. 260–261	■ **Reproducible Lesson Plan; Study Guide; Review Activity; Extension Activity** ■ **Chapter Test, Form A and Form B** ◉ **Understanding Psychology Testmaker**

PERFORMANCE ASSESSMENT ACTIVITY

Assign students to find magazine and newspaper articles that address the physical, sexual, and intellectual changes that occur during adulthood and old age. Have students contribute their articles to a classroom anthology on aging. Students should work in small groups to organize the material according to the stages of male and female development outlined in this chapter. Ask each student to write a one-paragraph summary to accompany the article they contributed. (Summaries should touch on all the main ideas contained in the article.)

CHAPTER RESOURCES

Readings for the Student

Bergquist, William, *et al. In Our Fifties: Voices of Men and Women Reinventing Their Lives.* San Francisco: Jossey-Bass, Inc., 1993.

Chown, Sheila M. *Human Aging.* Baltimore: Penguin, 1972.

Hamilton, M. and Reid, H. *A Hospice Handbook: A New Way to Care for the Dying.* Grand Rapids, MI: Eerdmans, 1980.

Readings for the Teacher

Henig, R. M. *The Myth of Senility.* New York: Anchor Press/Doubleday, 1981.

Kimmel, D. C. *Adulthood and Aging: An Interdisciplinary View.* New York: Wiley, 1980.

Thompson, E. H., Jr., *et al.* "Social Support and Caregiving Burden in Family Caregivers of Frail Elders." *Journal of Gerontological Social Work,* 48 (September 1993): 245–254.

Multimedia

Aging and Death. Wisconsin Foundation for Vocational Technical and Adult Education. This video examines the factors in aging successfully, presenting the stages of dying, and explores the need for ritual at the time of death.

Discrimination Against Women. Psychology Today (reader service). This is an audiotape of a discussion by Jo Ann Evans Gardner on the roles into which contemporary women are cast.

Margaret Mead (30 minutes). Modern Learning Aids. In this film anthropologist Margaret Mead discusses marriage, morality, and a woman's place in modern society.

For additional resources, see the bibliography beginning on page 530.

FOCUS

Motivating Activity

Ask students to share their ideas about the "perfect" age. Why do they feel this age is better than all other periods of life? In eliciting responses, explore students' attitudes and/or misperceptions regarding adulthood. Tell them that they will learn more about the aging process in this chapter. Suggest that students keep a section in their notebook in which they list ideas about adulthood and old age that were challenged or changed by material in the text.

Meeting Chapter Objectives.

Point out the objectives on page 243 to the students. Have students rephrase the objectives in question form. Then, assign students to answer the questions as they read Chapter 10.

Building Vocabulary.

Call on students to look up the definitions of the Key Terms in the Glossary and to read them aloud. Challenge volunteers to use each term in a sentence. Which term do they suspect is derived from the Greek word for "death"? *(thanatology)* Have students check their guesses in the dictionary.

FIGURE 10.1 Because of stereotypes that encourage us to fear aging, many of us tend to overlook the positive aspects of adulthood.

242

TEACHER CLASSROOM RESOURCES

- Chapter 10 Reproducible Lesson Plan
- Chapter 10 Study Guide
- Chapter 10 Review Activity
- Chapter 10 Application Activity
- Chapter 10 Extension Activity

- Transparency 19
  Transparency Strategies and Activities

- *Readings in Psychology:* Section 3, Readings 4, 5

- Chapter 10 Test, Form A and Form B

- Understanding Psychology Testmaker

Exploring Key Ideas
The Causes of Ageism.
As students read this chapter, they will encounter many references to stereotypes and societal attitudes that contribute to *ageism,* or prejudice against the old. Ask students to define *stereotype* and to offer some examples of stereotypic thinking about adolescence (see Chapter 9). Make sure they also recognize the main characteristics of *prejudicial thinking*—a tendency to form opinions or generalizations based on inadequate or faulty evidence. Encourage students to monitor their own thinking for stereotypic or prejudicial attitudes as they discuss the various topics in this chapter.

OBJECTIVES

After studying this chapter, you should be able to

- describe the physical, sexual, and intellectual changes that occur during adulthood.
- identify recent research related to older adults.
- identify, describe and critique the stages of dying.

KEY TERMS

ageism
closed awareness
decremental model of aging
generativity
menopause
mutual pretense awareness
open awareness
stagnation
suspected awareness
thanatology

In the preface to *The Seasons of a Man's Life* (1978), Yale researcher Daniel Levinson wrote: "Young adults often feel that to pass 30 is to be 'over the hill,' and they are given little beyond hollow clichés to provide a fuller sense of the actual problems and possibilities of adult life at different ages. The middle years, they imagine, will bring triviality and meaningless comfort at best, stagnation and hopelessness at worse. . . . Adults hope that life begins at 40—but the great anxiety is that it ends there. The result of this pervasive dread about middle age is almost complete silence about the experience of being adult."

As much as middle age is dreaded, old age is looked on with even greater fear and misunderstanding. Whereas in some cultures reaching old age is thought of as a blessing, in ours it is rarely thought about, but when it is, it's with anxiety. Everyone wants to look and act young. Gray hair must be dyed, faces lifted.

Much of our fear of aging is rooted in stereotypes of what it is to grow older. Middle age, it is thought, is a time of deterioration, both physical and mental. Many believe that sexual life declines markedly. In old age, many believe the process of deterioration only accelerates.

These are not true pictures of aging, however. Indeed, the positive side of adult life is one of the best-kept secrets in our society. By undermining some of the stereotypes about growing older, we hope to convey a true image of adult life.

IN YOUR JOURNAL

You have probably heard the saying, "You can't teach an old dog new tricks." In your journal, express this statement in your own words. Then, write whether you believe this saying is true, somewhat true, or false.

IN YOUR JOURNAL

Help students get started by explaining that the "old dog" in the axiom is usually applied to old people. To what extent do the students believe that old people are rigid and set in their ways?

EXTRA CREDIT ACTIVITY

Arrange for students to volunteer a few hours a week at a senior citizens' center, nursing home, or in a meals-on-wheels program in your community. Students should keep a personal journal of their experiences and impressions, with a focus on uncovering any preconceptions in their attitudes toward the old. Students should prepare an oral report describing their experiences for the class and assessing changes in their attitudes toward the elderly.

243

TEACH

Guided Practice

■ Analyzing Alternatives. After students read the margin feature, ask them to explain the two options open to psychologists studying the process of aging. What are the limitations of each? *(Longitudinal studies of aging follow one group of people over the course of their lives. Cross-sectional studies track various groups at different stages in their lives to develop a complete picture of the aging process. The first method is impractical because it takes decades to complete. The second method is limited by the fact that the different groups may have different backgrounds that will skew results.)*

■ Making a Chart. Have the students design a chart showing the similarities and differences between adolescence and old age. Column heads should include: Physical Changes, Developmental Tasks, Crises, and so on. Based on these charts, ask: What aspects of adjustment do the two stages have in common? What are the main differences? *(Answers will vary, but may include learning to accept adult responsibilities vs. learning to relinquish them.)* What, if any, strategies can adolescents and the elderly share to deal with bodily changes? (OBJECTIVE 1)

MORE about...

The Cohort Effect. Suppose you were asked to measure the performance of trains at various points along a busy route. How would you go about it?

You might adopt a *longitudinal* approach. You would board a train and stay with it for its entire journey, recording your observations along the way. Alternatively, you might employ a *cross-sectional* strategy. You would ask observers stationed at key points to report on the performance of various trains that pass by.

Psychologists who study the behavior of people as they progress through adulthood and old age face a similar task. Since this "journey" can last decades, few researchers adopt a purely longitudinal approach. Instead, most conduct cross-sectional studies in which they can measure different age groups, or *cohorts*, together at one time.

Unfortunately, people from different cohorts usually have different experiences in a number of important areas, including access to education, nutrition, career opportunities, and social values. Their different backgrounds make it difficult to determine how age affects human abilities, attitudes, and even health.

ADULTHOOD

What is adulthood like? For one thing, it is a period of great paradox. There is change and sameness, success and failure, crisis and stability, joy and sadness. Adulthood can be a time when a person matures fully into what he or she is. Or it can be a time when life closes in and what was once possibility is now limitation. How each of us reacts depends on circumstances and our general outlook on life.

In the past, more emphasis was placed on childhood and adolescence, and relatively little attention was given to the study of adulthood. Freud, for example, felt that the personality was set during childhood, and he did not consider the later development of the individual. As we saw in Chapter 8, Erikson does view development as a lifelong process. Yet his work, too, concentrates more on childhood and adolescence than on adulthood and old age.

Today, however, a growing number of psychologists are studying adult psychology. Much of what psychologists are learning emphasizes that adulthood is a period of changes and transitions. Among these changes are the new developmental tasks that adults must meet. These tasks include identifying and performing well in an occupation; taking on adult social and civic responsibilities; relating to one's husband or wife as a person; finding satisfying leisure activities; helping teenage children become responsible and satisfied adults; adjusting to the physical changes of adulthood; and relating to one's aging parents (Havighurst, 1972).

If you recall the developmental tasks of adolescence discussed in Chapter 9 (and some of your own experiences) you may recognize similarities between the years of adulthood and the adolescent years. During both periods bodily changes require psychological adjustments, relating well to others is an important goal (whether to parents, peers, spouses, or children), and meeting new responsibilities requires a good deal of effort. Teenagers often think they have nothing in common with their parents. Yet the tasks of adolescence and adulthood are similar enough that they can form the basis for improved communication between generations. In addition, understanding the problems and changes that accompany growing older can be good preparation for a time of life we all must enter.

Physical Changes

In general, human beings are at their physical peak between the ages of 18 and 25. This is the period when we are the strongest, healthiest, and have the quickest reflexes. One has only to think of the average age of professional athletes or dancers to verify this.

For most adults, the process of physical decline is slow and gradual—not at all noticeable, even month to month. Strength and stamina begin to decline in the late 20s. A 20-year-old manages to carry 4 heavy bags of groceries; a 40-year-old finds it easier to make 2 trips. What is lost physically may be replaced by experience. A 60-year-old racquetball player, well versed in the game's strategies, can compete with a faster, less experienced

CONNECTIONS: PSYCHOLOGY AND WORLD CULTURES

Other cultures and religions hold different views about old age and death. Some Asian cultures, for example, revere the elderly. Christianity, Judaism, Islam, Buddhism, and Hinduism hold somewhat different ideas about death. Assign students to research some of these cultural differences and prepare an oral report for the class. (OBJECTIVES 2, 3)

30-year-old player. In middle age appearance changes. The hair starts to turn gray and perhaps to thin out. The skin becomes somewhat dry and in-elastic; wrinkles appear. In old age, muscles and fat built up over the years break down, so that people often lose weight, become shorter, and develop more wrinkles, creases, and loose skin. The primary impact of aging on older adults is on their organ and muscle reserve. In daily activities—where the limits of our performance ability are rarely reached—the declines with age are rarely noticed. Muscle strength itself declines very slightly during the years 25–65.

With time the senses require more and more stimulation. During their 40s most people begin having difficulty seeing distant objects, adjusting to the dark, and focusing on printed pages, even if their eyesight has always been good. Many experience a gradual or sudden loss of hearing in their later years. In addition, reaction time slows. If an experimenter asks a young person and an older person to push a button when they see a light flash on, the older person will take longer to do so.

Health Problems.   Some of the changes we associate with growing older are the result of the natural processes of aging. Others result from diseases and from simple disuse and abuse. Two of the most common health prob-lems of middle age—heart disease and cancer—are related to obesity and smoking. Obesity can cause heart attacks and lead to hypertension and diabetes. In fact, for someone who is 30 percent overweight, the chance of dying during middle age is increased by 40 percent (Turner and Helms, 1979). Heavy smoking is related to cancer of the mouth, throat, and lungs, and to respiratory and heart problems. Smoking causes 400,000 deaths a year in the United States and increases the possibility of cardiovascular dis-ease, which is the leading cause of death during middle age (National Cen-ter for Health Statistics, 1991). The non-smoker, on the other hand, encounters only half the health problems of the heavy smoker. A person who eats sensibly, exercises, avoids cigarettes, drugs, and alcohol, and is not subjected to severe emotional stress will look and feel younger than someone who neglects his or her health. Muscle strength, which peaks at about age 30, is down 30 percent at age 70 for both men and women (Young, Stokes, & Crowe, 1984). A casual review of sports records will show that aging's main effect is on muscle strength, not endurance. Healthy older adults can exercise for long periods of time, little changed from their ability as younger adults (Spirduso & McRae, 1990).

The adulthood years are a time when lifestyle may set the stage for prob-lems that will show up then or in later life. Three of the most common caus-es of death in later adulthood—heart disease, cancer, and cirrhosis of the liver—may be encouraged by the fast-moving lifestyle of young adults. Drug abuse—likely to peak in late adolescence or young adulthood and drop sharply after that—is a problem. Other contributing factors are inad-equate diet and violent deaths. The deaths may result from accidents, a ten-dency, especially among males, to push the physical limits, and a social environment that encourages risk-taking among young adults (Miedzian, 1991). All three of these contributing factors are psychological, though their ultimate effects have biological consequences.

■ **Applying Data to New Situations.** Have the students brainstorm a list on the chalk-board of dos and don'ts for adults to follow as they age— for example, *"Don't* smoke" and *"Do* avoid unnecessary stress." Ask students to identi-fy how many of their dos and don'ts apply to adolescents as well. (OBJECTIVE 1)

■ **Identifying Faulty Assumptions.** Poll the class to find out how many students expect to live long healthy lives. Record the results on the chalkboard. Then, on a sheet of paper, have students an-swer the following questions anonymously.

1. Do you smoke cigarettes?
2. Do you worry excessively about tests or upcoming social situations such as a date?
3. Have you ever tried alcohol or drugs?
4. Do you enjoy taking risks— such as running a red light?
5. Have you ever trained be-yond your physical limit?
6. Do you sometimes eat more food than you need to eat?

Now have students reread "Health Problems" on this page, and reconduct the poll. How many students have changed their answer? With the class, explore how some of the habits detailed in the list can shorten life spans.

CONNECTIONS: PSYCHOLOGY AND HEALTH

Some recent research indicates that the rate at which we age and the age we ultimately attain may be linked to genetic programming (instead of be-havior and the environment). Have students research the genetic link to aging and prepare a written report on their findings. Students might also re-search recent attempts to find ways to slow down the aging process. For ex-ample, studies indicate that testos-terone therapy may significantly slow down the aging process in many men. Do students think that the genetic link to aging can be offset by good health care?

(For example, suppose a student's fam-ily has a history of heart disease. What preventive steps can students take to avoid a heart attack?)

Ask students to explain what unstated message the two photographs convey about marriage and middle age. *(that marriage for the middle aged can be a time of shared happiness)* You might request volunteers to explain if they share this attitude. **Answer to caption, Figure 10.2:** between the ages of 18 and 25

■ **Evaluating Stereotypes.**
Have students examine several issues of popular women's magazines. To what extent do these magazines reinforce stereotypical attitudes about menopause and life after 40? To what extent do they tear down these attitudes? (Refer students to *Lear's* as an example of the latter.) Based on their magazine survey, how do students think the press might influence women's attitudes on aging? (OBJECTIVE 1)

Readings in Psychology.
Have students read the Section 3, Reading 4 selection in *Readings in Psychology* and answer the questions that follow the selection.

FIGURE 10.2

A larger percentage of people in our society are living to more advanced ages. As a result, the elderly exert an increasing influence. **When are most people at their physical peak?**

Menopause. Between the ages of 45 and 50 in a woman's life is a stage called the *climacteric*, which represents all of the psychological and biological changes occurring at that time. A woman's production of sex hormones drops sharply—a biological event called **menopause.** The woman stops ovulating (producing eggs) and menstruating, and therefore cannot conceive children. However, menopause does not cause any reduction in a woman's sexual drive or sexual enjoyment.

Many women experience some degree of discomfort during menopause. However, the irritability and severe depression some women experience during the climacteric appear to have an emotional rather than physical origin.

One study shows that the negative effects of menopause are greatly exaggerated. Half of the women interviewed said they felt better, more confident, calmer, and freer after menopause than they had before. They no longer had to think about their periods or getting pregnant. Their relations with their husbands improved; they enjoyed sex as much as or more than they had before. Many said the worst part of menopause was not knowing what to expect (Neugarten *et al.*, 1963).

Men do not go through any biological change equivalent to menopause. The number of sperm a man's body produces declines gradually over the years, but men have fathered children at an advanced age.

Sexual Behavior. Is there sex after 40? According to one study, most college students believe their parents have intercourse no more than once a month and one-fourth of the students believed that their parents had had intercourse only once or not at all in the last year (Pocs *et al.*, 1977). Respondents to another survey believed that sex usually ends soon after age 60 (Reinisch & Beasley, 1990). In general, young people are uncomfortable with the idea that older people have sexual lives.

Despite younger people's beliefs, studies have shown that sexual activity does not automatically decline with age. Indeed, as sex researchers William Masters and Virginia Johnson point out, there is no physiological

You might test perceptions about middle-aged and older people by instructing students to poll opinion among their friends. Begin by distributing copies of the list of statements labeled a–g to students. Have students copy each statement on a sheet of paper with the following choice of responses beneath each statement.

Scale
1 = strongly agree
2 = slightly agree
3 = no opinion
4 = slightly disagree
5 = strongly disagree

Next, have students solicit two sets of responses from their peers: one response from their own point of view, the other from how students *think* a parent or grandparent might respond. Have students tally the data, and form conclusions about per- *(continued on page 247)*

reason for stopping sexual activity with advancing age (1970). Most older people who have an available partner maintain quite vigorous sex lives. Those who are inactive cite boredom with a partner of long standing, poor physical condition or illness (such as heart disease), or acceptance of the stereotype of loss of sex drive with aging (Mulligan & Mass, 1991).

It is true that there are changes in sexuality during adulthood. A man reaches his sexual peak in his late teens. From that time on, his sexual responsiveness declines. But the decline is very gradual and, except for the self-doubt it sometimes causes, does not usually interfere with normal sexual functioning. Kinsey measured this gradual decline of frequency of orgasm per week for males from 16 on, but found even at age 70 almost 70 percent of the males were still sexually active (Kinsey *et al.*, 1948). Women reach their sexual peak later than men; in addition, the decline in their sexual responsiveness occurs later.

Psychological factors may be a greater hindrance to a man's sexual activity than are physical factors. Preoccupation with his job and with making money may decrease a man's sexual drive. In addition, the decline in sexual responsiveness may arouse a "fear of failure" in some men that in turn affects their sexual responsiveness even more.

More so than age, then, good physical and mental health seem to be the key factors affecting sexual activity. Adults can and do continue to enjoy a healthy sex life. Sex after 40 is not only possible, it is a fact of life.

Intellectual Changes

People are better at learning new skills and information, solving problems that require speed and coordination, and shifting from one problem-solving strategy to another in their mid-20s than they were in adolescence (Baltes and Schaie, 1974). These abilities are considered signs of intelligence; they are among the skills intelligence tests measure.

At one time many psychologists thought that intellectual development reached a peak in the mid-20s and then declined. The reason was that people do not score as high on intelligence tests in middle age as they did when they were younger. Further investigation revealed that some parts of these tests measure speed, not intelligence (Bischof, 1969). As indicated above, a person's reaction time begins to slow after a certain age. Intelligence tests usually "penalized" adults for this fact.

One intelligence test, the Wechsler, takes this into account by testing two very different sorts of abilities. On the verbal portion, which measures facility with words and stored information, older people show little decline. However, on the performance parts of the test, which measure speed of reaction in performing tasks, their scores are lower. Schaie and Strother (1968) modified the normal cross-sectional technique to assess changes in intellectual functioning with age. They found that intelligence goes slowly upward as we age, peaking in the years just before normal retirement age.

Even with a decline in speed, people continue to acquire information and to expand their vocabularies as they grow older. The ability to comprehend new material and to think flexibly improves with the years and ex-

 LAB EXPERIMENTS AND DEMONSTRATIONS

ceived attitudinal differences among generations. Ask: Based on the text, are these sound perceptions? Why or why not?

Statements
a. People who publicly protest against the government should be punished.

b. It is too easy today to get a divorce.
c. Teenagers are not responsible enough to get married.
d. Young people have lost all respect for traditions and customs.
e. Without religion, life is meaningless.
f. Women have become too demanding in areas where they are unfit to

compete with men.
g. Until young people get married, it is better for them to live at home.

■ Making Comparisons.
Have the students number a piece of paper from 1 to 8. Tell them that number one represents the first decade of life, and so on. Ask them to write what they think is the most important task that individuals undertake in each decade. Then have them compare their responses with Levinson's model of adult development for men as illustrated in Figure 10.3 and described on pp. 249–252. Based on their own lists, do students think males and females go through the same stages of development? What, if any, differences can students suggest? (Review these answers against material on female development on pages 252–254.)
(OBJECTIVES 1, 2)

Like adolescents, adults must cope with new situations and developmental tasks.

perience. This is particularly true if a person has had higher education, lives in a stimulating environment, and works in an intellectually demanding career. One researcher studied more than 700 individuals who were engaged in scholarship, science, or the arts. Although the patterns varied from profession to profession, most of the subjects reached their peaks of creativity and productivity in their 40s (Dennis, 1966), but in the humanities such as history and foreign languages in their 60s.

Social and Personality Development

If life is a three-ring circus, one psychologist suggested child psychologists were seated too close to the entrance and gerontologists, who study the effects of old age, were seated too close to the exit. Both were missing a view of the main ring—adulthood. For a long time, psychologists commonly applied theories of childhood and adolescent development to the middle years (Botwinick, 1973). Only now are we beginning to find out how age affects personality. An individual's basic character—his or her style of adapting to situations—is relatively stable over the years. Researchers are also convinced, however, that personality is flexible and capable of changing as an individual confronts new tasks.

Many studies support the first point. A number of researchers have given the same attitude and personality tests to individuals in late adolescence and again 10 or 15 years later. Many of the subjects believed that they had changed dramatically, but the tests indicated that they had not. The degree of satisfaction they expressed about themselves and about life in gen-

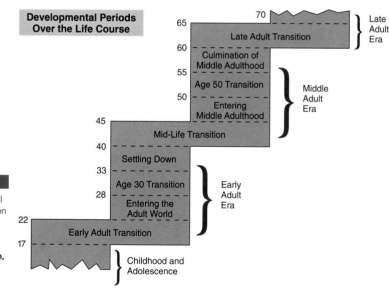

FIGURE 10.3

This model shows the developmental sequence of a man's life that Levinson proposed. The scheme emphasizes that development is an ongoing process that requires continual adjustment. **According to Levinson, what happens during "the age-thirty crisis"?**

CRITICAL THINKING ACTIVITY

Defining Goals. Assign students to develop a list of goals that they would like to achieve by each of the following ages: 30, 40, 50, 60, 70, 80. Tell students to think of goals related to their own personal relationships, education, choice of occupation, marriage, children, health, and so on. Students should next develop a time line identifying activities that will have to be performed or skills that will have to be developed in order to achieve these goals. Tell students that, after performing these preliminary assessments, they should write a short personal essay identifying one preeminent goal they would like to accomplish before they die and explain why it is important and how they will attempt to accomplish it.

eral in their middle years was consistent with their earlier views. Confident young people remained confident; self-haters, self-hating; passive individuals, passive—unless something upsetting had happened to them, such as a sudden change in economic status (Kimmel, 1980).

Despite the stability of character, people do face many changes in their lifetimes and adjust accordingly. Adults encounter new developmental tasks, just as adolescents do. They too must learn to cope with problems and deal with new situations. Learning the skills needed to cope with change seems to occur in stages for both adult males and females. One researcher who has studied personality development in males, Daniel Levinson, has developed a theory concerning the cycle of changes men go through.

Levinson's Theory of Male Development. The work of Daniel Levinson and his colleagues at Yale was not well known until 1976 when it was popularized in a national best-seller by Gail Sheehy entitled *Passages: Predictable Crises of Adult Life.* During his research, Levinson interviewed four groups of men between the ages of 35 and 45: 10 were executives, 10 were hourly workers in industry, 10 were novelists, and 10 were university biologists. He also based his theory on a number of other interviews of men both older and younger than this sample (Levinson, 1986).

A life structure was developed for each man based on these interviews. Each life structure was an account of the major periods of the man's life as determined by his activities, his associations, and his relationships. Analysis of these life structures revealed a pattern that seemed to apply to almost all the men sampled.

The model of adult development for men that Levinson and his colleagues proposed is shown in Figure 10.3. The three major eras are early adulthood (from about age 17 to about age 40), middle adulthood (40 to 60), and late adulthood (beginning at about 60). Notice the similarity between Levinson's eras and the last 3 of the 8 stages of Erikson's psychosocial theory, which was discussed in Chapter 8. Between these eras, Levinson identified important transition periods at ages 30, 40, 50, and 60, which last approximately 5 years. Levinson's research focused on the early adult era and the mid-life transition. The following discussion concentrates on what he learned about these stages.

Entering the adult world. From about age 22 to age 28, the young man is considered, both by himself and by society, to be a novice in the adult world—not fully established as a man, but no longer an adolescent. During this time he must attempt to resolve the conflict between the need to explore the options of the adult world and the need to establish a stable life structure. He needs to sample different kinds of relationships, to keep choices about career and employment open, to explore the nature of the world now accessible to him as an adult. But he also needs to begin a career and to establish a home and family of his own. The first life structure, then, may have a tentative quality. The young man may select a career or a job but not be committed to it. He may form romantic attachments and may even marry during this period; but the life structure of early adulthood often lacks a full sense of stability or permanence.

■ **Discussion.** A number of factors influence social and personality development in later life, including gender, occupation, and ethnic or cultural background. Have students discuss how these factors as well as personal habits, interests, worries, lifestyle, and opportunities affect the adjustments that people make as they age. Tell students to relate their comments to the models of male and female development presented on text pages 249–254.
(OBJECTIVE 2)

Teacher Note. Stress that recent research on the aging process has fostered a new assumption about development: that personality is flexible and capable of change at every stage in life.

WORKING WITH TRANSPARENCIES

Project Transparency 19 and use the guidelines provided in Teaching Strategies and Activities. Assign Student Worksheet 19.
Point out that Levinson's model challenges decremental attitudes that many people have about aging. Ask students how it does so.
Answer to caption, Figure 10.3:
reexamination of earlier commitments—e.g., questioning of choices of marriage partner, career, and life goals

CONNECTIONS: PSYCHOLOGY AND LITERATURE

Have the students locate and read the famous "All the world's a stage" speech from Shakespeare's *As You Like It* (Act II, Scene vii), in which the cynical character Jacques describes the "seven ages" of man. Arrange for a volunteer to deliver the speech with proper theatrical flourish to the class. Then have the students compare Jacques's seven ages to the stages that Daniel Levinson proposed and to the physical, sexual, and intellectual changes outlined at the beginning of this chapter. Point out that literature is often an excellent source of psychological insight.

■ **Discussion.** Ask students to discuss which of the changes described in Levinson's model may arise from the individual's need for change and achievement. Which may arise in response to changes in the individual's environment? *(Environment seems to be a factor in each period. For example, the BOOM phase may be influenced as much by society's changing attitudes toward the 36-to-40-year-old as by the individual's own developing sense of personal identity.)*
(OBJECTIVE 2)

The age-thirty crisis. Some years ago the motto of the rebellious, politically oriented young people who sought to change American society was "Never trust anyone over 30." Levinson's data reveal that the years between 28 and 30 are indeed often a major transition period. The thirtieth birthday can truly be a turning point; for most men in Levinson's sample, it could be called "the age-thirty crisis." During this transitional period the tentative commitments that were made in the first life structure are reexamined, and many questions about the choices of marriage partner, career, and life goals are reopened, often in a painful way. The man feels that any parts of his life that are unsatisfying or incomplete must be attended to now, because it will soon be too late to make major changes.

Settling down. The questioning and searching that are part of the age-thirty crisis begin to be resolved as the second adult life structure develops. Having probably made some firm choices about his career, family, and relationships, the man now begins actively carving out a niche in society, concentrating on what Levinson calls "making it" in the adult world. The man attempts to move up the ladder of prestige and achievement in his chosen career or profession and to be a full-fledged member of adult society.

Levinson found that near the end of the settling-down period, approximately between the ages of 36 and 40, there is a distinctive BOOM phase—"becoming one's own man." Whereas earlier the young man had looked to an older, more experienced man as a mentor, someone who would share his experience and wisdom, the relationship with the mentor is often fundamentally changed, or even broken off, in the process of becoming one's own man. Now it is time to become fully independent. During this period the man strives to attain the seniority and position in the world that he identified as his ultimate goal at the beginning of the settling-down period.

The mid-life transition. At about age 40, the period of early adulthood comes to an end and the mid-life transition begins. From about age 40 to age 45, the man begins again to ask questions, but now the questions concern the past as well as the future. He may ask: "What have I done with my life?" "What have I accomplished?" "What do I still wish to accomplish?" At age 30, the man had primarily looked ahead toward goals, but at the mid-life transition he is in a position to assess his accomplishments and to determine whether or not they have been satisfying. During this transition he begins to develop yet another life structure that will predominate during the period of middle adulthood.

During this period, the man often experiences a resurgence of interest in sex. In part this may be a result of his general reevaluation of his life to this point. In addition, he and his wife may have more time together alone, without the pressures of caring for small children. At the same time, however, his marriage may be at a low point (Rollins and Feldman, 1970) if he and his wife have developed different interests over the years of their marriage. Thus, the man's relationship with his wife—whether good or bad—is likely to be an important factor in the mid-life transition.

This may also be an important period in the relationship between the man and his adolescent children, since each is going through a period of transition. The man plays an important part in his children's lives as do the children in their father's (Vaillant, 1977). Some of the teenager's own experiences, may, in addition, rekindle feelings the parent had long forgotten. For example, a father may be reminded of his own youthful political ideals by a son who is active in protests against nuclear power plants.

Often a successful mid-life transition is accompanied by the man's becoming a mentor for a younger man. This event signals the attainment, in Erik Erikson's terms, of generativity. By **generativity,** Erikson means the desire to use one's accumulated wisdom to guide future generations—directly, as a parent, or indirectly. The opposite—**stagnation**—can also occur. A man may choose to hang on to the past, perhaps by taking part in the same sports. On the other hand, he may become preoccupied with his health or bitter about the direction his life has taken. Generativity or stagnation occurs for both men and women.

The mid-life transition has been the most discussed aspect of Levinson's work. About 80 percent of the men in his sample experienced the mid-life transition as a moderate to severe crisis, characterized by the questioning of virtually every aspect of their lives. It is a period of questioning, though, from which a new life structure must emerge.

Middle adulthood. The late 40s is a time when true adulthood can be achieved. The man who finds satisfactory solutions to his life crisis reaches a period of stability. He understands and tolerates others; he displays a sensitivity and concern for other people as people. He is able to strike a balance between the need for friends and the need for privacy.

■ **Analyzing a Quote.** Read aloud Erikson's definition of *generativity* as it applies to old age.

Old people can be generative in another way. . . . I'm convinced old people and children need each other and that there's an affinity between old age and childhood that, in fact, rounds out the life cycle. . . . [W]hen I say old people think like children, I do not mean childishly. But with wonder, joy, playfulness—all those things that adults often have to sacrifice for a while.

Based on this quote, how can adults avoid *stagnation* in old age? *(by seeing the world with new wonder; by letting go of some of the rigid conventions of adulthood)* What are some of the "affinities" that might exist between old age and childhood? *(As a tip, request volunteers to describe some of the bonds they had with an older friend or relative as a child.)* (OBJECTIVES 1, 2)

■ **Drawing a Cartoon.** You might request volunteers to draw a political cartoon showing a tongue-in-cheek look at the mid-life crises described by Levinson. Ask the rest of the class to explain how the student artists used humor to get across a serious—and sometimes painful—phase in many people's lives.

COOPERATIVE LEARNING ACTIVITY

Write each of Levinson's 10 stages on slips of paper, and have students draw one from a hat. Ask students to role-play a monologue in which they express the concerns, accomplishments, and frustrations of a man at that stage of development. After each performance, instruct the class to try to guess what stage was being portrayed.

■ **Expressing Opinions.** Ask students to respond to the assertion in the text that the late 40s can be the "prime of life" for a man (Stevens-Long, 1979). Do they agree? Might the same be true for women? Tell the students to support their opinions with evidence from the text or their own observations of life. (OBJECTIVE 2)

■ **Debating an Issue.** The woman in a two-worker family often remains responsible for housework and child care (Matlin, 1993). Have students debate the following issue: *Resolved*—Husbands in two-worker households should be equally responsible for all household chores, including caring for the children. Make sure that the two sides in the debate are composed of both males and females. (OBJECTIVE 1)

VISUAL INSTRUCTION

The word *syndrome* often has negative connotations. Ask students what, if any, negative connotations the phrase *"empty nest" syndrome* might have on attitudes toward women. Suppose men exhibited similar symptoms. Would the condition be given the same name?

Answer to caption, Figure 10.5: Some experience stress and readjustment. Others find new careers or resume prior interests.

For the man who is not as fortunate, this period can be a time of extreme frustration and unhappiness. Instead of generativity, there is stagnation; instead of change and improvement, there is a mood of resignation to a bad situation. The job is only a job. The individual may feel cut off from family and friends. The future holds no promise. By avoiding this life crisis, he is only inviting a later appearance of it, at age 50, with more crushing force (Rogers, 1979). For men and women, those who have a negative view of themselves tend to behave in such a way as to alienate those around them (Swann, Stein-Seroussi, & Gleiser, 1992).

Those who successfully adjust to middle age can find it a most gratifying period. The difficult early adulthood years are behind them; now they are looked to for leadership and expertise. In their work, marriage, and personal lives, they are happier than ever before. They are in the prime of life— a time that will someday be looked back upon as the best years of their lives (Stevens-Long, 1979). Keep in mind that Levinson's eras and transitions are based on averages from many individual interviews. No one's life is likely to match Levinson's divisions exactly.

Female Development. While there have been far more studies conducted among men than among women, some researchers have focused their attention on women's mid-life development. While many men experience a crisis at mid-life, married women at mid-life are facing fewer demands in their traditional task as mother. For many, this means greater personal freedom. As a result, they may be reentering the work force, going back to college, or starting or renewing careers outside the home. Rather than a time of crisis, it is a time of opportunity for those who opted to have a family first. For those women with both a career and a family, crises in one area tend to be balanced by successes in the other, and the evidence generally does not support the existence of a mid-life crisis for most women in today's world (Berger, 1994).

Career and family. Until about 1970, the traditional choice faced by a woman was to devote her time to a family *or* a career—not both. Today's woman—better educated, marrying at a later age, having her first child later—typically launches a career before starting a family. The financial picture has changed substantially, too. Two-worker families are the norm, not the exception. A year after giving birth, 57 percent of American mothers are working at their job outside the home (U.S. Bureau of the Census, 1992).

Despite these changes, the woman remains the one who is typically responsible for both housework and child care (Matlin, 1993), even if she also has a job outside the house. Changes are beginning to occur, however, that recognize the growing equality of men and women in dual-career households. In 1993, the United States Congress passed a law giving both men and women the opportunity to take time off from work without penalty for events such as the birth of a child.

Physical attractiveness in mid-life. Women have traditionally been more conscious of the aging process than men. This is perhaps because the male selection of a partner for courtship and marriage depended to a great extent on the physical attractiveness of the woman. Also, as a woman

FIGURE 10.5

Many women experience what is called the "empty nest" syndrome when grown children leave home and the 24-hour-a-day job in which they have been absorbed for decades is suddenly over. **How do women react to this change in their lives?**

COOPERATIVE LEARNING ACTIVITY

In connection with the class's discussion of female development, instruct students to work in small groups to develop a model that shows the developmental sequence of a woman's life. Tell students that they may adapt the model shown in Figure 10.3 if they wish, or create a more elaborate chart. Have the finished models displayed in class. Then ask a spokesperson from each group to explain how the group's model portrays current psychological theories related to the sequence of female development.

FIGURE 10.6

Many of our society's stereotyped attitudes about the elderly are not valid. Old people do not always become senile, they are not necessarily resistant to change, and they are not useless. **What is ageism?**

comes to be considered less attractive with age, she often faces the problem of adjusting to a different image of herself. There seems to be good reason for her concern. Declining physical attractiveness with age causes males to have less interest in their wives sexually; it does not impact females' interest in their husbands (Margolin & White, 1987).

The "empty nest" syndrome. A significant event in many women's lives is the departure from home of the last child. Contrary to popular belief, this event need not be traumatic. In fact, many women find that the period after the children are grown is one of the happiest of their lives. If they have not already done so, they reorganize their lives by focusing on new interests and activities (Grambs, 1989).

Of course, not all women experience the same sense of new freedom. Psychologists have found that a stable marriage makes a difference. If a woman has a warm relationship with her husband, she may find the adjustment easier because of his support. Conversely, if the woman is widowed or divorced, the transition can be much more difficult. How well her children adjust to their new independence can also affect a mother's happiness at this time (Harkins, 1978).

Depression in mid-life. In her book *Unfinished Business*, Maggie Scarf (1980) draws attention to another difference between men and women in their mid-life development. Statistically, women are from 2 to 6 times more likely than men to suffer from depression. Others have estimated the multiplier at 2 to 3 times more likely (cf., Nolen-Hoeksema, 1990). Depression can affect people of all ages, but it is most common among middle-aged women. In a survey conducted in New Haven, Connecticut (Boyd and Weissman, 1981), 7 percent of the women compared with 2.9 percent of the men aged 40 to 65 years old suffered from depression. Scarf believes that the reason for this difference in rate of depression is cultural. She views depression as the by-product of a traditional feminine sex-role stereotype. Early in life, young girls have been taught and encouraged to define them-

? FACT OR FICTION

The elderly need more sleep than younger adults.

Fiction. Studies show that as people progress from adulthood to old age, their need for sleep generally continues to decrease. However, sleep in elderly people is more disrupted and fragmented, so they need to spend more time in bed and take naps to get their required sleep. To the casual observer, the elderly appear to sleep longer.

VISUAL INSTRUCTION

Ask students to list other stereotypes that some people hold about the elderly. *(e.g., the elderly hold inflexible views)*
Answer to caption, Figure 10.6: prejudice against the old

■ **Demonstrating Reasoned Judgment.** Point out the various statistics indicating that women are more likely than men to suffer mid-life depression. Then tell students to imagine they are Maggie Scarf. Working in groups, have them write proposals for a new book to help women combat mid-life depression. The proposal should include the following items:

- a rationale, or statement of purpose, for the book
- a table of contents
- a description of the potential audience
- reasons a publisher should want to buy the proposal

Call on students to present their proposals aloud. Ask students to identify specific suggestions aimed at overturning the effects of stereotypic attitudes. (OBJECTIVES 1, 2)

■ **Readings in Psychology.** Have students read the Section 3, Reading 5 selection in *Readings in Psychology* and answer the questions that follow the selection.

COMMUNITY INVOLVEMENT

Arrange to have a clinical psychologist or other mental health professional visit the class to discuss the incidence of depression in middle-aged women. The speaker might describe the symptoms of depression, the causes, the dangers of ignoring depression when it occurs, current methods of treatment, and success rates in curing depression. Tell students to prepare questions for the speaker in advance of the appearance. (You might ask students to probe whether the professional thinks statistics on female depression are weighted by the reluctance of males to seek help for—or talk about—depression.)

■ **Identifying Ageism.** Bring in a collection of humorous birthday cards that deal with aging. Read these aloud to the class. Which of the cards reveal attitudes based on a decremental view of aging? Which cards use humor to underscore a positive view of aging? Use this activity to provoke a discussion of how humor can sometimes be used to mask prejudice. (Refer to the text discussion of myth vs. fact.) (OBJECTIVE 2)

Teacher Note. You might want to point out that such terms as "golden ager" are *euphemisms*—expressions meant to mask a harsher reality. Ask students to think of some other euphemisms connected to old age. *(e.g., "retirement community" for "old age home")*

Enrich. Have students complete the Chapter 10 Application Activity.

PSYCHOLOGY UPDATE

Alzheimer's Disease. Alzheimer's disease is an affliction more commonly seen among the elderly. About 4 million people have this disease, and it is the fourth leading cause of death among U.S. adults.

Alzheimer's is a neurological disease marked by a gradual deterioration of cognitive functioning. Early signs of the disease include frequent forgetting, poor judgment, increased irritability, and social withdrawal. Eventually Alzheimer's patients lose their ability to comprehend simple questions and to recognize friends and loved ones. Ultimately they require constant supervision and custodial care. Rarely do patients die from the disease itself, but their weakened state leaves them vulnerable to a variety of other potentially fatal problems.

The causes of Alzheimer's are complex and still not completely understood. Genetic susceptibility plays a role. Other causes may involve life events.

At present there is no cure for the disease. Many patients and their caretakers (usually their families) are offered supportive therapy that helps them learn to accept the relentless progression of the disease and the limitations it imposes on its victims.

selves as worthwhile through their relationships with other people. They feel good when they establish connections with people and are taught to look to others for approval and to be dependent.

Thus, during the early years of a woman's life, she may derive a sense of personal worth from her roles of daughter, lover, wife, and mother. These relationships change as children grow, parents die, or marriages fail. Some women begin to experience a sense of loss and personal worthlessness. Women not working outside the home may see themselves as failures compared with their husbands, who have experienced successes in their careers. The onset of menopause can trigger depression in some women. Those who have defined themselves as childbearers now view themselves as useless when they lose their ability to produce and care for children. On the other hand, many women welcome this time of life. Some women in their 50s find that the nature of their marriage changes when they no longer have to focus their attention on the needs of their children. The prospect of giving up the traditional roles of a dependent wife for a more independent role may be unsettling for a while, especially for those women who have spent a lifetime living according to a sex-role stereotype. Once those women become accustomed to their new role, however, many find that they enjoy the freedom that middle adulthood brings.

OLD AGE

In one big-city newspaper, the photograph of a man celebrating his ninetieth birthday was placed on the obituary page. Is this only the view on aging of one newspaper editor? Perhaps, but unfortunately, many people tend to regard old age as being just one step away from the grave. Indeed, some would rather die than grow old.

The fear of growing old is probably one of the most common fears in our society. We are surrounded with indications that aging and old age are negative—or at best something to ridicule. Birthday cards make light of aging; comedians joke about it. Advertisements urge us to trade in older products for the newer, faster model. We encourage older workers to retire— whether or not they want to retire—and replace them with younger people. Many do not even want to use the word *old* and instead refer to "golden agers" and "senior citizens."

Many of our attitudes about aging are based on a **decremental model of aging,** which holds that progressive physical and mental decline is inevitable with age. In other words, chronological age is what makes people "old." In fact, there are great differences in physical condition among the elderly, depending on their genetic makeup and environment. Many of us know people who are 80 and look and act 50, and vice versa. The prevalence of the decremental view in our society can be explained in part by ignorance and a lack of contact with older people. The result is a climate of prejudice against the old. A researcher coined the word **ageism** to refer to this prejudice. As with racism, and sexism, ageism feeds on myths rather than facts.

STUDY AND WRITING SKILLS

A number of organizations work to promote the welfare and improve the lives of older Americans. These include such groups as the Gray Panthers, the American Association of Retired Persons (AARP), and the National Council for Senior Citizens (NCSC). Have students research the activities of these and other organizations that help fulfill the ambitions and needs of the nation's elderly population. Students might write or interview representatives of the organization and gather brochures and other literature about the group. Ask students to prepare a brief oral report of their findings.

Young people tend to believe that the old suffer from poor health, live in poverty, and are frequent victims of crime. The elderly seldom see these as personal problems, though, interestingly, they tend to think of them as problems for other older people (Harris, 1978). Such beliefs, however, affect stereotypes of the elderly.

The notion that the aged tend to withdraw from life and sit around doing nothing is also very common. This, too, is a false picture. Comedian George Burns, actress Angela Lansbury, and musician B. B. King are good examples of active older individuals, and many less well-known older people follow their lead. The majority of older Americans work or wish to work either for pay or as volunteers.

Related to the idea that the elderly are unproductive is the notion that older people are inflexible or senile. Actually, rigidity is more a lifelong habit than a response to aging. The older person who tends to be rigid was probably rigid as a young adult. Senility, which affects only 10 percent of the aged, usually results from some disease rather than from the natural process of aging.

The opposite notion that old age is a time not of slippage but of stress-free bliss is also untrue (Butler, 1974). The aged are, in fact, subject to more stress than any other group, though many endure crises with remarkable strength.

Older people, however, do not think of themselves in terms of the myths mentioned above. They feel they are just as able as when they were younger. Most older people find their lives are as interesting as ever. Health, activities, and money have more to do with the happiness of the elderly than does their chronological age.

Changes in Health

Most people over 65 are in reasonably good health. Physical strength and the five senses do decline, of course, but 80 percent of the elderly are able to carry out their normal activities. (Fifteen percent are unable to do so, and 5 percent are in institutions.) For the most part, the health of an older person is related to his or her health when younger. Good health in adolescence and adult life carries over into old age.

All people, young and old, are subject to disease, though. About 40 percent of the elderly have at least one chronic disease (a permanent disability as opposed to an acute or temporary disability more common with younger people). The four most prevalent chronic diseases—heart disease, hypertension, diabetes, and arthritis—tend to afflict women more than men. In general, the major causes of death among the old are heart disease, cancer, and strokes.

The quality of health care for the elderly remains by and large inferior to that of the general population. The reasons for this are numerous. The elderly in the lower socioeconomic class tend not to take care of themselves or to seek out treatment when needed. Many doctors prefer to administer to younger patients with acute diseases rather than to older patients with long-term chronic conditions that can only be stabilized, not cured. Some

■ **Distinguishing Fact from Fiction.** Instruct students to prepare a two-column chart entitled the "Opinions of Old Age." Have them label one column "Fiction," the other column "Fact." As students read through material on old age, have them list commonly held myths in one column. In the other column, tell them to list a fact or statement that explodes the myth. An example of a myth might include: "Old age is a time . . . of stress-free bliss." The truth is: "The aged are, in fact, subject to more stress than any other group. . . ." Compile a master chart after students complete the activity. (OBJECTIVE 2)

■ **Evaluating a Generalization.** Ask students to evaluate the assertion in the text that "rigidity is more a lifelong habit than a response to aging." What examples from their own life can students cite to prove that rigidity is a habit sometimes formed in youth? (Ask students, for example, how they respond if their families or friends suddenly change an established routine.) (OBJECTIVES 1, 2)

BEYOND THE CLASSROOM

Almost every profession has success stories about people who "made it" very late in life. Have students develop a profile of a person who achieved a greater degree of success in old age than he or she did in younger years. Tell students to consider the full spectrum of professions—from artists to zoologists—before selecting a favorite subject and person to profile. Instruct students to keep profiles to one typed page. Ideally, the profiles should include a photograph of the person at work. Display the completed profiles in class. (Possible choices include poet William Carlos Williams, artist Georgia O'Keeffe, musician Pablo Casals, or "everyday heroes" of students' own choosing.)

■ Exploring Stereotypes.

The text asserts that some doctors hold stereotypical views of the aged. Ask the students if they are surprised by this claim. To demonstrate how easy it is to succumb to stereotypic thinking, ask students which doctor they would prefer to treat them—a doctor aged 40 or one aged 70? Of the males in class, how many would refuse to be examined by a female doctor? Do any of the females in class admit to a similar prejudice? Point out that everyone, even doctors, must be on guard against stereotypical thinking. Finally, ask students to identify some of the dangers and injustices that result from stereotyping old people. (e.g., misdiagnoses of illnesses, loss of employment) (OBJECTIVE 2)

MORE about...

Loose Jeans and Retirement. The average age in the United States and Canada continues to creep upward. We see evidence that baby boomers are aging everywhere, even in commercials. Blue jeans companies aimed ads at the boomers in the early 1990s that described jeans as being a "looser interpretation of the original."

That is bad news for the smaller number of children being born and growing up now as they plan for their own retirement. Today's retirees can count on Social Security for funds. Social Security, however, is not a personal retirement program. It is a tax-supported benefit. What we workers pay in as a salary tax is paid right back out to today's retirees as a benefit.

As the number of older people increases and the number in the workforce doesn't, one of two things has to happen. Taxes have to go up to continue supporting Social Security at its current levels. A more likely scenario, however, is a decrease in Social Security benefits. The public has too frequently demonstrated in recent years its intolerance for additional taxes. Today's workers need to be finding other funding sources for their retirement.

doctors hold stereotypical views of the aged that can lead to misdiagnosis and improper treatment.

For the 1 million old people who are no longer able to care for themselves, there are institutions. However, too many of these nursing homes have inadequate facilities. As more and more people each year reach late adulthood, it is paramount that there be a general overhaul of health care treatment and facilities for the elderly.

Changes in Life Situation

For younger people transitions in life—graduation, marriage, parenthood—are usually positive and create a deeper involvement in life. In late adulthood, transitions—retirement, widowhood—are often negative and reduce responsibilities and increase isolation. Perhaps the most devastating transition is the loss of a spouse. Over 50 percent of women and 20 percent of men are widowed by the age of 56. By the age of 80, one-third of men and 7 out of 10 women are alone (Stevens-Long, 1979). Across the entire age spectrum, there are 6 widows for every widower (Hess & Waring, 1983). All too often, the person loses not just a spouse but the support of friends and family, who cannot cope with the widowed person's grief or feel threatened by the survivor's new status as a single person.

The loss of self-esteem that comes with retirement and a diminished role in the community, or the grief over the loss of a spouse, can bring on a deep depression. One of every 4 suicides in the country is a person over 65, and older men commit suicide far more frequently than do women (Butler and Lewis, 1973). Unfortunately, the elderly receive only 2 percent of the available psychiatric services. To some extent, this is a result of societal attitudes toward old people. The adjustment and emotional problems of the old are often viewed by mental health personnel as natural and unavoidable results of aging. The same symptoms in younger people would more likely receive attention and treatment (Butler, 1963). A related problem is that modern medicine has developed some truly stunning measures for bringing people back from death's doorstep. Yet, much less effort has been targeted at reducing the deterioration aging causes. So people may survive a major trauma, only to return to the drudgery of a continuing loss of the skills and abilities required even to maintain daily living.

Most of the elderly have incomes of only half their preretirement income. Although the public believes that the lack of money is a major problem for the old, only 15 percent of the elderly find it a personal problem (Kalisy, 1977). Yet even though the percentage is smaller than many of us may have thought, it still indicates that lack of money is a problem for many of the elderly. Those who are living alone and without family are in the most precarious position. Of course, many old people do not stop working because they want to; quite frequently workers who are urged to retire would rather continue working. Societal prejudice against hiring and retaining people beyond the traditional retirement age will no doubt change as the life span of the general population increases—especially now that federal legislation prohibits forced retirement of workers based on their age.

CONNECTIONS: PSYCHOLOGY AND GOVERNMENT

The Clinton administration made health-care reform a domestic priority. Have students research the current state of the health-care debate and the progress that has been made thus far in overhauling the health-care system. What provisions have Congress and the administration made for ensuring adequate care for the elderly? What more needs to be done? Have students prepare either written or oral reports on their findings.

Changes in Sexual Activity

Just as young people tend to think sexual activity diminishes at mid-life, they often believe it ceases altogether in old age. Yet the majority of people over the age of 65 continue to be interested in sex, and healthy partners enjoy sexual activity into their 70s and 80s. Allgeier comments that, "Sexy young people mature into sexy middle-aged and elderly people" (1983, p. 144). As with so many humans behaviors, the best predictor of future behavior is past behavior. For the elderly with an available partner, the frequency and regularity of sexual activities during earlier years is the best overall predictor of such activities in later years. The reasons some do not engage in sexual activity apparently are related to poor health or the death of a spouse, rather than to a lack of interest or to sexual physiology and functioning. Societal attitudes are another factor that discourages sexual expression by the elderly. Old people are not supposed to be interested in sex or be sexually active. Sexual relationships in old age—and even displays of affection—are often considered silly, improper, or even morally wrong. People who grow old in this atmosphere may give up sexual activity because they are "supposed to." On a more personal level, older people often encounter opposition from family and friends if they want to remarry after the death of a spouse. Children and family, too, find the idea of love and sex in old age ridiculous or even vaguely disgusting. A change in our ideas may enable a large segment of our population to continue to enjoy a guilt-free, healthy sex life in old age.

Adjusting to Old Age

Many of the changes the elderly face make their adjustment to everyday life more difficult because they represent a loss of control over the environment. When older people are unable to maintain what they value most—good health, recognition in the community, visits from family and friends, privacy, leisure and work activities—the quality of their life suffers dramatically, along with their self-image.

The loss of control is usually gradual, and it may involve both physical changes (becoming sick or disabled) and external circumstances (moving to a nursing home). It is most devastating when it is cumulative (Schwartz and Proppe, 1970). Losing a husband is terrible enough, but the burden is only made worse by the further losses of friends and one's house. Those who experience a loss of control often develop a negative self-concept. They can regain their sense of control and a more positive self-image if they are helped to make the best of the options available to them. People with assertive personalities are often better at coping with life changes than more passive individuals because they are better able to demand and get the attention they need.

In order to help old people adjust, society must make some basic changes. Older people are beginning this process themselves by supporting organizations such as the Gray Panthers and the American Association of Retired Persons. These groups speak out and lobby on social issues of importance to them. Since the population over 65 is constantly growing,

■ **Identifying Alternatives.** Ask students to discuss how society could help make the experience of old age a more fruitful and happier time. What kinds of provisions could communities make for their retired and elderly adults? What services might the elderly provide to their communities? How could governments help the elderly achieve greater security and health? Suggest that students present their ideas in a letter to the editor of your regional newspaper. Ask students to support their recommendations by citing recent research related to older adults. (OBJECTIVE 2)

COOPERATIVE LEARNING ACTIVITY

Organize the class into 3 or 4 groups. Ask each group to develop ideas for an advertising campaign (either television or print) promoting the positive side of aging. Each group should prepare story boards (visual mockups) that describe their ads in detail: What is the setting? Who are the actors/actresses? How would the participants be dressed? Would they use humor? What would be said? Each group should then present their ad to the class. After all the presentations, ask the groups to discuss how difficult it was for them to come up with positive aspects of old age. Did any students feel differently about old age after preparing the ads?

PORTRAIT

B. F. Skinner
1904–1990
B.F. Skinner devoted his life to exploring how external causes shaped behavior. Therefore, it is understandable that one of the foremost promoters of operant conditioning (see Chapter 2) would propose behaviorist methods to help the elderly increase their mental performance. In *Enjoy Old Age*, Skinner recommended a number of techniques. He suggested that elderly people carry a notebook to jot down new ideas. Instead of searching through memory to retrieve these ideas, they could simply flip through the notebook. To avoid the embarrassment and unpleasantness of not remembering a person's name, Skinner suggested appealing graciously to age and accepting the shortcoming. He also recommended that the elderly rehearse or make mental notes of a discussion so that interruptions did not sidetrack them. As Skinner wrote, "thinking is behaving."

Teacher Note. You might read this profile to the class, and ask which of Skinner's tips might help them improve their memories.

MORE about...

Growing Old. America's old people may not be given much respect because they often lack status. Many then occupy the lower rungs of the economic ladder and go without adequate medical care. In Japan that situation rarely develops because the able-bodied continue to work or to help their families in the home. In addition, they are guaranteed a minimum income, receive free annual health examinations, and are eligible for completely free medical care after age 70. We could benefit by following Japan's lead here, especially in providing more job opportunities for the aged.

We Americans might also profit by copying the Japanese example of fully integrating the elderly in our daily lives. In Japan 75 percent of the old live with their children, as opposed to only 25 percent in the United States. For those who do live alone, the Japanese have established programs to assure that they receive daily visits or calls. To encourage the active involvement of all older citizens in social activities, the government subsidizes Elders Clubs and sports programs. Through these programs the aged supply each other with mutual support and gain a sense of self-pride.

social policy will have to take the elderly into consideration more and more. Attitudes toward old people are already slowly changing. Eventually a time will come when old age will be considered the culmination of life, not simply the termination.

Changes in Mental Functioning

As people age, there are also changes in many of the mental functions they use, although there is much less decline in intelligence and memory than people think. If you compare measures of intellectual ability for a group of elderly people with similar measures for younger people, you might see a difference—namely that older people do not score as well on intellectual tests. However, the older group of people will most likely be less educated and less familiar with test-taking than younger people. Furthermore, there are many different types of mental skills and abilities that combine to produce intellectual functioning, and these abilities do not develop at the same rate or time across the life span.

John Horn (1979) has proposed two types of intelligence, *crystallized* and *fluid* intelligence. Crystallized intelligence refers to the ability to use accumulated knowledge and learning in appropriate situations. This ability increases with age and experience, showing no decline in older adulthood. Fluid intelligence is the ability to solve abstract relational problems and to generate new hypotheses. This ability is not tied to schooling or education and gradually increases in development as the nervous system matures. As people age and their nervous systems decline, so does their fluid intelligence. Thus, older people may not be as good at problems that require them to combine and generate new information or ideas. A decline in the nervous system affects reaction time, visual motor flexibility, and memory. Elderly people have difficulty retrieving information from memory. If they are asked to recognize a familiar name or object, they cannot do so as well as younger people.

The ability of older people to remember and think clearly may also vary with their environment. B. F. Skinner maintained that older people do not receive as much reinforcement from the environment for their mental and verbal behaviors as younger people and so decline in their performance (Skinner and Vaughn, 1983). As their abilities to hear, taste, and see decline, as friends and relatives die, and as younger people become less responsive to their ideas, elderly people become less motivated to use their mental faculties. Recognizing the ways in which one's thinking is influenced by the circumstances of aging is a necessary first step toward changing these circumstances.

At age 79, Skinner wrote a book entitled *Enjoy Old Age* in which he suggested some practical ways to change one's environment to increase mental performance. Skinner noted that, just as physical abilities decline with physical fatigue, mental abilities decline with mental fatigue. Skinner suggests that older people protect themselves from mental fatigue by taking leisurely breaks in their mental activity and by working fewer hours a day on thought-related tasks.

CONNECTIONS: PSYCHOLOGY AND LANGUAGE ARTS

Many contemporary writers have produced works of fiction that have examined the changes a person goes through in adulthood. Ask students to consult with their language arts teacher and select a novel, short story, or play in which a major developmental crisis of adulthood is a central theme. Ask the students to write a short essay analyzing the character's psychological development in terms of the theories they have studied in this chapter. Ask several volunteers to share their papers with the class.

DEATH AND DYING

Should terminally ill patients be told they are going to die? What are the consequences for the family, the hospital staff, and the patient if the patient is informed? What if the patient is not informed? In their book *Awareness of Dying* (1965), Barney Glaser and Anselm Strauss have looked at these issues and their effects on dying patients, their families, and hospital staffs. Very often physicians decide not to tell patients that they are dying. Glaser and Strauss have called this **closed awareness;** the staff and family are aware of a patient's condition but the patient is not. Doctors often prefer this alternative because it minimizes demands on them. The patient's family and friends frequently support this decision because they are unable to confront the fact of death. Even when they are not informed, however, some patients begin to suspect that their illness is terminal. At this point, **suspected awareness,** they try to find out from the staff or their families whether their suspicions are correct.

If the patient does discover the seriousness of the illness, the hospital staff has two alternatives. They may pretend with the patient that neither knows that the disease is terminal (**mutual pretense awareness**), or they may openly acknowledge its gravity and perhaps even discuss the condition with the patient (**open awareness**). Nurses often prefer to be completely frank with patients from the start to avoid the distrust that sometimes develops when patients suspect they are dying but cannot discover the truth. The trend today is to inform patients of their condition, with the hospital staff given some discretion as to how much information to reveal.

Once patients have been informed of their condition, they must then cope with a truth that few of us want to face. Elizabeth Kübler-Ross (1969) did some pioneer work on how the terminally ill react to their impending death. Her investigations made a major contribution in establishing **thanatology**—the study of death and dying. Based on interviews with 200 dying patients, she identified five stages of psychological adjustment. The first stage is *denial*. People's most common reaction to learning that they have a terminal illness is shock and numbness, followed by denial. They react by saying, "No, it can't be happening to me," or "I'll get another opinion." They may assert that the doctors are incompetent or the diagnosis mistaken. In extreme cases, people may refuse treatment and persist in going about business as usual. Most patients who use denial extensively throughout their illness are people who have become accustomed to coping with difficult life situations in this way. Indeed, the denial habit may contribute to the seriousness of a condition. For example, a person might refuse to seek medical attention at the onset of the illness, denying that it exists.

During the second stage, *anger*, the reaction of dying people is "Why me?" They feel anger—at fate, at the powers that be, at every person who comes into their life. At this stage, they are likely to alienate themselves from others, for no one can relieve the anger they feel at their shortened life span and lost chances.

During the stage of *bargaining*, people change their attitude and attempt to bargain with fate. For example, a woman may ask God for a

■ **Debating an Issue.** Have students consider the ethical dilemma faced when doctors and family members withhold the fact that a patient is dying. Have the class debate the following issue: *Resolved*—that doctors and family should never withhold information regarding a terminal diagnosis. (Because this is an emotional subject, respect student wishes not to participate.) (OBJECTIVE 3)

Independent Practice

■ **Cooperative Learning Activity.** Tell students to imagine they are editors working on the premier issue of a newsletter for people entering middle and old age. Working in groups, assign students to design a four-page special edition entitled "So Now You're Over Forty." Instruct students to brainstorm a list of news stories and features to be included in the issue. Topics should explore expert opinion on the physical and intellectual changes of the post-40 years. Stories might also address the issues and fears of adults over 40. When students are done, have groups evaluate each other's newsletters for accuracy and clarity. (OBJECTIVES 1–3)

COOPERATIVE LEARNING ACTIVITY

Organize the class into four groups. Ask each to imagine they are counseling the family of one of the following: an 80-year-old man who is dying of cancer; a 50-year-old woman who has suffered a stroke; a 30-year-old who is dying of AIDS; a 20-year-old daughter who is dying from injuries sustained in a car accident. Instruct the members of each group to discuss their situation and to determine the advice they might offer to the family to help the patient face death. Have each group role-play the counseling session. (If possible, suggest that students talk with religious and/or social service personnel who have experience in dealing with such heartbreaking situations.)

Panel Discussion. Like racism and sexism, ageism can have detrimental effects on people. Ask students to participate in a panel discussion analyzing the various elements of ageism in American society. Panelists should discuss how ageism is expressed and in what ways attitudes have changed or are changing. (OBJECTIVES 1-3)

Using Psychology

After students have read the special feature, ask them to answer the following questions:

1. How does hospice care differ from traditional hospital care? *(Hospitals may use machines to prolong existence after a person has stopped living a normal life; hospices try to maintain a homelike atmosphere and do not try to prolong life.)*

2. What factors have contributed to the increase in hospice care in the United States? *(the move toward home-based care and the fact that many insurance companies now finance hospice services)*

Using Psychology

Hospices

The discussion of death is one of the few taboos left in twentieth-century America. The breakdown of extended families and the rise of modern medicine have insulated most people in our society from death. Many people have no direct experience with death, and, partly as a result, they are afraid to talk about it. In 1900, the average life span was less than 50 years, and most people died at home in their own beds. Today, most Americans live until at least 70, and they die in nursing homes and hospitals. Elaborate machines may prolong existence long after a person has stopped living a normal life.

FIGURE 10.7

A hospice patient during a visit with his family.

A movement to restore the dignity of dying revolves around the concept of the hospice—usually a special place where terminally ill people go to die. The hospice is designed to make the patient's surroundings pleasant and comfortable—less like a hospital and more like a home. Doctors in hospices do not try to prolong life but to improve the quality of life. A key component of hospice care is the use of tranquilizers and other drugs to ease discomfort and relieve pain.

COMMUNITY INVOLVEMENT

Arrange to have a speaker come to class to discuss death and dying. Possible sources for a speaker include a hospice worker, a "buddy" from an AIDS organization, or a nurse from a trauma center or nursing home. Among the topics the speaker might address are how terminal patients cope with dying, how families respond, and whether the dying go through Kübler-Ross's five stages. Following the presentation, allow time for student questions. Afterwards, ask students to summarize what they learned, orally or in writing.

The patient in a hospice leads the most normal life he or she is able to do, and is taken care of as much as possible by family members. If it can be arranged, a patient may choose to die at home.

The first and most famous hospice facility was St. Christopher's Hospice in London, England, established in 1967 to treat terminally ill cancer patients. In 1974, the first U.S. hospice was established in New Haven, Connecticut, and the numbers have grown since.

Another form of hospice service is becoming part of the mainstream of the health care system of the United States. This program features care for the elderly at home by visiting nurses, aides, physical therapists, chaplains, and social workers. Medicare now includes arrangements for providing and financing these hospice services. Many other insurance policies also include provisions for in-home hospice care. Many also provide for another form called "respite care." Growing rapidly in recent years, home-based hospice care is now a more frequently used service than inpatient hospice care in the United States.

certain amount of time in return for good behavior. She may promise a change of ways, even a dedication of her life to the church. She may announce that she is ready to settle for a less threatening form of the same illness and begin to bargain with the doctor over the diagnosis. For example, if she submits gracefully to some procedures, might she be rewarded by being spared the next stage of the illness? This stage is relatively short and is followed by the stage of *depression*.

During depression dying people are aware of the losses they are incurring (for example, loss of body tissue, loss of job, loss of life savings). Also, they are depressed about the loss that is to come: they are in the process of losing everybody and everything. Kübler-Ross suggests that it is helpful to allow such people to express their sadness and not to attempt to cover up the situation or force them to act cheerfully.

Finally, patients *accept* death. The struggle is over, and they experience a sense of calm. In some cases, the approach of death feels appropriate or peaceful. They seem to become detached intentionally so as to make death easier.

Not all terminal patients progress through the stages of Kübler-Ross describes. For example, a person may die in the denial stages because he or she is psychologically unable to proceed beyond it or because the course of the illness does not grant the necessary time to do so. Kübler-Ross notes that patients do not limit their responses to any one stage; a depressed patient may have recurring bursts of anger. She notes, too, that all patients in all stages persist in feeling hope. Even the most accepting and realistic patients leave open the possibility that they may live after all.

PSYCHOLOGISTS AT WORK

Within the broad field of developmental psychology, *gerontologists* are those who focus on the behaviors associated with old age. As a scientific pursuit, gerontology is still an expanding area of modern psychology. But the general study of old age is quite ancient, with roots in classical philosophy. The Roman statesman and philosopher Cicero, for example, wrote a famous treatise on the subject called *On Old Age*. As the baby boom generation ages, the study of gerontology promises to increase in importance.

ASSESS
Check for Understanding
Ask the class to look back to the objectives on p. 243 and to summarize the main points of the chapter orally or in writing.

Reteach
Have students complete the Chapter 10 Review Activity and share responses with each other.

Enrich
Ask students to complete the Chapter 10 Extension Activity and answer the questions that follow it.

Evaluate
Administer and grade the Chapter Test. Two forms are available should you wish to give different tests to different students/classes.

Use the Understanding Psychology Testmaker to create a customized test.

CLOSE

Remind students of their earlier discussion about the "perfect" age. Ask them whether their attitudes and expectations about adulthood have changed now that they have completed this chapter. In light of what they have learned, have students describe the lives they would like to lead as they grow older.

ANSWERS

Concepts and Vocabulary

1. Bodily changes require psychological adjustments. Relating well to others is an important goal, and meeting new responsibilities requires effort.

2. For descriptions see pp. 244–246.

3. better at comprehending new material and thinking flexibly; poorer at learning new skills; slower at coordination and shifting problem-solving strategies

4. For descriptions see pp. 249–252.

5. Around age 40 a man typically questions his accomplishments. He may also experience relationship problems.

6. Generativity is the desire to use one's accumulated wisdom to guide future generations. Stagnation is characterized by unhealthy preoccupation.

7. Mid-life problems faced by women may include conflicts over career vs. family; worries over attractiveness; the "empty nest" syndrome; depression, caused by lack of self-worth.

8. The decremental model suggests that progressive mental and physical decline is inevitable with age. It stereotypes older people, often leads to misdiagnoses, and limits the kind of care the elderly receive.

9. Health problems include a decline in physical strength and in the senses. Chronic illnesses also may increase.

CHAPTER 10 Review

SUMMARY

Use the following outline as a tool for reviewing this chapter. Copy the outline onto your own paper, leaving spaces between headings to make notes about key concepts.

   I. Adulthood

      A. Physical Changes

      B. Intellectual Changes

      C. Social and Personality Development

   II. Old Age

      A. Changes in Health

      B. Changes in Life Situation

      C. Changes in Sexual Activity

      D. Adjusting to Old Age

      E. Changes in Mental Functioning

   III. Death and Dying

CONCEPTS AND VOCABULARY

1. In what ways are adulthood and adolescence similar stages of development?

2. Describe the physical changes that occur during adulthood. What are the common health problems of adulthood?

3. Describe the changes that occur in intellectual abilities during adulthood. On what types of mental activities do adults perform more poorly? In what ways are adults better able to perform mental activities?

4. List Levinson's stages of adulthood. What occurs in each?

5. Define the "mid-life transition." What problems do men face during this transition?

6. Explain what Erikson means by generativity. What is stagnation?

7. List and summarize three mid-life problems faced by adult women.

8. Describe how the "decremental model of aging" leads to prejudiced attitudes toward the aged ("ageism").

9. What health problems are faced by the elderly? How many are able to lead normal lives? How many have a chronic illness? Does their sexual behavior change? If so, how?

10. Describe the kinds of life transitions or changes the elderly face.

11. What is crystallized intelligence? What is fluid intelligence? Which type of intelligence increases with age?

12. Name the field that studies death and dying.

13. Describe the different levels of awareness at which terminally ill persons can view their condition. Which do you think is the best approach?

14. Name Kübler-Ross's five stages of psychological adjustment to death. What behaviors would you expect of someone at each stage?

15. Explain the purpose of a hospice. What are two different forms of hospice care? What is one of the key components of hospice care?

CRITICAL THINKING

1. **Analyze.** In this chapter, it is suggested that self-esteem is vulnerable when it is based on only one aspect of identity—physical attractiveness. List other aspects of identity on which one could base his or her self-esteem in order to strengthen it. What do you think your self-esteem is based on? Can you think of any ways you could strengthen your self-esteem?

2. **Synthesize.** If someone were to ask you, "What can I do to stay mentally, emotionally, and physically young as long as possible," what would you tell this person?

About 80 percent of the elderly lead normal lives. About 40 percent have a chronic illness. Sexual behavior may change, but most people enjoy sexual activity late in life.

10. retirement, widowhood, adjustment to physical changes and changes in environment

11. Crystallized intelligence (increases with age): ability to use accumulated learning in appropriate situations.

Fluid intelligence: ability to solve abstract problems and generate hypotheses.

12. thanatology

13. These are closed awareness, suspected awareness, mutual pretense, open awareness. The trend today is to tell patients.

14. denial, anger, bargaining, depression, and acceptance; see pp. 259–261 for description

3. Synthesize. Death and dying have only recently become topics that are discussed openly. Given this growing openness, what changes do you see being made to make the adjustment to the prospect of dying less severe? What kinds of programs could hospitals and homes for the aged implement to help people make this adjustment?

4. Analyze. List several controversial questions, such as "Do you believe in fighting for your country no matter what the circumstances?" Ask people of different age groups to respond to your questions. Do you notice differences in the levels of reasoning? Use the explanations contained in this chapter and your own thoughts to account for the differences.

APPLYING KNOWLEDGE

1. Interview an adult who is more than 50 years old. Ask this person to describe himself or herself physically, socially, intellectually, and emotionally at the ages of 20, 30, 40, and 50. Before the interview, list specific questions that would provide this information. Ask which age was his or her favorite and why.

2. Arrange to interview a man and woman who are middle-aged. Interview them separately. Before you do the interviews, prepare a list of questions about work and family experiences. As you start the interview, explain to your subject what you are doing and ask for their understanding and cooperation. Inform them that you will be interviewing—or have already interviewed—a member of the opposite sex and will be comparing the answers. After you finish the interviews, think about how each person answered the questions. Did you find any differences between the man and the woman in attitudes or feelings about work? About attitudes toward the family? Do you think that men and women go through different stages of adult development? What are the dangers of generalizing from one set of interviews?

ANALYZING VIEWPOINTS

1. In some communities, elderly adults have the option of living in separate housing provided for senior citizens. Along with the benefits of this type of living arrangement go certain disadvantages. What are the benefits of separate housing for elderly adults? What disadvantages do you see? Write an article that makes the case that separate housing is the best solution for senior citizens. Then write an article that argues that senior citizens should live in the community, not in separate housing.

BEYOND THE CLASSROOM

1. Find out what services your community offers to its elderly adults. Look in the phone book to see if there are any special phone numbers for information on services for the elderly. You may want to ask the town or city hall or at your local library. Once you know what services are offered, try to visit a senior citizens' center or retirement home. If possible, tour the facility and talk with some of the senior citizens. How do you think these services could be improved to make the experience of old age a more fruitful and happier time? What services could the elderly provide to your community? Prepare a report describing your experiences.

In YOUR JOURNAL

1. Reread the entry in your journal that you wrote about the saying "You can't teach an old dog new tricks." Think about this statement in light of adult development and learning. What evidence is there that this statement is incorrect? Using what you have learned, write an entry in your journal that presents evidence supporting both sides of the issue.

15. A hospice is a homelike place where terminally ill people go to die. A second type provides at-home care. A key component of hospice care is the use of drugs to alleviate pain.

Critical Thinking

1. Encourage students to think of other aspects of identity that contribute to self-esteem.

2. Students' answers will vary. People can stay younger by leading healthy, active lives. Proper diet, exercise, and medical checkups contribute to physical health. Staying young mentally can be related to using and challenging one's mental abilities on a regular basis.

3. Students might suggest discussion groups for patients to share their concerns.

4. Answers will vary.

CHAPTER BONUS
Test Question

This question may be used for extra credit on the chapter test.
Choose the letter of the correct response.

Crystallized intelligence, or the ability to use our experience and accumulated knowledge,:

a. increases with age.
b. remains static throughout our lives.
c. decreases with age.
d. reaches its highest level at age 25.

Answer: **a**

Applying Knowledge

1. Answers will vary.

2. Answers will vary.

Analyzing Viewpoints

1. Answers will vary.

Beyond the Classroom

1. Answers will vary.

In Your Journal

If time permits, discuss journal entries individually with the students.

Personality and Individuality

CHAPTER 11

Personality Theory

CHAPTER 12

Psychological Testing

Your personality—your patterns of acting, thinking, and feeling—makes you unique.

264

INTRODUCING THE UNIT

The use of labels catches the attention of most people. Select short descriptions of the 12 astrological signs. Without revealing the astrological sign, read these descriptions aloud. Ask students to choose which of the 12 descriptions best fits their personality. Then compare the students' selections with their actual sign. Poll the class to find out how many students chose the correct birth sign based on description. *(Emphasize the generality of most astrological descriptions, hence their appeal to people who feel they are tailor-made for them.)*

Chapter 11 focuses on personality theories that attempt to explain similarities in the human temperament as well as reasons for individual differences.

Chapter 12 explores the uses—and pitfalls—of standardized testing. The chapter also provides students with strategies for reducing test-taking anxiety and for improving test performance.

Connecting to Past Learning
Ask students to name some of the various types of tests that they have taken in the past (both content-based and more standardized performance tests). List these tests on the chalkboard, and have students identify the ones that create the most apprehension. Solicit student opinion on the uses—and misuses—of tests as an evaluation tool.

265

UNIT PROJECT

Ask students to survey a representative group of students from each of the grades within your school (perhaps 20 per grade) about their understanding of the term *intelligent*. Suggest that students use the following incomplete sentence as a survey tool. "I consider a person intelligent, if he/she _____ ."

Have students sort through responses to identify and categorize the traits named. What, if any, common measures of intelligence did the survey reveal? Instruct students to reexamine these findings after the completion of Unit 4.

CHAPTER 11

Personality Theory

TEXT TOPICS	SPECIAL FEATURES	RESOURCE MATERIALS
What Personality Theorists Try to Do, pp. 267–270	**At a Glance:** Instant Personality Analysis and Astrology, p. 269	▰ Reproducible Lesson Plan; Study Guide; Review Activity ▯ *Readings in Psychology:* Section 4, Reading 1
Psychoanalytic Theories, pp. 270–277	**Fact or Fiction?,** p. 272 **Readings in Psychology:** On Basic Anxiety and Hostility, p. 277	▰ Reproducible Lesson Plan; ♟ Study Guide; Review Activity ▱ Transparency 20
Behavioral Theories, pp. 277–279	**More About Psychology,** p. 279	▰ Reproducible Lesson Plan; Study Guide; Review Activity
Cognitive Theory, pp. 279–280	**At a Glance:** Improving Your Self-Image, p. 280	▰ Reproducible Lesson Plan; Study Guide; Review Activity
Humanistic Psychology, pp. 281–284		▰ Reproducible Lesson Plan; ♟ Study Guide; Review Activity ▱ Transparency 21
Trait Theories, pp. 284–286	**Psychology Update,** p. 286	▰ Reproducible Lesson Plan; Study Guide; Review Activity; Application Activity; Extension Activity ▯ *Readings in Psychology:* Section 4, Readings 2, 3 ▰ Chapter Test, Form A and Form B ◉ Understanding Psychology Testmaker

PERFORMANCE ASSESSMENT ACTIVITY

Tell students that *personality* is derived from the Latin word *persona*—the term used to describe the masks worn in Greek theater. Roman actors adapted these masks, and they are still used today to identify the range of emotions portrayed in theater. As an example, have students recall the masks for tragedy or comedy. Or ask them to think of the masks painted on the face of a clown or mime. Working in groups, assign students to design or draw a mask that conveys a particular personality type, or *persona*. Encourage students to think in simple terms such as shy, angry, "devilish," happy, and so on. (Tell students to be prepared to select what they consider to be the two most important facial features used to convey the *persona*.)

CHAPTER RESOURCES

Readings for the Student
Kline, Nathan S. *From Sad to Glad.* New York: Ballantine Books, 1987.

Rogers, Carl. *A Way of Being.* Boston: Houghton Mifflin, 1980.

Sheehy, Gail. *Pathfinders.* New York: Bantam Books, 1982.

Readings for the Teacher
Hjelle, Larry A. and Ziegler, Daniel J. *Personality Theories* (3rd ed.). New York: McGraw-Hill, Inc., 1992.

Maslow, Abraham. *Toward a Psychology of Being.* New York: Van Nostrand Reinhold, 1968.

Schultz, Duane. *Theories of Personality* (4th ed.). Pacific Grove, CA: Brooks-Cole Publishing, 1990.

The Teaching of Personality Development, Parts 1 and 2. (Sociological Review Monographs). Millwood, NY: Kraus Reprints, 1974.

Multimedia
Maslow and Self-Actualization (two parts, 30 minutes each). Psychological Films. In this film Maslow discusses the dimensions of self-actualization and his subsequent research and theory.

Young Doctor Freud (98 minutes). Films for the Humanities. Produced by Austrian television, this German-language film with English subtitles explores Freud's childhood, youth, and early years as a physician-researcher.

For additional resources, see the bibliography beginning on page 530.

FOCUS

Motivating Activity

You might open this chapter by having students write down adjectives that describe their personality. Instruct them to include both positive and negative qualities. Encourage honesty by telling students that the lists will not be collected. Next, ask students to select the five adjectives that apply most consistently to their day-to-day public behavior (e.g., during school hours). Then have them pick the five adjectives that best apply to their private lives. Direct students to set their lists aside for future reference. (See Exploring Key Ideas.) Explain that in this chapter they will study some of the leading theories about factors that shape our personalities—both public and private.

Meeting Chapter Objectives.

Direct students to use the six reporter's words—*why? what? where? when? how? who?*—to form as many questions as possible for the objectives on page 267. To encourage creativity, tell students that the objectives can be broken apart and rephrased. Compile a master list of questions for students to answer as they read through the chapter.

Building Vocabulary.

Assign groups of students to prepare crossword puzzles using at least 15 of the Key Terms. Have the various groups exchange their puzzles with each other.

FIGURE 11.1 Psychologists who study personality explore whatever it is that makes one person think, feel, and act differently from another.

266

TEACHER CLASSROOM RESOURCES

Chapter 11 Reproducible Lesson Plan
Chapter 11 Study Guide
Chapter 11 Review Activity
Chapter 11 Application Activity
Chapter 11 Extension Activity

Transparencies 20, 21
Transparency Strategies and Activities

Readings in Psychology: Section 4, Readings 1, 2, 3

Chapter 11 Test, Form A and Form B

Understanding Psychology Testmaker

OBJECTIVES

After studying this chapter, you should be able to

■ identify the nature and aims of personality theory.

■ compare and contrast the personality theories discussed in this chapter.

■ describe the defense mechanisms and their role in psychoanalytic theory.

S helly and Deirdre both failed their semester examinations in psychology, but they reacted in very different ways. When Shelly saw her grade, she felt sick to her stomach and had to fight back tears. She rushed home, and shut herself up in her room to lie in bed, stare at the ceiling, and feel inadequate. Deirdre, on the other hand, was all bluster. She ran to the cafeteria to join her friends and make loud jokes about the stupid questions on the test.

Why did Shelly and Deirdre act so differently in similar situations? Speaking loosely, there is something inside people that makes them think, feel, and act differently, and that "something inside" is what we mean by personality.

When psychologists talk of aspects of personality, most are agreed that the elements of personality share the following features:

• *Characteristic:* Aspects of personality must occur in many or all people to be of much interest and use. For example, shyness is a characteristic of all human personalities to some degree.

• *Consistent:* Features must occur repeatedly in a variety of situations. Shy people, for example, generally act shy everywhere.

• *Unique:* The characteristics of personality combine in any of us in an unmatched manner. No two personalities are alike. The combination that defines *you* is identifiable.

KEY TERMS

archetype
behaviorism
collective unconscious
conditions of worth
contingencies of
   reinforcement
defense mechanisms
displacement
ego
extravert
factor analysis
fully functioning
humanistic psychology
id
inferiority complex
introvert
organism
positive regard
projection
reaction formation
regression
repression
self
self-actualization
superego
trait
unconditional positive regard
unconscious

IN YOUR JOURNAL

Think of a person you have had a chance to observe in a variety of social settings. Write an entry in your journal describing that person's characteristic way of interacting with people. How do others respond to this person?

267

Exploring Key Ideas

Defining Personality.
Ask students if they think there is any difference between the terms *personality* and *identity*. If so, how would students distinguish these terms? As a starting point, tell students that William James saw the self as comprised of two parts: the "I" and the "me". Which part do they think James would use to define personality? *(probably the "I")* Next, explain that many psychologists define personality as the characteristic ways a person responds to his or her environment—i.e., the social, public self. They define identity as the way someone sees himself or herself from the inside—i.e., the private self. Now ask students to refer to the lists compiled during the Motivating Activity. Did the activity confirm or disprove this theory of a dual self? (You might either request volunteers to share their experience or poll the class for a more general answer.)

IN YOUR JOURNAL

As a tip, tell students to think in terms of patterns of response. *(Patterns are what allow people to describe, or categorize, a person's personality.)*

EXTRA CREDIT ACTIVITY

Read aloud the following help-wanted ad: *Wanted: Sales Manager.* Established self-starter willing to accept responsibility for expanding business. Ability at creative staffing solutions and commitment to highest quality services highly desired. The ideal candidate will be a team player with successful sales and interpersonal skills. College degree required. Ask: What type of personality traits does the ad request? Why might these traits be useful for a sales manager? Assign students to collect a variety of help-wanted ads for various professions. What, if any, common traits turn up?

TEACH

Guided Practice

■ **Identifying Points of View.**
Although people share certain basic personality traits, each person has a unique combination of traits that defines him or her as an individual. To help students develop an awareness of individual differences, read aloud the following selection from *Walden* by Henry David Thoreau.

If a man does not keep pace with his companions, perhaps it is because he hears a different drummer. Let him step to the music which he hears, however measured or far away.

Ask: About what type of person is Thoreau writing? *(a person who follows a "different drummer" than his companions)* How might a team player view such a person? *(as a renegade or rebel)* How does Thoreau view this person? *(as someone who should—and must—follow his "drummer," or conscience)* What people in history or current life can students name who have followed a different drummer? What traits do they assign to such people? (OBJECTIVE 1)

Personality can be defined generally as characteristics consistently displayed and uniquely combined in each of us. It accounts for both the differences among people and for the consistencies in an individual's behavior over time and in different situations.

WHAT PERSONALITY THEORISTS TRY TO DO

First, personality theories provide a way of organizing the many characteristics you know about yourself and other people. You know people may be outgoing or shy, bossy or meek, quick-tempered or calm, witty or dull, fun-loving or gloomy, responsible or lazy.

All these words describe *personality traits*, or general ways of behaving that characterize an individual. Personality theorists try to determine whether certain traits go together, why a person has some traits and not others, and why a person might exhibit different traits in different situations. There is a good deal of disagreement among theorists as to which traits are significant. Nevertheless, all theorists share one common goal: to discover patterns in the ways people behave.

A second purpose of any personality theory is *to explain the differences* between individuals. In so doing, theorists probe beneath the surface. You might explain different behaviors in terms of motives: Kelly's primary goal, for example, may be to please others while Erica's may be to advance herself. These explanations are little more than descriptions, however. How did these two come to have different motives in the first place? Here, too, personality theorists disagree. One might suggest that Kelly had parents who encouraged altruistic (helping) behavior while Erica's parents encouraged achievement. Another theorist might seek less obvious causes—arguing, for example, that the roots of these differences could be traced back to toilet training.

A third goal of personality theory is to explore how people conduct their lives. It is no accident that most personality theorists began as psychotherapists. In working with people who had difficulty coping with everyday problems, they inevitably developed ideas about what it takes to live a relatively happy, untroubled life. Personality theorists try to explain why problems arise, and why they are more difficult for some people to manage than for others.

In addition, personality theorists are concerned with determining how life can be improved. It seems obvious that some people are dissatisfied with themselves, their parents, their husbands or wives and children, their home lives. People resign themselves to unrewarding jobs, and there is a widespread feeling that much is wrong with society and the world. Almost everyone recognizes that we need to grow and change, individually and collectively. But what are the proper goals of growth and change? How can we cope with the inevitable conflicts of life?

Personality psychologists attempt to answer these questions with systematic theories about human behavior. These theories are used to guide

At A Glance

INSTANT PERSONALITY ANALYSIS AND ASTROLOGY

Suppose someone handed you an astrological reading and told you it was specially written for you. Would you believe it? According to several studies, you probably would.

Subjects who were shown general personality assessments, which could have been written for almost anyone, readily believed they were prepared just for them. Believers—both men and women alike—rated the accuracy of the description at approximately 4.5 on a scale of 1 to 5, with 5 being the highest rating.

Researchers also found that the more personal facts an individual believes are used to compile a personality description, the greater his or her faith in its accuracy. Thus, an individual who thinks a horoscope is based on the year, month, and day of birth is more likely to believe its description than someone who thinks no personal information was used at all.

Our willingness to accept general descriptions of ourselves as accurate may be due to the universal human failing of being a bit too gullible. This is especially true when the words we hear are filled with praise.

For more details, see C. R. Snyder and Randee Jane Shenkel, "The P. T. Barnum Effect," *Psychology Today*, March 1975.

At A Glance

The writer in the selection from *Psychology Today* has a definite point of view, or opinion, on horoscopes. To help students identify and analyze this point of view, ask the following questions.
1. What was the original title of the article? *("The P. T. Barnum Effect")*
2. P. T. Barnum invented the circus. He is also known for the saying "A sucker is born every minute." How does the use of Barnum in the title give you a tip on the writer's opinion of horoscopes? *(Answers will vary, but students should note that the writer probably does not hold a high opinion of them.)*
3. What loaded, or emotion-filled, words does the writer use to weigh opinion? *(You might use "gullible" as an example.)*
4. What is the author's opinion of astrology? *(sees it as more-or-less empty generalizations)*
5. What is your opinion of astrology? *(Answers will vary.)*

research; and research, in turn, can test parts of a theory to see whether they are right or wrong. Thus, formal personality theories try to make ideas about why people act in certain ways more scientific by stating them very precisely and then testing them.

Psychology is still a young science, and development and testing of personality theories is still gaining sophistication. There are now many conflicting theories of personality, each with its friends and foes. In this chapter, we will describe four major schools of thought among personality theorists.

Psychoanalytic theories, developed by Sigmund Freud and his followers, emphasize the importance of motives hidden deep in the unconscious. B. F. Skinner and the behaviorists study the way rewards and punishments shape our actions. Humanistic theorists, like Abraham Maslow and Carl Rogers, stress our human potential growth, creativity, and spontaneity. Finally, trait theorists, like Gordon Allport and Hans Eysenck, emphasize the importance of understanding basic personality characteristics such as friendliness and aggression.

CONNECTIONS: PSYCHOLOGY AND HISTORY

Tell students that astrology has existed for thousands of years. Babylonian astrologers predicted wars and natural disasters, and ancient Greek astrologers used the stars to forecast the future for clients who visited them. In medieval Europe, people visited astrologers to search their charts for divine omens. Request interested students to prepare an oral report on the history of astrology, bringing it up to the present. They might mention, for example, the widely publicized astrological consultations among members of the Reagan White House.

■ **Making a Chart.** Working in groups, have students generate a chart to collect data on the following personality theorists: Freudians (or Neo-Freudians), Behaviorists, Cognitivists, Humanists, and Trait Theorists. Side column heads might include: Names of Famous Theorists, Beliefs or Premises, Data or Method to Establish Theories, and so on. Assign students to complete these charts as they make their way through the chapter. (You might want to post a master chart on the wall for students to fill out collectively at the end of each section.) (OBJECTIVE 2)

Teacher Note. You might want to review Freud's theory on the stages of personality development discussed in Chapter 8. (Consider assigning a student to prepare a mock instant "recap", similar to those used in sports reporting.)

■ **Readings in Psychology.** Have students read the Section 4, Reading 1 selection in *Readings in Psychology* and answer the questions that follow the selection.

Each of the theories we will discuss has a different image of human nature. What they have in common is a concern with understanding the differences among people.

PSYCHOANALYTIC THEORIES

Charming, spacious, homelike 1 rm. apts. Modern kitchenette. Hotel service. Weekly rats available.
—from classified advertisement, *The New York Times*

This advertisement was received and typeset by someone at the *Times*. The person who set the ad probably did not leave the "e" out of "rate" deliberately, but was it just an innocent mistake?

Slips like these are common. People usually laugh at them, even if they are meaningful. But sometimes they are disturbing. Everyone has made a remark that hurt a friend and has later asked himself, "Why did I say that? I didn't mean it." Yet, when he thinks about it, he may realize that he was angry at his friend and wanted to "get back" at him.

Sigmund Freud and the Unconscious

It was Sigmund Freud who first suggested that the little slips that people make, the things they mishear, and the odd misunderstandings they have are not really mistakes at all. Freud believed there was something behind these mistakes, even though people claimed they were just accidental and quickly corrected themselves. Similarly, when he listened to people describe their dreams, he believed the dreams had some meaning, even though the people who dreamed them did not know what they meant.

Freud was a neurologist who practiced in Vienna in the early 1900s. Since he specialized in nervous diseases, a great many people talked to him about their private lives, their conflicts, fears, and desires. At that time most people thought, as many still do, that we are aware of all our motives and feelings. But Freud reasoned that if people can say and dream things without knowing their meaning, they must not know as much about themselves as they think they do. He concluded that some of the most powerful influences on human personality are things we are *not* conscious of.

Freud was the first modern psychologist to suggest that every personality has a large **unconscious** component. Life includes both pleasurable and painful experiences. For Freud, experiences include feelings and thoughts as well as actual events. Freud believed that many of our experiences, particularly the painful episodes of childhood, are forgotten or buried in the unconscious. But although we may not consciously recall these experiences, they continue to influence our behavior. For example, a child who never fully pleases his demanding mother or father may feel unhappy much of the time and will doubt his abilities to succeed and to be loved. As an adult, the person may suffer from feelings of unworthiness and low self-esteem, despite his very real abilities. Freud believed that

> **Freud concluded that some of the most powerful influences on human personality are things we are not conscious of.**

PSYCHOLOGISTS AT WORK

The human personality has always intrigued philosophers and lay persons. Pseudosciences such as astrology, physiognomy, and Galen's humoral theory of temperament are all early examples of efforts to explain the "hows" and "whys" of human behavior. In recent years (i.e., in the post-Freud period), psychologists have applied the tools of science to generate new, more complicated theories of personality. Today, personality psychologists present survey data to support their views. They also formulate and/or use tests as methods of measurement (see Chapter 12). Training includes advanced work in psychological theory as well as courses in statistics and evaluative testing.

unconscious motives and the feelings people experience as children have an enormous impact on adult personality and behavior.

The Id, Ego, and Superego

Freud explained human personality by saying that it was a kind of energy system—like a steam engine or an electric dynamo. The energy in personality comes from two kinds of powerful instincts—the life instinct and the death instinct. Freud theorized that all of life moves toward death, and that the desire for a final end shows up in human personality as destructiveness and aggression. It is important to remember, however, the life instincts were more important in Freud's theory, and he saw them primarily as erotic or pleasure-seeking urges.

By 1923 Freud had described what became known as the structural concepts of the mind: id, ego, and superego (Figure 11.2). Though Freud often spoke of them as if they were actual parts of the personality, he introduced and regarded them simply as a *model* of how the mind works. In other words, the id, ego, and superego do not refer to actual portions of the brain. Instead, they explain how the mind functions and how the instinctual energies are regulated.

In Freud's theory the **id** is the reservoir or container of the instinctual and biological urges. At birth, you are all id, responding unconsciously to

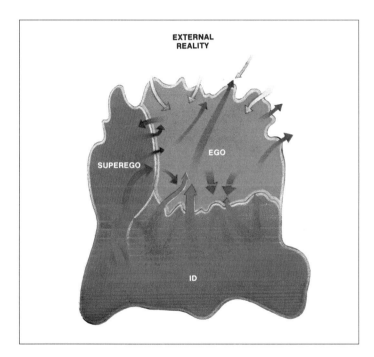

EXTERNAL REALITY

SUPEREGO

EGO

ID

FIGURE 11.2

This visual interpretation shows the Freudian theory of personality structure. The ego tries to balance the demands of the id and the superego against each other and the realities of the world. In doing this, it sometimes suppresses the irrational tendencies of the id, but it may also be able to deflect the id's energy into channels acceptable to both the superego and the outside world. These interactions and conflicts are represented by arrows in the figure. **Which of these components, according to Freud, is the source of guilt feelings?**

■ **Creative Writing.** Propose some type of decision making to the class. For example:

You're on a hike with a group of friends, and a rain storm suddenly hits. Everyone's food is destroyed in the downpour, except one person who wrapped her food in a plastic stuff sack. Night rolls in and you're starving. You notice that your friend has wandered away from her backpack. Part of you wants to steal her food—you need it to survive. Another part of you says the action is morally wrong. What will you do?

Challenge students to prepare a three-part dialogue in which the id, ego, and superego argue about the resolution of this moral dilemma. When students are done, request volunteers to read their dialogues aloud to the class. (OBJECTIVE 2)

■ **Categorizing Information.** Direct students to brainstorm a list of human traits. Record these on the chalkboard. Then, using descriptions in the text, have students categorize these traits as reflective of the id, ego, or superego. (Some traits might appear in more than one category.) (OBJECTIVE 2)

VISUAL INSTRUCTION

Make sure that students understand that Freud did not view the id, ego, and superego as separate entities or physical divisions of the brain. Instead, Freud used these as labels for strong psychological forces or motivations.
Answer to caption, Figure 11.2: the superego

CRITICAL THINKING ACTIVITY

Analyzing Information. Assign students to keep a personal diary of conflicts that they encounter each day. (To encourage honesty, emphasize that the diaries will not be collected.) At the end of the day, students should pretend they are Freudians. After each entry, they should analyze which Freudian principle was most operative in resolving the conflict: (1) interaction between the id and superego or (2) a defense mechanism. If a defense mechanism was at work, students should attempt to name it. At the end of the week, tell students to review methods of conflict resolution.

WORKING WITH TRANSPARENCIES

Project Transparency 20 and use the guidelines provided in Teaching Strategies and Activities. Assign Student Worksheet 20.

DID YOU KNOW?

Narcissism comes from a figure in Greek mythology (Narcissus) who fell in love with his own reflection in a pool of water.

■ **Developing Vocabulary.**
Before exploring the discussion of defense mechanisms, you might want to have students look up the meaning of each of the following terms: **fear** *(response to a real threat)*, **phobia** *(unreasonable fear of something that exists)*, and **anxiety** *(fear of the unknown)*. Challenge students to give examples of each term. Ask how each of these emotions or behaviors might produce avoidance in a person. What are some healthy forms of avoidance? *(fear-based escape from a burning building)* What are some unhealthy forms of avoidance? *(screaming at the sight of a garden snake)* (OBJECTIVE 3)

FACT OR FICTION

Self-centered people suffer from undeveloped egos.

Fiction. Narcissism is defined as a "self-love" marked by feelings of self-importance and superiority. According to Heinz Kohut, the psychiatrist who founded the theory of self-psychology, a certain degree of narcissism is necessary for the development of a healthy ego.

inborn instinctive urges for food and water. The id is the lustful or drive-ridden part of the unconscious. The demand of *Sesame Street's* Cookie Monster—"Me Want Cookie!"—is pure id. It operates in terms of the *pleasure principle*, seeking immediate gratification of desires, regardless of the consequences.

The personality process that is mostly conscious is called the **ego.** Gradually forming during the second and third years, and driven by psychic energy borrowed from the id, the ego is the rational, thoughtful personality process that operates in terms of the *reality principle*. If, for example, a person is hungry, the id might drive her to seek immediate satisfaction by dreaming of food or by eating all the available food at once instead of keeping some of it for a later time. The ego would recognize that the body needs real food and that it will continue to need food in the future. It would use the id's energy to preserve some of the food available now and to look for ways of finding more.

Suppose you thought of stealing the desired food from someone else. The part of the personality that would stop you is called the **superego.** The id is concerned with what the person *wants* to do and the ego is concerned with planning what she *can* do; the superego is concerned with what she *should* do. It is the moral part of the personality—the source of conscience and of high ideals—which operates in terms of a *moral principle*. But the superego can also create conflicts and problems. It is sometimes overly harsh, like a very strict parent. The superego, then, is also the source of guilt feelings which come from mild as well as serious deviations from what it defines as "right."

The id and the superego frequently come into conflict with each other. Because neither is concerned with reality, they may both come into conflict with the outside world as well. Freud saw the ego as part of the person that must satisfy the demands of the id without offending the superego. If the id is not satisfied, the person feels an intolerable tension of longing or anger or desire. If the superego is not obeyed, the person feels guilty and inferior. And if outside reality is ignored, the person suffers such outcomes as starvation or dislike by other people (Freud, 1943).

Defense Mechanisms

The ego's job is so difficult that unconsciously all people resort to psychological defenses. Rather than face intense frustration, conflict, or feelings of unworthiness, people deceive themselves into believing nothing is wrong. If the demands of the id and the ego cannot be resolved, it may be necessary to distort reality. Freud called these techniques **defense mechanisms** because they defend the ego from experiencing anxiety about failing in its tasks (Figure 11.3). Freud felt that these defense mechanisms stem mainly from the unconscious part of the ego. They ordinarily become conscious to the individual during a form of psychotherapy called psychoanalysis—and then only with great difficulty.

To some degree, defense mechanisms are necessary to psychological well-being. They relieve intolerable confusion, help people to weather intense emotional crisis, and give individuals time to work out problems they

CONNECTIONS: PSYCHOLOGY AND THE MEDIA

Review the Cookie Monster's id behavior. Then assign several students to view episodes of *Sesame Street*. What examples of the *pleasure principle, reality principle,* and *moral principle* can they identify at work in the puppets' personalities? (Sometimes the Cookie Monster's superego kicks in, for example, with the words "Me sorry.") Have students present the observances to the class. Or, if possible, have them put on their own puppet show with stuffed toys or dolls borrowed from their brothers and sisters. (If students think puppet shows are silly, point out (1) the long history of puppetry and (2) the use of puppets by some child psychologists.)

FIGURE 11.3

Freud discussed several defense mechanisms in his theory. Projection is a person seeing attributes of his own personality as though they were possessed by others. Repression is shown by a woman who is not only concealing and restraining a monstrous impulse, but also trying to conceal from herself the fact that she is doing so. The displacement of a widow's love for her lost husband and family onto her pets is another common defense mechanism. **In what ways are defense mechanisms helpful?**

might not be able to solve if they allowed themselves to feel all the pressures at work within them. However, if a person resorts to defense mechanisms all or most of the time, he will avoid facing and solving his problems realistically. A few of the defense mechanisms Freud identified are discussed below.

Repression. When a person has painful memories and unacceptable thoughts and motives that causes the ego too much anxiety, she may push that thought or urge out of consciousness down into the unconscious. This process is called **repression.** The person simply "forgets" the thing that disturbs her, or pushes it out of awareness without ever realizing it. For example, a grown woman whose father is meddling in her life may have the impulse to say "I hate you, Dad." But the woman may feel so anxious and afraid about having such an impulse that she unconsciously will come to believe that what she feels is not hatred. She replaces the feeling with

VISUAL INSTRUCTION

You might wish to review *sublimation* on page 208. Ask: What does this term mean? *(substitution of socially acceptable activities for unacceptable social impulses)* How does this term fit the definition of a *defense mechanism? (an ego defense against unacceptable or unpleasurable behavior)* **Answer to caption, Figure 11.3:** They relieve confusion, help individuals get through emotional troubles, and provide time to resolve problems.

Teacher Note. You might introduce students to other defense mechanisms not mentioned in the text.

Denial. Falsification of reality; the flip side of repression. ("You must be nuts. I'm not mad at you.")

Reversal. Turning the situation around. ("I'm not mad at you. You're mad at me.")

Isolation. Disconnection from the emotion. ("Yes, I guess I'm mad at you. Hey, did you see the game last night? What did you think?")

Rationalization. Overthink the problem to justify an action. ("I'm mad at you. But you'd be angry too if you had my rotten luck.")

Sublimation. Positive defense mechanism that channels energy into some useful activity. ("Mad at you? Sure, but let's work it out in a game of chess. We'll both feel better.")

ADDITIONAL INFORMATION

Reinforce that one of the central goals of psychoanalysis is to unlock the repression of memories or thoughts stored away during childhood. (Freud considered the concept of repression as the cornerstone of his whole system.) To unlock repression, a psychoanalyst "shrinks" a patient back to childhood.

The nickname "shrink" is derived from this process. You might ask students what the label "shrink" means to them. What stereotyped views of therapists does it trigger?

■ **Cooperative Learning Activity.** Organize the class into five groups, and assign each group one of the five defense mechanisms discussed in the text. Direct each group to design a skit illustrating the defense mechanism in action. (You might expand on this activity by including some of the defense mechanisms named in the side note on page 273.) After students present each skit, have other groups evaluate them in terms of the positive and negative effects of the defense mechanism on the characters involved.

■ **Analyzing a Quote.** Tell students that Elizabeth Loftus, professor of psychology and law at the University of Washington and authority on cognitive processes, offered the following evaluation of repression in 1993:

Repression definitions are so loose and varied, so abundant, so shifting that it is like trying to shoot a moving target. If repression is the avoidance in your conscious awareness of unpleasant experiences that come back to you, yes, I believe in repression. But if it is a blocking out of an endless stream of traumas that occur over and over that leave a person with absolutely no awareness that these things happen, that makes them behave in destructive ways and re-emerge decades later in some reliable form, I don't see any evidence for it. It flies in the face of everything we know about memory.

Ask: How does Loftus qualify Freud's use of repression? *(sees it as avoidance rather than subconscious blocking)* Review the information on memory in Chapter 3. Does repression as a subconscious drive "fl[y] in the face of everything we know about memory"? Why or why not?

274

apathy. She says, "I don't hate you. I have no special feelings at all about you." Nevertheless, the feelings of anger and hostility remain in the unconscious and may show themselves in cutting remarks or sarcastic jokes, slips of the tongue, or dreams. There is an element of repression in all defense mechanisms.

Projection. Another way the ego avoids anxiety is to believe that impulses coming from within are really coming from other people. For example, a boy who is extremely jealous of his girlfriend but does not want to admit to himself that he is threatened by her independence may claim, "I'm not jealous—she's the one who's always asking where I've been, who was that girl I was talking to. . ." This mechanism is called **projection** because inner feelings are thrown, or projected, outside. It is a common mechanism, which others might have pointed out in yourself from time to time. Many people, for example, feel that others dislike them, when in reality they dislike themselves.

Reaction Formation. **Reaction formation** involves replacing an unacceptable feeling or urge with its opposite. For example, a divorced father may resent having his child for the weekend. Unconsciously, he feels it is terribly wrong for a father to react that way, so he showers the child with expressions of love, toys, and exciting trips. A woman who finds her powerful ambitions unacceptable may play the role of a weak, helpless, passive female who wants nothing more than to please the men in her life—unconsciously covering up her true feelings.

Regression. **Regression** means going back to an earlier and less mature pattern of behavior. When a person is under severe pressure and his other defenses are not working, he may start acting in ways that helped him in the past. For example, he may throw a temper tantrum, make faces, cry loudly, or revert to eating and sleeping all the time the way he did as a small child. If you have ever been tempted to stick out your lower lip and pout when you know that you should really accept the fact that you cannot have your own way, you have experienced regression.

Displacement. **Displacement** occurs when the object of an unconscious wish provokes anxiety. This anxiety is reduced when the ego unconsciously shifts the wish to another object. The energy of the id is displaced from one object to another, more accessible, object. For example, if you wanted to hit your father but were afraid to, you might hit your kid brother instead. Your poor brother gets slapped around partly because he reminds you of your father and partly because he's not as likely to hit back.

In Summary. The recognition of the tremendous forces that exist in human personality and the difficulty of controlling and handling them was Freud's great contribution to understanding human life. After Freud, it became easier to understand why human life contains so much conflict. It is a matter, Freud thought, of a savage individual coming to terms with the rules of society. The id is the savage part, and the superego, the represen-

STUDY AND WRITING SKILLS

Explain that exposure to traumatic events sometimes produces the opposite effect of repression. People *cannot* forget the events. One of the most commonly cited examples of this form of *post-traumatic stress disorder* is the so-called Vietnam Syndrome. Request interested students to research the painful flashbacks experienced by many Vietnam veterans and nurses. If possible, you might encourage students to interview some vets about this experience. Have students share their findings in papers presented to the class. (Arrange for release forms and permission to quote from the interviews.)

tative of society. In a healthy person the ego, the "I," is strong enough to handle the struggle (Hall, 1954).

Freud was also the first psychologist to claim that infancy and childhood are critical times for forming a person's basic character structure. He felt that personality was well formed by the time the child entered school and that subsequent growth consisted of elaborating this basic structure.

Evaluating Freud's Contribution

Freud was the first major social scientist to propose a unified theory to understand and explain human behavior. No theory that has followed has been more complete, more complex, or more controversial. Some psychologists treat Freud's writings as a sacred text—if Freud said it, it must be so. At the other extreme, many have accused Freud of being unscientific—of proposing a theory that is too complex ever to be proved true or false.

In 1977, Seymour Fisher and Roger Greenberg published *The Scientific Credibility of Freud's Theories and Therapy,* a book that summarized more than 50 years of research on Freud's ideas. Some parts of his theory held up well. In one test of unconscious influences, a group of male subjects had electrodes attached to them and were told they would experience a painful shock at some time during the experiment. As you might expect, this raised their anxiety level considerably. While viewing a variety of word pairs such as *sham duck* or *worst cottage* presented briefly on a screen, these subjects were likely to make verbal slips such as *damn shock* or *cursed wattage.* Subjects in a control group not exposed to the threat of shock made no such slips (Motley, 1985). The finding has been confirmed in a number of other studies.

Other Freudian beliefs were not supported by evidence. For example, psychoanalysis (a form of therapy Freud proposed in which a person spends years examining the unconscious basis of his problems) seems to be no more effective than other forms of psychotherapy that are simpler, cheaper, and less time-consuming.

Fisher and Greenberg concluded: "When we add up the totals from our research, balancing the positive against the negative, we find that Freud has fared rather well. But like all theorists, he has proved in the long run to have far from a perfect score. He seems to have been right about a respectable number of issues, but he was also wrong about some important things" (p. 396).

In Freud's Footsteps

Freud's revolutionary ideas attracted many followers, and a number of these psychoanalysts came to develop important theories of their own.

Carl Jung. At one time, Carl Jung was Freud's closest associate. But when Freud and Jung started to argue about psychoanalytic theory, their personal relationship became strained. Finally, they stopped speaking to each other entirely, a mere seven years after they met.

Jung disagreed with Freud on two major points. First, he took a more positive view of human nature, believing that people try to develop their po-

FIGURE 11.4

Carl G. Jung was one of the most mystical and metaphysical of the pioneer theorists. **What are archetypes?**

CONNECTIONS: PSYCHOLOGY AND SOCIAL STUDIES

Tell students that the 20th century was turned upside down by the theories of two individuals—Sigmund Freud and Karl Marx. In commenting on these two historic figures, the director of the Freud Museum in London quipped: "Given world events, I'd say Freud is in better shape than Marx." Assign students to write a short paragraph assessing the meaning of this statement. Do they agree or disagree? Students should back up their opinions from articles written in the 1990s on the influence of these figures.

■ **Cooperative Learning Activity.** Organize students into small groups. Have each group explore some of the dreams that they have had personally or know about through friends. Instruct them to write down any common images that appear in these dreams. *(For example, some people dream that they are flying. Others experience a sense of swimming. Still others dream of heroic conquests.)* With the class, explore what, if any, images *all* the groups noted. Ask: Does this demonstration influence your opinion of Jung's theory of collective unconscious? Why or why not? What other experiments might you propose to evaluate this theory further? *(A possibility is a "dream poll" with forced-choice answers. For example: "Have you ever dreamed that you were flying?")*

FIGURE 11.5

Alfred Adler's writings on psychotherapy offer more optimism and practicality than those of Freud or Jung. His intuitive and common-sense approach to human life has greatly affected the thinking of psychologists throughout the century. **According to Adler, why did children develop an inferiority complex?**

tential as well as to handle their instinctual urges. Second, he distinguished between the personal unconscious, which was similar to Freud's idea of the unconscious, and the **collective unconscious,** which is a storehouse of instincts, urges, and memories of the entire human species down through history. He called these inherited, universal ideas **archetypes.** The same archetypes are present in every person. They reflect the common experiences of humanity with mothers, fathers, nature, war, and so on.

Jung went on to identify the archetypes by studying dreams and visions, paintings, poetry, folk stories, myths, and religions. He found that the same themes—the "archetypes"—appear again and again. For example, the story of Jack and the Beanstalk is essentially the same as the story of David and Goliath. Both tell how a small, weak, good person triumphs over a big, strong, bad person. Jung believed such stories are common and easy to understand because the situations they describe have occurred over and over again in human history and have been stored as archetypes in the unconscious of every human being (Jung, 1963).

Alfred Adler.   Like Jung, Alfred Adler was an associate of Freud who left his teacher in the early part of the twentieth century to develop his own approach to personality. Adler believed that the driving force in people's lives is a desire to overcome their feelings of inferiority. Classic examples are Demosthenes, who overcame a speech impediment by practicing speaking with pebbles in his mouth and became the greatest orator of ancient Greece; Napoleon, a short man who conquered Europe in the early 1800s; and Glenn Cunningham, an Olympic runner who lost his toes in a fire as a child and had to plead with doctors who wanted to amputate his legs because they thought he would never be able to use them again.

Everyone struggles with inferiority, said Adler. He describes a person who continually tries to compensate for their weakness and avoid feelings of inadequacy as having an **inferiority complex** (a term he introduced). Children first feel inferior because they are so little and so dependent on adults. Gradually they learn to do the things that older people can do. The satisfaction that comes from even such simple acts as walking or learning to use a spoon sets up a pattern of overcoming inadequacies, a pattern that lasts throughout life. Adler called these patterns *life styles*.

Adler believed that the way parents treat their children influences the styles of life they choose. Overpampering, in which the parents attempt to satisfy the child's every whim, tends to produce a self-centered person who has little regard for others and who expects everyone else to do what he or she wants. On the other hand, the child who is neglected by his or her parents may seek revenge by becoming an angry, hostile person. Both the pampered and the neglected child tend to grow into adults who lack confidence in their ability to meet the demands of life. Ideally, said Adler, a child should learn self-reliance and courage from the father and generosity and a feeling for others from the mother (Adler, 1959).

Other Theorists.   Although Jung and Adler were the first figures to break with Freud, many others followed. Erich Fromm's theory centered around the need to belong and the loneliness freedom brings. Karen Horney

■ **Readings in Psychology.** As a guide to the reading on page 277, ask students to answer the following questions: (1) What is the typical cause(s) of anxiety in children? *(dependency vs. hostile impulses toward parents)* (2) How does this view differ from the Freudian view of children? *(rejects psychosexual motivations of conflict)*

CONNECTIONS: PSYCHOLOGY AND LITERATURE

Some experts who adhere to Jung's concept of *collective unconscious* have used similarities among creation myths as proof of Jung's theory. For example, many creation myths include the story of a great flood (similar to the story told in the Bible). Request volunteers to collect examples of creation myths from various peoples and/or nations. (Encourage students to include at least one Native American myth.) What, if any, similarities, can they find? What is student opinion of myths as a source of evidence on the evolution of the human mind?

READINGS IN PSYCHOLOGY

On Basic Anxiety and Hostility

The typical conflict leading to anxiety in a child is that between dependency on the parents. . . and hostile impulses against the parents. Hostility may be aroused in a child in many ways: by the parents' lack of respect for him; by unreasonable demands and prohibitions, by injustice; by unreliability; by suppression of criticism; by the parents dominating him and ascribing these tendencies to love. . . . If a child, in addition to being dependent on his parents, is grossly or subtly intimidated by them and hence feels that any expression of hostile impulses against them endangers his security, then the existence of such hostile impulses is bound to create

anxiety. . . . The resulting picture may look exactly like what Freud describes as the Oedipus complex: passionate clinging to one parent and jealously toward the other or toward anyone interfering with the claim of exclusive possession. . . . *But the dynamic structure of these attachments is entirely different from what Freud conceives as the Oedipus complex. They are an early manifestation of neurotic* [anxiety-based] *conflicts rather than a primarily sexual phenomenon.*

From Karen Horney, *The Neurotic Personality in Our Time.* New York: Norton, 1937.

stressed the importance of basic anxiety, which a child feels because she is helpless, and basic hostility, a resentment of one's parents that generally accompanies this anxiety (Figure 11.6). She also attacked several basic beliefs of Freud, including his emphasis on the importance of penis envy in the development of women. Erik Erikson accepted Freud's basic theory, but outlined eight psychosocial stages (described in Chapter 8) that every person goes through from birth to old age. These and other neo-Freudians have helped to keep psychoanalytic theory alive and debated (Friman, Allen, Kerwin, & Larzelere, 1993).

FIGURE 11.6

Psychologist Karen Horney argued that we are shaped by our interpersonal relationships, not as Freud argued, by biological drives. **What does she say creates children's hostile impulses toward parents?**

BEHAVIORAL THEORIES

American psychology has long been dominated by the study of human and animal learning. In the 1940s, Yale psychologists John Dollard and Neal Miller used learning theory to analyze Freud's ideas, but behaviorists did not endorse Freud. **Behaviorism** holds that the proper subject matter of psychology is objectively observable behavior. Behaviorists believe that as individuals differ in their learning experiences, they acquire different behaviors and hence different personalities.

B. F. Skinner: Radical Behaviorism

Although his radical behaviorism was not proposed as a theory of personality, B. F. Skinner had a major impact on personality theory. Skinner saw no need for a general concept of personality structure. He focused instead on precisely what causes a person to act in a specific way. It is a very

CRITICAL THINKING ACTIVITY

Conducting an Opinion Poll. Tell students that a 1993 poll conducted by *U.S. News & World Report* revealed that 81 percent of Americans thought that therapy was helpful in solving personal problems. Challenge students to survey student opinion on this topic. Have them use a forced-choice question so that results may be easily tallied. (For example: How often would you be willing to seek help from a psychotherapist to solve a personal problem? (a) never (b) only in dire situations (c) whenever needed (d) all the time. Ask: How does the student poll compare to the poll conducted by *U.S. News?*

Point out that critics of Skinner contend that behavior modification is a cruel attempt to manipulate and control people. Have students discuss whether the critics have a valid argument.

Answer to caption, Figure 11.7: Practitioners are not as concerned with understanding behavior as they are with finding out how to predict and control behavior.

Teacher Note. You might assign students to prepare a mock "recap" of behavioral learning as discussed in Chapter 2.

■ **Debating an Issue.** You might organize two student panels to consider the following question: Is human behavior determined from within or from without? One panel, led by Sigmund Freud, should argue for the "within" position. The other panel, led by B. F. Skinner, should argue for the "without" position. In a follow-up discussion, have students decide what, if any, middle ground can be found between these two personality theories. (OBJECTIVE 2)

FIGURE 11.7

B. F. Skinner's pioneering work in behavioral psychology resulted in a number of therapeutic techniques that were markedly successful in treating certain kinds of problems. **Why is radical behaviorism often termed "pragmatic"?**

pragmatic approach, one that is less concerned with understanding behavior than with predicting it and controlling it.

Consider the case of Ruben, a college sophomore who has been rather depressed lately. Freud would likely seek the roots of Ruben's unhappiness in events in his childhood. Skinner's approach is more direct. First, Skinner would reject the vague label "depressed." Instead he would ask, exactly how does Ruben behave? The answer may be that Ruben spends most of the day in his room, cuts all his classes, rarely smiles or laughs, and makes little effort to talk to anyone.

Next, Skinner would try to understand the **contingencies of reinforcement.** What conditions are maintaining these behaviors? What reinforces Ruben for never leaving his room? One hypothesis is that Ruben's girlfriend Brandi has unintentionally reinforced this behavior by spending a lot of time with him, trying to cheer him up. Perhaps she didn't pay much attention to Ruben before he was depressed. Note that Skinner's approach immediately suggests a hypothesis that can be proved true or false. If paying attention to Ruben encourages his moroseness, then ignoring him should decrease the likelihood of this behavior. So Brandi might try ignoring Ruben for a few days. If he then starts leaving his room—which she should reinforce—she has discovered the contingencies of reinforcement that govern Ruben's behavior. If not, she will know that the hypothesis is wrong and can try something else. Perhaps Ruben is glued to the TV in his room all day and has become a game-show addict. Take away the TV and you will find out whether that is the reinforcer.

At first, radical behaviorism may seem to imply that Ruben is somehow faking his depression so that he can watch "Wheel of Fortune," see more of his girlfriend, or whatever. Skinner does not make this assumption. Ruben may be entirely unaware of the rewards that are shaping his behavior. In any case, Ruben's feelings are beside the point. What matters is not what's going on inside Ruben's head, but what he is doing. The point is to specify his behavior and then find out what causes it.

Skinner's approach has become very popular among psychologists, partly because it is so pragmatic. It is a very action-oriented, very American approach. It can be described in this way: Don't get all agitated about what's wrong; just jump in and try to fix it. Radical behaviorism often works. Skinnerians have applied the techniques to a wide range of behaviors, from teaching pigeons to play Ping-Pong to teaching severely retarded people to dress themselves and take part in simple activities once believed beyond their abilities.

Average human behavior, too, can be changed with rewards and punishments. The success of radical behaviorists with average people has been more limited, partly because our reinforcers are so complex. For example, in several studies juvenile delinquents have been placed in rehabilitation communities in which they are rewarded with special privileges or food for behaving in certain ways—taking classes, cleaning up their rooms, and so on. In one such study, Buehler, Patterson, and Furness (1966) found that delinquent girls reinforced each other for breaking the rules and talking back. Sometimes, peer approval can be a more powerful reinforcer than any reward a psychologist can offer.

Demonstrating Reasoned Judgment. Working with several students, generate a list of 5–10 personal dilemmas or conflicts commonly encountered by adolescents. Present each of these dilemmas or conflicts to the class as a whole. Ask: Which of the personality theorists mentioned in this chapter would *best* help an individual handle each dilemma? For example, suppose an individual had a problem with low self-esteem. He or she refused to have a birthday party because "nobody would come." Who would students recommend for help: a Freudian, a behaviorist, or a humanistic psychologist? Why?

Albert Bandura: Social Learning Theories

Skinner emphasizes reinforcement in his description and explanation of personality. However, Albert Bandura and his colleague Richard Walters (1963) argued that personality is acquired not only by direct reinforcement of behavior but also by *observational learning*, or imitation. In observational learning, a person acquires a new behavior by watching the actions of another person. For example, to teach a child how to hit a baseball with a bat, you could hand the child the bat and ball and reinforce him every time he used the bat and ball correctly (operant conditioning). However, you would probably demonstrate the correct way to hold the bat and swing at the ball instead because this way the child would acquire the behavior more quickly. Bandura and Walters believe that much of a young child's individual behavior and personality is acquired by exposure to specific everyday models.

In Bandura's view, people are capable of directing their own behavior by their choice of models. In part, when your parents object to the company you keep, they are trying to change the models you use. The most effective models are those who are the most similar to and most admired by the observer. Thus, you are more likely to learn new behaviors from your friends than from your parents' friends.

Bandura has made significant contributions to the development of behavioral theories of personality. His social cognitive theory (1986) recognizes the interaction—called *reciprocal determinism*—that occurs among the observing individual, the behavior of that individual, and the environment in which the behavior occurs. One important concept that governs our behavior is our view of our ability to succeed, which Bandura called *self-efficacy*. You decide whether to go on a date by assessing the environment—weather, your parents' current state of mind, your potential date's recent behaviors—the effects of your own past behavior, and your long-term past successes and failures. This leads to the development of an expectancy of success. As the behavior unfolds, you also develop *outcome expectations*. As long as they remain positive, you'll keep trying.

COGNITIVE THEORY

Bandura anticipated another form of personality theory. Cognitive theory is based on analysis of our own overt mental activity. George Kelly has gone one step further than those before him. He ignores the impact of hidden urges, unconscious determinants, drives, motivation, and emotion. Instead, he bases his theory simply on an analysis of our perception of ourselves and our environment. In Kelly's view, our personality is our cognitions about ourself.

The fundamental postulate of Kelly's *Personal Construct Theory* of personality is that our "processes are psychologically channelized by the ways in which (each of us) anticipates events" (Kelly, 1991, p. 32). He is concerned with individual people and their cognitive behavior. He emphasizes psychological processes within each of us, noting that these processes are

---

MORE about...

Interpersonal Theories of Personality. Most theories of personality consider the person as an individual. Some psychologists, however, regard personality as a function of a person's social environment. One of the first of these thinkers was Harry Stack Sullivan.

Sullivan's ideas have been organized into a two-dimensional model. One dimension is *power*, which ranges from dominance at one end of the scale to submissiveness at the other. The second dimension is *friendliness*, which ranges from friendliness to hostility. Most behaviors can be described as a combination of these two dimensions. For example, "helpfulness" is a combination of dominance and friendliness; "trusting" is a combination of submissiveness and friendliness.

Researchers also noticed that a person's actions tend to elicit specific responses from other people. A behavior and its most likely response are said to be *complementary*. For example, most people will respond to a request for help (trusting) by offering advice (helping), regardless of how "helpful" they are as individuals. Thus, many behaviors result not simply from a person's personality but also from that person's social environment.

■ **Demonstration.** If students think carefully, they can probably cite cases in which they used behavior to elicit a specific response from another person. That is, they've probably learned how to project aspects of their personality as a form of control. Request volunteers to role-play situations in which they use friendliness, anger, or some other personality trait to mold the behavior of another person. For example: A student spots an attractive person that he or she would like to date. What aspects of his or her personality would he or she project to convince the person to accept the date—even before asked? Use this activity to discuss the social learning and interpersonal theories of Albert Bandura and Harry Stack Sullivan. (OBJECTIVE 2)

DID YOU KNOW?

The Boy Scouts and Girl Scouts were originally founded to promote moral behavior in young people through social interaction. Request interested students to research the history of these two organizations. They might present their findings in a Past-to-Present poster.

MEETING SPECIAL NEEDS

Study Strategy. Students with reading problems often have difficulty differentiating main ideas from details. Teach students to skim for a main idea by skimming through the first paragraph of "Albert Bandura: Social Learning Theories" and "Cognitive Theory." Tell them that main ideas are often found at the beginning or end of each paragraph. Sometimes more than one sentence has to be put together to come up with the main idea. (In this case the second sentence of each paragraph states the main idea.) Have students apply this technique to the lead paragraphs underneath each of the other theories mentioned in the chapter.

At A Glance

After students read through the list of tips, challenge them to write definitions of the terms *success* and *failure* from the point of view of a humanistic psychologist.

VISUAL INSTRUCTION

Ask if any students have ever heard the expression "tough love." Evolve a meaning of the term with the class. *(Taking strong measures—including leaving a person to his or her own destructive behavior—to bring about change.)* Ask: How do you think Maslow and other humanists might view "tough love"? What, if any, alternatives might they suggest? Which approach do you think works best in curbing potentially destructive behavior?
Answer to caption, Figure 11.8: exceptional people who have coped with problems effectively

At A Glance

IMPROVING YOUR SELF-IMAGE

If your self-image can stand a boost, try taking these steps toward greater self-confidence. As you're reading this list, remember what humanistic personality theorists believe: a positive self-image is at the heart of successful adjustment.

- Base your personal goals on an honest appraisal of your strengths and weaknesses. Trying to be something you're not can only weaken your self-image.
- Don't let guilt and shame determine your goals. Let positive thinking guide your decision making.
- Don't blame everything that goes wrong on yourself. Sometimes external events can play an equally important role.
- When others dismiss your views, keep in mind that events are interpreted in different ways by different people.
- When things go wrong, don't be too hard on yourself. Never think of yourself as a failure, stupid, or ugly.
- Accept criticism of the things you do, but don't allow people to criticize you as a person.
- Use your failures in a constructive way. They may be telling you to readjust your goals and start over in a new direction.
- Don't stay in a situation that makes you feel inadequate. If you can't change the situation, move on to something new.

Try these suggestions and you'll soon see that there's no better feeling than feeling good about yourself.

For more details, see Philip Zimbardo, *Shyness: What It Is, What to Do About It,* Reading, Mass.: Addison-Wesley, 1990.

FIGURE 11.8

Abraham Maslow, along with Carl Rogers and others, helped create a humanistic orientation toward the study of behavior by stressing growth and the realization of an individual's potential. **Who did Maslow study to develop his theory of personality?**

channeled. By that he means that there is organization to how we behave, governed by a network of potential, but limited responses. The emphasis is on the individual and his or her plans—including their biases, errors, mistakes, and false conclusions. The primary feature of these personally constructed ideas about the world and how to behave in it is the individual's anticipations—or predictions—about his or her world. All of this is focused on governing the individual's behavior in real events.

Kelly goes on to develop 11 corollaries involving our individuality in how we develop our personal constructs. His view takes an optimistic view of humans. In his theory, we are masters rather than victims of our destiny. Our personal constructs tend to be stable, but we are able to change them in light of new evidence. All in all, Kelly's is a very flexible model of human behavior.

COOPERATIVE LEARNING ACTIVITY

Assign students to create an illustrated self-help book using the ten tips in the At a Glance feature. Using original sketches, staged photographs, or magazine clippings, assign students to compile a one- or two-page spread of pictures that conveys the meaning of each tip. Captions beneath each picture should explain its connection to the tip. Display these books for other students to examine.

HUMANISTIC PSYCHOLOGY

One might look at **humanistic psychology** as a rebellion against the rather negative, pessimistic view of human nature that dominated personality theory in the early 1900s. Psychoanalysts emphasized the struggle to control primitive, instinctual urges on the one hand, and to come to terms with the authoritarian demands of the superego or conscience on the other. The behaviorists, too, saw human behavior in mechanistic terms: our actions are shaped by rewards and punishments. Humanistic psychologists object to both approaches on the grounds that they demean human beings—Freud by emphasizing irrational and destructive instincts, Skinner by emphasizing external causes of behavior. In contrast, the humanists stress our relative freedom from instinctual pressures (compared to other animals) and our ability to create and live by personal standards.

Humanistic psychology is founded on the belief that all human beings strive for **self-actualization**—that is, the realization of our potentialities as unique human beings. Self-actualization involves an openness to a wide range of experiences; an awareness of and respect for one's own and other people's uniqueness; accepting the responsibilities of freedom and commitment; a desire to become more and more authentic or true to oneself; and an ability to grow.

Abraham Maslow: Growth and Self-Actualization

Abraham Maslow was one of the guiding spirits of the humanistic movement in psychology. He deliberately set out to create what he called "a third force in psychology" as an alternative to psychoanalysis and behaviorism. Maslow tried to base his theory of personality on studies of healthy, creative, self-actualizing people who fully utilize their talents and potential, rather than on studies of disturbed individuals.

When Maslow decided to study the most productive individuals he could find—in history as well as in his social and professional circles—he was breaking new ground. The theories of personality, discussed earlier, were developed by psychotherapists after years of working with people who could not cope with everyday frustrations and conflicts. In contrast, Maslow was curious about people who not only coped with everyday problems effectively, but who also created exceptional lives for themselves, people like Abraham Lincoln, Albert Einstein, and Eleanor Roosevelt.

Maslow found that, although these people sometimes had great emotional difficulties, they adjusted in ways that allowed them to become highly productive. Maslow also found that self-actualized individuals share a number of traits (Table 11.1). First, they *perceive reality accurately*, unlike most people who, because of prejudices and wishful thinking, perceive it rather inaccurately. Self-actualized people also *accept themselves*, other people, and their environments more readily than "average" people do. Without realizing it, most of us project our hopes and fears onto the world around us. We deny our own shortcomings and try to rationalize or change things we do not like about ourselves. Self-actualizing individuals accept themselves as they are.

CONNECTIONS: PSYCHOLOGY AND SOCIAL STUDIES

Explain that the study of history includes a subfield known as *psychohistory*. This field of inquiry applies personality theories to major figures from the past. Among those studied are Napoleon, Adolf Hitler, and Richard Nixon. Assign students to choose a figure from the past, male or female, and write a paper analyzing that person's life in psychological terms. (Instruct students to use one of the personality theories mentioned in this chapter.)

■ **Expressive Writing.** Tell students that one of the key concepts in Maslow's humanistic theory is the idea of *peak performance*—a moment when all one's personal powers, gratitude, and sense of fulfillment come together. To explore this concept further, instruct students to complete the following writing assignment as described by Maslow himself.

I would like you to think of the most wonderful experiences of your life; . . . perhaps from being in love, or from listening to music or suddenly 'being hit' by a book or painting, or some great creative moment. First list these. And then try to tell me how you feel in such acute moments, how you feel differently from the way you feel at other times, how you are at the moment a different person.

Request volunteers to share their writing. Ask: How does each experience described fit Maslow's definition of self-actualization? Would you describe the emotions of "peak performance" as an *altered state of consciousness*? (See Chapter 7.) Why or why not?

VISUAL INSTRUCTION

Point out that Rogers believed that a therapist should provide unconditional positive support to help a patient develop a positive sense of self-worth.
Answer to caption, Figure 11.9: an individual's image of who he or she is and important values

---

TABLE 11.1 • Characteristics of Self-Actualized Persons

They are realistically oriented.	They identify with humanity.
They accept themselves, other people, and the natural world for what they are.	Their intimate relationships with a few specially-loved people tend to be profound and deeply emotional rather than superficial.
They have a great deal of spontaneity.	Their values and attitudes are democratic.
They are problem-centered rather than self-centered.	They do not confuse means with ends.
They have an air of detachment and a need for privacy.	Their sense of humor is philosophical rather than hostile.
They are autonomous and independent.	They have a great fund of creativeness.
Their appreciation of people and things is fresh rather than stereotyped.	They resist conformity to the culture.
Most of them have had profound mystical or spiritual experiences although not necessarily religious in character.	They transcend the environment rather than just coping with it.

Source: Abraham Maslow, *Motivation and Personality* (New York: Harper & Row, 1970).

FIGURE 11.9

Carl Rogers had a considerable impact on modern psychology and on society. He emphasized personal experience rather than drives and instincts. **How did Rogers define "self"?**

Secure in themselves, healthy individuals are more *problem-centered* than self-centered. They are able to focus on tasks in a way that people concerned about maintaining and protecting their self-image cannot. They are more likely to base decisions on ethical principles than on calculations of the possible costs or benefits to themselves. They have a strong sense of *identity with other human beings,* and they have a strong *sense of humor,* but laugh with people, not at them.

Maslow also found that self-actualizing people are exceptionally *spontaneous.* They are not trying to be anything other than themselves, and they know themselves well enough to maintain their integrity in the face of opposition, unpopularity, and rejection. They are *autonomous.* They *value privacy* and frequently seek out solitude. This is not to say that they are detached or aloof. But rather than trying to be popular, they focus on deep, *loving relationships with the few people* to whom they are truly close.

Finally, the people Maslow studied had a rare ability to appreciate even the simplest things. They approached their lives with a *sense of discovery* that made each day a new day. They rarely felt bored or uninterested. Given to moments of intense joy and satisfaction, or "peak experiences," they got high on life itself. Maslow believed this to be both a cause and an effect of their creativity and originality (Maslow, 1970).

Maslow believed that to become self-actualizing a person must first satisfy his or her basic, primary needs—for food and shelter, physical safety, love and belonging, and self-esteem. Of course, to some extent the ability to satisfy these needs is often beyond our control. Still, no amount of wealth, talent, beauty, or any other asset can totally shield someone from frustration and disappointment. All people have to adjust to maintain themselves and to grow.

CRITICAL THINKING ACTIVITY

Synthesizing Information. Working in pairs, have students review Kohlberg's six levels of moral development in Chapter 8. Using this theory of human development, at what stage would students place the self-actualized persons described by Maslow? *(probably stage 6)* What items in Table 11.1 support students' choice? *(Answers will vary. Three examples of stage 6 thinking include: "They do not confuse the means with ends." "They resist conformity to the culture." "They transcend environment rather than just trying to cope with it.")*

Many psychologists have criticized Maslow's work. His claim that human nature is "good," for example, has been called an intrusion of subjective values into what should be a neutral science. The levels of specific needs, such as physical contact comfort, also discussed in Chapter 6, have not been defined (Feist, 1985). His study of self-actualizing people has been criticized because the sample was chosen on the basis of Maslow's own subjective criteria. How can one identify self-actualized people without knowing the characteristics of such people? But then, if one knows these characteristics to begin with, what sense does it make to list them as if they were the results of an empirical study?

Carl Rogers: Your Organism and Your Self

The people Carl Rogers counsels are "clients," not "patients." The word "patient" implies illness, a negative label that Rogers rejects. As a therapist, Rogers is primarily concerned with the detours on the path to self-actualization or "full functioning," as he calls it. Rogers believes that many people suffer from a conflict between what they value in themselves and what they learn other people value in them. He explains how this conflict develops this way: There are two sides or parts to every person. One is the **organism,** which is the whole of a person, including his or her body. Rogers believes that the organism is constantly struggling to become more and more complete and perfect. Anything that furthers this end is good: The organism wants to become everything it can possibly be. For example, children want to learn to walk and run because their bodies are built for these activities. People want to shout and dance and sing because their organisms contain the potential for these behaviors. Different people have different potentialities, but every person wants to realize them, to make them real, whatever they are. It is of no value to be able to paint and not to do it. It is of no value to be able to make witty jokes and not to do so. Whatever you can do, you want to do—and do as well as possible. This optimism about human nature is the essence of humanism.

Each individual also has what Rogers calls a **self.** The self is essentially your image of who you are and what you value—in yourself, in other people, in life in general. The self is something you acquire gradually over the years by observing how other people react to you. At first, the most significant other person in your life is your mother or whoever rears you. You want her approval or **positive regard.** You ask yourself, "How does she see me?" If the answer is, "She loves me. She likes what I am and what I do," you begin to develop positive regard for yourself.

But often this does not happen. The image you see reflected in your mother's eyes and actions is mixed. Whether or not she approves of you often depends on whether you spit up your baby food or do your homework on time. In other words, she places conditions on her love: *If* you do what she wants, she likes you. Young and impressionable, you accept these verdicts and incorporate **conditions of worth** into yourself. You begin to see yourself as good and worthy only if you act in certain ways. You've learned from your parents and from other people who are significant to you that unless you meet certain conditions you will not be loved.

■ **Debating an Issue.** You might assign students to debate the following topic: *Resolved*—That human beings have little free will in determining the shape of their personalities. Appoint some students to argue the *pro* position, using examples of defense mechanisms as evidence. Direct other students to argue the *con* position, using the ideas and experiments of Carl Rogers. (OBJECTIVES 2, 3)

■ **Writing an Advertisement.** Organize the students into groups, and assign them to review the major schools of personality theory discussed in the book. Then have each group design a 20-line advertisement in which a therapist from one of these schools announces the opening of a new clinic. Collect these advertisements, and read them aloud. Challenge students to guess the school of thought reflected by each ad. (OBJECTIVES 1–3)

STUDY AND WRITING SKILLS

Review Carl Rogers' ideas on self-image. Then have students complete the following statement: "My greatest potential as a person lies in my skill/ability/talent to _____ ." Tell students to list as many examples of potential as possible. Moreover, they can ask friends or families for their suggestions too. If suggestions feel comfortable, then students should use them. Based on this list and Rogers' definition of positive self-worth, have students write a description of themselves. (Tip: Do not be surprised if some students balk. Many people find it a far easier task to take a look at their negative features.)

■ **Cooperative Learning Activity.** Write the following list of traits on an overhead transparency.

Happy—Sad
Responsible—Irresponsible
Shy—Adventurous
Confident—Insecure
Warm—Cold
Friendly—Reserved
Relaxed—Tense
Active—Passive
Easygoing—Controlled
Serious—Happy-Go-Lucky
Sensitive—Callous
Open—Closed
Practical—Imaginative
Narrow-Minded—Broad-Minded
Honest—Devious

Show this list to students, and ask them to write down the word in each pair that best describes them most of the time. Next, ask students to pick someone to complete the same activity for them. (You might repeat this two or three times.) Ask students to compare their self-evaluation with the evaluation of others. What, if any differences, emerged? Encourage students to explore any discrepancies between the student's list of traits and the traits assigned by others. (OBJECTIVES 1, 2)

Rogers's work as a therapist convinced him that people cope with conditions of worth by rejecting or denying parts of their organism that do not fit their self-concept. For example, if your mother grew cold and distant whenever you became angry, you learned to deny yourself the right to express or perhaps even feel anger. Being angry "isn't you." In effect, you are cutting off a part of your organism or whole being; you are allowing yourself to experience and express only part of your being.

The greater the gap between the self and the organism, the more limited and defensive a person becomes. Rogers believes the cure for this situation—and the way to prevent it from ever developing—is **unconditional positive regard.** If significant others (parents, friends, a mate, perhaps a therapist) convey the feeling that they value you for what you are, in your entirety, you will gradually learn to grant yourself the same unconditional positive regard. The need to limit yourself declines or never develops in the first place. You will be able to accept your organism and become open to *all* your feelings, thoughts, and experiences—and hence to other people. This is what Rogers meant by **fully functioning.** The organism and the self are one: The individual is free to develop all his or her potentialities. Like Maslow and other humanistic psychologists, Rogers believes that self-regard and regard for others go together, and that the human potentials for good and for self-fulfillment outweigh the potentials for evil and despair (Rogers, 1951, 1961, 1980).

TRAIT THEORIES

Vijay spends many hours talking to other people, circulates freely at parties, and strikes up conversations while he waits in the dentist's office. Anjuli, though, spends more time with books than with other people and seldom goes to parties. In common-sense terms, we say that Vijay is friendly and Anjuli is not. Friendliness is a personality **trait** and some theorists have argued that studying such traits in detail is the best approach to solving the puzzle of human behavior.

One psychologist has defined a trait as "any relatively enduring way in which one individual differs from another" (Guilford, 1959). A trait, then, is a predisposition to respond in a certain way in many different kinds of situations—in a dentist's office, at a party, or in a classroom. More than any other personality theorists, trait theorists emphasize and try to explain the consistency of a normal, healthy individual's behavior in different situations.

Trait theorists generally make two basic assumptions about these underlying sources of consistency. First, every trait applies to all people. For example, everyone can be classified as more or less dependent. Second, these descriptions can be quantified. We might, for example, establish a scale on which an extremely dependent person scores 1 while a very independent person scores 10.

Thus, every trait can be used to classify people. Aggressiveness, for example, is a continuum: A few people are extremely aggressive or extreme-

---

CONNECTIONS: PSYCHOLOGY AND LITERATURE

Read aloud the following quotes.

- "The face is the image of the soul." (Cicero)
- "I am not much in fear of these fat, sleek fellows, but rather of those pale, thin ones." (Julius Caesar)
- "Cassius hath a lean and hungry look; he thinks too much: such men are

dangerous." (from *Julius Caesar,* by Shakespeare)

Ask: Upon what basis are each of these personality judgments based? *(physical appearance)* To what extent do people still judge personality by physical types? What are the limitations of this attitude?

ly unaggressive, and most of us fall somewhere in the middle. We understand people by specifying their traits, and we use traits to predict people's future behavior. If you were hiring someone to sell vacuum cleaners, you would probably choose Vijay rather than Anjuli. This choice would be based on two assumptions: that friendliness is a useful trait for salespeople and that a person who is friendly in the dentist's office and at parties will be friendly in another situation—namely, in the salesroom.

Trait theorists go beyond this kind of common-sense analysis to try to discover the underlying sources of the consistency of human behavior. What is the best way to describe the common features of Vijay's behavior? Is he friendly, or socially aggressive, or interested in people, or sure of himself, or something else? What is the underlying *trait* that best explains his behavior?

Most (but not all) trait theorists believe that a few basic traits are central for all people. An underlying trait of self-confidence, for example, might be used to explain more superficial characteristics like social aggressiveness and dependency. If this were true, it would mean that a person would be dependent because he or she lacked self-confidence. Psychologists who accept this approach set out on their theoretical search for basic traits with very few assumptions.

This is very different from the starting point of other personality theorists we have considered. Freud, for example, began with a well-defined theory of instincts. When he observed that some people were stingy, he set out to explain this in terms of his theory. Trait theorists would not start by trying to understand stinginess. Rather, they would try to determine whether stinginess was a trait. That is, they would try to find out whether people who were stingy in one type of situation were also stingy in others. Then they might ask whether stinginess is a sign of a more basic trait like possessiveness: Is the stingy person also very possessive in relationships? Thus, the first and foremost question for the trait theorists is: What behaviors go together?

Instead of theories telling them *where* to look, trait theorists have complex and sophisticated methods that tell them *how* to look. These methods begin with the statistical technique of correlation—discussed in Chapter 20—using one set of scores to predict another. If I know that someone talks to strangers in line at the supermarket, can I predict that he will be likely to strike up conversations in a singles bar? Such predictions are never perfect. Perhaps the reason Vijay is so outspoken in the dentist's office is that he's terrified, and jabbering to strangers is the only way he can distract himself from the image of a 16-foot drill. Sometimes, actions that look like the public demonstration of one trait may really reflect something else entirely.

Gordon Allport: Identifying Traits

Gordon W. Allport was an influential psychologist in his day. Many of his ideas of personality are similar to those of humanistic psychologists. For example, Allport emphasizes the positive, rational, and conscious reasons why we act the way we do. But he is most famous for his pioneering work on traits (Allport, 1961).

> **Most trait theorists believe a few basic traits are central for all people.**

■ **Research.** Some psychologists, such as Hans Eysenck and Ronald Grossarth-Maticek, see a strong connection between personality traits and some diseases. They connect worry and negative attitudes, for example, to cancer. You might request volunteers to research the recent interest in the mind-body connection in disease. (Suggest that students consult the *Readers' Guide to Periodical Literature* for articles listed under the heading of "Health." Also, they might read "The Late Word from the Personality Front" in *The Story of Psychology* by Morton Hunt.)

Have students report their findings in a news story format that might be distributed to the rest of the class.

■ **Writing an Advertisement.** Ask each student to pick the career or profession that most interests them at this time. Using the help-wanted ads collected in the Extra Credit Activity as a model, assign students to write a help-wanted ad for that position. Descriptions should include personality traits best suited for the field. Tell students to review the ads against their own personality. Do their interests match their personality? Why or why not? Using Maslow or Rogers as a guide, what techniques could students use to overcome personality "shortcomings"? (OBJECTIVES 1, 2)

LAB EXPERIMENTS AND DEMONSTRATIONS

Copy the following descriptions on an overhead transparency, and show them to the class:

Extravert: 1. needs and likes to be with people 2. energizes self through interaction with others 3. needs and wants many friends 4. interested in what is happening in the external world 5. tends to be expressive 6. tolerates criticism well 7. eager to jump into a new situation

Introvert: 1. needs to have "space" (territorial) 2. energizes self by being alone 3. limits friendships 4. interested in internal reactions 5. tends to be hesitant to express ideas/feelings 6. takes criticism "personally" 7. often reluctant to jump into a new situation

Ask: According to these traits, are you an extravert or an introvert? Or does it depend upon the situation you're in? If so, describe these situations.

ASSESS

Check for Understanding

Check for understanding by having students verbally explain the similarities and differences among the personality theories discussed in this chapter. Encourage them to refer to specific entries on the chart suggested in the margin note on page 270.

Reteach

▮▮▮ Have students complete the Chapter 11 Study Guide Activity. For extended review, assign the Chapter 11 Review Activity as homework or an in-class assignment.

Enrich

▮▮▮ Have students complete the Chapter 11 Application Activity.

Evaluate

▮▮▮ Administer and grade the Chapter Test. Two forms are available should you wish to give different tests to different students/classes.

▮ Use the Understanding Psychology Testmaker to create a customized test.

CLOSE

Write the name of a popular song title made famous by Sammy Davis, Jr. on the chalkboard: "I Gotta Be Me." Ask: According to what you have learned about personality theory, what is the "me" side of self? (*You might refresh student memory of the discussion of the "I" and "me" in the side margin note on page 267 of the TWE.*)

PSYCHOLOGY UPDATE

The Robust Five. Over the years, trait theorists have devised a number of ways to measure personality. Each involves a different number of traits or factors.

Trait psychologists have shown that five traits appear repeatedly in different research studies. Often called the "five robust factors," or "the big five," they are:

Extraversion is associated with warmth, talkativeness, being energetic. The opposite of this dimension is introversion, meaning quiet or reserved.

Agreeableness involves being sympathetic to others, kind, trusting. The opposite is cruel, nontrusting.

Conscientiousness identifies individuals who are dutiful, dedicated to completing tasks, organized and responsible.

Openness to experience describes people who are open-minded, willing to try intellectual experiences, new ideas, or creative experiences.

Emotional stability identifies individuals who experience things relatively easily and without upset (John, 1990; Costa, McCrae, & Dye, 1991).

Do these characteristics describe you? If not, what other characteristics would you want to add?

A trait, Allport said, makes a wide variety of situations "functionally equivalent"; that is, it enables a person to realize that many different situations call for a similar response. Thus, traits are responsible for the relative consistency of every individual's behavior. Allport provided classification schemes for distinguishing among kinds of traits. For example, he was concerned with emphasizing the differences between two major ways of studying personality. In the *nomothetic* approach, you study large groups of people in the search for general laws of personality. This can be contrasted with the *idiographic* approach, in which you study a particular person in detail, emphasizing his or her uniqueness. On the basis of this distinction, Allport defined *common* traits as those that apply to everyone and *individual* traits as those that apply more to a specific person.

An example of the latter is found in Allport's book *Letters from Jenny* (1965), which consists of 172 letters a woman whom Allport calls Jenny Masterson wrote to a friend. Jenny reveals herself in these letters, which she wrote between the ages of 58 and 70, as a complex and fiercely independent woman. In his preface to the book, Allport writes:

> [The] fascination of the *Letters* lies in their challenge to the reader (whether psychologist or layman) to "explain" Jenny—if he can. Why does an intelligent lady behave so persistently in a self-defeating manner?

Allport's own attempt to understand Jenny began with a search for the underlying traits that would explain the consistency of her behavior.

Hans Eysenck: Dimensions of Personality

More recent theorists have concentrated on what Allport called *common traits*, which they try to quantify in a precise, scientific manner. Their primary tool in this task has been an extremely sophisticated mathematical technique called **factor analysis** which describes the extent to which different personality variables are related.

Using factor analysis of personality data, Hans Eysenck (1970), an English psychologist, concluded that there are two basic dimensions of personality. The first dimension, *stability*, refers to the degree to which people have control over their feelings. At the emotionally-stable end of the personality spectrum is a person who is easy-going, relaxed, well adjusted, and even-tempered. At the anxiety-dominated end of the spectrum is the moody, anxious, and restless person. Eysenck's second dimension was actually identified years earlier by Carl Jung as *extraversion versus introversion*. **Extraverts** are sociable, outgoing, active, lively people. They enjoy parties and seek excitement. On the other end of the dimension are **introverts**, who are more thoughtful, reserved, passive, unsociable, and quiet.

Years after he identified the first two dimensions, Eysenck added a third, *psychoticism*. At this end of the dimension are self-centered, hostile and aggressive people, who act without much thought. Individuals at the other end of this dimension have what Freud might label high superego. They tend to be socially sensitive, high on caring and empathy, and easy people with whom to work (Eysenck, 1970, 1990).

CRITICAL THINKING ACTIVITY

Applying Concepts. Ask students to pick one of their favorite television or entertainment figures. Challenge them to describe the individual in terms of the "Big Five." Have students read their descriptions aloud, without naming the celebrity. Challenge the rest of the class to guess the person's identity based upon personality traits alone. (You might allow students to ask additional questions to probe for other clues. But all questions should be phrased in terms of behavioral characteristics. For example: "Is this person known for on-stage temper tantrums?")

SUMMARY

Use the following outline as a tool for reviewing this chapter. Copy the outline onto your own paper, leaving spaces between headings to make notes about key concepts.

I. What Personality Theorists Try to Do

II. Psychoanalytic Theories
  A. Sigmund Freud and the Unconscious
  B. The Id, Ego, and Superego
  C. Defense Mechanisms
  D. Evaluating Freud's Contribution
  E. In Freud's Footsteps

III. Behavioral Theories
  A. B. F. Skinner: Radical Behaviorism
  B. Albert Bandura: Social Learning Theories

IV. Cognitive Theory

V. Humanistic Psychology
  A. Abraham Maslow: Growth and Self-Actualization
  B. Carl Rogers: Your Organism and Your Self

VI. Trait Theories
  A. Gordon Allport: Identifying Traits
  B. Hans Eysenck: Dimensions of Personality

CONCEPTS AND VOCABULARY

1. Explain the functions that personality theories serve. List four major schools of thought among personality theorists.

2. According to Freud, what two factors have enormous impact on adult personality and behavior? Name the sources of the energy in the human personality. Explain Freud's three structures of the personality. Can you match the words *can*, *want*, and *should* to these three structures?

3. Give the techniques people use to defend against anxiety and to distort reality. What technique are you likely to be using if you pout? What technique might you be using if you think a teacher is angry at you because he or she gave a hard test but the teacher is not actually angry?

4. Who was the first major social scientist to propose a unified theory of human behavior? Who were two of his followers? How did they differ from him?

5. Give the name Jung gave to inherited, universal ideas. Explain their significance. What term did Adler introduce? Explain its significance.

6. What psychologist has had a major impact on personality theory without actually proposing a theory of personality? What was his approach called? Was he concerned about understanding behavior?

7. Why was B. F. Skinner's approach to personality popular among psychologists?

8. How do Bandura and Walters believe personality is acquired?

9. Name the branch of psychology that developed in reaction to psychoanalytic theory and behaviorism. This theory was founded on what belief? Who were the men who founded this approach?

10. List five characteristics of a self-actualized person.

11. According to Rogers there are two parts to every person. Name them. What situation creates a gap between these two parts? Explain the cure for this situation.

12. Why does Rogers object to the use of the term "patient" to refer to a person who seeks counseling?

13. What does Rogers mean by the term "fully functioning"?

14. Give the two basic assumptions behind trait theories. Explain.

287

11. organism and self; conditions of worth; unconditional positive regard

12. because it implies illness; negative label

13. refers to a situation where the organism and self are one

14. that every trait applies to all people; that these trait descriptions can be quantified

15. nomothetic, idiographic

16. see page 286

17. stability, extraversion vs. introversion, psychoticism

Critical Thinking

1. Request volunteers to share their lists. Note similarities and differences among lists. Encourage additional input from students.

2. Respect student privacy on this question. The goal is to distinguish between inherited and acquired characteristics. (You

ANSWERS

Concepts and Vocabulary

1. Functions: to discover patterns in the way people behave, to explain differences between individuals, to explore how people conduct their lives, and to determine how life can be improved; Schools: psychoanalytic, behaviorist, humanistic, trait theories

2. unconscious motives and feelings that people have as children; life drives and death drives; id, ego, and superego; id = want, ego = can, superego = should

3. defense mechanisms; regression; projection

4. Freud; Jung and Adler; Jung: distinguished two types of unconscious; Adler: replaced Freud's life and death drives with the drive to overcome feelings of inferiority

5. archetypes; inferiority complex; answers will vary

6. B. F. Skinner; radical behaviorism; more concerned with predicting and controlling behavior than understanding it

7. because it is pragmatic, action-oriented; because it often works

8. by observational learning or imitation as well as by direct reinforcement

9. humanistic psychology; that all human beings strive for self-actualization; Maslow and Rogers

10. see pages 281–282

might also talk about traits in terms of generational differences produced by the times.)

3. Answers will vary, but you might help students do the activity by encouraging them to research theories, noting what they accept and reject. This can form a basis for students' own system-building.

4. Traits will vary along with the magazine chosen. The goal of the activity is to identify personality patterns and to determine if any of these patterns apply to students' own lives.

Applying Knowledge

1. This activity requires students first to identify a "role model." Then they must apply three theories of personality as factors to explain the attributes of the person(s) chosen. Make sure students explain reasons they chose one theorist over the others.

2. You might explore whether the collages depict the social "I," private "me," or a combination of both.

3. Warn students not to violate privacy. The goal is to apply theoretical concepts to analyze human behavior. You might also allow some students to challenge the use of defense mechanisms to explain human behavior— some psychologists have questioned or modified them (especially as originally stated by Freud).

4. Descriptions will vary along with the theory and person chosen. The goal is to apply a theory as a tool of analysis.

5. Answers will vary. After each entry, students should cite reasons for selecting a comment.

288

15. What are Allport's two major ways of studying personality?

16. Explain the meaning of "the robust five."

17. Name and describe the three primary dimensions of Eysenck's theory of personality.

CRITICAL THINKING

1. **Analyze.** List the qualities and traits that you think comprise the "healthy" or "self-actualized" person. If this is done in class, you can see how your ideas of health and self-actualization differ from those of the other class members.

2. **Evaluate.** What are the key features of your own personality? What are the key features of the personalities of each of your parents? Compare your personality with those of your parents. There will be both similarities and differences. Because one's parents are necessarily such highly influential forces in a young person's development, it may be of greater interest to note the chief differences in personalities. Then try to identify the factors responsible for those differences. For example, what key individuals or events have influenced or redirected the course of your life or changed your habits of living? How have society's institutions affected you?

3. **Synthesize.** Develop your own theory of personality by answering the following questions. How does a person acquire a personality? What are the most important motivations for people? Why are people different? How can people change their personalities?

4. **Evaluate.** Read a weekly magazine that describes people and their lives and underline the adjectives used to describe the personalities of the people featured in the articles. Then make a list of these traits, noting how many times each trait or adjective was used in all of the magazine articles. Are there some traits that appear more frequently than others? How important would

288

you say these traits are in your own life? Are there characteristics that seem to be important to you but are not included in your list?

APPLYING KNOWLEDGE

1. The text contains a list of characteristics that Maslow found to be representative of people whom he described as "self-actualized." From among your acquaintances, choose a few whom you especially respect or admire for "doing their own thing," people who achieve satisfaction by being who and what they are. Ask them to list what they see as their distinguishing personality characteristics. Compare their answers and your observations with Maslow's list. In addition, compare this information with Jung's idea of individuation and Roger's fully functioning person. Do the theories adequately describe the characteristics you admire? Are they consistent with them?

2. Make a collage that depicts your personality, using pictures and words from magazines and newspapers. For example, include your likes, dislikes, hobbies, personality traits, appearance, and so on.

3. Listen to conversations of several friends, relatives, teachers, and so on. Try to identify their use of defense mechanisms and write down the circumstances surrounding their use. Try to listen to your own conversations and do the same for yourself. Why do you think people use defense mechanisms? Is it easier to identify defense mechanisms in yourself or in others? Why?

4. Select a newspaper or news magazine article that describes the activities or accomplishments of a person—for example, a popular sports figure, convicted criminal, politician, or business person. Then select a particular personality theory to describe the person's behavior and outlook on life. You may have to go beyond the material in the article to make a convincing argument for the theoretical view

6. The goal of this activity is to show differences between the two approaches. (One relies on environmental conditioning/retraining, the other relies on building a positive self-image.)

Analyzing Viewpoints

1. The goal of this activity is the use of labels as organizing tools—that is, as agents to arrange data. Students should note the limitations of any

label, especially the tendency to gloss over individual differences.

2. Student papers will vary. The goal is the effective use of evidence to support a premise or position.

Beyond the Classroom

1. Debaters should use arguments that accurately reflect the theories of each position chosen, rather than students' own personal theories.

you have selected. Then, enter into a classroom discussion with other students who have selected different personality theories to explain the same individual's personality. How do these theoretical views of the person differ? Decide which view best explains the person's actions.

5. Look and listen for "Freudian slips." Write them down and try to determine the reasons for each slip.

6. Imagine that you have a friend who is having problems in school. He is failing several subjects and spends very little time doing homework or studying for tests. He prefers to watch television. Your friend's parents do not understand why he is this way. Based on your knowledge of personality theories, answer these questions: How would Skinner explain your friend's behavior? How would Bandura explain his behavior?

ANALYZING VIEWPOINTS

1. Despite the many theories of personality developed by psychologists, many people rely more on a reading of their horoscope to interpret their personality. Are horoscopes any less valid than personality theories? How do the two differ? Is classifying someone as friendly or aggressive much different than classifying someone as an Aquarian? Write a paper that debates the merits of trait theories of personality versus horoscopes. In formulating your answer, consider how well each approach fulfills the four functions of personality theory discussed in the chapter.

2. Jung believed that people are unconsciously linked to their ancestral past. What evidence can you think of for or against the "collective unconscious" Jung described? Prepare a paper summarizing this evidence, pro and con. Be sure to use your own experiences as well as what you have learned from the chapter to develop your arguments.

BEYOND THE CLASSROOM

1. Go to your local library and do additional reading on two different personality theories. Arrange a class debate in which one group supports one theory and the other group supports the other theory. One lively debate would be between the behaviorists' position and the humanistic approach.

2. Both Jung and Eysenck talk about extraversion versus introversion as being a basic part of personality. Choose five people—include friends, acquaintances, or family members—and observe their behavior. If possible, observe them in public situations and in family situations. Classify each person as either extraverted, introverted, or unable to determine. Keep a record of your observations, including evidence for your classifications. Next, ask these five people whether they would say they are extraverted or introverted. What do the results tell you about extraversion/introversion as a personality trait? Is someone extraverted or introverted in all situations, or does it vary depending on the situation? Did you learn anything interesting about how people see themselves as compared to how others see them?

IN YOUR JOURNAL

1. Analyze the entry in your journal you wrote at the beginning of the study of this chapter. Now write another entry answering these questions: Does the person's behavior change depending on the setting? Explain your observations using a behavioral model of personality. What would you say are important reinforcers for this person?

2. In your journal, describe the theory of personality that is most appealing to you. Which seems to make the most sense? Why?

2. Answers will vary. The main focus of the task is to distinguish what, if any, differences exist between the private and the public self (or self-perceptions as opposed to the perceptions of others).

IN YOUR JOURNAL

If time permits, discuss journal entries individually with students.

CHAPTER BONUS
Test Question

This question may be used for extra credit on the chapter test.

Choose the letter of the correct response.

General ways of behaving that characterize an individual are known as:

a. instinctual drives.
b. reality principles.
c. archetypes.
d. personality traits.

Answer: **d**

CHAPTER 12
Psychological Testing

TEXT TOPICS	SPECIAL FEATURES	RESOURCE MATERIALS
Basic Characteristics of Tests, pp. 291–295		Reproducible Lesson Plan; Study Guide; Review Activity *Readings in Psychology:* Section 4, Reading 4
Intelligence Testing, pp. 295–298	**More About Psychology,** p. 295	Reproducible Lesson Plan; Study Guide; Review Activity
Test-Taking Strategies, pp. 299–302	**More About Psychology,** p. 299 **At a Glance:** Family Size and IQ, p. 301 **Using Psychology:** The SAT, pp. 302-303	Reproducible Lesson Plan; Study Guide; Review Activity; Application Activity Transparencies 22, 23
Measuring Abilities and Interests, pp. 303–306	**Psychology Update,** p. 303 **At a Glance:** Admissions Test Scores, p. 305	Reproducible Lesson Plan; Study Guide; Review Activity
Personality Testing, pp. 306–308		Reproducible Lesson Plan; Study Guide; Review Activity Transparency 24
Situational Testing, pp. 308–310	**Fact or Fiction?,** p. 310 **Using Psychology:** Test–Taking Tips, p. 310	Reproducible Lesson Plan; Study Guide; Review Activity; Extension Activity; Chapter Test, Form A and Form B Understanding Psychology Testmaker

PERFORMANCE ASSESSMENT ACTIVITY

Assign students to find reports in magazines and newspapers about issues and controversies related to test taking. Have students contribute articles, photographs, and graphs to a classroom display. Ask students to provide titles and captions to accompany any visual materials. As a follow-up activity, ask the students to write a one-paragraph statement about what they learned from information gathered by the class.

CHAPTER RESOURCES

Readings for the Student
Hoffman, Banesh. *The Tyranny of Testing.* New York: Collier, 1962.

Matarazzo, J. P. "Psychological Testing and Assessment in the 21st Century." *American Psychologist*, 47 (August 1992): 1007–1018.

Sternberg, R. J. and Detterman, D. *What is Intelligence?* Norwood, NJ: Ablex, 1986.

Weinberg, R. A. "Intelligence and IQ: Landmark Issues and Great Debates." *American Psychologist*, 44 (1991): 98–104.

Wilcox, Roger, ed. *The Psychological Consequences of Being a Black American.* New York: Wiley, 1971.

Readings for the Teacher
Anastasi, A. *Psychological Testing.* New York: Macmillan, 1982.

Angoff, W. H. "The Nature-Nurture Debate, Aptitudes, and Group Differences." *American Psychologist*, 43 (1988): 713–720.

Davidson, J. E. "Intelligence Recreated." *Educational Psychologist*, 25 (1990): 337–354.

Sternberg, R. J. *Beyond IQ: A Triarchic Theory of Human Intelligence.* New York: Cambridge University Press, 1985.

Multimedia
Intelligence—A Complex Concept. (28 minutes, 3/4″ or 1/2″ video). McGraw-Hill Films. This video presents different concepts of intelligence and several kinds of tests for measuring intelligence.

Intelligence Tests on Trial. (46 minutes, 3/4″ or Beta video). San Diego State College. This video recreates two federal court cases in which the use of intelligence tests for placement was challenged.

For additional resources, see the bibliography beginning on page 530.

FOCUS

Motivating Activity

Ask students to list the different kinds of tests they have taken. *(This list might include subject-specific tests in school, such as math, English, or history tests; written or road tests for a driver's license; IQ tests; ACTs; SATs; career interest tests; vocational aptitude tests; employment tests; and so on.)* Point out that these are all examples of psychological tests. Ask students to discuss the purpose of these various tests and to classify them as achievement tests, aptitude tests, interest tests, or personality tests. Have them discuss the advantages and disadvantages of each category of test. Tell students that they will learn more about psychological testing in this chapter.

Meeting Chapter Objectives.

Identify the main subjects in each objective on page 291. Have groups of students prepare data sheets on each of these subjects as they read through Chapter 12.

Building Vocabulary.

Have students read the glossary definitions and give examples of *objective personality tests* and *projective personality tests*. Ask them to identify ways these two tests might be distinguished. Ask: Can a test be both an objective personality test and a projective personality test? Why or why not?

Psychological Testing

FIGURE 12.1 Americans rely heavily on psychological testing because such tests promise to reveal a great deal about a person in a very short time.

290

TEACHER CLASSROOM RESOURCES

■ Chapter 12 Reproducible Lesson Plan
■ Chapter 12 Study Guide
■ Chapter 12 Review Activity
■ Chapter 12 Application Activity
■ Chapter 12 Extension Activity

📖 Transparencies 22, 23, 24
Transparency Strategies and
Activities

📑 *Readings in Psychology,* Section 4,
Reading 4

■ Chapter 12 Test, Form A and
Form B

◻ Understanding Psychology
Testmaker

Exploring Key Ideas

The Purpose of Testing.
Ask students to give examples of the types of tests used in different subjects they have taken. How do the tests given in one subject area compare to those in another? Ask students to explore how the various types of tests attempt to measure performance or knowledge. Challenge students to imagine they are instructors for a particular subject area. What type(s) of evaluation tools would they use? Tell students they will learn more about the variety and purposes of tests in this chapter. To try their hand at test-writing, assign students to write at least one question for a chapter test as they work their way through the text.

OBJECTIVES

After studying this chapter, you should be able to

- describe the concept of IQ and list several IQ tests.
- explain the application of aptitude tests, achievement tests, and interest tests.
- identify and describe the use of personality tests and situational testing.

KEY TERMS

achievement test
aptitude test
intelligence quotient (IQ)
interest test
norms
objective personality tests
percentile system
projective personality tests
reliability
situational test
validity

As a student, you are quite familiar with the use of tests to evaluate your academic performance. Testing has become an ever-present part of people's lives in our culture. In order to apply for a job as a mail carrier, firefighter, lawyer,or electrician, a person must take a standard civil service or licensing exam. In these cases, the tests are designed to measure what skills and knowledge the person has acquired. Other tests are designed to assess more general characteristics of personality. For example, a psychologist may want to assess your personality to help you select a suitable career or deal with an emotional problem.

Whether the test is designed to measure mental abilities or personality characteristics, its use and interpretation depend on how well it is constructed and the extent to which scores are related to actual performance. What does it mean when a person scores high on standardized written intelligence tests but earns poor grades in school? Can you actually select a mate by a computerized matching of your personality? Is it acceptable to screen job applicants by using personality tests or to place children in special programs on the basis of intelligence testing? What strategies are most useful in taking tests?

IN YOUR JOURNAL

Suppose you were asked to select the best person to be your teacher from among a group of applicants. How would you go about making the selection? Write your answer in your journal.

IN YOUR JOURNAL

Help students get started by suggesting that they compile a list of attributes a good teacher might possess. Ask them to analyze their completed list, and choose what they consider the three most important traits.

EXTRA CREDIT ACTIVITY

Ask students to devise a short psychological test to measure some area of knowledge, aptitude, achievement, interest, personality, or performance. Tell students that their tests can be fun. They may, for example, devise a test to measure sense of humor or how fast an individual can master juggling three tennis balls. Students should attempt to make their tests both reliable and valid, writing down how they approached these tasks. Have students summarize what they learned from this activity in a brief oral report to the class.

TEACH____

Guided Practice

■ **Discussion.** Explain that people often place a great deal of faith in what psychologists tell them—particularly in what psychological tests tell them. Point out that ethical issues sometimes arise when the results of a test may, for example, determine a person's future. Suppose a woman shows a high mechanical aptitude. She then chooses to become an aviation specialist without adequately exploring other career options. Is this a misuse of testing? Why or why not? Challenge students to cite what they considered to be potential examples of test misuse or abuse. *(Remind students that test results are descriptive of past experiences and current moods/interests rather than prescriptive.)* (OBJECTIVES 1–3)

The lure of tests is that they try to make it possible to find out a great deal about a person in a very short time.

FIGURE 12.2

Both school exams and aptitude tests can be considered psychological tests because both are intended to measure psychological variables (knowledge and skills). **What is the purpose of standardized tests?**

BASIC CHARACTERISTICS OF TESTS

Over the years, psychologists have developed a wide range of tools for measuring individual differences in intelligence, interests, skills, achievements, knowledge, and personality patterns. This chapter will describe the major types of tests in current use and discuss ways of dealing with them.

All tests have one characteristic that makes them both fascinating and remarkably practical: they try to make it possible to find out a great deal about a person in a short time. Tests can be useful in predicting how well a person might do in a particular career; in assessing an individual's desires, interests, and attitudes; and in revealing psychological problems. One virtue of standardized tests is that they can provide comparable data about many individuals. Further, psychologists can use some tests to help people understand things about themselves more clearly.

One of the great dangers of testing, however, is that we tend to forget that tests are merely *tools* for measuring and predicting human behavior. We start to think of test results (for example, an IQ) as things in themselves. The justification for using a test to make decisions about a person's future depends on whether a decision based on test scores would be fairer and more accurate than one based on other criteria. The fairness and usefulness of a test depend on several factors: its reliability, its validity, and the way its norms were established.

Test Reliability

The term **reliability** refers to a test's consistency—its ability to yield the same result under a variety of different circumstances. There are three basic ways of determining a test's reliability. First, if a person retakes the test, or takes a similar test, within a short time after the first testing, does he

or she receive approximately the same score? If, for example, you take a mechanical aptitude test three times in the space of six months and score 65 in January, a perfect score of 90 in March, and 70 in June, then the test is unreliable because it does not produce a measurement that is stable over time. This is assessing the measure's *test-retest* reliability.

The second measure of reliability is whether the test yields the same results when scored by different people. This is called *inter-scorer* reliability. If both your teacher and another teacher score an essay test that you have taken, and one gives you a B while the other gives you a D, then you have reason to complain about the test's reliability. The score you receive depends more on the grader than on you. On a reliable test, your score would be the same no matter who graded your paper.

One final way of determining a test's reliability is to find out whether, if you divide the test in half and score each half separately, the two scores are approximately the same. This is called *split-half* reliability. If a test is supposed to measure one quality in a person—for example, reading comprehension or administrative ability—then it should not have some sections on which the person scores high and others on which he or she scores low.

In checking tests for reliability, psychologists are trying to prevent variables from influencing a person's score. All kinds of irrelevant matters can interfere with a test. If the test taker is depressed because his pet goldfish is sick, or angry that he had to miss his favorite "Cheers" rerun to take the exam, or if a faulty thermostat has raised the temperature in the testing room to 114 degrees, he will probably score lower than if he is reasonably relaxed, comfortable, and content. No test can screen out all interferences, but a highly reliable test can do away with a good part of them.

Test Validity

A test may be reliable but still not valid. **Validity** is the ability of a test to measure what it is intended to measure (Figure 12.4). For example, a test that consists primarily of vocabulary lists will not measure aptitude for engineering. A history test will not measure general learning ability.

Determining the validity of a test is more complex than assessing its reliability. One of the chief methods for measuring validity is to find out how well a test *predicts* performance—its *predictive* validity. For example, a group of psychologists design a test to measure management ability. They ask questions about management systems, attitudes toward employees, and other relevant information. Will the people who score high on this test really make good managers?

Suppose the test makers decide that a good way to check the validity of the test is to find out how much a manager's staff improves in productivity in one year. If the staffs of those managers who scored high on the test produce more than the staffs of those managers who scored low on the test, the test may be considered valid. Corporations may then adopt it as one tool to use in deciding whom to hire as managers, assuming the test is also valid in their situation.

What if managers who are good at raising productivity are poor at decision making? It may be that this test measures talent for improving

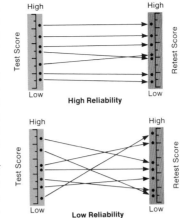

FIGURE 12.3

On the left, the test scores obtained by 7 individuals are ordered on a scale. On the right, the corresponding scores on a second version of the same test, given at a later time, are ordered. In the upper diagram, the two sets of scores correspond very closely. This pattern means the test is highly reliable. In the lower diagram, there is little relationship between the two. This scrambled pattern means the test has low reliability. **What is meant by saying a test is reliable?**

CONNECTIONS: PSYCHOLOGY AND THE LAW

Since the 1980s, many businesses have routinely administered "integrity tests" to their employees. Employers point to statistics that claim U.S. businesses lose as much as $25 billion a year through employee theft. Labor organizations, however, complain that integrity tests are neither reliable nor valid. They claim that many honest people have been ruined as a result of these tests. Several states have considered banning integrity tests—a move supported by the American Psychological Association. In 1991, the APA urged employers to discontinue using such tests since many of the tests examined (though not all) lacked predictive validity.

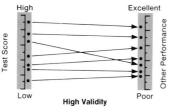

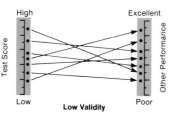

FIGURE 12.4

Reliability and validity are assessed in exactly the same way, except that assessment of validity requires that text scores be compared to some other measure of behavior. The lower diagram might represent the comparison of scores on the "head size" test of intelligence on the left with school grades on the right. The upper diagram might represent the result of comparing the Stanford-Binet Intelligence Scale scores with school grades. The Stanford-Binet is a valid test for predicting school grades; the head size measurement is not. **What defines a valid test?**

FIGURE 12.5

The range of possible raw scores on a test is shown in relation to an idealized curve that indicates the proportion of people who achieved each score. The vertical lines indicate percentiles, or proportions of the curve below certain points. Thus, the line indicated as the 1st percentile is the line below which only 1 percent of the curve lies. Similarly, 99 percent of the curve lies below the 99th percentile. **How do psychologists establish a scale for comparing test results?**

productivity, not general management ability. This is the kind of difficulty psychologists encounter in trying to assess the validity of a test. As the example shows, nothing can be said about a test's validity unless the *purpose* of the test is absolutely clear.

Establishing Norms

Once a test result is obtained, the examiner must translate the score into something useful. Suppose a child answers 32 of 50 questions on a vocabulary test correctly. What does this score mean? If the test is reliable and valid, it means that the child can be expected to understand a certain percentage of the words in a book at the reading level being tested. In other words, the score predicts how the child will *perform* at a given level.

But a "raw" score does not tell us where the child stands in relation to other children at his or her age and grade level. If most children answered 45 or more questions correctly, 32 is a low score. However, if most answered only 20 questions correctly, 32 is a very high score.

The method psychologists generally use to transform raw scores into figures that reflect comparisons with others is the **percentile system,** which resembles what is called "grading on the curve." In the percentile system, the scores actually achieved on the test are placed in order, ranging from the highest to the lowest. Each score is then compared with this list and assigned a percentile according to the percentage of scores that fall at or below this point. For example, if half the children in the above example scored 32 or below, then a score of 32 is at the 50th percentile. If 32 were the top score, it would be at the 100th percentile. In the example given in Figure 12.5, a score of 32 puts the child in the 75th percentile, since only 25 percent of the children scored higher than she did.

When psychologists design a test to be used in a variety of settings, they usually set up a scale for comparison by establishing norms. The test is given to a large representative sample of the group to be measured—for example, sixth graders or army privates or engineers. Percentiles are then es-

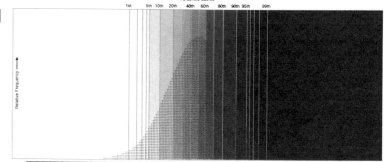

tablished on the basis of the scores achieved by this standardization group. These percentiles are called the test's **norms.** Most of the intelligence, aptitude, and personality tests you will encounter have been provided with norms in this way. Your percentile on an aptitude test such as the SAT, for example, reflects your standing among people of your age and grade who have taken these exams.

You should remember, however, that norms are not really standards—even though a norm group is sometimes misleadingly referred to as a "standardization group." Norms refer only to what has been found to be average for a particular group. If Johnny can read at the 50th percentile level, that does not mean that he has met some absolute standard for ability to read. It only means that he reads better than half the population and worse than the other half in his particular group.

In summary, when you take a test and obtain your score, you should consider the following questions in evaluating the results. (1) Do you think that if you took the same test again, you would receive a similar score? (2) Does your performance on this test reflect your normal performance in the subject? (3) If you were to compare your score with those of your classmates, would it reflect your general standing within that group?

INTELLIGENCE TESTING

Among the most widely used and widely disputed tests in the United States and Canada today are those that are designed to measure "intelligence" and yield an "IQ" score. This section will describe some of the major intelligence tests and present some of the issues that surround them.

The Development of Intelligence Tests

Alfred Binet, a French psychologist, was the first to develop a useful intelligence test. In 1904 Binet was asked by the Paris school authorities to devise a means of picking out "slow learners" so they could be placed in special classes from which they might better profit. Binet was unable to define intelligence, but he believed it was complex. He thought it was reflected in the things children do—make common-sense judgments, tell the meanings of words, and solve problems and puzzles. Binet assumed that whatever intelligence was, it increased with age; that is, older children had more intelligence than younger children. Therefore, in selecting items for his test he only included items on which older children did better than younger children. By asking the same questions of many children, Binet was able to determine the average age at which a particular question could be answered. For example, he discovered that certain questions could be answered by most 12-year-olds but not by most 11-year-olds. If a child of 11, or even 9, could answer these questions, he or she was said to have a *mental age* of 12. If a child of 12 could answer the 9-year-old-level questions

---

MORE about...

Multiple   Intelligences?
Many people believe that intelligence is primarily the ability to think logically. Psychologist Howard Gardner (1983) considers this view of intelligence to be inadequate, however, because it omits many other important skills. Gardner argues for a broader perspective that includes seven types of intelligence. The seven are: (1) verbal ability; (2) logical-mathematical reasoning skills; (3) spatial ability, or the ability to find your way around an environment and to form mental images of it; (4) musical ability, or the ability to create and perceive pitch and rhythm patterns; (5) body-kinesthetic ability, or skill at fine motor movements required for tasks such as gem cutting, surgery, and athletics; (6) interpersonal skills, involving understanding the feelings of others; and (7) intrapersonal skills, or knowledge of oneself.

Gardner's research on the results of brain disease convinced him that humans possess these seven different and often unrelated intellectual capacities or "intelligences." Moreover, he argues that the biological organization of the brain affects one's strength in each of the seven areas.

■ **Evaluating Concepts.**
After students read the margin feature, mention that intelligence is an elusive phenomenon. Many individuals who have not done well in school have gone on to make great intellectual or artistic contributions. An outstanding example is Albert Einstein. Conversely, many who have scored very high on intelligence tests have gone on to lead unproductive lives. Have students explain what the word *intelligence* means to them. What relation do they think exists between the following?

1. intelligence and success
2. intelligence and creativity
3. intelligence and moral substance

(OBJECTIVE 2)

ADDITIONAL INFORMATION

When Binet and his assistant, Theodore Simon, devised their intelligence tests, they often referred to "mental level." They rejected the term "mental age," introduced in 1911 by German psychologist Wilhelm Stern. To Binet, mental age represented something fixed and unchangeable, while mental level emphasized that a child's intelligence could change. Binet opposed the IQ, another of Stern's proposals, because he felt that representing human intelligence in a single number was misleading.

■ **Analyzing a Quote.** Read the following excerpt aloud. Tell students that it was written in 1922 by Walter Lippmann, one of the nation's leading political journalists.

If, for example, the impression takes root that these tests really measure intelligence, that they constitute a sort of last judgment on the child's capacity, that they reveal scientifically his predestined ability, then it would be a thousand times better if all the intelligence testers and all their questionnaires were sunk without warning into the Sargasso Sea. One only has to read the amount of literature on the subject, but more especially in the work of popularizers to see how easily the intelligence test can be turned into an engine of cruelty, how easily in the hands of blundering or prejudiced men it would turn into a method of stamping a permanent sense of inferiority upon the soul of a child.

Ask: What is Lippmann's main criticism of intelligence tests? Do you agree with Lippmann's contention? Explain.
(OBJECTIVE 2)

VISUAL INSTRUCTION

Point out that the photographs show the Stanford-Binet test being administered.
Answer to caption, Figure 12.6: by age levels

FIGURE 12.6

An examiner has built a tower of four blocks (top) and has told the child, "You make one like this." (bottom) The examiner shows the child the card with 6 small circles attached to it and says, "See all these things? Show me the dog," and so on. **How are test items grouped in the Stanford-Binet Intelligence Test?**

but not the questions for 10-year-olds and 11-year-olds, he or she was said to have a mental age of 9. Thus a slow learner was one who had a *mental age* that was less than his or her *chronological age*.

The Stanford-Binet. Binet's intelligence test has been revised many times since he developed it. The Binet test currently used in the United States is a revision created at Stanford University: the Stanford-Binet Intelligence Scale (Terman and Merrill, 1973). The Stanford-Binet, like the original test, groups test items by age level. To stimulate and maintain the child's interest, a variety of tasks are included, ranging from defining words to drawing pictures and explaining events in daily life. Children are tested one at a time. The examiner must carry out standardized instructions—at the same time putting the child at ease, getting him to pay attention, and encouraging him to try as hard as he can (Figure 12.6).

The **IQ,** or **intelligence quotient,** was originally computed by dividing a child's mental age (the average age of those who also received the same score as that child) by chronological (actual) age and multiplying by 100. Although the basic principles behind the calculation of IQ remain, scores are figured in a slightly different manner today. Researchers assign a score of 100 to the average performance at any given age. Then, IQ values are assigned to all the other test scores for this age group. If you have an IQ of 100, for example, this means that 50 percent of the test takers who are your age performed less well than you. In addition, test scores for several abilities are now reported instead of one general score, but the test is no longer widely used (Vernon, 1987).

The Wechsler Tests. Three frequently used intelligence tests are the revised versions of the Wechsler-Adult Intelligence Scale, now called WAIS-R (Wechsler, 1981) for adults, the Wechsler Intelligence Scale for Children, now called WISC-R (Wechsler, 1974) for children 6 to 16 years old, and the Wechsler Preschool and Primary Scale of Intelligence (WPPSI) for children 4 to 6½ years old.

Moreover, in addition to yielding one overall score, the Wechsler tests yield percentile scores in several areas—vocabulary, information, arithmetic, picture arrangement, and so on. These ratings are used to compute separate IQ scores for verbal and performance abilities. This type of scoring provides a more detailed picture of the individual's strengths and weaknesses than a single score does.

Group Tests. The Wechsler and Stanford-Binet tests, because they are given individually, are costly and time-consuming to administer. During World War I, when the United States Army found that it had to test nearly 2 million men, and quickly, individual testing was a luxury the army could not afford. Thus paper-and-pencil intelligence tests, which could be given to large groups of people at the same time, were developed. Current group IQ tests, such as the Army Alpha (standard) and Beta (nonverbal) tests, have proved to be convenient and effective and are used extensively in schools, employment offices, and many other institutions.

CONNECTIONS: PSYCHOLOGY AND MATHEMATICS

Psychologists must often be expert mathematicians in order to draw statistical conclusions from the raw data that they collect. Ask students to explain the original formula used for calculating the intelligence quotient: IQ = Mental Age divided by Chronological Age × 100. Have students work out several problems using the IQ formula. *(For example, a person with both a mental age and a chronological age of 17 would have an IQ of 100 (17/17 × 100 = 100), and a person with a mental age of 15 and a chronological age of 10 would have an IQ of 150 (15/10 × 100 = 150).*

General Information
1. How many wings does a bird have?
2. How many nickels make a dime?
3. What is steam made of?
4. Who wrote "Paradise Lost"?
5. What is pepper?

General Comprehension
1. What should you do if you see someone forget his book when he leaves his seat in a restaurant?
2. What is the advantage of keeping money in a bank?
3. Why is copper often used in electrical wires?

Arithmetic
1. Sam had three pieces of candy and Joe gave him four more. How many pieces of candy did Sam have altogether?
2. Three men divided eighteen golf balls equally among themselves. How many golf balls did each man receive?
3. If two apples cost 15¢, what will be the cost of a dozen apples?

Similarities
1. In what way are a lion and a tiger alike?
2. In what way are a saw and a hammer alike?
3. In what way are an hour and a week alike?
4. In what way are a circle and a triangle alike?

Vocabulary
"What is a puzzle?"
"What does 'addition' mean?"

FIGURE 12.7

These test items are similar to those included in the various Wechsler intelligence scales. (a) A sampling of questions from five of the verbal subtests. (b) A problem in block design, one of the performance subtests. (c) In another example of a performance subtest, the subject puts together puzzle pieces to form a familiar object, such as a duck. (Test items courtesy The Psychological Corporation, New York) **Why is IQ testing controversial?**

The Uses and Meaning of IQ Scores

In general, the norms for intelligence tests are established in such a way that most people score near 100. Out of 100 people, 16 will score above 115 and 16 will score below 85. About 2 in 100 score above 130 (very superior) and 2 score below 70. This means that a score of 130 places a person in the 98th percentile; a score of 70, in the 2nd percentile. Those who score below 70 have traditionally been classified as mentally retarded. More specific categories include: mildly retarded, but educable (55–69); moderately retarded, but trainable (40–54); severely retarded (25–39); and profoundly retarded (below 25).

What do these scores mean? What do the tests measure? IQ scores seem to be most useful when related to school achievement: They are quite accurate in predicting which people will do well in schools, colleges, and universities. Critics of IQ testing do not question this predictive ability. They do wonder, however, whether such tests actually measure "intelli-

■ **Identifying Bias.** The quote below by L. M. Terman may be construed as evidence for Walter Lippmann's contention that IQ tests can be turned into "an engine of cruelty." Before reading the quote aloud, warn students of its racist language. Then point out that these remarks once appeared in the instruction manual that accompanied Stanford-Binet tests:

[Low intelligence] *is very, very common among Spanish-Indian and Mexican families of the Southwest and also among negroes. Their dullness seems to be racial family stocks from which they come. . . .*

The writer predicts that . . . racial differences in general intelligence . . . cannot be wiped out by any scheme of mental culture.

VISUAL INSTRUCTION

Adrian Dove intentionally designed questions to be culturally biased against middle-class whites. Ask: How successful was Dove in this task? What was Dove's motivation? *(to prove that standard intelligence tests lacked validity because of pro-white cultural bias)*
Answer to caption, Figure 12.8: a test entirely without bias—which has turned out to be impossible

FIGURE 12.8

Psychologist Adrian Dove developed the Counterbalance Intelligence Test to stress the fact that cultural background can influence performance on an intelligence test. People from certain cultural backgrounds would get high scores on this test, whereas people from other cultural backgrounds would probably get very low scores. **What is a culture-fair test?**

The Dove Counterbalance Intelligence Test
by Adrian Dove

If they throw the dice and "7" is showing on the top, what is facing down?
(a) "Seven" (b) "Snake eyes"
(c) "Boxcars" (d) "Little Joes"
(e) "Eleven"

Jazz pianist Ahmad Jamal took an Arabic name after becoming really famous. Previously he had some fame with what he called his "slave name." What was his previous name?
(a) Willie Lee Jackson
(b) LeRoi Jones
(c) Wilbur McDougal
(d) Fritz Jones (e) Andy Johnson

In "C. C. Rider," what does "C. C." stand for?
(a) Civil Service
(b) Church Council
(c) County Circuit, preacher of an old-time rambler
(d) Country Club
(e) "Cheating Charley" (the "Boxcar Gunsel")

Cheap "chitlings" (not the kind you purchase at the frozen-food counter) will taste rubbery unless they are cooked long enough. How soon can you quit cooking them to eat and enjoy them?
(a) 15 minutes (b) 2 hours
(c) 24 hours
(d) 1 week (on a low flame)
(e) 1 hour

If a judge finds you guilty of "holding weed" (in California), what's the most he can give you?
(a) Indeterminate (life) (b) A nickel
(c) A dime (d) A year in county
(e) $100.00.

A "Handkerchief Head" is
(a) A cool cat (b) A porter
(c) An "Uncle Tom" (d) A hoddi
(e) A "preacher"

gence." Most psychologists agree that intelligence is the ability to acquire new ideas and new behavior, and to adapt to new situations. Is success in school or the ability to take a test a real indication of such ability? Generally, IQ tests measure the ability to solve certain types of problems. But they do not directly measure the ability to pose those problems or to question the validity of problems set by others (Hoffman, 1962). This is only part of the reason why IQ testing is so controversial.

The Controversy Over IQ

Much of the debate about IQ testing centers around one question: Do genetic differences or environmental inequalities cause two people to receive different scores on intelligence tests? A technique researchers use is studying the results of people with varying degrees of genetic relationship. We find that as genetic relationship increases—say from parent and child to identical twins—the similarity of IQ also increases. Correlation gauges the degree of relationship between two variables, .00 indicating no relationship, + (or −) 1.00 indicating a perfect relationship. The IQs of identical twins reared together correlates +.86, which is approaching the test-retest limits of intelligence tests. A parent and child's intelligence correlates +.40 (Bouchard & McGue, 1981). Generally, about half of all variation in IQs can be attributed to genetic factors. Regarding environment, studies show that brothers and/or sisters raised in the same environment are more likely to have similar IQs than siblings raised apart. Environment, therefore, does have an impact on IQ.

Some researchers study the effects of environment on IQ factors by focusing on preschool programs, such as Head Start, which exposes economically disadvantaged youths to enriching experiences. Some studies show that quality preschool programs help raise IQ initially, but the increase begins to fade after some years. Participating children, however, are less likely to be in special education classes, less likely to be held back, and more likely to graduate from high school than are children without such preschool experiences (Zigler, Styfco, & Gilman, 1993). Each year of school missed may drop a person's IQ as much as 5 points (Ceci, 1991). The richness of the home environment, the quality of food, the number of brothers and sisters in the family—all affect IQ.

Another concern is the bias of intelligence tests. Developing a valid, reliable test of IQ without bias—sometimes called a culture-free or culture-fair test—has turned out to be impossible. Consider the answer to a seemingly simple question such as "What color is a banana?" Many children raised on farms or in the suburbs would answer "yellow;" those who live in inner cities could realistically answer "brown;" and those who have known only poverty might respond "brown" or "black."

Both heredity and environment have an impact on intelligence. It seems unlikely that we will ever be able to develop a truly culture-free test. Advances in behavioral genetics research continue to refine results on the contributions heredity and experience have on IQ. It remains clear that these two factors are both contributing and interact in their effects.

CONNECTIONS: PSYCHOLOGY AND SOCIAL STUDIES

Tell students that the U.S. Congress approved funds for Head Start in 1964. It was part of a promise by President Lyndon Johnson to wipe out poverty and create a "Great Society." Some experts involved in Head Start claimed that improved test scores proved the value of what psychologists call environmental intervention. Assign interested students to prepare an oral report on the successes and setbacks of Head Start. In a follow-up discussion, challenge students to consider whether a similar program should be devised for the 1990s.

TEST-TAKING STRATEGIES

The difference in scores achieved by children of different cultural backgrounds on IQ tests reflects not only a difference in accumulated knowledge, but also a difference in skills for taking tests. Several researchers have coached disadvantaged children in test taking—with good results. It seems that many do not fully understand the tasks they are required to perform on the tests. They have not learned the strategies to solve test problems. When they do, their scores improve. This suggests that a person's IQ score also reflects his or her skill and experience in taking tests. In short, IQ tests are far from perfect measures of intelligence, because a variety of factors irrelevant to intelligence affects results.

Many educators and psychologists have studied the way people prepare themselves for tests and the way they respond in a testing situation. These strategies can be useful in preparation for any kind of test, whether it is a biology test, a civil service test, or a college entrance exam.

Studying for a Test

One of the differences between people who do well on tests or exams and those who do poorly is in the type and amount of studying they do. People who have developed good study habits often earn high grades and derive a general sense of accomplishment from their efforts. Knowing that they are adequately prepared for a test also reduces their anxiety. Like other skills, studying skills are acquired through practice and instruction.

Psychologists who study how people learn verbal or written material have shown that people master material better when they practice or rehearse the material several times. This means that if you read actively—raise questions and quiz yourself—about the assigned chapters for an exam several times you will remember more of the material than a student who studies by reading the assigned chapters only once. In terms of studying then, practice does make perfect. Furthermore, peoples' performance on a test will most likely improve if they space their study time over several intervals rather than cram all the studying into one session. It would be better to study an hour a night for five nights than to cram all of the studying into five hours on the night before the exam. When cramming is used as a substitute for planned study, test performance is not as good.

People should plan their study time so that they avoid studying materials that are similar to each other. Suppose, for example, that you are studying for a French exam and at the same time you have Spanish and geometry homework to do. Since French and Spanish are more similar than French and geometry, you should space your Spanish and French study time so that you reduce the possibility of one interfering with the other. You could do your Spanish homework early in the day, and set aside several short blocks of time in the late afternoon and evening to prepare for the French exam. In between the times set aside for studying French, you could do geometry homework, since this material is less likely to interfere with your memory of the French material.

MORE about . . .

New Views of Intelligence.
Robert Sternberg (1985) proposed a three-part theory of intelligence involving the kind of problem-solving traditionally associated with IQ tests. The three parts for processing information focus on:

Knowledge acquisition: the traditional means for learning new information;

Performance skills: the skills and strategies for solving problems;

Metacognition: strategies for applying knowledge and monitoring progress toward solving a problem; Partway through solving an algebra problem, this component may kick in to decide that the approach you've selected isn't working. At that point, a new one will be selected.

Sternberg, however, also identified two other aspects of intelligence:

Experiential intelligence: This involves creativity; key element is alternative views of reality—new ways to view the world;

Contextual intelligence: involves what is usually called "street smarts" or "business sense." The key element is adaptability in use of available resources.

Neither of the last two skills would be detected in normal tests of intelligence.

■ **Identifying Variables.**
Request volunteers to explain what is meant by a *self-fulfilling prophecy*. *(the idea that a person acts in such a way as to make his or her expectations come true)* Next, ask students to imagine a student with a history of "freezing" on exams. Ask: How might this experience affect the student's performance on an IQ test? *(leads the student to assume he or she will do poorly on this test as well)* Point out that IQ tests often become a part of students' permanent school record. What factors are *not* revealed by the raw numbers of the test? *(the student's history of anxiety)* What other variables do students think might affect performance on an IQ test?

As a follow-up activity, divide the class into two groups. Assign half the students to develop a list of helpful hints to prepare for an IQ test. Direct the other half to develop a feedback form that students might attach to the test to note factors that may have hindered their test-taking performance. (OBJECTIVE 1)

CONNECTIONS: PSYCHOLOGY AND SOCIAL STUDIES

Henry H. Goddard (1865–1957) made important contributions in the area of psychological testing, but he also played a part in one of psychology's sorrier episodes. Goddard set up a program in which a staff administered psychological tests to immigrants arriving at Ellis Island. In 1917, Goddard reported that 83% of the Jews, 80% of the Hungarians, 79% of the Italians, and 87% of the Russians tested were feeble-minded. He based these conclusions on tests with questions such as "What is Crisco?" and "Who is Christy Mathewson?" (a pitcher for the New York Giants). Today, we recognize these tests as culturally biased. At the time, however, Congress used such "scientific" evidence to back the restrictive immigration laws of 1924.

■ **Demonstration.** If possible, arrange to hold class for several days in an audiovisual room that can be easily set up for a hidden video camera. You might even tell students that they are being videotaped as part of an in-service training program for teachers. After students are comfortable in their new environment, announce you are giving a surprise quiz. Make sure the camera is running while students take the test. After students hand in the tests, turn on the videotape for them to assess. What examples of test anxiety can they identify? Did any students seem more nervous than others? Review material in the text that might reduce examples cited. (OBJECTIVES 1–3)

Teacher Note. Some students may be relatively relaxed when they enter an exam room but then suddenly find that they cannot remember anything they had learned for the exam. Point out that mental blocks happen when people temporarily panic. You might have students practice the following technique for dispelling mental blocks. Tell the students to close their eyes and slowly take a few deep breaths and to consciously let their bodies relax. This quick relaxation technique is often enough to counter temporary panic.

Reducing Test Anxiety

One of the biggest problems that people have in preparing for or taking an exam or test is anxiety. As the time draws near to the test, people generally experience an increase in tension. While some people can control their anxiety, others are so panic-stricken that they cannot perform well. Actually, a moderate amount of tension improves performance. A person who feels no tension at all is not as alert or attentive to details as he or she could be. When a person experiences a high level of tension, however, panic and disorganization set in and performance declines. Adequate preparation for a test helps reduce some of the anxiety. Beyond that, a person can learn specific techniques for reducing tension and relaxing before an exam. For example, allowing plenty of time to get to the testing site and having a good night's sleep beforehand will help reduce anxiety.

Since most tests are timed and many tests are designed to assess performance under pressure, one way you can reduce the stress of test-taking is to manage your time. Know how much time you will have and be sure to have a watch so that you can keep track. Divide your time so that you don't take too long on any one part. If you don't, you might discover that you have 10 minutes left to complete the second half of the test.

Another way to reduce your level of anxiety is to believe in yourself and tell yourself that you *can* do well on the test. Having a plan of action or a strategy for taking the test will increase your confidence in test-taking. Knowing how to take a test involves some familiarity with the different kinds of tests and questions you will be asked.

Preparing Yourself for a Test

With the increase in the use for job and college selection, a number of courses and books have been developed to help people prepare for specific exams. The courses usually have two goals. One is to familiarize the individual with testing strategies and to help the test taker develop a knowledge of testing procedures. The second goal is to provide specific instruction or coaching in the subject matter of the test.

If you have no experience with machine-scored multiple choice exams, you may not be as confident as a more experienced test taker. Thus, a familiarity with the question format and with the special answer sheets can be useful. Many courses offer sample items for practice. Sometimes, the answer sheets can be confusing to the inexperienced test taker because of the codes that are required to identify the person taking the test. Marking your answer correctly may also mean using a specific type of pencil, selecting an answer row, and completely filling in the space between two parallel lines or inside circles. When you do have to mark your answers in rows of circles or squares, make sure you are in the correct row.

In addition to the actual mechanics of taking tests, you can learn how to read and answer multiple-choice items. For example, it is important to know ahead of time whether there is a penalty for guessing. Some exams are scored only for correct answers ("rights only" scoring), in which case you would do better to guess than to leave a blank. Other exams are

COOPERATIVE LEARNING ACTIVITY

Encourage any students in your class who may have developed test-taking strategies on their own to share their ideas. Ask volunteers to prepare a brief presentation for the class. You might also ask the students to share their personal "disaster" stories relating to taking tests. Encourage the students to diagnose the cause of each "disaster" and suggest ways it might be avoided in the future. Suggest that students form test support groups to lend one another advice and encouragement before important tests.

scored by subtracting the number of wrong answers from the number of correct answers (formula scoring). Follow the test publisher's advice on guessing. You should also learn to read all of the multiple-choice options, not just the first one that seems right. Do not spend too much time on puzzling items, especially since most tests are timed. Later, if time permits, you can go back to difficult items and apply more specific strategies for deciding on the best answers. Also review the Test-Taking Tips box on page 310.

Some organizations offer courses that provide coaching for specific tests. They vary in cost and quality. Some are very expensive and very intensive, sometimes involving daily study for a period of up to six months. There is debate about the benefit of such courses. Often, the focus of coaching courses is on increasing a person's vocabulary and refreshing his or her knowledge of specific subjects. If a person has been out of school, these courses may be helpful. For a student who is currently taking English and mathematics courses, however, these programs may not prove beneficial.

At A Glance

FAMILY SIZE AND IQ

It wasn't that long ago that nearly everyone came from a large family. Now most couples have just one, two, or three children.

Instead of bemoaning the loss of the large family, psychologists tell us we should be happy it's gone because large families produce children with lower IQs. Psychologists also point to evidence that keeping a family small may increase the likelihood of having smart children and that a child's intelligence is affected by where in the birth order he or she was born.

The classic study of family size and IQ was conducted in the Netherlands. It was based on the military examinations of more than 386,000 Dutch people. Researchers found that the brightest subjects came from the smallest families and had few, if any, brothers and sisters when they were born. Thus, the first-born child in a family of 2 was usually brighter than the last child in a family of 10. The differences in IQ, however, from one birth order position to another average only about one-quarter point.

The effects of family size on intelligence may be explained by what a house full of children does to the home environment. It increases the amount of time a child spends with other children and decreases the amount of parental attention he or she receives. When this happens, and children have limited contact with adults, development of intelligence has been known to suffer.

For more details, see R. B. Zajonc and G. B. Markus, (1976). "Birth Order and Intellectual Development," Psychological Review, vol. 82, 74–88.

FIGURE 12.9

The General Aptitude Test Battery (GATB) consists of a number of different kinds of tests. Samples of items testing verbal and mathematical skills (top) and manual skills (bottom) are shown here. **What are some of the ways to reduce the anxiety of taking a test?**

1. Which two words have the same meaning?
   (a) open (b) happy (c) glad (d) green

2. Which two words have the opposite meaning?
   (a) old (b) dry (c) cold (d) young

3. A man works 8 hours a day, 40 hours a week. He earns $1.40 an hour. How much does he earn each week?
   (A) $40.00   (C) $50.60
   (B) $44.60   (D) $56.00

4. At the left is a drawing of a flat piece of metal. Which object at the right can be made from this piece of metal?
   A B C D

VISUAL INSTRUCTION

Ask volunteers to answer the four questions. Which took the longest for them to solve? Why? *(probably question 3, since it involves both verbal comprehension and mathematical calculation)* **Answer to caption, Figure 12.9:** Answers will vary, but might include: get plenty of rest beforehand, arrive at the testing site ahead of time, let your body relax, manage time effectively, be confident.

At A Glance

After students read the special feature, ask them to answer the following questions:
1. What were the results of the Dutch study? *(The smaller the family, the higher a child's IQ is likely to be; in large families, the last born's IQ will probably be lower than the first born's.)*
2. What factor, other than the amount of adult attention that children in large families receive, might contribute to their lower IQs? *(Answers will vary.)*

MEETING SPECIAL NEEDS

Test-taking Strategy. Students who are inefficient readers and prone to panicking on timed tests will often profit by using a form of rapid reading called *scanning*. This preview technique allows students to assess the overall scope of the material to plan their time. Tell the students you are going to demonstrate scanning to find the names of all the different kinds of personality tests mentioned on pp. 306-308. Using your finger, model scanning by snaking your finger rapidly down each page. Demonstrate finding the various names of the tests: Minnesota Multiphasic Personality Inventory, Rorschach inkblot test, and so on. Time students as they scan p. 296 for all the names of the various intelligence tests.

WORKING WITH TRANSPARENCIES

Project Transparencies 22 and 23 and use the guidelines provided in Teaching Strategies and Activities. Assign Student Worksheets 22 and 23.

Using Psychology

After students read the special feature, ask them the following questions:
1. What led to the development of college entrance examinations? *(the success of tests to screen prospects for the military during World War I)*
2. What is the purpose of the PSAT? *(to prepare juniors for the kinds of questions that they will encounter on the SAT, for early admission to college, or for scholarship applications)*
3. What change has occurred in SAT scores since 1972? *(From 1972 to 1982 they declined; they remained stable during the 1980s; recently, math scores have drifted upward and verbal scores downward.)*

Enrich. Have students complete the Chapter 12 Application Activity.

Using Psychology
The SAT

The tremendous success of mass testing to screen people for the army in World War I encouraged the College Board (a nonprofit membership association of schools and colleges) to develop objective tests to screen students for college admission. It developed a number of college entrance examinations, including the SAT—long called the Scholastic Aptitude Test, now the Scholastic Assessment Test. This test, along with achievement and other tests, makes up the College Board's Admissions Testing Program. The American College Testing Program (ACT) offers another, similar series of admission tests. The results of standardized tests are among several criteria that colleges use for selecting students.

More than 1 million high school students take SATs every year. Juniors take the PSAT (Preliminary Scholastic Aptitude Test) to prepare them for the kinds of questions they will encounter on SATs, for early admission to college, and for scholarship applications.

The three-hour SAT-I is, for the most part, a multiple-choice test that includes 75–90 minutes devoted to verbal reasoning, 60–75 minutes to mathematical reasoning, and 30 minutes to pretesting or "equating" questions. The verbal parts measure your ability to use words, and include questions on vocabulary, analogies, and reading comprehension. The math part stresses problem-solving in arithmetic, algebra, and geometry, data interpretation, and applied mathematics. The pretesting items are new questions being tested for difficulty. The "equating" questions are old questions from former tests that are used to standardize scores so that students are not penalized if their particular SAT is more difficult than former SATs.

You do not pass or fail SATs. Your score is compared with those of others who took similar tests over the years. Most colleges use these relative values, based on a national rather than a local standard, as part of their assessment of your academic ability.

The average scores of students taking the SATs dropped gradually over the first 10 years that national averages were recorded (beginning in 1972). There are many theories explaining this. One theory is that some schools lacked the traditionally strong emphasis on the basic academic skills. Another theory is that teachers were giving students higher grades than in the past for comparable work, so that students with lower capabilities were advancing through the grades.

COOPERATIVE LEARNING ACTIVITY

The SATs have become a rite of passage for more than one million students each year. To investigate the institutionalization of the SATs, request groups of students to study college catalogs in the guidance office or library. Of the total number of catalogs reviewed, how many requested submission of SAT scores? What were the mean verbal and math scores requested? Suppose students refused to take the SATs. How do they think their decision might limit college choices? (Hypothetically, do students think colleges would turn down a straight-A student without SATs? Why or why not?)

The year 1982 marked the low point; the national average scores started slowly back up, but were generally stable during the 1980s. Now, the math scores are drifting slowly upward again, while the verbal scores are drifting slowly downward. It is not immediately obvious why this is happening, although the changes from year to year are usually only a point or two.

The fact that different teachers and schools grade comparable work differently is a major rationale for nationally standardized tests such as the SATs. Many students have shown that SATs are a more accurate gauge of student ability than the subjective opinions of the students' teachers (Stanley, 1976).

MEASURING ABILITIES AND INTERESTS

Intelligence tests are designed to measure a person's overall ability to solve problems that involve symbols such as words, numbers, and pictures. Psychologists have developed other tests to assess special abilities and experiences. These include aptitude tests, achievement tests, and interest tests.

Aptitude Tests

Aptitude tests attempt to discover a person's talents and to predict how well he or she will be able to learn a new skill. They are assessed primarily in terms of their *predictive validity*. The two most widely known such tests are the Differential Aptitude Test (DAT) and the General Aptitude Test Battery (GATB). The GATB is the most widely used of these tests (Figure 12.9). Actually, the GATB comprises nine different tests, ranging from vocabulary to manual dexterity. Test results are used to determine whether a person shows promise for each of a large number of occupations. In addition to the GATB there are aptitude tests in music, language, art, mathematics, and other special fields.

Achievement Tests

Whereas aptitude tests are designed to predict how well a person will be able to learn a new skill, **achievement tests** are designed to measure how much a person has already learned in a particular area. Such tests not only enable an instructor to assess a student's knowledge, they also help students to assess their progress for themselves. They are validated in terms of their *content validity,* or how well they measure students' mastery of a set of knowledge.

PSYCHOLOGY UPDATE

Computerized Adaptive Testing (CAT). Computers are often used to administer ability tests. One computer-based method is called "adaptive testing" or "tailored testing" (Weiss & Vale, 1987). To understand adaptive testing, recall that in a standard test everyone gets the same questions in the same order. With an adaptive test, however, the order of questions is changed by the computer as it *adapts* the test to the individual's performance.

If you are taking the test and answer several problems correctly, the computer will begin to challenge you with harder problems. If you miss a question, the computer will follow it with an easier problem, and so on. The purpose of this testing method is to measure your ability by finding the difficulty level where you correctly answer most but not all of the problems (70 percent, for example). Adaptive testing is more accurate than standard testing, especially when test takers are either very high or very low in ability.

CHAPTER 12 Lesson Plan

■ **Applying Concepts.** Ask students to explain the difference between *predictive* and *content validity*. Ask: To which kind of test does each term apply? *(Aptitude tests are intended to be predictive of how well a person will be able to learn a new skill. Achievement tests are validated in terms of content and measure how well a person has mastered a set of knowledge.)* (OBJECTIVE 2)

Teacher Note. After students read the margin feature, you might refer them back to the discussion of computer-assisted instruction (CAI) in Chapter 2. Point out that in both situations, the computer adapts the programmed information to suit the individual's performance.

■ **Forming Hypotheses.** Tell students that, according to statistics compiled by the College Entrance Examination Board, mean scores on the verbal portion of the SAT have dropped from 460 in 1970 to 423 in 1992 (out of a maximum of 800). Math scores exhibit a smaller overall decline—from 488 in 1970 to 476 in 1992. Challenge students to speculate on reasons for the decline. If possible, allow students to use the *Readers' Guide to Periodical Literature* to locate articles on the declining scores. Ask: How did your hypotheses compare to hypotheses advanced in these articles? (OBJECTIVE 2)

CRITICAL THINKING ACTIVITY

Making Comparisons. Ask students to list all the different kinds of psychological tests that they have studied in this chapter and to rank them according to the following criteria: first, from most to least useful for the test giver; and then, from most to least useful for the test taker. Ask students to compare their two rankings. Which kinds of tests seem to benefit the test giver and the test taker equally? Which kinds of tests seem to be more useful to the test giver than the test taker? Ask students to suggest reasons for these discrepancies.

VISUAL INSTRUCTION

Explore the effect of environment on test taking by having students name various distractors. *(Possibilities include the hum and flickering of fluorescent lighting, heat or cold, noise, a cramped writing surface or—if any are left-handed—a writing surface designed for right-handers.)*
Answer to caption, Figure 12.10: to determine a person's preferences, attitudes, and interests

■ **Cooperative Learning Activity.** As a continuation of the question raised in the Visual Instruction, organize the class into small groups. Assign each to imagine it is a group of architects hired by the Educational Testing Service in Princeton, New Jersey. The group's goal is to draft a plan for the ideal testing environment. Offer the students the option of presenting their ideas in writing, in drawings, or in a combination of forms. Call on a member from each group to present its plan to the class as a whole.

FIGURE 12.10

A number of factors, including the individual's mood and the physical setup of the room, can influence test results. A person can sometimes do poorly one day in one setting and well on another day in different circumstances. **What is the purpose of an interest test?**

The distinction between achievement and aptitude tests has become somewhat blurred. What psychologists had thought were tests of aptitude—defined as *innate* ability or talent—turned out to measure experience as well, so that in part they were achievement tests. On the other hand, achievement tests often turned out to be the best predictors of many kinds of occupational abilities, so that they were in some sense aptitude tests. Because of this overlap, the distinction between the two types of tests rests more on purpose and validation than on content. If a test is used to predict future ability, it is considered to be an aptitude test; if it is used to assess what a person already knows, it is an achievement test.

Interest Tests

The instruments for measuring interests are fundamentally different from the instruments for measuring abilities. Answers to questions on an intelligence test indicate whether a person can, in fact, do certain kinds of thinking and solve certain kinds of problems. There are right and wrong answers. But the answers to questions on an interest or a personality test are not scored right or wrong. The question in this type of testing is not "How much can you do?" or "How much do you know?" but "What are you like?"

The essential purpose of an **interest test** is to determine a person's preferences, attitudes, and interests. The test taker's responses are compared to the responses given by people in clearly defined groups, such as professions or occupations. The more a person's interest patterns correspond to those of people in a particular occupation, the more likely that person is to enjoy and succeed in that profession.

CRITICAL THINKING ACTIVITY

Identifying Faulty Reasoning. Many people put so much faith in the results of psychological tests because the tests often purport to be based on scientific principles. In other words, people believe tests can measure such things as intelligence or achievement in much the same way that a thermometer can measure temperature. Ask students to explain the problem with this kind of reasoning. *(Remind students that tests are tools and that some tools are more efficient and accurate at measuring than others.)*

At A Glance

ADMISSIONS TEST SCORES

Every winter and spring, high school students go through an American rite of passage: they take their college entrance exams. How well they do may influence what happens in their lives. Most students believe that the colleges they attend, the jobs they get, the people they marry are all affected, to some degree, by their scores.

Little wonder, then, that most students try to do everything they can to do well on the exams. Although no one has discovered a magic formula for getting the top grades, many students repeat exams such as the SAT, usually taking it first in the spring of their junior year and then in the winter of their senior year. According to the Educational Testing Service, the writers of this test, 1 student in 20 will gain 100 points or more, and about 1 in 100 will lose 100 points or more. Generally speaking, the odds are with students to improve their scores. College admissions committees take this into account when they interpret the results.

Experts attribute this score gain to several factors. Students' intellectual capacities have increased between their junior and senior years, and a round of practice helped take the jitters out of exam time. In short, the students taking the test for the second time are a little older, a little smarter, and more experienced.

At A Glance

After students read the special feature, ask them to answer the following questions:
1. What are some of the effects that SAT scores can have on the lives of students? *(They may play a role in whether a student gets into college and where; indirectly, they affect, to some degree, a person's future job and choice of a marriage partner.)*
2. How can students improve their odds of getting a high score on the SAT? *(by taking the test a second time)*

VISUAL INSTRUCTION

Point out that the KPR often forces respondents to make a fine distinction among activities, all of which may be considered favorable or unfavorable. For example, a person who may not enjoy reading at all still must choose among a love story, a mystery, and science fiction. What do students think is being assessed in this question? *(Students may note emotional, investigative, and analytical preferences.)*
Answer to caption, Figure 12.11: what careers might be appropriate for people

		Most	Least
G.	Read a love story	● G.	●
H.	Read a mystery	● H.	●
I.	Read science fiction	● I.	●
J.	Visit an art gallery	● J.	●
K.	Browse in a library	● K.	●
L.	Visit a museum	● L.	●
M.	Collect autographs	● M.	●
N.	Collect coins	● N.	●
O.	Collect butterflies	● O.	●
P.	Watch television	● P.	●
Q.	Go for a walk	● Q.	●
R.	Listen to music	● R.	●

FIGURE 12.11

Shown are items from the Kuder Preference Record (KPR), a test that works like the Strong-Campbell Interest Inventory. The individual taking the test chooses from among three possible activities the one he or she would most like to do and the one he or she would least like to do. The test provides numerous sets of such alternatives. **What is the Kuder Preference Record designed to measure?**

COMMUNITY INVOLVEMENT

Challenge students to act as investigative reporters. Their assignment is to write an informative news story on the use of tests by employers in your community. Request volunteers to contact as many employers as possible. Have them ask the following questions: (1) Are tests part of the application process? If so, to what extent are they used in making hiring decisions? (2) Are tests used after hiring to determine promotions, reassignments, or pay raises? (3) What retraining do you offer employees who do poorly on a test? After students have compiled their data, have them write their news stories for class distribution. (Tip: Arrange for necessary release forms for all interviews.)

■ **Discussion.** Point out that achievement tests are not always a sure-fire indicator of a person's future achievement. Success in college, as in other endeavors in life, depends on other factors as well, such as motivation, mental health, emotional maturity, and creativity—things that the SAT does not measure. As an introduction to the section on personality testing, write the factors listed below on the chalkboard or distribute lists of them to the students. Ask students which of the factors might legitimately be used in assessing students for college admission. Which factors should not be used? Why?

1. Reading skills
2. Vocabulary skills
3. Logic skills
4. Math skills
5. Memory capacity
6. Creativity
7. Motivation
8. Common sense
9. Speaking ability
10. Emotional maturity
11. Interpersonal skills
12. Mental health
13. Violent behavior
14. Illness
15. Grooming
16. U.S. citizenship
17. Length of hair
18. Religion
19. Race
20. Handicap
21. Ability to pay
22. Gender
23. Athletic skills
24. Age
25. Criminal record
26. Cultural background
27. Political affiliation

(OBJECTIVE 2)

In constructing the widely used Strong-Campbell Interest Inventory (Campbell, 1977) for example, psychologists compared the responses of people who are successfully employed in different occupations to the responses of "people in general." Suppose most engineers said they liked the idea of becoming astronomers but would not be interested in a coaching job, whereas "people in general" were evenly divided on these (and other) questions. A person who responded as the engineers did would rank high on the scale of interest in engineering. The Kuder Preference Record, part of which is shown in Figure 12.11, is based on the same principle. The purpose of these measures is to help people find the career that is right for them.

PERSONALITY TESTING

Psychologists and psychiatrists use **personality tests** to assess personality characteristics and to identify problems. Some of these tests are **objective,** or forced choice—that is, a person must select one out of a small number of possible responses. Others are **projective tests**—they encourage test takers to respond freely, giving their own interpretations of various test stimuli.

Objective Personality Tests

One of the most widely used tests for general personality assessment is the Minnesota Multiphasic Personality Inventory (MMPI-2). Like other personality tests, the MMPI-2 has no right or wrong answers. The test consists of 550 statements to which a person can respond "true," "false," or "cannot say." Items include "I like tall women"; "I wake up tired most mornings"; "I am envied by most people"; "I often feel a tingling in my fingers."

The items on the MMPI-2 reveal habits, fears, delusions, sexual attitudes, and symptoms of mental problems. Although the statements that relate to a given characteristic (such as depression) are scattered throughout the test, the answers to them can be pulled out and organized into a single depression scale. There are 10 such clinical scales to the MMPI-2 (Graham, 1990). In scoring the MMPI-2 a psychologist looks for *patterns* of responses, not a high or low score on one or all of the scales. This is because the items on the test do not, by themselves, identify personality types.

In creating the original MMPI, the test makers did not try to think up statements that would identify depression, anxiety, and so on. Rather, they invented a wide range of statements about all sorts of topics; gave the test to groups of people already known to be well adjusted, depressed, anxious, and so on; and retained for the test those questions that discriminated among these groups—questions, for example, that people suffering from depression almost always answered differently from normal groups (Hathaway and McKinley, 1940). Many of the items on the MMPI-2 may sound like sheer nonsense. But they work, and for many psychologists that's all

PSYCHOLOGISTS AT WORK

Point out that for more than half a century, *school psychologists* have administered IQ and achievement tests to schoolchildren. More recently, school psychologists have also begun to focus on the mental health of students as well. Psychology has also been applied to education through the efforts of *edu-* *cational psychologists*. These psychologists conduct research on such topics as teacher-student relationships, the components of effective teaching, and the effects of cultural diversity upon a school system.

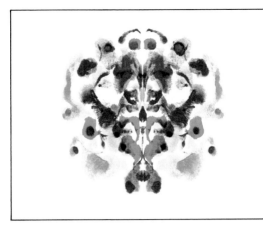 

FIGURE 12.12

In interpretation of a person's responses to the ink blots on the Rorschach test, as much attention may be paid to the style of the responses as to their content. **What are projective tests?**

that counts. One unique aspect of the MMPI-2 is that it has built-in "lie detectors." If an individual gives a false response to one statement, he or she may be caught by rephrasing of the same question at a later point.

The subject of thousands of studies, the MMPI-2 has been one of the most frequently used psychological tests (Lubin, Larsen, & Matarazzo, 1984; Costa *et al*, 1985). The MMPI-2 includes revisions aimed at modernizing the language, removing sexist terms or phrases, and adding items reflecting current issues such as alcohol and drug abuse and suicide. Introduced in 1989, the MMPI-2 is expected to be as useful as the original test (Graham, 1990). Both forms of the test have been used—and misused—in employment offices to screen job applicants. A person who is trying to get a job is likely to give answers he or she thinks the employer would like to see—thereby falling into some of the traps built into the test. Administering the MMPI-2 under such circumstances can produce misleading, even damaging results. Innocently trying to make a good impression, the job applicant ends up looking like a liar instead. As an aid to counseling and therapy, however, it can be a valuable tool.

Projective Personality Tests

Projective tests are open-ended examinations that invite people to tell stories about pictures, diagrams, or objects. The idea is that because the test material has no established meaning, the story a person tells must say something about his or her needs, wishes, fears, and other aspects of personality. In other words, the subject will project his or her feelings onto the test items.

Perhaps the best-known and most widely discussed projective measure is the Rorschach ink-blot test, developed by Swiss psychiatrist Hermann Rorschach in 1921. Rorschach created 10 cards with ink-blot designs and a system for interpreting responses. To administer the test, a psychologist

Independent Practice

■ **Research.** Assign students to examine back issues of *Reader's Digest, Family Circle*, or any magazine that is likely to run "tests" of intelligence, aptitude, or personal adjustment. Have students select a test and list the skills they think are being tested. Then have them take the test. Score their performance, and see how well they did. Next, ask them to reread the article closely to see if they can find out how the "normal" performance was defined. Ask them to analyze how well the article and test specify the reliability, validity, norms, objectivity, and efficiency of the test. Finally, ask them to rewrite any questions that would make the test more reliable and valid. (OBJECTIVES 1–3)

■ **Creating a Chart.** Ask students to imagine that they are the authors or editors of this textbook. What kind of chart do they think would help students gain an overview of all the different kinds of tests that are discussed in this chapter? Have students work independently or in small groups to design a chart summarizing the nature and purpose of IQ, aptitude, achievement, interest, personality, and situational tests. (OBJECTIVES 1–3)

hands the ink blots one by one to the subject, asking the person to say what he or she sees. The person might say that a certain area represents an airplane or an animal's head. This is the free-association period of the test. The psychologist then asks certain general questions in an attempt to discover what aspects of the ink blot determined the person's response (Figure 12.12).

There are a number of systems for scoring Rorschach responses. Some are very specific; for example, according to one system, a person who mentions human movement more often than color in the ink blots is probably introverted while an extravert will mention color more than movement. Other systems are far more intuitive—for example, noting whether the subject is open or hostile. Many researchers have criticized the Rorschach, charging that the scoring systems are neither reliable nor valid. But it continues to be used by therapists as an introduction to therapy.

The second most widely used projective measure was developed by Henry Murray. The Thematic Apperception Test (TAT) consists of a series of 20 cards containing pictures of vague but suggestive situations. The individual is asked to tell a story about the picture, indicating how the situation shown on the card developed, what the characters are thinking and feeling, and how it will end.

As with the Rorschach, there are many different scoring systems. The interpreter usually focuses on the themes that emerge from the story and the needs of the main characters. Are they aggressive? Do they seem to have needs for achievement, love, or sex? Are they being attacked or criticized by another person, or are they receiving affection and comfort?

SITUATIONAL TESTING

Is there any direct relationship between a person's responses to statements on the MMPI-2 and his everyday behavior? Do a person's perceptions of an ink blot really tell whether she will be able to remain calm under pressure? Many psychologists think not. They believe that the closer a test is to the actual situation the examiner wants to know about, the more useful the results will be. A test that measures an individual's performance in terms of emotional, attitudinal, and behavioral responses to "true life" situations is called a **situational test.** An example is a test for a driver's license, requiring that the person actually drive.

An early situational test for job placement was developed by the Office of Strategic Services (OSS) during World War II. The OSS wanted to evaluate candidates for assignment to military espionage, which requires a high degree of self-control and frustration tolerance. In order to judge the candidates, the OSS set up a three-day session of intensive testing during which candidates were required to live together in close quarters and were confronted with a number of complicated and frustrating problems.

In one procedure, a staff member instructed the candidate to build a certain type of cube with the help of two assistants. The helpers were actually psychologists who played prearranged roles. One was extremely lazy and passive, engaged in projects of his own, and offered no advice. The other

LAB EXPERIMENTS AND DEMONSTRATIONS

Remind students that the TAT is a projective test in which the test taker projects his or her thoughts onto the characters in a set of pictures. To demonstrate the open-ended nature of the TAT, find three pictures that show (1) a person opening a door and entering a room with suitcase in hand, (2) a man and woman in formal attire engaged in a conversation, and (3) a man looking in a window from outside a house. Instruct students to write a paragraph explaining what they think is going on in each of these pictures and what the characters are thinking. Collect, shuffle, and share some of the responses anonymously. Can the class identify the gender of the writers? What, if anything, do they think the stories reveal about the writers?

FIGURE 12.13

Using this airplane flight simulator, pilots are trained and tested before they are given the responsibility of flying a real airliner. The psychologists using standard tests described in this chapter would have difficulty predicting accurately whether a pilot would panic in such a situation. (United Air Lines photo) **What is a situational test?**

interfered with the work by making impractical suggestions, harassing the candidate, and asking embarrassing questions. The "assistants" succeeded so well in frustrating the candidates that not one finished the construction. But by placing the candidates in these situations, the examiners were able to predict how these men might respond to military intelligence work. The EEOC guidelines (1978) and court decisions based on them have had a significant effect on personnel testing. Job-selection and job-placement tests in many professions must now be demonstrably job relevant.

The widespread use of testing raises numerous ethical questions. We would all probably agree it is appropriate for the law to require that people pass driving tests before taking the wheel alone. But is it appropriate for a business organization to pry into an individual's fundamental beliefs before offering that person a job? Is it right for colleges to use attitude questionnaires to select their freshman classes? What does a student's attitude toward her mother, the opposite sex, or freedom of the press have to do with whether she will be able to pass French or Anthropology?

Such considerations lead to doubts about the use of tests in making major decisions about individual lives. Should people be denied a college education or be confined to a mental institution on the basis of test results? Should people be required to take tests at all, when many find it a traumatic, demanding experience of questionable value? The answers to these questions are not easy. Psychological tests, like other technological advances, have their uses and their limitations. Like automobiles, tranquilizers, and nuclear power, tests can be overused and badly used. But, as is the case with other technologies, they can be used well if people understand them. Muchinsky (1993) notes that "some authors . . . believe that psychological tests have outperformed all other types of predictors across the full spectrum of jobs" (p. 113).

VISUAL INSTRUCTION

Ask the class to brainstorm a list of situational tests. (*Possibilities include: training simulators at nuclear power plants or licensing procedures requiring an applicant to demonstrate actual competency (e.g., flying a plane to earn a pilot's license or instructing a high school class to earn a teaching certificate).* **Answer to caption, Figure 12.13:** a test that measures an individual's performance in terms of emotional, attitudinal, and behavioral responses to "true life" situations

■ **Forming Conclusions.** Arrange with the school guidance counselor to borrow a variety of tests. Try to obtain a sampling of the categories of tests covered in this chapter. Remind students that tests can reveal something about the biases, values, or thinking of a time period. Organize the class into groups, and instruct them to imagine they are historians from the year 2030. Distribute copies of the various tests. Based on these tests, what can they conclude about the American personality (or at least the personality of the test makers) in the 1990s? Call on students to share their conclusions with the class. (OBJECTIVES 1–3)

ASSESS

Check for Understanding

Ask students to summarize the differences among the various kinds of tests mentioned in the objectives on p. 291.

STUDY AND WRITING SKILLS

The widespread uses of psychological tests raise many ethical questions, especially concerning the fine line that often exists between the legitimate use of tests to weed out unsuitable candidates and their misuse that results in discrimination against whole classes of people. Have students consider some of these ethical issues and then write a "Testing Code of Ethics" for employers to follow.

Using Psychology

Review each of the 10 tips with the students. Ask them to identify the behaviors that already are part of their test-taking strategies. Suggest that they copy those tips on which they need to focus more strongly and to try to put them into practice the next time they take a test.

Reteach

Have students complete the Chapter 12 Study Guide Activity. For extended review, assign the Chapter 12 Review Activity as homework or an in-class assignment.

Enrich

Ask students to complete the Chapter 12 Extension Activity and answer the questions that follow it.

Evaluate

Administer and grade the Chapter Test. Two different forms are available should you wish to give different tests to different students/classes.

Use the Understanding Psychology Testmaker to create a customized test.

CLOSE

Ask the students whether, on the basis of their study of this chapter, they can suggest any alternatives to tests and grades as they are commonly used.

? FACT OR FICTION

It is good practice to review and change your answers on a multiple-choice test if you disagree with your first responses.

Fact. Although students often believe that their "first impression" is correct, this may not be the case. Studies show that students are likely to benefit from changing answers, especially if they are fairly confident that the new answer is the correct one (Benjamin, Cavell, & Shallenberger, 1984).

Using Psychology

Test-Taking Tips

The following tips will help you perform better on tests. Some of them have to do with studying for the test, some with taking the test, and some with your answers on particular types of tests.

1. Outline a plan to decide how much and how long you will study. Use any practice material that is available for the test.
2. Make yourself familiar with the format of standardized tests—multiple choice, verbal analogy, or essay.
3. When preparing for an essay question, review the major ideas. For short-answer tests, learn material such as dates, events, and formulas.
4. Get plenty of sleep the night before the test. Always arrive at the testing place on time. Bring a watch, but try not to focus on it.
5. Sit in a place where you will not be distracted by friends.
6. Read the instructions carefully and, if you are allowed to mark on the test, underline or circle key phrases in the directions. In essay questions, these might include "compare and contrast," "trace," "define," and "illustrate." Also underline important elements of a reading comprehension passage such as names, numbers, and dates so that you can locate them quickly. If the directions are not clear, ask any questions before the timing period begins.
7. Make sure you know what the penalty is for guessing.
8. Go through the test and plan how much time you will spend on each part. Answer the questions that are easy for you first, then concentrate on the harder ones if time permits.
9. In essay questions, always write an outline before you begin writing. Spend one-third to one-half of your time on the outline and the rest on the actual writing. If you run out of time, hand in the rest of the outline.
10. In a multiple-choice test, read every possible answer before making your choice. In rankings, one of the answers in the middle is usually right. In true-false questions, answers with absolute qualifiers, such as "always" or "never" are often wrong. In an "all of the above" question, if you know that at least two answers are correct, choose "all of the above."

COOPERATIVE LEARNING ACTIVITY

Humor can often get an important point across more effectively than a practical list. Organize the students into 10 teams of artists and writers. Assign each team to create a humorous or satirical cartoon that illustrates one of the 10 test-taking tips in the Using Psychology feature. For example, tip number 7, "Make sure you know what the penalty is for guessing," should appeal to any student with Gary Larson's "Far Side" mentality. Display the 10 completed cartoons in class or somewhere in the school.

SUMMARY

Use the following outline as a tool for reviewing this chapter. Copy the outline onto your own paper, leaving spaces between headings to make notes about key concepts.

I. Basic Characteristics of Tests

   A. Test Reliability

   B. Test Validity

   C. Establishing Norms

II. Intelligence Testing

   A. The Development of Intelligence Tests

   B. The Uses and Meanings of IQ Scores

   C. The Controversy Over IQ

III. Test-Taking Strategies

   A. Studying for a Test

   B. Reducing Test Anxiety

   C. Preparing Yourself for a Test

IV. Measuring Abilities and Interests

   A. Aptitude Tests

   B. Achievement Tests

   C. Interest Tests

V. Personality Testing

   A. Objective Personality Tests

   B. Projective Personality Tests

VI. Situational Testing

CONCEPTS AND VOCABULARY

1. Identify one characteristic that all tests have in common.

2. Explain several uses of psychological tests.

3. Define test reliability. Describe three ways of assessing reliability.

4. What is test validity? How is the validity of a test determined?

5. Explain what norms are. How are norms established?

6. An IQ test score is a poor predictor of musical ability. Does this mean the IQ test is not valid? Explain your answer.

7. How do psychologists compare scores obtained by different individuals?

8. Who was the first psychologist to develop an intelligence test? What is the name of the test he developed?

9. How was the first IQ test developed? How was the "intelligence quotient" calculated by Binet? How is it calculated now?

10. How does the Stanford-Binet IQ test differ from the Wechsler IQ tests?

11. Provide some ways you can prepare for taking a test besides studying a text and your notes. Give examples of ways to improve your general test-taking behavior.

12. Explain the main finding of the study of family size and IQ in the Netherlands.

13. Explain the difference between an aptitude test and an achievement test. Give an example of each type of test.

14. In what ways do interest tests differ from achievement tests? When are interest tests used?

15. What are the two basic types of personality tests? What are some of the differences between the types? Give an example of each type of test.

16. How is the situational test different from other forms of tests? What is the advantage of a situational test?

ANSWERS

Concepts and Vocabulary

1. All tests aim to find out a great deal about people in a very short time.

2. Answers include: measuring intelligence, skills, and knowledge; assessing an individual's desires, interests, and attitudes; predicting future success in a particular career.

3. Test reliability is a test's ability to yield the same result under a variety of circumstances. Three ways of assessing reliability are to see if retesting, having different scorers, and splitting the test in half yield the same results.

4. Test validity is a test's ability to measure what it is intended to measure. One way of determining validity is to find out how well a test predicts future performance.

5. Norms are percentiles established on the basis of the scores achieved by a large representative sample of the group to be tested.

6. If an IQ test is intended to measure intelligence, it is not valid in assessing musical ability. Validity would have to be determined by seeing if the IQ test predicts actual intelligence.

7. by establishing a percentile system for ranking scores

8. Alfred Binet; the Stanford-Binet Intelligence Scale

9. The first intelligence test was developed by selecting items on which older children did better than

younger children and by determining the average age at which a particular question could be answered. Individuals were then measured according to that scale. IQ was originally calculated by dividing mental age by chronological age × 100. Today, IQ is calculated on a basis similar to the percentile system.

10. Wechsler places more emphasis on performance tasks than Stanford-Binet. It also yields percentile scores in several areas.

11. Preparation includes techniques to reduce anxiety, rest, and alleviating mental blocks. Improving test-taking behavior includes becoming familiar with the test format, learning how to read and answer multiple-choice items, and managing time efficiently.

12. The brightest came from the smallest families.

13. Aptitude tests are designed to predict how well a person will be able to learn a new skill. Achievement tests are de-

signed to measure how much a person already knows about a particular subject.

14. Interest tests measure preferences, attitudes, and interests, and are intended to help people make informed career choices. Interest tests have no right or wrong answers.

15. *Objective* personality tests, such as the MMPI, require the individual to select one answer from a small number of given choices; they usually have only one method of scoring. *Projective* personality tests, such as the Rorschach inkblot test, consist of open-ended questions, to which individuals respond freely; they often have several possible methods of scoring.

16. Situational tests measure an individual's performance in "real-life" situations. By mimicking actual situations, they may predict success.

17. Answers will vary.

Critical Thinking

1. Begin by having students list the qualities they would like and dislike in a potential friend, and have them explain the criteria they would apply to determine whether the person "measures up."

2. Ask students to volunteer their own definitions of intelligence. Once intelligence has been fully defined, have students list criteria and methods.

3. Be sure students consider issues of reliability and validity in trying to determine a method of bias-free testing.

17. Describe the advantages and disadvantages of using tests to make decisions.

CRITICAL THINKING

1. **Analyze.** This chapter discusses a wide range of devices used to measure intelligence, aptitudes, personality traits, and so on. Think about and write down the criteria by which you "test" others. How crucial are these "tests" in determining whether or not you decide to pursue a friendship? Think about the ways in which you "test" yourself. Are the criteria you use for yourself the same as those you use for others? If not, what are the differences?

2. **Synthesize.** If you were asked to rate people on an intelligence scale of your own making, what criteria would you use, and how would you make your decision? What roles would such factors as memory, emotional maturity, creativity, morality, and intuition play in formulating your intelligence scale? How would you "test" for these factors?

3. **Synthesize.** One criticism of many tests is that they favor one particular segment of the population: usually white, middle- and upper-class, well-educated individuals. Is it possible to design a test that is truly objective, a test that favors no one group over another? What types of factors would you need to consider in the design of the test? How would you assess its reliability? Its validity? Assume you have been asked to design a test to measure athletic ability. How would you answer each of these questions?

4. **Evaluate.** Tests are widely used in education to assess students' intelligence and to predict future academic success. But only a small number of tests have been used to predict how happy people will be with their lives or how successful they will be in their careers. Explain why you think this may be the case. Are there certain things that testing cannot access or predict? Think of several examples.

APPLYING KNOWLEDGE

1. Can intelligence be learned? Try the following with two groups of subjects. For one group, give a series of problems like the following example: "Is this statement true or false? If gyuks are jogins and kuulls are jogins, then gyuks are kuulls." For the other group, give the same instructions, but also explain the first example by translating gyuks, jogins, and kuulls as cats, animals, and dogs. Then the statement will read, "If cats are animals and dogs are animals, then cats are dogs." The statement is obviously false. You can make other examples, like "If some chairs are made of wood, and some tables are made of wood, then chairs are tables." Experiment with a variety of these statements. Make some true and some false. Compare the results of the two groups. This is a question from an intelligence test. Can people learn to improve their scores on intelligence tests? Explain your answer.

2. Do you believe that test-taking strategies can make a major difference in how well a student performs on a test? Develop a 10-minute presentation on how to improve your test-taking skills. Be sure to include the following issues: how to study more effectively; how to reduce test anxiety; and how to take the test itself. How will you know if your course has been successful? Suggest different methods for assessing the success of your presentation.

3. Ask one of your academic teachers if you can spend some time after class talking about how he or she makes up a test. How does the teacher decide the number and type of questions? Does he or she prefer objective or subjective questions? Does the teacher consider the validity or reliability of the test? How is the test scored? Are the tests ever graded on a curve?

4. Choose several adults you know—they may be relatives, teachers, or acquaintances. Interview

4. Ask students to discuss the many variables that may influence happiness and career success.

Applying Knowledge

1. Answers will vary, but student responses should document the analogies that were used in their tests and an analysis of the results.

2. Answers will vary, but student responses should focus on ways to implement at least one of the tips presented on p. 310 and consider the issues of reliability and validity in testing the effectiveness of the presentation.

3. Answers will vary. Since some teachers might be reluctant to participate in such a study, you might make arrangements with teachers beforehand.

them about the types of tests they have taken in their lives. Classify the various types of tests (e.g., intelligence, personality, job-related). Ask whether they considered the test(s) fair. How do they feel about tests in general? Do we rely too much on testing in our society?

5. Imagine that you work for an insurance company and are trying to find out how likely it is for people of different ages to be involved in accidents. What criterion do you use? The number of accidents per year? Accidents per thousand miles of driving? Discuss what is right or wrong with these and other criteria.

6. Call or write for one of the questionnaires available from a computer dating service, (usually advertised in the classified sections of newspapers). Fill out or just look over the questionnaire. Into what general categories do the questions seem to fall? What does the questionnaire seek to measure? Do you think it might be a useful way to obtain meaningful information about people? Did the questionnaire ask the most informative questions about you? If not, what needs to be added?

ANALYZING VIEWPOINTS

1. Intelligence tests, such as the SAT, are supposed to measure a student's abilities gained over a lifetime of schooling. Many students, however, take advantage of one of the SAT preparatory courses that help them prepare for the test. These courses often "guarantee" higher scores for participating students. Because these courses often cost a good deal of money, not every student is able to take advantage of them. Are these SAT prep courses fair? Should they be allowed? Write an essay debating each side of the issue. Be sure to address the issue of how these courses affect the validity of the SAT test.

2. Psychological testing has been considered an invasion of privacy by some people. Others

maintain that psychological tests are an important means of gathering information. Write an essay that describes the pros and cons concerning the use of psychological testing.

3. In some cultures, people are assigned to jobs and provided educational opportunities based on their scores on IQ tests. Develop a list of the pros and cons of using IQ scores for job assignment and educational placement.

BEYOND THE CLASSROOM

1. Call a local business and set up an appointment with someone who hires new employees, such as a member of the personnel department or the owner of a small business. Tell the person you call that you are doing a project for a psychology class, and you would like to find out more about the use of tests in hiring. Find out if tests are used and, if so, what kinds of information the tests provide.

2. Invite a representative from your school guidance or counseling office to talk to the class about the tests used to measure people's interests or abilities. Ask him or her to explain what different tests are used in your school and how they are used. Suggest that the speaker identify or describe sample questions.

IN YOUR JOURNAL

1. Reread your journal entry about selecting the best teaching prospect from among a group of applicants. Devise a situational test to use in your assessment. Consider and list in your journal the behaviors you most want to evaluate in the applicants.

4. Answers will vary, but student responses should include documentation of the interviews they conducted and draw logical conclusions.

5. Answers will vary, but student responses should include an evaluation of several criteria for measuring accident risk.

6. Answers will vary, but student responses should include an analysis of its reliability and validity.

Analyzing Viewpoints

1. Answers will vary, but students should address both sides of the issue.

2. Answers will vary, but students should address the opposing views regarding psychological testing and the matter of an individual's right to privacy.

3. Answers will vary, but student responses should consider the predictive validity of using IQ tests to deter-

mine job assignments and educational placement.

Beyond the Classroom

1. Answers will vary, but students should demonstrate that they conducted the interviews and should provide a summary of their findings.

2. In conjunction with the speaker's presentation, you might arrange for the class to take an interest test.

IN YOUR JOURNAL

If time permits, discuss journal entries individually with the students.

CHAPTER BONUS
Test Question

This question may be used for extra credit on the chapter test.
Choose the letter of the correct response.

The measure of intelligence that takes into account both chronological and mental age is called:

a. practical intelligence.
b. fluid intelligence.
c. the Stanford scale.
d. the intelligence quotient.

Answer: **d**

Adjustment and Breakdown

CHAPTER 13
Stress and Health

CHAPTER 14
Adjustment in Society

CHAPTER 15
Abnormal Behavior

CHAPTER 16
Therapy and Change

314

Stress is a response to threatening or challenging conditions in our environment.

UNIT PROJECT

Refer students to the overview of Unit 5 in the Table of Contents. Ask: In terms of cause-and-effect, how are Chapters 13–15 related to Chapter 16? *(Chapters 13–15 show some of the adjustments and breakdowns—causes—that may lead people into therapy—effect.)* As an on-going project, set up a bulletin board display entitled "Surviving Life." Assign students to clip pictures—or bring in photographs—of ways people positively deal with the stresses and conflicts of everyday life. Each picture should include a caption identifying how the activity allows people to cope with stress, conflict, and change.

315

CONNECTING TO PAST LEARNING

In Chapter 11, students learned about the use of trait theories of personal behavior. Using this concept, challenge students to answer one of the key questions in Chapter 16: What makes a good therapist? Have students save their responses for review and revision at the end of the unit.

CHAPTER 13
Stress and Health

TEXT TOPICS	SPECIAL FEATURES	RESOURCE MATERIALS
Sources of Stress, pp. 317–324	**Fact or Fiction?,** p. 318 **More About Psychology,** p. 319 **Psychology Update,** p. 323 **Psychology and You,** p. 324	▬ **Reproducible Lesson Plan; Study Guide; Review Activity**
Reactions to Stress, pp. 324–332	**Psychology Update,** p. 327 **More About Psychology,** p. 329 **At a Glance:** Are You Type A?, p. 330 **Psychology and You,** p. 332	▬ **Reproducible Lesson Plan; Study Guide; Review Activity; Extension Activity Transparency 25**
Coping With Stress, pp. 333–337	**More About Psychology,** p. 337	▬ **Reproducible Lesson Plan; Study Guide; Review Activity; Application Activity; Chapter Test, Form A and Form B *Readings in Psychology:* Section 5, Readings 1, 2 Understanding Psychology Testmaker**

PERFORMANCE ASSESSMENT ACTIVITY

Assign students to create a photo montage or audiovisual presentation showing the connection between stress and physical and mental disorders. Students should work independently or in small groups to organize their visual displays around the three interrelated concepts of stressor, stress, and stress reaction. Exhibit the finished works in the classroom or in the school. Ask each student to write a "catalog description" to accompany their work. (Look for an understanding of the various sources of stress and reactions to it.)

CHAPTER RESOURCES

Readings for the Student
Frank, A. W. *At the Will of the Body: Reflections on Illness.* Boston: Houghton Mifflin, 1991.

Lazarus, R. S., and Folkman, S. *Stress, Appraisal, and Coping.* New York: Springer, 1984.

Readings for the Teacher
Chamberlain, K., and Zika, S. "The Minor Events Approach to Stress: Support for the Use of Daily Hassles." *British Journal of Psychology,* 81 (1990): 469–481.

Sarafino, E. P. *Health Psychology: Biopsychosocial Interactions.* New York: Wiley, 1990.

Scheier, M. F., and Carver, C. S. "Optimism, Coping, and Health: Assessment and Implications of Generalized Outcome Expectancies." *Health Psychology,* 4 (1985): 219–247.

Multimedia
Dealing with Stress. Sunburst Communications. This film examines the causes, effects, and handling of stress. It demonstrates that stress is a normal, necessary part of life and describes methods of coping with stress and stressful situations.

Managing Time (25 minutes, color). Division of the Bureau of National Affairs. In this film Peter Drucker draws on his experience as a management consultant and suggests solutions to the problems of wasted time.

Many Hear—Some Listen (12 minutes, color). Centrom Corporation. In this film the skill of listening to words, as opposed to just hearing them, is depicted.

Stress (11 minutes). National Film Board of Canada. In this film Hans Selye explains his theory that stress is the cause of many illnesses, especially in people not prepared to cope with it.

CHAPTER 13
Lesson Plan

FOCUS

Motivating Activity

Ask students to write down on a sheet of paper five common sources of stress in their daily lives. Tell them not to put their names on the paper. Collect the responses and then randomly list some of the sources on the chalkboard. Ask: What do you consider to be the three *most* serious sources of stress? Why? Tell students that Chapter 13 takes an in-depth look at stress—its causes, its links to health problems, and some of the ways to cope with it.

Meeting Chapter Objectives.

Identify the main subject in each objective on page 317. Have groups of students prepare data sheets on each of these subjects as they read Chapter 13.

Building Vocabulary.

Call on students to read aloud each of the Key Terms in the Glossary. Challenge volunteers to use each of these terms in a sentence.

CHAPTER 13
Stress and Health

FIGURE 13.1 Stress is our perception of an inability to cope with a difficult situation or event—a serious fight, for instance.

316

TEACHER CLASSROOM RESOURCES

- Chapter 13 Reproducible Lesson Plan
- Chapter 13 Study Guide
- Chapter 13 Review Activity
- Chapter 13 Application Activity
- Chapter 13 Extension Activity

- Transparency 25
  Transparency Strategies and
    Activities

- *Readings in Psychology:* Section 5,
    Readings 1, 2

- Chapter 13 Test, Form A and Form B

- Understanding Psychology
    Testmaker

OBJECTIVES

After studying this chapter, you should be able to

■ give examples of the psychological, physical, and behavioral reactions to stress.

■ identify various sources of stress.

■ explain different strategies of coping with stress.

B randon Leary, an ambitious high school junior, fails his final exam in French; he is terrified that his chances of getting into college have been ruined, and a day or two later he develops an unsightly rash. Juanita Collazos, Brandon's classmate, learns that her parents cannot afford to pay her tuition for her freshman year of college; her friends wonder why she has suddenly become so bad-tempered. Angela Ferrizi gets her first leading role in a high school play; while running to call her boyfriend, she realizes that she cannot remember his phone number. Brandon, Juanita, and Angela may all suffer from **stress.**

What exactly is stress? There are many definitions, and even researchers in the field use the term in several ways. To some experts, stress is an *event* that produces tension or worry. Others describe it as a person's physical or psychological *response* to such an event. Still other researchers regard stress as a person's *perception* of the event. A slight variation on these ideas is the definition we shall use in this chapter.

To refer to the stress-producing event or situation, we shall use the term **stressor.** It is important to note that an event that is a stressor for one person may not be for another. For example, traveling in an airplane may be a stressor for someone who has never flown, but not for a flight attendant. Stress, then, will be used to refer to a person's internal reactions—whether perceptual, cognitive, or emotional—to a stressor. To discuss the body's observable response to a stressor, we shall use the term **stress reaction.**

KEY TERMS

anger
anxiety
approach-approach conflict
approach-avoidance conflict
avoidance-avoidance conflict
biofeedback
conflict situation
cognitive appraisal
cognitive preparation
denial
depressant
distress
double approach-avoidance conflict
eustress
fear
frustration
intellectualization
learned helplessness
meditation
progressive relaxation
social support
stress
stressor
stress reaction

IN YOUR JOURNAL

What are the major sources of stress in school? Can you pinpoint specific occasions, times, and events when many students seemed to feel stressed? Answer these questions in your journal.

317

Exploring Key Ideas

The Mechanics of Stress. Stress-producing events or situations in the environment play an even greater role in physical health than experts previously thought. Researchers have found that many physical and mental disorders occur after a cluster of personal hardships, such as marital or business problems or changes in lifestyle. Apparently, the potential for certain physical illnesses lies dormant in a person and is precipitated only when that individual is under unusual stress. What, if any, examples can they cite from their own lives? (OBJECTIVE 1)

IN YOUR JOURNAL

Help students get started by having the class brainstorm a list of school-related events and situations. Tell students to select three items from the list as the major sources of stress in school.

EXTRA CREDIT ACTIVITY

Assign students to research occupations known for their high stress levels (e.g, police officers, firefighters, astronauts, miners, flight controllers, fighter pilots, oil field wildcatters). Students should select one occupation and prepare a "day in the life" profile of this stressful line of work. Encourage students to think of interesting ways to present their profiles. They might, for example, write a magazine feature article or record a radio commentary.

Teacher Note. Hans Selye was an endocrinologist with a career-long interest in the physiological effects of stress.

■ **Building Vocabulary.** In discussing the psychological meanings of *distress* and *eustress*, ask students to think of other words that begin with the Greek prefix *eu-* meaning "good" or "well." (*Students might mention the name of the rock group "The Eurythmics" or the terms "euthanasia" and "eugenics."*)

■ **Making a Chart.** Have students design a chart comparing the broad areas of conflict situations. Side column heads should include: Definition/ Explanation and Everyday Examples. Compile a master chart with the class on the chalkboard. (OBJECTIVE 2)

? FACT OR FICTION

People who manage stress well are free from conflict.

Fiction. Conflict is an inevitable and unavoidable part of life. Conflicts can be a source of much stress. It is unrealistic to believe that anyone can eliminate all conflicts from his or her life. Rather, the key is learning to deal with conflicts when they occur. People who deal successfully with stress are usually good at coping with life's ever-present conflicts.

SOURCES OF STRESS

Many people think of stress only as a condition to be avoided. However, Canadian researcher Hans Selye distinguished between two types of stress. Negative stress, or **distress,** stems from acute anxiety or pressure and can take a harsh toll on the mind and body. Positive stress, or **eustress,** results from the strivings and challenges that are the spice of life (Selye and Cherry, 1978; Selye, 1982).

Stress is a normal—even essential—part of life that goes hand in hand with working toward any goal or facing any challenge. In fact, as athletes gearing up for a game or students cramming for an exam can testify, stress can spur us on to greater effectiveness and achievement. In addition, whether we like it or not, we cannot escape stress; "complete freedom from stress," notes Selye (1974), "is death." But we can learn to cope with stress, so that it makes our lives interesting without overwhelming us.

Conflict Situations

In our daily lives, we often have to make difficult decisions between two or more options—for example, going to a movie with friends or staying home to study for tomorrow's exam. These alternatives tend to result from conflicting motives—say, the desire to socialize versus the desire to do well in school—and they are a major source of stress. These dilemmas are **conflict situations** (Miller, 1944), and they fall into four broad categories.

In an **approach-approach conflict,** the individual must choose between *two attractive alternatives*. For example, a high school senior has been accepted at two excellent colleges, and she must decide which one to attend. Such a conflict is generally easy to resolve. The student in this situation will find some reason to attend one college rather than the other— perhaps better climate or more courses in her intended major field. An approach-approach conflict is a "conflict" in name only. It does not produce a great deal of stress, since both choices are satisfying. After inserting your quarters, you do not stand for hours in front of a soft-drink machine trying to decide between Coke and Sprite.

An **avoidance-avoidance conflict** occurs when an individual confronts *two unattractive alternatives*. Consider the case of a college graduate unable to find a job after many months of searching. She is finally offered a position that has no future and does not pay well. Should she accept it, or should she continue to look for something better? Either course of action will be frustrating, and there is usually a high level of indecision and stress. The young woman in this example may decide that one option is "the lesser of two evils," or she may try to escape the decision; for instance, by registering with a temporary-employment agency until she gets the "right" job, or by applying to graduate school.

An individual who wants to do something but has fears or doubts or is repulsed by it at the same time is experiencing an **approach-avoidance conflict.** For example, a man wants to ask for a raise, but he is afraid he will be fired if he does. In cases like this, the degree of stress depends on the

PSYCHOLOGISTS AT WORK

Health psychologists identify psychological factors that are related to disease and apply principles of psychology to the prevention, diagnosis, and treatment of medical disorders. They believe that the mind plays an important role in many medical problems, and that people's health habits and ways they manage stress have a strong relation to staying healthy. Many health psychologists work in health-care institutions.

intensity of the desire or of the perceived threat. Resolution of this type of conflict is often very difficult and generally depends on the person's finding added reasons to choose one alternative over the other. The man in this example may learn that his boss thinks his work has been excellent, so he feels there is little risk of being fired if he asks for more money.

Probably the most common conflict situation is a **double approach-avoidance conflict,** in which the individual must choose between *two or more alternatives, each of which has attractive and unattractive aspects.* To use a simple illustration, a young woman working in Chicago cannot decide whether to spend her vacation in Paris or at her parents' home in North Carolina. She has never been to Paris, but the air fare and hotel bills will be more than she can really afford. Visiting her parents will be inexpensive and relaxing, but not very exciting. As in an approach-avoidance conflict, the degree of stress generated depends on the intensity of the attractions and repulsions. A double approach-avoidance conflict may be resolved in one of three ways: (1) finding new factors that make one option preferable—the young woman may hear about a reduced air fare to Paris; (2) finding a third alternative—she may decide to go to Quebec, which is closer and less expensive than Paris but still French in character; (3) choosing one of the alternatives in order to stop having to worry about the problem. In this last case, the person usually rationalizes his or her choice by emphasizing its good points and downplaying its drawbacks, as well as the advantages of the other option. So, the young woman may rationalize her decision to go to Paris by emphasizing that the trip will probably cost even more next year. Typically, in a double approach-avoidance, one drawback is the inability, if a person makes one choice, to have the other.

Life Changes

Major life changes—marriage, serious illness, a new job, moving away, and death in the family, for example—are important sources of stress. Common to most of these events is the separation of an individual from familiar friends, relations, or colleagues. Even marriage may involve breaking free from many longstanding ties.

Many stress researchers have concentrated on these life changes to determine how much stress they are likely to cause. Two of the foremost life-change researchers are Thomas H. Holmes and Richard H. Rahe (1967), who developed a scale to measure the effects of 43 common events, ranging from the death of a spouse to going on a vacation. Holmes and Rahe asked a cross-section of the population to rate each of these events on a scale of 1 to 100, with marriage assigned a value of 50, on the basis of how much adjustment the event required. The figures they obtained form the basis of their Social Readjustment Rating Scale (SRRS), which is shown in Table 13.1.

It is important to note that one life change can trigger others, thus greatly increasing the level of stress. Marriage, for example, may be accompanied by a change in financial status, a change in living conditions, and a change in residence.

MORE about...

What Did You Say? The avoidance-avoidance conflict is so much a part of our everyday lives that it is reflected in a number of popular sayings. Have you ever heard friends describe themselves as "caught between a rock and a hard place"? How about, "twixt the devil and the deep blue sea" or "out of the frying pan and into the fire"? Can you think of any other sayings that would describe one of the four conflicts we often encounter?

Life changes are among the most important sources of stress.

Teacher Note. Some examples of sayings that describe conflict situations include: (a) "Six of one, half dozen of another." [approach-approach] (b) "Between Scylla and Charybdis"; "darned if you do, darned if you don't." [avoidance-avoidance] (c) "Caught between heaven and hell." [approach-avoidance] (d) "You can't have your cake and eat it, too." [double approach-avoidance]

■ **Forming Generalizations.** In connection with discussion of Table 13.1 on page 320, have students check the latest almanacs and other statistical references to find as many statistics as they can relating to the various life events in Holmes and Rahe's list. For example, how many divorces were there in the United States last year? How many mortgages were granted (or foreclosed)? How many Americans were unemployed? Based on this research, ask: What generalizations can you form about the pervasiveness of stress in our society? (Tip: Have students look at stress-related statistics in terms of total population.) (OBJECTIVE 2)

COOPERATIVE LEARNING ACTIVITY

After students have read about the four conflict situations and discussed them in class, divide the students into four groups. Assign each group one of the four categories, and instruct them to create a five-minute skit that dramatizes a typical dilemma that might occur in their particular conflict situa-tion. Have the skits performed in class. Then lead the class in a critique of the various presentations. (Remind students that critiques point out good points as well as negative points. Recall, for example, the rating system of 1–5 stars for movies.)

■ Analyzing Data. Ask students to identify all the life events listed in the table that they have experienced within the last three months. Then have students add up their scores. Point out that Rahe's findings showed that 70 percent of men with scores over 300 became sick, whereas men with scores below 150 remained healthy. Request volunteers to discuss where their scores fall on the rating. Do they think the rating scale is valid? If not, what variables might this rating system fail to take into account?

Answer to caption, Table 13.1: change in work hours or conditions, change in residence, change in schools

■ Discussion. Point out that what all the items in the table have in common—other than causing stress—is that they involve change of some sort. The greater or more lasting the change, the greater the stress and their mean value. Have students describe the outlook of people who claim to dread change of any sort. In their experience, are such people better equipped to cope with stress than people who claim to welcome change in their lives? (You might review the discussion of flexibility in Chapter 3.) (OBJECTIVES 1, 2)

TABLE 13.1

The Social Readjustment Rating Scale lists 43 items that require individuals to make the most changes in their lives. **Which of the life events have a mean value of 20?**

	TABLE 13.1 • Social Readjustment Rating Scale	
Rank	*Life Event*	*Mean Value*
1	Death of spouse	100
2	Divorce	73
3	Marital separation	65
4	Jail term	63
5	Death of close family member	63
6	Personal injury or illness	53
7	Marriage	50
8	Fired at work	47
9	Marital reconciliation	45
10	Retirement	45
11	Change in health of family member	44
12	Pregnancy	40
13	Sex difficulties	39
14	Gain of new family member	39
15	Business readjustment	39
16	Change in financial state	38
17	Death of close friend	37
18	Change to different line of work	36
19	Change in number of arguments with spouse	35
20	Mortgage over $10,000	31
21	Foreclosure of mortgage or loan	30
22	Change in responsibilities at work	29
23	Son or daughter leaving home	29
24	Trouble with in-laws	29
25	Outstanding personal achievement	28
26	Wife begin or stop work	26
27	Begin or end school	26
28	Change in living conditions	25
29	Revision of personal habits	24
30	Trouble with boss	23
31	Change in work hours or conditions	20
32	Change in residence	20
33	Change in schools	20
34	Change in recreation	19
35	Change in church activities	19
36	Change in social activities	18
37	Mortgage or loans less than $10,000	17
38	Change in sleeping habits	16
39	Change in number of family get-togethers	15
40	Change in eating habits	15
41	Vacation	13
42	Christmas	12
43	Minor violations of the law	11

Reprinted with permission from T. H. Holmes and R. H. Rahe, "The Social Readjustment Rating Scale," *Journal of Psychosomatic Research*, 1967, Table 3, p. 216. © 1967, Pergamon Press Ltd.

Rahe (1975) administered this scale to thousands of naval officers and enlisted men and found that the higher a man's score, the more likely he

STUDY AND WRITING SKILLS

Have students write a short story, poem, or song developed around one or more of the life changes listed in the Holmes-Rahe Social Readjustment Rating Scale. Tell students that they should focus on the themes of *change* and *readjustment*. Their works should depict the various kinds of stress reactions that are involved in major life events. Have students read or perform their finished works in class. If your school has a literary magazine, suggest that they submit their work for publication.

was to become ill. Men with scores below 150 tended to remain healthy, while about 70 percent of those with scores over 300 became sick. There are problems, however. Some of the items on the SRRS may result from illness, rather than cause it (Brett, Brief, Burke, George, & Webster, 1990). Some of the items, such as marriage, are joyful events that are not related to illness (Taylor, 1991). Several studies suggest there is only a small relationship between stressful life events and illness (Brett, *et al.*, 1990).

As you read the list, it may occur to you that many of the items do not yet apply to you. So, another factor that should be considered is the age of the person. In one study, Chamberlain & Zika (1990) asked four groups of about 150 New Zealanders to rank the severity of various problems. They found that the different groups had very different rankings. Students were most troubled by the pressures of time, members of the community were most worried about future security, mothers by finances and household matters, and the elderly by their neighborhood and health—the least hassling issues for students.

Every one of us faces many daily hassles: traffic, arguments, car trouble. Could it be that the primary effects of stress are the accumulation of little things that just constantly seem to hassle us (Weinberger, Hiner, & Tierney, 1987)? Seventy-five married couples recorded their everyday hassles, and it turned out those were significantly correlated with health problems such as sore throats and headaches later experienced (DeLongis, Folkman, & Lazarus, 1988). In spite of these problems and variations in individual stress reactions, the Holmes-Rahe scale is a useful guideline for measuring stress.

Work

Most people spend more time at work than they do at any other activity. Not surprisingly, then, work can be a prime source of stress, and there is a great deal of evidence to show that on-the-job stress affects the physical and mental health of many employees. The statistics are staggering: one study estimated that cardiovascular disease, which is often linked to stress, accounts for 12 percent of worker absenteeism in the United States and adds up to an average loss of about $4 billion a year. Other health problems that often stem from stress—migraine headaches, for example—resulted in a loss of more than 20 million work days in one year.

What causes stress on the job? Researchers have identified more than 40 factors that can be occupational stressors. We can group these factors into seven general categories.

1. *The nature of the job.* A worker may suffer stress reactions as a result of *working conditions* (temperature, humidity, noise, vibration, and lighting, for example) or *work overload* (a workload that is too heavy or too difficult); *underload* (too little work) can also be a stressor.
2. *Role in the organization.* An employee may suffer from *role ambiguity* or *role conflict*. Role ambiguity arises when the worker is unclear about what is expected. Role conflict occurs when the job demands that the worker do things that (a) he or she dislikes or disapproves of

FIGURE 13.2

The birth of a child is a happy event, but it also creates stress for the baby's parents and siblings. **What is the mean value of gaining a new family member on the scale?**

VISUAL INSTRUCTION

Remind students that one life change, such as the birth of a child, can trigger others. Ask students to review Table 13.1 and to identify some repercussions that the arrival of a new child can bring to a family. *(e.g., change in financial state, revision of personal habits)* **Answer to caption, Figure 13.2:** 39

■ **Classifying Information.** In discussing the seven categories of occupational stressors, ask students to identify actual work situations that might fall under each category. For example, coal mining would fall under the first heading: the nature of the job. Declining union clout might fall under the fifth heading: organization structure and climate. (OBJECTIVE 2)

 LAB EXPERIMENTS AND DEMONSTRATIONS

After discussing the SRRS, have students work in pairs to develop a list of 25 life events that are stressful for teenagers. As a group, use these lists to create one master list of 25 items. (Items repeated by several groups are obvious candidates; votes may have to be taken on others.) In small groups, direct students to rate these 25 events in order, from the most stressful to the least stressful. (The criteria should be the difficulty in adjusting to a situation.) Next, tell them to assign a numerical value to each event, using the SRRS as a model. Discuss the difficulty of assessing the impact of life changes, noting times in which group members disagreed. Ask: What variables played a role in the disagreements?

Have students brainstorm a list of other occupations in which being responsible for the well-being of others might be a source of stress. *(e.g., flight controller, crane operator at a construction site)*
Answer to caption, Figure 13.3: Stress may affect young workers who want to advance rapidly and older workers who feel they can no longer advance.

■ **Identifying Alternatives.**
Ask students to discuss the implications of the study cited in the sixth category: family and outside activities. Ask: How can a supportive marriage help reduce on-the-job stress? Next, mention that many people live alone, which can also be a source of stress. What advice would students give to stressed unmarried workers who live alone? *(Answers will vary, but might include: confide in friends, keep busy with enjoyable after-work activities, relax with a pet.)* (OBJECTIVE 3)

FIGURE 13.3

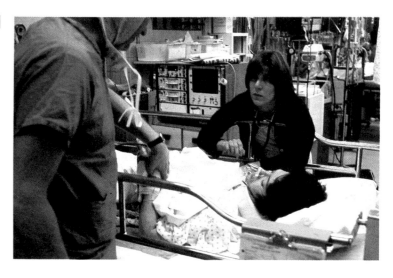

Feeling responsible for other people is one source of on-the-job stress. In a hospital, where one wrong decision can mean the difference between life and death, this particular stressor may affect many employees. **In what ways can career development lead to stress?**

or (b) he or she thinks are beyond the scope of the job description. *Responsibility for other people* is another important role-related stressor. People in "white-collar" (managerial and professional) positions seem most likely to be victims of this type of stress.

3. *Interpersonal relationships.* Research suggests that poor relationships between a worker and his or her superiors, subordinates, and colleagues may be stressful.

4. *Career development.* For many workers, especially those in the early phase of their careers, the desire to advance rapidly may be a stressor. For other workers, usually older ones, fear and frustration can result when they reach a "career ceiling," the point at which they can no longer advance within the organization.

5. *Organizational structure and climate.* An organization that does not encourage a sense of belonging, worker participation in decision making, and good communication within its ranks is likely to generate stress; and that stress often leads to illness (French, Caplan, & Van Harrison, 1982).

6. *Family and outside activities.* The worker's life away from the job can cause stress on the job. Burke and Weir (1977) found that a close, supportive marriage—in which an employee can informally discuss job problems with his or her spouse—is likely to prevent or reduce on-the-job stress and increase both occupational and marital satisfaction. In contrast, a less successful marriage can intensify, if not create, stress at work. Marital and family problems are among the most common problems reported by employees (Trice & Beyer, 1984).

7. *Miscellaneous.* As we have seen, life changes can be significant stressors. Many life changes are work-related—a change of jobs, unemployment, and retirement, for example.

Invite the manager of a fairly large local or regional business to visit the class to discuss how his or her company addresses stress among company employees via its organizational structure or climate. For example, does the company encourage a sense of belonging and involve workers in corporate decision making? Does the manager maintain an "open door" policy? Tell students to be prepared with questions.

Everyday Sources of Stress

Some stressors—notably the life changes we have discussed—are major events. However, there are many minor sources of stress that we must confront and cope with either on an everyday basis (rush-hour traffic, for example) or only once in a while (say, running out of gas).

Frustration.   **Frustration** is a common source of everyday stress. It is the feeling of bafflement or disappointment that results when progress toward a goal is blocked. It has a wide variety of causes—delays (a long checkout line at the supermarket), lack of resources (not enough money to buy new clothes), physical limitations (running for a bus and missing it), accidents (breaking a glass), other people (someone breaks a date at the last minute), or institutional regulations (an overdue fine for a library book).

Frustration is a daily occurrence; in fact, it would be possible for *all* of the examples given above to happen to one person in one day. Frustration is especially stressful when we feel that it has been caused by unreasonable circumstances (say, saving just enough money to buy a certain Father's Day present, only to learn that the store has raised its prices) or when the circumstances are unexpected. Constant frustration has been shown to cause stress reactions such as aggression, fantasy, and withdrawal.

Environmental Stressors.   As we have seen, environmental conditions such as noise may cause stress on the job, and these factors can have similar effects on the public at large. In fact, surveys have shown that Americans regard noise as one of the foremost irritants in their lives. Noise is particularly aggravating when it is loud, irregular, or uncontrollable. Constant exposure to unpleasant noise levels can lead to hearing loss and can interfere with learning. One study, for example, showed that children who lived in the lower, noisier floors of an apartment house built over a highway had a lower reading ability than did children living in the upper, quieter floors (Cohen *et al.*, 1973). There *are* some problems with this study, however. For example, apartments higher in a building usually cost more. Might not the higher-paid, better-educated families live on the higher floors?

It was long assumed that crowding was an environmental stressor. Indeed, most people dislike certain high-density situations and can feel stress when other people get too close. Crowding itself, however, is not the problem. The subway system in Tokyo hires people to push more people onto the subways during rush hours. It is an accepted part of Japanese culture to be able to function effectively within a small "personal space." People of Middle Eastern derivation tend to have markedly small personal spaces. As a result, they stand much closer in a conversation than is comfortable for most citizens of the United States or Canada. The problems occur not when you are crowded, but when you *feel* crowded (Taylor, 1991).

There is a positive side to crowding. Imagine, for example, that you and a friend go to a football game and find you are the only spectators in the stadium. You would probably feel quite peculiar, since we expect—and enjoy—the excitement of a cheering crowd in such a situation. Feeling

PSYCHOLOGY UPDATE

Hassles and Uplifts. In addition to the impact that major stressful events such as a divorce or death in the family can have, psychologists have studied the effects that relatively minor, day-to-day stressors can have on health. These more common stressors are called *hassles*. Examples of hassles include losing your car keys, being caught in a crowded elevator with a smoker, or being late for work because you were stuck in a traffic jam. Research has found a connection between hassles and health problems. It may be that hassles gradually weaken the body's defense system, making it harder to fight off potential health problems.

It has also been suggested that small, positive events—called *uplifts*—can protect against stress. Uplifts are things that make a person feel good, such as winning a few dollars in a lottery or doing well on an exam. Some psychologists claim that uplifts can have the opposite effect of hassles—they can reduce stress and protect a person's health.

■ **Discussion.** After students read the margin feature, ask them to brainstorm as many examples of everyday hassles and uplifts as they can. Which outnumbers the other—the hassles or uplifts? What explanations can students offer for this result? (You might save this list for use during a discussion of learned helplessness—and learned optimism—in Chapter 15.)

Teacher Note. Although there is overcrowding in many urban areas with a high crime rate, crowding alone does not seem to cause crime. Other stressors, such as poverty and unemployment, may be the causative agents.

COOPERATIVE LEARNING ACTIVITY

Bring into class a videotape of a popular TV sitcom involving young people. As the students watch the video, have them identify the stressors encountered by the characters. Ask: What coping strategies do the characters use? Do all the characters react in the same way to a stressful situation? What factors, or variables, do you think cause people to behave differently under stress? Which, if any, of the characters used coping mechanisms similar to your own?

■ **Debating an Issue.** Although urban life is often fast-paced, alienating, impersonal, and lonely, millions of people live there even though they could live elsewhere. What positive stressors do cities provide for them? To find out, have the class debate the following issue: *Resolved*—That city life may be hazardous to your health. (Appoint some students to speak from the perspective of urbanites from some of the nation's larger cities such as New York, Chicago, Los Angeles, Dallas, or Miami. Have others represent a small-town perspective.)

PSYCHOLOGY and YOU

Stress on the Battlefield. Waiting for battle to begin is extremely stressful on wartime troops. In the Persian Gulf War, American troops spent five months camping in the desert before hostilities began. They were isolated, bored and uninformed. In addition, most had never been in battle and were not prepared for the horror and carnage they were likely to see.

Mail from home provided the greatest relief from the stresses of waiting. Persian Gulf soldiers were inundated with cookies, candy, plastic Christmas trees, suntan oil, and other treats from family members back home. The military leased a cruise ship for troop furloughs. In addition, the soldiers were able to obtain news of the war from Armed Forces Radio.

The Army established a psychiatric ward in the desert where soldiers could come to talk about family problems and their own anxieties. Once battle commenced, the ward was used to treat battle fatigue.

unpleasantly crowded depends largely on our ability to maintain a degree of privacy and distance from others. You may enjoy being part of a crowd at a rock concert, for example, but you may hate it when everyone shoves to get out.

Jonathan Freedman (1975) has concluded that the effects of crowding depend on the situation. If the situation is pleasant, crowding makes people feel better; if the situation is unpleasant, crowding makes them feel worse. In other words, being packed together *intensifies* people's reactions, but it does not *create* them.

The United States is now an urban nation, and many areas are very crowded. Not only are our cities crowded, but they also are nuclei of noise, soot, traffic, crime, and fear—all of which are stressors. Stanley Milgram (1970) describes urban living as "stimulus overload"; the individual is barraged by more inputs than he or she can deal with. As a result, people in cities tend to ignore stimuli that do not directly concern them (a blind person trying to cross a busy street, for example). They identify others only as roles (the mechanic who does not have your car ready, rather than Mr. Jones whose wife was rushed to the hospital last night). The result of these behaviors is a fast-paced, alienating, impersonal, and lonely environment.

REACTIONS TO STRESS

A person who encounters a stressor that is intense or prolonged will react to it. There is a wide variety of stress reactions, and their effects range from beneficial to harmful. Many of the physiological responses are inborn methods that probably evolved to cope with stress effectively. In addition, many responses to stress are automatic. Just as the body reacts to a cut by producing new tissue, it has means to heal the wounds of stress—crying, for example.

Coping mechanisms that worked for our remote ancestors are not necessarily successful in our modern technological society. But human beings are often slow to give up anything that is well established. We are more likely to depend solely on these ancient stress responses than to make conscious attempts to modify them or adopt others that we now know are more appropriate to our twentieth-century life style.

The ways in which different people react to stress vary considerably; each person's response is the product of many factors. Stress reactions may be physical, psychological, or behavioral, but these categories are not clear-cut. The human body is a *holistic* (integrated) organism; our physical well-being affects how we think and behave, poor mental health can trigger physical illness, and so on.

Regardless of the stressor, the body reacts with immediate arousal. The adrenal glands are stimulated to produce (a) hormones that increase the amount of blood sugar for extra energy and (b) adrenalin, which causes rapid heartbeat and breathing and enables the body to use energy more quickly. These responses are designed to prepare a person for self-defense.

CRITICAL THINKING ACTIVITY

Identifying Cause and Effect. Ask students to list major problems and/or life changes that they have confronted during the last few years. Next, have them organize these events along a time line. When the time lines are done, have students recall periods of physical illness over the same time span. Direct them to record these illnesses on the time line in red. Instruct students to identify correlations between life events and periods of physical illness. Ask volunteers to discuss whether they think a cause-and-effect relationship exists between the two. (As an alternative, students might carry out this activity based upon the life events and illnesses of an older relative or friend. If no correlation exists, have students explore coping strategies used to survive hardships such as the loss of a spouse.)

a

c

d

b

FIGURE 13.4

Our reactions to various events depend on our own personalities, as well as on the severity of the event itself. The family facing the destruction of their home, the high school senior waiting for her college admissions interview, the man coping with the terminal illness of a loved one, and the family facing a financial crisis are all experiencing various levels of stress. **What happens during the resistance stage to stress?**

PORTRAIT

Teresa Bernárdez
1931-
Psychiatric treatment of and attitudes toward women have come a long way since Freud's historical analysis of Dora. Today many psychiatrists specialize in the stresses and problems faced by women, not only in the United States but on a worldwide basis. One such professional is Teresa Bernárdez. Bernárdez earned a medical degree in her native Argentina. Upon coming to the United States, she pursued advanced studies in psychiatry and went on to teach at such prestigious schools as Radcliffe and Michigan State. Today Bernárdez is known for her work in the mental and physical health of women. Her research and aid to international women's groups has earned Bernárdez many awards, including the Peace Award from the Pawlowski Foundation.

VISUAL INSTRUCTION

Ask students to note the visual indications of stress in the four photographs. What are some of the obvious physical signs that a person is under extreme stress? *(answers will vary, but might include: nervousness, difficulty in holding back tears)*
Answer to caption, Figure 13.4: An individual finds ways to cope with the stressor and to ward off, superficially at least, adverse reactions.

PSYCHOLOGISTS AT WORK

Good political diplomacy has always involved good psychology. But in today's conflict-ridden world diplomats and policy makers are being aided by *peace psychologists*. This new group of professionals specializes in studying ways to avoid wars and other conflicts. Peace psychologists, for example, use scientific methods to analyze the personalities of world leaders to work out negotiation strategies for when the leaders face each another across the bargaining table. It is the job of peace psychologists to provide tips on how to avoid personal confrontations that could scuttle a nuclear arms agreement, for example.

■ Applying Concepts. Write the following stages in the body's stress reaction on the chalkboard: Alarm, Resistance, and Exhaustion. Then have students pick one of the life events listed on Table 13.1 on page 320. Working individually or in small groups, assign them to write a scenario in which a fictitious character goes through one or all of these stages. (Tell students that it is appropriate to use humor.) Request volunteers to read their scenarios aloud. Ask students to identify the stages of stress reaction exemplified by the stories.
(OBJECTIVES 1, 2)

WORKING WITH TRANSPARENCIES

Project Transparency 25 and use the guidelines provided in Teaching Strategies and Activities. Assign Student Worksheet 25.

VISUAL INSTRUCTION

Have students analyze the photograph on this page and point out that maintaining unit cohesion and discipline is an important means of minimizing the effects of *battle fatigue*—the exhaustion caused by prolonged exposure to combat.
Answer to caption, Figure 13.5: The individual may be unable to think clearly and act decisively.

However, if stress persists for a long time, the body's resources are used up. The person becomes exhausted and, in extreme cases, dies.

Selye (1956, 1976) identified three stages in the body's stress reaction: alarm, resistance, and exhaustion. In the *alarm* stage, the body mobilizes its "fight-or-flight" defenses: heartbeat and breathing quicken, muscles tense, the pupils dilate, and hormones that sustain these reactions are secreted. The person becomes exceptionally alert and sensitive to stimuli in the environment and tries to keep a firm grip on his or her emotions. For example, a hiker who confronts a rattlesnake on a mountain trail freezes in his tracks, is suddenly aware of every sound around him, and tries not to panic. If the alarm reaction is insufficient to deal with the stressor, the person may develop symptoms such as anxiety.

In the *resistance* stage, the person often finds means to cope with the stressor and to ward off, superficially at least, adverse reactions. Thus an airline passenger who recovers from the shock and frustration of losing her luggage may tell herself to keep calm when reporting its disappearance to airline officials, calling her insurance company, and so on. At this stage, the person may suffer psychosomatic symptoms, which result from strain that he or she pretends is nonexistent.

If exposure to the stressor continues, the individual reaches the stage of *exhaustion*. At this point, the adrenal and other glands involved in the "fight-or-flight" response have been taxed to their limit and become unable to secrete hormones. The individual reaches the breaking point: He or she

FIGURE 13.5

A soldier subjected to extreme and prolonged stress may reach the stage that Hans Selye calls exhaustion. **What happens during this stage?**

 ## LAB EXPERIMENTS AND DEMONSTRATIONS

You might demonstrate how unexpected behavior can become a stressor in group situations by trying this experiment: At some time during class, stop what you are doing. Sit thoughtfully at your desk, perhaps exhibiting a facial expression indicative of some sort of distress. Do not respond to any questions the students may have. After a few minutes, ask them how they felt. Did they experience an increase in stress and any accompanying physical reactions (such as nervousness or fear)? If so, tell them that their bodies were reacting to the first of Selye's three stages—alarm.

becomes exhausted and disoriented and may develop delusions—of persecution, for example—in an effort to retain some type of coping strategy. The problem is that the very responses that were good for immediate resistance to stress—such as reducing digestion and boosting blood pressure—are detrimental in the long run. Think about the importance of control over environmental stressors in keeping stress at bay discussed earlier. Some investigators have found that assembly-line workers in repetitive jobs over which they exercise very little control are likely to show the effects of stress. It is not surprising that the corporate executives running the company—who can control their own destiny to some degree—are less likely to show such stress (Karasek & Theorell, 1990).

Let us now examine some of the major psychological, behavioral, and physical reactions to stress. We shall discuss both short-term and long-term responses in each category.

Psychological Reactions

Short-term Reactions. Short-term psychological stress reactions may be either emotional or cognitive. The most common response to a sudden and powerful stressor is **anxiety,** which is a feeling of imminent but unclear threat. An employee whose boss passes by in the hall without saying hello may develop anxiety about her future on the job. **Anger** is likely to result from frustration. A college student who does not make the lacrosse team may fly into a rage when he puts his favorite CD in the player and it skips. **Fear** is usually the reaction when a stressor involves real danger—a fire, for example. Fear directs the individual to withdraw or flee, but in severe cases he or she may panic and be unable to act. Common examples of short-term emotional stress reactions are overreacting to minor irritations, getting no joy from daily pleasures, and doubting one's own abilities.

Cognitive reactions include difficulty in concentrating or thinking clearly. A student who must give an oral presentation may worry about it but find himself unable to prepare for it. Another student wants to surprise her father with the news that she has been admitted to her first-choice college, but cannot recall where his office is. Another type of cognitive stress reaction is unjustified suspicion or distrust of others.

Long-term Reactions. Prolonged stress, in combination with other factors, affects mental health. It does not necessarily cause mental illness, but it may contribute to the severity of mental illness. There is an increased likelihood of psychiatric disorder following a major life change, for example. Among those who attempt suicide, and those with depression, schizophrenia, or anxiety-based disorders, there seems to be quite a definite link between stress and subsequent symptoms.

Behavioral Reactions

Short-term Reactions. There are many short-term behavioral changes that result from stress. A person may develop nervous habits (trembling or

PSYCHOLOGY UPDATE

The Bad News about Bad News. Hans Selye (1976) viewed stress as one of life's events that contributes to aging. Whereas we can replace lost sleep, it was Selye's opinion that resisting stress takes something out of us that is never recoverable; we are permanently altered.

Talking with the victims of tragedies can provide a sense of what Selye meant. The victims of the nuclear accident in 1979 at Three Mile Island were still suffering after-effects five years later. In comparison with others from a similar town not threatened by the disaster, the nearby residents were experiencing higher blood pressure. The Three Mile Islanders also reported that thoughts of the disaster and its implications persisted (Davidson & Baum, 1986).

Witnesses and victims of violent accidents or natural disasters often report similar effects after the disaster and its immediate threat are long past.

■ **Discussion.** After students read the margin feature, discuss Selye's contention that long-term resistance to stress may permanently alter people and/or contribute to aging. What evidence can students cite to support this theory? *(One way that a person might be altered is by developing a fatalistic attitude about life in general.)*

■ **Demonstrating Reasoned Judgment.** A saying describes suicide as "a long-term solution to a short-term problem." Explore the link between stress and suicide. Then have students consider a hypothetical case in which someone is so overwhelmed by the loss of a job that he or she threatens suicide. What short-term remedies can students recommend to help the person get through this extreme short-term reaction to job loss? *(Suicide is a serious subject for students today. For more on this topic, see Chapters 15 and 16.)* (OBJECTIVES 1, 3)

BEYOND THE CLASSROOM

Invite a guest speaker from a local suicide hot line to address the class. Request that the speaker explain the nature of calls received by the hot line and techniques used to "talk down" the callers. The speaker might also discuss some of the symptoms of severe stress. Finally, ask the speaker to explain the type of training that hot line workers receive. After the presentation, assign students to summarize what they have learned.

■ **Making a Chart.** Assign groups of students to design a chart comparing the following categories: Psychological Reactions, Behavioral Reactions, and Physical Reactions. Side column heads should include: Short-Term and Long-Term. Direct students to complete the chart with data drawn from text pages 327–329. (OBJECTIVE 1)

■ **Representing an Idea Visually.** Request interested students to select a high-stress job, such as the air-traffic controllers mentioned on this page. Then, challenge them to design a poster that might be displayed on the job site to warn workers of the health hazards of stress. Posters can be informational, inspirational, or humorous. (OBJECTIVES 1–3)

Research is confirming that stress is a major cause of disease today.

pacing, for example), gulp meals, smoke or drink more, take drugs, or feel tired for no reason. There may be changes in his or her posture. He or she may temporarily lose interest in eating, grooming, bathing, and so on.

Some behavioral reactions are positive, however. In a tornado, for example, some people will risk their lives to help others. Such stressors often create attitudes of cooperation that override individual differences and disagreements.

Escape is another behavioral stress reaction, and it is often the best way to deal with frustration. For example, a woman who is on a bus that is caught in snarled traffic may get off and walk to her destination.

Long-term Reactions.   While many people can endure great amounts of stress without marked behavioral responses, others may be seriously affected. Severe stress can be significant to the development of escapist personality styles—alcoholism, drug addiction, chronic unemployment, and attempted suicide, for example. Stress has also been noted as a contributing cause of aggressive personalities, delinquency, and criminal behavior. In addition, people with high scores on the Holmes-Rahe scale appear to be more accident-prone than average.

Physical Reactions

Short-term Reactions.   As we have mentioned, the physiological "fight-or-flight" response—accelerated heart rate and so on—is the body's immediate reaction to stress. This response is geared to prepare human beings to fight or run from an enemy such as a savage animal or band of warriors, and it was probably useful earlier in human history. But we cannot deal with most modern stressors—a financial problem, for instance—in this manner, and physical responses to stress are now generally inappropriate. In fact, prolonged physical arousal can cause health problems including difficulty in breathing, insomnia, migraine headaches, urinary and bowel irregularities, muscle aches, sweating, and dryness of mouth.

Long-term Reactions.   Stress is certainly a contributing cause of illness. We have already discussed the study by Rahe (1975) linking low scores on the Holmes-Rahe scale to reports of good health for the following year, while those with high scores became sick.

Emotional stress is clearly related to such illnesses as peptic ulcers, hypertension, certain kinds of arthritis, asthma, and heart disease. Those who work in high-stress occupations may pay a high price. Air-traffic controllers, for example, spend their days juggling the lives of hundreds of people on air routes where a minor error can mean mass death. They are said to suffer from the highest incidence of peptic ulcers of any professional group (Cobb and Rose, 1973). Similarly, a student may come down with flu on the day before an important exam, or a director may have an asthma attack on the opening night of a play.

Stress can be at least partly responsible for almost *any* disease, as shown by the scope of illness associated with high Holmes-Rahe scores. Stress can contribute to disease in several ways. Sometimes it can be the

STUDY AND WRITING SKILLS

Read the following excerpt from a *New York Times* editorial entitled "Stress, Cops and Suicide" (12/1/93):

Few [police officers] *share details of their workday with their families for fear of frightening them. Inhabitants of a world where toughness is prized, even fewer feel free to reveal emotional fragility to their colleagues, let alone their superiors. . . . In killing themselves police officers may be, quite simply, relieving a stress about which they find it impossible to talk.*

Ask students to imagine they are the police commissioner of New York. What kind of program would they institute to curb suicides among police? (You might persuade one of your more curious students to locate the complete editorial to find out what the commissioner actually did.)

direct cause of illness. A migraine headache, for example, is usually a physical reaction to stress. Stress may also contribute to illness indirectly. It reduces our resistance to infectious disease by tampering with the immune defense system (O'Leary, 1990).

In one experiment, researchers gave neutral nose drops to a control group, and gave other subjects viruses known to cause a cold. After a week's isolation, subjects given the virus who reported they were under high stress were roughly twice as likely to come down with a cold as those reporting little or no stress (Cohen, Tyrrell, & Smith, 1991). Furthermore, stress can lower our resistance to disease if we react by neglecting our diet, not exercising, or smoking or drinking too much.

Animal studies suggest that psychological stress may contribute to some forms of cancer. One study involved a group of mice vulnerable to cancer. Some of the mice were kept in housing that exposed them to stressful noises, while other mice were kept in quieter housing. At the end of the experiment, 92 percent of the high-stress mice had developed cancer compared with only 7 percent of the low-stress animals (Anderson, 1982).

Some people smoke in order to reduce tension, but smoking increases their risk of lung and mouth cancer. Having any form of cancer is in itself highly stressful. The degree to which a person is able to cope with this stress can be an important factor in his or her recovery (Taylor, 1983).

Factors Influencing Reactions to Stress

Personality Differences. In some cases, the individual's personality may make him or her more vulnerable to stress. For example, two researchers have suggested that persons who exhibit a behavior pattern they call "Type A" are very likely to have coronary artery disease, often followed by heart attacks, in their thirties and forties. Those who do not have this pattern (Type B people) almost never have heart attacks before the age of 70 (Friedman and Rosenman, 1974).

The Type A person's body is in a chronic state of stress, with an almost constant flow of adrenalin into the bloodstream. This adrenalin apparently interacts with cholesterol or other chemical agents to block the coronary arteries, which lead to the heart. It may be that high levels of adrenalin prevent the normal chemical breakdown of cholesterol in the blood.

Type A people are always prepared for fight or flight. They have a great deal of "free-floating" hostility—that is, anger that has no real object or focus. They are extremely irritable, and one of the things that irritates Type A people most is delay of any kind. They become impatient waiting in line, always move and eat rapidly, often try to do two or three things at once (such as reading while eating), and feel guilty when they aren't doing *something*. They are also extremely competitive. In short, Type A people are always struggling—with time, other people, or both. Note that we have been describing an extreme version of the Type A personality. Most people respond to the world with Type A behavior at times, but are not in a constant state of stress. Carson and Butcher (1992) noted that many studies indicated that aggression and hostility, as well as insecurity and the inability or unwillingness to express anger, can increase susceptibility to coronary

MORE about...

Stress and Natural Disasters. A very stressful life event was experienced by the victims of the 1980 Mount St. Helens volcanic eruption in the state of Washington.

One study looked at the effects of the eruption on the residents of Othello, Washington. The researchers compared data gathered from community records for a six-month period after the disaster with the same time the previous year. The records indicated large increases in alcohol abuse, domestic violence, and physical illnesses. The death rate increased by nearly 19 percent.

The long-lasting impact of the Mount St. Helens disaster can be seen from the results of a three-year study that compared the residents of Castle Rock, Washington, which had been greatly affected by the volcano, with those living in another town that was not affected by the disaster. The adult residents of Castle Rock were nearly 12 times as likely to suffer from a psychological disorder. Many of the Castle Rock residents were suffering from post-traumatic stress, depression, and severe anxiety.

■ **Research.** Have students research other natural disasters that have led to short-term and long-term stress reactions. Direct them to investigate methods that communities and health organizations have tried to help people cope with the stress. *(Examples include the Chernobyl nuclear disaster in Ukraine, Hurricane Hugo in Florida, or the 1993 floods along the Mississippi River.)* (OBJECTIVES 1–3)

Teacher Note. Underscore that most research does not suggest that stress causes cancer. Instead, researchers believe that stress may affect the course of cancer by draining the strength of the immune system. The study of the relationship between psychological factors and the immune system has given rise to a fast-growing new specialty: *psychoneuroimmunology*. Investigators in this field suggest that mental imagery can alter the workings of the immune system. (For example: Imagine the white blood cells as a powerful army waging battle against the weak germs.) You might have interested students further research this field.

Enrich. Have students complete the Chapter 13 Extension Activity.

CONNECTIONS: PSYCHOLOGY AND HEALTH

Have the students work in teams to prepare a brief oral presentation about one of the major chronic diseases that have been linked to stress: peptic ulcers, hypertension, and certain kinds of asthma, arthritis, and heart disease. Students should research and describe the symptoms as well as the methods of diagnosis and treatment of each disorder. Encourage the students to include visual aids in their presentations to the class.

At A Glance

Have students complete this informal self-assessment test in class, and discuss their responses. Point out that Type A personalities become more than irritated when they are made to wait—they become outraged. In short, even mild stress provokes extreme reactions among some Type A personalities.

Next, explain that recent research has zeroed in on *hostility* as a deadly component in the Type A personality. Some researchers (Eliot & Buell, 1983) have suggested that unrelenting hostility and the negative emotions that accompany it tax the heart by constricting the arteries and making the heart beat faster. Hostility also floods the body with "fight-or-flight" hormones. Over the long term, the arteries break down under the constant wear and tear, leading to the blockages that cause heart attacks. Brainstorm ways Type A personalities might control anger and hostility. (Tip: Studies have proven relaxation, self-control, and goal-setting effective.)

At A Glance

ARE YOU TYPE A?

Are you high-strung, tense, and always concerned about time? Then you might have a Type A personality. To find out for sure, ask yourself the following questions. Your answers will tell you whether you're giving your heart a hard time.

- Are you continually aware of time? Type A people live by the clock and measure their day in terms of how much they accomplish each minute.
- Are you always in a rush? Type A people do everything very quickly. They eat, move, walk, and talk at a speeded-up pace.
- Do you lose your patience when things take too long? Type A people get outraged when a sales clerk spends an extra minute ringing up a sale.
- Do you always try to do more than one thing at the same time? Type A people feel that one of the best ways to get more accomplished is to do two or more things at once.
- Do you tend to use nervous gestures to emphasize your point? Type A people express their tension by clenching their fists, pointing their fingers, and banging on the desk.
- Do you evaluate your life in terms of how much you accomplish rather than what you accomplish? Type A people emphasize such quantitative measures as the number of A's they got in school or the number of sales they made during the month.

If you answered yes to most of these questions, it may be time to slow down. Not because slower is better, but because slower is less taxing on your heart.

For more details, see Meyer Friedman and Diane Ulmer. *Treating Type A Behavior—and Your Heart.* New York: Alfred A. Knopf, 1984.

heart disease. Booth-Kewley and Friedman confirmed that Type A behavior increased the chances of heart disease, but also found that depression, anger, hostility, aggression, and anxiety contributed. They concluded that it is not hurry and impatience that lead to heart problems, but the negative emotions accompanying our daily activities (1987).

Another personality trait that can affect the strength of a stress reaction is emotional expressiveness. Some research suggests that people who neither express nor admit to strong feelings of despair, depression, and anger are more likely to develop cancer than those who can give vent to their emo-

BEYOND THE CLASSROOM

Ask students to go to a library and explore back issues of the *New Yorker* and other magazines that feature a variety of sophisticated cartoons. Tell students to find examples that depict classic Type A personalities, such as the fuming boss and the always-in-a-hurry worker. Have students contribute their cartoons to a classroom display along with a caption that identifies the Type A behavior depicted in the cartoon.

tions. Some investigators have proposed a Type C—cancer-prone—behavior pattern. People who deny their negative emotions, tend to express feelings less freely, and show a high tendency toward social conformity, have a greater risk of getting cancer (Baltrusch, Stangel, & Titze, 1991). Negative life events such as those measured by the Holmes and Rahe scale do seem to be related to an increased likelihood of cancer in later life (Forsen, 1991).

Perceived Control over Stressors.   In the late 1950s, Joseph Brady and his colleagues (1958) published the results of their classic (but now questioned) experiment on the effects of controlling stressful events. They linked two monkeys to a machine that gave them an equal number of shocks. One could prevent the shocks by pushing a lever and the other could not. The monkey who could control the shocks—later named the "executive monkey"—developed ulcers. Brady theorized that constant worry about when to press the lever produced higher levels of stress for the executive monkey than inability to act did for the powerless one.

Later attempts to achieve similar results with other animals were not successful. According to J. M. Weiss (1972), when Brady's research team set up the original study, there was a bias in the selection of subjects. The monkeys who were selected to be the "executive monkeys" had shown themselves to be more likely to push the lever than the monkeys who were selected for the no-control situation. Thus, these monkeys may have been more reactive and, consequently, possibly more prone to develop ulcers.

The accepted view today is that physical disorders are more likely when we do *not* have control over stressors. Most evidence to support this theory comes from experiments on animals. Weiss (1972), for example, gave two groups of rats identical electric shocks. In one group, a rat could avoid the shock by touching its nose to a panel; the other group had no control over the shocks. The group that could regulate the shocks developed far fewer ulcers than those that could not.

Subsequent experiments showed that feedback is also an important factor. Animals that responded to avoid shock and then heard a tone to signal that they had done the "right" thing suffered fewer ulcers than those that responded to avoid the shock but were given no feedback.

Weiss (1971) found that lack of feedback can harm human beings as well. His research showed that people develop ulcers when they have to make large numbers of responses but receive no feedback about their effectiveness. This lack of feedback is a factor in role ambiguity.

Another study that used human subjects (Hokanson *et al.*, 1963) punished errors on cognitive tasks with mild electric shocks. Subjects who were allowed to take breaks when they wanted to showed less increase in blood pressure than did those who were assigned for breaks. This and other research supports the conclusion that we respond to a stressor more intensely when we cannot control it (Loudenslager, 1988).

Social Support.   Sidney Cobb (1976) has defined **social support** as information that leads someone to believe that he or she is cared for, loved,

■ **Analyzing Information.**
In discussing the effect of perceived control and social support on stress reactions, ask: Do you think young adults experience more stress today than 100 years ago? Why or why not? Then have students think ahead to the 21st century. Do they think stress will increase or decrease? To provoke discussion, you might read the following passage from the Fall 1992 Special Issue of *TIME* entitled "Beyond the Year 2000."

The century to come . . . will be complex, fast-paced, and turbulent. Human beings everywhere have learned to live with, even thrive on, explosive increases in the volume of knowledge. . . . Change has become almost addictive, a jolt to energy and creativity.

Ask: Does the reporter think people will have more or less control over events? *(less)* Why? *(pace of change will pick up)* How does the reporter view this stressor? *(It prods creativity.)* How do you think your generation will handle the fast-paced life of the 2000s? *(Answers will vary.)* (OBJECTIVES 2, 3)

ADDITIONAL INFORMATION

Stress sometimes results in the development of *psychosomatic disorders*—physical disorders that are attributable to emotional or other psychological causes. Research suggests that psychosomatic disorders are adaptive insofar as they reduce a person's need for action during a time of stress. One long-term effect of this behavior is the person's inability to resolve psychological problems in any effective way. (For more on this type of mental disorder, see Chapter 15.)

DID YOU KNOW?

According to the *Journal of the American Medical Association*, the mortality rates for major chronic illnesses, such as heart disease, cancer, and lung disease, are 25–33 percent lower for Hispanics than for other white Americans. Researchers cite the strong social support provided by Hispanic families as the reason.

■ **Role Playing.** Ask the students to describe in their own words the four kinds of support that social groups offer. Then ask the class to consider the following scenario:

Since dropping out of college, a young man has worked for 10 years as a reporter for a small town newspaper. He has never earned much, but does own a house, which is heavily mortgaged. He is unmarried, but has a girlfriend and many other close friends. Now, however, the newspaper has gone out of business. Because he doesn't have a college degree, the young man has been unable to find another reporter's job. The bills are piling up, and the bank is threatening to foreclose on his house.

Ask volunteers to role-play (or write) four scenes, showing how each of the four kinds of social support—emotional, appraisal, informational, and instrumental—can work to help the young man deal with his stressful situation. (OBJECTIVE 3)

PSYCHOLOGY and YOU

Stress on the Home Front. War creates tremendous stresses not only on soldiers in the field, but also on loved ones back home. The Persian Gulf War was particularly stressful on military families because more than 25,000 of the armed forces sent to Saudi Arabia were women.

The women soldiers were forced to leave their children behind with their husbands, parents, or other family members. Husbands had to take a leave of absence from their jobs or arrange for day care for their children. Many children of troops in the Gulf suffered from nightmares and loss of appetite.

One way that the husbands and wives of combat troops coped with wartime stresses was to form support groups among themselves so they could talk about their problems and fears. Military bases offered family members various kinds of help, such as psychological counseling and financial support. Schools with large numbers of military children also provided counseling and special programs to help students cope.

respected, and part of a network of communication and mutual obligation. He has found that social support can reduce both the likelihood and the severity of stress-related diseases—a finding often replicated (Cohen, 1988).

Cobb's and Cohen's conclusions have been backed up by many other studies. A study of pregnant women (Nuckolls, Cassel, and Kaplan, 1972), for example, noted that 91 percent of those with high Holmes-Rahe scores and low social support experienced complications in pregnancy, as compared with only 33 percent of those with high Holmes-Rahe scores and high social support. In fact, the high-stress and high-support group suffered fewer complications than did women who reported *low* Holmes-Rahe scores. Social groups seem to offer at least four kinds of support. First, *emotional* support involves concerned listening, which forms a basis for offering affection and concern, and bolstering the stressed person's self-confidence. Second, *appraisal* support is interactive. The listener feeds back information and probing questions to the stressed person as an aid in sorting out and understanding the sources of the stress. A third kind, *informational* support, emerges from appraisal support. Here the listener responds to what he or she has learned, evaluating the manner in which the person is dealing with his or her stressors. Finally, *instrumental* support represents active, positive support in the form of direct help such as money or living quarters. Yet there is evidence that some friends, despite the best intentions, may be more of a strain than a help in a crisis (Rook, 1990).

Yet some sources of social support can be especially helpful. One study of male blue-collar workers (Wells, 1977) reported that social support from wives and supervisors counteracted the health consequences of stress more effectively than did support from co-workers, friends, or relatives.

Amount of Stress. You have read that high amounts of stress can have serious effects on health, but *low* stress at work—underload—may trigger similar reactions. One group of researchers (Caplan *et al.*, 1975) studied more than 2,000 men in many different occupations. They found that as on-the-job boredom increases, so does the probability of psychological and physical complaints and illnesses. Assembly-line workers rated their jobs as most boring and suffered the most stress-related disorders. Accountants, engineers, and computer programmers reported average amounts of boredom. Professors and physicians expressed the lowest levels of boredom and had the fewest stress-related problems.

Another study (Harrison, 1976), however, drew different conclusions. Work overload corresponded to greater job dissatisfaction in all the occupations under consideration. Underload, however, caused discontent mostly among white-collar workers; it had little effect on the job dissatisfaction of assembly-line workers. One possible explanation is that on-the-job gratification is more important to white- than to blue-collar workers, and underload does not allow for much job gratification (House, 1972).

In spite of these somewhat inconsistent findings, we can basically describe the relationship between stress and health as a bell curve. At both extremes of the curve—very low and very high stress—illness is most probable. At the curve's center, a person feels challenged without being overwhelmed, and is most likely to be healthy and effective.

BEYOND THE CLASSROOM

Guide the class in developing a questionnaire that they can use to survey local residents about the main environmental stressors in your neighborhood or town. Factors to consider include: weather, noise, crime, litter, industrial pollution, over- or underdevelopment, and demographics. Have students tabulate their findings and discuss the survey results in class. (For guidelines on conducting a survey, you might have students borrow a government text used in your school.)

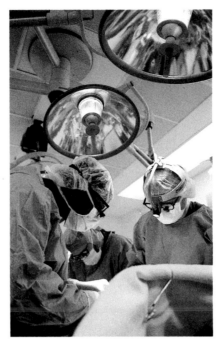

FIGURE 13.6

Low stress and boredom on the job can damage health as much as high stress can. One study found that assembly-line workers rated their jobs as most boring and suffered the most stress-related disorders. **How did physicians rate their jobs?**

COPING WITH STRESS

The best overall recommendation for coping with stress is to bring it under control before it is too late. Richard Rahe and Ransom J. Arthur (1968) have divided the process by which stress can cause disease into six stages:

1. *Perception of the situation.* The person is aware that something is challenging him or her.
2. *Psychological responses.* The person denies or minimizes the situation or represses its effects.
3. *Physiological responses.* The person undergoes the "fight-or-flight" re-action, which we have discussed.

■ **Discussion.** Draw a continuum line on the chalkboard. Along this line, organize the six stages in the process by which stress develops into disease. Challenge students to identify a stressor and to explain how it might affect a person at each of the six stages. Write the students' responses under the appropriate segment of the continuum. Next, challenge students to identify a course of action that could be applied at each stage along the continuum to counter the effects of the stress.
(OBJECTIVES 2, 3)

4. *Protective behavior.* The person tries to deal with the situation.
5. *Signs of illness.* The person begins to act sick—staying home from work or school, for example.
6. *Frank disease.* A doctor confirms the illness, and the person is officially sick.

Rahe and Arthur believe that dealing with stress during the first four stages can generally—and relatively easily—prevent disease. If a person has reached the final two stages, though, the process is hard to stop or reverse.

To break the chain of events that can cause a stress-related disease, it is necessary for a person either to alter his or her awareness of the problem and of the potential consequences or, if stress is unavoidable, to modify its physical and psychological effects. Let us now look at some specific coping strategies that people use to combat stress.

Psychological Coping Strategies

Our interpretation or evaluation of an event—a process psychologists call **cognitive appraisal**—helps to determine its stress impact. Drugs can affect cognitive appraisal. For example, drinking may help to convince a man who has been fired that his troubles are not serious, or that he will enjoy unemployment, or that getting drunk is the best solution for the time being.

We can also try to influence our cognitive appraisals by means of psychological coping strategies, and stress reactions are more likely to occur when these strategies fail. Common defense mechanisms (see Chapter 11) are **denial,** in which a person decides that the event is not really a stressor, and **intellectualization,** in which the person watches the situation from an emotionally detached standpoint.

Both denial and intellectualization can prevent physical reactions to stress. In one study (Lazarus *et al.*, 1965), three groups of subjects viewed a film that showed gruesome accidents at a sawmill. One group was told that the injuries were not real, but were staged by the actors (denial); a second group was advised that they were seeing an educational film about the importance of safety measures (intellectualization); the third group was told nothing. The levels of physical reaction were lower in the first two groups than in the third. Thus, if a person does not evaluate an event or situation as stressful, a stress reaction will not occur. But that's really failing to deal with what could be a legitimate stressor (Holahan & Moos, 1985).

When a person knows that stress is unavoidable, though, **cognitive preparation** can be the most successful strategy. Irving Janis (1958) studied patients before and after surgery to analyze the relationship between fear before the event and coping afterward. He found that patients who expressed moderate fear recovered most successfully; those who showed extreme fear or little or no fear before surgery did not cope as well. Janis believes that cognitive preparation, which he terms "the work of worrying," enables a person to mentally rehearse possible outcomes. In this way, he or she is better prepared for whatever does happen than is someone who has used denial or intellectualization beforehand.

 LAB EXPERIMENTS AND DEMONSTRATIONS

You might want to lead the class through the following exercises to demonstrate the technique involved in progressive relaxation. Tell students that the technique relaxes the mind by relaxing the body through a sequence of easy exercises. Request volunteers to lie on the floor. Tell them to slowly contract and relax the following muscle groups a few times until no tension is felt:
Feet: Point feet straight out and curl toes tightly. Release and relax.
Lower legs: Point feet toward face as high as they go. Relax.
(continued on page 335)

Modifying Physical Reactions to Stress

Drugs. Many people use drugs—both legal and illegal—as a way to reduce stress and the physical symptoms, as well as the tension, boredom, and depression, that accompany it. Physicians often prescribe mild sedatives (Valium, for example) for people who complain of stress. Some of these drugs may indeed relieve stress temporarily, but most do not. In addition, all of these drugs carry varying risks of dangerous side effects, including physical dependence. If you must use drugs to cope with stress, do so only as a temporary measure to help you through a crisis. *Do not* use them to deal with normal, everyday stress.

Alcohol is the most widely used and abused drug today, and is involved in about 10 percent of all deaths (Smith, 1989). It is a **depressant,** which means that it reduces the activity of the central nervous system (see Chapter 7). As a result, drinking will reduce tension quickly. However, Miller (1976) has demonstrated that the more often a person drinks to escape stress, the more dependent he or she will become on alcohol. Among chronic alcoholics in particular, drinking may actually *increase* depression or anxiety (Nathan and O'Brien, 1971), and can lead to very high rates of suicide in comparison to other disorders (Gomberg, 1989). Alcoholism is a critical health problem in the United States; the National Institute on Alcohol Abuse and Alcoholism estimates that between 9 and 10 million adults in America are alcoholics or problem drinkers.

Tobacco is the second most commonly used drug. Many smokers claim that cigarettes relieve various stressors; they will smoke more at work, at parties, or when anxious or nervous. Studies (Silverstein, 1976; Perlick, 1977) indicate that smoking does not reduce anxiety or irritability; *not* smoking, however, tends to aggravate the smoker's stress reaction. Not only are cigarettes useless against stress, but they greatly increase the risk of lung cancer and other illnesses. Although cigarette use declined steadily during the 1980s in the United States, it was up slightly from mid-decade levels among both male and female high school seniors (Ray & Ksir, 1993).

Relaxation. Many techniques of relaxation have been developed specially to cope with stress. More than half a century ago, Dr. Edmond Jacobson devised a method called **progressive relaxation** to reduce muscle tension. This involves lying down comfortably and tensing and then learning how to relax each major muscle group in turn. Jacobson later added exercises for mental relaxation in which a person conjures up images and then lets them go. **Meditation** is a relaxation technique that has been shown to counteract both physical and psychological responses to stress (see Chapter 7). Experienced meditators quickly reach an alpha-wave mental state related to that of Stage I sleep and are able to resume their activities feeling refreshed.

Biofeedback. As explained in Chapter 7, **biofeedback** is a technique for bringing specific body processes—blood pressure and muscle tension, for example—under a person's conscious control. The subject is hooked up to an electronic device that measures the process he or she wants to regulate

Independent Practice

■ **Weighing Alternatives.** Ask students to imagine a world without stress—both the advantages and the disadvantages. (You might have them draw up a balance sheet to weigh the alternatives more clearly.) Next, assign students to present their opinion of such a world in one of the following forms: essay, poem, short story, song, drawing, or photo montage. Request volunteers to present their creations. Ask: What opinion(s) does the work express about life in a stress-free world? (OBJECTIVE 1)

■ **Autobiographical Writing.** Instruct students to recall an incident in which stress affected their judgment and caused them to behave in an unsafe manner. Ask them to write a brief autobiographical essay in which they describe the event and reflect on the outcome of their behavior. (To encourage honesty, tell the students that the assignment will not be collected.) Under the same circumstances, how would they behave based on what they have learned in this chapter? (OBJECTIVES 1, 2)

 LAB EXPERIMENTS AND DEMONSTRATIONS

Upper legs: Keeping legs straight, lift feet off floor 10 inches. Relax.
Stomach: Take a deep breath and tighten stomach muscles as you hold breath. Relax.
Chest: Push shoulders back and hold as you exhale slowly. Relax.
Upper arms: Tighten muscles in both

of the upper arms. Relax.
Lower arms: Tighten muscles as you move hands toward arms. Relax.
Hands: Make tight fists and hold. Relax.
Neck: Smile broadly and tighten neck muscles. Relax.
Forehead: Push eyebrows up and

tighten. Relax.
At the end of the exercises, ask volunteers to describe their feelings. Ask: When would you be most likely to use progressive relaxation techniques?

■ **Research.** Have students interview two people in each of the following age groups: 8–12, 13–18, 19–25, 26–35, 36–45, 46–55, and 55 and older. Ask students to find out what the interviewees' greatest stressors are and what, if anything, they do to manage stress. Have students make a chart comparing stressors of various age groups. What conclusions can they draw about age-related stress? Do the causes of stress change with age? If so, how? What, if any, changes took place in coping mechanisms?
(OBJECTIVES 2, 3)

■ **Cooperative Learning Activity.** Organize the students into small productions teams. Ask each group to develop a videotape, public service announcement, or brochure titled "Stress and Survival." The focus should be on effective ways for people to cope with everyday stress.
(OBJECTIVE 3)

VISUAL INSTRUCTION

Put the headings *Mild, Moderate,* and *Strenuous* on the chalkboard. Then ask the students to brainstorm as many examples as they can of exercises and place them under one of the categories. Review the lists and eliminate any that might cause negative stress for some people *(e.g., rappelling).* Finally, have the students identify those forms of exercise that most people could easily squeeze into a busy schedule.
Answer to caption, Figure 13.7: may burn off stress hormones; aids in respiratory and cardiovascular fitness

and plays that process back, in the form of either sounds or visual patterns. This feedback enables many, though not all, people to learn to control various bodily responses. Biofeedback has been used most successfully to train tense people to relax.

Behavioral Coping Strategies

Controlling Stressful Situations. There are several ways in which we can control our exposure to stressful events and thereby reduce levels of stress. As noted earlier, escape or withdrawal, when possible, can be an effective coping strategy. A young woman who is not enjoying herself at a party, for example, can leave. When avoiding an event is not practical, controlling its timing may be helpful; you can try to space out stress-producing events. A couple who are planning to have a baby in the summer, for instance, may postpone looking for a new house.

Problem Solving. Sometimes neither avoiding nor spacing events is possible. A high school senior may face a deadline for a college application and an important exam on the same day. In cases like this, problem solving, or confronting the matter head-on, can be the best way to cope. Regarding frustrations or conflicts as problems to be solved means the situation becomes a positive challenge rather than a negative setback. Problem solving involves a rational analysis of the situation that will lead to an appropriate decision. The student in our example may map out the remaining days and allocate specific times to work on the application and others to study for the test; he may also decide that he can gain more time for these activities by skipping band practice or postponing a date. Problem solving is a very healthy strategy that tends to sharpen insights and attention to detail and develop flexibility.

Explanatory Style. Martin Seligman (1991) describes two very different styles of thinking. The *optimist* typically puts the best face on any set of events. Following a loss, an optimistic quarterback will suggest, "What's done is done. Start thinking about next week!" The *pessimist* always sees the dark side. After becoming ill and missing the senior prom, the pessimist will say, "This always happens to me! I never get to. . . . " Seligman performed a study of baseball players, grouping them as optimists or pessimists from their quotes in the sports pages. He found the pessimists were much more likely to die at a younger age.

Exercise. Physical exercise is another constructive way to reduce stress. It stimulates and provides an outlet for physical arousal, and it may burn off stress hormones. Continuous rhythmic exercise—running or swimming, for example—is not only effective against stress but also ideal for respiratory and cardiovascular fitness. David Holmes and colleagues have performed experiments that indicate aerobic exercise reduces cardiovascular response and arousal following both stressful life events and immediate stress (Roth & Holmes, 1987; Holmes & Roth, 1988).

FIGURE 13.7

Physical exercise reduces stress, so find a way of introducing a regular exercise program into your schedule. You don't need to become an athlete; many people exercise by walking to and from work every day. **In what other ways is exercise healthful?**

CONNECTIONS: PSYCHOLOGY AND PHYSICAL EDUCATION

As your students probably already know, physical exercise provides an excellent way to reduce mental stress. Ask students to talk with coaches and/or physical education teachers about the reasons for this. For example, what physical changes occur in the body to help trigger stress reduction? What, if any, activities are more effective than others? Have students present their findings in a brief oral report to the class.

Support Groups and Professional Help. We have discussed the positive role that social support plays in reducing stress. There are groups that operate beyond ordinary personal networks to help people with specific stress-related problems—Alcoholics Anonymous, Weight Watchers, crisis intervention centers, and so on. Professionals such as psychologists, doctors, social workers, and ministers can also be consulted.

Training. A situation can be stressful because we are unsure we can deal with it; it may be new, unfamiliar, or dangerous. Training to prepare for such a situation can ease the stress. For instance, a student who is nervous about going to a friend's country club because she does not play tennis might take a few tennis lessons. Exposure to moderate stressors in a relatively safe but challenging environment allows a person to gain experience and confidence in coping; Outward Bound, which trains young people in wilderness survival, illustrates this strategy.

Improving Interpersonal Skills. Much of the stress we undergo results from interpersonal relations. Developing skill in dealing with others—family, friends co-workers—is thus one of the best ways to manage stress. There are several advantages to being able to interact well with others: increased self-confidence and self-esteem, less chance of loneliness or interpersonal conflict, and development of social support systems.

A Lifelong Challenge

Although you have read about the problems and difficulties that stress can cause, you should not forget that stress is not necessarily "bad." As you have seen, too little stress can be has harmful as too much stress under some circumstances.

Throughout our lives, stress is a challenge that we will inevitably and repeatedly encounter. It is thus best to develop a range of coping strategies that we can apply to different situations, and it is important to learn when each strategy is most suitable. Coping strategies that are used inappropriately can actually increase stress.

Some people respond to setbacks in coping by learning *not* to try to cope at all. Psychologists call this condition **learned helplessness** (Seligman, 1975; see Chapter 2). In learned helplessness, a person suffers from an event or situation so severely or so often that he or she comes to believe that it is uncontrollable and that any effort to cope will fail. The person also begins to apply the same attitude to other situations; for example, a man who feels continually frustrated and thwarted on the job may give up trying to cope with difficulties in other areas of his life as well.

We *can* learn to cope if we try. Albert Ellis (1978) sums up perhaps the most positive way to deal with stress:

I feel determined to strive to use whatever power I have to change the unpleasant stresses of life that I can change, to dislike but realistically accept those that I cannot change, and to have the wisdom to know the difference between the two.

MORE about...

Bad Memories. One among many unfortunate reminders from the Vietnam War is a psychological condition called *post-traumatic stress disorder*. It is a condition that involves personally unpleasant behavior and experiences caused by a traumatic stress, the effects of which tend to show up after the event has passed.

With some returning Vietnam War veterans, nightmares, flashbacks, feelings of paranoia, and feelings of guilt about having survived did not appear until months after returning to the United States. More startling was the fact that in some instances the symptoms did not occur for as long as five years.

In women, events such as rape, witnessing a violent accident or death, or being in a serious accident can cause a post-traumatic stress disorder, but the responses usually start immediately after the traumatizing event.

In these instances, the effects of stress actually follow the removal of the stressor, but may continue for a long time afterward.

ASSESS

Check for Understanding

Ask students to summarize the principal causes of stress, the ways people react to it, and strategies for coping with it.

Reteach

Have students complete the Chapter 13 Study Guide Activity. For extended review, assign the Chapter 13 Review Activity as homework or an in-class activity.

Enrich

Readings in Psychology. Have students read the Section 5, Reading 1 and Reading 2 selections in *Readings in Psychology* and answer the questions that follow the selections.

Evaluate

Administer and grade the Chapter Test. Two forms are available should you wish to give different tests to different students/classes.

Use the Understanding Psychology Testmaker to create a customized test.

CLOSE

Remind students of the five common sources of stress in their lives that they identified in the opening activity. Now that they have studied the chapter, ask them to suggest practical ways to cope with each stressor.

COMMUNITY INVOLVEMENT

Contact your county departments of social services and mental health. Ask them to advise you about support groups in your area that might be willing to send representatives to speak to your class. Speakers should describe how their group's program is designed to help people cope with stress-related problems. If possible, arrange to have representatives come from support groups that cater to young adults.

ANSWERS

Concepts and Vocabulary

1. The most common is double approach-avoidance conflict. It can be resolved by finding new factors that make one option preferable, by finding a third alternative, or by choosing one of the alternatives in order to stop having to worry about the problem.

2. separation of an individual from friends, relatives, or colleagues, or break from longstanding ties

3. It examines only a small percentage of the large number of possible stressors. It does not take into account cultural differences in what are regarded as stressors.

4. Hans Selye; alarm, resistance, exhaustion

5. clearly linked to peptic ulcers, hypertension, certain kinds of arthritis, asthma, and heart disease; partly related to almost any disease

6. A negative effect is coronary artery disease, often followed by heart attacks. Type A personalities are in a constant state of stress because of their general hostility and anger.

7. People who repress strong emotions are more likely to develop cancer. The research is inconclusive thus far.

8. The accepted view is that physical disorders result when we do not have control over stressors. The results of Brady's study, in

which a monkey that could control the stressor developed ulcers, have never been duplicated, and so the differences remain unreconciled.

9. A good recommendation is to control stress before it is too late. With unavoidable stress, cognitive preparation can help. Worrying can be beneficial.

10. controlling stressful situations, problem solving, exercise, support groups

---

SUMMARY

Use the following outline as a tool for reviewing this chapter. Copy the outline onto your own paper, leaving spaces between headings to make notes about key concepts.

I. Sources of Stress
  A. Conflict Situations
  B. Life Changes
  C. Work
  D. Everyday Sources of Stress

II. Reactions to Stress
  A. Psychological Reactions
  B. Behavioral Reactions
  C. Physical Reactions
  D. Factors Influencing Reactions to Stress

III. Coping with Stress
  A. Psychological Coping Strategies
  B. Modifying Physical Reactions to Stress
  C. Behavioral Coping Strategies
  D. A Lifelong Challenge

CONCEPTS AND VOCABULARY

1. What is the most common conflict situation? In what ways can this conflict be resolved?

2. What do many major life changes share in common?

3. Identify at least two criticisms of the Holmes-Rahe scale.

4. Who identified three stages in the body's response to stress? What are the three stages?

5. To what illnesses is emotional stress clearly related? To what illnesses is stress at least partly related?

6. Describe the negative effects of "Type A" behavior. Why do people exhibit "Type A" behavior?

7. How can emotional expressiveness affect the development of cancer? Are the research findings conclusive in this area?

8. What is the accepted view on the relationship between degree of control over stressors and its effect on physical disorders? Brady's famous study does not agree with the accepted view. How is this difference reconciled?

9. What is the best overall recommendation for coping with stress? When stress is unavoidable, what is the most successful coping strategy? Is worrying beneficial when a person faces an *unavoidable* stress?

10. Identify at least three behavioral ways to cope with stress.

11. If a person does not learn to cope with stress, what condition may result?

CRITICAL THINKING

1. **Analyze.** Some studies have found that high levels of stress can lead to both physical and mental illness. Do you believe this is true? What evidence do you have? Are all individuals equally susceptible to stress-related illnesses? Are some people better able to cope with stress than others? What does this say about stress as a *cause* of illness?

APPLYING KNOWLEDGE

1. Study your own family, and try to identify stressors affecting each family member. Do these stressors result from the roles that family members have, from their ages, from their contacts with the outside world, from the ways that family members relate to each other, or from some other sources? Are there ways in which you contribute to family stress? Are there ways in which you do (or could) help reduce stress?

---

and professional help, improving interpersonal skills

11. Answers will vary, but students might note that the person may learn not to cope at all—i.e., learned helplessness.

Critical Thinking

1. Have students discuss whether all people are equally susceptible to stress-related illness.

2. The Holmes-Rahe "Social Readjustment Rating Scale" lists life events deemed to be stressful to adults. Assume your job is to develop a similar scale for teenagers only. In what ways would your scale be different? What would you add to or delete from the list?

3. Short-term reactions to stress often include physical responses—in other words, illness and other health problems. Ask a variety of people to give you examples of times when they have suffered from short-term health problems that they believe were associated with stress. You may have to prompt them with specific questions—for example: "Did you or your spouse get sick on your honeymoon?" "How did you feel on the first day of school this year?" "The last time you stayed home from school (or work) because of illness, was there anything stressful happening in your life?" Try to list a number of examples of stresses and corresponding health problems.

4. Try a systematic program of relaxation to see if physical relaxation helps you deal with stress. For example, deliberately try to relax your muscles for a minute or two between each of your classes, at lunch time, and during other breaks. Do this consistently for a week. At the end of the week, evaluate your mental attitude. Do you feel less stressed?

5. Go to a local shopping center or mall and observe a few cigarette smokers. Many smokers claim that smoking cigarettes relieves stress. Do the smokers you observe seem to smoke more in stressful conditions, such as waiting in line? Do the smokers seem relaxed? Do you believe that smoking relieves tension and stress?

ANALYZING VIEWPOINTS

1. Is stress always "bad"? Can stress ever be positive? Write a paper that presents both viewpoints. To gather additional information on this topic, you may want to read books and re-cent magazine articles on stress. Be sure to give examples in support of both positions.

BEYOND THE CLASSROOM

1. The Holmes-Rahe "Social Readjustment Rating Scale" is designed to measure the effects of various stressful life events, ranging from the death of a family member to changes at work or school. Holmes and Rahe assigned relative values to each event with the idea that the higher the value, the more stressful the event. Interview five people you know, asking each person how stressful the past year has been. Ask them to rate the past year's stress on a 1-to-10 scale, with 1 being least stressful and 10 being most stressful. When they tell you what rating they would assign to the past year's stress, write it down. Then, using the list that appears on page 320, ask these same people to look at the list of stressful events. Ask them to circle the events that have occurred in their lives over the past year. Study the five lists. Compare the results of the list with the person's 1-to-10 rating of how stressful the past year has been. What do the results say about the relationship between stress and major life events?

IN YOUR JOURNAL

1. Reread the journal entry you made at the beginning of the chapter. Next, consider these questions: Do students seem more stressed prior to tests or exams? Can you discover any common elements among these sources of stress? What might be done to alleviate stress in school? Would stress be reduced or eliminated if there were no grades? What if there were no tests? What would school be like without stress? Should stress in school be eliminated? Write your answers to these questions in your journal.

Applying Knowledge

1. Answers will vary. Students might respond in the form of a journal entry, an informative report, or a chart.

2. Answers will vary, but student responses should use the scale as a basis.

3. Answers will vary. Students should document the findings.

4. Answers will vary, but students should describe the techniques they used and evaluate the effects.

5. Answers will vary, but students should keep a log of their observations and draw logical conclusions.

Analyzing Viewpoints

1. Answers will vary, but students should cite sources in support of their arguments.

Beyond the Classroom

1. Answers will vary, but students should document the interview procedure and provide an analysis of their findings.

IN YOUR JOURNAL

If time permits, discuss journal entries individually with the students.

CHAPTER BONUS
Test Question

This question may be used for extra credit on the chapter test.
Choose the letter of the correct response.

An event or a circumstance that produces threats to an individual's health or well-being is called:

a. resistance.
b. a stressor.
c. an uplift.
d. coping.

Answer: **b**

CHAPTER 14
Adjustment in Society

TEXT TOPICS	SPECIAL FEATURES	RESOURCE MATERIALS
Love and Marriage, pp. 341–348	More About Psychology, p. 344	Reproducible Lesson Plan; Study Guide; Review Activity *Readings in Psychology:* Section 5, Reading 3
Parent-Child Relationships, pp. 348–352		Reproducible Lesson Plan; Study Guide; Review Activity; Extension Activity
College Life, pp. 353–355	Psychology and You, p. 355	Reproducible Lesson Plan; Study Guide; Review Activity *Readings in Psychology:* Section 5, Reading 4
Working, pp. 355–359	Fact or Fiction?, p. 358	Reproducible Lesson Plan; Study Guide; Review Activity; Application Activity; Chapter Test, Form A and Form B Understanding Psychology Testmaker

PERFORMANCE ASSESSMENT ACTIVITY

Arrange for a group of alumni from your school to visit the class and participate in a panel discussion. Ask students to work in small groups to prepare a list of questions to serve as a basis for interviewing the panel about their adjustments to and during adulthood. Questions should address methods of coping with change and such issues as leaving home, college experiences, first jobs, career advancements or moves, marriage and romance, and relationships with parents and siblings. Students should summarize what they learn from the panel by drawing up a series of statements: "Adjustment to _____ means having to _____ ." (Students' statements should reflect the experiences of alumni.)

CHAPTER RESOURCES

Readings for the Student
Ruddick, Sara, and Daniels, Pamela, eds. *Working It Out: 23 Women Writers, Artists, Scientists, and Scholars Talk About Their Lives and Work.* New York: Pantheon, 1977.

Terkel, Studs. *Working.* New York: Avon Books, 1974.

Turgenev, Ivan. *Fathers and Sons.* Baltimore: Penguin Books, 1975.

Readings for the Teacher
Ainsworth, M. D. S. "Attachments Beyond Infancy." *American Psychologist,* 44 (1989): 709–716.

Aldwin, C. M., and Revenson, T. A. "Does Coping Help? A Reexamination of the Relation Between Coping and Mental Health." *Journal of Personality and Social Psychology,* 53 (1987): 337–348.

Barling, J. *Employment, Stress, and Family Functioning.* New York: Wiley, 1990.

Katzell, R. A., and Thompson, D. E. "Work Motivation: Theory and Practice." *American Psychologist,* 45 (1990): 144–153.

Lamb, M. E. "Paternal Influences on Early Socio-Economic Development." *Journal of Child Psychology and Psychiatry and Allied Disciplines,* 23 (1982): 185–190.

Whitbourne, S. K. *Adult Development.* New York: Praeger, 1986.

Multimedia
Love and Marriage (1/2" video). Ohio University Telecommunications Center. This video presents three couples for study: newlyweds, a couple married for 50 years, and a remarried couple.

For additional resources, see the bibliography beginning on page 530.

FOCUS

Motivating Activity

Write the phrase *well-adjusted* on the chalkboard. Ask: What do people generally mean when they say someone "has it all together"? What are the attributes of such a person? Do these attributes conform to your understanding of well-adjusted? Why or why not? (Some students may think the phrase is used to describe someone who has an edge of arrogance to them. Explore whether this arrogance is a cover.) Tell students that Chapter 14 describes how a person can become well adjusted in life. Have students write down in their journals some of the attributes of a well-adjusted person as defined by the text.

Meeting Chapter Objectives.
Point out the objectives on page 341. Have students rephrase the objectives in question form. Then, assign students to answer the questions as they read Chapter 14.

Building Vocabulary.
Have students use a dictionary to identify the etymologies and word parts for *autonomy* and *resynthesis*. Then call on students to read aloud the definitions in the Glossary.

Adjustment in Society

FIGURE 14.1 Adjustment is adapting to as well as actively shaping one's environment. It is coping with the ordinary experiences as well as the stresses of life.

340

TEACHER CLASSROOM RESOURCES

Chapter 14 Reproducible Lesson Plan
Chapter 14 Study Guide
Chapter 14 Review Activity
Chapter 14 Application Activity
Chapter 14 Extension Activity

Chapter 14 Test, Form A and Form B

Understanding Psychology Testmaker

Readings in Psychology: Section 5, Readings 3, 4

Exploring Key Ideas

The Challenge of Adjustment. A seagull or hawk may seem to hover or glide effortlessly in the air, but the apparent poise of the bird's flight is actually the result of dozens of moment-by-moment adjustments of the wings, tail, feet, and head to the ever-changing air currents. Ask your students to consider this metaphor, and explain how it applies to human adjustment. Challenge students to brainstorm some of the behavior adjustments that they make on a daily basis to "fly right." *(Many adjustments are done almost unconsciously. As an example, have students think of the mental shifts that occur as they end a conversation with a friend and head into a classroom.)*

OBJECTIVES

After studying this chapter, you should be able to

■ describe a variety of styles and types of marriages.

■ define the nature of parental-child interactions and conflicts.

■ identify some of the issues related to adjustment to college life.

■ explain various issues related to working.

KEY TERMS

adjustment
autonomy
career
developmental friendship
resynthesis

The McCaslins and their five children live in a rural area of eastern Kentucky. The father is a tall, gangly man who broke his back several years ago while working in construction. He is not able to perform any kind of physical labor and has been unable to find other work. The company refused to give him a disability pension, and probably because he is too proud to apply, his family does not receive welfare. Consequently, the family is forced to survive on garden vegetables and what little food they can buy with assistance from relatives.

In spite of this hard, meager existence, the McCaslins work to maintain a close, loving relationship. The parents do not touch each other very much in front of strangers or their children, but "they give each other long looks of recognition, sympathy, and affection. They understand each other in that silent, real lasting way that defies . . . labels," writes psychiatrist Robert Coles (1971). Because they have learned to cope with the stresses of disability and poverty, we can say that the McCaslins are well adjusted.

By **adjustment,** psychologists mean the process of adapting to and actively shaping, one's environment. When psychologists call a person well adjusted, they do *not* mean that he or she has managed to avoid stress, problems, and conflicts. They *do* mean that the person has learned to deal with frustration, disappointment and loss, as well as achievements, joys, and gains.

IN YOUR JOURNAL

Have you heard the phrase "love at first sight"? Write a paragraph in your journal explaining what you think this phrase means.

341

IN YOUR JOURNAL

To help students get started, you might ask them to recall a famous "love at first sight" story, such as Shakespeare's *Romeo and Juliet*. (You might also consider showing them the scene from Franco Zeffirelli's movie when the lovers first meet at the Capulets' feast.)

EXTRA CREDIT ACTIVITY

Greek and Roman myths are a rich source for stories about love. Ask students to read several myths that focus on loving relationships, such as the myths of Pyramus and Thisbe, Dido and Aeneas, Cupid and Psyche, and Theseus and Ariadne. With their knowledge of psychology in mind, have students select a myth of their choice and write a critical analysis of the love relationship. How do the lovers adjust or fail to adjust to each other? Tell students to draw from information in the chapter when presenting their analyses.

VISUAL INSTRUCTION

After students read the sampling from Rubin's questionnaire, point out that the two categories of "liking" and "loving" are not mutually exclusive. Successful friendships and marriages include a mixture of sentiments from each category. In fact, people in successful marriages usually claim that their spouse is their best friend, and successful friendships usually involve sentiment that Rubin associates with loving.
Answer to caption, Figure 14.2: distinguishing between liking and loving

DID YOU KNOW?

In Russia it is the custom to give flowers on a first date—but they must be given in odd numbers. An even number would symbolize a funeral.

FIGURE 14.2

The numbered labels, such as "Favorable evaluation," were developed after analyzing subjects' responses. They were not part of Rubin's original questionnaire, but are included here to identify typical questions. **What was the purpose of Rubin's study?**

Liking

1. *Favorable evaluation.*
   I think that _____ (my boyfriend or girlfriend) is unusually well adjusted.
   It seems to me that it is very easy for _____ to gain admiration.
2. *Respect and confidence.*
   I have great confidence in _____ 's good judgment.
   I would vote for _____ in a class or group election.
3. *Perceived similarity.*
   I think that _____ and I are quite similar to each other.
   When I am with _____ , we are almost always in the same mood.

Loving

1. *Attachment.*
   If I could never be with _____ , I would feel miserable.
   It would be hard for me to get along without _____ .
2. *Caring.*
   If _____ were feeling badly, my first duty would be to cheer him (her) up.
   I would do almost anything for _____ .
3. *Intimacy.*
   I feel that I can confide in _____ about almost anything.
   When I am with _____ , I spend a good deal of time just looking at him (her).

Psychologists who study adjustment try to understand not only how people cope with extreme hardship but also how to handle more ordinary experiences of life. Love and marriage, parent-child relationships, college, and work are potential sources of stress. Adjusting to each of these experiences involves unique challenges and difficulties.

LOVE AND MARRIAGE

The idea of love without marriage is no longer shocking. The fact that a couple is developing a close and intimate relationship, or even living together, does not necessarily mean that they are contemplating marriage. Still the idea of marriage without love remains unpopular in Western thought. Marrying for convenience, companionship, financial security, or *any* reason that doesn't include love strikes most of us as impossible or at least unfortunate.

This, according to psychologist Zick Rubin (1973), is one of the main reasons it is difficult for many people to adjust to love and marriage. Exaggerated ideas about love may also help to explain the growing frequency of divorce. Fewer couples who have "fallen out of love" are staying together for the sake of the children or to avoid gossip than did in the past. But let us begin at the beginning, with love.

Love

Reflecting on almost two decades of studies, Hatfield (1988) identifies two common types of love. *Passionate love* is very intense, sensual, and all-consuming. It has a feeling of great excitement, of intense sexuality, yet there is almost an element of danger—that it may go away at any moment. In fact, it does usually fade in any romance. When passionate love subsides, it may grow into *companionate love*, which includes friendship, liking someone, mutual trusting, and wanting to be with them. Companionate love is a more stable love, which includes the commitment and intimacy identified by Sternberg (1988). There are other views of love, however.

Some years ago Rubin (1973) covered the University of Michigan campus with requests for student volunteers. The top line of his posters—"Only dating couples can do it!"—attracted hundreds of students, so many that he had to turn most away. Those who remained—couples who had been going together for anywhere from a few weeks to six or seven years—filled out questionnaires about their feelings toward their partners and their same sex friends. The answers enabled Rubin to distinguish between liking and loving (see Figure 14.2).

Liking is based primarily on respect for another person and the feeling that he or she is similar to you. Loving is rather different. As Rubin writes, "There are probably as many reasons for loving as there are people who love. In each case there is a different constellation of needs to be gratified, a different set of characteristics that are found to be rewarding, a different ideal to be fulfilled" (pp. 228–229). However, looking beyond these differ-

CONNECTIONS: PSYCHOLOGY AND LANGUAGE ARTS

In their book *Metaphors We Live By*, George Lakoff and Mark Johnson outline several categories of metaphors that people use to organize their thoughts about love. These categories include:
1. Love is a Journey. ["We're not going anywhere."]
2. Love is a Physical Force. ["They gravitated toward each other."]
3. Love is a Patient. ["They have a healthy marriage."]
4. Love is Madness. ["I'm crazy about him/her."]
5. Love is Magic. ["I was spellbound."]
(continued on page 343)

ences, Rubin identified three major components of romantic love: *need* or *attachment*, *caring* or *the desire to give*, and *intimacy*.

People in love feel strong desires to be with the other person, to touch, to be praised and cared for, to fulfill and be fulfilled. The fact that love is so often described as a longing, a hunger, a desire to possess, a sickness that only one person can heal, suggests the role need plays in romantic love.

Equally central is the desire to give. Love goes beyond the cost-reward level of human interaction. It has been defined as "the active concern for the life and growth of that which we love" (Fromm, 1956: p. 26), and as "that state in which the happiness of another person is essential to our own"

FIGURE 14.3

It is easy to think of love in a narrow context and consider only the sexual relationship that exists between a man and a woman. This view, however, omits the kinds of love that exist between children and grandparents, between people and their pets, between siblings, and between parents and their children. **Why are caring and need important in love?**

CONNECTIONS: PSYCHOLOGY AND LANGUAGE ARTS

6. Love is War. ["He won her hand in marriage."]
Working in groups, have students come up with other metaphors that fall in these categories. Ask: What other categories can you suggest? Ask members from each group to present its metaphors.

■ **Analyzing a Passage.** Ask students to respond to the following quotation from *Is Marriage Necessary?* by psychologist Lawrence Casler:

I don't believe love is part of human nature, not for a minute. There are social pressures at work.

Do students agree with Casler that love is not "part of human nature"? How might Charles Darwin have responded to Casler?

As an extending activity, you might consider these questions: If love is indeed part of human nature, is marriage? Or is marriage more a social convention? To provoke discussion, you might have students consider weddings among enslaved Africans. Slaveholders made no effort to promote marriages, rather enslaved couples devised them as a method of promoting family unity. Ask: To what extent were slave weddings an effort to satisfy a basic human need for family bonding? (OBJECTIVE 1)

VISUAL INSTRUCTION

Ask students to consider the interactions that they imagine occurring in each photograph in terms of caring and need. How is caring being expressed in each? How are needs being fulfilled for everyone pictured?
Answer to caption, Figure 14.3: Need without caring becomes self-centered and demanding. Caring without need is charity or merely kindness.

■ **Analyzing Ideals.** The idea of "romantic love" is often fostered in popular songs, novels, films, and advertisements. Ask students to cite specific examples from each of these media. Ask: What romantic ideal is illustrated by each example? How do these images affect people's expectations about love and marriage? What, if any, purpose does an ideal serve? *(An ideal might serve as a model toward which to strive—promoting good behavior. People might also harshly judge themselves and life for not measuring up to the ideal.)* (OBJECTIVE 1)

■ **Analyzing Concepts.** After students read the margin feature, draw a large equilateral triangle on the chalkboard. Then, from the center, draw a line to each apex, thus dividing the triangle into three equal parts. Label the parts *Intimacy, Passion,* and *Commitment.* Now ask students to describe different love relationships. *(Answers might include: parent-child, newlywed, a couple on the verge of a breakup.)* Explain how the lines within the triangle should be adjusted to accommodate each relationship. *(For example, in a parent-child relationship, commitment may be the largest component from the parent's point of view.)* (OBJECTIVES 1, 2)

MORE about. . .

Triangular Theory of Love. Love comes in many sizes and shapes. A theory that accounts for the many forms of love has been proposed by psychologist Robert Sternberg (1986). Sternberg's triangular theory of love contends that love is made up of three parts: intimacy, passion, and commitment. The various combinations of these parts account for why love is experienced in many different ways.

Intimacy refers to the feeling part of love—as when we feel close to another. Passion is love's motivating aspect, which drives us to seek romance. Commitment is the thinking component of love—when we realize that a relationship is love and we desire to maintain the relationship over time.

Using Sternberg's model, we can see how different kinds of love are made up of different degrees of intimacy, passion, and commitment. The "love at first sight" felt on a first date has lots of passion but little commitment, whereas the love felt by a couple celebrating their fiftieth wedding anniversary has much intimacy and commitment but probably less passion.

(Heinlein, in Levinger and Snoek, 1972). This kind of love is very altruistic, very giving. Without caring, need becomes a series of self-centered, desperate demands; without need, caring is charity or kindness. In love, the two are intertwined.

Need and caring take various forms, depending on individual situations. What all people in love share is intimacy—a special knowledge of each other derived from uncensored self-disclosure. Exploring your "true self" to another person is always risky. It doesn't hurt so much if a person rejects a role you are trying to play. But it can be devastating if a person rejects the secret longings and fears you ordinarily disguise or keep hidden. It hurts deeply if he or she uses that private information to manipulate you. This is one of the reasons why love so often brings out violent emotions—the highs and lows of our lives.

Rubin conducted a number of experiments to test common assumptions about the way people in love feel and act. He found that couples who rated high on his "love scale" did, indeed, spend more time gazing into each other's eyes (while waiting for the experimenter) than other couples did. However, he was unable to prove that lovers sacrifice their own comfort for that of their partners.

Perhaps the most interesting discoveries in "love research" concern the differences between men and women. Rubin found that most couples were equal on the love scale: the woman expressed the same degree of love for her partner as he did for her. However, women tended to *like* their boyfriends—to respect and identify with them—more than their boyfriends liked them. Women also tended to love and share intimacies with their same-sex friends more often than men did with theirs.

This is not surprising. As Rubin suggests, women in our society tend to specialize in the social and emotional dimensions of life. However, the revelation that men are significantly more romantic than women is surprising, though perhaps it should not have been. At a time when women usually worked at home, who they married basically determined their style of living. Now earning power is no longer such a powerful concern. With more than half of all married women working outside the home, both men and women contribute to family finance, and with that ability comes the ability to be more romantic. In fact, Fehr and Russell (1991) reported that women are no longer different from men as to how romantic they are, or their ability to participate equally in widely varying forms of passionate or companionate love.

A follow-up questionnaire, sent a year after Rubin's original study, indicated that when both a man and a woman are romantic, the relationship is likely to progress—that is, they become more intimate and committed to each other. The implication of this finding? That love is not something that happens *to* you; it is something you seek and create.

Marriage

A couple decides to make a formal and public commitment to each other. They marry. Will they "live happily ever after"? Their chances are good if they come from similar cultural and economic backgrounds, have about

STUDY AND WRITING SKILLS

Ask students to develop a marriage contract for themselves, setting out the partners' mutual responsibilities and expectations. The contract should include clauses defining how the couple will make decisions, share responsibilities around the house, deal with rearing children, and celebrate holidays. It should also address such issues as social activities that include the spouse and activities that can exclude the spouse. Have students discuss and compare their contracts in class. What common themes and original ideas emerge?

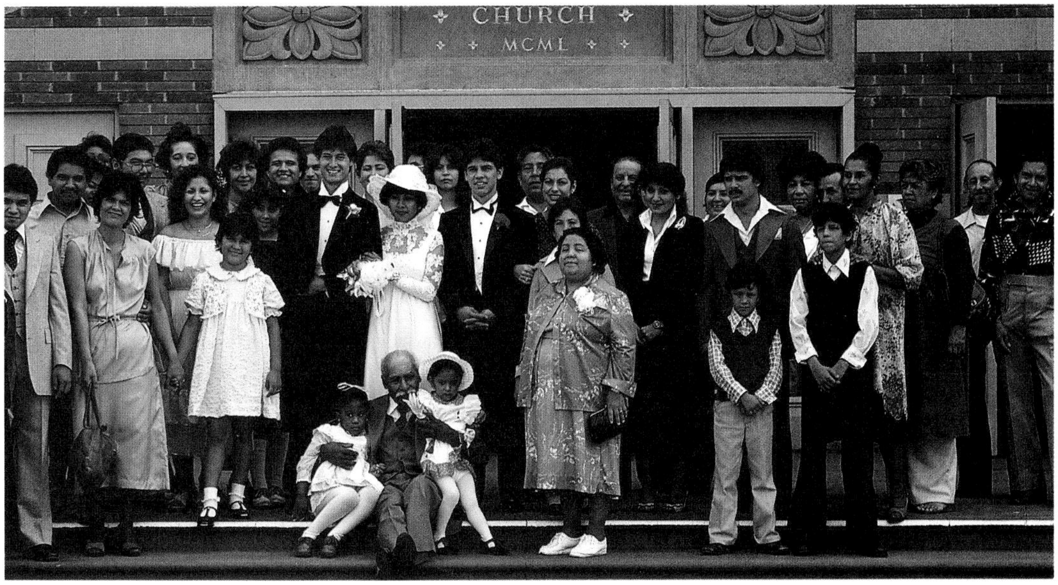

FIGURE 14.4

Healthy adjustment to marriage seems to depend on whether the couple's needs are compatible, on whether their image of themselves coincide with their images of each other, and on whether they agree on what their roles should be. **Which period of married life do many couples report is the happiest?**

the same level of education, and practice (or fail to practice) the same religion. Their chances are better still if their parents were happily married, they had happy childhoods, and they maintain good relations with their families. All of these are good predictors of marital success. Two principles tend to govern behavior leading to successful marriages: endogamy and homogamy. *Endogamy* identifies the tendency to marry someone who is from one's own social group. Marriages are more likely to be successful when we marry those like us (Buss, 1985). In addition, *homogamy* identifies our tendency to marry someone who has similar attributes, including physical attractiveness, age, and physique, to our own. A common observation is that people who marry tend to look similar to one another. It is now suspected that social processes operate that tend to cause this matching to happen. At a dance held at the University of Minnesota a number of years ago, a computer randomly matched students. Physical attractiveness was the best predictor of the likelihood that two randomly matched people would continue dating (Walster, Aronson, Abrahams, & Rottman, 1966).

Married life proceeds through a predictable series of events, with accompanying stresses and joys. The *newlywed* period represents shedding the responsibilities and pressures of your role in your families of origin. You assume a new and very different role. Often, couples report the newlywed period as one of the two happiest times in a marriage. The *children* period usually starts with the new mother experiencing depression in the days immediately following the birth of a child. Generally, married couples' ratings of happiness may reach their lowest levels during this time. One reason is that new responsibilities are thrust on both new parents. Another is that they have considerably less mobility and freedom. Nearly

CHAPTER 14 Lesson Plan

VISUAL INSTRUCTION

Write the heading *Compatibility* on the chalkboard and underneath it the three subheadings *Needs, Images, and Roles.* Request volunteers to suggest examples of how incompatibility in any one of the subheadings might pose problems in a marriage. For example, what happens when the "honeymoon" is over and a couple starts to see each other as humans—complete with good *and* bad points?
(OBJECTIVE 1)

Answer to caption, Figure 14.4: the newlywed period; the empty nest period

Teacher Note. Some sociologists predict that, as the number of divorces increase and become more socially acceptable, "serial monogamy" will become more common. The anthropologist Margaret Mead, for example, claimed to have had three "successful" marriages, each suited to the different needs she had at different stages of her life. You might point out to the students that compatibility at the beginning of a marriage is no guarantee that the marriage will last. Ask: What adjustments can couples make to ensure ongoing compatibility?

CRITICAL THINKING ACTIVITY

Analyzing a Quote. You might explore the changing role of fatherhood within a marriage by reading aloud the following advice from the revised edition of Dr. Spock's *Baby and Child Care:*

The father—any father—should be sharing with the mother the day-to-day care of their child from birth onward. . . . This is the natural way for the father to start the relationship, just as it is for the mother.

Ask: What role does this book assign to men within the marriage? How does the role differ from the role of fatherhood in prior decades?

Additional Information.
Levinger and Snoek (1972) studied manager-worker relations and developed an incremental theory of human interaction that also applies in interpersonal attraction or love:

Strangers: Any two people, neither of whom knows the other; no contact.
Unilateral awareness: "Who was that masked man?" captures this level of contact—one person is aware of the other at some level.
Surface contact: Physical attractiveness and the physical closeness of the two people are important here.
Mutuality—minor: A small level of interaction, such as going out for soft drinks.
Mutuality—major: By now, shared attitudes, values, and a growing knowledge of the other person are becoming increasingly important.
Total unity: This represents a blending of values and desires. According to this theory, a woman and a man should achieve this level of interaction before entertaining thoughts of marriage.

You might present this theory to the class, and ask volunteers to role-play (or write) a skit demonstrating the interpersonal dynamics at each level.
(OBJECTIVE 1)

every decision, no matter how mundane, has to be planned around the child or children.

Children's adolescence is the third phase. At this age, children are at least manageable. As their adolescent children grow toward adulthood, parents shift increasing amounts of responsibility to them. This phase is not without its problems, however. One special problem is that, as the children reach adolescence, the parents may themselves be going through a stage of examining their own life, goals, and priorities.

Couples enter another stage when the children leave home and are on their own—the *empty nest*. Almost always presented as a depression period, usually it is not. The regained freedom and the extra time now available for self-betterment more than counteracts the negative emotions (Reinke, Holmes, & Harris, 1985). This is often one of the happiest times in a marriage.

Finally, couples reach the *alone again* period. Many older couples report that the retirement years are a satisfying period. Yet, at the same time, these couples increasingly face the likelihood of illness and the eventual death of a partner (Carter & McGoldrick, 1988).

Surveying couples who have been married 15 years or longer, Lauer & Lauer (1985) identified a number of reasons men and women listed for the success of their marriages. Interestingly, the first seven reasons, including (number 1) "My spouse is my best friend" and (number 4) "Marriage is a long-term commitment," are cited identically by men and women.

Marital Problems and Divorce

The marriage of today is quite different from the marriages of yesteryear. More than half of all married women work, and with that status comes financial and personal independence. One factor likely contributing to the growing number of divorces in this nation is the increasing financial independence of working women.

Are housework and child care shared by couples who both work outside the home? One study shows that women with full-time jobs spend an average of 42.5 hours per week on work related to child care at home, while their husbands spend 26.7 hours (Jump & Hass, 1987). Martin and Osborne (1993) note that husbands agree that the household chores should be split more evenly when wives work outside the home. Yet while women in the marketplace spend less time on chores than women who do not have outside jobs, their husbands do not spend more time on chores.

In general, healthy adjustment to marriage seems to depend on three factors: whether the couple's needs are compatible; whether the husband's and wife's images of themselves coincide with their images of each other; and whether they agree on what the husband's and wife's roles in the marriage are.

External factors may make it impossible for one or both to live up to their own role expectations. A man who is unemployed cannot be the good provider he wants to be and may take his frustrations out on his family, who constantly remind him of this. A woman trying to hold a job and raise

ADDITIONAL INFORMATION

Here are the top reasons that married men and women gave to explain why their marriages had lasted at least 15 years (adapted from Lauer & Lauer, 1985). The first seven reasons are the same for both men and women. These are:

My spouse is my best friend.

I like my spouse as a person.
Marriage is a long-term commitment.
Marriage is sacred.
We agree on aims and goals.
My spouse has grown more interesting.
I want the relationship to succeed.

Men's Reasons 8–15:
(continued on page 347)

a family in a slum tenement cannot keep the kitchen with a broken sink clean, provide good meals for her family, or keep her children safe.

Often couples just grow apart: the husband becomes totally engrossed in his work or in a hobby; the wife, in her career, children, or community affairs. One day they wake up and realize that they stopped communicating years ago (Arkoff, 1968).

Let us suppose they are unable or unwilling to fill each other's needs and role expectations through accommodation or compromise. Perhaps they cannot face their problems. For example, many people have a taboo about discussing—much less seeking help for—sexual problems. Perhaps they have sought professional help, talked their difficulties out with each other and with friends, and come to the conclusion that they want more from life than their current marriage allows. For whatever reasons, they decide on divorce. What then?

In many ways, adjusting to divorce is like adjusting to death—the death of a relationship. Almost inevitably, divorce releases a torrent of emotions: anger (even if the person wanted a divorce), resentment, fear, loneliness, anxiety, and above all the feeling of failure. Both individuals are suddenly thrust into a variety of unfamiliar situations. A man may find himself cooking for the first time in years; a woman, fixing her first leaky faucet. Dating for the first time in 5 or 10 years can make a formerly married person feel like an adolescent. Friends may feel they have to choose sides. Some divorcing people may find it unsettling to think of giving up on a marriage or being unattached and free to do whatever they like. One of the biggest problems may be time—the free time a person desperately wanted but now has no idea what to do with.

All of this adds up to what Mel Krantzler calls "separation shock." The shock may be greatest for individuals who saw divorce as liberation and did not anticipate difficult times. But whatever the circumstances, most divorced people go through a period of mourning that lasts until the person suddenly realizes that he or she has survived. This is the first step toward adjusting to divorce. Resentment of his or her former spouse subsides. The pain left over from the past no longer dominates the present. The divorced person begins calling old friends, making new ones, and enjoying the fact that he or she can base decisions on his or her own personal interests. In effect, the divorcee has begun to construct a new identity as a single person (Krantzler, 1973).

Children and Divorce

The traditional American family is under assault. Divorces are on the rise, and as a consequence, so is the number of single-parent families and the number of children subjected to the stresses of divorce. Within the foreseeable future, as many as 3 in 10 children will be born to parents who divorce before their child is 18, and about the same ratio of children will be born to unmarried mothers. Only about 40 percent of newborns will live with their natural parents through their eighteenth birthday (Furstenberg & Cherlin, 1991).

Adjusting to a divorce tends to be harder for children than for their parents.

■ **Analyzing Data.** Census figures prove that the popular notion of the "typical" American family as consisting of a married couple with two children is just that—a notion. Ask students the following questions about the state of the "American family." Then have them compare their answers to statistics from the 1990 census (included in parentheses after each question). Based on this exercise, challenge students to form generalizations.

1. The 1990 census counted 91.9 million households in the United States. What percentage of these households do you think were maintained by married couples? *(55%)*

2. What percentage of households with children under age 18 included a married couple? *(26%)*

3. What can you infer about the number of households with children that were headed by a single parent? *(probably the majority; 29%)*

(OBJECTIVE 1)

ADDITIONAL INFORMATION

An enduring marriage is important to social stability.
We laugh together.
I am proud of my spouse's achievements.
We agree on a philosophy of life.
We agree about our sex life.
We agree on how and how often to

show affection.
I confide in my spouse.
We share outside hobbies and interests.

Women's Reasons 8–15:
We laugh together.
We agree on a philosophy of life.
We agree on how and how often to show affection.

An enduring marriage is important to social stability.
We have a stimulating exchange of ideas.
We discuss things calmly.
We agree about our sex life.
I am proud of my spouse's achievements.

■ **Identifying Alternatives.**
Ask students to brainstorm to generate a list of things that a couple might do to avoid a divorce. *(Answers will vary, but might include: working to maintain mutual patience and understanding, developing good communications, seeking outside help).* Next, ask students to develop a list of behaviors that they believe divorcing couples should observe to ease the transition out of married life, both for themselves and for any children involved. *(e.g., avoid pettiness and the urge to inflict pain)* Because some of your students may come from households involving divorce, respect privacy and sensitivity on this last question.
(OBJECTIVE 1)

■ **Readings in Psychology.**
Have students read the Section 5, Reading 3 selection in *Readings in Psychology* and answer the questions that follow the selection.

Adjusting to divorce is usually far more difficult for children than for their parents. First, rarely do the children want the divorce to occur: the conflict is not theirs, but their parents'. Second, while the parents may have good reasons for the separation, the children (especially very young children) are unlikely to understand those reasons. Third, the children themselves rarely have any control over the outcome of the divorce. Such decisions as whom they live with and how frequently they will be able to see the separated parent are out of their hands. Finally, children, especially young ones, can't muster as much emotional maturity as their parents to help them through such an overwhelming experience.

A child of parents who divorce may exhibit behaviors ranging from being visibly upset to depression to rebellion. Berger (1994) argues that the longevity of these behaviors is determined by "the harmony of the parents' ongoing relationship, the stability of the child's life, and the adequacy of the caregiving arrangement" (p. 348).

Adolescents experience special problems as a result of their parents' divorce, for their developmental stage already involves the process of breaking family ties. When that separation takes place before the adolescent is ready to play his or her own hand in it, the experience can be terribly unsettling. As one young person said, "[It was] like having the rug pulled out from under me" (Wallerstein and Kelly, 1974, p. 486).

Like their parents, most children do eventually come to terms with divorce. They learn to put some distance between themselves and their parents' conflict, and they learn to be realistic about the situation and make the best of it. Adjustment is made easier when parents take special care to explain the divorce and allow children to express their feelings.

Divorce is becoming a problem with which more and more children will have to cope. Marital problems, however, are not the only area of family conflict. Just as there are discrepancies between expectations and reality for husbands and wives, disillusionments and disagreements also exist between children and parents. Parents expect certain behaviors and attitudes from their children, but these expectations sometimes are not met. Children and their parents do often disagree. They must search for ways to resolve their conflicts.

PARENT-CHILD RELATIONSHIPS

The scene: Son enters living room, bouncing a basketball.

Mother: Get out of here with that. You'll break something!

Son: No, I won't!

(The ball hits a lamp.)

Mother: You never listen to anything I say. You had to break something, didn't you? You're so stupid sometimes.

Son: You broke the washing machine. What does that make you?

Mother: Floyd, you know better than to be rude.

CONNECTIONS: PSYCHOLOGY AND THE LAW

Divorce almost invariably involves lawyers. Arrange for a divorce lawyer to visit the class and talk about the legal issues that must be considered in divorce proceedings in your state. Encourage the speaker to speculate about the possible connection between rising divorce rates and the widespread availability of "no-fault" divorces. The lawyer might also be asked to talk about the psychological skills he or she must have to be successful in the profession.

FIGURE 14.5

Conflict and power struggles between parents and children are inevitable, especially when expectations of behavior or desires differ. **What are common areas of disagreement between parents and adolescents?**

Son: You were rude first. You called me stupid.
Mother: I don't want to hear another word from you. Go to your room this minute!
Son: Quit trying to boss me around. I'm not a kid anymore.
Mother: To your room this instant!
Son: Go ahead, make me.

—Adapted from Haim G. Ginott, *Between Parent and Teenager* (1971).

As this scene illustrates, conflict, whether between husband and wife or child and parent, is a process that can escalate with surprising quickness from contradictory desires to a bitter power struggle. In our society, parent-child conflict is particularly common and may be explosive during adolescence. Adolescence is a period of inner struggles—goals versus fear of inability to accomplish them, desire for independence versus the realization that they are "only human." The adolescent thus needs parents who are sure of themselves, their identities, and their values. Such parents serve not only as models but also as sources of stability in a world that has become complicated and full of choices.

Sources of Parent-Adolescent Conflict

"The generation gap" is an expression that most of us have heard and used. It refers to a simple fact: adolescents and their parents tend to think differently about things. Some of the specific issues may change from one generation to the next. For example, in the days of World Wars I and II, many

PORTRAIT

Margaret Mahler
1897–1985
Giving credence to Milton's line that "childhood shows the man, / As morning shows the day," Margaret Mahler spent much of her career charting how children interact with their mothers through an inevitable and often turbulent process in order to become individuals in their own right. In books such as *The Psychological Birth of the Human Infant* (1975), Mahler showed that the way in which very young children manage to separate themselves psychologically from their mothers will determine how well they will adjust in later life. According to Mahler, the mother's role is crucial in her child's development of "separation-individuation": If she hurries the process or resists it, the child is likely to adjust poorly to intimate relationships throughout life.

■ **Evaluating a Generaliza-tion.** During the 1960s, the media helped promote a popu-lar generalization: A *generation gap* exists between people over 30 and under 30. The genera-tions supposedly differed on everything from values and morals to their taste in cloth-ing and music. Ask students if they think a generation gap ex-ists today or if they see some common ground among the generations. (OBJECTIVE 2)

■ **Debating an Issue.** Wher-ever there is inequality, there will be double standards. Some we expect and tolerate (e.g., adults get to stay up late; children are put to bed early); others are considered unjust. The females in your class should be well armed with in-stances of double standards in American society, but they may be surprised that males, too, often feel they are the vic-tims of double standards. (For example, how many men can get away with crying in public or even expect sympathy from close friends when they do?) To encourage discussion of double standards, debate the following topic: *Resolved—* That U.S. society still forces men to follow a "tough-guy" role while blasting them for male "chauvinism." (OBJECTIVES 1, 2, 4)

parents were upset and frightened because their sons wanted to join the armed forces. But during the Vietnam War, parents were hurt and angered because some of their sons refused to "serve their country."

One of the most frequently discussed areas of disagreement between adolescents and their parents is sex. Parents accustomed to thinking of sex as something for married people are likely to find their children in active disagreement. In part as a result of the Pill, more young people are having sexual relations at a younger age than in the past. Among college students the issue is complex. A survey indicated that males and females showed no difference in their agreement with the appropriateness of a wide variety of sexual activities, such as heavy petting on a first date (Sprecher, 1989). When rating *people* rather than *actions*, however, differences emerged. For example, it was considered less appropriate for a female to engage in sexu-al activity in a casual relationship than a male (Sprecher, McKinney, & Or-buch, 1987). So, some forms of a double standard for male and female sexual behavior do still exist, even among young adults.

Another common area of disagreement is drugs. A national survey con-ducted annually by the Institute for Social Research at the University of Michigan reveals that 37 percent of its sample of high school seniors had tried marijuana, 63 percent had tried cigarettes, and 88 percent had tried alcohol at least once. Illicit drug use peaked in 1978–80, but since then, has been on a slow, steady decline among 18 to 25 year olds. Yet, in the same sample, 54 percent of high school seniors had used alcohol within the pre-vious month (Johnston, Bachman, & O'Malley, 1992). Another survey cal-culated that 64 percent of those ages 18 to 25 had consumed alcohol in the preceding 30 days (NIDA, 1992).

The list of issues on which adolescents and parents can disagree could go on for pages, for it is seemingly endless. But there are other sources of conflict between parents and children of all ages.

Parental Expectations

In her book *Peoplemaking*, Virginia Satir describes a case from her experi-ence as a family therapist:

. . . [J]ust after Christmas . . . a young mother whom I will call Elaine came to see me. She was in a rage at her six-year-old daughter, Pam. It seems that Elaine had scrimped and saved many months to buy Pam a very fancy doll. Pam reacted with indifference to the doll her mother had worked so hard to get. Elaine felt very crushed and disappointed, inside. Outside she acted angry (1972, p. 205).

Elaine had done something many parents do. She had taken a childhood dream of her own (she never had a fancy doll when she was growing up) and projected it onto her daughter—who already had several dolls and re-ally would have preferred a sled.

It is easy for parents to take their own unfulfilled dreams—not just for a little girl to have a doll but for a grown daughter or son to be a doctor or go to college—and wish for their child to fulfill them instead. It is also easy for parents to expect children to share their own interests and goals. Many

PSYCHOLOGISTS AT WORK

Marriage counseling is perhaps one of the psychology fields with which the general public is most familiar. Al-though requirements vary from state to state, marriage counselors often must hold advanced degrees in psy-chology. They may also have back-grounds in sociology and social work. Working in private practices or in so-cial agencies and hospital clinics, marriage counselors seldom have the luxury of a 9-to-5 schedule. Instead, they must usually work evenings and weekends when their clients have free time. These professionals often use behavioral conditioning and cognitive techniques to help people alter their counterproductive behaviors and im-prove their interpersonal communica-tion skills.

fathers, for example, just assume that their sons will want to continue in the family business, whether or not the young man has ever expressed any such interest. But it is not always easy for parents to remember that because of different circumstances, different times, and different personalities, children frequently don't have the same dreams as their parents.

The Power Struggle: Escalating Conflict

There is no question that there are many potential sources of conflict within the family. Fathers and mothers play different roles and have different expectations for themselves and each other. They also have values, goals, and expectations that they try to instill in their children—even though the effort may sometimes be reminiscent of putting a shoe on the wrong foot. Both children and adults may become stuck in their roles: parents sometimes forget how it felt to be a child, and children often have difficulty imagining what it is like to be a parent. Each family member experiences personal stresses, too, that relate to life outside the family, in jobs, school, or dating. All these pressures demand some understanding or at least tolerance from other members of the family.

As differences between family members persist, it may be difficult for individuals to keep trying to listen and understand each other's point of view. A father and son can argue the point of whether the bicycle belongs in the garage or on the street just so many times before their words become a monotonous dialogue with no one listening.

FIGURE 14.6

When real communication is achieved in the family, family members are able to trust and be open with each other. They can be secure in the knowledge that they are understood. **Why is there less chance for problems escalating in democratic families?**

■ **Discussion.** In discussing the problem of unwarranted parental expectations, ask the students if the opposite situation is also true: Can conflicts also arise when children, especially teenagers, unreasonably expect too much of their parents? Call on volunteers to describe some instances when children end up feeling "crushed and disappointed" and "angry" like the young mother, Elaine, that Virginia Satir describes in her book. (One possible example is the teenager who thinks his parents "owe" it to him to buy him a new car.) (OBJECTIVE 2)

VISUAL INSTRUCTION

Remind students of the three ways that parents and children relate to one another—authoritarian, permissive, and democratic—that they read about in Chapter 9. **Answer to caption, Figure 14.6:** because democratic families communicate to make decisions

CONNECTIONS: PSYCHOLOGY AND THE MEDIA

Assign students to watch television situation comedies and dramas for examples of the various kinds of blame-shifting that can occur in disputes between parents and children, or wives and husbands—such as shaming or psychoanalyzing. Have students videotape several examples for presentation and discussion in class. Ask the students to explain how the characters who resort to these blame-shifting methods try to avoid responsibility for the conflicts.

■ **Analyzing Conflict.** Write the four headings *Judging, Diagnosing, Teaching,* and *Shaming* on the chalkboard. Ask two volunteers to improvise a parent-child conflict in which all four kinds of blame-laying are involved. Have the class discuss why such tactics are usually counterproductive. Next, call on two other volunteers to role-play the original improvised scene. This time, however, direct students to avoid inflammatory rhetoric as a way of working toward resolution of the conflict.

As a follow-up exercise, write the labels *Parents* and *Teenage Children* on the chalkboard. Challenge students to identify words or phrases that each can use to provoke a fight—either intentionally or unintentionally. Request volunteers to design a poster entitled "Fighting Words."

VISUAL INSTRUCTION

Point out all the smiling faces in the photograph, and remind students that adjustment is not just learning to deal with frustration, disappointment, and loss. It's also adjusting to life's achievements, joys, and gains. **Answer to caption, Figure 14.7:** organizing one's time, meeting new people, confronting ideas that challenge old assumptions

Instead of making a constructive effort to work out a solution to differences, parents and children, or wives and husbands, may take an easier but counterproductive route—that of blaming the other person. There are several ways of doing this. One is *judging*, or *criticizing*, accusing the other person of being at fault ("You're being selfish!"); another is *diagnosing*, or *psychoanalyzing*, by commenting on a person's possible psychological motives for an action ("You're taking it out on me because you had a rough day at work"). Other common tactics include *teaching* ("We don't put our elbows on the dinner table"); and *name-calling*, or *shaming*, humiliating another, thus making him or her feel ashamed, embarrassed, or guilty ("Don't you feel like a baby for storming around like that?"). In each instance, when one person tries to avoid responsibility for the conflict, the result is likely to be its escalation rather than its resolution.

In parent-child conflict the general pattern of family interactions also has a great deal to do with whether disagreements and disappointments reach the stage of war we witnessed earlier in the basketball episode. Described in Chapter 9, parents and children relate to one another according to three patterns—authoritarian, permissive, or democratic.

Both dominant and permissive parents have good chances of developing conflict-ridden relationships with their children. In the first case, as we have seen, children are bound to rebel as they grow up and learn to think for themselves; and in the second case, parents themselves may eventually feel like rebelling as their children keep testing the parents' limits. In democratic families, though, the chances for conflict to escalate are not so great because these families communicate to make decisions.

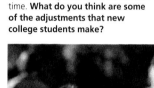
FIGURE 14.7

College life means many changes for students away from home for the first time. **What do you think are some of the adjustments that new college students make?**

LAB EXPERIMENTS AND DEMONSTRATIONS

Request a volunteer to take part in a mock college interview. Acting as the interviewer, ask the "candidate" about personal interests, favorite books and magazines, work experience, career goals, academic record, and interpersonal skills. After the interview, request volunteers to share their experiences on any admission interviews that they may have had. Were they similar to the one just observed? How might a job interview be different? Ask: Is the interviewee passively adapting to an environment or actively shaping an environment?

COLLEGE LIFE

We have been talking about the things that happen within the family, when children, wives, and husbands live together in the same household. Families, however, don't stay together forever. Children grow up and leave home to set up new households and start their own families.

Growing up involves gaining a sense of **autonomy**—the ability to take care of oneself—and independence. Each person learns to make decisions, develop a value system, be responsible, and to care for himself or herself. Growing up is a process that starts long before an individual leaves home to live as a self-sufficient adult. But ultimately, it means separating from the family, both physically and emotionally.

For millions of young Americans, college is one of the first big steps toward this separation. College students are freer than they ever have been or may ever be again. This can be a personally liberating and stimulating experience. But it also requires adjustment. The emotional upheaval many freshmen feel has been called "college shock."

Peter Madison spent nearly 10 years collecting data on how several hundred students adjusted to college. Each student provided a detailed life history and kept a weekly journal. Madison had classmates write descriptions of some of the students, and tested and retested some at various points in their college careers. The results?

Madison found that many students approach college with high, and often unrealistic, aspirations. For example, Bridget wanted to be an astronomer. She liked the idea of being different, and she considered astronomy an elite and adventuresome field. But she didn't know how many long, hard, unadventuresome hours she would have to spend studying mathematics to fulfill her dream. Keith planned to become a physician for what he described as "humanitarian" reasons. But he had never thought about working in a hospital or watching people sicken and die.

These two students, like many others, based their goals on fantasy. They didn't have the experience to make realistic choices or the maturity to evaluate their own motives and needs. Their experiences during the first semesters of college led them to change both their minds and their images of themselves.

Sources of Change

How does going to college stimulate change? First, college may challenge the identity a student has established in high school. A top student who does extremely well on the College Boards is likely to go to a top college. Nearly everyone there is as bright and competitive as she is. Within a matter of weeks the student's identity as a star pupil has evaporated; she may have to struggle to get average grades. Young people who excelled in sports, drama, or student politics may have similar experiences. The high school student-body president discovers two other high school presidents in his dormitory alone.

Second, whether students come from small towns or big cities, they are likely to encounter greater diversity in college than they ever have be-

---

Many students approach college with unrealistically high expectations.

Teacher Note. You might point out that "college shock" affects parents, too—and not just financially. It can be as liberating, satisfying, and frightening for the parent as it is for the college-bound child. In a 1992 special issue of *Life* magazine entitled "Getting at the Heart of the American Family," one mother used birth imagery to describe her daughter's departure: "a real cutting of the cord."

■ **Discussion.** Have students discuss the key idea, which is highlighted in the sidebar on this page. What is the difference between "high expectations" and "unrealistically high expectations"? *(The one is motivating; the other is bound to lead to disappointment and confusion.)* Challenge students to give examples of both kinds of expectations. (OBJECTIVE 3)

CRITICAL THINKING ACTIVITY

Analyzing Conflict. Ask students to consider the many kinds of unproductive behaviors that can intensify parent-child conflicts. Tell them to imagine that they are "psychological referees" hired to mediate between a parent and a child. Instruct them to draw up a rule book defining what kinds of behaviors are and are not fair play in a parent-child dispute. (OBJECTIVE 2)

VISUAL INSTRUCTION

You might explore the concept of change by repeating the following saying: "Show me a thing that does not change." As the students have already seen in earlier chapters, change is something people must often learn to embrace—or risk constant negative stress.
Answer to caption, Figure 14.8: Answers will vary, but might include: tightening up, redoubling their efforts, detaching themselves emotionally, resynthesis.

Readings in Psychology. Have students read the Section 5, Reading 4 selection in *Readings in Psychology* and answer the questions that follow the selection.

FIGURE 14.8

After completing a year or two of college, students may find that the career goals they had as high school seniors no longer suit their interests. The average college student changes majors twice before finding the right one. **In what ways do students cope with change?**

fore—diversity in religious and ethnic backgrounds, family income levels, and attitudes. During his first quarter, Bob dated a Catholic woman, a Jewish woman, and an Asian woman; a history major, a music major, an English major, and a math major. Fred found that the students living in his dorm ranged from "grinds," who did nothing but study, to "liberals," who were involved in all sorts of causes; from athletes, who cared more about physical than intellectual competition, and business types, who saw college as a place to get vocational training and make contacts for future use, to guys who just wanted to have a good time.

A student who develops a close relationship with another, then discovers that the person holds beliefs or engages in behavior he or she has always considered immoral, may be badly shaken. You are faced with a choice—abandon deeply held values or give up an important friendship. Madison (1969) calls close relationships between individuals who force each other to reexamine their basic assumptions **developmental friendships.** He found that developmental friendships in particular and student culture in general have more impact on college students than professors do.

However, if instructors and assigned books clarify thoughts that have been brewing in a student's mind, they can make all the difference. This was true of Keith. Keith did extremely well in the courses required for a pre-med student, but found he enjoyed his literature and philosophy classes far more. He began reading avidly. He felt as if each of the authors had deliberately set out to put all his self-doubts into words. In time Keith realized that his interest in medicine was superficial. He had decided to become a doctor because it was a respected profession that would give him status, security, and a good income—and would guarantee his parents' love. The self-image Keith had brought to college was completely changed.

CRITICAL THINKING ACTIVITY

Weighing Alternatives. Organize the class into small groups. Instruct each group to prepare a balance sheet weighing the advantages and disadvantages of living at home while attending college versus living in a campus dorm. The list should include emotional as well as practical considerations. Request a member from each group to share its balance sheet. Based on this exercise, what choices would students make? (Point out that comparing advantages and disadvantages is one of the important steps in the decision-making process. Explore with students some of the potential negative outcomes if this step is skipped.)

Coping with Change

Madison found that students cope with the stress of going to college in several different ways. Some "tighten up" when their goals are threatened by internal or external change. They redouble their efforts to succeed in the field they have chosen and avoid people and situations that might bring their doubts to the surface. Troy, for example, stayed with a chemical-engineering program for three years, despite a growing interest in social science. By the time he realized that engineering was not the field for him, it was too late to change majors. He got the degree, but left college with no idea where he was heading.

Others avoid confronting doubt by frittering away their time, going through the motions of attending college but detaching themselves emotionally.

Some students manage to keep their options open until they have enough information and experience to make a choice. Keith is an example. In June of his freshman year he wrote in his diary,

> I must decide between philosophy and medicine. If I have enough confidence in the quality of my thought, I shall become a philosopher; if not, a comfortable doctor (quoted in Madison, 1969, p. 58).

By June of the following year he had decided.

> Sitting on a tennis court I had the very sudden and dramatic realization that my life was my own and not my parents', that I could do what I wanted and did not necessarily have to do what they wanted. I think I correlated this with dropping out of the pre-med program. Material values became less and less important from then on (p. 58).

Madison calls this third method of coping **resynthesis.** For most students this involves a period of vacillation, doubt, and anxiety. The student tries to combine the new and old, temporarily abandons the original goal, retreats, heads in another direction, retreats again—and finally reorganizes his or her feelings and efforts around an emerging identity. Thus Bridget changed her major to psychology and found that she was now able to combine her desire to be a scientist with her interest in people.

WORKING

For one person work means loading 70,000 pounds on his five-axle truck, driving alone for several hours a day, perhaps for several days, with only a few stops for food and fuel, talk, relief, and sleep. While he is alone in the cab, tension is constant: it is hard to brake suddenly carrying thousands of pounds, so he must always think ahead. The work is wearing, yet he likes the odd hours and the independence.

For another person work means spending eight or nine hours a day at an advertising agency, dealing with clients and supervising commercial writers. She earns good money, spends a great deal of time talking with people, and has plenty of opportunities to exercise her talents as a

PSYCHOLOGY and YOU

Coping with Dorm Life. "I need my space," says the cartoon character Garfield the Cat in a TV commercial. Just as animals like their space, so do humans. We do better when we can control who moves in and out of our territory.

As the time approaches for college, you may be faced with choosing a dormitory. The most common types of dorms are the suite style, which consists of two or three double rooms in which four to six students share a common bathroom and lounge area, and the corridor style, which houses two to a room in a double-loaded corridor with a common bathroom.

Psychologists have found that corridor residents reported feeling more crowded and had impaired social relationships. They frequently avoided other people on their floor. Suite residents, in contrast, reported that most of their friends lived on the same floor. Corridor residents more often avoided eye contact with others. In addition, corridor residents were more competitive; suite dwellers were more cooperative.

■ **Analyzing Information.** After students read the margin feature, call on two volunteers to go to the chalkboard and draw floor plans of the two dorm designs. Ask the class to discuss why they think the suite design allows the students to feel more control over their environment and promotes adjustment to dorm life. Point out that good architects are always concerned with the psychological effects of the spaces they create. (OBJECTIVE 3)

■ **Discussion.** Ask students to identify Madison's three methods of coping with change. *("tightening up" by redoubling efforts, avoiding confronting doubts by wasting time, and resynthesizing)* Lead a discussion of the three college-related examples given in the text, and then ask the students if they think Madison's theory can be applied to other life endeavors as well. *(Students may find that the theory can be applied to the way people make certain career choices.)* (OBJECTIVE 3)

BEYOND THE CLASSROOM

Point out to students that there are many guides published annually to help students and parents select a suitable college. For example, *U.S. News & World Report* publishes an annual issue called "America's Best Colleges," which, along with feature articles, includes rankings of national, regional, and specialty schools. Have students find and bring several of these guides to class. Arrange with the school's guidance counselor to speak to the class about how these publications should be used.

VISUAL INSTRUCTION

Ask students to speculate whether creative or performing artists find their jobs personally satisfying and, if so, why. *(Answers will vary, but might include they can often pursue a stimulating variety of challenges.)*
Answer to caption, Figure 14.9: Answers will vary, but might include: Work may be performed in a variety of settings, under different schedules, under different managerial organizations, and for different reasons.

■ **Analyzing a Case Study.**
Read the following hypothetical case to the students. Then ask them to answer the questions that follow.
Richard's first job was as a landscaper's assistant—mowing lawns, trimming shrubs, and caring for flower beds—a job he kept throughout high school and college. It was often back-breaking work and didn't pay well, but Richard found it satisfying because he enjoyed working outdoors and making things grow. He often fantasized about the ideal gardens he would like to create. Now, fresh from college, Richard works in the publicity department of a large corporation. He has a good starting salary, some pleasant coworkers, and moderate challenges, but whenever he looks out the window and sees the landscapers, he feels a bit envious. He wishes he had gotten a degree in landscape design rather than communications.

1. What practical advice would you give to Richard to help him adjust to his present job?
2. What long-term advice would you give to Richard? Would you advise him to change careers?

FIGURE 14.9

Few careers offer as much personal satisfaction as that of a creative or performing artist. **In what ways are each individual's work experience different?**

manager. All three are qualities she likes about her job. Yet she must also deal with deadlines and worry about whether millions of dollars worth of ads will sell the products or not—and, subconsciously, whether it's worth the effort if they do.

For a third person work means training severely handicapped children to use their muscles to grasp a spoon, to gesture in sign language, and perhaps to take a few steps. The job is often depressing and frustrating, but there are also moments of intense personal satisfaction when a child makes progress.

The point is, each person's work experience is different. Jobs are performed in different settings: offices, stores, schools, hospitals, mines, trucks. Some occupations have structured time schedules; others are more flexible. Some workers are self-employed; most must answer to one or more higher-ups. Some workers are "in it for the money"; for others the job is a vehicle for more important personal satisfactions. Some workers do an entire task from beginning to end; others, like factory workers and copy editors, are only part of a larger process. Each person reacts differently to a job as a result of his or her own personality.

The First Job

For most people, getting their first full-time job is the major step into adulthood. It is exciting but frightening. Most students have vague notions about the world of work, pieced together from hearsay, brief glimpses during interviews, and the employer's sales pitch. The new secretary in publishing does not know what proofreaders and editors actually do. More important, she does not know what will be expected of her. Will the other workers accept her? The unknown is always frightening, and the first days and weeks on a job are often stressful. The ex-student finds herself completely exhausted at the end of the day.

Although some individuals receive training in job skills in school, few are taught all they will need to know in their first job: how to handle office politics, for instance, or cope with trivial problems, such as getting a typewriter repaired. Work also involves "psychological skills," such as common sense, an ability to deal with people, and an ability to cope with minor crises on a day-to-day basis. Few students are prepared for this.

In addition, the actual tasks a new employee is required to perform may be unexpected and disappointing. In school a student may have been writing papers about world food crisis and the symbolist poets. At work in a publishing house she may find herself typing letters, filling out forms, and taking messages. She may get little or no feedback on her performance. A memo she spent hours writing may lie unread on her boss's desk. She dreamed of guiding young authors through their first novel, but in reality she rarely even meets an author. In short, she finds she is neither growing personally nor making a meaningful contribution to literature. The job falls considerably short of her expectations, in part because they were unrealistic from the start (Morris, 1990).

CONNECTIONS: PSYCHOLOGY AND SOCIAL STUDIES

Organize the students into teams to develop lessons on the following skills needed to finding a job: using the help-wanted section of the newspaper, completing a job application, developing a resume, devising a suitable cover letter. Each team should prepare a resource packet to distribute to the class, and give a presentation on the best way to approach and complete their assigned job-related skill. (Suggest that students consult the school guidance office, the county employment services office, and the local library for information.)

FIGURE 14.10

A young person's first job often requires a period of adjustment. Hopes for an exciting, interesting job may have to be deferred until after serving an apprenticeship. **What are Quinn's five sources of work satisfaction?**

Work Satisfaction and Dissatisfaction

The Ability to Adjust. As a rule people do not become stars, editors, or company vice-presidents overnight. A young employee may know he could handle some things better than his boss does three weeks after taking a job. But if he becomes too impatient or if he makes the boss look foolish, he is likely to lose the opportunity to put his ideas into practice in the future. The emphasis here is on compromise: long-term personal goals should not be forsaken, but patience and an ability to tolerate frustration and delay are needed. A young woman may dream of acting, but waiting on tables may be the best job she can get. In this case, she will be happiest if she accepts this job as a short-term solution.

Adjusting to work also means being able to take the good with the bad. No job is all glamour. A model may have to pose in a bathing suit in 40-degree weather; a corporation vice-president may have to deal with distasteful office politics and boring correspondence; a baseball player must attend practice sessions and stay on a strict diet. As one chemist has stated: "Most of my job I do for free, because I enjoy it. The parts I don't like are what I do for the money."

Sources of Work Satisfaction. Some workers may seek high salaries, pleasant working conditions, and low-pressure jobs; others may be concerned only with finding personal fulfillment at work. Most workers, however, have both economic and personal goals. One study (Quinn *et al.*, 1971) has identified five major sources of work satisfaction.

1. *Resources.* The worker feels that he or she has enough available resources—help, supplies, and equipment—to do the job well.

Independent Practice

Beyond the Classroom.

Assign the students to interview someone who has been successfully married for 20 years or more. Tell them to ask the following questions and record the answers: What factors have kept you together for so long? What one thing is most important to a good marriage? What would you do differently if you were going to be married today? How does love change in a long marriage? What advice would you give about marriage? Have the students share their findings in class and identify any common themes that emerge from their interviews. (Arrange for release forms granting permission for students to share the interviews.) (OBJECTIVE 1)

CRITICAL THINKING ACTIVITY

Setting Priorities. Ask students to evaluate the work expectations upon graduation from high school or college. To help students, distribute copies of the list below. Ask students to rank the items from most to least important. Next, have students tally the individual rankings. What norms can they identify from males, females, and the combined responses? What conclusions regarding work satisfaction can students draw from this exercise? **Items to be ranked:**
Salary
Vacation
Fringe benefits
Chances for advancement
Coworkers
Variety of task
Work routine
Sex of immediate supervisor
Individualized work
Benefits to society
Challenge of assignments

■ **Research.** Have students select a famous twentieth-century personality who has been the subject of biography. Instruct students to research the life of this person, focusing especially on the adjustments—or maladjustments—the person made at college (if applicable) or in the first stages of his or her career. What behaviors led to success or problems later in life? Have students report their findings to the class, either orally or in writing. Tell students to be prepared with at least one interesting anecdote that relates to psychological development and adjustment.
(OBJECTIVES 3, 4)

VISUAL INSTRUCTION

Point out that many retirees who are financially secure find volunteer work to keep them active and involved socially.
Answer to caption, Figure 14.11: Have students check resources for current figures.

ASSESS

Check for Understanding

Ask students to define what is meant by adjustment. Then have them identify the different kinds of adjustments required in each of the following: love and marriage, parent-child relations, college, and work.

? FACT OR FICTION

■ **People who are most satisfied with their work do the best job.**

Fiction. In general, work satisfaction is not associated with how productive a person is on the job. People who dislike their jobs are often as productive as those with high levels of work satisfaction. However, work satisfaction is related to turnover. Employees who are unhappy with their jobs are the most likely to quit.

FIGURE 14.11

Many people continue to work after their retirement, but they are likely to change the kind of work they do. Someone who has worked in an office for many years, for instance, may relish the chance to work outdoors. **What percentage of workers change jobs in an average year?**

2. *Financial reward.* The job pays well, offers good fringe benefits, and is secure.
3. *Challenge.* The job is interesting and enables the worker to use his or her special talents and abilities.
4. *Relations with co-workers.* The worker is on good terms professionally and socially with colleagues.
5. *Comfort.* Working conditions and related factors—hours, travel to and from the job, work environment, and so on—are attractive.

Job satisfaction has been on the decline for many years in the United States. One problem is that the number of jobs requiring a college education has not risen as rapidly as the number of college graduates, and as a result, some people find themselves overeducated for their position (Mottaz, 1984). In addition, college-educated employees place more emphasis on the significance of their job and their involvement in the task itself in rating job satisfaction.

Changing Careers

Some theorists predict that in the future, people will change their **career**—a vocation in which a person works at least a few years—several times in their lifetimes. As we saw earlier, people today live longer than ever before, and so they have a longer work life. It is not uncommon for a person to retire from one job at the age of 60 or 65, then embark on a new career as a real-estate salesperson, travel broker, writer, or consultant. Some employers (especially some local governments) have early-retirement programs that allow people to leave jobs with partial pay at a relatively young age; alumni of these programs have been especially good candidates for "second wind" careers. Many women also split their careers by stepping out of the job market to raise children, then reentering the working world for a second full career.

There is some evidence that people are changing careers because they are not so easily satisfied as they once were. There have been periods in our history, like the Great Depression, when work of any sort could attract and hold steady workers simply because of the great need for money, but times have changed. As we have seen, people want work that is psychologically as well as financially rewarding. If a person is unhappy at a job, changing careers may provide the answer, through better pay, better working conditions, or more interesting tasks. "Job shopping," or trying out several careers, is most common among people who have recently entered the labor force and are still trying to get a feel for the work that suits them best. Across all ages, however, worker satisfaction is affected by the availability of *other* jobs. Research indicates that, during periods when jobs are hard to find, workers tolerate more dissatisfaction with their present job (Carsten & Spector, 1987).

Does this mean you should forget about career training, since you probably will not stick with your first job? Not at all. You should acquire as many abilities and interests as you can—in and out of school; you should work to develop your interpersonal skills; and you should look at change as

COMMUNITY INVOLVEMENT

Have students visit a state-sponsored or private employment agency to learn about the current availability of jobs in your community or region. Instruct students to investigate employment opportunities in their field of interest. Also, have them identify the jobs with the highest employment potential. (That is, which job categories are most open?) What are the minimum qualifications needed for entry-level positions in the various fields? Based on their research, have students present an oral report on the overall job market in your area.

desirable and challenging. In these ways, more occupations will be open to you, and the better your chances of employment will be, both now and in the future.

Comparable Worth

Consider the following two cases. Tonya is employed as a day-care supervisor for a state government. In order to qualify for this job, she needed three years of experience as well as college credit. In her job, she is responsible for not only the care and well-being of the children but also the supervision of several subordinates. Trent, also a state worker, is in charge of a storeroom and is responsible for supplying goods to various departments in his building as well as supervising several subordinates. In order to qualify for his job, Trent needed four years of experience. In terms of actual job demands, Trent's and Tonya's jobs might seem to be quite comparable. However, Trent is paid more than Tonya, despite the fact that Tonya's job requires college credit. In theory, jobs of comparable training, skill, and importance should be compensated at the same rate. In practice, however, the market value of many jobs traditionally held by females is considerably lower than that of comparable jobs traditionally held by males. Moreover, as Juanita Kreps, Secretary of Labor in the Carter Administration, pointed out, "Many of the occupational groups in which women are concentrated pay low wages while requiring higher-than-average educational achievement."

Many groups have been working to achieve equal pay for comparable work. The National Organization for Women has made the upgrading of traditionally female jobs one of its highest priorities. Labor unions have also been addressing the issue of pay equity. Delegates at the 1981 national convention of the AFL-CIO were urged to press for equal pay for comparable work in all future contract negotiations.

It may seem surprising that such demands were necessary. After all, the Civil Rights Act, passed by Congress in 1964, had included Title VII, which prohibits discrimination on the basis of sex in hiring, firing, terms of compensation, and work conditions. Moreover, the Equal Employment Opportunity Commission (EEOC) was set up to enforce Title VII. The fact is that, for economic reasons, many employers are unwilling to raise salaries, especially if they are able to find workers who will accept the low wages that they do offer. It is up to the workers, therefore, to demand the wages to which they are entitled.

A 1981 Supreme Court decision opened the door for workers to bring lawsuits for equal pay for comparable work under Title VII. Affirmative action programs assist in equalizing the recruitment and hiring efforts of American organizations. However, if poorly implemented, affirmative action can produce negative psychological effects. Hiring women because they are women rather than for their specific expertise sometimes plays down the value of their leadership, their group's accomplishments, and their inclination to want to continue to lead (Heilman, Simon, & Repper, 1987).

Reteach

Have students complete the Chapter 14 Study Guide Activity. For extended review, assign the Chapter 14 Review Activity as homework or an in-class assignment.

Enrich

Have students complete the Chapter 14 Extension Activity.

Evaluate

Administer and grade the Chapter Test. Two forms are available should you wish to give different tests to different students/classes.

Use the Understanding Psychology Testmaker to create a customized test.

CLOSE

Ask students to write a paragraph in their journals, applying what they have learned to a specific problem they are having or have recently had. Tell students they will not be asked to share with the class what they have written. Explain that the purpose is for them to enhance their own personal adjustment to some aspect of life.

CONNECTIONS: PSYCHOLOGY AND SOCIAL STUDIES

Have students research the socially and legally charged issue of comparable worth. Suggest that they contact such groups as the National Organization for Women, the NAACP, and the AFL-CIO to find out what their most recent findings are on this subject. Students should also research recent newspaper and magazine reports to try to determine pay discrepancies between various groups of citizens. Based on this research, what conclusions can students form about the pay scales offered to women, members of minority groups, and so on? Ask: What obstacles still exist to achieving equal economic opportunity within the United States?

ANSWERS

Concepts and Vocabulary

1. Adjustment is the process of adapting to as well as actively shaping one's environment. Students' examples will vary.

2. Liking is, in part, respect for another and the feeling that he or she is similar to you. Loving is a complex constellation of needs, rewards, and different ideals to be fulfilled. Three major components: need, caring, and intimacy. Answers will vary.

3. Stages of typical marriage include: newlywed, children, children's adolescence, empty nest, retirement, alone again.

4. Answers will vary. Marital happiness depends on the partners' having compatible needs, images of themselves that coincide with their images of each other, and a clear understanding of each other's role.

5. Divorce releases a torrent of emotions: anger, resentment, fear, loneliness, anxiety, and a feeling of failure. Children's reactions range from upset to rebellion.

6. Answers will vary.

7. may result in hurt feelings and anger, leaving the child no choice but to submit or rebel; include blame-shifting (judging, diagnosing, teaching, shaming)

8. Authoritarians make decisions for their children. Permissive enforce only

SUMMARY

Use the following outline as a tool for reviewing this chapter. Copy the outline onto your own paper, leaving spaces between headings to make notes about key concepts.

I. Love and Marriage

  A. Love

  B. Marriage

  C. Marital Problems and Divorce

  D. Children and Divorce

II. Parent-Child Relationships

  A. Sources of Parent-Adolescent Conflict

  B. Parental Expectations

  C. The Power Struggle: Escalating Conflict

III. College Life

  A. Sources of Change

  B. Coping with Change

IV. Working

  A. The First Job

  B. Work Satisfaction and Dissatisfaction

  C. Changing Careers

  D. Comparable Worth

CONCEPTS AND VOCABULARY

1. Describe what psychologists mean by "adjustment." Give an example of an adjustment you have recently made.

2. In what ways are liking and loving different? What are three major components of liking and loving? How do males and females differ in their feelings of love?

3. Name the stages through which a typical marriage will develop.

4. Identify several factors that marital happiness depends upon. What leads to marital conflict?

5. How do spouses react to divorce? How are children affected by divorce?

6. Describe some common sources of parent-adolescent conflict.

7. How can parental expectations result in parent-child conflict? What are some of the counterproductive reactions to conflict displayed by parents and children?

8. How do authoritarian parents deal with their children? How about permissive parents? Democratic parents?

9. List at least two of the new experiences and challenges that a student faces when entering college. How do students cope with stress at college?

10. What new challenges are faced in work? List the factors that determine job satisfaction. What leads to career changes?

CRITICAL THINKING

1. Synthesize. Some experts believe that one out of two marriages today will end in divorce. How do you account for this trend? What do you think could be done to slow the rise in the divorce rate?

2. Analyze. Write a short paper entitled "My Most Difficult Adjustment in Life." Relate an experience that required an adjustment. What were your feelings at the time? How did you eventually make the adjustment? How did you feel once you made the adjustment? What did you learn from this experience that could help you adjust to future changes in your life?

3. Synthesize. Pretend someone has just asked you, "How do I know if I'm in love?" How would you respond?

those rules that their children will allow. Democratic parents interact, guide, but do not dominate.

9. College students meet new people, encounter new ideas, question old beliefs, and may find their expectations are unrealistic. They may cope with stress by redoubling efforts to maintain past choices, avoiding doubts, or resynthesizing their feelings.

10. Work-related challenges include:

unanticipated demands, unrealistic expectations, need for "psychological skills." Answers will vary.

Critical Thinking

1. Students should consider various ways that people fail to adjust to the challenges of marriage. They should also consider recent societal changes that make it easier to obtain a divorce as well as the changing role of women

1. The idea of "romantic love" is fostered in fairy-tales like "Cinderella" and "Sleeping Beauty" and in popular songs, novels, short stories, and TV commercials. Take examples from one or two of these areas, and discuss how they express the romantic ideal of falling in love with the perfect stranger.

2. It has been suggested that marriages go through several stages as a couple grows older. Identify the stages from your reading, and study your family, neighbors, or friends. Do they fit this suggestion, and if so, what stage are they experiencing currently? Why do you think they do or do not fit within one of the described stages?

3. If any of the marriages of people you know have ended in divorce, make some notes on why you think this occurred. If some of these people are available, ask them how they adjusted to being divorced and what kind of problems they had. What did they do to help their children adjust to the divorce?

4. The chapter mentions two potential sources of parent-adolescent conflict (drugs and sex). Ask several adults that you know what conflicts they had with their parents when they were adolescents. Were the conflicts ever resolved, or did they just go away over time? Ask several of your friends what conflicts they have with their parents. Are any of their conflicts the same as the conflicts mentioned by the adults you talked to? Do you think there are certain parent-adolescent conflicts that every generation experiences?

ANALYZING VIEWPOINTS

1. For many young adults, college is the first major step toward gaining a sense of autonomy. The separation from the family often provides the young adult with opportunities for growth and personal development. In recent years, however, many young adults have been moving back home after they graduate from college. How do you think this might affect their developing sense of autonomy? Write a paper that argues both sides of the issue. Include reasons why moving back home should have little impact on the young adult's sense of autonomy, and reasons why the move home may hinder the young adult's development into adulthood.

BEYOND THE CLASSROOM

1. Talk to several adults about their first job. What were their expectations? Were these expectations met? Did they enjoy the job? How long did they work at this particular job? What did they learn from their first job about the world of work? What did they learn about themselves? Did this job lead to a career in the same field? Go to the library and read any of Studs Terkel's books on working. (Ask your teacher or librarian for a reference.) Compare the experiences of the adults you talked to with several of the adults you read about in Terkel's book. What do you now know about individuals' experiences in their first jobs?

IN YOUR JOURNAL

1. One of the enduring myths involving love and marriage is the idea of "love at first sight." Psychologists often do not take the idea seriously, pointing out that most people learn to love and cherish another person over a period of time. Is there such a thing as love at first sight? Or is this just a romantic myth perpetuated by images from the movies and television? Write answers to these questions in your journal. Use what you have learned from the chapter, as well as any magazine articles you can find on the topic of love. Be sure to give examples. You may include people you know or people who are public figures.

age them to apply their knowledge of psychology to ways of reducing the divorce rate.

2. Allow students the option of keeping their responses to this assignment private.

3. Students should consider Zick Rubin's research in formulating their responses.

Applying Knowledge

1. Answers will vary, but student responses should note that most are based on the ideal of physical attraction.

2. Answers will vary, but students should include a description of each stage and explain why their subjects fit the categories.

3. Answers will vary.

4. Answers will vary, but students should present the results and draw valid conclusions.

Analyzing Viewpoints

1. Answers will vary, but student responses should address both sides of the issue concerning autonomy.

Beyond the Classroom

1. Answers will vary, but students should demonstrate firsthand research with several adults.

IN YOUR JOURNAL

If time permits, discuss journal entries individually with the students.

CHAPTER BONUS
Test Question

This question may be used for extra credit on the chapter test.
Choose the letter of the correct response.

Close relationships between individuals who force one another to examine their basic assumptions are called:

a. autonomic relationships.

b. resynthesis.

c. developmental friendships.

d. endogamy.

Answer: **c**

CHAPTER 15

Abnormal Behavior

TEXT TOPICS	SPECIAL FEATURES	RESOURCE MATERIALS
What is Abnormal Behavior? pp. 363–368 **The Problem of Classification,** pp. 368–369	**Using Psychology:** Legal Definitions of Sanity, pp. 366–367	Reproducible Lesson Plan; Study Guide; Review Activity
Anxiety-Based Disorders, pp. 369–372 **Somatoform Disorders,** pp. 372–373 **Dissociative Disorders,** pp. 373–374 **Mood Disorders,** pp. 374–378 **Schizophrenia,** pp. 378–382 **Personality Disorders,** pp. 382–383	**More About Psychology,** p. 373 **More About Psychology,** p. 378 **Psychology Update,** p. 380	Reproducible Lesson Plan; Study Guide; Review Activity *Readings in Psychology:* Section 5, Readings 6, 7, 8
Drug Addiction, pp. 383–385	**Fact or Fiction?,** p. 384	Reproducible Lesson Plan; Study Guide; Review Activity; Extension Activity
DSM-IV: New Ways to Categorize Mental Illness, pp. 386–388	**Psychology Update,** p. 386	Reproducible Lesson Plan; Study Guide; Review Activity; Application Activity; Chapter Test, Form A and Form B Understanding Pychology Testmaker

PERFORMANCE ASSESSMENT ACTIVITY

As an ongoing project, assign students to clip articles from your local newspapers that describe some kind of abnormal behavior. Direct them to paste each article on a separate sheet of paper. Below the article, students should identify the category (or categories) of abnormal behavior that it exemplifies. (For example, a report on drunk driving would illustrate possible addiction or alcoholism.) Have students compile these articles in a notebook or binder for use in the Cooperative Learning activity on page 385. (Categorization of the clippings should reflect the classifications used in the text.)

CHAPTER RESOURCES

Readings for the Student
Green, Hannah. *I Never Promised You a Rose Garden.* New York: New American Library, 1964.

Sheehan, S. *Is There No Place on Earth for Me?* Boston: Houghton Mifflin, 1982.

Sizemore, C. C., and Pittillo, E. S. *I'm Eve.* New York: Doubleday, 1977.

Readings for the Teacher
Blashfield, R., Sprock, J., and Fuller, A. "Suggested Guidelines for Including/Excluding Categories in the DSM-IV." *Comp. Psychiatry,* 31 (1990): 15–19.

Feyerabend, P. *Farewell to Reason.* New York: Verso, 1987.

Neale, J. M., Oltmann, T. F., and Davison, G. C. *Case Studies in Abnormal Psychology.* New York: Wiley, 1982.

Tischler, G., ed. *Diagnosis and Classification in Psychiatry.* New York: Cambridge University Press, 1987.

Multimedia
Personality Disorders—Failures of Adjustment (45 minutes, 1/2" video). IBIS Media. This video surveys many personality disorders through dramatization and shows the causes and the effective treatments.

For additional resources, see the bibliography beginning on page 530.

CHAPTER 15
Lesson Plan

FOCUS

Motivating Activity

Assign students two tasks. First, on a sheet of paper, have them write a definition of the term *mental illness*. Second, beneath this definition, direct students to list the traits, behaviors, or symptoms that they associate with mentally ill people. (For example, suppose students were psychiatrists. What "diagnostic bell ringers" might catch their attention?) Next, have students put their papers in sealed envelopes with their names on the outside. Collect the envelopes for redistribution at a later time. Then tell students that this chapter will give them the tools to review their statements for accuracy and stereotypes. (See Close on page 388.)

Meeting Chapter Objectives.

Point out the five objectives on p. 363. Then have students skim the heads and the boldfaced or italicized terms to find the pages on which each of these objectives will be covered. Assign groups of students to carry out the direction(s) in each objective as they read the chapter.

Building Vocabulary.

Have students preview the list of key terms, and offer definitions for any terms they feel they already know, such as *anxiety*. After each guess, look up the term in the Glossary. How close did students come to the real meanings? Assign remaining terms for groups of students to define.

Abnormal Behavior

FIGURE 15.1 For psychologists, defining abnormality is neither simple nor sure. Much depends on the approach one uses and on the behavior's setting.

362

TEACHER CLASSROOM RESOURCES

- Chapter 15 Reproducible Lesson Plan
- Chapter 15 Study Guide
- Chapter 15 Review Activity
- Chapter 15 Application Activity
- Chapter 15 Extension Activity

- *Readings in Psychology:* Section 5, Readings 6, 7, 8

- Chapter 15 Test, Form A and Form B

- Understanding Psychology Testmaker

OBJECTIVES

After studying this chapter, you should be able to

- distinguish between the concepts of normality and abnormality.
- identify the behavioral patterns psychologists label anxiety disorders.
- identify the behavioral patterns psychologists label mood disorders.
- describe the concept of schizophrenia and give possible explanations for its origin.
- describe how a personality disorder differs from anxiety disorders, mood disorders, and schizophrenic disorders.

A man living in the Ozark Mountains has a vision in which God speaks to him. He begins preaching to his relatives and neighbors, and soon he has the whole town in a state of religious fervor. People say he has a "calling." His reputation as a prophet and healer spreads, and in time he is drawing large audiences everywhere he goes. However, when he ventures into St. Louis and attempts to hold a prayer meeting, blocking traffic on a main street at rush hour, he is arrested. He tells the policemen about his conversations with God, and they hurry him off to the nearest mental hospital.

A housewife is tired all the time, but she has trouble sleeping. The chores keep piling up because she has no energy. Applications for evening courses and "help wanted" clippings from the classified ads lie untouched in a drawer. She consults the family doctor, but he says she's in perfect health. One night she tells her husband that she's thinking of seeing a psychotherapist. He thinks this is ridiculous. According to him, all she needs is to get up out of her chair and get busy.

KEY TERMS

- addiction
- antisocial personality
- anxiety
- bipolar disorder
- conversion disorder
- delusion
- depressive-type reaction
- dissociative disorder
- double bind
- DSM-III-Revised
- DSM-IV
- hallucination
- major depressive disorder
- manic-type reaction
- multiple personality
- panic disorder
- personality disorder
- phobia
- post-traumatic stress disorder
- psychogenic amnesia
- psychogenic fugue
- psychological dependence
- schizophrenia
- somatoform disorder
- tolerance
- withdrawal

IN YOUR JOURNAL

What is a phobia? Write its definition as well as the definitions of the following terms in your journal: *acrophobia, xenophobia, ergasiophobia, monophobia.* Use a dictionary to help you with the assignment.

363

Exploring Key Ideas

Defining Abnormal Behavior. Brainstorm with the class examples of what they consider to be "normal" adolescent behavior. List these items on the chalkboard. Then ask students to imagine the following settings: (1) a rural village in India, (2) a presidential inaugural, (3) a funeral, (4) a courtyard in the city of Beijing (China). Which of the behaviors named would be "abnormal" in each of these settings? Why? Use this activity to underscore that defining "normal" is neither simple nor easy. It depends upon such variables as behavioral setting, cultural perspective, public expectations, and so on.

IN YOUR JOURNAL

As a tip, point out that *phobia* is a root in all the italicized terms. Explain that *phobia* comes from the Greek *phobos* for "fear." What can students assume about the four terms based upon this derivation? *(that they all involve some kind of fear)*

EXTRA CREDIT ACTIVITY

Assign interested students to research how other cultures have treated people often labeled mentally ill or "deviant" in the present-day United States. Encourage some students to investigate traditional Native American cultures. Request others to research cultures in Asia, Africa, Latin America, or the Middle East. Have students present their findings in brief oral reports.

TEACH

Guided Practice

■ **Demonstration.** As a quick illustration of the thin line that often separates normal from abnormal behavior, organize the students into three groups. Tell each group to adopt one of the following behaviors: (1) Reach out to shake hands with friends, but hold onto hands much longer than usual. (2) Make direct eye contact with someone on the bus or in the cafeteria, and prolong the gaze for 10 seconds. (3) When asked "How are you doing?" (or some similar greeting), say "Why do you want to know?" Instruct students to write down reactions. What signals did people use to indicate that students were acting "abnormally"? (OBJECTIVE 1)

■ **Applying Concepts.** Review the three common methods for distinguishing normal from abnormal behavior—the deviance approach, the adjustment approach, and the psychological health approach. Then have students review the two examples on page 363. Which approach might best be used to analyze the "prophet" and the "housewife"? *(Answers will vary, but students might note: deviance approach, adjustment approach.)* (OBJECTIVE 1)

Who is right? The "prophet" or the policemen? The housewife or her husband? It is often difficult to draw a line between normal and abnormal behavior. Behavior that some people consider normal seems abnormal to others. Many feel that having visions and hearing voices is an important part of a religious experience. Other people believe these are symptoms of mental disorder. The man in the example above was interviewed by psychiatrists, diagnosed as "paranoid schizophrenic," and hospitalized for mental illness. Had he stayed home, he could have been considered perfectly normal. Indeed, more than normal—popular.

WHAT IS ABNORMAL BEHAVIOR?

Behavior some people consider normal seems abnormal to others.

In our example, the man was classified as mentally troubled because his behavior was so different from what other people felt was "normal." Yet the fact that a person is different does not necessarily mean that he or she is suffering from a mental illness. Indeed, going along with the crowd may at times be self-destructive. Most readers—and most psychologists—would agree that a teenager who uses cocaine because nearly everyone in his social circles does has problems.

In the case of the housewife, she was the one who decided she was psychologically troubled, simply because she was so unhappy. Yet unhappiness and even genuine depression are certainly not foolproof signs of psychological disturbance or of impending breakdown. Everyone feels low from time to time.

How, then, do psychologists distinguish the normal from the abnormal? There are a number of ways to define abnormality, none of which is entirely satisfactory. We will look at the most popular ways of drawing the line between normal and abnormal in terms of deviance, adjustment, and psychological health. Then, we will look at the application of these principles in legal definitions of abnormality. Finally, we will consider the criticism that in all these models people are arbitrarily labeled mentally ill.

Deviation From Normality

One approach to defining abnormality is to say that whatever most people do is normal. Abnormality, then, is any deviation from the average or from the majority. It is normal to bathe periodically, to express grief at the death of a loved one, and to wear warm clothes when going out in the cold, because most people do so. Because very few people take 10 showers a day, or laugh when a loved one dies, or wear bathing suits in the snow, those who do so may be considered abnormal.

However, the deviance approach, as commonly used as it is, has serious limitations. If most people cheat on their income-tax returns, are honest taxpayers abnormal? If most people are noncreative, was Shakespeare abnormal? Because the majority is not always right or best, the deviance approach to defining abnormality is not a generally useful standard.

ADDITIONAL INFORMATION

Make sure that students understand that there is no absolute list of symptoms of mental disorder. Most psychologists define normal behavior as the ability to cope with stress and conflict, and abnormal behavior as the failure to adjust to the stresses of life.

FIGURE 15.2

The line between normal and abnormal is sometimes a fine one and depends very much on the observer and the standard being used. What some people consider deviant, others may see as just a little odd. **What are three approaches that are used to distinguish between the normal and the abnormal?**

FIGURE 15.3

Chaim Soutine painted *The Madwoman* in 1920. Many people believe that those who are mentally ill are always recognizable by their bizarre appearance and behavior— that they are somehow fundamentally different from the rest of us. **What are limitations to defining abnormal behavior as "deviating from what most people do"?**

Adjustment

Another way to distinguish normal from abnormal people is to say that normal people are able to get along in the world—physically, emotionally, and socially. They can feed and clothe themselves, work, find friends, and live by the rules of society. By this definition, abnormal people are the ones who fail to *adjust*. They may be so unhappy that they refuse to eat or so lethargic that they cannot hold a job. They may experience so much anxiety in relationships with others that they end up avoiding people, living in a lonely world of their own.

Psychological Health

The terms "mental illness" and "mental health" imply that psychological disturbance or abnormality is like a physical sickness—such as the flu or tuberculosis. Although many psychologists think that "mental illness" is different from physical illness, the idea remains that there is some ideal

CONNECTIONS: PSYCHOLOGY AND SOCIAL STUDIES

Tell students that the first well-known mental health pioneer in the present-day United States was Benjamin Rush (1745–1813). Nicknamed the "father of American psychiatry," Rush wrote the first American treatise on mental health. Entitled *Medical Inquiries and Observations Upon the Diseases of the Mind*, the book became the basis for the first organized course in psychiatry. Request interested students to prepare an illustrated biography or poster celebrating Rush's many achievements, emphasizing his work in psychiatry.

■ **Defining Terms.** Point out the loose use of the word *crazy* in everyday language. Ask students to cite some of the "crazy" behaviors of well-known celebrities. Then ask students if they consider any of these people *mentally ill.* Why or why not? What do students think constitutes *sanity* and *insanity?* Use student discussion as a bridge into the Using Psychology feature.

U sing Psychology

As a guide to reading, ask these questions:
1. What is the definition of "criminal insanity"? *(not responsible for actions because of a mental disease/defect)*
2. In what type of cases is the court most likely to rule in favor of insanity? *(noncriminal, commitment proceedings)*
3. Why do you think the insanity plea is so rarely successful in criminal cases? *(Students may note the reluctance of juries to allow a criminal to escape punishment on the basis of a hard-to-prove defense.)*

VISUAL INSTRUCTION

Ask students to define the term *assassin. (a murderer who strikes suddenly and by surprise; usually used for the killer of a politically important person)* Why might the defense in the Hinckley case have been eager to avoid this label? *(because of its purposeful, political connotations)*
Answer to caption, Figure 15.4: insanity

---

way for people to function psychologically, just as there is an ideal way for people to function physically. Some psychologists feel that the normal or healthy person would be one who is functioning ideally or who is at least striving toward ideal functioning. Personality theorists such as Carl Jung

U sing Psychology

Legal Definitions of Sanity

When John Hinckley was tried for shooting President Ronald Reagan in 1981, he was found "not guilty by reason of insanity" and sent to a mental hospital. This widely publicized case raised some concern among psychiatrists and lawyers about the legal definition of sanity. The terms "sane" and "insane" are legal, rather than psychological, terms.

FIGURE 15.4

President Reagan waves to the crowd moments before being shot by John Hinckley. **What was Hinckley's attorney's defense in court?**

STUDY AND WRITING SKILLS

Ask groups of students to research the lives of other assassins and would-be assassins. Choices include John Wilkes Booth, Lee Harvey Oswald, James Earl Ray, Sirhan Sirhan, "Squeaky" Fromme, and David Chapman. Tell students to focus on family/environmental backgrounds, personality profiles, and stated motives behind the shootings. Have students present their findings in oral reports. What, if any, features/traits did these individuals share in common? Did any of the figures fit the definition of criminally insane? If so, why?

While there is no single definition of criminal insanity, the most widely used set of guidelines was developed by the American Law Institute in 1962. It emphasized that people are not responsible for their criminal acts if "as a result of mental disease or defect" they do not know that what they did was wrong or if they were unable to act differently. The guidelines also noted that "the terms 'mental disease or defect' do not include an abnormality manifested only by repeated criminal or otherwise antisocial conduct."

It is often difficult to apply these guidelines to real people. In *United States* v. *Brawner* (1972), the American Law Institute guidelines were defined more precisely by noting that "mental disease or defect includes any abnormal condition of the mind, which substantially impairs behavior controls" (Holmes, 1991). As in the Hinckley case, expert witnesses are usually called on both sides. The defense lawyer maintains that his or her client is insane, and the prosecutor tries to prove the defendant sane. The jurors decide which set of expert witnesses is correct. A person who is judged insane may spend more time in a mental hospital than he or she would have spent in prison if judged sane.

Although an insanity defense generates publicity, this plea is used rarely and is usually unsuccessful. The courts judge people insane much more often for purposes of commitment to mental institutions.

Laws vary from state to state, but generally a person can be committed to a mental hospital if he or she is judged to be (1) mentally ill and (2) dangerous to himself or herself or others.

In *formal commitment* proceedings, a friend or relative usually asks a judge to order a mental health examination. *Informal commitment* occurs when, for example, the police bring in a person who is acting wildly. In most states, a person can be held against his or her will for a specified period of time for observation ranging from 1 to 20 days. In some states, this detention does not even require the certification of a mental health professional that the action is needed. Following that short observational period, there must be formal commitment proceedings in order for a person to be held against his or her will.

and Abraham Maslow (see Chapter 11) have tried to describe this striving process, which is often referred to as *self-actualization*. According to this line of thinking, to be normal or healthy involves full acceptance and expression of one's own individuality and humanness.

PORTRAIT

Dorothea Dix
1802–1887
Dorothea Dix grew up in a frontier town in present-day Maine. Like Erik Erikson, Dix never earned a degree in psychology. Nonetheless, she won fame for her crusading efforts on behalf of the mentally ill. A school teacher by trade, Dix offered to teach Sunday school in a Boston prison. There she got a firsthand look at the horrible treatment of mentally ill people locked away in jail. The experience sent Dix into nearly 1,000 prisons, jails, and poorhouses. In 1843, armed with volumes of evidence, Dix went before the Massachusetts legislature. She declared:

I proceed, Gentlemen, briefly to call your attention to the state of Insane Persons confined within this Commonwealth in cages, closets, cellars, stalls, pens: Chained, naked, beaten with rods, and lashed into obedience.

Dix extended her campaign across the United States and into Canada and Scotland. History credits her with founding and funding 32 of the nation's first mental hospitals.

CONNECTIONS: PSYCHOLOGY AND THE LAW

Review the debate over song lyrics, written materials, and films charged with obscene or violent words or actions. Then conduct a panel discussion in which students explore whether there is a connection between these materials and deviant behavior (as some people charge). When, if ever, should materials be censored? As an extension activity, you might formally debate the following topic: *Resolved*—That freedom of speech and press extends to all forms of expression.

The phrase "mad as a hatter" became widely used because many hatmakers suffered from tremors, slurred speech, and confusion. Scientists discovered that this condition was caused by mercury-laden vapors inhaled by the hatmakers while they worked on felt hats.

■ **Interpreting a Point of View.** In condemning the use of the term *mentally ill,* Thomas Szasz declared: *Whenever we try to give a definition of what mental health is, we simply state our preference for a certain type of cultural, social, and ethical order.* Ask: (1) On what grounds did Szasz oppose use of the term *mentally ill? (It grew out of personal bias.)* (2) How do you think Szasz might have viewed conformity? *(probably would oppose it)* (3) The text states: "The fact that it is difficult to define abnormality does not mean that no such thing exists." With which point of view do you agree—that of Szasz or that of the text? *(Encourage students to support their answers with well-reasoned arguments.)* (OBJECTIVE 1)

One problem with this approach to defining abnormality is that it is difficult to determine whether or not a person is doing a good job of actualizing himself or herself. How can you tell when a person is doing his or her best? What are the signs that he or she is losing the struggle? Answers to such questions must often be arbitrary.

The definitions of abnormality are somewhat arbitrary. This fact has led some theorists to conclude that labeling a person as "mentally ill" simply because his or her behavior is odd is a mistake as well as cruel and irresponsible. The foremost spokesperson of this point of view is the American psychologist Thomas Szasz (1961).

Szasz argues that most of the people whom we call mentally ill are not ill at all. They simply have "problems in living"—serious conflicts with the world around them. But instead of dealing with the patient's conflict as something that deserves attention and respect, psychiatrists simply label him as "sick" and shunt him off to a hospital. The society's norms remain unchallenged, and the psychiatrist remains in a comfortable position of authority. The one who loses is the patient, who is deprived both of responsibility for his behavior and of his dignity as a human being. As a result, Szasz claims, the patient's problems intensify. Szasz's position is a minority stand. Most psychologists and psychiatrists would agree that a person who claims to be God or Napoleon is truly abnormal and disturbed.

The fact that it is difficult to define abnormality does not mean that no such thing exists. What it does mean is that we should be very cautious about judging a person to be "mentally ill" just because he or she acts in a way that we cannot understand. It should also be kept in mind that mild psychological disorders are common. It is only when a psychological problem becomes severe enough to disrupt everyday life that it is thought of as "abnormality" or "illness."

THE PROBLEM OF CLASSIFICATION

For years psychiatrists have been trying to devise a logical and useful method for classifying emotional disorders. This is a difficult task, for psychological problems do not lend themselves to the same sort of categorizing that physical illnesses do. The causes and symptoms of psychological disturbances and breakdowns, and the cures for those breakdowns, are rarely obvious or clearcut.

All of the major classification schemes have accepted the medical model—they assume that abnormal behavior can be described in the same manner as any physical illness. The physician diagnoses a specific disease when a person has certain specific symptoms.

In 1952, the American Psychiatric Association agreed upon a standard system for classifying abnormal symptoms, which it published in the *Diagnostic and Statistical Manual of Mental Disorders*, or DSM. This has been revised four times as the DSM-II (1968), the DSM-III (1980), and **DSM-III-Revised** (1987). The most recent revision, the **DSM-IV,** was published in 1994.

LAB EXPERIMENTS AND DEMONSTRATIONS

Mention that some people hold stereotypes about mentally disturbed people. Often these biases grow out of fear or lack of information. A common example is the tendency to equate neurosis with psychosis. Review these two terms. Point out these terms are used by psychologists today only to refer to a broad range of disorders rather than single categories. Then instruct students to conduct a random survey of attitudes toward neurotic behavior. As a survey tool, have students prepare a form with the following incomplete sentence at the top: "A person with a neurosis . . ."

Beneath the sentence students should copy these statements. The continuum included with item 1 should be repeated for all the choices.

(continued on page 369)

The revisions were made for a number of reasons. The DSM-II was criticized as too vague: two psychologists often gave different diagnoses for the same patient. The DSM-III and DSM-III-R systems listed more concrete and specific symptoms for a diagnosis. As a result, their diagnoses proved far more reliable. Reflecting the fact that changes in society affect what behaviors are viewed as abnormal, diagnoses based on DSM-IV should be even more reliable. Prior to DSM-III, disorders were classified not only by symptoms but also by assumed causes. This made consistent diagnoses difficult. A large number of disorders were added to DSM-III and DSM-III-R. Moreover, individual cases are now diagnosed on five axes or dimensions—detailed near the end of this chapter—which make it possible to assign multiple diagnoses.

A major change occurred in the shifts from DSM-II to DSM-IV. Before 1980, the two most commonly used diagnostic distinctions were neurosis and psychosis. Though the terms *neurosis* and *psychosis* have been replaced by more specific ones, they are still used by many psychologists. However, the conditions originally identified under neurosis and psychosis have been expanded into more detailed categories, including anxiety-based disorders, somatoform disorders, dissociative disorders, mood disorders, and schizophrenia.

ANXIETY-BASED DISORDERS

Fifteen percent of adults have endured symptoms typical of the anxiety-based disorders (Regier, *et al.*, 1988). These disorders share certain characteristics, including feelings of anxiety and personal inadequacy and an avoidance of dealing with problems. People with anxiety-based disorders often have unrealistic images of themselves. People who are deeply anxious doubt and seem unable to free themselves of recurring worries and fears. Their emotional problems may be expressed in constant worrying, sudden mood swings, or a variety of physical symptoms (for example, headaches, sweating, muscle tightness, weakness, and fatigue). Anxious people often have difficulty forming stable and satisfying relationships. Even though their behavior may be self-defeating and ineffective in solving problems, those driven by anxiety often refuse to give up their behaviors in favor of more effective ways of dealing with anxiety. In the DSM-IV, the anxiety-based disorders include *generalized anxiety disorder, phobic disorder, panic disorder, obsessive-compulsive disorder,* and *post-traumatic stress disorder.*

Generalized Anxiety Disorder

Once in a while, everyone feels nervous for reasons he or she cannot explain, but a severely anxious person almost always feels this way. **Anxiety** is a generalized apprehension—a vague feeling that one is in danger. This anxiety rarely blossoms into full-fledged panic attacks, which may include choking sensations, chest pain, dizziness, trembling, and hot flashes. Unlike fear, which is a reaction to real and identifiable threats, anxiety is a reaction to vague or imagined dangers.

Teaching Note. To discourage self-diagnosis on the part of students, you might hand out the following information.

If the Label Fits . . .
A medical student read about Bella's Syndrome—a skin condition that occurs as chigger-like, scratchable spots—and his chest started itching.
Then he read about Ursala's Complex—a loss of motor control that leads the upper extremities to tremble—and his hands started shaking. He read on.
Next, he learned about lung infarction—a collapsing of the lungs that can occur because of impeded blood circulation—and he noticed that his increasingly red chest seemed more concave than usual.
This created an intense feeling of latent melancholia—brought on by worrying about the other three conditions.
This individual was suffering from Medical Student Syndrome. The conditions? Not real. His afflictions? The same as those he had read.
As you read about mental illnesses, don't self-diagnose. Are you ill? If you think so, form the acronym from the first four conditions above—BULL! It's very unlikely you're sick. But if you're worried, talk with a professional—not with yourself.

LAB EXPERIMENTS AND DEMONSTRATIONS

1. is strongly out of touch with reality.

strongly				strongly
agree				disagree
1	2	3	4	5

2. is incapable of holding a position of responsibility.
3. should be placed in an institution.
4. probably has a brain disorder.
5. tends to hear voices.
6. generally has a low IQ.
7. is a weak person trying to slide by on a disability.
8. should not be around children.
9. can often be spotted by looks.
10. has a family history of neurosis.

Have students tally individual and collective scores. Based on these numbers, what generalizations can students form about attitudes toward neurosis? (Tip: The lower the score, the more stereotyped the view of the respondent.)

■ **Demonstration.** Tell students to conduct a "fear poll." Have them hand out lists of the following widely held fears: heights, open spaces, flying, lightning, closed spaces, insanity, reptiles, death, strangers, darkness, germs, mice, driving, spiders, bridges. If possible, encourage students to include several generations of respondents. Direct students to have each person polled rank the fears, assigning 1 to the most fearful item, 2 to the second-most fearful item, and so on. Have students tally the results. What item topped the list overall? Were there wide differences in generational rankings? If so, what were these differences? (OBJECTIVE 2)

Teacher Note. You might name the phobia for each of the fear-based stimuli named in the poll.

acrophobia—heights
aerophobia—flying
agoraphobia—open spaces
amaxophobia—driving
arachniphobia—spiders
astraphobia—lightning
claustrophobia—closed spaces
dementophobia—insanity
gephyrophobia—bridges
herpetophobia—reptiles
mikrophobia—germs
murophobia—mice
nyctophobia—darkness
thanatophobia—death
xenophobia—strangers

Answer to caption, Figure 15.5: fear of closed spaces

■ **Readings in Psychology.** Have students read the Section 5, Reading 6 selection in *Readings in Psychology* and answer the questions that follow the selection.

FIGURE 15.5

A person suffering from agoraphobia would fear going into a crowded shopping center such as this one. **What is claustrophobia?**

Some people experience a continuous, generalized anxiety. Fearing unknown and unforeseen circumstances, they are unable to make decisions or enjoy life. They may become so preoccupied with their internal problems that they neglect their social relationships. People who experience generalized anxiety often have trouble dealing with their family and friends and fulfilling their responsibilities, and this adds to their anxiety. They are trapped in a vicious cycle. The more they worry, the more difficulty they have; the more difficulty they have, the more they worry.

Often, the experience of generalized anxiety is accompanied by physical symptoms: muscular tension; an inability to relax; a furrowed brow; and a strained face. Poor appetite, indigestion, diarrhea, and frequent urination are also commonly present. Because anxious people are in a constant state of apprehension, they may have difficulty sleeping or, once asleep, may wake up suddenly in the night. As a result, they may feel tired when they wake up in the morning.

Why are some people so anxious? Some theorists stress the role of learning. If a man feels very anxious on a date, for example, even the thought of another date may make him nervous, so he learns to avoid having dates and there is never a chance to unlearn the anxiety. His anxiety may then generalize to other situations and become a worse problem.

Phobic Disorder

When severe anxiety is focused on a particular object, activity, or situation that seems out of proportion to the real dangers involved, it is called a phobic disorder, or **phobia.** Phobias may be classified as simple phobias, social phobias, and agoraphobia. A *simple phobia* can focus on almost anything, including high places (acrophobia), enclosed spaces (claustrophobia), and darkness (nyctophobia). Victims of *social phobias* fear that they will embarrass themselves in a public place or a social setting. Perhaps the most common specific fear is of speaking in public, but others include eating in public, using public bathrooms, meeting strangers, and going on a first date.

Phobic individuals develop elaborate plans to avoid the situations they fear. For example, people suffering from an extreme fear of crowds (*agoraphobia*) may stop going to movies or shopping in large, busy stores. Some reach the point where they will not leave their houses at all.

Phobias range in intensity from mild to extremely severe. Most people deal with their phobias by avoiding the thing that frightens them. Thus the phobias are learned and maintained by the reinforcing effects of avoidance. One common form of treatment for phobias involves providing the phobic person with opportunities to experience the feared object under conditions in which he or she feels safe.

Panic Disorder

Another kind of anxiety disorder is **panic disorder.** During a panic attack, a victim experiences sudden and unexplainable attacks of intense fear, leading the individual to feel a sense of inevitable doom or even the fear that

COOPERATIVE LEARNING ACTIVITY

Copy each of the phobias listed on this page onto pieces of poster board. Add any additional phobias that you might find in a medical dictionary. Using these cards, request three volunteers to take part in a game of psychological Jeopardy. The topic on which students will compete is *phobias*. Every time you hold up a poster board, a student must form a question that accurately identifies the phobia. An incorrect guess receives a minus one, a correct guess a plus one. (You might expand this game to include other categories mentioned in the text.)

A B C

FIGURE 15.6

Shown here are an artist's representations of several phobias. **What phobias are shown in the drawings?**

he or she is about to die. Although symptoms of panic disorder differ from individual to individual, they may include a sense of smothering, choking, or difficulty breathing, faintness or dizziness, nausea, and chest pains. Although panic attacks sometimes last for an hour or more, they usually last just a few minutes.

Obsessive-Compulsive Disorder

A person suffering from acute anxiety may find himself thinking the same thoughts over and over again. Such an uncontrollable pattern of thoughts is called *obsession*. Or someone may repeatedly perform irrational actions. This is called a *compulsion*. The neurotic person may experience both these agonies together—a condition called *obsessive-compulsive disorder*.

A compulsive person may feel compelled to wash his hands 20 or 30 times a day, or to avoid stepping on cracks in the sidewalk when he goes out. An obsessive person may be unable to rid herself of unpleasant thoughts about death, or of a recurring impulse to make obscene remarks in public. The obsessive-compulsive may wash her hands continually *and* torment herself with thoughts of obscene behavior.

Everyone has obsessions and compulsions. Love might be described as an obsession; so might a hobby that occupies most of a person's spare time. Striving to do something "perfectly" is often considered to be a compulsion. But if the person who is deeply engrossed in a hobby or who aims for perfection enjoys this intense absorption and can still function effectively, he or she is usually not considered disabled by anxiety. Psychologists consider it a problem only when such thoughts and activities interfere with what a person wants and needs to do. Someone who spends so much time double-checking every detail of her work that she can never finish a job is considered more anxious than conscientious.

Why do people develop obsessions and compulsions? Possibly because they serve as diversions from a person's real fears and their origins and thus may reduce anxiety somewhat. In addition, compulsions provide a disturbed person with the evidence that she is doing something well, even if it is only avoiding the cracks on a sidewalk.

FIGURE 15.7

A still from the film *The Caine Mutiny*, in which Humphrey Bogart played Captain Queeg, an individual who was obsessed with order. Any disruption of Queeg's routine sent him into panic. **What is a compulsion?**

DID YOU KNOW?

Anxiety declines in middle-aged people. Some researchers claim this is because of the death of cells in the locus ceruleus, a portion of the medulla oblongata, which in turn forms part of the brain stem. This "burn out" of brain cells, claim some psychologists, coincides with a decline in panic attacks, addiction, and bulimia in people over age 40.

CONNECTIONS: PSYCHOLOGY AND LITERATURE

Read this passage from *Macbeth*. Tell students that it describes a sleepwalking Lady Macbeth.
Doctor: You see, her eyes are open.
Gentlewoman: Ay, but their sense is shut.
Doctor: What is it she does now? Look, how she rubs her hands.

Gentlewoman: It is an accustomed action with her, to seem thus washing her hands. I have known her continue in this a quarter of an hour.
Lady Macbeth: Yet here's a spot.
Doctor: Hark! She speaks. . . .
Lady Macbeth: Out, damned spot! out, I say!

Ask: What disorder possesses Lady Macbeth? Based on what you've learned, what might have caused it?

Have students read the play to find out. Tell them to identify other examples of mental disorders used in this Shakespearean tragedy.

■ Analyzing Literature.

Read aloud the following lines from *Dulce et decorum est,* by Wilfred Owen.

Gas! Gas! Quick, boys—An
*   ecstasy of fumbling,*
Fitting the clumsy helmets
*   just in time,*
But someone still was yelling
*   out and stumbling*
And flound'ring like a man in
*   fire or lime.*
Dim through the misty panes
*   and thick green light,*
As under a green sea, I saw
*   him drowning.*
In all my dreams before my
*   helpless sight*
He plunges at me, guttering,
*   choking, drowning.*

Ask: What traumatic event is the poet describing? *(death in war)* What lines exhibit that the poet suffers from post-traumatic stress? *(dreams of the death)* What might have produced the disorder? *(perhaps helpless to save the person)*

VISUAL INSTRUCTION

Ask students to identify the cause(s) of the conditions in the pictures. *(conversion of emotional distress into physical distress; preoccupation with imaginary ailments)*
Answer to caption, Figure 15.8: conversion reactions and hypochondriasis

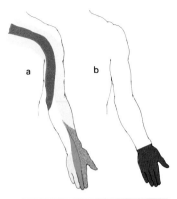

FIGURE 15.8

A patient who complained to a doctor that his right hand had become numb might be diagnosed as suffering from a conversion reaction, depending on the exact pattern of the numbness. The skin areas served by different nerves in the arm are shown in (a). The "glove" numbness shown in (b) could result from damage to these nerves.
What are the two kinds of somatoform disorders?

Post-Traumatic Stress Disorder

Post-traumatic stress disorder is a condition in which a person who has experienced a traumatic event feels severe and long-lasting aftereffects. This disorder is common among veterans of military combat; survivors of natural disasters, such as floods or tornadoes; and victims of human aggression, such as rape and assault, and unnatural catastrophes, such as a plane crash. The event that triggers the disorder overwhelms a person's normal sense of reality and ability to cope. Typical symptoms include involuntary "flashbacks" or recurring nightmares during which the victim re-experiences the ordeal, insomnia, and feelings of guilt. Post-traumatic stress disorder can be extremely long-lasting. Studies show that survivors of Nazi concentration camps and soldiers returning from war may display symptoms decades after the traumatic event.

SOMATOFORM DISORDERS

Anxiety can create a wide variety of physical symptoms for which there is no apparent physical cause. This phenomenon is known as a **somatoform disorder,** or hysteria. The term *hysteria* was more commonly used in Freud's time to refer to unexplainable fainting, paralysis, or deafness. Today the term *somatoform disorder* is preferred. There are two major types of somatoform disorders that psychologists identify: *conversion reactions* and *hypochondriasis.*

Conversion Disorders.   A **conversion disorder** is the conversion of emotional difficulties into the loss of a specific physiological function. While the loss is real, there is no actual physical damage. Many people occasionally experience mild conversion reactions, as when someone is so frightened he or she cannot move, but a conversion disorder is not simply a brief loss of functioning due to fright. It persists.

A conversion reaction results in a real and prolonged handicap—the person literally cannot hear or feel anything in his left hand or move his legs or exercise some other normal physical function (Figure 15.8). For example, a man might wake up one morning and find himself paralyzed from the waist down. The normal reaction to this would be panic. However, he might accept the loss of function with relative calm—called *la belle indifférence.* This is one sign that a person is suffering from a psychological rather than a physiological problem. Most psychologists believe that people suffering from conversion reactions unconsciously invent physical symptoms to gain freedom from unbearable conflict. For example, a woman who lives in terror of blurting out things that she does not want to say may lose the power of speech. This "solves" the problem. Conversion reactions are comparatively rare.

Hypochondriasis.   Conversion disorders must be distinguished from *hypochondriasis,* in which a person who is in good health becomes preoccupied with imaginary ailments. The hypochondriac spends a lot of time

CONNECTIONS: PSYCHOLOGY AND THE MEDIA

Many newspapers and magazines regularly run humorous cartoons that capture or satirize psychological disorders of some kind. (For example, "Pigpen" in Peanuts looks visually abnormal. But is he mentally abnormal? Charlie Brown regularly battles with bouts of low self-esteem or what Seligman would call "learned helplessness.") Assign students to clip cartoons, and analyze the behavior depicted from a psychological point of view.

looking for signs of serious illness and often misinterprets minor aches, pains, bruises or bumps as early signs of a fatal illness. Despite negative results in medical tests and physical evaluations, the hypochondriac typically continues to believe that a disease or malfunction exists. Hypochondriasis occurs mainly during young adulthood and is equally common to men and women.

DISSOCIATIVE DISORDERS

A **dissociative disorder** involves a disturbance in conscious experience such as a loss of memory or identity. These psychological phenomena fascinate many people, so we hear a good deal about amnesia and "multiple personalities." Actually, they are very rare.

Loss of identity, or **psychogenic amnesia,** may be an attempt to escape from problems by blotting them out completely. Amnesiacs remember how to speak and usually retain a fund of general knowledge, but they may not know who they are, where they live and work, or who their family is (Levant, 1966). This amnesia should be distinguished from other losses of memory that result from organic brain damage, normal forgetting, or drug abuse.

In **psychogenic fugue,** another type of dissociative reaction, amnesia is coupled with active flight to a different environment. For example, a woman may suddenly disappear and "wake up" three days later in a restaurant 200 miles from home. She may actually establish a new identity—assume a new name, marry, take a job, and so forth—in a new place. She may repress all knowledge of a previous life. A fugue state may last for days or for decades. However long it lasts, the individual, when she comes out of it, will have no memory of what she has done in the interim. Fugue, then, is a sort of traveling amnesia, and it probably serves the same psychological function as amnesia: escape from unbearable conflict or anxiety.

In **multiple personality,** a third type of dissociative reaction, someone seems to have two or more distinct identities. Eve White, a young woman who sought psychiatric treatment for severe headaches and blackouts, has become a famous example. Eve White was a conscientious, self-controlled, rather shy person. However, during one of her therapy sessions, her expression—and her personality—suddenly changed. Eve Black, as she now called herself, was childlike, fun-loving, and irresponsible—the opposite of the woman who originally walked into the psychiatrist's office. Eve Black was conscious of Eve White's existence, but considered her a separate person. Eve White did not know about Eve Black, however, and neither was she conscious of Jane, a third personality that emerged during the course of therapy. (This case served as the basis for the book and film *The Three Faces of Eve.*) Some psychologists believe that this dividing up of the personality is the result of the individual's effort to escape from a part of himself or herself that he or she fears. The "secret self" then emerges in the form of a separate personality. It is an extremely rare disorder.

MORE about...

Women and Depression. Statistics show that women are twice as likely as men to suffer from depression. Does this indicate that depression has a sex-linked genetic component? Not necessarily. Researchers have found that women are more likely than men to report depressive symptoms.

First, in most cultures women show a greater awareness of their emotions than men do. Second, women are more likely to express their emotions to others, making them more likely than men to *report* that they feel depressed. Third, women and men show different reactions to stress. Women often direct their frustrations inward, whereas men frequently react to their frustrations with behavior directed outward—showing aggression or drinking heavily (Nolen-Hoeksema, 1987).

In short, the sex differences in depression may say more about the way people deal with their feelings than about the causes of depression. With changing sex roles and increasing opportunities for women, this sex difference may decrease in the future.

DID YOU KNOW?

In 1691, eight young girls in the town of Salem, Massachusetts, began exhibiting disorderly speech, odd postures, bizarre gestures, and convulsive fits. Doctors were unable to explain the phenomenon or prescribe a cure. When some of the girls claimed they were bewitched, hysteria spread far and wide. Puritan courts sentenced hundreds of accused witches to be hanged. Some researchers (Linda Caporael, 1976, and Mary Matossian, 1982) claim that ergot poisoning caused the girls' behavior. Ergot poisoning results from a fungus that grows on damp grain crops. Many of the girls exhibited the symptoms of ergotism—convulsions, sensations of being pricked or bitten, and temporary loss of hearing, sight, and speech.

■ **Evaluating Conclusions.** Have students reread the last sentence in the margin feature on this page. Then have them reread the information on sexual attitudes and roles on pages 230–232 of Chapter 9. Ask: Does information on these pages support or refute the conclusion in the margin note? *(tends to support)*

CONNECTIONS: PSYCHOLOGY AND MATHEMATICS

Assign interested students to rent a copy of *The Three Faces of Eve* from the "Film Classics" section of a video store. (If the film is not available, suggest they locate the book in the library.) Then tell students to imagine they are movie (book) reviewers in the late 1950s. Have them write a critique of the film (book) that might have run in magazines at the time. For models, you might show students some of the reviews run each week in magazines such as *TIME* or *Newsweek.*

Chris Sizemore published a book many years later (Sizemore & Pittillo, 1977), explaining that Eve ultimately had 21 separate personalities, though never more than 3 at a time. Her case is often confused with Sybil—a woman whose 16 personalities were also described in a book and a film. However, Sybil was depicted sometimes as wandering in a field hallucinating. That loss of contact with reality makes her diagnosis more likely that of borderline disorder, closer to a schizophrenic condition.

While cases like Eve and Sybil are fascinating, they are extremely rare and somewhat controversial. One researcher (Abse, 1966) reviewed the entire psychological literature and was able to find published accounts of only 200 people who supposedly suffered from any dissociative reaction.

MOOD DISORDERS

We all experience mood swings. Sometimes we are happy or elated, while at other times we feel dejected, miserable, or depressed. Yet, even when we are discouraged, most of us still feel we can control our emotions and that these feelings will pass. Occasional depression is a common experience. In some people, however, these moods are more intense and tend to last for longer periods. These individuals often get the sense that their depression will go on forever and that there is nothing they can do to change it. As a result, their emotions hamper their ability to function effectively. In extreme cases, a mood may cause individuals to lose touch with reality or seriously threaten their health or lives.

Major Depressive Disorder

Major depressive disorder occurs in two forms. *Single-episode* depression strikes deeply and seriously in one dramatic episode. *Recurrent depression* is an extended pattern shared with single-episode depression, of sadness, anxiety, fatigue, agitated behavior, and reduced ability to function and interact with others. It may also interfere with sleep patterns and the ability to concentrate. It ranges from mild feelings of uneasiness, sadness, and apathy to intense suicidal despair. Blatt, D'Afflitti, and Quinlan (1976) found that men and women experience depression similarly, sharing three primary elements—*dependency*: a sensed need for others' help and support; *self-criticism*: a negative assessment of one's own worth; and *inefficacy*: being bothered by the idea that "nothing I do matters."

The cognitive theories of Aaron Beck and Martin Seligman have often served as the basis for research on depression. Beck (1983) believes that depressed people draw illogical conclusions about themselves—they blame themselves for normal problems and consider every minor failure a catastrophe. As described in Chapter 2, Martin Seligman (1975) believes that depression is caused by a feeling of learned helplessness. The depressed person learns to believe that he has no control over events in his life and that it is useless to even try.

Psychologists developed theories to provide a physiological or biological explanation of depression. One theory—that a deficit of the chemical norepinephrine leads to depression—was promising, but turned out to be too simplistic. Unfortunately, no better model has been proposed. Given the impact that some medicines have in treating depression and that basic physiological functions such as sleep are influenced by depression, a possible role for physiological mechanisms cannot be eliminated.

Bipolar Disorder

A common type of mood disorder is a **bipolar disorder** in which individuals are excessively and inappropriately happy or unhappy. These reactions may take the form of high elation, hopeless depression, or an alternation between the two.

In a **manic-type reaction,** a person experiences elation, extreme confusion, distractibility, and racing thoughts. Often, the person has an exaggerated sense of self-esteem and engages in irresponsible behavior such as shopping sprees, insulting remarks, or the following type of behavior.

On admission she slapped the nurse, addressed the house physician as God, made the sign of the cross, and laughed loudly when she was asked to don the hospital garb. This she promptly tore to shreds. . . . She sang at the top of her voice, screamed through the window, and leered at the patients promenading in the recreation yard (Karnash, 1945).

This state is not as easy to detect as some others because the person is optimistic, seeming to be in touch with reality, and blessed with an unending sense of optimism. During a manic episode, a person may behave as if

■ **Analyzing a Quote**. Read aloud the following quote from Martin Seligman.

People become depressed when their explanatory style is internal ('I'm to blame'), stable ('I'll always be this way') and global ('Nothing I do turns out right'). . . .

Ask: How does Seligman believe that depressed people see themselves? *(as the cause of all problems; as unable to change or succeed)* According to the theory of learned helplessness, how do such individuals see the external world? *(as beyond their control)* Next, tell students that Seligman offered his antidote to depression in a book entitled *Learned Optimism*. Challenge students to rewrite the quote to express the way an optimist might view life's events. *(You might get students started by writing the following incomplete version of the quote on the chalkboard: "People become optimistic when their explanatory style is external ['I'm not to blame'], flexible. . . .")* (OBJECTIVE 3)

CONNECTIONS: PSYCHOLOGY AND THE ARTS

Assign interested students to research some famous figures in the arts who suffered from bouts of depression. Choices include Vincent van Gogh, Robert Schumann, Hector Berlioz, and Gustav Mahler. Tell students to write case studies of each of these figures for a chapter in a psychology text on bipolar disorders. Have students share their case studies with the rest of the class.

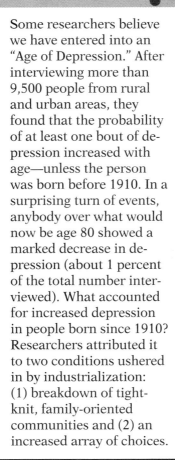

FIGURE 15.11

A male patient diagnosed as a schizophrenic with paranoid tendencies did both these paintings. Both illustrations are characterized by the symbolism of watchful eyes, grasping hands, and the self as subject matter. **What are delusions?**

he or she needs less sleep, and the activity level typically increases, as does the loudness and the frequency with which he or she speaks.

In the **depressive-type reaction,** the individual is overcome by feelings of failure, sinfulness, worthlessness, and despair. In contrast to the optimism and high activity of a manic-type reaction, a depressive-type reaction is marked by lethargy, despair, and unresponsiveness. The behavior of someone with a major depressive disorder is essentially the same as someone who is depressed in a bipolar disorder (Perris, 1982).

The patient lay in bed, immobile, with a dull, depressed expression on his face. His eyes were sunken and downcast. Even when spoken to, he would not raise his eyes to look at the speaker. Usually he did not respond at all to questions, but sometimes, after apparently great effort, he would mumble something about the "Scourge of God" (Morris, 1990).

In some cases, a patient will alternate between frantic action and motionless despair. Some people experience occasional episodes of a manic type or depressive type reaction, separated by long intervals of relatively normal behavior. Others exhibit almost no normal behavior, cycling instead from periods of manic-type reactions to equally intense depressive type reactions. Some theorists have speculated that the manic periods serve as an attempt to ward off the underlying hopelessness. Others believe that mania can be traced to the same biochemical disorder responsible for depression.

Suicide and Depression

Not all people who commit suicide are depressed, and not all depressed people attempt suicide. But many depressives do think about suicide, and some of them translate these thoughts into action.

People may take their lives for any number of reasons. It may be to escape from physical or emotional pain—perhaps a terminal illness or the loneliness of old age. It might be an effort to end the torment of unacceptable feelings, to punish themselves for wrongs they feel they have committed, or to punish others who have not perceived their needs (Mintz, 1968). In many cases we simply do not know why the suicide occurred.

But we do know that every year about 30,000 Americans end their lives—about 1 every 18 minutes. More women than men attempt suicide, but more men than women succeed. Suicide is most common among the elderly, but also ranks as the second most common cause of death among college students. Contrary to popular belief, people who threaten suicide or

FIGURE 15.12

This is a portrait of a "suicidal melancholic" done in England in the 1800s. This woman, only 34, suffered from the delusion that she would be murdered and eventually began to attempt suicide to escape the danger. **What are the symptoms of simple schizophrenia?**

CHAPTER 15 Lesson Plan

■ **Making a Bar Graph.** Distribute copies of the following statistics on suicide rates released by the U.S. Department of the Census, 1990.

Age Group	Rate Per 100,000 of Population
15–24	12.8
25–34	15.9
35–44	14.3
45–54	14.8
55–64	15.7
65–74	16.8
75–84	28.9
over 85	19.7

Assign students to plot this information in the form of a bar graph. When students are done, ask the following questions: Which age group has the largest percentage of suicides? *(75–84)* the lowest? *(15–24)* Applying Seligman's theory of learned helplessness, what factors or conditions might account for the high rate of suicide among the elderly? *(Answers will vary, but might include: age-related health problems, death of spouse/peers, loneliness, lack of income and opportunities to work, and so on.)* (OBJECTIVE 3)

▮ **Readings in Psychology.** Have students read the Section 5, Reading 7 selection in *Readings in Psychology* and answer the questions that follow the selection.

VISUAL INSTRUCTION

Point out some of the physical effects of depression on aging. *(The woman looks older than her 34 years.)* **Answer to caption, Figure 15.12:** loss of interest in the world; apathy and noncommunication

ADDITIONAL INFORMATION

Winter can be a dreary time for many people. But for people who suffer from Seasonal Affective Disorder (SAD) it is a time of low spirits, sleepiness, and overall depression. According to the DSM classification system, a diagnosis of SAD must satisfy two requirements: (1) symptoms must reoccur consecutively for two years, and (2) symptoms must clear up after 60 days in a non-winter season. You might assign students to research some of the theories and proposed treatments for SAD. Have them present their findings in the form of a poster.

■ **Analyzing a Quote.** Tell students that the term *schizophrenia* was devised by Swiss psychiatrist Eugen Bleuler in 1911. Prior to this time, the psychosis had been called *dementia praecox*. Read aloud Bleuler's explanation of the term's origin.

I call the dementia praecox "schizophrenia" from the Greek words schizein, *meaning "to split," and* phren, *meaning "mind" because the "splitting" of the different psychic functions is one of its most important characteristics. For the sake of convenience, I use the word in the singular although it is apparent that the group includes several diseases.*

Ask: How closely does Bleuler's description of schizophrenia match the description in the text? What similarities and/or differences can you spot? What distinguishes schizophrenia from other mood and personality disorders? (OBJECTIVES 3, 4)

▌ **Readings in Psychology.** Have students read the Section 5, Reading 8 selection in *Readings in Psychology* and answer the questions that follow the selection.

MORE about...

Living with Schizophrenia. Incoherence is one of the symptoms associated with people who have schizophrenia. One patient described the experience as losing the ability to focus his thoughts.

"I can't concentrate. It's diversion of attention that troubles me. I am picking up different conversations. It's like being a transmitter. The sounds are coming through to me but I feel my mind cannot cope with everything. It's difficult to concentrate on any one sound."

Another symptom is diverted attention, perhaps brought on by cognitive flooding or an inability to choose among various stimuli competing for attention. Another patient told of being unable to organize his perceptions.

"Everything is in bits. You put the picture up bit by bit into your head. It's like a photograph that's being torn to bits and put together again. You have to absorb it again. If you move, it's frightening. The picture you had in your head is still there but it's broken up" (McGhie and Chapman, 1961).

make an unsuccessful attempt usually *are* serious. Studies show that about 70 percent of people who kill themselves threaten to do so within the 3 months preceding the suicide, and an unsuccessful attempt is often a trial run (Alvarez, 1970; Davis & Sandoval, 1991).

Anxiety, phobias, obsessions, compulsions, somatoform disorders, mania, depression, and suicide—all are ways people use, in various combinations, to escape problems in themselves or the world in which they live. With the obvious exception of suicide, these anxiety reactions do not shut people off completely from daily life. Schizophrenia does.

SCHIZOPHRENIA

Depression we can understand. Anxiety most of us have experienced. In addition, we can appreciate how people with these problems strive to overcome them as best they can. An individual with schizophrenia, however, who withdraws from normal life and whose distorted perceptions and behavior reach an irrational, fantastic, fear-laden, unimaginable level, does so in ways that are hard to understand. Yet, we are making progress in furthering our understanding of schizophrenia—the most complex and severe psychological problem we encounter.

While the disorders we have discussed so far are primarily problems of emotion, schizophrenia is a problem of cognition. A person's thought processes are somewhat disturbed and those with schizophrenia have lost contact with reality to considerable extent. One expert noted that someone with depression or severe anxiety problems dreams in an unreal way about life, while a person with schizophrenia lives life as an unreal dream. Schizophrenia is not a single problem; it has no single cause or cure. Rather, it is a collection of symptoms that indicates an individual has serious difficulty trying to meet the demands of life.

Approximately half the patients in United States mental hospitals have been diagnosed as schizophrenic (Regier *et al.*, 1988). What distinguishes this disorder from other types of psychological disturbance? **Schizophrenia** involves confused and disordered thoughts and perceptions.

Suppose a psychiatrist is interviewing a patient who has just been admitted to a hospital. The individual demonstrates a wide assortment of symptoms. He is intensely excited, expresses extreme hostility toward members of his family, and at the same time claims that he loves them, showing conflicting feelings. One minute he is extremely aggressive, questioning the psychiatrist's motives and even threatening her. The next minute he withdraws and acts as if he does not hear anything she says. Then he begins talking again. "Naturally," he says, "I am growing my father's hair." Although all of the person's other behavior indicates psychological problems, this last statement would be the "diagnostic bell ringer." It reveals that the man is living in a private, disordered reality.

Many people with schizophrenia experience **delusions**—false beliefs maintained in the face of contrary evidence—and **hallucinations**—sensations in the absence of appropriate stimulation. A person with schizophre-

CONNECTIONS: PSYCHOLOGY AND THE MEDIA

Arrange for several mental health professionals to visit the class. Then show relevant clips from a film that portrays some form of mental illness—e.g., *One Flew Over the Cuckoo's Nest, Clean and Sober,* or *I Never Promised You a Rose Garden.* After the film clip, ask the visitors to discuss the behavior of the characters from a mental health perspective. How accurate were the portrayals? What, if any, misinformation about mental health was imparted by the film?

nia may show a number of other symptoms as well. One is *incoherence* or a marked decline in thought processes. The language of someone with schizophrenia may be speeded; sometimes, it is described as "word salad." Another symptom is *disturbances of affect*, or emotions that are inappropriate for the circumstances. In addition, an individual with schizophrenia may display severe *deterioration in normal movement*, which may occur as slowed movement, non-movement, or as highly agitated behavior. Another symptom is a marked *decline in previous levels of functioning;* for example, a sharp dropoff in productivity at work. Yet another is *diverted attention*, perhaps brought about by cognitive flooding, as if the person is unable to focus his or her attention.

Psychologists classify schizophrenia into several subtypes. One, the *paranoid type* involves delusions, including *grandeur*: "I am the savior of my people," or *persecution*: "Someone is always watching me." The *catatonic type* may remain motionless for long periods, exhibiting "waxy flexibility" in which limbs in unusual position may take a long time returning to the resting, relaxed position—exactly as if melting a wax statue. Symptoms of the *disorganized type* include incoherent language, inappropriate emotions, giggling for no apparent reason, generally disorganized motor behavior, and hallucinations and delusions. An individual with *undifferentiated type* schizophrenia exhibits symptoms that prominently include hallucinations and delusions, scrambled speech and thought processes, or motor performances that would qualify under more than one of the other types of schizophrenia—or none of them.

Schizophrenia is a very complex condition and treatment is long-term and usually requires hospitalization. Long-term institutionalization sometimes leads to a patient who is *burned-out;* one who is unlikely to function

FIGURE 15.13

Although they are in the same place, each of these autistic children is in his own world, and there is no interaction. **What causes autism?**

■ **Discussion.** Tell students that other schizophrenic delusions (beside grandeur and persecution) include:

- Delusions of control: Belief that other people or beings (e.g., extraterrestrials) are controlling one's actions.
- Delusions of reference: Belief that unrelated events (e.g., a TV program) are referring to one's self.
- Delusions of sin and guilt: Belief that one has committed an unforgivable sin.
- Hypochondriacal delusions: Belief in infliction by bizarre diseases.
- Nihilistic delusions: Belief that the world does not exist.

Ask: Based on the text, what are some of the possible causes of such delusions? (*Lead students to understand the complex nature of schizophrenia.*) (OBJECTIVE 4)

VISUAL INSTRUCTION

Refer students to the margin feature on page 380. Ask: What feature do schizophrenia and autism share? *(detachment)* Assign students to research some of the ways the two conditions differ.
Answer to caption, Figure 15.13: No known cause exists at the present.

BEYOND THE CLASSROOM

Tell students that simple schizophrenia often first appears in the teenage years. It also tends to strike more males than females. Request volunteers to research the symptoms, suspected causes, and treatment of simple schizophrenia. If possible, urge students to interview professionals familiar with the disorder at the county mental health department. Based on their investigation, have students prepare a mock news report. (Volunteers can role-play professionals in the field.) If students have access to a video camera, you might have them tape and edit a film version of their report.

■ **Making a Chart.** Working individually or in small groups, assign students to compare the various theories on the causes of schizophrenia. Top column heads should identify the specific theory (e.g., Biological Influences). Side column heads should include: Description of Theory, Supporting Evidence, Limitations of Theory. Call on students to share their charts. Based on this information, what generalizations can they form about the causes of schizophrenia? (OBJECTIVE 4)

DID YOU KNOW?

In 1959, Milton Rokeach moved three patients claiming to be Jesus Christ into the same ward. Rokeach wanted to see whether "their delusional systems of belief and their behavior might change if they were confronted with the ultimate contradiction conceivable for human beings: more than one person claiming the same identity." After more than two years, each patient remained convinced that he had created the world (and the other two patients).

PSYCHOLOGY UPDATE

Schizophrenia and Autism. The detachment is similar. The appearance of being in a different world is there in both conditions, but psychologists, after long debate, have concluded that autism and schizophrenia are different conditions.

Obvious to the parents in haunting ways soon after birth, *infantile autism* causes children to differ from normal children in three ways. First, they do not respond to other people. If you pick up an autistic child, he or she is stiff or limp; the child will not cling to you as normal children will. Second, an autistic child is very slow in developing language and communication skills. By age 5 or 6, they may simply repeat what has been said: a condition called *echolalia*. Third, autistic children are very limited in their interests and behavior. They may abuse themselves or repeat a simple hand motion for hours without ceasing.

Explaining autism's cause has been difficult. Learning-based and psychoanalytic attempts have failed. The best guess is that genetics play no role (Smalley, 1991), but an inborn defect may interact with later environmental or biological events (Carson & Butcher, 1992) to produce autism.

---

normally in society. Schizophrenia is considered in the DSM-IV to be a permanent condition. It may go into remission—in which the symptoms disappear and the person seems quite normal—but the DSM-IV comments that adjustment tends to deteriorate between successive episodes of the reappearance of symptoms.

Anyone reading the diagnostic criteria in DSM-IV for treating schizophrenia is aware that no real cure exists, and once an individual is diagnosed with schizophrenia, he or she never escapes it. That leads to the final form of schizophrenia, the *remission type*. This diagnostic label is applied to anyone whose symptoms are completely gone. The expectation is clearly that those symptoms will return, so the schizophrenia is simply viewed as "in remission."

What is the actual cause of schizophrenia? There are many theories, and just as certainly, there is disagreement. In all likelihood, the ultimate cause is an interaction of environmental, genetic, and biochemical factors.

Biological Influences. Genetics is almost certainly involved. Gottesman (1991) summarized the results of more than 35 studies done in western Europe, 1920–1987. He found that there is a 1 percent likelihood that anyone in the general population will develop schizophrenia. What's more, as the degree of genetic relationship increases, so do the odds that, if one member of a pair of humans develops schizophrenia, the other will, too. Yet, even among identical twins, if one twin develops schizophrenia, only 42 percent of the other twins will develop it. This finding argues that other factors in addition to heredity also have a role.

In trying to define the role of genetics more precisely, researchers have studied children born to schizophrenic mothers who are separated from their mothers at birth and raised in different homes. Using an *adoption study*, Kety (1983) found 17 percent of 47 children of schizophrenic mothers developed schizophrenia; none of 50 control children whose natural mother did not have schizophrenia developed it, though they were also raised in foster homes. Even studies of children raised in natural families where both parents were later diagnosed as having schizophrenia reveal that as much as 28 percent of the children are completely normal. In summary, these studies show that psychologists cannot specify the exact contribution hereditary factors make to schizophrenia (Carson & Sanislow, 1992).

Biochemistry and Physiology. The proper working of the brain depends on the presence of right amounts of many different chemicals, from oxygen to proteins. Some psychologists believe that psychosis is due largely to chemical imbalances in the brain. According to one theory, some people are born with a nervous system that gets aroused very easily and takes a long time to return to normal. Such people might be particularly likely to get upset when they are stressed (Zubin and Spring, 1977).

Chemical problems may also be involved in schizophrenia. A number of researchers think that the basic problem in schizophrenia is that too much or too little of certain chemicals has "knocked out of kilter" the brain's mechanisms for processing information, perhaps interfering with normal

---

MEETING SPECIAL NEEDS

Modeling. An effective technique for teaching students with problems in reading comprehension is *modeling*—having a teacher or tutor verbally talk a student through the reading process. Working in pairs, you might assign students to take turns reading "Schizophrenia and Autism" aloud. The "modeler" should tell the reader exactly what his or her thinking/analysis process is as he or she works through the passage. (For example: "The first sentence tells me that I'm going to learn one way that schizophrenia and autism are similar. I've prepared my mind to spot that similarity.")

FIGURE 15.14

A child born with a biochemically unusual nervous system that reacts very strongly to stimulation may have pronounced hallucinations during an early childhood illness that has no lasting effect on most children. As he grows older, he may try to discuss his memories of that time with his parents. Being insecure themselves, they may become uneasy and respond in ways that make him feel he is wrong or bad in some way. His unusual biochemistry causes him to react very strongly to this rebuff, and he now has further troubling experiences he needs to make sense of. He then feels a conflict between his need to talk to his parents about these experiences and his fear of their cold response. He is well on the way to becoming psychologically disordered unless the links in this chain are somehow broken. **What are three factors that are used to explain the causes of schizophrenia?**

synaptic transmission. The *dopamine hypothesis* suggests that an excess of dopamine at selected synapses is related to a diagnosis of schizophrenia. Carlsson (1988) notes that correlational studies are not enough to demonstrate a direct role for dopamine in schizophrenia. It seems likely that chemicals play a role, but it is hard to tell whether these chemicals are the cause of schizophrenia or the result of it. They may even be caused by the fact that people with schizophrenia tend to live in hospitals, where they get little exercise, eat institutional food, and are generally given daily doses of tranquilizers. Living under such conditions, anyone might begin to show chemical imbalances and abnormal behavior. The use of CT and MRI (see Chapter 4) has led to the discoveries that the brains of people with schizophrenia often show signs of deteriorated brain tissue (Pearlson, *et al.*, 1989). One consistent result is that women who at some time develop schizophrenia, are likely to have difficult pregnancies and difficulties giving birth. Yet researchers are not sure what role these difficulties have in determining whether the children develop schizophrenia. This problem emphasizes that the environment may play an important role in fostering the development of schizophrenia.

Family and Interactions. From Freud onward, it has been tempting to blame the family situation in childhood for problems that develop during adulthood. Paul Meehl (1962, 1989) suggests that bad experiences during childhood are not enough, in and of themselves, to lead to schizophrenia, but being part of a *pathogenic*, or unhealthful family, may contribute to problems in the adult years.

Studies show that families of individuals who later develop schizophrenia are often on the verge of falling apart. Another frequent finding is that family members organize themselves around—or in spite of—the very unusual, demanding, or maladaptive behavior of one member of the family.

VISUAL INSTRUCTION

Ask students to identify details in the picture that some people might read as antisocial. *(motorcycles, dark sunglasses, and so on)* How do students perceive the picture? *(If students ride motorcycles or have members of their family who do so, the picture may not seem abnormal or threatening at all.)* **Answer to caption, Figure 15.15:** Answers will vary, but may include: irresponsible, selfish, guiltless, destructive, and so on.

■ **Applying Concepts.** Read aloud the following hypothetical case study.

Jillian's parents neither spoiled her nor treated her harshly. They bought her more than she needed. But Jillian persistently charged items to their credit card without asking. She also showed little regard for traffic laws, taping speeding tickets to her mirror like badges of honor. Even her father's tears did not move Jillian to remorse. When he cried, she declared: "Dad, get it together. You're boring me." In desperation, Jillian's parents turned to a psychologist for help.

Ask: Based on behavioral disorders discussed in the text, what preliminary diagnosis might the psychologist offer to Jillian's parents? What evidence supports your hypothesis? *(Lead students to see the antisocial aspects of the case such as irresponsibility, selfishness, lack of shame or guilt, and so on.)* (OBJECTIVE 5)

FIGURE 15.15

Many psychologists would classify these gang members as antisocial. **What are characteristics of the antisocial individual?**

Communication, too, often seems disorganized in the early family life of people who later develop schizophrenia.

A child's ability to think and to communicate with others can be undermined if his or her parents repeatedly communicate contradictory messages. For example, a mother may resent her child and feel uncomfortable around him, yet also feel obligated to act lovingly toward him. She tells the child how much she loves him, but at the same time she stiffens whenever he tries to hug her. Thus the child is given one message in words and another in action.

As a result, the child is placed in an impossible situation. If he reaches out to his mother, she shows him (in her actions) how much she dislikes this. If he avoids her, she tells him (in words) how much she dislikes that. He wants very much to please her, but no matter what he does, it is wrong. He is caught in a *double bind*.

According to **double-bind** theory, childhoods full of such contradictory messages result in adults who perceive the world as a confusing, disconnected place and believe that their words and actions have little significance or meaning. Consequently, they develop the kind of disordered behaviors and thoughts we have been describing.

In Summary. Which of these theories is correct? At this point, we do not know. It may be that each is partially true. Perhaps people who inherit a tendency toward psychological disorders react more strongly to a double bind than others would. Perhaps people who are caught in a double bind are especially vulnerable to chemical imbalances. The *diathesis-stress hypothesis* states that an individual may have inherited a predisposition toward schizophrenia. For schizophrenia to develop, however, that person must contact an environment with certain stressors before the schizophrenia will develop. Explaining the causes of schizophrenia is perhaps the most complex research problem psychologists face.

PERSONALITY DISORDERS

Personality disorders are different from the problems we have been discussing. People with personality disorders generally do not suffer from acute anxiety; nor do they behave in bizarre, incomprehensible ways. Psychologists consider these people "abnormal" because they seem unable to establish meaningful relationships with other people, to assume social responsibilities, or to adapt to their social environment. This diagnostic category includes a wide range of self-defeating personality patterns, from painfully shy, lonely types to vain, pushy show-offs. In this section we focus on the **antisocial personality,** sometimes called the sociopath or psychopath.

Antisocial individuals are irresponsible, immature, emotionally shallow people who seem to court trouble. Extremely selfish, they treat people as objects—as things to be used for gratification and to be cast coldly aside when no longer wanted. Intolerant of everyday frustrations and unable to

CRITICAL THINKING ACTIVITY

Forming Conclusions. Assign students to clip pictures of teenagers from magazines that some adults might consider to be antisocial. (You might ask students to review the material on how adults view adolescents in Chapter 9.) Have students present these pictures, pointing out the details that led them to select each item. Then ask students to show the pictures again. As teenagers, do they view these same pictures as antisocial? Why or why not? Based on this exercise, challenge students to form conclusions on differences between adult and adolescent definitions of antisocial behavior in the teen years.

save or plan or wait, they live for the moment. Seeking thrills is their major occupation. If they should injure other people along the way or break social rules, they do not seem to feel any shame or guilt. It's the other person's tough luck. Nor does getting caught seem to rattle them. No matter how many times they are reprimanded, punished, or jailed, they never learn how to stay out of trouble. They simply do not profit from experience.

Many antisocial individuals can get away with destructive behavior because they are intelligent, entertaining, and able to mimic emotions they do not feel. They win affection and confidence from others whom they then take advantage of. This ability to charm while exploiting seemed to help David Koresh dominate the religious followers of the Branch Davidian compound in Waco, Texas, with tragic results in early 1993.

If caught, antisocial individuals will either spin a fantastic lie or simply insist, with wide-eyed sincerity, that their intentions were utterly pure. Guilt and anxiety have no place in the antisocial personality. A fine example is that of Hugh Johnson, a con man caught after having defrauded people out of thousands of dollars in 64 separate swindles. When asked why he had victimized so many people, "he replied with some heat that he never took more from a person than the person could afford to lose, and further, that he was only reducing the likelihood that other more dangerous criminals would use force to achieve the same ends" (Nathan and Harris, 1975, pp. 406–407).

How do psychologists explain such a lack of ordinary human decency and shame? According to one theory, the psychopath has simply imitated his or her own antisocial parents. Others point to lack of discipline or inconsistent discipline during childhood. Finally, some researchers believe that psychopaths have a "faulty nervous system." While most of us get very aroused when we do something that we've been punished for in the past, psychopaths never seem to learn to anticipate punishment.

DRUG ADDICTION

In American society, drug abuse has become a major psychological problem. Millions of Americans depend so heavily on drugs that they hurt themselves physically, socially, and psychologically.

Abuse of drugs invariably involves **psychological dependence.** Users come to depend so much on the feeling of well-being they obtain from the drug that they feel compelled to continue using it. People can become psychologically dependent on a wide variety of drugs, including alcohol, caffeine, nicotine (in cigarettes), cocaine, marijuana, and amphetamines. When deprived of the drug, a psychologically dependent person becomes restless, irritable, and uneasy.

In addition to psychological dependence, some drugs lead to physiological **addiction.** A person is addicted when his system has become so used to the drug that the drugged state becomes the body's "normal" state. If the drug is not in the body, the person experiences extreme physical discomfort, as he would if he were deprived of oxygen or water.

Independent Practice

■ **Research.** Read aloud the following lines from the lead story on the end of the Branch Davidians from the May 3, 1993, issue of *TIME:*
The sun didn't blacken, nor the moon turn red, but the world did come to an end, just as their prophet had promised.
Tell students that "The End" came in a burst of flames as a ball of fire consumed the compound—and most of the followers—of David Koresh. Assign students to use the *Readers' Guide to Periodical Literature* to locate articles on the Branch Davidians and Koresh's hold. Based on these articles, have students prepare a paper on how the religious cult fulfilled the psychological definition of *abnormal.* Also, tell them to identify specific examples of behavioral disorders mentioned in this chapter. (OBJECTIVES 1–5)

■ **Debating an Issue.** Many psychologists say drug addiction is a disease. The law says drug use is a crime. Ask students to consider this controversial issue by debating the following topic: *Resolved—* That all drug offenders should be assigned to a rehabilitation center for drug-induced offenses. (OBJECTIVE 5)

CRITICAL THINKING ACTIVITY

Analyzing a Quote. Read aloud the following analysis of antisocial behavior:

There are very definite aspects of our cultural pattern which give [antisocial personalities] *encouragement. In America we put great value on the acquisition of material gain. . . . At the other end, . . . our machine civilization tends to level and strangle individuality, leaving large groups within our culture fearful. . . . In such an atmosphere,* [antisocial behavior] *. . . grows and fattens.* (Gough, 1948)

Ask students to identify the causes of antisocial behavior cited in this passage. Then, discuss whether they agree or disagree.

■ **Discussion.** You might want to distribute a list of the warning signs of problem drinking.

- *Increased Desire:* Urge to drink more often and/or centering a day's or week's activities around a drink.
- *Increased Tolerance:* Need to drink more alcohol to reach the desired "high."
- *Extreme Mood Changes:* Acting in ways uncharacteristic with past behavioral patterns.
- *Black Outs (or "Brown Outs"):* Total lapses of memory or only partial recall of behavior while drinking.
- *Morning Drinking:* Picking up a drink to start the day or ease a hangover. (Not just in the morning, but at any inappropriate time.)

Ask students to distinguish between dependence, tolerance, and addiction. Ask: At which stage might these warning signs become pronounced? *(at all three stages, but most likely at the stage of tolerance and/or addiction)* (OBJECTIVES 1, 5)

Enrich. Have students complete the Chapter 15 Extension Activity and answer the questions following it.

? FACT OR FICTION

■ *Alcoholism can lead to permanent memory loss.*

Fact. Some alcoholics suffer from Korsakoff's syndrome, a form of organic amnesia in which the person is unable to remember any newly acquired information. For example, even after years of treatment, one patient did not recognize his therapist and introduced himself whenever they met.

Just as dependence causes a psychological need for the drug, addiction causes a physical need. Furthermore, once a person is addicted to a drug, he develops **tolerance;** that is, his body becomes so accustomed to the drug that he has to keep increasing his dosage in order to obtain the "high" that he achieved with his earlier doses. With certain sleeping pills, for example, a person can rapidly develop a tolerance for up to 15 times the original dose. Further, an addict must have his drug in order to retain what little physical and psychological balance he has left. If he does not get it, he is likely to go through the dreaded experience of withdrawal.

Withdrawal is a state of physical and psychological upset during which the body and the mind revolt against, and finally get used to, the absence of the drug. Withdrawal symptoms vary from person to person and from drug to drug. They range from a mild case of nausea and "the shakes" to hallucinations, convulsions, coma, and death.

Alcoholism

This country's most serious drug problem is alcoholism. Researchers estimate that 88 percent of all high school seniors have consumed alcohol at some time since entering adolescence, and that 54 percent have consumed it within the past month (Johnston, Bachman, & O'Malley, 1992). More than half of the students entering high school have already tried alcohol; by the time of graduation, 92 percent have tried it. An estimated 35 percent report having consumed 5 or more drinks in a row within the previous 2 weeks, and 4 percent of graduating seniors are drinking alcohol daily (Payne, Hahn, & Pinger, 1991). Ten percent of drinking adults consume about one-half of all the alcohol sold in the United States (Kinney & Leaton, 1987). Fifty percent or more of the deaths in automobile accidents each year can be traced to alcohol; in half of all murders either the killer or the victim has been drinking. In addition, the cost in human suffering to the alcoholic and his or her family is impossible to measure.

In small doses, alcohol might be called a social wonder drug. The first psychological function that it slows down is our inhibitions. Two drinks can make a person relaxed, talkative, playful, even giggly. It is for this reason that many people consider alcohol a stimulant—it is really a depressant.

As the number of drinks increases, the fun decreases. One by one, the person's psychological and physiological functions begin to shut down. Perceptions and sensations become distorted, and behavior may become obnoxious. The person begins to stumble and weave, speech becomes slurred, and reactions—to a stop sign, for example—become sluggish. If enough alcohol accumulates in the body, it leads to unconsciousness—and in some cases coma and death. It all depends on how much and how rapidly alcohol enters the bloodstream—which, in turn, depends on a person's weight, body chemistry, how much he or she drinks how quickly, and his or her past experience with drinking.

Alcohol can produce psychological dependence, tolerance, and addiction. One researcher has outlined three stages of alcoholism. In the first stage, the individual discovers that alcohol reduces her tensions, gives her

ADDITIONAL INFORMATION

Because of the high incidence of teen abuse of alcohol, many schools have a substance abuse counselor on staff or can make a referral. Find out if such a resource exists in your school. If so, arrange to obtain pamphlets and books that deal with the subject of alcoholism. You might use these materials as part of a lesson on recognition of the signs of dependency, tolerance, or addiction.

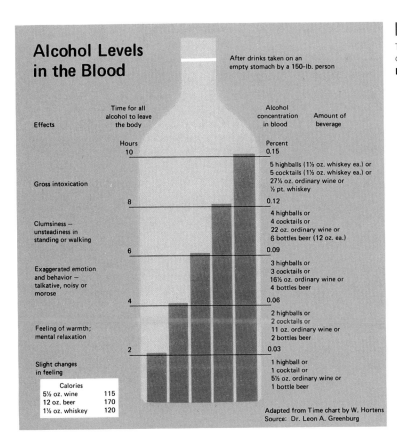

Alcohol Levels in the Blood

After drinks taken on an empty stomach by a 150-lb. person

FIGURE 15.16

This chart shows the effects of alcohol on a 150-pound person. **What are problems caused by drinking?**

Effects | Time for all alcohol to leave the body | Alcohol concentration in blood | Amount of beverage

Hours

| 10 | 0.15 |

Gross intoxication — 5 highballs (1½ oz. whiskey ea.) or 5 cocktails (1½ oz. whiskey ea.) or 27½ oz. ordinary wine or ½ pt. whiskey

| 8 | 0.12 |

Clumsiness — unsteadiness in standing or walking — 4 highballs or 4 cocktails or 22 oz. ordinary wine or 6 bottles beer (12 oz. ea.)

| 6 | 0.09 |

Exaggerated emotion and behavior — talkative, noisy or morose — 3 highballs or 3 cocktails or 16½ oz. ordinary wine or 4 bottles beer

| 4 | 0.06 |

Feeling of warmth; mental relaxation — 2 highballs or 2 cocktails or 11 oz. ordinary wine or 2 bottles beer

| 2 | 0.03 |

Slight changes in feeling — 1 highball or 1 cocktail or 5½ oz. ordinary wine or 1 bottle beer

Calories
5½ oz. wine 115
12 oz. beer 170
1½ oz. whiskey 120

Adapted from Time chart by W. Hortens
Source: Dr. Leon A. Greenburg

self-confidence, and reduces social pressures. Drinking makes her feel better. In the second stage, the beverage becomes a drug. The individual begins to drink so heavily that she feels she has to hide her habit. Thus she begins "sneaking" drinks. In this stage she may also begin to suffer from blackouts—she is unable to recall what happened during a drinking episode. In the final stage, she drinks compulsively, beginning in the morning. She becomes inefficient at work and tends to go on drinking sprees that may last for weeks. She is now an alcoholic, drinking continuously, eating infrequently, and feeling sick when deprived of her drug. Her health deteriorates rapidly (Jellinek, 1960).

The first step in treating the alcoholic is to see her through the violent withdrawal—called *delirium tremens*—typical of alcohol addiction, and then to try to make her healthier. She may be given a variety of treatments—from drugs to psychotherapy. Alcoholics Anonymous, an organization for alcoholics run by people who have had a drinking problem, has been more successful than most organizations. There is no certain cure for alcoholism. One problem is that our society tends to encourage social drinking and to tolerate the first stage of alcoholism.

■ **Creative Writing.** Tell students that many soap opera writers take psychology courses to get tips on character development. Challenge students to write an episode for one of their favorite soap operas in which an established character—or a new character—grapples with some psychological disorder.

Encourage students to act out these episodes for the class as a whole. Ask: What disorder did this episode address? What behavior characteristics served as "diagnostic bell ringers"?

PSYCHOLOGY UPDATE

DSM-IV. Psychologists, psychiatrists, and other researchers conduct studies called clinical trials to see whether the DSM classification system is helpful and useful. However, clinical trials take several years to design, run, and report. For this reason the organizers of the DSM system try not to change the system too often.

In 1987, the American Psychiatric Association published a revised manual called DSM-III-R. However, since relatively little time had elapsed since the publication of DSM-III, most changes were minor. For example, *affective disorders* are now called *mood disorders*, to be consistent with popular usage. The personality disorders now include two additional categories (sadistic and self-defeating) as "proposed personality disorders."

DSM-IV, published in 1994, offers few major changes from DSM-III-R. One controversial addition is the inclusion of premenstrual syndrome (PMS) as a distinct category. Overall, the greater specificity that came with DSM-III and DSM-III-R was well received by most practitioners, and refinements to make descriptions of diagnostic categories even more specific are offered in DSM-IV.

DSM-IV: NEW WAYS TO CATEGORIZE MENTAL ILLNESS

As mentioned earlier, there were several problems with the DSM-II classification scheme, including use of such general terms as neurosis and psychosis.

The DSM-III, DSM-III-R, and DSM-IV solved some of these by emphasizing behavior patterns that were found to occur in particular clusters rather than emphasizing the causes of various disorders. Furthermore, each diagnostic disorder is distinguished from other, similar diagnoses that a psychologist or psychiatrist may be considering.

Within each diagnostic category, the following descriptions are included:
1. *essential features* of the disorder—those that "define" the disorder;
2. *associated features*—features that are usually present;
3. information on *differential diagnosis*—that is, how to distinguish this disorder from other disorders with which it might be confused; and
4. *diagnostic criteria*—a list of symptoms, taken from the lists of essential and associated features, that must be present for the patient to be given this diagnostic label.

These more precise diagnostic criteria reduce the chances that the same patient will be classified as schizophrenic by one doctor and manic-depressive by another. Since researchers often rely on diagnostic labels to study underlying factors that may cause disorders, it is particularly important for their work that patients with similar symptoms be classified in the same diagnostic category.

The DSM-IV also recognizes the complexity of classifying people on the basis of mental disorders. Often, a person may exhibit more than one disorder or may be experiencing other stresses that complicate the diagnosis. In early classification systems, it was difficult to give a patient more than one label. The DSM-III-R and now DSM-IV overcame this problem by using five major dimensions, or *axes*, to describe a person's mental functioning. Each axis reflects a different aspect of a patient's case. Because the DSM-IV uses five axes to evaluate individuals, it is referred to as a multiple-axial system.

Axis I is used to classify current symptoms into explicitly defined categories. These categories range from disorders that are usually first evident in infancy, childhood, or adolescence (such as conduct disorders) to substance-use disorders (such as alcoholism), to schizophrenia. Table 15.1 shows a more detailed listing of the Axis I categories.

Axis II is used to describe developmental disorders and long-standing personality disorders or maladaptive traits such as compulsiveness, overdependency, or aggressiveness. Axis II is also used to describe specific developmental disorders for children, adolescents, and, in some cases, adults. Examples of developmental problems that would be classified under Axis II are language disorders, reading or writing difficulties, mental retardation, autism, and speech problems.

CRITICAL THINKING ACTIVITY

Applying Concepts. After students have developed the soap opera episodes suggested in the side margin on this page, have them categorize the various disorders described according to the DSM classification system. (If you did not use the writing exercise, have students watch a soap opera and write a review that makes use of DSM.)

TABLE 15.1 • DSM-IV Axis I and Selected Axis II Categories

Axis I

Disorders usually first evident in infancy, childhood, or adolescence

1. **Developmental disorders (NOTE: These are coded on Axis II.)**
   Mental Retardation
   Pervasive developmental
       disorders
       Autistic disorder
   Specific developmental
       disorders
       Academic skills
   Language and speech disorders
   Disruptive behavior disorders
       Attention-deficit hyper-
           activity disorder
       Conduct disorder
   Anxiety disorders of childhood
       or adolescence
   Eating disorders
       Anorexia nervosa
       Bulimia nervosa
   Gender identity disorders
   Tic disorders
   Elimination disorders
       Functional enuresis
   Speech disorders not elsewhere
       classified

2. **Organic mental disorders**
   Dementias arising in the senium
       and presenium
       Senile dementia
       Presenile dementia
   Psychoactive substance-induced
       organic mental disorder

3. **Psychoactive substance-induced organic disorder**

4. **Schizophrenia**
   Catatonic
   Disorganized
   Paranoid
   Undifferentiated
   Residual

5. **Delusional (paranoid) disorder**

6. **Psychotic disorders not elsewhere classified**

7. **Mood disorders**
   Bipolar disorder
   Depressive disorders
       Dysthymia

8. **Anxiety disorders**
   Panic disorder with agoraphobia
   Panic disorder without
       agoraphobia
   Social phobia
   Simple phobia
   Generalized anxiety disorder
   Obsessive-compulsive disorder
   Post-traumatic stress disorder

9. **Somatoform disorders**
   Conversion disorder
   Hypochondriasis
   Somatization disorder
   Somatoform pain disorder

10. **Dissociative disorder**
    Multiple personality disorder
    Psychogenic fugue
    Psychogenic amnesia
    Depersonalization disorder

11. **Sexual disorders**

12. **Sleep disorders**

13. **Factitious disorders**

14. **Impulse control disorders not elsewhere classified**

15. **Adjustment disorder**

Personality disorders (NOTE: These are coded on Axis II.)
   Cluster A
       Paranoid
       Schizoid
       Schizotypal
   Cluster B
       Antisocial
       Borderline
       Histrionic
       Narcissistic
   Cluster C
       Avoidant
       Dependent
       Obsessive-compulsive
       Passive-aggressive

CHAPTER 15 Lesson Plan

■ **Reading a Table.** Refer students to Table 15.1. Ask: (1) What information is organized on the table? *(types of mental disorders)* (2) Based on the text, what is Axis II used to describe? *(development disorders or long-standing personality disorders)* (3) What do the boldface headings indicate? *(categories into which the disorders are broken)*

As further reinforcement, you might reread the mock case study in the side note on page 382. Ask students what category (or categories) psychiatrists might use to label Jillian? *(The most obvious choice is: Personality disorder, Cluster B, Antisocial. Students might come up with other choices, too. In all cases, have them explain their rationale.)*

DID YOU KNOW?

The World Health Organization (WHO) has its own classification system for mental disorders known as the *International Classification of Diseases,* or *ICD-10.* This is the world's only international classification system for psychological disturbances.

CONNECTIONS: PSYCHOLOGY AND SCIENCE

Point out to students that the psychology profession developed the DSM classification system as a way of organizing data on a wide range of behaviors. Other fields of science have devised their own way of classifying, categorizing, or ordering data. Request volunteers to collect information on classification in other fields such as biology, chemistry, physics, and the environmental sciences. Suggest that they talk to the science teachers in your school for suggestions.

ASSESS

Check for Understanding

Organize the students into groups, and assign each group to fill in details in one of the major categories of information in the Summary outline on page 389.

Reteach

Have students complete the Chapter 15 Study Guide Activity. For extended review assign the Chapter 15 Review Activity as homework or an in-class assignment.

Enrich

Have students complete the Chapter 15 Application Activity.

Evaluate

Administer and grade the Chapter 15 Test. Two forms are available should you wish to give different tests to different students/classes.

Use the Understanding Psychology Testmaker to create a customized test.

CLOSE

Return the envelopes that you collected from students in the Motivating Activity. (See page 362). Challenge students to reassess their definitions and traits of mental illness. What, if any, stereotyped thinking can they identify? What modifications would they now make to the list? Do students think *mental illness* is even a term that should be used at all? If not, what term would they use?

It is possible for an individual to have a disorder on both Axis I and Axis II. For example, an adult may have a major depression noted on Axis I and a compulsive personality disorder noted on Axis II. A child may have a conduct disorder noted on Axis I and a developmental language disorder on Axis II. In other cases, a person may be seeking treatment primarily for a condition noted on Axis I or Axis II alone. The use of both Axes I and II permits multiple diagnoses and allows the clinician flexibility in making provisional diagnoses when there is not enough information available on the patient to make a firm diagnosis.

Axis III is used to describe physical disorders or medical conditions that are potentially relevant to understanding or managing the person. In some cases, a physical disorder may be causing the syndrome diagnosed on either Axis I or II. In other cases, the physical disorder may be important in the overall management of the individual, as in the case of a diabetic child with a conduct disorder.

Axis IV is a measurement of the current stress level at which the person is functioning. The rating of stressors is based on what the person has experienced within the past year. A seven-point code is used to describe stressors ranging from no apparent stressors (a rating of 1), or 0, meaning there is inadequate information for a rating, to catastrophic levels of stress (6). The prognosis may be better for a disorder that develops following a severe stressor than for one that develops after no stressor or a minimal stressor.

Axis V is used to describe the highest level of adaptive functioning present within the past year. Adaptive functioning refers to three major areas: social relations, occupational functioning, and the person's use of leisure time. *Social relations* refer to the quality of a person's relationships with family and friends. *Occupational functioning* involves functioning as a worker, student, or homemaker and the quality of the work accomplished. *Use of leisure time* includes recreational activities or hobbies and the degree of involvement and pleasure a person has in them. Ninety means good functioning in all areas, 50 means serious difficulty, and 10 means there is persistent danger.

With DSM-II, a patient's diagnosis might have been simply "alcohol addiction." Under the DSM-IV system, however, he or she might be diagnosed as follows:

Axis I:	alcohol dependence;
Axis II:	avoidant personality disorder;
Axis III:	diabetes;
Axis IV:	3: loss of job, one child moved out of house, marital conflict;
Axis V:	45: major impairment in several areas.

This offers a good deal more information about the patient—information that may be useful in devising a treatment program. Furthermore, this five-part diagnosis may be extremely helpful to researchers trying to discover connections among psychological disorders and other factors such as stress and physical illness.

CRITICAL THINKING ACTIVITY

Demonstrating Reasoned Judgment. Have students discuss the individual and community responsibility for treating mental illness. On the chalkboard, have them speculate on some of the "helpers" (both professional and nonprofessional) to whom a person might turn. How should these avenues of help be advertised? Use students' answers to these questions as a bridge into Chapter 16: "Therapy and Change."

SUMMARY

Use the following outline as a tool for reviewing this chapter. Copy the outline onto your own paper, leaving spaces between headings to make notes about key concepts.

- **I.** What is Abnormal Behavior?
    - **A.** Deviation from Normality
    - **B.** Adjustment
    - **C.** Psychological Health
- **II.** The Problem of Classification
- **III.** Anxiety-Based Disorders
    - **A.** Generalized Anxiety Disorder
    - **B.** Phobic Disorder
    - **C.** Panic Disorder
    - **D.** Obsessive-Compulsive Disorder
    - **E.** Post-Traumatic Stress Disorder
- **IV.** Somatoform Disorders
- **V.** Dissociative Disorders
- **VI.** Mood Disorders
    - **A.** Major Depressive Disorder
    - **B.** Bipolar Disorder
    - **C.** Suicide and Depression
- **VII.** Schizophrenia
- **VIII.** Personality Disorders
- **IX.** Drug Addiction
    - **A.** Alcoholism
- **X.** DSM-IV: New Ways to Categorize Mental Illness

CONCEPTS AND VOCABULARY

1. Describe three ways of defining abnormality. Describe one shortcoming of each definition.

2. What is the legal definition of insanity? Is pleading insanity highly successful as a means of defense in criminal cases?

3. What system do psychologists use to classify abnormal behavior? In what ways is this system different from the one that preceded it?

4. List some differences between anxiety-based disorders and schizophrenia. What is the difference between symptoms (for example, depression) that a psychologically healthy person might experience and the symptoms of a psychologically disturbed person?

5. Describe the symptoms associated with anxiety. Give two explanations for the cause of anxiety.

6. How do phobias differ from normal fears? Give one explanation for the causes of phobias.

7. What is an obsession? What is a compulsion? Why do people develop obsessions and compulsions?

8. What do psychologists mean when they refer to someone as having a somatoform disorder?

9. What is a conversion disorder? What do psychologists believe causes a conversion disorder?

10. How do conversion disorders and hypochondriasis differ?

11. What is a psychogenic fugue? What psychological function might it serve? How does it differ from psychogenic amnesia?

12. What is multiple personality? How common a disorder is it? From what do psychologists think multiple personality may come?

13. Describe the contemporary theories that explain the causes of depression.

389

ANSWERS

Concepts and Vocabulary

1. (a) deviation approach; majority not always right (b) adjustment approach; no guarantee anyone will adjust to all situations (c) mental health approach; no set definition on what constitutes mental health

2. not responsible as the result of a mental illness; not usually

3. DSM; less vague

4. Differences should underscore the complete detachment for reality that characterized schizophrenia. (For example, a depressed person can respond more or less coherently. A schizophrenic cannot.)

5. muscular tension; inability to relax, furrowed brow, strained face, poor appetite, indigestion, diarrhea, frequent urination, and difficulty sleeping; learned behavior, physiological shortcomings, suppression of unconscious desires

6. intense, obsessive irrational fears that prompt situational avoidance; learned behavior reinforced by avoidance

7. uncontrollable pattern of thoughts; repeated pattern of irrational actions; to serve as diversions from fears (including fear of success)

8. psychological difficulties that take on physical (somatic) form

9. physical symptoms for conversion of emotional difficulties into the loss of a particular physical function; desire to gain freedom from unbearable anxiety

10. conversion disorders: may develop symptoms; hypochondriasis: preoccupation with imaginary ailments

11. dissociative reaction in which amnesia is coupled with active flight to a different environment; an escape from unbearable fear or anxiety; involves different location and life apart from prior life

12. type of dissociative reaction; rare; an escape from part of self that has been hurt or causes fear

13. result of guilt and need for self-punishment (Freud); result of illogical conclusions about self (Beck); result of learned helplessness (Seligman)

14. disorder that involves confused and distorted thoughts; delusions and hallucinations; simple schizophrenia (withdrawal from world) and catatonia (physical standstill)

15. manic: elation confusion, racing thoughts, exaggerated self-esteem; depressive: feelings of failure, worthlessness, and despair; bipolar: alternating feelings of high or excessive elation and hopeless depression

16. cause unknown; exploring genetic components, family environment, and chemical imbalances

17. inherited predisposition, chemical imbalance in the brain, long-term exposure to double-bind

18. usually do not suffer from anxiety despite sometimes bizarre behavior; able to form relationships in the real world

19. irresponsible, immature, emotionally shallow, thrill-seekers, etc.

20. dependence upon drug-induced sense of well-being; drugged state is the "normal" state; need to use increasingly higher amounts of drugs to get "high"

21. (a) 88 percent of all high school seniors have tried; 10 percent of population consume one-half of all alcohol sold; some 50 percent of auto accidents related to alcohol (b) depressant (c) dependence, tolerance, addiction (d) supervised withdrawal and physiological treatment/ group support (more in Chapter 16)

Critical Thinking

1. Point out the subjective/cultural influences on the definition of mental illness.

---

14. What is schizophrenia? What are two common experiences of people with schizophrenia? Summarize two types of schizophrenic reactions.

15. What is a manic reaction? What is a depressive reaction? What is a bipolar disorder?

16. Do psychologists know what causes autism? What avenues are they exploring?

17. What are the three major causes given for schizophrenic reactions?

18. How do personality disorders differ from anxiety-based disorders and schizophrenia?

19. How would you describe someone who is classified as having an antisocial personality disorder?

20. What are the differences between drug dependency, drug addiction, and drug tolerance?

21. What evidence is there that heavy drinking is a serious problem in America? Is alcohol a stimulant or a depressant? What are the stages of alcoholism? What can be done to help alcoholics?

CRITICAL THINKING

1. **Synthesize.** Develop your own definition of mental illness. Is your definition free of social values, or are values a necessary part of every definition of mental illness? Explain.

2. **Analyze.** It is thought that one of the conditions that produces mental disorders is overexposure to double-bind situations. Everyone has faced these situations at various times. How many examples from your own experiences can you think of that illustrate various forms of the double-bind situation? How did you resolve the conflicts? Can you see patterns of behavior responses developing?

3. **Evaluate.** Whenever you dismiss certain people as "creeps," for example, you are really saying more about yourself than about the people you are labeling. For example, people who are nervous in social gatherings often may not like other people who are nervous in social gatherings. For a possible indication of your own problems, make a list of people you don't like and the reason(s) why you don't like them. Take a hard, honest look at those traits you have written down and see how many of them apply to you as well.

4. **Analyze.** What are you afraid of? Do you fear high places, or water, or maybe snakes or spiders? Try to think back to when you first had these fears. Can you state rationally why you have each of your fears?

5. **Analyze.** What makes you anxious? Consider the times you have experienced a general apprehension and try to list the particular settings or situations in which you are most likely to feel this way. What ways have you developed to help you cope with anxiety? Are there times when anxiety has hindered your behavior? Are there times when anxiety has helped your behavior? If you answered the last two questions in the affirmative, how do you explain the difference?

APPLYING KNOWLEDGE

1. Watch television for a week. Keep a journal of programs which have some psychological theme. What examples of mental breakdown are described? How common are they made to appear? Are simple solutions given? How is the psychologist or psychiatrist shown? Does this person have ready answers? What are they? How do they compare to what you have learned?

2. Cut out about 15 pictures of people from magazines and paste them on a large piece of paper. Include among the pictures several of people with long or mussed up hair and untidy clothes. Ask several friends or classmates if they can determine whether any the people in the pictures

---

2. Respect student privacy. Explore concept of double-bind, then request volunteered examples.

3. Explore the use of labels as a defense mechanism. (See Chapter 11.)

4. Work only with fears that students are willing to share. Share a personal example of a fear that you or a friend overcame.

5. Focus on the concept of anxiety, respecting student privacy. Explore the conceptual idea of anxiety as a negative and positive force. Volunteered responses can be used as examples.

Applying Knowledge

1. Student responses will vary with the program. Descriptions of disorders should match those in the text.

2. You might review the shortcomings of physical traits as a method of personality analysis. (See Chapter 11.)

are mentally ill. How many select the people with unkempt appearances? What conclusions can you draw from this demonstration?

3. Study a book of paintings and drawings by Vincent van Gogh. Can you tell which were done when he was mentally healthy and which were done when he may have been suffering from a severe psychological disorder? How?

4. Read newspapers and news magazines for articles dealing with mental illness. Keep a record of the maladaptive behavior that is identified and who makes the diagnosis. In what contexts is mental illness discussed? Do the articles address legal issues? What can you learn about treatment of mental illness from your collection of articles?

ANALYZING VIEWPOINTS

1. In many states, temporary insanity can be used as a defense in a criminal trial. As mentioned in the chapter, John Hinckley was found not guilty by reason of insanity of attempting to assassinate then-President Reagan. Write a paper that argues for and against the legitimacy of the insanity defense in criminal cases. Before you begin writing, spend some time researching the insanity defense at your local library. Look for books, magazines, articles, and newspaper articles on the topic. Find information concerning a particular case in which the insanity defense was used. Use the information you find as the basis for your paper.

2. Individuals who are defined as mentally incompetent or as dangers to themselves or society can, in many states, be held in an institution against their will for up to 72 hours. Is this a reasonable policy? Does it matter who is classifying the individuals? Is there any potential for abuse? In an essay, debate both sides of the issue: yes, there is a need for authorities to be able to confine individuals who may do themselves or others harm; and no, confining an individual based on someone's subjective

judgment violates the individual's freedom and personal rights.

BEYOND THE CLASSROOM

1. Find out more about the treatment and care of mental health patients in your community. First ask your school nurse or school psychologist to give you a list of places in the community that provide treatment for mental health problems. Possibilities are a community mental health center, a halfway house, or a local hospital. Working with your teacher, choose one of the places, then call and explain that you are doing a project for a high school psychology class and ask if someone could come to your class and talk about mental health services in your community. Work with other students to prepare a list of questions you can ask the speaker. Questions might focus on identifying the most common types of problems; the duration of treatment programs; and the effectiveness of different kinds of treatment.

IN YOUR JOURNAL

1. Read the definitions of the four phobias that you wrote in your journal at the beginning of your study of Chapter 15. Choose one of these phobias and write a paragraph that describes how it can adversely affect an individual.

2. Some phobias are simple phobias, or fears connected to one thing or to a specific activity. Other phobias are social phobias, or the fear of suffering embarrassment or humiliation in a social situation. The fear of public speaking is among the most common social phobias. Make an entry in your journal explaining why you think many people dislike speaking in public.

3. You might suggest that students research a biography of van Gogh to develop a frame of reference.

4. Conclusions should reflect the different categories of data studied: type of maladaptive behavior, person/agency making the judgment, factors influencing judgment, most common legal issues raised.

Analyzing Viewpoints

1. Papers should follow the format for persuasive writing: statement of position, evidence in support of position, conclusion/restatement of position.

2. Essays should address protection of individual rights vs. protection of the public welfare.

CHAPTER BONUS
Test Question

This question may be used for extra credit on the chapter test.
Choose the letter of the correct response.

Which of the following statements regarding use of the DSM-IV is false?

a. It is more specific in describing disorders than earlier editions.

b. Its categories change with changing times and attitudes.

c. Its usefulness probably outweighs the disadvantages.

d. The new edition does not include schizophrenia.

Answer: **d**

Beyond the Classroom

1. Because of the confidentiality guaranteed by most institutions, students should obtain all the necessary authorization and release forms.

IN YOUR JOURNAL

If time permits, discuss journal entries individually with students

CHAPTER 16
Therapy and Change

TEXT TOPICS	SPECIAL FEATURES	RESOURCE MATERIALS
What is Psychotherapy?, pp. 393–397	Psychology and You, p. 395	Reproducible Lesson Plan; Study Guide; Review Activity
Kinds of Psychotherapy, pp. 397–409	More About Psychology, p. 401; p. 402; pp. 409–410 Fact or Fiction?, p. 406	Reproducible Lesson Plan; Study Guide; Review Activity; Application Activity Transparency 26
Biological Approaches to Treatment, pp. 410–411		Reproducible Lesson Plan; Study Guide; Review Activity
Does Psychotherapy Work?, pp. 411–413	At a Glance: All About Valium, p. 412	Reproducible Lesson Plan; Study Guide; Review Activity; Extension Activity Readings in Psychology: Section 5, Reading 7
Mental Institutions, pp. 413–414	Psychology and You, p. 413	Reproducible Lesson Plan; Study Guide; Review Activity
Community Mental Health, pp. 415–419	Using Psychology: Crisis Intervention Programs, pp. 417–419	Reproducible Lesson Plan; Study Guide; Review Activity Chapter Test, Form A and Form B Understanding Psychology Testmaker

PERFORMANCE ASSESSMENT ACTIVITY

Tell students that psychotherapists have to be experts at reading *body language*, or the nonverbal clues that people send by physical gestures or movements. Assign students to locate photos that illustrate some form of body language. Direct them to write a short caption for each photo indicating what they "read" from the nonverbal clues. (Students should be able to support their interpretations with details from the photos.)

CHAPTER RESOURCES

Readings for the Student
Bandura, A. *Principles of Behavior Modification*. New York: Holt, Rinehart & Winston, 1969.

Barton, A. *Three Worlds of Therapy*. Palo Alto, CA: National Press Books, 1974.

Goffman, Erving. *Asylums*. Garden City, NY: Doubleday, 1961.

Szasz, Thomas, (ed.). *The Age of Madness*. Garden City, NY: Doubleday Anchor, 1973.

Readings for the Teacher
Brenner, D. *The Effective Psychotherapist*. New York: Pergamon Press, 1981.

Corsini, Raymond J., *Current Psychotherapies*. Itasca, IL: Peacock, 1984.

Garfield, Sol L., and Bergin, Allen E. *Handbook of Psychotherapy and Behavior Change: An Empirical Analysis*. New York: Wiley, 1986.

Multimedia
Psychotherapy (26 minutes, 3/4" or 1/2" video). McGraw-Hill Training System. This video uses dramatizations of several psychotherapy sessions to show the basic concepts and techniques of therapists.

Three Approaches to Psychotherapy, No. 1—Dr. Carl Rogers (48 minutes). Psychological Films. This film describes Rogers' methods of therapy.

Three Approaches to Psychotherapy, No. 2—Dr. Frederick Perls. (32 minutes). Psychological Films. This film describes Gestalt therapy as practiced by Perls.

Three Approaches to Psychotherapy, No. 3—Dr. Albert Ellis (50 minutes). Psychological Films. This film describes rational-emotive psychotherapy as practiced by Ellis.

For additional resources, see the bibliography beginning on page 530.

FOCUS

Motivating Activity

You might open the chapter by asking students to write down the conditions under which they might seek counseling or therapy. (To encourage honesty, tell students that the papers will not be collected.) Underneath this list or statement, have them indicate the qualities that they would look for in a therapist. For example, what level of training would they expect? What school of therapy would most appeal to them? (Encourage students to review these schools in Chapter 11, if necessary.) Tell students to save this material for reexamination at the end of the chapter. (See Close on page 419.)

Meeting Chapter Objectives.

Identify the main subjects or topics in each objective on page 393. Have groups of students prepare data sheets on each of these objectives as they read Chapter 16.

Building Vocabulary.

Assign students to draw on prior knowledge or familiar word parts to guess the definition of each of the key terms on page 393. After each guess, have students look up the term in the Glossary. How close did they come to the real meaning?

Therapy and Change

FIGURE 16.1 The primary goal of each of the many different kinds of therapy is strengthening the person's control over his or her life.

392

TEACHER CLASSROOM RESOURCES

- Chapter 16 Reproducible Lesson Plan
- Chapter 16 Study Guide
- Chapter 16 Review Activity
- Chapter 16 Application Activity
- Chapter 16 Extension Activity

- Transparency 26
  Transparency Strategies and Activities

- *Readings in Psychology:* Section 5, Reading 7

- Chapter 16 Test, Form A and Form B

- Understanding Psychology Testmaker

OBJECTIVES

After studying this chapter, you should be able to

- explain the nature of psychotherapy and trace its historical development.
- describe psychoanalysis and its aims.
- describe the processes and goals of behavior therapy, cognitive therapies, and humanist / existential therapies.
- give examples of various forms of group therapy.

A t certain times of transition and crisis in life, we may feel an urgent need to find someone trustworthy with whom to share our doubts and problems. A parent, relative, or close friend is often helpful in such times of need. Many psychological problems, however, are too bewildering and complex to be solved in this way. When people become dissatisfied or distraught with life and suspect that the reason lies within themselves, they are likely to seek help from someone with training and experience in such matters. People who have been trained to deal with the psychological problems of others include psychologists, psychiatrists, and social workers. The special kind of help they provide is called **psychotherapy.**

Presented in this chapter are some of the major approaches to therapy and what it is like to undergo therapy. In addition, we will explore various types of group therapy, probe the current situation in America's mental institutions, and touch on the trend toward community mental health.

KEY TERMS

behavior therapy
contingency management
eclectic approach
ego states
empathy
encounter group
family therapy
free association
gestalt therapy
group therapy
human potential movement
insight
person-centered therapy
placebo effect
psychoanalysis
psychotherapy
rational-emotive therapy
resistance
self-help groups
systematic desensitization
transactional analysis
transference
unconditional positive regard

Exploring Key Ideas

Defining Psychotherapy.
Read aloud the following definition of psychotherapy offered by Lewis Wolberg (1977):

Psychotherapy is the treatment, by psychological means, of problems of an emotional nature in which a trained person deliberately establishes a professional relationship with the patient with the object of (1) removing, modifying, or retarding existing symptoms, (2) mediating disturbed patterns of behavior, and (3) promoting positive personality growth and development.

Ask: What does Wolberg see as the main function of a psychotherapist? *(promoting positive personality growth and development)* Then point out that, although all psychotherapists share this goal, they differ in the techniques to achieve it. Tell students that Chapter 16 explores some of these methods. It also investigates some alternatives to psychotherapy that are available to individuals today.

IN YOUR JOURNAL

Recommend a treatment for the following problems: compulsive overeating, inability to finish work, severe depression. Write your recommendations in your journal.

393

IN YOUR JOURNAL

You might recommend that students look back at Chapter 15 for some of the symptoms and causes of compulsive behavior, lethargy, and depression.

EXTRA CREDIT ACTIVITY

Assign interested students to prepare a time line showing major events in the historic development of psychotherapy. Explain to students that they might break their time lines with a zig-zag line to indicate big jumps in time. However, within each block, intervals should be in equal units of measure. Also suggest that students construct a wall-size time line, using strips of computer paper. Possible sources of information include: (1) *The Story of Psychology*, by Morton Hunt, and (2) *Psychology in America,* by Ernest R. Hilgard.

TEACH

Guided Practice

■ **Analyzing a Quote.** To illustrate the changes that have taken place in the treatment of mental disorders in recent times, read aloud the following 18th-century account of London's Bethlehem Hospital.

It seems strange that any should recover here, the cryings, screechings, roarings, brawlings, shaking of chains, swarings, frettings, chaffing, are so many, so hideous, so great, that they are more able to drive a man that hath his witts, rather out of them, than to help one that . . . hath lost them to finde them againe.

Ask students what this passage tells them about the treatment of mental disorders little more than 200 years ago. Mention that the term *bedlam* was derived from conditions at Bethlehem. What does *bedlam* mean? *(uproar)* Did the term fit mental institutions at that time? Why or why not? (OBJECTIVE 1)

WHAT IS PSYCHOTHERAPY?

Psychotherapy literally means "healing of the soul," and in early times psychological disturbances were often thought to represent some sort of moral or religious problem. Troubled people were sometimes viewed as being inhabited by devils or demons, and treatment consisted of exorcism—the driving out of these demons by religious ceremonies or by physical punishment. Within the last 200 years, however, views of psychological disorders have changed. Mental disorders came slowly to be thought of as diseases, and the term "mental illness" was applied to many psychological problems.

The fact that psychological disturbance is seen as the symptom of a disease has helped to reduce the stigma associated with such problems, and it has done much to convince society that troubled people need care and treatment. Nevertheless, many psychotherapists feel that the term "mental illness" has outlived its usefulness and that, in fact, it may now be doing more harm than good.

The trouble with letting a person think of himself as mentally ill is that he sees himself in a passive, helpless position. He sees his troubles as being caused by forces over which he has no control. By thinking of himself in this way, the person can avoid taking responsibility for his own situation and for helping himself change.

One of the functions of psychotherapy is to help people realize that they are responsible for their own problems and that, even more importantly, they are the only ones who can really solve these problems. This approach does not imply that people become disturbed on purpose or that no one should need outside help. People often adopt certain techniques for getting along in life that seem appropriate at the time but that lead to trouble in the long run. Such patterns can be difficult for the individual to see or change. The major task of the therapist, therefore, is to help people examine their way of living, to understand how their present way of living causes problems, and to start living in new, more beneficial ways. The therapist can be thought of as a guide who is hired by the individual to help him find the source of his problems and some possible solutions.

Characteristics of Psychotherapy

There are many different kinds of therapy, only a few of which will be described in this chapter. Each one is based on different theories about how human personality works, and each one is carried out in a different style. Some psychotherapists stick rigorously to one style and consider the others useless. Other psychotherapists use an **eclectic approach** to therapy, choosing methods from many different kinds of therapy and using whatever works best. But whatever the style or philosophy, all types of psychotherapy have certain characteristics in common.

The primary goal of psychotherapy is to strengthen the patient's control over his or her life. People seeking psychotherapy feel trapped in behavior patterns. Over the years they have developed not only certain feelings about themselves, but behaviors that reinforce those feelings. Such people

CONNECTIONS: PSYCHOLOGY AND THE LAW

Request students to research the case of Joyce Brown—the first homeless person chosen by New York City health officials to be hospitalized under a program for mentally ill street people. With the help of lawyers from the American Civil Liberties Union, Brown successfully fought for her right to live free (Barbanel, 1988). Have students present their findings in an oral report. Advise them to take into account the rights of the individual vs. the rights of the public at large. In a general discussion, explore student opinion on the Brown case.

lack freedom and have limited options in choosing the direction their lives will take. Their behavior and feelings make it impossible for them to reach their goals. For example, a man who is severely critical of himself may feel others are equally harsh in their judgments of him. Rather than risk feelings of rejection, he avoids social gatherings. A person who is uncomfortable meeting other people will, no doubt, feel lonely and rejected. His critical feelings about himself will be strengthened, and he may come to feel that he will remain unloved for life.

The aim of psychotherapy for such a person would be to free him of his burden of self-hate. With a more positive self-image, the man would not be locked into the cycle of avoidance, rejection, and despair. For perhaps the first time, he could feel in control of his life. His behavior would be based on *choice*, and not on the necessity that goes with fixed behavior patterns.

In order to change, it is necessary for the patient to achieve some *understanding* of his troubles. One of the first tasks of therapy, therefore, is to examine the patient's problem closely.

The man in our example will, in the course of his therapy, discover the origin of his self-critical, despairing feelings. He may also realize that, although these feelings developed from real situations, perhaps during his childhood, they no longer apply to his adult capabilities. Gradually the patient's view of himself will become more realistic.

Another major task of therapy is to help the patient find meaningful *alternatives* to his present unsatisfactory ways of behaving. The patient we have been discussing may look for ways to meet new people rather than avoid them.

One of the most important factors in effective treatment is the patient's belief or hope that he *can* change. The influence that a patient's hopes and expectations have on his improvement is often called the **placebo effect.** This name comes from giving medical patients *placebos*—harmless sugar pills—when they complain of ailments that do not seem to have any physiological basis. The patients take the tablets and their symptoms disappear.

The placebo effect does not imply that problems can be solved simply by fooling the patient. It does demonstrate, however, the tremendous importance of the patient's attitude in finding a way to change. A patient who does not believe he can be helped probably cannot be. A patient who believes he can change and believes he has the power to change will find a way. Therapy goes beyond the placebo effect. It combines the patient's belief that he can change with hard work and professional guidance.

What Makes a Good Therapist?

In American society, there are many people who practice psychotherapy. Some, like clinical neuropsychologists, are trained in psychology and physiology; others, like counseling psychologists, have different forms of formal training. The various kinds of professional therapists and the training that each goes through before practicing psychotherapy are shown in Table 16.1.

Before going to a professional therapist, most people first turn to a friend or other nonprofessional for help and advice. Sometimes, this is exactly

PSYCHOLOGY and YOU

How to Be Assertive. It's hard to be assertive all the time in every situation. You may find it easy to ask a favor of a friend but impossible to make a similar request of a stranger. If you want to spread your assertiveness over more situations, try following these simple suggestions:

• Begin your attempts at developing assertiveness in the least threatening situations.

• Increase your nonverbal assertiveness. Stand erect, look at a person straight in the eyes during conversation, eliminate any nervous habits and smile.

• Work up to a difficult task in a series of gradual steps.

• If you're afraid to tell people how you feel when you disagree, start by expressing your opinion when you're asked. Once you feel confident in your ability to disagree, you're ready to volunteer your feelings.

• If you find it hard to begin a conversation with a person you've just met, try asking open-ended questions: ones that cannot be answered just "yes" or "no."

By following these suggestions, you probably won't increase your assertiveness overnight. But each day will bring you closer to your goal.

■ Analyzing Information. Focus student attention on the tips in the feature for nonverbal assertiveness. Ask students how skilled they are at reading body language. Next, read the following selection from "How Well Do You Read Body Language?" by Dane Archer and Robin M. Akert, in the October 1977 issue of *Psychology Today.*

Our society places a great deal of emphasis on words, with early and intensive training in spelling, vocabulary, writing, reading, and even foreign languages. Nonverbal communication, by contrast, appears less frequently in a school curricula than even a vanished language like Latin. Since we now know that an understanding of nonverbal clues is indispensable to understanding other people, perhaps we need to explore new ways . . . to read these rich, unspoken languages.

Ask: Why do the authors think a course should be offered in body language? *(to improve our understanding of people)* If this school offered such a course, would you sign up? Why or why not? Why do you think the ability to read body language might be an invaluable tool for therapists? (OBJECTIVES 1, 2)

BEYOND THE CLASSROOM

For students interested in learning more about body language, assign them to research additional articles in past issues of *Psychology Today* or to read books such as Edward T. Hall's *The Silent Language* or Dane Archer's *How to Expand Your Social Intelligence Quotient.* Challenge these students to offer a 15-minute lesson in this "silent language" to the rest of the class.

■ **Creating a Reference Book.** Assign groups of students to create a class reference book on various types of psychological professions. Each entry should be prepared on separate pages so that it can be inserted into a binder alphabetically. Encourage students to illustrate items and expand as necessary. The items on this page provide a start. (Lay analysts, psychiatric social workers, and paraprofessionals may be subdivided into individual entries.) Other professions can be found in the "Psychologists at Work" in the Bottom Notes of each chapter in the Teacher's Wraparound Edition and in the narrative of the chapters themselves.
(OBJECTIVES 1, 2)

Teacher Note. Point out mention of the clergy in the Paraprofessional section of Table 16.1. You might tell students that some clergy train as *pastoral counselors*. These paraprofessionals have a college background in both psychology and theology. They intern in mental health facilities as chaplains.

TABLE 16.1 • Kinds of Therapists

Clinical psychologists are therapists with a Ph.D. degree. They have completed a three- to four-year research-oriented program in psychology, plus a one-year predoctoral or postdoctoral supervised internship in psychotherapy and psychological assessment. Some clinical psychologists have a Psy.D.: a *Doctor of Psychology*. Their education covers the same courses as a Ph.D. program, without a research-based doctoral dissertation. The dissertation hours are spent learning additional skills in testing, interviewing, and offering psychotherapy.

Counseling psychologists generally have a master's or Ph.D. degree in counseling psychology. They usually work in educational institutions, where they are available for consultation about personal problems. They customarily refer clients with serious problems to clinical psychologists or psychiatrists.

Clinical Neuropsychologists have Ph.D. degrees with education similar to clinical psychologists. However, they also have extensive education in neurophysiology regarding the mechanisms and operation of the brain. They typically work with patients who have brain injury that is interfering with normal behavior. Such damage may result from drug use, accident, or normal aging. Their primary role has been in assessing neurological damage; some are now involved in therapy.

Psychiatrists are medical doctors who specialize in the treatment of mental illness. They take post-graduate training in abnormal behavior. Because of their medical background, psychiatrists are the primary group licensed to prescribe medicines and the only group that can perform operations, but pilot programs in which psychologists with education in physiology and neurology are prescribing medications have been introduced.

Psychoanalysts are usually medical doctors who have taken special training in the theory of personality and techniques of psychotherapy of Sigmund Freud, typically at a psychoanalytic institute. They must themselves be psychoanalyzed before they can practice.

Lay analysts are psychoanalysts who do not have degrees in medicine but who have studied with established psychoanalysts. Psychoanalysts and lay analysts are the only types of psychotherapists who are labeled specifically in terms of their theoretical orientation and form of therapy.

Psychiatric social workers are people with a master's degree in social work. They generally receive supervised practical training coupled with two years of graduate-level courses in psychology.

Paraprofessionals include clergy, physicians, teachers, and others who dispense a great deal of advice despite the fact that they have had little or no formal training in therapy or counseling. Nevertheless, more troubled people turn to paraprofessionals than to professionals. Rape Crisis hot lines and Battered Women's hot lines are often staffed by paraprofessionals.

what's needed. But professional therapists are likely to be more skillful in encouraging the person to examine uncomfortable feelings and problems. In the process of therapy, the patient may feel frustrated because he cannot push the burden of responsibility onto someone else the way he can with a friend.

The process of therapy is often difficult and upsetting, and patients frequently become heavily dependent on the therapist while they are trying to make changes. A patient may become angry or hurt, for example, if his

PSYCHOLOGISTS AT WORK

Throughout many treatment facilities—rehabilitation centers, hospitals, clinics, halfway houses, and more—*psychiatric nurses* have grown in number. These nurses hold standard nursing licenses, but most have gone beyond their RN (Registered Nurse) degree to do advanced training in psychology. Some even hold a master's degree.

A psychiatric nurse dispenses medication or acts as a "contact" in the long hours between counseling sessions. Their words and gestures help patients and clients deal with the day-to-day problems of emotional recovery. Often psychiatric nurses work hand in hand with therapists providing detailed observations of patients. They are in a very real sense "the therapy in between the therapy."

therapist goes on vacation. The therapist, therefore, has to be careful not to betray the trust that the patient has placed in her. On the other hand, she must not let the patient lean on her or take out his problems on her. Patients often try to avoid their problems by using the therapist as a substitute parent or by blaming her for their misfortunes.

Whether psychotherapy will be beneficial to a person depends on both the patient and the therapist. Patients who get the most out of psychotherapy are people with high intelligence, a good education, and a middle-class background. Such people have much in common with most therapists, and this similarity seems to help. In addition, the people who benefit most from psychotherapy are those who have relatively mild problems about which they have considerable anxiety or depression. Severely disturbed, apathetic patients are much more difficult to change. Therapy will also be more effective with people who are introspective and who can withstand frustration. Therapy is neither easy nor fast; it demands as much from the patient as it does from the therapist.

There are three characteristics that are found in effective therapists. First, a therapist needs to be psychologically *healthy*. A therapist who is anxious, defensive, and withdrawn will not be able to see his patient's problems clearly. A second important characteristic is **empathy**—a capacity for warmth and understanding. Troubled people are usually fearful and confused about explaining their problems. The therapist needs to be able to give the patient confidence that he is capable of caring and understanding. Finally, a good therapist must be *experienced* in dealing with people—in understanding their complexities, seeing through the games they play to trick the therapist and themselves, and judging their strengths and weaknesses. Only by having worked with many people can a therapist learn when to give support, when to insist that the patient stand on his own feet, and how to make sense of the things people say.

KINDS OF PSYCHOTHERAPY

Although there are many approaches to psychotherapy, only some of the more influential approaches will be discussed: psychoanalysis, humanistic approaches to treatment, cognitive approaches to treatment, and behavioral approaches to treatment. In addition to these types of individual therapy, several kinds of group therapy will be described.

Psychoanalysis

For a long time **psychoanalysis** was the only formalized psychotherapy practiced in Western society. It was this type of therapy that gave rise to the classic picture of a bearded Viennese doctor seated behind a patient who is lying on a couch.

Psychoanalysis is based on the theories of Sigmund Freud. According to Freud's views, psychological disturbances are due to anxiety about hid-

Teacher Note. You might tell students the following old joke: "How many psychotherapists does it take to change a light bulb? One—but the light bulb has to want to change." Ask students to identify the grain of truth behind this joke. *(that therapy will not work unless a patient/client wants it to work)*

■ **Making a Chart.** Assign students to design a chart to compare the following treatments: *Psychoanalysis, Person-centered Therapy, Existential Therapy, Gestalt Therapy, Transactional Analysis, Rational-Emotive Therapy, Cognitive-Behavioral Therapy*, and *Behavioral Therapy*. Vertical side heads should include: *Origins, Techniques, Advantages,* and *Disadvantages*. Have students fill out the charts as they read the chapter. Encourage students to include their own ideas in the entries for *Advantages* and *Disadvantages*.

COMMUNITY INVOLVEMENT

Mention to students that one study (Cowan, 1982) identified nonprofessional "helpers" to whom many people take their problems. They include: hairdressers, divorce lawyers, and industrial supervisors. The study revealed that these "helpers" recognized their role as "therapists," and accepted it. Request students to invite one or more of these nonprofessional helpers to speak to the class. Instruct students to ask them about the following topics: (1) their most common problems, (2) how they respond, and (3) their feelings about being "community therapists."

■ **Demonstration.** To demonstrate free association, instruct students to write down every thought that comes into their head for five minutes. Caution students to suspend all judgment and analysis. When the five minutes are up, allow students to do some self-analysis of their writing. What, if any, patterns or surprising thoughts turn up? Request volunteers to share entries or to talk about feelings of resistance that they might have had during the exercise. (OBJECTIVE 2)

■ **Making a Flowchart.** Organize students into small groups and direct them to design a flowchart illustrating the main steps or stages in the psychoanalytical process. Encourage students to illustrate the flowchart, showing the patient-therapist relationship at the various stages. (OBJECTIVE 2)

den conflicts between the unconscious components of one's personality. (Freud's theory of personality is described in Chapters 8 and 11.) One job of the psychoanalyst, therefore, is to help make the patients aware of the unconscious impulses, desires, and fears that are causing the anxiety. Psychoanalysts believe that if patients can understand their unconscious motives, they have taken the first step toward gaining control over their behavior and freeing themselves of their problems. Such understanding is called **insight.**

Psychoanalysis is a slow procedure. It may take years of fifty-minute sessions several times a week before the patient is able to make fundamental changes in her life. Throughout this time, the analyst assists his patient in a thorough examination of the unconscious motives behind her behavior. This task begins with the analyst telling the patient to relax and talk about everything that comes into her mind. This method is called **free association.** The patient may consider her passing thoughts too unimportant or too embarrassing to mention. But the analyst suggests that she express everything—the thought that seems most inconsequential may, in fact, be the most meaningful upon closer examination.

As the patient lies on the couch, she may describe her dreams, discuss private thoughts, or recall long-forgotten experiences. The psychoanalyst often says nothing for long periods of time. The psychoanalyst also occasionally makes remarks or asks questions that guide the patient, or he may suggest an unconscious motive or factor that explains something the patient has been talking about, but most of the work is done by the patient herself.

The patient is understandably reluctant to reveal painful feelings and to examine lifelong patterns that need to be changed, and as the analysis proceeds, she is likely to unconsciously try to hold back the flow of information. This phenomenon—in fact, any behavior that impedes the course of therapy—is called **resistance.** The patient may have agreed to cooperate fully, yet she finds at times that her mind is blank, that she feels powerless and can no longer think of anything to say. At such times the analyst will simply point out what is happening and wait for the patient to continue. The analyst may also suggest another line of approach to the area of resistance. By analyzing the patient's resistances, both the therapist and the patient can understand how the patient deals with anxiety-provoking material.

Sooner or later, the analyst begins to appear in the patient's associations and dreams. The patient may begin feeling toward the analyst the way she feels toward some other important figure in her life. This process is called **transference.**

If the patient can recognize what is happening, transference may allow her to experience her true feelings toward the important person. But often, instead of experiencing and understanding her feelings, the patient simply begins acting toward the therapist in the same way she used to act toward the important person, usually one of her parents.

The therapist does not allow the patient to resort to these tactics. Remaining impersonal and anonymous, the therapist always directs the patient back to herself. The therapist may ask, for example, "What do you see when you imagine my face?" The patient may reply that she sees the ther-

CONNECTIONS: PSYCHOLOGY AND ART

Tell students that psychoanalytic methods encourage patients to report their dreams and then free-associate on their meaning. The therapist uses these associations for clues into the patient's subconscious. Request a volunteer to bring into class a copy of either *The Nightmare,* by John Henry Fuseli, or *The* *Dream,* by Max Beckman. Request a volunteer to free-associate on the images called up by this nightmare/dream. Challenge the rest of the class to form opinions on what, if anything, they can infer from these associations.

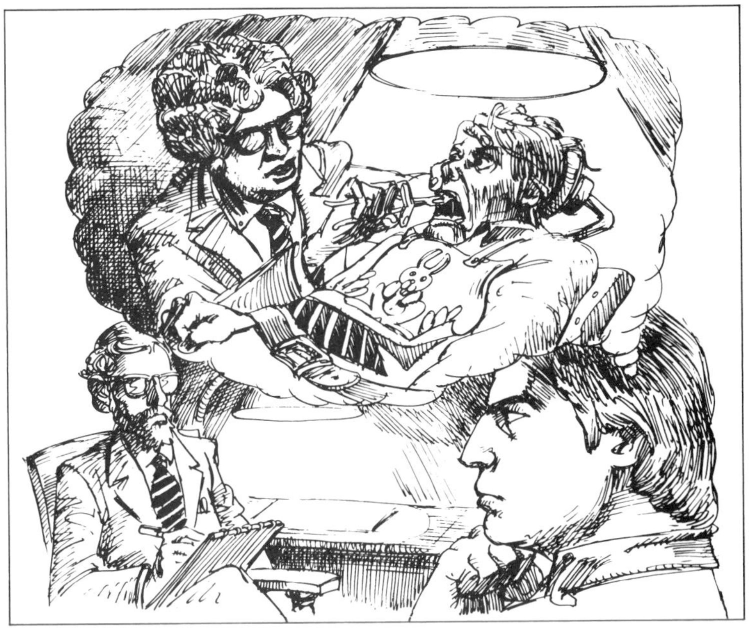

FIGURE 16.2

The patient's resistance is shown in the fact that he is seeing the therapist as a menacing dentist. At the same time, the "dentist" seems to him like an impersonal frightening mother. **What is transference?**

apist as an angry, frowning, unpleasant figure. The therapist never takes this personally. Instead, he may calmly say, "What does this make you think of?" Gradually, it will become clear to both patient and therapist that the patient is reacting to the neutral therapist as though he were a threatening father.

By understanding why she is engaging in transference, the patient becomes aware of her real feelings and motivations. She may begin to understand, for example, why she has trouble with her boss at work: she may be seeing her boss, her therapist—and indeed any man in a position of authority—in the same way that as a child she saw her father.

Existential/Humanist Therapies

Humanistic psychology has given rise to several new approaches to psychotherapy, known collectively as the **human potential movement.** We discussed these schools of psychology in Chapter 11. To review, humanistic psychologists stress the actualization of one's unique potentials through personal responsibility, freedom of choice, and authentic relationships.

Person-centered Therapy. **Person-centered therapy** is based on the theories of Carl Rogers (1951, 1977; see Chapter 11). The use of the term "person" or "client" instead of "patient" gives one an insight into the reasoning behind Rogers's method. "Patient" may suggest inferiority, whereas "person" or "client" implies an equal relationship between the therapist and the individual seeking help.

VISUAL INSTRUCTION

Have students cover up the caption. Ask them to identify examples of resistance and transference in the drawing.

Answer to caption, Figure 16.2: process, experienced by the patient, of feeling toward an analyst or therapist the way he or she feels toward some other important figure in his or her life

■ **Representing Ideas Visually.** Write the names of the different approaches to treatment mentioned in the text on 3 x 5 cards. Organize the students into groups, and give each group one of the cards. Tell the students to draw sketches showing the setting in which each of these therapies might occur. Special attention should be given to the position and/or attitude of the therapist. Ask each group to show its sketch, and have the rest of the class guess the therapy shown. (OBJECTIVES 2, 3)

LAB EXPERIMENTS AND DEMONSTRATIONS

To illustrate the listening-talking interchange that takes place during psychoanalysis, divide the class into pairs. Direct one student to play the part of the listener. For three minutes, the student should silently pay attention to everything the other student says. Direct the listener to keep eye contact and to make no judgments or facial expressions. When the three minutes are up, have students change roles. In a follow-up discussion, ask students to share how they felt in each role. For example, how did the talker respond to having someone's undivided attention—with discomfort or with a feeling of importance?

VISUAL INSTRUCTION

Without reading the caption, ask students if they can identify the type of therapist in this picture. After reading the caption, request volunteers to compare the role of a therapist in an encounter group with the role of a therapist in psychoanalysis. **Answer to caption, Figure 16.3:** the attitude of emotional support provided by the therapist in person-centered therapy

Teacher Note. Rogers originally called his therapy *client-centered.* He later changed it to *person-centered* to indicate his belief that the same principles employed in counseling applied to all human interactions.

■ **Discussion.** Tell students that a *person-centered* therapist often uses the expression "I hear you" during therapy sessions. Ask: Why do you think this phrase is an important part of the humanistic approach to counseling? *(Lead students to understand that therapists use the phrase to validate the importance of what a person has said. They also use the phrase to mirror back a conversation to avoid miscommunication.)*

Person-centered therapists assume that people are basically good and that they are capable of handling their own lives. Psychological problems arise when the true self becomes lost and the individual comes to view himself according to the standards of others. One of the goals of therapy, therefore, is to help him recognize his own strength and confidence so that he can learn to be true to his own standards and ideas about how to live effectively.

In the course of an interview, the client is encouraged to speak freely about intimate matters that may be bothering him. He is told that what he talks about is up to him. The therapist listens and encourages conversation but tries to avoid giving opinions. Instead, she tries to echo back as clearly as possible the feelings the client has expressed. She may try to extract the

FIGURE 16.3

Many encounter group leaders feel that their role in the group is the same as that of any other member. Only if the group as a whole or any one of its members gets into trouble will the leader intervene to rescue the situation. Typically, other group members will exhibit leadership or therapeutic skills and the designated leader will remain in the background. **What is unconditional positive regard?**

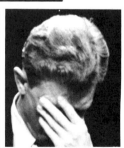

CRITICAL THINKING ACTIVITY

Developing Empathy. Request volunteers to write a mock transcript from a person-centered therapy session. (If possible, have students locate an actual transcript from a collection of case studies to use as a model.) Then divide the class into pairs, and distribute copies of the transcript. Instruct students to role-play the session. Explore the feelings experienced by the "patient." Next, assign volunteers to rewrite the transcript from the perspective of another therapy approach. (This will take a day or two.) Using the new transcripts, conduct another role play, *(continued on page 401)*

main points from the client's hesitant or rambling explanations. For example, a male client may tell a long story about an incident with his father, and the therapist may respond by saying, "This kind of thing makes you feel very stupid." The client may in turn say, "No, not stupid, angry. It's really he who is being stupid." And the therapist will say, "Oh, I see, you really feel angry at him when he acts this way." Between them, they form a clearer and clearer picture of how the client really feels about himself, his life, and the people around him.

Person-centered therapy is conducted in an atmosphere of emotional support that Rogers calls **unconditional positive regard.** As in psychoanalysis, the therapist never says that she thinks the client or what the client has said is good or bad. But she shows the client that she will accept anything that is said without embarrassment, reservation, or anger. The therapist's main responsibility is creating a warm and accepting relationship between herself and her client.

This acceptance makes it easier for the client to explore thoughts about himself and his experiences. He is able to abandon old values without fear of disapproval, and he can begin to see himself, his situation, and his relationships with others in a new light.

As he reduces his tensions and releases his emotions, the client feels that he is becoming a more complete person. He gains the courage to accept parts of his personality that he had formerly considered weak or bad, and, by recognizing his self-worth, he can set up realistic goals and consider the steps necessary to reach them. The client's movement toward independence signals the end of the need for therapy—he can assume the final steps to independence on his own.

Existential Therapy.   Like Rogers, all therapists in the human potential movement see their role as helping individuals to achieve self-determination. Existential therapists believe that for most people, freedom and autonomy are threatening. To acknowledge that you are a unique and independent person is to acknowledge that you are alone. These therapists argue that many people avoid this realization unconsciously, burying their feelings and desires. Therapists like Rollo May (1969, 1975, 1977) attempt to help patients overcome the fear of freedom, get in touch with their true feelings, and accept responsibility for their lives.

Viktor Frankl (1970) is also an existentialist, but approaches therapy somewhat differently. After listening to a patient express despair, he might ask, "Why don't you commit suicide?" Frankl is not being cruel or sarcastic. He is trying to help the individual find meaning in life. The patient's answer (whether it is "my husband and children," "my religion," or "my work") provides clues about what the person values.

In Frankl's view, feelings of emptiness and boredom are the primary source of emotional problems.

Mental health is based on a certain degree of tension between what one has already achieved and what one still ought to accomplish, or the gap between what one is and what one should become. Such a tension is inherent in the human being and is therefore indispensable to mental well-

MORE about. . .

Carl Rogers and Unconditional Positive Regard. One of the fundamental aspects of Carl Rogers's person-centered therapy (originally called "client-centered therapy) is to show the client unconditional positive regard. However, this ideal is difficult to reach in practice.

Rogers was not content merely to theorize about psychological processes. He believed in conducting research to verify his hypotheses. To that end he often recorded therapy sessions he conducted (with the client's permission, of course), so that his methods could be studied scientifically. One of his students, Charles Truax, did just that.

Truax analyzed Rogers's responses to a client during the course of therapy. He found that Rogers displayed frequent verbal and nonverbal reinforcements to statements that indicated optimism or self-assuredness. He provided relatively few reinforcements after the client complained of symptoms and frustrations.

It seems that there is a strong pull to support ideas we agree with and to ignore those we disagree with. Apparently, even the master of unconditional positive reinforcement is not immune from this motive.

■ **Forming Hypotheses.**
Focus on the use of the term *hypothesis* in the second paragraph of the margin feature. Then read aloud the following description by Neal Miller (1972) on the state of mind necessary for forming a hypothesis:

I am quite freewheeling and intuitive—follow hunches, vary procedures, try out wild ideas, and take short-cuts. During it [the hypothesis stage], *I am usually not interested in elaborate controls.*

Ask: How would Miller define a hypothesis? *(Answers will vary, but students might say as an original thought or theory about a problem.)* Do students agree with his approach to forming a hypothesis? Why or why not? *(You might encourage students to review the data on creativity in Chapter 3.)* According to the feature, what stage comes next? *(verifying the hypothesis)* Why might controls be necessary at this stage? *(to ensure the accuracy of data collection)*
(OBJECTIVES 1–3)

CRITICAL THINKING ACTIVITY

using the same pairs and same "patients." Challenge students to compare the different emotions, thoughts, and/or resistance evoked by the two different

therapies. Which did each "patient" prefer? Why?

PORTRAIT

Rollo May
1909–

Rollo May pioneered the humanistic psychology movement. May also took the lead in introducing European *existentialism* to the United States. He derived his ideas from philosophers such as Sören Kierkegaard, Friedrich Nietzsche, Edmund Husserl, and Martin Heidegger.

The German name for existential psychiatry is *Daseinanalysis*. The rough translation of *Dasein* is "being-in-the-world." As defined by May, the person develops a sense of "being-in-the-world" by abandoning a state of helplessness and embracing life as it exists. As practiced by May and other existential psychologists, mental health rests upon a self-determined personality.

■ **Analyzing a Quote.** Read aloud the "The Gestalt Prayer," by Fritz Perls (1969):

I do my thing, and you do your thing.
I am not in this world to live up to your expectations
And you are not in this world to live up to mine.
You are you and I am I.
And if we find each other, it's beautiful.
If not, it can't be helped.

Ask: How does this "prayer" illustrate the principles of Gestalt mentioned in the text? It has been said that these lines reflected Perls' belief in the Golden Rule. Do you agree? (OBJECTIVE 3)

MORE about...

Irrational Thinking. Albert Ellis (1961) asserts that the irrational ideas we believe stand in the way of achieving lives that are free of anxiety. Some of the most common irrational beliefs identified by Ellis are:

Everything I do must be approved and loved by virtually everybody.

I have to be completely competent, totally in control and successful in everything I do.

It is catastrophic when things are not going the way I want them to go.

My unhappiness is not my fault. People and events over which I have no control are responsible.

Any time I encounter something that I fear, I need to be consumed with worries and be upset about it.

It is easier to avoid life's difficulties and responsibilities than to develop a better system for meeting them.

My life and the people with whom I work should be changed from the way they are.

The best I can do for myself is to relax and enjoy life. Inaction and passivity are the best bet to maximize my own enjoyment.

Ellis believes we need to overcome each of these false assumptions to move toward rational living.

being . . . .What people actually need is not a tensionless state but rather the striving and struggling for some worthy goal (1970, pp. 165–166).

Frankl believes a therapist should help to open the patient's eyes to the possibilities in life and guide him or her toward challenges.

Gestalt Therapy. Developed by Fritz Perls in the 1950s and 1960s, **gestalt therapy** emphasizes the relationship between the patient and therapist in the here and now (Perls, Hefferline, and Goodman, 1965). Suppose that toward the middle of a session a patient runs out of problems to discuss and sits mute, staring blankly out the window. Instead of waiting for the patient to speak up, a gestalt therapist would say what he feels. "I can't stand the way you just sit there and say nothing. This is very frustrating for me. You are impossible. . . . There, now I feel better" (Kempler, 1973, p. 272). The therapist is not blowing off steam in an unprofessional way. He does this to encourage (by example) the patient to express his feelings, even if it means risking a relationship.

Gestalt therapy is based on the belief that many individuals are so concerned with obtaining approval that they become strangers to themselves. For example, an individual may always defer to authority figures, but he may be detached from the part of himself that has fantasies of rebelling. Neither part acknowledges the other. Gestalt therapists attempt to help a person fit the pieces together. The word *gestalt* comes from the German word for "form" or "shape."

Transactional Analysis. Introduced by Eric Berne (1964) in the early 1950s, **transactional analysis** is both a theory of personality and a method of therapy. The central assumption of transactional analysis (often referred to as TA) is that people function and experience their world from one of three perspectives, or ego states. **Ego states** represent the ways people organize their thoughts, feelings, and actions. Sometimes adults think, feel, and act from a *child ego* state. For example, a man who has been stopped by a police officer for speeding may feel and act as he did when he was a boy and was caught doing something wrong by his parents. Other times, people may act, think, and feel like one of their parents, close friends, or teachers—from a *parent ego* state. For example, a person who acts in a judgmental and opinionated way is most likely functioning from the parent ego state.

The *adult ego* state represents people's thoughts, feelings, and behaviors that are rationally related to their experience of the present. Reactions in the child or parent ego states are shaped and sometimes distorted by past experiences with other people. Reactions in the adult ego state allow people to deal effectively and responsibly with their everyday problems.

If a friend tells you "you should carry an umbrella today—it might rain," he or she is probably speaking from a parent ego state. If you say or think "Mind your own business," you are probably reacting from a child ego state. What would an adult ego state reaction be? It would be to look around and see whether it looks like rain and act accordingly.

STUDY AND WRITING SKILLS

Repeat a Lakota saying to students: "Today is a good day to die." Explain that this was not a death wish. Instead, it was a reminder to live well—as if the day might be the last. Ask: How does this attitude reflect the thinking of existential psychology? (*Both Rollo May and Victor Frankl emphasized the importance of a life lived meaningfully.*) Next, tell students to imagine they had a second chance to begin life anew. What three things would they change, intensify, or keep the same? Request volunteers to share their list. Ask: How might this approach to life open one's eyes to new possibilities?

Berne believed that these three personality parts develop through people's interactions with significant people in their lives. Furthermore, he believed that while people are growing up they develop specific plans that define how they will act toward other people and how other people are expected to act toward them. People learn to "play games" or engage in predictable exchanges with other people to fit their life plan.

One goal of the TA therapist is to help people identify maladaptive transactions or strategies for living (usually from the parent or child ego state). Another is to help them develop more effective adult ego state responses. The TA therapist usually begins therapy by establishing a contract with the client. The contract states what the client wants to change and what the therapist will or will not do to help the client achieve his or her goal.

One woman sought TA therapy to help her deal with her relations with men. She found that on a first date with someone, she would always make a point of saying that she just wanted to be friends, but then she would act in a flirtatious way that gave the opposite impression. If the man made a pass at her, she would be outraged. By exploring and discussing her behavior with the therapist, she discovered that she had been playing games from her child ego state. This insight helped her recognize what she wanted in her relationships, and helped her learn how to behave. In most cases, transactional analysis focuses on the individual's assuming responsibility for his or her actions (Holland, 1973). This theory had tremendous appeal, especially to the public, when it first appeared. However, it is not used as widely now, having been supplanted by forms of cognitive therapy.

Cognitive Therapies

Until the mid-1960s, the emphasis of most therapies was on changing people's external behavior. Since that time, however, this has changed. Unlike behavior therapists who attempt to change external behavior, cognitive therapists focus on changing the way people think (Beck, 1991). Basic assumptions that cognitive therapies share are that faulty cognitions—our irrational or uninformed beliefs, expectations, and ways of thinking—distort our actions, attitudes, and emotions, and, in order to improve our lives, we need to change our thinking patterns.

In what other ways are cognitive therapies similar? According to Ross (1977), all these theories follow one or more of the 3 principles: disconfirmation, reconceptualization, and insight. *Disconfirmation* means clients may be confronted with evidence that directly contradicts their existing beliefs. In *reconceptualization*, clients work toward an alternative belief system to explain their experiences or current observations. In *insight*, clients work toward understanding how they derived these new or revised beliefs.

Rational-Emotive Therapy. **Rational-emotive therapy (RET)** is a form of therapy developed by Albert Ellis in the late 1950s (Ellis, 1973). Ellis believes that people behave in deliberate and rational ways, given their

---

CRITICAL THINKING ACTIVITY

Analyzing a Quote. Read aloud the following selection from an interview with Albert Ellis printed in *Psychology Today.*

Patients temporarily felt better from all the talk and attention but didn't seem to get better. . . . I began to wonder why I had to wait passively for weeks or months until a client showed . . . his or her own interpretive initiative. . . . Why . . . couldn't I help them with some pointed questions or remarks? So I began to become more eclectic.

Ask: Why did Ellis question psychoanalysis? What is an eclectic approach to therapy? In what ways is RET different from psychoanalysis?

CHAPTER 16 Lesson Plan

■ **Writing a Contract.** With the class, recall some of the situations that cause stress in teenagers. (See Chapter 13.) List these on the chalkboard. Then organize the class into groups, and assign each group one of these situations. Next, tell students to imagine they have entered transactional analysis to find ways of dealing with this situation more effectively. Assign students to write a contract that might be drawn up between themselves and a TA therapist. *(Contracts should follow the guidelines established on this page. They should also reflect the principles of TA therapy.)*

■ **Analyzing Information.** Berne believed that children acquired feelings about themselves between ages 3–7 and that these feelings served as a script for later life. The script, said Berne, rested upon the way children saw their position in relation to others. The four main positions included:

1. I'm not O.K.—You're O.K.
2. I'm not O.K.—You're not O.K.
3. I'm O.K.—You're not O.K.
4. I'm O.K.—You're O.K.

Challenge students to speculate on some of the development problems faced by children in the first three positions. What techniques might Berne or a TA therapist employ to "rewrite the script" so that a person sees himself or herself from the fourth position? Is the fourth position that of a child, parent, or adult? *(adult)* (OBJECTIVE 3)

▬ **Enrich.** Have students complete the Chapter 16 Application Activity.

Teacher Note. You might tell students about some of the following additional approaches to therapy.

- *Morita therapy.* Developed in Japan and based on Zen; begins by having a patient stay in bed 4–7 days in isolation; thereafter, therapy focuses on the patient directing his or her thoughts to the here-and-now of the outside world.
- *Ordeal therapy.* Assigns a patient a more difficult task than the one faced.
- *Primal therapy.* Requires a patient to let go of infantile rage through screaming.
- *Paradoxical therapy.* Pushes patient to keep doing, or even step up, troubling behavior to force a break-through.
- *Orgone therapy.* Has a patient sit in a box and concentrate on absorbing the energy from a benevolent universe.
- *Miscellaneous therapies.* Dozens of others such as: dance therapy, miracles therapy, and so on.

Challenge students to explore why these fringe therapies may work for some people. *(e.g., gives the patient a sense of taking some action to provoke a change)*

assumptions about life. Emotional problems arise when an individual's assumptions are unrealistic.

Suppose a man seeks therapy when a woman leaves him. He cannot stand the fact that she has rejected him. Without her his life is empty and miserable. She has made him feel utterly worthless. He must get her back. An RET therapist would not look for incidents in the past that are making the present unbearable for this man, as a psychoanalyst would. RET therapists do not probe; they reason. Like a spoiled child, the man is demanding that the woman love him. He expects—indeed, insists—that things will always go his way. Given this assumption, the only possible explanation for her behavior is that something is dreadfully wrong, either with him or with her.

What is wrong, in the therapist's view, is the man's thinking. By defining his feelings for the woman as need rather than desire, he—not she—is causing his depression. When you convince yourself that you need someone, you will in fact be unable to carry on without that person. When you believe that you cannot stand rejection, you will in fact fall apart when you encounter rejection.

The goal of rational-emotive therapy is to correct these false and self-defeating beliefs. Rejection is unpleasant, but it is not unbearable. The woman may be very desirable, but she is not irreplaceable. To teach the individual to think in realistic terms, the RET therapist may use a number of techniques. One is role playing so that the person can see how his beliefs affect his relationships. Another technique is modeling to demonstrate other ways of thinking and acting. A third is humor to underline the absurdity of his beliefs. Still another technique is simple persuasion. The therapist may also make homework assignments to give the man practice in acting more reasonably. For example, the therapist may instruct him to ask women who are likely to reject him out on dates. Why? So that he will learn that he can cope with things not going his way.

Ellis believes that the individual must take three steps to cure or correct himself. First, he must realize that some of his assumptions are false. Second, he must see that he is making *himself* disturbed by acting on false beliefs. Finally, he must work to break old habits of thought and behavior. He has to practice, to learn self-discipline, to take risks.

Cognitive-Behavioral Therapy. Aaron T. Beck (1970, 1967) first introduced a form of cognitive therapy that is similar to Ellis's rational emotive therapy. The primary difference is Beck's insistence that therapists—through using persuasion and logic to change existing beliefs—also encourage clients to engage in actual tests of their own beliefs, consistent with Ross's principle of disconfirmation. Behavioral assignments for a client include homework, organized as experiments to allow the client to assess the truth value of his or her beliefs. Therapists also develop alternate belief systems—other explanations for the client's current beliefs—representing Ross's principle of reconceptualization, often as a set-up for the "experiment" the client is to do at home. Finally, cognitive therapists focus on the client's distortions in processing information—an application of Ross's principle of insight (Hollon & Beck, 1986).

Behavior therapists believe a disturbed person has learned to behave in the wrong way.

COOPERATIVE LEARNING ACTIVITY

Request a volunteer to compile a list of all the different therapists mentioned in the text. Then assign students to represent each one of these people. Conduct a mock panel discussion in which members of the class pose questions about the therapists' various approaches to treatment, attitudes toward patients, and expected time frame for change.

FIGURE 16.4

The behavior therapy approach to the treatment of infantile autism involves the use of contingency management, also known as operant conditioning (see Chapter 2). The therapist rewards the child with affection for performing desirable activities. Unfortunately, the early success measures reported using behavior modification techniques were not maintained by the children once formal behavior modification techniques were terminated. Haloperidol, a medicine used to treat schizophrenia, has removed some symptoms, but the basic problems remain. As children with autism age, more and more permanently end up in institutions. At this time, there is no broadly effective therapeutic strategy that works. **In what other settings is contingency management used?**

Behavior Therapies

Psychoanalysis and the human potential movement have sometimes been criticized for being "all talk and no action." In **behavior therapy** there is much more emphasis on action. Rather than spending large amounts of time going into the patient's past history or the details of his or her dreams, the behavior therapist concentrates on finding out what is specifically wrong with the patient's current life and takes steps to change it.

The idea behind behavior therapy is that a disturbed person is one who has *learned* to behave in the wrong way. The therapist's job, therefore, is to "reeducate" the patient. The reasons for the patient's undesirable behavior are not important; what is important is to change the behavior. To bring about such changes, the therapist uses certain conditioning techniques first discovered in animal laboratories.

One technique used by behavior therapists is **systematic desensitization.** This method is used to overcome irrational fears and anxieties the patient has learned (Smith, 1990). The goal of desensitization therapy is to encourage people to imagine the feared situation while relaxing, thus extinguishing the fear response. For example, suppose a student is terrified of speaking in front of large groups—that, in fact, his stage fright is so tremendous that he is unable to speak when called upon in class. How would desensitization therapy effectively change this person's behavior?

The therapist might have the student make a list of all the aspects of talking to others that he finds frightening. Perhaps the most frightening aspect

■ **Demonstration.** You might request a volunteer to perform the steps in desensitization as described in the text. Have the "subject" name a situation that he or she finds frightening, such as riding in an airplane, taking a test, or going out on a date. On a large sheet of paper, have the student draw a ladder. Direct him or her to rank items associated with the situation chosen, recording the most fearful on the top rung and the least fearful on the bottom rung. Then, lower the lights and use relaxation techniques suggested in Chapter 7 to relax the student. Then have the subject visualize each rung on the ladder and talk his or her way up. When the demonstration is over, ask the subject to describe the experience. Or, if possible, have the subject report back when he or she actually faces the fear. What, if any, effect did desensitization have? (OBJECTIVE 3)

DID YOU KNOW?

More than 16 million Americans seek mental health treatment each year. The majority of people who need treatment, however, never go.

? FACT OR FICTION

■ *Behaviorists are cold and manipulative.*

Fiction. Many popular portrayals depict behaviorists as cold, unfeeling scientists. But surveys show the opposite. Clients consistently rate behaviorist therapists as equally or more caring than their colleagues. Perhaps their focus on topics of immediate concern to the client contributes to this impression.

is actually standing before an audience, whereas the least frightening is speaking to a single other person. The client ranks his fears, from the most frightening on down. Then, the therapist begins teaching the patient to relax. Once he knows how to relax completely, the client is ready for the next step. The client tries to imagine as vividly as possible the least disturbing scene on his list. As he thinks about speaking to a single stranger, the student may feel a mild anxiety. But because the therapist has taught him how to relax, the patient learns to think about the experience without feeling afraid. The basic logic is that a person cannot feel anxious and relaxed at the same time. The therapist attempts to replace anxiety with its opposite, relaxation, through counterconditioning.

This procedure is followed step by step through the list of anxiety-arousing events. The patient reaches a point where he is able to imagine the situations that threaten him the most without feeling anxiety. Now the therapist starts to expose the person to real-life situations that have previously frightened him. Therapy finally reaches the point where the student is able to deliver an unrehearsed speech before a full auditorium.

Another form of behavior therapy is called **contingency management.** In this method the therapist and patient decide what old, undesirable behavior needs to be eliminated and what new, desirable behavior needs to appear (Figure 16.4). Arrangements are then made for the old behavior to go unrewarded and for the desired behavior to be reinforced. In its simplest form, contingency management consists of the therapist agreeing with the patient, "If you do X, I will give you Y." This form of agreement is similar to systems of reward that people often use on themselves or parents use on children. For instance, a student may say to himself, "If I get a good grade on the exam, I'll treat myself to a great dinner." The reward is *contingent* (dependent) upon getting a good grade.

Contingency management is used in prisons, mental hospitals, schools, and army bases, as well as with individual patients. In these situations it is possible to set up whole miniature systems of rewards, called token economies. For example, psychologists in some mental hospitals select behavior they judge desirable. Patients are then rewarded for these behaviors with "hospital," or token, money. Thus if a patient cleans his room or works in the hospital garden, he is rewarded with token money. The patients are able to cash in their token money for things they want, such as candy or cigarettes, for certain privileges, such as time away from the ward. These methods are successful in inducing mental patients to begin leading active lives. They learn to take care of themselves and to take on responsibility instead of having to be cared for constantly.

Group Therapies

In the forms of therapy described thus far, the troubled person is usually alone with the therapist. In **group therapy,** however, she is in the company of others. There are several advantages to this situation. Group therapy gives the troubled person practical experience with one of her biggest problems—getting along with other people. A person in group therapy also has a chance to see how other people are struggling with problems similar to

LAB EXPERIMENTS AND DEMONSTRATIONS

Review the behavioral approach to therapy, with emphasis upon contingency management. Then divide the class into small groups. Have one member from each group volunteer a bad habit that he or she would like to change. Challenge the rest of the group to develop a reward/reinforcement schedule that will help break this habit. If any volunteers choose to try the program, have them regularly report their progress to the class. (At some point, you might explore how these reports serve as a positive or negative stressor.)

FIGURE 16.5

Therapists use various techniques to get the members of a group therapy session to help one another see themselves and others more clearly. **What are advantages to group therapy?**

FIGURE 16.6

In a family therapy session, the therapist observes the interactions in order to discern, describe, and treat the patterns that contribute to the disturbance of one or more of its members. **What does a skilled therapist provide in a family therapy session?**

her own, and she discovers what other people think of her. She, in turn, can express what she thinks of them, and in this exchange she discovers where she is mistaken in her views of herself and of other people and where she is correct (Drum, 1990).

Another advantage to group therapy is the fact that one therapist can help a large number of people. Most group-therapy sessions are led by a trained therapist who makes suggestions, clarifies points, and keeps activ-

---

VISUAL INSTRUCTION

Ask students to compare Figures 16.5 and 16.6. What do the types of therapy share in common? *(Most students will emphasize the importance of social interaction and the presence of a therapist as a member of both groups.)*
Answer to caption, Figure 16.5: gives a troubled person practical experience in getting along with others; gets a chance to see how others are struggling with similar problems; receives feedback from peers; offers therapist a chance to help a large number of people
Answer to caption, Figure 16.6: points out what is wrong from an objective viewpoint and can suggest ways of improving communication and fairness within the family

Teacher Note. Another benefit of group therapy is its low cost. Because a number of patients contribute to the therapist's fee, counseling is within financial reach of more people.

ADDITIONAL INFORMATION

Tell students about two distinct approaches to family therapy.

- *Conjoint family therapy.* Therapist places emphasis on self-esteem of all family members and on improving interpersonal relationships.
- *Structural family therapy.* Therapist attempts to modify the organization-

al structure of the family.

Review the types of family structures mentioned in Chapter 9 (authoritarian, democratic, permissive/laissez-faire). Ask: Which approach to family therapy might a therapist use to treat each of these types of families? Why?

Researchers have cited 11 factors that help make group therapy effective (Yalom, 1985). Distribute a copy of these factors to students.

- *Hope.* Instills hope that change is possible.
- *Universality.* Relieves feelings of uniqueness—and often shame—when others talk about similar problems.
- *Information.* Provides data about the disorder and corrective behavior from both the therapist and group members.
- *Altruism.* Shows that clients have something to offer to others.
- *Corrective recreation of primary family.* Provides a new kind of "family" to help heal wounds.
- *Social skills.* Corrects interpersonal flaws through group feedback.
- *Modeling.* Offers examples of new behavior.
- *Interpersonal learning.* Offers a "social laboratory" to try out a "new self."
- *Group cohesiveness.* Imparts a sense of "belonging."
- *Catharsis.* Allows people to express feelings and vulnerability.
- *Existential factors.* Teaches that ultimately each person must address his or her own problems.

Ask students what three factors would be *most* important to them if they entered group therapy. Have them weigh group therapy against individual therapy. Which do they find most attractive? **Answer to caption, Figure 16.7:** role playing, speaking, effective leadership, etc. (OBJECTIVE 4)

ities from getting out of hand. In this way, her training and experience are used to help as many as 20 people at once, although 8-10 is a more comfortable number.

Family Therapy.   Therapists often suggest, after talking to a patient, that the entire family unit should work at group therapy. This method is particularly useful because the members of the group are all people of great importance in one another's lives. In **family therapy** it is possible to untangle the twisted web of relationships that have led one or more members in the family to experience emotional suffering.

Often family members are unhappy because they are mistreating or are being mistreated by other family members in ways no one understands or wants to talk about. The family therapist can point out what is going wrong from an objective viewpoint and can suggest ways of improving communication and fairness in the family.

Not all group therapies are run by professionals, however. Some of the most successful examples are provided in nonprofessional organizations, such as self-help groups.

Self-Help Groups.   An increasing number of **self-help groups** have emerged in recent years. These voluntary groups, composed of people who share a particular problem, are often conducted without the active involvement of a professional therapist. During regularly scheduled meetings, members of the group come together to discuss their difficulties and to provide support and possible solutions.

FIGURE 16.7

The purpose of an encounter group session is to provide experiences that will help people to live more intense lives; the methods used are intended to increase sensitivity, openness, and honesty. **What are common techniques used in encounter group sessions?**

Request volunteers to visit bookstores and libraries to compile a list of some of the self-help books currently available. Assign them to prepare an annotated bibliography of as many of these titles as possible. Annotations should explain the purpose and approach of the book. Direct students to bind their collection of titles into a class reference entitled: "Patient, Heal Thyself." Use this reference to explore the benefits and drawbacks of self-help as a form of therapy.

Self-help groups have been formed to deal with problems ranging from alcoholism, overeating, and drug addiction, to child abuse, widowhood, single parenting, adjusting to cancer, and gambling. The best known self-help group is Alcoholics Anonymous (AA) which was founded in 1935. Far more people find treatment for their drinking problems through AA than in psychotherapy or treatment centers. Many self-help groups have based their organizations on the AA model in which individual members can call on other members for help and emotional support.

The purpose of Alcoholics Anonymous is "to carry the AA message to the sick alcoholic who wants it." According to AA, the only way for alcoholics to change is to admit publicly that they are powerless over alcohol and that their lives have become unmanageable. Alcoholics must come to believe that only some power greater than themselves can help them. Those who think they can battle out the problem alone will not be successful.

Members of AA usually meet at least once a week to discuss the meaning of this message, to talk about their experiences with alcohol, and to describe the new hope they have found with AA. Mutual encouragement, friendship, and an emphasis on personal responsibility are used to keep an individual sober.

Encounter Groups.   The power of group interaction to affect and change people gave rise to the controversial **encounter group.** Encounter groups are primarily for people who function adequately in everyday life but who, for some reason, feel unhappy, dissatisfied, or stagnant.

The purpose of encounter groups (which are also known as T-groups or sensitivity training) is to provide experiences that will help people live more intense lives. Being in a small group (between 7 and 20 people) for this express purpose is bound to teach an individual something about interpersonal relations. Techniques are often used in groups to overcome the restrictions people live by in everyday life. A typical exercise requires each person to say something to every other person and at the same time to touch him or her in some way. Such methods are intended to increase sensitivity, openness, and honesty.

Role playing is another common encounter-group technique. It is a form of theater in which the goal is to help people expose and understand themselves. A person may try acting out the role of a character in one of his dreams; another person may pretend to be herself as a child talking to her mother, played by another member. By switching roles and placing themselves in each other's situation, group members are better able to see themselves as others see them. The advice, the support, the common basis for understanding the good and the bad in one another, and the seeking of higher, more mature levels of development can make such groups very helpful (Galanter, 1990).

Key to a group functioning well is its leader. Some group members, unprepared for the intense emotional exposure that may occur, have suffered long-lasting psychological distress. It is important to have leaders sensitive to the long-term implications of the group's activities who are prepared to deal with these possibilities.

MORE about...

Self-Help Groups. Founded in 1935, Alcoholics Anonymous (AA) was the first of a vast number of self-help groups now formed and functioning. One of the unique features of AA is its 12-step program that members are encouraged to learn and practice.

The Twelve Steps of Alcoholics Anonymous

1. We admitted we were powerless over alcohol—that our lives had become unmanageable.
2. Came to believe that a Power greater than ourselves could restore us to sanity.
3. Made a decision to turn our will and our lives over to the care of God *as we understood Him.*
4. Made a searching and fearless moral inventory of ourselves.
5. Admitted to God, to ourselves, and to another human being the exact nature of our wrongs.
6. Were entirely ready to have God remove all these defects of character.
7. Humbly asked Him to remove our shortcomings.

(Continued on page 410)

Teacher Note. Before reading the Twelve Steps, tell students that AA is not a religion. Nor does it require members to hold any established religious beliefs. (The program states: "The only requirement for membership is a desire to stop drinking.") It uses the word "God" to stand for a "Higher Power," a force that can remove the obsession of alcohol.

■ **Analyzing Information.** Organize the students in small groups, and have them find features in the Twelve Steps that correspond with one or more of the therapies mentioned in this book. Request members to share their findings. In a follow-up discussion, tell students that AA is the most popular—and most successful—form of self-help for alcoholics. Most rehabilitation centers suggest strongly that people enter AA as part of their recovery. Challenge students to speculate on reasons for the program's success. (OBJECTIVE 4)

WORKING WITH TRANSPARENCIES

Project Transparency 26 and use the guidelines provided in Teaching Strategies and Activities. Assign Student Worksheet 26.

CONNECTIONS: PSYCHOLOGY AND THE MEDIA

Tell students that one form of drug therapy employs the use of a video camera. The patient sits alone and talks to the camera about his or her addiction problem for up to 30 minutes. The patient and therapist later view the video together. Then the patient views it alone. Challenge students to explore how this technique promotes acceptance and responsibility for drug addiction. Why is this acceptance necessary for recovery?

Independent Practice

■ **Debating an Issue.** "I feel so normal that I have to use tricks to remember whether I've taken it," says one user of Prozac. But not all Prozac users have the same reaction. Some have reported bouts of insomnia, violent behavior, and suicidal thoughts. Tell students at one time Prozac was considered the "wonder drug" of psychotherapy. Many therapists thought—and still do—that it was the key to unlocking severe chronic depression. Request volunteers to research the Prozac controversy, including a 1991 petition to ban the drug (which the FDA turned down). Suggest that students use the *Readers' Guide to Periodical Literature* to locate some of the articles written about the drug in the last few years. Based on this research, have students formally debate the following topic: *Resolved*—That Prozac is a good drug with serious side effects for only a minority of people.

Instruct the rest of the class to take down points made by each side. Using this information, assign them to write essays expressing their opinion on the Prozac controversy. (OBJECTIVE 1)

MORE about. . .

8. Made a list of all persons we had harmed and became willing to make amends to them all.
9. Made direct amends to such people wherever possible, except when to do so would injure them or others.
10. Continued to take moral inventory and when we were wrong promptly admitted it.
11. Sought through prayer and meditation to improve our conscious contact with God *as we understood Him,* praying only for knowledge of His will for us and the power to carry that out.
12. Having had a spiritual awakening as a result of these steps, we tried to carry this message to alcoholics, and to practice these principles in all our affairs.

BIOLOGICAL APPROACHES TO TREATMENT

The various "talking" and "learning" therapies described so far in this chapter have been aimed primarily at patients who are still generally capable of functioning within society. But what of those people who are not capable of clear thinking or who are dangerous to themselves or others? For a long time the most common method of keeping dangerous or overactive schizophrenic patients in check was physical restraint—the strait jacket, wetsheet wrapping, isolation. The patient was also calmed down by means of psychosurgery (see Chapter 4) or electroconvulsive shock. From the mid-1950s on, however, the use of medication made it possible to virtually eliminate these forms of restraint.

Neuroleptic (also called *antipsychotic* or *psychoactive*) drugs are used in the treatment of schizophrenia. The most popular of these medicines have been the phenothizines—including Thorazine (chlorpromazine), and Stelazine (trifluoperazine). Now a butyrophenone by the name of Haldol is being widely prescribed. High levels of dopamine activity (a major neurotransmitter) are associated with schizophrenia. These medicines have their effect by blocking dopamine receptor sites on neurons. Patients with schizophrenia who take these medications improve in a number of ways: they become less withdrawn, become less confused and agitated, have fewer auditory hallucinations, and are less irritable and hostile (Cole, 1964). Comparing use of neuroleptic drugs to the use of placebos makes it quite clear that the neuroleptics reduced symptoms and intensity of schizophrenia in more than 90 percent of the cases; less than 3 percent were worse (Davis *et al.*, 1980).

Although the patient who takes antipsychotic drugs is often improved enough to leave the hospital, he or she may have trouble adjusting to the outside world. Many patients now face the "revolving door" syndrome of going to a mental hospital, being released, returning to the hospital, being released again, and so on. Phenothiazines also have a number of unpleasant side effects, including a dry mouth, blurred vision, grogginess, constipation, and muscle disorders.

Another class of drugs, called *antidepressants* (including Elavil, Tofranil, and Parnate), relieve depression. Interestingly, they do not affect the mood of nondepressed people. It is almost as if these medicines supply a chemical that some depressed people lack. Some of the antidepressants have such severe side effects that they can lead to death, so they must be given under close medical supervision. However, Prozac was introduced in 1987 and within just a few years became the most popular antidepressant. Unlike other antidepressants, Prozac tends to produce weight loss instead of gain and is typically much safer than other antidepressants (Ray & Ksir, 1993).

Lithium carbonate is now widely used to return manic-depressive patients to a state of equilibrium in which extreme mood swings disappear. While all of the other medicines described here are synthetic, lithium is a natural chemical element. It, too, can cause side effects if it is not taken under proper medical supervision. The finding that lithium salt reduces the symptoms of someone with a bipolar disorder, more so than of those with

CONNECTIONS: PSYCHOLOGY AND THE LAW

Tell students that in Berkeley, California, voters passed a law to ban the use of ECT in their area. The courts later overturned the law. Have students review information on ECT on page 413. What are the pros and cons of its use? Working individually or in small groups, challenge students to write a position paper on the use of ECT in their community. What, if any, legal restrictions should be applied to this controversial form of treatment?

a unipolar depression, suggests to researchers that these may be two different illnesses (Pokorny & Prein, 1974).

DOES PSYCHOTHERAPY WORK?

In 1952 Hans Eysenck published a review of 5 studies of the effectiveness of psychoanalytic treatment and 19 studies of the effectiveness of "eclectic" psychotherapy, treatment in which several different therapeutic approaches are combined. Eysenck concluded that psychotherapy was no more effective than no treatment at all. According to his interpretation of these 24 studies, only 44 percent of the psychoanalytic patients improved with treatment, while 64 percent of those given eclectic psychotherapy were "cured" or had improved.

Most startling, Eysenck argued that even this 64-percent improvement rate did not demonstrate the effectiveness of psychotherapy, since it has been reported that 72 percent of a group of hospitalized neurotics improved *without* treatment. If no treatment at all leads to as much improvement as psychotherapy, the obvious conclusion is that psychotherapy is not effective. Eysenck (1966) vigorously defended his controversial position, which generated a large number of additional reviews and a great many studies of the effectiveness of psychotherapy.

One of the most thoughtful and carefully reasoned reviews was written by Allen Bergin (1971). Bergin made the following points in reply to Eysenck. First, he demonstrated that when some different but equally reasonable assumptions about the classification of patients were made, the effectiveness of psychoanalytic treatment was much greater than Eysenck had reported; perhaps as many as 83 percent of the patients improved or recovered. Second, he reviewed a number of studies which showed that the rate of improvement without treatment was only about 30 percent.

Bergin's review leads one to question the validity of Eysenck's sweeping generalization that psychotherapy is no more effective than no treatment at all. But much of Bergin's argument is based on differences of opinion about how patients should be classified. Precise criteria for "improvement" are difficult to define and apply. The nature of "spontaneous remission" (sudden disappearance) of symptoms in persons who have not received help from unacknowledged sources—family, friends, relatives, religious advisors, family physicians. Additionally, if, as some researchers believe, the prime ingredient in therapy is the establishment of a close relationship, then "spontaneous remission" in people who have received continuing help from such sources is not spontaneous at all.

An analysis of nearly 400 studies of the effectiveness of psychotherapy, conducted by Mary Lee Smith and Gene V. Glass (1977), used elaborate statistical procedures to estimate the effects of psychotherapy. They found that therapy is generally more effective than no treatment, and that on the average most forms of therapy have similar effects.

Will any therapy do for any client? Probably not. Smith and Glass were able to show that for some specific clients and situations, some forms

COOPERATIVE LEARNING ACTIVITY

Explain to students that one of the problems of determining the effectiveness of psychotherapy is the lack of agreed-upon criteria for success. Challenge groups of students to attempt to design such criteria. Remind them that their criteria should be in measurable form so that a data base can be collected. As a guiding question, have students contemplate when a therapist or patient might know that it is time to end the relationship—i.e., the client is "well." *(If students get frustrated, point out the lack of universal answers is the problem faced by the psychotherapeutic community as a whole.)*

At A Glance

To guide students' reading of the feature, ask the following questions:
1. What are some of the uses of Valium? *(to reduce stress, anxiety, and seizures; to relieve muscle spasms; to control hypertension; to aid delivery of babies)*
2. How does Valium work? *(depresses the central nervous system)*
3. What are its drawbacks? *(may encourage dependency; may prevent people from using nondrug-oriented ways of stress reduction)*

■ **Applying Concepts.** Read aloud the description of the following individuals, and ask students to determine which therapy they would recommend and why.

1. Anne finds it hard to express her feelings to her husband and children. Her parents were distant, too. Anne never remembers being hugged as a child.
2. Debbie loves to ski but is terrified of the ski lift. Her fear of heights prevents her from fully enjoying the sport.
3. John's father is an alcoholic. He wants to help his father—and himself—but doesn't know how.
4. Chris has suffered from mood swings for over a year. He feels depressed and has trouble sleeping and dealing with job-related pressures.

(As students suggest therapies most effective for each case, underscore the variety of processes and goals available for treatment.) (OBJECTIVES 1–4)

At A Glance

ALL ABOUT VALIUM

Valium is one of the most frequently prescribed brands of the drug diazepam. More than 25 million Americans use this minor tranquilizer to help them cope with the pressures in their lives. Approximately 80 percent of the Valium prescribed is consumed by ordinary people who have trouble dealing with today's fast-paced society. Only about 20 percent is taken by patients in hospitals and institutions.

Valium acts as a central nervous system depressant to reduce the amount of anxiety and arousal a person feels. It is also used for such varied purposes as the relief of muscle spasms, the emergency control of seizures, the control of hypertension, and the relief of anxiety and unwanted muscle spasms during labor. Most doctors believe that Valium serves these functions in a way that no other minor tranquilizer can.

Doctors who have analyzed the use and overuse of Valium agree, however, that it is a drug that can never be taken for granted and that it needs careful watching. Many people who use it could probably deal with their anxiety more effectively by determining and eliminating the source of the anxiety. If this is not effective, they might try other ways of handling stress, such as counseling, support groups, and exercise programs before resorting to drugs.

of therapy would be expected to have a greater effect than others. For example, if the client is a 30-year-old of average intelligence, with what was traditionally called a neurosis, seen in individual sessions by a therapist with 5 years of experience, psychodynamic therapy would be expected to have a greater effect than systematic desensitization. But in the case of a highly intelligent 20-year-old with a phobia, systematic desensitization would be expected to have a greater impact. However, these are educated guesses based on the interpretation of some complex statistical manipulations. One drawback is that most physical therapies are a treatment, but not a cure for various mental and behavioral disorders. Once physical therapy has done all it can for the patient, then the search begins for the appropriate form of psychotherapy to achieve a cure.

Commonly known as sedatives or mild tranquilizers, *anti-anxiety drugs* are used to reduce excitability and cause drowsiness. The barbiturates, then Miltown (meprobamate), and eventually the benzodiazepines have been very popular prescriptions in recent decades. At one time Valium was the most popular prescription drug in the country. Now several benzodi-

CRITICAL THINKING ACTIVITY

Interpreting Statistics. Hand out copies of the bar graph on the opposite page. Then ask students the following questions.

1. What is the subject of the graph? *(effectiveness of the various types of psychotherapy)*
2. Which are the two most effective therapies according to this set of data? *(systematic desensitization, behavioral modification)*
3. Which is the least successful? *(gestalt)*
4. How might a psychotherapist use this data to refute the Eysenck report? *(Statistics show a significant rate of recovery in most cases.)*

azepines—including Xanax (alprazolam)—have joined it among the 50 most prescribed drugs.

While these drugs are effective for helping normal people cope with difficult periods in their lives, they are also prescribed for the alleviation of various neurotic symptoms, psychosomatic problems, and symptoms of alcohol withdrawal. The major effect of Valium, Librium, and Miltown is to depress the activity of the central nervous system. If the drugs are taken properly, the side effects are few and consist mainly of drowsiness. However, prolonged use may lead to dependence, and heavy doses taken along with alcohol can result in death. They do reduce anxiety, but the best use seems to be not for chronic anxiety, but for dealing with acute (one-time) anxiety (Mellinger, Balter, & Uhlenhuth, 1985).

"Shock treatment," as *electroconvulsive therapy* is commonly called, has proved extremely effective in the treatment of depression, though no one understands exactly how it works (Kalinowsky, 1975). It involves administering, over several weeks, a series of brief electrical shocks of approximately 70–150 volts for 0.1–1.0 seconds. The shock induces a convulsion similar to an epileptic seizure that may last up to a minute. As it is now applied, electroconvulsive therapy entails very little discomfort for the patient. Prior to treatment, the patient is given a sedative and injected with a muscle relaxant to alleviate involuntary muscular contractions and prevent physical injury. Even with these improvements, however, electroconvulsive therapy is a drastic treatment and must be used with great caution. Its use has declined somewhat, but it remains a highly effective treatment for depression (Thienhaus, *et al*, 1990).

MENTAL INSTITUTIONS

When the demands of everyday life cannot be met, the mentally disturbed person may face the prospect of institutionalization. There are institutions to handle many different social problems: prisons for criminals, hospitals for the physically ill, and mental institutions for people who are considered unable to function in normal society.

Commitment

The process of placing a person in a mental hospital is called *commitment*. It is estimated that two out of five mental patients are committed against their will. Involuntary commitment is a controversial legal and ethical issue. It has been argued that a committed mental patient has fewer rights than a convicted criminal.

Whether a person ends up in a mental hospital depends on a number of factors beyond his or her mental state. People with family and friends who are willing to care for them are less likely to be institutionalized. Money is also a factor. With budget cutbacks leading to more limited public

PSYCHOLOGY and YOU

The Revolving Door: A Legacy of Deinstitutionalization. Homelessness is a major problem in the United States, and it is likely that you come into contact with the homeless at least occasionally. When you do, chances are good that you may be observing a person with a psychiatric disorder.

It is estimated that 33 percent of the homeless are mentally ill, overlapping partially with 33 percent of the homeless estimated to be severely addicted (Rossi, 1990). This seems to be a direct result of deinstitutionalization.

Since the introduction of psychoactive drugs in the 1950s, the number of patients confined to mental institutions has steadily dropped. Unfortunately, most psychoactive drugs do not cure disorders. Rather, they merely control the more obvious symptoms of mental illness so that patients are no longer dangerous. Thus, there is no longer any reason to keep these people institutionalized.

A majority of mental inmates have been released from institutions, but they often find it impossible to hold steady jobs or to live on their own. In this way, the noble goal of deinstitutionalization has contributed to the problem of homelessness and has affected all our lives.

■**Identifying Cause and Effect.** Assign students to read the margin feature on homelessness. Ask: What relationship does the feature establish between deinstitutionalization and homelessness? *(that deinstitutionalization has contributed to the problem)* Next, organize students into action committees. Instruct each group to investigate the issue of homelessness today, looking at the programs started in major cities such as New York. Based on their research, challenge each committee to submit a recommendation about how to handle this problem. Each group, for example, should decide between reinstitutionalization or establishment of more shelters and/or group homes. If they decide in favor of group homes, what efforts should be made to educate the public? (For a statement of the issue, refer students to "The Plight of the Deinstitutionalized Mental Patient," in *Science*, 1977, p. 1366.) (OBJECTIVES 1, 4)

Enrich. Have students complete the Chapter 16 Extension Activity.

Readings in Psychology. Have students read the Section 5, Reading 7 selection in *Readings in Psychology* and answer the questions that follow the selection.

CRITICAL THINKING ACTIVITY

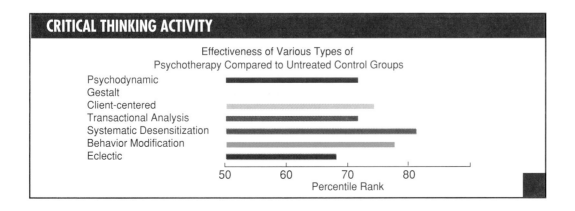

Effectiveness of Various Types of Psychotherapy Compared to Untreated Control Groups

Psychodynamic
Gestalt
Client-centered
Transactional Analysis
Systematic Desensitization
Behavior Modification
Eclectic

50   60   70   80
Percentile Rank

■ Identifying the Central Issue.

Read aloud the sidebar stating the goal of health care provided by mental hospitals. Then, based on the text, assign students to list obstacles to achieving this goal. In students' opinion, what is the central issue or problem that prevents many mental hospitals from fulfilling their purpose? *(Some students may cite a lack of funding.)*

■ Study and Writing Skills.

Organize the students into small groups. Using information in the text, challenge each group to draft a bill of rights for patients confined to mental institutions. Have a member from each group read the draft aloud. Next, compile a master document on the chalkboard. Request volunteers to contact a mental health agency in your community or region to see if such a document already exists. If possible, students should arrange to get a copy of it. Ask: How do the provisions compare with the document drawn up by the class? (OBJECTIVE 1)

A mental hospital should be a place where a person is temporarily freed from social pressures he or she cannot bear.

---

facilities, it is now getting harder for a person to stay in a mental hospital for any length of time.

Conditions

The quality and cost of care in mental institutions vary greatly. There are more than 4,000 mental health facilities in the United States. About half of them offer inpatient care. Among these, private institutions offer more concentrated care and a better environment, but many of them are very expensive. The majority of people go to state mental hospitals or cheaper private institutions. The quality of treatment in these hospitals varies tremendously. It is possible, in fact, for a patient's condition to worsen or remain unchanged because the patient comes to depend on the hospital environment and loses social and vocational skills, in addition to losing a role in their former home environment. When patients fail to improve, they remain institutionalized year after year. This situation exists because most public hospitals lack funds for adequate nursing staffs, equipment, and therapists. In many cases, the patients' day-to-day care is left to attendants who do little more than clean and feed the patients and keep order.

Ideally, a mental hospital should be a place where the patient is temporarily freed from social pressures he or she cannot bear. Limited and carefully planned demands should be made by a staff capable of understanding and concern for the individual. Unfortunately, the reality of many state hospitals does not fit this ideal. Patients can become molded into a pattern of obedience, dependence, and conformity by a deadening routine of sleep, meals, and ways of filling time (Goffman, 1961).

As the patients become increasingly apathetic and resigned, they lose all ties with the outside world. In order to survive the boredom of each day, they rely on fantasy, dreams, and sleep, and they stop thinking about returning to outside life. Nevertheless, many patients welcome this routine—they prefer to be taken care of and to avoid the responsibilities of the outside world.

Individual and group psychotherapy are provided in mental hospitals, but this type of therapy is slow and expensive. It does not work well with hospital patients, who are often beyond caring whether they improve or not, or who are exhibiting such unique bizarre behavior that individual psychotherapy is a must if there is ever to be any hope of recovery. Partly as a result, mental hospitals tend to stress physical treatments.

There are certain dangers inherent in the use of psychiatric drugs. They are often administered to make up for the lack of staff at mental hospitals. In many institutions it is common policy to administer a tranquilizer to every patient early in the morning, so that throughout the day there is very little activity among patients, thus reducing the workload required of an already overworked staff.

Most psychiatric drugs, when given in high doses over long periods, have undesirable side effects, such as extreme lethargy or peculiar losses of coordination. For such reasons, it is not uncommon for mental patients to flush some of their drugs down the toilet.

CRITICAL THINKING ACTIVITY

Weighing Advantages and Disadvantages. Direct students to review information on the biological treatment of behavioral disorders with drugs. Organize a panel discussion in which students debate the use of drug therapy in mental hospitals. Assign panelists to represent the following points of view: a psychiatrist, a behavioral psychologist, a health care worker, and several patients.

FIGURE 16.8

In a hospital where the goal is to restore the person to normal functioning, every effort is made to duplicate real settings and real situations and to involve the person in his or her treatment. This patient is meeting with her doctor to discuss her treatment and evaluate how she is doing and what should happen next. **Why does the quality of treatment in mental hospitals vary so greatly?**

COMMUNITY MENTAL HEALTH

Since the nineteenth century, extremely deviant behavior has been viewed as an illness to be treated by medical personnel in a hospital setting. Large mental hospitals were built in rural areas, where space could be obtained cheaply and patients could be concealed from the public, who thought them unsightly and dangerous. But the social isolation of patients, their removal from familiar surroundings and family life, often made later re-adjustment to society even more difficult. Released patients found them-selves too far from the hospital for any supplementary care and too fragile to cope independently with the pressures of the outside world. Eventually it became apparent that if these patients were to make a successful return to the community, the community was going to have to provide some support.

Community Mental Health Centers

The Community Mental Health Centers Act of 1963 was designed to solve some of the problems faced by patients trying to reenter society. One mental health center was required for every 50,000 members of the U.S. population, to supply needed psychological services for the ex-patient at-tempting to function within the community. These centers were also sup-posed to educate community workers such as police, teachers, and clergy in the principles of preventive mental health, to train paraprofessionals, and to carry out research. A countrywide system of mental health centers has not yet been achieved, and funding for existing centers has been cut

VISUAL INSTRUCTION

Challenge students to read the patient's body language. What emotions or thoughts do they think the young woman might be experienc-ing? Next, have students se-lect one of the therapy approaches mentioned in this text. What treatment might the therapist recom-mend to the young woman? *(Treatment plans should re-flect the school chosen.)* **Answer to caption, Figure 16.8:** mainly from differ-ences in funding

■ **Research.** Using the tele-phone book, request students to identify community mental health centers in your area. (These can often be found in the yellow pages or in special sections at the front of the tele-phone book.) You might also have students contact some hot lines to find out where the less-publicized support groups meet. Based on their research, have students compile a men-tal health directory that might be made available for the gen-eral school population through the guidance office. (OBJECTIVE 4)

What principles of group therapy can students identify in this photo? How do such settings provide people with an opportunity to develop new skills in interpersonal relations?
Answer to caption, Figure 16.9: provide a way for patients to ease their way back into society

Teacher Note. You might tell students that police are the personnel most commonly called to intervene in family quarrels. These domestic squabbles are dangerous not only to the family members involved, but also to the police who handle them. New York City has taken the lead in offering sensitivity workshops to its police force. Training includes lectures, demonstrations, and role playing to help the police "rehearse" intervention strategies. The program has proven so successful that police departments throughout the United States have adopted it. (OBJECTIVES 1, 3)

FIGURE 16.9

This group of ex-hospital patients meets to discuss problems and help one another make the adjustment to becoming functioning members of the community. **What purpose do halfway houses serve?**

back in many cities; but those centers that are in operation supply important services.

Outpatients can walk into a clinic and receive therapy once, twice, or several times a week, without leaving school, job, or family, and without feeling stigmatized as institutionalized mental patients. The centers also serve as a bridge between hospitalization and complete independence by giving care to patients after they are released from hospitals.

For the more severely disturbed, hospitalization can be provided within the community. Friends and family have easy access to patients, who feel less isolated and more accepted. Many centers have arrangements for day hospitals, in which patients take advantage of the hospital during the day and go home at night.

Many community mental health centers also maintain storefront clinics that are open around the clock to deal with such emergencies as acute anxiety attacks, suicide attempts, and bad drug trips. The centers may have teams of psychologically trained personnel on call to go to city hospital emergency rooms to deal with psychological traumas.

Mental health centers provide qualified personnel to serve as consultants to other community workers, such as teachers, police, and clergy, advising them on how to handle psychological problems in the classroom and within the community. Sensitivity workshops give instruction on such matters as how to intervene in family quarrels, how to talk to potential suicide victims, and how to keep truants from dropping out of school. Somewhat surprisingly, one of the effects of expanded Medicare coverage was to make nursing homes the largest national caretaker for the mentally ill. It is estimated that there were 668,000 in such facilities who were mentally ill in the mid-1980s (Goldman, Feder, & Scanlon, 1986).

Request a volunteer to have several members of the police department visit the class. (Ideally, at least one male and one female will attend.) Instruct students to tell the speakers that the topic of discussion is the handling of and intervention in family quarrels. Arrange for students to write at least one question apiece to ask the officers.

Halfway Houses.   There are thousands of people who spend time in mental hospitals, prisons, and homes for delinquents and who, when finally released, are psychologically unprepared to return to life in society. They may be able to behave well under structured conditions, but they find the freedom and immensity of society confusing and overwhelming. Such people can ease back into society through halfway houses.

Often operating in large, older homes that have been divided into a series of living quarters, halfway houses encourage residents to take part in cooperative activities such as cooking, cleaning, and maintaining the yard. It is all part of an effort to place the residents back into the larger community as productive, contributing citizens.

DID YOU KNOW?

One of the best known halfway houses is Daytop Village, a program for recovering drug addicts.

Using Psychology

To help students read the feature, you might ask the following questions:
1. What are some of the approaches commonly used by crisis intervention counselors? *(provide general support by listening and offering encouragement; help people assess their situation realistically; help individuals work out coping mechanisms)*
2. What problems do hot lines handle? *(Answers include: suicide, substance abuse, rape, physical and sexual abuse, compulsive gambling.)*
3. What is the purpose of the National AIDS Hot Line? *(to provide medical information to people who fear they might have the disease or who need help dealing with the emotional turmoil of coping with AIDS)*
4. What technique do crisis workers use to deal with stress? *(role playing)*

Using Psychology

Crisis Intervention Programs

An active approach to mental health is the development of community-based crisis intervention programs, which help individuals and families deal with emergencies or highly stressful situations. Typically, during a period of emotional turmoil, people feel overwhelmed and cannot deal with their everyday affairs. The crisis may be the death of a loved one, the loss of a job, a rape or mugging, a family breakup, or an attempted suicide. The intervention is generally short-term, lasting for no more than five or six sessions. It is like psychological first aid.

Crisis intervention counselors use four approaches. First, they provide general support by listening to the person's concerns and by providing encouragement and hope that the crisis will pass. Second, counselors help people assess their situation realistically; identify what they can do to help themselves; and look directly into their emotions, thoughts, and behavior to gain a clearer assessment of the problem. Third, counselors help individuals work out adaptive ways of coping with present and future crises. Fourth, counselors help people make some permanent changes in their lives. They may, for example, help people change jobs, move to a safer neighborhood, or establish stable friendships and support groups.

Crisis intervention may take the form of a telephone hot line. People who are in trouble can telephone at any time and receive immediate counseling, sympathy, and comfort. The best known of these systems is the Los Angeles Suicide Prevention Center, which

STUDY AND WRITING SKILLS

Assign interested students to find out more about the operation and procedures in a halfway house. Recommend that they interview substance abuse counselors at the county mental health agency. If possible, have students visit a halfway house. (In all cases, the visit should be carefully arranged to protect client privacy.) If a halfway house is not an option, the counselor might agree to set up an interview with a former client. Based on this research, assign students to write a short story entitled: "A Day in the Life of a Halfway House." (Suggest that they use first names only.)

ASSESS

Check for Understanding

Challenge students to brainstorm a list of mental disorders. (Allow students to review Chapter 15, if necessary.) Record these on the chalkboard, and have students identify the therapy that might be most appropriate for each disorder.

was established in 1958. Similar hot lines have been set up for alcoholics, rape victims, battered women, runaway children, gamblers, sexually abused people, and lonely people who just need a shoulder to cry on or someone to listen to them. In addition to providing sympathy, hot line volunteers across the United States and Canada give information on community services that can help callers with their problems.

One type of hot line responds to issues and problems concerning AIDS (Acquired *I*mmune *D*eficiency *S*yndrome). The National AIDS Hot Line is affiliated with the Centers for Disease Control in Atlanta. Its phones are answered 24 hours a day by information specialists who are trained to answer callers' questions and to use crisis intervention techniques. There are also many state AIDS hot lines. Some are staffed by medical personnel including physicians, nurses, and pharmacists. The reason for this is that some of the people who call in ask about symptoms they are experiencing. Counselors need to be able to answer effectively.

AIDS hot lines are not only for people who suspect they have AIDS. Since AIDS is an infectious and terminal disease, many people are confused and frightened about its spread. Hot lines encourage such people to call and ask questions about the disease. Can I get infected just by sitting next to someone with AIDS? If I do not know anyone with AIDS, should I still be concerned about the disease? These and other questions are answered by information specialists at the hot lines. The hot lines also provide referrals to treatment and assessment centers, counseling facilities, and support groups. People who call are not asked for their names. All callers remain anonymous.

FIGURE 16.10

Crisis intervention counselors are trained to deal with people who are going through critical periods in their lives. This counselor works in a shelter for battered women. **What are the main purposes of hot lines?**

Hot lines are usually staffed by volunteers. After dealing with the immediate emotional turmoil over the telephone, the volunteer urges the caller to go to a community facility and meet with a crisis intervention counselor who can provide more assistance. If necessary, long-term help (more than five or six sessions) is set up so the person can develop more effective ways of coping.

Many of the people who staff the crisis intervention hot lines or community centers are not mental health specialists. Rather, they are concerned and caring individuals who have been trained—often in programs lasting 40 hours or more—to provide help to people who are going through crises. Even trained counselors and therapists require specialized skills to deal with their clients' emotional turmoil during an emergency.

Crisis intervention workers are taught to listen to and understand what people are saying, even when the situation may be highly emotional or chaotic. The skilled attention of a concerned listener sometimes helps a person in crisis become aware of feelings that contribute to his or her sense of panic.

In order to be effective in their helping role, crisis workers must learn how to deal with their own emotional reactions to common crisis situations through role playing and other methods. By practicing their reactions beforehand, the trainees become more relaxed and less anxious in real-life crises. In addition, role playing allows the workers to become aware of their own feelings and biases.

The Rise of the Paraprofessional

Professionals who traditionally treat mental disorder have always been in short supply. Moreover, they tend to be white and middle class, which may inhibit free communication with nonwhite or poorly educated patients. To overcome both problems, increasing numbers of mental health workers called paraprofessionals are being trained. Margaret Rioch (1967) showed that housewives with no previous psychological training but with well-balanced and sympathetic natures made excellent mental health counselors after two years of intensive training. In recent years, paraprofessionals have been providing a wide variety of mental health services, including interviewing, testing, counseling, and making home visits. When they are carefully screened and trained, and because they often are close in ethnic background to their clients, they have been effective.

Mental health centers are now in a time of change. Community resistance, budgetary cutbacks, and controversy over the effectiveness of programs are major forces that will shape the future of community psychology.

Reteach

Have students complete the Chapter 16 Review Activity and share responses with each other.

Enrich

Ask students to complete the Chapter 16 Study Guide Activity.

Evaluate

Administer and grade the Chapter 16 Test. Two forms are available should you wish to give different tests to different students/classes.

Use the Understanding Psychology Testmaker to create a customized test.

CLOSE

Have students review the list of conditions that might prompt them to seek therapy and the characteristics of the therapist they would seek. (See Motivating Activity, page 392.) What, if any, revisions would students make in this material? Request volunteers to share how Chapter 16 reshaped their opinions of therapy.

STUDY AND WRITING SKILLS

Request interested students to prepare a career handbook for the various paraprofessionals who work in the field of psychology. Each occupation mentioned should include a description of psychology-related job duties, type of training or experience needed for the job, and the monetary and personal rewards a person might expect. Students might contact the following for information: state employment office, county mental health agency, personnel office of a local hospital, and/or career guidance office at a community college. Encourage students to present their handbook to the rest of the class.

ANSWERS

Concepts and Vocabulary

1. method used to assist people in dealing with their problems; realize they are responsible for their own lives and to help them solve problems

2. psychiatric social workers, clinical psychologists, psychiatrists, lay analysts, counselors; good mental health, warmth and understanding, interpersonal experience; varied characteristics, but most important is a willingness to change

3. make the patient aware of unconscious motives and desires; free association and talk over a long period

4. to help individuals recognize their own inner strength; both accept whatever the patient says

5. to correct people's false and self-defeating beliefs; steps include realization of false assumptions, an awareness of how these assumptions affect behavior

6. focuses on changing specific behaviors through conditioning; extinguish fear through visualization and relaxation; arrange ways to leave old behavior unrewarded and to reinforce new behavior

7. family therapy; self-help groups tackle a problem through sharing with therapist and peers; encounter groups help people live more intense lives

16 Review

SUMMARY

Use the following outline as a tool for reviewing this chapter. Copy the outline onto your own paper, leaving spaces between headings to make notes about key concepts.

    I. What Is Psychotherapy?

        A. Characteristics of Psychotherapy

        B. What Makes a Good Therapist?

    II. Kinds of Psychotherapy

        A. Psychoanalysis

        B. Existential/Humanist Therapies

        C. Cognitive Therapies

        D. Behavior Therapies

        E. Group Therapies

   III. Biological Approaches to Treatment

   IV. Does Psychotherapy Work?

    V. Mental Institutions

        A. Commitment

        B. Conditions

   VI. Community Mental Health

        A. Community Mental Health Centers

        B. The Rise of the Paraprofessional

CONCEPTS AND VOCABULARY

1. Define psychotherapy and state its goal. What two goals should the client achieve during therapy?

2. What kinds of professionals see persons with behavioral problems? What characteristics of the therapist have been found to increase effectiveness? What client characteristics are associated with favorable outcomes in therapy?

3. State the goal of psychoanalysis. What does the therapist do to achieve this goal?

4. State the goal of humanistic psychotherapy. What similarities are there between this type of therapy and psychoanalysis?

5. State the goal of rational-emotive therapy (RET). What steps does RET expect the client to take to solve his or her problem?

6. How does behavior therapy differ from the other therapies in its approach to correcting an individual's problem? Describe the behavioral therapeutic techniques of systematic desensitization and contingency management.

7. Describe three types of group therapy.

8. Describe the results of studies that have attempted to evaluate the effectiveness of psychotherapy.

9. Identify the effects of antipsychotic drugs, antidepressants, and antianxiety drugs. When is each used? What are the side effects and dangers of each?

10. What are community mental health centers and how do they operate? What is a halfway house?

CRITICAL THINKING

1. **Analyze.** On a sheet of paper, draw a large thermometer ranging from 0 to 100 degrees. Think of the most fearful thing you can imagine, and write it down at the 100-degree mark. Write down the least fearful thing you can think of near the 0-degree mark. Continue to list your fears on the thermometer according to their severity. If they agree to do so, have several friends make similar lists of their fears. Compare lists, looking for differences and similarities. Do you think any of your fears are based on conditioning? Can you think of a method of reconditioning that would remove the fear or make it less intense?

2. **Evaluate.** Transactional analysis distinguishes among three different ways of experiencing ourselves: parent, adult, and child ego states.

---

8. Students should focus on the Eysenck study and other studies that refute or modify its results.

9. antipsychotics with schizophrenia, antidepressants with depression, antianxiety with stress disorders; side effects and dangers are listed on pp. 410–413

10. provide a variety of noninstitutional services to help people function within the community and to train para-

professionals in the field of mental health; offer a short-term solution for patients seeking to reenter society

Critical Thinking

1. Explore how this exercise helps students to identify and rank their fears.

2. You might provide students with a specific problem to discuss, such as walking into a party where they do not know anyone. Ask how each of the ego

Think back to a recent crisis or difficult time you experienced. Then imagine how you would have reacted to the situation as a 6-year-old. Your response to this reflects your child ego state reactions. What would your mother and father have told you to do in that situation? This represents a possible parent ego state reaction. Finally, how do you feel about the situation now? Your answer will most likely reflect your adult ego state. Which ego state helps you deal with the crisis most effectively?

APPLYING KNOWLEDGE

1. With your teacher's guidance, ask several people in different businesses if they would hire someone they knew had undergone psychotherapy. Do their responses indicate to you that society has matured to where it now understands and accepts emotional problems in the same way it accepts medical problems? Do you believe a person should be barred from high public office because he or she has sought psychotherapy?

2. Begin assertiveness training by trying the following exercise. Engage a friend in a casual conversation. During part of the conversation, raise or lower your voice. Experiment with the amount of eye contact you have during the conversation. Try staring at your friend, then not making any eye contact at all. Change the rate of your speaking from very fast to very slow. What kind of reactions in your friend do you notice with each change? What new insights about yourself did you gain by doing this exercise?

ANALYZING VIEWPOINTS

1. Within the field of psychology there is conflicting evidence about the effectiveness of psychotherapy. Some studies have concluded that psychotherapy is really no more effective than no treatment at all. Other studies have found just the opposite—that psychotherapy *is* gener-

ally more effective than no treatment at all. What do you think? Does psychotherapy work? Write a paper that presents a sound argument for both sides of the issue. Use what you have learned from the chapter and look for additional information in magazine articles and books on the topic.

BEYOND THE CLASSROOM

1. Make plans to attend an open meeting of one of the following self-help support groups: Alcoholics Anonymous, Alanon, Alateen, Smokenders, Narcotics Anonymous, Weight Watchers, or Overeaters Anonymous. Go with a classmate so that you can share your observations and experiences. At the meeting, notice the ways in which the group provides support for people.

2. Go to your local library or video store to find a movie that portrays life in a mental institution, such as *One Flew Over the Cuckoo's Nest* or *Awakenings*. Watch the film carefully. How do these portrayals match with your text's description? In a paper, describe some of the patients' symptoms and how you would classify them. What kind of treatment(s) were being administered?

In Your Journal

1. Reread the recommendations for treatment that you wrote in your journal. How do the techniques you suggest resemble the therapies described in this chapter? Answer this question in your journal.

Beyond the Classroom

1. Advise students that some meetings are "closed" to observers to protect the privacy of participants.

2. You might have students present their ideas in the form of a case study.

In Your Journal

If time permits, discuss journal entries individually with students.

---

states might respond to this situation.

Applying Knowledge

1. Before conducting this activity, make sure you secure the necessary release forms for interviews. You might also have students investigate new laws that protect the right of patients to ignore questions dealing with mental health.

2. Request volunteers to explain how these exercises increased their assertiveness.

Analyzing Viewpoints

1. You might have students present their findings in the form of an oral report.

CHAPTER BONUS
Test Question

This question may be used for extra credit on the chapter test.
Choose the letter of the correct response.

Which of the following statements best fits the ideas of behavioral therapy?

a. Observational learning is the best form of treatment.

b. Both abnormal and normal behavior are learned.

c. Therapy should be based on drugs and other medical procedures.

d. The best treatment is group therapy that involves two or more members of the same family.

Answer: **b**

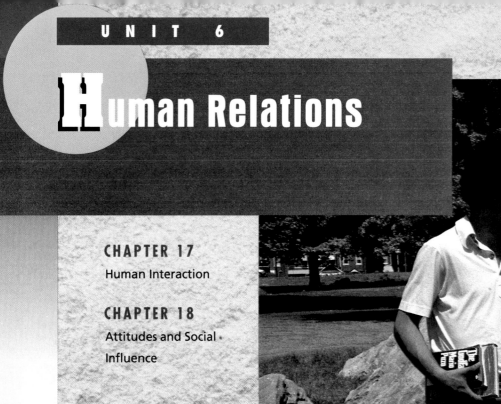

UNIT 6

Human Relations

CHAPTER 17

Human Interaction

CHAPTER 18

Attitudes and Social
Influence

422

Our behavior is shaped to a large degree by
the social situations and settings in which
we find ourselves.

INTRODUCING THE UNIT

Challenge students to write down two or three adjectives that characterize their attitude toward life. (To encourage honesty, tell students that their lists will not be collected.) Then ask students to trace the origins of these attitudes. If any students say "I was born this way," ask for examples of similar attitudes in family members. Suggest that students record their theories in their journal for examination as they progress through Chapters 17 and 18.

Unit 6 in Perspective

Chapter 17 explores the dynamics of interpersonal relationships, focusing on factors that hold together or drive apart couples and group members.

Chapter 18 looks in depth at some of the attitudes—negative and positive—that shape society. It also examines techniques that can change attitudes, with emphasis upon the persuasion process.

Connecting to Past Learning
Have students list all of the personal and group interactions in which they are involved during a given day. What percentage of their time do students estimate is spent with groups? What percentage with only 1–2 individuals? What percentage is spent alone? Use this activity to underscore the importance of understanding the dynamics of social relationships.

423

UNIT PROJECT

Assign students to draw a large calendar for the time period you plan to spend on Unit 6. Instruct students to allow space for taking daily notations on the calendar. Before each class session, allow 5 minutes for students to write down some of the people or forces that influenced their attitudes or beliefs during the prior 24-hour period. Tell students to look for examples of peer pressure, advertisements, parental pressure, and so on. At the end of the unit, challenge students to assess how this activity made them more aware of the persuasion processes that touch their lives.

CHAPTER 17
Human Interaction

TEXT TOPICS	SPECIAL FEATURES	RESOURCE MATERIALS
Needing Other People, pp. 425–427		▰ **Reproducible Lesson Plan; Study Guide; Review Activity**
Choosing Friends, pp. 428–432	**At a Glance:** Who Is Shy?, p. 429 **Psychology and You,** p. 430	▰ **Reproducible Lesson Plan; Study Guide; Review Activity; Application Activity**
Personal Relationships, pp. 432–437	**Psychology and You,** p. 434	▰ **Reproducible Lesson Plan; Study Guide; Review Activity** ▯ *Readings in Psychology:* **Section 6, Reading 1**
How People Perceive One Another, pp. 437–441	**Psychology Update,** p. 439	▰ **Reproducible Lesson Plan; Study Guide; Review Activity** ▮ **Transparency 27** ▯ *Readings in Psychology:* **Section 6, Reading 2**
What Are Groups?, pp. 441–443	**More About Psychology,** p. 442	▰ **Reproducible Lesson Plan; Study Guide; Review Activity**
How Groups Are Held Together, pp. 443–444		▰ **Reproducible Lesson Plan; Study Guide; Review Activity**
Interactions Within Groups, pp. 444–451	**Fact or Fiction?,** p. 445 **Using Psychology,** pp. 447–450	▰ **Reproducible Lesson Plan; Study Guide; Review Activity** ▮ **Transparencies 28, 29**
Group Conflict Versus Cooperation, pp. 451–452		▰ **Reproducible Lesson Plan; Study Guide; Review Activity; Extension Activity Chapter Test, Form A and Form B** ▣ **Understanding Psychology Testmaker**

PERFORMANCE ASSESSMENT ACTIVITY

Instruct students to imagine that they are curators of a museum planning to mount an exhibit entitled "Human Interaction." Organize the class into three groups, and assign each group responsibility for finding works of art related to one of the three chapter objectives. Students should find photographs or reproductions of paintings and sculptures that depict people interacting in various ways. Students should prepare captions to accompany the works. (Captions should reflect principles discussed in this chapter.)

CHAPTER RESOURCES

Readings for the Student

Aronson, Elliot. *The Social Animal*. New York: W. H. Freeman, 1988.

Hall, Edward T. *The Hidden Dimension*. Garden City, NY: Doubleday, 1966.

Hatfield, E., and Sprecher, S. *Mirror, Mirror: The Importance of Looks in Everyday Life*. Albany, NY: State University of New York Press, 1986

Readings for the Teacher

Feldman, R. S., and Rime, B., eds. *Fundamentals of Nonverbal Behavior*. Cambridge, England: Cambridge University Press, 1991.

Harvey, J. H., and Weary, G. *Perspectives on Attributional Processes*. Dubuque, IA: W. C. Brown, 1981.

Lindzey, G., and Aronson, E., eds. *Handbook of Social Psychology*. New York: Random House, 1985.

Shaw, Marvin E. *Group Dynamics: The Psychology of Small Group Behavior*. New York: McGraw-Hill, 1976.

Multimedia

Rights and Responsibilities (29 minutes, 3/4″ video). Public Television Library. This video shows the processes high school students deal with while setting up a student government.

The Social Animal (30 minutes). Indiana University. This video illustrates the work of Asch on group pressure to conform, Sherif on group exclusion, and Deutsch on the effects of threat on interpersonal relations.

For additional resources see the bibliography beginning on page 530.

Human Interaction

FOCUS

Motivating Activity

Challenge students to consider this question: If you were a shoe, what kind of shoe would you be? Tell students to select a type of footwear that typifies their personality and to write a few sentences explaining the reasons for their choice. Next, request a volunteer to come to the front of the class. Challenge other students to identify what type of shoe they imagine the volunteer as being. (For example, students might describe an easy-going, relaxed person as a comfortable moccasin.)

Encourage members of the class to agree or disagree with each assessment. Repeat this process with several volunteers. Finally, have the volunteers identify how they view themselves. How do their assessments compare with those of their classmates? Explain that the impressions we have of ourselves and others affect the way we interact in society. Tell the class that they will learn more about how people interact in this chapter.

Meeting Chapter Objectives.

Point out the objectives on page 425. Have students rephrase the objectives in question form. Then assign students to answer the questions as they read Chapter 17.

Building Vocabulary.

Call on students to read aloud the definitions of each of the Key Terms in the Glossary. Challenge volunteers to use these terms in sentences.

FIGURE 17.1 How much we need other people varies, but interaction with others is a way of satisfying the needs we all have for praise, respect, love, and affection.

424

TEACHER CLASSROOM RESOURCES

- Chapter 17 Reproducible Lesson Plan
- Chapter 17 Study Guide
- Chapter 17 Review Activity
- Chapter 17 Application Activity
- Chapter 17 Extension Activity

- Transparencies 27, 28, 29 Transparency Strategies and Activities

- *Readings in Psychology:* Section 6, Readings 1, 2

- Chapter 17 Test, Form A and Form B

- Understanding Psychology Testmaker

OBJECTIVES

After studying this chapter, you should be able to

- describe the basic human need for interaction with others.
- discuss the ways individuals form impressions of one another.
- describe the interactive patterns within groups.

P eople vary considerably in their need for social contact and in their desire and ability to be alone. You have probably heard or read stories of hermits and recluses who voluntarily isolate themselves, but most people would not welcome a solitary life. Why do people choose to interact with certain people and not with others? What is so important about being around other people? What do psychologists know about human interaction? This chapter will answer these questions and provide insights into group interactions.

KEY TERMS

actor-observer bias
attribution theory
body language
complementarity
diffusion of responsibility
ego-support value
fundamental attribution error
group
ideology
implicit personality theory
nonverbal communication
norms
physical proximity
self-serving bias
social functions
social rules
sociogram
stereotype
stimulation value
task functions
utility value

IN YOUR JOURNAL

Write down the first 10 or 15 words or phrases that come to mind when you ask yourself "Who am I?"

425

Exploring Key Ideas

Interaction and Socialization. Remind students that they have already studied many theories about the ways in which humans learn to interact in society. (Have students skim through the Table of Contents to identify some of these theories.)

Next, tell students that Chapter 17 focuses on social interactions once behaviors are already fairly well developed. Point out that a central issue in any human interaction is *perception*. That is, is our perception of others a true indicator of their actual intentions and personality? Do others perceive us as we perceive ourselves? Another central issue is *conformity*. To what extent must individuals sacrifice autonomy in order to belong to a group? Tell students to keep these two issues (and the related questions) in mind as they read this chapter.

IN YOUR JOURNAL

Tell students to consider the question "Who am I?" by looking at it from two angles: "Am I who *I* think I am, or am I who *other people* think I am?"

EXTRA CREDIT ACTIVITY

Ask students to imagine that they are in the process of founding a task- or social-oriented organization (e.g., a community volunteer group to provide services for home-bound patients, an amateur puppet theater for children, a stamp-and-coin club). Based on the concepts and theories discussed in this chapter, instruct students to draw up bylaws to govern their proposed organization. (The bylaws should help ensure group cohesiveness and address such issues as norms, ideology, and commitment. They should also outline the communication patterns that will operate within the group and set guidelines on the selection and responsibilities of leaders.)

TEACH

Guided Practice

■ **Analyzing Information.**
Schachter set out to test the old saying "Misery loves company." He found out that misery not only loves company—it loves *miserable* company. Ask students to explain how the following old saying might also apply to Schachter's findings:

"There's strength in numbers." *(Companionship can offer people a feeling of security when they are feeling vulnerable.)* Ask students to cite examples from movies that seem to support Schachter's findings. (OBJECTIVE 1)

Low Anxiety   High Anxiety

● Women who chose to be alone or did not care
● Women who chose to affiliate

FIGURE 17.2

These graphs show the results of Schachter's experiment about the effects of anxiety on affiliation. **Which group was more likely to seek company?**

NEEDING OTHER PEOPLE

From infancy we depend on others to satisfy our basic needs. In this relationship we learn to associate close personal contact with the satisfaction of basic needs. In later life we seek personal contact for the same reason, even though we can now care for ourselves.

Being around other human beings, interacting with others, has become a habit that would be difficult to break. Moreover, we have developed needs for praise, respect, love and affection, the sense of achievement, and other rewarding experiences. These needs, acquired through social learning, can only be satisfied by other human beings (Bandura and Walters, 1963).

Anxiety and Companionship

Social psychologists are interested in discovering what circumstances intensify our desire for human contact. It seems that we need company most when we are afraid or anxious, and we also need company when we are unsure of ourselves and want to compare our feelings with other people's.

Psychologist Stanley Schachter (1959) decided to test the old saying "Misery loves company." His experiment showed that people suffering from a high level of anxiety are more likely to seek out company than those who feel less anxious. He arranged for a number of college women to come to his laboratory. One group of women was greeted by a frightening-looking man in a white coat who identified himself as Dr. Gregor Zilstein of the medical school. Dr. Zilstein told each woman that she would be given electric shocks in order to study the effect of electricity on the body. He told the women, in an ominous tone, that the shocks would be extremely painful. With a devilish smile, he added that the shocks would cause no permanent skin damage. For obvious reasons, this group of women was referred to as the high-anxiety group.

The doctor was friendly to the other group, and told them that the shocks would produce only ticklish, tingling sensations, which they might even find pleasant. These women formed the low-anxiety group.

Zilstein told each subject that she would have to leave the laboratory while he set up the equipment. He then asked each woman to indicate on a questionnaire whether she wished to wait alone in a private room or with other subjects in a larger room. Most women in the low-anxiety group chose to wait alone. However, the majority of high-anxiety women preferred to wait with others. Thus, the experiment demonstrated that high anxiety tends to produce a need for companionship (Figure 17.2).

Comparing Experiences and Reducing Uncertainty

People also like to get together with one another to reduce their uncertainties about themselves. For example, when you get tests back, you probably ask your friends how they did. You try to understand your own situation by comparing it to other people's. You learn your strengths and weaknesses by asking: Can other people do it, too? Do they do it better or worse? Many individuals use the performance of others as a basis for self-evaluation. According to this theory, one of the reasons why the women in the shock experiment sought company was to find out how they should respond to Dr. Zilstein. Should they feel fear or anger, or should they take the whole thing in stride? One way to get this information was to talk to others.

Schachter conducted another experiment to test this idea. It was essentially the same as the Dr. Zilstein experiment, but this time *all* the women were made anxious. Half of them were then given the choice between waiting alone and waiting with other women about to take part in the same experiment. The other half were given the choice between waiting alone and passing the time in a room where students were waiting to see their academic advisers.

As you might expect, the women who had a chance to be with other women in the same predicament seized the opportunity. These women wanted to compare their dilemma with others. But most of the women in the second group chose to spend the time alone rather than with the unconcerned students. As the experimenter put it, "Misery doesn't love just any kind of company, it loves only miserable company."

Other researchers have shown that the more uncertain a person is, the more likely he or she is to seek out other people. Like Schachter, Harold Gerard and J.M. Rabbie recruited volunteers for an experiment. When the volunteers arrived, some of them were escorted to a booth and attached to a machine that was supposed to measure emotionality. The machine was turned on, and the subjects were able to see not only their own ratings but the ratings of three other participants as well. In each case the dial for the subject registered 82 on a scale of 100; the dials for the other participants registered 79, 80, and 81. (As you've undoubtedly guessed, the machine was rigged.) A second group of subjects was attached to a similar machine and shown their own ratings but not those of other participants. A third group was not given any information about themselves or other participants in the experiment. When asked whether they wanted to wait alone or with other subjects, most of the people in the first group chose to wait alone. They had seen how they compared to others and felt they were reacting appropriately. However, most of the subjects in the other two groups, who had no basis for evaluating themselves, chose to wait with other people (Gerard and Rabbie, 1961).

Friendship also offers support in trying times. Friends may serve as mediators if you have problems with another person. Friends are there to react to your ideas. In your social network, friends are your connections to a broad array of available support.

Yet, as we will see, predicting the effects of friendship can be quite complex. In Karen Rook's study (1987), she found that having friends who offer support helped reduce very high stress. On the other hand, friends were no significant help in dealing with average amounts of stress. Perhaps, most surprisingly, the support of friends actually hindered people's ability to deal with low levels of stress. Rook theorizes that reviewing smaller problems again and again with your friends may actually increase your sensitivity to them.

■ **Drawing Conclusions.** Ask students to consider the role that gossip plays in human interaction. What connection can they see between gossip and people's need to compare experiences or reduce uncertainty? *(Gossip can fulfill both functions.)* When can gossip serve as a negative social reinforcement? *(spreads incorrect information, promotes cliques, and so on)* (OBJECTIVE 1)

■ **Discussion.** Ask students how often they avoid discussing a problem of theirs with friends by saying "I don't want to talk about it anymore." What prompts people to avoid interacting with well-intentioned friends who want to help in solving a problem? Ask: Do you think that reviewing problems again and again with friends becomes counterproductive? (OBJECTIVE 1)

LAB EXPERIMENTS AND DEMONSTRATIONS

Ask students to keep a "contact log" for at least one week. Instruct students to record each time that a friend initiates contact, whether by telephone, letter, or in person. Tell students to identify the motivating factor underlying each contact: Was it to alleviate anxiety, compare experiences, or reduce uncertainty?

Have students analyze their findings and prepare brief oral reports on their findings for the class.

FIGURE 17.3

A set of apartments such as this was used in a study of friendship choice. It was found that the fewer doors there were between people, the more likely they were to become friends. **What is physical proximity?**

CHOOSING FRIENDS

Most people feel they have a great deal of latitude in the friends they choose. Easy transportation, telephones, and the spare time available to most Americans would all seem to ease communication among them and, therefore, to permit them a wide range of individuals from whom to choose companions, friends, and lovers. But in fact, we rarely venture beyond the most convenient methods in making contact with others.

Proximity

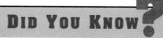

One of the most important factors in choosing friends is physical proximity.

Would it surprise you to learn that one of the most important factors in determining whether two people will become friends is **physical proximity**—the distance from one another that people live or work? In general, the closer two individuals are geographically to one another, the more likely they are to become attracted to each other. And it is more than just the opportunity for interaction that makes the difference.

Psychologists have found that even in a small two-story apartment building where each resident was in easy reach of everyone else, people were more likely to become close friends with the person next door than with anyone else (Figure 17.3). Psychologists believe that this is a result of the fears and embarrassments most people have about making contact with strangers. When two people live next door to one another, go to the same class, or work in the same place, they are able to get used to one another and to find reasons to talk to one another without ever having to seriously risk rejection. To make friends with someone whom you do not see routinely is much more difficult. You have to make it clear that you are interested and thus run the risk of making a fool of yourself—either because the

At A Glance

WHO IS SHY?

If you would rather disappear into the wallpaper than go to the class dance, you're shy. If you prefer to spend evenings at home instead of risking the possibility of meeting new people, you're shy too. But contrary to what you probably think, you are not alone. More than 80 percent of people questioned in one survey on shyness said they had been shy at some time in their lives. Out of this number, 40 percent said they felt shy now.

This does not mean that everyone is equally shy: There are degrees of shyness ranging from slight discomfort to some situations to sheer panic in all situations. Only 25 percent of the sample approached the far end of the scale, considering themselves to be chronically shy. An even smaller group—4 percent—said they were shy all the time in all situations.

If you are shy, it may give you some comfort to know that shyness is not a purely American trait. It is found to differing degrees in cultures throughout the world. In fact, right at this moment, 60 percent of Asians would say they were shy, too.

For more details, see Philip G. Zimbardo, *Shyness: What It Is, What to Do About It,* Reading, Mass.: Addison-Wesley, 1990.

other person turns out to be less interesting than he or she seemed at a distance or because that person expresses no interest in you. Of course, it may turn out that both of you are very glad someone spoke up.

Reward Values

Proximity helps people make friends, but it does not ensure lasting friendship. Sometimes people who are forced together in a situation take a dislike to one another that develops into hatred. Furthermore, once people have made friends, physical separation does not necessarily bring an end to their relationship. What are the factors that determine whether people will like each other once they come into contact?

One reward of friendship is stimulation. A friend has **stimulation value** if he or she is interesting or imaginative or can introduce you to new ideas or experiences. A friend who is cooperative and helpful, who seems willing to give his or her time and resources to help you achieve your goals, has **utility value.** A third type of value in friendship is **ego-support value:** sympathy and encouragement when things go badly, appreciation and approval

At A Glance

After students read the special feature, ask them to answer the following questions:
1. What percentage of people in one particular study admitted to being shy at some point in their lives? *(80%)*
2. How many admitted to still feeling shy? *(40%)*
3. In contrast to Americans, what percentage of Asians admit to feeling shy? *(60%)*
4. What factor does the feature suggest may sometimes promote shyness? *(culture norms, as in Asia)*

■ **Discussion.** Ask students to consider friendships that they have formed in the past. Call on volunteers to describe the circumstances under which the friendships formed. Was physical proximity the most important factor? Have the students identify which of the three reward values—stimulation, utility, and ego support— were factors in the formation of the friendship. (OBJECTIVE 2)

Teacher Note. So that students understand that ego support has its limits as a reward value, you might read them the following philosophical observation from Cicero's treatise *On Friendship*: "There is no greater bane to friendship than adulation, fawning, and flattery."

STUDY AND WRITING SKILLS

Assign students to find quotations that attempt to define what a friend or friendship is. They might explore books of quotations (such as *Bartlett's*), review entries in the library card catalog, and check the indexes in biographies and autobiographies of famous people (especially those who were known to have strong or stormy friendships). Students might also take a look at greeting card racks. After they have gathered several quotations, direct students to categorize them according to the three kinds of reward values: stimulation, utility, and ego support. Students might present their findings in a short informative essay.

■ **Role Play.** Call on pairs of volunteers to role-play the four reciprocal reinforcement techniques described in the margin feature. Tell each pair to engage in two conversations: one that purposely ignores the four recommended techniques, and one that incorporates one or more of the them. After each performance, ask the class to assess the effectiveness of reciprocal reinforcement in promoting good interpersonal relationships. (OBJECTIVE 2)

Teacher Note. According to a 1983 Roper Organization poll, men and women differ somewhat on what they first notice when they meet someone of the opposite sex for the first time. Forty-five percent of men reported that they first notice a woman's figure and build. Thirty-five percent notice the face, 29 percent how she is dressed, 24 percent her smile, and 22 percent her eyes. Of the women polled, 35 percent first notice how a man dresses. Thirty percent notice his eyes, 29 percent his build, 27 percent his face, and 27 percent his smile. Sixteen percent of both men and women first notice one another's hair, and 11 percent other features. (Tip: You might use this background to help students organize their own survey of gender preferences. Compare the results with the findings cited in this survey.)

How to Relate to People.
If you're like most people, you want others to like you, but knowing exactly how to make them like you is not always that easy. Most psychologists believe that the principle of *reciprocal reinforcement* has a great deal to do with how you get along with others. In simple terms, this principle states that people will like you if your behavior makes them feel good about themselves.

Here are some reinforcement techniques you can use to get a head start on winning and keeping friends:

• When you're talking to another person, try to spend at least 50 percent of the time listening to what the other person says.

• Be an active rather than a passive listener. By commenting directly on what the other person says, you will show that you are really interested.

• Instead of focusing only on your own accomplishments, ask questions about the person you are with.

• Approval is one of the best reinforcers if it is used correctly, but another person is easily turned off if it is not sincere. Be sure to praise only those things the other person considers important.

when things go well. These three kinds of rewards— stimulation, utility, and ego support—are evaluated consciously or unconsciously in every friendship. A man may like another man because the second man is a witty conversationalist (stimulation value) and knows a lot about gardening (utility value). A woman may like a man because he values her opinions (ego-support value) and because she has an exciting time with him (stimulation value).

By considering the three kinds of rewards that a person may look for in friendship, it is possible to understand other factors that affect liking and loving.

Physical Appearance. A person's physical appearance greatly influences others' impressions of him or her. People feel better about themselves when they associate with people others consider desirable. This is true of same-sex as well as opposite-sex relationships. Physical attractiveness influences our choice of friends as well as lovers.

In one study (Dion, Berscheid, and Walster, 1972), subjects were shown pictures of men and women of varying degrees of physical attractiveness and were asked to rate their personality traits. The physically attractive people were consistently viewed more positively than the less attractive ones. They were seen as more sensitive, kind, interesting, strong, poised, modest, and sociable, as well as more sexually responsive. It seems, therefore, that although we have heard that "beauty is only skin deep," we act as if it permeates one's entire personality.

People who do not meet society's standards for attractiveness are often viewed in an unfavorable light. Research has shown that obese adults are often discriminated against when they apply for jobs. Even children are targets of prejudice (Figure 17.4). An unattractive child is far more likely to be judged "bad" or "cruel" for an act of misbehavior than is a more attractive peer (Dion, Berscheid, and Walster, 1972).

Interestingly, psychologists have found that both men and women pay much less attention to physical appearance when choosing a marriage partner or a close friend than when inviting someone to go to a movie or a party. But neither men nor women necessarily seek out the most attractive member of their social world. Rather, people usually seek out others whom they consider their equals on the scale of attractiveness (Folkes, 1982).

Approval. Another factor that affects a person's choice of friends is approval. All of us tend to like people who agree with and support us because they make us feel better about ourselves—they provide ego-support value.

The results of one experiment suggest that other people's evaluations of oneself are more meaningful when they are a mixture of praise and criticism than when they are extreme in either direction. No one believes that he or she is all good or all bad. As a result, one can take more seriously a person who sees some good points and some bad points. But when the good points come first, hearing the bad can make one disappointed and angry at the person who made them. When the bad points come first, the effect is opposite. One thinks, "This person is perceptive and honest. At

PSYCHOLOGISTS AT WORK

Are we genetically predisposed to be attracted to good-looking people? Is jealousy something in our genes? *Evolutionary psychologists* would say yes, claiming that our most basic behaviors concerning physical attractiveness, approval, and similarity evolved in response to biological challenges faced by our distant ancestors. Although researchers in this field admit culture helps shape behavior, they believe we often act as we do because we are inherently motivated to pass our genes on to future generations. These psychologists see jealousy, for example, as an instinctive way to counter a perceived threat to our survival and that of our children. As might be expected, this field provokes a great deal of controversy among people who question or reject the theory of evolution.

FIGURE 17.4

In one experiment, adult women were shown reports about and photographs of children participating in a variety of antisocial behaviors. The adults tended not only to see the behaviors committed by the unattractive children as more generally antisocial, but to attribute a more inherently negative moral character to these children than to the attractive ones (Adapted from Dion, 1972). **What were the findings in the study in which adults rated the personality traits of other adults of varying physical attractiveness?**

first she was critical but later she saw what I was really like" (Aronson and Linder, 1965).

Similarity. People tend to choose friends whose backgrounds, attitudes, and interests are similar to their own. Often, husbands and wives have similar economic, religious, and educational backgrounds.

There are several explanations for the power of shared attitudes. First, agreement about what is stimulating, worthwhile, or fun provides the basis for sharing activities. People who have similar interests are likely to do more things together and to get to know one another better.

FIGURE 17.5

These two men obviously enjoy one another's company. **What reward values does friendship provide?**

Teacher Note. Psychologist David Buss of the University of Michigan surveyed more than 10,000 people in 37 cultures on every continent except Antarctica. Everywhere, the men consistently valued physical attractiveness and youth in a mate more than women did. The women consistently preferred a prospective mate to have ambition, status, and resources. Evolutionary psychologists theorize that since such gender-specific preferences are uniform across cultures they are innate behaviors and not primarily the result of social forces.

VISUAL INSTRUCTION

Ask the students to consider the information in the caption to Figure 17.4 from a different point of view. Are the unattractive children really being judged too harshly, or are the attractive children actually being treated too leniently? In other words, did the mothers misjudge only the behaviors of the unattractive children? (People generally tend to associate beauty with goodness and less attractive features with negative moral character.)
Answer to caption, Figure 17.4: Physically attractive people were consistently viewed more positively than the less attractive ones.
Answer to caption, Figure 17.5: stimulation, utility, and ego support

STUDY AND WRITING SKILLS

Assign students to research the psychological evidence that people are instinctively biased against unattractive people. Ask them to write an essay, drawing on their research and their general knowledge of psychology. Tell students to suggest ways people might learn to recognize this bias in themselves and to overcome it. You might have the students participate in a panel discussion of this topic in which they present their findings and recommendations.

Enrich. Have students complete the Chapter 17 Application Activity.

■ **Applying a Concept.** In discussing the concept of complementarity, remind students of the characters in the long-running sitcom *The Odd Couple*. Ask students to identify some other examples of "odd couples." As an extending activity, request volunteers to write or act out a skit in which the "odd couple" demonstrates its complementarity. (OBJECTIVE 2)

Second, most of us feel uneasy around people who are constantly challenging our views, and we translate our uneasiness into hostility or avoidance. We are more comfortable around people who support us. A friend's agreement bolsters your confidence and contributes to your self-esteem. In addition, most of us are self-centered enough to assume that people who share our values are basically decent and intelligent.

Finally, people who agree about things usually find it easier to communicate with each other. They have fewer arguments and misunderstandings; they are better able to predict one another's behavior and thus feel at ease with each other (Carli *et al*, 1991).

Complementarity—an attraction between opposite types of people— is not unusual, however. For example, a dominant person might be happy with a submissive mate. Still, most psychologists agree that similarity is a much more important factor. Although the old idea that opposites attract seems reasonable, researchers continue to be unable to verify it (Berscheid and Walster, 1978; Brehm, 1992).

PERSONAL RELATIONSHIPS

Your personal relationships with others bring meaning and substance to your everyday experiences. Knowing that you have loved ones who care about you and are willing recipients of your affection contributes to the quality of your life and your overall sense of well-being—and to theirs. Throughout life, you establish different kinds of personal relationships. Your first meaningful relationships were established within the family.

Parent-Child Relationships

Noted psychologists, including Erik Erikson, believed that early and persistent patterns of parent-child interaction can influence people's later adult expectations about their relationships with the significant people in their lives. If a young infant's first relationship with a caregiver is loving, responsive, and consistent, the child will develop a trust in the ability of other people to meet his or her needs. This trusting, in turn, will encourage the person to be receptive to people. On the other hand, a child who has experienced unresponsive, inconsistent, or unaffectionate care in infancy will most likely be more wary or mistrustful of other people. Within the parent-child relationship, we learn how to manipulate others to have our needs met. A parent is likely to satisfy the wishes of a child who acts "good," that is, who does what the parent asks. The child may also learn to get attention by pouting or having temper tantrums.

As children develop and form relationships with people outside their family, they apply what they have learned about relationships. As a result of childhood experiences, an individual might, for example, believe that the only way to establish and maintain good relationships with friends is always to say what pleases them rather than speak the truth.

STUDY AND WRITING SKILLS

Assign students to evaluate the theory that family violence perpetuates itself in successive generations. Have the students research magazine and newspaper articles as well as psychological studies. Instruct students to consider the danger of a self-fulfilling prophecy. (For example, "I grew up in an atmosphere of family violence; therefore, my future family life will probably be violent, too.") Tell students to present their findings in a brief informative essay that cites their sources.

Your parents influence the quality of your adult relationships in other ways. They provide you with your first model of a marital relationship. As you watched your mother and father interacting with each other as husband and wife, you were most likely forming some tentative conclusions about the nature of relationships. Later on, you might use their example as a guide in selecting a future mate or in evaluating your relationships. If your parents have a happy marriage, you will most likely seek to duplicate it by imitating their patterns. Sadly, the reverse may also be true. Evidence suggests that being part of a violent family in childhood increases the likelihood that someone will perpetuate that mode of behavior against his or her children and spouse (Rice, 1993).

Love Relationships

While most people say that they love their parents, their friends, and maybe even their brothers and sisters, they attach a different meaning to *love* when referring to a boyfriend, girlfriend, or spouse. Love means different things to different people and within different relationships.

Psychologist Zick Rubin (1973) distinguished between *liking* and *loving*. According to Rubin, liking usually involves respect or high regard for another person. Love usually involves liking plus three other elements: great attachment to and dependency on the person; a caring for or desire to help the person; and the desire for an exclusive, intimate relationship with the person. You may remember from Chapter 14 that Sternberg (1988) writes of the roles of passion, intimacy, and commitment in love. Other researchers (Berscheid, 1983; Davis, 1985; and Hatfield and Walster, 1981) have distinguished between two types of love. *Passionate love* is an intensely emotional and sexual fascination with a mate and a strong desire for exclusiveness. Feelings of excitement, anxiety, tenderness, and jealously are all common in passionate love. Passionate love is what is commonly referred to as "romantic love" in which lovers long for their partners and seek to capture their affection. In contrast to the relatively short-lived passionate love is *companionate love*, which is defined as the affection we feel for those with whom our lives are deeply intertwined. People who share a mutual concern and care for each other and who have strong, frequent, and long-term interactions are likely to experience companionate love. Friendship, understanding, and the willingness to make sacrifices for each other are characteristic of companionate love.

The differences between passionate and companionate love can be further examined by reviewing the development of each type of love. Psychologists Ellen Berscheid and Elaine Walster (1974) maintain that three criteria must be met for passionate love to occur. First, there must be a culturally held expectation that one will fall in love or be smitten by passionate desire for a person. People who believe in "love at first sight" or "falling head over heels in love" are likely to experience it. Second, there must be an appropriate "love object," someone who is "right."

The third criterion is the presence of an emotional arousal, which the person interprets as love. This emotional arousal can be experienced in a number of different ways, ranging from sexual arousal to anxiety or

FIGURE 17.6

What makes people fall in love? Is there such a thing as love at first sight? Does romantic love endure? Romance has inspired poets, painters, and playwrights through the ages. Psychologists are also interested in learning more about what causes people to fall in and out of love. **What are the characteristics of companionate love?**

COOPERATIVE LEARNING ACTIVITY

Organize the class into two teams and give them a few days to prepare strategies for a debate on the following question: What is the ideal relationship to which people should aspire—passionate love or companionate love? Tell each team that they will not be informed of the position that they will argue until the day of the debate. Therefore, they should prepare arguments both for and against each of the two kinds of love relationships. On the day of the debate, have the teams select debate leaders, who should flip a coin to determine which side each team will support.

■ Analyzing Information.

Ask students to consider the familiar saying, "Absence makes the heart grow fonder." According to the margin feature, under what circumstances is this saying true? *(when the relationship is already strong)* As a creative writing exercise, request volunteers to prepare short stories of students separated by distance and summer vacations. Read these stories aloud. Ask the rest of the class to predict whether the relationships will survive the separation. Why or why not? (OBJECTIVES 1, 2)

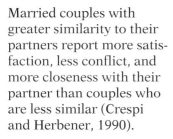

DID YOU KNOW?

Married couples with greater similarity to their partners report more satisfaction, less conflict, and more closeness with their partner than couples who are less similar (Crespi and Herbener, 1990).

Teacher Note. Mature, companionate love is characterized by empathy for the loved one (experiences are shared); deep concern for the welfare and happiness of the loved one (the partner will alter his or her own plans to make the loved one happy); finding pleasure in working for the loved one's welfare; and allowing the loved one freedom to do whatever he or she wishes (mature love is not possessive). (D. A. Prescott, 1957) Based on this background, you might challenge students to design a list of Dos and Don'ts for engaged couples.

PSYCHOLOGY and YOU

Love and Separation. Suppose you were involved in a serious romance and your partner had to move away. What would happen to your relationship?

Psychologists have studied couples who endure many different types of separation: college students who separate during vacations, college students who attend different schools, traveling executives and their spouses, military couples separated by active tours of duty, and prisoners of war and their families. Two findings consistently emerge from these studies: (1) all separations are stressful; and (2) strong relationships generally endure separations, whereas weak relationships generally do not. In fact, some college students report that they use separations (during the summer break or a semester abroad) specifically to test the strength of their relationships. On the other hand, people dissatisfied with their relationships often seek separations by accepting jobs requiring frequent travel or requesting transfers to new locations.

Will your relationship survive a separation? The answer depends more on the strength of your relationship than on the length or distance of separation itself.

anger. In fact, the source of a person's emotional arousal or love feelings may not even be the loved one, but another source. An attractive female interviewed males on a high, narrow swinging foot bridge over a deep ravine. After the experiment, she gave them her telephone number and asked them to call her if they wanted to learn additional details about the experiment. These men were significantly more likely to call her than were men interviewed by the same person and given the same invitation on a low, wide bridge over a very shallow culvert (Dutton & Aron, 1974). Apparently, their fear was misinterpreted as love for the researcher! According to Berscheid and Walster's theory, the emotional arousal you have experienced from the fright will channel itself into what feels like romantic love. Similarly, if you are going on a date and are anxious or excited about going to a new place, you may interpret the emotional arousal you feel as love for your date.

The onset of romantic or passionate love is fairly swift and sudden. It is quite fragile compared with companionate love. Passionate love, marked by strong, emotional upswings, rarely lasts long. Some passionate love relationships turn into longer lasting companionate love relationships.

The development of companionate love is less dramatic than that of passionate love. It begins as a mutual attraction between two people and changes as they build their relationship together. The development of a more intimate relationship may be stable and uneventful, stable but increasingly satisfying, or unstable and conflict-ridden. There are many variations in relationship patterns. Relationships that seem unstable often find stability, and seemingly unchanging relationships sometimes deteriorate into separation.

The development of a close companionate relationship is influenced by the degree to which each person is willing to reveal personal and private information about himself or herself. Couples who are willing to trust each other and who communicate their feelings and ideas freely are likely to have a close relationship that endures. Ordinarily, the more personal information a person discloses to a companion, the more personal information the companion is likely to disclose in return. This mutual disclosure serves to deepen the relationship.

Nonverbal Communication

Central to the development and maintenance of a relationship is the willingness to communicate aspects of yourself to others. Communication involves at least two people: a person who sends a message and a person who receives it. The message sent consists of an idea and some emotional component. Messages are sent verbally and nonverbally. "I like to watch you dance" is a verbal message; a warm smile is an example of **nonverbal communication.**

Although most people are aware of what they are saying verbally, they are often unaware of their nonverbal messages. They are more aware of the nonverbal messages when they are on the receiving end of them. You have probably heard someone say, "It doesn't matter," speaking in a low voice and looking away; the unspoken message is "My feelings are hurt." You do not need to be told in so many words that a friend is elated or

CONNECTIONS: PSYCHOLOGY AND LITERATURE

Assign each student to find two love poems—one that celebrates or bemoans passionate love, and one that praises or laments companionate love. Ask students to look for poems from a variety of time periods and cultures. Tell the students to bring copies of their poems to class. Select a group of volunteers to work as editors to sort and organize the poems into an anthology. Arrange to have copies of the anthology distributed to the class.

depressed, angry or pleased, nervous or content. You sense these things. People communicate nonverbally not only through facial expressions but also through their use of space and body language (posture and gestures).

Personal Space. Anthropologist Edward T. Hall became acutely aware of the importance people attach to space when he found himself backing away from a colleague he particularly liked and respected. The associate was not an American, which led Hall to wonder whether people from different cultures had different ideas about the proper distance at which to hold an informal conversation. He decided to pursue the question.

After much observation, Hall concluded that Americans carry a "bubble" of privacy around them—their personal space. If another person invades this bubble, we feel slightly threatened, imposed upon, and generally uncomfortable. For Germans, the bubble of privacy is much larger; for Arabs, much smaller (Hall, 1959). Thus, an Arab man talking to a German man, for example, may try to establish his accustomed talking distance and move closer. The German may conclude that the Arab is "pushy." When the German moves back to what he feels is a normal distance, the Arab may take this as a sign of coldness and conclude that the man is aloof.

There are four distances or zones within which we communicate with each other. Our *intimate* distance is up to about 18 inches. The only people whom we let within that zone—our personal bubble—are members of our immediate family, relatives, close friends, and lovers. With few exceptions—such as being at a play with a friend—those are the only people with whom you exchange information in whispers or a very soft voice. When we are forced to stand very close to non-intimates, as in a crowded elevator, we try to hold our bodies immobile and avoid eye contact.

Our *personal* distance is about 4 feet. We use a soft or low voice in this zone, such as when we are talking with only one other person. People at this distance from us are usually our friends or acquaintances. A teacher and a pupil would stand up to 4 feet apart in a conversation.

Our *social* distance is 4 to 12 feet. If you and a friend were joined by other friends at a party, the circle would simply grow bigger. Once the distance across the circle reaches about 12 feet, however, the group would tend to break into smaller circles. Using a moderate or full voice, it would be hard to be heard comfortably across that distance saying the kinds of things friends like to say to one another. Business relationships are rarely conducted with more than 12 feet between the people doing business. In business or formal relations, distance can be a very important dimension. If you visit a university professor, a department head, a dean, and the school's president, your chair will probably be further removed from the person with each move up the administrative hierarchy. Is such distancing obvious in your school? If you step back when someone at a party comes within 2 feet, you're discouraging further intimacy even though you may not be aware of the nonverbal message you're sending.

Finally, our *public* distance is anything over 12 feet (Figure 17.7). At this distance, you will typically use your loudest voice. You will be at least this far removed from your teacher in many teaching situations and from the singer or the group in most rock concerts (Hall, 1966; Hall & Hall, 1971).

■ **Demonstration.** Have students identify their preferred personal space within each of the four zones described in the text: intimate, personal, social, and public. Then request volunteers to demonstrate the various distance ranges. Have them indicate the distance at which somebody "invades their space." Ask: Do ranges differ from person to person? (Contrast, for example, the ranges comfortable for an extravert as opposed to an introvert.) (OBJECTIVES 1–3)

Teacher Note. You might point out that American and Northern European tourists are often puzzled to see men in Italy and other Mediterranean countries walking arm in arm in public. This degree of intimacy is culturally acceptable for friends engaged in conversation. Similar intimacy among men can be observed in many Middle Eastern countries, such as Turkey.

Readings in Psychology. Have students read the Section 6, Reading 1 selection in *Readings in Psychology* and answer the questions that follow the selection.

CONNECTIONS: PSYCHOLOGY AND ART

Assign a group of students to research several art books or museum catalogs to find examples of paintings and drawings that illustrate each of the four kinds of personal space: intimate, personal, social, and public. Arrange to have copies of the paintings assembled in a classroom display. Have the students write appropriate captions, identifying the work, the artist, the period, and the medium.

Ask students to describe other occasions when a "public distance" is maintained as long as possible. For example, call on students to describe how a movie theater fills up, or how people select their seats in a doctor's waiting room or in an airport lounge. Can they recall observing people using subtle, or perhaps not-so-subtle, body language to protect their personal space in public? (OBJECTIVE 3)

Answer to caption, Figure 17.7: back away or become immobile and avoid eye contact

Answer to caption, Figure 17.8: social rules

Teacher Note. In discussing the social rules surrounding touching, you might point out the uproar that Australian Prime Minister Paul Keating created when he put his arm around Queen Elizabeth during a public reception. Not even someone with the status of prime minister can claim that privilege. Another example might be the "Clinton hug." Upon victory, the President-elect hugged his Vice President, Al Gore. Never before had a U.S. President embraced a man on public television. The action made front-page news.

FIGURE 17.7

Many of these people place themselves more than 12 feet apart, a signal that they desire minimal direct personal communication. **How do we react when someone enters our "bubble" of privacy?**

How people use space to communicate will become clear if you keep this scheme in mind.

Body Language. The way you carry your body also communicates information about you. This is your **body language.** If you stand tall and erect, you convey the impression of self-assurance. If you sit and talk with your arms folded and legs crossed—a closed body position—you communicate that you are protecting yourself. When you unfold your arms and stretch out, your open body position may be saying that you are open to people.

One group of researchers found that women who adopt an open body position are better liked and are listened to more closely than women who assume a closed position. A number of students were given a questionnaire that measured their opinions on everything from the legalization of marijuana to the custom of tipping. A few weeks later, they were invited back and asked to evaluate other students' responses to the same questions. Some students were shown a slide of this female student sitting in a closed position; others saw a slide of her sitting in a neutral or open position. A high percentage of those who saw the open-looking picture indicated that they liked her and changed many of their opinions to agree with hers when they filled out the questionnaire a second time. On the other hand, the group that saw the closed-looking picture tended to stick with their original responses (McGinley, LeFevre, and McGinley, 1975).

FIGURE 17.8

Our body language includes the postures we adopt and the gestures we make to convey messages. **What rules govern body language?**

Although the use of body language is often unconscious, many of the postures we adopt and gestures we make are governed by **social rules** (Figure 17.8). These rules are very subtle. *Touching,* for example, has rules—not just where, but who (Duncan, 1969). Your teacher or boss is much more likely to touch you than you are to touch him or her. Touching is considered a privilege of higher status.

Have the students work in teams of writers and artists to develop a glossary of body language. Instruct the teams to decide on a consistent style and format for their glossary. For example, should it be organized like a standard illustrated dictionary—A to Z with the pictures added as supplements—or should the visual elements determine how the glossary is organized (e.g., facial cues followed by posture cues, and so on)? Assign a team of editors to compile the glossary and oversee its publication. Distribute copies to all the class members.

There are cultural differences in body language, just as there are in the use of space. For example, Americans move their heads up and down to show agreement and shake them back and forth to show disagreement. The Semang of Malaya thrust their heads sharply forward to agree and lower their eyes to disagree, while the Dayak of Borneo agree by raising their eyebrows and disagree by bringing them together. You read earlier about the Germans' expanded personal space. Their smiles are also governed by different rules; they smile less frequently. That leaves the Germans thinking Americans are deceptive—using a smile to hide their true feelings. Americans often view Germans as cold or distant. It's all in the absence of a smile (Hall & Hall, 1990).

You do not have to go to Borneo or Europe to observe cultural variations in nonverbal communication. In a field study conducted in hospitals, airports, and restaurants, LaFrance and Mayo (1976) found that African Americans and white Americans use eye contact in very different ways. Although people of both races looked at each other for the same proportion of time during a conversation, the timing was different. African Americans tend to look at their partner when they are speaking, and to look away while listening; whites do just the opposite. These unconscious differences may sometimes make African Americans and whites uncomfortable when they talk to each other.

HOW PEOPLE PERCEIVE ONE ANOTHER

It takes people very little time to make judgments about one another. From one brief conversation, or even by watching a person across a room, you

**Very Warm
Industrious
Critical
Practical
Determined**

FIGURE 17.9

What is your impression of this person? Do you think you would like him? What do you think of the way he is dressed? What sort of expression does he have on his face? When you have formed an impression, turn to Figure 17.10 and do the same.

CHAPTER 17 Lesson Plan

■ **Applying Concepts.** Have students list as many examples of cultural differences in body language as they can. Discuss these examples in connection with one of the key ideas of this chapter: that people often misinterpret the behaviors of other people. Challenge students to suggest ways that people from different cultures can overcome such misreadings of one another's intentions. (OBJECTIVE 2)

VISUAL INSTRUCTION

Figures 17.9 and 17.10 test the validity of the implicit personality theory. Have the students answer the questions posed in this caption before they turn to Figure 17.10.

Answer to caption, Figure 17.9: Answers will vary, but according to the implicit personality theory the students' impressions should be influenced by the words "very warm" in the illustration.

BEYOND THE CLASSROOM

Assign students to research examples of cultural differences in body language. Tell students that tourist guides and travel memoirs as well as books of cultural anthropology might be valuable sources of information on this topic. Have students present their findings in brief oral reports to the class. Suggest that they enliven their presentations with visual aids and interesting anecdotes about cultural misunderstandings related to body language.

■ **Discussion.** Lead the students in a discussion of the implicit personality theory, especially its usefulness in helping us predict with some degree of accuracy how the people we meet will behave. Point out, too, the importance of social introductions in light of this theory. For example, when a host says to a guest, "I know you'll enjoy meeting Kevin. He's so warm and witty," the guest will generally become predisposed to perceiving Kevin favorably when the two eventually meet. (OBJECTIVE 2)

VISUAL INSTRUCTION

Tell the students not to look back to Figure 17.9 while they are considering this figure. How many actually think the person pictured here looks different from the one on page 437? Ask students to consider the old saying "What you see is what you get" in light of this experiment. Do they think it should be reworded as *"How you see is what you get"*? Why or why not? **Answer to caption, Figure 17.10:** If the students' impressions have changed, the reason is in the change of words—from "very warm" to "rather cold"; otherwise, the two figures are identical.

may form an impression of what someone is like, and first impressions influence the future of a relationship. If a person *seems* interesting, he or she becomes a candidate for future interaction. A person who seems to have nothing interesting to say—or much too much to say—does not. We tend to be sympathetic toward someone who seems shy; to expect a lot from someone who impresses us as intelligent; to be wary of a person who strikes us as aggressive.

Forming an impression of a person is not a passive process in which certain characteristics of the individual are the input and a certain impression is the automatic outcome. If impressions varied only when input varied, then everyone meeting a particular stranger would form the same impression of him or her. This, of course, is not what happens. One individual may judge a newcomer to be "quiet," another may judge the same person to be "dull," and still another person may think the person "mysterious." These various impressions lead to different expectations of the newcomer and to different patterns of interaction with him or her.

Implicit Personality Theory

One reason different people develop different impressions of the same stranger is that we each have our own **implicit personality theory**—our own set of assumptions about how people behave and what traits or characteristics go together. When you meet someone who seems unusually intelligent, you may assume she is also active, highly motivated, and conscientious. Another person in the group may have an altogether different "theory" about highly intelligent people—that they are boring, boastful,

**Rather Cold
Industrious
Critical
Practical
Determined**

FIGURE 17.10

Are your impressions of this person different from your impressions of the person in Figure 17.9? **If so, why are your impressions different?**

LAB EXPERIMENTS AND DEMONSTRATIONS

Arrange to have a "stranger" interrupt your class, supposedly to deliver you a message. Interact with the "stranger" for a few moments where all of the students can see. After the "stranger" is gone, ask students to write down what impressions they formed. Call on students to read their impressions aloud and to compare them among themselves. Discuss why different students formed different impressions.

unfriendly, and the like. Whatever the person does provides "evidence" for both theories. You are impressed by how animated she becomes when talking about her work; the other person does not care for how little attention she pays to other people. Both of you are filling in gaps in what you know about the person, fitting her into a type you carry around in your head.

Experiments indicate that our impressions are strongly influenced by a few traits (Figures 17.9, 17.10). For example, one researcher invited a guest lecturer to a psychology class. Beforehand all the students were given a brief description of the visitor. The descriptions were identical in all traits but one. Half the students were told that the speaker was rather cold, the other half that he was very warm. After the lecture the researcher asked all the students to evaluate the lecturer. Reading their impressions, you would hardly know that the two groups of students were describing the same person. The students who had been told he was cold saw a humorless, ruthless, self-centered person. The other students saw a relaxed, friendly, concerned person. Changing one adverb and one adjective—substituting "rather cold" for "very warm"—had a dramatic effect on the student's perception of the lecturer, as described in Figure 17.10. The process illustrates a primacy effect. The students interpreted the last neutral words in terms of the first one, giving it greater—or primary—impact. Thus, to be warm and determined was perceived as dedicated; to be cold and determined was perceived as rigid. It also affected their behavior. Students in the "warm group" were warm themselves, initiating more conversations with the speaker than did the students in the other group (Kelley, 1950).

Stereotypes. The line between applying implicit personality theories to people (as the students did) and thinking in stereotypes is a very thin one. A **stereotype** is an exaggerated set of assumptions about an identifiable group of people. The belief that males are dominant and independent or that females are nurturing and emotional are examples. Stereotypes may contain positive or negative information, but primacy effects may cause stereotypes to bias us. If stereotypes influence our information about people, then they may become self-fulfilling prophecies (Hamilton & Sherman, 1989).

Implicit personality theories are useful because they help us to predict with *some* degree of accuracy how people will behave. Without them, we would spend considerable energy observing and testing people to find out what they are like, whether we want to pursue a relationship with them, and so on. Like stereotypes, if the assumptions we make about people from our first impressions don't weaken as we get to know them better, then we are guilty of harboring prejudice.

Personality Versus Circumstance: Attribution Theory

You're waiting at a traffic light. Somebody behind you honks and gestures frantically for you to get out of the way. Not sure what's happening, you move your car—slowly, so they won't think you're a pushover—to allow the driver to pull even with you. As he does, the driver looks across at you and says, "Thanks. My wife's in labor. We're in a hurry!"

PSYCHOLOGY UPDATE

Stereotyping Bias in Psychiatric Diagnosis. Psychiatric professionals are trained to be objective observers of human behavior, but they are not immune to stereotyping their patients. Researchers have identified biases involving several groups, including the mentally retarded, the elderly, and people of low socioeconomic status (SES).

Mentally retarded people were consistently *underdiagnosed*; that is, they were not given a diagnosis when their symptoms indicated that a disorder in fact existed. Specifically, retarded patients frequently showed symptoms of depression, anxiety, and other disorders, but these problems were rarely diagnosed.

Frequently people of low SES and elderly patients were *overdiagnosed*, that is, given diagnoses that were not warranted by their behavior. In the absence of clear symptoms, some low-SES patients were falsely labeled as schizophrenic. Often physical and cognitive deterioration expected of elderly patients was labeled depression or dementia (disorganized thinking).

These findings have prompted psychiatric professionals to take a closer look at the symptoms of these patients and the conditions that may contribute to their problems.

CONNECTIONS: PSYCHOLOGY AND SOCIAL STUDIES

Have students research history books to find stereotypical images that were used to reinforce cultural fears and prejudices. Tell students to look especially for political cartoons and war propaganda posters. (Many cartoons appear in the chapters on World War I and World War II in U.S. history textbooks.) Instruct students to identify the source and date of each stereotypical image and to explain its cultural context. Lead the class in a discussion of how stereotypes can be both hateful and hurtful.

WORKING WITH TRANSPARENCIES

Project Transparency 27 and use the guidelines provided in Teaching Strategies and Activities. Assign Student Worksheet 27. Make sure students understand the nature of the interactions occurring among the characters in the illustration. **Answer to caption, Figure 17.11:** an analysis of how we interpret and understand other people's behavior

■ **Role Play.** Before class begins, arrange for three volunteers to role-play the following scene:

A young man in a leather jacket is walking down a street, past a line of parked cars. It begins to rain heavily. The young man notices that one of the parked cars has all its windows open. He looks around and then opens the car door. As he leans inside and begins rolling up the windows, the owner comes running up, shouting "Stop! Thief! Someone call the police!" The young man protests, but the owner—a well-dressed, older man—continues his accusations. Just then, a shopkeeper steps out onto the sidewalk and says, "I saw the whole thing. That young man was just trying to roll up your windows and save your car from getting ruined by the rain."

Have the class analyze the behaviors of the young man and the owner in terms of attribution theory and stereotyping. (OBJECTIVE 2)

FIGURE 17.11

Who attributes what to whom? In this first part of an experiment, actors A and B were talking while observers C and D watched B and A, respectively. Both actors later rated their own behavior in terms of personal characteristics about themselves or characteristics of the situation. Observers C and D similarly rated each of their target actors. The results showed that actors attributed their own behavior more to situational factors than to enduring personality factors. Observers, however, saw the actors' behavior more in terms of personality factors. **What is attribution theory?**

> **How we interpret another's behavior depends just as much on how we perceive it as on what it is.**

If you're like most of us, you feel foolish, but everyone has moments like that. You were facing a situation that many social psychologists study—trying to interpret and explain people's behavior by identifying what caused the behavior (Jones, 1990). The focus of study in this circumstance is called **attribution theory** (Heider, 1958; Kelley, 1967; Jones & Nisbett, 1972), an analysis of how we interpret and understand other people's behavior. When you first heard the horn, you undoubtedly attributed the man's pushiness to personal characteristics—often called *dispositional factors*. Once he thanked you and gave a valid reason for his urgency, your analysis immediately changed to credit his behavior to the needs of his wife—often called *situational factors*.

Typically, we explain our own behavior in terms of situational factors, but we—as in the example at the traffic light—attribute others' behavior to their dispositions. That represents what psychologists call a **fundamental attribution error** (Ross, 1977). This is a common occurrence. For example, turn to the sports pages of a newspaper and read the interviews of the winners and losers in an important football game. More often than not, the winning team will laud the brilliance of their quarterback, their defense, or their game plan—disposition is credited. The losing team will blame the "breaks," a key injury, or some other uncontrollable factor—the situation is blamed (Lau & Russell, 1980).

When there's glory to be claimed, we often demonstrate another form of error called a **self-serving bias.** In victory, we are quick to claim personal responsibility; in defeat, we pin the blame on circumstances beyond our control. Another factor that influences our ability to judge people's behavior is the **actor-observer bias** (Jones & Nisbett, 1972). How we interpret another's behavior depends just as much on how we perceive it as on what

ADDITIONAL INFORMATION

The tendency to attribute other people's behavior to personality rather than to situational forces is so pervasive that it often overrides common sense. For example, Gilbert and Jones (1986) found that even when people knew for certain that a writer had been assigned to argue a particular point of view on a topic, they nevertheless assumed that the opinions expressed were truly the writer's own. Accordingly, it is not uncommon for people to assume that defense lawyers are as corrupt as the criminals whom they may be required to defend.

it is. For example, researchers set up an experiment in which observers watched two participants in conversation. Observers standing behind Participant A thought B dominated the conversation. Observers standing behind Participant B thought A dominated the conversation. A neutral observer to the side of the conversation thought both A and B contributed equally (Taylor & Fiske, 1975). When able to see only one actor, the observers of A or B commit the fundamental attribution error, the neutral observer does not. See Figure 17.11 for another version of this experiment.

The point is that we all actively perceive other people's actions. What we conclude about other people depends not just on what they do, but also on our interpretations. This is true not just when we deal with individuals, but also when we react to groups.

WHAT ARE GROUPS?

What do the Rolling Stones, the St. Stanislaus Parish Bowling Team, the American Association of Retired Persons (AARP), and country music's Alabama have in common? Each can be classified as a **group.** In general, the features that distinguish a group from a nongroup are interdependence, shared goals, and communication.

Interdependence

All the people in the world who have red hair and freckles make up a category of people, but they are not a group. The people in this collection

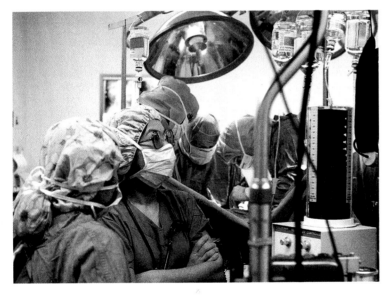

FIGURE 17.12

Whether or not the members of this surgical team are friendly outside the operating room does not matter. Their main purpose as a group is do a certain job. **What are the features that groups share?**

■ **Demonstration.** Have students explain in their own words what is meant by "norms of behavior." Then call on two volunteers to act out the various scenarios described in the margin feature. After the demonstrations, have the class discuss which kind of behavior is the norm in your community. At which point in the scenarios did the students feel that eye contact became more than a socially acceptable form of behavior? At which point did it become overtly threatening? (OBJECTIVE 3)

MORE about. . .

The Eyes Have It. Visual behavior illustrates the effects of norms on our behavior. When you are passing someone in the hallway whom you do not know, you have two choices: to speak or not to speak. If you say hello, or nod, or otherwise acknowledge the other person, and they respond, then what? If you decide not to speak, then what?

In both instances, when you are 10 to 18 feet in front of the person, you are expected to divert your eyes to the right. You develop an intense interest in a bulletin board you've looked at a hundred times, or you look at the ceiling or the floor.

If you continue looking at the person until your head is turned 90 degrees, it would be considered "pushy." If you turned and continued viewing a member of the opposite sex as he or she (and you) continued walking down the hallway, it would border on sexual harassment.

In an elevator, it is customary for riders to redistribute the floor space more or less equally each time someone gets on or off. These norms are the unwritten "rules of the road" that govern our social behavior.

are not interdependent. Interdependence occurs when any action by one of them will affect or influence the other members or when the same event will influence each one. For instance, in groups of athletes, entertainers, or roommates, each member has a certain responsibility to the rest of the group; if he or she does not fulfill it, the other members will be affected. For the athletes, the consequence may be losing the game; for the entertainers, a bad show; for the roommates, a messy apartment.

In small groups, members usually have a direct influence on one another: one member communicates directly with another. In larger groups, the influence may be indirect. The interdependence between you and the President of the United States is not a result of personal contact. Nevertheless, one of the things that make the people of the United States a group is the fact that the President's actions affect you and that your actions, together with those of many other Americans, affect the President.

Common Goals

Group members become interdependent because they see themselves as sharing certain common goals. Groups are usually created to perform tasks or to organize activities that no individual could handle alone. Members of a consumer group, for example, share the common goal of working for consumer protection. Members of ethnic and religious groups desire to perpetuate a common heritage or set of beliefs.

The purposes groups serve are of two general kinds: **task functions,** those directed toward getting some job done; and **social functions,** those directed toward filling the emotional needs of members. In most groups, task and social functions are naturally combined and cannot easily be separated, although one dominates in any given group.

Political parties, teams of surgeons, and crews of construction workers are all task-oriented groups (Figure 17.12). Although social interactions occur within each of these groups, their main purpose is to complete a project or achieve some change in the environment. Social functions are emphasized in more informal, temporary groups. When people take walks together, attend parties, or participate in conversations, they have formed a group to gain such social rewards as companionship and emotional support. But again, every group involves both task and social functions, at least to some degree.

Whether it's boys or girls engaged in a neighborhood tug-of-war contest, a college football team preparing for the big game, or a NASA lunar launch team spread around the world, communication is crucial to the functions of a group. In some cases, the communication is directed outward as a declaration of group membership, such as when a member of the band wears a T-shirt or jacket with the school's logo or name.

In other instances, the communication is internal, intended primarily for group members, announcing group activities. Direct communication aids members' feelings of belonging. It increases the likelihood that group members will respond differently to one another than to those who do not belong to the group. It encourages debate among members regarding goals,

LAB EXPERIMENTS AND DEMONSTRATIONS

To demonstrate some unwritten "rules of the road" that govern our social behavior, use tape to outline an 8′ x 8′ square on the floor in front of the class. Tell students that the square represents an elevator. Then designate a side of the square as the doorway. Call on students one at a time to enter the "elevator." Tell them to behave like strangers. Ask the rest of the class to observe the students' movements as the "elevator" fills to capacity. Have all of the "passengers" arranged themselves facing the door? Have the males gravitated toward the back? After the "elevator" is full, call on two more students to enter. Do they try to force their way inside, or do they decide to back away? After the students return to their seats, have them discuss the unwritten rules that govern elevator etiquette.

and increases members' feelings of commitment to group goals through processes of communication.

HOW GROUPS ARE HELD TOGETHER

The factors that work to hold groups together—that increase the group's *cohesiveness*—include the attitudes and standards they share, and their commitment to them.

Norms

One way in which groups keep their members going in the same direction is by developing group norms. **Norms** are rules for the behavior and attitudes of group members. These rules are not necessarily rigid laws. They may be more like tendencies or habits. But group members are expected to act in accordance with group norms and are punished in some way if they do not. If a college student shaved her hair off, her friends would not hesitate to say something about it. Strangers might point and giggle—simply because she violated the norm that hair should be a certain length and style. Thus, the punishment may take the form of coldness or criticism from other group members. If the norm is very important to the group, a member who violates it may endure a more severe social reaction or may be excluded from the group.

Ideology

For a group to be cohesive, members must share the same values. In some cases, people are drawn together because they discover they have common ideas, attitudes, and goals—that is, a common **ideology.** In other instances, people are attracted to a group because its ideology provides them with a new way of looking at themselves and interpreting events, and a new set of goals and means for achieving them. The National Organization for Women (NOW), for example, has provided a focal point for resistance to discrimination on the basis of sex. The American Association of Retired Persons (AARP) lobbies for the rights of older people and retirees. Leaders, heroes and heroines, rallies, books and pamphlets, slogans, and symbols all help to popularize an ideology, win converts, and create feelings of solidarity among group members.

Commitment

One factor that increases individual commitment is the requirement of personal sacrifice. If a person is willing to pay money, endure hardship, or undergo humiliation to join a group, he or she is likely to continue with it. For example, college students who undergo embarrassing initiation rites to join sororities or fraternities tend to develop a loyalty to the group that lasts

■ Writing a Case Study.
Have students identify various groups within your school. List responses on the chalkboard. Then divide the class into groups. Assign each group to prepare a case study analyzing how one of the groups is held together. Ask the students to identify the norms that pertain to each group. Do certain norms apply to all the groups that the class listed? What particular norms distinguish each group from all the others? Next, have students identify each group's distinguishing ideology. Finally, direct students to assess the commitment of individual members to the group. Have students share their case studies with the class as a whole.
(OBJECTIVE 3)

CONNECTIONS: PSYCHOLOGY AND LITERATURE

Fiction often provides keen insights into how norms govern social behavior. Assign students to research and find an example of a novel, short story, or fairy tale in which a character breaks a norm and suffers social consequences. (Nathaniel Hawthorne's *The Scarlet Letter* is one example.) Have students prepare a synopsis of their chosen work and present it orally to the class.

■ **Writing a Case Study.** Fol-low up your discussion of how groups are held together with a discussion of how they disin-tegrate. Ask students to con-sider a failed school group or community organization with which they are familiar. Work-ing in groups, assign students to write a second case study analyzing the group's disinte-gration in terms of each of the three elements that contribute to cohesiveness—norms, ideol-ogy, and commitment.
(OBJECTIVE 3)

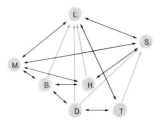

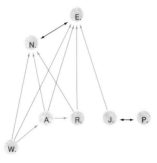

FIGURE 17.13

In these sociograms, the blue arrows indicate admiration that is not returned; the black arrows indicate a two-way friendship. The more a person is liked, the higher in the pattern he or she appears. The pattern of the bottom group shows a hierarchical structure. **Who are the leaders in the bottom group?**

well beyond their college years. Cohesiveness will be high if members are committed to their group.

Another factor that strengthens group commitment is participation. When people actively participate in group decisions and share the rewards of the group's accomplishments, their feeling of membership increases—they feel that they have helped make the group what it is. For example, social psychologists have compared groups of workers who participate in decisions that affect their jobs with other workers who elect representa-tives to decision-making committees or workers who are simply told what to do. Those who participate have higher morale and accept change more readily than the other workers (Coch and French, 1948). Other studies have highlighted the importance of supportive managers in maintaining such worker involvement (Locke, Latham, & Erez, 1988).

The processes that hold a group together must work both ways. The individual must be responsive to the norms of the group, subscribe to its ideology, and be prepared to make sacrifices in order to be part of it. But the group must also respond to the needs of its members. It cannot achieve cohesiveness if its norms are unenforceable, if its ideology is inconsistent with the beliefs of its members, or if the rewards it offers do not outweigh the sacrifices it requires.

INTERACTIONS WITHIN GROUPS

Providing an individual with values and a sense of identity is only one aspect of the group's meaning to him or her. The particular role he or she plays in the group's activities is also important. Each group member has certain unique abilities and interests, and the group has a number of dif-ferent tasks that need to be performed. The study of the roles various members play in the group, and of how these roles are interrelated, is the study of *group structure*.

There are many different aspects to group structure: the personal rela-tionships between individual members, such as liking relationships and trusting relationships; the rank of each member on a particular dimension, such as power, popularity, status, or amount of resources; and the roles various members play. A *role* is behavior expected of an individual because of his or her membership in a particular group. Thus, when your class meets, someone has the role of teacher, others have the role of students. Is someone a student leader in your class? Does someone always remain silent? Is another person always making jokes?

Each of us has *multiple roles* that shift as we merge with different groups. Occasionally, we may find ourselves in *role conflict* such as if you switch schools and your old school plays your new school in football.

Communication Patterns

One technique psychologists use to analyze group structure is the **socio-gram.** All members of a group are asked to name those people with whom they would like to interact on a given occasion or for a specific purpose, those they like best, and so on. For example, the members may be asked with whom they would like to go to a party, to discuss politics, to spend a vacation, or to complete a task. Their choices can then be diagrammed, as shown in Figure 17.13. Sociograms can help psychologists predict how that individual is likely to communicate with other group members. Another way to discover the structure of a group is to examine the communication patterns in the group—who says what to whom, and how often.

One experiment on communication patterns was done by Harold Leavitt in 1951. He gave a card with several symbols on it to each person in a group of five. Leavitt put each person in a separate room or booth and allowed the members to communicate only by written messages. In this way he was able to create the networks shown in Figure 17.14. Each circle represents a person; the lines represent open channels. Subjects placed in each position could exchange messages only with the person to whom they were connected by channels.

The most interesting result of this experiment was that the people who were organized into a "circle" were the slowest at solving the problem but the happiest at doing it. In this group everyone sent and received a large number of messages until someone solved the problem and passed the information on. In the "wheel," by contrast, everyone sent a few messages to

FACT OR FICTION

Group decisions are always conservative.

Fiction. Often group decisions are more extreme than the choice any individual member would make on his or her own. The process—at one time called a *risky shift*—is better called a *shift toward extremity*. Psychologists believe that this shift toward an extreme occurs because people listen to arguments in group discussions and add new ones they had not previously considered to justify their original position. This, combined with their desire to appear better than average, encourages the shift toward extremity.

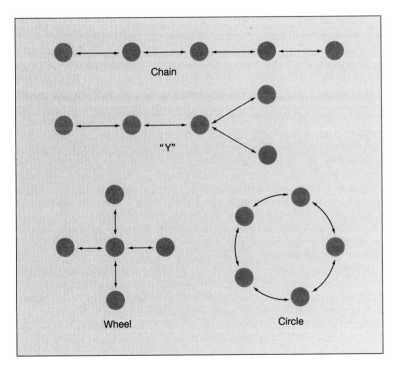

Chain

"Y"

Wheel

Circle

FIGURE 17.14

This illustration shows Harold Leavitt's communication network system. **What were Leavitt's findings regarding centralized organizations?**

CHAPTER 17 Lesson Plan

■ **Interpreting Diagrams.** Reproduce the models for the "Wheel" and "Circle" communication networks on the chalkboard. First, ask students to explain the kind of interaction that occurs in each model. Next, instruct them to explain why the "Circle" network is slower, but more satisfying than the "Wheel" network for solving tasks. *(The "Wheel" is faster because it uses a centralized command; in effect, one person makes all the decisions. This may be unsatisfying for anyone outside the hub. The "Circle" is slower because it involves greater intercommunication, which in itself may prove to be more satisfying.)* (OBJECTIVE 3)

VISUAL INSTRUCTION

Have students identify the dot in each figure that represents the group leader. *(The center dots in the "Chain," "Y," and "Wheel" models represent the group leaders. The "Circle" model has no primary leader.)* **Answer to caption, Figure 17.14:** more useful for task-oriented groups

WORKING WITH TRANSPARENCIES

Project Transparencies 28 and 29 and use the guidelines provided in Teaching Strategies and Activities. Assign Student Worksheets 28 and 29.

COMMUNITY INVOLVEMENT

Invite the general manager of a local business to visit the class to talk about how his or her company is organized. The speaker should be asked specifically to discuss the company's chain of command and communication patterns as outlined in its business plan. Students should prepare questions in advance to try to ascertain if the speaker's company employs communication networks similar to those identified by Harold Leavitt and pictured in Figure 17.14.

FIGURE 17.15

Lee Iacocca was fired from his job at one automobile company, yet he went on to become the Chairman of the Board of the Chrysler Corporation. Iacocca's leadership skills were put to the test at Chrysler, and he was widely credited with having steered the company away from bankruptcy to success. **According to Blake and Mouton, what are two areas of concern for leaders?**

one center person, who figured out the answer and told the rest what it was. These groups found the solution quickly, but the people on the outside of the wheel did not particularly enjoy the job.

Following the experiment, the members in each group were asked to identify the leader of their group. In the centralized groups (wheel, Y, and chain), the person in the center was usually chosen as the group leader. But in the circle network half the group members said they thought there was no real leader, and those who did say there was a leader disagreed on who that leader was. Thus a centralized organization seems more useful for task-oriented groups, whereas a decentralized network is more useful in socially oriented groups.

Leadership

All groups, whether made up of gangsters, workers, Girl Scouts, or politicians, have leaders. A leader embodies the norms and ideals of the group and represents the group to outsiders. Within the group, a leader initiates action, gives orders, makes decisions, and settles disputes. In short, a leader is one who has a great deal of influence on the other members.

Leadership may be defined in several ways. Most of us think of leadership as a *personality trait*. To an extent, this is true. Stogdill (1974), summarizing years of experiments and research, identified leadership as being an aspect of personality, the ability to get people to comply. It can be thought of as skills in social influence or persuasion, or simply as social power. It has been found that leaders tend to be better adjusted, more self-confident, more energetic and outgoing, and slightly more intelligent than other members of their group (Gibb, 1969). Often, we view leaders as either task leaders or social leaders, but Blake and Mouton (1985) proposed a different model. They argue that leaders are concerned to some degree with both output (that is, the task) and the welfare of the people. Each dimension is separate, and any leader can be at any level on either dimension. A leader deeply concerned with both output and welfare would likely develop a team management program, so that workers contribute to the group's goals. A leader concerned solely with output would stress obedience; a leader whose primary concern was the worker might create a stress-free atmosphere with a friendly organization. A leader who cared little for output or welfare might encourage workers to do the minimum to keep things functioning (Blake & McCanse, 1991).

Another way to think of leadership is as the *end product of the reinforcements of the group* being led (Berry & Houston, 1993). In this way, leadership is simply the center or focus of group action, an instrument for achieving the group's goal(s), or a result of group interaction (Stogdill, 1974). In this sense, the nature of the group in part determines who will lead. Different circumstances call for different kinds of leaders. A group that is threatened by internal conflict requires a leader who is good at handling people, settling disputes, soothing tempers, and the like. A group that has a complex task to perform needs a leader with special experience to set goals and plan strategies for achieving them (Fiedler, 1969).

Diffusion of Responsibility

Sometimes, several people are faced with a common problem although they have no leader and may not even see themselves as a group. There have been many famous examples of muggings, rapes, and murders that were committed in public while a large group of people watched without intervening or calling for help.

Psychologists have tried to find out why these people didn't act by studying artificial crises. In one experiment, college students were asked to participate in a discussion of personal problems. They were asked to wait in separate rooms. Some were told that they would be communicating with

Using Psychology

The Peer Group

In the early years of a child's life, parents play an important and influential role. As children grow older, however, the influence of their peers becomes increasingly strong. Peer groups are made up of people who have similar interests, frequent contact, and a mutual influence on each other. Peer interactions are different from parent-child or teacher-student interactions in that peer interactions are usually initiated for companionship and amusement, whereas parent or teacher interactions are more often based on a need for protection, care, or instruction (Damon, 1983). People generally choose their peer groups, whereas they do not choose their parents, siblings, or teachers.

Research on infants and preschool children indicates that peer interactions through play help children develop important social skills. By the time children reach school age, they spend almost as much of their time with peers as they do with their parents. By the second grade, most children have at least three or four good friends among their same-sex peers (Reisman and Shorr, 1978). During the transition from childhood to adolescence, peers become the central focus of attention (Feiring & Lewis, 1989). The peer group remains a major source of socialization during adolescence and adulthood. Unlike peer groups in grade school, which are made up primarily of same-sex friends of the same age, adolescent and adult peer groups consist of members of both sexes and include a wider range of ages.

The peer group serves a number of important functions in a person's life. To begin with, peers provide *companionship*—people with whom to spend time and talk. The way peers provide this closeness changes with development.

Teacher Note. Another term used in psychology for *peer group* is *reference group*. You might point this out, especially if your students are researching books and articles on this topic.

Using Psychology

After students read the special feature, have them answer the following questions:
1. At what stage of life do peers first become the central focus of attention for a person? *(during the transition from childhood to adulthood)*
2. In what area of personal behavior is the influence of the peer group generally the strongest? *(in matters of personal preference and taste)*
3. How does peer group affiliation encourage adolescents to become more independent? *(by providing an opportunity for the adolescent to try out and discuss new behaviors)*

CONNECTIONS: PSYCHOLOGY AND THE MEDIA

Besides its status as an American musical classic, the movie version of *West Side Story* offers students a chance to study the various characteristics of peer groups as outlined in the Using Psychology feature. The movie also illustrates the concepts involved in group conflicts and touches on the value of cooperation. (The filmmakers built in stereotypes and prejudice as well.) Assign students to view *West Side Story* from the perspective of a film critic for a popular psychology journal. Have them critique the movie's portrayal of peer group interaction. In addition, suggest that students mention stereotypes reflective of the era in which the film was made.

PORTRAIT

Theodore M. Newcomb
1903–1984

When Theodore Newcomb joined the faculty at Bennington College in 1934, he embarked on the study destined to make him famous. At the time, Bennington was a newly founded women's college known for its liberal views. Most of the students, however, came from largely conservative backgrounds.

Newcomb, though socially liberal, was the son of a clergyman and had studied theology before deciding to earn his doctorate in psychology. At Bennington, he became intrigued by the problem that these conservative young women faced upon entering the college. How did they go about adjusting to their new environment? What Newcomb found was that most of the women changed their social attitudes and adopted the liberal views of the peer group already established on campus. By adopting liberal attitudes, the newcomers were able to fit in and gain peer acceptance.

Twenty-five years later, Newcomb conducted a follow-up to his original Bennington study. Did the women resume their conservative attitudes after leaving college? Newcomb found that the alumni continued to hold on to their liberal views, even though their peer group had long ago disintegrated.

(For more on the Bennington study, see Chapter 18.)

Sociologist Dexter Dunphy (1963) observed the changes in the way teenagers in an urban setting spend time with each other. In early adolescence, teenagers spend most of their time with same-sex friends in cliques of three or four people. Then, these friendships expand to include additional same-sex friends. By the mid-teens, these friendships have evolved into organized crowds in which cliques engage in group-to-group interaction. The crowds soon include both sexes and include social activities such as dances and parties. By late adolescence, people begin to date within these crowds and form more intimate relationships. By young adulthood, the peer crowd has disintegrated, to be replaced by loosely organized groups of couples.

Another important psychological feature of peer groups is *peer acceptance*. Peer friendships and peer group acceptance are compelling forces. The extent to which you are liked and accepted by your peers can affect the way you feel about yourself as well as the way your peers treat you. In an effort to be accepted and admired, members of peer groups conform to the standards and values of the group.

In adolescence, conformity to peer group standards generally increases with age, but the level of conformity depends on the tasks or behavior demanded. If a person is uncertain about an issue or has mixed feelings, he or she is more likely to go along with the group opinion. In matters involving a firm personal conviction, however, the older adolescent is more likely to take an individual stand, even when the opinion conflicts with peer group standards.

Peer group influence is generally strongest in matters of *personal preference and taste*. Peers shape a teenager's preference for music, hairstyles, clothes, recreation, and choice of friends. Peers are also much more influential than parents or teachers in shaping sexual attitudes and behavior. The use of drugs and alcohol is heavily influenced by peer group activities. Despite this, the peer group for most adolescents has values and beliefs very similar to the parents of its members (Fasick, 1984).

While parents, older adults, and teachers are more likely than peers to influence a person's political views and academic and career choices, the socioeconomic status of the peer group does influence an adolescent's *vocational plans*. For example, lower-class teenagers with middle-class friends generally aspire to higher-status careers. One reason for this influence may be that people seek others who share their goals and values. Parents of any class who encourage their children to do well in school and to aspire to high-status careers also influence their children's choice of friends based on these values.

 LAB EXPERIMENTS AND DEMONSTRATIONS

To test the power of peer and social pressure and the effect it has on determining norms of behavior, suggest that a few of your students adopt some subtle form of "abnormal" behavior for a day, such as socially unacceptable dress or grooming. (Discuss each student's plan ahead of time and alert the school authorities to the nature of this experiment.) Tell the students to keep a log of how people react to their "abnormal" behavior and whether they feel others treated them differently. Have the students report the results of their experiment to the class.

FIGURE 17.16

Peer groups are an important part of a teenager's life. Group members are likely to dress alike, talk alike, and share similar interests and goals. **What are the negative aspects of peer pressure?**

Peer group affiliation can encourage adolescents to become more independent of their parents. Peers provide an opportunity for people to try out or discuss new behaviors that are not encouraged or are discouraged by parents. For example, most parents do not discuss or encourage adolescents' sexuality, but peers readily exchange ideas and information on this subject. The peer group is a major source of support when a date or an attempted date leads to rejection. It is a means by which an adolescent can reaffirm his or her own worth and ideas, dispel confusion, and maintain self-confidence. Peers are crucial in guiding the process (Schlegal & Barry, 1991). Family ties become less intense as adolescents identify with their peer group and try out new behaviors and ideas.

The shift in interest toward the peer group helps to encourage a separateness between parent and adolescent. Sometimes, the pressure to conform to peer group standards instead of parental standards results in overt rebellion and antisocial behavior. For most people, however, independence from parents is achieved without

VISUAL INSTRUCTION

Ask students to distinguish between *belonging* and *conforming*. Can an individual belong to a peer group without conforming? Challenge the students to explain. **Answer to caption, Figure 17.16:** Answers will vary, but may include: disruptive behavior; prejudicial nature of the "in group"; tendency to discredit members of the "out group."

■ **Debating an Issue.** After students read the special feature on the peer group, organize two teams to debate the following issue: *Resolved—* Cliques should be banned in school because they hinder healthy socialization. (OBJECTIVE 3)

CRITICAL THINKING ACTIVITY

Analyzing Ideas. Ask students to analyze the peer group with which they are most closely affiliated. What norms must each member follow in order to gain memberships or remain part of the group? How does the peer group reward or punish its members to maintain the norms that operate within the group? Ask students to identify a situation when their peer group, or an individual within the group, rewarded or punished them because of their actions. Did they conform or rebel? Ask students to summarize their analyses in a brief essay.

■ **Analyzing Media.** Have students recall scenes from the film *The Time Machine*, based on H. G. Wells's classic science-fiction novel about time travel. In particular, remind students of the scene in which people called the Eloi ignore the cries for help of a companion who is drowning. Discuss this scene in terms of diffusion of responsibility. Ask students to supply other instances—either from films, novels, or real life.
(OBJECTIVE 3)

Independent Practice

■ **Conducting a Survey.** Ask students to poll people in the community to find out how many have ever struck up conversations or friendships with complete strangers. Tell students to ask those who respond affirmatively to describe the circumstances that led them to "break the ice." Have students present their findings in brief oral reports to the class. (OBJECTIVE 1)

■ **Assessing Personality.** Request volunteers to bring in a collection of personal photographs that show them in all kinds of moods and poses. (They can be at different ages—even early childhood.) Have volunteers indicate on a slip of paper the photograph that they think *most* typifies their personality. Then request the rest of the class to examine the photographs. (If possible, use an opaque projector.) What photo or photos would students choose? Why? Have each volunteer show the slip of paper identifying the photo he or she chose. How did the choices compare? Encourage students to discuss the difference between their public and private personalities.
(OBJECTIVE 2)

450

extreme disruption. Most adolescents and young adults accept their parents' values as their own once they establish independence.

The influence of peers can sometimes produce unpleasant effects. While almost everyone wants to be accepted and liked by peers, not everyone is. Some people experience peer rejection or neglect. Usually the people who achieve high peer status (those liked by a number of peers) are friendlier, more physically attractive, more socially outgoing, cooperative, and do better in school (Dodge, 1983). As a rule, the unpopular people lack the social skills necessary for acceptance and often engage in socially undesirable actions such as aggressive and antagonistic behavior. People who are neglected or rejected by their peers may withdraw and feel very lonely and isolated. Frequently they are shy and unhappy and lack self-confidence. Some individuals go to extreme lengths to please a group in order to earn acceptance or avoid rejection. This desire to please can, in turn, lead to further disruptive behavior. Adolescents who try to adjust to a peer group whose views oppose those held by their families may also face considerable conflict and stress (Newman, 1982).

Adolescents derive more than just "fun" from participating in their peer group activities. Peer groups satisfy an emotional need—the need to belong. The members of a peer group feel a bond that distinguishes "us" from "them." It is somewhat paradoxical that this way of finding out who "we" are helps the individual find out who he or she is.

The negative aspect of peer group unity is the prejudicial nature of the "in group" and the tendency to discredit members of the "out group." The positive side of this unity is the security and strength that it gives, for example, to minorities dealing with prejudices from a majority. In this way, peer groups serve the same psychological function as support groups.

only one other person; others were given the impression that they would be talking with as many as five other people. All communication, the psychologist told each student, was to take place over microphones so that everyone would remain anonymous and thus would be able to speak more freely. Each person was to talk in turn.

In reality, there were no other people—all the voices the subjects heard were on tape. As the discussion progressed, the subject heard one of the participants go into what sounded like an epileptic seizure. The victim

CONNECTIONS: PSYCHOLOGY AND SOCIETY

Have students research the psychology of bystander intervention by examining examples of violence occurring in public before a large crowd that failed to intervene. (The murder of Kitty Genovese in Queens, New York, in the 1960s is one such case. More than 30 neighbors and bystanders heard her when she screamed for help, but did not come to her aid.) Have students prepare oral reports in which they describe the incident chosen and how psychologists interpreted the behavior of the bystanders.

began to call for help, making choking sounds. The experimenters found that 85 percent of the people who thought they were alone with the victim came out of their room to help him. But of those who believed there were four other people nearby, only 31 percent did anything to help.

The experimenters suggested that this behavior was the result of **diffusion of responsibility.** In other words, because several people were present, each subject assumed someone else would help. The researchers found that in experiments where people could see the other participants, the same pattern emerged. In addition, bystanders reassured one another that it would not be a good idea to interfere. These findings on diffusion of responsibility suggest that the larger the crowd or group of bystanders, the more likely any given individual is to feel that he or she is not responsible for whatever is going on (Darley and Latané, 1968).

Another influence that inhibits action is the tendency to minimize the *need* for any response. To act, you must admit that an emergency exists. But you may not know exactly what is going on when you hear screams or loud thumps upstairs. You are likely to wait before risking the embarrassment of rushing to help where help is not needed or wanted. It is easier to persuade yourself that nothing needs to be done if you look around and see other people behaving calmly. Not only can you see that they think nothing is wrong, but you can see that not doing anything is entirely proper. You are able to minimize the need to act and shift any responsibility to those around you. However, the presence of a leader or being familiar with the person needing help both increase the likelihood and speed of help being offered. The same is true of *knowing* what kind of help is required, seeing the correct form of assistance being modeled, or the expectation of future interactions with the person needing help. These situations increase the chances that assistance will be offered when it is most needed (Baron & Byrne, 1991).

GROUP CONFLICT VERSUS COOPERATION

Conflicts between groups are a fact of everyday life: some level of hostility exists between women and men, young and old, workers and bosses, African Americans and whites, Catholics and Protestants, students and teachers. Why do these conflicts exist, and why do they persist? In the next chapter, we discuss prejudice, discrimination, and related issues. But first let us consider the findings of a group of psychologists who created a boys' camp in order to study intergroup relations. The camp at Robber's Cave offered all the usual activities, and the boys had no idea that they were part of an experiment.

From the beginning of the experiment, the boys were divided into two separate groups. The boys hiked, swam, and played baseball only with members of their own group, and friendships and group spirit soon developed. After a while the experimenters (working as counselors) brought the groups together for a tournament. The psychologists had hypothesized

FIGURE 17.17

During the Robber's Cave experiment, the boys competed against one another in such activities as tug-of-war. The considerable hostility that developed between the two groups was expressed in drawings like the one above. **How did the experimenters try to eliminate the hostility?**

CONNECTIONS: PSYCHOLOGY AND LITERATURE

Nobel laureate William Golding's famous novel *The Lord of the Flies* traces how a planeload of schoolboys degenerates into two savagely competitive groups after they become stranded on a deserted island. The novel is rich in symbolism that lends itself to various psychological interpretations (e.g., that all the characters represent aspects of the personality of the central character, Ralph). Some of your students may enjoy reading, or rereading, this book for its insights into the psychological origin of group conflicts.

ASSESS
Check for Understanding
Ask students to summarize what they have learned in this chapter regarding why and how human beings interact.

Reteach
Have students complete the Chapter 17 Study Guide Activity. For extended review assign the Chapter 17 Review Activity as homework or an in-class assignment.

Enrich
Ask students to complete the Chapter 17 Extension Activity and answer the questions following it.

Evaluate
Administer and grade the Chapter 17 Test. Two forms are available should you wish to give different tests to different students/classes.

Use the Understanding Psychology Testmaker to create a customized test.

CLOSE
Ask students to think back to the activity in which they were asked to describe themselves as a type of footwear. Now that they have finished Chapter 17, would they want to reconsider their original choice? Can one kind of shoe still adequately represent their personality as they themselves and others view it? Challenge students to write down their personal reactions in a narrative essay entitled "Walk in My Shoes." (Tip: Tell students that the use of humor is appropriate.)

that when these two groups of boys were placed in competitive situations, where one group could achieve its goals only at the expense of the other, hostility would develop. They were right.

Although the games began in a spirit of good sportsmanship, tension mounted as the tournament continued. Friendly competition gave way to name calling, fistfights, and raids on enemy cabins. The psychologists had demonstrated the ease with which they could produce unity within the two boys' groups and hatred between them. The experimenters then tried to see what might end the conflict and create harmony between the two groups. They tried to bring the groups together for enjoyable activities, such as a movie and a good meal. This approach failed. The campers shoved and pushed each other, threw food and insults, and generally used the opportunity to continue their attacks.

Next, the psychologists deliberately invented a series of "emergencies" so that the boys would either have to help one another or lose the chance to do or get something they all wanted. For instance, one morning someone reported that the water line to the camp had broken. The boys were told that unless they worked together to find the break and fix it, they would all have to leave camp. By afternoon, they had jointly found and fixed the damage. Gradually, through such cooperative activities, intergroup hostility and tensions lessened. Friendships began to develop between individuals of the opposing groups, and eventually the groups began to seek out occasions to mingle. At the end of the camp period, members of both groups requested that they ride home together on the same bus.

The results of this experiment were striking. A group of boys from identical backgrounds had developed considerable hostility toward each other, simply because they were placed in competition. The crucial factor in eliminating group hostility was cooperation (Sherif *et al.*, 1961).

The question of conflict is not confined just to small groups. It applies to large communities too, but then the possibility of a social trap is greater. A *social trap* occurs when individuals in a group decide not to cooperate. Instead, they act selfishly and create a bad situation for all.

An illustration of the social trap can be seen in the way Americans have responded to the problems of pollution. We know that automobile exhaust pollutes the air. We know that one way to reduce air pollution is to carpool or use public transportation. Yet the driver who commutes 30 miles a day, alone, and who knows that he or she is polluting the air, thinks: "Yes, I know my car exhaust is bad, but I am only one person. If I stop driving, it won't make any difference." As long as we fall into that social trap, we shall continue to destroy our environment.

Psychologists have been exploring ways to overcome social traps such as this one. One approach is to use laws to bring about behavior changes, such as the law requiring special exhaust systems in cars. Another way to change people's behavior is to educate them concerning the issues and also to communicate the idea that "Yes, you do make a difference." By publicizing the problems and solutions, and organizing groups to act, individuals begin to feel that what they do does have an impact. And their actions are reinforced by the group. In this way, people find it more beneficial to cooperate than to act in a purely selfish manner.

CRITICAL THINKING ACTIVITY

Synthesizing Information. Ask students to identify some of the various social traps that affect American society today—i.e., instances of individuals acting selfishly and thereby creating a bad situation for all. An example might include the person who neglects to recycle newspapers, thinking that it will have no effect on the environment. Have students think of ideas and slogans for an advertising campaign to convince such individuals to change their behavior.

SUMMARY

Use the following outline as a tool for reviewing this chapter. Copy the outline onto your own paper, leaving spaces between headings to make notes about key concepts.

CONCEPTS AND VOCABULARY

1. In what situations do we want to be with other people?

2. Is the saying "Misery loves company" accurate?

3. What is the most important factor in determining the start of a friendship? Why is this an important factor?

4. Describe the three kinds of rewards that a friendship offers.

5. At what stage of a relationship is physical attractiveness of a partner an important concern? Are you likely to ask a very attractive person for a date?

6. Which person is likely to make a better impression on you—one who praises you first and then criticizes you or someone who points out your faults and then discusses your good points?

7. In general, are you likely to choose as a friend a person who is similar to you or a person who complements your strengths and weaknesses?

8. How do passionate love and companionate love differ?

9. How far would you stand from someone to indicate that you would like to talk to that person? Explain why this is so.

10. What theory do you use when you form an impression of a stranger? If that judgment is based on the stranger's similarity to other people in a given category, what set of assumptions are you using?

11. If you want people to think that you are smart, should you try to do your best on the first, second, or last test in a class? What theory does this illustrate?

12. What features distinguish a group from a nongroup? What are the purposes of a group?

13. What factors work to hold a group together? What factors increase the commitment of a person to the group?

14. What technique do psychologists use to study group structure? In what types of group structures will a leader be easily recognized?

453

ANSWERS

Concepts and Vocabulary

1. when we are afraid, anxious, unsure, or want to compare our feelings to those of others

2. Yes. Schachter's experiment found that people suffering from high anxiety are more likely to seek out company.

3. The most important is physical proximity. It increases the likelihood that two people will become attracted to one another.

4. stimulation (the friend is interesting); utility (the friend is helpful); and ego support (the friend is encouraging)

5. in the early stage, when impressions are first formed; yes, if you are attractive yourself

6. the one who criticizes first then praises

7. one who is similar to you

8. Passionate love is intensely emotional, sexual, exclusive, and short-lived. Companionate love is the lasting affection for those with whom our lives are deeply intertwined.

9. Generally, you would stand about three feet away—between the person's personal and social zones. The distance may vary from culture to culture.

10. implicit personality theory; stereotypes

11. on the first test; attribution theory

12. interdependence, shared goals, and communication; tasks or social functions

13. shared norms, a common ideology, and high commitment and participation of group members; Commitment increases when the individuals can share in group decisions and share the rewards.

14. They use the sociogram technique; leaders are easily recognized in the wheel, Y, and chain structures.

15. social leaders and task leaders; social leaders usually command more loyalty; through aspects of personality (charisma), skills in social influence or persuasion (expertise), or social power

16. diffusion of responsibility and minimizing the need for any response to a problem

17. You would involve them in some cooperative work to solve a crisis that concerns both groups.

453

Critical Thinking

1. Answers will vary. Make certain that student responses include a good understanding of what altruism is. Students may note that we are most likely to help someone in need when "costs" are low, the person in need is similar to us, the need for help is obvious, and other people have helped or are in the process of helping.

2. Begin discussion by asking students why people "put on acts" with different groups. Is this necessarily negative behavior, or normal adjustment to changes in social environment?

3. Start by having students give definitions of jealousy and describing the feelings and physical responses involved. Then have them discuss the causes of jealousy and whether males and females react differently. (In matters of love, studies show that males are more jealous when they suspect the partner of sexual infidelity; women when they suspect the partner of emotional attachments to someone else.)

4. Encourage students to explore their ideas about love and friendship, and respect any hesitancy they may have about discussing in public such a sensitive issue.

Applying Knowledge

1. Answers will vary, but student responses should demonstrate an understanding of both the advantages and disadvantages of stereotypes.

2. Answers will vary, but students should keep a careful

15. What are the two kinds of group leaders? Which type will command the loyalty of the group? What are three ways to become a group leader?

16. What are two factors that inhibit group action?

17. If you wanted to reduce conflict between two opposing groups of students, what kinds of activities would you ask them to participate in?

CRITICAL THINKING

1. **Synthesize.** Think about what you have learned from your reading and classroom discussions about altruistic or helping behavior. How might it be possible to increase altruistic behavior in people? What factors might prevent this from occurring? If you were asked to lecture on this topic, what would you tell your listeners?

2. **Apply.** Describe several situations in which you "put on an act" for your family or peer group. Is putting on an act more likely to occur around peers or family? Why do people behave differently around different groups?

3. **Analyze.** Have you ever been jealous of a boyfriend, girlfriend, sibling, friend, or parent? Recall a time when you were jealous of another person. What was the nature of your relationship with this person? How did you feel about yourself? What made you feel jealous? What effect did your responses to the jealousy have on your relationship with the person? Ask several of your friends (both male and female) to respond to these questions. Compare your experience of jealousy with your friends' reactions. Do you notice any similarities? Are there differences between your male and female friends' jealous reactions? If you had it to do over again within the relationship, would you respond the same way?

4. **Analyze.** Friendship and love are often combined in personal relationships, yet loved ones

and friends are often selected for different reasons, and we often act differently toward each one. Think of people whom you consider your friends. What type of behavior do you expect from them? What do you do with them that you can't do with people you do not call friends? Be as specific as you can. Do different friends fulfill different roles in your life? Think of someone you love now or loved at one time. How would you describe this person? What are or were your expectations of him or her? In what ways do you act similarly toward your loved one and friends? Share your ideas and insights with a classmate, friend, or loved one and get reactions.

APPLYING KNOWLEDGE

1. We may think that stereotyping does not influence us. Watch a television program about (a) a detective, (b) an African American family, (c) a white family, (d) an independent woman. What character traits does each have? Do we laugh at some of these characterizations when they do not fit the stereotypes? Which stereotypes do we not laugh at?

2. Examine the interactions between members of your family, your friends, or even strangers, paying as little attention as possible to verbal interaction and noting instead proximity, posture, gesture, facial expression, eye contact, relative position, and nonlinguistic verbal cues. Are you able to interpret the body language? Does this nonverbal communication conflict with what people communicate verbally? What happens if you reply verbally to nonverbal messages?

3. People tend to see other people's behavior as determined by personality traits, while they see their own behavior as a function of the situation they are in. To demonstrate this phenomenon, you will need the help of a friend. Give your friend a sheet of paper and ask him or her to list the following traits across the top of the sheet: sincere, conscientious, aggressive, friendly, in-

log of their observations and analyze the behaviors they observed.

3. Answers will vary, but students should demonstrate that they completed the experiment and report their findings.

4. Answers will vary, but the students should keep a log of their observations during the experiment and present an analysis of their findings.

5. Answers will vary, but student responses should include a description of the

friend's personal space, how it was "invaded," and how the friend reacted.

6. Answers will vary, but student responses should include a personal list and a comparison to the lists of the two friends.

7. Answers will vary, but each leadership profile should address the three areas of charisma, expertise, and power.

dependent, and mature. Then have your friend list the following names of people down the left side of the paper: the president, a public figure he or she dislikes, himself or herself, the name of a neighbor he or she hardly knows, and his or her best friend. Then ask your friend to fill in the chart by rating each person on each trait, giving a plus if the person has the trait listed across the top, a minus if the person does not have the trait, and a zero if it depends on the situation. When your friend is finished, sum up the number of pluses, minuses, and zeros for each person, including himself or herself. If your friend is like most people, you will notice that more traits, both positive and negative, were assigned to other people. Share your observations with your friend.

4. Get on an elevator and stand facing the back wall. Have a friend watch the other riders to see how they react to the violation of this simple social norm.

5. Conduct an experiment on personal space by going to the library and sitting at a table where a friend is seated. After a few minutes, begin to "invade" his or her space by placing your books and papers across the imaginary line that divides the space between the two of you. Describe your friend's reactions to your encroachments.

6. List in detail the main things you look for when you choose close friends. What are your reasons for rejecting certain people as either close friends or acquaintances? Ask two of your friends to make similar lists. After they have made their lists, share your list with them. Discuss the similarities and differences.

7. In the groups to which you belong (clubs, your school, and so on) you have undoubtedly had leaders or people with influence over you. Pick a few such leaders and answer these questions about them. Are they experts? Are they socially attractive? How much power do they have? How have they obtained it?

ANALYZING VIEWPOINTS

1. Some people claim that nonverbal communication is a more accurate indicator of an individual's true thoughts and feelings than verbal communication. Others disagree, arguing that verbal communication is most accurate—people are rational beings, and they generally say what they mean. Which viewpoint do you agree with? Write an essay that argues both sides of the issue.

BEYOND THE CLASSROOM

1. Choose a person in your community whom you consider to be a leader. This could be a politician, a member of the clergy, the coach of a sports team, or any other individual you consider to be a leader. What qualities does this person have that make him or her a leader? How does the person demonstrate the characteristics of leadership? Arrange an interview with the individual. Ask him or her the following questions: What is your personal definition of leadership? What do you consider to be the qualities of a good leader? With your teacher's assistance, find out if the person would be willing to come and talk to your class about leadership. If you are unable to arrange a class visit, prepare a report based on your interview.

IN YOUR JOURNAL

1. Analyze the items in your journal entry that you wrote at the beginning of the chapter. Now, categorize these items as either physical traits, psychological characteristics, or group affiliations. How much of your self-concept is built on your identification with groups? Write your answer in your journal.

455

Analyzing Viewpoints

1. Answers will vary, but the students' essays should address both sides of the issue regarding nonverbal communication before drawing a conclusion.

Beyond the Classroom

1. Answers will vary, but students' reports should document their interview questions and address such leadership issues as charisma, expertise, and power.

IN YOUR JOURNAL

If time permits, discuss journal entries individually with the students.

CHAPTER BONUS
Test Question

This question may be used for extra credit on the chapter test.
Choose the letter of the correct response.

A friendship in which two individuals provide sympathy and encouragement to one another when things go badly is based on:

a. physical proximity.
b. stimulation value.
c. actor-observer bias.
d. ego-support value.

Answer: **d**

Attitudes and Social Influence

TEXT TOPICS	SPECIAL FEATURES	RESOURCE MATERIALS
Where Attitudes Come From, pp. 457–459		▰ Reproducible Lesson Plan; Study Guide; Review Activity
Attitude Formation, pp. 459–461	**Psychology and You,** p. 461	▰ Reproducible Lesson Plan; Study Guide; Review Activity
Prejudice, pp. 461–465		▰ Reproducible Lesson Plan; Study Guide; Review Activity; Application Activity
Cognitive Consistency and Changing Attitudes, pp. 465–466		▰ Reproducible Lesson Plan; Study Guide; Review Activity
Attitudes and Actions, pp. 466–469	**More About Psychology,** p. 469	▰ Reproducible Lesson Plan; Study Guide; Review Activity
Persuasion, pp. 469–477	**At a Glance:** Sex in Advertising, p. 471 **Psychology and You,** p. 473 **Fact or Fiction?,** p. 475 **Using Psychology:** Promoting Energy Conservation, pp. 476–477	▰ Reproducible Lesson Plan; Study Guide; Review Activity ▯ *Readings in Psychology:* Section 6, Reading 3
Social Influence, pp. 478–482	**Psychology and You,** p. 477	▰ Reproducible Lesson Plan; Study Guide; Review Activity; Extension Activity ▯ *Readings in Psychology:* Section 6, Reading 4 ▰ Chapter Test, Form A and Form B ▣ Understanding Psychology Testmaker

PERFORMANCE ASSESSMENT ACTIVITY

Assign students to collect letters to the editor from their local newspaper or a national magazine. Working in groups, have students identify the issue addressed in each letter. Then direct them to identify the writer's attitude on this issue. Challenge students to go one step further. Ask: What beliefs underlie this attitude? For example, if a letter criticizes pay discrepancies between men and women, the letter writer probably believes in equality. Request a member from each group to share their analyses with the class. (Students should avoid interjecting any of their own attitudes or beliefs in the presentation—unless they clearly label them as such.)

CHAPTER RESOURCES

Readings for the Student
Brown, Roger. *Social Psychology.* New York: The Free Press, 1985.

Cialdini, R. B. *Influence: How and Why People Agree to Do Things.* New York: Morrow, 1984.

Lifton, Robert Jay. *Home from the War.* New York: Simon & Schuster, 1973.

Readings for the Teacher
Festinger, L. *A Theory of Cognitive Dissonance.* Stanford, CA: Stanford University Press, 1957.

McGuire, W. J. "Attitudes and Attitude Change." In G. Lindsey and E. Aronson (Eds.), *Handbook of Social Psychology* (pp. 233–346), Reading, MA: Addison-Wesley, 1985.

Milgram, S. *Obedience to Authority.* New York: Harper & Row, 1974.

Zimbardo, P. G., and Leippe, M. R. *The Psychology of Attitude Change and Social Influence.* New York: McGraw-Hill, 1991.

Multimedia
Coping with Peer Pressure—Getting Along Without Going Along (3/4" or 1/2" video). Guidance Associates. This video demonstrates the forces of peer pressure and some resistance techniques.

Obedience (45 minutes). New York University. This includes actual films of the Milgram experiment.

For additional resources, see the bibliography beginning on page 530.

FOCUS

Motivating Activity

Write the following categories on the chalkboard:

- politics
- education
- clothing styles
- dating choices
- personal values

Ask students to spend a few minutes thinking about the people or forces that have influenced their attitudes, opinions, or beliefs in each of these areas. Using this as a basis, have students brainstorm a generalized list of influences on the five categories of attitudes. Ask: Do the sources of influence differ from area to area? Or do some sources exert weight in all areas? For example, what role does parental or peer pressure play? What role does the media play? Save student responses for use in the Close activity on page 482.

Meeting Chapter Objectives.

Using the six "reporter's questions" *(Who? What? Where? Why? When? and How?)*, have students write the objectives on page 457 as questions. Assign them to answer the questions as they read the chapter.

Building Vocabulary.

Assign groups of students to prepare crossword puzzles using at least 10 of the Key Terms. Have the groups exchange their puzzles with each other.

Attitudes and Social Influence

FIGURE 18.1 Our attitudes, opinions, and beliefs can be strongly reinforced and supported by being with others who share them.

456

TEACHER CLASSROOM RESOURCES

- Chapter 18 Reproducible Lesson Plan
- Chapter 18 Study Guide
- Chapter 18 Review Activity
- Chapter 18 Application Activity
- Chapter 18 Extension Activity

- *Readings in Psychology:* Section 6, Readings 3, 4

- Chapter 18 Test, Form A and Form B

- Understanding Psychology Testmaker

Exploring Key Ideas
Describing Attitudes.
Challenge students to discuss what is meant by the expressions "good attitude" and "bad attitude." Tell students that the use of "good" or "bad" implies a value or moral judgment. Ask: Who or what sets the standards on what is "good" or "bad" about an attitude? Suppose a person holds an attitude that is contrary to popular opinion. Does that mean the individual's attitude is ethically incorrect? Why or why not? Tell students that Chapter 18 provides possible answers to these and other questions. It also explains how attitudes can be changed. Suggest that students write down any personal attitudes that are questioned or changed by information in this chapter.

OBJECTIVES

After studying this chapter, you should be able to
- trace the origin and composition of attitudes.
- describe prejudice and its relationship to stereotypes and roles.
- cite the sources of attitude change.
- explain the different types of persuasion processes.

Are you convinced that vitamin C is the best cure for the common cold? Did the oil companies cause the energy crisis? How do you feel about atheism, patriotism, and the Dallas Cowboys? Each of us has a wide variety of opinions, attitudes, and beliefs. Some of them are worth dying for, and others aren't worth the time it takes to explain them.

This chapter is about our attitudes, opinions, and beliefs—where they come from and how they change. It is also about the subtle and complex relationships between what we think, what we say, and what we do.

KEY TERMS

attitude
audience
boomerang effect
brainwashing
channel
cognitive dissonance
compliance
discrimination
identification
inoculation effect
internalization
message
obedience
persuasion
prejudice
scapegoat
self-fulfilling prophecy
self-justification
sleeper effect
source

IN YOUR JOURNAL

Write a definition of prejudice in your journal. In addition, list at least four examples of prejudiced thinking.

IN YOUR JOURNAL

You might begin this journal-writing exercise by requesting volunteers to name some of the prejudices that are being challenged in the closing years of this century. Focus, for example, on the broad-based rights movement that has encompassed groups from ethnic minorities and women to the aged and the handicapped. Request students to name some of the prejudices that these and other groups have faced in our society.

EXTRA CREDIT ACTIVITY

Assign interested students to obtain a copy of the Bill of Rights. Tell students to copy the ten amendments onto a series of poster boards, leaving space below each one. Working together, instruct students to list the values, ideals, and beliefs explicitly stated or implied by each amendment. Display the poster boards around the classroom. Ask students how the Bill of Rights has influenced the attitudes of the American people. Challenge them to name other documents that have an effect on our beliefs. (Refer to these poster boards during the discussion of inoculation on page 477.)

457

TEACH

Guided Practice

■ **Analyzing Viewpoints.**
Read aloud the following statements, and ask students to write down whether they agree or disagree.

1. Rock music should be censored for use of profanity.
2. Employers should have the right to test employees at random for drug use.
3. Parents should have the right to approve all their children's decisions until age 18.
4. People with AIDS should be quarantined from the rest of society.
5. The federal government should have the right to ban violent television programs from prime time.

Next, tell students that their responses to each of these controversial statements involved an attitude or belief. Slowly read each statement again. Instruct students to write down how their parents and friends might have responded to each statement. Request volunteers to report the results. Ask: On which, if any, of these issues might you and your parents disagree? Why? Do you think your friends would hold the same opinion as you? *(To check this answer, you might poll volunteers on their responses. Was there uniform student opinion on each of these issues?)* (OBJECTIVE 1)

WHERE ATTITUDES COME FROM

An **attitude** is a predisposition to respond in particular ways toward specific things. It has three main elements: (1) a belief or opinion about something; (2) feelings about that thing; and (3) a tendency to act toward that thing in certain ways. For example, what is your attitude toward the senators from your state? Do you *believe* they are doing a good job? Do you *feel* you trust or distrust them? Would you *act* to vote for them?

We have very definite beliefs, feelings, and responses to things about which we have no firsthand knowledge. Where do these attitudes come from? The culture in which you grew up, the people who raised you, and those with whom you associate—your peers—all shape your attitudes.

Culture. Culture influences everything from our taste in food to our attitudes toward human relationships and our political opinions. For example, most (if not all) Americans would consider eating grubs, curdled milk spiced with cattle blood, or monkey meat disgusting. Yet in some parts of the world these are considered delicacies. Some Americans believe eating meat is essential for good health. Hindus consider anyone's desire for thick, juicy steaks or hamburgers disgusting.

Almost all Americans would agree that in polygamous societies, where a man is allowed to have more than one wife, women are oppressed. But women in polygamous societies feel nothing but pity for a woman whose husband hasn't acquired other wives to help with the work and to keep her company.

Most of us would also agree that parents who interfere in their children's choice of a marriage partner are behaving outrageously and that a person should be able to marry the person he or she loves. However, in many parts of India, parents choose husbands for their daughters, and the girls are relieved not to have to make such an important choice:

"We girls don't have to worry at all. We know we'll get married. When we are old enough our parents will find a suitable boy and everything will be arranged. We don't have to go into competition with each other. . . . Besides how would we be able to judge the character of a boy? . . . Our parents are older and wiser, and they aren't deceived as easily as we would be. I'd far rather have my parents choose for me" (Mace and Mace, 1960, p. 131).

The list of culturally derived attitudes is endless. Indeed, it is only by traveling and reading about other ways of life that we discover how many of the things we take for granted are *attitudes*, not facts.

Parents. There is abundant evidence that all of us acquire many basic attitudes from our parents. How else would you account for the finding that 80 percent of a national sample of elementary school children favored the same political party as their fathers (Hess and Torney, 1967), and 83 percent of high school seniors in a nationwide sample also preferred the same presidential candidate as both their parents (Jennings and Niemi,

---

ADDITIONAL INFORMATION

Have students analyze what attitudes are. Lead students to understand that an attitude is a readiness to respond in a positive or negative way to a class of people, objects, or ideas. Point out that attitudes are composed of three parts: belief, like or dislike, and behavior. Ask students to provide concrete examples of each of the elements of an attitude.

1974)? Parental influence wanes as children get older, of course. A sample of college students selected the same party as their father only 50 to 60 percent of the time (Goldsen *et al.*, 1960). Despite the decline, this study still suggests significant parental influence even after a person has become an adult.

Peers. It is not surprising that parental influence declines as children get older and are exposed to many other sources of influence. In a now classic study, Newcomb (1943) questioned and requestioned students at Bennington College about their political attitudes over a period of 4 years. Most of the young women came from wealthy, staunchly conservative families. In contrast, most Bennington faculty members were outspoken liberals. Newcomb found that many of the students were "converted" to the liberal point of view. In 1936, 54 percent of the juniors and seniors supported Franklin D. Roosevelt and the New Deal—although praising Roosevelt to their families would have produced about the same reactions as praising Muammar al-Qaddhafi to Bill Clinton. Indeed, nearly 30 percent of the students favored Socialist or Communist candidates. Newcomb contacted the subjects of his study 25 years after they had graduated and found that most had maintained the attitudes they had acquired in college. One reason was that they had chosen friends, husbands, and careers that supported liberal values (Newcomb *et al.*, 1967). People tend to adopt the likes and dislikes of groups whose approval and acceptance they seek.

ATTITUDE FORMATION

Having suggested where attitudes come from, we can now look at how they develop. The three main processes involved in forming or changing attitudes are compliance, identification, and internalization (Kelman, 1961).

If you praise a certain film director because everyone else does, you are complying. If you find yourself agreeing with everything a friend you particularly admire says about the director, you are identifying with the friend's attitudes. If you genuinely like the director's work and, regardless of what other people think, regard it as brilliant, you are expressing an internalized attitude.

Compliance

One of the best measures of attitude is behavior. If a man settles back into "his chair" after dinner, launches into a discussion of his support of the women's movement, then shouts to his wife—who is in the kitchen washing the dishes—to bring more coffee, you probably wouldn't believe what he had been saying. His actions speak louder than his words. Yet the same man might hire women for jobs he has always considered "men's work" because the law requires him to do so. He also might finally accept his wife's going to work because he knows that she, their children, and many of their friends would consider him old-fashioned if he didn't.

■ **Discussion.** Challenge students to brainstorm the main socializing forces on people under age 18. Then rank these in order. In what order do parents or family appear? Next, have students analyze the Bennington College study. Ask: What does this study imply about the effect college faculty have on student opinion? *(that the opinions of faculty can influence students or challenge long-standing family values)* Would a similar study done in the mid-1990s yield the same results? *(Answers will vary. Students may note that today's students would be less likely to accept the faculty's views, perhaps because today's young people have been exposed to a variety of opinions and views at a younger age.)*

■ **Evaluating Generalizations.** Direct students to write down four of their strongest beliefs. Next to each item, have students list some of the ways that these beliefs influence their behavior. For example, after Bennington students "converted" to liberalism, how did this belief influence their voting patterns? Request volunteers to share their responses. Based on this exercise, ask students to evaluate the validity of the following text statement: "One of the best measures of attitude is behavior." (OBJECTIVE 1)

CONNECTIONS: PSYCHOLOGY AND SOCIAL STUDIES

Tell students to imagine they are cross-cultural trainers hired by a major United States multinational corporation. Their job is to relocate employees in one of the following nations: Japan, India, Kenya, Turkey, or Colombia. Assign students to research culturally derived attitudes of which the employees must be aware. Students should present their findings in the form of a relocation handbook. At least one item in the booklet should be a list of "Dos" and "Don'ts." (For example: "Do not wear your shoes in a traditional Turkish household or Muslim mosque." "Do carry business cards in Japan.") Make the booklets available for the rest of the class to examine.

■ **Debating an Issue.** Request volunteers to cite examples of legal compliance. *(The text mentions a man who hires a woman for "men's work" because the law requires it. Another example might be obeying a 30-mile-an-hour speed limit on a little-traveled road rather than risking a ticket.)* List these items on the chalkboard. Then explore the difference between *compliance* and *internalization.* Based on this discussion, have students debate the following topic: *Resolved*—Changes in attitude cannot be legislated. (OBJECTIVES 1, 3)

■ **Analyzing a Passage.** Read aloud the following passage from a profile on social psychologist Thomas Pettigrew from the December 1986 issue of *Psychology Today.*

Pettigrew was influenced early in life by his Scottish-born grandmother. She was critical of some aspects of American society and chose not to become a U.S. citizen. When young Tom returned from a school trip to Richmond's St. John's Church and exuberantly recounted how Patrick Henry had uttered his immortal line, "Give me liberty or give me death!" his grandmother admonished him. . . . "Ah yes, 'tis a fine story, lad. . . . Did they happen to mention that he owned 22 slaves?" . . . The question . . . [stayed with Pettigrew] into adulthood.

Tell students that today Pettigrew is one of the nation's leading experts in race relations. Ask: How do you think identification played a role in his career decision? (OBJECTIVES 1, 2)

People often adapt their actions to the wishes of others, in order to avoid discomfort or rejection and to gain support. This is called **compliance.**

But under such circumstances, social pressure often results in only temporary compliance and attitudes do not really change. Later in this chapter, however, we shall see that compliance can sometimes affect one's beliefs. We shall also discuss in detail how group pressure can lead to conformity.

Identification

One way in which attitudes may really be formed or changed is through the process of **identification.** Suppose you have a favorite uncle who is everything you hope to be. He is a successful musician, has many famous friends, and seems to know a great deal about everything. In many ways you identify with him and copy his behavior. One night, during an intense conversation, your uncle asks you why you do not vote. At first, you feel defensive and argumentative. You contend that it does not matter, that your vote would not make a difference. However, as you listen to your uncle, you find yourself starting to agree with him. If a person as knowledgeable and respectable as your uncle believes it is important to vote, then perhaps you should, too. Later you find yourself eager to take part in the political process. You have adopted a new attitude because of your identification with your uncle.

Identification occurs when a person wants to define himself or herself in terms of a person or group, and therefore adopts the person's or group's attitudes and ways of behaving. Identification is different from compliance because the individual actually believes the newly adopted views. But because these attitudes are based on emotional attachment to another person or group rather than the person's own assessment of the issues, they are fragile. If the person's attachment to that person or group fades, the attitudes may also weaken.

Previously, you read that adolescents move away from peer groups and toward independence as they grow older. If this is true, do attitudes stabilize with age? Krosnick and Alwin (1989) studied the political and social attitudes of groups of people of various ages over an extended period. Those in the 18 to 25 age group were the most likely to change their attitudes, those age 34 and older held attitudes that were essentially stable. So, as identification with peer groups declines through late adolescence and into adulthood, attitudes become more stable.

Internalization

Internalization is the wholehearted acceptance of an attitude: it becomes an integral part of the person. Internalization is most likely to occur when an attitude is consistent with a person's basic beliefs and values and supports his or her self-image. The person adopts a new attitude because he or she believes it is right to do so—not because he or she wants to be like someone else.

BEYOND THE CLASSROOM

Request interested students to investigate further the story of Thomas Pettigrew. If possible, have them locate the article "A Prejudice Against Prejudice," in *Psychology Today* (December 1986) or *The Best of Psychology Today* (McGraw-Hill, 1990). Assign them to analyze the steps leading to Pettigrew's internalization of his grandmother's antiracist views. Have students present their findings in the form of an oral report. Suggest that students also focus on the positive and negative use of "prejudice" in the story title.

Internalization is the most lasting of the three sources of attitude formation or change. Your internalized attitudes will be more resistant to pressure from other people because your reasons for holding these views have nothing to do with other people: They are based on your own evaluation of the merits of the issue. A Bennington student put it this way:

"I became liberal at first because of its prestige value; I remain so because the problems around which my liberalism centers are important. What I want now is to be effective in solving problems" (Newcomb, 1943, p. 136).

As this example suggests, compliance or identification may lead to the internalization of an attitude. Often the three overlap. You may support a political candidate in part because you know your friends will approve, in part because someone you admire speaks highly of the candidate, and in part because you believe his or her ideals are consistent with your own.

PREJUDICE

Prejudice means, literally, prejudgment. It means deciding beforehand what a person will be like instead of withholding judgment until it can be based on his or her individual qualities. To hold stereotypes about a group of people is to be prejudiced about them. Prejudice is not necessarily negative—men who are prejudiced against women are often equally prejudiced in favor of men, for example.

Stereotypes and Roles

Prejudice is strengthened and maintained by the existence of stereotypes and roles. A stereotype is an oversimplified, hard-to-change way of seeing people who belong to some group or category. African Americans, scientists, women, Mexicans, and the rich, for example, often have been seen in certain rigid ways, rather than as individuals. A role is an oversimplified, hard-to-change way of acting. Stereotypes and roles can act together in a way that makes them difficult to break down. For example, many whites once had a stereotype of African Americans, believing them to be irresponsible, superstitious, and unintelligent. Whites who believed this expected African Americans to act out a role that was consistent with a stereotype. African Americans were expected to be submissive, deferential, and respectful toward whites, who acted out the role of the superior, condescending parent. In the past, many African Americans and whites accepted these roles and looked at themselves and each other according to these stereotypes. In the past several decades, however, many African Americans and whites have worked to step out of these roles and drop these stereotypes, and to some extent they have been successful.

Stereotypes are also preserved in the communications media, which have traditionally portrayed Native Americans as violent, Italians as greasy

Protest Demonstrations. At the start of the Persian Gulf War, thousands of people marched in antiwar demonstrations in American cities. Some carried signs that said "No blood for oil," or "No corpses for crude."

The antiwar demonstrators marched because they believed that the war was morally wrong or that it was not worth the loss of American lives. Others feared that they or their friends or family members would be called upon to fight. By demonstrating, the protesters both publicly declared their own stand on the war and hoped to persuade others to adopt their view.

The protests helped stimulate public debate about whether the war was necessary and the causes were just. The demonstrators also reflected the divisions and doubts among the American public over the war.

■ **Building Vocabulary.** Have students explain the relationship among the terms *prejudice, stereotype,* and *role.* Then challenge them to write a sentence in which they use all three terms correctly. Request volunteers to read their sentences aloud. (OBJECTIVE 2)

■ **Identifying Stereotypes.** Copy the following occupations in a horizontal list across the chalkboard: construction worker, hairdresser, elementary school teacher, lawyer, model, sanitation worker, truck driver, nurse, surgeon, and television news anchor. Next, have students brainstorm stereotypes associated with each of these jobs. *(Remind students that some stereotypes are positive.)* With the class, explore the accuracy of each set of stereotypes. In a follow-up discussion, ask: Does every stereotype hold a grain of truth? Why or why not? (OBJECTIVE 2)

Enrich. Have students complete the Chapter 18 Application Activity.

CRITICAL THINKING ACTIVITY

Identifying Stereotypes. Have students collect advertisements that use children to sell products. Tell them to study the way in which the child actors depict the role(s) of children. What kind of clothes do they wear? In what situations do they appear? What attitudes or behaviors do the ads assign to children? How might these ads affect the way children see themselves? How might they affect the way adults see children? Using these questions, have students distinguish the positive and negative stereotypes in the various ads.

VISUAL INSTRUCTION

Point out the use of gestalt art. Challenge students to suggest links between the art and the lines from Baldwin's book. (Underscore the perceptual flips in both the art and the written selections.) **Answer to caption, Figure 18.2:** ability to inhibit negative attitudes

■ **Identifying a Point of View.** Read aloud the following quote by social psychologist R. Brown:

Stereotypes are not objectionable because they are generalizations about categories; such generalizations are valuable when they are true. . . . What is objectionable about them? I think it is their ethnocentrism and the implication that important traits are inborn for a large group.

Begin by asking students to define *ethnocentrism.* *(emotional attitude that one's own nation or ethnic group is superior to all others)* Then have students identify Brown's opinion of stereotypes. *(It is mixed. It can be a positive organizing tool or can incorrectly imply that a group has an inborn, or fixed, character.)* Ask: Do you agree with Brown's opinion of stereotypes? Why or why not? (OBJECTIVE 2)

FIGURE 18.2

These lines from James Baldwin's novel *Nobody Knows My Name* express the impossible dilemma of being black in a white world and the way it feels to try to break free of the roles and prejudices that are part of the situation. **According to Patricia Devine's studies, what elements separate prejudiced from nonprejudiced individuals?**

gangsters, Jews as misers, and teenagers as car-crazy rock fans. Many of these stereotypes are changing now, with new ones replacing them. The charming, husband-dominated housewives of the 1960s are now the independent, career-seeking, often single, moms of the 1990s. A critical look at television programs and movies reveals a lot about what is widely believed in American society.

Patricia Devine (1989) proposed a model to explain the relationships between stereotypes and prejudice. She theorizes that if a specific stimulus is encountered, it automatically activates your stereotype mechanism. For example, if you see a Mexican man or woman, it activates your stereotype of Mexicans. Devine suggests that what separates prejudiced from nonprejudiced people is their ability to inhibit negative attitudes. If you can do so, your response will be nonprejudiced; if you cannot restrain your negative beliefs, you will behave in a prejudiced manner.

Another psychologist, Thomas Pettigrew, suggests that in situations where members of a dominant and a submissive group can be identified, each group may play a role that fosters and maintains its respective position. A member of a dominating group, for example, will speak first, interrupt more often, and talk louder and longer. A member of the submissive group will show deference and concern for the dominant member and do more listening and less interrupting.

Prejudice and Discrimination

There are many possible causes for prejudice. Psychologists have found that people tend to be prejudiced against those less well-off than them-

CONNECTIONS: PSYCHOLOGY AND SOCIAL STUDIES

During wars, each side typically views the other in stereotyped ways, leading to extreme prejudice. During World War II, the anger and fear generated by Pearl Harbor fell heaviest upon Japanese Americans living in California and other parts of the western United States. Request volunteers to research the forced relocation of thousands of Japanese Americans to internment camps. (One highly readable source is *Desert Exile* by Yoshiko Uchida.) Ask students to prepare oral reports on the causes and effects of misdirected prejudice. Advise them to conclude their reports with the 1988 Senate apology and tax-free payment of $20,000 to each of the 60,000 surviving *Nisei* (U.S. citizens born of Japanese parents).

selves—they seem to justify being on top by assuming that anyone of lower status or income must be inferior. People who have suffered economic setbacks also tend to be prejudiced—they blame others for their misfortune. Prejudice also arises from "guilt by association." People who dislike cities and urban living, for example, tend to distrust people associated with cities. Also, people tend to be prejudiced in favor of those they see as similar to themselves and against those who seem different.

Whatever the original cause, prejudice seems to persist. One reason is that children who grow up in an atmosphere of prejudice conform to the prejudicial norm. That is, they are encouraged to conform to the thoughts and practices of their parents and other teachers.

Prejudice, which is an attitude, should be distinguished from **discrimination,** the unequal treatment of members of certain groups. It is possible for a prejudiced person not to discriminate. He or she may recognize his or her prejudice and try not to act on it. Similarly, a person may discriminate, not out of prejudice, but in compliance with social pressures. Personal discrimination may take the form of refusing to rent to African Americans or allowing only men to frequent a particular club or paying migrant workers substandard wages.

Scapegoating

One of the most popular theories to explain prejudice is the scapegoat theory (Allport, 1954; Hovland and Sears, 1940). According to this view, prejudice and the associated discrimination are the result of displaced aggression. When people are prevented from achieving their goals, they often react by being aggressive. When there is no obvious target for their aggression, they displace their frustration onto other people who are not responsible for the problem but who cannot strike back or cause them social disapproval. The target of displaced aggression is called a **scapegoat.**

African Americans in this country have been the scapegoats for the economic frustrations of lower-income white Americans who felt exploited and powerless themselves. The anger they felt could not be expressed on an appropriate target (say, the government), so instead they directed their hostility toward those whom they viewed as less powerful than themselves—the African Americans. Between 1882 and 1930, the number of lynchings per year in southern states varied according to the price of cotton. When prices were low, indicating economic hard times, the number of lynchings increased (Hovland and Sears, 1940).

Members of a group often become the targets of discrimination because of one or more of several features (Berkowitz, 1962). Among these are safety, visibility, strangeness, and prior dislike. For example, the object of discrimination is a safe target because he or she is too weak to return the attack. The target is visible or easily differentiated from others. In addition, the target is unfamiliar or different in some way. From the time we are old enough to express ourselves, we all tend to react by withdrawing from the new, the strange, or the unknown. In situations where we are empowered, that rejection may take even stronger forms. Finally, once we have developed a prejudice against a group, aggression that we might later target at a

■ Analyzing Categories.
Organize the students into groups and have each group develop a list of ways dominant and submissive roles might be informally established in business, school, and society in general. *(Answers will vary. Sample answers follow: business—assigning executive parking lots, keeping employees waiting; school—a popular student dominating the conversation, a table where the "in group" always eats—and others respecting it; society—name dropping, being seated at a table before anyone else.)*

DID YOU KNOW?

The term *scapegoat* comes from the chapter of Leviticus in the Bible. As originally translated, the passage read: "This is the escape goat upon which the sins of the people are laid, and which is then let go in the wilderness." A later edition, translated by Tindale, substituted *scapegoat* for *escape goat.* In the New Testament, the divine scapegoat for humanity is Jesus Christ. The term has since been applied to any person, group, or thing blamed for the crimes or misfortunes of others.

CONNECTIONS: PSYCHOLOGY AND SOCIAL STUDIES

Scapegoating presented a hideous face in World War II when Adolf Hitler blamed the Jews for Germany's problems. Even in his final days in power, Hitler clung to this bold lie. Wrote Hitler just before taking his own life:

It is untrue that I or anybody else in Germany wanted a war in 1939. It was wanted and provoked exclusively by those international statesmen who either were of Jewish origin or worked for Jewish interests.

With students explore how scapegoating opened the door to the hatreds of the Holocaust, the Nazi attempt to wipe out the Jews of Europe. (For an award-winning film and book on individual resistance to the Holocaust, see *The Courage to Care* or *Schindler's List.*)

VISUAL INSTRUCTION

Before students read the caption, have them form inferences about the self-image of the child who drew each picture on pages 464 and 465. Record answers on the chalkboard. Then tell students that the same child drew both pictures—within one day of each other. To find out the reason for such different self-images, have students read the caption. Ask: What can you infer from this experiment about some of the causes and effects of prejudice? **Answer to caption, Figure 18.3:** conformity to the social norm

■ **Demonstration.** You might illustrate how integration can be furthered in the classroom by using the "jigsaw groups," first developed by Elliot Aronson (1978). Organize the students into six groups, and assign each group one of the paragraphs in "Integration" (pages 464–465). Give each group a question related to its paragraph. However, assign the whole class to answer *all* six questions. To complete this task, the various groups must work together. Ask: How does this learning task help break down the barriers of prejudice? (OBJECTIVES 2, 3)

Teacher Note. You might tell students Aronson and his colleagues first applied "jigsaw groups" as a method of furthering cooperation among Latino and Anglo children in California.

FIGURE 18.3

After the assassination of Martin Luther King, Jr., a third-grade teacher gave her students a lesson in discrimination. On the basis of eye color, the teacher organized the students into two groups and favored one group (the blue-eyed children) the first day with privileges. The next day she reversed the situation, favoring the brown-eyed children. On the day they were favored the blue-eyed children reportedly "took savage delight" in keeping "inferiors" in their place and said they felt "good inside," "smarter," and "stronger." On that day, one child drew the picture shown on the right. The next day, the same child, now one of the "inferiors," drew the picture on the left. The children who had felt "smart" and "strong" on their favored day became tense, lacked confidence, and did badly on the day they were discriminated against. They said they felt "like dying" and "like quitting school." **Why does prejudice persist?**

disliked person (or the group he or she represents) may be displaced onto the previously disliked group.

Integration

Centuries of racial prejudice in the United States and throughout the world seem to indicate that racial hatred poses an extremely complicated problem. One barrier to cooperation between the races is segregation. In one research project, a group of psychologists reasoned that if people of different races had the opportunity to meet as equals, they might come to recognize that their prejudices had no basis. Therefore, they interviewed people who had been placed in integrated and segregated buildings of a housing project just after World War II. The results showed clearly that the amount and type of contact between African American and white neighbors greatly influenced their opinions toward each other.

The integrated housing situation gave the housewives a chance to have contact with one another and to interact informally and casually. The housewives were likely to encounter each other in the elevators, hallways, and laundry room. In this informal climate they did not have to worry that trying to strike up a conversation might be misinterpreted. In contrast, contact in the segregated buildings would have to be more deliberate and might be considered suspicious.

In the integrated buildings more than 60 percent of the white housewives reported having "friendly relations" with African Americans. In the segregated buildings less than 10 percent reported friendships, and more than 80 percent reported no contact at all. In the integrated buildings, 2 out of 3 white women expressed a desire to be friendly with African Americans. In the segregated buildings only 1 in 11 expressed such a desire. Similar effects occurred in the attitudes of African American women toward whites (Deutsch and Collins, 1951).

Contacts reduce intergroup hostility in some instances but not in others. Several factors seem to be involved. First, the need to cooperate forces people to abandon negative stereotypes. Second, contact between people who occupy the same status is more likely to break down barriers than contact between people who do not perceive themselves as equals. Frequent contact with a white landlord is not likely to change an African American's stereotype of whites; nor is the relationship between a white executive and an African American chauffeur likely to change the white person's stereotype. The housewives in the integrated buildings were social equals: they had about the same incomes, lived under similar conditions, faced the same problems, and so on. Finally, when social norms support intergroup cooperation, people are likely to turn contacts into friendships.

In their study on changing trends in race relations, Sears, Peplau, and Taylor (1991), noted the decline of *old-fashioned racism*. The researchers stated this form included prejudices regarding the laziness of African Americans or those of Hispanic lineage. At its worst, old-fashioned racism promoted segregation in schools, jobs, housing, and transportation. Although most of the remnants of old-fashioned racism are gone now, a new form, what Sears, Peplau, and Taylor call *modern racism*, raises new barri-

CONNECTIONS: PSYCHOLOGY AND THE LAW

In 1954, the Supreme Court unanimously struck down segregation in the landmark decision of *Brown* v. *Board of Education of Topeka, Kansas*. Read aloud part of the majority opinion delivered by Chief Justice Earl Warren:

To separate [children] *from others of similar age and qualifications solely be-* *cause of their race generates a feeling of inferiority as to their status in the community that may affect their hearts and minds in a way unlikely ever to be undone. . . . Separate education facilities are inherently unequal.*

Ask how this decision helped tear down barriers to racial cooperation.

ers. The researchers theorize that this kind of racism takes several forms. *Illusory change* identifies the tendency of whites to shy away from openly supporting the traditional forms of racism. Yet, at the same time, whites fail to support ways to fight racism. The researchers suggest that *ambivalence,* sometimes called *aversive racism,* is another form. In this scenario, while whites endorse genuinely egalitarian systems, many harbor negative feelings toward African Americans. Another form of modern racism is *realistic group conflict* in which groups fight implementation of programs that will change the status quo.

Each of these explanations contains elements of truth. The costs of achieving true integration are substantial. Social psychology contributes specific suggestions such as the lessons from the Robber's Cave experiment discussed in Chapter 17: Have common goals with mutual benefits to get antagonistic groups working together. In Chapter 17, you read that groups are interdependent collections of individuals. It seems appropriate to end this section by noting that social psychological research suggests that successful cooperative interdependence holds our best hope for overcoming the remaining problems of racism.

COGNITIVE CONSISTENCY AND CHANGING ATTITUDES

Many social psychologists have theorized that people's attitudes change because they are always trying to get things to fit together logically inside their heads. Holding two opposing attitudes can create great conflict in an individual, throwing him or her off balance. A doctor who smokes and a parent who is uncomfortable with children have one thing in common: they are in conflict.

According to Leon Festinger (1957) people in such situations experience cognitive dissonance (Figure 18.4). **Cognitive dissonance** is the uncomfortable feeling that arises when a person experiences contradictory or conflicting thoughts, beliefs, attitudes, or feelings. To reduce dissonance, it is necessary to change one or both of the conflicting attitudes.

Some people attempt to evade dissonance by avoiding situations or exposure to information that would create conflict. For example, they may make a point of subscribing to newspapers and magazines that uphold their political attitudes, of surrounding themselves with people who share the same ideas, and of attending only those speeches and lectures that support their views. It is not surprising that such people get quite upset when a piece of conflicting information finally does get through.

The process of dissonance reduction does not always take place consciously, but it is a frequent and powerful occurrence. In fact, remarkably long-lasting changes in attitudes were produced in an experiment in which students were made aware that their emphasis on freedom was inconsistent with their indifference to equality and civil rights. In the initial 40-minute session, students ranked a number of values by importance to

■ **Applying Concepts.** After students understand the idea of *cognitive dissonance,* have them list examples of cognitive dissonance in their own lives. *(An example might be the mostly vegetarian student who occasionally sneaks a hamburger or an athlete who smokes.)* When the listing is completed, tell students to put an X by the types of dissonance with which they are willing to live. Then instruct them to put an R next to types that they are motivated to change. Request volunteers to share their "R" list. With the rest of the class, propose a workable solution to end the dissonance. *(You might encourage students to review Chapter 16 on some psychological methods of change.)* (OBJECTIVE 3)

■ **Synthesizing Information.** Write the following saying on the chalkboard: "Birds of a feather flock together." Ask students how the theory of cognitive dissonance might explain the truth behind this saying. Then challenge students to cite exceptions to the rule. *(Tip: Repeat another saying, "Opposites attract.")* Explore reasons some people can tolerate—and may even search for—dissonance in their relationships.

BEYOND THE CLASSROOM

Following the decision in *Brown* v. *Board of Education,* a movement took shape to *mainstream* mentally and physically disabled students into the regular school systems. Legal clout was put into the effort with passage of the 1975 Individuals with Disabilities Education Act (IDEA). Request volunteers to prepare a balance sheet on the strides made toward integrating disabled individuals into the "mainstream" of American education. In chart form, have students present some of the victories—and unfinished challenges—of special education. Direct researchers to focus on how mainstreaming affects attitudes of both disabled and non-disabled students.

■ **Discussion.** Read aloud the conclusion from the experiment on dissonance reduction:

If such socially important values as equality and freedom can be altered to become more important to human subjects, they can surely be altered to become less important. Who shall decide. . . ?

Call on students to summarize how researchers used cognitive dissonance to increase the importance of equality and freedom among the group tested. *(Once cognitive dissonance was raised, the subjects took action to reduce it—i.e., donated money to the NAACP.)*

Challenge students to suggest ways that "socially important values" could be made less important. *(You may wish to refer students back to the discussion of stereotypes and prejudice.)* (OBJECTIVE 2)

themselves—including the key variables "freedom" and "equality." They were also asked to express their attitudes toward civil rights. The students then compared their answers with a table of typical answers, which was interpreted for them by the researchers. The researchers said that the typical tendency to rank freedom high and equality low showed that students in general are "much more interested in their own freedom than in other people's." The students were also told that such rankings are consistent with a lack of concern for civil rights. Finally, students were asked whether their results left them satisfied or dissatisfied. The control group, who did not receive the researchers' explanation, simply filled out their rankings and went home, oblivious to any inconsistencies in attitude they might have expressed.

Three to five months after the initial test, the researchers sent out a solicitation for donations or memberships on NAACP stationery to test whether students tested would act on the values they expressed. They received many more replies from students in the experimental group than in the control group. They concluded that the test had somehow made the first group of students more receptive to civil-rights issues. On tests 15 to 17 months later, changes in attitude were much more likely in subjects who had been dissatisfied with what they had been told about the results of their original test than in subjects who had not been dissatisfied. This suggests that cognitive dissonance spurred changes in attitudes toward civil rights.

This is a powerful and lasting impact from a simple 40-minute session and a few follow-up tests. One of the researchers was disturbed by the implications, for "If such socially important values as equality and freedom can be altered to become more important to human subjects, they can surely be altered to also become less important. Who shall decide. . . ?" (Rokeach, 1971, p. 458).

ATTITUDES AND ACTIONS

Social psychologists have discovered several interesting relationships between attitudes and actions. Obviously, your attitudes affect your actions: if you like Fords, you will buy a Ford. Some of the other relationships are not so obvious.

Doing Is Believing

It turns out, for example, that if you like Fords but buy a Chevrolet for some reason (perhaps you can get a better deal on a Chevy), you will end up liking Fords less. In other words, actions affect attitudes.

In many instances, if you act and speak as though you have certain beliefs and feelings, you may begin to *really* feel and believe this way. For example, people accused of a crime have confessed to crimes they did not commit. They confessed to relieve the pressure; but having said that they did the deed, they begin to believe that they really *are* guilty.

CONNECTIONS: PSYCHOLOGY AND SOCIAL STUDIES

To help students understand cognitive dissonance, present the following activity. Tell students that, as the 1960s opened, the civil rights movement exploded across the United States. On June 12, 1963, President John F. Kennedy went on nationwide television and radio to deliver the strongest

civil rights message ever given by a President. Read part of this message aloud:

We preach freedom around the world, and we mean it, and we cherish our freedom here at home, but are we to say to the world, and much more importantly, to each other that this is a land

of the free except for the Negroes; that we have no second-class citizens except Negroes; that we have no class or caste system, no ghettoes, no master race except with respect to Negroes?

Next week I shall ask the Congress of the United States to act, to make a (continued on page 467)

FIGURE 18.4

In the cartoon, Mary has a positive attitude toward Bill and a negative attitude toward certain clothing styles. She can maintain both attitudes until a situation arises in which they are brought into conflict. Then she is faced with a state of dissonance that can be reduced only by a change in attitude. **In what ways can she resolve the conflict?**

One explanation for this phenomenon comes from the theory of cognitive dissonance. If a person acts one way but thinks another, he or she will experience dissonance. To reduce the dissonance, the person will have to change either the behavior or the attitude. A similar explanation is that people have a need for **self-justification**—a need to justify their behavior.

In an experiment that demonstrated these principles, subjects were paid either $1 or $20 (roughly $5 and $100 in mid-1990s currency) to tell another person that a boring experiment in which they both had to participate was really a lot of fun. Afterward, the experimenters asked the subjects how they felt about the experiment. They found that the subjects who had been paid $20 to lie about the experiment continued to believe that it had been boring. Those who had been paid $1, however, came to believe that the experiment had actually been fairly enjoyable. These people had less reason to tell the lie, so they experienced more dissonance when they did so. To justify their lie, they had to believe that they had actually enjoyed the experiment (Festinger and Carlsmith, 1959).

VISUAL INSTRUCTION

Organize the class into groups. Instruct two people within each group to role-play the parts of Mary and Bill. In recommending suggestions to end Mary's cognitive dissonance, remind students to avoid creating cognitive dissonance in Bill. Have each group present its solution to the class. Challenge other students to evaluate whether the solution would affect a change through compliance, identification, or internalization. **Answer to caption, Figure 18.4:** Answers will vary, but may include: through avoiding the situation.

■ **Discussion.** Pose the following situation to students: A friend has just bought a new car. However, she is experiencing cognitive dissonance because the car has some undesirable features that she had failed to spot prior to purchase. Challenge students to suggest ways the woman might reduce the cognitive dissonance. At least one method should include the use of self-justification. (For example: "I looked at other models, and they were much worse than this car.")

CONNECTIONS: PSYCHOLOGY AND SOCIAL STUDIES

commitment it has not fully made in this century to the proposition that race has no place in American life or law. . . .

Ask: What ideal does Kennedy highlight? *(freedom)* How does he create cognitive dissonance in listeners? *(by citing examples of the lack of freedom within the U.S.)* Why do you think

Kennedy chose to address people by TV and radio? *(brought his message into American homes)*

Next, tell students that five months after Kennedy's speech, he was killed. Upon becoming President, Lyndon Johnson pledged to push through Kennedy's civil rights bill. Within

months, Congress passed the Civil Rights Act of 1964. Challenge students to offer psychological reasons people backed the law. *(Lead students to understand how Kennedy's assassination increased cognitive dissonance triggered by his speech.)*

PORTRAIT

Carolyn Robertson Payton
1925–

The actions of individual African Americans have inspired countless young people to shake off the burdens of prejudice. Rather than bow under the weight of racial stereotypes, they now look to a growing number of successful role models in all walks of life. In the field of psychology, Carolyn Robertson Payton is such an example.

Payton grew up in Norfolk, Virginia. She earned a home economics degree at Bennett College in Greensboro, North Carolina. She then went on to earn an M.S. degree in psychology from the University of Wisconsin at Madison, and a Ph.D. in counseling from the Columbia University Teachers College.

Upon graduation, Payton accepted teaching and counseling positions at such prestigious schools as Howard University in Washington, D.C. She also served in the Peace Corps from 1961–1977. In 1977, President Jimmy Carter appointed Payton the first woman—and first African American—director of the Peace Corps.

After struggling to open the doors to more women in the Peace Corps, Payton returned to Howard University as director of counseling. On behalf of Payton's humanitarian efforts at home and around the world, the Capitol Press Club honored her as its 1978 "Woman of the Year."

> If you speak and act as if something is true, you yourself may come to believe it.

The phenomenon of self-justification has serious implications. For example, how would you justify to yourself the fact that you had intentionally injured another human being? In another psychological experiment, subjects were led to believe that they had injured or hurt other subjects in some way (Glass, 1964). The aggressors were then asked how they felt about the victims they had just harmed. It was found that the aggressors had convinced themselves that they did not like the victims of their cruelty. In other words, the aggressors talked themselves into believing that their defenseless victims had deserved their injury. The aggressors also considered their victims to be less attractive after the experiment than before—their self-justification for hurting another person was something like, "Oh well, this person doesn't amount to much, anyway."

Self-Fulfilling Prophecy

Another relationship between attitudes and actions is rather subtle—but extremely widespread. It is possible, it seems, for a person to act in such a way as to make his or her attitudes come true. This phenomenon is called **self-fulfilling prophecy.** Suppose, for example, you are convinced that you are a bad cook. Every time you go into the kitchen, you start thinking poorly of yourself. Because you approach the task of baking a cake with great anxiety, you fumble the measurements, pour in too much milk, leave out an ingredient, and so on. As a result, your cake is a flop. You thus confirm that you *are* a bad cook, by scripting a disaster each time you cook.

Self-fulfilling prophecies can influence all kinds of human activity. Suppose you believe that people are basically friendly and generous. Whenever you approach other people, you are friendly and open. Because of your smile and positive attitude toward yourself and the world, people like you. Thus your attitude that people are friendly produces your friendly behavior, which in turn causes people to respond favorably toward you. But suppose you turn this example around. Imagine that you believe people are selfish and cold. Because of your negative attitude, you tend to avert your eyes from other people, to act gloomy, and to appear rather unfriendly. People think your actions are strange and, consequently, they act coldly toward you. Your attitude has produced the kind of behavior that makes the attitude come true (Fiske & Taylor, 1991).

Practical Implications

The psychological findings related to self-justification and self-fulfilling prophecy show that there is truth in the saying "Life is what you make it." What you do affects you directly, and it affects the way the world acts toward you. The fact that all people tend to justify their actions by changing their attitudes has several practical consequences. If you give in to pressure and act against your better judgment, you will be undermining your own beliefs. The next time you are in a similar situation, you will find it even harder to stand up for what you believe in because you will have begun to wonder whether you believe it yourself. If you want to strengthen

---

CRITICAL THINKING ACTIVITY

Analyzing a Quote. Read the following quote in which civil rights worker Dorothy Cotton recalls a segregated South at the start of the 1950s.

In those days when a black person from another country, from Africa, visited the U.S., they said they could recognize when a black person had grown up under our system, because they always walked with a little bit of stoop, a little bit of shame.

Ask: What does Cotton's remark reveal about the effect of prejudice on behavior? How would segregation promote a self-fulfilling prophecy of despair?

your convictions about something, it is a good idea to speak and act on your beliefs at every opportunity. If you do make a mistake and act against your beliefs, you should admit that you are wrong and not try to justify yourself.

The phenomenon of self-fulfilling prophecy shows that the way the world seems to you may be a result of your own actions. Other people, who act differently, will have different experiences and produce different effects. When you find the world unsatisfactory, remember that to some extent, you are creating it. When you find the world a joyful place, remember, too, that it is making you happy partly because you believe that it can.

PERSUASION

Persuasion is a direct attempt to influence attitudes. At one time or another everyone engages in persuasion. When a smiling student who is working her way through college by selling magazine subscriptions comes to the door, she attempts to persuade you that reading *Newsweek* or *Sports Illustrated* or *Ms.* will make you better informed and give you lots to talk about at parties. Parents often attempt to persuade a son or daughter to conform to their values about life. Similarly, some young people try to persuade their parents that all their friends' parents are buying them home computers. In each case, the persuader's main hope is that by changing the other person's attitudes he or she can change that person's behavior as well.

The Communication Process

Enormous amounts of time, money, and effort go into campaigns to persuade people to change their attitudes and behavior. Some succeed on a grand scale; others seem to have no effect. One of the most difficult questions social psychologists have tried to answer is: What makes a persuasive communication effective?

The communication process can be broken down into four parts. The **message** itself is only one part. It is also important to consider the **source** of the message, the **channel** through which it is delivered, and the **audience** that receives it.

The Source.   How a person sees the source, or originator, of a message may be a critical factor in his or her acceptance or rejection of it. The person receiving the message asks himself or herself two basic questions: Is the person giving the message trustworthy and sincere? Does he or she know anything about the subject? If the source seems reliable and knowledgeable, the message is likely to be accepted (McGuire, 1985).

Suppose, for example, that you have written a paper criticizing a short story for your English class. A friend who reads the paper tells you about an article that praises the story and asks you to reconsider your view. The article was written by Agnes Stearn, a college student. You might change

MORE about...

Behavioral Confirmation.
The text describes how beliefs can change actions through processes such as self-justification and the self-fulfilling prophecy. Our expectations can also affect other people's actions. This process is called *behavioral confirmation.*

For example, suppose you are led to believe that another person is friendly and outgoing. To find out more about that person, you would most likely ask that person questions an outgoing person would answer. "What kinds of things do you do with your friends?" "What do you do to have fun?"

Most likely you would get answers that describe the person's outgoing activities. Even a shy person who has only a few friends will think of some outgoing things, though probably not as many as an extraverted person would.

Furthermore, by discussing these activities, the person will actually start to *feel* and *act* more outgoing than he or she usually does. In this way the person's behavior will start to confirm your initial impression, even if that impression was not particularly accurate.

■ **Demonstration.** Read aloud the following list of products to students. Have them copy down each item. Then instruct them to list as many brand names after the product as possible.

soft drinks	soap
cars	blue jeans
shampoo	cereal

Call on volunteers to read the brand names for each product aloud. Explore how students learn about and/or choose a brand. *(If students watch television, they often have a favorite commercial. Ask how influential such commercials are.)* Ask: Which of the following *most* influences you to buy a product for the first time: advertising appeal, the opinions of friends, product quality, or some other reason? (OBJECTIVE 4)

■ **Demonstration.** After students read the margin feature, request a few volunteers to conduct an experiment. For several days, have them make it a point to smile and greet everyone warmly. Tell them to observe people's reactions carefully. How do their physical attitudes change after a few days? Do people look like they expect a smile? Are they more willing to talk? What, if any, evidence of behavioral confirmation did the test reveal? (OBJECTIVES 3, 4)

PSYCHOLOGISTS AT WORK

In the post-World War II era, a broad field known as industrial psychology has grown in importance. *Industrial psychologists* study all aspects of behavior that relate to the workplace. Organizational psychologists, for example, focus on human relationships within the corporate structure. Personnel psychologists concern themselves with screening, hiring, assigning, promoting, and firing workers. Another group of specialists, the consumer psychologists, studies the persuasion techniques discussed in this chapter.

Industrial psychologists work in the public and private sectors. Some freelance as independent consultants. Although job requirements vary greatly, most companies look for a doctoral degree in some area of industrial psychology.

■ **Making a Chart.** With the class, brainstorm some of the features of an effective message. *(clarity, pertinence to the subject, appropriate language, and so on)* Then explore factors that ensure delivery, or communication, of the message. Based on this discussion, assign small groups of students to design illustrated flowcharts showing the four main parts in the communication process. Direct students to create descriptive labels or captions that explain the "flow" of information. (OBJECTIVE 4)

VISUAL INSTRUCTION

Instruct students to read the explanation of the *boomerang effect* on page 470. Then read the following information that appeared in the advertisement below the headline: "Doctors need to know about current issues relevant to the medical profession. Subscribe to *Medical World News.*" Ask students how the emotional wallop of the ad might boomerang.
Answer to caption, Figure 18.5: Answers will vary, but students may mention the attention-grabbing headline or elements of the photo.

your opinion—and you might not. But suppose your friend tells you the same critique was written by Stephen King. Chances are that you would begin to doubt your own judgment. Three psychologists tried this experiment. Not surprisingly, many more students changed their minds about a piece of writing when they thought the criticism was written by a famous writer (Aronson, Turner, and Carlsmith, 1963).

A person receiving the message also asks: Do I like the source? If the communicator is respected and admired, people will tend to go along with the message, either because they believe in his or her judgment or because they want to be like him or her. The identification phenomenon explains the frequent use of athletes in advertisements. Football players and Olympic champions are not (in most cases) experts on deodorants, electric razors, or milk. Indeed, when an athlete endorses a particular brand of deodorant on television, we all know he or she is doing it for the money. Nevertheless, the process of identification makes these sales pitches highly effective (Kanner, 1989).

However, attempts to be friendly and personal can backfire. When people dislike the individual or group delivering a message, they are likely to respond by taking the opposite point of view. This is known as the **boomerang effect.**

The Message.   Suppose two people with opposing viewpoints are trying to persuade you to agree with them. Suppose further that you like and trust both of them. In this situation the message becomes more important than the source. The persuasiveness of a message depends on the way in which it is composed and organized as well as on the actual content.

Should the message arouse emotion? Are people more likely to change their attitudes if they are afraid or angry or pleased? The answer is yes, but

FIGURE 18.5

Major factors in a successful advertisement campaign include a clear picture of the characteristics of the target or recipient and the characteristics of the message source. **Why is this advertisement persuasive?**

🧪 LAB EXPERIMENTS AND DEMONSTRATIONS

Invite a guest speaker to participate in an experiment with the class. If possible, contact a person knowledgeable in advertising or marketing techniques. (Examples might be a person who sells ad space in the local newspaper or a member of a local advertising agency.) Arrange for students to come to class in two shifts. For the first shift, ask the speaker to deliver a warm, friendly, and/or humorous message on "ad talk." For the second shift, have the speaker deliver the same message in a cold, matter-of-fact manner. In the next class session, request students to write a review of the talk, including the main impact points. After comparing results, discuss the importance of the source in audience acceptance of a message.

At A Glance

SEX IN ADVERTISING

Pick up any newspaper or magazine and you'll see dozens of scantily-clad women and rugged, sensual he-men trying to sell products in the best way they know how. As they drape themselves over automobiles and puff provocatively on their cigarettes, they tell consumers that sex and their product are a package deal.

This may sound like a message few of us could resist, but according to some researchers, our willpower is stronger than advertisers think. Research has shown that sexy ads get readers' attention, but the wrong audience actually reads the message. More women than men read the ads in which a sexy woman appears, and more men than women read ads showing attractive men.

Researchers have also found that sex does not increase product recall and may in fact get in the way of remembering a brand name. In one study, subjects were shown some ads containing sexy pictures and some without. One week after seeing the ads, subjects could remember more about the "nonsexy" products than they could about the "sexy" ones.

Results like these are sure to change at least some advertisers' approaches. But it will take a lot more than this to convince others that sex is not the advertiser's best friend.

the most effective messages combine emotional appeal with factual information and argument. A moderately arousing message typically causes the largest shift of opinion. Similarly, a message that deviates moderately from those of the target audience will tend to move that audience furthest. A communication that overemphasizes the emotional side of an issue may boomerang. If the message is too upsetting, people may reject it. For example, showing pictures of accident victims to people who have been arrested for drunken driving may convince them not to drive when they've been drinking. But if the film is so bloody that people are frightened or disgusted, they may also stop listening to the message. On the other hand, a communication that includes only logic and information may miss its mark because the audience does not relate the facts to their personal lives.

When presenting an argument, is it more effective to present both sides of an issue or only one side? For the most part, a two-sided communication is more effective because the audience tends to believe that the speaker is objective and fair-minded. A slight hazard of presenting opposing arguments is that they might undercut the message or suggest that the whole issue is too controversial to make a decision about.

People usually respond positively to a message that is structured and delivered in a dynamic way. But a communication that is forceful to the

At A Glance

To guide student reading of the feature, ask the following questions:
1. Why do many advertisers use sexy ads? *(to gain attention of readers)*
2. What does research reveal about the target audience as opposed to the audience that actually receives the message? *(According to the feature, the sex opposite the intended audience usually reads the ad.)*
3. What reasons can you suggest why so many men and women read ads that feature their own gender? *(Answers will vary, but lead students to understand people's fascination with the "ideal body type.")*
4. Are such ads effective? *(Answers will vary, but students may note that they are ineffective if they block recall of the brand's name.)*

■ **Evaluating Propaganda.** Students may think of propaganda as negative because of some of the uses to which it has been put—for example, support of wartime goals, indoctrination, and so on. However, some experts argue that propaganda is neither good nor bad. It is simply a method of communication intended to influence, or sway, opinion.

You might have students identify examples of positive and negative uses of propaganda. *(For a list of propaganda techniques, see the Bottom Note on page 111 of Chapter 5.)*

LAB EXPERIMENTS AND DEMONSTRATIONS

With the class, choose an item of clothing that is popular among students. Next, appoint a survey team to poll students on reasons they wear the item. *(Questions should elicit responses on the influence of peers, advertising campaigns, and so on.)* Have students report their findings to the class. Then, organize students into small groups and challenge them to design an advertising campaign for another clothing product intended to replace the popular clothing item originally selected. Caution students to keep their audience in mind when preparing their campaigns.

FIGURE 18.6

In 1940 Prime Minister Winston Churchill spoke these words in an address to the British House of Commons. Churchill's long record as a soldier and as a political leader made him a source whose knowledge and trustworthiness were beyond question by the time he was needed to lead the fight against Hitler. **What are two questions that listeners often ask themselves about the source of a message?**

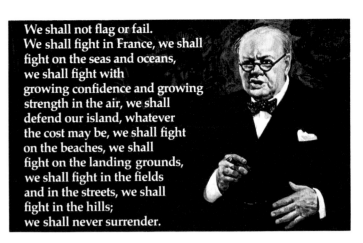

We shall not flag or fail. We shall fight in France, we shall fight on the seas and oceans, we shall fight with growing confidence and growing strength in the air, we shall defend our island, whatever the cost may be, we shall fight on the beaches, we shall fight on the landing grounds, we shall fight in the fields and in the streets, we shall fight in the hills; we shall never surrender.

point of being pushy may produce negative results. People generally resent being pressured. If listeners infer from a message that they are being left with no choice but to agree with the speaker's viewpoint, they may reject an opinion for this reason alone.

The Channel. Where, when, and how a message is presented also influences the audience's response. In general, personal contact is the most effective approach to an audience. For example, in one study in Ann Arbor, Michigan, 75 percent of voters who had been contacted personally voted in favor of a change in the city charter. Only 45 percent of those who had received the message in the mail and 19 percent of those who had only seen ads in the media voted for the change (Eldersveld and Dodge, 1954).

However, as we saw earlier, personal contact may boomerang: people may dislike the communicator or feel that they are being pressured. Besides, you can reach a great many more people through mailings and radio and television broadcasts than you can in person.

There is some evidence that television and films are more effective media of persuasion than printed matter. People tend to believe what they see and hear with their own senses (even if they know the information has been edited before it is broadcast). In one experiment, 51 percent of people who had watched a film could answer factual questions about the issue in question—compared to 29 percent of those who had only seen printed material. In addition, more of the people who had viewed the film altered their viewpoints than did people who had read about the issue (Hovland, Lumsdaine, and Sheffield, 1949). But the most effective channel also depends in part on the audience.

The Audience. The audience includes all those people whose attitudes the communicator is trying to change. Being able to persuade people to alter their views depends on knowing who the audience is and why they hold the attitudes they do (Figure 18.7). Suppose, for example, you are involved in a program to reduce the birthrate in a population that is outgrowing its food supply. The first step would be to inform people of various methods of birth control as well as how and where to obtain them. However, the fact that people know how to limit their families does not mean that they will do so. To persuade them to use available contraceptives, you need to know why they value large families. In some areas of the world, people have as many children as they can because they do not expect most babies to survive early childhood. In this case you might want to tie the family-planning campaign to programs of infant care. In some areas, children begin working at odd jobs at an early age and bring in needed income. In this case, you might want to promote an incentive system for families who limit themselves to two or three children.

If the people are not taking advantage of available means of birth control, you will want to know who is resisting. Perhaps men believe fathering a child is a sign of virility. Perhaps women consider motherhood an essential element of femininity. Perhaps both sexes see parenthood as a symbol of maturity and adulthood (Coale, 1973). Knowing who your audience is and what motivates them is crucial.

One way to maximize the chances of persuasion is to capitalize on the audience's emotional needs. For example, one advertising researcher was able to help the Red Cross collect blood donations from men by analyzing their fears. He thought that men associated loss of blood with weakness and loss of manliness. He suggested that the Red Cross publish ads telling prospective donors how manly they were and offer donors pins shaped like drops of blood as medals for bravery. The campaign worked: blood donations from men increased sharply (Dichter, 1964).

Several strategies effectively involve the audience. One strategy that has been studied extensively is the *foot-in-the-door technique*, which involves first making a very small request that someone is almost sure to agree to, and then making a much more demanding request (Dillard, 1991). In one experiment, researchers Freedman and Fraser (1966) asked residents of Palo Alto, California, for permission to place a small sign reading "Be a Safe Driver" in a window of their homes. Two weeks later, another person asked residents for permission to stake a large "Drive Carefully" sign in the front yard. Nearly 56 percent of those who had agreed to the first request also agreed to the second request. However, only 17 percent of the residents who only heard the second request, but not the first, agreed to put the sign in their yard.

Another strategy is sometimes called the *door-in-the-face technique*. It works like this: To encourage people to agree to a moderate request that might otherwise be rejected, you make a major request—likely to be rejected. When it is, you follow up immediately with a more minor request. For example, you might ask a friend "I'm helping my parents move this weekend. Would you come over and help us Saturday and Sunday until we're done?" "No? Well, then, could you come over Saturday morning and just help me move our grand piano?" You have a much higher likelihood of success on the second request following the first than if you had made only the second request (Dillard, 1991).

PSYCHOLOGY and YOU

The Anchoring Effect. Most research on persuasion focuses on large efforts such as political and advertising campaigns. How can you, as an individual, persuade others?

One technique is *anchoring*. When people make judgments under conditions of uncertainty, they are often swayed by suggestions of what is appropriate. One study asked two groups of subjects how many African countries were in the United Nations. One group was asked, "Is it more or less than 65?" The other group was asked, "Is it more or less than 15?" On the average, the first group estimated about 40, the second group about 25. The suggested number serves as an anchor, or starting point, for people's estimates.

Examples of anchors are common. When street performers begin their acts, they often line their hats with dollar bills. People selling cars and houses start with a high price.

Independent Practice

■ **Research.** Tell students about two unusual nonprofit groups: Population Communications International (PCI) and Population Communication Services (PCS). Today these groups are using television advertising to influence population growth in Mexico, India, and Kenya. Explain that the cultures in all three of these nations value large families. To change this attitude, PCI and PCS have turned to psychology.

The most effective method of achieving this goal has proven to be soap operas such as Kenya's *Tushuriane* ("Let's Talk About It") and Mexico's *Ven Conmigo* ("Come With Me"). Request interested students to look up articles on this project in the *Readers' Guide to Periodical Literature* (under the heading Population). Then assign them to write a soap-opera episode that PCI or PSC might run to change attitudes on family size. *(Remind students that the most effective episodes will take into account cultural factors that shape attitudes.)* (OBJECTIVES 1, 3, 4)

🧪 LAB EXPERIMENTS AND DEMONSTRATIONS

Request volunteers to select a worthy charity or volunteer organization in your community. Direct them to approach the group to explain that the class is conducting an experiment on the *foot-in-the-door technique* and that the money raised by the experiment will be donated to the charity. (Caution students not to use the charity's name without the organization's knowledge.) Next, have students draw up a petition in favor of government sponsorship of the charity. Direct students to go to a block of houses, asking people to sign the petition. A week later have them return to the same houses, this time asking for a donation to the charity. As a control, students should also go to an equal number of houses with no knowledge of the petition. Which group gave more donations—the petition group or the control group?

Organize the students into groups to analyze the different techniques used to attract recruits into the military. Have students consider the target audience for the ad on the right. What conclusions can students draw about troops recruited for the military in the 1990s? *(Underscore the idea of diversity.)*
Answer to caption, Figure 18.7: (left): appeal to patriotism; use of Uncle Sam as a spokesperson; (right): lure of occupational opportunity and training; features diverse, youthful, and happy individuals

■ **Comparing Past and Present.** Focus on the use of the expression "Today's Army" in the advertisement on the right. Assign interested students to investigate the composition and policies of the Army prior to World War II and in the 1990s. Have them summarize their findings in the form of a chart entitled: "The U.S. Army—Yesterday and Today." *(To guide students, tell them that the biggest changes revolve around integration of minorities and women.)* Use the chart in a general class discussion of how prejudice shaped military policy prior to World War II. Ask: What factors have reshaped attitudes in this area? (OBJECTIVES 1–4)

FIGURE 18.7

Audiences change from generation to generation, so the means of persuading them must also change. Attitudes toward the armed services, for example, have changed markedly since World War I, thus requiring army recruiters to alter their approach. **What strategies have been devised to involve the audience?**

Models of Persuasion. Social psychologists study many elements of the communication process. Some focus on the cognitions that accompany attitudes and attitude change. Their goals are to determine what cognitive processes occur when an attitude is being examined and how these processes affect attitude changes (Baron & Byrne, 1991).

The basis of the *elaboration likelihood model* (ELM), proposed by Petty and Cacioppo (1986), is that a message leads to thinking, but how much and at what depth is determined both by the message and the needs of the person receiving it. Two different levels of activity are possible. *Central route processing* occurs when the recipient thoughtfully considers the issues and arguments. *Peripheral route processing* is characterized by considering other cues rather than the message itself. Some of the cues are: Is the speaker knowledgeable? Do I like the speaker? Is the message conveyed in an interesting, compelling way? Another model of persuasion that shares some of the elements of ELM is the *heuristic model* (Chaiken, 1987). A *heuristic* is a rule of thumb or a shortcut that may lead to, but doesn't guarantee, a solution.

Like ELM, the heuristic model proposes two ways in which attitudes may be changed. If an individual is not interested in an issue under discussion, he or she is likely to rely on *heuristic processing*, a very casual, low-attention form of analyzing evidence. In this kind of processing, the recipient tunes in to the peripheral aspects of the message—the likability of the source, the number of arguments, and the tone of voice.

On the other hand, if the recipient is deeply interested or curious about the topic of a message, the likely result is what Chaiken calls *systematic processing*. Systematic processing shares many of the same features with central route processing. What's an example? You know that when you go to

Debating an Issue. Research has revealed that children watch an average of 20,000 commercials a year (Shaffer, 1989). Of these ads, nearly 80 percent concentrate on selling some kind of sugared food product (Berk, 1989). Some of the most successful spokespersons in children's ads are cartoon figures or animated toys. Provide this background to students. Then organize two teams to debate the following topic: *Resolved*—That television ads take unfair advantage of children.

hear a comedian, if no one in the audience laughs, you are less likely to do so yourself. If you do find yourself laughing when no one else is, you quickly suppress it. At your house, if you are alone, you are less likely to laugh out loud at something funny on radio or television than if someone is with you who is laughing. A comedian's performance is seldom centrally involving, so you are likely to rely on heuristics.

In one test of the heuristic model, Axsom, Yates, and Chaiken (1987) set up a situation in which subjects listened to a speech advocating probation rather than jail for convicted criminals. The researchers instituted several variables. Some subjects, for example, listened to a debate—supposedly recorded live earlier—interrupted by rounds of enthusiastic applause. Others heard only scattered applause and occasionally vehement disagreement. The experimenters expressed the importance of the topic to some subjects while they told others to relax as they listened. In addition, some subjects listened to a debate that included valid and strong arguments while others heard weak arguments.

The researchers drew several conclusions from the experiment. Subjects who were deeply interested in the topic were more likely to consider the arguments. Subjects who were not interested were more easily swayed by the audience's reactions. When the audience was unreceptive, the subjects' attitudes changed very little. Whether they heard strong or weak arguments did not make much difference. For interested subjects, the quality of the arguments was the key, whether or not the audience was receptive.

The Sleeper Effect

Changes in attitudes are not always permanent. In fact, efforts at persuasion usually have their greatest impact immediately and then fade away. However, sometimes people seem to reach different conclusions about a message after a period of time has elapsed. This curious **sleeper effect** has been explained in several ways.

One explanation of the delayed-action impact depends on the tendency to retain the message but forget the source. As time goes by, a positive source no longer holds power to persuade nor does a negative source undercut the message. When the source is negative and the memory of the source fades, the message then "speaks for itself" and more people may accept it (Kelman and Hovland, 1953).

The problem is that this requires forgetting of one thing and retention of another, with no obvious reason why that should occur. Researchers (Pratkanis *et al.*, 1988) conducted experiments to verify their *differential decay hypothesis*. They argued that if the message is heard first, followed by a discounting cue (such as a low-credibility source), the two balance each other out—no effect is observed. At the same time, however, the negative aspects of the cue dissipate more rapidly than the impact of the highly elab-

? FACT OR FICTION

People expect other people to think like they do.

Fact. Common sense tells you that people are unique and hold different values and attitudes. Yet we often expect other people to think and act like we do and are surprised when they do not. This process is called the *false consensus effect.*

The most vulnerable attitudes are those you have never had to defend.

■ **Demonstration.** Request a volunteer to take a book of jokes out of the library or to search for jokes in popular magazines such as *Reader's Digest.* Instruct them to write down the corniest jokes possible (ones that would make students grimace instead of laugh). On a tape recording, prepare a laugh track. (You might ask the school drama teacher for some volunteer "laughers.") At the start of a class period, give a straightforward reading of the jokes without the sound track. Then read them a second time with comical intonation and use of the laugh track. After discussing the different responses, ask students to identify the type of processing illustrated by this demonstration. *(heuristic processing)* (OBJECTIVE 4)

Teacher Note. To illustrate people's unconscious awareness of the *sleeper effect,* you might point out the use of such expressions as "Let me think about it" or "Let me sleep on it." What other similar phrases can students suggest? Do they feel most people need time for the message to "sink in"? Why or why not?

Modeling. Some learning disabled students might have trouble following the flow of information in each type of message processing discussed on pages 474–475. Organize the class into small groups, and assign a student tutor to model a reading of "Models of Persuasion." An example of modeling might be: "I've just read the sentence on *elaboration likelihood* (p. 474). This sentence tells me that people process messages at different levels of thought. The sentence also tells me that they process messages differently when they need the information. I expect that the next sentences will tell about the various levels of information processing."

Using Psychology

To guide student reading of the feature, ask the following questions:

1. What is the topic of the feature? *(methods used to convince Americans to conserve energy)*

2. What three techniques did Kohlenberg and his colleagues use to convince consumers to change their energy-consuming habits? *(dissemination of information, feedback, and financial incentives)*

3. Which method was most successful? *(financial incentives)*

4. Based on this feature, what conclusions can you draw about reasons people change attitudes or habits? *(Answers will vary, but lead students to understand that people are most likely to change their attitudes if they personally benefit from the change.)*

---

orated message. It's easier to remember your own position than the details of an argument. If the cue decays rapidly and the argument more slowly, what remains is the effect on an attitude.

Using Psychology

Promoting Energy Conservation

Americans use—and waste—more energy than any other people on earth. The fuel crisis, ad campaigns on the need to conserve energy, and the steadily rising cost of gasoline, oil, and electricity have hardly made a dent in our rate of energy use. How can Americans be persuaded to conserve energy? Kohlenberg, Phillips, and Proctor (1976) attempted to answer this question. The demand for electricity peaks in the morning and again in the late afternoon, when people take showers and use vacuum cleaners, washing machines, and other electrical appliances. Unlike other forms of energy, electricity cannot be stored. Power companies therefore have to maintain generators that are in full use for only a few hours each day. One solution to the growing demand for electricity is to build more generators. The other solution is to change people's habits, cutting back the peak demand.

Kohlenberg and his colleagues tried three techniques for convincing volunteer families to reduce their electricity use during peak periods. The first was to provide information. Researchers explained the problem, asked the families to try to cut back, and suggested how they might do so. Monitors installed in each house indicated that this approach had little or no effect. Considering that all the families were conservation-minded, this was surprising.

Next, the researchers tried feedback. A bulb that lit up whenever the family approached peak consumption levels was placed in each house. Immediate and direct evidence of electricity overuse was expected to help the families cut back. Although somewhat more effective than information alone, feedback did not break the families' habits of electricity use.

Finally, the researchers declared that families would earn twice the amount of their electricity bill if they reduced their peak use 100 percent, the full amount if they cut back 50 percent, and so on. This strategy worked. None of the families reduced their peak use 100 percent, but all did cut back. A follow-up revealed that all returned to the convenience of using appliances during peak hours after the incentive was removed.

What this simple experiment demonstrated was that campaigns to reduce the use of electricity during peak periods are largely inef-

---

COOPERATIVE LEARNING ACTIVITY

Review the conclusion of researchers involved in the dissonance reduction experiment on page 466:
The researchers said that the typical tendency to rank freedom high and equality low showed that students in general are "much more interested in their own freedom than in other people's."

Ask: How does the study discussed in the Using Psychology feature indicate that people tend to favor their own personal interests over the public interest? Next, have students identify a social issue that concerns them such as the plight of the homeless, AIDS research, and so on. Organize students

into groups and have them use information in this chapter to devise a campaign to promote individual involvement in this issue.

fective. However, if power companies were to provide incentives—say, reduced rates for families that cut back during the peaks—they might save themselves the cost of building and maintaining partially used plants.

In the 1980s, a New England power company encouraged customers to take part in a plan in which they would not control the heating of their homes during some of the morning and afternoon hours. Then, during the 1990s, a Texas power company developed a device that allowed the company to turn off a user's air conditioner during the summer months in periods of peak usage. Both programs were, for the most part, successful, but the driving force again was rewards to the customer for limiting power consumption during peak periods. The New England customers paid less for their power while the Texas power company paid its customers a flat fee for having the device installed.

It may also be that it simply takes time for people to change their minds. As the message "sinks in," attitudes change more. A dramatic example of this was the experiment mentioned earlier in which students who were made aware of inconsistencies in their values concerning civil rights changed their ideas more after 15 to 17 months than after 3 weeks.

The Inoculation Effect

What can you do to resist persuasion? Research has shown that people can be educated to resist attitude change. This technique can be compared to an inoculation (McGuire, 1970). Inoculation against persuasion works in much the same way as inoculation against certain diseases. When a person is vaccinated he is given a weakened or dead form of the disease-causing agent, which stimulates his body to manufacture defenses. Then, if that person is attacked by a more potent form of the agent, his defenses make him or her immune to infection. Similarly, a person who has resisted a mild attack on his or her beliefs is ready to defend them against an onslaught that might otherwise have been overwhelming.

The **inoculation effect** can be explained in two ways: it motivates individuals to defend their beliefs more strongly, and it gives them some practice in defending those beliefs. The most vulnerable attitudes you have, therefore, are the ones that you have never had to defend. For example, you might find yourself hard put to defend your faith in democracy or in the healthfulness of vegetables if you have never had these beliefs questioned.

PSYCHOLOGY and YOU

Psychological Warfare. Psychological warfare refers to any activities and techniques designed to demoralize enemy troops and persuade them to give up the fight. Both sides used psychological warfare extensively in the Persian Gulf War.

As American troops waited in the Saudi Arabian desert for the war to begin, an Iraqi radio announcer nicknamed "Baghdad Betty" tried to persuade them that they would be crushed by Iraqi might. After the war started, Iraq forced captured Allied pilots to denounce the war on TV.

The Allied forces dropped leaflets on Iraqi soldiers and issued false reports of Iraqi defections in an attempt to convince Iraqi soldiers to surrender. In addition, underground radio stations broadcast war news into Iraq. Allied forces also armed resistance fighters in Iraqi-occupied Kuwait so they could wage a secret war against Iraq. No one knows how effective psychological warfare is, but military leaders consider it an essential part of modern warfare.

■ **Applying a Concept.** Refer students to the posters developed in the Extra Credit activity assigned in the Bottom Note on page 457. After reviewing the values demonstrated by these posters, ask students to identify ways in which a belief in the American system of government is promoted in the United States. (*Examples will vary widely. Students might mention use of the national anthem at baseball games, celebration of the Fourth of July, required courses in civics and government, and so on.*) Ask students to consider how such techniques help "inoculate" Americans against demagogues and/or totalitarian practices. (OBJECTIVES 1–4)

■ **Research.** To introduce the material on Social Influence, have a volunteer read the margin feature on psychological warfare aloud to the rest of the class. Then direct students to investigate the religious beliefs and anti-Americanism among Iraqi troops involved in the Persian Gulf War. Have them present their findings to the class in an oral report. Ask: How did these attitudes inoculate Iraqi soldiers against leaflets dropped by the Allies? How do dictators such as Saddam Hussein use such attitudes to perpetuate their governments? (*You may wish to review the effect of scapegoating. In the Persian Gulf War, Hussein used the United States as a scapegoat.*) (OBJECTIVES 1–4)

CRITICAL THINKING ACTIVITY

Weighing Pros and Cons. Point out to students that the "Pledge of Allegiance" is read in many schools. Explain that opinion remains divided over this practice. To quiet the debate, federal courts ruled that students (or anyone else) have the right to remain silent during the Pledge. Challenge students to weigh the pros and cons of this practice. List these items on the chalkboard. Then have students write an essay entitled: "The Pledge of Allegiance—Inoculation or Indoctrination?" (Tip: This is an emotional issue. Allow students to devise an essay of their own choosing if they object to discussing this topic.)

DID YOU KNOW?

An American journalist coined the word *brainwash* in 1951. It was a translation of the Chinese expression *hsinao*—"wash brain" or "cleanse the mind." The Chinese used the term *hsinao* to describe the reeducation of youth after the communist takeover and the policy toward U.S. prisoners of war captured in Korea.

SOCIAL INFLUENCE

Brainwashing

The most extreme means of changing attitudes involves a combination of psychological gamesmanship and physical torture, aptly called **brainwashing.** The most extensive studies of brainwashing have been done on Westerners who had been captured by the Chinese during the Korean War and subjected to "thought reform." Psychiatrist Robert Jay Lifton interviewed several dozen prisoners released by the Chinese, and, from their accounts, he outlined the methods used to break down people's convictions and introduce new patterns of belief, feeling, and behavior (1963).

The aim in brainwashing is as much to create a new person as to change attitudes. So the first step is to strip away all identity and subject the person to intense social pressure and physical stress. Prison is a perfect setting for this process. The person is isolated from social support, is a number not a name, is clothed like everyone else, and can be surrounded by people who have had their thoughts "reformed" and are contemptuous of "reaction-

FIGURE 18.8

Members of Hare Krishna spread their message. **What problems do many members of cults face when they try to return to their former way of life?**

MEETING SPECIAL NEEDS

Learning Strategy. Students with learning problems may need concrete mental images to understand an abstract concept. To explain brainwashing, you might tell students that it involves three basic steps: unfreezing, pouring into a new mold, and refreezing. During the unfreezing stage, a subject's confidence in prior attitudes and behavior is thoroughly shaken (melted). To restore psychological and emotional balance, a new attitude or behavior is suggested to the subject (a new thought mold). If the subject accepts the suggestion, he or she receives a reward to "freeze" the attitude or behavior in place.

aries." So long as the prisoner holds out, he is treated with contempt or exhorted to confess by his fellow prisoners. He is interrogated past the point of exhaustion by his captors, and is humiliated and discomfited by being bound hand and foot at all times, even during meals or elimination. Any personal information the prisoner uses to justify himself is turned against him as evidence of his guilt.

At some point, the prisoner realizes that resistance is impossible; the pressures are simply intolerable. Resistance gives way to cooperation, but only as a means of avoiding any more demoralization. The prisoner is rewarded for cooperating. Cooperation involves confessing to crimes against the people in his former way of life.

Throughout the process his cell mates are an integral part of the brainwashing team, berating him at first, then warming to him after his confession. For most of his waking hours, the prisoner is part of a marathon group therapy session built on Marxist ideology. The prisoner is asked not only to interpret his current behavior that way but also to reinterpret his life before capture. Guilt is systematically aroused and defined by Marxist standards. What the prisoner does is to learn a new version of his life, and his confession, provided at first to get some relief from the isolation and pain, becomes more elaborate, coherent, and ideologically based. And with every "improvement" in his attitudes, prison life is made a little more pleasant. Finally, by a combination of threat, peer pressure, systematic rewards, and other psychological means, the prisoner comes to believe his confession. But as one survivor recalled, "it is a special kind of belief . . . you accept it—in order to avoid trouble—because every time you don't agree, trouble starts again" (Lifton, 1963, p. 31). These techniques appear to succeed only as long as the person remains a prisoner.

It's hard to say where persuasion ends and brainwashing begins. Some researchers believe that brainwashing is just a very intense form of persuasion. Drawing this line has become particularly important to the courts—especially in cases such as lawsuits regarding the deprogramming of members of religious cults.

Margaret Thaler Singer (1979) has studied more than 300 former members of religious cults. Many had joined during periods of depression and confusion. The cults offered structure and gave life meaning: they provided friends and ready-made decisions about marriage and careers, dating and sex. Being cut off from the outside world, an intensive indoctrination often increased the new member's sense of commitment.

When people become dissatisfied and quit, many have trouble readjusting to the world they left behind. Among the problems Singer has observed are depression, loneliness, indecisiveness, passivity, guilt, and blurring of mental activity. The average person takes 6 to 18 months to return to normal.

Group Pressure to Conform

Have you ever come home and surprised your parents by wearing the latest fad in clothing? Possibly the conversation that followed went something like this:

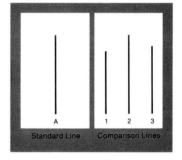

FIGURE 18.9

These two cards were shown to subjects in one trial of Asch's experiment on conformity. The actual discrimination is easy. **What was the purpose of Asch's experiment?**

A
Standard Line
1 2 3
Comparison Lines

■ **Analyzing a Quote.** Read aloud the following quotes by Norman Alexander, one of the African American POWs held in North Vietnam.

[T]hey put me in a concrete cell that was about 6 by 9 feet. You either had a board or a concrete pallet for a bed. . . . [T]he first couple of weeks I couldn't put it all together. . . . The interrogations and beatings [just kept coming].

When Dr. King was assassinated, they . . . wanted me to tell black soldiers not to fight. . . . I would tell them no. . . . Although black people [in the U.S.] are kind of behind the power curtain, . . . America is still the . . . best hope.

Ask: What brainwashing techniques did the Vietcong use against Alexander? What special tactic did they apply to African American POWs? What values do you think enabled Alexander to resist the brainwashing?

VISUAL INSTRUCTION

To set the stage for the series of photos on page 480, ask students to identify which comparison line in the right box matches the line in the left box. **Answer to caption, Figure 18.9:** to test conformity to pressure from one's peers

COOPERATIVE LEARNING ACTIVITY

Organize the students into groups. Then tell them to imagine they are psychologists interested in "deprogramming" former cult members. Challenge them to devise the most effective strategies for helping the individuals readjust. Have students share their suggestions. As a follow-up activity, request students to research some of the methods actually used by psychologists such as Margaret Thaler Singer.

■ **Creative Writing.** To illustrate the influence of social norms on individual behavior, tell students to imagine that they have found a way to be invisible for 24 hours. Next, assign students to write a short story in which they describe how they would spend that day. (To encourage honesty, mention that the stories will not be collected.) Next, tell students that a similar activity was conducted by social psychologist David K. Dodd (1985). The study revealed that 36 percent of the stories involved antisocial activities such as "rob a bank." Conduct an anonymous paper ballot to determine how your class compared to the Dodd study. Ask: What does this activity (and/or the Dodd experiment) reveal about the effect of peer pressure on curbing antisocial behavior? (OBJECTIVES 3, 4)

FIGURE 18.10

These photographs were taken during Asch's experiment on conformity. Subject 6 is the only real subject; the others are confederates of the experimenter. The subject listens to the others express identical judgments that differ from his own. He is in a dilemma: Does he express the judgment he knows to be correct and risk being different from the group, or does he conform to the group's judgment? **What were Asch's findings?**

"How can you go around looking like that?"
"But everyone dresses like this."

Psychologist Solomon Asch (1952) designed what has become a classic experiment to test conformity to pressure from one's peers. He found that people may conform to other people's ideas of the truth, even when they disagree. The following is what you would have experienced if you had been a subject in this experiment.

You and six other students meet in a classroom for an experiment on visual judgment. You are shown a card with one line on it. You are then shown another card containing three lines and are asked to pick the one that is the same length as the first line. One of the three is exactly the same length and is easy to determine. The other two lines are obviously different (Figure 18.9). The experiment begins uneventfully. The subjects announce their answers in the order in which they are seated in the room. You happen to be sixth, and one person follows you. On the first comparison, every person chooses the same matching line. The second set of cards is displayed, and once again the group is unanimous. The discriminations seem simple and easy, and you prepare for what you expect will be a rather boring experiment.

On the third trial, there is an unexpected disturbance. You are quite certain that line 2 is the one that matches the standard. Yet the first person in the group announces confidently that line 1 is the correct match. Then, the second person follows suit and he, too, declares that the answer is line 1. So do the third, fourth, and fifth subjects. Now it is your turn. You are suddenly faced with two contradictory pieces of information: the evidence of your own senses tells you that one answer is clearly correct, but the unanimous and confident judgments of the 5 preceding subjects tell you that you are wrong.

The dilemma persists through 18 trials. On 12 of the trials, the other group members unanimously give an answer that differs from what you clearly perceive to be correct. It is only at the end of the experimental session that you learn the explanation for the confusion. The 6 other subjects were all actors, and they had been instructed to give incorrect answers on those 12 trials (Figure 18.10).

How do most subjects react to this situation? Asch found that almost one-third of his 50 subjects conformed at least half the time. These conformers he called the "yielders." Most yielders explained to Asch afterward that they knew which line was correct but that they yielded to group pressure in order not to appear different from the others. Asch called those who did not conform "independents." They gave the correct answer despite group pressure. Why so much conformity? According to one theory, most children are taught the overriding importance of being liked and of being accepted. Conformity is the standard means of gaining this approval.

One of the most important findings of Asch's experiment was that if even one person among the first five failed to conform to the group's judgment, the subject was able to stick to his own perceptions. It seems that it is hardest to stand alone. Later researchers have shown that, under some conditions, a minority view can come to win over the larger group (Moscovici, 1985).

Obedience to Authority

The influence other people have on your attitudes and actions is considerable. Sometimes this influence is indirect and subtle; at other times it is quite direct. People may simply tell you what to believe and what to do. Under what conditions do you obey them?

Everyone in this society has had experiences with various authorities, such as parents, teachers, police officers, managers, judges, clergy, and military officers. **Obedience** to these authorities can be either useful or destructive. For instance, obeying the orders of a doctor or firefighter in an emergency would be constructive. Psychologists are more interested, however, in the negative aspects of obedience. They know from such cases in history as German Nazism and American atrocities in Vietnam that individuals frequently obey irrational commands. In fact, people often obey authority even when obedience goes against their conscience and their whole system of morality.

The most famous investigation of obedience was conducted in 1963 by social psychologist Stanley Milgram. The experiment was set up as follows. Two subjects appeared for each session. They were told that they would be participating in an experiment to test the effects of punishment on memory. One of the subjects was to be the "teacher" and the other, the "learner." In reality, the learner was not a volunteer subject; he was Milgram's accomplice. The teacher was to read a list of words into a microphone to be memorized by the learner, who would be in a nearby room. If the learner failed to recite the list back correctly, the teacher was to administer an electric shock. The alleged purpose of the experiment was to test whether the shock would have any effect on learning. In actuality, however, Milgram wanted to discover how far the teacher would follow his instructions; how much shock would he be willing to give a fellow human being?

FIGURE 18.11

In Stanley Milgram's experiment on obedience, the "learner" (b) is connected to the shock apparatus. (c) Milgram explains the procedure to the "teacher." (d) This subject refuses to administer shocks any further and angrily rises in protest. (e) Milgram explains the truth about the experiment. (© 1965 by Stanley Milgram. From the film *Obedience*. Distributed by New York University Film Library.) **Why did many of the subjects continue to administer shocks to the learner?**

a

b

c

d

e

CONNECTIONS: PSYCHOLOGY AND SOCIAL STUDIES

Tell students that at the Nuremberg Trials, former Gestapo officer Adolf Eichmann offered the following defense:

I am not the monster I am made out to be. This mass slaughter [the Holocaust] *is solely the responsibility of political leaders. My guilt lies in my obedience, my respect for discipline, my allegiance to the colors and the service* [of Germany].

Ask: How does the Eichmann quote illustrate the negative aspect of obedience? *(obeyed authority even when obedience defied the whole system of human morality)* When do human beings have an obligation to disobey authority? *(To help students assess this question, you might refer them to the discussion of ethical behavior in Chapter 9.)*

ASSESS

Check for Understanding

Organize the students into seven groups, and assign them to devise a list of the most important main ideas for each major topic in the outline on page 483. Have members from each group share their lists with the class as a whole.

Reteach

Have students complete the Chapter 18 Study Guide Activity. For extended review assign the Chapter 18 Review Activity as homework or an in-class assignment.

Enrich

Ask students to complete the Chapter 18 Extension Activity and answer the questions that follow it.

Evaluate

Administer and grade the Chapter 18 Test. Two forms are available should you wish to give different tests to different students/classes.

Use the Understanding Psychology Testmaker to create a customized test.

CLOSE

Have students review the list of attitudinal influences compiled in the Motivating Activity (see page 456). Based on information in the chapter, how would students modify or revise influences in each category named? What do students think are the most important influences on their own belief system?

As the experiment began, the learner continually gave wrong answers, and the teacher began to administer the prescribed shocks from an impressive-looking shock generator. The generator had a dial that ranged from 15 volts, which was labeled "Slight Shock," to 450 volts, which was labeled "Danger: Severe Shock." After each of the learner's mistakes, the teacher was told to increase the voltage by one level. The teacher believed that the learner was receiving these shocks because he had seen the learner being strapped into a chair in the other room and had watched electrodes being attached to the learner's hands. In reality, however, the accomplice was receiving no shocks at all from the equipment.

As the experiment progressed, the learner made many mistakes and the teacher was instructed to give increasingly severe shocks. At 300 volts the learner pounded on the wall in protest and refused to provide any further answers. At this point the experimenter instructed the subject to treat the absence of an answer as a wrong answer and to continue the procedure. The experiment ended either when the maximum 450 volts was administered or when the teacher refused to administer any more shocks. If at any point the teacher indicated that he wanted to stop, the experimenter calmly told him to continue: "Whether the learner likes it or not, you must go on until he has learned all the word pairs correctly."

These subjects were not sadists. Many of them showed signs of extreme tension and discomfort during the session, and they often told the experimenter that they would like to stop. Despite these feelings, they continued to obey the experimenter's commands. They were ordinary people—salespersons, engineers, postal workers—placed in an unusual situation.

What accounts for this surprisingly high level of obedience? Part of the answer is that the experimenter represents a legitimate authority. People assume that such an authority knows what he is doing, even when his instructions seem to run counter to their own standards of moral behavior.

Milgram's subjects could have walked out at any time—they had nothing to lose by leaving. Nevertheless, social conditioning for obeying legitimate authorities is so strongly ingrained that people often lack the words or the ways to do otherwise. Simply getting up and leaving would have violated powerful unwritten rules of acceptable social behavior.

Another experiment that caused ordinary people to act in extraordinary ways was performed by Philip Zimbardo and his colleagues. Zimbardo randomly divided male volunteers into two groups: "prisoners" and "prison guards." He sent both groups to live in a simulated "prison" set up in the basement of a Stanford University building. He gave the "guards" instructions to maintain order. Within two days, most of the "guards" had become intoxicated with power; they acted cruelly toward the prisoners, often without reason. At the same time, the "prisoners" began showing signs of extreme stress, often acting subdued and depressed. The emotional reactions were so extreme that the two-week experiment was ended after only six days. It seems that the prison environment was much stronger than individual personalities. Although the subjects in this experiment were emotionally mature and stable, the roles these individuals adopted changed the way they acted. There may be other situations in everyday life that may cause us and those around us to act in ways we do not expect.

BEYOND THE CLASSROOM

Assign students to sit near a handicapped parking area at a busy shopping area. Over a period of at least an hour, have them log the following information: the number of disabled people who use the parking area, the number of nondisabled people who use the area, the number of people who pull into the area and leave when they see the sign. Besides conducting an experiment on obedience, you might ask students how their activities may have created cognitive dissonance among violators.

SUMMARY

Use the following outline as a tool for reviewing this chapter. Copy the outline onto your own paper, leaving spaces between headings to make notes about key concepts.

I. Where Attitudes Come From

II. Attitude Formation
   A. Compliance
   B. Identification
   C. Internalization

III. Prejudice
   A. Stereotypes and Roles
   B. Prejudice and Discrimination
   C. Scapegoating
   D. Integration

IV. Cognitive Consistency and Changing Attitudes

V. Attitudes and Actions
   A. Doing Is Believing
   B. Self-Fulfilling Prophecy
   C. Practical Implications

VI. Persuasion
   A. The Communication Process
   B. The Sleeper Effect
   C. The Inoculation Effect

VII. Social Influence
   A. Brainwashing
   B. Group Pressure to Conform
   C. Obedience to Authority

CONCEPTS AND VOCABULARY

1. What is an attitude? What are the three elements of an attitude?

2. What are the three processes involved in changing an attitude? Which process is based on emotional attachment to another person?

3. Can prejudice be defined as a negative judgment toward another group of people? What is the name given by researchers to prejudiced persons who share a number of traits in common? According to these researchers, why do these people use stereotypes? Can a person discriminate against another person without being prejudiced?

4. What factors are important in reducing intergroup hostility through integration?

5. What is the name Leon Festinger gave to the uncomfortable feelings that arise when a person experiences conflicting thoughts, beliefs, attitudes, or feelings?

6. Which cognitive act are people engaging in when they convince themselves that they did not like the victim of their aggressive act?

7. What are the four parts of the communication process? What two questions do people ask themselves about the source of a communication? If you listen to the argument of a person whom you dislike and then take the opposite point of view, what effect has just taken place?

8. What will be the effect on listeners if you use a very emotional appeal or if you pressure them to adopt your point of view?

9. How can the sleeper effect be explained? The inoculation effect?

10. What are the steps used to brainwash a person?

11. What percentage of people were "yielders" in Solomon Asch's conformity experiments? Why do people conform? What event will reduce conformity?

12. What are the three ways in which subjects were helped to resist the authoritative experimenter in Stanley Milgram's experiment?

483

ANSWERS

Concepts and Vocabulary

1. enduring set of beliefs, feelings, and tendencies toward people or things in predisposed ways; a belief or opinion about something, feelings about the thing, a tendency to act toward that thing in certain ways

2. compliance, identification, internalization; identification

3. Prejudice cannot be defined as a negative judgment toward another group of people. Answers will vary. A person may discriminate against another person without being prejudiced.

4. abandonment of negative stereotypes; support of social norms; similarity in background

5. cognitive dissonance

6. self-justification

7. Four components are message, source, channel, and audience. People receiving a message ask themselves: "Is the person giving the message trustworthy and sincere?" and "Does he or she know anything about the subject?" The boomerang effect will occur.

8. may take opposite point of view (boomerang effect) or stop listening

9. sleeper effect: by the tendency to retain a message but forget the source (allowing message "to speak for itself"); by need for message to "sink in;" inoc-

ulation effect: by the motivation to defend beliefs; by practice in defending beliefs

10. Answers include: strip away identity, subject person to intense personal pressure and stress, punishment for "unreformed behavior," breakdown of resistance, cooperation to avoid further demoralization, reward for cooperation, and inculcation of new attitudes.

11. about one-third; perhaps taught to conform as a child, need for acceptance; if more than one person refuses to conform

12. the removal of the physical presence of the experimenter, putting the subject face to face with the victim, providing other "teachers" to support the subject's defiance

Critical Thinking

1. In assessing the effect of advertising on purchasing decisions, students should use specific examples. Encourage students to cite commercials in their assessment of obnoxious advertising (or name successful products linked with such campaigns).

2. In evaluating the results of this activity, have students take into account the different developmental stages of life (i.e., the adolescence for independence) and the historic/environmental factors that affected each generation.

3. In analyzing the stereotypes generated by this activity, refer students to "Views of Adolescence" in Chapter 9.

Applying Knowledge

1. Encourage students to assess the effect of gender-related adjectives on the survey results. (They might have respondents indicate their gender.)

2. Student analyses should accurately reflect details in the ads.

3. Before beginning work, suggest that students review the "Using Psychology" feature on page 476.

4. One of the goals of the test is to determine the power of suggestion vs. actual sensory preference.

5. Most prejudices grow out of fear or ethnocentrism. Reduction of prejudice relies upon information and contact and cooperation among groups.

CRITICAL THINKING

1. **Analyze.** One of the primary objectives of advertising is to get the viewers/listeners to remember the product. To what extent do you think familiarity with brand names influences your choices in the market? How many television commercials do you find obnoxious? Do you find that you remember the products advertised in "obnoxious" commercials better than you remember products that appear in less offensive advertisements? Do you think there is a possibility that some commercials are deliberately offensive?

2. **Evaluate.** Parents have an early influence on their children's attitudes and beliefs. Check the degree of similarity between your parents' views and your views on selected issues. First, generate a list of ten statements on issues such as political affiliation, nuclear energy, mandatory retirement, equal pay, and paternity leave. Then develop a questionnaire based on these issues in which a person can respond by agreeing or disagreeing with the statements. Use a five-point scale ranging from 1 (strongly agree) to 5 (strongly disagree). Ask your parents to complete the same questionnaire. Notice the similarity or dissimilarity between your responses and those of your parents.

3. **Apply.** A stereotype is a shorthand, overly simplified description of a group of people, which influences attitudes. People can acquire stereotypes from their social interactions with others, from watching television, or elsewhere. Examine the stereotypes that have emerged about teenagers by asking a group of adults to describe teenagers. Have them complete the open-ended statement, "Teenagers are . . . ," as many times as they can. Ask at least eight to give you responses. Then compile the statements and see whether you can pick out stereotypes. Did you detect any stereotypes? If so, how might adults' stereotyped views of teenagers affect the way they act toward them? How can stereotypes be changed?

APPLYING KNOWLEDGE

1. Collect magazine ads of 10 different brands of detergent. Using a scale of 0 to 10, have subjects rate the detergent as being weak or strong—0 being the weakest and 10 being the strongest. Have different subjects rate the same brands on the same scale for masculinity or femininity—0 being the most feminine and 10 being the most masculine. Now average your scores. What conclusions can you draw from your results?

2. Collect samples of advertising that depict various techniques of persuasion—identification, social approval, fear of disaster, and so on. Analyze each ad on the basis of effectiveness and the type of person to whom it might appeal.

3. Choose some issue on which you have a strong opinion. If you were given an unlimited budget, how would you go about persuading people to agree with you? Describe the sources you would employ, the channels you would use, the content of your message, and the audience you would try to reach.

4. To what extent does advertising influence your choice of foods? Find several people who prefer butter to margarine. Ask them why they prefer butter. If they say it tastes better, then ask them to participate in an experiment to test their claims. Get several brands of both butter and margarine and spread them lightly on the same kind of relatively tasteless crackers or toast. Blindfold your subjects and provide them with a glass of water to rinse their mouths whenever they wish. Ask them to identify the samples. Run through the series about four times, varying the order of presentation. Try similar experiments with people who prefer certain brands of orange juice, cola, or coffee.

5. Make a list of 10 or more nationalities, religions, races, and occupations. Have friends or family members list five things that come to mind when these groups are mentioned. What are your conclusions? Do you detect any prejudices? How might prejudices be reduced?

6. Point out that this activity not only measures the attitudes of other people, it also requires students to look at traits they have assigned to them.

7. To encourage self-appraisal, have students prepare their checklist anonymously. Explore whether the activity created cognitive dissonance in any students.

Analyzing Viewpoints

1. Use this activity to explore the need for "debriefing" after emotionally charged experiments such as the Milgram project.

2. You might encourage students to do additional research into forced integration, citing specific evidence in support of their opinion. (Research can extend back as far as the forced

6. Choose a controversial topic, such as abortion, drug abuse, war, or women's rights, and devise 10 questions to measure people's attitudes toward this issue. Give the questionnaire to a number of people and see whether your results make sense in terms of what you already know about these people.

7. Write the following list on a separate sheet of paper:
   a sightless person
   a child abuser
   a thief
   an elderly person
   a recovering alcoholic
   a wrestler with one leg
   a drug addict
   a homeless man
   a homeless child
   a mentally ill person
   Place a ✓ by each person on the list you would consider having as a friend. Place a — by each person you would be unlikely to have as a friend. Compare your selections with those of your classmates. Argue against or support the statement: "Everyone has some prejudices." Discuss ways to change prejudices toward others.

ANALYZING VIEWPOINTS

1. Do researchers have the right to fool their subjects, even in the name of science? Consider, for example, the effects on Milgram's subjects of believing they had harmed a fellow subject by following the order of a stranger. Do you think this experiment was valuable for allowing the subjects to realize the extent of their conformity? Write an essay that argues both sides of the issue. Be sure to use what you have learned from the chapter.

2. Experiments have shown that enforced integration in housing has resulted in less interracial hostility. What is your opinion of legally enforcing racial integration in housing, employment, and schools? Write a paper that lists the pros and cons of legally enforced racial integration.

3. Research psychologists seek to understand and control human behavior; their overall goal is to promote healthy psychological development of individuals. Through their efforts, however, they have identified a variety of tools that are effective in socially controlling people through persuasion. Write a paper that debates both sides of this question: Is it ethically acceptable for people to use techniques of psychological control to sell merchandise? Look for additional information on the topic in books, magazines, and newspapers.

BEYOND THE CLASSROOM

1. Write down your attitudes about people who receive welfare. Put this piece of paper aside. Contact your local department of human/social services and set up an interview. Tell them you are doing a project for a high school psychology class. Ask them to describe the backgrounds and family situations of people who receive social services. Now look at what you wrote earlier. Have any of your attitudes changed? Why or why not?

In Your Journal

After reading the chapter and class discussions, would you revise the definition of prejudice that you wrote at the beginning of this chapter's study? In your journal, write a one-page paper explaining whether or not prejudice is inevitable.

485

---

integration of the high school in Little Rock, Arkansas.)

3. Encourage students to cite ways in which individuals might resist the persuasive techniques used by advertisers. (One of the first steps is an awareness—and the ability to recognize—various advertising tactics.)

Beyond the Classroom

1. One of the goals of this activity is to assess the effect of information upon firmly held prejudices.

In Your Journal

If time permits, discuss journal entries individually with students.

CHAPTER BONUS
Test Question

This question may be used for extra credit on the chapter test.
Choose the letter of the correct response.

The processes involved in attitude formation include compliance, identification, and:
a. self-justification.
b. cognitive dissonance.
c. internalization.
d. positive regard.

Answer: **c**

Psychology: Careers and Statistics

CHAPTER 19

Psychology: Present and Future

CHAPTER 20

Psychological Research and Statistics

Psychologists' research findings help us better understand our behaviors, perceptions, and attitudes.

486

INTRODUCING THE UNIT

Brainstorm a list of inventions or procedures developed after World War II. *(Student responses may include: space vehicles, personal computers, mobile telephones, CDs, laser surgery, turbo cars, etc.)* Then read the following selection from *Megatrends*, by John Naisbitt:

We are living in the time of parenthesis, the time between eras. . . . Although the time between eras is uncertain, it [is] *. . . filled with opportunity. If we can learn to make uncertainty our friend, we can achieve much more than in stable eras. . . . My God! What a fantastic time to be alive!*

Ask: According to Naisbitt, why do we live in an uncertain time? Do you agree? Why or why not? How does uncertainty contribute to stress—and, as Naisbitt suggests, creativity? What role do you think psychologists can play in helping people survive "the time of parenthesis"?

Chapter 19 leads students into the future by taking a look at trends in the field of psychology. An overview of psychology-related careers provides the unifying thread.

Chapter 20 examines the tools that help psychologists form and evaluate theories. Through the use of research and statistical analysis, psychologists continue to expand the boundaries of our knowledge of human behavior.

Connecting to Past Learning
Students are near completion of their course of study. Ask: Suppose you were considering a career in some area of psychology. What are some of the jobs or occupations from which you could choose? List student responses on the chalkboard. Add to and/or revise the list as students work their way through Unit 7.

487

UNIT PROJECT

Assign students to imagine they are *futurists,* or people who predict trends in the decades ahead. Suggest students use the *Readers' Guide to Periodical Literature* and future-oriented publications such as *The Futurist* or *Omni* to compile a list of trends predicted for the early 2000s. (Tip: Some magazines have put out special issues on the approaching millennium. See, for example, the Fall 1992 Special Issue of *TIME.*) Underneath each item, instruct students to write a short paragraph describing the trend. Post these descriptive lists on the bulletin board. As students go through Unit 7, challenge them to predict which fields of psychology will grow or develop because of these trends. *(Answers will vary, but might include: gerontology, space psychology, and cross-cultural psychology.)*

CHAPTER 19

Psychology: Present and Future

TEXT TOPICS	SPECIAL FEATURES	RESOURCE MATERIALS
Psychology's Contributions, pp. 489–492		▰ Reproducible Lesson Plan; Study Guide; Review Activity
Psychology Today, pp. 492–494		▰ Reproducible Lesson Plan; Study Guide; Review Activity
Psychology's Future, pp. 494–499	**More About Psychology,** p. 495 **Psychology Update,** p. 498	▰ Reproducible Lesson Plan; Study Guide; Review Activity; Application Activity; Extension Activity ▯ *Reading in Psychology:* Section 7, Readings 1, 2 ▰ Chapter Test, Form A and Form B ◉ Understanding Psychology Testmaker

PERFORMANCE ASSESSMENT ACTIVITY

Organize the students into several small groups, and assign them to pick two of the divisions listed in Table 19.1. Instruct students to design a coat of arms for each of the divisions chosen. Suggest that the students find out more about their chosen divisions before they begin their designs. They might also find it helpful to consult a book on heraldry to learn about the various components that typically make up a coat of arms. Tell students that each coat of arms should include a motto that embodies the division's outlook or purpose. Display the finished coats of arms in the classroom. (Look for an understanding of each division's specialty in the students' designs.)

CHAPTER RESOURCES

Readings for the Student

Gould, S. J. *The Mismeasure of Man.* New York: Norton, 1981.

Norman, D. A. *The Psychology of Everyday Things.* New York: Basic Books, 1988.

Sabin, Theodore, and Coe, William. *The Student Psychologist's Handbook: A Guide to Sources.* Cambridge, MA: Schenkman, 1969.

Sternberg, Robert F. *The Psychologist's Companion: A Guide to Scientific Writing for Students and Researchers.* New York: Cambridge University Press, 1988.

Readings for the Teacher

Baars, Bernard. *The Cognitive Revolution in Psychology.* New York: Guilford Press, 1986.

Bronstein, Phyllis, and Quina, Kathryn, eds. *Teaching a Psychology of People: Resources for Gender and Sociocultural Awareness.* Washington, D.C.: American Psychological Association, 1988.

Goldstein, A. P., and Krasner, L. *Modern Applied Psychology.* New York: Pergamon Press, 1987.

Haugeland, John, ed. *Mind Design.* Cambridge, MA: MIT Press, 1987.

Multimedia

In Space, Towards Peace (30 minutes). Discovering Psychology. This video discusses new horizons in psychology, including the ways in which psychologists are preparing astronauts for space travel and insight into the psychology of peace.

The Infinite Voyage: Fires of the Mind (60 minutes). PBS. This documentary introduces viewers to the functions of the brain and how they are studied.

Past, Present, and Promise (30 minutes). Discovering Psychology. This is an introduction to psychology as a science at the crossroads of many disciplines, from philosophy and anthropology to biochemistry and artificial intelligence.

For additional resources see the bibliography beginning on page 530.

CHAPTER 19
Lesson Plan

FOCUS

Motivating Activity

Ask the students to brainstorm to generate a list of jobs or careers that they have considered entering after they complete their education. Record their ideas on the chalkboard, and have them discuss which of the careers are either directly or indirectly related to psychology. For example, a football coach might apply the concepts of sports psychology to improve player performance. A union contract negotiator might apply the concepts of group interaction and group conflict to negotiations between union and management. Try to connect each career that the students listed to some aspect of psychology. Tell students that they will be learning more about psychology-related careers in this chapter.

Meeting Chapter Objectives.

Point out the objectives on page 489 to the students. Note that the first objective pertains to the present, and the second pertains to the future. Assign students to look for present and future applications and opportunities in the field of psychology as they read Chapter 19.

Building Vocabulary.

Call on a volunteer to look up the word *forensic* in a dictionary and to read the definition and etymology aloud. Ask students to venture a guess as to what forensic psychology would entail. Then have them look up the meaning in the Glossary.

Psychology: Present and Future

FIGURE 19.1 Psychology plays an increasingly important role in the space exploration program.

488

TEACHER CLASSROOM RESOURCES

- Chapter 19 Reproducible Lesson Plan
- Chapter 19 Study Guide
- Chapter 19 Review Activity
- Chapter 19 Application Activity
- Chapter 19 Extension Activity

- *Readings in Psychology:* Section 7, Readings 1, 2

- Chapter 19 Test, Form A and Form B

- Understanding Psychology Testmaker

OBJECTIVES

After studying this chapter, you should be able to

■ identify and describe ways in which psychology is used to improve the workplace.

■ identify and describe new areas of research in psychology.

KEY TERMS

engineering psychology
forensic psychology
gerontology
industrial-organizational psychology
sports psychology
visualization

"What are you going to do when you get out of school?"

"Beats me. My grandparents want me to learn the shoe business and take over when they retire. Mom and Dad want me to think about law as a career. I was leaning toward business administration, but my sister just graduated with an MBA. I don't want to be just like her. I've got more choices than I can handle."

This conversation is imaginary, but typical for juniors and seniors in high school. You *do* have many options. Because you have spent a period of time studying psychology, it may be beneficial to respond to questions about psychology: What will I do with what I have learned? Was it worth it if this is the only psychology course I ever take? What careers in psychology are open to me? To help you find answers to these questions, this chapter has several points to consider, beginning with some of the ways psychology contributes to society.

IN YOUR JOURNAL

What do you think will be the most serious problem or problems in the United States and in the world in the twenty-first century? Write your answer in your journal.

489

EXTRA CREDIT ACTIVITY

Various professional organizations are mentioned throughout this chapter. Request volunteers to write to each of these groups, explaining that they are psychology students interested in obtaining promotional literature or background articles on the organization. The students should then prepare a short oral report about each organization and contribute the materials that they collected to a classroom resource display.

Exploring Key Ideas
Psychology—Today and Tomorrow.

Tell students that in ending his book *The Story of Psychology,* Morton Hunt asked: "Where do we go from here?" Challenge students to predict what new frontiers they think psychology will cross in the years ahead. Remind them of the recent questions raised about the psychoanalytical theories of Freud. Do students expect to see a new theory replace Freudian analysis? Or do they think psychology will be more like a "Chinese menu" from which patients (clients) can chose? Next, read aloud the answer that Hunt provided to his own question:

It is likely that many of the discoveries of the future will, like those of the past, prove useful to humankind in ways ranging from the trivial to the consequential—from tips on child care and memory improvement, say, to the radical improvement of education and the reduction of racist and ethnic hatreds.

Instruct students to keep this vision of psychology in mind as they read Chapter 19. What conclusions can they form?

IN YOUR JOURNAL

Help students get started by suggesting various categories of problems for them to contemplate, such as the environment, employment, crime, population, education, racial and ethnic conflict, international relations, and so on.

TEACH
Guided Practice

VISUAL INSTRUCTION

Request students to research nations in which patients with mental disorders still receive inadequate care. Challenge them to write a speech that Dix might have given before the United Nations in behalf of these patients. In addition to citing poor conditions, the speech should recommend specific suggestions for reform. **Answer to caption, Figure 19.2:** Her crusade led to more enlightened treatment of the mentally ill in Canada and Great Britain as well as in the United States.

■ **Illustrating an Idea.** Organize the students into nine groups, and assign them the task of creating posters that illustrate the title of this section: "Psychology's Contributions." Assign three of the groups to focus on contributions to the work environment. Three other groups should concentrate on contributions to the development of mental health care. The other three groups should explore new areas of research. (Encourage students to skim through the entire book for ideas.) When students have completed their tasks, have each group present its posters to the class.

(OBJECTIVES 1, 2)

FIGURE 19.2

Dorothea L. Dix campaigned vigorously for improving care for the mentally ill. **What effect did Dix have on reform?**

PSYCHOLOGY'S CONTRIBUTIONS

Since psychology's beginnings as a separate discipline, psychologists have made many contributions to society. Below are some of the ways psychology promotes human welfare, clarifies methods of assessment, and helps individuals better understand their environment and themselves.

Psychology's Role in Mental Illness

Of all of psychology's contributions, perhaps its most significant is the development of forms of professional helping, including psychotherapy. An early step forward came in the 1790s through the pioneering efforts of Philippe Pinel, a French physician and a founder of psychiatry. Pinel unchained patients who were held in mental wards, some of whom had been restrained for more than 20 years. Pinel argued against the prevailing belief that the mentally ill were possessed by demons. Moreover, Pinel thought mental illness could be treated. Mainly due to his efforts, France became a leader in improving conditions for the mentally ill.

Despite the progress in France, more than half a century passed before similar efforts were exerted in the United States. After discovering that the mentally ill were being jailed along with criminals, teacher and social reformer Dorothea Dix became the chief spokesperson for reform. Her personal crusade in the 1840s aroused interest in the problems of mental illness and led to more enlightened treatment of the mentally ill in Canada and Great Britain as well as in the United States.

A former mental patient, Clifford Beers, was the guiding force in the early growth of the modern mental health movement. Beers's own account of his illness and recovery, *A Mind That Found Itself,* first published nearly 90 years ago, has motivated students, mental health workers, and concerned individuals to promote better psychiatric care in communities, in schools, and in hospitals. The book set into motion Beers's plan to improve conditions. Beers in 1908 founded the Connecticut Society for Mental Hygiene, the first organization of its type. In its charter, the Connecticut Society pledged to eliminate restraints on patients, improve standards of care for the mentally retarded, prevent mental disorder, preserve mental health, and provide information on mental illness to the public. Beers's vigorous efforts also played an important role in forming the National Committee for Mental Hygiene, which in turn was instrumental in organizing the National Association for Mental Health in 1950.

Psychology's Role in Testing

You probably had your first encounter with a psychologist while in elementary school. Most students are given IQ tests or other tests at an early age. You have probably taken one or more of the Iowa Tests of Basic Skills, which provide scores on reading, vocabulary, language, arithmetic, and work-study skills, or perhaps the Stanford Achievement Test, which measures progress in grammar and word and paragraph meaning.

PSYCHOLOGISTS AT WORK

Since World War II, the world has become increasingly interdependent. Today the nations of the world are linked by trade, travel, communication, immigration, and more. At one time, the work of promoting cooperation belonged to diplomats. But today they are joined by *cross-cultural psychologists*— professionals who investigate the similarities and differences in the psychological functioning of different cultures and ethnic groups. These professionals study everything from child-rearing practices to perceptions of beauty. In addition to a degree in psychology, *(continued on page 491)*

Psychologists have played a leading role devising and updating these tests, as well as other tests in higher education that assess personal skills. Many of you have taken or will take one or both of the two major standardized college entrance exams: the Scholastic Assessment Test (SAT-I) and the American College Testing Proficiency Examination Program (ACT). Developed in 1959, the current ACT (1989) places greater stress on scientific concepts and abstract reading skills than the earlier version and less emphasis on factual material. Nearly 1 million high school seniors take the ACT each year. The SAT, taken by about 1.2 million high school seniors annually, was redesigned in 1994 to give more weight to abstract thinking skills. Current technology also affects testing. The 1994 version of the SAT allowed the use of hand calculators for the first time ever.

Psychology's Role in the Workplace

Almost every activity of our daily lives depends in some way on machines. Researchers in **engineering psychology** apply psychological principles to human-machine interaction. These psychologists play a part in designing machines, including selecting and training people to operate machines so they can be used efficiently. Consider the problem posed in Figure 19.3 before you read any further.

Why did the apartment dweller walk up the last several floors rather than take the elevator? Some of you guessed correctly that some of the buttons were too high for her to reach. The elevator designer had not anticipated that some people would not be able to operate the elevator without assistance. The controls in many modern elevators are placed at lower levels so that people who are physically challenged can reach all the buttons.

The photograph on page 488 shows another example of engineering in terms of behavior. Designing work spaces and equipment control panels requires knowledge of vertical and horizontal reach measurements and a knowledge of normal and maximum work areas. Controls are positioned first based on importance to system functioning, then frequency of use. Controls with related use are positioned together, and controls used in a sequence are positioned in that sequence (Berry & Houston, 1993).

Next, consider examples on a simpler level: common tools and utensils. Think about how differently the handles of a knife, a screwdriver, pliers, and a hammer are shaped. Why is this so? Designers take into account the direction of force being applied through the handle, the position of the hand when doing so, as well as other factors for efficient use of the implement.

Psychology's Role in Everyday Living

There are so many different careers in psychology that you may wonder what they have in common. In most cases, the answer is behavior. The desire to understand behavior links psychologists, regardless of their specialty.

Rearing children.   With more than half of all mothers and an even higher percentage of fathers working outside the home, day-care and out-of-

FIGURE 19.3

A young girl always rode the elevator down from her family's apartment on the 37th floor on her way to school. Every evening when she returned home, however, she rode to the 31st floor and then walked the rest of the way. Why did she always walk the last six floors? **What areas does an engineering psychologist study?**

VISUAL INSTRUCTION

Have students imagine how a team of engineering psychologists might go about designing an interior and dashboard for a new car model. What other kinds of design projects do students think might benefit from the input of engineering psychologists? (Tip: Refer students to the More About feature on page 495.) **Answer to caption, Figure 19.3:** An engineering psychologist applies psychological principles to human-machine interaction.

Teacher Note. Make sure students recognize that the common bond among all the different branches of psychology is "the desire to understand behavior."

PSYCHOLOGISTS AT WORK

people seeking to enter this field need proficiency in a foreign language, training in global studies, and living experience abroad. Cross-cultural psychology is predicted to become one of the fastest-growing psychological fields of the 2000s.

■ **Comparing Points of View.**
The cover story of the June 28, 1993, issue of *TIME* studied the changing role of father-hood—an area of everyday life keenly studied by social psychologists. Read aloud the following passage, and then ask the questions that follow:

Go to a park and watch father and mother next to a child on a jungle gym. The father encourages the kid to challenge himself by climbing to the top; the mother tells him to be careful. What's most important is to have the balance of encouragement along with a warning.

William Maddox, director
Family Research Council

[A] cultural imperative—fathers must do it this way and mothers must do it that way—only creates problems for the vast number of people who don't fit those tendencies, without benefiting the children at all.

Anthony Rotundo,
historian

1. What is Maddox's point of view on parenting? *(that the role of father and mother complement each other and must strike a balance)*
2. What is Rotundo's point of view? *(that cultural imperatives don't benefit parents or children)*
3. On what areas might the two disagree? *(on the roles assigned by Maddox)*
4. Given current social trends, what tips would you offer to parents today? How do you think Maddox and Rotundo might respond to your suggestions? Explain. (OBJECTIVE 2)

home nurturing and learning are significant issues. Researchers note that day care appears to have few negative effects on children and actually promotes development of social skills (Bukatko & Daehler, 1992). Interestingly, children with experience in day care tend to be more assertive and aggressive. Alison Clarke-Stewart (1989) has suggested that this may simply result from the fact that day-care children think at a more advanced level, but have not yet developed the social skills with which to implement their plans smoothly.

Harry Harlow's work led to the idea that the attachment of children to their caregivers is made stronger by physical contact. That, in turn, led to the demonstration that breast-feeding versus bottle-feeding—long a hotly debated topic—really makes no difference in the parent-child attachment. It is the holding, not the feeding, that is important.

Improving Learning. Psychologists play a role in designing and assessing tools for learning in a variety of media: for example, their understanding of the principles of learning contributed to the development of the PBS series "Sesame Street." Studies show that almost 60 percent of the children who watch that program at least 5 times a week can recite the entire alphabet correctly. Originally designed to provide creative ways to educate children with skills required in school—such as spelling, counting, and new words—this program, as the data indicate, has met its goal.

Aging. The work of many psychologists led to a clearer understanding about challenges facing men and women as they age. Daniel Levinson's work reported in *The Season's of a Man's Life* (1978) details the various stages and crises that unfold in a typical man's life. There is considerable interest in seeing the long-promised seasons of a woman's life.

Increased understanding of the abilities of the aged is an area in which psychology must make continued contributions. Census Bureau data indicate continued growth in the number of elderly citizens. Projections suggest that the number of men and women between the ages of 60 and 79 will grow to 14.2 million by 2000, and to 22.8 million by 2050. Those more than 80 years old will increase to 2.8 million by the end of the century and to 7.4 million by 2050. The latest census placed the percentage of citizens 65 years old and older at 12.5 percent, compared to 8.1 percent in 1950.

PSYCHOLOGY TODAY

Contemporary psychology can be grouped into experimental fields and applied fields. Experimental psychologists use a variety of scientific methods to study psychological processes. Applied psychologists put knowledge of psychology to work solving human problems. Yet this distinction is not always sharp. Both the experimental and the applied psychologist gather the available evidence and offer the best they find. Both study behavior, and both use similar processes in similar situations. A major difference is that applied psychologists search for immediate solutions, experimental psychologists for long-range answers.

STUDY AND WRITING SKILLS

Assign students to research the current and projected demographics of aging in the United States. What changes in America's politics, social programs, health-care systems, and businesses do futurists foresee as the elderly become a larger segment of the overall population? Tell students that they should present their findings either in the form of a written report or in a series of annotated graphs and charts.

Current Trends

The American Psychological Association (APA) is a scientific and professional society of psychologists and educators. Founded in 1892, it is the major psychological association in the United States and is made up of 45 divisions, each representing a specific area, type of work or research setting, or activity. The divisions include Teaching of Psychology, Clinical, Development, Educational, and Experimental. There are Divisions of Psychotherapy, Psychologists in Private Practice, and Psychological Hypnosis. Some divisions are research-oriented, while others are advocacy groups. Together they are a cross-section of the diverse nature of psychology.

Looking at what the typical psychologist does, between 1975 and 1977, 27 percent were engaged in teaching, 51 percent in mental health services. By 1993 that had shifted to 29 percent in teaching, 55 percent in mental health services. Research and teaching jobs have been declining since 1980. By contrast, jobs in various environments, offering psychotherapy and other clinically related services such as testing, have been a growth area. Estimates note that the number of university research jobs will rise starting around the year 2000 as those hired in the 1960s and 1970s retire.

The United States Bureau of Labor places psychology among the fastest-growing fields into the twenty-first century. In addition, the number of women in psychology has been increasing rapidly. In the early 1990s, women held 60 percent of the civilian jobs in psychology, and women received more than two-thirds of the bachelor and master's degrees conferred during that time. Moreover, the proportion of women in psychology is greater than in most other scientific disciplines (Simonton, 1992).

TABLE 19.1

Many people believe that all psychologists analyze and treat abnormal behavior. As you have learned, however, the range of the field of psychology is much broader. **What is the American Psychological Association?**

TABLE 19.1 • DIVISIONS OF THE APA

1. Division of General Psychology
2. Division of the Teaching of Psychology
3. Division of Experimental Psychology
5. Division on Evaluation and Measurement
6. Division on Physiological and Comparative Psychology
7. Division on Developmental Psychology
8. Division of Personality and Social Psychology
9. The Society for the Psychological Study of Social Issues
10. Division of Psychology and the Arts
12. Division of Clinical Psychology
13. Division of Consulting Psychology
14. Society for Industrial and Organizational Psychology
15. Division of Educational Psychology
16. Division of School Psychology
17. Division of Counseling Psychology
18. Division of Psychologists in Public Service
19. Division of Military Psychology
20. Division of Adult Development and Aging
21. The Society of Engineering and Applied Psychologists
22. Division of Rehabilitation Psychology
23. Division of Consumer Psychology
24. Division of Theoretical and Philosophical Psychology
25. Division for the Experimental Analysis of Behavior
26. Division of the History of Psychology
27. Division of Community Psychology
28. Division of Psychopharmacology
29. Division of Psychotherapy
30. Division of Psychological Hypnosis
31. Division of State Psychological Association Affairs
32. Division of Humanistic Psychology
33. Division of Mental Retardation
34. Division of Population and Environmental Psychology
35. Division of the Psychology of Women
36. Psychologists Interested in Religious Issues
37. Division of Child, Youth, and Family Services
38. Division of Health Psychology
39. Division of Psychoanalysis
40. Division of Clinical Neuropsychology
41. Division of American Psychology—Law Psychology
42. Division of Psychologists in Independent Practice
43. Division of Family Psychology
44. Society for the Psychological Study of Lesbian and Gay Issues
45. Society for the Psychological Study of Ethnic Minority Issues
46. Media Psychology
47. Exercise and Sport Psychology

Note: There is no Division 4 or Division 11.

DID YOU KNOW?

In 1990, 40 percent of doctoral-level psychologists were women. If current trends continue, women will soon account for 60 percent of new doctorates in this profession.

Teacher Note. If students have ever wondered how so many reports of new psychological discoveries manage to find their way into the news media, chances are the reports originated in the APA's Public Affairs Office. Each year this office generates thousands of news releases about psychological advances that could benefit individuals and society.

VISUAL INSTRUCTION

Have the students suggest the areas studied or treated by the various APA divisions listed in Table 19.1. For example, what kinds of concerns might Division 36--Psychologists Interested in Religious Issues—explore? *(e.g., cult phenomena)* **Answer to caption, Table 19.1:** a scientific and professional society of psychologists and educators, founded in 1892

COOPERATIVE LEARNING ACTIVITY

Have students work in pairs to research one of the APA divisions listed in Table 19.1. Suggest that they begin by writing a letter to the chairperson of their chosen division in care of the APA. (P.O. Box 2710, Hyattsville, MD 20784) Tell students to request a description of the division's interests and mission. As an alternative, students might interview a psychologist who works in the chosen area of specialization. Request students to present their findings in the form of a news story (or a "Psychologists at Work" feature).

Point out that 75 percent of the APA's 118,000 members hold doctorates and that, of these, about a third work in educational institutions. The rest are largely self-employed or work in industry, government, and other places. Many psychologists who hold BA and MA degrees do not belong to the APA, however. These professionals are more likely to be self-employed or work as testers, counselors, or therapists in hospitals, industry, or schools.
Answer to caption, Figure 19.4: a branch of applied psychology that studies and makes practical suggestions about the workings of the law

FIGURE 19.4

Psychologists are employed in many different settings. Some work in educational institutions, others work at hospitals and health centers, while still others work as independent practitioners. **What is forensic psychology?**

DID YOU KNOW?

Of all employed psychologists holding doctorates in 1990, fewer than 2 percent were African Americans, fewer than 2 percent were Hispanics, and roughly 9 percent were Asians. You might encourage students to investigate historical factors that account for this development.

One area in which psychology lags is in the number of minorities in the profession. Some basic demographic statistics show this inequity. In 1991, Hispanic Americans held less than 4 percent of the civilian jobs in psychology, African Americans less than 8 percent. These figures do not reflect the proportion of minorities in society.

It is important that psychology reach a more adequate representation of racial and ethnic minorities for several reasons. First, it limits the discipline because it leaves out the perspective and talents that minorities can provide. In addition, it can hamper growth because lack of minority representation may discourage other minority group members from studying psychology and entering the field. Finally, it may prevent minority individuals from seeking treatment because members of minority groups often prefer to receive care from psychologists who are part of their own racial or ethnic group.

Professional Organizations

Increasingly during the 1970s and 1980s, some members expressed dissatisfaction with the direction of the APA. As a result, a new organization, the American Psychological Society (APS), was founded in 1988; in 5 years it had grown to a membership of 15,000. By 1993, the American Psychological Association had 118,000 members (including 43,000 student members and teacher-associates).

Among the major sciences, psychology is the only one that has traditionally had both practitioners and researchers using the same name. Medical doctors and dentists apply the principles of biology. Engineering serves as the applications discipline of physics; pharmacy or chemical engineering for chemistry. No such division has previously existed for psychologists.

Another important organization for American psychologists is the Canadian Psychological Association (CPA). Founded in 1939, it had grown to 4,500 members by 1993. The CPA is dedicated to representing psychology's interests in the Canadian legislature and Canada in somewhat the same way as the APA and APS represent psychology in the United States.

PSYCHOLOGY'S FUTURE

You have studied the foundation from which psychology grew and evolved, but what does the future hold in store? Predicting the course of psychology is difficult, yet several trends seem likely to emerge.

Fields of Psychology

Elizabeth Loftus published a revealing article in 1974 on the susceptibility of eyewitness testimony to alteration by questioning and use. Since that time, there has been growing interest in psychology and the law. **Forensic**

Interpreting Statistics. Hand out copies of the following statistics:

Independent Practice 29.1%
University/College 28.6%
Hospitals 11.2%
Other Educational Settings 4.5%
Other Human Services 6.5%
Clinics 6.5%

Government 3.5%
Business and Industry 2.4%
Other 7.7%

Assign students to present this data in the form of a circle or bar graph entitled: "Where Psychologists Work." Based on these graphs, ask the following questions: In what employment setting(s) do most psychologists work? In which setting do you think each of the following might seek work: (a) experimental psychologist, (b) psychoanalyst, (c) mental health assistant, (d) personnel psychologist? Explain each of your choices.

psychology is a branch of applied psychology that studies and makes practical suggestions about the workings of the law. Many forensic psychologists study criminal behavior. Still others do work on the reliability of eyewitnesses, the effects on children who appear in court, counseling victims, and the jury selection process. A lawyer-psychologist often has both a Ph.D. and a law degree (Hofer, 1991).

Work and the working environment is the province of **industrial-organizational psychology,** or, as the field is often called, organizational psychology (Coutts, 1991). Psychologists in this field apply their findings to help businesses and industries operate more efficiently and humanely through improving methods of selection and training, and developing new organizational and management strategies. Other industrial-organizational psychologists concentrate on such issues as labor-union relations, rules defining harassment, job satisfaction, and worker motivations and incentives.

Sports psychology, a field that developed during the 1980s, is an important part of training for many amateur and professional athletes. Sports psychologists apply the principles of psychology to sports activities. Some focus on maximizing athletic performance through **visualization**—mentally rehearsing the steps of a complete, successful performance—improving concentration or relaxation, or reducing negative thoughts that may interfere with performance. Other areas of study include the psychological and physiological benefits of sports participation, violence, ethics in sports, and the design of safe equipment (Durkin, 1991).

The Challenges for Psychology

The American Psychological Association focused its 1969 annual convention on addressing what psychology can do to help solve our most pressing social problems. In his address to the convention, president George A. Miller sounded a rallying cry for psychologists. He suggested that the best thing psychology could do was to open up its findings to the broader world. He urged that "scientific psychology" be used to inform "public psychology"—broadly meaning popular beliefs about human behavior. In that address, Miller first sounded a phrase heard many times since. He was advocating that the collective responsibility of psychologists was "... less to assume the role of experts and try to apply psychology ourselves than to give it away to the people who really need it." The issues addressed at that convention—social change, urban problems, early learning, psychology and minorities, the reduction of violence, society's future—remain psychology's challenges today.

In what other ways can psychology's coming challenges be pinpointed? This can be done by analyzing the kinds of problems psychologists study and the activities in which psychologists are now engaged. A good starting point is a journal published by the American Psychological Society, *Current Directions in Psychological Science.* Its primary intent is to publish articles "... spanning the entire spectrum of scientific psychology and its applica-

MORE
about...

Psychology and Human Factors Engineering. Human factors engineers help design machines and equipment such as computer systems, automobiles, office equipment, and household appliances to match human abilities and limitations so that they can be operated efficiently and safely. Human factors engineers draw on physics, anatomy, psychology, and sociology as well as contributions from teachers and communications experts to analyze and solve a problem. Consider this example: Why is the gas pedal on the right side of your car's floor rather than on the left? The reason is more efficient use. Most people are right-side dominant and use the gas pedal more than the brake. This is only one of the areas of research for human factors engineers.

■ **Debating an Issue.** One concern for forensic psychologists is the controversial legal issue of recovered memories, in which people supposedly remember criminal events that they had repressed and forgotten for many years. How reliable are such memories, and should they be allowed to be entered as evidence in criminal trials? As *U.S. News & World Report* observed in a cover story exploring this issue (Nov. 29, 1993), "The entanglement of psychology and the law is not an entirely easy marriage." Organize students into two teams, and assign them to debate the following topic: *Resolved*—That the application of psychology has no place in an impartial court of law. (For a pro and con treatment of this issue, refer students to Morton Hunt's *Story of Psychology.*) (OBJECTIVE 2)

■ **Readings in Psychology.** Have students read the Section 7, Reading 1 and 2 selections in *Readings in Psychology* and answer the questions that follow the selection.

COMMUNITY INVOLVEMENT

Arrange for a sports psychologist to visit the class—perhaps a coach from a local college or a trainer from a regional ice-skating or gymnastics center. Ask the speaker to discuss the various psychological techniques that are employed to enhance athletic performance. Tell students to have questions ready in advance. If the speaker has no objections, you might want to videotape the presentation for later discussion.

■ Cooperative Learning Activity.

Organize the students into 9 teams, and assign each team one of the job categories in Table 19.2. Instruct students to write a short monologue in which a person describes what he or she does for living. Tell students to avoid using the job title or any words that directly refer to it. When students have prepared the activity, call on a member from each group to deliver the monologue. Challenge other students to guess the job. (OBJECTIVES 1, 2)

■ Role Play.

Bring a telephone directory to class, and point out the listings for the various kinds of hot lines that serve your community. Call on various pairs of volunteers to improvise the crises that different kinds of hot line advisers might be expected to handle. After each role play, ask the participants to discuss how they felt: What, if any, stress did the adviser experience? How did the caller feel about the effect of the conversation? Encourage the class to offer their observations. (OBJECTIVES 1, 2)

TABLE 19.2 • Jobs and Education

Crisis Hot Line Adviser
Employer: A large hospital
Can you do it? A person holding this job might even be a senior in high school. For most crisis intervention programs, applicants must complete a training program. A county hospital, for instance, might offer such training over three weekends. Following training, a typical assignment would involve two 4-hour shifts a week.
What's involved? Crisis hot line personnel respond primarily to two kinds of problems. One involves the immediate, possibly life-threatening situation that can arise as a result of a personal or family crisis—perhaps an argument or the unexpected death of a loved one. Drugs—whether from withdrawal or overdoses—can also bring about an immediate need for help. The other type of problem is the crisis evolving from long-term stress, such as that experienced in the family, on the job, or in a failure to develop one's career. Crises like these are not as threatening but still need to be resolved.
A person handling a hot line will have a list of psychologists and psychiatrists as well as information about a wide array of treatment facilities and programs operating in the vicinity. This job requires being able to calm the caller, identifying his or her problem, and helping that caller to see the wisdom—once the immediate crisis has been dealt with—of contacting the most appropriate agency for long-term follow-up.

Word Processor Salesperson
Employer: A local computer dealer
Can you do it? People with an interest in psychology are likely to have a higher-than-average interest in behavior—both theirs and others. That interest—even if only backed by a high school diploma—is a vital element of the successful salesperson. One report suggests that the best salespersons are motivated by the need for status, control, respect, routine, accomplishment, stimulation, and honesty. With those needs met, a salesperson—regardless of level of education—will feel happy. A basic understanding of people's driving forces—their needs for achievement, affiliation, and safety—is but one aspect of psychology that would aid someone seeking a career in sales.
What's involved? The key requirement may be experience. One psychologist has suggested that you cannot educate someone to be good in sales—but sensitivity to others can be improved by training. You must also be persistent, skillful at language, able to query prospective customers, and relate their needs to those answered by the product you are offering.

Ward Attendant
Employer: A state mental hospital
Can you do it? The successful applicant need not have a high school diploma, but he or she should have stronger-than-average commitment to helping people often not able to help themselves. Simple concern for humanity may be the key ingredient.
What's involved? On a typical day, the attendant helps the ward staff run the basic hospital facilities and programs. This means making beds, bathing patients, and cleaning the recreational and living areas. Also, the worker might participate in recreational activities with the patients, such as music, art, or sports events, or visits outside the hospital.

Mental Health Assistant
Employer: A senior citizen service center
Can you do it? This is a new career field, usually requiring at least an associate degree. An associate degree is awarded after a two-year course preparing for paraprofessional occupations in nursing homes, community mental health centers, centers dealing with mental retardation, or even special-education centers for the variously disabled in public schools.
What's involved? Typically supervised by a staff psychologist, an assistant helps with or conducts admission interviews. He or she may be responsible—under supervision—for administering various psychological tests, either to new patients or to assess the progress of those already admitted.

High School Psychology Teacher
Employer: The local Board of Education
Can you do it? What's required is a commitment to teaching. Since teaching is not a source of great financial reward, it is important to be able to find rewards in the job itself. Teaching requires a bachelor's degree, and current rules (and the recent pressures for competency testing) make it likely you will continue your education, working gradually toward a master's degree over the first 7 to 10 years or so in this position.
What's involved? A high school teacher has total responsibility for teaching five or six courses, but rarely are all courses in the same subject area. Thus, a student planning to teach psychology would do well to develop another major teaching strength—perhaps in sociology, economics, mathematics, or biology.

COMMUNITY INVOLVEMENT

Arrange with the guidance department and administrative staff to conduct a Psychology Career Day at your school. With the class, brainstorm a list of places in the community where people with psychological backgrounds might work. Possible choices include mental health agencies, hospitals, personnel departments, private clinics, day care centers, colleges, and your own guidance department. Assign a committee to contact each of these places to invite participants to take part. Instruct another committee to design a program. Direct a third committee to set up booths for each participant.

Personnel Director

Employer: A large department store

Can you do it? The successful applicant is likely to have a bachelor's degree in psychology, having concentrated on courses involving interviewing, test construction and interpretation, statistics, and—perhaps surprisingly to you—law. Such a person might also have taken a minor in management courses in a university's College of Business Administration. He or she would stress organizational and quantitative skills. This is not an entry-level job, however. Some prior experience with the employer's policies is a definite requirement.

What's involved? A personnel director may participate in a wide array of activities depending on the nature and interest of his or her employer.

Clearly, the decisions to hire and fire would be this person's responsibility, especially for the support staff in any organization. Such a person might also develop programs to improve or maintain staff skills—in sales, interpersonal sensitivity, or any other skill involved in conducting the company's business.

School Psychologist

Employer: A city school system

Can you do it? A master's degree is a must for this position; an undergraduate major in psychology is desirable. In addition, most school psychologists must be licensed or certified in their state of employment, which involves taking a test.

What's involved? In bigger districts, you might stay in one school, but many school psychologists divide their time among a number of schools. They are usually working with children experiencing the normal array of problems in school. A school psychologist might give reading, aptitude, interest, or intelligence tests, and must be skillful in interpreting them. At other times he or she might work directly with the children or young adults in school or with the families of those students.

Clinical Psychologist

Employer: Yourself

Can you do it? To use this title in most states requires a Ph.D. (a Doctor of Philosophy) or a Psy.D. (a Doctor of Psychology). The Psy.D. is a degree developed in the 1970s. In a Psy.D. program, a student gains skill in psychotherapy, undergoing intensive training in testing, interviewing, and giving supervised therapy.

What's involved? A practicing clinical psychologist is often self-employed. Thus, required skills include those needed to run any small business, in addition to knowledge of testing and practical experience with the limits and strengths of various forms of therapy. He or she must develop working relations with other clinicians in the area—psychiatrists, medical doctors, and other contacts in local hospitals and mental health facilities. From such sources come the patient/client referrals that are vital to one's success as a psychotherapist.

A typical day might involve 8 to 10 hours in various stages of psychotherapy with different individuals. The hours have to be offered at times when clients are free to visit, so this may be not a traditional 9-to-5 job. Other types of therapy a clinical psychologist might offer are group therapy or consultation with other therapeutic organizations such as Alcoholics Anonymous. It is also possible, of course, to utilize the same skills as a clinical psychologist in a state-supported mental hospital, a Veterans Administration hospital, or a community mental health center.

Consulting Psychologist

Employer: A management consulting firm

Can you do it? A Ph.D. is required for this job. Such a person might spend graduate school in an industrial-organizational psychology program learning management practices, testing strategies, interpersonal behavioral strategies, and intervention techniques in complex organizations.

What's involved? A consultant—by the very nature of his or her job—must offer an array of skills not normally represented among the full-time employees of companies that hire consultants. Thus, a consultant's job tends to be short-term. A consultant might, for instance, advise a company's top management on how to take human performance limits into account in the design of a control board for a nuclear power plant. He or she might be involved in all aspects of the design of an interstate highway—signs, bridges and crossover devices, and lane-flow control.

In conclusion

Employers are most likely to hire someone who offers special skills. In psychology, as in many other fields, job choices are limited if you have only a high school diploma. Surprisingly, when you have a Ph.D. you also have relatively few choices, but by that time you have chosen to fine-tune your education and experience to a specific kind of job—you are a specialist.

Those with a bachelor's degree in psychology may have the most options with the widest array of possible employers. Moreover, psychology is a logical undergraduate major for those planning graduate work in such fields as sociology, social work, law, medicine, or education. Human behavior plays a key role in all these areas.

PORTRAIT

Kenneth Bancroft Clark
1914–
Born in 1914 in the Panama Canal Zone, Kenneth B. Clark made a mark as head of an executive consulting firm that specialized in affirmative action in matters of race relations. As a consulting psychologist, Clark performed important psychological research that was cited in the 1954 landmark Supreme Court decision of *Brown* v. *Board of Education of Topeka, Kansas*, which outlawed segregation in the schools. Known as a gifted scholar, Clark is the author of *Dark Ghetto: Dilemmas of Social Power*, as well as a contributor of articles to many professional journals. He was also one of the principal organizers of Harlem Youth Opportunities Unlimited.

BEYOND THE CLASSROOM

Have students research colleges or universities that offer majors in psychology. The students should consult college catalogs to determine each school's general admissions policies and to learn whether the psychology department specializes in any particular area of psychology. If possible, students should also consult a description of the department's course offerings. Have students present their findings to the class and contribute any materials they gathered to a classroom display.

The writers of "Star Trek: The Next Generation" included a psychologist among the crew of the starship *Enterprise*. By the year 2000, about 1,000 people will have traveled into space. As more humans head into space and flights become longer, psychology will also reach for the stars. Issues will concern such things as: screening of astronauts for long, dangerous missions; causes and treatment of space sickness (perhaps through biofeedback); creation of a livable environment; avoidance of "groupthink"; and perhaps even love and marriage aboard a space station. (Tip: Assign interested students to find out more about the training and credentials needed to become a "space psychologist.")
(OBJECTIVE 1)

■ **Writing a Job Description.**
Ask students to imagine that they are involved in the space station program in which United States astronauts and Russian cosmonauts will take part. What kinds of psychological expertise might NASA and the Russians want to have available at various stages of the project—e.g., design, training, launch, and deployment? Ask students to present their ideas in the form of a detailed job description for "Space Station Psychologist." Have students model their job descriptions after entries in Table 19.2.
(OBJECTIVE 2)

PSYCHOLOGY UPDATE

Human Growth Hormone.
Scientists are now able to create human growth hormone, a chemical produced naturally by the pituitary gland. Although most bodies can produce the chemical, production generally declines during adulthood. In one experiment, gerontologist Daniel Rudman gave injections of the hormone to a control group of elderly individuals. After six months, the group had lost 14 percent of their body fat, gained nearly 9 percent in muscle mass, and their skin thickness and bone density had increased dramatically. Some who have taken the hormone are enthusiastic. One noted, "I don't know how else to put it: You just stop aging." Many scientists, however, including Rudman, warn that hormone injection is not a fountain of youth. They warn that no one can say what the long-term effects are and note that substantial research still needs to be done.

tions . . ." which ". . . focus on emerging trends, controversies, and issues of enduring importance to the science of psychology." *Current Directions* is only one of many good sources. Any other broad-based journal—such as the APA's *American Psychologist*—will show the same pattern. Psychology is concerned with a broad array of human areas of growth, development, personality, performance, and performance limits.

Another way to determine future directions of psychology is analyzing the trends of age in the population. The average age of the citizens in this country is going steadily upward; there are more people over age 65 in the United States and Canada now than at any time in the history of either country. That creates new problems for psychologists to study, and new careers in both research and service. This makes lifetime sports equipment manufacturers a good investment on the stock market. It also suggests a growing field in a specialty such as sports psychology, and another in developmental psychology: **gerontology**—the study of aging.

At the other end of the age spectrum are other factors that may impact future jobs for psychologists. Consider the traditional killers of children—measles, chicken pox, scarlet fever, rheumatic fever, mumps, tuberculosis, polio. All of these problems—assuming a child has his or her proper injections—are gone. The top three killers of children up through adolescence in our society now are accidents, violence, and drugs. These are not physiological problems like our old enemies—they're *psychological* problems.

Many of the problems that face society today are behavioral problems; that is, they can only be solved through changing behavior and attitudes. AIDS mandates a change in sexual practices. Counteracting violence requires either a change in laws or an alteration of traditional practices.

The introduction of tranquilizers in the mid-1950s revolutionized treatment of mental and personal pathologies. This revolution, however, has created in some mental hospitals what is called a revolving door: patients brought into the hospital are diagnosed, stabilized, and released with a balanced drug program. Once they feel better, however, they take their medicine irregularly, or stop it altogether—which results in their becoming once more symptomatic and they are readmitted to the hospital. The side effect is that many homeless people today would have traditionally been fed and sheltered in mental hospitals. Again, the solutions to such problems are behavioral. The behavioral sciences are a logical place to turn for help in dealing with the problems of the homeless.

Studies of the impact of the Head Start program have provided evidence that money invested in educating economically disadvantaged children was more than offset by savings in subsequent welfare payments, criminal activities, and jail sentences (Zigler & Muenchow, 1992). The education created more effective citizens better able to maintain themselves—a problem solved through modifying human behavior.

The explosive growth in the size of prison populations has created another revolving door. People convicted of crimes are being paroled earlier. Many are now put on probation rather than serve time. This is a complex series of problems that will require behavioral solutions—whether in retraining or post-sentencing activities to improve the lives of those caught up in the consequences of their criminal behavior.

CONNECTIONS: PSYCHOLOGY AND HEALTH

As the text explains, the traditional killers of children and adolescents—measles, mumps, polio—have been replaced by a new set of killers. Request volunteers to research the growth of random acts of violence and AIDS among young people at the start of the 1990s. Tell students to present their findings in the form of a news report to the class. Advise students to include relevant statistics and any firsthand accounts that they might uncover in their research. With the class as a whole, explore solutions to these problems. In which of these solutions can psychologists play a part?

Where Are We Headed?

Psychology stands now—relative to its founding—about where physics stood 100 years after Galileo dropped the bullet and cannon ball from the tower in Pisa (Krauskopf & Beiser, 1960). For society to expect psychology to have delivered benefits so soon after its founding might justifiably be called premature. Yet the need for such contribution is certainly there, as is the potential for greater need.

One way to think about psychology's direction is to consider what behavioral scientists themselves express about the future. Two original and provocative thinkers are B.F. Skinner and Alvin Toffler.

B.F. Skinner. B.F. Skinner wrote what became one of the most widely read as well as widely misunderstood books in the history of modern literature: *Beyond Freedom and Dignity* (1971). Skinner expressed the idea that we have created a society in which our behavior is largely controlled through the use of punishers. Speed and get a ticket; disturb the peace and be put in jail.

He argued that the operant principles of behavior management could be used to better match people to their jobs and to improve the satisfaction of human desires. Expressed in Chapter 2 was the idea that punishment will only suppress behavior. The old saying "While the cat's away, the mice will play" is a fitting acknowledgment of that fact. The problem is that punishment offers no hints as to more desirable behavior. Reinforcers, however, inform organisms when they have performed a correct response. Skinner basically argued that we should use positive reinforcers to lead people toward desired behaviors, rather than just punishing undesirable behaviors.

Some worried as to who would control the dispensing of reinforcers. The answer seems pretty obvious—society. Exactly the same control process would be in place as now operates to control police, military, and law enforcement officials.

Alvin Toffler. Toffler's *Future Shock* (1970) offered a frightening vision of a world of depleted resources he thought might be only decades away. Toffler noted that our society manufactures products that are designed to wear out. When they no longer work, we buy new ones—thus wasting most of the materials in the original product. He pleaded for a markedly increased humanization of planning—whether of commercial development or political changes. He argued that it is necessary to shift from a consumption-based economy to a service-based economy. Toffler's view was that equipment and products should be built to last. Thus, fewer manufacturing jobs would be available, but the difference, he argued, would easily be made up by creating many more service jobs to keep equipment working. Servicing consumes minimum resources and extends the useful life of products that consume raw materials.

It is not at all clear whether either Toffler's or Skinner's view will alter the way we live. But if shifts in our economy and society occur as suggested by these thinkers, it would mean a significant increase in the amount of person-to-person contact in our everyday life. It would also mean new areas of psychological research and study.

CRITICAL THINKING ACTIVITY

Analyzing Information. Read this passage from *Future Shock*:

Insurance companies may offer not merely to pay death benefits, but to care for the widow or widower for several months after bereavement, providing nurses, psychological counseling. . . . [T]hey may offer a computerized mating service to help the survivor locate a new life partner.

Ask students to explain where, according to Toffler, psychology is headed. Do they agree? Why or why not?

ANSWERS

Concepts and Vocabulary

1. Answers include: Iowa Tests of Basic Skills, Stanford Achievement Test.

2. They apply psychological principles to human-machine interaction.

3. Day care appears to have few negative effects and promotes social skills.

4. Answers will vary. Psychologists play a role in designing learning tools in various media.

5. In the U.S., the number of men and women between the ages of 60 and 79 is projected to grow from 14.2 million in 2000 to 22.8 million by 2050, and those 80 and older from 2.8 million to 7.4 million.

6. Applied psychologists search for immediate solutions by putting the knowledge of psychology to work. Experimental psychologists search for long-range answers by using scientific methods to study psychological processes.

7. American Psychological Association, American Psychology Society, Canadian Psychological Association

8. Since 1980 clinical psychology has grown.

9. In 1993, 29 percent of psychologists were in teaching; 55 percent in mental health services.

10. studies and makes practical suggestions about the workings of the law

---

CHAPTER 19 Review

---

11. They help businesses and industries operate more efficiently and humanely.

12. the study of aging

13. Toffler envisioned a future world depleted of resources and urged a shift to a service-based economy.

Critical Thinking

1. Answers will vary. Students should consider such factors as stimulation and rewards.

2. Answers will vary.

3. Answers will vary.

4. Students should begin by imagining the kinds of stressors workers are likely to encounter, especially regarding human-machine interaction.

5. Answers will vary.

6. Have students refer to the APA divisions listed in Table 19.1, and ask them to make logical inferences about the activities in each of the areas they select for discussion.

6. **Synthesize.** Name three areas of psychology and identify the sort of activity you expect of a psychologist working in each area.

7. **Synthesize.** Technology allows scientists and medical practitioners to study individuals and unlock secrets of the human body and mind. Despite the tremendous progress that has been made in understanding the workings of the human body and mind, there is still much to be discovered. List some of the mysteries of the human body and mind that require further study. What role can psychology play in the process of discovery?

8. **Evaluate.** You have probably given some thought to the kind of job you would like to have when you finish school. Name three jobs that you think will offer good opportunities for employment and explain why. Name three jobs that you think will offer few opportunities and explain why.

9. **Synthesize.** There are many types of mental health professionals. What common characteristics do they all share?

10. **Analyze.** Compare and contrast the educational requirements and the responsibilities of a crisis hotline advisor, a mental health assistant, and a consulting psychologist.

APPLYING KNOWLEDGE

1. Look around your dwelling and count the number of electronic appliances and other pieces of electronic equipment. Compare this to the number of similar devices your grandparents had. What differences have these devices made in your life? Have they made your life easier or more difficult? Explain. Now consider what technologies will be available to your grandchildren. How might this affect them?

2. List jobs or tasks that are performed by a machine or computer but that were performed by people in the past. After each listing, describe the new roles or tasks that human workers now have with regard to the machines or computers. Describe also how machines and computers have changed the nature of work. How have the skill requirements of human workers changed as a result? What advantages and disadvantages have machines and computers brought to the world of work? How might the systems being developed now change the nature of work in the future and the effect they will have on the workforce?

3. A psychiatrist once said that the line between mental health and mental illness is a thin one that we cross over many times each day. Do you agree? Why or why not?

BEYOND THE CLASSROOM

1. Make a list of five of your friends who work. Ask them to describe the hiring process they went through. Were their interviews structured? Did they have to take tests? If so, what types of tests were they? Did the tests seem appropriate to the nature of the job? Did your friends think the hiring process was fair?

2. Analyze Alvin Toffler's book *Future Shock.* List some of the major premises that Toffler presents in the book. Then, list at least four of Toffler's conclusions. Analyze whether the conclusions are valid, faulty, or may or may not be true.

IN YOUR JOURNAL

1. Analyze your journal entry in which you wrote about the most serious problems we face. Do you feel optimistic or pessimistic that those problems can be solved? Why or why not? In what specific ways might psychology help to solve these problems? Write answers to these questions in your journal.

7. Answers will vary.

8. Begin by having students define what they understand "good opportunities" to mean.

9. Help students realize that they share an interest in human behavior and a concern for people's welfare.

10. Have students begin by reviewing the three applicable job descriptions in Table 19.2.

Applying Knowledge

1. Answers will vary, but students should recognize that technology will continue to boom and affect the way people live.

2. Student responses should include an understanding of human-machine interaction.

3. Answers will vary.

CHAPTER BONUS
Test Question

This question may be used for extra credit on the chapter test.
Choose the letter of the correct response.

Work productivity, employee morale, and training methods are probably of greatest interest to the
a. forensic psychologist.
b. sports psychologist.
c. engineering psychologist.
d. industrial-organizational psychologist.

Answer: **d**

Beyond the Classroom

1. Answers will vary.

2. Answers will vary.

IN YOUR JOURNAL

If time permits, discuss journal entries individually with the students.

CHAPTER 20

Psychological Research and Statistics

TEXT TOPICS	SPECIAL FEATURES	RESOURCE MATERIALS
Gathering Data, pp. 503–507	**Fact or Fiction?,** p. 505; p. 506 **Psychology and You,** p. 507	Reproducible Lesson Plan; Study Guide; Review Activity Transparency 30
Avoiding Errors in Doing Research, pp. 507–508		Reproducible Lesson Plan; Study Guide; Review Activity
Statistical Evaluation, pp. 508–513	**Psychology Update,** p. 508	Reproducible Lesson Plan; Study Guide; Review Activity; Application Activity; Extension Activity; Chapter Test, Form A and Form B *Readings in Psychology:* Section 7, Readings 3, 4, 5 Transparencies 31, 32 Understanding Psychology Testmaker

PERFORMANCE ASSESSMENT ACTIVITY

Assign students to collect examples of graphic presentations of statistics from newspapers and magazines. *(circle graphs, bar graphs, line graphs, tables, charts, and so on)* Direct them to organize the clippings on posters that identify the method of presentation—i.e., a poster depicting bar graphs. Challenge students to explain the strengths of each form of presentation.

For example, which method shows percentages most clearly? Which method best illustrates trends? Next, have students write down their heights on a sheet of paper. Challenge each student to select a method of organizing this data graphically. *(The method chosen should take into account both the range of heights and the number of respondents.)*

CHAPTER RESOURCES

Readings for the Student

Huff, Darrell. *How to Lie with Statistics*. New York: Norton, 1954.

Lehman, Richard S. *Statistics and Research Design in the Behavioral Sciences*. Belmont, CA: Wadsworth, 1991.

Runkel, Philip J. *Casting Nets and Testing Specimens: Two Grand Methods of Psychology*. Westport, CT: Greenwood Press, 1990.

Readings for the Teacher

Cowels, Michael. *Statistics in Psychology: A Historical Perspective*. Hillsdale, NJ: Erlbaum, 1989.

Estes, W. K. *Statistical Methods in Psychological Research*. Hillsdale, NJ: Erlbaum, 1991.

Lovie, A. D. *New Developments in Statistics for Psychology and the Social Sciences*. London: Routledge Chapman and Hall, 1990.

Maxwell, Scott E., and Delaney, Harold. *Designing Experiments and Analyzing Data: A Model Comparison Perspective*. Belmont, CA: Wadsworth, 1990.

May, Richard B. *Application of Statistics in Behavioral Research*. New York: Harper Collins, 1990.

Multimedia

Hypothesis Testing (28 minutes, 3/4" or 1/2" video). Media Guild. This video shows how statistics are used to analyze a large population by means of a control group and random assignments.

Interpreting Your Own Self-Perception Profile (24 minutes, 3/4" or 1/2" video). American Management Association. This video shows how to do a personality self-inventory and interpret the results.

Methodology—The Psychologist and the Experiment (31 minutes, 3/4" or 1/2" video). McGraw-Hill Films. This video uses two experiments to present common methods and basic rules of psychological experiments.

Statistics and Graphs (2 parts of 20 minutes each, 3/4" video). Great Plains Instructional TV Library. Part 1 explains different types of statistics and the kinds of graphs that represent them. Part 2 shows how to design clear, readable graphs.

For additional resources see the bibliography beginning on page 530.

Psychological Research and Statistics

FOCUS

Motivating Activity

Brainstorm a list of subjects (other than psychology) that students are currently taking in school. Record these on the chalkboard. Suppose a problem or issue comes up in each of these areas. What method of research would students use to solve it? (Tip: To get students started, you might pose the following examples. In math, people often use *formulas* to solve a problem; in science, they often use a *lab experiment;* in auto mechanics, they might refer to *engine specs* or *computer diagnostics.*) Tell students that in Chapter 20 they will learn about the methods of research used in psychology. Ask them to note methods that overlap with those used in other disciplines. *(For instance, surveys are a valuable tool of the political scientist.)*

Meeting Chapter Objectives.

Point out the objectives on page 503. Have students rephrase them in question form. Then assign each question to a group of students to answer as they read Chapter 20.

Building Vocabulary.

Assign groups of students to prepare crossword puzzles using at least 20 of the Key Terms. Have the groups exchange their puzzles with each other.

FIGURE 20.1 Statistics have a variety of applications.

502

TEACHER CLASSROOM RESOURCES

- Chapter 20 Reproducible Lesson Plan
- Chapter 20 Study Guide
- Chapter 20 Review Activity
- Chapter 20 Application Activity
- Chapter 20 Extension Activity
- Transparencies 30, 31, 32 Transparency Strategies and Activities

- *Readings in Psychology:* Section 7, Reading 3, 4, 5
- Chapter 20 Test, Form A and Form B
- Understanding Psychology Testmaker

OBJECTIVES

After studying this chapter, you should be able to

- describe the process of psychological research.
- name the different types of psychological research and some of the methodological hazards of doing research.
- describe descriptive and inferential statistics.
- name specific research methods used to organize data.

I n this chapter we go behind the scenes to see how psychologists learn about what they don't already know. We poke into laboratories where they are conducting experiments, follow them on surveys, and expose some of the problems psychologists have in conducting research.

The surprise is that psychologists collect information somewhat like most people do in everyday life—only more carefully and more systematically. When you turn on the television and the picture is out of focus, you *experiment* with different knobs and dials until you find the one that works. When you ask a number of friends about a movie you are thinking of seeing, you are conducting an informal *survey*. Of course, there is more to doing scientific research than turning dials or asking friends what they think. Over the years psychologists, like other scientists, have transformed these everyday techniques for gathering and analyzing information into more precise tools.

As described in Chapter 1, researchers must begin by asking a specific question about a limited topic. The next step is to look for evidence.

KEY TERMS

case study
central tendency
control group
correlation
correlation coefficient
cross-sectional studies
dependent variable
descriptive statistics
experimental group
frequency distribution
histogram
independent variable
inferential statistics
longitudinal studies
mean
median
mode
naturalistic observation
normal curve
population
range
sample
self-fulfilling prophecy
standard deviation
statistics
survey
validity
variable
variance

IN YOUR JOURNAL

For the next seven days, observe how statistics are used in the media. In your journal, describe the examples you find.

Exploring Key Ideas

Defining Statistics.
Ask students to complete the following statement: "When I hear the word statistics, I think of _____ ." *(Most students will probably use a number-related term.)* As a creative writing assignment, you might ask students to write a humorous account entitled: "My Life as a Statistic." In the essay, students should think of ways they are counted or measured. *(For example, students are counted in census reports. Their educational scores on standardized tests go into a data bank. Their buying patterns might also be tallied. If students call into a radio straw poll, their vote becomes a statistic.)* Request volunteers to read their essays aloud.

IN YOUR JOURNAL

Remind students that media includes all the mass information sources: television, radio, newspapers and magazines, billboards, and so on.

EXTRA CREDIT ACTIVITY

Request volunteers to investigate the variables that influence how well students perform in school. Tell them to consider the following questions: What exactly are we studying? *(definition of problem)* Who are we being asked to study? *(sample)* How will we study this group? *(selection of sample)* How will data be collected? *(method of research)* How will the data be interpreted? *(evaluation)* Have the volunteers present their plans to the rest of the class for review. Then challenge them to put the finalized plan into action.

TEACH

Guided Practice

■ **Discussion.** Before reading the material on pages 504–507, brainstorm answers to the opening question: How do psychologists collect information about the topic they've chosen to study? Record student responses on the chalkboard. As they progress through the chapter, correct and add to the list. (You might also assign a team of students to evaluate the list against research methods described in earlier chapters of the text.) (OBJECTIVE 1)

VISUAL INSTRUCTION

Without referring to the caption, have students write down a brief description of what they think is happening in the series of pictures. Call on volunteers to read their answers aloud. Ask: What *biases* might have influenced your interpretation?

Answer to caption, Figure 20.2: degree of relatedness between two sets of data

---

DID YOU KNOW?

In the 1960s, Neal Miller and Leo Dicara (1967) stunned the psychological and medical world by reporting that they had trained rats to control their heart rates. All attempts to replicate Miller and DiCara's study failed, however—including their own. What went wrong? To date, nobody has found an answer.

FIGURE 20.2

This series of drawings show a correlation between the woman's sadness and the man's anger. However, is one causing the other? Perhaps, but they may both be responding to a third factor. **How do psychologists define correlation?**

GATHERING DATA

How do psychologists collect information about the topic they've chosen to study? The method a researcher uses partly depends on the research topic. For example, a social psychologist who is studying the effects of group pressure is likely to conduct an experiment. A psychologist who is interested in personality theories might begin with intensive case studies of individuals. But whatever approach to gathering data a psychologist selects, he or she must make certain basic decisions in advance.

Validity

Look at a major fashion magazine. It will include advertisements for products that "guarantee" thicker hair, freedom from wrinkles, and huge weight losses in "just two weeks!" Check the psychology section of a large bookstore. Shelves of books are devoted to self-help—how to achieve the perfect relationship, how to get out of bad relationships, how to find inner talents, how to bring up your children. On TV, a trusted actor, who has become famous playing a doctor, makes commercials praising a particular product and is perceived as an "expert." Are any of the claims made for these products, diets, and methods valid?

One of the tasks of psychologists is to determine **validity**—verifying that a claim is correct or disproving it. As described in Chapter 1, a claim, hypothesis, or theory cannot be accepted until it has been repeatedly tested and found to be true.

Samples

Suppose a psychologist wants to know how the desire to get into college affects the attitudes of high-school juniors and seniors. It would be impossible to study every junior and senior in the country. Instead, the researcher would select a **sample,** a relatively small group out of the total **population** under study—in this case, all high-school juniors and seniors.

Choosing a sample can be tricky. A sample must be *representative* of the population a researcher is studying. For example, if you wanted to know how tall American men are, you would want to make certain that your sample did not include a disproportionately large number of professional basketball players. Such a sample would be *biased*; it would not represent American men in general.

There are two ways to avoid a biased sample. One is to take a purely *random sample*, so that each individual within the scope of the research has an *equal chance* of being represented. For example, a psychologist might choose every twentieth name on school enrollment lists for a study of schoolchildren in a particular town. Random sampling is like drawing names or numbers out of a hat while blindfolded.

The second way to avoid bias is deliberately to pick individuals who represent the various subgroups in the population being studied. For example, the psychologist doing research on schoolchildren might select students of both sexes, of varying ages, of all social classes, and from all neighborhoods. This is called a *stratified sample.*

ADDITIONAL INFORMATION

During the discussion of naturalistic observation, point out that a researcher using this method records or writes down only what can be seen. Emphasize that the researcher must not make inferences about what the behaviors mean or what the subject might be feeling. Ask students to use this method to observe an individual or a group. Stress that recording behaviors, without making inferences, takes patience and hard work.

Correlations and Explanations

A researcher may simply want to observe people or other animals and record these observations in a descriptive study. More often, however, researchers want to examine the *relationship* between two sets of observations—say, between students' grades and the number of hours they sleep.

Scientists use the word **correlation** to describe the degree of relatedness between two sets of data. For example, there is a *positive correlation* between IQ scores and academic success. High IQ scores tend to go with high grades; low IQ scores tend to go with low grades. On the other hand, there is a *negative correlation* between smoking cigarettes and living a long, healthy life. The more a person smokes, the fewer years he or she may live. In this case, a high rank on one measure tends to go with a low rank on the other.

Experiments

Why would a researcher choose experimentation over other research methods? Experimentation enables the investigator to *control* the situation and to decrease the possibility that unnoticed, outside factors will influence the results.

Remember that an experiment is designed to prove or disprove a hypothesis. This is the main purpose of psychological studies and experiments—to develop a hypothesis or refine and test previous ones.

In designing and reporting experiments, psychologists think in terms of **variables**—that is, conditions and behaviors that are subject to variation or change. There are two types of variables: independent and dependent. The **independent variable** is the one experimenters manipulate so they can observe its effects. The **dependent variable** is the one that researchers believe will be affected by the independent variable.

Of course, there is always a chance that the very fact of participating in an experiment will change the way the subjects act. Subjects who undergo the experimental treatment are called the **experimental group.** For this reason, experimenters set up two groups. Subjects who are treated the same way as the experimental group, except that the experimental treatment is not applied, make up the **control group.**

A control group is necessary in all experiments. Without it, a researcher cannot be sure the experimental group is reacting to what he or she thinks it is reacting to—a change in the independent variable. By comparing the way control and experimental groups behaved in this experiment, the researchers can determine whether the independent variable influences behavior and how it does so.

The results of any experiment do not constitute the final word on the subject, however. Psychologists do not fully accept the results of their own or other people's studies until they have been *replicated*—that is, duplicated by at least one other psychologist with different subjects. Why? Because there is always a chance that some unnoticed factor in the original experiment was atypical.

■ **Demonstration.** Select a volunteer to take part in an experiment, without the knowledge of other students. Tell the volunteer that you will be distributing two paper cups of the identical soft drink to two test groups. In one test group, the volunteer will respond immediately and confidently to a distinction between the *two* brands. When class meets, organize the students into two groups. Ask one group to stand outside the room. With the first group, conduct a taste test in which students indicate if they prefer Brand X or Brand Y. The volunteer will quickly identify a preference and the reasons. Ask other respondents to indicate their preference. (If students can't decide, list that result also.) Now bring in the second group, and reconduct the test without a student prompter. Ask: What effect, if any, did the power of suggestion have on the first group? Use this activity to discuss the importance of a control group to any psychological experiment. For example, could students have answered the question *without* a control group?

LAB EXPERIMENTS AND DEMONSTRATIONS

Bring several spools of thread and needles to class. Then request an equal number of male and female students to take part in an experiment. Write the following question on the chalkboard: Who can thread a needle faster—men or women? Conduct a quick straw poll to determine student answers. Then test these responses by having the subjects carry out the test. (To increase stress, stand next to each student with a stop watch. Also, with either the males or females, talk in an animated fashion about a recent television program.) Now answer the question based on the experiment. Challenge students to suggest variables that might have affected the results. *(Answers will vary, but might include: traditional gender roles that give females more practice in threading needles, presence of a stop watch, chatter, and so on.)*

■ Conducting a Survey.

Tell students to imagine that a local pizzeria has asked them to conduct a survey on the preferences of high school students for pizza; for example, type of crust, favorite toppings, amount of cheese, and so on. Tell students that the pizzeria wants to use the results to design an advertising campaign to lure students away from another popular competitor. Working in small groups, have students design a survey using the following tips.

1. Define the topic. Usually, the narrower the topic, the more precise the research.
2. Select a sample. Determine which sample would be most effective for the study—a random sample or a representative sample. (e.g., a random poll in the cafeteria vs. a questionnaire distributed to several social studies classes at each grade level in the school)
3. Write the questions. Are forced-choice or open-ended questions best for the survey? (Forced-choice are easier to add up.)
4. Conduct the survey. To avoid biasing respondents, prepare a standard introduction used for everyone.
5. Tally data. Be sure to choose the best format for organizing the numbers.
6. Analyze results. Form generalizations based upon the data. Ask yourself: What does this survey tell me about the topic under research?

Request volunteers to conduct the survey. Using statistical results from the survey, have the rest of the class design advertisements that the pizzeria might use to win new patrons. Each ad should use statistics in some way. (OBJECTIVE 2)

? FACT OR FICTION

Controlled experiments are better than naturalistic observation.

Fiction. Many psychologists prefer the greater degree of control that is possible in experiments. However, this control comes at the price of environmental realism, what psychologists term *ecological validity*. Psychology needs many types of studies, including experiments and natural observations, to prosper as a science.

Naturalistic Observation

Researchers need to understand the way people and animals behave naturally, when they are not conscious of being the subjects of an experiment. To obtain such information, a psychologist uses **naturalistic observation.** For example, a social psychologist might join a commune or participate in a therapy group to study how leadership develops in these settings. A developmental psychologist might position himself or herself behind a two-way mirror to watch youngsters at play. Ethologists (scientists who specialize in studying animal behavior) often spend years observing members of a species before even considering an experiment. The cardinal rule of naturalistic observation is to avoid disturbing the people or animals you are studying, by concealing yourself or by acting as unobtrusively as possible. Otherwise, you may observe a performance produced for the researcher's benefit rather than natural behavior.

Case Studies

A **case study** is a scientific biography of an individual or group. Many case studies focus on a particular disorder, such as schizophrenia, or a particular experience, such as being confined to prison. Most combine long-term observation by one or more researchers, self-reports such as diaries, tapes of therapy sessions, and the results of psychological tests.

In the hands of a brilliant psychologist, case studies can be a powerful research tool. Sigmund Freud's theory of personality development, discussed in Chapter 11, was based on case studies of his patients. Jean Piaget's theory of intellectual development, described in Chapter 8, was based in part on case studies of his own children. By itself, however, a case study does not prove or disprove anything. You cannot generalize the results to anyone else without testing others. The sample is too small, and there is no way of knowing if the researcher's conclusions are correct.

What, then, is the value of case studies? They provide a wealth of descriptive material that may generate new hypotheses that researchers can then test under controlled conditions with comparison groups.

Surveys

Surveys may be impersonal, but they are the most practical way to gather data on the attitudes, beliefs, and experiences of large numbers of people. A survey can take the form of interviews, questionnaires, or a combination of the two.

Interviews allow a researcher to observe the subject and modify questions if the subject seems confused by them. On the other hand, questionnaires take less time to administer and the results are more uniform because everyone answers the same questions. Questionnaires also eliminate the possibility that the researcher will influence the subject by unconsciously frowning at an answer he or she does not like. Of course, there is always a danger that subjects will give misleading answers in order to make

LAB EXPERIMENTS AND DEMONSTRATIONS

Raise the following research problem. Eating satisfies a basic physiological need, but it also performs valuable social and psychological functions. What are these functions? To answer this question, suggest that students engage in a naturalistic observation activity. Assign teams of students to observe behavior in the following settings: the school cafeteria, a fast-food restaurant, a family meal, a fancy restaurant. Caution students to remain as unobtrusive as possible. Allow time for each team to report its findings. Ask: Why is naturalistic research better suited to answer this question than lab research?

themselves "look good." One way to detect this is to phase the same question in several different ways. A person who says yes, she believes in integration, but no, she would not want her child to marry someone of another race, is not as free of prejudice as the first answer implied.

Longitudinal Studies

Longitudinal studies cover long stretches of time. The psychologist studies and restudies the same group of students at regular intervals over a period of years to determine whether their behavior and feelings have changed, and if so, how.

Longitudinal studies are time-consuming and precarious; subjects may disappear in mid-study. But they are an ideal way to examine consistencies and inconsistencies in behavior over time.

Cross-sectional Studies

An alternative approach to gathering data is **cross-sectional studies.** In a cross-sectional study, psychologists organize individuals into groups on the basis of age. Then, these groups are randomly sampled, and the members of each group are surveyed, tested, or observed simultaneously. If you were conducting a cross-sectional study of intelligence, for example, you might give an IQ test to individuals—some 30 years old, some 40, some 60, and so forth—compare the average scores, and then draw conclusions about intelligence at various ages. Advantages of cross-sectional studies include that they are less expensive than longitudinal studies and reduce the amount of time necessary for the study. There is a problem, however. One study similar to our example concluded that intelligence declines with age. Yet, age may not have been the primary cause of the decline. The older subjects sampled have had very different educations and life experiences from the younger ones. These differences can easily influence the results.

All the methods for gathering information we've described have advantages and disadvantages; no one technique is better than the others for all purposes. The method a psychologist chooses depends on what he or she wants to learn. It also depends on practical matters such as the amount of money available for research and the researcher's training.

AVOIDING ERRORS IN DOING RESEARCH

In describing the methods and statistical techniques psychologists use, we have made research appear much simpler and much more straightforward than it actually is. Science is a painstaking, exacting process. Every researcher must be wary of numerous pitfalls that can trap him or her into mistakes. Next, we look at some of the most common problems psychological researchers confront and how they cope with them.

Psychologists are only human, and like all of us they prefer to be right. No matter how objective they try to be in their research, there is always a

---

PSYCHOLOGY and YOU

Baseball Statistics. Let us look at how statistics are used in one of our most popular sports, baseball. A batting average is the number of hits per official "at bats" (walks do not count). If a player has a batting average of .250, it means that he gets a hit every fourth time at the plate.

The earned run average represents the number of runs a pitcher allows per 9 innings of play. Consider the pitcher who pitches 180 innings in a season and allows 60 runs. On the average, this pitcher allows one run every 3 innings (180 innings divided by 60 runs). One run every 3 innings equals 3 runs every 9 innings, so the earned run average is 3. The next time you watch your favorite sport, think about the part that statistics plays in it.

WORKING WITH TRANSPARENCIES

Project Transparency 30 showing the results of a longitudinal study. Tell students it was conducted to find out how much continuity existed between an individual's behavior in childhood and behavior as an adult (Kagan and Moss, 1962). Tell students that researchers concluded that traditional sex roles had a strong influence on whether a childhood behavior pattern died out or survived in adulthood. Assign students to identify data on the graph that support this conclusion. (Note, for example, the traditional passive role assigned to females.)

Assign Student Worksheet 30.

Readings in Psychology. Have students read the Section 7, Readings 3, 4, and 5 selections in *Readings in Psychology* and answer the questions that follow the selections.

People sometimes think of a correlation as a cause-and-effect relationship. Some years ago, for example, medical researchers discovered a high correlation between cancer and drinking milk. It seemed that the number of cancer cases was increasing in areas where people drink large quantities of milk (e.g., New England) but that cancer was rare where people did not (e.g., Ceylon). So does milk cause cancer? Further research revealed a third, more important factor. Cancer usually strikes in middle age or later. As a result, it is more common in places where people enjoy a high standard of living—and can afford to drink quantities of milk. Therefore, milk may be correlated to cancer, but it does not *cause* it.

■ **Analyzing Statistics.** Organize the students into small groups, and give each group a different newspaper or different issues of the same newspaper. Next, direct each group to identify three or four different examples of statistics. Examples might range from the average daily temperature to the results of surveys or polls. Instruct students to analyze how the various statistics are used. Are any of the statistics used to present a misleading picture or to slant an argument? Which statistics are the most objective? Which statistics open the door for speculation beyond the written material? Have members of each group present their findings. As a follow-up activity, assign students to write a narrative essay entitled: "Numbers Don't Lie, Do They?" (OBJECTIVE 2)

VISUAL INSTRUCTION

Based on information from the table on page 509, have students form tentative conclusions on the effect of television watching upon quiz performance. Ask: Have you identified a correlation, a solid cause-and-effect relationship, or both? (See Bottom Note on page 507.)
Answer to caption, Figure 20.3: .5 hour and 1 hour

Cross-cultural Studies. Cross-cultural studies are comparisons of the way people in different cultures behave, feel, and think. These studies attempt to find whether a behavior pattern is universal or reflects people's experiences as children and adults in their culture.

In Stanley Milgram's original study (see Chapter 18), more than half of the subjects (26 of 40, or 65 percent) administered the highest level of shock.

Researchers at Swarthmore College hypothesized that Milgram's findings were due, in part, to the fact that his subjects were mostly middle-aged, working-class men. Most had probably served in the military during World War II and thus had experience taking orders and obeying authority. Young, liberal, highly educated Swarthmore students would obey less. Surprisingly, 88 percent of the Swarthmore undergraduates administered the highest level of shock!

Eventually, Milgram's experiment was conducted in Germany and Japan. The German and Japanese subjects also showed a high rate of obedience—over 80 percent in both groups.

chance that they will find what they want to find, unwittingly overlooking contrary evidence. This is what we mean by the **self-fulfilling prophecy.**

One way to avoid the self-fulfilling prophecy is to use the double-blind technique. Suppose a psychologist wants to study the effects of a particular tranquilizer. She might give the drug to an experimental group and a placebo (a harmless substitute for the drug) to a control group. The next step would be to compare their performances on a series of tests. This is a *single-blind* experiment. The subjects are "blind" in the sense that they do not know whether they have received the tranquilizer or the placebo.

As a further guarantee of objectivity, the researcher herself doesn't know who takes the drug or the placebo. (She may ask the pharmacist to number rather than label the pills.) *After* she scores the tests, she goes back to the pharmacist to learn which subjects took the tranquilizer and which took the placebo. This is a *double-blind experiment.* Neither the subjects nor the experimenter know which subjects received the tranquilizer. This eliminates the possibility that the researcher will unconsciously find what she expects to find about the effects of the drug.

Psychologists, like everyone else, have attitudes, feelings, and ideas of their own, and their reactions to different subjects may distort the results of a study. Researchers may unknowingly react differently to male and female subjects, short and tall subjects, subjects who speak with an accent or who remind them of someone they particularly like. These attitudes, however subtly expressed, may influence the way subjects behave.

In addition, subjects may behave differently than they would otherwise just because they know they are being studied. The presence of an observer may cause them to change their behavior, just as the presence of a photographer can transform a bunch of unruly children into a peaceful, smiling group. Under observation, people are apt to try to please or impress the observer—to act as they think they are expected to act. The use of a control group helps to correct for this, but does not totally eliminate the "observer effect."

Finally, a researcher may not have the equipment to study a subject adequately. For example, psychologists would never have been able to identify the stages of sleep (see Chapter 7) if the electroencephalograph had not been invented. Psychology is a relatively young science, and the tools and techniques psychologists possess may not always be equal to the questions they ask.

STATISTICAL EVALUATION

How many times have you been told that, in order to get good grades, you have to study? A psychology student named Kate has always restricted the amount of TV she watches during the week, particularly before a test. She has a friend, though, who does not watch TV before a test but who still does not get good grades. This fact challenges Kate's belief. Although Kate hypothesizes that, among her classmates, those who watch less TV get better grades, she decides to conduct a survey to test the validity of her hypothesis. Kate asks 15 students in her class to write down how many hours of TV they watched the night before their weekly psychology quiz and how many

COMMUNITY INVOLVEMENT

Invite a psychologist in your community to speak to the class. Ask the speaker to describe his or her job, focusing on what research he or she has done or expects to do in the future. Request that the speaker indicate some of the difficulties in conducting human research. Also have him or her discuss the qualities necessary for someone to be an effective researcher. Have students summarize the talk by writing a job description for a research psychologist. Suggest that students follow the model provided by entries in Table 19.2 on pages 496–497.

hours they watched on the night after the quiz. Kate collects additional data. She has her subjects check off familiar products on a list of 20 brand-name items that were advertised on TV the night before the quiz. Kate also asks her subjects to give their height.

When the data is turned in, Kate finds herself overwhelmed with the amount of information she has collected. Her data are presented in Figure 20.3. How can she organize it all so that it makes sense? How can she analyze it to see whether it supports or contradicts her hypothesis? The answers to these questions are found in **statistics,** a branch of mathematics that enables researchers to organize and evaluate the data they collect. We will explore the statistical procedures that help psychologists make sense out of the masses of data they collect.

Descriptive Statistics

When a study such as Kate's is completed, the first task is to organize the data in as brief and clear a manner as possible. For Kate, this means that she must put her responses together in a logical format. When she does this, she is using **descriptive statistics,** the listing and summarizing of data in a practical, efficient way, such as graphs and averages. In this section we will discuss the different forms of descriptive statistics.

Distributions of Data. One of the first steps that researchers take to organize their data is to create frequency tables and graphs. Tables and graphs provide a rough picture of the data. Are the scores bunched up or spread out? What score occurs most often? Frequency distributions and graphs provide researchers with their initial "peek" at the data.

Before	After	Grade*	Products	Height
0.0	1.5	5	2	71
0.5	2.5	10	4	64
0.5	2.5	9	6	69
1.0	2.0	10	14	60
1.0	2.5	8	10	71
1.0	1.5	7	9	63
1.5	3.0	9	7	70
1.5	2.5	8	12	59
1.5	2.5	8	9	75
1.5	3.0	6	14	60
2.0	3.0	5	13	68
2.5	2.5	3	17	65
2.5	3.5	4	10	72
3.0	3.0	0	18	62
4.0	4.0	4	20	67

* Highest grade possible is 10.

FIGURE 20.3

Kate's data shows the number of hours of television watched before and after the quiz, the grade on the quiz, the number of products recognized, and height in inches. **How much television did the two students with the best grades watch the night before the quiz?**

PORTRAIT

Herbert A. Simon
(1916–

Herbert Simon decided to follow a different career than his engineer-attorney father. His love of mathematics, however, eventually led Simon to walk in his father's footsteps. A brilliant student, Simon skipped grades and graduated with honors in economics from the University of Chicago. At age 20, he embarked on a distinguished career that led to a Nobel prize in economics. Invention of the computer, however, led Simon into psychology. Fascinated by artificial intelligence, Simon tried to find ways to duplicate human thinking. His efforts led Simon into the APA and back into graduate school, where he earned a Ph.D. in psychology. Simon's innovative studies in computer programming led him to receive the APA Distinguished Scientific Contribution Award in 1969.

PSYCHOLOGISTS AT WORK

In recent years, research psychologists have attempted to solve problems through the use of artificial intelligence (AI), the science of having computers perform tests that would ordinarily require human cognitive abilities. In the years ahead, this field promises to increase in importance. One of the functions of *artificial intelligence psychologists* is to develop computer programs that mimic human thought processes. Goals include teaching computers to make decisions, recognize visual patterns, understand language, and even offer creative insights. AI is already being applied in a wide range of activities from the diagnosis of human illness to the diagnosis of car problems.

■ Distinguishing Descriptive and Inferential Statistics.

Have students work in pairs and assign each student to view the graphics on pages 510 and 513. Ask: If you wanted a full picture (description) of the data compiled by Kate, which figure would you use? *(Figure 20.4)* Suppose you wanted to draw a conclusion on the relationship between height and TV viewing time before the quiz. Which figure would provide the quickest and easiest-to-read answer? *(Figure 20.9)* What can you conclude from Figure 20.9? *(that there was no relationship between height and viewing time)* As an extension activity, have each pair of students draw a scatterplot showing the number of TV hours before the quiz and grades on the quiz. What conclusions can students form on the basis of this scatterplot? *(that high grades were correlated with low TV viewing time before the exam)* (OBJECTIVES 3, 4)

VISUAL INSTRUCTION

Review with any learning disabled students the methods to read a chart and line graph.
Answer to caption, Figure 20.4: 2
Answer to caption, Figure 20.5: frequency polygon

FIGURE 20.4

A frequency distribution shows how often a particular observation occurs. **How many students watched 3 or more hours of television the night before the quiz?**

Hours	Frequency Before*	Frequency After*
0.0	1	0
0.5	2	0
1.0	3	0
1.5	4	2
2.0	1	1
2.5	2	6
3.0	1	4
3.5	0	1
4.0	1	1
Total	15	15

* Number of students.

FIGURE 20.5

This graph shows the number of hours of TV watched the night before the quiz. **What is this kind of graph called?**

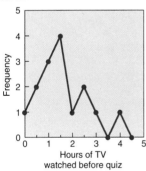

Hours of TV watched before quiz

Kate is interested in how many hours of TV her subjects watched the night before and the night after the quiz. She uses the numbers of hours of TV viewing as categories, and then she counts how many subjects reported each category of hours before and after the quiz. She has created a table called a frequency distribution (see Figure 20.4). A **frequency distribution** is a way of arranging data so that we know how often a particular score or observation occurs.

What can Kate do with this information? A commonly used technique is to figure out percentages. This is done simply by dividing the frequency of subjects within a category by the total number of subjects. So, before the quiz, about 13 percent of her subjects (2 divided by 15) watched TV for 2.5 hours. On the night after the quiz, 40 percent of her subjects watched 2.5 hours of TV (6 divided by 15). You are familiar with the use of percentages; test grades are often expressed as percentages (the number of correct points divided by 100). Sometimes frequency distributions include a column giving the percentage of each occurrence.

It is often easier to visualize frequency information in the form of a graph. Since Kate is most interested in how much TV her classmates watched, she decides to graph the results. Kate constructs a histogram. **Histograms** are very similar to bar graphs except that histograms are always vertical, and the bars touch.

Another kind of graph is the frequency polygon or frequency curve. Figure 20.5 is a frequency polygon. It shows the same information presented in a different way. The X axis and Y axis are exactly the same. Instead of drawing boxes, however, a mark is placed on the graph where the midpoint of the top of each histogram bar would be. Then the marks are connected with straight lines.

Frequency polygons are useful because they provide a clear picture of the shape of the data distribution. Another important feature is that more than one set of data can be graphed at the same time. For example, Kate might be interested in comparing how much TV was watched the night before the quiz with the amount watched the evening after the quiz. She can graph the "after quiz" data using a different kind of line. The comparison is obvious; in general, her subjects watched more TV on the night after the quiz than on the night before the quiz.

Imagine that Kate could measure how much TV everyone in Chicago watched one night. If she could graph that much information, her graph would probably look something like Figure 20.7. A few people would watch little or no TV, a few would have the TV on all day, while most would watch a moderate amount of TV. Therefore, the graph would be highest in the middle and taper off toward the tails, or ends, of the distribution, giving it the shape of a bell.

This curve is special. It is called the **normal curve** (or bell-shaped curve). Many variables, such as height, weight, and IQ, fall into such a curve if enough people are measured. The normal curve is symmetrical. This means that if a line is drawn down the middle of the curve, one side of the curve is a mirror image of the other side. It is an important distribution because of certain mathematical characteristics. We can divide the curve into sections and can predict how much of the curve, or what percentage of

---

CONNECTIONS: PSYCHOLOGY AND THE MEDIA

Assign students to observe television commercials over a week's period. Instruct them to pay particular attention to commercials that report the results of studies or that cite statistics. Have students write down specific examples of vague claims such as "the brand that doctors prefer." In an information-sharing session, call on students to report their findings. As a follow-up activity, direct students to write a list of guidelines that a government agency might write for the use of statistics in TV advertising.

cases, falls within each section. We shall return to this idea later and discuss the importance of the information shown on the curve.

Measures of Central Tendency.   Most of the time, researchers want to do more than organize their data. They want to be able to summarize information about the distribution into statistics. One of the most common ways of summarizing is to use a measure of **central tendency**—a number that describes something about the "average" score. We shall use Kate's quiz grades (refer back to Figure 20.3) in the examples that follow.

The **mode** is the most frequent score. In a graphed frequency distribution, the mode is the peak of the graph. The most frequently occurring quiz grade is 8; that is, the most students, in this case three, got a score of 8. Distributions can have more than one mode. The data for height presented in Figure 20.3 has two modes: 60 and 71. Distributions with two modes are called "bimodal."

When scores are put in order from least to most, the **median** is the middle score. Since the median is the midpoint of a set of values, it divides the frequency distribution into two halves. Therefore, 50 percent of the scores fall below the median, and 50 percent fall above the median. For an odd number of observations, the median would be the exact middle value. Here are the psychology quiz grades, in order: 0, 3, 4, 4, 5, 5, 6, 7, 8, 8, 8, 9, 9, 10, 10. The median is 7. As the middle score it divides the distribution in half: There are seven scores above it and seven scores below it. With an even number of observations, the median would be the midpoint between the two most central scores.

The **mean** is what most people think of as an "average" and is the most commonly used measure of central tendency. To find the mean, you add up all the scores and then divide by the number of scores you add.

The mean equals the sum of the scores on variable X divided by the total number of observations. For the quiz grades, the sum of the scores is 96, and the number of scores is 15. The mean equals 96 divided by 15, to give us a mean quiz grade of 6.4.

The mean can be considered the balance point of the distribution, like the middle of a seesaw, since it does reflect all the scores in a set of data. If the highest score in a data set is shifted higher, the mean will shift upward also. If we change the highest quiz grade from 10 to 20, the mean changes from 6.4 to 7.1.

Measures of Variance.   Distributions differ not only in their "average" score but also in terms of how "spread out" or how variable the scores are. Figure 20.8 shows two distributions drawn on the same axis. Each is symmetrical and each has the same mean. However, the distributions differ in terms of their variance. Measures of **variance** provide an index of how spread out the scores of a distribution are.

Two commonly used measures of variance are the range and the standard deviation. To compute the **range,** subtract the lowest score in a data set from the highest score. The highest quiz grade is 10 and the lowest is 0,

FIGURE 20.6

Many curves are not "normal" because scores pile up on one end of the distribution. These are called *skewed distributions.* Take a look at Figure 20.5 again. Most of the students fell into the lower range of the distribution (they did not watch much TV), and so it is positively skewed (the tail of the distribution points to the right, or positive, end of the X axis). If the students had watched many hours of TV, the graph would have been skewed in the other direction, or negatively skewed. **If everyone in your class took a sixth grade math test and you graphed the results, what kind of distribution would most likely occur?**

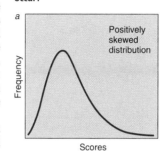

a   Positively skewed distribution
Frequency
Scores

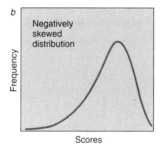

b   Negatively skewed distribution
Frequency
Scores

Independent Practice

■ **Applying the Research Process.** To apply statistical research processes to students' own lives, distribute copies of the test scores from a quiz. (To protect privacy, you might select the scores from a prior academic year.) Assign students to determine the mode, median, and mean for these scores. Then assign them to write a paragraph explaining what these measures of central tendency tell them about student performance. Next, instruct students to determine the range and standard deviation to measure variance. Ask: How do these data help summarize information about grades? In a follow-up activity, request volunteers to plot data in the form of a chart or graph. Present these graphic representations to the class. Call on students to explain whether they depict descriptive statistics or inferential statistics. *(descriptive statistics)* (OBJECTIVES 1–4)

Answer to caption, Figure 20.6: Since most students will get high scores, the graph will be negatively skewed.

MEETING SPECIAL NEEDS

Additional Practice. Students with learning disabilities may have trouble distinguishing the terms *mode, median,* and *mean.* You might help reinforce information in the text by asking students to complete the following activities. (Answers appear in parentheses.)

1. Mode, median, and mean are alike in that all three measure _____ . *(central tendency)*

2. Which of the following relationships expresses a mean, median, and mode?

_____ 3, 5, 10, 11, 15, 16 → 10.0 *(mean)*

_____ 2, 8, 10, 11, 12, 13, 18 → 11.0 *(median)*

_____ 4, 5, 12, 12, 12, 12, 16 → 12.0 *(mode)*

Answer to caption, Figure 20.7: The normal curve is symmetrical.

Answer to caption, Figure 20.8: a measure of variability that describes an average distance of every score from the mean of scores

Answer to caption, Figure 20.9: that there was no correlation between height and TV viewing time prior to the test

WORKING WITH TRANSPARENCIES

For further review on statistics and graphs, project Transparencies 31 and 32. Assign Student Worksheets 31 and 32.

■ **Research.** Review the importance of replication as a means of determining the validity of any experiment (see page 505). Then request a group of students to organize a study similar to the one performed by Kate. Instruct students to review information on conducting a survey, especially selection of a sample. Direct them to present their findings in graphics to match those depicted in the text. Did the student survey validate Kate's findings? Why or why not? (OBJECTIVES 1–4)

FIGURE 20.7

A normal curve may measure many different variables. **What is an important characteristic of normal curves?**

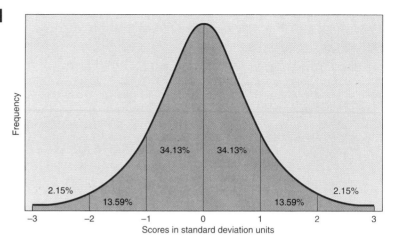

so the range is 10. The range uses only a small amount of information, and it is used only as a crude measure of variance.

The **standard deviation** is a better measure of variance because, like the mean, it uses all the data points in its calculation. It is the most widely used measure of variance. The standard deviation is like (but not exactly like) an "average" distance of every score to the mean of the scores. This distance is called a "deviation" and is written: $X - \overline{X}$ (which means a score minus the mean). Scores above the mean will have a positive deviation, and scores below the mean will have a negative deviation. The size of the "average" deviation depends on how variable, or spread out, the distribution is. If the distribution is very spread out, deviations tend to be large. If the distribution is bunched up, deviations tend to be small.

The standard deviation is a measure of distance, describing an "average" distance of every score to the mean. The larger the standard deviation, the more spread out the scores are.

Correlation Coefficients. A **correlation coefficient** describes the direction and strength of the relationship between two sets of observations. The most commonly used measure is the Pearson correlation coefficient (r). A coefficient with a plus ($+$) sign indicates a *positive correlation*. This means that as one variable *increases*, the second variable also *increases*. For example, the more you jog, the better your cardiovascular system works. A coefficient with a minus ($-$) sign indicates a *negative correlation*; as one variable *increases*, the second variable *decreases*. For example, the more hours a person spends at an after-school job, the fewer hours are available for studying. Correlations can take any value between $+1$ and -1 including 0. An r near $+1$ or -1 indicates a strong relationship (either positive or negative), while an r near 0 indicates a weak relationship. Generally, an r from 0.60 to 1.0 indicates a strong correlation, from 0.30 to 0.60 a moderate correlation, and from 0 to 0.30 a weak correlation. A correlation of 1.0 indicates a perfect relationship between two variables and is very rare.

COMMUNITY INVOLVEMENT

Invite the school psychologist to describe the way in which he or she uses or has used statistics for educational purposes. Center the discussion around the interpretation of some of the tests with which students may be familiar, such as PSATs. What, if any, biases does the speaker think may creep into standardized tests? Besides statistical data, what other information does the school psychologist use to evaluate students?

To get an idea of how her data looks, Kate draws some scatterplots. A *scatterplot* is a graph of subjects' scores on the two variables, and it demonstrates the direction of the relationship between them. Figure 20.9 illustrates the different kinds of correlations Kate looks at. Note that each point represents one person's score on two variables.

Inferential Statistics

The purpose of descriptive statistics is to describe the characteristics of a sample. But psychologists are not interested only in the information they collect from their subjects. They want to make generalizations about the population from which the subjects come. To make such generalizations, we need the tools of inferential statistics. Using **inferential statistics,** researchers can determine whether the data they collect support their hypotheses, or whether their results are merely due to chance outcomes.

Probability and Chance. If you toss a coin in the air, what is the probability that it will land with heads facing up? Since there are only two possible outcomes, the probability of heads is 0.50. If you toss a coin 10 times, you would expect 5 heads and 5 tails. What if in 9 flips you toss 9 heads and no tails? What is the probability that your next toss will be heads? It will still be 50-50. Each toss has the same probability no matter how many times you toss it. Each toss is independent of the other.

Statistical Significance. The normal curve (Figure 20.7) is one of many distributions psychologists use to evaluate the results of their studies. For example, Kate wants to know if her classmates watch more TV than the "average American." Since daily TV viewing is probably normally distributed, she can compare her results to the normal distribution, if she knows the population's mean number of TV viewing hours. There is a distribution to use when two groups are compared, a distribution when three or more groups are studied, and a distribution for correlations. All inferential statistics are associated with a distribution. Therefore, all possible outcomes or results are associated with a probability, just as with the normal curve. When psychologists evaluate the results of their studies, they ask: Could the results be due to chance? What researchers really want to know is whether the results are extreme enough so that they are more likely to be due to the variables being studied.

The problem is that this question cannot be answered with a yes or no. This is why researchers use some guidelines to evaluate probabilities. Many researchers say that if the probability that their results were due to chance is less than 5 percent (.05), then they are confident that the results are not due to chance. Some researchers want to be even more sure, and so they use 1 percent (.01) as their level of confidence. When the probability of a result is 0.05 or 0.01 (or whatever level the researcher sets), we say that the result is *statistically significant*. It is important to remember that probability tells us how *likely* it is that an event or outcome is due to chance, but not whether the event is *actually* due to chance.

FIGURE 20.8

Shown are two distributions with the same mean and different standard deviations. **What is standard deviation?**

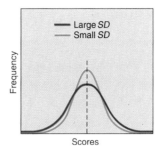

FIGURE 20.9

When there is little or no relationship between two variables, the points in the scatterplot do not seem to fall into any pattern. **What conclusions can you draw from this scatterplot?**

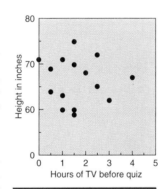

CRITICAL THINKING ACTIVITY

Analyzing Statistics. Assign volunteers to select an issue in the news that interests them. Then challenge students to use statistics to develop both a pro and con position on the issue. Advise students to consider only those statistics that support their position. Next, call on two students to present each position.

Direct the rest of the class to take notes on how each person makes use of numbers and surveys. In a follow-up discussion, brainstorm a list of questions that students might ask themselves whenever they read or hear statistics used to support a point of view.

ANSWERS

Concepts and Vocabulary

1. taking a purely random sample; deliberately picking a representative sample

2. to develop a hypothesis or refine and test previous hypotheses

3. independent variable; dependent variable

4. use of a survey; through interviews, questionnaires, or a combination of the two

5. longitudinal studies

6. to determine whether a behavior pattern is universal or whether it reflects the uniqueness of a particular culture

Critical Thinking

1. Begin by discussing the first hypothesis presented. Ask students to brainstorm ideas on how this theory could be disproved. Then have students organize their ideas into a process of research, such as those described in this chapter. *(e.g., define the problem, identify method of research, and so on)* Repeat this process for each item presented.

2. Answers will vary. Students might argue that the statement means that, even if two variables are correlated, a cause-and-effect relationship cannot be established without further research. (For example: On a hot day, many people at the beach bought cold drinks. At least 50 percent of the people who bought the drinks suffered heat exhaustion. The

---

CHAPTER 20 Review

SUMMARY

Use the following outline as a tool for reviewing this chapter. Copy the outline onto your own paper, leaving spaces between headings to make notes about key concepts.

    I. Gathering Data

        A. Validity

        B. Samples

        C. Correlations and Explanations

        D. Experiments

        E. Naturalistic Observation

        F. Case Studies

        G. Surveys

        H. Longitudinal Studies

        I. Cross-sectional Studies

    II. Avoiding Errors in Doing Research

   III. Statistical Evaluation

        A. Descriptive Statistics

        B. Inferential Statistics

CONCEPTS AND VOCABULARY

1. Indicate the two ways that a biased sample can be avoided.

2. Describe the main purpose of an experiment.

3. Name the variable that experimenters can control. Which variable is affected by the other?

4. Describe the most practical way to gather data on the attitudes, beliefs, and experiences of large numbers of people. How can this method obtain data?

5. What type of studies obtain data from people at regular intervals over a span of several years?

6. Describe the main purpose of a cross-sectional study.

CRITICAL THINKING

1. **Synthesize.** Several hypotheses are presented below. How could you attempt to disprove each one? Are there any that could not be disproved?

    a. A person will remember an unfinished task.
    b. Love reduces hate.
    c. You can raise blood pressure by making a subject anxious.
    d. Motivation increases learning.
    e. Making a rat hungry will cause the rat to require less training to find its way through a maze.

2. **Analyze.** Explain the following statement: "Correlation does not imply causation." Give an example that supports this statement. Then give another example where a correlation *might* imply causation.

3. **Apply.** How are statistics used within your classroom? Within your school? Give specific examples of the different types of statistics discussed in this chapter.

4. **Analyze.** What kinds of statistics are used in sports? Explain your answer with examples from different sports.

APPLYING KNOWLEDGE

1. Measurement is the assignment of numbers to observations. Psychologists face many problems in trying to measure behaviors and feelings. For example, how might the following factors be measured: (1) the number of people in a room; (2) height; (3) the proportion of votes a candidate will receive; (4) hunger; (5) love; (6) liberty. What makes each phenomenon difficult or easy to measure? What can you predict from this exercise regarding the difficulties of measuring such things as personality and intelligence?

2. Collect weights from twenty women and twenty men. Create a frequency distribution for each group. Since there are likely to be many differ-

---

drinks, however, did not cause the condition.)

3. Answers will vary. Most students will name tests—both content and standardized. However, encourage them to think of statistics used in other ways— sports, student elections, and so on.

4. Examples: baseball—batting average, earned-run average; basketball—free-throw percentage; football—yards per carry; boxing—knock-out percentages

Applying Knowledge

1. You might center this discussion around the use of forced-choice and open-ended questions. Discuss question format as a tool for measurement.

2. Student methodology should mirror the standards discussed in the text. You might turn evaluation over to students, encouraging them to review and modify each other's work.

ent weights, group them in 5-pound intervals before counting. For example: 110–114, 115–119, 120–124, 125–129, etc. Graph your data for men and women separately as frequency polygons on the same axis. Compute means, medians, modes, ranges, and standard deviations for women and men separately. How are the two distributions alike? How are they different? What would a frequency polygon look like if you combined the data for women and men into one sample? Write an essay summarizing your results.

ANALYZING VIEWPOINTS

1. One controversy surrounding the use of surveys is the role they can play in influencing future events. For example, political polls have often been criticized because they may cause people to switch their votes or even not vote at all. Television networks survey the viewing habits of select samples of people to determine which shows will be renewed for the following season. This can result in the cancellation of a program that does not fare well in the survey. List the pros and cons of using survey research to predict future events.

2. Does smoking cause lung cancer? Some scientists cite animal studies as proving that substances in cigarettes cause cell changes, which, in turn, lead to the development of cancer. Representatives of the tobacco industry state that animal studies cannot be generalized to humans. For humans, then, only correlational data is available, and correlations do not necessarily indicate causes. While there seems to be a correlation between smoking and lung cancer, not everyone who smokes get cancer, and non-smokers can develop lung cancer. Write an essay supporting both viewpoints. Be sure to include what you have learned from the chapter about correlations and inferential statistics. Read recent magazine and newspaper articles for more information about this controversy.

BEYOND THE CLASSROOM

1. Choose a traffic intersection near your home or school that has a stop sign. Design an experiment to assess the compliance of motorists with the posted stop sign. Spend several hours at different times of the day observing traffic at the intersection. Some of the research questions you should be considering include: What time of day will I conduct my observations? How will I determine whether motorists comply with the stop sign? How much information do I need to record? For example, do you need to record the number of vehicles, type of vehicles, whether the car stopped, time of day, or gender of the driver? Conduct your experiment and record your observations. Once you have completed your experiment, summarize the results. What are your findings? How many vehicles stopped at the stop sign? How many did not? What percentage of the total number of vehicles stopped? What percentage did not? Do these results vary based on the time of day (for example, rush hour versus midday)? Do the results vary based on the make of car? What other factors seemed to differentiate between cars that stopped and cars that did not? What are your conclusions?

IN YOUR JOURNAL

1. For each of the examples of statistics you listed in your journal, indicate whether you feel that enough information was provided to evaluate the validity of any reported claims or conclusions. What other information should have been provided? How might additional information change the reported conclusions?

IN YOUR JOURNAL

If time permits, discuss journal entries individually with students.

Analyzing Viewpoints

1. To get students started, ask them to consider the "bandwagon" syndrome when election predictions are made before polls have closed across the country. Also, you might point out historic election predictions proven wrong. Famous examples include Truman's narrowly won election over Dewey.

2. Make sure that student research is based on the guidelines provided in the chapter.

Beyond the Classroom

1. Discuss the value of naturalistic observation for this simple experiment on obedience. Encourage students to present their findings in two forms—descriptive statistics and inferential statistics. (Models of each method of organization can be found within the text.)

CHAPTER BONUS
Test Question

This question may be used for extra credit on the chapter test.
Choose the letter of the correct response.

You are analyzing correlations and your study shows that the taller people are, the more they weigh. Which of the following figures is the best estimate of the correlation coefficient between height and weight?

a. +.55
b. −.33
c. −.68
d. 0.00

Answer: **a**

Glossary

absolute threshold: The lowest level of physical energy that can be detected in half the trials. (p. 109)

accommodation: In Piaget's theory of cognitive development, the adjustment of one's scheme for understanding the world to fit newly observed events and experiences. (p. 190)

achievement test: An instrument used to measure how much an individual has learned in a given subject or area. (p. 303)

actor-observer bias: Tendency to attribute one's own behavior to outside causes rather than to a personality trait. (p. 440)

addiction: An altered psychological state in the body that causes physical dependence on a drug. (p. 383)

adjustment: The process of adapting to, as well as actively shaping, one's environment. (p. 341)

adrenal glands: Glands that secrete hormones and adrenalin. (p. 95)

ageism: Prejudice against the old. (p. 254)

anal stage: According to Freud, the stage at which children associate erotic pleasure with the elimination process. (p. 206)

androgynous: Combining or confusing traditionally male and female characteristics. (p. 232)

anger: The irate reaction likely to result from frustration. (p. 327)

antisocial personality: A personality disorder characterized by irresponsibility, shallow emotions, and lack of conscience. (p. 382)

anxiety: A vague, generalized apprehension or feeling that one is in danger. (pp. 327, 369)

applied science: Discovering ways to use scientific findings to accomplish practical goals. (p. 9)

approach-approach conflict: The situation in which the individual must choose between two attractive alternatives. (p. 318)

approach-avoidance conflict: The situation in which the individual wants to do something but fears or dislikes it at the same time. (p. 318)

aptitude test: An instrument used to estimate the probability that a person will be successful in learning a specific new skill or skills. (p. 303)

archetype: According to Jung, an inherited idea, based on the experiences of one's ancestors, that shapes one's perception of the world. (p. 276)

assimilation: In Piaget's theory of cognitive development, the process of fitting objects and experiences into one's scheme for understanding the environment. (p. 190)

asynchrony: The condition during the period of adolescence in which the growth or maturation of bodily parts is uneven. (p. 224)

attitude: Predisposition to act, think, and feel in particular ways toward a class of people, objects, or ideas. (p. 458)

attribution theory: A collection of principles based on the assumption that emotion results from the combined impact of the state of arousal, the interpretation we make of this state, and the causal link we make connecting the arousal and our interpretation. (p. 440)

audience: In the communication process, the person or persons receiving a message. (p. 469)

516

auditory nerve: Carries impulses from the inner ear to the brain, resulting in the sensation of sound. (p. 117)

authoritarian families: Families in which parents are the "bosses." (p. 236)

authoritative families: Families in which adolescents participate in decisions affecting their lives. (p. 236)

autonomic nervous system: Part of the peripheral nervous system that controls internal biological functions such as heart rate and digestion. (p. 83)

autonomy: Ability to take care of self and make own decisions. (p. 353)

aversive control: The process of influencing behavior by means of unpleasant stimuli. (p. 34)

avoidance-avoidance conflict: The situation in which the individual must choose between two unattractive alternatives. (p. 318)

avoidance conditioning: The training of an organism to remove or withdraw from an unpleasant stimulus before it starts. (p. 35)

B

basic science: The pursuit of knowledge about natural phenomena for its own sake. (p. 9)

behavior modification: The systematic application of learning principles to change people's actions and feelings. (p. 43)

behavior therapy: A form of therapy aimed at changing undesirable behavior through conditioning techniques. (p. 405)

behaviorism: The school of psychology that holds that the proper subject matter of psychology is objectively observable behavior—and nothing else. (p. 277)

binocular fusion: The process of combining the images received from the two eyes into a single, fused image. (p. 117)

biofeedback: The process of learning to control bodily states with the help of machines that provide information about physiological processes. (pp. 173, 335)

bipolar disorder: Disorder in which an individual alternates between feelings of euphoria and depression. (p. 375)

body language: Nonverbal communication through gestures, positions, and movements of the body. (p. 436)

boomerang effect: A change in attitude or behavior opposite to the one desired by the persuader. (p. 470)

brainwashing: The most extreme form of attitude change, accompanied through peer pressure, physical suffering, threats, rewards for compliance, manipulation of guilt, intensive indoctrination, and other psychological means. (p. 478)

C

Cannon-Bard theory: A theory introduced by psychologists Cannon and Bard that attributed emotion to the simultaneous activity of the brain and "gut" reactions. (p. 148)

career: A vocation in which a person works at least a few years. (p. 358)

case study: An intensive investigation of an individual or group, usually focusing on a single psychological phenomenon. (p. 506)

central nervous system (CNS): The brain and spinal cord. (p. 83)

central processing: The second stage of information processing—storing (in memory) and sorting (by thought) information in the brain. (p. 53)

central tendency: A number that describes something about the "average" score of a distribution. (p. 511)

cerebellum: A lower portion of the brain which controls posture and balance and regulates the details of motor commands from the cerebral cortex. (p. 84)

cerebral cortex: The gray mass surrounding the subcortex, which controls most of the higher brain functions, such as reading and problem solving. (p. 84)

cerebrum: The inner part of the brain, in front of and above the cerebellum. (p. 84)

channel: In the communication process, the means by which a message is transmitted from the source to the audience. (p. 469)

classical conditioning: A learning procedure in which a stimulus that normally elicits a given response is repeatedly preceded by a neutral stimulus (one that usually does not elicit the response). Eventually, the neutral stimulus will evoke a similar response when presented by itself. (p. 25)

closed awareness: The situation in which the medical staff and the family are aware of the patient's terminal condition but the patient is not. (p. 259)

517

cognitive: Mental (p. 4)

cognitive appraisal: The interpretation of an event that helps to determine its stress impact. (p. 334)

cognitive dissonance: The uncomfortable feeling that arises when a person experiences contradictory or conflicting thoughts, attitudes, beliefs, or feelings. (p. 465)

cognitive preparation: The coping strategy in which the person mentally rehearses possible outcomes. (p. 334)

collective unconscious: According to Jung, that part of the mind that contains inherited instincts, urges, and memories common to all people. (p. 276)

complementarity: The attraction that often develops between opposite types of people because of the ability of one to supply what the other lacks. (p. 432)

compliance: A change of behavior in order to avoid discomfort or rejection and gain approval; a superficial form of attitude change. (p. 460)

concept: A label for a class of objects or events that share common attributes. (p. 69)

conditioned response (CR): In classical conditioning, the learned reaction to a conditioned stimulus. (p. 25)

conditioned stimulus (CS): In classical conditioning, a once-neutral event that has come to elicit a given response after a period of training in which it has been paired with an unconditioned stimulus (UCS). (p. 25)

conditions of worth: Rogers's term for the conditions a person must meet in order to regard himself or herself positively. (p. 283)

cones: Receptor cells in the retina sensitive to color. Because they require more light than rods to function, they are most useful in daytime vision. (p. 115)

confabulation: The act of filling in memory with statements that make sense but that are, in fact, untrue. (p. 64)

conflict situations: The situation in which a person must choose between two or more options that tend to result from opposing motives. (p. 318)

conformity: Acting in accordance with some specified authority. (p. 238)

consciousness: A state of awareness, including a person's feelings, sensations, ideas, and perceptions. (p. 157)

conservation: The principle that a given quantity does not change when its appearance is changed. The discovery of this principle between the ages of five and seven is important to the intellectual development of the child. (p. 192)

constancy: The tendency to perceive certain objects in the same way, regardless of changing angle, distance, or lighting. (p. 125)

contingencies of reinforcement: Skinner's term for the occurrence of a reward or punishment following a particular behavior. (p. 278)

contingency management: A form of behavior therapy in which undesirable behavior is not reinforced, while desirable behavior is reinforced. (p. 406)

control group: In an experiment, a group of subjects that is treated in the same way as the experimental group, except that the experimental treatment (or independent variable) is not applied. (p. 505)

conversion disorder: A form of hysteria characterized by changing emotional difficulties into a loss of a specific body function. (p. 372)

corpus callosum: A band of nerves that connects the two hemispheres of the cortex and carries messages back and forth between them. (p. 87)

correlation: The degree of relatedness between two sets of data. (p. 505)

correlation coefficient: A statistic that describes the direction and strength of the relationship between two sets of observations. (p. 512)

creativity: The capacity to use information and/or abilities in such a way that the results are new, original, and meaningful. (p. 72)

critical period: A specific time in development when certain skills or abilities are most easily learned. (p. 201)

cross-sectional studies: Acquiring comparable data subgroups on the basis of certain criteria for the purpose of studying similarities and differences. (p. 507)

D

decibels: Measures of the physical intensity of sound, which is lawfully related to the sensation of loudness. (p. 117)

decremental model of aging: This holds that progressive physical and mental decline is inevitable with age. (p. 254)

defense mechanisms: According to Freud, certain specific means by which the ego unconsciously protects itself against unpleasant impulses or circumstances. (p. 272)

delusion: A false belief that a person maintains in the face of contrary evidence. (p. 378)

democratic families: Families in which all members participate in decisions affecting their lives. (p. 236)

denial: A coping mechanism in which a person decides that the event is not really a stressor. (p. 334)

dependent variable: The factor, chosen by the experimenter, that may or may not change when the independent variable is changed. Its actual value is determined by responses of the subject being studied. (p. 505)

depressant: A drug that reduces the activity of the central nervous system. (p. 335)

depressive-type reaction: A response pattern in which a person is overcome by feelings of failure, sinfulness, worthlessness, and despair. (p. 376)

descriptive statistics: The listing and summarizing of data in a practical, efficient way, such as graphs and averages. (p. 509)

developmental friendship: The type of friendship in which the partners force one another to re-examine their basic assumptions and perhaps adopt new ideas and beliefs. (p. 354)

developmental psychology: The study of changes that occur as an individual matures. (p. 183)

difference threshold: The smallest change in a physical stimulus that can be detected in half the trials. (p. 111)

diffusion of responsibility: The tendency of the presence of others to lessen an individual's feelings of responsibility for his or her actions or failure to act. (p. 451)

directed thinking: Systematic, logical, goal-directed thought. (p. 70)

discrimination: (1) The ability to respond differently to similar but distinct stimuli. (2) The unequal treatment of individuals on the basis of their race, ethnic group, class, age, sex, or membership in another category, rather than on the basis of individual characteristics. (pp. 25, 463)

displacement: The redirection of desires, feelings, or impulses from their proper object to a substitute. (p. 274)

dissociative disorder: A form of hysteria in which a person experiences a loss of memory or identity, or exhibits two or more identities. (p. 373)

distress: The type of stress that stems from acute anxiety or pressure. (p. 318)

double approach-avoidance conflict: The situation in which the individual must choose between two or more alternatives, each of which has attractive and unattractive aspects. (p. 319)

double bind: A situation in which a person receives conflicting demands, so that no matter what he or she does, it is wrong. Example: "Do not read this." (p. 382)

drive reduction theory: A theory formulated by psychologist Clark Hull that states that physiological needs drive an organism to act in random or habitual ways until its needs are satisfied. (p. 136)

DSM-III-R: Version of the American Psychiatric Association's *Diagnostic and Statistical Manual of Mental Disorders* published in 1987. This classification scheme for mental illness is far more specific than its predecessors. (p. 368)

DSM-IV: The fourth version of the American Psychiatric Association's *Diagnostic and Statistical Manual of Mental Disorders*. This 1994 version of the classification scheme for mental illness continues the detailed specification of symptoms from DSM-III-R. (p. 368)

E

eclectic approach: Method that combines many different kinds of therapy. (p. 394)

ego: According to Freud, the part of the personality that is in touch with reality. The ego strives to meet the demands of the id and the superego in socially acceptable ways. (p. 272)

ego states: Phrase used in transactional analysis theory to describe ways people organize their thoughts, feelings, and actions. (p. 402)

ego-support value: The ability of a person to provide another person with sympathy, encouragement, and approval. (p. 429)

eidetic memory: The ability to remember with great accuracy visual information on the basis of short-term exposure; also called "photographic memory." (p. 64)

Electra complex: One of the controversial tenets of Freudian theory; according to Freud, it is the daughter's wish to possess her father sexually, coupled with hostility toward her mother. After a brief period of primary attachment to the father, the girl again begins to identify with her mother, partly in order to reduce her fear of punishment from her mother. (p. 208)

empathy: Capacity for warmth and understanding. (p. 397)

encounter group: A type of therapy for people who function adequately in everyday life but who feel unhappy, dissatisfied, or stagnant; aimed at providing experiences that will help people increase their sensitivity, openness, and honesty. (p. 409)

endocrine system: A chemical communication system, using hormones, by which messages are sent through the bloodstream to particular organs of the body. (p. 93)

engineering psychology: The branch of psychology that applies psychological principles to human-machine interaction. (p. 491)

escape conditioning: The training of an organism to remove or terminate an unpleasant stimulus. (p. 35)

ethology: The study of animal behavior in its natural environment. (p. 97)

eustress: Positive stress, which results from the strivings and challenges that are the spice of life. (p. 318)

experimental group: The group of subjects to which an independent variable is applied. (p. 505)

extinction: The gradual disappearance of a conditioned response because the reinforcement is withheld or because the conditioned stimulus is repeatedly presented without the unconditioned stimulus. (p. 27)

extrasensory perception (ESP): An ability to gain information by some means other than the ordinary senses (such as taste, hearing, and vision). (p. 127)

extravert: An outgoing, active person who directs his or her energies and interests toward other people and things. (p. 286)

F

factor analysis: A complex statistical technique used to identify the underlying reasons variables are correlated. (p. 286)

family therapy: A form of therapy aimed at understanding and improving relationships that have led one or more members in a close social unit to experience emotional suffering. (p. 408)

fear: The usual reaction when a stressor involves real or imagined danger. (p. 327)

feature extraction: The identification and analysis of specific elements of a sensory input. (p. 55)

feedback: Information received after an action as to its effectiveness or correctness. (p. 37)

fixed-interval schedule: A schedule of reinforcement in which a specific amount of time must elapse before a response will elicit reinforcement. (p. 32)

fixed-ratio schedule: A schedule of reinforcement in which a specific number of correct responses is required before reinforcement can be obtained. (p. 31)

forebrain: Part of the brain that includes the thalamus and the hypothalamus. (p. 84)

forensic psychology: The branch of psychology that focuses on legal issues. (p. 494)

free association: A method used by psychoanalysts to examine the unconscious. The patient is instructed to say whatever comes into his or her mind. (p. 398)

frequency distribution: An arrangement of data that indicates how often a particular score or observation occurs. (p. 510)

frustration: The feeling of bafflement, agitation, or disappointment that results when a person's progress toward a goal is blocked. (p. 323)

fully functioning: Rogers's term for an individual whose organism and self coincide, allowing him or her to be open to experience, to possess unconditional positive regard, and to have harmonious relations with others. (p. 284)

fundamental attribution error: Inclination to attribute others' behavior to dispositional factors but to attribute our own behavior to situational factors. (p. 440)

520

fundamental needs: In Maslow's hierarchy-of-needs theory, these are the biological drives that must be satisfied in order to maintain life. (p. 143)

G

generalization: Responding similarly to a range of similar stimuli. (p. 25)

generativity: According to Erikson, the desire, in middle age, to use one's accumulated wisdom to guide future generations. (p. 251)

genital stage: According to Freud, the stage during which an individual's sexual satisfaction depends as much on giving pleasure as on receiving it. (p. 208)

gerontology: The study of aging. (p. 498)

Gestalt: In perception, the experience that comes from organizing bits and pieces of information into meaningful wholes. (p. 120)

gestalt therapy: A form of therapy that emphasizes the relationship between the patient and therapist in the here and now. The aim is to encourage the person to recognize all sides of his or her personality. (p. 402)

grasping reflex: An infant's clinging response to a touch on the palm of his or her hand. (p. 184)

group: An aggregate of people characterized by shared goals, a degree of interdependence, and some amount of communication. (p. 441)

group therapy: A form of therapy in which patients work together with the aid of a leader to resolve interpersonal problems. (p. 406)

H

hallucination: Perceptions that have no direct external cause. (pp. 165, 378)

hallucinogens: Drugs that often produce hallucinations. (p. 170)

hindbrain: Part of brain that contains medulla and pons. (p. 84)

histogram: A graph similar to a bar graph that indicates how often a particular score or observation occurs. (p. 510)

homeostasis: The tendency of all organisms to correct imbalances and deviations from their normal state. (p. 134)

hormones: Chemical substances that carry messages through the body in the blood. (p. 93)

human potential movement: An approach to psychotherapy that stresses the actualization of one's unique potentials through personal responsibility, freedom of choice, and authentic relationships. (p. 399)

humanistic psychology: An approach to psychology that stresses the uniqueness of the individual; focuses on the value, dignity, and worth of each person; and holds that healthy living is the result of realizing one's full potential. (p. 281)

hypertension: High levels of blood pressure, which are unhealthful. (p. 176)

hypnosis: A naturally altered state of consciousness resulting from a narrowed focus of attention and characterized by heightened suggestibility. (p. 163)

hypothalamus: A small area located below the thalamus that regulates the autonomic nervous system and motivates behavior such as eating, drinking, and temperature regulation. (p. 95)

hypothesis: An educated guess about the relationship between two variables. (p. 8)

I

id: According to Freud, that part of the unconscious personality that contains our needs, drives, and instincts as well as repressed material. The id strives for immediate satisfaction. (p. 271)

identification: (1) The process by which a child adopts the values and principles of the same-sex parent. (2) The process of seeing oneself as similar to another person or group, and accepting the attitudes of another person or group as one's own. (pp. 207, 460)

identity crisis: According to Erikson, a time of storm and stress during which adolescents worry intensely about who they are. (p. 228)

ideology: The set of principles, attitudes, and defined objectives for which a group stands. (p. 443)

illusions: Perceptions that misrepresent physical stimuli. (p. 126)

image: A mental representation of specific events or objects (the most primitive unit of thought). (p. 69)

implicit personality theory: A set of assumptions each person has about how people behave and what personality traits or characteristics go together. (p. 438)

imprinting: A social learning capacity in some species by which attachments are formed to other organisms or to objects very early in life. (p. 201)

independent variable: In an experiment, the factor that is deliberately manipulated by the experimenters to test its effect on another factor; the cause in a functional relationship of change. (p. 505)

industrial-organizational psychology: The branches of psychology that study the psychology of the workplace. (p. 495)

inferential statistics: Numerical methods used to determine whether research data support a hypothesis or whether results were due to chance. (p. 513)

inferiority complex: According to Adler, a pattern of avoiding feelings of inadequacy and insignificance rather than trying to overcome their source. (p. 276)

initiation rites: Ceremony or ritual in which an individual is admitted to new status or accepted into a new position. (p. 219)

innate: Part of one's biological inheritance. (p. 145)

inoculation effect: A method of developing resistance to persuasion by exposing a person to arguments that challenge his or her beliefs so that he or she can practice defending them. (p. 477)

input: The first stage of information processing—receiving information through the senses. (p. 53)

insight: The sudden realization of the solution to a problem. (pp. 75, 398)

intellectualization: A coping mechanism in which the person analyzes a situation from an emotionally detached viewpoint. (p. 334)

intelligence quotient (IQ): Originally, a measure of a person's mental development obtained by dividing his or her mental age (the score achieved on a standardized intelligence test) by his or her chronological age and multiplying by 100; now, any standardized measure of intelligence based on a scale in which 100 is defined to be average. (p. 296)

interest test: An instrument designed to measure a person's preferences, attitudes, and interests in certain activities. (p. 304)

internalization: The process of incorporating the values, ideas, and standards of others as a part of oneself. (p. 460)

introspection: A method of self-observation in which subjects report on their thoughts and feelings. (p. 11)

introvert: A reserved, withdrawn person who is preoccupied with his or her inner thoughts and feelings. (p. 286)

J

James-Lange theory: A theory formulated by psychologists James and Lange that suggests that emotions result from the perception of bodily changes. (p. 148)

K

kinesthesis: The sense of movement and body position, acquired through receptors located in and near the muscles, tendons, and joints. (p. 119)

L

laissez-faire families: Families in which children have the final say; permissive families. (p. 236)

latency stage: According to Freud, the stage at which sexual desires are pushed into the background and the child becomes involved in exploring the world and learning new skills. (p. 208)

lateral hypothalamus (LH): The part of the hypothalamus that produces hunger signals. (p. 135)

learned helplessness: The condition in which the person suffers from a situation so severely or so often that he or she comes to believe that it is uncontrollable and that any effort to cope will fail. (p. 337)

learning: A lasting change in behavior that results from experience. (p. 23)

lens: A flexible, transparent structure in the eye that changes its shape to focus light on the retina. (p. 115)

lobes: The different regions into which the cerebral cortex is divided. (p. 85)

longitudinal studies: Repeatedly gathering data on the same group of subjects over a period of time for the purpose of studying consistencies and changes. (p. 507)

long-term memory: Information storage that has unlimited capacity and often may last indefinitely. (p. 56)

LSD: An extremely potent psychedelic drug that produces hallucinations and distortions of perception and thought. (p. 171)

M

major depressive disorder: Severe form of depression that interferes with functioning, concentration, and mental and physical well-being. (p. 375)

manic-type reaction: A psychotic reaction characterized by extreme elation, agitation, confusion, disorientation, and incoherence. (p. 375)

marijuana: The dried leaves and flowers of Indian hemp (*Cannabis sativa*) that produces an altered state of consciousness when smoked or ingested. (p. 166)

maturation: The internally programmed growth of a child. (p. 185)

mean: The arithmetic average; a measure of central tendency. (p. 511)

median: The score that divides a distribution of rank-ordered observations in half; the middle score. (p. 511)

meditation: Focusing of attention on an image, thought, bodily process, or external object with the goal of clearing one's mind and producing an "inner peace." (pp. 174, 335)

medulla: Part of brain that controls several important functions including breathing. (p. 84)

memory: The complex mental function of storage and retrieval of what has been learned or experienced. (p. 56)

menarche: The first menstrual period. (p. 223)

menopause: The biological event in which a woman's production of sex hormones is sharply reduced. (p. 246)

message: In the communication process, the actual content transmitted from the source to the audience. (p. 469)

metacognition: The awareness of one's own cognitive processes. (p. 71)

midbrain: Part of brain that integrates sensory information. (p. 84)

mnemonic devices: Methods for remembering items by relating them to information already held in the brain. (p. 68)

mode: The most frequent score in a distribution of observations. (p. 511)

motion parallax: The apparent movement of stationary objects relative to one another that occurs when the observer changes position. Near objects seem to move greater distances than far objects. (p. 124)

multiple personality: A rare condition in which one person shows two or more separate consciousnesses with distinct personalities. (p. 373)

mutual pretense awareness: The situation in which both the medical staff and the patient pretend they do not know that the patient's disease is terminal. (p. 259)

N

naturalistic observation: Studying phenomena as they occur in natural surroundings, without interfering. (p. 506)

negative reinforcement: Increasing the strength of a given response by removing or preventing a painful stimulus when the response occurs. (p. 35)

neurons: The long, thin cells that constitute the structural and functional unit of nerve tissue, along which messages travel to, from, and within the brain. (p. 82)

neutral stimulus: A stimulus that does not initially elicit a response. (p. 24)

nondirected thinking: The free flow of images and ideas, occurring with no particular goal. (p. 70)

nonverbal communication: The process of communicating through the use of space, body language, and facial expression. (p. 434)

normal curve: A symmetrical, bell-shaped curve with known mathematical properties. (p. 510)

norms: (1) Shared standards of behavior accepted by and expected from group members. (2) Standards of comparison for test results developed by giving the test to large, well-defined groups of people. (pp. 295, 443)

O

obedience: A change in attitude or behavior brought about by social pressure to comply with people perceived to be authorities. (p. 481)

object permanence: A child's realization, developed between the ages of one and two, that an object exists even when he or she cannot see or touch it. (p. 191)

objective personality tests: Forced-choice tests (in which a person must select one of several answers) designed to study personal characteristics. (p. 306)

Oedipal conflict: According to Freud, a boy's wish to possess his mother sexually, coupled with hostility toward his father. In order to reduce his or her fear of punishment from the same-sex parent, the child begins to identify with the parent of the same sex. (p. 207)

olfactory nerve: The nerve that carries smell impulses from the nose to the brain. (p. 118)

open awareness: The situation in which the medical staff and patient publicly admit to the knowledge of the patient's terminal disease. (p. 259)

operant conditioning: A form of learning in which a certain action is reinforced or punished, resulting in corresponding increases or decreases in the likelihood that similar actions will occur again. (p. 30)

optic nerve: The nerve that carries impulses from the retina to the brain. (p. 115)

oral stage: According to Freud, the stage at which infants associate erotic pleasure with the mouth. (p. 206)

organism: Rogers's term for the whole person, including all of his or her feelings, thoughts, and urges as well as body. (p. 283)

output: The final stage of information processing—acting on the basis of information. (p. 53)

P

panic disorder: Anxiety that manifests itself in the form of panic attacks. (p. 370)

percentile system: A system for ranking test scores that indicates the ratio of scores lower and higher than a given score. (p. 294)

perception: The organization of sensory information into meaningful experiences. (p. 107)

peripheral nervous system (PNS): Two networks of nerves branching out from the spinal cord that conduct information from the bodily organs to the central nervous system (sensory nerves) and takes information back to the organs (motor nerves). (p. 83)

permissive families: Families in which children have the final say; laissez-faire families. (p. 236)

personality disorder: A wide array of psychological disturbances characterized by lifelong maladaptive patterns that are relatively free of anxiety and other emotional symptoms. (p. 382)

person-centered therapy: A form of therapy aimed at helping individuals recognize their own strengths and gain confidence so they can be true to their own standards and ideas about how to live effectively. (p. 399)

persuasion: The direct attempt to influence attitudes. (p. 469)

phallic stage: According to Freud, the stage at which children associate sexual pleasure with their genitals. (p. 207)

phobia: A form of severe anxiety in which a person focuses on a particular object or situation. (p. 370)

physical proximity: The physical nearness of one person to another person. (p. 428)

physiological: Physical (p. 4)

pitch: The experience associated with a sound's frequency; the "highness" or "lowness" of a sound. (p. 117)

pituitary gland: The center which secretes a large number of hormones to control the endocrine system. (p. 95)

placebo effect: The influence that a patient's hopes and expectations have on his or her improvement during therapy. (p. 395)

polygraph: A machine used to measure physiological changes, particularly in lie detection. (p. 149)

pons: Part of brain that helps coordinate muscles, movements, and a variety of other functions. (p. 84)

population: In psychological research, any group of people, animals, concepts, or events that are alike in at least one respect; the total group of subjects from which a sample is drawn. (p. 504)

positive regard: Rogers's term for viewing oneself in a positive light because of positive feedback received from interaction with others. (p. 283)

posthypnotic suggestion: A suggestion made during a hypnotic trance that influences the subject's behavior after the trance is ended. (p. 164)

post-traumatic stress disorder: Phenomenon in which victims of catastrophes experience again the original event in the form of dreams or flashbacks. (p. 372)

prejudice: Preconceived attitudes toward a person or group that have been formed without sufficient evidence and are not easily changed. (p. 461)

primary reinforcers: Stimuli that are naturally (innately) rewarding, such as food or water. (p. 33)

proactive interference: The hampering of recall of more recently learned material by the recall of previously learned material. (p. 65)

progressive relaxation: Lying down comfortably and tensing and releasing the tension in each major muscle group in turn. (p. 335)

projection: Ascribing one's own undesirable attitudes, feelings, or thoughts to others. (p. 274)

projective personality tests: Unstructured tests of personality in which a person is asked to respond freely, giving his or her own interpretation of various ambiguous stimuli. (p. 306)

psychiatry: A medical specialty that involves the study, diagnosis, and treatment of mental disorders. (p. 15)

psychoanalysis: A form of therapy aimed at making patients aware of their unconscious motives so that they can gain control over their behavior and free themselves of self-defeating patterns. (p. 397)

psychogenic amnesia: A failure to remember past experiences. (p. 373)

psychogenic fugue: Condition in which individuals sometimes assume a new identity. (p. 373)

psychological dependence: Use of a drug to such an extent that a person feels nervous and anxious without it. (p. 383)

psychological needs: In Maslow's hierarchy-of-needs theory, these include the urge to belong and to give and receive love, and the urge to acquire esteem through competence and achievement. If these urges are frustrated, it will be difficult for the person to strive for fulfillment of the next level in the hierarchy—*self-actualization needs*. (p. 143)

psychology: The scientific study of the mental processes and behavior of organisms. (p. 7)

psychophysics: The study of the relationships between sensory experiences and the physical stimuli that cause them. (p. 108)

psychotherapy: A general term for any treatment used by psychiatrists, social workers, or psychologists to help troubled individuals overcome their problems. The goal of psychotherapy is to break the behavior patterns that lead to unhappiness. (p. 393)

puberty: Sexual maturation; it is the biological event that marks the end of childhood. (p. 223)

pupil: The opening in the iris that regulates the amount of light entering the eye. (p. 115)

R

range: A measure of variability; the lowest score in a distribution subtracted from the highest score. (p. 511)

rational-emotive therapy: A form of therapy aimed at changing unrealistic assumptions about oneself and other people. It is believed that once a person understands that he or she has been acting on false beliefs, self-defeating thoughts and behaviors will be avoided. (p. 403)

rationalization: A process whereby an individual seeks to explain an often unpleasant emotion or behavior in a way that will preserve his or her self-esteem. (p. 226)

reaction formation: Replacing an unacceptable feeling or urge with its opposite. (p. 274)

recall: The type of memory retrieval in which a person reconstructs previously learned material. (p. 64)

recognition: The type of memory retrieval in which a person is required to identify an object, idea, or situation as one he or she has or has not experienced before. (p. 63)

recombination: Mentally rearranging the elements of a problem in order to arrive at a novel solution. (p. 73)

referred pain: The sensation of pain in an area away from the actual source; most commonly experienced with internal pain. (p. 120)

regression: A return to an earlier stage of development or pattern of behavior in a threatening or stressful situation. (p. 274)

reinforcement: Immediately following a particular response with a reward in order to strengthen that response. (p. 31)

reliability: The ability of a test to give the same results under similar test conditions. (p. 292)

REM sleep: The period of sleep during which the eyes dart back and forth (rapid eye movement) and dreaming usually occurs. (p. 159)

representational thought: The intellectual ability of a child to picture something in his or her mind. (p. 191)

repression: The exclusion from conscious awareness of a painful, unpleasant, or undesirable memory. (pp. 66, 273)

resistance: The reluctance of a patient either to reveal painful feelings or to examine long-standing behavior patterns. (p. 398)

response chains: Learned reactions that follow one another in sequence, each reaction producing the signal for the next. (p. 41)

resynthesis: The process of combining old ideas with new ones and reorganizing feelings in order to renew one's identity. (p. 355)

retina: The innermost coating of the back of the eye, containing the light-sensitive receptor cells. (p. 115)

retinal disparity: The differences between the images stimulating each eye. (p. 117)

retrieval: The process of obtaining information that has been stored in memory. (p. 63)

retroactive interference: The hampering of recall of learned material by the recall of other material learned more recently. (p. 65)

rods: Receptor cells in the retina that are sensitive to light, but not to color. Rods are particularly useful in night vision. (p. 115)

role taking: An important aspect of children's play that involves assuming adult roles, thus enabling the child to experience different points of view firsthand. (p. 212)

rooting reflex: An infant's response in turning toward the source of touching that occurs anywhere around his or her mouth. (p. 184)

rule: A statement of the relationship between two or more concepts (the most complex unit of thought). (p. 70)

S

sample: The small portion of data, out of the total amount available, that a researcher collects. (p. 504)

scapegoat: A person (or group of people) who becomes the target of another person's displaced anger or aggression. (p. 463)

schemes: Plans for knowing. (p. 189)

schizophrenia: A group of disorders characterized by confused and disconnected thoughts, emotions, and perceptions. (p. 378)

secondary reinforcer: A stimulus that becomes reinforcing through its link with a primary reinforcer. (p. 33)

selective attention: Focusing one's awareness on a limited segment of the total amount of sensory input one is receiving. (p. 54)

self: Rogers's term for one's experience or image of oneself, developed through interaction with others. (p. 283)

self-actualization: The humanist term for realizing one's unique potential. (p. 281)

self-actualization needs: The top of Maslow's hierarchy-of-needs. These include the pursuit of knowledge and beauty, or whatever else is required for the realization of one's unique potential. Before these needs can be satisfied, people must first meet their *fundamental* and *psychological* needs. (p. 143)

self-fulfilling prophecy: A belief, prediction, or expectation that operates to bring about its own fulfillment. (pp. 226, 468, 508)

self-help groups: Groups of individuals that share a problem and meet to discuss it without the active involvement of professional therapists. (p. 408)

self-justification: The need to rationalize one's attitude and behavior. (p. 467)

self-serving bias: Tendency to claim success is due to our efforts while failure is due to circumstances beyond our control. (p. 440)

sensation: What occurs when a stimulus activates a receptor. (p. 107)

sensory storage: Very brief (0–1 seconds) memory storage immediately following initial reception of a stimulus. (p. 56)

separation anxiety: A phase many children experience after twelve months, characterized by fear and anxiety at any prolonged absence of the primary caregiver. (p. 193)

set: A habitual strategy or pattern of problem solving. (p. 71)

sex identity: One's biological inheritance; it includes genetic traits and may include some sex-linked behaviors. (p. 231)

sex role: Defined partly by genetic makeup, but mainly by the society and culture in which the individual lives, it is a description of how a person with a given identity is supposed to behave. (p. 231)

shaping: A technique of operant conditioning in which the desired behavior is "molded" by first rewarding any act similar to that behavior and then requiring closer and closer approximations to the desired behavior before giving the reward. (p. 40)

short-term memory: Memory that is limited in capacity to about seven items and in duration by the subject's active rehearsal. (p. 56)

signal-detection theory: A summary of mathematical relationships between motivation, sensitivity, and sensation. (p. 114)

situational test: A simulation of a real event designed to measure a person's performance under such circumstances. (p. 308)

sleeper effect: The delayed impact on attitude change of a persuasive communication. (p. 475)

social functions: In groups, those responses directed toward satisfying the emotional needs of members. (p. 442)

social learning theory: Bandura's view of human development, emphasizing interaction. (p. 229)

social rules: Agreements among members of a society about how members should act in particular situations; also called *norms*. (p. 436)

social support: Information that leads someone to believe that he or she is cared for, loved, respected, and part of a network of communication and mutual obligation. (p. 331)

socialization: The process of learning the rules of behavior of the culture within which an individual is born and will live. (p. 205)

sociobiology: The study of the biological basis of social behavior. (p. 98)

sociogram: A diagram representing relationships within a group, especially likes and dislikes of members for other members. (p. 444)

somatic nervous system: The half of the peripheral nervous system that controls sensory and motor aspects of voluntary movement of skeletal muscles. (p. 83)

somatoform disorder: A mental disorder marked by physical symptoms for which there is no apparent physical cause. (p. 372)

source: In the communication process, the person or group from which a message originates. (p. 469)

species-specific behaviors: Responses that are characteristic of a particular animal species. (p. 97)

spermarche: Period during which males achieve first ejaculation. (p. 223)

spinal cord: The bundle of nerves that run down the length of the back and transmit most messages back and forth between the body and the brain. (p. 83)

sports psychology: The branch of psychology that studies athletics and athletic performance. (p. 495)

stagnation: According to Erikson, a discontinuation of development and a desire to recapture the past, characteristic of some middle-aged people. (p. 251)

standard deviation: A measure of variability that describes an average distance of every score from the mean of the scores. (p. 512)

statistics: The branch of mathematics concerned with summarizing and making meaningful inferences from collections of data. (p. 509)

stereopsis: The use by the visual system of retinal disparity to give depth information—providing a three-dimensional appearance to the world. (p. 117)

stereotype: A set of assumptions about people in a given category often based on half-truths and non-truths. (p. 439)

stimulation value: The ability of a person or subject to interest or to expose you to new ideas and experiences. (p. 429)

527

stress: A person's perception of his or her inability to cope with a certain tense event or situation. (p. 317)

stressor: A stress-producing event or situation. (p. 317)

stress reaction: The body's response to a stressor. (p. 317)

sublimation: The process of redirecting sexual impulses into learning tasks that begins at about the age of five. (p. 208)

subliminal advertising: Attempt to influence people with messages that are below normal thresholds of detection. (p. 109)

superego: According to Freud, the process of the personality that inhibits the socially undesirable impulses of the id. The superego may cause excessive guilt if it is overly harsh. (p. 272)

survey: Sampling of data, obtained through interviews and questionnaires. (p. 506)

suspected awareness: The situation in which some patients begin to sense that their illness is terminal and endeavor to find out from a medical staff or from their families whether their suspicions are true. (p. 259)

symbol: An abstract unit of thought that represents an object, event, or quality. (p. 69)

synapses: The gaps between individual nerve cells. (p. 82)

systematic desensitization: A technique used by behavior therapists to help a patient overcome irrational fears and anxieties. The goal is to teach the person to relax so that he or she will not feel anxious in the presence of feared objects. (p. 405)

T

task functions: In groups, those functions directed toward getting a job done. (p. 442)

telegraphic speech: The kind of verbal utterances offered by young children. Words are left out, but the meaning is usually still clear. (p. 200)

thalamus: The portion of the brain that sorts incoming impulses and directs them to various parts of the brain. It also relays messages from one part of the brain to another. (p. 86)

thanatology: The study of death and dying. (p. 259)

thyroid gland: The part of the endocrine system that produces several hormones, including thyroxin. (p. 95)

token economy: A form of conditioning in which desirable behavior is reinforced with valueless objects or points, which can be accumulated and exchanged for various rewards. (p. 46)

tolerance: Physical adaptation to a drug, so that a person needs an increased dosage in order to produce the original effect. (p. 384)

trait: A tendency to react to a situation in a way that remains stable over time. (p. 284)

transactional analysis: A form of therapy aimed at helping clients become more flexible by discovering the scripts they play and replay in their lives. (p. 402)

transfer: The effects of past learning on the ability to learn new tasks. (p. 37)

transference: The process, experienced by the patient, of feeling toward an analyst or therapist the way he or she feels or felt toward some other important figure in his or her life. (p. 398)

U

unconditional positive regard: In person-centered therapy, the atmosphere of emotional support provided by the therapist. The therapist shows the person or client he or she accepts anything the person says and does not become embarrassed or angry. (pp. 284, 401)

unconditioned response (UCR): In classical conditioning, an organism's automatic (or natural) reaction to a stimulus. (p. 24)

unconditioned stimulus (UCS): An event that elicits a certain predictable response without previous training. (p. 24)

unconscious: According to Freud, the part of the mind that contains material we are unaware of, but that strongly influences conscious processes and behaviors. (p. 270)

utility value: The ability of a person or subject to help another achieve his or her goals. (p. 429)

V

validity: The ability of a test to measure what it is intended to measure; verifying a theory. (pp. 293, 504)

variable: In an experimental situation, any factor that is capable of change. (p. 505)

variable-interval schedule: A schedule of reinforcement in which changing amounts of time must elapse before a response will obtain reinforcement each time. (p. 32)

variable-ratio schedule: A schedule of reinforcement in which a different number of responses are required before reinforcement can be obtained each time. (p. 31)

variance: Difference or variation. (p. 511)

ventromedial hypothalamus (VMH): The part of the hypothalamus that causes one to stop eating. (p. 135)

vestibular system: Three semicircular canals located in the inner ear and connected to the brain by the vestibular nerve. They provide the sense of balance. (p. 119)

visualization: Mentally rehearsing the steps involved in a successful performance or process. (p. 495)

W

Weber's law: The principle that the larger or stronger a stimulus, the larger the change required for an observer to notice a difference. (p. 111)

withdrawal: The symptoms that occur after a person discontinues the use of a drug to which he or she had become addicted. (p. 384)

Bibliography

A

AARONSON, B., AND OSMOND, H. *Psychedelics: The Uses and Implications of Hallucinogenic Drugs*. Garden City, NY: Doubleday, 1970.

ABRAMSON, L. Y., SELIGMAN, M., AND TEASDALE, J. D. "Learned Helplessness in Humans: Critique and Reformulation." *Journal of Abnormal Psychology*, 87 (1978): 49–74.

ABSE, D. W. *Hysteria and Related Mental Disorders*. Baltimore: Williams & Wilkins, 1966.

ADAMS, J. A. *Human Memory*. New York: McGraw-Hill, 1967.

ADLER, A. *What Life Should Mean to You*. New York: Putnam, 1959 (paper).

AHRENS, R. "Beitrag zur Entwicklung des Physiognomie-und Mimikerkennens." *Z. exp. angew. Psychol.*, 2 (1954): 412–454.

ALEXANDER, C. N., RAINFORTH, M. V., AND GELDERLOOS, P. "Transcendental Meditation, Self-actualization, and Psychological Health: A Conceptual Overview and Statistical Meta-analysis." *Journal of Social Behavior and Personality*, 6 (1991): 189–247.

ALLGEIER, A. R. "Sexuality and Gender Roles in the Second Half of Life." In *Changing Boundaries*, ed. by Allgeier and N. McCormick. Palo Alto, CA: Mayfield, 1983.

ALLPORT, G. *Personality: A Psychological Interpretation*. New York: Henry Holt, 1937.

_____. *The Nature of Prejudice*. Garden City, NY: Doubleday, 1954 (paper).

_____. *Pattern and Growth in Personality*. New York: Holt, Rinehart and Winston, 1961.

_____(ED.). *Letters from Jenny*. New York: Harcourt, Brace & World, 1965.

ALVAREZ, A. *The Savage God: A Study of Suicide*. New York: Random House, 1970.

AMERICAN ENTERPRISE INSTITUTE FOR PUBLIC POLICY RESEARCH. *Public Opinion*, 6, 34, Survey by the Roper Organization (Roper Report 83–5), April 23–30, 1983; reported in F. P. Price, *Intimate Relationships, Marriages, and Families*, 2nd ed. Mountain View, CA: Mayfield Publishing Company, 1993.

AMERICAN LAW INSTITUTE. *Model Penal Code: Proposed Official Draft*. Philadelphia: American Law Institute, 1962.

AMERICAN PSYCHIATRIC ASSOCIATION. *Diagnostic and Statistical Manual of Mental Disorders*. 2nd ed. Washington, D.C.: American Psychiatric Association, 1968.

AMERICAN PSYCHOLOGICAL ASSOCIATION. *1993 Profile of APA Membership*. Washington, D.C.: Author (Office of Demographic, Employment and Educational Research), 1993.

ANASTASI, A. *Psychological Testing*. 3rd ed. New York: Macmillan, 1968.

ANDERSON, A. "How the Mind Heals." *Psychology Today*, 16 (December 1982): 51–56.

ANGOFF, W. H., AND DYER, H. S. "The Admissions Testing Program." In *The College Boards Admissions Testing Program*, ed. by W. H. Angoff. New York: College Entrance Examination Board, 1971, pp. 1–13.

ANTHONY, J. "The Reactions of Adults to Adolescents and Their Behavior." In *Adolescence: Psychological Perspectives*, ed. by G. Caplan and S. Lebovici. New York: Basic Books, 1969.

ARIETI, S. (ED.) *American Handbook of Psychology*. 3 vols. New York: Basic Books, 1959.

ARKOFF, A. *Adjustment and Mental Health*. New York: McGraw-Hill, 1968.

ARNHEIM, R. *Art and Visual Perception: A Psychology of the Creative Eye*. Berkeley: University of California Press, 1974.

ARONSON, E., AND LINDER, D. "Gain and Loss of Esteem as Determinants of Interpersonal Attractiveness." *Journal of Experimental Social Psychology*, 1 (1965): 156–171.

_____, TURNER, J., AND CARLSMITH, M. "Communicator Credibility and Communicator Discrepancy as Determinants of Opinion Change." *Journal of Abnormal and Social Psychology*, 67 (1963): 31–36.

___, ET AL. "Busing and Racial Tension: The Jigsaw Route to Learning and Liking." *Psychology Today*, 9 (February 1975): 43–50.

ASCH, S. *Social Psychology*. New York: Prentice-Hall, 1952.

_____. "Effects of Group Pressure upon the Modification and Distortion of Judgments." In *Basic Studies in Social Psychology*, ed. by J. Proshansky and B. Seidenberg. New York: Holt, Rinehart and Winston, 1965, pp. 393–401.

ASH, P., AND KROEKER, L. P. "Personnel Selection, Classification, and Placement." In *Annual Review of Psychology*. Palo Alto, CA: Annual Reviews, 1975, pp. 481–507.

ATKINSON, J. W. (ED.). *Motives in Fantasy, Action, and Society*. New York: Van Nostrand Reinhold, 1958.

AVERILL, J. "Studies on Anger and Aggression: Implications for Theories of Emotion." *American Psychologist*, 38 (1983): 1145–1160.

AXSOM, D., YATES, S., AND CHAIKEN, S. "Audience Response as a Heuristic Cue in Persuasion." *Journal of Personality and Social Psychology*, 53 (1987): 30–40.

B

BACHRACH, A. J. *Psychological Research: An Introduction*. 2nd ed. New York: Random House, 1965.

BACK, K. W. *Beyond Words: The Story of Sensitivity Training and the Encounter Movement*. New York: Basic Books, 1972.

BAILLERGEON, R., GRABER, M., DECOPS, J., AND BLACK, J. "Why Do Young Infants Fail to Search for Hidden Objects?" *Cognition*, 36 (1990): 255–284.

BALDWIN, A. A. *Theories of Child Development*. New York: Wiley, 1967.

BALTES, P. B., AND SCHAIE, K. W. "Aging and IQ—The Myth of the Twilight Years." In *Readings in Aging and Death: Contemporary Perspectives*, ed. by S. H. Zarit, New York: Harper & Row, 1977.

BALTRUSCH, H. J., STANGEL, W., AND TITZE, I. "Stress, Cancer, and Immunity: New Developments in Biopsychosocial and Psychoneuroimmunologic Research." *Acta Neurologica*, 13 (1991): 315–327.

BANDURA, A. "The Stormy Decade: Fact or Fiction?" *Psychology in the Schools*, 1 (1964): 224–231.

_____. "Influence of Models' Reinforcement Contingencies on the Acquisition of Imitative Responses." *Journal of Personality and Social Psychology*, 1 (1965): 589–595.

_____. "Analysis of Modeling Processes." In *Psychological Modeling: Conflicting Theories*, ed. by A. Bandura. Chicago: Aldine-Atherton, 1971, pp. 1–62.

_____. "The Psychology of Chance Encounters and Life Paths." *American Psychologist*, 37 (1982): 747–755.

_____. *Social Foundations of Thought and Action: A Social Cognitive Theory*. Englewood Cliffs, NJ: Prentice-Hall, 1986.

_____, AND WALTERS, R. H. *Social Learning and Personality Development*. New York: Holt, Rinehart and Winston, 1963.

BARBER, T. X. "Measuring 'Hypnoticlike' Suggestibility with and Without 'Hypnotic Induction': Psychometric Properties, Norms, and Variables Influencing Response to the Barber Suggestibility Scale (BSS)." *Psychological Reports*, 16 (1965): 809–844.

BARD, P. "On Emotional Expression After Decortication with Some Remarks of Certain Theoretical Views: Part I." *Psychological Review*, 41 (1934), 309–329, "Part II," 41 (1934), 424–449.

BARON, R. A., AND BYRNE, D. *Social Psychology: Understanding Human Interaction*, 6th ed. Boston: Allyn and Bacon, 1991.

BARROW, G. M., AND SMITH, P. A. *Aging, Ageism and Society*. St. Paul, MN: West Publishing Co., 1979.

BASS, B. M. *Stogdill's Handbook of Leadership: A Survey of Theory and Research*, Rev. ed. New York: Free Press, 1981.

BAUM, A., AND VALINS, S. *Architecture and Social Behavior*. Hillsdale, N.J.: Lawrence Erlbaum Associates, 1977.

BAUMRIND, D. "Current Patterns of Parental Authority." *Developmental Psychology Monographs*, 4 (1971): 1, Pt. 2.

BECK, A. T. *Depression: Causes and Treatment*. Philadelphia: University of Pennsylvania Press, 1967.

_____. "Cognitive Therapy: Nature and Relation to Behavior Therapy." *Behavior Therapy*, 1 (1970): 184–200.

BEEBE-CENTER, J. G. "Standards for the Use of Gust Scale." *Journal of Psychology*, 28 (1949): 411–419.

BELSKY, J. "The Determinants of Parenting: A Process Model." *Child Development*, 55 (1984): 83–96.

BEM, D. J. *Beliefs, Attitudes and Human Affairs*. Belmont, CA.: Brooks/Cole, 1970.

BEM. S. L. "Androgyny vs. the Little Lives of Fluffy Women and Chesty Men." *Psychology Today*, 8 (September 1975): 59–62.

_____. "Gender Schema Theory: A Cognitive Account of Sex Typing." *Psychological Review*, 88 (1981): 354–364.

_____. "Androgyny and Gender Schema Theory: A Conceptual and Empirical Integration." In *Nebraska Symposium on Motivation: Psychology and Gender*, ed. by T. B. Sonderegger. Lincoln, NE: University of Nebraska Press, (1985): 179–266.

_____. *The Lenses of Gender: Transforming the Debate on Sexual Inequality*. New Haven, CT: Yale University Press, 1993.

BENSON, H. *The Relaxation Response*. New York: Avon, 1975.

_____, AND WALLACE, R. K. "Decreased Drug Abuse with Transcendental Meditation: A Study of 1862 Subjects." In *Drug Abuse: Proceedings of the International Conference*, ed. by C. J. D. Arafonetis. Philadelphia: Lea & Febiger, 1972.

BERGER, K. S. *The Developing Person through the Life Span*, 3rd ed. New York: Worth Publishers, 1994.

BERGIN, A. E. "The Evaluation of Therapeutic Outcomes." In *Handbook of Psychotherapy and Behavior Change: An Empirical Analysis*, ed. by A. E. Bergin and S. L. Garfield. New York: Wiley, 1971.

BERKOWITZ, L. *Aggression: A Social Psychological Analysis*. New York: McGraw-Hill Book Company, 1962.

BERNARD, J. *The Future of Marriage*. New York: Bantam, 1973.

BERNE, E. *Games People Play*. New York: Grove Press, 1964.

_____, AND WALSTER, A. "A Little Bit of Love." In *Foundations of Interpersonal Attraction*, ed. by T. L. Huston. New York: Academic Press, 1974.

BERRY, L. M., AND HOUSTON, J. P. *Psychology at Work: An Introduction to Industrial and Organizational Psychology*. Madison, WI: WCBrown and Benchmark Publishers, 1993.

BERSHEID, E. "Emotion." In *Close Relationships*, ed. by H. H. Kelley. New York: Freeman, 1983.

_____. "Physical Attractiveness." In *Advances in Experimental Social Psychology*, ed. by Leonard Berkowitz. New York: Academic Press, 1974.

_____. *Interpersonal Attraction*. 2nd ed. Reading, MA: Addison-Wesley, 1978.

BINDER, A., GEIS, G., AND BRUCE, D. *Juvenile Delinquency: Historical, Cultural, and Legal Perspectives*. New York: Macmillan, 1988.

BISCHOF, L. *Adult Psychology*. New York: Harper & Row, 1969.

BLAKE, R. R. AND MCCANSE, A. A. *Leadership Dilemmas—Grid Solutions*. Houston, TX: Gulf Publishing Company, 1991.

_____, AND MOUTON, J. S. *The Managerial Grid III: The Key to Leadership Excellence*, 3rd ed. Houston, TX: Gulf Publishing Company, 1985.

BLATT, S. J., D'AFFLITTI, J. P., AND QUINLAN, D.M. "Experiences of Depression in Normal Young Adults." In *Journal of Abnormal Psychology*, 85 (1976): 383–389.

BLOWERS, G. H., AND TURTLE, A. M. *Psychology Moving East: The Status of Western Philosophy in Asia*. Boulder, CO: Westview Press, 1987.

BOOTH-KEWLEY, S. AND FRIEDMAN, H. S. "Psychological Predictors of Heart Disease: A Quantitative Review." *Psychological Bulletin*, 101 (1987): 343–362.

BORNSTEIN, R. F. "Subliminal Techniques as Propaganda Tools; Review and Critique." *Journal of Mind and Behavior*, 10 (1989): 231–262.

BOUCHARD, T. J., JR., AND MCGUE, M. "Familial Studies of Intelligence: A Review." *Science*, 212 (1981): 1055–1059.

BOWER, G. "Mood and Memory." *American Psychologist*, 36 (1981): 129–148.

BOWLBY, J. "Separation Anxiety: A Critical Review of the Literature." *Journal of Child Psychology and Psychiatry*, 1 (1960–1961): 251–269.

_____. *Child Care and Growth of Love*. 2nd ed. Baltimore: Penguin, 1965.

BOYD, J., AND WEISSMAN, M. "The Epidemiology of Psychiatric Disorders of Middle Age: Depression, Alcoholism, and Suicide." In *Modern Perspectives in the Psychiatry of Middle Age*, ed. by J. G. Howels. New York: Brunner/Mazel, 1981.

BRADY, J. V. "Ulcers in 'Executive' Monkeys." *Scientific American*, 199 (October 1958): 95–100.

BREAN, H. "Hidden Sell Technique Almost Here." *Life* (March 31, 1958): 102–114.

BRECHER, E. M. *The Sex Researchers*. New York: American Library, 1971.

_____, AND THE EDITORS OF *Consumer Reports*. *Licit and Illicit Drugs*. Boston: Little, Brown, 1972.

BRETT, J. F., BRIEF, A. P., BURKE, M. J., GEORGE, J. M., AND WEBSTER, J. "Negative Affectivity and the Reporting of Stressful Life Events." *Health Psychology*, 9 (1990): 57–68.

BRITTAIN, C. V. "Adolescent Choices and Parent-Peer Cross Pressures." *American Sociological Review*, 28 (1963): 385–391.

_____. "A Comparison of Urban and Rural Adolescence with Respect to Peer Versus Parent Compliance." *Adolescence*, 4 (1969): 59–68.

BROWN, B. S., WIENCKOWSKI, L. A., AND BIVENS, L. W. *Psychosurgery: Perspectives on a Current Issue*. Washington, D.C.: U.S. Department of Health, Education, and Welfare, Public Health Service, 1973.

BROWN, R. *A First Language: The Early Stages*. Cambridge, MA: Harvard University Press, 1973.

BRUNER, J. S., GOODNOW, J. J., AND AUSTIN, G. A. *A Study of Thinking*. New York: Wiley, 1956 (paper).

BUCK, L., AND AXEL, R. "A Novel Multigene Family may Encode Odorant Receptors: A Molecular Basis for Odor Recognition." *Cell*, 65 (1991): 175–187.

BUDZYNSKI, T. H., ET AL. "EMG Biofeedback and Tension Headache: A Controlled Outcome Study." *Psychosomatic Medicine*, 35 (1973): 484–496.

BUEHLER, R. E., PATTERSON, G. R., AND FURNESS, R. M. "The Reinforcement of Behavior in Institutional Settings." *Behavior Research and Therapy*, 4 (1966): 157–167.

BUKATKO, D., AND DAEHLER, M. W. *Child Development: A Topical Approach*. Boston: Houghton-Mifflin Company, 1992.

BURKE, R. J., AND WEIR, T. "Marital Helping Relationships: The Moderators Between Stress and Well-Being." *The Journal of Psychology*, 95 (1977): 121–130.

BUSS, D. M. "Human Mate Selection." *American Scientist*, 73 (1985): 47–51.

BUTLER, R. N. "Psychiatric Evaluation of the Aged." *Geriatrics*, 18 (1963): 220–232.

_____. "Successful Aging and the Role of the Life Review." *Journal of the American Geriatrics Society*, 1974.

_____, AND LEWIS, M. I. *Aging and Mental Health: Positive Psychosocial Approaches*. St. Louis: Mosby, 1973.

BUTTERFIELD-PICARD, H., AND MAGNO, J. "Hospice, The Adjective Not the Noun: The Future of National Priority." *American Psychologist*, 37 (1982): 1254–1259.

C

CAMPBELL, D. P. *Manual for the Strong-Campbell Interest Inventory T325* (merged form). Stanford, CA: Stanford University Press, 1977.

CANN, A., SHERMAN, S. J ., AND ELKES, R. "Effects of Initial Request Size and Timing of a Second Request on Compliance: The Foot-in-the-door and the Door-in-the-face." *Journal of Personality and Social Psychology*, 32 (1975): 774–782.

CAPLAN, G. *Principles of Preventive Psychiatry*. New York: Basic Books, 1965.

CAPLAN, R. D., COBB, S. FRENCH, J. R. P., VANHARRISON, R., AND PINNEAU, R. *Job Demands and Worker Health: Main Effects and Occupational Differences*. Washington, D.C.: National Institute for Occupational Safety and Health, 1975.

CAREY, S. "The Child as Word Learner." In *Language Theory and Psychological Reality*, ed. by M. Halle, J. Bresnan, J., and G. A. Miller. Cambridge, MA: MIT Press, 1978.

CARLSSON, A. "The Current Status of the Dopamine Hypothesis of Schizophrenia." *Neuropsychopharmacology*, 1 (1988): 179–186.

CARRINGTON, P. *Releasing: The New Behavioral Science Method for Dealing With Pressure Situations*. New York: William Morrow and Company, Inc., 1984.

CARSON, R. C. AND BUTCHER, J. N. *Abnormal Psychology and Modern Life*, 9th ed. New York: Harper Collins Publishers, 1992.

_____, AND SANISLOW, C. A., III. "The Schizophrenias." In *Comprehensive Handbook of Psychopathology*, 2nd ed., ed. by H. E. Adams and P. B. Surkur. New York: Plenum, 1992.

CARSTEN, J. M. AND SPECTOR, P. E. "Unemployment, Job Satisfaction, and Employee Turnover: A Meta-analytic Test of the Muchinsky Model." *Journal of Applied Psychology*, 72 (1987): 374–381.

CARTER, E. A., AND MCGOLDRICK, M. "Overview: The Changing Family Life Cycle—A Framework for Family Therapy." In *The Changing Family Cycle: A Framework for Family Therapy*, 2nd ed., ed. by E. A. Carter and M. McGoldrick. New York: Gardner Press, 1988.

CECI, S. J. "How Much Does Schooling Influence General Intelligence and its Cognitive Components? A Reassessment of the Evidence." *Developmental Psychology*, 27 (1991): 703–722.

CENTERS FOR DISEASE CONTROL. "Premarital Sexual Experiences among Adolescent Women—United States, 1970–1988." *Morbidity and Mortality Weekly Report*, 39 (January 4, 1991): 929–932.

CENTERS FOR DISEASE CONTROL. "Sexual Behavior among High School Students—United States, 1990." *Morbidity and Mortality Weekly Report*, 40 (January 3, 1992): 885–888.

CHAIKEN, S. "The Heuristic Model of Persuasion." In M. P. Zanna, J. M. Olson, and C. P. Herman (Eds.), Social Influence: The Ontario symposium (Vol 5) 1987: pp. 3–39. Hillsdale, NJ: Lawrence A. Eribaum.

CHAMBERLAIN, K., AND ZIKA, S. "The Minor Events Approach to Stress: Support for the Use of Daily Hassles." *British Journal of Psychology*, 81 (1990): 469–481.

CHANCE, P. "Telepathy Could Be Real." *Psychology Today*, 9 (February 1976): 40–44, 65.

CHAND, I. P., CRIDER, D. M., AND WILLETS, F. K. "Parent-Youth Disagreement as Perceived by Youth: A Longitudinal Study." *Youth and Society*, 6 (1975): 365–375.

CHERRY, F., AND DEAUX, K. "Fear of Success Versus Fear of Gender-Inappropriate Behavior." *Sex Roles*, 4 (1978): 97–102.

CHILMAN, C. S. *Adolescent Sexuality in a Changing American Society*, 2nd ed. New York: John Wiley and Sons, 1983.

CHUKOVSKY, K. *From Two To Five*. Berkeley: University of California Press, 1963.

CLARE, A. *Psychiatry in Dissent: Controversial Issues in Thought and Practice*. Philadelphia: Institute for the Study of Human Issues, 1979.

CLARKE-STEWART, K. A. "Infant Day Care: Maligned or Malignant?" *American Psychologist*, 44 (1989): 266–273.

COALE, A. J. "The Demographic Transition Reconsidered." In *International Population Conference*, Liège, 1973.

COBB, S. "Social Support as a Moderator of Life Stress." *Psychosomatic Medicine*, 38 (September-October 1976): 300–314.

_____, AND ROSE, R. "Hypertension, Peptic Ulcers, and Diabetes in Air Traffic Controllers." *Journal of the American Medical Association*, 224 (1973): 489–492.

COCH, L., AND FRENCH, J. R. P., JR. "Overcoming Resistance to Change." *Human Relations*, 1 (1948): 512–532.

COFER, C. N. *Motivation and Emotions*. Glenview, IL: Scott, Foresman, 1972.

COHEN, A. R. *Attitude Change and Social Influence*. New York: Basic Books, 1964.

COHEN, H., AND FILIPCZAK, J. *A New Learning Environment*. San Francisco: Jossey-Bass, 1971.

COHEN, S. "Psychosocial Models of the Role of Social Support in the Etiology of Physical Disease." *Health Psychology*, 7 (1988): 269–297.

COHEN, S., GLASS, D., AND SINGER, J. "Apartment Noises, Auditory Discrimination and Reading Ability in Children." *Journal of Experimental Social Psychology*, 9 (1973): 407–422.

_____, TYRRELL, D. A., AND SMITH, A. P. "Psychological Stress and Susceptibility to the Common Cold." *New England Journal of Medicine*, 325 (1991): 606–612.

COLBY, A., KOHLBERG, L., GIBBS, J., AND LIEBERMAN, M. "A Longitudinal Study of Moral Judgment." *Monographs of the Society for Research in Child Development*, 48 (1983): 1–124.

COLE, J. O. "Phenothiazine Treatment in Acute Schizophrenia: Effectiveness." *Archives of General Psychiatry*, 10 (1964): 246–261.

COLEMAN, J. C. *Abnormal Psychology and Modern Life*. 5th ed. Glenview, IL: Scott, Foresman, 1976.

_____. *Contemporary Psychology and Effective Behavior*. 4th ed. Glenview, IL: Scott, Foresman, 1979.

COLEMAN, J. S. *The Adolescent Society*. New York: Free Press, 1961.

COLES, R. "Life in Appalachia: The Case of Hugh McCaslin." *Life at the Bottom*, ed. by G. Armstrong. New York: Bantam, 1971, pp. 26–42.

CONGER, J. J. *Adolescence and Youth: Psychological Development in a Changing World*. New York: Harper & Row, 1973.

CORDER, E. H., SAUNDERS, A. M., STRITTMATTER, W. J., SCHMECHEL, D. E., GASKELL, P. C., SMALL, G. W., ROSES, A. D., HAINES, J. L., AND PERICAK-VANCE, M. A. "Gene Dose of Apolioprotein E Type 4 Allele and the Risk of Alzheimer's Disease in Late Onset Families." *Science*, 261: 921–923.

CORSINI, R. J. (ED.). *Current Psychotherapies*. Itasca, IL: Peacock, 1973.

COSTA, P. T., JR., MCCRAE, R. R., AND DYE, D. A. "Facet Scales for Agreeableness and Conscientiousness: A Revision of the NEO Personality Inventory." *Personality and Individual Differences*, 12 (1991): 887–898.

COUTTS, L. M. "The Organizational Psychologist." In *Applied Psychology: Variety and Opportunity*, ed. by R. Gifford. Boston: Allyn and Bacon, 1991.

CRONBACH, L. J. *Essentials of Psychological Testing*. 3rd ed. New York: Harper & Row, 1970.

CULLITON, B. J. "Psychosurgery: National Commission Issues Surprisingly Favorable Report." *Science*, 194 (1976): 299–301.

D

DACEY, J. S. *Adolescents Today*. Santa Monica, CA: Goodyear, 1979.

DAMON, W. *Social and Personality Development*. New York: Norton, 1983.

DARLEY, J. M., AND LATANÉ, B. "Bystander Intervention in Emergencies: Diffusion of Responsibility." *Journal of Personality and Social Psychology*, 8 (1968): 377–383.

DARWIN, C. *The Expression of Emotions in Man and Animals*. Chicago: University of Chicago Press, 1967; originally published in 1872.

DASEN, P. R., AND HERON, A. "Cross-Cultural Tests of Piaget's Theory." In *Handbook of Cross-Cultural Psychology*. Vol. 4: Developmental Psychology, ed. by H. Triandis. Boston: Allyn and Bacon, 1981.

DAVIS, A. "Socio-Economic Influences upon Children's Learning." *Understanding the Child*, 20 (1951): 10–16.

DAVIS, J. M., SCHAFFER, C. B., KILLIAN, G. A., KINARD, C., AND CHAN, C. "Important Issues in the Drug Treatment of Schizophrenia." *Schizophrenia Bulletin*, 6 (1980): 70–87.

DAVIS, K. "Near and Dear. Friendship and Love Compared." *Psychology Today*, 19 (February 1985): 22–30.

DE BONO, E. *New Think: The Use of Lateral Thinking in the Generation of New Ideas*. New York: Basic Books, 1968.

DECI, E. L. "Effects of Externally Mediated Rewards on Intrinsic Motivation." *Journal of Personality and Social Psychology*, 18 (1971): 105–115.

_____, AND RYAN, R. M. "The Support of Autonomy and the Control of Behavior." *Journal of Personality and Social Psychology*, 53 (1987): 1024–1037.

DEIKMAN, A. J. "Experimental Meditation." *Journal of Nervous and Mental Disease*, 136 (1963): 329–373.

DELGADO, J. M. R. *Physical Control of the Mind*. New York: Harper & Row, 1969.

DELONGIS, A., FOLKMAN, S., AND LAZARUS, R. S. "The Impact of Daily Stress on Health and Mood: Psychological and Social Resources as Mediators." *Journal of Personality and Social Psychology*, 54 (1988): 486–495.

DEMENT, W. *Some Must Watch While Some Must Sleep*. New York: Norton, 1976.

_____, AND WOLPERT, E. "Relation of Eye Movements, Bodily Mobility, and External Stimuli to Dream Content." *Journal of Experimental Psychology*, 55 (1958): 543–553.

DENNIS, W. "Creative Productivity Between the Ages of Twenty and Eighty Years." *Journal of Gerontology*, 21 (1966): 1–8.

DENNIS, W. "Causes of Retardation Among Institutional Children: Iran." *Journal of Genetic Psychology*, 96 (1960): 47–59.

DEUTSCH, A. R. *How to Hold Your Job: Gaining Skills and Becoming Promotable in Difficult Times*. Englewood Cliffs, NJ: Prentice-Hall, 1984.

DEUTSCH, M., AND COLLINS, M. *Interracial Housing: A Psychological Evaluation of a Social Experiment*. Minneapolis: University of Minnesota Press, 1951.

DEVINE, P. G. "Stereotypes and Prejudice: Their Automatic and Controlled Components." *Journal of Personality and Social Psychology*, 56 (1989): 5–18

DIAMOND, A. "Development of the Ability to Use Recall to Guide Action, as Indicated by Infants' Performance on AB." *Child Development*, 56 (1985): 868–883.

DICHTER, E. *Handbook of Consumer Motivations*. New York: McGraw-Hill, 1964.

DILLBECK, M. C., AND ORME-JOHNSON, D. W. "Physiological Differences Between Transcendental Meditation and Rest." *American Psychologist*, 42 (1987): 879–881.

DION, K. L., BERSCHEID, E., AND WALSTER, E. "What Is Beautiful Is Good." *Journal of Personality and Social Psychology*, 24 (1972): 285–290.

DODGE, K. "Behavioral Antecedents of Peer Social Status." *Child Development*, 54 (1983): 1386–1389.

DOWNS, A. C. "The Social Biological Constraints of Social Competency." In *Developing Social Competency in Adolescence*, ed. by T. P. Gullotta, G. R. Adams, and R. R. Montemayor. Newbury Park, CA: Sage, 1990.

DUBAS, J. S., GRABER, J. A., AND PETERSEN, A. C. "A Longitudinal Investigation of Adolescents' Changing Perceptions of Pubertal Timing." *Developmental Psychology*, 27 (1991): 580–589.

DU BOIS, P. H. "Review of Scholastic Aptitude Test." In *The Seventh Mental Measurements Yearbook*, ed. by O.K. Buros. Highland Park, N.J.: Gryphon Press, 1972, pp. 646–648.

DUNCKER, K. "On Problem Solving." Trans. by L. S. Lees. *Psychological Monographs*, 58, no. 270 (1945).

_____. *The Mechanism of the Mind*. New York: Simon & Schuster, 1969.

DUNPHY, D. "The Social Structure of Urban Adolescent Peer Groups." *Sociometry*, 26 (1963): 230–246.

DURKIN, J. "The Sports Psychologist." In *Applied Psychology: Variety and Opportunity*, ed. by R. Gifford, Boston: Allyn and Bacon, 1991.

DUTTON, D. G., AND ARON, A. P. "Some Evidence for Heightened Sexual Arousal under Conditions of High Anxiety." *Journal of Personality and Social Psychology*, 30 (1974): 510–517.

DWYER, J., AND MAYER, J. "Psychological Effects of Variations in Physical Appearance During Adolescence." *Adolescence* (1968–1969): 353–368.

E

EDWARDS, J. N., AND BRAUBURGER, M. B. "Exchange and Parent-Youth Conflict." *Journal of Marriage and the Family*, 35 (1973): 101–107.

EKMAN, P., FRIESEN, W. V., AND ELLSWORTH, P. *Emotion in the Human Face: Guidelines for Research and an Integration of Findings*. Elmsford, N.Y.: Pergamon, 1972.

ELDERSVELD, S., AND DODGE, R. "Personal Contact or Mail Propaganda? An Experiment in Voting Turnout and Attitude Change." In *Public Opinion and Propaganda*, ed. by D. Katz, *et al*. New York: Dryden Press, 1954, pp. 532–542.

ELKIN, I., ET AL. "National Institute of Mental Health Treatment of Depression Collaborative Research Program: General Effectiveness of Treatments." *Archives of General Psychiatry*, 46 (1989): 971–982.

ELKIND, D. "Egocentrism Redux." *Developmental Review*, 5 (1985): 218–226.

ELKIND, D., AND WEINER, I. B. *Development of the Child*. New York: Wiley, 1978.

ELLIS, A. "Rational-Emotive Theraphy." In *Current Psychotherapies*, ed. by R. Corsini. Itasca, IL.: Peacock, 1973, pp. 167–206.

_____. "What People Can Do for Themselves to Cope with Stress." In *Stress at Work*, ed. by C. L. Cooper and R. Payne. New York: Wiley, 1978.

ELLIS, A., AND HARPER, R. A. *A Guide to Rational Living*. North Hollywood, CA: Wilshire Book Company, 1961.

EPPLEY, K. R., ABRAMS, A. I., AND SHEAR, J. "Differential Effects of Relaxation Techniques on Trait Anxiety: A Meta-analysis." *Journal of Clinical Psychology*, 45 (1989): 957–974.

ERIKSON, E. *Childhood and Society*. New York: Norton, 1950.

_____. *Identity: Youth and Crisis*. New York: Norton, 1968.

535

EWEN, R. B. *An Introduction to Theories of Personality*. Hillsdale, NJ: Erlbaum, Lawrence, and Associates, 1993.

EYSENCK, H. J. "The Effects of Psychotheraphy: An Evaluation." *Journal of Consulting Psychology*, 16 (1952): 319–324.

_____. *The Dynamics of Anxiety and Hysteria*. London: Routledge & Kegan Paul, 1957.

_____. *The Effects of Psychotherapy*. New York: International Science Press, 1966.

_____. *The Structure of Human Personality*, London: Metheun, 1970.

_____. "Biological Dimensions of Personality." In *Handbook of Personality Theory and Research* (pp. 244–276), ed. by L. A. Pervin. New York: Guilford Press, 1990.

F

FARADAY, A. *The Dream Game*. New York: Harper & Row, 1974.

FASICK, F. A. "Parents, Peers, Youth Culture, and Autonomy in Adolescence." *Adolescence*, 19 (1984): 143–157.

FEHR, B., AND RUSSELL, J. A. "The Concept of Love Viewed from a Prototype Perspective." *Journal of Personality and Social Psychology*, 60 (1991): 425–438.

FEIRING, C., AND LEWIS, M. "Changing Characteristics of the U.S. Family: Implications for Family Networks, Relationships, and Child Development." In *Beyond the Dyad*, ed. by Michael Lewis. New York: Plenum, 1989.

FEIST, J. *Theories of Personality*. New York: Holt, Rinehart and Winston, 1985.

FESTINGER, L. *A Theory of Cognitive Dissonance*. Stanford, CA.: Stanford University Press, 1957.

_____, AND CARLSMITH, J. M. "Cognitive Consequences of Forced Compliance." *Journal of Abnormal and Social Psychology*, 58 (1959): 203–210.

FIEDLER, F. E. "Style or Circumstance: The Leadership Enigma." *Psychology Today*, 2 (1969): 38–43.

FISCHER, K. W. *Piaget's Theory of Learning and Cognitive Development*. Chicago: Markham, 1973.

_____. *The Organization of Simple Learning*. Chicago: Markham, 1973.

FISHER, S., AND GREENBERG, R. P. *The Scientific Credibility of Freud's Theories and Therapy*. New York: Basic Books, 1977.

FITTS, P. M., AND POSNER, M. I. *Human Performance*. Belmont, CA.: Brooks/Cole, 1967.

FITTS, W. H. *The Experience of Psychotherapy*. New York: Van Nostrand, 1965.

FLAVELL, J. H. *The Developmental Theory of Jean Piaget*. New York: Van Nostrand, 1963.

FORSEN, A. "Psychosocial Stress as a Risk for Breast Cancer." *Psychotherapy and Psychosomatics*, 55 (1991): 176–185.

FOULKES, D. *The Psychology of Sleep*. New York: Scribner's, 1966.

FOUTS, R. (1993) Personal communication.

FOX, L. J. "Effecting the Use of Efficient Study Habits." In *Control of Human Behavior*, ed. by R. Ulrich, T. Stachnik, and J. Mabry, Vol. 1 Glenview, IL: Scott, Foresman, 1966.

FRANCIS, G. J., AND MILBOURN, G. *Human Behavior in the Work Environment: A Managerial Perspective*. Santa Monica, CA: Goodyear, 1980.

FRANKL, V. *Man's Search for Meaning: An Introduction to Logotherapy*. New York: Clarion, 1970.

FREEDMAN, J. L. *Crowding and Behavior*. San Francisco: Freeman, 1975.

FREEDMAN, J. L., AND FRASER, S. C. "Compliance without Pressure: The Foot-in-the-door Technique." *Journal of Personality and Social Psychology*, 4 (1966): 195–202.

FREUD, S. *An Outline of Psychoanalysis*. Ed. and trans. by James Strachey. New York: Norton, 1949; originally published 1940.

_____. *A General Introduction to Psychoanalysis*. Trans. by Joan Riviere. Garden City, N.Y.: Garden City Publishing, 1943.

FRIED, P. A., AND WATKINSON, B. "36- and 48-month Neurobehavioral Follow-up of Children Prenatally Exposed to Marijuana, Cigarettes, and Alcohol." *Development and Behavioral Pediatrics*, 11 (1990): 49–58.

FRIMAN, P. C., ALLEN, K. D., KERWIN, M. L. E., AND LARZELERE, R. "Changes in Modern Psychology: A Citation Analysis of the Kuhnian Displacement Thesis." *American Psychologist*, 48 (1993): 658–664.

FROMM, E. *Man for Himself: An Inquiry into the Psychology of Ethics*. New York: Holt, Rinehart and Winston, 1947.

_____. *The Art of Loving*. New York: Harper & Row, 1956.

FURSTENBERG, F. F., BROOKS-GUNN, J., MORGAN, S. *Adolescent Mothers in Later Life*. New York: Cambridge University Press, 1987.

_____, AND CHERLIN, A. J. *Divided Families: What Happens to Children When Parents Part*. Cambridge, MA: Harvard University Press, 1991.

FURTH, H. *Piaget and Knowledge*. Englewood Cliffs, N.J.: Prentice-Hall, 1969.

G

GALANTER, M. "Cults and Zealous Self-help Movements: A Psychiatric Perspective." *American Journal of Psychiatry*, 147 (1990): 543–551.

GALTON, SIR FRANCIS. *Hereditary Genius: An Inquiry into Its Laws and Consequences*. London: Macmillan, 1869.

GARCIA, J., AND KOELLING, R. A. "The Relation of Cue to Consequence in Avoidance Learning." *Psychonomic Science*, 4 (1966): 123–124.

GARDNER, R. A., AND GARDNER, B. T. "Teaching Sign Language to a Chimpanzee." *Science*, 1965 (1969): 644–672.

GELDARD, F. A. *The Human Senses*. 2nd ed. New York: Wiley, 1972.

GERARD, H. B., AND RABBIE, J. M. "Fear and Social Comparison." *Journal of Abnormal and Social Psychology*, 62 (1961): 586–592.

GERGEN, K. J., GERGEN, M. M., AND BARTON, W. H. "Deviance in the Dark." *Psychology Today*, 7 (October 1973): 129, 130.

GERST, M. S. "Symbolic Coding Processes in Observational Learning." *Journal of Personality and Social Psychology*, 19 (1971): 9–17.

GESELL, A., AND THOMPSON, H. "Learning and Growth in Identical Twin Infants." *Genetic Psychological Monograph*, 6 (1929): 1–124.

GIBB, C. "Leadership." In *The Handbook of Social Psychology*, ed. by G. Lindsey and E. Aronson, Vol. 4, 2nd ed. Reading, MA.: Addison-Wesley, 1969.

GILLIGAN, C. *In a Different Voice: Psychological Theory and Women's Development*. Cambridge, MA: Harvard University Press, 1982.

_____, AND ATTANUCCI, J. "Two Moral Orientations: Gender Differences and Similarities." *Merrill-Palmer Quarterly*, 34 (1988): 223–237.

GINSBURG, H., AND OPPER, S. *Piaget's Theory of Intellectual Development: An Introduction*. Englewood Cliffs, N.J.: Prentice-Hall, 1969.

GLASS, D. C. "Changes in Linking as a Means of Reducing Cognitive Discrepancies Between Self-Esteem and Aggression." *Journal of Personality*, 32 (1964): 531–549.

GLENN, N. D., AND SUPANCIC, M. "The Social and Demographic Correlates of Divorce and Separation in the United States: An update and reconsideration." *Journal of Marriage and the Family*, 47 (1984): 652–741.

GOFFMAN, E. *Asylums*. Garden City, N.J.: Doubleday, 1961 (paper).

GOLDMAN, H. H., FEDER, J., AND SCANLON, W. "Chronic Mental Patients in Nursing Homes: Reexamining Data from the National Nursing Home Survey." *Hospital and Community Psychiatry*, 37 (1986): 269–272.

GOLDSEN, R., ET AL. *What College Students Think*. New York: Van Nostrand, 1960.

GOLEMAN, D. "Who's Mentally Ill?" *Psychology Today*, 11 (January 1978): 34–41.

GOMBERG, E. S. "Suicide Rates Among Women with Alcohol Problems." *American Journal of Public Health*, 79 (1989): 1363–1365.

GOODENOUGH, F. L. "Expression of the Emotions in a Blind-Deaf Child." *Journal of Abnormal and Social Psychology*, 27 (1932): 328–333.

GOTTESMAN, I. I. *Schizophrenia Genesis: The Origins of Madness*. New York: W. H. Freeman, 1991.

_____, AND SHIELDS, J. *Schizophrenia: The Epigenetic Puzzle*. Cambridge, England: Cambridge University Press, 1982.

GRAHAM, J. R. *MMPI-2: Assessing Personality and Psychopathology*. New York: Oxford University Press, 1990.

GRAMBS, J. D. *Women Over Forty: Visions and Realities*, Rev. ed. New York: Springer, 1989.

GREEN, D. M., AND SWETS, J. A. *Signal Detection Theory and Psychophysics*. New York: Wiley, 1966.

GREENBLATT, M., ET AL. (EDS.) *Drugs and Social Therapy in Chronic Schizophrenia*. Springfield, IL.: Charles C. Thomas, 1965.

GREGORY, R. L. *The Intelligent Eye*. New York: McGraw-Hill, 1970 (paper).

GUILFORD, J. P. *Personality*. New York: McGraw-Hill, 1959.

GUSTAVSON, C. R., ET AL. "Coyote Predation Control by Aversive Conditioning." *Science*, 184 (1974): 581–583.

H

HAAN, N., AND DAY, D. "A Longitudinal Study of Change and Sameness in Personality Development: Adolescence to Later Adulthood." *International Journal of Aging and Human Development*, 5 (1974): 11–39.

HABER, R. N. "How We Remember What We See." *Scientific American*, 222 (1970): 104–112.

HALACY, D. R., JR. *Man and Memory*. New York: Harper & Row, 1970.

HALL, C. S. *A Primer of Freudian Psychology*. Cleveland: World, 1954 (paper).

_____, AND VAN DE CASTLE, R. L. *The Content Analysis of Dreams*. New York: Appleton-Century-Crofts, 1966.

HALL, E. T. *The Silent Language*. Garden City, N.Y.: Doubleday, 1959.

_____. *The Hidden Dimension*. Garden City, N.Y.: Doubleday, 1966.

_____, AND HALL, M. *Understanding Cultural Differences*. Yarmouth, ME: Intercultural Press, Inc. 1990.

HALL, G. S. "The Moral and Religious Training of Children." *Princeton Review* (January 1882): 26–48.

_____. *Adolescence*. New York: Appleton, 1904.

HAMILTON, D. L., AND SHERMAN, S. J. "Illusory Correlations: Implications for Stereotype Theory and Research." In *Stereotyping and Prejudice: Changing Conceptions*, ed. by D. Bar-Tal, C. R. Graumann, A. W. Kruglanski, and W. Stroebe. New York: Springer-Verlag, 1989.

HANNAY, H. J., AND LEVIN, H. S. "Electronic Explorations of the Brain." *National Forum*, LXVII (Spring, 1987): 9–10.

HARDIN, G. "The Tragedy of the Commons." *Science*, 162 (1968): 1243–1248.

HARKINS, E. B. "Effect of Empty Nest Transition on Self-Report of Psychological and Physical Well-Being." *Journal of Marriage and the Family*, 40 (1978): 549–556.

HARLOW, H. F. "The Formation of Learning Sets." *Psychological Review*, 56 (1949): 51–65.

_____. "The Development of Affectional Patterns in Infant Monkeys." In *Determinants of Infant Behavior*, ed. by B. M. Foss. New York: Wiley, 1961, pp. 75–100.

_____, AND ZIMMERMAN, R. R. "Affectional Responses in the Infant Monkey." *Science*, 140 (1959): 421–432.

HARRIS, B. "Whatever Happened to Little Albert?" *American Psychologist,* 34 (1979): 151–160.

HARRIS, C. S. *Fact Book on Aging: A Profile of America's Older Population*. Washington, D.C.: National Council on the Aging, 1978.

HARTMAN, B. J. "An Exploratory Study of the Effects of Disco Music on the Auditory and Vestibular Systems." *Journal of Auditory Research*, 22 (1982): 271–274.

HARTUP, W. W. "Peer Interation and Social Organization." In *Carmichael's Manual of Child Psychology*, ed. by P. H. Mussen, Vol. 3. New York: Wiley, 1970.

HASS, A. *Teenage Sexuality: A Survey of Teenage Sexual Behavior*. New York: Macmillan, 1979.

HASSETT, J. *A Primer of Psychophysiology*. San Francisco: Freeman, 1978a.

_____. "Teaching Yourself to Relax." *Psychology Today*, 12 (August 1978b): 28–40.

HASSETT, J. "Checking the Accuracy of Pupil Scores in Standardized Tests." *English Journal*, 67 (October 1978): 30–31.

HASTORF, A. H., SCHNEIDER, D. J., AND POLEFKA, J. *Person Perception*. 2nd ed. Reading, MA.: Addison-Wesley, 1979.

HATFIELD, E., AND WALSTER, G. *A New Look at Love*, Reading, MA.: Addison-Wesley, 1981.

HATHAWAY, S. R., AND MC KINLEY, J. C. "A Multiphasic Personality Schedule (Minnesota): I. Construction of the Schedule." *Journal of Psychology*, 10 (1940): 249–254.

HAVIGHURST, R. J. *Developmental Tasks and Education*. 3rd ed. New York: McKay, 1972.

HAYS, W. L. *Statistics for Psychologists*. New York: Holt, Rinehart and Winston, 1963.

HEBB, D. O. "What Psychology Is About." *American Psychologist*, 29 (1974): 71–79.

HEILMAN, M. E., SIMON, M. C., AND REPPER, D. P. "Intentionally Favored, Unintentionally Harmed? Impact of Sex-based Preferential Selection in Self-perceptions and Self-evaluations." *Journal of Applied Psychology*, 72 (1987): 62–68.

HELD, R., AND HEIN, A. "A Movement-produced Stimulation in the Development of Visually Guided Behavior." *Journal of Comparative Physiology and Psychology*, 56 (1963): 606–613.

HENNING, H. "Die Qualitätenreihe des Geschmacks." *Zeitschrift für Psychologie*, 74 (1916): 203–219.

HERON, W. "The Pathology of Boredom." *Scientific American*, 196 (January 1957): 57–62.

HERRNSTEIN, R. "I.Q." *Atlantic*, 228 (1971): 43–64.

HERRON, J. "Southpaws: How Different Are They?" *Psychology Today* (March 1976): 50–56.

HESS, B., AND WARING. J. "Family Relationships of Older Women: A Women's Issue." In *Older Women, Issues and Prospects*, ed. by E. W. Markson. Lexington, MA: Lexington Books, 1983.

HESS, E. H. "'Imprinting' in Animals." *Scientific American*, 198 (1958): 81–90.

_____. "'Imprinting' in a Natural Laboratory." *Scientific American*, 227 (1972): 24–31.

HESS, R., AND TORNEY, J. *The Development of Political Attitudes in Children*. Chicago: Aldine, 1967.

HIGGINS-TRENK, A., AND GAITE, A. J. H. "Elusiveness of Formal Operational Thought in Adolescents." *Proceedings of the Seventy-ninth Annual Convention of the American Psychological Association*, 1971.

HILGARD, E. R. *Hypnotic Susceptibility*. New York: Harcourt Brace Jovanovich, 1965.

_____. *Divided Consciousness: Multiple Controls in Human Thought and Action*, expanded ed. New York: Wiley-Interscience, 1986.

_____. *Psychology in America: A Historical Survey*. New York: Harcourt Brace Jovanovich, 1987.

HIROTO, D. S. "Locus of Control and Learned Helplessness." *Journal of Experimental Psychology*, 102 (1974): 187–193.

HIRST, W. "The Amnesic Syndrome: Descriptions and Explanations." *Psychological Bulletin*, 91 (1982): 435–460.

HOBSON, J. A. *Sleep*. New York: Scientific American Library, 1989.

HOCHBERG, J. *Perception*. Englewood Cliffs, N.J.: Prentice-Hall, 1964 (paper).

HOFER, P. "The Lawyer-Psychologist." In *Applied Psychology: Variety and Opportunity*, ed. by R. Gifford. Boston: Allyn and Bacon, 1991.

HOFFMAN, B. *The Tyranny of Testing*. New York: Collier, 1962 (paper).

HOFFMAN, L. W. "Effects of Maternal Employment on the Child—A Review of the Research." *Developmental Psychology*, 10 (1974): 204–228.

HOKANSON, J. E., DEGOOD, D. E., FORREST, M. S., AND BRITTAIN, T. M. "Availability of Avoidance Behaviors for Modulating Vascular-Stress Responses." *Journal of Personality and Social Psychology*, 67 (1963): 60–68.

HOLAHAN, C. J., AND MOOS, R. H. "Life Stress and Health: Personality, Coping, and Family Support in Stress Resistance." *Journal of Personality and Social Psychology*, 49 (1985): 739–747.

HOLBORN, H. *A History of Modern Germany* 1850–1945. New York: Knopf, 1969.

HOLDEN, C. "Identical Twins Reared Apart." *Science*, 207 (1980): 1323–1328.

HOLLAND, G. A. "Transactional Analysis." In *Current Psychotherapies*, ed. by R. Corsini. Itasca, IL: Peacock, 1973, pp. 353–400.

HOLLON, S. D., AND BECK, A. T. "Cognitive and Cognitive-Behavioral Therapies." In *Psychotherapy and Behavior Change*, 3rd ed., ed. by S. L. Garfield and A. E. Bergin. New York: Wiley, 1986.

HOLMES, D. *Abnormal Psychology*. New York: Harper Collins Publishers, 1991.

HOLMES, D. L. AND MORRISON, F. J. *The Child: An Introduction to Developmental Psychology*. Monterey, CA: Brooks/Cole, 1979.

HOLMES, D. S., AND ROTH, D. L. "Effects of Aerobic Exercise on Cardiomuscular Activity during Psychological Stress." *Journal of Psychosomatic Research*, 32 (1988): 469–474.

HOLMES, T. H., AND RAHE, R. H. "The Social Readjustment Scale." *Journal of Psychosomatic Research*, 11 (1967): 213.

HONIG, W. H. (ED.). *Operant Behavior: Areas of Research and Application*. New York: Appleton-Century-Crofts, 1966.

HORN, J. L. "The Aging of Human Abilities." In *Handbook of Developmental Psychology*, Englewood Cliffs, N.J.: Prentice Hall, 1982, pp. 847–870.

HORNER, M. S. "Femininity and Successful Achievement: A Basic Inconsistency." In *Feminine Personality and Conflict*, ed. by J. Bardwick, E. M. Douvan, M. S. Horner, and D. Gutman. Belmont, CA: Brooks/Cole, 1970.

_____. "Towards an Understanding of Achievement-related Conflicts in Women." *Journal of Social Issues*, 28 (1972): 157–175.

HORROCKS, J. E., AND BENIMOFF, M. "Isolation from the Peer Group During Adolescence." *Adolescence*, 2 (1967): 41–52.

_____. *Work Stress and Social Support*. Reading, MA: Addison-Wesley, 1981.

_____, LANDIS, K. R., AND UMBERSON, D. "Social Relationships and Health." *Science*, 241 (1988): 540–545.

HOVLAND C., LUMSDAINE, A., AND SHEFFIELD, F. *Experiments on Mass Communication*. Princeton, N.J.: Princeton University Press, 1949.

_____, AND SEARS, R. "Minor Studies of Aggression: Correlation of Lynching with Economic Indices." *Journal of Psychology*, 9 (1940): 301–310.

HRDY, S. B. "Raising Darwin's Consciousness: Females and Evolutionary Theory," pp. 161–171. In *The Evolution of Sex* (Nobel Conference), ed. by R. Belig and G. Stevens. San Francisco: Harper and Row, 1988.

HUBEL, D. H., AND WIESEL, T. N. "Receptive Fields, Binocular Interaction, and Functional Architecture in the Cat's Visual Cortex." *Journal of Physiology*, 160 (1962): 106–154.

HULL, C. *Principles of Behavior: An Introduction to Behavior Theory*. New York: Appleton-Century-Crofts, 1943.

HURLOCK, E. B. *Developmental Psychology: A Life-Span Approach*. 5th ed. New York: McGraw-Hill, 1980.

HUSTON, A., ET AL. "Communicating More than Content: Formal Features of Children's Television Programs." *Journal of Communication*, 31 (1981): 32–48.

HUSTON, A. C., WATKINS, B. A., AND KUNKEL, D. "Public Policy and Children's Television." *American Psychologist*, 44 (1989): 424–433.

I

INHELDER, B. "Memory and Intelligence in the Child." In *Studies in Cognitive Development*, ed. by D. Elkind and J. F. Flavell. New York: Oxford University Press, 1969, pp. 337–364.

_____, AND PIAGET, J. *The Early Growth of Logic in the Child*. New York: Harper & Row, 1964.

IZARD, C. E. *The Face of Emotion*. New York: Appleton-Century-Crofts, 1971.

_____. *Patterns of Emotions: A New Analysis of Anxiety and Depression*. New York: Academic Press, 1972.

J

JAMES, W. *The Principles of Psychology*. Vol. 2. New York: Holt, 1890.

JELLINEK, E. M. *The Disease Concept of Alcoholism*. New Brunswick, N.J.: Hillhouse Press, 1960.

JENNINGS, M., AND NIEMI, R. "The Transmission of Political Values from Parent to Child." *American Political Science Review*, 62 (1968): 169–184.

JÉQUIER, E. "Energy Utilization in Human Obesity." *Annals of the New York Academy of Sciences*, 499 (1987): 73–83.

JOHN, O. P. "The Big Five" Factor Taxonomy: Dimensions of Personality in the Natural Language and in Questionnaires." In *Handbook of Personality Theory and Research* (pp. 67–100), ed. by L. A. Pervin. New York: Guilford Press, 1990.

JOHNSON, E. S., AND WILLIAMSON, J. B. *Growing Old: The Social Problems of Aging*. New York: Holt, Rinehart and Winston, 1980.

JOHNSTON, L. D., BACHMAN, J. B., AND O'MALLEY, P. M. *Monitoring the Future: Questionnaire Responses from the Nation's High School Seniors* (1978 Vol.). Ann Arbor, MI: Institute for Social Research, 1980.

_____. "Summary of the 1991 Drug Study Results," press release. Ann Arbor, MI: Institute for Social Research, University of Michigan, 1992.

JONES, E. E. *Interpersonal Perception*. New York: W.H. Freeman, 1990.

JONES, E. E., AND DAVIS, K. E. "From Acts to Dispositions: The Attribution Process in Person Perception." In *Advances in Experimental Social Psychology*, ed. by Leonard Berkowitz. Vol. 2. New York: Academic Press, 1965, pp. 219–266.

_____, AND NISBETT, R. E. "The Actor and the Observer: Different Perceptions of the Cause of Behavior." In *Attribution: Perceiving the Causes of Behavior*, ed. by E. E. Jones, D. E. Karouse, H. H. Kelley, R. E. Nisbett, S. Valins, and B. Weiner. Morristown, NJ: General Learning Press, 1972.

JONES, F. H. "A Four-Year Follow-Up of Vulnerable Adolescents." *Journal of Nervous and Mental Disease*, 159 (1974): 20–39.

JONES, M. C. "The Elimination of Children's Fears." *Journal of Experimental Psychology*. 29 (1924): 383–390.

_____. "Psychological Correlates of Somatic Development." *Child Development*, 36 (1965): 899–911.

_____. "Albert, Peter, and John B. Watson." *American Psychologist*, (August 1974): 581–583.

JOSSELSON, R. "Ego Development in Adolescence." In *Handbook of Adolescent Psychology*, ed. by J. Adelson. New York: Wiley, 1980.

JOURARD, S. M. *The Transparent Self*. 2nd ed. New York: Van Nostrand, 1971 (paper).

JOUVET, M. "The Stages of Sleep." *Scientific American*, 216 (1967): 62–72.

JUNG, C. G. *Memories, Dreams, Reflections*. Ed. by A. Jaffe, trans. by R. and C. Winston, New York: Pantheon, 1963.

K

KALAT, J. W. *Introduction to Psychology*, 3rd ed. Belmont, CA: Wadsworth Publishing, 1993.

_____. *Biological Psychology*, 4th ed. Belmont, CA: Wadsworth Publishing Company, 1992.

KALINOWSKY, L. B. "The Convulsive Therapies." In *Comprehensive Textbook of Psychiatry*, ed. by A. M. Freedman, H. I. Kaplan, and B. J. Saddocks. Baltimore: Williams & Wilkins, 1975.

KALISY, R. A. "Attitudes and Aging: Myths and Realities." In *The Later Years: Social Applications of Gerontology*, ed. by R. A. Kalisy. Monterey, CA: Brooks/Cole, 1977.

KALMIS, I. V., AND BRUNER, J. S. "The Coordination of Visual Observation and Instrumental Behavior in Early Infancy." *Perception*, 2 (1973): 304–314.

KANDEL, D. B., AND LESSER, G. S. "Parental and Peer Influences on Educational Plans of Adolescents." *American Sociological Review*, 34 (1969): 213–223.

_____. "The Role of Parents and Peers in Adolescent Marijuana Use." *Science*, 181 (1973): 1067–1070.

KAPLAN, B. (ED.). *The Inner World of Mental Illness*. New York: Harper & Row, 1964 (paper).

KAPLAN, H. I., AND SADDOCK, B. J. *Modern Synopsis of Comprehensive Textbook of Psychiatry*, 4th ed. Baltimore: Williams & Wilkins, 1985.

KARASEK, R., AND THEORELL, T. *Healthy Work: Stress, Productivity, and the Reconstruction of Working Life*. New York: Basic Books, 1990.

KELLEY, H. H. "The Warm-Cold Variable in First Impressions of Persons." *Journal of Personality*, 18 (1950): 431–439.

_____. "Attribution Theory in Social Psychology." In *Nebraska Symposium on Motivation*, ed. by D. Levine. pp. 192–238. Lincoln, NE: University of Nebraska Press, 1967.

KELLEY, G. A. *The Psychology of Personal Constructs, Volume One: A Theory of Personality*. London: Routledge, 1991.

KELMAN, H. C. "Processes of Opinion Change." *Public Opinion Quarterly*, 21 (1961): 57–78.

_____, AND HOVLAND, C. I. "'Reinstatement' of the Communicator in Delayed Measurement of Opinion Change." *Journal of Abnormal and Social Psychology*, 48 (1953): 327–335.

KEMPLER, W. "Gestalt Therapy." In *Current Psychotherapies*, ed. by R. Corsini. Itasca, IL: Peacock, 1973, pp. 251–286.

KIMMEL, D. C. *Adulthood and Aging*. 2nd ed. New York: Wiley, 1980.

KINNEY, J., AND LEATON, G. *Loosening the Grip: A Handbook of Alcohol Information*, 3rd ed. St. Louis: Times Mirror/Mosby, 1987.

KINSEY, A. C., POMEROY, W. B., AND MARTIN, C. E. *Sexual Behavior in the Human Male*. Philadelphia: Saunders, 1948.

_____, ET AL. *Sexual Behavior in the Human Female*. Philadelphia: Saunders, 1953.

KLAPPER, J. T. *The Effects of Mass Communications*. New York: Free Press, 1960.

KLEINMUNTZ, B., AND SZUCKO, J. J. "Lie Detection in Ancient and Modern Times: A Call for Contemporary Scientific Study." *American Psychologist*, 39 (1984): pp. 766–776.

KLEITMAN, N. "Patterns of Dreaming." *Scientific American*, 203 (November 1960): 82–88.

_____. *Sleep and Wakefulness*. Rev. ed. Chicago: University of Chicago Press, 1963.

KLESGES, R. "Effects of Television on Metabolic Rate: Potential Implications for Childhood Obesity." *Pediatrics*, 91 (2), (1993).

KLINEBERG, O. "Emotional Expression in Chinese Literature." *Journal of Abnormal and Social Psychology*, 33 (1938): 517–520.

KLÜVER, H., AND BUCY, P. C. "Psychic Blindness and Other Symptoms Following Bilateral Temporal Lobectomy in Rhesus Monkeys." *American Journal of Physiology*, 119 (1937): 532–535.

KOESTLER, A. *The Act of Creation*. New York: Macmillan, 1964.

KOFFKA, K. *Principles of Gestalt Psychology*. New York: Harcourt Brace Jovanovich, 1963.

KOHLBERG, L. "The Child as Moral Philosopher." *Psychology Today*, 2 (September 1968): 25–30.

_____. "The Development of Children's Orientations Toward a Moral Order: I. Sequence in the Development of Moral Thought." *Vita Humana*, 6 (1969): 11–33.

_____. "Stage and Sequence: The Cognitive-Developmental Approach to Socialization." In *Handbook of Socialization Theory and Research*, ed. by D.A. Goslin. Chicago: Rand-McNally, 1969.

_____, AND KRAMER, R. "Continuities and Discontinuities in Child and Adult Moral Development." *Human Development*, 12 (1969): 93–120.

_____, AND TUNEL, E. *Research in Moral Development: The Cognitive-Developmental Approach*. New York: Holt, Rinehart and Winston, 1971.

KOHLENBERG, R., PHILLIPS, T., AND PROCTOR, W. "A Behaviorial Analysis of Peaking in Residential Electrical Energy Consumers." *Journal of Applied Behaviorial Analysis*, 9 (1976): 13–18.

KOHLER, W. *The Mentality of Apes*. New York: Liveright, 1976.

KORTEN, F. F., COOK, S. W., AND LACEY, J. I. (EDS.). *Psychology and the Problems of Society*. Washington, D.C.: American Psychological Association, 1970.

KRAMER, M. "Statistics of Mental Disorders in the United States: Some Urgent Needs and Suggested Solutions." *Journal of the Royal Statistical Society*, Series A, 132 (1969): 353–407.

KRANTZLER, M. *Creative Divorce*. New York: Evans, 1973.

KREPS, J. *Sex in the Marketplace. American Women at Work*. Baltimore: Johns Hopkins University, 1971.

KROSNICK, J. A., AND ALWIN, D. F. "Aging and Susceptibility to Attitude Change." *Journal of Personality and Social Psychology*, 57 (1989): 416–425.

KÜBLER-ROSS, E. *On Death and Dying*. New York: Macmillan, 1969.

L

LA FRANCE, M., AND MAYO, C. "Racial Differences in Gaze Behavior During Conversations: Two Systematic Observation Studies." *Journal of Personality and Social Psychology*, 33 (1976): 547–552.

LAING, R. D. *The Politics of Experience*. New York: Pantheon, 1967.

_____, AND ESTERSON, A. *Sanity, Madness, and the Family*. 2nd ed. New York: Basic Books, 1971.

LANGE, C. G., AND JAMES, W. *The Emotions*. Ed. by Knight Dunlap, trans. by I. A. Haupt. Baltimore: Williams & Wilkins, 1922.

LASHLEY, K. S. *Brain Mechanisms and Intelligence*. Chicago: University of Chicago Press, 1929.

LAU, R. R. AND RUSSELL, D. "Attributions in the Sports Pages." *Journal of Personality and Social Psychology*, 39 (1980): 29–38.

LAUER, J., AND LAUER, R. "Marriages Made to Last." *Psychology Today*, 16(6) (1985): 22–26.

LAZARUS, R. S., ET AL. "The Principle of Short-Circuiting of Threat: Further Evidence." *Journal of Personality*, 3 (1965): 622–635.

LEARMAN, L. A., AVORN, J., EVERITT, D.E., AND ROSENTHAL, R. "Pygmalion in the Nursing Home: The Effects of Caregiver Expectations on the Patient Outcomes." *Journal of the American Geriatrics Society*, 38 (1990): 797–803

LEAVITT, H. J. "Some Effects of Certain Communication Patterns on Group Performance." *Journal of Abnormal Social Psychology*, 46 (1951): 38–50.

LERNER, R. M., AND KNAPP, J. R. "Actual and Perceived Intrafamilial Attitudes of Late Adolescents and Their Parents." *Journal of Youth and Adolescence*, 4 (1975): 17–36.

_____, AND SPANIER, G. B. *Adolescent Development: A Life-Span Perspective*. New York: McGraw-Hill, 1980.

LEVINGER, G., AND SNOEK, J. D. *Attractions in Relationship: A New Look at Interpersonal Attraction*. Morristown, N.J.: General Learning Press, 1972.

LEVINSON, D. J., "Living with Dying." *Newsweek* (May 1, 1978): 52–61.

_____. "A Conception of Adult Development." *American Psychologist*, 41 (1986): 31.

_____, DARROW, C. M., KLEIN, E. G., LEVINSON, M. H., AND MCKEE, B. *The Seasons of a Man's Life*. New York: Alfred A. Knopf, 1978.

541

LIEBERT, R., SPRAFKIN, J., AND DAVIDSON, E. *The Early Window: Effects of Television on Children and Youth.* 2nd ed. New York: Pergamon, 1982.

LIFTON, R. J. *Thought Reform and the Psychology of Totalism: A Study of "Brainwashing" in China.* New York: Norton, 1963 (paper).

_____. *Home from the War.* New York: Simon & Schuster, 1973.

LINDNER, R. *The Fifty-Minute Hour.* New York: McGraw-Hill, 1974.

LITTENBERG, R., TULKIN, S., AND KAGAN, J. "Cognitive Components of Separation Anxiety." *Developmental Psychology*, 4 (1971): 387–388.

LOCKE, E. A., LATHAM, G. P., AND EREZ, M. "The Determinants of Goal Commitment." *Academy of Management Review*, 13 (1988): 23–29.

LOFTUS, E. "Reconstructing Memory: The Incredible Eyewitness." *Psychology Today*, 8, no. 7 (1974): 116–119.

_____. *Eyewitness Testimony*, Cambridge, MA: Harvard University Press, 1979.

_____. "Trial by Data: Psychological Research as Legal Evidence." *American Psychologist*, 35 (1980): 270–283.

_____. *Memory: Surprising New Insights into How We Remember and Why We Forget.* Reading, MA: Addison-Wesley, 1980.

_____, AND LOFTUS, G. R. "On the Performance of Stored Information in the Human Brain. *American Psychologist*, 35 (1980): 409–420.

_____, AND PALMER, J. C. "Reconstruction of Automobile Destruction: The Influence of the Wording of a Question." *Journal of Verbal Learning and Verbal Behavior*, 13 (1974): 585–589.

LOGUE, A. "Waiter, There's a Phobia in My Soup." *Psychology Today*, 12 (1978): 36.

_____. *The Psychology of Eating and Drinking.* New York: W.H. Freeman, 1986.

LORAYNE, H., AND LUCAS, J. *The Memory Book*. New York: Ballantine, 1974 (paper).

LORENZ, K. Z. *Studies in Animal and Human Behavior*, trans. by Robert Martin, 2 vols. Cambridge, MA: Harvard University Press, 1972.

LORENZ, S. *Our Son, Ken.* New York: Dell, 1969 (paper).

LOVAAS, O. I., ET AL. "Establishment of Imitation and Its Use for the Development of Complex Behavior in Schizophrenic Children." *Behavior Research and Therapy*, 5 (August 1967): 171–181.

_____, KOEGEL, R. L., SIMMONS, J. Q., AND LONG, J. S. "Some Generalizations and Follow-up Measures on Autistic Children in Behavior Therapy." *Journal of Applied Behavior Analysis*, 6 (1973): 131–165.

LUBIN, B., LARSEN, R. M., AND MATARAZZO, J. D. "Patterns of Psychological Test Usage in the United States: 1935–1982." *American Psychologist*, 39 (1984): 451–454.

LUCE, G. G., AND SEGAL, J. *Sleep.* New York: Coward, McCann & Geoghegan, 1966.

LURIA, A. R. *The Mind of a Mnemonist.* New York: Basic Books, 1968.

LYKKEN, D. T. "Psychology and the Lie Detector Industry." *American Psychologist*, 29 (1974): 725–739.

_____. "Detection of Guilty Knowledge: A Commitment on Forman and McCauley." *Journal of Applied Psychology*, 73 (1988): 303–304.

M

MACCOBY, E. E., AND MARTIN, J. "Socialization in the Context of the Family. In *Handbook of Child Psychology* (4th ed., Vol. 4), ed. by P. Mussen; *Socialization, Personality, and Social Development*, ed. by E. M. Hetherington. New York: Wiley, 1983.

MACCOBY, E., AND MASTERS, J. C. "Attachment and Dependency." In *Manual of Child Psychology*, ed. by Paul H. Mussen. Vol. 2. New York: Wiley, 1970, pp. 159–260.

MACE, D., AND MACE, V. *Marriage: East and West.* New York: Doubleday, 1960.

MACKAY, C. *Extraordinary Popular Delusions and the Madness of Crowds.* New York: Farrar, Straus & Giroux, 1932.

MADISON, P. *Personality Development in College.* Reading, MA: Addison-Wesley, 1969.

MARCIA, J. E. "Development and Validation of Ego Identity Status." *Journal of Personality and Social Psychology*, 3 (1966): 551–558.

MARGOLIN, L., AND WHITE, L. "The Continuing Role of Physical Attractiveness in Marriage." *Journal of Marriage and the Family*, 49 (1987): 21–27.

MARLATT, G., AND ROHSENOW, D. "The Think-Drink Effect." *Psychology Today*, 15 (December 1981): 60–70.

MARLER, P. "On Animal Aggression: The Roles of Strangeness and Familiarity." *American Psychologist*, 31, no. 3 (March 1976): 239–246.

MARTIN, T. C., AND BUMPAS, L. L. "Recent Trends in Marital Disruption." *Demography*, 26 (1989): 37–51.

MASLOW, A. H. *Motivation and Personality*, Rev. ed. New York: Harper and Row, 1970.

MASTERS, W. H., AND JOHNSON, V. E. *Human Sexual Inadequacy.* Boston: Little, Brown, 1970.

_____, "The Symptomatic Adolescent Five Years Later: He Didn't Grow Out of It." *American Journal of Psychiatry*, 123 (1967): 1338–1345.

MATLIN, M. W. *The Psychology of Women*, 2nd ed. Fort Worth, TX: Harcourt Brace Jovanovich, 1993.

MAY, R. *Existential Psychology.* 2nd ed. New York: Random House, 1969.

_____. *The Courage to Create*. New York: Norton, 1975.

_____. *The Meaning of Anxiety*, Rev. ed. New York: Norton, 1977.

MC CARLEY, R. W. "Where Dreams Come From: A New Theory." *Psychology Today*, 12 (December 1978): 54–65.

MC CLELLAND, D. C. "Need Achievement and Entrepreneurship: A Longitudinal Study." *Journal of Personality and Social Psychology*, 1 (1965): 389–392.

MC CLELLAND, D. C. "Risk Taking in Children with High and Low Need for Achievement." In *Motives in Fantasy, Action, and Society*, pp. 306–321, ed. by J. W. Atkinson. Princeton, NJ: Van Nostrand, 1958.

_____, AND HARRIS, T. G. "To Know Why Men Do What They Do: A Conversation with David C. McClelland." *Psychology Today*, 4 (January 1971): 35–39.

_____ ET AL. *The Achievement Motive*. New York: Appleton-Century-Crofts, 1953.

MC COY, K. *Coping with Teenage Depression*. New York: Mosby, 1982.

MC GHIE, A., AND CHAPMAN, J. "Disorders of Attention and Perception in Early Schizophrenia." *British Journal of Medical Psychiatry*, 34 (1961): 103–116.

MC GINLEY, H., LE FEVRE, R., AND MC GINLEY, P. "The Influence of a Communicator's Body Position on Opinion Change in Others." *Journal of Personality and Social Psychology*, 31 (1975): 686–690.

MC GUIRE, W. J. "A Vaccine for Brainwash." *Psychology Today*, 3 (February 1970): 36–39, 62–64.

MC KENZIE, S. C. *Aging and Old Age*. Glenview, IL: Scott, Foresman, 1980.

MEEHL, P. "Schizotaxia, Schizotype, Schizophrenia." *American Psychologist*, 17 (1962): 827–832.

MEEHL, P. "Schizotaxia Revisited." *Archives of General Psychiatry*, 46 (1989): 935–944.

MELLINGER, G. D., BALTER, M. B. AND UHLENHUTH, E. H. "Insomnia and its Treatment: Prevalence and Correlates." *Archives of General Psychiatry*, 42 (1985): 225–232.

MELZACK, R. "Phantom Limbs and the Concept of a Neuromatrix." *Trends in Neurosciences*, 13 (1990): 88–92.

_____, AND WALL, P. D. "Pain Mechanisms: A New Theory." *Science*, 150 (1965): 971–979.

MEYER, W. J., AND DUSEK, J. B. *Child Psychology: A Developmental Perspective*. Lexington, MA: Heath, 1979.

MIDDLEBROOK, P. N. *Social Psychology and Modern Life*. 2nd ed. New York: Knopf, 1980.

MIEDZIAN, M. *Boys Will Be Boys: Breaking the Link between Masculinity and Violence*. New York: Doubleday, 1991.

MILGRIM, S. *Obedience to Authority*. New York: Harper & Row, 1964.

_____. "The Experience of Living in Cities." *Science*, 167 (1970): 1461–1468.

MILLER, G. A. "The Magical Number Seven, Plus or Minus Two: Some Limits on Our Capacity for Processing Information." *Psychological Review*, 63 (1956): 81–97.

_____, "Psychology as a Means of Promoting Human Welfare." In *Psychology and the Problems of Society*. ed. by F. F. Korten, S. W. Cook, and J. I. Lacey. Washington, D.C.: American Psychological Association, 1970.

_____, GALANTER, E., AND PRIBRAM, K. H. *Plans and the Structure of Behavior*. New York: Holt, Rinehart and Winston, 1960.

MILLER, G. R., AND FONTES, N. E. "Trial by Videotape." *Psychology Today*, 12 (May 1979): 92–101.

MILLER, L. K. "Behavioral Principles and Experimental Communities." In *Behavior Modification: Principles, Issues, and Applications*, ed. by W. E. Craighead, A. E. Kazdin, and M. J. Mahoney. Boston: Houghton Mifflin, 1976.

_____, AND SCHNEIDER, R. "The Use of a Token System in Project Headstart." *Journal of Applied Behavior Analysis*, 3 (1970): 213–220.

MILLER, N. E. "Experimental Studies of Conflict." In *Personality and the Behavior Disorders.*, ed. by J. Hunt. New York: Ronald Press, 1944.

MILLER, N. E., AND DI CARA, L. "Instrumental Learning of Heart Rate Changes in Curarized Rats: Shaping and Specificity to Discriminative Stimulus." *Journal of Comparative and Physiological Psychology*, 63 (1967): 12–19.

_____, AND DWORKIN, B. R. "Visceral Learning: Recent Difficulties with Curarized Rats and Significant Problems for Human Research." In *Cardiovas Psychophysiology*, ed. by Paul A. Obrist, *et al*. Chicago: Aldine-Atherton, 1974.

MILLER, S., AND SELIGMAN, M. "The Reformulated Model of Helplessness and Depression: Evidence and Theory." In *Psychological Stress and Psychopathology*, ed. by N. W. Newfield. New York: McGraw-Hill, 1982.

MINER, J. B. "Psychological Testing and Fair Employment Practices." *Personnel Psychology*, 27 (1974): 49–62.

MINTZ, R. S. "Psychotherapy of the Suicidal Patient." In *Suicidal Behaviors*, ed. by H. L. P. Resnik. Boston: Little, Brown, 1968.

MITCHELL, J. E., AND ECKERT, E. D. "Scope and Significance of Eating Disorders." *Journal of Consulting and Clinical Psychology*, 55 (1987): 628–634.

MOESSINGER, A. C. "Mothers who Smoke and the Lungs of their Offspring." In *Prenatal Abuse of Licit and Illicit Drugs*, ed. by Donald Hutchings. New York: New York Academy of Science, 1989.

MORRIS, C. G. *Contemporary Psychology and Effective Behavior*, 7th ed. New York: HarperCollins Publishers, 1990.

MOSCOVICI, S. "Social Influence and Conformity." In *Handbook of Social Psychology*, 3rd ed., ed. by G. Lindsay and E. Aronson. New York: Random House, 1985.

MOTLEY, M. T. "Slips of the Tongue." *Scientific American*, 253 (1985): 116–127.

MOWRER, O. H., AND MOWRER, M. "Enuresis: A Method for Its Study and Treatment." *American Journal of Orthopsychiatry*, 8 (1938): 436–459.

MUCHINSKY, P. M. *Psychology Applied to Work*, 4th ed. Pacific Grove, CA: Brooks/Cole Publishing Company, 1993.

MUNNS, M. "The Values of Adolescents Compared with Parents and Peers." *Adolescence*, 7 (1972): 519–524.

MURRAY, H. A., ET AL. *Exploration in Personality*. New York: Oxford University Press, 1934.

MUSSEN, P. H., CONGER, J. J., AND KAGAN, J. *Child Development and Personality*, 4th ed. New York: Harper & Row, 1974.

_____. *Essentials of Child Development and Personality*. Philadelphia: Harper & Row, 1980.

N

NARAJANO, C., AND ORNSTEIN, R. *On the Psychology of Meditation*. New York: Viking, 1971.

NATHAN, P. E., AND HARRIS, S. L. *Psychopathology and Society*, New York: McGraw-Hill, 1975.

_____, AND O'BRIEN, J. S. "An Experimental Analysis of the Behavior of Alcoholics and Nonalcoholics During Prolonged Experimental Drinking: A Necessary Precursor of Behavior Therapy?" *Behavior Therapy*, 2 (1971): 455–476.

NATIONAL CENTER FOR HEALTH STATISTICS. *Health, United States, 1990*. Hyattsville, MD: Public Health Service, 1991.

NEHER, A. "Maslow's Theory of Motivation: A Critique." *Journal of Humanistic Psychology*, 31 (1991): 89–112.

NEISSER, ULRIC. *Cognitive Psychology*. New York: Appleton-Century-Crofts, 1967.

NEUGARTEN, B., ET AL. "Women's Attitudes Toward the Menopause." *Vita Humana*, 6 (1963): 140–151.

New York Times, "Parents on the Brink of Child Abuse Get Crisis Aid," April 17, 1983, pp. 1, 29.

NEWCOMB, T. *Personality and Social Change*. New York: Dryden Press, 1943.

_____, ET AL. *Persistence and Change: Bennington College and Its Students After 25 Years*. New York: Wiley, 1967.

NEWMAN, G., AND NICHOLS, C. R. "Sexual Activities and Attitudes in Older Persons." *Journal of the American Medical Association*, 173 (1960): 33–35.

NEWMAN, O. *Defensible Space*. New York: Macmillan, 1972.

NEWMAN, P. "The Peer Group." In *Handbook of Developmental Psychology*, ed. by B. B. Wolman. Englewood Cliffs, NJ: Prentice Hall, 1982.

NOLEN-HOEKSEMA, S. "Sex Differences in Unipolar Depression: Evidence and Theory." *Psychological Bulletin*, 101 (1987): 259–282.

NUCKOLLS, K., CASSEL, J., AND KAPLAN, B. H. "Psychological Assets, Life Crisis, and the Prognosis of Pregnancy." *American Journal of Epidemiology*, 95 (1972): 431–444.

O

OAKES, P. J., AND TURNER, J. C. "Is Limited Information Processing Capacity the Cause of Social Stereotyping?" *European Review of Social Psychology*, 9 (1990): 147–152.

OFFER, D., AND OFFER, J. *From Teenage to Young Manhood*. New York: Basic Books, 1975.

OLDS, J., AND OLDS, M. E. "Drives, Rewards and the Brain." In *New Directions in Psychology II*, ed. by F. Barron, *et al.* New York: Holt, Rinehart and Winston, 1965.

O'LEARY, A. "Stress, Emotion, and Human Immune Function." *Psychological Bulletin*, 108 (1990): 363–382.

ORNE, M. T. "The Nature of Hypnosis: Artifact and Essence." *Journal of Abnormal and Social Psychology*, 58 (1959): 277–299.

ORNSTEIN, R. *The Psychology of Consciousness*. 2nd ed. New York: Harcourt Brace Jovanovich, 1977.

P

PALMORE, E. "What Can the USA Learn from Japan about Aging?" In *Readings in Aging and Death: Contemporary Perspectives*, ed. by S. H. Zarit. New York: Harper & Row, 1977.

PALUDI, M. A. "Psychometric Properties and Underlying Assumptions of Four Objective Measures of Fear of Success." *Sex Roles*, 10 (1984): 765–781.

PARKE, R., AND SLABY, R. "Aggression: A Multilevel Analysis." In *Handbook of Child Psychology. Vol. 14. Socialization, Personality and Social Development*. 4th ed., ed. by P. H. Mussen and M. E. Hetherington. New York: Wiley, 1983.

_____, AND LEWIS, N. "The Family in Context: A Multilevel Interactional Analysis of Child Abuse." In *Parent-Child Interaction: Theory, Research and Prospect*. ed. by R. W. Henderson. New York: Academic Press, 1980.

PATCH, V. D. "Methadone." *New England Journal of Medicine*, 286 (1972): 43–45.

PAVLOV, I. P. *Conditioned Reflexes*. Trans. by G. V. Anrep. London: Oxford University Press, 1927.

PAYNE, W. A., HAHN, D. B., AND PINGER, R. R. *Drugs: Issues for Today*. St. Louis, MO: Mosby-Year Book, Inc., 1991.

PEARL, D., BOUTHILET, L., AND LAZAR, J. (EDS.). *Television and Behavior: Ten Years of Scientific Progress and Implications for the Eighties*. Vols. 1 and 2. Washington, D.C.: U.S. Government Printing Office, 1982.

PEARLSON, G. D., KIM, W. S., KUBOS, K., MOBERG, P., JARAYAM, G., BASCOM, M., CHASE, G., GOLDFINGER, A., AND TUNE, L. "Ventricle-Brain Ratio, Computed Tomographic Density, and Brain Area in 50 Schizophrenics." *Archives of General Psychiatry*, 46 (1989).

PELLEGRINI, A. D. "Rough and Tumble Play: Developmental and Educational Significance." *Educational Psychologist*, 22 (1987): 23–43.

PENFIELD, W. "Consciousness, Memory, and Man's Conditioned Reflexes." In *On the Biology of Learning*, ed. by K. H. Pribram. New York: Harcourt Brace Jovanovich, 1969.

PERLICK, D. "The Withdrawal Syndrome: Nicotine Addiction and the Effects of Stopping Smoking in Heavy and Light Smokers." Unpublished doctoral dissertation. Columbia University, 1977.

PERLS, F. HEFFERLINE, R. F., AND GOODMAN, P. *Gestalt Therapy*. New York: Dell, 1965.

PERRIS, C. "The Distinction between Bipolar and Unipolar Affective Disorders." In *Handbook of Affective Disorders*, ed. by E. S. Paykel. New York: Guilford Press, 1982.

PETERSON, A. C. "Adolescent Development." *Annual Review of Psychology*, 39 (1988): 583–607.

PETTY, R. E., AND CACIOPPO, J. T. "The Elaboration Likelihood Model of Persuasion." In *Advances in Experimental Social Psychology* (Vol. 19, pp. 123–205), ed. by L. Berkowitz. New York: Academic Press, 1986.

PIAGET, J. *The Language and Thought of the Child*. London: Routledge & Kegan Paul, 1926.

PILBEAM, D. "An Idea We Could Live Without—the Naked Ape." *Discovery*, 7, no. 2 (Spring 1972): 63–70.

PINES, M. "Infants Are Smarter Than Anybody Thinks." *The New York Times Magazine* (November 29, 1970).

PLOMIN, R. "The Role of Inheritance in Behavior." *Science*, 248 (1990): 183–188.

POCS, O., ET AL. "Is There Sex After 40?" *Psychology Today*, 10 (June 1977): 54–57.

POKORNEY, A. D., AND PREIN, R. F. "Lithium in Treatment and Prevention of Affective Disorder." *Diseases of the Nervous System*, 35 (1974): 327–333.

POLIVY, J., AND HERMAN, C. P. "Diagnosis and Treatment of Normal Eating." *Journal of Consulting and Clinical Psychology*, 55 (1987): 635–644.

PSYCHOSURGERY: AN NAMH POSITION STATEMENT. *Mental Hygiene*, 58 (1974): 22–24.

Q

QUINN, R., SEASHORE, S., KAHN, R., MANGIONE, T., CAMPBELL, D., STAINES, G., AND MCCULLOUGH, M. *Survey of Working Conditions*. Washington, D.C.: U.S. Government Printing Office, 1971.

R

RABKIN, L. (ED.). *Psychopathology and Literature*. San Francisco: Chandler, 1966.

RAHE, R. H. "Life Changes and Near-Future Illness Reports." In *Emotions: Their Parameters and Measurement*, ed. by L. Levi. New York: Raven Press, 1975.

_____, H., AND ARTHUR, R. J. "Life Change Patterns Surrounding Illness Experience." *Journal of Psychosomatic Research*, 11 (1968): 341–345.

RAY, O., AND KSIR, C. *Drugs, Society, & Human Behavior*, 6th ed. St. Louis: Mosby-Year Book, Inc., 1993.

REGIER, D. A., BOYD, J. H., BURKE, J. D., MYERS, J. K. KRAMER, M., ROBINS, L. N., GEORGE, L. K., KARNO, M., AND LOCKE, B. Z. "One-month Prevalence of Mental Disorders in the United States." *Archives of General Psychiatry*, 45 (1988): 877–896.

REID, D. W., HAAS, G., AND HAWKINGS, D. "Locus of Desired Control and Positive Self-Concept of the Elderly." *Journal of Gerontology*, 32 (1977): 441–450.

REINISCH, J., AND BEASLEY, R. *The Kinsey Institute New Report on Sex*. New York: St. Martin's Press, 1990.

REINKE, B., HOLMES, D. S., AND HARRIS, R. "The Timing of Psychosocial Changes in Women's Lives: The Years 25 to 45." *Journal of Personality and Social Psychology*, 48 (1985): 1353–1365.

REISMAN, D., GLAZER, N., AND DENNEY, R. *The Lonely Crowd*. New Haven, Conn.: Yale University Press, 1953 (paper).

REISMAN, J., AND SHORR, S. "Friendship Claims and Expectations Among Children and Adults." *Child Development*, 49 (1978): 913–916.

REPPUCCI, N. D., AND SAUNDERS, J. T. "Social Psychology of Behavior Modification." *American Psychologist*, 29 (1974): 649–660.

REYNOLDS, G. S. *A Primer of Operant Conditioning*. Glenview, IL.: Scott, Foresman, 1968.

RHINE, J. B. *Extra-Sensory Perception*. Boston: Branden, 1964.

RHINE, L. E. *Hidden Channels of the Mind*. New York: Apollo, 1961 (paper).

RICE, F. P. *The Adolesent: Development, Relationships, and Culture*, 6th ed. Boston: Allyn and Bacon, pp. 434–441, 1990.

_____. *Intimate Relationships, Marriages, and Families*, 2nd ed. Mountain View, CA: Mayfield Publishing Company, 1993.

RICE, M. "The Role of Television in Language Acquisition." *Developmental Review*, 3 (1983): 221–224.

RICHMAN, A. L., MILLER, P. M., AND LE VINE, R. A. "Cultural and Educational Variations in Maternal Responsiveness." *Developmental Psychology*, 28 (1992): 614–621.

RIERDEN, J., KOFF, E., AND STUBBS, M. "Gender, Depression, and Body Image in Early Adolescents." *Journal of Early Adolescence*, 8 (1988): 109–117.

RILEY, V. "Psychoneuroendocrine Influences on Immunocompetence and Neoplasia." *Science*, 212 (1981): 1100–1109.

ROEDIGER, H. L. III "Implicit Memory: Retention without Remembering. *American Psychologist*, 45 (1990): 1043–1056.

ROGERS, C. *Client-centered Therapy*. Boston: Houghton Mifflin, 1951.

_____. *On Becoming a Person*. Boston: Houghton Mifflin, 1961.

ROGERS, C. R. *On Personal Power: Inner Strength and its Revolutionary Impact*. New York: Delacorte, 1977.

ROGERS, C. R. *A Way of Being*. Boston: Houghton Mifflin, 1980.

ROGERS, D. *The Psychology of Adolescence*. 3rd ed. Englewood Cliffs, NJ: Prentice-Hall, 1977.

_____. *The Adult Years: An Introduction to Aging*. Englewood Cliffs, NJ: Prentice-Hall, 1979.

ROKEACH, M. "Long-Range Experimental Modification of Values, Attitudes, and Behavior." *American Psychologist*, 26 (1971): 453–459.

ROLLINS, B. C., AND FELDMAN, H. "Marital Satisfaction over the Family Life Cycle." *Journal of Marriage and the Family*, 32 (1970): 20–28.

ROOK, K. S. "Social Support Versus Companionship: Effects on Life Stress, Loneliness, and Evaluations by Others." *Journal of Personality and Social Psychology*, 52 (1987): 1132–1147.

_____. "Parallels in the Study of Social Support and Social Strain." *Journal of Social and Clinical Psychology*, 9 (1990): 118–132.

ROSENTHAL, R. *Environmental Effects in Behavioral Research*. New York: Appleton-Century-Crofts, 1966.

_____, AND ROSNOW, R. L. (EDS.). *Artifact in Behavioral Research*. New York: Academic Press, 1969.

ROSS, L. "The Intuitive Psychologist and His Shortcomings." In *Advances in Experimental Social Psychology* (Vol. 10), ed. by L. Berkowitz. New York: Academic Press, 1977.

ROSSI, P. H. "The Old Homeless and the New Homelessness in Historical Perspective." *American Psychologist*, 45 (1990): 954–959.

ROTH, D. L., AND HOLMES, D. S. "Influence of Aerobic Exercise Training and Relaxation Training on Physical and Psychologic Health Following Stressful Life Events." *Psychosomatic Medicine*, 49 (1987): 355–365.

RUBIN, I. "Sex over 65." In *Advances in Sex Research*, ed. by H. G. Beigel. New York: Harper & Row, 1963.

RUBIN, Z. "Measurement of Romantic Love." *Journal of Personality and Social Psychology*, 16 (1970): 265–273.

_____. *Liking and Loving*. New York: Holt, Rinehart and Winston, 1973.

RUSSELL, M. J., SWITZ, G. M., AND THOMPSON, K. "Olfactory Influence on the Human Menstrual Cycle." *Pharmacology, Biochemistry, and Behavior*, 13 (1980): 737–738.

S

SAHAKIAN, W. S. *Psychology of Learning*. Chicago: Markam, 1970.

SALK L. "Mother's Heartbeat as an Imprinting Stimulus." *Transactions of the New York Academy of Sciences*, 24 (1962): 753–763.

SARASON, I. G., AND SARASON, B. R. *Abnormal Psychology*. 3rd ed. Englewood Cliffs, NJ: Prentice-Hall, 1980.

SARBIN, I., AND COE, W. *Hypnosis: A Social Psychological Analysis of Influence Communication*. New York: Holt, Rinehart and Winston, 1972.

_____. "Hypnosis and Psychopathology: Replacing Old Myths with Fresh Metaphors." *Journal of Abnormal Psychology*, 88 (1979): 506–526.

SAUL, S. *Aging: An Album of People Growing Old*. New York: Wiley, 1974.

SCARF, M. *Unfinished Business: Pressure Points in the Lives of Women*. New York: Ballentine Books, 1980.

SCHACHTER, S. *The Psychology of Affiliation*. Stanford, CA.: University Press, 1959.

_____. *Emotion, Obesity, and Crime*. New York: Academic Press, 1971.

_____. "Second Thoughts on Biological and Psychological Explanations of Behavior." In *Cognitive Theories in Social Psychology*, ed. by L. Berkowitz. New York: Academic Press, 1978.

_____, AND LATANÉ, B. "Crime, Cognition, and the Autonomic Nervous System." In *Nebraska Symposium on Motivation*, ed. by M. Jones. Lincoln, NE: University of Nebraska Press, 1964.

_____, AND SINGER, J. "Cognitive, Social, and Physiological Determinants of Emotional State." *Psychological Review*, 69 (1962): 379–399.

SCHAIE, W. K., AND STROTHER, C. "A Cross-sectional Study of Age Changes in Cognitive Behavior." *Psychological Bulletin*, 70 (1968): 671–680.

SCHLEGAL, A., AND BARRY, H. *Adolescence: An Anthropological Inquiry*. New York: Free Press, 1991.

SCHNEIDER, K. "The Cognitive Basis of Task Choice in Preschool Children." *Advances in Motivation and Achievement*, 3 (1984): 57– 72.

SCHREIBER, F. R. *Sybil*. New York: Warner, 1973.

SCHULMAN, J., ET AL. "Recipe for a Jury," *Psychology Today*, 6 (May 1973): 37–44.

SCHULTES, R. E. *Hallucinogenic Plants*. New York: Golden Press, 1976.

SCHWARTZ, A. N., AND PETERSON, J. A. *Introduction to Gerontology*. San Francisco: Holt, Rinehart and Winston, 1979.

_____, AND PROPPE, H. G. "Toward Person/Environment Transactional Research in Aging." *Gerontologist*, 10 (1970): 228–232.

SCHWARTZ, G. E., DAVIDSON, R., AND MAER, R. "Right Hemisphere Lateralization for Emotion in the Human Brain: Interactions with Cognition." *Science*, 190 (1975): 286–288.

SEARS, D. O., PEPLAU, L. A., AND TAYLOR, S. E. *Social Psychology*, 7th ed. Englewood Cliffs, NJ: Prentice-Hall, 1991.

SEARS, R., MACCOBY, E., AND LEVIN, H. *Patterns of Child Rearing*. New York: Harper & Row, 1957.

SEIGEL, R. K. "Hallucinations." *Scientific American*, 237 (October 1977): 132–140.

SELIGMAN, M. E. P. *Helplessness*. San Francisco: Freeman, 1975.

_____. *Learned Optimism*. New York: Alfred A. Knopf, 1991.

SELYE, H. *The Stress of Life*. New York: McGraw-Hill, 1956.

_____. *Stress in Health and Disease*. Woburn, MA: Butterworth, 1976.

_____. "History and Present Status of the Stress Concept." In *Handbook of Stress: Theoretical and Clinical Aspects*, ed. by L. Goldberger and S. Breznitz. New York: Free Press, 1982.

_____. *Stress Without Distress*. Philadelphia: Lippincott, 1974.

_____, AND CHERRY, L. "On the Real Benefits of Eustress." *Psychology Today*, 11 (March 1978): 60–70.

SEXTON, V. AND HOGAN, J. D. (EDS.). *International Psychology: Views from Around the World*. Omaha: University of Nebraska Press, 1992.

SHAPIRO, D. "Preface." In *Biofeedback and Self-Control 1972*, ed. by D. Shapiro, *et al*. Chicago: Aldine-Atherton, 1973.

SHAPIRO, E. (ED.). *PsychoSources: A Psychology Resource Catalog*. New York: Bantam, 1973 (paper).

SHAVER, P. "Questions Concerning Fear of Success and Its Conceptual Relatives." *Sex Roles*, 2 (1976): 305–320.

SHEEHY, G. *Passages*. New York: Dutton, 1976.

SHOR, R. E., AND ORNE, M. T. (EDS.). *The Nature of Hypnosis*. New York: Holt, Rinehart and Winston, 1965.

SILVERMAN, J. "When Schizophrenia Helps." *Psychology Today*, 4 (September 1970): 62–65.

SILVERSTEIN, B. "An Addiction Explanation of Cigarette-Induced Relaxation." Unpublished doctoral dissertation, Columbia University, 1976.

SIMONS, R. L., AND WHITBECK, L. B., CONGER, R. D., AND WU, C. I. "Intergenerational Transmission of Harsh Parenting." *Developmental Psychology*, 27 (1991): 159–171.

SINGER, J., AND SINGER, D. "Psychologists Look at Television: Cognitive, Developmental, Personality and Social Policy Implications." *American Psychologist*, 38 (1983): 826–834.

SINGER, J. N. "Job Strain as a Function of Job and Life Stress." Unpublished doctoral dissertation, Colorado State University, 1975.

SINGER, M. T. "Coming Out of the Cults." *Psychology Today*, 12 (January 1979): 72–82.

SIZEMORE, C. C., AND PITTILLO, E. S. *I'm Eve*. Garden City, NY: Doubleday Books, 1977.

SKINNER, B. F. *The Behavior of Organisms*. New York: Appleton-Century-Crofts, 1961.

_____. *Walden Two*. New York: Macmillan, 1962; originally published 1948.

_____. *Beyond Freedom and Dignity*. New York: Knopf, 1971.

_____. *About Behaviorism*. New York: Knopf, 1974.

_____. "Intellectual Self-Management in Old Age." *American Psychologist*, 38 (1983): 239–244.

_____, AND VAUGHN, M. E. *Enjoy Old Age*. New York: Norton, 1983.

SMALLEY, S. L. "Genetic Influences in Autism." *Psychiatric Clinics of North America*, 14 (1991): 125–139.

SMITH, M. L., AND GLASS, G. V. "Meta-Analysis of Psychotherapy Outcome Studies." *American Psychologist*, 32 (1977): 752–760.

SMITH, W. *A Profile of Health and Disease in America*. New York: Facts on File, 1989.

SNELLGROVE, L. *Psychological Experiments and Demonstrations*. New York: McGraw-Hill, 1967.

SNYDER, S. H. *Madness and the Brain*. New York: McGraw-Hill, 1973.

SOLOMON, R. L., AND CORBIT, J. D. "An Opponent-Process Theory of Motivation." *Psychological Review*, 81 (1974): 119–145.

SPERLING, G. "The Information Available in Brief Visual Presentations." *Psychological Monographs*, 74, no. 11 (1960).

SPIRDUSO, W. W., AND MACRAE, P. G. "Motor Performance and Aging." In *Handbook of the Psychology of Aging*, 3rd ed., ed. by J. E. Birren and K. W. Schaie. San Diego, CA: Academic Press, 1990.

SPITZ, R., AND WOLFF, K. M. "Anaclitic Depression: An Inquiry into the Genesis of Psychiatric Conditions in Early Childhood, II." In *The Psychoanalytic Study of the Child*, ed. by A. Freud, *et al.* Vol. II. New York: International Universities Press, 1946, pp. 313–342.

_____. "The Smiling Response: A Contribution to the Ontogenesis of Social Relations." *Genetic Psychology Monographs*, 34 (1956): 57–123.

SPRECHER, S. "Premarital Sexual Standards for Different Categories of Individuals." *Journal of Sex Research*, 26 (1989): 232–248.

_____, MCKINNEY, K., AND ORBUCH, T. L. "Has the Double Standard Disappeared?: An Experimental Test." *Social Psychology Quarterly*, 50 (1987): 24–31.

SQUIRE, L. R. *Memory and Brain*. New York: Oxford University Press, 1987.

STANLEY, J. C. "Test Better Finder of Great Math Talent Than Teachers Are." *American Psychologist*, 31 (1976): 313–314.

STARR, C., AND TAGGART, R. *Biology: The Unity and Diversity of Life*, 5th ed. Belmont, CA: Wadsworth Publishing Company, 1989.

STERNBERG, R. *Beyond IQ: A Triarchic Theory of Human Intelligence*. New York: Cambridge University Press, 1985.

_____. "A Triangular Theory of Love." *Psychological Review*, 93 (1986): 119–135.

_____. *The Triangle of Love: Intimacy, Passion, Commitment*. New York: Basic Books, 1988.

STEVENS, S. S. "The Measurement of Loudness." *Journal of the Acoustical Society of America*, 27 (1955): 815–819.

_____. "The Surprising Simplicity of Sensory Metrics." *American Psychologist*, 17 (1962): 29–39.

STEVENS-LONG, J. *Adult Life Developmental Processes*. Palo Alto, CA: Mayfield, 1979.

STOGDILL, R. M. *Handbook of Leadership: A Survey of Theory and Research*. New York: Free Press, 1974.

STROMEYER, C. F. "Eidetikers." *Psychology Today*, 4 (1970): 76–80.

SURWIT, R. S., SHAPIRO, D., AND GOOD, M. I. "Comparison of Cardiovascular Feedback, Neuromuscular Feedback, and Meditation in the Treatment of Borderline Essential Hypertension." *Journal of Consulting and Clinical Psychology*, 46 (1978): 252–263.

SWANN, W. B., STEIN-SEROUSSI, A., AND GLEISER, R. B. "Why People Self-verify." *Journal of Personality and Social Psychology*, 62 (1992): 392–401.

SZASZ, T. *The Myth of Mental Illness*. New York: Harper and Row, Publishers, 1966; Dell, 1967.

_____. *The Age of Madness*. Garden City, NY: Doubleday Anchor, 1973 (paper).

T

TANNER, J. M., WHITEHOUSE, R. H., AND TAKAISHI, M. "Standards from Birth to Maturity for Height, Weight, Height Velocity, and Weight Velocity for British Children, 1965, Parts I and II." *Archives of Disease in Childhood*, 41 (1966).

TART, C. T. (ED.). *Altered States of Consciousness*. 2nd ed. New York: Wiley, 1972.

TAYLOR, S. "Adjustment to Threatening Events." *American Psychologist*, 38 (1983): 1161–1173.

TAYLOR, S. E. *Health Psychology*, 2nd ed. New York: McGraw-Hill, 1991.

_____, AND FISKE, S. T. "Point of View and Perception of Causality." *Journal of Personal and Social Psychology*, 32 (1975): 439–445.

TERMAN, L. M. *The Measurement of Intelligence*. Boston: Houghton Mifflin, 1916.

_____, AND MERRILL, M. A. *Measuring Intelligence*. Boston: Houghton Mifflin, 1937.

_____. *Stanford-Binet Intelligence Scale: Manual for the Third Revision. Form L-M*. Boston: Houghton Mifflin, 1973.

THOMPSON, R. F. (ED.). *Physiological Psychology*. San Francisco: Freeman, 1971.

_____. "The Neurobiology of Learning and Memory." *Science*, Vol. 23 (August 29, 1986): 941.

THOMPSON, W. R., AND GRUSEC, J. "Studies of Early Experience." In *Manual of Child Psychology*, ed. by Paul H. Hussen. Vol. 2. New York: Wiley, 1970, pp. 565–656.

_____. "Studies in Early Experience." In *Carmichael's Manual of Child Psychology*, 5th ed. New York: Wiley, 1970.

THORNBURG, H., AND ARAS, Z. "Physical Characteristics of Developing Adolescents." *Journal of Adolescent Research*, 1 (1986): 47–78.

TOFFLER, A. *Future Shock*. New York: Random House, 1970.

TREISMAN, A. M. "Verbal Cues, Language, and Meaning in Selective Listening." *American Journal of Psychology*, 77 (1964): 206–219.

_____, AND GORMICAN S. "Feature Analysis in Early Vision: Evidence from Search Asymmetries." *Psychological Review*, 95 (1988): 15–48.

TRICE, H. M., AND BEYER, J. M. "Employee Assistance Programs: Blending Performance-oriented and Humanitarian Ideologies to Assist Emotionally Disturbed Employees." In *Research in Community and Mental Health: A Research Annual*, Vol. 4, ed. by J. R. Greenley. Greenwich, CT: JAI Press, 1984.

TROTTER, R. "Baby Face." *Psychology Today*, 17 (August 1983): 15–20.

TULVING, E. "Episodic and Semantic Memory." In *Organization of Meaning*, ed. by E. Tulving and W. Donaldson. New York: Academic Press, 1972.

TURNER, J. S., AND HELMS, D. B. *Contemporary Adulthood*, Philadelphia: Saunders, 1979.

TYLER, L. E. *The Psychology of Human Differences*, 3rd. ed. New York: Appleton-Century-Crofts, 1965.

_____. "Human Abilities." In *Annual Review of Psychology*. Palo Alto, CA: Annual Reviews, 1975, pp. 177–206.

U

U.S. BUREAU OF THE CENSUS. *Statistical Abstract of the United States*, 98th ed. Washington, D.C.: U.S. Government Printing Office, 1978; cited in Bukatko & Daehler.

U.S. BUREAU OF THE CENSUS. *Statistical Abstract of the United States*, 110th ed. Washington, D.C.: U.S. Government Printing Office, 1990; cited in Bukatko & Daehler.

U.S. DEPARTMENT OF JUSTICE. *Crime in the United States*. Washington, D.C.: Federal Bureau of Investigation, 1990.

UNITED STATES V. BRAWNER, 471 F.2d 969 (D.C. 1972).

V

VAILLANT, G. E. *Adaption to Life*. Boston: Little, Brown, 1977.

VALENSTEIN, E. S. *Great and Desperate Cures: The Rise and Fall of Psychosurgery and other Radical Treatments for Mental Illness*. New York: Basic Books, 1986.

VANDELL, D. L., HENDERSON, V. K., AND WILSON, K. S. "A Longitudinal Study of Children with Day Care Experiences of Varying Quality." *Child Development*, 59 (1988): 1286–1292.

VAN HARRISON, R. "Person-Environment Fit and Job Stress." In *Stress at Work*, ed. by C. L. Cooper and R. Payne. New York: Wiley, 1978.

VERNON, P. E. "The Demise of the Stanford Binet Scale." *Canadian Psychology*, 28 (1987): 251–258.

VICTOR, M., AND ADAMS, R. D. "Opiates and Other Synthetic Analgesic Drugs." In *Harrison's Principles of Internal Medicine*, ed. by M. M. Wintrobe, *et al*. New York: McGraw-Hill, 1970, pp. 677–681.

VOKEY, J. R., AND READ, J. D. "Subliminal Messages, Between the Devil and the Media." *American Psychologist*, 40 (1985): 1231–1239.

W

WADE, C., AND CIRESE, S. *Human Sexuality*, 2nd ed. San Diego, CA: Harcourt Brace Jovanovich, 1991.

WADE, N. "Sociobiology: Troubled Birth for a New Discipline." *Science*, 191 (March 19, 1976): 1151–1155.

WALD, G. "The Receptors of Color Vision." *Science*, 145 (1964): 1007–1016.

WALLACE, R. K. "Physiological Effects of Transcendental Meditation." *Science*, 167 (1970): 1751–1754.

WALLERSTEIN, J., AND KELLY, J. "The Effects of Parental Divorce: The Adolescent Experience." In *The Child in His Family: Children at Psychiatric Risk*, ed. by J. Anthony and C. Koupernik. New York: Wiley 1974, pp. 479–505.

WALSTER, E., ARONSON, V., ABRAHAMS, D., AND ROTTMAN, L. "Importance of Physical Attractiveness in Dating Behavior." *Journal of Personality and Social Psychology*, 4 (1966): 508–516.

WASHBURN, S. L. "Human Behavior and the Behavior of Other Animals." *American Psychologist*, 33 (May 1978): 405–418.

WATERSON, E. J., AND MURRAY-LYON, I. M. "Preventing Alcohol Related Birth Damage: A Review." *Social Science and Medicine*, 30 (1990): 349–364.

WATSON, D. L., AND THARP, R. G. *Self-directed Behavior: Self-modification for Personal Adjustment*. Monterey, CA: Brooks/Cole, 1972.

WATSON, J. B. *Behaviorism*. New York: Norton, 1970; originally published 1924.

_____, AND RAYNER, R. "Conditioned Emotional Reactions." *Journal of Experimental Psychology*, 3 (1920): 1–14.

WECHSLER, D. *Wechsler Intelligence Scale for Children—Revised*. New York: Psychological Corp., 1974.

_____. *Manual for the Wechsler Adult Intelligence Scale—Revised*. New York: Psychological Corp., 1981.

WEIL, A. *The Natural Mind*. Boston: Houghton Mifflin, 1972.

_____, ZINBERG, N., AND NELSEN, J. M. "Clinical and Psychological Effects of Marijuana in Man." *Science*, 162 (1968): 1234–1242.

WEINBERGER, M., HINER, S. L., AND TIERNEY, W. M. "In Support of Hassles as a Measure of Stress in Predicting Health Outcomes." *Journal of Behavioral Medicine*, 10 (1987): 19–31.

WEISS, D. J., AND VALE, C. D. "Adaptive Testing." *Applied Psychology: An International Review*, 36 (1987).

WEISS, J. M. "Influence of Psychological Variables on Stress-Induced Pathology." In *Physiology, Emotion and Psychosomatic Illness* (Ciba Foundation Symposium 8). New York: American Elsevier, 1972.

_____. "Effects of Coping Behavior in Different Warning-Signal Conditions on Stress Pathology in Rats." *Journal of Comparative and Physiological Psychology*, 77 (1971): 1–13.

WHITE, B. L. "Child Development Research: An Edifice Without a Foundation." *Merrill-Palmer Quarterly of Behavior and Development*, 15 (1969): 49–79.

WHITE, R. "Motivation Reconsidered: The Concept of Competence." *Psychological Review*, 66 (1959): 297–333.

_____. *The Abnormal Personality*. New York: Ronald, 1964.

_____. *Lives in Progress: A Study of the Natural Growth of Personality*. 2nd ed. New York: Holt, Rinehart and Winston, 1966.

_____, RIGGS, M. M., AND GILBERT, D. C. *Case Workbook in Personality*. New York: Holt, Rinehart and Winston, 1976.

WILD, B. S., AND HAYNES, C. A. "A Dynamic Conceptual Framework of Generalized Adaptation to Stressful Stimuli." *Psychological Reports*, 38 (1976): 319–334.

WILL, G. F. "A Good Death." *Newsweek* (January 9, 1978): 72.

WILLIAMSON, J. B., EVANS, L., AND MUNLEY, A. *Aging and Society*. New York: Holt, Rinehart and Winston, 1980.

WILSON, E. O. *Sociobiology: A New Synthesis*. Cambridge, MA: Harvard University Press, 1975a.

_____. "Human Decency Is Animal." *The New York Times Magazine* (October 12, 1975b): 38–49.

WILSON, T. D., KRAFT, D., AND DUNN, D. S. "The Disruptive Effects of Explaining Attitudes: The Moderating Effects of Knowledge about the Attitude Object." *Journal of Experimental Social Psychology*, 25 (1989): 379–400.

WITELSON, S. F. "The Brain Connection: The Corpus Callosum Is Larger in Left-handers." *Science*, 229 (1985): 665–668.

WOLFE, J. B. "Effectiveness of Token-Rewards for Chimpanzees." *Comparative Psychological Monographs*, 12 (1936): whole no. 5.

WOLMAN, B. B. (ED.). *Handbook of General Psychology*. Englewood Cliffs: NJ: Prentice-Hall, 1973.

_____ (ED.). *Handbook of Clinical Psychology*. New York: McGraw-Hill, 1965.

WOODS, S. C. "The Eating Paradox: How We Tolerate Food." *Psychological Review*, 98 (1991): 488–505.

WOOLFOLK, R. L. "Psychophysiological Correlates of Meditation." *Archives of General Psychiatry*, 32 (1975): 1326–1333.

WRIGHT, J., AND HUSTON, A. "A Matter of Form: Potentials of Television for Young Viewers." *American Psychologist*, 38 (1983): 835–843.

_____, SIGELMAN, C. K., AND SANFORD, F. H. *Psychology: A Scientific Study of Human Behavior*. 5th ed. Monterey, CA: Brooks/Cole, 1979.

Y

YARROW, L. J. AND GOODWIN, M. S. "The Immediate Impact of Separation Reactions of Infants to a Change in Mother Figures." In *The Competent Infant*, ed. by L. J. Stone, T. J. Smith, and L. B. Murphy. New York: Basic Books, 1973.

YOUNG, A., STOKES, M., AND CROWE, M. "Size and Strength of the Quadricep Muscles of Old and Young Women." *European Journal of Clinical Investigation*, 14 (1984): 282–287.

Z

ZARIT, S. H. (ED.). *Readings in Aging and Death: Contemporary Perspectives*. New York: Harper & Row, 1977.

ZIGLER, E., AND MUENCHOW, S. *Head Start: The Inside Story of America's Most Successful Educational Experiment*. New York: Basic Books, 1992.

_____, STYFCO, S. J., AND GILMAN, E. "The National Head Start Program for Disadvantaged Preschoolers." In *Head Start and Beyond: A National Plan for Extended Childhood Intervention*, ed. by E. Zigler, and S. J. Styfco. New Haven, CT: Yale University Press, 1993.

ZIMBARDO, P. G. *Psychology and Life*. 10th ed. Glenview, IL: Scott, Foresman, 1979.

_____, EBBESEN, E. B., AND MASLACH, C. *Influencing Attitudes and Changing Behavior*. 2nd ed. Reading, MA: Addison-Wesley, 1977.

ZUBIN, J., AND MONEY, J. (EDS.). *Contemporary Sexual Behavior: Critical Issues in the 1970s*. Baltimore: Johns Hopkins University Press, 1973.

Italicized page numbers refer to graphic illustrations. Preceding the page number, abbreviations refer to a graph (g), table or chart (t), illustration (i), or photograph or painting (p). The index is organized into two parts: a subject index and a name index.

553

Photo Credits

Cover,(puzzle)(c)Comstock Stock Photography, (sunset) (c)Uniphoto,Inc.; iii—Robert McElroy/Woodfin Camp & Associates; iii—B.Losh/FPG International; iv—Arthur Tress/Photo Researchers; iv—Julie Marcotte/Tony Stone Images; iv—Nathan Bilow/Stock Imagery; ix—Nathan Bilow/Stock Imagery; v—Custom Medical Stock; v—Steve McCarroll; v—Tibor Hirsch/Photo Researchers; vi—Ellan Young/Photo Researchers; vi—Joel Gordon; vii—James L. Ballard; vii—Steinmetz/Custom Medical Stock; viii—Frank Siteman/The Picture Cube; viii—Kindra Clineff/The Picture Cube; x—Bob Daemmrich/Stock Boston; x—Cary Wolinsky/Stock Boston; xi—James L. Ballard; xi—Ted Horowitz/Stock Market; xii—Doug Martin; xii—Burton McNeely/The Image Bank; 1—D.C. Lowe/FPG International; 2—Hickson & Associates; 4—Tom Dunham/Visual Education Corporation; 10—M.C. Escher—Escher Foundation, Haags Gemeentemuseum, The Hague; 13—(t) The Bettmann Archive; 13—(b) The Granger Collection; 15—Wide World Photos; 17—(bc) Robert McElroy/Woodfin Camp & Associates; 17—(bl) NASA; 17—(br) D.C.Lowe/FPG International; 17—(tc) Kindra Clineff/The Picture Cube; 17—(tcc) file photo; 17—(tcl) file photo; 17—(tcr) file photo; 17—(tl) file photo; 17—(tr) file photo; 20–21—Mugshots/Tony Stone Images; 22—B. Losh/FPG International; 30(t)—Steve McCarroll; 30(b)—Suzanne Szasz/Photo Researchers; 32—Bill Boyarshy; 34—Yerkes Regional Primate Research Center; 41—Thomas Jefferson School/Roger Bean; 42—(l) Dave Stoecklien/The Stock Market; 42—(c) David Madison /DUOMO; 42—(r) David Madison/DUOMO; 45—Friedman/The Picture Cube; 49—Arnold & Brown; 52—Arthur Tress/Photo Researchers; 54—Frederica Georgia/Photo Researchers; 62—Jim Anderson/Woodfin Camp & Associates; 72—Werner Kalber/PPS; 74—Werner Kalber/PPS; 75—Frank Siteman/The Picture Cube; 78–79—FPG International; 80—Julie Marcotte/Tony Stone Images; 90—Brian Brake/Photo Researchers; 91—(t) James Olds; 91—(b) Larry Mulvehill/Photo Researchers; 92—Steve McCarroll; 96—Loren McIntyre/Woodfin Camp & Associates; 99—Jack Prelutsky/Stock Boston; 100—M.P. Kahl/Photo Researchers; 102—Lowell J. Georgia/Photo Researchers; 103—Mariette Pathy Allen; 106—Tim Courlas; 113—Dohdan Hrynewych/Stock Boston; 115—Adam Hart-Davis/Science Photo Library, Photo Researchers; 116—Tom Suzuki; 121—First Image; 122—Steve McCarroll; 125—Philip Clark; 126—Baron Wolmon/Woodfin Camp & Associates; 127—Courtesy, Foundation for Research on the Nature of Man; 132—Custom Medical Stock; 137—Ted Russell/The Image Bank; 138—courtesy R.A. Butler; 140—Harry Crosby; 146—reproduced from *Darwin and Facial Expressions*, Academic Press, 1973; 149—M. Kowal/Custom Medical Stock Photo; 156—Tibor Hirsch/Photo Researchers; 158—(t),Bruce Roberts/Photo Researchers; 158—(b),D.P.I.; 161—Allan Hobson/Photo Researchers; 167—Michael Tamborrino/FPG International; 171—D&I MacDonald/The Picture Cube; 173—Will & Deni McIntyre/Photo Researchers; 175—courtesy the Newark Museum; 180–181—Ellan Young/Photo Researchers; 182—David Hundley/The Stock Market; 184—(l) Bill MacDonald; 184—(r) Jason Laure/Woodfin Camp & Associates; 185—Jason Laure/Woodfin Camp & Associates; 189—George Zimbel/Monkmeyer Press Photo; 190—George Zimbel/Monkmeyer Press Photo; 191—Bill MacDonald; 192—Steve Wells; 195—Frank Siteman/The Picture Cube; 198—Gaye Hilsenrath (MR)/The Picture Cube; 200—Thomas McAvoy/Time-Life Picture Agency; 201—Harry F. Harlow, University of Wisconsin Primate Center; 202—Harry F. Harlow, University of Wisconsin Primate Center; 204—Nancy Sheehan/The Picture Cube; 205—Ruth Dixon; 207—Edward Lettau/FPG International; 211—Cleo Photo/The Picture Cube; 218—Fotopic/Stock Imagery; 221—Malcolm Kirk/Peter Arnold, INC.; 224—Tom Dunham/Visual Education Corporation; 230—Joel Gordon; 242—Steinmetz/Custom Medical Stock Photo; 246—Anthony Edgeworth/The Stock Market; 250—Richard T. Nowitz/FPG International; 252—Diana Mara Henry; 253—Burton McNeely/The Image Bank; 260—Scott Thode/International Stock Photo; 264–265—Henry Diltz; 266—James L. Ballard; 275—The Bettmann Archives; 276—World Wide Photos; 278—Ted Polumbaum; 280—The Bettmann Archive; 282—John Oldenkamp; 290—Kindra Clineff/The Picture Cube; 292—(l) Blair Seitz/Photo Researchers; 292—(r) James Amos/Photo Researchers; 296—John Oldenkamp, with permission of the Houghton Mifflin Company, from Herman and Merrill Stanford Binet Intelligence Scale; 297—Werner Kalber/PPS; 301—Steve McCarroll; 304—Stephen Frisch/Stock Boston; 309—courtesy United Airlines; 314–315—Brent Jones; 316—Pallas Photo/Stock Imagery; 321—Michal Heron/Woodfin Camp & Associates; 322—Eugene Richard/Magnum Photos; 325—(bl) Frank Siteman/The Picture Cube; 325—(cl) Dave Schaefer/The Picture Cube; 325—(r) First Image; 325—(tl) Chris Brown/Stock Boston; 326—Larry Burrows/Life Pictures Service; 333—(tl) Jan Halaska/Photo Researchers; 333—(r) O'Brien & Mayo/FPG International; 333—(bl) David R. Frazier; 336—Frank Siteman/The Picture Cube; 340—James L. Ballard; 343—(tl) Robert C. Dawson/Stock Imagery; 343—(tr) David R. Frazier; 343—(cr) Pictures Unlimited; 343—(bl) Joseph Nettis/Tony Stone Images; 343—(bc) file photo; 343—(br) David/Lissy/Stock Imagery; 345—Lester Sloan/Woodfin Camp & Associates; 349—Vivienne/D.P.I.; 351—Avrom Laverne/D.P.I.; 352—Nathan Bilow/Stock Imagery; 354—Frank Siteman/The Picture Cube; 357—Michal Heron; 358—George Ancona/International Stock Photo; 362—Nathan Bilow/Stock Imagery; 365—(t) Diane Tong; 365—(b) The National Museum of Western Art, Tokyo; 366—Sygma; 370—Leonard Freed/Magnum Photos; 371—Columbia Pictures Inc., A Stanley Kramer Production, 1953; 374—(t) Rick Smolan/Stock Boston; 374—(b) Michal Heron; 376—courtesy Al Vercoutere, Camerillo State Hospital; 377—file photo; 379—Stephen J. Potter/Stock Boston; 382—Paul Fusco/Magnum Photos; 392—Julie Marcotte/Stock Boston; 399—Jeff Kaufman/FPG International; 400—Lee Pratt; 405—Will & Deni McIntyre/Photo Researchers; 407—(t) Stacy Pick/Stock Boston; 407—(b) Bob Daemmrich/Stock Boston; 408—Bob Daemmrich/Stock Boston; 415—Peter Berndt,MD/Custom Medical Stock Photo; 416—David York/Medichrome; 418—Mark Antman/Stock Boston; 422–423—John Colwell /Grant Heilman; 424—Cary Wolinsky/Stock Boston; 431—Pete Robinson; 433—Robert Eckert/Stock Boston; 436—(t) Dennis Stock/Magnum Photos; 436—(b) Tim Courlas; 441—M. Feinberg/The Picture Cube; 446—Ted Thai/Sygma; 449—Paul Fusco/Magnum Photos; 451—from M. Sherif and C.W. Sherif, *Social Psychology*, Harper Row, Publishers, Inc. 1969; 456—James L. Ballard; 464—courtesy Jane Elliot; 465—courtesy Jane Elliot; 470—courtesy Medical World News; 474—courtesy Department of the Army; 478—Alex Borodulin/Peter Arnold Inc.; 480—Willam Vandivert; 481—file photo; 486–487—Arthur Tilley/FPG International; 488—Ted Horowitz/Stock Market; 490—The Bettmann Archive; 491—The Bettmann Archive; 494—SuperStock; 502—Michael Melford/The Image Bank